SCHOLARSHIPS

FELLOWSHIPS

AND LOANS

ISSN 1058-5699

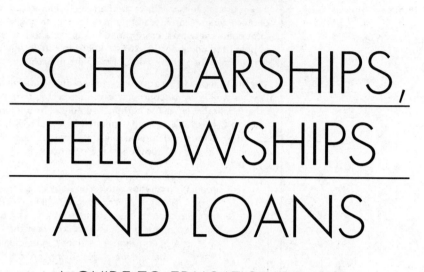

SCHOLARSHIPS, FELLOWSHIPS AND LOANS

A GUIDE TO EDUCATION-RELATED
FINANCIAL AID PROGRAMS FOR
STUDENTS AND PROFESSIONALS

Volume Two
Sponsors and Their Scholarships: I–T

Thirty-Third Edition

GALE
CENGAGE Learning·

Farmington Hills, Mich • San Francisco • New York • Waterville, Maine
Meriden, Conn • Mason, Ohio • Chicago

GALE
CENGAGE Learning®

Scholarships, Fellowships and Loans, 33rd Edition

Project Editor: Bohdan Romaniuk

Editorial Support Services: Wayne Fong

Composition and Electronic Prepress: Gary Leach

Manufacturing: Rita Wimberley

For product information and technology assistance, contact us at
Gale Customer Support, 1-800-877-4253.
For permission to use material from this text or product,
submit all requests online at **www.cengage.com/permissions.**
Further permissions questions can be emailed to
permissionrequest@cengage.com

Gale
27500 Drake Rd.
Farmington Hills, MI, 48331-3535

ISBN-13: 978-1-4103-1532-8 (3 vol. set)
ISBN-13: 978-1-4103-1533-5 (vol. 1)
ISBN-13: 978-1-4103-1534-2 (vol. 2)
ISBN-13: 978-1-4103-1535-9 (vol. 3)

ISSN 1058-5699

This title is also available as an e-book.
ISBN-13: 978-1-4103-1536-6
Contact your Gale sales representative for ordering information.

Printed in the United States of America
1 2 3 4 5   19 18 17 16 15

Contents

Volume 1

Highlights vii

Introduction ix

User's Guide. xiii

Federal Programs xvii

AmeriCorps xix

State Higher Education Agencies xxi

Abbreviations xxv

Sponsors and Their Scholarships: A-H 1

Volume 2

Highlights vii

Introduction ix

User's Guide. xiii

Federal Programs xvii

AmeriCorps xix

State Higher Education Agencies xxi

Abbreviations xxv

Sponsors and Their Scholarships: I-T 645

Volume 3

Highlights vii

Introduction ix

User's Guide. xiii

Federal Programs xvii

AmeriCorps xix

State Higher Education Agencies xxi

Abbreviations xxv

Sponsors and Their Scholarships: U-Z. 1231

Field of Study Index 1343

Legal Residence Index. 1437

Place of Study Index 1509

Special Recipient Index 1579

Sponsor and Scholarship Index 1601

This edition of *Scholarships, Fellowships and Loans (SFL)* provides access to more than 7,500 sources of education-related financial aid for students and professionals at all levels. *SFL*'s scope ranges from undergraduate and vocational/technical education through post-doctoral and professional studies. Students and others interested in education funding will find comprehensive information on a variety of programs in all educational areas, including:

- Architecture
- Area and Ethnic Studies
- Art
- Business
- Communications
- Computer Science
- Education
- Engineering
- Health Science
- Humanities
- Industrial Arts
- Language

- Law
- Literature
- Liberal Arts
- Library Science
- Life Science
- Medicine
- Mathematics
- Performing Arts
- Philosophy
- Physical Sciences
- Social Sciences
- Theology and Religion

SFL Provides Detailed Information on Awards

SFL provides all the information students need to complete their financial aid search. Entries include: administering organization name and address; purpose of award; qualifications and restrictions; selection criteria; award amount and number of awards granted; application details and deadlines; detailed contact information.

Additionally, look for the section on federal financial aid following the User's Guide for a quick summary of programs sponsored by the U.S. government, as well as information on the AmeriCorps program. There is also a section that lists higher education agencies by state.

Five Indexes Allow Quick and Easy Access to Awards

Whether you are a high school student looking for basic undergraduate financial aid, a scientist investigating research grants, or a professional attempting to finance additional career training, SFL aids your search by providing access to awards through the following indexes:

Field of Study Index categorizes awards by very specific subject fields.

Legal Resident Index targets awards restricted to applicants from specific geographic locations.

Place of Study Index provides a handy guide to awards granted for study within specific states, provinces, or countries.

Special Recipient Index lists awards that are reserved for candidates who qualify by virtue of their gender, organizational affiliation, minority or ethnic background.

Sponsor and Scholarship Index provides a complete alphabetical listing of all awards and their administering organizations.

Catchwords

SFL includes catchwords of the organization on each corresponding page, to aid the user in finding a particular entry.

As we make our way through difficult economic times, there is a growing need for a more highly-trained and educated work force. From political discussions and debates to reports from future-oriented think tanks and other groups, there is agreement that postsecondary education is a key to success. Yet how are students and their families to afford the already high (and constantly rising) cost of higher education? Searching for financial aid can be very tedious and difficult, even though hundreds of millions of dollars in aid reportedly go unclaimed every year.

Scholarships, Fellowships and Loans (SFL), the most comprehensive single directory of education-related financial aid available, can save you time, effort, and money by helping you to focus your search within the largest pool of awards and avoid pursuing aid for which you do not qualify. In most cases, the detailed descriptions contain enough information to allow you to decide if a particular scholarship is right for you to begin the application process. *SFL* lists more than 7,500 major awards available to U.S. and Canadian students for study throughout the world. Included are:

- scholarships, fellowships, and grants, which do not require repayment;

- loans, which require repayment either monetarily or through service;

- scholarship loans, which are scholarships that become loans if the recipient does not comply with the award's terms;

- internships and work study programs, which provide training, work experience, and (usually) monetary compensation; and

- awards and prizes that recognize excellence in a particular field.

Also included are other forms of assistance offered by associations, corporations, religious groups, fraternal organizations, foundations, and other private organizations and companies. *SFL* includes a broad representation of government-funded awards at the national and state levels, as well as a representative sampling of lesser-known and more narrowly focused awards, such as those of a strictly local nature or programs sponsored by small organizations. Financial aid programs administered and funded by individual colleges or universities are not included in *SFL*. Both need- and merit-based awards are included. Competition-based awards and prizes are included when they offer funds that support study or research and are intended to encourage further educational or professional growth.

Students of All Types Can Benefit

Traditional students as well as those returning to school, non-degree learners, those in need of retraining, and established professionals can use the funding sources listed in *SFL* for formal and non-formal programs of study at all levels:

- high school

- vocational

- undergraduate

- graduate

- postgraduate

- doctorate

- postdoctorate

- professional development

Content and Arrangement

Scholarships, Fellowships and Loans is organized into a main section containing descriptive listings of award programs and their administering organizations, and five indexes.

The main section, Sponsors and Their Scholarships, is arranged alphabetically by name of administering organization. Entries for each organization's awards appear immediately following the entry on the organization. Each entry contains detailed contact and descriptive information, often providing users with all the information they need to make a decision about applying.

The indexes provide a variety of specific access points to the information contained within the organization and award listings, allowing users to easily identify awards of interest.

Practical Tips on How to Find Financial Aid

While there are many education-related financial aid programs for students of all types and study levels, the competition for available funds is steadily increasing. You will improve the likelihood of meeting your financial aid goals if you:

- carefully assess your particular needs and preferences;

- consider any special circumstances or conditions that might qualify you for aid; and

- carefully research available aid programs.

The following pages list some general guidelines for making your way through the search and application process.

Start Your Search Early

Any search for financial aid is likely to be more successful if you begin early. If you allow enough time to complete all of the necessary steps, you will be more likely to identify a wide variety of awards for which you qualify with plenty of time to meet their application deadlines. This can increase your chances of obtaining aid.

Some experts recommend that you start this process up to two years before you think you will need financial assistance. While you will probably be able to obtain some support if you allow less time, you might overlook some important opportunities.

Some awards are given on a first-come, first-served basis, and if you do not file your application early enough, the aid will already be distributed. In many cases, if your application is late you will not be considered, even if you have met all of the other criteria.

An early start will also allow you to identify organizations that offer scholarships to members or participants, such as student or professional associations, in time to establish membership or otherwise meet their qualifying criteria.

Assess Your Needs and Goals

The intended recipients for financial aid programs and the purposes for which awards are established can vary greatly. Some programs are open to almost anyone, while others are restricted to very specific categories of recipients. The majority of awards fall somewhere in between. Your first step in seeking financial aid is to establish your basic qualifications as a potential recipient. The following are some general questions to ask yourself to help define your educational and financial needs and goals:

- What kinds of colleges or universities interest me?

- What careers or fields of study interest me?

- Do I plan to earn a degree?

- Am I only interested in financial aid that is a gift, or will I consider a loan or work study?

- In what parts of the country am I willing to live and study?

Leave No Stone Unturned

After you have defined your goals, the next step is to identify any special factors that might make you eligible for aid programs offered only to a restricted group. Examine this area carefully, and remember that even minor or unlikely connections may be worth checking. The most common qualifications and restrictions involve:

- citizenship
- community involvement or volunteer work
- creative or professional accomplishment
- employer
- financial need
- gender
- merit or academic achievement
- military or veteran status
- organization membership (such as a union, association, or fraternal group)
- place of residence
- race or ethnic group
- religious affiliation

With many awards, you may be eligible if your spouse, parents, or guardians meet certain criteria by status or affiliations. You should be aware of your parents' affiliations even if you don't live with one (or both) of them, or if they are deceased. And given enough lead time, it may be possible for you (or your parents) to join a particular organization, or establish necessary residence, in time for you to be eligible for certain funds.

Contact Financial Aid Offices

Most colleges, universities, and other educational institutions offer their own financial aid programs. Their financial aid offices may also have information on privately sponsored awards that are specifically designated for students at those institutions. Contact their respective financial aid offices to request applications and details for all of the aid programs they sponsor and/or administer.

Use *SFL* to Identify Awards Sponsored by Private Organizations and Corporations

Scholarships, Fellowships and Loans (SFL) is the most comprehensive single source of information on major education-related financial aid programs sponsored and administered by private organizations and companies for use by students and professionals. Using *SFL* as a starting point, you can quickly compile a substantial list of financial aid programs for which you may qualify by following these simple steps:

- Compile an initial list of awards offered in your field of study.

- If you have already chosen your field of study, look in the Field of Study Index to find listings of awards grouped by more precise disciplines (such as Accounting or Journalism). If you choose this approach, your initial list is likely to be shorter but more focused. Eliminate awards that cannot be used at your chosen level of study or that do not meet your financial needs. Are you an undergraduate only interested in scholarships? Are you a graduate student willing to participate in an internship or take out a loan? Consult the User's Guide to determine which of the study level categories and award types apply to your particular situation. Both indexes clearly note the study levels at which awards may be used. The Field of Study Index also lists the type of financial aid provided.

- Eliminate awards by citizenship, residence, and other restrictions (minority status, ethnic background, gender, organizational affiliation) that make you ineligible.

- If your list is based on the Field of Study Index, you will need to look under the section for qualifications in each descriptive listing to see what requirements apply.

- Read the descriptive listings for each of the award programs left on your list. The descriptive listings should contain all the information you need to decide if you qualify and should apply for each of the awards on your list.

Expand Your List of Possibilities

If you are willing to take the initiative and do a little extra digging, you should be able to add to your list of institution-related and privately sponsored programs. In most cases, the best possibilities fall into these two areas:

Government Agencies and Programs. The Sponsors and Their Scholarships main section includes a broad representation of award programs sponsored by federal and state governments. Since these listings are not meant to be exhaustive, you should be able to identify additional programs by contacting the government agencies responsible for education-related financial aid programs listed here. On the federal level, contact the U.S. Department of Education at 400 Maryland Ave., SW, Washington, DC 20202, or on their website at http://www.ed.gov, for up-to-date information on U.S. Government award programs. For a broad overview of federal financial aid, consult the Federal Programs section. Similarly, you may contact your state department of education for details on what is offered in your particular state. Please see the State Higher Education Agencies section for state-by-state listings.

Local Sources of Awards. A surprisingly large number of financial aid programs are sponsored by small and/or local organizations. *SFL* contains a representative sampling of such programs to encourage you to seek similar programs in your own geographic area. High school guidance counselors are often aware of local programs as well, and they can usually tell you how to get in touch with the sponsoring or administering organizations. Local newspapers are also rich sources of information on financial aid programs.

Allow Enough Time for the Application Process

The amount of time needed to complete the application process for individual awards will vary, so you should pay close attention to application deadlines. Some awards carry application deadlines that require you to apply a year or more before your studies will begin. In general, allow plenty of time to:

- Write for official applications. You may not be considered for some awards unless you apply with the correct forms.

- Read all instructions carefully.

- Take note of application deadlines.

- Accurately and completely file all required supporting material, such as essays, school transcripts, and financial records. If you fail to answer certain questions, you may be disqualified even if you are a worthy candidate.

- Give references enough time to submit their recommendations. Teachers in particular get many requests for letters of recommendation and should be given as much advance notice as possible.

Make Sure You Qualify

Finally, don't needlessly submerge yourself in paperwork. If you find you don't qualify for a particular award, don't apply for it. Instead, use your time and energy to find and apply for more likely sources of aid.

Available in Electronic Format

Scholarships, Fellowships and Loans is also available online as part of the Gale Directory Library. For more information, call 1-800-877-GALE.

Comments and Suggestions Welcome

We welcome reader suggestions regarding new and previously unlisted organizations and awards. Please send your suggestions to:

Scholarships, Fellowships and Loans

Gale, Cengage Learning

27500 Drake Rd.

Farmington Hills, MI 48331-3535

Phone: (248) 699-4253

Toll-free: 800-347-4253

Fax: (248) 699-8070

Email: Bob.Romaniuk@cengage.com

Scholarships, Fellowships and Loans is comprised of a main section containing descriptive listings on award programs and their administering organizations, and five indexes that aid users in identifying relevant information. Each of these sections is described in detail below.

Sponsors and Their Scholarships

SFL contains two types of descriptive listings:

- brief entries on the organizations that sponsor or administer specific award programs

- descriptive entries on the award programs themselves

Entries are arranged alphabetically by administering organization; awards administered by each organization follow that organization's listings. Entries contain detailed contact and descriptive information. Users are strongly encouraged to read the descriptions carefully and pay particular attention to the various eligibility requirements before applying for awards.

The following sample organization and award entries illustrate the kind of information that is or might be included in these entries. Each item of information is preceded by a number, and is explained in the paragraph with the same number on the following pages.

Sample Entry

❚ 1 ❚ 3445
❚ 2 ❚ Microscopy Society of America
❚ 3 ❚ 4 Barlows Landing Rd., Ste. 8 Woods Hole, MA 02543
❚ 4 ❚ *Ph:* (508) 563-1155
❚ 5 ❚ *Fax:* (508) 563-1211
❚ 6 ❚ *Free:* 800-538-3672
❚ 7 ❚ *E-mail:* businessofficemsa.microscopy.com
❚ 8 ❚ *URL:* http://www.msa.microscopy.com
❚ 9 ❚ 3446
❚ 10 ❚ MSA Presidential Student Awards
❚ 11 ❚ *(Graduate, Undergraduate/*
❚ 12 ❚ *Award*

❚ 13 ❚ Purpose: To recognize outstanding original research by students. ❚ 14 ❚ Focus: Biological Clinical Sciences—Microscopy, Physical Sciences—Microscopy. ❚ 15 ❚ Qualif.: Candidate may be of any nationality, but must be enrolled at a recognized college or university in the United States at the time of the MSA annual meeting. ❚ 16 ❚ Criteria: Selection is done based on the applicant's

career objectives, academic record, and financial need. ❚ 17 ❚ Funds Avail.: Registration and round-trip travel to the MSA annual meeting, plus a stipend to defray lodging and other expenses. ❚ 18 ❚ Duration: Annual. ❚ 19 ❚ Number awarded: 5. ❚ 20 ❚ To Apply: Write to MSA for application form and guidelines. ❚ 21 ❚ Deadline: March 15. ❚ 22 ❚ Remarks: Established in 1979. ❚ 23 ❚ Contact: Alternate phone number: 800-538-EMSA.

Descriptions of Numbered Elements

❚ 1 ❚ **Organization Entry Number.** Administering organizations are listed alphabetically. Each entry is followed by an alphabetical listing of its awards. All entries (organization and award) are numbered in a single sequence. These numbers are used as references in the indexes.

❚ 2 ❚ **Organization Name.** The name of the organization administering the awards that follow.

❚ 3 ❚ **Mailing Address.** The organization's permanent mailing address is listed when known; in some cases an award address is given.

❚ 4 ❚ **Telephone Number.** The general telephone number for the administering organization. Phone numbers pertaining to specific awards are listed under "Contact" in the award description.

❚ 5 ❚ **Fax Number.** The facsimile number for the administering organization. Fax numbers pertaining to specific awards are included under "Contact" in the award description.

❚ 6 ❚ **Toll-free Number.** The toll-free number for the administering organization. Toll-free numbers pertaining to specific awards are included under "Contact" in the award description.

❚ 7 ❚ **E-mail Address.** The electronic mail address for the administering organization. Electronic mail addresses pertaining to specific awards are included under "Contact" in the award description.

❚ 8 ❚ **URL.** The web address for the administering organization.

❚ 9 ❚ **Award Entry Number.** Awards are listed alphabetically following the entry for their administering organizations. All entries (organization and award) are numbered in a single sequence. These numbers are used as references in the indexes.

❚ 10 ❚ **Award Name.** Names of awards are always listed. Organization titles or acronyms have been added to generic award names (for example, MSA Undergraduate Scholarships, Canadian Council Fiction Writing Grant, etc.) to avoid confusion.

❚ 11 ❚ Study Level. The level of study for which the award may be used. One or more of the following terms will be listed:

- All: not restricted to a particular level.
- High School: study at the secondary level.
- Vocational: study leading to postsecondary awards, certificates, or diplomas requiring less than two years of study.
- 2 Year: study leading to a bachelor's degree within two years
- 4 Year: study leading to a bachelor's degree within four years
- Undergraduate: study immediately beyond the secondary level, including associate, colleges and universities, junior colleges, technical institutes leading to a bachelor's degree, and vocational technical schools.
- Graduate: study leading to an M.A., M.S., LL.B., LL.M., and other intermediate degrees.
- Master's: study leading specifically to a master's degree, such as a M.A., M.S., or M.B.A.
- Postgraduate: study beyond the graduate level not specifically leading to a degree.
- Doctorate: study leading to a Ph.D., Ed.D., Sc.D., M.D., D.D.S., D.O., J.D., and other terminal degrees.
- Postdoctorate: study beyond the doctorate level; includes awards intended for professional development when candidates must hold a doctoral degree to qualify.
- Professional Development: career development not necessarily restricted by study.

❚ 12 ❚ Award Type. The type or category of award. One or more of the following terms will be listed:

- Award: generally includes aid given in recognition and support of excellence, including awards given through music and arts competitions. Non-monetary awards and awards given strictly for recognition are not included.
- Fellowship: awards granted for graduate- or postgraduate-level research or education that do not require repayment.
- Grant: includes support for research, travel, and creative, experimental, or innovative projects.
- Internship: training and work experience programs. Internships that do not include compensation of some type are not included.
- Loan: aid that must be repaid either monetarily or through service. Some loans are interest-free, others are not.
- Prize: funds awarded as the result of a competition or contest. Prizes that are not intended to be used for

study or to support professional development are not included.

- Scholarships: support for formal educational programs that does not require repayment.
- Scholarship Loan: a scholarship that becomes a loan if the recipient does not comply with the terms.
- Work Study: combined study and work program for which payment is received.
- Other: anything that does not fit the other categories, such as a travel award.

❚ 13 ❚ Purpose. The purpose for which the award is granted is listed here when known.

❚ 14 ❚ Focus. The field(s) of study that the recipient must be pursuing.

❚ 15 ❚ Qualif. Information regarding applicant eligibility. Some examples of qualification requirements include the following: academic record, citizenship, financial need, organizational affiliation, minority or ethnic background, residency, and gender.

❚ 16 ❚ Criteria Information concerning selection criteria.

❚ 17 ❚ Funds Avail. The award dollar amounts are included here along with other relevant funding information, such as the time period covered by the award, a breakdown of expenses covered (e.g., stipends, tuition and fees, travel and living allowances, equipment funds, etc.), the amount awarded to the institution, loan repayment schedules, service-in-return-for-funding agreements, and other obligations.

❚ 18 ❚ Duration. Frequency of the award.

❚ 19 ❚ Number awarded. Typical number of awards distributed.

❚ 20 ❚ To Apply. Application guidelines, requirements, and other information.

❚ 21 ❚ Deadline. Application due dates, notification dates (the date when the applicant will be notified of receipt or denial of award), disbursement dates, and other relevant dates.

❚ 22 ❚ Remarks. Any additional information concerning the award.

❚ 23 ❚ Contact. When contact information differs from that given for the administering organization, relevant addresses, telephone and fax numbers, and names of specific contact persons are listed here. When the address is that of the administering organization, the entry number for the organization is provided.

Indexes

Field of Study Index classifies awards by one or more of 450 specific subject categories, allowing users to easily target their search by specific area of study. Citations are arranged alphabetically under all appropriate subject terms. Each citation is followed by the study level and award type, which appear in parentheses and can be used to narrow the search even further.

Legal Residence Index lists awards that are restricted by the applicant's residence of legal record. Award citations are arranged alphabetically by country and subarranged by region, state or province (for U.S. and Canada). Each citation is followed by the study level and award type, which appear in parentheses and can be used to eliminate inappropriate awards.

Place of Study Index lists awards that carry restrictions on where study can take place. Award citations are arranged alphabetically under the following geographic headings:

- United States
- United States—by Region
- United States—by State
- Canada
- Canada—by Province
- International
- International—by Region
- International—by Country

Each citation is followed by the study level and award type, which appear in parentheses.

Special Recipient Index lists awards that carry restrictions or special qualifying factors relating to applicant affiliation. This index allows users to quickly identify awards relating to the following categories:

- African American
- Asian American
- Association Membership
- Disabled
- Employer Affiliation
- Ethnic Group Membership
- Fraternal Organization Membership
- Hispanic American
- Military
- Minority
- Native American
- Religious Affiliation
- Union Affiliation
- Veteran

Awards are listed under all appropriate headings. Each citation includes information on study level and award type, which appear in parentheses and can be used to further narrow the search. Users interested in awards restricted to particular minorities should also look under the general Minorities heading, which lists awards targeted for minorities but not restricted to any particular minority group.

Sponsor and Scholarship Index lists, in a single alphabetic sequence, all of the administering organizations, awards, and acronyms included in *SFL*.

Federal aid for college students is available through a variety of programs administered by the U.S. Department of Education. Most colleges and universities participate in federal programs, but there are exceptions. Contact a school's financial aid office to find out if it is a participating institution. If it participates, the student works with financial aid counselors to determine how much aid can be obtained.

Aid for students comes in three forms: grants (gifts to the student), loans (which must be repaid), and work-study jobs (a job for the student while enrolled in which his/her pay is applied to his school account). These types of aid are further explained below. More information can be found at http://www.ed.gov.

Grants

Pell Grants are intended to provide funds for any undergraduate student (who does not already have a degree) who wishes to attend college regardless of family financial background. They are available through the financial aid office at the school. The maximum Pell Grant award for the 2015-2016 award year (July 1, 2015 to June 30, 2016) is $5,775.

Federal Supplemental Educational Opportunity Grants (FSEOG) are intended for students with exceptional financial need, these grants are typically for smaller amounts (between $100 and $4,000) than Pell Grants. They are available on a limited basis.

Loans

Student loans are available a variety of ways. Loans may not be taken out for more than the cost of attendance at the school, which is determined by the financial aid administrator. Grants and other forms of aid are taken into consideration when determining the amount a student will be allowed to borrow. Loan amounts may be reduced if a student receives other forms of aid. Loans are divided into two types, subsidized and unsubsidized:

Subsidized loans: the federal government pays the interest on the loan until after schooling is complete.

Unsubsidized loans: the student incurs the interest charges while in school, but payment of the charges may be deferred until schooling is complete. The advantage of unsubsidized loans is that there are usually fewer restrictions against obtaining them. Amounts available through these programs vary depending on academic level. The total debt a student or a student's parents may accumulate for that student is $31,000 for a dependent undergraduate student, $57,500 for an independent undergraduate student (with a limit of $23,000 in subsidized loans), and $138,500 for a graduate or professional student (with a limit of $65,500 in subsidized loans) or $224,000 for health professionals.

Available Funding Programs Direct Loan Program

These low-interest loans bypass lending institutions such as banks. They are a direct arrangement between the government and the student (administered by the school). There are four repayment options for the Direct Loan program: the Income Contingent Repayment Plan, the Extended Repayment Plan, the Graduated Repayment Plan, and the Standard Repayment Plan.

Direct subsidized loans may be taken out for a maximum of $3,500 by incoming freshmen, $4,500 for sophomores, and $5,500 for juniors and seniors. The amounts for independent undergraduate students range from $9,500 to $12,500 per year for direct loans. Independent students face some restrictions on the amount of subsidized funds they can receive from the program. At least half of the funds borrowed through the Direct Loan program by independent students must come from unsubsidized loans. Graduate students may borrow up to $20,500 directly in unsubsidized loans.

Direct PLUS Loans Direct PLUS loans are federal loans that graduate or professional degree students and parents of dependent undergraduate students can use to help pay education expenses. The U.S. Department of Education makes Direct PLUS loans to eligible borrowers through schools participating in the program. The Maximum amount to be borrowed is the cost of attending the shool minus other forms of aid already obtained. For 2015-2016 the fixed rate for a Direct PLUS loan is 6.84%.

With the Direct PLUS loan, students or parents fill out a Direct PLUS Loan Application, available at the school's financial aid office. The funds are disbursed to the school. Students and parents may choose from three repayment plans: Standard, Extended, or Graduated.

Perkins Loan Program The Perkins Loan program allows students who have unusual financial need to borrow funds not otherwise available from other loan or grant programs. Up to $5,500 is available to undergraduates each year (up to $8,000 for graduate students). These loans have a fixed interest rate of 5%. Perkins Loans must be repaid within ten years.

Federal Work-Study Program Work-study is an arrangement that allows students to work on campus while they are enrolled to help pay their expenses. The federal government pays the majority of the student's wages, although the department where the student works also contributes. The employment must be relevant to the student's field of study and only so much time per semester may be devoted to the job. If the student earns the amount of aid prior to the end of the semester, work is terminated for the duration of the award period.

Other Considerations

Application: Applying for federal student aid is free. All federal aid is obtained by first completing a Free Application for Federal Student Aid (FAFSA). After the application is submitted, it will be processed by the Department of Education. The student then receives a Student Aid Report (SAR), which contains a figure for Expected Family Contribution. This is the amount that the student should plan on providing from non-federal sources in order to attend school.

Dependency: If a student is eligible for independent status, more money may be available in the form of loans. The interest rates and the programs for repayment, however, are the same. Independent status provides more financial aid for students who do not have the benefit of parental financial contributions.

Deadline: FAFSA deadlines are set by federal and state agencies, as well as individual schools, and vary widely. Applicants are encouraged to apply as soon as possible after January 1 of the year they plan to enroll, but no earlier.

Special Circumstances: The financial aid counselor at the school will often listen to extenuating circumstances such as unexpected medical expenses, private education expenses for other family members, or recent unemployment when evaluating requests for assistance.

Contact Information for Federal Financial Aid Programs

Call (800)433-3243 to have questions answered or to request the *Student Guide to Financial Aid*; (319) 337-5665 to find out if your application has been processed; (800) 730-8913 (TTY) if you are hearing impaired; (800) 647-8733 to report fraud, waste, or abuse of federal student aid funds; or visit http://www.ed.gov for application forms, guidelines, and general information.

President Clinton launched this volunteer community service program in September 1993 through the *National and Community Service Trust Act*, aimed at helping college-bound young people pay for their education while serving their communities. AmeriCorps volunteers receive minimum wage, health benefits, and a grant toward college for up to two years.

Funds for the program are distributed by the federal government in the form of grants to qualifying organizations and community groups with the goal of achieving direct results in addressing the nation's critical education, human services, public safety, and environmental needs at the community level. The program provides meaningful opportunities for Americans to serve their country in organized efforts, fostering citizen responsibility, building community, and providing educational opportunities for those who make a substantial commitment to service.

The AmeriCorps programs are run by not-for-profit organizations or partnerships, institutions of higher learning, local governments, school or police districts, states, Native American tribes, and federal agencies. Examples of participating programs include Habitat for Humanity, the American Red Cross, Boys and Girls Clubs, and local community centers and places of worship. Volunteers have nearly 1,000 different groups from which to choose. The AmeriCorps Pledge: "I will get things done for America to make our people safer, smarter, and healthier. I will bring Americans together to strengthen our communities. Faced with apathy, I will take action. Faced with conflict, I will seek a common ground. Faced with adversity, I will persevere. I will carry this commitment with me this year and beyond. I am an Ameri-Corps Member and I am going to get things done."

Eligibility and Selection for Service in AmeriCorps

Citizens and legal resident aliens who are 17 years of age or older are eligible to serve in AmeriCorps before, during, or after post-secondary education. In general, participants must be high school graduates or agree to achieve their GED prior to receiving education awards. Individual programs select service participants on a nondiscriminatory and nonpolitical basis. There are national and state-wide recruiting information systems and a national pool of potential service volunteers.

Term of Service

One full-time term of service is a minimum of 1,700 hours over the course of one year or less; or a part-time term, which can range from 300 hours to 900 hours. Short-term service (such as a summer program) provides eligibility for reduced part-time status.

Compensation

You will receive a modest living allowance, health insurance, student loan deferment, and training. After you complete your term of service, you will receive an education award to help pay for your education. Serve part-time and you will receive a portion of the full amount. The amount is tied to the maximum amount of the U.S. Department of Education's Pell Grant. Prior to fiscal year 2010, the amount of an education award had remained the same since the AmeriCorps program began. In fiscal year 2016, which begins October 1, 2015, the award is $5,805 for a year of full-time service, and is pro-rated for part-time service.

How Can I Use an Award?

These awards may be used to repay qualified existing or future student loans, to pay all or part of the cost of attending a qualified institute of higher education (including some vocational programs), or to pay expenses while participating in an approved school-to-work program. Awards must be used within seven years of completion of service.

Contact

Individuals interested in participating in AmeriCorps national service programs should apply directly. For basic program information, individuals can call the AmeriCorps Information Hotline at 1-800-942-2677 or visit their Web site at http://www.nationalservice.gov/programs/americorps.

The following is an alphabetic state-by-state listing of agencies located in the United States. Many of these agencies administer special federal award programs, as well as state-specific awards, such as the Tuition Incentive Program (TIP) offered by the state of Michigan for low-income students to receive free tuition at community colleges. Financial aid seekers should contact the agency in their home state for more information.

ALABAMA

Alabama Comm. on Higher Education
100 N. Union St.
P.O. Box 302000
Montgomery, AL 36104
(334)242-1998
http://www.ache.state.al.us

ALASKA

Alaska Comm. on Postsecondary Education
P.O. Box 110505
Juneau, AK 99811-0505
(907)465-2962
http://
www.alaskadvantage.state.ak.us/

ARIZONA

Arizona Comm. for Postsecondary Education
2020 N. Central Ave.,
Ste. 650
Phoenix, AZ 85004-4503
(602)258-2435
http://highered.az.ogov

ARKANSAS

Arkansas Dept. of Higher Education
423 Main St., Ste. 400
Little Rock, AR 72201
(501)371-2000
http://www.adhe.edu

CALIFORNIA

California Student Aid Comm.
PO Box 419026
Rancho Cordova, CA 95741-9026

(888)224-7268
http://www.csac.ca.gov

COLORADO

Colorado Dept. of Higher Education
1560 Broadway, Ste. 1600
Denver, CO 80202
(303)862-3001
http://highered.colorado.gov

CONNECTICUT

Connecticut Dept. of Higher Education
61 Woodland St.
Hartford, CT 06105-2326
(860)947-1800
http://www.ctdhe.org

DELAWARE

Delaware Dept. of Higher Education Scholarship/ incentive Loan Program
The Townsend Building
401 Federal St.
Dover, DE 19901
(302)735-4000
http://www.doe.k12.de.us/Page/316

DISTRICT OF COLUMBIA

District of Columbia Office of the State Superintendent of Education
810 1st St., NE, 9th Fl.
Washington, DC 20002
(202)727-6436
http://osse.dc.gov

FLORIDA

Office of Student Financial Assistance
Dept. of Education
325 W. Gaines St.

Turlington Bldg., Ste. 1514
Tallahassee, FL 32399-0400
(800)336-3475
http://
www.floridastudentfinancialaid.org

GEORGIA

Georgia Student Finance Comm.
2082 E. Exchange Pl.
Tucker, GA 30084
(770)724-9000
http://www.gsfc.org/gsfcnew/index.cfm

HAWAII

Hawaii Board of Regents
2444 Dole St., Bachman 207
Honolulu, HI 96822-2302
(808)956-8753
http://www.hawaii.edu/offices/bor/

IDAHO

Idaho State Board of Education
PO Box 83720
Boise, ID 83720-0037
(208)334-2270
http://www.boardofed.idaho.gov

ILLINOIS

Illinois Student Assistance Comm.
1755 Lake Cook Rd.
Deerfield, IL 60015-5209
(800)899-4722
http://www.isac.org

INDIANA

Indiana Comm. for Higher Education
101 W. Ohio St., Ste. 550
Indianapolis, IN 46204-1984

(888)528-4719
http://www.in.gov/che

IOWA

Iowa College Student Aid Comm.
430 E. Grand Ave., Fl. 3
Des Moines, IA 50309-1920
(877)272-4456
http://www.iowacollegeaid.gov

KANSAS

Kansas Board of Regents
1000 SW Jackson St., Ste. 520
Topeka, KS 66612-1368
(785)296-3421
http://www.kansasregents.org

KENTUCKY

Kentucky Higher Education Assistance Authority
100 Airport Rd.
Frankfort, KY 40602-0798
(800)928-8926
http://www.kheaa.com

LOUISIANA

Louisiana Office of Student Financial Assistance
602 N. Fifth St.
Baton Rouge, LA 70802
(225)219-1012
http://www.osfa.state.la.us

MAINE

Finance Authority of Maine (FAME)
5 Community Dr.
P.O. Box 0949
Augusta, ME 04332-0949
(207)623-3263
http://www.famemaine.com

MARYLAND

Maryland Higher Education Comm.
6 N. Liberty St.
Baltimore, MD 21201
(410)767-3301
http://www.mhec.state.md.us

MASSACHUSETTS

Massachusetts Dept. of Higher Education
One Ashburton Pl., Rm. 1401
Boston, MA 02108-1696

(617)994-6950
http://www.mass.edu

MICHIGAN

Michigan Higher Education Student Loan Authority
Student Scholarships and Grants
P.O. Box 30462
Lansing, MI 48909-7962
(888)447-2687
http://www.michigan.gov/mistudentaid

MINNESOTA

Minnesota Office of Higher Education
1450 Energy Park Dr., Ste. 350
St. Paul, MN 55108-5227
(651)642-0567
http://www.ohe.state.mn.us/index.cfm

MISSISSIPPI

Mississippi Institutions of Higher Learning
3825 Ridgewood Rd.
Jackson, MS 39211
(601)432-6198
http://www.ihl.state.ms.us

MISSOURI

Missouri Dept. of Higher Education
205 Jefferson St.
P.O.Box 1469
Jefferson City, MO 65102-1469
(573)751-2361
http://www.dhe.mo.gov/

MONTANA

Montana Board of Regents
Office of Commissioner of Higher Education
Montana University System
2500 Broadway St.
PO Box 203201
Helena, MT 59620-3201
(406)444-6570
http://www.mus.edu

NEBRASKA

Nebraska Coordinating Comm. for Postsecondary Education
P.O. Box 95005
Lincoln, NE 68509-5005
(402)471-2847

http://www.ccpe.state.ne.us/
PublicDoc/CCPE/Default.asp

NEVADA

Nevada Department of Education
700 E. Fifth St.
Carson City, NV 89701
(775)687-9200
http://www.doe.nv.gov

(Southern Office)
9890 S. Maryland Pkwy., 2nd Fl.
Las Vegas, NV 89183
(702)486-6458

NEW HAMPSHIRE

New Hampshire Higher Education Comm.
101 Pleasant St.
Concord, NH 03301-3494
(603)271-3494
http://www.state.nh.us/postsecondary

NEW JERSEY

Higher Education Student Assistance Authority
P.O. Box 545
Trenton, NJ 08625-0545
(800)792-8670
http://www.hesaa.org

NEW MEXICO

New Mexico Higher Education Dept.
2048 Galisteo St.
Santa Fe, NM 87505-2100
(505)476-8400
http://www.hed.state.nm.us

NEW YORK

New York State Higher Education Svcs. Corp.
99 Washington Ave.
Albany, NY 12255
(888)697-4372
http://www.hesc.ny.gov

NORTH CAROLINA

North Carolina State Education Assistance Authority
PO Box 14103
Research Triangle Park, NC 27709

(919)549-8614
http://www.ncseaa.edu

NORTH DAKOTA

North Dakota University System

North Dakota Student Financial Assistance Program
10th Fl., State Capitol
600 E. Boulevard Ave., Dept. 215
Bismarck, ND 58505-0230
(701)328-2960
http://www.ndus.edu

OHIO

Ohio Department of Higher Education

25 S. Front St.
Columbus, OH 43215
(614)466-6000
http://www.ohiohighered.org

OKLAHOMA

Oklahoma State Regents for Higher Education

Oklahoma Guaranteed Loan Program
655 Research Pkwy.
Suite 200
Oklahoma City, OK 73104
(405)225-9100
http://www.okhighered.org

OREGON

Oregon Student Access Comm.

1500 Valley River Dr., Ste. 100
Eugene, OR 97401
(541)687-7400
http://www.osac.state.or.us

PENNSYLVANIA

Pennsylvania Higher Education Assistance Agency

1200 N. 7th St.
Harrisburg, PA 17102-1444
(800)233-0557
http://www.pheaa.org

RHODE ISLAND

Rhode Island Higher Education Assistance Authority

560 Jefferson Blvd., Ste. 100
Warwick, RI 02886-1304

(401)736-1100
http://www.riheaa.org

SOUTH CAROLINA

South Carolina Comm. on Higher Education

1122 Lady St., Ste. 300
Columbia, SC 29201
(803)737-2260
http://www.che.sc.gov/

SOUTH DAKOTA

South Dakota Board of Regents

306 E. Capitol Ave., Ste. 200
Pierre, SD 57501
(605)773-3455
http://www.sdbor.edu/

TENNESSEE

Tennessee Higher Education Comm.

Parkway Towers
404 James Robertson Pkwy., Ste. 1900
Nashville, TN 37243-0830
(615)741-3605
https://www.state.tn.us/thec

TEXAS

Texas Higher Education Coordinating Board

P.O. Box 12788
Austin, TX 78711-2788
(512)427-6101
http://www.thecb.state.tx.us

UTAH

Utah State Board of Regents

Board of Regents Building, The Gateway
60 South 400 West
Salt Lake City, UT 84101-1284
(801)321-7101
http://higeredutah.org

VERMONT

Vermont Student Assistance Corp.

10 E. Allen St.
P.O. Box 2000

Winooski, VT 05404
(800)642-3177
http://www.services.vsac.org/wps
/wcm/connect/vsac/VSAC

VIRGINIA

State Council of Higher Education for Virginia

James Monroe Bldg.
101 N. 14th St., 10th Fl.
Richmond, VA 23219
(804)225-2600
http://www.schev.edu

WASHINGTON

Washington Student Achievement Council

917 Lakeridge Way
Olympia, WA 98502
(360)753-7800
http://www.hecb.wa.gov

WEST VIRGINIA

West Virginia Higher Education Policy Comm.

1018 Kanawha Blvd., E., Ste. 700
Charleston, WV 25301
(304)558-2101
http://www.hepc.wvnet.edu

WISCONSIN

Wisconsin Higher Education Aids Board

131 W. Wilson St., Ste. 902
P.O. Box 7885
Madison, WI 53707-7885
(608)267-2206
http://heab.state.wi.us

WYOMING

Wyoming Community College Comm.

2300 Capitol Ave., 5th Fl., Ste. B
Cheyenne, WY 82002
(307)777-7763
http://www.communitycolleges.wy.edu

U.S. State Abbreviations

AK	Alaska
AL	Alabama
AR	Arkansas
AZ	Arizona
CA	California
CO	Colorado
CT	Connecticut
DC	District of Columbia
DE	Delaware
FL	Florida
GA	Georgia
GU	Guam
HI	Hawaii
IA	Iowa
ID	Idaho
IL	Illinois
IN	Indiana
KS	Kansas
KY	Kentucky
LA	Louisiana
MA	Massachusetts
MD	Maryland
ME	Maine
MI	Michigan
MN	Minnesota
MO	Missouri
MS	Mississippi
MT	Montana
NC	North Carolina
ND	North Dakota
NE	Nebraska
NH	New Hampshire
NJ	New Jersey
NM	New Mexico
NV	Nevada
NY	New York
OH	Ohio
OK	Oklahoma
OR	Oregon
PA	Pennsylvania
PR	Puerto Rico
RI	Rhode Island
SC	South Carolina
SD	South Dakota
TN	Tennessee
TX	Texas
UT	Utah
VA	Virginia
VI	Virgin Islands
VT	Vermont
WA	Washington
WI	Wisconsin
WV	West Virginia
WY	Wyoming

Canadian Province Abbreviations

AB	Alberta
BC	British Columbia
MB	Manitoba
NB	New Brunswick
NL	Newfoundland and Labrador
NS	Nova Scotia
NT	Northwest Territories
ON	Ontario
PE	Prince Edward Island
QC	Quebec
SK	Saskatchewan
YT	Yukon Territory

Other Abbreviations

ACT	American College Testing Program
B.A.	Bachelor of Arts
B.Arch.	Bachelor of Architecture
B.F.A.	Bachelor of Fine Arts
B.S.	Bachelor of Science
B.Sc.	Bachelor of Science
CSS	College Scholarship Service
D.D.S.	Doctor of Dental Science/Surgery
D.O.	Doctor of Osteopathy
D.Sc.	Doctor of Science
D.S.W.	Doctor of Social Work
D.V.M.	Doctor of Veterinary Medicine
D.V.M.S.	Doctor of Veterinary Medicine and Surgery
D.V.S.	Doctor of Veterinary Science
FAFSA	Free Application for Federal Student Aid
FWS	Federal Work Study
GED	General Education Development Certificate
GPA	Grade Point Average
GRE	Graduate Record Examination
J.D.	Doctor of Jurisprudence
LL.B.	Bachelor of Law
LL.M.	Master of Law
LSAT	Law School Admission Test
M.A.	Master of Arts
M.Arch.	Master of Architecture
M.B.A.	Master of Business Administration
M.D.	Doctor of Medicine
M.Div.	Master of Divinity
M.F.A.	Master of Fine Arts
MIA	Missing in Action
M.L.S.	Master of Library Science
M.N.	Master of Nursing
M.S.	Master of Science
M.S.W.	Master of Social Work
O.D.	Doctor of Optometry
Pharm.D.	Doctor of Pharmacy
Ph.D.	Doctor of Philosophy
POW	Prisoner of War
PSAT	Preliminary Scholastic Aptitude Test
ROTC	Reserve Officers Training Corps
SAR	Student Aid Report
SAT	Scholastic Aptitude Test
Sc.D.	Doctor of Science
TDD	Telephone Device for the Deaf
Th.d.	Doctor of Theology
U.N.	United Nations
U.S.	United States

4795 ■ Ice Skating Institute (ISI)
6000 Custer Rd., Bldg. 9
Plano, TX 75023
Ph: (972)735-8800
Fax: (972)735-8815
URL: www.skateisi.com/site

4796 ■ Ice Skating Institute of America Education Foundation Scholarships *(Undergraduate/ Scholarship)*

Purpose: To promote the intellectual growth of ISI member skaters. **Focus:** General studies/Field of study not specified. **Qualif.:** Applicants must have completed at least three years of high school or equivalent, with a minimum 3.0 grade point average (based on a 4.0 system) during the last two years; must be a current individual or professional member of the Ice Skating Institute and have been for a minimum of four years; must have participated in the ISI Recreational Skater Program at an ISI Administrative member (rink or club) program for a minimum of four years; must have participated in ISI group classes or ISI Endorsed Competitions within the last two years. Must have completed 120 hours of volunteer service, of which at least 60 hours must be in association with an ISI member facility; must enroll and carry the minimum number of credit hours necessary to be a full time undergraduate student. Teachers or instructors must be a current Professional Member of the Ice Skating Institute, teaching the ISI program at an ISI Administrative Member (rink or club). Instructor status must be verified by the ISI Administrative Member. **Criteria:** Final selection will be made by the Trustees of the ISIA Education Foundation.

Funds Avail.: $4,000. **Duration:** Entire length of undergraduate study. **Number Awarded:** Varies. **To Apply:** Applicants must submit completed application form, two evaluation forms (one from the supervisor at the site where a majority of the volunteer service took place and the second from an adult not associated with ice skating and not a relative of the applicant) and a statement of 500 words or less, typed or printed explaining "Why I should receive an ISIA Education Foundation Scholarship." **Deadline:** March 1.

4797 ■ Idaho Association of Legal Secretaries (IDALS)
c/o Sheila D. Rhodes
PO Box 698
Lewiston, ID 83501
URL: idals.org

4798 ■ Monna Mawson Scholarships
(Undergraduate/Scholarship)

Purpose: To award scholarship to an individual entering the legal field. **Focus:** Law; Paralegal studies. **Qualif.:** Applicant's course of study must be paralegal, legal secretary/ assistant, law or pre-law; must be Idaho resident; must be attending Idaho school. **Criteria:** Award will be based in GPA, goals and need.

Funds Avail.: No specific amount. **Number Awarded:** 1. **To Apply:** Applicant must submit a completed application and must attach the following: two letters of recommendation, at least one should be from an educator, the second may be from a business or personal friend; and a copy of applicant's transcript of grades. **Deadline:** March 30. **Contact:** Sheila Rhodes at 208-746-3646, ara@aralawoffice.com.

4799 ■ Idaho Chapter of the American Fisheries Society (ICAFS)
c/o Jim Chandler, President
1221 W Idaho St.
Boise, ID 83702
Ph: (208)388-2974
URL: www.idahoafs.org

4800 ■ Ted Bjornn University of Idaho Graduate Student Scholarships *(Graduate/Scholarship)*

Purpose: To promote the conservation, development and wise use of the fisheries. **Focus:** Fisheries sciences/ management. **Qualif.:** Applicants must be graduate students working towards a degree in fisheries or aquatic sciences at the University of Idaho. **Criteria:** Selection will be made on the basis of academic promise and potential contribution to the profession.

Funds Avail.: $500. **Duration:** Annual. **Number Awarded:** 1. **To Apply:** Applicants must submit a one to two page curriculum vitae or resume, listing experience and pertinent education up to this point; a written statement of how the applicant sees himself/herself working and contributing in the profession to advance the goals of the American Fisheries Society; a written statement of why the applicant wants the scholarship; and a letter of support from a faculty advisor which includes current academic standing in a degree program.

4801 ■ Ted Bjornn University of Idaho Undergraduate Student Scholarships *(Undergraduate/ Scholarship)*

Purpose: To promote the conservation, development and wise use of the fisheries. **Focus:** Fisheries sciences/

Awards are arranged alphabetically below their administering organizations

management. **Qualif.:** Applicants must be undergraduate students working towards a degree in fisheries or aquatic sciences at the University of Idaho. **Criteria:** Selection will be made on the basis of academic promise and potential contribution to the profession.

Funds Avail.: $500. **Duration:** Annual. **Number Awarded:** 1. **To Apply:** Applicants must submit a one to two page curriculum vitae or resume, listing experience and pertinent education up to this point; a written statement of how the applicant sees himself/herself working and contributing in the profession to advance the goals of the American Fisheries Society; a written statement of why the applicant want the scholarship; and a letter of support from a faculty advisor which includes current academic standing in a degree program.

4802 ■ ICAFS Idaho Graduate Student Scholarships
(Graduate/Scholarship)

Purpose: To assist with college education costs of graduate students whose professional goals support the mission and objectives of the society. **Focus:** Fisheries sciences/management. **Qualif.:** Applicant must be a graduate student at any Idaho college/university during the next academic year, and must have a career goal that advances the mission and objectives of the American Fisheries Society. **Criteria:** Selection is based on academic record; career goals; experiences that enhance the student as a professional; and letter of recommendation from a biology professor, faculty advisor, or administrator.

Funds Avail.: $1,000. **Duration:** Annual; One year. **Number Awarded:** 1. **To Apply:** Applicants must submit a completed application form and resume; a statement of career goals (300 words or less); a letter of recommendation from a biology professor, faculty advisor, or administrator; and a copy of college transcript(s). **Deadline:** January 31. **Remarks:** Established in 2005. **Contact:** Lauri Monnot at 208-373-0461 or lauri.monnot@deq.idaho.gov.

4803 ■ ICAFS Idaho High School Student Scholarships *(Undergraduate/Scholarship)*

Purpose: To assist with college education costs of high school students whose professional goals support the mission and objectives of the Society. **Focus:** Fisheries sciences/management. **Qualif.:** Applicant must be a senior enrolled in an Idaho high school; have a GPA of at least 3.0; planning to attend a college/university located in Idaho; and have career goals that advance the mission and objectives of the American Fisheries Society. **Criteria:** Selection is based on career goals; course work; GPA; and letter of recommendation from a biology or science teacher

Funds Avail.: $500. **Duration:** Annual; One year. **Number Awarded:** 1. **To Apply:** Applicants must submit a completed application form; a statement of career goals (300 words or less); a letter of recommendation from a biology or science teacher; and a copy of high school transcript(s). **Deadline:** January 31. **Remarks:** Established in 2005. **Contact:** Lauri Monnot at 208-373-0461, or lauri.monnot@deq.idaho.gov.

4804 ■ ICAFS Idaho Undergraduate Student Scholarships *(Undergraduate/Scholarship)*

Purpose: To assist with college education costs of graduate students whose professional goals support the mission and objectives of the society. **Focus:** Fisheries sciences/management. **Qualif.:** Applicant must be an undergraduate student enrolled at any Idaho college/university the next academic year; have a GPA of at least 3.0; and have career

goals that advance the mission and objectives of the American Fisheries Society. **Criteria:** Selection is based on academic record; career goals; GPA; letter of recommendation from a biology professor, faculty advisor, administrator or employer; and relevant experiences that enhance the student as a professional.

Funds Avail.: $1,000. **Duration:** Annual; One year. **Number Awarded:** 1. **To Apply:** Applicants must submit a completed application form and resume; a statement of your career goals (300 words or less); a letter of recommendation from a biology professor, faculty advisor, or administrator; and a copy of college transcript(s). **Deadline:** January 31. **Remarks:** Established in 2005. **Contact:** Lauri Monnot at 208-373-0461 or lauri.monnot@deq.idaho.gov.

4805 ■ Susan B. Martin Memorial Scholarships
(Graduate/Scholarship)

Purpose: To assist with college education costs of graduate students whose professional goals support the mission and objectives of the society. **Focus:** Fisheries sciences/management. **Qualif.:** Applicant must be a graduate student at any Idaho college/university during the next academic year, and must have a career goal that advances the mission and objectives of the American Fisheries Society. **Criteria:** Selection is based on academic record; career goals; experiences that enhance the student as a professional; letter of recommendation from a biology professor, faculty advisor, or administrator; and demonstrated examples of mentoring and inspiring the growth and development of aquatic scientists.

Funds Avail.: $2,000. **Duration:** Annual. **To Apply:** Applicants must submit a completed application form and resume; a statement of career goals (300 words or less); a letter of recommendation from a biology professor, faculty advisor, or administrator; and a copy of college transcript(s). **Deadline:** January 31. **Remarks:** Established in 2008. **Contact:** Lauri Monnot at 208-373-0461 or lauri.monnot@deq.idaho.gov.

4806 ■ Idaho Community Foundation (ICF)
210 W State St.
Boise, ID 83702-6052
Ph: (208)342-3535
Fax: (208)342-3577
Free: 800-657-5357
E-mail: info@idcomfdn.org
URL: www.idcomfdn.org

4807 ■ Mike Crapo Math and Science Scholarship Fund *(Undergraduate/Scholarship)*

Purpose: To assist Idaho students who are interested in pursuing math and science degrees at Idaho college and universities. **Focus:** Mathematics and mathematical sciences. **Qualif.:** Applicants must be students, pursuing math and science degrees at Idaho colleges and universities, that are residents of Idaho and enrolled as a full-time student at the freshman level at a public or private four-year college or university in the state of Idaho. They must also have a cumulative GPA of 3.0 or above for all class work prior to the application. **Criteria:** Recipients are selected based on financial need and academic performance.

Funds Avail.: No specific amount. **Duration:** Annual. **To Apply:** Applicants must submit a "300-word or less" original essay discussing the value of math and science to an

Awards are arranged alphabetically below their administering organizations

individual and society as a whole; most recent certified transcript from high school and higher education institution; two letters of reference from teacher/professor of math or science and from two members of the community who are not relatives and ACT/SAT Assessment Report. **Deadline:** April 1. **Contact:** Elly Davis, Idaho Community Foundation, 210 W. State Street, Boise, Idaho 83702; Phone: 208-342-3535; E-mail: edavis@idcomfdn.org.

4808 ■ Alois and Marie Goldmann Scholarship Fund (Undergraduate/Scholarship)

Purpose: To promote greater understanding of the Holocaust among high school students in Idaho. **Focus:** General studies/Field of study not specified. **Qualif.:** Applicants must be senior students in an accredited high school or home school in Idaho; must have plans to attend an accredited Idaho Institution of higher learning during the academic year. **Criteria:** Recipients are selected based on originality of an essay or research paper.

Funds Avail.: Approximately $1,000. **Duration:** Annual. **To Apply:** Applicants must submit a formal research paper, bibliography and references. Completed application must be submitted to: Goldmann Scholarship Committee. **Deadline:** March 15. **Remarks:** Established in 1997. **Contact:** Elly Davis, Idaho Community Foundation, 210 W. State Street, Boise, Idaho 83702; Phone: 208-342-3535; E-mail: edavis@idcomfdn.org.

4809 ■ Idaho Nursing and Health Professions Scholarships (Undergraduate/Scholarship)

Purpose: To assist recipients with educational expenses at any Idaho accredited nursing program. **Focus:** Nursing. **Qualif.:** Applicant must be a student that has been accepted by an accredited Idaho nursing or health professions program, including but not limited to respiratory therapy, physical therapy, and others. **Criteria:** Preference will be given to a student in the top third of the academic ranking of the class.

Funds Avail.: No specific amount. **Duration:** Annual. **To Apply:** Applicants must send three copies of signed and completed application form. **Deadline:** April 1. **Contact:** Elly Davis, Idaho Community Foundation, 210 W. State Street, Boise, Idaho 83702; Phone: 208-342-3535; E-mail: edavis@idcomfdn.org.

4810 ■ Idaho Society of CPA's Scholarships (Undergraduate/Scholarship)

Purpose: To attract the best and brightest students to the profession pursuing an accounting degree at an Idaho school. **Focus:** Accounting. **Qualif.:** Applicants must be residents of Idaho that are enrolled as full-time students at the junior or senior level of public or private college or university in the state of Idaho majoring in accounting, and have a cumulative GPA of 2.75 or above for all class work prior to the application. **Criteria:** Recipients are selected based on GPA or academic standing, individual achievement as evidenced through participation in outside and activities, leadership roles, work experience and sincere desire for further education or training.

Funds Avail.: Amount varies. **Duration:** Annual. **Number Awarded:** Varies. **To Apply:** Applicants must submit a completed application form along with most recent college/university transcript and copy of most recent grades (if not reflected on transcript). **Deadline:** April 10. **Remarks:** Established in 2003. **Contact:** Idaho Community Foundation, at the above address.

4811 ■ Jim Poore Memorial Scholarships (Undergraduate/Scholarship)

Purpose: To encourage and promote the attainment of higher education goals for students who have demonstrated an aptitude for and an interest in writing. **Focus:** Writing. **Qualif.:** Applicants must be graduating seniors from public or private school of Ada, Adams, Boise, Canyon, Elmore, Gem, Payette, Valley, Washington or a high school serving the Marsing, Homedale, Bruneau or Riggins communities. They must also be residents of Idaho, and have a minimum of 2.5 GPA. **Criteria:** Recipients are selected based on general school record, community activities, writing sample and an oral interview in Boise by Committee Members.

Funds Avail.: $1,000. **Duration:** Annual. **To Apply:** Applicants must submit a completed application along with creative writing sample, recent certified grade transcript and community activities verification. **Deadline:** April 1. **Contact:** Elly Davis, Idaho Community Foundation, 210 W. State Street, Boise, Idaho 83702; Phone: 208-342-3535; E-mail: edavis@idcomfdn.org.

4812 ■ Roger C. Sathre Memorial Scholarship Fund (Undergraduate/Scholarship)

Purpose: To recognize and encourage outstanding Idaho students pursuing first certificates or degree in professional-technical education or professional-technical teacher education at Idaho Schools. **Focus:** General studies/Field of study not specified. **Qualif.:** Applicants must be residents of Idaho; must have graduated from an accredited public or private high school in Idaho or equivalent; must have maintained a cumulative GPA of 2.5 or better during the previous two years of school at an accredited high school or post-secondary school; must be enrolled as full-time students as defined by the school in a professional-technical or professional-technical teacher education program at an accredited college or university in Idaho; must be pursuing an undergraduate course of consecutive attendance and leading to a first degree, technical certificate or other approved award. **Criteria:** Recipients are selected based on financial need.

Funds Avail.: Amount varies. **Duration:** Annual. **To Apply:** Applicants must submit a completed application form; must write an essay identifying the reasons for wanting to pursue the chosen field; must obtain two letters of recommendation, report documenting financial need and portfolio of academic and technical achievement; official transcript and attendance reports from previous two years of school. **Deadline:** April 1. **Contact:** Elly Davis, Idaho Community Foundation, 210 W. State Street, Boise, Idaho 83702; Phone: 208-342-3535; E-mail: edavis@idcomfdn.org.

4813 ■ W.L. Shattuck Scholarships (Undergraduate/Scholarship)

Purpose: To further the education of students at an accredited college, university or technical college. **Focus:** General studies/Field of study not specified. **Qualif.:** Applicants must be high school graduate students of Idaho Falls School District 91 or 93 who are not younger than 16 years of age or older than 26, and accepted and enrolled at an accredited higher education or technical education program. **Criteria:** Recipients are selected based on financial need.

Funds Avail.: No specific amount. **Duration:** Annual. **To Apply:** Applicants must submit a completed application form; an official high school transcript; two letters of recommendation; resume and short statement of educational goals; must also submit the names and addresses of higher

Awards are arranged alphabetically below their administering organizations

education or technical education programs to be attended and three copies of an original completed application form. **Deadline:** April 1. **Contact:** Elly Davis, Idaho Community Foundation, 210 W. State Street, Boise, Idaho 83702; Phone: 208-342-3535; E-mail: edavis@idcomfdn.org.

4814 ■ Idaho Nursery and Landscape Association (INLA)

c/o Ann Bates, Executive Director
PO Box 2065
Idaho Falls, ID 83403
Ph: (208)681-4769
Fax: (208)529-0832
URL: www.inlagrow.org

4815 ■ Idaho Nursery and Landscape Association Scholarships *(Undergraduate/Scholarship)*

Purpose: To encourage the study of Horticulture, Floriculture, Plant Pathology, Landscape Design, Turfgrass Management, Botany and allied subjects that pertain to the Green Industry. **Focus:** Horticulture. **Qualif.:** Applicants must be Idaho residents and students in an accredited two or four-year program in the State of Idaho pursuing studies in the Green Industry. **Criteria:** Recipients are selected based on scholastic record, students' ability and sincerity in pursuing employment in the Green Industry.

Funds Avail.: $750. **Duration:** Annual. **Number Awarded:** 2. **To Apply:** Applicants must submit "one-page, typed" essay stating their reasons for interest in this particular field of endeavor, future plans and goals; must submit a letter of recommendation from someone in the community who will evaluate citizenship; must submit school transcript and letter of recommendation from a professor in the applicant's major field of study. **Deadline:** November 1. **Contact:** Ann Bates, Executive Director, at the above address.

4816 ■ Idaho State Board of Education

650 W State St., 3rd Fl.
Boise, ID 83702
Ph: (208)334-2270
Fax: (208)334-2632
E-mail: board@osbe.idaho.gov
URL: www.boardofed.idaho.gov/index.asp

4817 ■ Tschudy Family Scholarships *(Undergraduate/Scholarship)*

Purpose: To encourage educational pursuits among less capable students by providing educational assistance. **Focus:** General studies/Field of study not specified. **Qualif.:** Applicants must be residents of Idaho; must be graduating Emmett High School seniors or have graduated within the last seven years from Emmett High School; and must be full-time academic students (at least 14 credit hours) at BSU, ISU, LCSC or UI. **Criteria:** Selection is based on academic merit and financial need.

Funds Avail.: $2,500. **Duration:** Annual. **To Apply:** Applicants must accomplish a general application available at the website. **Deadline:** February 15.

4818 ■ Idaho State Broadcasters Association (ISBA)

1674 W Hill Rd., Ste. 3
Boise, ID 83702-4741

Ph: (208)345-3072
Fax: (208)343-8046
E-mail: isba@qwestoffice.net
URL: bestinbroadcasting.com/i5ba2/

4819 ■ ISBA General Scholarships *(Undergraduate/Scholarship)*

Purpose: To further the interests of broadcasters in Idaho. **Focus:** Broadcasting. **Qualif.:** Applicants must be enrolled in an Idaho college or university as a full-time student; must have exhibited superior potential in studies or activities relative to broadcasting; must be recognized and respected by his/her peer group; must have a GPA of 2.0 in the first two years of school and a GPA of 2.5 in the last two years of school. **Criteria:** Selection will be based on the committee's criteria.

Funds Avail.: $1,000. **Duration:** Annual. **Number Awarded:** 2. **To Apply:** Applicants must submit a completed application form, letter of recommendation from the GM of an ISBA member station, transcripts and an essay (one page is sufficient) explaining the applicant's reasons for applying for the scholarship as well as career plans. **Deadline:** March 15.

4820 ■ Illinois Association of Chamber of Commerce Executives (IACCE)

PO Box 9436
Springfield, IL 62791-9436
Ph: (217)585-2995
URL: www.iacce.org

4821 ■ Illinois Association of Chamber of Commerce Executives Scholarships *(Professional development/Scholarship)*

Purpose: To provide trainings that will help the members to continue their education. **Focus:** General studies/Field of study not specified. **Qualif.:** Applicants must be students enrolled in a Master's degree program. Scholarship will be available only to Chamber professionals that have been employed in the industry for one year or more. **Criteria:** Recipients are selected based on rating scale which include the thoroughness of comments, information, verification and explanation, presentation of materials and financial need.

Funds Avail.: Up to $5,000. **Duration:** Annual. **To Apply:** Applicants must complete the application form; resume of professional and education experiences; and letter of reference from Chamber's current board president or executives.

4822 ■ Illinois Business Education Association (IBEA)

8536 E Jackson St. Rd.
Du Quoin, IL 62832-3802
Ph: (618)542-5528
Fax: (618)542-5528
E-mail: president@ibea.org
URL: www.ibea.org

4823 ■ IBEA Graduate Scholarships *(Graduate/Scholarship)*

Purpose: To provide financial assistance to qualified students enrolled in an Illinois teacher education program.

Awards are arranged alphabetically below their administering organizations

Focus: Business. **Qualif.:** Applicants must be IBEA members who are enrolled in an Illinois college or university business teacher education program or related business area with an emphasis in business education at the graduate level; must have completed at least two graduate courses in his/her program; must be Illinois residents who plan to teach in the field of business education. **Criteria:** Recipients are selected based on academic performance and financial need.

Funds Avail.: $2,500. **Duration:** Annual. **To Apply:** Applicants must complete the application form available online; must provide an essay stating the reasons for choosing business education as a career; must have officially sealed high school, community college, and/or university transcripts; must have two letters of recommendation and proof of enrollment. **Deadline:** May 15.

4824 ■ IBEA Undergraduate Scholarships
(Undergraduate/Scholarship)

Purpose: To provide financial assistance to qualified students enrolled in an Illinois teacher education program. **Focus:** Business; Computer and information sciences; Education; Marketing and distribution. **Qualif.:** Applicants must be community college or university students; must be enrolled in an Illinois teacher education program with an emphasis in business education leading to certification in business, marketing, and/or computer education; must be sponsored by an IBEA member and must be enrolled in undergraduate classes during the fall semester following the application. **Criteria:** Recipients are selected based on academic performance and financial need.

Funds Avail.: $5,000. **To Apply:** Applicants must complete the application form available online; must provide an essay stating the reasons for choosing business education as a career; must have officially sealed high school, community college, and/or university transcripts; must have at least 30 semester hours or equivalent of community college or university credit; must have two letters of recommendation. **Deadline:** May 15.

4825 ■ Illinois City County Management Association (ILCMA)
Center for Governmental Studies
Northern Illinois University
148 N 3rd St.
DeKalb, IL 60115
Ph: (815)753-5424
Fax: (815)753-7278
URL: www.ilcma.org

4826 ■ James M. Banovetz Illinois Local Government Fellowships *(Graduate, Master's/Fellowship)*

Purpose: To finance studies leading to a Master's in Public Administration (MPA) or equivalent degree. **Focus:** Public administration. **Qualif.:** Applicants must be graduate students, in good academic standing, at an institution of higher learning in Illinois who are accepted into a degree program that is designed to prepare them to enter the field of city/county management, and have completed at least nine hours of coursework, not including internship or capstone hours, necessary to complete their degree. **Criteria:** Applicants will be selected on the basis of their commitment to serve the public through a career in either municipal or county management.

Funds Avail.: $2,000. **To Apply:** Applicants should submit

the complete fellowship application consists of: completed application form; a sealed letter of recommendation from their graduate dean or program director; a sealed recommendation letter from their supervisor; and transcripts of grades from their undergraduate and graduate institutions (photocopies are acceptable). **Deadline:** April 15. **Contact:** Dawn Peters at ILCMA, at the above address.

4827 ■ Illinois Lake Management Association (ILMA)
PO Box 20655
Springfield, IL 62708
Fax: (815)653-5097
Free: 800-338-6976
E-mail: ilma@ilma-lakes.org
URL: www.ilma-lakes.org

4828 ■ Robert Esser Student Achievement Scholarships *(Graduate, Undergraduate/Fellowship, Scholarship)*

Purpose: To financially assist students who want to pursue their studies in lake management and watershed ecosystem. **Focus:** Water resources. **Qualif.:** Applicants must be Illinois residents; must be attending an Illinois accredited college or university; must be full time junior or senior undergraduate students or graduate students; must be enrolled in a lake-related curriculum with clearly articulated personal goals and objectives geared toward Illinois lakes. **Criteria:** Applicants will be selected based on the primary selection criteria: (1) academic achievements; (2) major field of study; (3) statement of career goals and student special interest.

Funds Avail.: $500. **To Apply:** Applicants must complete the application form available in the website; must attach 2 letter of recommendation; must provide official transcripts; must include a project description, budget, and description of how the scholarship money will be spent. **Deadline:** December 31. **Contact:** Illinois Lake Management Association at the above address.

4829 ■ Illinois Lake Management Association Undergraduate/Graduate Scholarships *(Graduate, Undergraduate/Fellowship, Scholarship)*

Purpose: To financially assist students who want to pursue their studies in lake management and watershed ecosystem. **Focus:** Water resources. **Qualif.:** Applicants must be full time undergraduate or graduate students; must have a cumulative GPA of at least 2.5 on an undergraduate 4.0 scale and 3.0 on a graduate 4.0 scale; must be enrolled in a natural resource discipline related to lake and/or lake watershed management; must be Illinois residents enrolled in accredited colleges and universities in Indiana, Michigan, Minnesota, Ohio, Wisconsin and/or students enrolled in an accredited Illinois college or university. **Criteria:** Applicants will be selected based on the primary selection criteria: (1) academic achievements; (2) major field of study; (3) statement of career goals and student special interest.

Funds Avail.: $1,000. **To Apply:** Applicants must complete the application form available on the website; must attach 2 letter of recommendation; must provide official transcripts; must include a project description, budget, and description of how the scholarship money will be spent. **Deadline:** December 31. **Contact:** Illinois Lake Management Association at the above address.

Awards are arranged alphabetically below their administering organizations

4830 ■ Illinois Landscape Contractors Association (ILCA)

2625 Butterfield Rd., Ste. 104S
Oak Brook, IL 60523-1234
Ph: (630)472-2851
Fax: (630)472-3150
E-mail: information@ilca.net
URL: www.ilca.net

4831 ■ Illinois Landscape Contractors Association Scholarships (Undergraduate/Scholarship)

Purpose: To support the education of students pursuing a career in horticulture. **Focus:** Horticulture. **Qualif.:** Applicants must be either: residents of Illinois and enrolled full-time in an accredited two or four-year college horticultural program, with course work toward a degree in a horticultural program; or, residents of Illinois and enrolled part-time in an accredited two- or four-year college horticultural program, and attending a school located in Illinois, Wisconsin, Michigan, Indiana, Missouri or Iowa. **Criteria:** Recipients are selected based on academic performance and financial need.

Funds Avail.: One $10,000; two $5,000; one $2,500. **Duration:** Annual. **Number Awarded:** Varies. **To Apply:** Applicants must submit a completed application form; a letter describing their goals and aspirations in the field of horticulture, a transcript of records; must attach evaluation/letters from employers, internships, work study or any horticulture/landscape experience. **Deadline:** March 16.

4832 ■ Illinois Society of Professional Engineers (ISPE)

100 E Washington St.
Springfield, IL 62701
Ph: (217)544-7424
Fax: (217)528-6545
E-mail: info@IllinoisEngineer.com
URL: www.illinoisengineer.com

4833 ■ ISPE/M.E. Amstutz Memorial Awards (Undergraduate/Scholarship)

Purpose: To provide financial assistance for the education of students for the advancement and betterment of human welfare and the engineering profession. **Focus:** Engineering. **Qualif.:** Applicants must be enrolled in an ABET accredited engineering program; be at least juniors maintaining B average or better; and demonstrate financial need. **Criteria:** Recipients are judged based on financial need; extracurricular activities; interest in engineering and the applicants' essays.

Funds Avail.: $1,500. **Number Awarded:** 1. **To Apply:** Applicants must submit official transcripts of all college and university work; two letters of reference from the department chair or department faculty member from past employer or other character reference; and a typewritten essay in 200 words or less discussing why they want to become a professional engineer. **Deadline:** April 1. **Contact:** ISPE Foundation, Info@IllinoisEngineer.com.

4834 ■ ISPE Foundation Scholarships (Undergraduate/Scholarship)

Purpose: To provide financial assistance for the education of students who are sons or daughters of ISPE members. **Focus:** Engineering. **Qualif.:** Applicants must be attending an Illinois university; enrolled in an engineering program accredited by the Accreditation Board of Engineering and Technology (ABET); have at least junior standing; a B average or better in courses which are credited toward the engineering degree. **Criteria:** Recipients are judged based on financial need, extracurricular activities, interest in engineering and the applicants' essays.

Funds Avail.: $1,000. **Duration:** Annual. **To Apply:** Applicants must submit official transcripts of all college and university work; two letters of reference from the department chair or department faculty member; from past employer or other character reference; and typewritten essay in 200 words or less discussing why they want to become a professional engineer. **Deadline:** April 1. **Contact:** Illinois Society of Professional Engineers Foundation, www.illinoisengineer.com.

4835 ■ Illinois State Dental Society (ISDS)

1010 S 2nd St.
Springfield, IL 62704-3005
Ph: (217)525-1406
Fax: (217)525-8872
Free: 800-475-4737
E-mail: info@isds.org
URL: www.isds.org

4836 ■ Paul W. Clopper Scholarship Grant for Junior Dental Students (Undergraduate/Scholarship)

Purpose: To support qualified dental students who are succeeding academically and who have committed themselves to community involvement. **Focus:** Dental laboratory technology. **Qualif.:** Applicants must be incoming junior students in the fall semester of dental school. **Criteria:** Selection will be based on the committee's criteria.

Funds Avail.: $3,000. **Duration:** Annual. **Number Awarded:** 3. **To Apply:** Applicants must complete and submit the application form available at the website. Two written faculty letters of recommendation attesting the applicants' progress as students and their activity as community volunteers must be mailed directly to the Clopper Scholarship Committee. A transcript for three completed semester, along with the cumulative GPA must be mailed directly to the ISDS Foundation Scholarship Committee. **Deadline:** May 19.

4837 ■ Illinois Student Assistance Commission (ISAC)

1755 Lake Cook Rd.
Deerfield, IL 60015-5209
Fax: (847)831-8549
Free: 800-899-4722
E-mail: isac.studentservices@isac.illinois.gov
URL: www.isac.org

4838 ■ Allied Health Care Professional Scholarships (Undergraduate/Scholarship)

Purpose: To increase the number of nurse practitioners, physician assistants and certified nurse midwives practicing in areas of Illinois; to provide financial support to a qualified allied healthcare professional students. **Focus:** Health sciences. **Qualif.:** Applicant must be a nurse practitioner, physician assistant or certified nurse midwife student; must be accepted or enrolled in a school located in Illinois and accredited in its field; must be a full-time or part-time

Awards are arranged alphabetically below their administering organizations

student; must demonstrate financial need; and must apply to the school's financial aid department on or before the designated application deadline date. A part-time student must be enrolled for at least one-third of the number of hours required per term by the school. **Criteria:** Preference will be given to an applicant who demonstrates: (1) Previous experience with medically underserved populations; (2) Greatest financial need; and (3) Academic capabilities.

Funds Avail.: $7,500. **Duration:** Up to two years. **Number Awarded:** 12. **To Apply:** Applicant must complete the application forms available online; must have the financial aid award information; must have the proof of enrollment or letter of acceptance into the program. **Deadline:** June 30. **Contact:** Allied Health Care Professional Scholarship Program, Illinois Department of Public Health, Center for Rural Health, 535 W Jefferson St., Springfield, IL 62761; Bronwyn Jones-Leach at 217-782-1624.

4839 ■ Robert C. Byrd Honors Scholarships
(Undergraduate/Scholarship)

Purpose: To provide financial support to deserving individuals who have outstanding academic achievements. **Focus:** General studies/Field of study not specified. **Qualif.:** Applicant must be a U.S citizen or an eligible non-citizen; must be an Illinois resident; must be an Illinois high school graduate; must be enrolled, or accepted for enrollment on a full-time basis as an undergraduate student at a U.S Department of Education-approved college in the United States. **Criteria:** Selection of awardees within each Illinois geographic district will be based on their academic performance data reported by the high school at the end of the third semester prior to graduation and by the ACT, SAT, or Prairie State Achievement Exam scores reported by the end of the third semester before high school graduation.

Funds Avail.: $1,500. **Duration:** Annual; Four years. **To Apply:** Applicant must complete the eligibility certification form and must be sent to ISAC, 1775 Lake Cook Rd., Deerfield, IL 60015-5209. **Deadline:** July 15.

4840 ■ Illinois Future Teacher Corps Scholarships
(Undergraduate/Scholarship)

Purpose: To provide financial support to deserving individuals intending to pursue their careers as teachers. **Focus:** Teaching. **Qualif.:** Applicant must be a U.S citizen or an eligible non-citizen; must be a resident of Illinois; must be a high school graduate or person who has received a General Education Development certificate; must be enrolled or accepted for enrollment as a junior or above on at least a half-time basis in a Teacher Education Program at an eligible Illinois public or private college, seeking initial teacher certification; must be pursuing additional coursework needed to gain Illinois State Board of Education approval to teach, including alternative teacher certification; must maintain a cumulative grade point average of 2.5 on a 4.0 scale; must maintain satisfactory academic progress as determined by the college; must comply with Federal Selective Service registration requirements; must not be in default on any student loans, nor owe a refund on any state or federal grant; not have previously received funds from the IFTC program for the equivalent of two academic years; and not yet received funds from the Minority Teachers of Illinois (MTI) Scholarships or Illinois Special Education Teacher Tuition Waiver (SETTW) programs during the same term(s). **Criteria:** Selection will be based on academic performance and eligibility requirements. Priority is given to individuals intending to pursue a teacher shortage discipline and/or making a commitment to teach at a hard-to-staff school and minority students.

Funds Avail.: $5,000 - $10,000. **Duration:** Annual; One academic year. **To Apply:** Applicant must complete the application for Teacher Education Scholarship Programs; must sign the application's Teaching Agreement/Promissory Note promising to fulfill the teaching commitment or repay funds received, plus interest. **Deadline:** March 1.

4841 ■ Illinois Special Education Teacher Tuition Waiver Scholarships (SETTW) *(Undergraduate/ Scholarship)*

Purpose: To provide support to deserving individuals intending to pursue their career in special education programs. **Focus:** Education, Special. **Qualif.:** Applicant must be a U.S. citizen or an eligible non-citizen; must be an Illinois resident; must have graduated from an approved high school in the academic year in the upper half of their graduating class according to performance-based academic data provided by the high school; or graduated from an approved high school prior to the academic year in which the award is made; and must hold a valid teaching certificate that is not in the discipline of special education; must be enrolled or accepted for enrollment at one of the eligible public four-year colleges in Illinois as an undergraduate or graduate student seeking initial certification in any area of special education; must be enrolled in a program of special education within ten days after the beginning of the term for which the waiver was initially awarded; must comply with federal Selective Service registration requirements. **Criteria:** Selection will be based on the applicant's academic standing and eligibility requirements.

Funds Avail.: No specific amount. **Duration:** Annual; One academic year. **To Apply:** Application forms are available online at the College Zone. **Deadline:** March 1.

4842 ■ Illinois Student Assistance Commission Medical Student Scholarships *(Undergraduate/ Scholarship)*

Purpose: To financially support qualified medical students. **Focus:** Medical technology; Medicine, Osteopathic. **Qualif.:** Applicants must be enrolled in an approved allopathic or osteopathic medical school in Illinois; must agree to work in an identified physician-shortage area in Illinois; must be Illinois residents; must demonstrate financial need and be committed to primary care; must be students waiting for confirmation of acceptance to medical school. **Criteria:** Preference will be given to applicants who demonstrate: (1) A commitment to primary health care; (2) Financial need; and (3) Prior experience with populations whose healthcare needs are underserved.

Funds Avail.: No specific amount. **To Apply:** Applicants must complete the application form available online; must provide an autobiographical profile; must have one of the following: (1) For students entering medical school: First year student must submit a copy of AMCAS application or AACOMAS applicant profile; (2) For all other medical student-a transcript or verification from the college of the GPA or academic standing. **Deadline:** May 15. **Contact:** Tom Yocum at 217-782-1624.

4843 ■ Illinois Student Assistance Commission Merit Recognition Scholarships (MRS)
(Undergraduate/Scholarship)

Purpose: To provide financial support to qualified individuals intending to pursue their education. **Focus:** General studies/Field of study not specified. **Qualif.:** Applicants must be U.S citizens or an eligible non-citizens; must be residents of Illinois; must be in the top five percent of their

Awards are arranged alphabetically below their administering organizations

high school class; must take the ACT, SAT or Prairie State Achievement Exam; must attend an approved, Illinois post-secondary institution as undergraduates on at least a half-time basis, or attend one of the nation's four approved Military Science Academies; must comply with federal Selective Service registration requirements. **Criteria:** Applicants will be selected based on the eligibility requirements.

Funds Avail.: $1,000. **Duration:** Annual; One academic year. **To Apply:** Applicants are advised to contact the Illinois Student Assistance Commission Office for application forms and other required materials. **Deadline:** June 15. **Contact:** Scholarship application and application documents must be sent to ISAC, 1775 Lake Cook Rd., Deerfield, IL 60015-5209.

4844 ■ Illinois Student Assistance Commission Nurse Educator Scholarships (NESP)
(Undergraduate/Scholarship)

Purpose: To provide financial support to a qualified individual intending to pursue a career in professional or practical nursing education in Illinois. **Focus:** Nursing. **Qualif.:** Applicant must be a U.S citizen or an eligible noncitizen; must be an Illinois resident; must be a recipient of at least a bachelor's degree; must be enrolled, or accepted for enrollment, on at least a half-time basis in an approved program of practical nursing education at the graduate level at an eligible Illinois college; must have a satisfactory academic progress as determined by the college; must comply with federal Selective Service registration requirements. **Criteria:** Selection will be based on the following criteria: (1) Cumulative GPA (converted to a 4.0 scale) are prioritized from highest to lowest; (2) EFCs are prioritized from lowest to highest; (3) Renewal applicants receive priority consideration provided that they: maintain their qualified applicant status by continuing to meet all criteria listed under the eligibility section that appears earlier on this page and submit the renewal application on a timely basis. Priority consideration is given to the qualified applicant who submits a complete application on the earliest date.

Funds Avail.: No specific amount. **Duration:** Annual; One academic year. **To Apply:** Application forms are available to download and print from College Zone. **Deadline:** May 31.

4845 ■ Illinois Student Assistance Commission Nursing Education Scholarships *(Undergraduate/Scholarship)*

Purpose: To provide financial assistance to qualified individuals pursuing an associate degree in nursing, an associate degree in applied sciences in nursing, a hospital-based diploma in nursing, a baccalaureate degree in nursing, a graduate degree in nursing or a certificate in practical nursing. **Focus:** Nursing. **Qualif.:** Applicant must be a resident of Illinois for at least one year prior to application; must be a citizen or lawful permanent resident alien of the United States; must be enrolled in or accepted for enrollment on at least a half-time basis in an approved program of graduate professional nursing education or practical nursing at an eligible Illinois college; must have applied for Federal Student Financial Aid to determine the expected family contribution (EFC); not be in default on any student loan, nor owe a refund in any state or federal grant; must comply with federal Selective Service registration requirements; must be in need of financial assistance based on applicant's Student Aid Report. **Criteria:** Recipients will be selected based on the following criteria: (1) Renewal

recipients will receive preference; (2) If the number of qualified applicants exceeds the number of scholarships to be awarded, priority in awarding scholarships will be given to students who: (a) Have the greatest financial need per the Student Aid Report; (b) Are full-time or closest to full-time students; (c) Have the fewest number of credit hours remaining to complete their nursing degree; (c) Already have an associate degree or hospital-based diploma in nursing or a certificate in practical nursing and are pursuing a higher degree; (d) Have the highest cumulative grade point average as documented on an official transcript or other official school form.; (3) When all criteria are equal, a lottery may be used to determine scholarships.

Funds Avail.: No specific amount. **Duration:** Annual. **To Apply:** Applicant must submit a completed, signed and dated application form prior to the deadline; must have a copy of his/her Illinois-registered professional nurse license or Illinois practical nurse license; must include a current copy of an official transcript or other current official school form that indicates a cumulative grade point average; must include a copy of a current Student Aid Report (SAR) that indicates an estimated financial contribution. A current SAR is required, even if you are not eligible for or have not applied for other financial assistance. **Deadline:** May 31.

4846 ■ Minority Teachers of Illinois Scholarships (MTI) *(Undergraduate/Scholarship)*

Purpose: To provide financial support to the qualified individuals intending to pursue their careers as a preschool, elementary or secondary school teacher. **Focus:** Teaching. **Qualif.:** Applicant must be a U.S citizen or an eligible noncitizen; must be a resident of Illinois; must be either a African American/Black, Hispanic American, Asian American or of Native American origin; must be a high school graduate, or hold a General Educational Development certificate; must be enrolled at least on a part-time basis as an undergraduate or graduate student; must be enrolled or accepted for enrollment at a qualified Illinois institution of higher education in a course of study which, upon completion, qualifies to be certified as a preschool, elementary or secondary school teacher by the Illinois State Board of Education, including alternative teacher certification; must maintain a cumulative grade point average of 2.5 on a 4.0 scale; must maintain a satisfactory academic progress as determined by the college; must comply with federal Selective Service registration requirements. **Criteria:** Applicant will be selected based on the academic standing and eligibility requirements.

Funds Avail.: $5,000. **Duration:** Annual; One academic year. **Number Awarded:** Varies. **To Apply:** Applicant must submit the complete application form for the Teacher Education Scholarship Programs (available online); must sign the application's Teaching Agreement or Promissory Note promising to fulfill the teaching commitment or repay funds received plus interest. **Deadline:** March 1.

4847 ■ Image
3307 3rd Ave. W
Seattle, WA 98119
Ph: (206)281-2988
Fax: (206)281-2979
Free: 866-481-0688
E-mail: image@imagejournal.org
URL: imagejournal.org

Awards are arranged alphabetically below their administering organizations

4848 ■ Milton Center Fellowships (Postgraduate/Fellowship)

Purpose: To support writers of poetry, fiction and creative nonfiction who seek to animate the Christian imagination, promote intellectual integrity, and explore the human condition with honesty and compassion. **Focus:** Creative writing. **Qualif.:** Applicant must be a U.S. citizen, or be able to show proof of permanent residency, unexpired temporary residency, or a current valid visa, and possess at least an M.A. in English Literature, Creative Writing, or the humanities, or an MFA in Creative Writing. **Criteria:** Fellowships will be awarded to applicants who present a clearly formulated proposal, a high quality of writing, and a demonstrated ability to complete the project.

Funds Avail.: $16,000. **Duration:** nine months. **To Apply:** Applicants must submit a book proposal, including synopsis and description of its audience (limit 2000 words); an autobiographical essay about the applicant's development as a writer and a person of faith (limit 2000 words); 30 to 50 double-spaced pages of prose or 8 to 12 poems; a brief explanation of what the applicant aim to accomplish next year at the Center; and a $25 application fee (make check payable to Image). **Deadline:** March 15.

4849 ■ Luci Shaw Fellowship (Undergraduate/Fellowship)

Purpose: To expose a promising undergraduate student to the world of literary publishing and the nonprofit arts organization. **Focus:** Literature. **Qualif.:** Applicant must be currently enrolled in a four-year undergraduate institution. **Criteria:** Selection is based on the application.

Funds Avail.: No specific amount. **To Apply:** Applicants must submit a completed application form along with a letter of introduction; a resume; a writing sample of 10-15 pages (this could be a term paper, a personal essay, or creative writing. It can include poetry, but it shouldn't be all poetry); and two letters of recommendation from teachers, work or volunteer supervisors, or other mentors who know you well. **Deadline:** February 15. **Contact:** Tyler McCabe, at programs@imagejournal.org.

4850 ■ Imagine America Foundation (IAF)

12001 Sunrise Valley Dr., Ste. 203
Reston, VA 20191
Ph: (571)267-3012
URL: www.imagine-america.org

4851 ■ Career Colleges Scholarships (Undergraduate/Scholarship)

Purpose: To help thousands of high school seniors each year pursue postsecondary career education at hundreds of career schools across the United States. **Focus:** General studies/Field of study not specified. **Qualif.:** Applicants must be high school graduates who are pursuing postsecondary career education at participating career colleges across the United States. **Criteria:** Recipients are selected based on financial need.

Funds Avail.: $1,000. **Duration:** Annual. **To Apply:** Application details and process shall be determined by the scholarship program officers. **Deadline:** December 31.

4852 ■ High School Counselors Scholarships (Undergraduate/Scholarship)

Purpose: To help high school seniors each year pursue postsecondary career education at hundreds of career schools across the United States. **Focus:** General studies/Field of study not specified. **Qualif.:** Applicants must be high school graduates who are pursuing postsecondary career education at participating career colleges across the United States; Applicants must have a high school grade point average of 2.5 or greater. **Criteria:** Recipients are selected based on financial need.

Funds Avail.: $1,000. **Duration:** Annual. **Number Awarded:** 5. **To Apply:** Application details and process shall be determined by the scholarship program officers.

4853 ■ Imagine America Scholarships (Undergraduate/Scholarship, Grant)

Purpose: To support and promote the benefits of career colleges to the general public. **Focus:** General studies/Field of study not specified. **Qualif.:** Applicants must be high school seniors, military personnel and adult students planning to attend one of the participating career school campuses. **Criteria:** Selection will be based on the committee's criteria.

Funds Avail.: $1,000. **Duration:** Annual. **Number Awarded:** Up to 5. **To Apply:** Applicants may visit the website for the online application process and other details.

4854 ■ Immigration and Ethnic History Society (IEHS)

c/o Tinothy D. Draper, Secretary
Waubonsee Community College
Div. of Social Science and Education
Rte. 47, Waubonsee Dr.
Sugar Grove, IL 60554-9454
Ph: (630)466-7900
URL: www.iehs.org

4855 ■ John Higham Travel Grants (Graduate/Grant)

Purpose: To provide travel grants to graduate students to be used toward costs of attending the OAH/IEHS Annual Meeting. **Focus:** History, American; Immigration. **Qualif.:** Candidates must be graduate students with a preferred area of concentration in American Immigration and/or American Ethnic and/or American Intellectual history. **Criteria:** Selection will be based on the committee's criteria.

Funds Avail.: No specific amount. **Duration:** Annual. **Number Awarded:** 3. **To Apply:** Applicants must provide the following documents: current and permanent addresses; educational background; degrees achieved and expected; current institution attending; current status; travel funds from other sources; publications and papers presented. Applicants will be required to include a short statement of no more than 500 words about how they envision attending the annual meeting will help prepare them for a career in history. Applicants will need to indicate if other travel monies will be made available. One complete copy of each application must be mailed directly to each committee member. **Deadline:** December 2. **Contact:** Andrew K. Sandoval-Strausz, Department of History, MSC06 3760, One University of New Mexico, Albuquerque, NM 87131-1181; Julio Capo, Jr., History Dept., Herter Hall, University of Massachusetts, 161 Presidents Dr., Amherst, MA 01003-9312; Maddalena Marinari, Department of History, Doyle Hall 135, St. Bonaventure University, 3261 W State Rd., St. Bonaventure, NY 14778.

4856 ■ Immune Deficiency Foundation (IDF)

110 West Rd., Ste. 300
Towson, MD 21204

Awards are arranged alphabetically below their administering organizations

Fax: (410)321-9165
Free: 800-296-4433
E-mail: info@primaryimmune.org
URL: primaryimmune.org

4857 ■ The Eric Marder Scholarships
(Undergraduate/Scholarship)

Purpose: To improve the diagnosis and treatment of patients with primary immune deficiency diseases through research, education and advocacy. **Focus:** General studies/Field of study not specified. **Qualif.:** Applicants must be undergraduate students living with primary immune deficiency diseases planning to complete their secondary education. **Criteria:** Recipients are selected based on financial need.

Funds Avail.: No specific amount. **Duration:** Annual. **To Apply:** Applicants must complete the application form. **Deadline:** May 1. **Remarks:** Established in 2001.

4858 ■ Incorporated Society of Irish American Lawyers (ISIAL)
40 N Main St., Ste. 435
Mount Clemens, MI 48043
Ph: (586)468-2940
Fax: (586)468-6926
E-mail: president@irish-lawyers.org
URL: www.irish-lawyers.org

4859 ■ Thomas P. Thornton Scholarships
(Undergraduate/Scholarship)

Purpose: To support junior and senior students enrolled in any law schools. **Focus:** Law. **Qualif.:** Applicants must be currently junior or senior students; must have an overall GPA of at least 2.50; must be of Irish decent. **Criteria:** Selection will be based on the committee's criteria.

Funds Avail.: $2,000. **Duration:** Annual. **Number Awarded:** 2. **To Apply:** Applicants must submit their resume and a letter stating why they should be awarded the scholarship. Applicants must also include information pertaining to their Irish heritage and financial need, and must attach a copy of transcript of grades from the latest semester. **Deadline:** April 16. **Contact:** Frances G. Murphy at fmurphy@garanlucow.com.

4860 ■ Independent Accountants Association of Illinois (IAAI)
PO Box 1506
Galesburg, IL 61402-1506
Free: 800-313-2270
E-mail: iaai@grics.net
URL: www.illinoisaccountants.com

4861 ■ IAAI Scholarship Foundation Accounting Scholarships (Undergraduate/Scholarship)

Purpose: To support deserving college students who have indicated a firm intention of pursuing their accounting studies at a successful conclusion and plan to enter the accounting profession. **Focus:** Accounting. **Qualif.:** Applicants must be residential college students interested in pursuing a career in the field of accounting throughout the State of Illinois. **Criteria:** Selection will be based on the committee's criteria.

Funds Avail.: $1,000. **Duration:** Annual. **Number**

Awarded: 2. **To Apply:** Qualified students should complete the scholarship application. Submit official transcripts from colleges attended, along with a letter of recommendation from an accounting professor or head of the accounting department. Documents may be submitted together or separately. **Deadline:** June 30.

4862 ■ Independent Lubricant Manufacturers Association (ILMA)
400 N Columbus St., Ste. 201
Alexandria, VA 22314-2264
Ph: (703)684-5574
Fax: (703)836-8503
E-mail: ilma@ilma.org
URL: www.ilma.org

4863 ■ Independent Lubricant Manufacturers Association Scholarships (Undergraduate/Scholarship)

Purpose: To provide financial assistance to deserving students. **Focus:** General studies/Field of study not specified. **Qualif.:** Applicant must be a citizen in a North American country; must attend or be enrolled in a college or university in North America; must be registered as a full-time student (12 credit hours or more per semester, 9 credit hours per trimester or more); must have a minimum of 3.0 cumulative GPA. **Criteria:** Selection of applicants will be based on financial need and GPS. Preference will be given to those with major in Math, Science or Engineering.

Funds Avail.: $1,000. **Duration:** Four years. **To Apply:** Applicant must have a letter of recommendation from teacher or advisor. Application forms are available online. **Deadline:** June 30.

4864 ■ Independent Order of Foresters
789 Don Mills Rd.
Toronto, ON, Canada M3C 1T9
Free: 800-828-1540
E-mail: service@foresters.com
URL: www.foresters.com

4865 ■ Foresters Scholarships (Undergraduate/Scholarship)

Purpose: To provide opportunity for Foresters members to pursue higher learning through financial support. **Focus:** General studies/Field of study not specified. **Qualif.:** Applicants must be eligible members, their spouses and dependent children, including grandchildren who will be continuing their postsecondary education. Eligible students of any age with a minimum GPA of 2.8 or 70% may apply. **Criteria:** Scholarship recipients will be selected based on proof of registration; completed application; and academic performance. The Selection Committee takes note of balanced geographical representation.

Funds Avail.: $8,000. **To Apply:** Applicants must have the Forester life, Foresters annuity, Social Fraternal membership and a registered non-voting member; must submit an application form together with official transcripts; community service achievement list; two letters of reference; and a member consent form. **Deadline:** February 28.

4866 ■ Independent Professional Seed Association (IPSA)
2504 Alexander Dr.
Jonesboro, AR 72401

Awards are arranged alphabetically below their administering organizations

Ph: (870)336-0777
Fax: (888)888-5058
Free: 888-888-5058
E-mail: info@independentseeds.com
URL: www.independentseeds.com

4867 ■ Myron Asplin Foundation Scholarships
(Undergraduate/Scholarship)

Purpose: To support a high school seniors pursuing agriculture related degree. **Focus:** Agricultural sciences. **Qualif.:** Applicants must be active students continuing their education in an agriculture-related field of study. **Criteria:** Applicants will be selected based on combination of academic achievement; community and agricultural involvement.

Funds Avail.: $1,000. **Duration:** Annual. **Number Awarded:** 1. **To Apply:** Applicants must submit application form (available at the website) with high school transcript; list of courses taken and grades received during senior year (if not included in transcript); recent photo (name printed at the back); two letters of recommendation from non-relatives; one reference form from an employer or instructor; and a 300-word essay. **Deadline:** May 15.

4868 ■ Independent Professional Seed Association Student Recognition Awards *(Undergraduate/ Scholarship)*

Purpose: To promote education in the field of agriculture. **Focus:** Agriculture, Economic aspects. **Qualif.:** Applicants must be active student entering junior/senior year or graduate students studying agriculture or related field. **Criteria:** Preference will be given to the dependents of an IPSA member and associates.

Funds Avail.: $1,000. **Duration:** Annual. **Number Awarded:** Varies. **To Apply:** Application form is available at the website. Applicants must attach student transcript; two recommendation letters from professors; a statement about personal and professional goals and objectives; work experience for the last two years; and recommendation from the nominator along with any relationship to IPSA member or Associate member company. **Deadline:** May 15. **Remarks:** The Award was created in 1997 with donations from Independent Corn Breeders Association. **Contact:** IPSA, P.O. Box 241312, Omaha, NE 68124-5312; Ph. 402-991-3550 Fax: 877-415-1306 info@ independentseeds.com.

4869 ■ Independent University Alumni Association at Lowell
PO Box 242
Lowell, MA 01853-0242
Ph: (978)454-6335
Fax: (978)452-7889
E-mail: alumnioffice@iuaal.org
URL: www.iuaal.org

4870 ■ Gehring Memorial Foundation Scholarships
(Graduate, Undergraduate/Scholarship)

Purpose: To support graduate and undergraduate students who are pursuing education at Lowell. **Focus:** General studies/Field of study not specified. **Qualif.:** Applicant must be a Lowell graduate or undergraduate student. **Criteria:** Selection is based on scholarship record, personality, and ability in leadership, extracurricular activities, and financial need.

Funds Avail.: No specific amount. **To Apply:** Applicants must submit a completed application form together with the required supporting materials.

4871 ■ Barnett D. Gordon Scholarships *(Graduate, Undergraduate/Scholarship)*

Purpose: To support graduate and undergraduate students who are pursuing education at Lowell. **Focus:** General studies/Field of study not specified. **Qualif.:** Applicant must be a Lowell graduate or undergraduate student. **Criteria:** Selection is based on the application.

Funds Avail.: No specific amount. **To Apply:** Applicants must submit a completed application form together with the required supporting materials.

4872 ■ Independent University Alumni Association Scholarships *(Graduate, Undergraduate/Scholarship)*

Purpose: To support graduate and undergraduate students who are pursuing education at Lowell. **Focus:** General studies/Field of study not specified. **Qualif.:** Applicant must be a Lowell graduate or undergraduate student. **Criteria:** Selection is based on the application.

Funds Avail.: No specific amount. **To Apply:** Applicants must submit a completed application form together with the required supporting materials. **Contact:** Independent University Alumni Association at Lowell, at the above address.

4873 ■ Joseph Kaplan Fund *(Graduate, Undergraduate/Scholarship)*

Purpose: To support graduate and undergraduate students who are pursuing education at Lowell. **Focus:** General studies/Field of study not specified. **Qualif.:** Applicant must be a Lowell graduate or undergraduate student. **Criteria:** Selection is based on the application.

Funds Avail.: No specific amount. **To Apply:** Applicants must submit a completed application form together with the required supporting materials.

4874 ■ Jacob Ziskind Memorial Fund for Upperclassmen *(Graduate, Undergraduate/Scholarship)*

Purpose: To support graduate and undergraduate students who are pursuing education at Lowell. **Focus:** General studies/Field of study not specified. **Qualif.:** Applicant must be a Lowell graduate or undergraduate upperclassman student. **Criteria:** Selection is based on the application.

Funds Avail.: No specific amount. **To Apply:** Applicants must submit a completed application form together with the required supporting materials. **Contact:** Independent University Alumni Association at Lowell, at the above address.

4875 ■ Indiana Bar Foundation (IBF)
615 N Alabama St., Ste. 122
Indianapolis, IN 46204
Ph: (317)269-2415
Fax: (317)536-2271
Free: 800-279-8772
E-mail: info@inbf.org
URL: inbf.org

4876 ■ Joseph T. Helling Scholarship Fund
(Undergraduate/Scholarship)

Purpose: To provide scholarships to young attorneys in Indiana. **Focus:** Law. **Qualif.:** Applicant or nominee must

Awards are arranged alphabetically below their administering organizations

be actively practicing law in Indiana; must be admitted to the practice of law less than five years; must be a member of the Indiana State Bar Association. **Criteria:** Selection will be based on the following traits and principles: community involvement; public service, including a demonstrated dedication to work related endeavors that benefit the less fortunate in society; demonstrated commitment to professionalism and civility in the legal profession and an interest in promoting the profession through local and state bar associations and bar foundations; dedication to the legal profession equaled to his/her dedication to family.

Funds Avail.: No specific amount. **Duration:** Annual. **To Apply:** Applicants must submit a completed application/nomination form. Applicants must also submit a concise typewritten paragraph describing the accomplishments, contributions and/or initiatives of the nominee in the areas addressed by the award criteria indicating the significance of their impact. **Deadline:** July 15.

4877 ■ Indiana Broadcasters Association (IBA)
14074 Trade Center Dr., Ste. 141
Fishers, IN 46038
Ph: (317)770-0970
Fax: (317)770-0972
Free: 800-342-6276
E-mail: iba@indianabroadcasters.org
URL: www.indianabroadcasters.org

4878 ■ Indiana Broadcasters Association College Scholarship Program *(Undergraduate/Scholarship)*

Purpose: To promote cooperation and understanding among broadcasters, both radio and television as well as among businesses and other organizations associated with the broadcast industry; to foster and promote the development of the art of broadcasting; to encourage and promote customs and practices which will be in the best interests of the public and the broadcasting industry; to protect members in every lawful and proper manner from injuries and unjust actions; and to act as a contact with other broadcast associations. **Focus:** Broadcasting. **Qualif.:** Applicants must have an overall 3.0 GPA on a 4.0 scale; must be residents of Indiana; must be current college students; and must be actively participating in a college broadcast facility or working for a commercial broadcast facility while attending an IBA Member Educational Institution. **Criteria:** Recipients are selected based on academic performance.

Funds Avail.: No specific amount. **Duration:** Annual. **To Apply:** Applicants must complete the Transcript Request Form and application form and send them to the College Records Office. **Deadline:** March 1.

4879 ■ Indiana Broadcasters Association High School Scholarship Program *(Undergraduate/Scholarship)*

Purpose: To promote cooperation and understanding among broadcasters, both radio and television as well as among businesses and other organizations associated with the broadcast industry; to foster and promote the development of the art of broadcasting; to encourage and promote customs and practices which will be in the best interests of the public and the broadcasting industry; to protect members in every lawful and proper manner from injuries and unjust actions; and to act as a contact with other broadcast associations. **Focus:** Broadcasting. **Qualif.:** Applicants must have an overall 3.0 GPA on a 4.0 scale; must

be residents of Indiana; must be second-semester seniors at an Indiana High school planning to attend an Indiana post-secondary school; must be actively participating in a high school broadcast facility while attending an Indiana high school; and must have received credit in a High School Broadcasting, Telecommunications or Broadcast Journalism course. **Criteria:** Recipients are selected based on academic performance. Applicant's essay will be used for evaluating their interest in continuing an education in telecommunications or broadcast journalism.

Funds Avail.: No specific amount. **Duration:** Annual. **To Apply:** Applicants must complete the application form and the High School Transcript Request Form and send them to the high school records office. **Deadline:** March 1.

4880 ■ Indiana FFA Association
1 N Capitol Ave., Ste. 600
Indianapolis, IN 46204
Ph: (317)407-7926
URL: inffa.org/association

4881 ■ Indiana FFA Association State Fair Scholarship *(Undergraduate/Scholarship)*

Purpose: To support individuals who benefited themselves and the Indiana FFA by contributing to the Indiana FFA Pavilion and its activities at the State Fair. **Focus:** General studies/Field of study not specified. **Qualif.:** Applicants must be active FFA members. **Criteria:** Selection will be based on the committee's criteria.

Funds Avail.: $500. **Duration:** Annual. **To Apply:** Applicants must complete and submit the application form available online and must provide some required materials. **Deadline:** May 31. **Contact:** Lisa Chaudion; Address: P.O. Box 9 Trafalgar, IN 46181.

4882 ■ Indiana Library Federation (ILF)
941 E 86th St., Ste. 260
Indianapolis, IN 46240
Ph: (317)257-2040
Fax: (317)257-1389
E-mail: askus@ilfonline.org
URL: www.ilfonline.org

4883 ■ Esther Schlundt Memorial Scholarships *(Graduate/Scholarship)*

Purpose: To foster the professional growth of its members and the promotion of all libraries in Indiana. **Focus:** Library and archival sciences. **Qualif.:** Applicants must be entering or currently enrolled in an ALA-accredited graduate degree program in library and information science; or must be entering or currently enrolled in an Indiana State Library-approved library certification program. **Criteria:** Recipients are selected based on academic performance.

Funds Avail.: $750; $1,000. **To Apply:** Applicants must submit three letters of recommendation from which one must come from a librarian; must submit a transcript or copy of official grade report for any library science courses already completed for masters candidates, all undergraduate transcripts and a copy of official grade report for any course already taken toward library certification. School library media candidates must submit transcripts of any education and/or library science courses completed. **Contact:** Application form and supporting documents should be sent to Scholarship Committee at the above address.

Awards are arranged alphabetically below their administering organizations

4884 ■ Sue Marsh Weller Memorial Scholarships
(Graduate, Postgraduate, Undergraduate/Scholarship)

Purpose: To provide financial assistance to the needs of the members for their professional growth. **Focus:** Library and archival sciences. **Qualif.:** Applicants must be entering or currently enrolled in an ALA-accredited program of graduate study specializing in children librarianship; must be legal residents of Indiana; must accept employment in an Indiana library within one year after completing their library education; and must continue to work in an Indiana library for at least one year after accepting employment. If recipients are unable to comply with these conditions, scholarship must be repaid as a loan. **Criteria:** Recipients are selected based on interest in librarianship as a profession; personality and character; academic record; economic need; and references and/or a personal interview.

Funds Avail.: No specific amount. **To Apply:** Applicants must submit three letters of recommendation from which one must come from a librarian. Masters candidates must submit (a) transcript or copy of official grade report for any library science courses already completed, (b) transcripts of all undergraduate education and (c) transcripts from other graduate work (may be included, but are not required). Public library certification candidates must submit (a) a copy of the approved public library certification program, (b) transcripts from undergraduate education and/or high school and (c) transcript or copy of official grade report for any course already taken toward library certification. School library media candidates must submit (a) official grade report for any education and/or library science courses already completed (undergraduate and/or high school), (b) a transcript for all undergraduate or graduate work completed and (c) transcripts from high school may be included by candidates that have not yet completed any graduate or undergraduate work. **Deadline:** June 30.

4885 ■ Indiana State University
200 N 7th St.
Terre Haute, IN 47809-1902
Ph: (812) 237-6311
Free: 800-468-6478
URL: www.indstate.edu

4886 ■ Warren M. Anderson Scholarships
(Undergraduate/Scholarship)

Purpose: To support the educational pursuit of underrepresented minority students. **Focus:** General studies/ Field of study not specified. **Qualif.:** Applicants must be Indiana and out-of-state residents who are underrepresented minorities with a cumulative GPA of 3.5 on a 4.0 scale. **Criteria:** Selection is based on academic and financial need.

Funds Avail.: $5,000 each. **Duration:** Annual. **Number Awarded:** 10. **To Apply:** Applicants may visit the website to verify the application process and other pieces of information. **Deadline:** March 1.

4887 ■ Indiana State University Academic Excellence Scholarships *(Undergraduate/Scholarship)*

Purpose: To support incoming ISU students in their pursuit of higher education. **Focus:** General studies/Field of study not specified. **Qualif.:** Applicants should be incoming freshmen who are admitted to the ISU by December 1 and must have the combination of two of the following three: a cumulative GPA of at least 3.75 on a 4.0 scale; an 1200 SAT (combined critical reading and mathematics) or 26 ACT (composite); and/or, ranking in the top 10% of the senior high school class. **Criteria:** Selection will be based on the committee's criteria.

Funds Avail.: $2,000. **Duration:** Annual; up to three years. **To Apply:** Applicants who are admitted to the University will be automatically qualified for the scholarship. The application for admission serves as the scholarship application. **Deadline:** December 1 (fall); December 15 (spring).

4888 ■ Indiana State University Incentive Scholarships *(Undergraduate/Scholarship)*

Purpose: To support incoming ISU students in their pursuit of higher education. **Focus:** General studies/Field of study not specified. **Qualif.:** Applicants must be residents outside Indiana and not qualify for a reduced tuition rate offered through the Illinois Student Scholarship, Kentucky Student Scholarship, Midwest Consortium Scholarship, or Ohio Student Scholarship. They also must have a cumulative high school grade point average of at least 3.0 on a 4.0 scale and earn a college-prep diploma. **Criteria:** Selection will be based on the committee's criteria.

Funds Avail.: $5,000 (out-of-state tuition). **Duration:** Annual. **To Apply:** Applicants who are admitted to the University will be automatically qualified for the scholarship. The application for admission serves as the scholarship application. **Deadline:** June 15.

4889 ■ Indiana State University President's Scholarships *(Undergraduate/Scholarship)*

Purpose: To support incoming ISU students in their pursuit of higher education. **Focus:** General studies/Field of study not specified. **Qualif.:** Applicants should be incoming freshmen who are admitted to the ISU by December 1 and must have the combination of two of the following three: a cumulative GPA of at least 3.75 on a 4.0 scale; an 1200 SAT (combined critical reading and mathematics) or 26 ACT (composite); and/or, ranking in the top 10% of the senior high school class. **Criteria:** Selection will be based on the committee's criteria.

Funds Avail.: Amount varies. **Duration:** Annual. **Number Awarded:** Approximately 20. **To Apply:** Applicants who are admitted to the University will be automatically qualified for the scholarship. The application for admission serves as the scholarship application. **Remarks:** No additional application required.

4890 ■ Indiana State University Rural Health Scholarships *(Graduate/Scholarship)*

Purpose: To prepare and support students from rural Indiana to go back to their hometown as a primary care physician. **Focus:** Medicine. **Qualif.:** Applicants should be residents of Indiana and be incoming freshmen who are admitted to the ISU by December 1 and must have the combination of two of the following three: a cumulative GPA of at least 3.5 on a 4.0 scale; an 1200 SAT (combined critical reading and mathematics on one test date) or a 27 ACT. **Criteria:** Selection is highly competitive and based upon academic and personal accomplishments, as well as performance in a winter interview competition.

Funds Avail.: No specific amount. **Duration:** Annual. **Number Awarded:** 10. **To Apply:** Applicants may visit the website to verify the application process and other pieces of information. **Deadline:** December 1. **Remarks:** The program is developed by Indiana State University and Indiana University School of Medicine.

Awards are arranged alphabetically below their administering organizations

4891 ■ Indiana State University Transfer Student Scholarships (Undergraduate/Scholarship)

Purpose: To support transfer students in their pursuit of higher education. **Focus:** General studies/Field of study not specified. **Qualif.:** Applicants must be Indiana and out-of-state residents, including on-campus and online-only students. All incoming transfer students who are admitted to the University by the deadline listed below will be automatically considered for the scholarship. **Criteria:** Selection will be based on the committee's criteria.

Funds Avail.: $2,000. **Duration:** Annual. **Number Awarded:** 60 (30 need-based; 30 non-need based). **To Apply:** Applicants who are admitted to the University will be automatically qualified for the scholarship. The application for admission serves as the scholarship application. **Deadline:** April 1 (admission deadline).

4892 ■ ISU Gongaware Scholarships (Undergraduate/Scholarship)

Purpose: To support incoming ISU students in their pursuit of higher education. **Focus:** Insurance and insurance-related fields; Risk management. **Qualif.:** Applicants should be admitted as incoming freshmen who are admitted to the ISU and must have the combination of two of the following three: a cumulative GPA of at least 3.5 on a 4.0 scale; a 1070 SAT (combined critical reading and mathematics) or 23 ACT (composite); and/or, ranking in the top 15% of the senior high school class. **Criteria:** Selection is based on academic, personal accomplishments, and performance in an interview.

Funds Avail.: $6,500 and additional $3,000 for professional development account. **Duration:** Annual; up to three years. **Number Awarded:** 4. **To Apply:** Applicants may visit the website to verify the application process and other pieces of information. **Deadline:** December 3. **Contact:** Call 1-888-269-4460.

4893 ■ ISU Networks Scholarships College of Business (Undergraduate/Scholarship)

Purpose: To support those who are pursuing business-related education. **Focus:** Business administration; Finance. **Qualif.:** Applicants should be admitted as incoming freshmen who are admitted to the ISU-Scott College of Business and must have the combination of two of the following three: a cumulative GPA of at least 3.5 on a 4.0 scale after seven semesters; at least 1070 SATV + SATM or 23 ACT; and/or, ranking in the top 15% of the senior high school class. **Criteria:** Selection shall be based on the demonstrated leadership in high school and in the community, as well as on the aforesaid qualifications and compliance with the application process.

Funds Avail.: Amount varies. **Duration:** Annual; up to four years. **Number Awarded:** Varies. **To Apply:** Applicants must submit the completed application form; (one-page) essay outlining their interests in financial services industry; resume; two letters of recommendation; and high school transcripts in a sealed envelope. **Deadline:** December 5. **Contact:** Call 812-237-2442 or Email nfi@indstate.edu.

4894 ■ Noyce Scholarships for Secondary Math and Science Education (Undergraduate/Scholarship)

Purpose: To support transfer students in their pursuit of higher education and teaching of secondary mathematics and science education. **Focus:** Education, Secondary; Mathematics and mathematical sciences; Science. **Qualif.:** Applicants must be transfer students and have a cumula-tive grade point average of 2.75 and a 3.0 cumulative grade point average in all science and mathematics course work. **Criteria:** Selection will be based on the committee's criteria.

Funds Avail.: $10,000; additional $2,000 award available based on academic need. **Duration:** Annual. **Number Awarded:** Varies. **To Apply:** Applicants who are admitted to the University will be automatically qualified for the scholarship. The application for admission serves as the scholarship application.

4895 ■ Phi Theta Kappa Scholarships (Undergraduate/Scholarship)

Purpose: To support students who are members of the Phi Theta Kappa in their pursuit of higher education. **Focus:** Art; Science. **Qualif.:** Applicants are Indiana and out-of-state residents, including on-campus and online-only students and must have earned a minimum of 60 transferable credits. Other requirements include a minimum cumulative grade point average of 3.5 and membership in Phi Theta Kappa National Honor Society. **Criteria:** Selection will be based on the committee's criteria,

Funds Avail.: $6,000 each. **Duration:** Annual. **Number Awarded:** 10. **To Apply:** Applicants who are admitted to the University will be automatically qualified for the scholarship. The application for admission serves as the scholarship application. In addition, students must provide a documentation of honor society membership and a letter of recommendation together with the admission application. **Deadline:** April 1.

4896 ■ Indiana State University Alumni Association (ISUAA)

Indiana State University
30 N 5th St.
Terre Haute, IN 47807
Ph: (812)514-8400
Fax: (812)237-8157
Free: 800-258-6478
E-mail: alumni@indstatefoundation.org
URL: www.indstate.edu/alumni

4897 ■ Indiana State University Academic Promise Scholarships (Undergraduate/Scholarship)

Purpose: To support students for showing academic promise and for them to obtain higher education degree. **Focus:** General studies/Field of study not specified. **Qualif.:** Applicants must be enrolled as full-time students each semester (minimum of 12 credits) and successfully complete a minimum of 30 credit hours each academic year. This will enable them to successfully progress toward graduation within four years. They must also achieve a minimum cumulative grade point average of 3.00. **Criteria:** Selection will be based on the committee's criteria.

Funds Avail.: Total value of $4,000 ($2,000 per academic year). **Duration:** Annual. **To Apply:** Applicants may visit the website to verify the application process and other pieces of information.

4898 ■ Indiana State University Creative and Performing Arts Awards (Undergraduate/Scholarship)

Purpose: To support students in their pursuit of higher education in creative and performing arts. **Focus:** Art; Dance; Education, Physical; English language and literature; Music; Theater arts. **Qualif.:** Applicants must be Indiana and out-of-state residents and have at least a 2.5

Awards are arranged alphabetically below their administering organizations

cumulative grade point average on a 4.0 scale. **Criteria:** Selection is based on academic and personal accomplishments.

Funds Avail.: $3,000 per year. **Duration:** Annual; up to three years. **Number Awarded:** Varies. **To Apply:** Applicants should contact the department of the area in which they are applying for specific information. **Deadline:** March 1. **Contact:** Art: 812-237-3697; Music: 812-237-27771; English Creative Writing: 812-237-3161; Kinesiology, Recreation, and Sport-Dance Minor: 812-237-2183; Theater: 812-237-3342.

4899 ■ ISU Child of Alumni Book Voucher Awards
(Undergraduate/Scholarship)

Purpose: To support the educational pursuits of dependents of alumni. **Focus:** General studies/Field of study not specified. **Qualif.:** Applicants must be enrolled full-time with 12 or more credit hours in both Fall and Spring semesters at ISU. **Criteria:** Selection will be based on the committee's criteria.

Funds Avail.: $500 ($250 in fall and another in spring). **Duration:** Annual. **To Apply:** Applicants may visit the website to verify the application process and other pieces of information.

4900 ■ Indigenous Bar Association (IBA)
c/o Anne Chalmers
70 Pineglen Crescent
Ottawa, ON, Canada K2G 0G8
Ph: (613)224-1529
URL: www.indigenousbar.ca

4901 ■ IBA Law Student Scholarship Foundation Scholarships *(Undergraduate/Scholarship)*

Purpose: To provide assistance to qualified individuals who want to pursue their education. **Focus:** Law. **Qualif.:** Applicant must be an Indigenous law student currently enrolled in law school who, at a minimum, has substantially completed their first year of legal studies; must have demonstrated interest in serving the Indigenous community and the creator with honor and integrity. **Criteria:** Recipient will be selected based on financial need, academic merit and commitment to Indigenous legal matters.

Funds Avail.: $2,000. **Duration:** Annual. **Number Awarded:** 1. **To Apply:** Applicant must complete the application form available online; must submit a short personal essay describing why they should receive the scholarship, including financial need, community involvement, as well as his/her goals and career aspirations; must enclose two letters of recommendations. Application form and other supporting documents must be sent to Anne Chalmers. **Deadline:** June 30. **Contact:** Anne Chalmers, Phone: 613-224-1529; email: achalmers@indigenousbar.ca.

4902 ■ Indspire
Box 5
50 Generations Dr., Ste. 100
Ohsweken, ON, Canada N0A 1M0
Ph: (519)445-3021
Free: 866-433-3159
E-mail: education@indspire.ca
URL: indspire.ca

4903 ■ Indspire Health Careers Bursary and Scholarships *(Graduate, Undergraduate/Scholarship)*

Purpose: To support students pursuing accredited health studies leading to employment in the health professions and who have demonstrated the potential for academic success. **Focus:** Biology; Chemistry; Dentistry; Medical laboratory technology; Medicine; Nursing; Pharmacy. **Qualif.:** Applicant must be a Canadian resident First Nation (status and non-status), Metis or Inuit student enrolled in a full-time post-secondary study. **Criteria:** Selection is based on financial need, academic performance, connection to the aboriginal community and commitment to the field of study.

Funds Avail.: No specific amount. **Duration:** One academic year. **To Apply:** Applicants must submit a completed current NAAF Aboriginal Health Careers Bursary and Scholarship Application form along with proof of First Nation, Inuit or Metis ancestry; official transcripts from present or most recent academic program; two completed Applicant Assessment Forms; letter of personal introduction (750-1,500 words); an updated resume or curriculum vitae; a recent photograph; letter of confirmation of admission into a program or proof of continuing enrollment; letter from a Band/Post Secondary Education Office or Support Organization if funding is not available; verification of tuition and fees; and Financial Report Form (if a previous recipient and has not yet forwarded it to NAAF). **Deadline:** June1 and November 2. **Contact:** education@indspire.ca.

4904 ■ Indspire Post-Secondary Education Scholarships *(Graduate, Undergraduate/Scholarship)*

Purpose: To meet the increasing needs of First Nations, Inuit and Metis students for financial support and to assist them in the pursuit of excellence in every discipline. **Focus:** Business; Education; Engineering; Information science and technology; Law; Science; Social sciences; Social work. **Qualif.:** Applicant must be a Canadian resident First Nation (status and non-status), Metis or Inuit student enrolled in a full-time post-secondary study. **Criteria:** Selection is based on financial need, academic performance, connection to the aboriginal community and commitment to the field of study.

Funds Avail.: No specific amount. **Duration:** One academic year. **To Apply:** Applicants must submit a completed current NAAF Post-Secondary Education Bursary Awards Application form along with proof of First Nation, Inuit or Metis ancestry; official transcripts from present or most recent academic program; two completed Applicant Assessment Forms; letter of personal introduction (750-1,500 words); an updated resume or curriculum vitae; a recent photograph; letter of confirmation of admission into a program or proof of continuing enrollment; letter from the Band/Post Secondary Education Office or Support Organization if funding is not available; verification of tuition and fees; and Financial Report Form (if a previous recipient and has not yet forwarded it to NAAF). **Deadline:** June 1 and November 2. **Contact:** education@indspire.ca.

4905 ■ Oil and Gas Trades and Technology Bursary and Scholarships *(Undergraduate/Scholarship)*

Purpose: To provide financial support to aboriginal people interested in pursuing studies in the Oil and Gas trades and technology sector in Alberta and Alberta Aboriginal apprentices. **Focus:** Industry and trade. **Qualif.:** Applicant must be a Canadian resident aboriginal who is either First Nation status or non-status, Inuit or Metis; accepted or has applied for part-time or full-time studies in Alberta at an accredited training institute, college or university; an aboriginal across Canada taking Certificate, Diploma or Applied Degree Programs in Alberta. **Criteria:** Selection is based on demonstrated financial need; involvement with the aboriginal community; suitability and commitment to trades; and academic performance.

Awards are arranged alphabetically below their administering organizations

Funds Avail.: No specific amount. **Duration:** One month to four years. **To Apply:** Applicant must submit a completed NAAF OGTT Application form together with a proof of First Nation, Inuit or Metis ancestry; official transcripts from present or most recent academic program; letter of recommendation from elder, treachery, principal, employer, coach or community leader; a recent photograph; current resume; letter of confirmation of admission into a program or proof of continuing enrollment; and Financial Report Form (if a previous recipient and has not yet forwarded it to NAAF). **Deadline:** April 30 and November 30. **Contact:** education@indspire.ca.

4906 ■ Industrial Designers Society of America (IDSA)

555 Grove St., Ste. 200
Herndon, VA 20170
Ph: (703)707-6000
Fax: (703)787-8501
URL: www.idsa.org

4907 ■ IDSA Gianninoto Graduate Scholarships
(Graduate, Undergraduate/Scholarship)

Purpose: To recognize excellence in the industrial design field. **Focus:** Industrial design. **Qualif.:** Applicants must be in their final year of study in an undergraduate industrial design program and currently applying to graduate school; must be currently enrolled in an industrial design graduate program or a practicing professional applying to return to graduate school; must be a member of an IDSA student chapter; must be a US citizen or US resident. **Criteria:** Selection of applicants will be based on the application materials.

Funds Avail.: No specific amount. **Number Awarded:** 1. **To Apply:** Applicants must complete the application form available on the website. **Deadline:** May 18.

4908 ■ Industrial Supply Association (ISA)

100 N 20th St., Ste. 400
Philadelphia, PA 19103-1462
Ph: (215)320-3862
Fax: (215)963-9785
Free: 877-460-2365
E-mail: info@isapartners.org
URL: www.isapartners.org

4909 ■ Gary L. Buffington Memorial Scholarships
(Undergraduate/Scholarship)

Purpose: To recognize members who embody the values fostered by Gary L. Buffington while performing his duty for the industry. **Focus:** Education, Industrial. **Qualif.:** Applicant must be a rising senior in an established college or university industrial distribution channel. **Criteria:** Recipient will be selected based on criteria of high educational performance, leadership and community service.

Funds Avail.: $10,000. **To Apply:** Applicant must submit a completed application.

4910 ■ Information Age Publishing Inc. (IAP)

7500 E McCormick Pkwy.
Scottsdale, AZ 85258
Ph: (704)752-9125
Fax: (704)752-9113

E-mail: infoage@infoagepub.com
URL: www.infoagepub.com

4911 ■ Information Age Publishing Graduate Student Book Scholarships *(Doctorate, Graduate/Scholarship)*

Purpose: To assist students with their graduate education finances. **Focus:** General studies/Field of study not specified. **Qualif.:** Applicant must be a full-time Master's or doctoral level student, and must be nominated by any faculty member. **Criteria:** Selection is based on the nomination letter.

Funds Avail.: No specific amount. **To Apply:** Any full-time tenure track faculty member may nominate a student. Nominating letter should include: the nominating faculty member's name, rank, department and college affiliation; the nominated student's name, department and college affiliation, and email address; and a brief description of the student's need.

4912 ■ Infusion Nurses Society (INS)

315 Norwood Park S
Norwood, MA 02062
Ph: (781)440-9408
Fax: (781)440-9409
Free: 800-694-0298
E-mail: ins@ins1.org
URL: www.ins1.org

4913 ■ Leslie Baranowski Scholarships for Professional Excellence *(Professional development/Scholarship)*

Purpose: To support and recognize commitment in improving and enhancing the quality of infusion care. **Focus:** Health care services; Nursing. **Qualif.:** Applicants must be members of Infusion Nurses Society (INS). **Criteria:** Applicants will be selected based on Scholarship Committee's review of the application materials.

Funds Avail.: $2,500. **Number Awarded:** Up to 2. **To Apply:** Applicants must submit a completed application form; (two-page, double-spaced) summary on how they would use the scholarship award to demonstrate/facilitate leadership in the community of infusion.

4914 ■ Gardner Foundation Infusion Nurses Society Education Scholarships *(Professional development/Scholarship)*

Purpose: To support and recognize a commitment to continuing education. **Focus:** Health care services; Nursing. **Qualif.:** Applicants must be members of Infusion Nurses Society (INS). **Criteria:** Applicants will be selected based on the Scholarship Committees' review on the application materials.

Funds Avail.: $1,000. **Number Awarded:** 2. **To Apply:** Applicants must submit a completed application form available at the website; an evidence of acceptance into a collegiate program; and (two-page, double-spaced) summary of professional goals and how continuing education (collegiate, post-collegiate) will enhance their practice.

4915 ■ Institut de Recherche Robert-Sauve en Sante et en Securite du Travail (IRSST)

505, boul. De Maisonneuve Ouest
Montreal, QC, Canada H3A 3C2

Awards are arranged alphabetically below their administering organizations

Ph: (514)288-1551
Fax: (514)288-7636
E-mail: humanresources@irsst.qc.ca
URL: www.irsst.qc.ca

4916 ■ IRSST Doctoral Scholarship *(Doctorate/ Fellowship)*

Purpose: To financially assist graduate students who want to enhance their research programs which deal with the prevention of industrial accidents and occupational diseases or the rehabilitation of affected workers. **Focus:** Occupational safety and health. **Qualif.:** Applicants must be Canadian citizens within the meaning of the Citizenship Act (R.S.C. 1985, c. C-29) or permanent residents of Canada within the meaning of the Immigration and Refugee Protection Act (S.C. 2001, c. 27); must be permanent residents of Quebec within the meaning of the Health Insurance Act and be domiciled in Quebec. **Criteria:** Selection of applicants will be based on the following scholarship criteria: (1) Applicant's performance; (2) Scientific merit of the research project; (3) Quality and relevance of the research environment.

Funds Avail.: $19,000. **Duration:** Annual. **To Apply:** Applicants must complete the application form available on the website; must submit the official transcripts of all university grades, including those for completed programs and those under way; must provide an evaluation form from each of two scientists other than the research supervisor, who have participated in the applicant's education; must provide a letter of recommendation written by the research supervisor. **Deadline:** October. **Contact:** Michel Asselin, Research Advisor, Coordinator of the Graduate Scholarship Program; e-mail: bourses@irsst.qc.ca.

4917 ■ IRSST Doctoral Scholarships Abroad *(Doctorate/Fellowship)*

Purpose: To financially assist graduate students who want to enhance their research programs which deal with the prevention of industrial accidents and occupational diseases or the rehabilitation of affected workers. **Focus:** Occupational safety and health. **Qualif.:** Applicants must be preparing to start or currently enrolled in a full-time master's or doctoral program leading to obtention of a PhD or a research doctorate; have at least one academic year left to complete if applying for a new scholarship; and have a GPA of at least B+ or the equivalent for all studies completed for their undergraduate degree. **Criteria:** Selection of applicants will be based on the following scholarship criteria: (1) Applicant's performance; (2) Scientific merit of the research project; (3) Quality and relevance of the research environment.

Funds Avail.: $25,000. **Duration:** Annual. **To Apply:** Applicants must complete the application form available on the website; must submit the official transcripts of all university grades including those for completed programs and those under way; must provide an evaluation form from each of two scientists other than the research supervisor who have participated in the applicant's education; must provide a letter of recommendation written by the research supervisor. **Deadline:** October. **Contact:** Michel Asselin, Research advisor, Coordinator of the Graduate Scholarship Program; e-mail: bourses@irsst.qc.ca.

4918 ■ IRSST Doctoral Scholarships Supplement *(Doctorate/Fellowship)*

Purpose: To financially assist graduate students who want to enhance their research programs which deal with the prevention of industrial accidents and occupational diseases or the rehabilitation of affected workers. **Focus:** Occupational safety and health. **Qualif.:** Applicants must be Canadian citizens within the meaning of the Citizenship Act (R.S.C. 1985, c. C-29) or a permanent resident of Canada within the meaning of the Immigration and Refugee Protection Act (S.C. 2001, c. 27); must be permanent residents of Quebec within the meaning of the Health Insurance Act and be domiciled in Quebec. **Criteria:** Selection of applicants will be based on the following scholarship criteria: (1) Applicant's performance; (2) Scientific merit of the research project; (3) Quality and relevance of the research environment.

Funds Avail.: $5,000. **Duration:** Annual. **To Apply:** Applicants must complete the application form available on the website; must submit the official transcripts of all university grades, including those for completed programs and those under way; must provide an evaluation form from each of two scientists other than the research supervisor, who have participated in the applicant's education; must provide a letter of recommendation written by the research supervisor. **Deadline:** October. **Contact:** Michel Asselin, Research advisor, Coordinator of the Graduate Scholarship Program; e-mail: bourses@irsst.qc.ca.

4919 ■ IRSST Masters Scholarships *(Master's/ Fellowship)*

Purpose: To financially assist graduate students who want to enhance their research programs which deal with the prevention of industrial accidents and occupational diseases or the rehabilitation of affected workers. **Focus:** Occupational safety and health. **Qualif.:** Applicants must be Canadian citizens within the meaning of the Citizenship Act (R.S.C. 1985, c. C-29) or permanent residents of Canada within the meaning of the Immigration and Refugee Protection Act (S.C. 2001, c. 27); must be permanent residents of Quebec within the meaning of the Health Insurance Act and be domiciled in Quebec. **Criteria:** Selection of applicants will be based on the following scholarship criteria: (1) Applicant's performance; (2) Scientific merit of the research project; (3) Quality and relevance of the research environment.

Funds Avail.: $14,250. **Duration:** Annual. **To Apply:** Applicants must complete the application form available on the website; must submit the official transcripts of all university grades, including those for completed programs and those under way; must provide an evaluation form from each of two scientists other than the research supervisor, who have participated in the applicant's education; must provide a letter of recommendation written by the research supervisor. **Deadline:** October. **Contact:** Michel Asselin, Research advisor, Coordinator of the Graduate Scholarship Program; e-mail: bourses@irsst.qc.ca.

4920 ■ IRSST Masters Scholarships Supplement *(Master's/Fellowship)*

Purpose: To financially assist graduate students who want to enhance their research programs which deal with the prevention of industrial accidents and occupational diseases or the rehabilitation of affected workers. **Focus:** Occupational safety and health. **Qualif.:** Applicants must be Canadian citizens within the meaning of the Citizenship Act (R.S.C. 1985, c. C-29) or permanent residents of Canada within the meaning of the Immigration and Refugee Protection Act (S.C. 2001, c. 27); must be permanent residents of Quebec within the meaning of the Health Insurance Act and be domiciled in Quebec. **Criteria:** Selection of applicants will be based on the following scholarship criteria:

Awards are arranged alphabetically below their administering organizations

(1) Applicant's performance; (2) Scientific merit of the research project; (3) Quality and relevance of the research environment.

Funds Avail.: $3,750. **Duration:** Annual. **To Apply:** Applicants must complete the application form available on the website; must submit the official transcripts of all university grades, including those for completed programs and those under way; must provide an evaluation form from each of two scientists other than the research supervisor, who have participated in the applicant's education; must provide a letter of recommendation written by the research supervisor. **Deadline:** October. **Contact:** Michel Asselin, Research advisor, Coordinator of the Graduate Scholarship Program; e-mail: bourses@irsst.qc.ca.

4921 ■ IRSST Postdoctoral Scholarships
(Postdoctorate/Fellowship)

Purpose: To financially assist graduate students who want to enhance their research programs which deal with the prevention of industrial accidents and occupational diseases or the rehabilitation of affected workers. **Focus:** Occupational safety and health. **Qualif.:** Applicants must have PhD for no more than four years or successfully defended their doctoral thesis by no later than August 15; have a research which will be completed at a location other than where they obtained their doctorate; and not have submitted more than two prior applications regardless of whether the applicant has been accepted or rejected. **Criteria:** Selection of applicants will be based on the following scholarship criteria: (1) Applicant's performance; (2) Scientific merit of the research project; (3) Quality and relevance of the research environment.

Funds Avail.: $30,000. **Duration:** Annual. **To Apply:** Applicants must complete the application form available on the website; must submit the official transcripts of all university grades, including those for completed programs and those under way; must provide an evaluation form from each of two scientists other than the research supervisor, who have participated in the applicant's education; must provide a letter of recommendation written by the research supervisor; a proof of Canadian citizenship and a copy of valid Quebec health insurance card. **Deadline:** October. **Contact:** Michel Asselin, Research advisor, Coordinator of the Graduate Scholarship Program; e-mail: bourses@irsst.qc.ca.

4922 ■ IRSST Postdoctoral Scholarships Abroad
(Postdoctorate/Fellowship)

Purpose: To financially assist graduate students who want to enhance their research programs which deal with the prevention of industrial accidents and occupational diseases or the rehabilitation of affected workers. **Focus:** Occupational safety and health. **Qualif.:** Applicants must be Canadian citizens within the meaning of the Citizenship Act (R.S.C. 1985, c. C-29) or permanent residents of Canada within the meaning of the Immigration and Refugee Protection Act (S.C. 2001, c. 27); must be permanent residents of Quebec within the meaning of the Health Insurance Act and be domiciled in Quebec; must have held a PhD. for no more than four year. **Criteria:** Selection of applicants will be based on the following scholarship criteria: (1) Applicant's performance; (2) Scientific merit of the research project; (3) Quality and relevance of the research environment.

Funds Avail.: $36,000. **Duration:** Annual. **To Apply:** Applicants must complete the application form available on the website; must submit the official transcripts of all

university grades, including those for completed programs and those under way; must provide an evaluation form from each of two scientists other than the research supervisor, who have participated in the applicant's education; must provide a letter of recommendation written by the research supervisor. **Deadline:** October. **Contact:** Michel Asselin, Research advisor, Coordinator of the Graduate Scholarship Program; e-mail: bourses@irsst.qc.ca.

4923 ■ Institut des Sciences Mathematiques (ISM)
University of Quebec in Montreal
201, ave. du President-Kennedy, office PK-5211
Montreal, QC, Canada H2X 3Y7
Ph: (514)987-3000
Fax: (514)987-8935
E-mail: ism@uqam.ca
URL: ism.uqam.ca/~ism/?language=default

4924 ■ ISM Doctoral Fellowships *(Doctorate/ Fellowship)*

Purpose: To provide financial support for outstanding, new students intending to pursue a doctoral program at one of the ISM member universities. **Focus:** Mathematics and mathematical sciences. **Qualif.:** Applicant must hold (at the time of the award) a degree in mathematics or statistics from a recognized university. **Criteria:** Selection is based on submitted application and materials.

Funds Avail.: $20,000/year. **Duration:** two years. **To Apply:** Applicants must complete the application online and must submit a curriculum vitae, all university transcripts, names and email addresses of two to five persons who will write the letters of recommendation; and Mathematics GRE results (optional). **Deadline:** January 16.

4925 ■ ISM Scholarships for Graduate Studies
(Graduate/Scholarship)

Purpose: To support students who wish to complete a PhD in mathematics. **Focus:** Mathematics and mathematical sciences. **Qualif.:** Applicant must be enrolled to a graduate study program in mathematics at one of the member universities. **Criteria:** Selection is based on excellent academic record and research aptitude and experience.

Funds Avail.: No specific amount. **To Apply:** Applicants must submit up-to-date university transcripts (graduate and undergraduate); a curriculum vitae; and two letters of recommendation. The applicant must submit application materials to his/her host departments. **Deadline:** March 2.

4926 ■ Institute for Anarchist Studies
PO Box 15586
Washington, DC 20003
E-mail: info@anarchiststudies.org
URL: www.anarchist-studies.org

4927 ■ Institute for Anarchist Studies Grants for Radical Writers and Translators *(Professional development/Grant)*

Purpose: To support writers and translators in the development of theoretical tools, contemporary anarchist theory and practice. **Focus:** General studies/Field of study not specified. **Qualif.:** Applicants must be essay writers and translators. **Criteria:** Applicants will be evaluated based on content of the submitted work, ability to complete the project and publishing plans.

Awards are arranged alphabetically below their administering organizations

Funds Avail.: $4,000. **Duration:** Annual. **To Apply:** Applicants must complete the application form and mail 14 copies; must provide an essay or translation project. **Deadline:** January 15.

4928 ■ Institute for Diversity in Health Management

155 N Wacker Ave.
Chicago, IL 60606
Ph: (312)422-2630
Fax: (312)278-0893
E-mail: institute@aha.org
URL: www.diversityconnection.org

4929 ■ Cathy L. Brock Memorial Scholarships
(Graduate/Scholarship)

Purpose: To provide financial support to help fund graduate education for students preparing for a career as health administrators. **Focus:** Health education; Health services administration. **Qualif.:** Applicant must be a first or second year graduate student pursuing a degree in healthcare administration or a comparable degree program (MBA, MPH, MHA, MPA, MSN or BSN); must demonstrate financial need and a commitment to community service; must excel academically (minimum 3.0 GPA); must be a member of a federally classified ethnic minority group and have proof of U.S. citizenship. **Criteria:** Selection is based on leadership potential, academic achievement, community involvement, commitment to health care administration, financial need and overall professional maturity.

Funds Avail.: $1,000. **Duration:** Annual. **Number Awarded:** 1. **To Apply:** Applicants are required to complete the application online. **Deadline:** January 9. **Contact:** Chris O. Biddle, Education Specialist; Phone: 312-422-2658; Email:cbiddle@aha.org.

4930 ■ Elliott C. Roberts Scholarships *(Graduate/Scholarship)*

Purpose: To provide financial support to help fund graduate education for students preparing for a career as health administrators. **Focus:** Health education; Health services administration. **Qualif.:** Applicant must be a first or second year graduate student pursuing a degree in healthcare administration or a comparable degree program (MBA, MPH, MHA, MPA, MSN or BSN); must demonstrate financial need and a commitment to community service; must excel academically (minimum 3.0 GPA); must be a member of a federally classified ethnic minority group and have proof of U.S. citizenship. **Criteria:** Selection is based on leadership potential, academic achievement, community involvement, commitment to health care administration, financial need and overall professional maturity.

Funds Avail.: $1,000. **Duration:** Annual. **Number Awarded:** 1. **To Apply:** Applicants are required to complete the application online. **Deadline:** January 9. **Contact:** institutescholarship@aha.org.

4931 ■ Transamerica Retirement Solutions Leaders in Health Care Scholarships *(Graduate/Scholarship)*

Purpose: To provide financial support to help fund graduate education for students preparing for a career as health administrators. **Focus:** Health education; Health services administration. **Qualif.:** Applicant must be a first or second year graduate student pursuing a degree in healthcare administration or a comparable degree program (MBA,

MPH, MHA, MPA, MSN or BSN); must demonstrate financial need and a commitment to community service; must excel academically (minimum 3.0 GPA); must be a member of a federally classified ethnic minority group and have proof of U.S. citizenship. **Criteria:** Selection is based on leadership potential, academic achievement, community involvement, commitment to health care administration, financial need and overall professional maturity.

Funds Avail.: $5,000. **Duration:** Annual. **Number Awarded:** 2. **To Apply:** Applicants are required to complete the application online. **Deadline:** January 9. **Contact:** Chris O. Biddle, Education Specialist; Phone: 312-422-2658; Email:cbiddle@aha.org.

4932 ■ Institute of Food Technologists (IFT)

525 W Van Buren St., Ste. 1000
Chicago, IL 60607
Ph: (312)782-8424
Fax: (312)782-8348
Free: 800-438-3663
E-mail: info@ift.org
URL: www.ift.org

4933 ■ Institute of Food Technologists Graduate Scholarships *(Graduate/Scholarship)*

Purpose: To support and encourage outstanding research and education in food science and technology. **Focus:** Food science and technology. **Qualif.:** Applicants must possess a minimum of a 3.0 GPA and an exemplary interest in food science and research together with demonstrated scientific aptitude. Applicants' research must be in such disciplines as genetics, horticulture, nutrition, microbiology, biochemistry, engineering, chemistry, etc. Program is also open to students who are enrolled in graduate studies leading to an M.S. or PhD at the time the scholarship becomes effective. **Criteria:** Recipients are selected based on scholastic standing, leadership ability and demonstrated diversity in the food industry.

Funds Avail.: Varies. **Duration:** Annual. **Number Awarded:** Varies. **To Apply:** Applicants must submit an application stating their name and contact information; degrees held; date received; department and institution where degrees were received; degree; department and institution where study will be conducted; statement outlining student's career objectives; list of extracurricular activities and hobbies; list of awards, honors and scholarship received; detailed information regarding publications and presentations; summary of work experience; and a typewritten outline of proposed field of research. Applicants must also submit an official transcript of records. **Deadline:** February 20.

4934 ■ Institute of Food Technologists Junior/ Senior Scholarships *(Undergraduate/Scholarship)*

Purpose: To encourage and support undergraduate students intending to pursue a career in the field of food science/technology and in other related areas. **Focus:** Food science and technology. **Qualif.:** Program is open to sophomores, juniors or seniors with a 3.0 GPA or above, pursuing a curriculum in food science or food technology in an educational institution having an IFT approved degree program. **Criteria:** Recipients are selected based on scholastic standing, leadership ability and demonstrated diversity in food industry.

Funds Avail.: No specific amount. **Duration:** Annual. **Num-**

Awards are arranged alphabetically below their administering organizations

ber Awarded: Varies. **To Apply:** Applicants must submit an application form including name and contact information, degree and department where the study will be conducted; statement outlining students career objectives; list of extracurricular activities and hobbies; list of awards, honors and scholarship received; summary of work experience. Applicants must submit an official transcript of all college courses completed. Applicants must submit two letters of recommendation from a faculty member who is familiar with the applicant. **Contact:** Institute of Food Technologists at info@ift.org.

4935 ■ Institute of Food Technologists Sophomore Scholarships *(Undergraduate/Scholarship)*

Purpose: To inspire careers in the field of food science/technology. **Focus:** Food science and technology. **Qualif.:** Applicants must be freshmen students intending to enroll in an approved food science/technology program and who have maintained at least 3.0 GPA for the first term of study and are recommended by the department head. **Criteria:** Recipients are selected based on scholastic eligibility.

Funds Avail.: No specific amount. **Duration:** Annual. **To Apply:** Applicants must complete the application form; must submit an official transcript of record; letter of recommendation from a faculty member in the food science/food technology department who is familiar with the applicant's eligibility; a one-page essay stating why they desire to continue their studies in food science and/or food technology. **Deadline:** February 10. **Contact:** Institute of Food Technologists at info@ift.org.

4936 ■ Institute of Food Technologists - Alamo Section

c/o Scott McCormick, Golf Sceretary
C.H. Guenther and Son
2201 Broadway St.
San Antonio, TX 78230
Ph: (210)351-6261
E-mail: info@alamoift.org
URL: www.alamoift.org

4937 ■ Alamo IFT Scholarship *(Undergraduate/Scholarship)*

Purpose: To provide assistance for local students pursuing their studies. **Focus:** General studies/Field of study not specified. **Qualif.:** The student must be an undergraduate that is currently enrolled and pursuing a degree in Food Science and Technology or the Culinary Arts. **Criteria:** Selection will be based on the committee's criteria.

Funds Avail.: No specific amount. **Duration:** Annual. **To Apply:** Interested applicants must contact the IFT Alamo Section for the application details.

4938 ■ Institute of Food Technologists - Great Lakes Section

c/o John Bailey, Treasurer
232 Hidden Forest Rd.
Battle Creek, MI 49014
E-mail: greatlakesift@gmail.com
URL: www.greatlakesift.org

4939 ■ Clifford L. Bedford Scholarship Award *(Undergraduate/Scholarship)*

Purpose: To support an undergraduate student pursuing a career in food industry. **Focus:** Food science and technol-

ogy. **Qualif.:** Applicants must be undergraduate students who intend to pursue a career in the food industry; must have at least 3.0 GPA; must be active members of IFT and GLS-IFT; must be enrolled in an accredited Michigan college or university. **Criteria:** Selection shall be made on the basis of both academic and non-academic performance.

Funds Avail.: $1,000. **Duration:** Annual. **To Apply:** Applicants may visit the website for the online application; must submit two signed letters of recommendation (in pdf form) emailed or uploaded directly by persons who are recommending the students; letters must be from faculty members or employers familiar with the scholarship applicants' training and other abilities. **Deadline:** February 28. **Contact:** Todd A. Van Thomme, GLS-IFT Scholarship Award Committee Chair: Phone: 616-949-9610.

4940 ■ Great Lakes Section Diversity Scholarship *(Graduate, Undergraduate/Scholarship)*

Purpose: To support students pursuing careers in the food industry. **Focus:** Food science and technology. **Qualif.:** Applicant must have a student membership in IFT; enrolled in an accredited Michigan college or university; with at least 3.0 GPA. **Criteria:** Selection of all award recipients will be made by the Scholarship Awards Committee as outlined by the GLS-IFT by-laws.

Funds Avail.: $1,000. **Duration:** Annual. **To Apply:** Applicants may visit the website for the online application; must submit Two signed letters of recommendation (in pdf form) emailed or uploaded directly by the person who is recommending the student; letters must be from faculty members or employers familiar with the scholarship applicant's training and other abilities. **Deadline:** February 28. **Contact:** Todd A. Van Thomme, GLS-IFT Scholarship Award Committee Chair: Phone: 616-949-9610.

4941 ■ Institute for Health Metrics and Evaluation (IHME)

2301 5th Ave., Ste. 600
Seattle, WA 98121
Ph: (206)897-2800
Fax: (206)897-2899
E-mail: ihme@healthdata.org
URL: www.healthdata.org

4942 ■ Institute for Health Metrics and Evaluation Post Bachelor Fellowships *(Graduate/Fellowship)*

Purpose: To provide opportunities for recent college graduates with strong quantitative skills to train with faculty and senior researchers on a variety of global health projects. **Focus:** Public health. **Qualif.:** Applicant must have a Bachelor's degree and proven quantitative and analytical skills, with high academic potential and a strong interest in pursuing an academic or professional career related to global health. **Criteria:** All submitted application materials will be reviewed by a team of faculty, senior researchers and the Education and Training Office at IHME.

Funds Avail.: 1st year fellow - $40,008; 2nd year fellow - $44,004; 3rd year fellow - $45,324. **Duration:** 2 years. **To Apply:** Applicants must submit a resume (two-page limit); official copy of academic transcripts; one letter of reference from a professor or professional familiar with the applicant's coursework or research; and a brief personal statement (500-word max) on how the applicant's skills, experience and long-term career goals contribute to his/her candidacy. **Deadline:** January 10. **Contact:** Please contact us at: pbfs@healthdata.org.

Awards are arranged alphabetically below their administering organizations

4943 ■ Institute for Health Metrics and Evaluation Post Graduate Fellowships *(Doctorate, Postdoctorate/ Fellowship)*

Purpose: To provide opportunities both for self-directed research and interdisciplinary collaboration in health metrics. **Focus:** Public health. **Qualif.:** Applicant must be have a PhD or MD; have a strong quantitative background, with advanced research experience, especially with data analysis and statistical methods. **Criteria:** Candidate selection includes a phone interview and final interview, usually held at IHME offices.

Funds Avail.: $50,000. **Duration:** One year. **To Apply:** Applicants must submit a cover letter; curriculum vitae or resume; a personal statement; three sealed letters of recommendation; highest degree attained transcript; English reprint of most significant publication or research paper; and proof of proficiency in English for candidates whose native language is not English. **Deadline:** November 1. **Contact:** pgf@healthdata.org.

4944 ■ Institute for Humane Studies (IHS)
George Mason University
3434 Washington Blvd., MS 1C5
Arlington, VA 22201
Ph: (703)993-4880
URL: www.theihs.org

4945 ■ Humane Studies Fellowships *(Graduate/ Fellowship, Scholarship)*

Purpose: To provide financial assistance to support the work of outstanding students interested in exploring the principles, practices and institutions necessary for a free society through their academic work. **Focus:** General studies/Field of study not specified. **Qualif.:** Applicants must be full-time graduate students or undergraduate juniors or seniors during academic year; must clearly demonstrate research interest in the intellectual and institutional foundations of a free society. **Criteria:** Candidates will be evaluated based on academic or professional performance, potential for success in chosen field and relevance of work to the advancement of a free society.

Funds Avail.: $2,000-$15,000. **Duration:** Annual. **To Apply:** Applicants must submit applications online which include completed application form; college transcripts; admission test scores; two recommendations; essays; writing sample; dissertation proposal; and a non-refundable $25.00 application fee. **Deadline:** Applications must be submitted on December 31.

4946 ■ Institute of Industrial Engineers (IIE)
3577 Parkway Ln., Ste. 200
Norcross, GA 30092
Ph: (770)449-0460
Fax: (770)441-3295
Free: 800-494-0460
E-mail: executiveoffices@iienet.org
URL: www.iienet2.org

4947 ■ John S.W. Fargher Scholarships *(Graduate/ Scholarship)*

Purpose: To recognize academic excellence and noteworthy contribution to the development of the industrial engineering profession. **Focus:** Engineering, Industrial. **Qualif.:** Applicants must be graduate students enrolled in

any school in the United States and its territories, provided that the school's engineering program or equivalent is accredited by an accrediting agency recognized by IIE and the students are pursuing a course of study in industrial engineering or engineering management. **Criteria:** Applicants will be selected based on GPA, IIE student chapter involvement and nomination letter.

Funds Avail.: $1,000. **Duration:** Annual. **Number Awarded:** 1. **To Apply:** Applicants must submit a nomination letter, along with an official transcript to IIE. **Deadline:** September 1. **Contact:** Bonnie Cameron, headquarters operations administrator, 770-449-0461, ext. 105; email: bcameron@iienet.org.

4948 ■ Dwight D. Gardner Scholarships *(Undergraduate/Scholarship)*

Purpose: To recognize undergraduate industrial engineering students for academic excellence and campus leadership. **Focus:** Engineering, Industrial. **Qualif.:** Candidates must be undergraduate students enrolled in any school in the United States and its territories, Canada and Mexico, provided that the school's engineering program or equivalent is accredited by an agency or organization recognized by IIE and the student is pursuing a course of study in industrial engineering. Candidates must be active Institute members and have an overall average of 3.40 on a scale of 0-4.00. **Criteria:** Scholarship recipient will be selected based on scholastic ability, character, leadership, potential service to the industrial engineering profession and need for financial assistance. Preference will be given to applicants who have demonstrated an interest in management consulting.

Funds Avail.: $3,000. **Duration:** Annual. **Number Awarded:** 3. **To Apply:** Candidates must be nominated by IE department heads and mailed to the Institute headquarters. After the review of nominations, eligible candidates will receive an application package that must be completed and sent back to IIE. **Deadline:** February 1.

4949 ■ Gilbreth Memorial Fellowships *(Graduate/ Scholarship)*

Purpose: To recognize graduate industrial engineering students for academic excellence and campus leadership. **Focus:** Engineering, Industrial. **Qualif.:** Candidates must be graduate students enrolled in any school in the United States and its territories, Canada and Mexico, pursuing and advanced degree in industrial engineering or equivalent. Candidates must be active Institute members and have an overall average of 3.40 on a scale of 0-4.00. **Criteria:** Scholarship recipient will be selected based on scholastic ability, character, leadership, potential service to the industrial engineering profession and need for financial assistance. Preference will be given to applicants who have demonstrated an interest in management consulting.

Funds Avail.: $3,000. **Number Awarded:** 2. **To Apply:** Candidates must be nominated by IE department heads and mailed to the Institute headquarters. After review of nominations, eligible candidates will receive an application package that must be completed and sent back to IIE. **Deadline:** February 1.

4950 ■ IIE Council of Fellows Undergraduate Scholarships *(Undergraduate/Scholarship)*

Purpose: To reward outstanding academic scholarship and leadership at the undergraduate level. **Focus:** Engineering, Industrial. **Qualif.:** Applicants must be undergraduate students enrolled in any school provided that the school's

Awards are arranged alphabetically below their administering organizations

industrial engineering program or equivalent is accredited by an agency or organization recognized by IIE and the students are pursuing a course of study in industrial engineering. **Criteria:** Selection shall be based on scholastic ability, character, leadership, potential service to the industrial engineering profession and need for financial assistance.

Funds Avail.: $1,000 each. **Duration:** Annual. **Number Awarded:** 2. **To Apply:** Applicants must be nominated by IE department heads and mailed to the Institute headquarters by the deadline fixed by the Institute. After the review of nominations, eligible candidates will receive an application package that must be completed and sent back to IIE. **Deadline:** November 15. **Contact:** Bonnie Cameron, headquarters operations administrator, 770-449-0461, ext. 105; email: bcameron@iienet.org.

4951 ■ IIE Presidents Scholarships *(Undergraduate/Scholarship)*

Purpose: To recognize excellence in scholarly activities and leadership of the industrial engineering profession. **Focus:** Engineering, Industrial. **Qualif.:** Applicants must be undergraduate students pursuing a course of study in industrial engineering who are active in a student chapter, and have demonstrated leadership and promoted IIE involvement on campus. **Criteria:** Selection shall be based on the aforementioned applicants' qualifications and compliance with the application details.

Funds Avail.: $1,000. **Duration:** Annual. **Number Awarded:** 1. **To Apply:** Applicants must be nominated by IE department heads and mailed to the Institute headquarters by the deadline fixed by the Institute. After the review of nominations, eligible candidates will receive an application package that must be completed and sent back to IIE. **Deadline:** November 15. **Contact:** Bonnie Cameron, headquarters operations administrator, 770-449-0461, ext. 105; email: bcameron@iienet.org.

4952 ■ John L. Imhoff Scholarships *(Graduate, Undergraduate/Scholarship)*

Purpose: To recognize and support a student pursuing an industrial engineering degree who, by academic, employment and/or professional achievements, has made noteworthy contributions to the development of the industrial engineering profession through international understanding. **Focus:** Engineering, Industrial. **Qualif.:** Candidates must be pursuing a BS in an accredited IE program, or have a BS in IE and pursuing a master's or doctorate degree in an accredited IE program. **Criteria:** Selection shall be based on the aforementioned candidates' qualifications and compliance with the application details.

Funds Avail.: $1,000. **Duration:** Annual. **Number Awarded:** 1. **To Apply:** Candidates must submit a completed application form; a written essay describing candidate's international contributions to, or experience in, industrial engineering; and three references reinforcing applicant's contributions to the industrial engineering profession through international understanding. **Deadline:** November 15. **Contact:** Bonnie Cameron, headquarters operations administrator, 770-449-0461, ext. 105; email: bcameron@iienet.org.

4953 ■ Harold and Inge Marcus Scholarships *(Undergraduate/Scholarship)*

Purpose: To recognize undergraduate industrial engineering students for academic excellence and noteworthy contribution to the development of the industrial engineer-

ing profession. **Focus:** Engineering, Industrial. **Qualif.:** Applicants must be undergraduate students enrolled in any school in the United States, provided that the school's engineering program is accredited by an agency recognized by IIE and the student is pursuing a course of study in industrial engineering. **Criteria:** Selection shall be based on scholastic ability, character, leadership, potential service to the industrial engineering profession and need for financial assistance.

Funds Avail.: $1,000. **Duration:** Annual. **Number Awarded:** 1. **To Apply:** Applicants must be nominated by IE department heads and mailed to the Institute headquarters by the deadline fixed by the Institute. After the review of nominations, eligible candidates will receive an application package that must be completed and sent back to IIE. **Deadline:** November 15. **Contact:** Bonnie Cameron, headquarters operations administrator, 770-449-0461, ext. 105; email: bcameron@iienet.org.

4954 ■ Marvin Mundel Memorial Scholarships *(Undergraduate/Scholarship)*

Purpose: To support the education of industrial engineering students for academic excellence and campus leadership. **Focus:** Engineering, Industrial. **Qualif.:** Applicants must be undergraduate students enrolled in any school in the United States and its territories, Canada and Mexico, provided that the school's industrial engineering program or equivalent is accredited by an agency or organization recognized by IIE and the students are pursuing a course of study in industrial engineering. **Criteria:** Selection shall be based on scholastic ability, character, leadership, potential service to the industrial engineering profession and need for financial assistance. Preference will be given to applicants who have demonstrated an interest in work measurement and methods engineering.

Funds Avail.: $1,000 each. **Duration:** Annual. **Number Awarded:** 2. **To Apply:** Applicants must be nominated by IE department heads and mailed to the Institute headquarters by the deadline fixed by the Institute. After the review of nominations, eligible candidates will receive an application package that must be completed and sent back to IIE. **Deadline:** November 15. **Contact:** Bonnie Cameron, headquarters operations administrator, 770-449-0461, ext. 105; email: bcameron@iienet.org.

4955 ■ A.O. Putnam Memorial Scholarships *(Undergraduate/Scholarship)*

Purpose: To support the education of industrial engineering students for academic excellence and campus leadership. **Focus:** Engineering, Industrial. **Qualif.:** Applicants must be undergraduate students enrolled in any school in the United States and its territories, Canada and Mexico, provided that the school's industrial engineering program or equivalent is accredited by an agency or organization recognized by IIE and the students are pursuing a course of study in industrial engineering. **Criteria:** Selection shall be based on scholastic ability, character, leadership, potential service to the industrial engineering profession and need for financial assistance. Preference will be given to applicants who have demonstrated an interest in management consulting.

Funds Avail.: $700. **Duration:** Annual. **Number Awarded:** 1. **To Apply:** Applicants must be nominated by IE department heads and mailed to the Institute headquarters by the deadline fixed by the Institute. After the review of nominations, eligible candidates will receive an application package that must be completed and sent back to IIE. **Deadline:**

Awards are arranged alphabetically below their administering organizations

November 15. **Contact:** Bonnie Cameron, headquarters operations administrator, 770-449-0461, ext. 105; email: bcameron@iienet.org.

4956 ■ E.J. Sierleja Memorial Fellowships (Graduate/ Fellowship)

Purpose: To recognize graduate students for academic excellence and campus leadership. **Focus:** Transportation. **Qualif.:** Candidates must be graduate students pursuing advanced studies in the area of transportation. **Criteria:** Preference will be given to students pursuing advanced studies on rail transportation.

Funds Avail.: $700. **Duration:** Annual. **Number Awarded:** 1. **To Apply:** Candidates must be nominated by IE department heads. Nominations must be mailed to the Institute headquarters. Candidates must submit a completed application package to IIE. **Deadline:** February 1. **Contact:** Bonnie Cameron at the above address.

4957 ■ United Parcel Service Scholarships for Female Students (Undergraduate/Scholarship)

Purpose: To support the education of industrial engineering students for academic excellence and campus leadership. **Focus:** Engineering, Industrial. **Qualif.:** Applicants must be undergraduate students enrolled in any school in the United States and its territories, Canada and Mexico, provided that the school's industrial engineering program or equivalent is accredited by an agency or organization recognized by IIE and the students are pursuing a course of study in industrial engineering. **Criteria:** Selection shall be based on scholastic ability, character, leadership, potential service to the industrial engineering profession and need for financial assistance. Preference will be given to applicants who have demonstrated an interest in management consulting.

Funds Avail.: $4,000. **Duration:** Annual. **Number Awarded:** 1. **To Apply:** Applicants must be nominated by IE department heads and mailed to the Institute headquarters by the deadline fixed by the Institute. After the review of nominations, eligible candidates will receive an application package that must be completed and sent back to IIE. **Deadline:** November 15. **Contact:** Bonnie Cameron, headquarters operations administrator, 770-449-0461, ext. 105; email: bcameron@iienet.org.

4958 ■ United Parcel Service Scholarships for Minority Students (Undergraduate/Scholarship)

Purpose: To support the education of industrial engineering students for academic excellence and campus leadership. **Focus:** Engineering, Industrial. **Qualif.:** Applicants must be undergraduate students enrolled in any school in the United States and its territories, Canada and Mexico, provided that the school's industrial engineering program or equivalent is accredited by an agency or organization recognized by IIE and the students are pursuing a course of study in industrial engineering. **Criteria:** Selection shall be based on scholastic ability, character, leadership, potential service to the industrial engineering profession and need for financial assistance. Preference will be given to applicants who have demonstrated an interest in management consulting.

Funds Avail.: $4,000. **Duration:** Annual. **Number Awarded:** 1. **To Apply:** Applicants must be nominated by IE department heads and mailed to the Institute headquarters by the deadline fixed by the Institute. After the review of nominations, eligible candidates will receive an application package that must be completed and sent back to IIE.

Deadline: November 15. **Contact:** Bonnie Cameron, headquarters operations administrator, 770-449-0461, ext. 105; email: bcameron@iienet.org.

4959 ■ Lisa Zaken Awards For Excellence (Graduate, Undergraduate/Scholarship)

Purpose: To recognize excellence in scholarly activities and leadership related to the industrial engineering profession on campus. **Focus:** Engineering, Industrial. **Qualif.:** Candidates must be undergraduate and graduate students enrolled in any school, and pursuing a course of study in industrial engineering. Candidates must also be active in a student chapter having demonstrated leadership, as well as having promoted IIE involvement on campus, and have an overall grade point average of 3.00 on a scale of 0-4.00. **Criteria:** Candidates will be selected based on GPA, IIE student chapter involvement and nomination letter.

Funds Avail.: $700. **Duration:** Annual. **Number Awarded:** 1. **To Apply:** Candidates must submit a nomination letter, along with an official transcript to IIE. **Deadline:** November 15. **Contact:** Bonnie Cameron, headquarters operations administrator, 770-449-0461, ext. 105; email: bcameron@iienet.org.

4960 ■ Institute of International Education (IIE)

IIE New York City
809 United Nations Plz.
New York, NY 10017-3503
Ph: (212)883-8200
Fax: (212)984-5452
E-mail: membership@iie.org
URL: www.iie.org

4961 ■ David L. Boren Fellowships (Graduate/ Fellowship)

Purpose: To support graduate students to add an important international and language component to their graduate education through specialization in area study, language study or increased language proficiency. **Focus:** Area and ethnic studies; International affairs and relations. **Qualif.:** Applicants must be American graduate students. **Criteria:** Selection will be based on the committee's criteria.

Funds Avail.: $30,000. **Duration:** Annual. **To Apply:** Interested applicants may contact the IIE for the application process and other information. **Deadline:** January 28.

4962 ■ David L. Boren Scholarships (Undergraduate, College/Scholarship)

Purpose: To support students who wish to study abroad in areas of the world that are critical to the nation's interests and underrepresented in study abroad. **Focus:** Area and ethnic studies; International affairs and relations. **Qualif.:** Applicants must be American undergraduate students. **Criteria:** Selection will be based on the committee's criteria.

Funds Avail.: $20,000. **Duration:** Annual. **To Apply:** Interested applicants may contact the IIE for the application process and other information. **Deadline:** February 5. **Remarks:** Funded by the National Security Education Program.

4963 ■ Institute for International Law and Justice (IILJ)

New York University School of Law
139 MacDougal St., 3rd Fl.
New York, NY 10012

Awards are arranged alphabetically below their administering organizations

Ph: (212)998-6709
Fax: (212)995-3825
E-mail: iilj@exchange.law.nyu.edu
URL: www.iilj.org

4964 ■ IILJ Scholarships *(Doctorate/Scholarship)*

Purpose: To promote the study of law. **Focus:** Law. **Qualif.:** Applicants must be law school students with outstanding academic backgrounds and strong international law interests. **Criteria:** Selection will be based on the committee's criteria.

Funds Avail.: No specific amount. **To Apply:** Applicants must complete the appropriate section of the JD application. Interested applicants are asked to submit a one-page essay, of no more than 500 words, with the JD application. The essay should explain how their approach and commitment to scholarship and to their intended study of international law make them a suitable candidate for the Scholars Program. **Deadline:** March. **Contact:** iilj@juris.law.nyu.edu.

4965 ■ IILJ Visiting Fellowships and Research *(Postdoctorate/Fellowship)*

Purpose: To promote the study of law. **Focus:** Law. **Qualif.:** Applicants must be postdoctoral scholars or professorial visitors holding academic positions in other universities who are in full-time residence at the Law School. Full-time doctoral students of non-law departments of universities in the greater New York area, whose work is directly focused on central concerns of the program, may also be invited to participate informally in activities of the program. **Criteria:** Selection will be on a competitive basis.

Funds Avail.: No specific amount. **Duration:** Annual. **To Apply:** Applicants must complete and submit the application to the Hauser Global Law School program office. **Contact:** iilj@juris.law.nyu.edu.

4966 ■ Institute of Management Accountants (IMA)

10 Paragon Dr., Ste. 1
Montvale, NJ 07645-1774
Ph: (201)573-9000
Free: 800-638-4427
E-mail: ima@imanet.org
URL: www.imanet.org

4967 ■ Stuart Cameron and Margaret McLeod Memorial Scholarships (SCMS) *(Graduate, Undergraduate/Scholarship)*

Purpose: To help student members of IMA offset the high cost of education and pursue further studies in preparation for careers in accounting, management and finance. **Focus:** Accounting; Finance; Management. **Qualif.:** Applicants must be IMA student members (membership number must be indicated in the application); may either be full or part-time students with strictly 12 credits per semester; must be physically located in the United States or Puerto Rico studying at regionally accredited institutions; have minimum GPA of 3.0 throughout undergraduate/graduate academic career; pursuing a career in management accounting, financial management or information. **Criteria:** Selection of applicants will be based on academic merit, IMA participation, quality of presentation and other materials provided.

Funds Avail.: $5,000 and a maximum of $1,000 for the combined cost of lodging and transportation to attend both events. **To Apply:** Applicants must submit (one-page) resume; official university transcripts with school seal enclosed in a sealed envelope; two recommendations (from current or past employer, professor or an IMA member); should be in an attached form with reference's signature across the envelope seal; and (two-page) written statement indicating: reasons for applying for scholarship, why she/he deserves the award, specific contributions to IMA and ideas on how he/she will promote awareness, increase membership and certification within IMA. **Deadline:** February 15.

4968 ■ IMA Memorial Education Fund Scholarships (MEF) *(Graduate, Undergraduate/Scholarship)*

Purpose: To help student members of IMA offset the high cost of education and pursue further studies in preparation for careers in accounting, management and finance. **Focus:** Accounting; Finance; Management. **Qualif.:** Applicants must be IMA student members (membership number must be indicated in the application); must be physically located in the United States or Puerto Rico and is currently studying at regionally accredited institutions; must have minimum GPA of 3.0 throughout undergraduate/graduate academic career; pursuing a career in management accounting, financial management, or information; and must carry at least six credits per semester. **Criteria:** Selection of applicants will be based on academic merit; IMA participation; quality of presentation; and strength of recommendation.

Funds Avail.: $1,000-$2,500. **Duration:** Annual. **To Apply:** Applicants must submit (one-page) resume; official university transcripts with school seal enclosed in a sealed envelope; two letters of recommendations (from current or past employer, professor or an IMA member). Should be in an attached form with reference's signature across the envelope seal; and (two-page) written statement indicating: career goals and objectives; reasons for applying the scholarship, statements why the applicant deserves the award, specific contributions to IMA, suggestions on promoting awareness, increasing membership and certification within IMA. **Deadline:** February 15.

4969 ■ Institute of Management Accountants FAR Doctoral Student Grants Program *(Doctorate/Grant)*

Purpose: To financially assist accounting doctoral students who are pursuing research for the advancement of management accounting profession. **Focus:** Accounting. **Qualif.:** Applicant must be an accounting doctoral student. **Criteria:** Proposals will be reviewed and evaluated by the FAR Board of Trustees and Directors.

Funds Avail.: No specific amount. **To Apply:** Applicants must prepare a research plan; a letter from the researcher's dissertation chair or faculty advisor; and a letter from student indicating: a) completion of the doctoral program; b) plans for submitting the research to academic journal; c) discussion of research; d) budget proposal. Materials should be submitted electronically (PDF or Word document). **Remarks:** Established in 2005.

4970 ■ Institute for Public Relations (IPR)

2096 Weimer Hall
Gainesville, FL 32611-8400
Ph: (352)392-0280
Fax: (352)846-1122
URL: www.instituteforpr.org

4971 ■ IPR Pathfinder Award *(Advanced Professional/Recognition, Grant)*

Purpose: To recognize an original program of scholarly research that has made a significant contribution to the

Awards are arranged alphabetically below their administering organizations

body of knowledge and practice of public relations. **Focus:** Public relations. **Qualif.:** Applicants must be professionals who are conducting or writing research related to the public relations. **Criteria:** The selection committee is particularly interested in scholarly contributions resulting in the publication of major articles, chapters and/or books that integrates this program of research or articulates its importance to public relations research and practice.

Funds Avail.: $2,000. **Duration:** Annual. **Number Awarded:** 1. **To Apply:** Application details can be found at the program website.

4972 ■ Ketchum Excellence in Public Relations Research Award (Graduate/Fellowship, Internship)

Purpose: To bring the recipient onto Ketchum's premises for an important work experience, allowing the grad student to have a major practical experience and learn what "research that matters to the practice" means. **Focus:** Public relations.

Funds Avail.: $7,500 for ten-week PR research internship with Ketchum in New York City during summer; $2,500 stipend for the research paper after it has been accepted for publication by IPR. **Duration:** Annual. **Number Awarded:** 1. **Deadline:** February 26.

4973 ■ Institute of Real Estate Management (IREM)
430 N Michigan Ave.
Chicago, IL 60611
Fax: (800)338-4736
Free: 800-837-0706
E-mail: getinfo@irem.org
URL: www.irem.org

4974 ■ George M. Brooker, CPM Diversity Collegiate Scholarship (Graduate, Undergraduate/Scholarship)

Purpose: To attract young people from underrepresented populations into the real estate management business. **Focus:** Management; Real estate. **Qualif.:** Applicants must: be members of a minority (non-Caucasian) group; be citizens of the United States; be beginning in their junior or senior years of undergraduate work or pursuing graduate or post-graduate studies; have declared a major in real estate or a related field; have a minimum GPA of 3.0 on a 4.0 scale within their major; and have completed two courses in real estate or have indicated the intent to complete such courses. **Criteria:** Recipients are chosen based on merit.

Funds Avail.: $2,500 (undergraduate); $5,000 (graduate). **Duration:** Semiannual. **Number Awarded:** Varies. **To Apply:** Applicants must submit complete application (available in the website), three letters of recommendation of which one must come from the college dean, written essay (not to exceed 500 words) explaining the applicants' interest in the industry, and a letter of recommendation from local IREM chapter president or officer. **Deadline:** June 30; December 31.

4975 ■ Donald M. Furbush Professional Development Grants (Other/Grant)

Purpose: To provide funding for individuals to follow the institute's entire curriculum required to qualify for the CPM designation, ARM certification and Accredited Commercial Manager certification, thus promoting professional development. **Focus:** Management; Real estate. **Qualif.:** Nominees

must be of legal age in the country in which the nominee resides; and must be actively employed in the real estate management industry. **Criteria:** Selection is based on commitment to professional excellence, financial need, strength of recommendation and personal commitment in gaining CPM designation.

Funds Avail.: up to $6,000. **To Apply:** Applicants must submit complete application (available in the website). **Deadline:** June 30.

4976 ■ Paul H. Rittle Sr. Professional Development Grants (Other/Grant)

Purpose: To provide financial assistance to individuals exploring a career in real estate management. **Focus:** Management; Real estate. **Qualif.:** Applicants must be of legal age and currently employed in some aspect of the real estate field. **Criteria:** Recipients are selected on the basis of financial need; commitment to real estate management as a career; and character as demonstrated by community involvement.

Funds Avail.: $3,000. **Duration:** Quarterly. **Number Awarded:** Varies. **To Apply:** Applicants must submit official application form; employer affidavit and financial status form; personal letter describing the objectives and information of the applicant; for U.S. citizen: a letter support from the local president or officer supporting your application; a copy of applicant's signed federal income tax return and Form W-2 for previous year; for international applicants: letter from employee or client if self-employed and total income indicated in Annual Income Statement for the previous year (if married include your spouse). **Deadline:** Monthly between the 15th and last day of the month except during the last quarter of the year.

4977 ■ Institute of Transportation Engineers (ITE)
1627 Eye St. NW, Ste. 600
Washington, DC 20006
Ph: (202)289-0222
Fax: (202)289-7722
E-mail: ite_staff@ite.org
URL: www.ite.org

4978 ■ Institute of Transportation Engineers - Texas District Fellowships (Graduate/Fellowship)

Purpose: To support students wishing to pursue a graduate study in transportation engineering. **Focus:** Transportation. **Qualif.:** Applicant must be planning to pursue a Master's degree in transportation engineering with a principal course work in traffic engineering, geometric design and/or transportation planning; have earned, or will earn a bachelor's degree and must be qualified for unconditional admission to the graduate study program at the chosen host university; must not be a previous recipient of the fellowship; and must be from Texas and pursuing study at one of the universities within the district. **Criteria:** Selection is based on applicant's past academic performance, the proposed program of study, an essay discussing the reasons for pursuing a graduate degree in transportation and outlining career objectives, as well as recommendations from three references.

Funds Avail.: $1,000. **Duration:** Annual. **Number Awarded:** Up to 2. **To Apply:** Applicants must submit an application along with the essay; a copy of resume; and a list of proposed courses taken in working toward the degree for each university/college listed. In addition, applicants

Awards are arranged alphabetically below their administering organizations

must submit, under separate cover, a completed reference form from each of the reference named in the application and an official transcript from each college/university attended prior or is currently attending. **Deadline:** April 1.

4979 ■ Institute of Transportation Engineers - Western District Fellowships (Graduate/Fellowship)

Purpose: To support students wishing to pursue a graduate study in transportation engineering. **Focus:** Transportation. **Qualif.:** Applicant must be planning to pursue a Master's degree in transportation engineering with principal course work in traffic engineering, geometric design and/or transportation planning; have earned, or will earn a bachelor's degree and must be qualified for unconditional admission to a graduate study program at the chosen host university; must not be a previous recipient of the fellowship; a resident of the Western District (Alaska, Arizona, California, Colorado, Hawaii, Idaho, Montana, Nevada, New Mexico, Oregon, Utah, Washington, Wyoming and all U.S. territories except Puerto Rico); and planning to study at one of the universities within the district. **Criteria:** Selection is based on applicant's past academic performance, the proposed program of study, an essay discussing the reasons for pursuing a graduate degree in transportation and outlining career objectives as well as recommendations from three references.

Funds Avail.: $1,000. **Duration:** Annual. **Number Awarded:** 1. **To Apply:** Applicants must submit an application along with the essay; a copy of resume; and a list of proposed courses taken in working toward the degree for each university/college listed. In addition, applicants must submit, under separate cover, a completed reference form from each of the reference named in the application and an official transcript from each college/university attended prior or is currently attending. **Deadline:** April 1.

4980 ■ Transoft Solutions, Inc. Ahead of the Curve Scholarships (AOTC) (Graduate, Undergraduate/ Scholarship)

Purpose: To encourage students to pursue studies in transportation and/or traffic engineering. **Focus:** Transportation. **Qualif.:** Applicant must be a transportation engineering student within the U.S. or Canada, and must not be a previous recipient of the scholarship. **Criteria:** Selection is based on the student's current academic performance, proposed program of study, an essay outlining career objectives, as well as recommendations from three references.

Funds Avail.: $2,000. **Duration:** Annual. **Number Awarded:** 1. **To Apply:** Applicants must submit an application along with the essay; a copy of resume; and a list of proposed courses taken in working toward the degree for each university/college listed. In addition, applicants must submit, under separate cover, a completed reference form from each of the reference named in the application, and an official transcript from each college/university attended prior or is currently attending. **Deadline:** April 1.

4981 ■ Institute of Turkish Studies (ITS)

Georgetown University
Intercultural Ctr. 305R
Washington, DC 20057-1033
Ph: (202)687-0292
Fax: (202)687-3780
E-mail: itsdirector@turkishstudies.org
URL: www.turkishstudies.org

Awards are arranged alphabetically below their administering organizations

4982 ■ Institute of Turkish Studies Dissertation Writing Grants (Graduate/Grant)

Purpose: To provide partial support for travel and research to Turkey for those who hold a Ph.D. in a social sciences or humanities discipline. **Focus:** Turkish studies. **Qualif.:** Applicants must be: graduate students in any field of the social sciences and/or humanities; U.S. citizens or permanent residents at the time of the application; currently enrolled in a Ph.D. degree program in the United States; and, expecting to complete all Ph.D. requirements except their dissertations by March the following year. **Criteria:** Recipients will be selected by the expert panels.

Funds Avail.: $5,000 to $15,000. **Duration:** Annual. **To Apply:** Applicants must send a two-page grant application cover sheet (available at the website); a maximum of six pages project proposal, double-space; budget; three letters of recommendation; curriculum vitae; and an academic transcript send by university registrar. Applications and supporting documents must be sent electronically in MS Word or PDF format or by regular mail. **Deadline:** March 2.

4983 ■ Institute of Turkish Studies Post-Doctoral Summer Travel-Research Grants (Postdoctorate/ Grant)

Purpose: To provide partial support for travel and research to Turkey for those who hold a Ph.D. in a social sciences or humanities discipline. **Focus:** Humanities; Social sciences; Turkish studies. **Qualif.:** Applicants must be U.S. citizens or permanent residents who are currently working in the United States and holding a Ph.D. in social science or humanities. **Criteria:** Recipients will be selected by the expert panels.

Funds Avail.: No specific amount. **Duration:** Annual. **To Apply:** Applicants must send a (two-page) grant application cover sheet available at the website; a project proposal (maximum of five pages, double-spaced); budget; three letters of recommendation; and a curriculum vitae. Applications and supporting documents must be sent electronically in MS Word or PDF format or by regular mail. **Deadline:** March 2.

4984 ■ Institute of Turkish Studies Sabbatical Research Grants (Other/Grant)

Purpose: To support faculty research during the course of their sabbaticals. **Focus:** Turkish studies. **Qualif.:** Applicants must be faculty members in the field of social sciences and/or humanities; must be U.S. citizens or permanent residents. **Criteria:** Recipients will be selected by the expert panels.

Funds Avail.: $25,000 each. **Duration:** Annual. **Number Awarded:** Varies. **To Apply:** Applicants must send a two-page grant application cover sheet available at the website; a project proposal (maximum of six pages, double-spaced); and a curriculum vitae. Applications must be sent electronically in MS Word or PDF format or by regular mail. **Deadline:** March 2.

4985 ■ Institute of Turkish Studies Summer Language Study Grants in Turkey (Graduate/Grant)

Purpose: To provide summer travel to Turkey in preparation for graduate research in language study. **Focus:** Humanities; Social sciences; Turkish studies. **Qualif.:** Applicants must be: U.S. citizens or permanent residents; graduate students in the field of social science or humanities; and, enrolled in a university within United States. **Criteria:** Recipients will be selected based on the final decision of the expert panels.

Funds Avail.: $1,000 to $3,000. **Duration:** Annual. **To Apply:** Applicants must send a (two-page) grant application cover sheet (available at the website); a project proposal (maximum of three pages, double-spaced); budget; three letters of recommendation; curriculum vitae; academic transcript send by university registrar. Applications and supporting documents must be sent electronically in MS Word or PDF format or by regular mail. **Deadline:** March 2. **Remarks:** Established in 1983.

4986 ■ Institute for Women's Policy Research (IWPR)

1200 18th St. NW, Ste. 301
Washington, DC 20036
Ph: (202)785-5100
Fax: (202)833-4362
E-mail: iwpr@iwpr.org
URL: www.iwpr.org

4987 ■ Mariam K. Chamberlain Fellowships in Women and Public Policy *(Graduate/Fellowship)*

Purpose: To provide training and experience to graduate students. **Focus:** Social sciences; Statistics; Women's studies. **Qualif.:** Applicants should have at least a bachelor's degree in a social science discipline, statistics, or women's studies; have strong quantitative and library research skills and knowledge of women's issues; familiarity with Microsoft Word and Excel; knowledge of STATA, SPSS, SAS, and graphics software; with qualitative research skills. **Criteria:** Selection is based on the application.

Funds Avail.: $27,000. **Duration:** Annual. **Number Awarded:** 1. **To Apply:** Applicants must submit a cover letter, a resume, a list of relevant classes taken (this list can be included with the resume), a 3-7 page writing sample, and two confidential (sealed) letters of recommendation. **Deadline:** February 28. **Contact:** Lindsey Reichlin at MKCfellowship@iwpr.org.

4988 ■ Insurance Scholarship Foundation of America (ISFA)

PO Box 866
Hendersonville, NC 28793-0866
E-mail: foundation@inssfa.org
URL: www.inssfa.org

4989 ■ CPCU Loman Education Foundation Scholarships *(Other/Scholarship)*

Purpose: To support professional scholarship applicants who demonstrate the desire to enhance their career by becoming a CPCU. **Focus:** Insurance and insurance-related fields. **Qualif.:** Applicants must have minimum of two years employment in the insurance industry; must be studying the CPCU program; and must not receive full reimbursement for the course, books, etc. from their employer or any other outside source. **Criteria:** Recipients are selected based on academic performance.

Funds Avail.: No Specific amount. **To Apply:** Applicants must submit completed application form.

4990 ■ Founders Circle Professional Scholarships *(Other/Scholarship)*

Purpose: To support exceptional commitment to the insurance industry. **Focus:** Insurance and insurance-related

fields. **Qualif.:** Applicants must have at least five years continuous insurance industry employment; must have demonstrated excellence in educational and career endeavors; and must engage in a course of study designed to improve knowledge and skills in performing employment responsibilities. **Criteria:** Recipients are selected based on academic performance.

Funds Avail.: $1,000 - $2,000. **To Apply:** Applicants must submit a completed application form.

4991 ■ Insurance Scholarship Foundation of America College Scholarships *(Undergraduate, Graduate/Scholarship)*

Purpose: To promote excellence in the insurance industry by underwriting the education of current and future employees. **Focus:** Insurance and insurance-related fields. **Qualif.:** Applicants must be candidates for a bachelor's or higher degree with a major in insurance, risk management or actuarial science; must be currently attending a college or university and be completing or have completed the second year of college; must have successfully completed two insurance, risk management or actuarial science courses having minimum of three credit hours each; and must have achieved at least 3.0 grade point average on a 4.0 scale. **Criteria:** Recipients are selected based on academic performance.

Funds Avail.: $1,000 - $5,000. **To Apply:** Applicants must submit a completed application form. **Contact:** Insurance Scholarship Foundation of America at the above address.

4992 ■ Insurance Scholarship Foundation of America Professional Scholarships *(Other/Scholarship)*

Purpose: To promote excellence in the insurance industry by underwriting the education of current and future employees. **Focus:** Insurance and insurance-related fields. **Qualif.:** Applicants must have at least two years of insurance industry employment; must be engaged in a course of study to improve knowledge and skills in performing employment responsibilities; must not be receiving full reimbursement for the expenses of tuition, books etc. from an employer or from any other outside source; and must have background that indicates the applicant's motivation. **Criteria:** Recipients are selected based on academic performance.

Funds Avail.: Up to $1,000. **To Apply:** Applicants must submit completed application form. **Contact:** Insurance Scholarship Foundation of America at the above address.

4993 ■ Marsh College Scholarships *(Undergraduate/Scholarship)*

Purpose: To promote excellence in the insurance industry by underwriting the education of current and future employees. **Focus:** Insurance and insurance-related fields. **Qualif.:** Applicants must be candidates for a bachelor's or higher degree with a major in insurance, risk management or actuarial science; must be currently attending a college or university and be completing or have completed the second year of college; must have successfully completed two insurance, risk management, or actuarial science courses having a minimum of three credit hours each; and must have achieved at least 3.0 grade point of average on a 4.0 scale. **Criteria:** Recipients are selected based on academic performance.

Funds Avail.: No specific amount. **To Apply:** Applicants must submit a completed application form.

Awards are arranged alphabetically below their administering organizations

4994 ■ Inter-American Foundation (IAF)

1331 Pennsylvania Ave. NW, Ste. 1200 N
Washington, DC 20004-1766
Ph: (202)360-4530
Fax: (703)306-4365
E-mail: inquiries@iaf.gov
URL: www.iaf.gov

4995 ■ IAF Fellowships *(Doctorate/Fellowship)*

Purpose: To support dissertation research of doctoral students regarding grassroots development issues in Latin America and the Caribbean. **Focus:** Culture; Government; Latin American studies; Physical sciences; Social sciences. **Qualif.:** Applicants must be doctoral (Ph.D.) students currently enrolled in a U.S. university and must have advanced candidacy before initiating IAF-funded field research; must be U.S. citizens and citizens of independent Latin American and Caribbean countries (except Cuba); must speak and read the language(s) appropriate to the research proposal; and must demonstrate a planned, substantive collaboration, during the field research period, with an affiliated development or applied research institution in the Latin American or Caribbean country. **Criteria:** Fellowships are based on both development and scholarly criteria. Selection will be based on the applicants' eligibility and their research proposals.

Funds Avail.: $3,000 research allowance; $1,500 monthly stipend for 12 months. **To Apply:** Applicants should primarily submit their respective research proposals. Proposed research should have a focus on grassroots development and only in exceptional cases will the IAF support proposals reflecting a primary interest in macro questions of politics and economics as they relate to the environment of the poor. They may also contact the IAF for the other materials necessary for the submission of applications. **Remarks:** The IAF Fellowships are currently administered with the support of the Institute for International Education (IIE). **Contact:** Any inquiries should be addressed to the Institute of International Education at iaffellowships@iie.org.

4996 ■ Inter American Press Association (IAPA)

Jules Dubois Bldg.
1801 SW 3rd Ave.
Miami, FL 33129
Ph: (305)634-2465
Fax: (305)635-2272
E-mail: info@sipiapa.org
URL: www.sipiapa.com

4997 ■ Inter American Press Association Scholarships *(Undergraduate/Scholarship)*

Purpose: To defend and promote the right of the peoples of the Americas to be fully and freely informed through an independent press. **Focus:** Journalism. **Qualif.:** Applicants must be journalists or journalism seniors or graduates between 21 to 35 years of age with a good command of the language they are to use; must have completed their degree before beginning the scholarship year; must have taken at least three years of professional journalism. Language ability for U.S. and Canadian candidates must be attested to by a recognized authority in Spanish or Portuguese. Latin American candidates must take a TOEFL test (Test of English as a Foreign Language). U.S. and Canadian scholars must take minimum of three university courses; must have participated in the Scholarship Fund's

Reporting Program; and must undertake a major research project. **Criteria:** Recipients are selected based on academic achievement and financial need.

Funds Avail.: $20,000. **Duration:** Annual. **To Apply:** Applicants must complete the application form and submit along with an autobiography; transcripts of the university studies; three letters of recommendation; and proof of certification. **Deadline:** January 30. **Contact:** Mauricio J. Montaldo, Coordinator; becas@sipiapa.org.

4998 ■ Intercollegiate Studies Institute (ISI)

3901 Centerville Rd.
Wilmington, DE 19807-1938
Ph: (302)652-4600
Fax: (302)652-1760
Free: 800-526-7022
E-mail: info@isi.org
URL: home.isi.org

4999 ■ Salvatori Fellowships *(Graduate/Fellowship)*

Purpose: To improve the ability of the American people to understand their heritage, to distinguish its principles, and to choose well so that, through self-governance, they may protect their nation and preserve their liberties for themselves and the generations to come. **Focus:** United States studies. **Qualif.:** Applicant must be a U.S. citizen and member of the Intercollegiate Studies Institute; must be a college senior or graduate student; must engage in graduate studies for the purpose of teaching at the college level. **Criteria:** Applicant must meet the requirements specific to the fellowship.

Funds Avail.: $10,000. **Duration:** Annual; One year. **Number Awarded:** 2. **To Apply:** Application forms may be obtained from the. Applicant must submit the following: (1) Four brief statement; (2) Three essays; (3) Three letters of academic recommendation; (4) College transcript; (5) 2x3 photo or headshot. **Deadline:** January 16. **Contact:** Graduate Fellowship Program, awards@isi.org.

5000 ■ Richard M. Weaver Fellowships *(Graduate/ Fellowship)*

Purpose: To assist motivated future teachers, similar to Professor Weaver, by the need to integrate the idea of liberal education with their teaching efforts, and in doing so, to restore to university studies their distinction and worth. **Focus:** Education. **Qualif.:** Applicant must be a U.S. citizen and member of the Intercollegiate Studies Institute; must be a college senior or graduate student; must engage in graduate studies for the purpose of teaching at the college level. **Criteria:** Applicant must meet the requirements specific to the fellowship.

Funds Avail.: Stipend of $5,000 and awards $1,000 in ISI Books. **To Apply:** Application form is available at the website. Applicant must submit the following: (1) Four brief statements; (2) Three essays; (3) Three letters of academic recommendation; (4) College transcript; (5) 2x3 photo or headshot. **Deadline:** January 16. **Contact:** Graduate Fellowship Program, awards@isi.org.

5001 ■ Western Civilization Fellowships *(Graduate/ Fellowship)*

Purpose: To support students in the graduate level in the study of the institutions, values and history of the West. **Focus:** Western European studies. **Qualif.:** Applicant must be a U.S citizen and member of the Intercollegiate Studies

Awards are arranged alphabetically below their administering organizations

Institute; must be a college senior or graduate student; must engage in graduate studies for the purpose of teaching at the college level. **Criteria:** Applicant must meet the requirements specific to the fellowship.

Funds Avail.: $20,000. **Duration:** Annual; One year. **Number Awarded:** 3. **To Apply:** Application forms may be obtained from the website. Applicant must submit the following: (1) Four brief statement; (2) Three essays; (3) Three letters of academic recommendation; (4) College transcript; (5) 2x3 photo or headshot. **Deadline:** January 16. **Contact:** Graduate Fellowship Program, awards@isi.org.

5002 ■ Intermediaries & Reinsurance Underwriters Association, Inc. (IRU Inc.)

c/o The Beaumont Group, Inc.
3626 E Tremont Ave., Ste. 203
Throggs Neck, NY 10465
Ph: (718)892-0228
URL: www.irua.com

5003 ■ Intermediaries and Reinsurance Underwriters Association Internship Program *(Undergraduate/ Internship)*

Purpose: To provide an opportunity for college juniors and seniors to learn about the reinsurance industry and gain practical experience in its operation. **Focus:** Insurance and insurance-related fields. **Qualif.:** Applicants must be full-time students enrolled in an undergraduate program at an accredited four-year college or university; have at least one term remaining following completion of the intern program; have an overall GPA of at least 3.0 and two recommendations from faculty advisor, dean or department chairman; must be enrolled in degree program with a major in insurance, economics, business or a related field; and must be U.S. citizens of at least 18 years of age. **Criteria:** Applicants will be evaluated by the Internship Selection Committee.

Funds Avail.: $2,500. **Duration:** Annual. **To Apply:** Applicants may apply online and must submit a resume, two faculty recommendations and a certified copy of transcript. **Deadline:** February 1.

5004 ■ Intermountain Section American Water Works Association

c/o Alane E. Boyd, Executive Director
3430 E Danish Rd.
Sandy, UT 84093
Ph: (801)712-1619
URL: www.ims-awwa.org

5005 ■ IMS AWWA Graduate Science and Engineering Scholarships *(Graduate/Scholarship)*

Purpose: To support students pursuing studies in the field of water quality, supply, and treatment in the Intermountain West. **Focus:** Water resources; Water supply industry. **Qualif.:** Applicants must be students pursuing education in science and engineering related to the field of water quality, supply, resources or treatment in the Intermountain West. **Criteria:** Selection will be based on the committee's criteria.

Funds Avail.: $1,500. **To Apply:** Interested applicants may contact the Intermountain Section for the application process and other information. **Deadline:** November 14.

5006 ■ Eva Nieminski Honorary Graduate Science and Engineering Scholarships *(Graduate/ Scholarship)*

Purpose: To support students pursuing studies in the field of water quality, supply, and treatment in the Intermountain West. **Focus:** Water resources; Water supply industry. **Qualif.:** Applicants must be students pursuing education in science and engineering related to the field of water quality, supply, resources or treatment in the Intermountain West. **Criteria:** Selection will be based on the committee's criteria.

Funds Avail.: $1,000. **To Apply:** Interested applicants may contact the Intermountain Section for the application process and other information. **Deadline:** November 14.

5007 ■ International Anesthesia Research Society (IARS)

44 Montgomery St., Ste. 1605
San Francisco, CA 94104-4703
Ph: (415)296-6900
Fax: (415)296-6901
E-mail: info@iars.org
URL: www.iars.org

5008 ■ IARS Mentored Research Awards (IMRA) *(Professional development/Grant)*

Purpose: To support investigations that will further the understanding of clinical practice in anesthesiology and related sciences. **Focus:** Anesthesiology. **Qualif.:** Applicants must be investigators with IARS membership who have yet to establish substantial independent research funding or who are initiating a new area of research. They must also have completed their clinical training or Ph.D. for under ten years, and have a minimum of 45% protected non-clinical time. **Criteria:** Selection will be based on the submitted applications, which will be reviewed on the basis of scientific merit, adequate preliminary data, career potential of the investigators, and importance of the investigation to the specialty of anesthesiology.

Funds Avail.: Maximum of $150,000 each. **Duration:** Annual; up to two years. **Number Awarded:** 4. **To Apply:** Applicants must check the website for more information. **Deadline:** January 30. **Contact:** Questions can be sent to awards@iars.org.

5009 ■ International Association of Administrative Professionals (IAAP)

10502 N Ambassador Dr., Ste. 100
Kansas City, MO 64153
Ph: (816)891-6600
Fax: (816)891-9118
URL: www.iaap-hq.org

5010 ■ IAAP Wings Chapter Scholarships *(Undergraduate/Scholarship)*

Purpose: To provide financial assistance for qualified individuals from the Greater Miami Valley area who are pursuing careers as office professionals. **Focus:** Business. **Qualif.:** Applicants must have applied and have been accepted or be currently attending an accredited university, college, junior college, community college, or technical or vocational school. **Criteria:** Applicants are evaluated based on academic merit.

Funds Avail.: No specific amount. **To Apply:** Applicants

Awards are arranged alphabetically below their administering organizations

must submit all the required application information.

5011 ■ International Association of Arson Investigators (IAAI)

2111 Baldwin Ave., Ste. 203
Crofton, MD 21114
Ph: (410)451-3473
Fax: (410)451-9049
Free: 800-468-4224
URL: firearson.com

5012 ■ John Charles Wilson Scholarships
(Undergraduate/Scholarship)

Purpose: To foster, support and promote fire prevention and arson awareness through education and training. **Focus:** Fires and fire prevention. **Qualif.:** Applicants must be members or immediate family members in good standing of the International Association of Arson Investigators (AIIA); must be recommended and sponsored by an IAAI member; and be enrolled in a two or four-year accredited college or university that offers courses in police or fire science including fire investigation and related subjects. **Criteria:** Recipients are selected based on academic performance, financial need and recommendation.

Funds Avail.: $1,000. **Duration:** Annual. **Number Awarded:** 2 or more. **To Apply:** Applicants must submit completed the application form; certified transcripts; and an original essay of 500 words or less providing background information and future plans in police and fire sciences and related-fields. Essay must be typed or handwritten and be on 8 1/2"x 11" plain white paper. **Deadline:** February 15. **Contact:** IAAI Foundation Scholarships at iaaifoundation@firearson.com.

5013 ■ International Association of Black Actuaries (IABA)

PO Box 369
Windsor, CT 06095
Ph: (860)906-1286
Fax: (860)906-1369
E-mail: iaba@blackactuaries.org
URL: www.blackactuaries.org

5014 ■ International Association of Black Actuaries Scholarships *(Undergraduate/Scholarship)*

Purpose: To provide scholarships among undergraduates or graduate level for qualified black students who are interested in pursuing actuarial careers. **Focus:** Actuarial science. **Qualif.:** Applicants must be permanent residents or U.S./Canadian citizens; must be admitted to college or university which offers either a program in actuarial science or courses that will serve to prepare the students for actuarial career; must have demonstrated mathematical ability an interest in an actuarial career; must have at least 3.0 GPA on a 4.0 scale, a Math SAT score of at least 600 or an ACT Math score of at least 28; must have completed the calculus and probability courses; must be juniors, seniors or graduate students attempting or already passed the exam; must have completed or completing the validation by educational experience(VEE) requirements; must have determination, self-motivation, excellent recommendations from mathematics-related instructors and familiarity with an actuarial profession demands. **Criteria:** Recipients are selected based on broader math background, high GPA

and Math SAT/ACT scores, merit and financial need.

Funds Avail.: $500-$4,000. **To Apply:** Applicants must submit a completed online application form, two nomination forms completed by instructors and/or advisors at educational institution, an official, sealed record of any educational examination scores, Student Aid Report (SAR) showing the financial date and a copy of college or university catalog or information sheet showing an estimated expenses. **Deadline:** May 31. **Contact:** Kate Weaver at iabafdvp@blackactuaries.org.

5015 ■ International Association for Dental Research (IADR)

1619 Duke St.
Alexandria, VA 22314-3406
Ph: (703)548-0066
Fax: (703)548-1883
URL: www.iadr.com

5016 ■ IADR John Clarkson Fellowship
(Postdoctorate/Fellowship)

Purpose: To allow investigators in the field of public dental health to obtain training and experience at a center of excellence. **Focus:** Dentistry. **Qualif.:** Applicants must hold a degree in dentistry or in a scientific discipline (dental, masters, or PhD degrees); must be members of IADR; and must be actively engaged in research in public dental health. **Criteria:** Recipients are selected based on merit.

Funds Avail.: Up to $15,000 covering accommodation, subsistence and travel. **To Apply:** Applications should be made individually and should include the following details: name, address, current place of work, and position; IADR Division/Section membership; full curriculum vitae and reprints of three relevant publications; references from two recognized scientists and the principal Dean/Chair of the institution where the applicant is employed; and an outline (3 pages maximum, single-spaced) by the applicant describing how his/her experience and interests qualify him/her as a candidate for the Fellowship, including: detailed description of the subject areas to be covered in the training program; practical use to which the training acquired would be put, proposed duration and dates of the fellowship; institutes and country it is proposed to visit; reasons for selection of particular institutes(s); previous Fellowships/awards; and detailed budget for program. Applications are sent electronically. **Deadline:** October 13. **Contact:** Sheri S. Herren, email at sherren@iadr.org.

5017 ■ IADR John Gray Fellowship *(Other/Fellowship)*

Purpose: To allow dental or postgraduate students to obtain training and experience in dental or related research. **Focus:** Dentistry. **Qualif.:** Applicants must be registered students in an accredited or acceptable dental school or in a recognized formal postgraduate program; must be in a training program in the division in which the fellowship is awarded; must be sponsored by their faculty advisor/direct supervisor or the Dean of the School; and must be IADR members. **Criteria:** Recipients are selected based on merit.

Funds Avail.: $10,000. **Duration:** Biennial; in odd-numbered years. **To Apply:** Applicants must submit a proposal to the division secretary outlining: the precise title of the subject to be studied; detailed description of the subjects to be covered in the training program; practical use to which the training acquired would be put; proposed

Awards are arranged alphabetically below their administering organizations

duration and dates of the fellowship; institute(s) and country it is proposed to visit; reasons for particular institute(s); previous fellowships or awards; and budget for program. The division officers will select the fellowship recipient and will then send the candidate's name to the Central Office for presentation to the IADR Board of Directors for approval. **Contact:** Sheri S. Herren, Strategic Programs Manager at sherren@iadr.org.

5018 ■ IADR Toshio Nakao Fellowship *(Other/ Fellowship)*

Purpose: To allow young investigators in the area of dental materials science to obtain training and experience at a center of excellence. **Focus:** Dentistry. **Qualif.:** Applicants must hold a degree in dentistry or in a scientific discipline; must be within five years of obtaining their dental or scientific degree on or at the fellowship proposal deadline; and must be members of IADR and are actively engaged in research. **Criteria:** Recipients are selected based on merit as evaluated by the IADR Fellowships Committee. Preference will be given to applicants from regions with less developed research programs in the field of materials science.

Funds Avail.: Up to $15,000. **Duration:** Biennial; in odd-numbered years. **To Apply:** Applications should be made individually and should include the following details (in English): name, address, date of birth, current place of work, and position; IADR Division/Section membership; full curriculum vitae with list and reprints of three relevant publications; references from two recognized scientists, one of whom should be from the principal (Dean/Chair) of the institution where the applicant is employed; and an outline by the applicant of how his/her experience and interests qualify him/her as a candidate for the fellowship (no more than three single spaced pages), including: detailed description of the subject areas to be covered in the training program; practical use to which the training acquired would be put; proposed duration and dates of the fellowship; institutes and/or country it is proposed to visit; reasons for particular institutes(s); previous fellowships/ awards; and budget for program. **Contact:** Sheri S. Herren, Strategic Programs Manager at sherren@iadr.org.

5019 ■ IADR Norton Ross Fellowship *(Postgraduate/ Fellowship)*

Purpose: To allow dental or postgraduate students to obtain training and experience in dental or related research. **Focus:** Dentistry. **Qualif.:** Applicants must be registered in an accredited or acceptable dental school or in a recognized formal postgraduate program; must be sponsored by their faculty advisor, direct supervisor, or the Dean of the school; may have a college or advanced degree in a discipline other than dentistry; and must be IADR members. **Criteria:** Recipients are selected based on merit.

Funds Avail.: $2,800. **Duration:** Biennial; in even-numbered years. **To Apply:** Applicants must submit a proposal directly to their division outlining: the precise title of the subject to be studied; detailed description of the subjects to be covered in the training program; practical use to which the training acquired would be put; proposed duration and dates of the fellowship; institute(s) and country it is proposed to visit; reasons for particular institute(s); previous fellowships or awards; and budget for program. **Deadline:** October 13. **Contact:** Sheri S. Herren, Strategic Programs Manager at sherren@iadr.org.

5020 ■ IADR David B. Scott Fellowship *(Undergraduate/Fellowship, Award)*

Purpose: To improve knowledge on oral health by advancing and supporting research projects; to support and represent the oral health research community; and to facilitate the communication and application of research findings. **Focus:** Dental hygiene. **Qualif.:** Program is open to dental students; must be registered in an accredited or acceptable dental school; and must be sponsored by a dental researcher with the approval of their school's dean. Candidates may not have received their dental degree nor should they be due to receive their degree in the year of the award; may have a college or advanced degree in a discipline other than the industry; and must be IADR members. **Criteria:** Recipients are selected based on the submitted project proposal as reviewed by the IADR Board of Directors.

Funds Avail.: $2,500. **Duration:** Annual. **To Apply:** Applicants and their sponsors must submit a research project proposal to the division not exceeding eight pages (including references), typed and double-spaced. Proposal should include aims, objectives and significance of the proposal; rationale and background to the study; materials and methods; statistical treatment of data; facilities and equipment; and budget. **Deadline:** October 13. **Remarks:** Established in 1987. **Contact:** Sheri S. Herren, Strategic Programs Manager at sherren@iadr.org.

5021 ■ International Association of Emergency Managers (IAEM)

201 Park Washington Ct.
Falls Church, VA 22046-4527
Ph: (703)538-1795
Fax: (703)241-5603
E-mail: info@iaem.com
URL: iaem.com

5022 ■ International Association of Emergency Managers Scholarships *(Undergraduate/Scholarship)*

Purpose: To assist the profession by identifying and developing students with the intellect and technical skills that can advance and enhance emergency management or disaster management. **Focus:** Emergency and disaster services. **Qualif.:** Applicants must be students studying the field of emergency management, disaster management or a related program. **Criteria:** Selection will be based on merit.

Funds Avail.: No specific amount. **To Apply:** Interested applicants may contact the International Association of Emergency Managers Scholarship Program for the application process and other information. **Contact:** Dawn M. Shiley, IAEM Communications Manager & Scholarship Program Director at shiley@iaem.com.

5023 ■ International Association for Food Protection (IAFP)

6200 Aurora Ave., Ste. 200W
Des Moines, IA 50322-2864
Ph: (515)276-3344
Fax: (515)276-8655
Free: 800-369-6337
E-mail: info@foodprotection.org
URL: www.foodprotection.org

Awards are arranged alphabetically below their administering organizations

---

5024 ■ International Association for Food Protection - Student Travel Scholarship Program
(Undergraduate, Graduate/Scholarship)

Purpose: To provide travel funding for full-time students to attend the Annual Meeting of the International Association for Food Protection and to encourage developing scientists to participate in association activities. **Focus:** Food science and technology; Microbiology; Toxicology. **Qualif.:** Applicants must be members of IAFP; must demonstrate interest in and commitment to food safety and quality as undergraduate or graduate students enrolled full-time in a food science, microbiology, toxicology or other program related to food microbiological or toxicological safety at a college or university at the time of the application deadline. **Criteria:** Selection will be based on the committee's criteria.

Funds Avail.: No specific amount. **To Apply:** Applicants must submit an application in one electronic file that includes the following documents: completed application form; statement of interest explaining the applicants' interest in food safety and quality, career aspirations, reasons to attend the IAFP Annual Meeting, and current research projects: how the project will enhance food safety or quality and who will benefit from the work. One letter of recommendation from faculty member or department head to include: outstanding qualifications/contributions made throughout the students' academic career; potential value the students possesses toward making significant future contributions in the food safety profession. Applicants must also include one-page maximum, additional information: list of received awards, honors, travel grants, scholarships, etc.; schools attended; involvement in local affiliate; other relevant supporting materials. **Deadline:** February 26. **Contact:** scholarship@foodprotection.org.

5025 ■ International Association for Great Lakes Research (IAGLR)
c/o Wendy L. Foster, Business Manager
4840 S State Rd.
Ann Arbor, MI 48108
Ph: (734)665-5303
Fax: (734)741-2055
E-mail: office@iaglr.org
URL: www.iaglr.org

5026 ■ Norman S. Baldwin Fishery Science Scholarship *(Doctorate, Graduate/Scholarship)*

Purpose: To promote academic excellence by encouraging young scientists to undertake graduate research in fishery biology and to enter the field of Great Lakes science. **Focus:** Fisheries sciences/management. **Qualif.:** Applicants must be full-time MSc or PhD students who have proposed research topics that are relevant to Great Lakes fish research; must not be in their final years of study at the time of application; and must not have previously received the award. **Criteria:** Selection shall be based on scientific merit, presentation, originality and contribution to the understanding of Great Lakes fisheries.

Funds Avail.: $6,000. **Duration:** Annual. **Number Awarded:** 1. **To Apply:** Applicants must submit a complete application which is composed of four parts: a letter of application (one page); a supervising professor's letter of endorsement; a brief title and extended abstract of proposed research (maximum of 2 single-spaced pages); and a statement on how and why the research will make a significant contribution to understanding the biology of Great Lakes fishes or improving Great Lakes fishery management (maximum of 1 single-spaced page). **Deadline:** March 1. **Contact:** scholarships@iaglr.org.

5027 ■ Paul W. Rodgers Scholarship *(Undergraduate, Master's, Doctorate/Scholarship)*

Purpose: To support the advancement of knowledge relating to Great Lakes aquatic ecosystem health and management. **Focus:** Conservation of natural resources.

Funds Avail.: $2,000. **Duration:** Annual. **Deadline:** March 1. **Remarks:** Established in 1999.

5028 ■ International Association of Healthcare Central Service Materiel Management (IAHCSMM)
55 W Wacker Dr., Ste. 501
Chicago, IL 60601
Ph: (312)440-0078
Fax: (312)440-9474
Free: 800-962-8274
E-mail: mailbox@iahcsmm.com
URL: www.iahcsmm.org

5029 ■ IAHCSMM-Purdue University Scholarship Awards *(Other/Scholarship)*

Purpose: To financially support individuals who are pursuing their educational and individual growth. **Focus:** General studies/Field of study not specified. **Qualif.:** Applicants must be employed in the Steering Processing profession in a non-management position for a minimum of one year. **Criteria:** Applicants will be evaluated based on financial need; interest in pursuing educational and individual growth goals; participation in activities (association, hospital department, community); and years of service in Central Service.

Funds Avail.: No specific amount. **To Apply:** Applicants must complete the application form available at the website with a reference letter and personal essay attached. **Deadline:** February 1.

5030 ■ SPSmedical CS Scholarships *(Other/Scholarship)*

Purpose: To give individuals the opportunity to work towards certification by providing all the study materials needed to prepare for the certification exam. **Focus:** Medical technology. **Qualif.:** Applicants must be employed in the CS profession for at least of six months. **Criteria:** Scholarships will be awarded to applicants who will fulfill the requirements.

Funds Avail.: No specific amount. **Number Awarded:** 3. **To Apply:** Applicants must complete the application form available at the website and submit along with recommendation from supervisor/manager.

5031 ■ International Association of Law Enforcement Intelligence Analysts (IALEIA)
PO Box 13857
Richmond, VA 23225
Fax: (804)565-2059
URL: www.ialeia.org

5032 ■ Jorge Espejal Contreras Memorial Scholarships *(Graduate, Undergraduate/Scholarship)*

Purpose: To strive for professionalism in the intelligence field by promoting career development and continued

Awards are arranged alphabetically below their administering organizations

education. **Focus:** Criminal justice; Intelligence service; Statistics. **Qualif.:** Program is open to active IALEIA members or immediate family members enrolled in an intelligence, analysis, criminal justice or other related undergraduate or graduate program at an accredited academic institution; must be based on full-time or part-time enrollment in an accredited college/university and can be on campus or via distance-learning. **Criteria:** Recipients are selected based on the eligibility status evaluated through the quality of the essay (minimum of 1,000 words), its originality and its complete response to addressing the required topic, complete check for grammar, punctuation and spelling.

Funds Avail.: $1,500. **Duration:** Annual. **Number Awarded:** 1. **To Apply:** Applicants should download application from the IALEIA website and submit to the IALEIA Training, Education, and Career Development Committee. Eligible submissions must be provided in English. Applicants must submit their work electronically to the attention of the TE&CD Director and a signed original copy to be mailed. Application must include a mandatory 1,000-1,500-word essay on: The Future of Law Enforcement Intelligence as a Profession. **Deadline:** March 14.

5033 ■ The Henley Putnam University Scholarships
(Other/Scholarship)

Purpose: To promote career development and continued education in the intelligence field by providing educational assistance. **Focus:** Intelligence service. **Qualif.:** Applicants must be active IALEIA members or immediate family members. **Criteria:** Applicants will be evaluated by the IALEIA Director of Training, Education and Career Development and TE&CD committee members.

Funds Avail.: No specific amount. **To Apply:** Applicants should download and submit an application from the IALEIA website to the Training, Education and Career Development Committee along with (1,000-1,500 words) essay on "The Future of Online Distance Learning in Law Enforcement". **Contact:** Nancy A. Reggio, Director of Admissions, Henley-Putnam University at nreggio@henley-putnam.edu.

5034 ■ International Association of Law Libraries (IALL)
c/o Barbara Garavaglia, Secretary
University of Michigan Law Library
801 Monroe St.
Ann Arbor, MI 48109
E-mail: bvaccaro@umich.edu
URL: iall.org

5035 ■ International Association of Law Libraries Scholarship Program *(Other/Scholarship)*
Purpose: To enable law librarians who are normally unable to benefit from the association's activities to attend the Annual Course in International Law Librarianship that forms the annual conference of the association. **Focus:** Law. **Qualif.:** Applicants must be in current employment in librarianship with significant legal context to their work; applicants need not to be members of the association. **Criteria:** Recipients are selected based on demonstrated promise to make a significant contribution to the profession of law librarianship. Preference is given to applicants who cannot otherwise attend the conference without the scholarship; who have not yet received in IALL bursary or scholarship in the past years of the program; and who have not attended a conference outside their own country. Program is not open to officers or members of the Board of the Association.

Funds Avail.: Up to $1,500. **Duration:** One year. **To Apply:** Applicants must submit a full resume including name and qualifications; full contact details including an e-mail address; letter of application and personal statement; at least two reference letters; an itemized estimate of expenses for attending the conference including airfare, ground transportation, hotel and food. **Contact:** Barbara Garavaglia, Chair of the IALL Scholarships Committee at bvaccaro@umich.edu.

5036 ■ International Association of Lighting Designers (IALD)
440 N Wells St., Ste. 210
Chicago, IL 60654
Ph: (312)527-3677
Fax: (312)527-3680
E-mail: iald@iald.org
URL: www.iald.org

5037 ■ IALD Education Trust Scholarship Program
(Graduate, Undergraduate/Scholarship)

Purpose: To promote the study of architectural lighting design. **Focus:** Architecture; Lighting science. **Qualif.:** Applicants must be student members of the IALD, or have their applications pending, currently enrolled in an undergraduate or graduate program and pursuing architectural lighting design as their course of study. **Criteria:** Applicants will be judged based on grades, extracurricular activities, portfolio of work and personal recommendations.

Funds Avail.: No specific amount. **Duration:** Annual. **To Apply:** Applicants must complete and submit the following materials: an application form (available at the website); a copy of official transcript; resume; two letters of recommendation; statement of personal experience with lighting, reasons for studying lighting or why deserve the scholarship (maximum of 2 pages); and examples of work in 8.5x11 format (maximum of 10 images). **Deadline:** March 15. **Contact:** trustscholarships@iald.org.

5038 ■ International Association for the Study of Pain (IASP)
1510 H St. NW, Ste. 600
Washington, DC 20005-1020
Ph: (202)524-5300
Fax: (202)524-5301
E-mail: IASPdesk@iasp-pain.org
URL: www.iasp-pain.org//am/template.cfm?Section=home

5039 ■ Phillip A. Spiegel IASP Congress Trainee Scholarship *(College, Graduate, Undergraduate/Scholarship)*

Purpose: To support IASP trainees who need financial assistance in furthering their education in the study of pain. **Focus:** General studies/Field of study not specified. **Qualif.:** Applicants must be trainees of IASP. **Criteria:** Selection will be based on the following criteria: enrollment in a full-time degree program or in full-time study in the area of pain and/or employment status and location; presentation at a national or international scientific meeting; applicants' self-selected best publication; involvement in research, lab experience, or hospital or university teaching.

Awards are arranged alphabetically below their administering organizations

Funds Avail.: No specific amount. **Duration:** Annual. **To Apply:** Interested applicants may contact the Association for the application process and other informations. **Remarks:** Established in 2011. **Contact:** grants@iasp-pain.org; 202-524-5300.

5040 ■ International Association of Wildland Fire (IAWF)

1418 Washburn St.
Missoula, MT 59801
Ph: (406)531-8264
Free: 888-440-4293
E-mail: execdir@iawfonline.org
URL: www.iawfonline.org

5041 ■ International Association of Wildland Fire Graduate-Level Scholarships *(Doctorate, Graduate/ Scholarship)*

Purpose: To financially assist graduate students in obtaining their graduate level degree in a wildland fire or any related topics. **Focus:** Fires and fire prevention. **Qualif.:** Applicants must be IAWF members who are enrolled full-time in graduate school; must be Master's of Science or Ph.D. students. **Criteria:** Selection of applicants will be based on the criteria of the selection committee.

Funds Avail.: $3,000. **Duration:** Annual. **Number Awarded:** 2. **To Apply:** Applicants must complete the application form available on the website; must provide a 500-750 word essay that includes three components: (1) a description of how they have or will overcome challenges and/or barriers associated with their academic program and associated research; (2) a description of how the international fire community will benefit from completion of their work; (3) a statement of the anticipated benefit the scholarship would bring to the student with particular emphasis on how scholarship fund would be used to further their research goals and/or allow the dissemination of research to the fire management community; must arrange the letter of support to be submitted on behalf of their primary thesis supervisor. The letter of support must confirm that the student is enrolled in an MSc or PhD program; has at least eight months remaining in the program at the time of application; the content of the essay is accurate; and has the ability to complete the work. **Deadline:** January 29 and March 15. **Contact:** Nancy HF French, Chair, IAWF Scholarship Committee, Michigan Tech Research Institute; Email: nhfrench@mtu.edu.

5042 ■ International Association of Women Police (IAWP)

PO Box 13485
Portland, OR 97213
Ph: (301)464-1402
Fax: (301)560-8836
E-mail: firstvicepresident@iawp.org
URL: www.iawp.org

5043 ■ IAWP International Recognition and Scholarship Awards *(Other/Scholarship)*

Purpose: To increase the understanding about the roles of women officers in various countries; to encourage participation in the International Association of Women Police by all countries of the world; to promote membership through the recipient of this award within the region; to increase the understanding and awareness of women in law enforcement and the International Association of Women Police; and to recognize the accomplishments of a women officer from outside North America. **Focus:** Law enforcement. **Qualif.:** Applicants must be women and members of the police organization. **Criteria:** Recipients are selected based on pre-selected criteria including completeness of application, evidence of policing skills, interest in increasing awareness and understanding of the role of women in law enforcement, willingness to network and ability to communicate with other conference attendees.

Funds Avail.: $500. **Duration:** Annual. **To Apply:** Applicants must submit a personal information including the name, rank, assignment, police organization and contact information; biography including education, employment history and interest; a letter of support from the applicant's senior officer or administrator indicating how long they have known the applicant and the basis of the recommendation; and a letter of application written by applicants showing why they deserve to receive the scholarship award. **Deadline:** April 1. **Contact:** IAWP, International Recognition and Scholarship Committee at the above address.

5044 ■ International Association of Workforce Professionals (IAWP)

1801 Louisville Rd.
Frankfort, KY 40601
Ph: (502)223-4459
Free: 888-898-9960
E-mail: iawp@iawponline.org
URL: www.iawponline.org

5045 ■ W. Scott Boyd Group Grants *(Advanced Professional/Grant)*

Purpose: To provide financial assistance for IAWP chapters and subchapters, as well as chapters working with their agencies for the presentation of group educational and training programs. **Focus:** General studies/Field of study not specified. **Qualif.:** Applicants must be IAWP full members. **Criteria:** Recipients are selected on a first-come-first-serve basis.

Funds Avail.: $1,000. **Duration:** Annual. **To Apply:** Applicants must complete the application form and attach a brief explanation of how this course relates to their work or promotional chances. **Contact:** International Association of Workforce Professionals at the above address.

5046 ■ Logan S. Chambers Individual Scholarships *(Other/Scholarship)*

Purpose: To provide financial assistance for IAWP full members who wish to increase their knowledge, skills and abilities in a course of study that pertains to employment and training work, or toward a degree program that relates to job performance and/or promotional possibilities. **Focus:** General studies/Field of study not specified. **Qualif.:** Applicants must be IAWP full members. **Criteria:** Recipients are selected on a first-come-first-serve basis.

Funds Avail.: $100 - $350. **Duration:** Annual. **To Apply:** Applicants must complete the application form and attach a brief explanation of how this course relates to their work or promotional chances.

5047 ■ Freddy L. Jacobs Scholarships *(Undergraduate/Scholarship)*

Purpose: To provide financial assistance for IAWP student members or dependents of IAWP full members who wish to

Awards are arranged alphabetically below their administering organizations

increase their knowledge, skills and abilities in the area of leadership or workforce development. **Focus:** General studies/Field of study not specified. **Qualif.:** Applicants must be pursuing an associate, undergraduate degree or other certification who are required to complete an extracurricular educational or training to program to obtain high school diploma; and must be dependents of IAWP members. **Criteria:** Recipients are selected based on a first-come-first-serve basis.

Funds Avail.: $75 - $250. **Duration:** Annual. **To Apply:** Applicants must complete the scholarship application form and attach a brief explanation of how this course will increase their knowledge, skills and abilities in the area of leadership or workforce development. **Deadline:** December 31.

5048 ■ International Bowling Media Association (IBMA)

c/o Joan Romero, President
6544 Gloria Ave.
Van Nuys, CA 91406
Ph: (818)787-2310
URL: www.bowlingmedia.org

5049 ■ Chuck Pezzano Scholarships
(Undergraduate/Scholarship)

Purpose: To provide financial support for students pursuing a career in communications that involves the sport of bowling. **Focus:** Communications; Sports writing. **Qualif.:** Applicants must have a minimum of 2.5 GPA; must be high school or vocational school seniors or college students. **Criteria:** Awards are given based on academic merit, civic and bowling participation.

Funds Avail.: Maximum of $3,000. **Duration:** Annual. **Number Awarded:** 3. **To Apply:** Applicants must send an application form (available at the website); transcript; at least one reference letter; maximum of 1000 words essay; and any other information to support your application. **Deadline:** May 21.

5050 ■ International Catacomb Society (ICS)

38 Montvale Ave., Ste. 120
Stoneham, MA 02180
E-mail: info@catacombsociety.org
URL: www.catacombsociety.org

5051 ■ Shohet Scholars Program *(Professional development/Grant)*

Purpose: To support significant, innovative research that can be completed and reported within the award period as regards to the catacombs. **Focus:** Art, Roman. **Qualif.:** Applicants must be scholars of all institutional affiliations who are US citizens and possess a doctoral degree or equivalent; must be in their early post-doctoral or launching stage of their careers; must be independent, unaffiliated scholars without doctoral credentials but equivalent in experience, competence and accomplishments of other candidates. **Criteria:** Applications will be evaluated by a jury of academic experts who take into account the quality and feasibility of the research project submitted, the time required to meet the objectives sought, the anticipated impact of the findings, and the excellence of the applicants' skills as attested by diplomas obtained, letters of recommendation, and publications, papers, and presentations.

Funds Avail.: $5,000 up to $30,000. **Duration:** Annual. **To Apply:** Applicants must submit the following materials: information sheet; curriculum vitae; maximum of 2,500 words (10 pages, double-spaced) research proposal; 100-word abstract and significance of the proposed research; budget proposal; letters of recommendation from three individuals; and letter from applicants' Department Chairperson or other institutional officer. If applicants will conduct an archaeological fieldwork or project involving items in museum collections, they must submit a statement of permission. **Deadline:** January 15. **Remarks:** Established in 2001. **Contact:** ahoek@hds.harvard.edu.

5052 ■ International Center for Not-for-Profit Law (ICNL)

1126 16th St. NW, Ste. 400
Washington, DC 20036-4837
Ph: (202)452-8600
Fax: (202)452-8555
E-mail: infoicnl@icnl.org
URL: www.icnl.org

5053 ■ ICNL Fellowships *(Advanced Professional, Professional development/Fellowship)*

Purpose: To provide opportunities to engage practitioners and scholars to advance the legal environment for civil society by providing them with the support and expertise of ICNL's international staff; access to extensive library of NGO legal materials; and meetings with NGO representatives, academics and others in Washington, DC. **Focus:** Law. **Qualif.:** Applicants must be residents from all countries in Asia and the Pacific, the Middle East and North Africa, Sub-Saharan Africa, Europe and Eurasia, and Latin America and the Caribbean. **Criteria:** Entries will be evaluated based on compliance with eligibility requirements and application procedures and on demonstrated interest and experience relating to the legal environment for civil society.

Funds Avail.: No specific amount. **Duration:** Annual. **To Apply:** Applicants must accomplish all required documents in English: application coversheet; proposal; resume, curriculum vitae, or other statement of work history and education. **Deadline:** March 10. **Contact:** ICNL Program Assistant Brittany Grabel at: bgrabel@icnl.org.

5054 ■ International Centre for Diffraction Data (ICDD)

12 Campus Blvd.
Newtown Square, PA 19073-3273
Ph: (610)325-9814
Fax: (610)325-9823
Free: 866-378-9331
E-mail: info@icdd.com
URL: www.icdd.com

5055 ■ Ludo Frevel Crystallography Scholarships
(Graduate/Scholarship)

Purpose: To encourage promising graduate students to pursue crystallographically oriented research. **Focus:** Mineralogy. **Qualif.:** Applicant must be a graduate student enrolled in a graduate degree program with major interest in crystallography (crystal structure analysis, crystal morphology, modulated structures, correlation of atomic structure with physical properties, systematic classification of crystal structures, phase identification and materials

Awards are arranged alphabetically below their administering organizations

characterization). **Criteria:** Selection is based on the proposal (impact, innovativeness, originality, efficacy of approach, and relationship to crystallography) and the student (recommendation letter, educational track record, prior work and/or research, honors, awards and professional activities).

Funds Avail.: $2,500. **Duration:** Annual; One year (renewable). **To Apply:** Applicants are required to complete the application online. **Deadline:** October 22. **Contact:** Eileen Jennings, jennings@icdd.com; 610-325-9814.

5056 ■ International City/County Management Association (ICMA)

777 N Capitol St. NE, Ste. 500
Washington, DC 20002-4201
Ph: (202)289-4262
Fax: (202)962-3500
E-mail: customerservices@icma.org
URL: www.icmarc.org

5057 ■ ICMA Local Government Management Fellowships *(Master's/Fellowship)*

Purpose: To generate interest in local government careers among recent master's program graduates. **Focus:** Local government. **Qualif.:** Applicants must be students holding or earning a master's degree in public administration/management, public policy, public affairs, or related fields from an academic institution that is a member of the Network of Schools of Public Policy, Affairs and Administration. **Criteria:** Applicants will be selected on the basis of their academic performance, demonstrated leadership potential, commitment to public service, communication skills, initiative, creativity, and positive attitude.

Funds Avail.: Amount varies. **To Apply:** The application has two parts: online and supplemental. Applicants must complete all the questions in the online application and must submit the following supplemental materials: official graduate and undergraduate transcripts; three letters of recommendation which are the two must be from professors/program directors, and one professional recommendation, sealed and signed across the envelope by the recommendation writer. **Deadline:** December 8. **Contact:** Email at lgmfprogram@icma.org for questions.

5058 ■ International Code Council (ICC)

500 New Jersey Ave. NW, 6th Fl.
Washington, DC 20001-2070
Ph: (202)370-1800
Fax: (202)783-2348
Free: 888-422-7233
URL: www.iccsafe.org

5059 ■ C.D. Howard Scholarships *(Undergraduate/ Scholarship)*

Purpose: To provide financial assistance for children of ICC governmental members. **Focus:** General studies/Field of study not specified. **Qualif.:** Applicants must be children of code enforcement agency personnel. The jurisdiction authority must be an active Governmental Member of the International Code Council. Children must be dependents as defined by the Internal Revenue Service. **Criteria:** Selection will be based on merit and demonstrated need for financial assistance.

Funds Avail.: $1,000. **Duration:** Annual. **Number**

Awarded: 1. **To Apply:** Applicants must complete the scholarship application; must submit a financial information along with the details of any other financial assistance they are receiving; must also provide evidence of satisfactory scholastic achievement including grades, test scores and teacher recommendations. A one-page narrative on why the applicant should be awarded the scholarship is also required. **Deadline:** June 28. **Contact:** International Code Council, Attn: Scholarships c/o: Elise Craig, ecraig@iccsafe.org.

5060 ■ International Code Council Foundation General Scholarship Fund *(Undergraduate/ Scholarship)*

Purpose: To provide financial assistance for children of ICC governmental members. **Focus:** General studies/Field of study not specified. **Qualif.:** Applicants must be children of code enforcement agency personnel. The jurisdiction authority must be an active Governmental Member of the International Code Council. Children must be dependents as defined by the Internal Revenue Service. Typically, this includes birth children, stepchildren, legally adopted children or a legal ward financially supported by the employee. **Criteria:** Scholarship is given to those who are pursuing educational opportunities beyond the high school level at a recognized and/or accredited institution. Selection is done on the basis of satisfactory scholastic achievement and demonstrated need for financial assistance.

Funds Avail.: $2,500 each. **Duration:** Annual. **Number Awarded:** 2. **To Apply:** Applicants must complete the application form and must submit a one-page narrative on why they deserve the scholarship. **Deadline:** June 28. **Contact:** International Code Council, Attn: Scholarships c/o: Elise Craig, ecraig@iccsafe.org.

5061 ■ J.W. "Bill" Neese Scholarships *(Undergraduate/Scholarship)*

Purpose: To provide financial assistance for children of ICC governmental members. **Focus:** Engineering, Architectural. **Qualif.:** Applicants must be children of code enforcement agency personnel. The jurisdiction authority must be an active governmental member of the International Code Council. Children must be dependents as defined by the Internal Revenue Service. Typically, this includes birth children, stepchildren, legally adopted children or a legal ward financially supported by the employee. **Criteria:** Scholarship is given to those who are pursuing educational opportunities beyond the high school level at a recognized and/or accredited institution. Selection is done on the basis of satisfactory scholastic achievement and demonstrated need for financial assistance.

Funds Avail.: $1,000. **Duration:** Annual. **Number Awarded:** 1. **To Apply:** Applicants must complete the application form and must submit a one-page narrative stating why they deserve the scholarship. **Deadline:** June 28. **Contact:** International Code Council, Attn: Scholarships c/o: Elise Craig, ecraig@iccsafe.org.

5062 ■ Charlie O'Meilia Scholarships *(Undergraduate/Scholarship)*

Purpose: To provide financial assistance for children of ICC Governmental Members. **Focus:** General studies/Field of study not specified. **Qualif.:** Applicants must be children of code enforcement agency personnel. The jurisdiction authority must be an active Governmental Member of the International Code Council; children must be dependents as defined by the Internal Revenue Service. Typically, this

Awards are arranged alphabetically below their administering organizations

includes birth children, stepchildren, legally adopted children or a legal ward financially supported by the employee. **Criteria:** Recipients will be selected based on scholastic achievement and demonstrated need for financial assistance.

Funds Avail.: $1,000. **Duration:** Annual. **Number Awarded:** 1. **To Apply:** Applications and instructions are available in the ICC and ICCF websites. Applicants must provide evidence of satisfactory scholastic achievement including grades, test scores and teacher recommendations. Applicants must complete the scholarship application. A one-page narrative on why the applicant should be awarded the scholarship is also required. **Deadline:** June 28. **Contact:** International Code Council, Attn: Scholarships c/o: Elise Craig, ecraig@iccsafe.org.

5063 ■ William J. Tangye Scholarships
(Undergraduate/Scholarship)

Purpose: To provide financial assistance for children of ICC members intending to pursue higher education. **Focus:** Engineering, Architectural. **Qualif.:** Applicants must be children of code enforcement agency personnel. The jurisdiction authority must be an active Governmental Member of the International Code Council. Children must be dependents as defined by the Internal Revenue Service. Typically, this includes birth children, stepchildren, legally adopted children or a legal ward financially supported by the employee. Applicants must be enrolled in engineering, architecture or construction technology programs in a recognized and/or accredited school such as a university, trade school, business college or other institutions as approved by the ICC prior to distribution of the award. **Criteria:** Selection will be based on merit.

Funds Avail.: $2,500. **Duration:** Annual. **Number Awarded:** 1. **To Apply:** Applications and instructions are available at the ICC and ICCF websites. **Deadline:** June 28. **Contact:** International Code Council, Attn: Scholarships c/o: Elise Craig, ecraig@iccsafe.org.

5064 ■ International Council for Canadian Studies (ICCS)
Holland Cross RO
1620 Scott St., Unit 8
Ottawa, ON, Canada K1Y 4V1
Ph: (819)205-0359
Fax: (613)789-7830
URL: www.iccs-ciec.ca

5065 ■ Canadian Studies Postdoctoral Fellowships
(Postdoctorate/Fellowship)

Purpose: To enable young Canadian and foreign academics to visit a Canadian or foreign university with a Canadian Studies program for a teaching or research fellowship. **Focus:** Canadian studies. **Qualif.:** Applicants must be in post-doctoral level that have completed a doctoral thesis on a topic primarily related to Canada and are not employed as a full-time; must obtain a formal commitment from such universities concerning the services and teaching and/or research opportunities which would be available to them. **Criteria:** Selection will be based on the committee's criteria.

Funds Avail.: $2,500. **Duration:** Minimum of one month and maximum of three months. **To Apply:** Applicants must submit the following materials: up-to-date curriculum vitae; copy of the doctoral thesis; full description of the project proposed by the applicant during his/her fellowship; an of-

ficial letter from the host university indicating its support of the young researcher (availability of research tools, library, archives, computer, office, accommodation, teaching load and other responsibilities); two letters of reference from university professors knowledgeable with the candidates' studies; and letter from the senior researcher's host outlining the research project and the work to be assigned to the young researcher during the fellowship. For applicant applying for a research fellowship, they must include a budget detailing travel expenses, material, photocopies, etc. and for applicant applying for a teaching fellowship, they must also include a course outline maximum of two pages. Application files must be submitted to the ICCS with a recommendation from the national Canadian Studies Association. **Deadline:** November 24.

5066 ■ International Council for Canadian Studies Graduate Student Scholarships *(Postgraduate/ Scholarship)*

Purpose: To support the works of young scholars, by enabling successful candidates for their research related to their thesis or dissertation in the field of Canadian Studies. **Focus:** Canadian studies. **Qualif.:** Applicant must be a student in the social sciences or humanities who is in the process of preparing a graduate thesis or doctoral dissertation in Canada; must be at the thesis or dissertation stage; and must obtained in writing the support of a faculty member at a Canadian University who has agreed to act as the student's academic sponsor during the tenure of his/her award. **Criteria:** Applicants will be evaluated based on clarity of the proposal and its methodology; the proposal's potential contribution; must demonstrate the need for the research to be carried out in Canada and by the strength of the letter of support. Nominations will be evaluated and ranked by the adjudication committee appointed by the International Council for Canadian Studies.

Funds Avail.: No specific amount. **Number Awarded:** 6. **To Apply:** Applicants must submit a two-page proposal outlining the thesis/dissertation project; an official university transcript; copy of a letter from the faculty member in a Canadian University indicating their willingness to act as the student's academic sponsor; and a letter of support from the student's thesis/dissertation supervisor. **Deadline:** November 24.

5067 ■ International Council of Shopping Centers Foundation
1221 Avenue of the Americas, 41st Fl.
New York, NY 10020-1099
Ph: (646)728-3800
Fax: (732)694-1755
E-mail: foundation@icsc.org
URL: www.icsc.org/foundation

5068 ■ Harold E. Eisenberg Foundation Scholarships *(Other/Scholarship)*

Purpose: To support graduates and real estate practitioner an educational scholarships. **Focus:** Management; Marketing and distribution. **Qualif.:** Applicant must be a member of ICSC and employed by a member company in good standing; actively employed in the retail real estate industry for a minimum of one year or is a recent graduate of a college/university with an emphasis in real estate. **Criteria:** Scholarship will be given to applicant who works in the mid-west of the United States.

Funds Avail.: No specific amount. **To Apply:** Applicants

Awards are arranged alphabetically below their administering organizations

must complete the online scholarship application; in addition, applicants must submit two letters of recommendation.

5069 ■ Mary Lou Fiala Fellowships (Other/Fellowship)

Purpose: To support an outstanding professional with passion and commitment to retail real estate, and has the potential to make a lasting contribution to the industry. **Focus:** Real estate. **Qualif.:** Applicant must be 35 years of age or younger at the application close date; be a United States citizen or permanent resident; a professional in the retail real estate industry for a minimum of 2 years and be committed to a career in retail real estate; and have a passion for learning and giving back. **Criteria:** Selection is based on professional excellence and active commitment to helping others through service in their communities, profession or fields of research.

Funds Avail.: No specific amount. **To Apply:** Applicant must be nominated to complete the application.

5070 ■ Charles Grossman Graduate Scholarships (Graduate/Scholarship)

Purpose: To assist and encourage extraordinary students to select retail real estate as their career path. **Focus:** Real estate. **Qualif.:** Applicant must be an active ICSC member who is or will be a graduate degree seeking candidate enrolled at an accredited college/university; be a full time student or a part time student who is working full time; have minimum overall 3.0 GPA and an ICSC member; and must be dedicated to the industry with a proven track record of involvement and participation. **Criteria:** Selection is based on the application

Funds Avail.: $10,000. **To Apply:** All application materials are to be sent electronically with the exception of school transcripts and letters of reference. **Deadline:** May 21. **Contact:** International Council of Shopping Centers Foundation, at the above address.

5071 ■ John T. Riordan Professional Education Scholarships (Other/Scholarship)

Purpose: To support retail estate professionals who wants to further their education and career development. **Focus:** Management; Marketing and distribution. **Qualif.:** Applicant must be a member of ICSC and employed by a member company in good standing; actively employed in the retail real estate industry for a minimum of one year or is a recent graduate of a college/university with an emphasis in real estate. **Criteria:** Selection is based on the application.

Funds Avail.: No specific amount. **To Apply:** Applicants must complete the online scholarship application; in addition, applicants must submit two letters of recommendation. **Contact:** International Council of Shopping Centers Foundation, at the above address.

5072 ■ Schurgin Family Foundation Scholarships (Undergraduate/Scholarship)

Purpose: To provide tuition assistance to undergraduate students who are studying retail real estate or a related field. **Focus:** Real estate. **Qualif.:** Applicant must be a U.S. Citizen who is or will be a junior or senior undergraduate degree seeking candidate enrolled full time at an accredited college/university; have a minimum of 3.0 GPA; with strong interest in the industry and a record of participation and involvement. **Criteria:** Selection is based on the application.

Funds Avail.: $5,000. **Duration:** Annual. **Number**

Awarded: 2. **To Apply:** All application materials are to be sent electronically with the exception of school transcripts and letters of reference. **Deadline:** May 21.

5073 ■ International Council on Systems Engineering (INCOSE)
7670 Opportunity Rd., Ste. 220
San Diego, CA 92111-2222
Ph: (858)541-1725
Fax: (858)541-1725
Free: 800-366-1164
E-mail: info@incose.org
URL: www.incose.org

5074 ■ Johns Hopkins University/Applied Physics Laboratory Alexander Kossiakoff Scholarships (Doctorate, Graduate, Master's/Scholarship)

Purpose: To encourage promising applied systems engineering research by students in a Masters or Doctoral program. **Focus:** Systems engineering. **Qualif.:** Applicant must be a U.S. citizen and must be an admitted student in a Masters or Doctoral Program in Systems Engineering at an accredited university. **Criteria:** Selection will be based on the following criteria: rigor and creativity of proposed applied research; potential application to Applied Physics Laboratory systems engineering interests; strength of resume and bio sketch; strength of academic recommendations; additional attributes noted in the applicant's materials that go beyond the application requirements.

Funds Avail.: $5,000. **Duration:** Annual. **To Apply:** Each applicant must submit an application package to include a complete resume/vitae, a brief bio-sketch, description of the study/research areas of interest (at least three to four pages), and a discussion of the contribution and expected outcomes that will benefit applications of interest to the Laboratory; must have two faculty references submit recommendation letters on their behalf. **Remarks:** Established in 2009.

5075 ■ James E. Long Memorial Post Doctoral Fellowships (Postdoctorate/Fellowship)

Purpose: To inspire innovative post-doctorate level research that has the potential to produce major improvements in advancing the practice of systems engineering and systems thinking. **Focus:** Systems engineering. **Qualif.:** Status as someone engaged in promising post-doctoral research at an accredited university or research institute. **Criteria:** Selection will be based on the following criteria: advance the state of the practice of systems thinking or the systems perspective; demonstrate potential for rapid theory to practice especially in improving systems approaches to solving complex problems; serve as a catalyst for additional research in the area of systems thinking.

Funds Avail.: $5,000. **Duration:** Annual. **To Apply:** Applicant must submit an application package to include complete resume/vitae, a brief bio-sketch, description of the study/research area of interest and a discussion of the contributions and expected outcomes that will benefit applications to advance the state of the practice; must have two professional references familiar with the applicant's research, submit recommendation letters on their behalf outlining the potential benefits and application toward solving complex problems. **Deadline:** May 1.

5076 ■ Stevens Doctoral Awards (Doctorate/Award)
Purpose: To inspire and recognize innovative doctoral-level research to the field of systems engineering and

Awards are arranged alphabetically below their administering organizations

integration. **Focus:** Systems engineering. **Qualif.:** Applicant must be a qualified PhD student in a degree program with an approved research proposal and many not receive more than one award. **Criteria:** Selection will be based on the advancement of the state-of-the-knowledge in systems engineering and integration; potential for the advancement of the state-of-the-practice of systems engineering and integration within the next five to ten years.

Funds Avail.: $5,000. **Duration:** Annual. **To Apply:** Applicant may visit the website to download the Doctoral Award Application.

5077 ■ International Dairy-Deli-Bakery Association (IDDBA)
636 Science Dr.
Madison, WI 53711-1073
Ph: (608)310-5000
Fax: (608)238-6330
E-mail: iddba@iddba.org
URL: www.iddba.org

5078 ■ International Dairy-Deli-Bakery Association Undergraduate/Graduate Scholarships *(Graduate, Undergraduate/Scholarship)*

Purpose: To support employees of IDDBA-member companies. **Focus:** Business; Culinary arts; Food service careers. **Qualif.:** Applicants must have an academic field of study in a food-related field such as culinary arts, baking/pastry arts or food science, business or marketing program. Applicants must also have a 2.5 grade-point average on a 4.0 scale, or equivalent which may be waived for first-time returning adult students. **Criteria:** If financial resources run low, priority will be given to supermarket dairy, deli and bakery employees.

Funds Avail.: $100-$1,000. **Duration:** One semester. **To Apply:** Applicants must submit a completed application form together with at least one letter of reference on letterhead from a department/store manager and/or professional academic contact. Incomplete or illegible applications will not be considered. **Deadline:** January 1; April 1; July 1; October 1. **Contact:** scholarships@iddba.org.

5079 ■ Undergraduate/Graduate Scholarships *(Undergraduate, Graduate/Scholarship)*

Purpose: To provide an academic support to high school seniors and current or returning college or vocational/technical school students. **Focus:** Business; Food science and technology; Marketing and distribution. **Qualif.:** Applicants must be current full- or part-time employees of an IDDBA-member company; must work a minimum of 13 hours per week during the school year for an IDDBA-member company; must have academic field of study in a food-related field, business or marketing program; and must have a 2.5 grade-point average on a 4.0 scale, or equivalent. **Criteria:** Priority will be given to supermarket dairy, deli and bakery employees.

Funds Avail.: $100 to $1,000 per semester. **Duration:** Annual. **Number Awarded:** 2. **To Apply:** Applicants may apply online by visiting the IDDBA's website, or download the application form provided by IDDBA. **Deadline:** January1; April 1; July 1; October 1. **Contact:** scholarships@iddba.org.

5080 ■ International Dance Teachers' Association (IDTA)
International House
76 Bennett Rd.

East Sussex
Brighton BN2 5JL, United Kingdom
Ph: 44 1273 685652
Fax: 44 1273 674388
URL: www.idta.co.uk

5081 ■ IDTA Freestyle Scholarships *(Undergraduate/ Scholarship)*

Purpose: To provide assistance for students who wants to pursue a dance career; to further the knowledge about the art of dance and all its forms. **Focus:** General studies/Field of study not specified. **Qualif.:** Applicants must be members of IDTA. **Criteria:** Selection will be based on the committee's criteria.

Funds Avail.: No specific amount. **Duration:** Annual. **To Apply:** Interested applicants must contact IDTA for the application details.

5082 ■ International Desalination Association (IDA)
94 Central St., Ste. 200
Topsfield, MA 01983-1838
Ph: (978)887-0410
Fax: (978)887-0411
E-mail: info@idadesal.org
URL: www.idadesal.org

5083 ■ Channabasappa Memorial Scholarships *(Graduate, Doctorate/Scholarship)*

Purpose: To provide assistance for graduate students intending to further their education in subjects related to desalination. **Focus:** Engineering; Engineering, Hydraulic; Science; Water resources. **Qualif.:** Applicant must be a graduate of an accredited university; must be from the top 10% of the class in science or engineering; must prove admission to a graduate program in desalination/water reuse; must demonstrate leadership and achievement potential; and must be an IDA member. **Criteria:** Recipients will be selected based on the undergraduate and graduate transcripts, references and motivation for a career in desalination.

Funds Avail.: $10,000 maximum grant per student. **To Apply:** Applicants must submit a completed application form available at the website; a transcript of undergraduate academic records indicating grade point average or rank in the class; four letters of recommendation, one from a director or a distinguished IDA member; a description of the applicant's objectives and plans for graduate study; an evidence of other sources of funding to complete the applicant's degree objective; proof of acceptance to a graduate program at an accredited university; a faculty sponsor statement indicating the nature and scope of the research. **Contact:** Ms. Leslie Merrill, lmerrill@idadesal.org.

5084 ■ IDA Fellowship Awards *(Other/Fellowship)*

Purpose: To promote development in the desalination and water reuse industry. **Focus:** Engineering; Engineering, Hydraulic; Science; Water resources. **Qualif.:** Applicant must be an IDA member who has 8-10 years of work experience in the field of desalination or water reuse. **Criteria:** Applicants will be selected based on the following: high professional achievements; relevance of the experience; responsible career goals for advancement in the chosen field; potential to make a contribution in the field of water reuse; benefits of the attachment to the applicants;

Awards are arranged alphabetically below their administering organizations

assurance that the applicant will remain connected to the desalination water-reuse industry through future work.

Funds Avail.: $10,000. **To Apply:** Applicants must submit a completed application form; a single copy of resume/ curriculum vitae; a fellow's proposal (single copy, maximum of five pages, double-spaced); two letters of recommendations from either of the advisors, instructors or individuals who know the applicant's work and personal character; and must pass the oral interview. Letters should be sealed in an envelope, signed across by the recommender. Finalists will be interviewed by the selection Committee. **Contact:** Questions regarding the fellowship should be forwarded to Leslie Merrill at lmerrill@idadesal.org.

5085 ■ International Development Research Centre (IDRC)

150 Kent St.
Ottawa, ON, Canada K1P 0B2
Ph: (613)236-6163
Fax: (613)238-7230
E-mail: info@idrc.ca
URL: www.idrc.ca

5086 ■ The Bentley Cropping Systems Fellowship
(Graduate/Fellowship)

Purpose: To provide funding for field research aimed at increasing the yield of food crops, improving farmers' livelihoods, and improving soil fertility. **Focus:** Agricultural sciences; Food science and technology. **Qualif.:** Applicant must be a citizen or permanent resident of Canada, or a citizen of a developing country; be enrolled full-time at a recognized university at the master's, doctoral, or post-doctoral level in Canada or in a developing country for the duration of the award period. **Criteria:** Selection shall be based on the qualifications of the applicant, as well as to the submitted proposal of the person.

Funds Avail.: 30,000 Candian Dollars. **Duration:** Biennial. **To Apply:** Applicant must be able to submit a research proposal focusing on very simple cropping-systems research that can benefit smallholder farmers in developing countries, especially rural women farmers. For more information, visit the program page or website. **Deadline:** October 1.

5087 ■ International Door Association (IDA)

PO Box 246
West Milton, OH 45383
Ph: (937)698-8042
Fax: (937)698-6153
Free: 800-355-4432
E-mail: info@longmgt.com
URL: www.doors.org

5088 ■ International Door Association Scholarship Foundation Program *(Undergraduate, Vocational/ Occupational/Scholarship)*

Purpose: To support advanced educational opportunities for scholastically eligible students. **Focus:** General studies/ Field of study not specified. **Qualif.:** Applicant must be a high school with senior standing, community college, an associate degree program, vocational school or similar certification/diploma program, undergraduate college or university; have a cumulative grade point average equal to or greater than 3.0 on a 4.0 scale (or equivalent); must be

an immediate family member, an employee, or an immediate family member of an employee of an IDA Installing/ Servicing Dealer Member or an IDA Primary Industry Manufacturer/Vendor Member in good standing. **Criteria:** Applicants will be selected based on their grades, community and school involvement, recommendations and character determined through narrative.

Funds Avail.: $2,000 for full-time; for part-time, award amount is to be determined by semester hours or equivalent taken, and not to exceed $1,000. **Duration:** One academic year. **To Apply:** Applicants must submit a completed and signed application; an official transcript; personal statement; three letters of recommendation; list of leadership activities; and brochure of accredited schools (optional). **Deadline:** July 15. **Remarks:** Scholarship has two criteria: Primary Full-Time and Secondary Part-Time. **Contact:** Peggy Sanders, Scholarship Administrator, psanders@ longmgt.com.

5089 ■ International Executive Housekeepers Association (IEHA)

1001 Eastwind Dr., Ste. 301
Westerville, OH 43081-3361
Ph: (614)895-7166
Fax: (614)895-1248
Free: 800-200-6342
E-mail: excel@ieha.org
URL: www.ieha.org

5090 ■ International Executive Housekeepers Association Education Foundation Scholarship Awards *(Undergraduate/Scholarship)*

Purpose: To financially support students who are continuing their education to enhance their knowledge in their chosen field. **Focus:** General studies/Field of study not specified. **Qualif.:** Applicants must be IEHA members enrolled in an undergraduate or associate degree or IEHA approved certification program. **Criteria:** Selection will be based on the committee's criteria.

Funds Avail.: Up to $80,000. **To Apply:** Applicants must submit application form, a letter from your school official, your official school transcript, and a manuscript describing the applying for the scholarship and an explanation letter of career goals. **Deadline:** January 10.

5091 ■ International Executive Housekeepers Association Spartan Scholarship Awards *(Undergraduate/Scholarship)*

Purpose: To provide educational assistance to those who are in need. **Focus:** General studies/Field of study not specified. **Qualif.:** Applicant must be an IEHA member or an immediate family of an IEHA member. **Criteria:** Scholarship recipient will be selected based on the IEHA Education Committee's review of the application materials.

Funds Avail.: $1,500. **To Apply:** Applicants must submit a completed application form and a letter stating: reasons for applying the funds, the use of the award and explanation of career goals.

5092 ■ International Facility Management Association Foundation

800 Gessner Rd., Ste. 900
Houston, TX 77024-4257
Ph: (713)623-4362

Awards are arranged alphabetically below their administering organizations

Fax: (713)623-6124
E-mail: ifma@ifma.org
URL: www.ifmafoundation.org

5093 ■ IFMA Foundation Scholarships *(Undergraduate, Graduate/Scholarship)*

Purpose: To fund and promote education and research for the advancement of facility management. **Focus:** Management; Materials handling. **Qualif.:** Applicants must be full time graduate or undergraduate students at the time of submission and of receiving the scholarship; enrolled in a facility management (or related field) degree curriculum, in an accredited four-year Bachelor (undergraduate) program or an accredited Master/Doctoral (graduate) program; and may not be employed full time. Undergraduate student must have completed two years of university and have a minimum GPA of 3.20. Graduate student must have a minimum GPA of 3.5. **Criteria:** Selection shall be based on achievements/accomplishments, involvement, letter of intent, resume and recommendation.

Funds Avail.: $1,500 to $5,000. **Duration:** Annual. **To Apply:** Applicants are required to apply online. **Deadline:** May 31. **Contact:** Cara Johnson, IFMA Foundation Administrator at: cara.johnson@ifma.org.

5094 ■ International Food Service Executives Association (IFSEA)

4955 Miller St., Ste. 107
Wheat Ridge, CO 80033
Free: 800-893-5499
URL: www.ifsea.com

5095 ■ IFSEA Worthy Goal Scholarships *(Two Year College, Undergraduate, Vocational/Occupational/Scholarship)*

Purpose: To provide assistance to deserving individuals intending to receive food service management or vocational training beyond the high school level. **Focus:** Food service careers. **Qualif.:** Applicant must be enrolled or accepted as a full time student in a Food Service-related major at a 2 or 4 year college or university for the fall term following the award. **Criteria:** Recipient is chosen based on merit as reviewed by the IFSEA Scholarship Committee.

Funds Avail.: $250-$1,500. **Duration:** Annual. **To Apply:** Applicant must provide a summary of projected 1-year expenses and income/ fundraising beginning with the fall semester or a summary of financial statement; a statement (maximum of 500 words) on personal background focusing on aspects regarding food service and future goals; documentation of work experience, student organizations, transcript of grades, three letters of recommendation, and a statement (maximum of 250 words) on how receiving the scholarship would help you in reaching the goals you have set for yourself. Applicants may also visit the website for further information and instructions. **Contact:** Forward complete application package to: Worthy Goal Scholarship Fund, c/o Brian Kunihiro, Trustee, 94-870 Lumiauau St. P106, Waipahu, HI 96797.

5096 ■ International Foodservice Editorial Council (IFEC)

7 Point Pl.
Hyde Park, NY 12538
Ph: (845)229-6973

Fax: (845)229-6973
E-mail: ifec@ifeconline.com
URL: ifeconline.com

5097 ■ International Foodservice Editorial Council Scholarships *(Graduate, Undergraduate/Scholarship)*

Purpose: To assist students pursuing careers as writers, editors, public relation and marketing communication practitioners and closely related areas within the foodservice industry. **Focus:** Communications; Culinary arts; Food science and technology; Food service careers; Graphic art and design; Hotel, institutional, and restaurant management; Journalism; Nutrition; Photography; Public relations. **Qualif.:** Applicants must be currently enrolled and in good standing in a post-secondary, degree-granting educational institution; must have an expected graduation date; and must show an evidence of training, skills and interest in food service and communication arts. **Criteria:** Recipients will be selected based on academic record, character references, and financial need.

Funds Avail.: Varies. **Number Awarded:** Varies. **To Apply:** Applicants must submit a complete application together with academic transcript and two letters of recommendation from a supervisor, teacher, advisor or other foodservice or communications professional familiar with applicants' skills. Application requirements must be typewritten and submitted using U.S. Postal Service's Return Receipt Service. **Deadline:** March 15.

5098 ■ International Foundation for Ethical Research (IFER)

53 W Jackson Blvd., Ste. 1552
Chicago, IL 60604
Ph: (312)427-6025
Fax: (312)427-6524
E-mail: ifer@navs.org
URL: www.ifer.org

5099 ■ Graduate Fellowships in Alternatives in Scientific Research *(Doctorate, Graduate/Fellowship)*

Purpose: To provide monetary assistance to graduate students. **Focus:** Science technologies. **Qualif.:** Applicant must be a student enrolled in Master's and Ph.D programs in the sciences, humanities, psychology and journalism. **Criteria:** Selection of applicant will be based on the application form and other supporting documents.

Funds Avail.: A stipend of $12,500 and up to $2,500 for supplies. **Duration:** Annual. **To Apply:** Application forms are available and can be downloaded at the website. **Deadline:** March 30. **Remarks:** Fellowships are renewable annually for up to three years.

5100 ■ International Franchise Association (IFA)

1501 K St. NW, Ste. 350
Washington, DC 20005
Ph: (202)628-8000
Fax: (202)628-0812
Free: 800-543-1038
E-mail: ifa@franchise.org
URL: www.franchise.org

5101 ■ Don Debolt Franchising Scholarship Program *(Undergraduate/Scholarship)*

Purpose: To provide financial support to those students who are acquiring knowledge about franchising. **Focus:**

Awards are arranged alphabetically below their administering organizations

Business. **Qualif.:** Applicant must be the overall winner of the Delta Epsilon Chi Entrepreneurship Academy Competitive. **Criteria:** Preference will be given to those students who meet the criteria.

Funds Avail.: No specific amount. **To Apply:** Applicants may visit the website to verify the application process and other pieces of information.

5102 ■ Franchise Law Diversity Scholarship Awards
(Undergraduate/Scholarship)

Purpose: To support minority law students in pursuing their careers in franchise law. **Focus:** Law. **Qualif.:** Applicants must be enrolled in an ABA-accredited law schools. Applicants must have 2L or 3L status during the period of the scholarship, and they must be enrolled in at least one course oriented towards franchise law (e.g., Torts, Unfair Trade Practices, Trade Secrets, Antitrust, Trademarks, Contracts, Agency, Securities). Applicants must be considered members of diverse groups (African American, American Indian, Hispanic American, Asian American or Gay/Lesbian). **Criteria:** Preference will be given to those students who are in need.

Funds Avail.: $4,000. **Duration:** Annual. **To Apply:** Applicants may visit the website to verify the application process and other pieces of information. **Contact:** John Reynolds at jreynolds@franchise.org.

5103 ■ International Furnishings and Design Association (IFDA)
610 Freedom Business Ctr., Ste. 110
King of Prussia, PA 19406
Ph: (610)992-0011
Fax: (610)992-0021
E-mail: info@ifda.com
URL: www.ifda.com

5104 ■ International Furnishings and Design Association Educational Foundation Student Scholarships *(Undergraduate/Scholarship)*

Purpose: To foster educational and philanthropic activities which will benefit individuals and institutions; to promote, develop or enhance the furnishings and design industries and the practice of these professions. **Focus:** Interior design. **Qualif.:** Applicants must be post-secondary students majoring in Interior Design or closely related-field; must have completed four design-related courses and be enrolled at an accredited school or college. **Criteria:** Committees will review the applications based on uniqueness and creativity of work.

Funds Avail.: No specific amount. **Duration:** Annual. **To Apply:** Applicants must submit official transcript of records verifying a student's enrollment and GPA; a letter of recommendation from a design educator; must provide four copies of the following: (1) essay describing personal long and short term goals, awards and achievements in no more than 300-400 words; two digital photos of student's own original work preferably in color or in one page. **Deadline:** March 31. **Contact:** Sue Williams, Director of Scholarships & Grants at colleaguesinc@earthlink.net.

5105 ■ International Furnishings and Design Association Part-time Student Scholarships
(Undergraduate/Scholarship)

Purpose: To promote, develop or enhance the furnishings and design industries and the practice of these profes-

sions. **Focus:** Interior design. **Qualif.:** Applicants must have completed four courses in interior design or related field; must be enrolled as part-time students and be currently enrolled in at least two courses. **Criteria:** Recipients will be selected based on submitted application.

Funds Avail.: $1,500. **Duration:** Annual. **To Apply:** Applicants must submit certified, sealed transcript of course work that verifies enrollment with GPA. It may be sent by the school or college; a separate letter of recommendation from a professor or instructor on official school stationery; four copies of the following: (1) 200-400 word essay explaining long and short-term goals, achievements, awards or accomplishments; (2) two different examples of digital works; (3) completed application form. Send application packet to Merry Mabbett Dean. **Deadline:** March 31. **Contact:** Sue Williams, Director of Scholarships & Grants at colleaguesinc@earthlink.net.

5106 ■ International Grenfell Association (IGA)
81 Kenmount Rd., 2nd Fl.
Saint John's, NL, Canada A1B 3P8
Ph: (709)745-6162
Fax: (709)745-6163
E-mail: iga@nfld.net
URL: www.grenfellassociation.org

5107 ■ International Grenfell Association Bursary
(Undergraduate/Scholarship)

Purpose: To support the education of students with financial need who have been accepted into or are currently attending a post-secondary education institution. **Focus:** General studies/Field of study not specified. **Qualif.:** Applicant must be a Canadian citizen in the IGA region (must have graduated from a high school within the region); must not already possess a post-secondary degree; and must complete at least four courses per semester. **Criteria:** Selection will be based on the committee's criteria.

Funds Avail.: No specific amount. **To Apply:** Application forms and information can be obtained from the Grenfell Scholarship Committee or may be obtained online. Applications must be completed by the student and returned to the committee on or before the deadline. **Deadline:** February 15.

5108 ■ International Grenfell Association Secondary/High School Bursaries *(Undergraduate/Scholarship)*

Purpose: To support the education of high achievers who are planning to pursue college education. **Focus:** General studies/Field of study not specified. **Qualif.:** Applicants must be Canadian citizens residing in the IGA region; must be in regular attendance at high schools in the IGA region; must have achieved superior results in the previous year's final exams and the current year's midterms; must complete Level III examinations achieving grades consistent with previous attainment; must be eligible for entrance to a university; and must have taken a full course load (normally a minimum of 5 courses per semester). **Criteria:** Selection will be based on the committee's criteria.

Funds Avail.: No specific amount. **Duration:** Annual. **To Apply:** Applications must be completed by the student and returned to the principal on or before the deadline. Application form can be downloaded online. **Deadline:** February 15.

Awards are arranged alphabetically below their administering organizations

5109 ■ International Grenfell Association University/Post-Secondary Bursaries (Undergraduate/Scholarship)

Purpose: To support the education of high achievers and/or those with financial need who have completed one or more years of post-secondary education with one renewable scholarship. **Focus:** General studies/Field of study not specified. **Qualif.:** Applicant must be a Canadian citizen residing in the IGA region (must have graduated from a high school within the region); have completed one or more years of post-secondary education in a program leading to an undergraduate degree from a recognized university or diploma from a minimum of a three-year program at a recognized college; must achieve superior results in the current fall and winter semesters; must not already possess a post-secondary degree; and must undertake a full course load (minimum of 5 courses per semester). **Criteria:** Selection will be based on the committee's criteria.

Funds Avail.: No specific amount. **Duration:** Annual. **To Apply:** Application forms and information can be obtained from the Grenfell Scholarship Committee or may be obtained online. The application must be completed by the student and returned to the committee on or before the deadline. **Deadline:** Apri 1.

5110 ■ International Harvester Collectors (IHC)

c/o Emmett Webb, Membership Chair
PO Box 35
Dublin, IN 47335-0035
Ph: (765)478-6179
E-mail: ihcclub@aol.com
URL: www.nationalihcollectors.com

5111 ■ International Harvester Collectors Scholarships (Undergraduate/Scholarship)

Purpose: To provide a worldwide collector's network for the preservation of history, products, literature and memorabilia of the International Harvester Company. **Focus:** General studies/Field of study not specified. **Qualif.:** All applicants must be members, children of members or grandchildren of members of the International Harvester Collectors Inc., Club; must be enrolled or accepted for enrollment in an accredited college, university, junior college, trade, or technical school, or other similar post-high school educational institution; must be graduating high school seniors on the year of the application. **Criteria:** Award is given based on a review of properly submitted essays done by the Board of Directors of the International Harvester Collectors Inc., Club.

Funds Avail.: $1,000 - 1st prize; $750 - 2nd price. **Duration:** Annual. **Number Awarded:** 2. **To Apply:** Applicants are required to submit an essay of not less than 1,000 but not more than 2,000 words discussing on the topic given by the scholarship in-charge. Applicants must also provide separate information regarding the educational institution which includes the complete mailing address and telephone number of that educational institution's financial aid office; an annotated bibliography that lists the sources of information for the essay; a cover letter stating the institution the applicants will be attending, how the scholarship will be used in achieving the students' goals, and the process by which applicants acquired the information for the essay. **Deadline:** June 1. **Contact:** Darell Darst, farmall130@socket.net.

5112 ■ International Horn Society (IHS)

c/o Heidi Vogel, Executive Secretary
PO Box 630158
Lanai City, HI 96763-0158
Ph: (808)565-7273
Fax: (808)565-7273
E-mail: exec-secretary@hornsociety.org
URL: www.hornsociety.org

5113 ■ Paul Mansur Scholarships (Undergraduate/Scholarship)

Purpose: To provide opportunities for full-time students attending the IHS international symposium to receive a lesson from a world-renowned artist or teacher. **Focus:** Music. **Qualif.:** Applicants must be full-time students 18 years or younger and 19-26 years old at the time of the symposium. **Criteria:** Candidates' essays will be evaluated for both content and grammar by the appointed Committee of the IHS President.

Funds Avail.: No amount mentioned. **Number Awarded:** 1. **To Apply:** Those applicants must submit applications to the IHS Executive Secretary, either on print or by email; proof of full-time public or private school, conservatory, or university enrollment; and essay on the subject of how attending and receiving a lesson during the symposium will enhance his/her education. For those applicants whose native language is not English may submit application in their native language but translation is required. **Deadline:** May 15. **Contact:** Heidi Vogel, IHS Executive Secretary at the above address.

5114 ■ Barry Tuckwell Scholarships (All/Scholarship)

Purpose: To encourage and support worthy horn students to pursue education and performance by attending and participating in masterclasses and workshops throughout the world. **Focus:** Music. **Qualif.:** Applicants must be age 18 to 24. **Criteria:** Recipients will be selected by the appointed Committee of IHS Scholarship Chairs based on combination of ability, character, motivation, goals and opportunities available at the selected venue.

Funds Avail.: $500. **Number Awarded:** 1. **To Apply:** Applicants must submit a completed Tuckwell Scholarship application, available online or from the executive secretary; three copies of two brief essays outlining the applicant's experience and plan to study and perform at a specific event; three copies of a CD-format recording of one movement of a concerto or sonata (with piano), one etude and two orchestral excerpts; and two letters of recommendation including an assessment of need. **Deadline:** April 1. **Contact:** Heidi Vogel at the above address.

5115 ■ International Information Systems Security Certification Consortium (ISC2)

311 Park Place Blvd., Ste. 400
Clearwater, FL 33759
Ph: (727)785-0189
Fax: (727)683-0157
Free: 866-331-4722
E-mail: membersupport@isc2.org
URL: www.isc2.org

5116 ■ (ISC)2 Foundation Information Security Scholarships (All/Scholarship)

Purpose: To provide educational assistance to future information security professionals to prepare them for a

Awards are arranged alphabetically below their administering organizations

rewarding career in the said important field. **Focus:** Computer and information sciences; Information science and technology; National security. **Qualif.:** Applicants must be pursuing a course of study, and/or have a declared major/minor, with an information assurance (IA) or cyber security concentration and enrolled at a regionally accredited college or university (or equivalent for non-US applicants). Studies may be full-time, part-time, study online or on campus. **Criteria:** Selection shall be based on the aforementioned applicants' qualifications and compliance with the application details.

Funds Avail.: Amount varies. **Duration:** Annual. **Number Awarded:** Varies. **To Apply:** Applicants may visit the scholarship section of the bestowing organization's website for further information regarding the application details. **Remarks:** The scholarships being offered are the following: Undergraduate Scholarship; Graduate Scholarship; Women's Scholarship; Harold Tipton Memorial Scholarship; U.S.A. Cyber Warrior Scholarship; University of Phoenix (ISC)2 Scholarship; and the Faculty Vouchers. Each of them have individual guidelines and/or requirements as well, so be sure to visit each scholarship page to learn more. **Contact:** Inquiries can be sent to scholarships@ isc2.org.

5117 ■ International Institute for Municipal Clerks (IIMC)

8331 Utica Ave., Ste. 200
Rancho Cucamonga, CA 91730
Ph: (909)944-4162
Fax: (909)944-8545
Free: 800-251-1639
URL: www.iimc.com

5118 ■ Certified Municipal Clerk Scholarships (CMC) (Other/Scholarship)

Purpose: To enhance the job performance of the Clerk in small and large municipalities. **Focus:** General studies/Field of study not specified. **Qualif.:** Applicants must be IIMC members in good standing who are municipal clerks or deputy clerks (or related titles) on the date of application. **Criteria:** Applications are evaluated by the scholarship selection committee based on their designed criteria.

Funds Avail.: No specific amount. **To Apply:** Application forms are available on-line. Applicants must submit a letter indicating the municipality's commitment to grant time off to attend the Certification Program.

5119 ■ Master Municipal Clerks Academy Scholarships (Other/Scholarship)

Purpose: To support municipal clerks and deputy clerks to improve their professional performance. **Focus:** General studies/Field of study not specified. **Qualif.:** Applicants must be members in good standing of IIMC who are Certified Municipal Clerks or Deputy Clerks (or related titles) on the date of application. **Criteria:** Applicants are evaluated based on the criteria designed by the scholarship selection committee. Preference will be given to applicants who have plans to attend an Academy program.

Funds Avail.: No specific amount. **To Apply:** Applicants must submit all the required application information. Application forms are available on-line.

5120 ■ International Law Students Association (ILSA)

701 13th St. NW, 6th Fl.
Washington, DC 20005-3962

Ph: (202)639-9355
Fax: (202)639-9355
E-mail: ilsa@ilsa.org
URL: www.ilsa.org

5121 ■ ILSA Internships (Graduate/Internship)

Purpose: To support law students in their career development. **Focus:** Law. **Qualif.:** Applicants must be law students who are motivated, friendly, and detail oriented, and should be lawfully in the United States. **Criteria:** Selection will be based on ILSA's criteria.

Funds Avail.: No specific amount. **To Apply:** Applicants must submit a cover letter and resume to the ILSA Executive Office.

5122 ■ International Literacy Association (ILA)

800 Barksdale Rd.
Newark, DE 19714-8139
Ph: (302)731-1600
Fax: (302)731-1057
Free: 800-336-7323
E-mail: customerservice@reading.org
URL: www.literacyworldwide.org

5123 ■ Jeanne S. Chall Research Fellowship (Doctorate, Graduate/Fellowship)

Purpose: To honor reading research by promising scholars in areas of beginning reading, readability, reading difficulty, stages of reading development, relation of vocabulary to reading, and diagnosing those with limited ability. **Focus:** Reading. **Qualif.:** Applicants must be members of the International Reading Association; may either be doctoral students who are planning or beginning their dissertations; or a university based graduate students embarking on independent research studies. **Criteria:** Applications and proposals will be reviewed by the members of the International Reading Association Studies and Research based on: significance of research question; rationale for the research; adequacy of methods and data treatment; significance of project impact; clarity and specificity.

Funds Avail.: $6,000. **Duration:** Annual. **To Apply:** Applicants are advised to visit the website for the online application process and must submit the following requirements: curriculum vitae; reference letter; academic letters; and project proposal. **Deadline:** January 15. **Remarks:** The program was founded in honor of Dr. Jeanne S. Chall. Established in 1998.

5124 ■ Elva Knight Research Grants (Professional development/Grant)

Purpose: To support promising research that addresses significant questions for the discipline of reading/literacy research and practice. **Focus:** Reading. **Qualif.:** Applicants must be members of the International Reading Association. **Criteria:** Applications and proposals will be reviewed by the members of the International Reading Association Studies and Research based on: significance of research questions; rationale for the research; adequacy of methods and data treatment; significance of project impact; clarity and specificity.

Funds Avail.: $8,000. **To Apply:** Applicants must visit the website for the online application process. Applicants are required to provide a project proposal. **Deadline:** November 1.

Awards are arranged alphabetically below their administering organizations

5125 ■ Helen M. Robinson Grants *(Doctorate/Award, Monetary, Grant)*

Purpose: To assist doctoral students at the early stages of their dissertation research in the area of reading and literacy. **Focus:** Reading. **Qualif.:** Applicants must be members of the International Reading Association; must be doctoral students in the early stages of the dissertation research in areas of reading and literacy. **Criteria:** Applications and proposals will be reviewed by the members of the International Reading Association Studies and Research based on: significance of research question; rationale for the research; adequacy of methods and data treatment; significance of project impact; clarity and specificity.

Funds Avail.: $1,200. **Duration:** Annual. **To Apply:** Applicants are advised to visit the website for the online application process. Applicants are required to provide a project proposal. **Deadline:** January 15.

5126 ■ Steven A. Stahl Research Grants *(Graduate/ Grant)*

Purpose: To provide graduating students the opportunity to conduct their classroom research in reading. **Focus:** Reading. **Qualif.:** Applicants must be graduate students who are members of the International Reading Association; and have at least three years of pre-K-12 teaching experience. **Criteria:** Evaluations will be reviewed by the members of International Reading Association Steven A. Stahl Research Grant Committee based on: significance of the research questions; rationale for the research; appropriateness and adequacy of the methodology; clarity and cohesion of the text.

Funds Avail.: $1,000. **Duration:** Annual. **To Apply:** Applicants are advised to visit the website for the online application process. **Deadline:** January 15.

5127 ■ International Military Community Executives Association (IMCEA)

PO Box 7946
Round Rock, TX 78683-7946
Ph: (940)463-5145
Fax: (866)369-2435
E-mail: imcea@imcea.org
URL: imcea.org

5128 ■ Robert W. Brunsman Memorial Scholarship *(Professional development/Scholarship)*

Purpose: To assist MWR professionals in continuing their education. **Focus:** General studies/Field of study not specified. **Qualif.:** Applicants must be IMCEA MWR/Services Professional Members in good standing who are currently enrolled in a higher learning institution, whether in-class or on-line. **Criteria:** Selection shall be based on the aforementioned applicants' qualifications and compliance with the application details.

Funds Avail.: $1,000. **Duration:** Annual. **To Apply:** Applicants must mail the application form and attach a two-page, double spaced essay discussing how each area of MWR/Services (clubs, bowlings, golf, child care, etc.) might work together to create synergy and enhance the mission of IMCEA. Each area has its own distinct challenges and opportunities. Submit the said documents along with a copy of the current college transcript to the Scholarship Committee. **Deadline:** May 15.

5129 ■ Roy C. and Dorothy Jean Olson Memorial Scholarships *(Undergraduate/Scholarship)*

Purpose: To assist young men and women in furthering their education beyond secondary level. **Focus:** General

studies/Field of study not specified. **Qualif.:** Applicants must be family members of current IMCEA Professional Members who are graduating from high school and continuing their education, or who are already enrolled in college. **Criteria:** Selection shall be based on the aforementioned applicants' qualifications and compliance with the application details.

Funds Avail.: $1,000. **Duration:** Annual. **To Apply:** Applicants must mail the application form, along with the following: a two-page essay discussing the question "How do social networking and media outlets affect the US Military mission in a wartime environment?"; a letter of acceptance to the college or university that the applicants are planning to attend; and/or, a transcript from the college or university currently attended. **Deadline:** May 15.

5130 ■ International Narcotics Interdiction Association (INIA)

PO Box 1757
Spring Hill, TN 37174
Free: 866-780-4642
E-mail: info@inia.org
URL: www.inia.org

5131 ■ INIA Scholarship Program *(Undergraduate/ Scholarship)*

Purpose: To support a given charity or other non-profit agencies and events. **Focus:** General studies/Field of study not specified. **Qualif.:** Applicants must be children of INIA members who will be in their senior year of high school; the parent INIA member must be current in his/her membership, or deceased. **Criteria:** Recipients will be selected based on submitted essay which will be judged based on its content, form and grammar.

Funds Avail.: Up to $1,000 each. **Duration:** Annual. **To Apply:** Applicants must submit their completed application form along with an essay not exceeding 500 words on the topic described on the application form. It must be accompanied by the signed certification statement indicating that the parent/guardian had monitored the essay. Prior to receiving the funds, applicants are required to provide a proof of admission to an accredited institute in a full-time status. **Deadline:** April 30. **Contact:** INIA Scholarship Award; P.O. Box 1757 Springhill, TN 37174; E-mail: info@inia.org phone: 866-780-4642.

5132 ■ International Nurses Society on Addictions (IntNSA)

3416 Primm Ln.
Birmingham, AL 35216
Ph: (205)823-6106
E-mail: intnsa@primemanagement.net
URL: www.intnsa.org

5133 ■ Lois Widley Student Scholarships *(Graduate, Undergraduate/Scholarship)*

Purpose: To financially assist IntNSA members to further their professional education. **Focus:** Nursing. **Qualif.:** Applicant must be a current full time student in a nursing undergraduate or graduate program; must be sponsored by a current IntNSA member. **Criteria:** Selection of applicants will be based on the Scholarship application criteria.

Funds Avail.: $2,000. **Number Awarded:** 4. **To Apply:** Applicants must complete the application form available

Awards are arranged alphabetically below their administering organizations

online; must submit a recommendation letter, letter of support from their sponsor, and essay about their interest in attending the conference and what they plan to do with the knowledge gained (250-300 word). **Deadline:** June 30.

5134 ■ International Order of the King's Daughters and Sons (IOKDS)

34 Vincent Ave.
Chautauqua, NY 14722
Ph: (716)357-4951
Fax: (716)357-3762
URL: www.iokds.org

5135 ■ Chautauqua Scholarships Program
(Undergraduate/Scholarship)

Purpose: To strengthen faith, build confidence and increase leadership skills. **Focus:** Art; Religion. **Qualif.:** Applicants must be Christians between 19-25 years old who have at least two years of college or university and who have an interest in learning and the arts. **Criteria:** Recipients are selected based on applicant's Christian beliefs and practice; an inquiring mind; energy and enthusiasm; and respect and responsibility.

Funds Avail.: No specific amount. **Duration:** Weekly; four times a week. **To Apply:** Applicants must submit a letter of recommendation from the pastor; copy of completed application form. Applicants must also pass the telephone interview with the Director of Chautauqua Department. **Deadline:** March 15. **Contact:** Chautauqua Scholarship Program Director, Vicki Carter, at chqscholars@gmail.com.

5136 ■ International Organic Inspectors Association (IOIA)

PO Box 6
Broadus, MT 59317
Ph: (406)436-2031
E-mail: ioia@ioia.net
URL: www.ioia.net

5137 ■ IOIA Organic Community Initiative Scholarships *(Other/Scholarship)*

Purpose: To provide full tuition for an IOIA Basic Inspector Training Course. **Focus:** Education, Vocational-technical. **Qualif.:** Applicants must be individuals residing outside of the United States and Canada. **Criteria:** Recipients will be selected based on their potential to effect change in their organic community and financial need.

Funds Avail.: No amount mentioned. **Duration:** Annual. **To Apply:** Applicants must submit a completed application form, cover letter, current resume, and list of three references. **Deadline:** October 1. **Contact:** Margaret Scoles, IOIA Executive Director at the above address.

5138 ■ IOIA Andrew Rutherford Scholarships *(Other/Scholarship)*

Purpose: To provide full tuition for an IOIA Inspector Training Course. **Focus:** Education, Vocational-technical. **Qualif.:** Applicants must come from outside of the US or Canada; prospective and experienced inspectors are eligible to apply for the Scholarship. **Criteria:** Selection will be based on the applicants' potential and financial need.

Funds Avail.: No amount mentioned. **Duration:** Annual. **To Apply:** Applicants must submit completed application

form, cover letter, current resume, and list of references. **Deadline:** October 1. **Contact:** Margaret Scoles, 406-436-2031, ioia@ioia.net.

5139 ■ International Paralegal Management Association (IPMA)

980 N Michigan Ave., Ste. 1400
Chicago, IL 60611
Ph: (312)214-4991
Free: 888-662-9155
E-mail: info@paralegalmanagement.org
URL: www.paralegalmanagement.org

5140 ■ Therese A. Cannon Educational Scholarships *(Other/Scholarship)*

Purpose: To assist members in continuing their education through advanced formal training. **Focus:** Paralegal studies. **Qualif.:** Applicants must be regular, associate, life or emeritus IPMA members. **Criteria:** Selection shall be based on Content, Writing Skills and Persuasiveness.

Funds Avail.: No specific amount. **To Apply:** Applicants must complete the application form (available at the website) and submit it along with a one page essay. **Remarks:** The scholarship was created to honor Teri Cannon's dedicated service to the IPMA and to recognize her commitment to the education of paralegal and paralegal management.

5141 ■ International Personnel Management Association (IPMA-HR)

1617 Duke St.
Alexandria, VA 22314
Ph: (703)549-7100
Fax: (703)684-0948
E-mail: publications@ipma-hr.org
URL: www.ipma-hr.org

5142 ■ IPMA-HR Graduate Study Fellowships *(Graduate, Master's/Fellowship)*

Purpose: To allow recipients to pursue graduate study in public administration, business administration, the law or a related field. **Focus:** Business administration; Law; Public administration. **Qualif.:** Applicants must have a minimum of five years of full-time professional experience of excellent quality and depth. At least two of these years must be in an HR-related area; must have a strong academic record; must have demonstrated leadership, management or creativity; strong commitment to public sector human resources; must have a current national membership in the Association of at least one year, other than as student members. **Criteria:** Selection will be based on the committee's criteria.

Funds Avail.: No specific amount. **Duration:** Annual. **To Apply:** Applicants must provide the following: letter indicating acceptance to graduate school for a law degree or a master's degree in public administration, business administration or a related field; and official copies of all undergraduate and graduate transcripts. **Deadline:** June 1.

5143 ■ International Radio and Television Society Foundation (IRTS)

1697 Broadway, 10th Fl.
New York, NY 10019
Ph: (212)867-6650

Awards are arranged alphabetically below their administering organizations

URL: irtsfoundation.org

5144 ■ International Radio and Television Society Foundation Summer Fellowships Program
(Undergraduate, Graduate/Fellowship)

Purpose: To assist students in their professional development. **Focus:** General studies/Field of study not specified. **Qualif.:** Applicants must be college juniors, seniors or graduate students from all majors (including math, computer science, business, marketing, communications, etc.), as of April of the current year. **Criteria:** Selection shall be based on the aforementioned qualifications and compliance with the application details.

Funds Avail.: No specific amount. **Duration:** Annual. **To Apply:** Applicants must fill-up the provided application form which is available at the website. Additional document must also includes one-page resume (Word document or PDF). **Deadline:** November 2.

5145 ■ International Research and Exchanges Board (IREX)
1275 K St. NW, Ste. 600
Washington, DC 20005
Ph: (202)628-8188
Fax: (202)628-8189
E-mail: irex@irex.org
URL: www.irex.org

5146 ■ Educational and Cultural Affairs Alumni Small Grants Program (ECA) *(Other/Grant)*

Purpose: To bring outstanding secondary school teachers from around the globe to the United States to further develop expertise in their subject areas, enhance their teaching skills, and increase their knowledge about the United States. **Focus:** European studies. **Qualif.:** Applicants must be alumni of the Edmund S. Muskie Graduate Fellowship Program (MUSKIE) or the Eurasian Undergraduate Program (UGRAD). **Criteria:** Selection is based on the applications.

Funds Avail.: No specific amount. **To Apply:** Applicants must contact their local IREX office for application details.

5147 ■ Individual Advanced Research Opportunities Program For Master's Students *(Graduate, Master's/Fellowship)*

Purpose: To support in-depth, primary source research in policy-relevant subjects related to Southeast Europe and Eurasia. **Focus:** European studies. **Qualif.:** Applicants must be U.S. citizens who are currently enrolled in a Master's program. **Criteria:** Selection will be based on the following criteria: overall strength of proposals, reference and proposed methodology; importance of topic towards foreign policy community; value of research to community; demonstrated serious preparatory work; well-argued need to conduct the research; language skills adequate for proposed research; feasibility of project and timeframe; demonstrated career commitment to the field; and few previous opportunities to conduct the research. Preference will be given to research projects on the countries of Central Asia and the Caucasus.

Funds Avail.: No specific amount. **Duration:** from one to three months. **To Apply:** Applicants must complete an application form; must submit a research proposal; five-page curriculum vitae; transcript of records; Professional/

Academic Reference and one Language Proficiency Form (to be sent directly by referee). Other information on the research proposal can be verified at the website. **Deadline:** November 16. **Contact:** iaro@irex.org.

5148 ■ IREX Individual Advanced Research Opportunities Program For Pre-doctoral Students
(Doctorate/Fellowship)

Purpose: To support in-depth, primary source research in policy-relevant subjects related to Southeast Europe and Eurasia. **Focus:** European studies. **Qualif.:** Applicants must be U.S. citizens who are currently enrolled in a Ph.D. program. **Criteria:** Selection will be based on the following criteria: overall strength of proposals, reference and proposed methodology; importance of topic towards foreign policy community; value of research to community; demonstrated serious preparatory work; well-argued need to conduct the research; language skills adequate for proposed research; feasibility of project and timeframe; demonstrated career commitment to the field; and few previous opportunities to conduct the research. Preference will be given to research projects on the countries of Central Asia and the Caucasus.

Funds Avail.: No specific amount. **Duration:** from two to nine months. **To Apply:** Applicants must complete an application form; must submit a research proposal; five-page curriculum vitae; transcript of records; Professional/ Academic Reference and one Language Proficiency Form (to be sent directly by referee). Other information on the research proposal can be verified at the website. **Deadline:** November 16. **Contact:** iaro@irex.org.

5149 ■ IREX Individual Advanced Research Opportunities Program For Professionals *(Other/Fellowship)*

Purpose: To support in-depth, primary source research in policy-relevant subjects related to Southeast Europe and Eurasia. **Focus:** European studies. **Qualif.:** Applicants must be U.S. citizens who have one of the following degrees (MA, MS, MFA, MBA, MPA, MLIS, MPH, JD, or MD). They must not be enrolled as students during the grant period. **Criteria:** Selection will be based on the following criteria: overall strength of proposals, reference and proposed methodology; importance of topic towards foreign policy community; value of research to community; demonstrated serious preparatory work; well-argued need to conduct the research; language skills adequate for proposed research; feasibility of project and timeframe; demonstrated career commitment to the field; and few previous opportunities to conduct the research. Preference will be given to research projects on the countries of Central Asia and the Caucasus.

Funds Avail.: No specific amount. **Duration:** from two to nine months. **To Apply:** Applicants must complete an application form; must submit a research proposal; five-page curriculum vitae; transcript of records; Professional/ Academic Reference and one Language Proficiency Form (to be sent directly by referee). Other information on the research proposal can be verified at the website. **Deadline:** November 16. **Contact:** iaro@irex.org.

5150 ■ IREX Individual Advanced Research Opportunities Program for Postdoctoral Scholars
(Postdoctorate/Fellowship)

Purpose: To support in-depth, primary source research in policy-relevant subjects related to Southeast Europe and Eurasia. **Focus:** European studies. **Qualif.:** Applicants

Awards are arranged alphabetically below their administering organizations

must be U.S. citizens who are Ph.D. holders. **Criteria:** Selection will be based on the following criteria: overall strength of proposals, reference and proposed methodology; importance of topic towards foreign policy community; value of research to community; demonstrated serious preparatory work; well-argued need to conduct the research; language skills adequate for proposed research; feasibility of project and timeframe; demonstrated career commitment to the field; and few previous opportunities to conduct the research. Preference will be given to research projects on the countries of Central Asia and the Caucasus.

Funds Avail.: No specific amount. **Duration:** from two to nine months. **To Apply:** Applicants must complete an application form; must submit a research proposal; five-page curriculum vitae; transcript of records; Professional/Academic Reference and one Language Proficiency Form (to be sent directly by referee). Other information on the research proposal can be verified at the website. **Deadline:** November 16. **Contact:** iaro@irex.org.

5151 ■ The International Research Foundation for English Language Education (TIRF)

177 Webster St., No. 220
Monterey, CA 93940
Fax: (831)647-6650
E-mail: info@tirfonline.org
URL: www.tirfonline.org

5152 ■ Doctoral Dissertation Grants *(Doctorate/Grant)*

Purpose: To support students completing their doctoral research on topics related to the foundation's priorities. **Focus:** General studies/Field of study not specified. **Qualif.:** Applicants must be enrolled in a legitimate doctoral program; must be advanced to candidacy and have had a research plan approved by a faculty committee at their university; must have a research supervisor. **Criteria:** Selection will be based on the committee's criteria.

Funds Avail.: $5,000. **To Apply:** Applicants must write a proposal which is clearly related to TIRF's research priorities; must follow specific instructions located in the call for proposals. Applicants' research supervisor must submit an official letter of support attesting to the applicants' readiness to complete the doctoral dissertation. **Deadline:** April 22. **Remarks:** Established in 2002.

5153 ■ International Rett Syndrome Foundation (IRSF)

4600 Devitt Dr.
Cincinnati, OH 45246
Ph: (513)874-3020
Fax: (513)874-2520
Free: 800-818-7388
E-mail: admin@rettsyndrome.org
URL: www.rettsyndrome.org

5154 ■ Mentored Training Fellowships *(Advanced Professional, Postdoctorate/Fellowship)*

Purpose: To assist post-doctoral research scientists and clinical scientists establish careers in the fields relevant to Rett syndrome research. **Focus:** Neuroscience. **Qualif.:** Applicants must be post-doctoral research scientists or clinical scientists. **Criteria:** Selection will be based on the committee's criteria.

Funds Avail.: $100,000. **Duration:** Two years. **To Apply:** Applicants must visit the website to create an account and for the online submission process. Applicants must submit a maximum of two pages letter of intent or expression of interest through the IRSF's website describing the project in a succinct manner. The letter of intent should include objective and specific aims of the proposal, research design and methods, qualifications of the principal investigator, mentor, and other principal investigators involved in the project. Preliminary data must be included within the page limitations. Applicants must also submit a copy of their CV, available at the website, and that of their mentor.

5155 ■ International Safety Equipment Association (ISEA)

1901 N Moore St.
Arlington, VA 22209-1762
Ph: (703)525-1695
Fax: (703)528-2148
URL: safetyequipment.org

5156 ■ Lincoln C. Bailey Memorial Scholarship Fund *(Undergraduate/Scholarship)*

Purpose: To provide financial assistance to the promising dependant of its members in the final year in college or universities. **Focus:** General studies/Field of study not specified. **Qualif.:** Applicants must be in the first year or second year in college; a dependant of ISEA members. **Criteria:** Scholarship winner is selected by an independent panel, based on academic achievement, extracurricular activity and financial need.

Funds Avail.: No specific amount. **Duration:** Annual. **To Apply:** Applicants must submit transcript and financial information.

5157 ■ International Sanitary Supply Association (ISSA)

7373 N Lincoln Ave.
Lincolnwood, IL 60712-1799
Ph: (847)982-0800
Fax: (847)982-1012
Free: 800-225-4772
E-mail: info@issa.com
URL: www.issa.com

5158 ■ International Sanitary Supply Association Foundation Scholarships *(Undergraduate/Scholarship)*

Purpose: To provide scholarship assistance to qualified Canadian students who will be attending college or university in Canada. **Focus:** General studies/Field of study not specified. **Qualif.:** Applicants must be entering or continuing studies at a fully accredited four-year college or university; **Criteria:** Applicants will be judged on the basis of merit, individual accomplishments, and evidence of leadership. Preference will be given to those with financial need and other special circumstances.

Funds Avail.: No specific amount. **To Apply:** Applicants must provide a resume with personal information; an essay; academic activity and leadership record; official high school or college/university transcript; must also submit official SAT, ACT, GRE, GMAT or LSAT test scores; two evaluations from current or past professors or teaching assistants. **Deadline:** March 1.

Awards are arranged alphabetically below their administering organizations

5159 ■ International Society of Air Safety Investigators (ISASI)

107 E Holly Ave., Ste. No. 11
Sterling, VA 20164
Ph: (703)430-9668
Fax: (703)430-4970
E-mail: isasi@erols.com
URL: www.isasi.org

5160 ■ The ISASI Rudolf Kapustin Memorial Scholarships *(Undergraduate/Scholarship)*

Purpose: To encourage and assist college-level students interested in the field of aviation safety and aircraft occurrence investigation. **Focus:** Aviation. **Qualif.:** Applicant must be a member of ISASI and enrolled as a full-time student in a recognized education program, which includes courses in aircraft engineering and/or operations, aviation psychology, aviation safety or aircraft occurrence investigation, etc., with major or minor subjects that focus on aviation safety/investigation. **Criteria:** Scholarship Fund Committee will review submitted materials.

Funds Avail.: $2000. **To Apply:** Applicants must submit an application form and a 1000 word paper in English addressing "the challenges for air safety investigators". Paper must be countersigned by applicant's tutor/academic supervisor as authentic, original work. **Deadline:** April 15.

5161 ■ International Society for Disease Surveillance (ISDS)

26 Lincoln St., Ste. 3
Brighton, MA 02135
Ph: (617)779-0880
E-mail: syndromic@syndromic.org
URL: www.syndromic.org

5162 ■ ISDS Graduate Student Scholarships *(Doctorate, Graduate/Scholarship)*

Purpose: To provide ISDS members the opportunity to disseminate innovative research and practice and to create network with the broader surveillance community. **Focus:** General studies/Field of study not specified. **Qualif.:** Applicants must be ISDS members; must be Master's or PhD candidates in surveillance-related field; must be in need of funding to attend the conference. **Criteria:** Applicants will be judged based on abstract acceptance by review committee, innovation of work described in the abstract and personal statement.

Funds Avail.: No specific amount. **To Apply:** Applicants must submit the contact information with name, address, institutional affiliation and position title; proof of student status (scanned copy of unofficial transcript and student ID); estimated cost of attendance, including travel, accommodations and conference registration; short statement on why attending the ISDS 10th Annual Conference; abstract for the ISDS 10th Annual Conference accepted by the 2011 Scientific Program Committee. **Deadline:** August 19.

5163 ■ International Society of Explosives Engineers (ISEE)

30325 Bainbridge Rd.
Cleveland, OH 44139
Ph: (440)349-4400
Fax: (440)349-3788

E-mail: isee@isee.org
URL: www.isee.org

5164 ■ SEE Education Foundation Scholarships *(Undergraduate, Graduate, Doctorate/Scholarship)*

Purpose: To support students pursuing a technical undergraduate, graduate or doctorate degree in the fields of education related to the commercial explosives industry. **Focus:** Engineering, Chemical; Engineering, Nuclear. **Qualif.:** Applicants must be pursuing technical, undergraduate, graduate or doctorate degrees in fields of education related to the commercial explosives industry; and able to demonstrate financial need. **Criteria:** Students will be assessed on their financial need, academic and professional achievements and goals related to the industry.

Funds Avail.: Close to $60,000. **Duration:** Annual. **Number Awarded:** Varies. **To Apply:** Applicants must submit a completed scholarship application together with a documentation of income; two letters of recommendation; college transcript(s); and a personal challenge and goal statement. Applicants must provide contact information for the university financial aid/scholarship representative. First year college students must enclose a letter of acceptance from the university for the upcoming academic year. **Deadline:** June 1. **Remarks:** The scholarships are offered in various memorial funds. **Contact:** International Society of Explosives Engineers, at the above address.

5165 ■ International Society for Human Ethology (ISHE)

c/o Dori LeCroy, Treasurer
1824 Kanuga Rd.
Hendersonville, NC 28739-6732
URL: www.ishe.org

5166 ■ Owen F. Aldis Scholarship Fund *(Doctorate/Scholarship)*

Purpose: To nurture excellence in human ethology by supporting students who are undertaking empirical research in human behavior, drawing on the repertoire of methods developed in biology and the human behavioral sciences. **Focus:** Behavioral sciences. **Qualif.:** Applicants must be graduate (pre-doctoral) students, in any academic discipline related to human ethology, who are in good standing as certified by their academic advisor or director at a recognized educational or scientific institution. **Criteria:** Selection shall be based on the premises that the applicants' respective research proposals on human behavior are able to meet the "scientific quality" and "ethological relevance".

Funds Avail.: Up to $8,000. **Duration:** Annual. **To Apply:** Applications must be submitted in English. Applications should consist of the title of the study, the applicant's name and institutional affiliation; a letter from the applicant's institution giving permission for the applicant to conduct the proposed research at that institution; short CV's of the applicant and his/her mentor (with publications); an outline of the planned study, of maximum length 12 double-spaced pages, with the following sections: aims, concentrating on innovative aspects; theoretical background; methodological issues and procedure; schedule. Applications should be sent to Maryanne Fisher, ISHE Secretary. **Deadline:** November 1.

5167 ■ International Society for Humor Studies (ISHS)

Holy Names University
3500 Mountain Blvd.
Oakland, CA 94619

Awards are arranged alphabetically below their administering organizations

Ph: (510)436-1532
E-mail: ishs@hnu.edu
URL: www.hnu.edu/ishs

5168 ■ International Society for Humor Studies Graduate Student Awards (GSA) *(Graduate/Award, Scholarship)*

Purpose: To recognize outstanding scholars and promising graduate students conducting research in humor studies with either a Scholarly Contribution or a Graduate Student Award. **Focus:** Humanities. **Qualif.:** Applicants must be graduate students working toward master's or doctorate degrees and doing noteworthy research within humor studies and/or all ISHS graduate student members planning to attend the Society's annual conference. **Criteria:** Candidates will be evaluated by ISHS Awards Committee based on merit.

Funds Avail.: No specific amount. **To Apply:** Applicants must submit a letter of intent to compete for a GSA, a description of their research program within humor studies, a presentation proposal, and all required registration materials and fees. **Remarks:** Established in 2006.

5169 ■ International Society for Humor Studies Scholarly Contribution Awards (SCA) *(Other/Award)*

Purpose: To recognize outstanding scholars and promising graduate students conducting research in humor studies with either a Scholarly Contribution or a Graduate Student Award. **Focus:** Humanities. **Qualif.:** Applicants must be researchers doing important work but lacking international recognition due to limited opportunities to travel or to publish outside of their region of the world and scholars involved in humor research through high quality publications, conference presentations, and other scholarly activities. **Criteria:** Candidates will be evaluated by the ISHS Awards Committee.

Funds Avail.: No specific amount. **To Apply:** Applicants must submit complete application form. **Remarks:** Established in 2006.

5170 ■ International Society for Infectious Diseases (ISID)

9 Babcock St., 3rd Fl.
Brookline, MA 02446
Ph: (617)277-0551
Fax: (617)278-9113
E-mail: info@isid.org
URL: www.isid.org

5171 ■ ISID Small Grant *(Postdoctorate, Professional development/Grant)*

Purpose: To support and foster the professional development of individuals in the field of human infectious diseases research. **Focus:** Infectious diseases. **Qualif.:** Applicants must be nationals or residents of resource-limited countries, in the early stages of their research career, and have not previously received major research funding or who have not had an opportunity to work or study outside their region. **Criteria:** Selection will be based on the committee's criteria.

Funds Avail.: $6,000 each. **Duration:** Annual. **Number Awarded:** Up to 5. **To Apply:** Interested applicants must submit the following documents: completed application form; research plan (up to 5 pages); current curriculum vitae; letter of recommendation from the applicants' home/

sponsoring institution. Applicants who wish to use their ISID Grant to do training and research in a setting outside of their own region should include curriculum vitae of the research sponsor and letter of agreement from the sponsor. **Deadline:** April 1.

5172 ■ International Society of Offshore and Polar Engineers (ISOPE)

495 N Whisman Rd., Ste. 300
Mountain View, CA 94043-5711
Ph: (650)254-1871
Fax: (650)254-2038
E-mail: info@isope.org
URL: www.isope.org

5173 ■ ISOPE Offshore Mechanics Scholarships for Outstanding Students *(Graduate/Scholarship)*

Purpose: To provide students the opportunity to engage in research in the field of Offshore Mechanics. **Focus:** Mechanics and repairs. **Qualif.:** Applicants must be graduate students; or admitted to a graduate program (verified by the Department Chairman or the supervising professor); must have demonstrated scholastic achievement; must be individuals of integrity, good character and strict morals. **Criteria:** Preference is given to applicants whose papers are accepted at the council-supported technical meetings.

Funds Avail.: No specific amount. **To Apply:** Applicants must fill up the application form available at the website and submit a hard copy of the application form at the ISOPE Office together with official college academic transcripts; a statement of personal professional objectives; and a recommendation letter from the supervising professor.

5174 ■ International Society for Reef Studies (ISRS)

c/o Schneider Group Meeting and Marketing Services
5400 Bosque Blvd., Ste. 680
Waco, TX 76710-4446
Ph: (254)776-3550
E-mail: isrs@sgmeet.com
URL: www.coralreefs.org

5175 ■ ISRS Graduate Fellowships *(Doctorate, Graduate/Fellowship)*

Purpose: To help PhD students develop skills and address problems related to coral reef ecosystem research and management. **Focus:** Biology, Marine. **Qualif.:** Applicants must be students or full members of the ISRS; must be already admitted to a PhD program at an accredited university. **Criteria:** Applicants will be selected based on submitted documents.

Funds Avail.: Up to $2,500. **Duration:** Annual. **Number Awarded:** 2. **To Apply:** Applicants must submit a five-page proposal as a PDF document using 12-point font which includes: applicants' details, overview, methods, relevance and implications, detailed budget, literature cited, curriculum vitae (maximum of two pages), letter of support, contributions to ISRS. The completed proposal must be combined into a single document and emailed as an attachment in PDF format. Applicants must check the format available on the website. **Deadline:** January 9. **Contact:** Rupert Ormond, at the above address, or Email: rupert.ormond.mci@gmail.com.

Awards are arranged alphabetically below their administering organizations

5176 ■ International Society for Therapeutic Ultrasound (ISTU)

14750 Sweitzer Ln., Ste. 100
Laurel, MD 20707-5906
Ph: (301)498-4100
Fax: (301)498-4450
E-mail: admin@istu.org
URL: www.istu.org

5177 ■ William and Francis Fry Honorary Fellowships for Contributions to Therapeutic Ultrasound *(Professional development/Fellowship)*

Purpose: To award individuals who have made outstanding contributions to therapeutic ultrasound. **Focus:** Medicine. **Qualif.:** Applicants must have contributions to therapeutic ultrasound. **Criteria:** Recipients will be selected based on the impact of their contributions.

Funds Avail.: No specific amount. **Duration:** Annual; One year. **To Apply:** Applicants must visit the website for further information.

5178 ■ ISTU Student Prize *(Undergraduate/Prize)*

Purpose: To recognize students who exhibit strong potential to impact the world of therapeutic ultrasound. **Focus:** Medicine. **Qualif.:** Applicants must be students who have potential in the field of therapeutic ultrasound. **Criteria:** Applicants will be evaluated based on committee's criteria.

Funds Avail.: No specific amount. **Duration:** Annual. **To Apply:** Applicants must visit the website for further information.

5179 ■ Nadine Barrie Smith Student Awards *(Undergraduate/Award)*

Purpose: To recognize student achievements in the field of therapeutic ultrasound. **Focus:** Medicine. **Qualif.:** Applicants must be interested in the field of therapeutic ultrasound. **Criteria:** Award will be given to applicants who best meet the judges' criteria.

Funds Avail.: No specific amount. **Duration:** Annual; One year. **To Apply:** Applicants must visit the website for procedures and required materials.

5180 ■ International Society of Travel and Tourism Educators (ISTTE)

23220 Edgewater St.
Saint Clair Shores, MI 48082
Ph: (586)294-0208
Fax: (586)294-0208
URL: www.istte.org

5181 ■ ISTTE Scholarships *(Graduate, Undergraduate/Scholarship)*

Purpose: To assist students affiliated with ISTTE member schools in their education. **Focus:** Travel and tourism. **Qualif.:** Applicants must be students affiliated with ISTTE member schools during the current academic year. **Criteria:** Selection will be based on the submitted applications, particularly essays. ISTTE member faculty will judge the essays using the following five criteria: comprehension; organization; creativity; conclusions; and writing.

Funds Avail.: $500 each. **Number Awarded:** 4. **To Apply:** Applicants must submit a word-processed, double-spaced, 3-5 page original essay on a topic relevant to this year's conference theme. ISTTE's 2015 Conference theme is "Contemporary Issues in Tourism and Hospitality Education" and the essay should reflect this theme or other sustainable tourism planning and development niches. Applications should be submitted on the deadline. **Deadline:** May 30. **Remarks:** The committee will award the scholarships in the following categories: Graduate School; Four-Year College/University; Two-Year College/University; and High School or Non-degree Proprietary School (Certificate). **Contact:** Questions should be forwarded to: Wayne Smith Ph.D., College of Charleston HTM Dept./School of Business, 5 Liberty St., Charleston, SC 29424; Phone: 842-953-6663; Email: smithww@cofc.edu.

5182 ■ International Technology and Engineering Educators Association (ITEEA)

1914 Association Dr., Ste. 201
Reston, VA 20191-1539
Ph: (703)860-2100
Fax: (703)860-0353
E-mail: iteea@iteea.org
URL: www.iteea.org

5183 ■ ITEEA Greer/FTE Grants *(Other/Grant)*

Purpose: To recognize and encourage individual achievement and ability in any aspect of technology and engineering. **Focus:** Engineering; Teaching; Technology. **Qualif.:** Recipients must be ITEEA members and register for the ITEEA annual conference; must be a technology and engineering education teachers or supervisors for secondary education grades 6-12; must not have attended more than three previous ITEEA conferences. **Criteria:** Recipients are selected based on application materials.

Funds Avail.: $1,000. **To Apply:** Applicants must submit the following required materials: (1) applicant's name, address, phone, fax, email, school name, grade level, subject(s) taught, previous ITEEA/ITEA conferences attended, and other pertinent data; (2) brief history of the applicant's professional participation activities, includes curriculum projects, professional association memberships, position held, grants/scholarships received, and awards; (3) explanation of why the applicant is seeking the grant; (4) knowledge/experience the applicant expect to gain from attending the ITEEA conference. **Deadline:** December 1. **Contact:** GREER/FTEE GRANT, Foundation for Technology and Engineering Educators; Email: iteea@iteea.org.

5184 ■ Litherland/FTEE Scholarships *(Undergraduate/Scholarship)*

Purpose: To promote the study of technology and engineering education teacher preparation. **Focus:** Technology. **Qualif.:** Applicant must be a member of ITEA; Applicant must not be a senior by application deadline; Applicant must be a current, full-time undergraduate majoring in technology education teacher preparation. **Criteria:** The award is given based upon interest in acting, academic ability, need and faculty recommendation.

Funds Avail.: $1,000. **Duration:** Annual. **To Apply:** Applicants must submit the following requirements: Letter of application that includes statement about personal interest in teaching technology and applicant's address with day and night telephone numbers; Applicant's resume; A photocopy of applicant's college transcript. A grade point average of 2.5 or more is required; Three faculty recommendations. **Deadline:** December 1.

Awards are arranged alphabetically below their administering organizations

5185 ■ Maley/FTE Scholarships (Graduate/Scholarship)

Purpose: To enhance education and careers in technology and engineering education. **Focus:** Engineering; Teaching; Technology. **Qualif.:** Applicant must be a member of the ITEEA; must be a technology and engineering teacher at any grade level who is beginning and continuing graduate study. **Criteria:** ITEEA scholarship committee will review all the application and materials based on the following criteria: (1) evidence of teaching success; (2) plans for action research; (3) recommendation; (4) plans for professional development; (5) the applicant's need.

Funds Avail.: $1,000. **Duration:** Annual. **To Apply:** Applicant must submit a letter of application with clear explanation of: (a) plans for graduate study, (b) plans for action research, (c) the applicant's need, and (d) identification details - school name, grade level, address, telephone, and home address; must provide resume not exceeding four pages that describes current position, professional activities, and achievements; must provide a college transcript, and documentation of acceptance into graduate school; must have three recommendation letters from among the following: undergraduate faculty, graduate faculty and school administration. **Deadline:** December 1. **Contact:** MALEY/FTEE SCHOLARSHIP, Foundation for Technology and Engineering Educators; Email: iteea@iteea.org.

5186 ■ Maley/FTEE Teacher Scholarships (Graduate/Scholarship)

Purpose: To promote the study of technology and engineering education teacher preparation. **Focus:** Technology. **Qualif.:** Applicant must be a member of ITEA; must not be a technology teacher at any grade level who is beginning or continuing graduate study. **Criteria:** Scholarship is given based on the committee's criteria.

Funds Avail.: $1,000. **Duration:** Annual. **To Apply:** Applicant must submit the following requirements: letter of application with clear explanation of: (a) plans for graduate study, (b) plans for action research, (c) the applicant's need, and (d) identification details -school name, grade level, address, telephone, and home address; resume not exceeding four pages that describes current position, professional activities, and achievements; official college transcript(s); Documentation of acceptance into graduate school; and three recommendation letters. **Deadline:** December 1.

5187 ■ International Textile and Apparel Association (ITAA)

PO Box 70687
Knoxville, TN 37938-0687
Ph: (865)992-1535
E-mail: info@itaaonline.org
URL: www.itaaonline.org

5188 ■ ITAA Faculty Awards, Honors, Grants and Fellowships (Undergraduate, Graduate, Advanced Professional, Professional development/Award, Fellowship, Grant, Monetary, Recognition, Scholarship)

Purpose: To recognize individuals for their outstanding contributions to the Association. **Focus:** Design; Textile science. **Qualif.:** Applicants must be faculty members. **Criteria:** Selection will be based on the committee's criteria.

Funds Avail.: $30,000. **Duration:** Annual. **To Apply:** Applicants should visit the website for requirements pertaining to specific programs (i.e. awards, honors, grants and fellowships). **Deadline:** February 1.

5189 ■ International Thomas Merton Society (ITMS)

2001 Newburg Rd.
Louisville, KY 40205
Ph: (502)272-8177
Fax: (502)272-8452
URL: merton.org

5190 ■ Daggy Youth/Student Scholarships (Undergraduate, Professional development/Scholarship)

Purpose: To enable young people to participate in an International Thomas Merton Society Conference. **Qualif.:** Applicants must be young individuals (ages 14-29) who are interested in learning about Thomas Merton. **Criteria:** Scholarships will be awarded to qualified candidates based on their personal statement.

Funds Avail.: No specific amount. **Duration:** Biennial. **To Apply:** Applicants must submit a statement explaining why they are interested in learning more about Thomas Merton and how they think they would benefit from attending the ITMS Conference; must have the recommendation from a youth minister, campus minister, pastor, teacher, or other qualified adult. **Deadline:** March 15. **Remarks:** The scholarships were established to honor the late Robert E. Daggy, founding member and second President of the ITMS. **Contact:** Jamie Fazio, at: jfazio1@naz.edu.

5191 ■ William H. Shannon Fellowships (Graduate, Undergraduate/Fellowship)

Purpose: To enable qualified researchers to visit the Thomas Merton Center archives. **Focus:** General studies/Field of study not specified. **Qualif.:** Applicants must be researchers, students or young scholars without academic affiliation; must be members of the ITMS who are engaged in research for thesis and dissertations. **Criteria:** Awards will be based on (1) the quality of the proposal submitted and on (2) the need for consulting archival materials at the site proposed.

Funds Avail.: $750. **Duration:** Annual. **Number Awarded:** 5. **To Apply:** Applicants must submit a detailed proposal (500-750 words) explaining the subject and goals of the applicant's research and the rationale for consulting primary sources at the Merton collection selected by the applicant; must have a letter of recommendation from a scholar familiar with the applicant's qualifications and research interest; and a proposed expense budget. Successful applicants are required to submit an expense account and a report summarizing the results of their research. **Deadline:** July 15. **Remarks:** Awards are named in honor of William H. Shannon, founding President of the International Thomas Merton Society. **Contact:** Return application to: Dr. Paul M. Pearson at the above address.; E-mail: merton@bellarmine.edu.

5192 ■ International Trademark Association (INTA)

655 3rd Ave., 10th Fl.
New York, NY 10017-5617
Ph: (212)642-1700
Fax: (212)768-7796
E-mail: info@inta.org

Awards are arranged alphabetically below their administering organizations

URL: www.inta.org

5193 ■ International Trademark Association-Ladas Memorial Awards *(Other, Undergraduate/Award)*

Purpose: To provide incentives to students and professionals to further develop their interest in the field of trademark law. **Focus:** Law. **Qualif.:** Awards are open to students, practitioners and academics interested in trademarks and trademark law. **Criteria:** Recipients will be selected based on nature, breadth and timeliness of the subject(s) addressed; originality of the subject and thought; extent of the research and scholarship; and quality of writing.

Funds Avail.: $2,500 each. **Duration:** Annual. **To Apply:** Applicants must submit an original unpublished manuscript or published articles that are submitted or otherwise come to the attention of INTA no longer than one year prior to the deadline. The subject of the paper must affect or be related to trademarks. Applicants must include a cover page. Foreign students must submit proof of university enrollment. **Deadline:** February 6.

5194 ■ International Transplant Nurses Society (ITNS)

8735 W Higgins Rd., Ste. 300
Chicago, IL 60631
Ph: (847)375-6340
Fax: (847)375-6341
E-mail: info@itns.org
URL: www.itns.org

5195 ■ ITNS Research Grants *(Other/Grant)*

Purpose: To encourage qualified transplant health care providers to contribute to the advancement of transplantation through research by providing financial aid. **Focus:** Medical research. **Qualif.:** Investigator must be member of ITNS; have submitted a complete research application package; are ready to begin the research project immediately upon obtaining funding; and have signed an ITNS research agreement. **Criteria:** Preference is given to studies that address scholarly work such as clinical outcomes and quality improvement; program evaluation projects are encouraged.

Funds Avail.: $2,500. **Duration:** One year. **To Apply:** Applicants must send application form; four copies of the proposal contains title page, abstract, proposal narrative maximum of 5 singled-spaced pages, appendices, budget and biographical sketch maximum of two pages. Scholarship information and instructions are available in the website. **Deadline:** July 1. **Contact:** Application form should be e-mailed to Cynthia Russell at russellc@health.missouri.edu.

5196 ■ International Union of Bricklayers and Allied Craftworkers (BAC)

620 F St. NW
Washington, DC 20004
Ph: (202)783-3788
Free: 888-880-8222
E-mail: askbac@bacweb.org
URL: www.bacweb.org

5197 ■ Union Plus Scholarship Program *(Undergraduate/Scholarship)*

Purpose: To assist students pursuing their post-secondary education. **Focus:** General studies/Field of study not speci-fied. **Qualif.:** Applicant must be a current or retired members of unions participating in any Union Plus program, their spouses and their dependent children (including foster children, step children, and any other child for whom the individual member provides greater than 50% of his or her support) can apply for a Union Plus Scholarship; must be accepted into an accredited college or university, community college or recognized technical or trade school. **Criteria:** Applicants for scholarships are evaluated according to academic ability, social awareness, financial need and appreciation of labor. Scholarship applications are judged by a committee of impartial post secondary educators.

Funds Avail.: $500 - $4,000. **Duration:** Annual. **To Apply:** Application forms are available at the website. **Deadline:** January 31.

5198 ■ U.S. Bates Scholarship Program *(Undergraduate/Scholarship)*

Purpose: To assist the children of BAC members in pursuing a college education. **Focus:** General studies/Field of study not specified. **Qualif.:** Applicant must be a son or daughter of U.S BAC members (in good standing) of U.S. BAC locals who will be juniors in high school; must take or plan to take the standardized PSAT exam in the fall of their junior year. **Criteria:** Selection of recipients is administered through the National Merit Scholarship Corporation.

Funds Avail.: $2,500. **Duration:** Annual; One year. **Number Awarded:** 3. **To Apply:** Applicant must apply during their junior year in high school. **Deadline:** February 28. **Contact:** BAC's Educational Department at askbac@bacweb.org or call 888880-8222 ext. 3111.

5199 ■ International Union of Operating Engineers - Local 564

2120 N Brazosport Blvd. N
Richwood, TX 77531-2306
Ph: (979)480-0003
Fax: (979)480-0509
Free: 800-IUO-E564
URL: local564.com

5200 ■ Local 564 Scholarship Award *(High School/Scholarship)*

Purpose: To provide support to members' dependent children that are graduating High School Seniors. **Focus:** General studies/Field of study not specified. **Qualif.:** Applicants must be dependent children whose parent or guardian is a member of the union with good standing. **Criteria:** Selection criteria will be determined by the committee.

Funds Avail.: $500. **Duration:** Annual. **Number Awarded:** 2. **To Apply:** Interested applicants may contact the union for further information.

5201 ■ International Women's Fishing Association (IWFA)

PO Box 31507
Palm Beach Gardens, FL 33420-1507
E-mail: webmaster@iwfa.org
URL: www.iwfa.org

5202 ■ International Women's Fishing Association Scholarship Trust *(Graduate/Scholarship)*

Purpose: To support students in attaining graduate degrees in marine science. **Focus:** Biology, Marine. **Qua-

Awards are arranged alphabetically below their administering organizations

lif.: Applicant must be matriculated at a recognized University; pursuing a study leading to a graduate degree in marine sciences. **Criteria:** Selection is based on character, academic accomplishments, ability and the need for the award.

Funds Avail.: $2,000. **To Apply:** Applicant must submit a completed application form; transcript of college records; recent photo with reverse sign; letter including: description of research in Marine Science, explanation of choosing graduate institution, career goals and financial need; and letters of recommendation from instructor in major field, advisor or other school officials; and completed summary sheet. **Deadline:** March 1. **Remarks:** Established in 1965. **Contact:** Diane Locke.

5203 ■ International Women's Media Foundation (IWMF)
1625 K St. NW, Ste. 1275
Washington, DC 20006
URL: www.iwmf.org

5204 ■ Elizabeth Neuffer Fellowships (Other/Fellowship)
Purpose: To provide a woman journalist with a transformative experience that will impact her career by offering her the opportunity to conduct research at leading academic institutions and build journalistic skills. **Focus:** Journalism. **Qualif.:** Applicants must be female journalists whose work focuses on human rights and social justice, and must have a minimum of three years of experience in journalism. **Criteria:** Selection is based on the applicant's completed applications, the caliber and promise of the applicant's work on human rights and social justice, and on personal statements explaining how the fellowship would be a transformative experience.

Funds Avail.: No specific amount. **Duration:** Annual. **Number Awarded:** 1. **To Apply:** Applicants must complete the application form online. **Deadline:** April 11.

5205 ■ Internet Society (ISOC)
1775 Wiehle Ave., Ste. 201
Reston, VA 20190-5158
Ph: (703)439-2120
Fax: (703)326-9881
E-mail: isoc@isoc.org
URL: www.internetsociety.org

5206 ■ Internet Society Fellowships to the IETF (Doctorate, Master's/Fellowship)
Purpose: To increase the diversity of inputs to, and global awareness of the IETF's vital work. **Focus:** Computer and information sciences. **Qualif.:** Applicants must be Masters or PhD students; must be employed in a technical or technical management capacity with a data network provider (including university networks), a technology vendor, local technical association, or other similar organization; or must hold a university level in computer science, information technology, or similar degree; and must demonstrate similar and relevant work experience. **Criteria:** Recipients will be selected based on submitted applications.

Funds Avail.: No specific amount. **To Apply:** Applicants must submit a filled-out application form. **Deadline:** July 15.

5207 ■ Iowa Association for Justice (IAJ)
505 5th Ave., Ste. 630
Des Moines, IA 50309

Ph: (515)280-7366
Fax: (515)280-3745
Free: 800-373-4852
E-mail: info@iowajustice.org
URL: www.iowajustice.org

5208 ■ Byard Braley Scholarship (Undergraduate/Scholarship)
Purpose: To assist injured workers or their family members in the pursuit of further education. **Focus:** General studies/Field of study not specified. **Qualif.:** Applicants must be injured Iowa workers or their family members who aspire to further their education. **Criteria:** Selection will be based on the committee's criteria.

Funds Avail.: $500. **Duration:** Semiannual. **To Apply:** Interested applicants may contact IAJ workers' compensation section for the application process and other information. **Deadline:** July 15; November 15.

5209 ■ Iowa Choral Directors Association (ICDA)
c/o Jason Rausch
317 Pershing Ave.
Decorah, IA 52101
Ph: (319)329-4089
E-mail: president@iowachoral.org
URL: www.iowachoral.org

5210 ■ ICDA Graduate Scholarships (Graduate/Scholarship)
Purpose: To provide financial assistance to ICDA members in their pursuit of graduate work. **Focus:** General studies/Field of study not specified. **Qualif.:** Applicants must be active or life members of ACDA/ICDA; must be studying towards graduate degree; must be full-time graduate students or completing a minimum of four-weeks summer term. **Criteria:** Selection will be based on evaluation of submitted documents and specific criteria.

Funds Avail.: Up to $750. **Duration:** Annual. **To Apply:** Applicants must submit a completed application form; a letter stating educational plans and why applicants deserve the award; must submit the tuition costs, validated by the institution. **Deadline:** May 1. **Remarks:** Established in 1987. **Contact:** Joleen Nelson Woods, ICDA Executive Secretary/Treasurer, at the above address.

5211 ■ ICDA Research Grants (Graduate/Grant)
Purpose: To provide financial assistance to ICDA members in their pursuit of graduate work. **Focus:** General studies/Field of study not specified. **Qualif.:** Applicants must be active or life members of ACDA/ICDA; must pursue a project involving an in-depth study of a particular aspect of the choral art. **Criteria:** Selection will be based on evaluation of submitted documents and specific criteria.

Funds Avail.: $500. **Duration:** Annual. **To Apply:** Applicants must submit a completed application form; breakdown of projected costs; must include a personal statement of the candidates' worthiness of the award. Monograph required within one calendar year of receiving the grant. **Deadline:** May 1. **Remarks:** Established in 1987. **Contact:** Joleen Nelson Woods, ICDA Executive Secretary/Treasurer, at the above address.

5212 ■ Iowa Court Reporters Association (ICRA)
2944 Miami St.
Osceola, IA 50213-8317

Awards are arranged alphabetically below their administering organizations

Ph: (515)966-7881
E-mail: info@iacra.org
URL: www.iacra.org

5213 ■ Mary L. Brown High School Student Scholarships *(Undergraduate/Scholarship)*

Purpose: To promote and advance the interest of individuals engaged in the profession of shorthand reporting throughout the state of Iowa; to develop greater awareness and appreciation for the profession through public education and to promote the shorthand reporting industry. **Focus:** Broadcasting. **Qualif.:** Applicants must be enrolled as a Realtime Reporting major in either Judicial or Captioning/ CART service; must attend AIB College of Business; and must be graduates of an Iowa high school. **Criteria:** Recipients are selected based on grades, community and school activities.

Funds Avail.: $1,000. **To Apply:** Applicants must submit a completed application form along with two letters of recommendation and a 250-word essay. **Deadline:** March 1.

5214 ■ Iowa Library Association (ILA)
6919 Vista Dr.
Des Moines, IA 50309
Ph: (515)273-5322
Free: 800-452-5507
URL: www.iowalibraryassociation.org

5215 ■ Iowa Library Association Foundation Scholarships *(Graduate/Scholarship)*

Purpose: To assist outstanding students who are pursuing a graduate degree in school library studies at the University of Northern Iowa. **Focus:** Information science and technology; Library and archival sciences. **Qualif.:** Applicants must have been fully admitted into the graduate program in school library studies at the University of Northern Iowa and enrolled continuously for three semesters of study. Applicants must have at least a 3.25 grade point average (on a 4.0 scale) for their undergraduate program of study or previous graduate studies of at least 8 credit hours. **Criteria:** Recipients will be chosen based on demonstrated academic excellence, potential to become a successful librarian, evidence of the ability to work well with others, and demonstrated communication skills. Selection shall be made solely on the basis of stated criteria without regard to sex, creed, race, national origin.

Funds Avail.: $1,500. **To Apply:** Applicants must accomplish proper completion and filing of the application form (available online) and submit along with three letters of recommendation from persons working in the library science/information science field. **Deadline:** September 11. **Contact:** President Mike Wright; Phone: 515-282-8192; or 800-452-5507; E-mail: mwright@dbqco.org.

5216 ■ Jack E. Tillson Scholarships *(Graduate/Scholarship)*

Purpose: To assist outstanding students who are pursuing a graduate degree in Library Science or Information Science at the University of Iowa. **Focus:** Information science and technology; Library and archival sciences. **Qualif.:** Applicants must have been admitted as regular students in the graduate program in library science/information science and be enrolled at least half-time in that program at the University of Iowa. Applicants must have at least a 3.25 grade point average (on a scale of 4.0) for their undergradu-

ate program of study or previous graduate work of at least 8 credit hours. **Criteria:** Applicants will be evaluated based on academic excellence, potential to become a successful librarian, ability to work well with others, and demonstrated communication skills. Selection shall be made solely on the basis of stated criteria without regard to sex, creed, race, national origin.

Funds Avail.: $1,500. **Duration:** Annual. **To Apply:** Applicants must accomplish proper completion and filing of the application form (available online) and submit along with three letters of recommendation from persons working in the library science/information science field. **Deadline:** September 11. **Contact:** President Mike Wright; Phone: 515-282-8192; or 800-452-5507; E-mail: mwright@dbqco.org.

5217 ■ Iowa Newspaper Association (INA)
319 E 5th St.
Des Moines, IA 50309-1927
Ph: (515)244-2145
Fax: (515)244-4855
E-mail: ina@inanews.com
URL: www.inanews.com

5218 ■ INF Scholarships *(Undergraduate/Scholarship)*

Purpose: To champion the quality and future of Iowa's newspaper enterprises and the communities they serve. **Focus:** Journalism. **Qualif.:** Applicants must be Iowa college students preparing for a career in the newspaper industry. High school seniors and students currently enrolled at a college or university are encouraged to apply. **Criteria:** Recipients are selected based on academic records, financial need, demonstrated talent and desire to work for an Iowa newspaper.

Funds Avail.: No specific amount. **To Apply:** Applicants must attach two letters of reference including one from a teacher or guidance counselor; must attach a one-page statement about self, educational and career goals; two samples of writing or other examples of works which attest to the applicant's abilities. Samples should be printed on or affixed to 8.5" x 11" sheets of white copy paper. **Deadline:** February 13.

5219 ■ Iowa Journalism Institute Scholarships *(Undergraduate/Scholarship)*

Purpose: To champion the quality and future of Iowa's newspaper enterprises and the communities they serve. **Focus:** Communications; Journalism. **Qualif.:** Applicants must be students studying journalism, communications, mass communications, photojournalism, graphic design, marketing or public relations at a college or university in Iowa, Illinois, or Wisconsin. **Criteria:** Recipients are selected based on academic records, financial need, demonstrated talent and desire to work for an Iowa newspaper.

Funds Avail.: No specific amount. **To Apply:** Applicants must attach two letters of reference including one from a teacher or guidance counselor; must attach a one-page statement about self, educational and career goals; two samples of writings or other examples of work which attest to the abilities of applicants in their intended career field. These samples should be printed on or affixed to 8.5" x 11" sheets of white copy paper. **Deadline:** February 13.

5220 ■ Carter Pitts Scholarships *(Undergraduate/Scholarship)*

Purpose: To champion the quality and future of Iowa's newspaper enterprises and the communities they serve.

Awards are arranged alphabetically below their administering organizations

Focus: Journalism. Qualif.: Applicants must be Iowa college students preparing for a career in the newspaper industry. High school seniors and students currently enrolled at a college or university are encouraged to apply. Criteria: Recipients are selected based on academic records, financial need, demonstrated talent and desire to work for an Iowa newspaper.

Funds Avail.: $500. To Apply: Applicants must attach two letters of reference including one from teacher or guidance counselor; must attach a one-page statement about self, educational and career goals; two samples of writings or other examples of work that attest to their abilities in the journalism field. Samples should be printed on or affixed to 8.5″ x 11″ sheets of white copy paper.

5221 ■ Iranian American Bar Association (IABA)
5185 MacArthur Blvd. NW, Ste. 624
Washington, DC 20016
E-mail: info@iaba.us
URL: www.iaba.us

5222 ■ Iranian American Bar Association Scholarships (Graduate/Scholarship)

Purpose: To support law students for their commitment to the advancement of the Iranian American community. Focus: Law. Qualif.: Applicants must be of Iranian heritage or committed to the advancement of the Iranian American community and IABA's mission; must be enrolled in an accredited law school in U.S.; must be in the position to accept the scholarship in the school year for which it is being awarded; and must be full-time students. Criteria: Applicants will be judged based on merit and financial need.

Funds Avail.: Varies. Duration: Annual. To Apply: Applicants must submit a duly completed National Scholarship Application Form; a detailed resume; a statement or essay written by the applicant (no more than one single-sided 1.5-spaced typewritten page); and official law school and college transcripts. Deadline: March 31. Contact: Email: scholarship@iaba.us.

5223 ■ Iranian Scholarship Foundation (ISF)
PO Box 320204
Los Gatos, CA 95032
Ph: (650)331-0508
E-mail: info@theisf.org
URL: www.iranianscholarships.com

5224 ■ ISF Excellence in Community Service Scholarships (Undergraduate/Scholarship)

Purpose: To provide financial assistance to qualified individuals who want to pursue their studies. Focus: General studies/Field of study not specified. Qualif.: Applicants must be enrolled or accepted at a four-year accredited American University; must possess and maintain a GPA of 3.5 or higher; must have a portfolio of community service; must have a minimum SAT score of 1850 or 27 for ACT. Criteria: Selection will be based on the submitted application and financial need.

Funds Avail.: No specific amount. Duration: Annual. To Apply: Applicant must provide two letters of recommendation, one from a teacher and one from an organization for which the student has performed community work; must write a 750-1000 words essay about his/ her dreams and aspirations. Deadline: May 31.

5225 ■ ISF Undergraduate Scholarships (Undergraduate/Scholarship)

Purpose: To provide financial support to qualified Iranian-American students in America. Focus: General studies/ Field of study not specified. Qualif.: Applicant must be enrolled or accepted at a four-year accredited American University; must be in need of financial assistance; must have participated in community service; must possess and maintain a GPA of 3.5 or higher; must have a minimum SAT score of 1850 or 27 for ACT. Criteria: Selection will be based on the submitted application and financial need.

Funds Avail.: No specific amount. Duration: Annual. To Apply: Applicant must provide two letters of recommendation, one from a teacher and one from an organization for which the student has performed community service; must write a 750-1000 words essay about his/her dreams and aspirations. Deadline: May 31.

5226 ■ Dr. Ali Jarrahi Merit Scholarships (Undergraduate/Scholarship)

Purpose: To provide financial assistance to top Iranian American students in the United States. Focus: General studies/Field of study not specified. Qualif.: Applicant must be accepted at one of the top American Universities; must possess a GPA of 4.0 or higher; must have a portfolio of community service; must have a minimum SAT score of 2300 or ACT 31. Criteria: Selection will be based on the submitted application and financial need.

Funds Avail.: $2,000. Duration: Annual. To Apply: Applicant must provide two letters of recommendation, one from a teacher and one from an organization for which the student has performed community work; must write a 750-1000 words essay about his/ her dreams and aspirations. Deadline: May 31.

5227 ■ ISA -The International Society of Automation (ISA)
67 Alexander Dr.
Research Triangle Park, NC 27709
Ph: (919)549-8411
Fax: (919)549-8288
E-mail: info@isa.org
URL: www.isa.org

5228 ■ ISA Aerospace Industries Division - William H. Atkinson Scholarships (Graduate, Undergraduate/ Scholarship)

Purpose: To support outstanding students pursuing careers in the area pertinent to the Division's activity. Focus: Automotive technology; Systems engineering. Qualif.: Applicant must be currently enrolled in a graduate or undergraduate program in an instrumentation, systems, or automation discipline (2-year program or 4-year baccalaureate program or its equivalent). Two-year program applicants must have completed at least one academic semester or its equivalent. Four-year degree program applicants must be in sophomore year or higher at the time of application. Applicants must be full-time students in an educational institution and have at least an overall GPA of 3.0 on a 4.0 scale. Criteria: Preference is given to students who are enrolled in a degree program in instrumentation, systems, and automation or other closely related field.

Funds Avail.: No specific amount. To Apply: Applicants must submit completed application (with Department Head Signature); two reference letters; original transcript (with

Awards are arranged alphabetically below their administering organizations

raised seal); list of awards and honors; extracurricular activities; employment history; and an essay. Mail the original and ten copies of the complete application with attachments unfolded in an envelope. **Deadline:** February 15. **Contact:** Dennis Coad at Dennis.l.coad@boeing.com.

5229 ■ Norman E. and Mary-Belle Huston Scholarships (Graduate, Undergraduate/Scholarship)

Purpose: To promote education in an instrumentation, systems, or automation discipline. **Focus:** Automotive technology; Systems engineering. **Qualif.:** Applicant must be currently enrolled in a graduate or undergraduate program in an instrumentation, systems, or automation discipline (2-year program or 4-year baccalaureate program or its equivalent). Two-year program applicants must have completed at least one academic semester or its equivalent. Four-year degree program applicants must be in sophomore year or higher at the time of application. Applicants must be full-time students in an educational institution who have at least an overall GPA of 2.5 on a 4.0 scale. **Criteria:** Preference is given to students who are enrolled in a degree program in instrumentation, systems, and automation or other closely related field.

Funds Avail.: No specific amount. **To Apply:** Applicants must submit a completed application (with Department Head Signature); two reference letters; original transcript (with raised seal); list of awards and honors; extracurricular activities; employment history; and an essay. Mail the original and ten copies of the complete application with attachments unfolded in an envelope. **Deadline:** February 15.

5230 ■ ISA Educational Foundation Scholarships (Graduate, Undergraduate/Scholarship)

Purpose: To support students tuition and related expenses and research activities and initiatives. **Focus:** Automotive technology; Systems engineering. **Qualif.:** Applicant must be a full-time college/university student in either a graduate, undergraduate, or 2-year degree program; must have an overall GPA of at least 3.0 on a 4.0 scale; and must be enrolled in a program in automation and control or a closely related field. **Criteria:** Preference is given to students who are enrolled in a degree program in instrumentation, systems, and automation or other closely related field.

Funds Avail.: $5,000. **Number Awarded:** 2. **To Apply:** Applicants must submit completed application (with Department Head Signature); two reference letters; original transcript (with raised seal); list of awards and honors and extracurricular activities; employment history; and an essay. Mail the original and ten copies of the complete application with attachments unfolded in an envelope. **Deadline:** February 15.

5231 ■ ISA Executive Board Scholarships (Graduate, Undergraduate/Scholarship)

Purpose: To support college or university students who demonstrate outstanding potential for long-range contribution to the fields of automation and control. **Focus:** Automotive technology; Systems engineering. **Qualif.:** Applicants must be currently enrolled in a graduate or undergraduate program in an instrumentation, systems, or automation discipline (2-year program or 4 year baccalaureate program or its equivalent). Two-year program applicants must have completed at least one academic semester. Four-year degree program applicants must be in sophomore year or higher at the time of application. Applicants must be full-time students in an educational institution who have at

least an overall GPA of 3.0 on a 4.0 scale. **Criteria:** Preference is given to applicants with demonstrated leadership capabilities.

Funds Avail.: Amount varies. **To Apply:** Applicants must submit a completed application (with Department Head Signature); two reference letters; original transcript (with raised seal); list of awards and honors; extracurricular activities; employment history; and an essay. Mail the original and ten copies of the complete application with attachments unfolded in an envelope. **Deadline:** February 15. **Contact:** Scholarship Committee; Phone: 919-549-8411.

5232 ■ ISA Section and District Scholarships - Birmingham (Graduate, Undergraduate/Scholarship)

Purpose: To support college or university students who demonstrate outstanding potential for long-range contribution to the fields of automation and control. **Focus:** Automotive technology; Systems engineering. **Qualif.:** Applicants must be currently enrolled in a graduate or undergraduate program in an instrumentation, systems, or automation discipline (2-year program or 4-year baccalaureate program or its equivalent). Two-year program applicants must have completed at least one academic semester or its equivalent. Four-year degree program applicants must be in sophomore year or higher at the time of application. Applicants must be full-time students in an educational institution and have at least an overall GPA of 3.0 on a 4.0 scale. **Criteria:** Preference is given to students who are enrolled in a degree program in instrumentation, systems, and automation or other closely related field.

Funds Avail.: No specific amount. **To Apply:** Applicants must submit completed application (with Department Head Signature); two reference letters; original transcript (with raised seal); list of awards and honors; extracurricular activities; employment history; and an essay. Mail the original and ten copies of the complete application with attachments unfolded in an envelope. **Deadline:** February 15. **Contact:** Catherine Andrews at candrews@hilealabama.com.

5233 ■ ISA Section and District Scholarships - Houston (Graduate, Undergraduate/Scholarship)

Purpose: To support college or university students who demonstrate outstanding potential for long-range contribution to the fields of automation and control. **Focus:** Automotive technology; Systems engineering. **Qualif.:** Applicants must be currently enrolled in a graduate or undergraduate program in an instrumentation, systems, or automation discipline (2-year program or 4-year baccalaureate program or its equivalent). Two-year program applicants must have completed at least one academic semester or its equivalent. Four-year degree program applicants must be in sophomore year or higher at the time of application. Applicants must be full-time students in an educational institution and have at least an overall GPA of 3.0 on a 4.0 scale. **Criteria:** Preference is given to students who are enrolled in a degree program in instrumentation, systems, and automation or other closely related field.

Funds Avail.: No specific amount. **To Apply:** Applicants must submit completed application (with Department Head Signature); two reference letters; original transcript (with raised seal); list of awards and honors; extracurricular activities; employment history; and an essay. Mail the original and ten copies of the complete application with attachments unfolded in an envelope. **Deadline:** February 15. **Contact:** Chan Miller at cmiller@technip.com.

Awards are arranged alphabetically below their administering organizations

5234 ■ ISA Section and District Scholarships - Lehigh Valley (Graduate, Undergraduate/Scholarship)

Purpose: To support college or university students who demonstrate outstanding potential for long-range contribution to the fields of automation and control. **Focus:** Automotive technology; Systems engineering. **Qualif.:** Applicant must be currently enrolled in a graduate or undergraduate program in an instrumentation, systems, or automation discipline (2-year program or 4-year baccalaureate program or its equivalent). Two-year program applicants must have completed at least one academic semester or its equivalent. Four-year degree program applicants must be in sophomore year or higher at the time of application. Applicants must be full-time students in an educational institution and have at least an overall GPA of 3.0 on a 4.0 scale. **Criteria:** Preference is given to students who are enrolled in a degree program in instrumentation, systems, and automation or other closely related field.

Funds Avail.: No specific amount. **To Apply:** Applicants must submit completed application (with Department Head Signature); two reference letters; original transcript (with raised seal); list of awards and honors; extracurricular activities; employment history; and an essay. Mail the original and ten copies of the complete application with attachments unfolded in an envelope. **Deadline:** February 15. **Contact:** Charles Longo at cblongo@pplweb.com.

5235 ■ ISA Section and District Scholarships - New Jersey (Graduate, Undergraduate/Scholarship)

Purpose: To support college or university students who demonstrate outstanding potential for long-range contribution to the fields of automation and control. **Focus:** Automotive technology; Systems engineering. **Qualif.:** Applicants must be currently enrolled in a graduate or undergraduate program in an instrumentation, systems, or automation discipline (2-year program or 4-year baccalaureate program or its equivalent). Two-year program applicants must have completed at least one academic semester or its equivalent. Four-year degree program applicants must be in sophomore year or higher at the time of application. Applicants must be full-time students in an educational institution and have at least an overall GPA of 3.0 on a 4.0 scale. **Criteria:** Preference is given to students who are enrolled in a degree program in instrumentation, systems, and automation or other closely related field.

Funds Avail.: No specific amount. **To Apply:** Applicants must submit completed application (with Department Head Signature); two reference letters; original transcript (with raised seal); list of awards and honors; extracurricular activities; employment history; and an essay. Mail the original and ten copies of the complete application with attachments unfolded in an envelope. **Deadline:** February 15. **Contact:** Bob Linder at boblindner@aol.com.

5236 ■ ISA Section and District Scholarships - Niagara Frontier (Graduate, Undergraduate/Scholarship)

Purpose: To support college or university students who demonstrate outstanding potential for long-range contribution to the fields of automation and control. **Focus:** Automotive technology; Systems engineering. **Qualif.:** Applicants must be currently enrolled in a graduate or undergraduate program in an instrumentation, systems, or automation discipline (2-year program or 4-year baccalaureate program or its equivalent). Two-year program applicants must have completed at least one academic semester or its equivalent. Four-year degree program applicants must be in sopho-

more year or higher at the time of application. Applicants must be full-time students in an educational institution and have at least an overall GPA of 3.0 on a 4.0 scale. **Criteria:** Preference is given to students who are enrolled in a degree program in instrumentation, systems, and automation or other closely related field.

Funds Avail.: No specific amount. **To Apply:** Applicants must submit completed application (with Department Head Signature); two reference letters; original transcript (with raised seal); list of awards and honors; extracurricular activities; employment history; and an essay. Mail the original and ten copies of the complete application with attachments unfolded in an envelope. **Deadline:** February 15. **Contact:** Maxwell Bennett at maxwell33@adelphia.net.

5237 ■ ISA Section and District Scholarships - Northern California (Graduate, Undergraduate/Scholarship)

Purpose: To support college or university students who demonstrate outstanding potential for long-range contribution to the fields of automation and control. **Focus:** Automotive technology; Systems engineering. **Qualif.:** Applicants must be currently enrolled in a graduate or undergraduate program in an instrumentation, systems, or automation discipline (2-year program or 4-year baccalaureate program or its equivalent). Two-year program applicants must have completed at least one academic semester or its equivalent. Four-year degree program applicants must be in sophomore year or higher or its equivalent at the time of application. Applicants must be full-time students in an educational institution and have at least an overall GPA of 3.0 on a 4.0 scale. **Criteria:** Preference is given to students who are enrolled in a degree program in instrumentation, systems, and automation or other closely related field.

Funds Avail.: No specific amount. **To Apply:** Applicants must submit completed application (with Department Head Signature); two reference letters; original transcript (with raised seal); list of awards and honors; extracurricular activities; employment history; and an essay. Mail the original and ten copies of the complete application with attachments unfolded in an envelope. **Deadline:** February 15. **Contact:** Terry Molloy at tvmolloy@cmes.net.

5238 ■ ISA Section and District Scholarships - Richmond Hopewell (Graduate, Undergraduate/Scholarship)

Purpose: To support college or university students who demonstrate outstanding potential for long-range contribution to the fields of automation and control. **Focus:** Automotive technology; Systems engineering. **Qualif.:** Applicants must be currently enrolled in a graduate or undergraduate program in an instrumentation, systems, or automation discipline (2-year program or 4-year baccalaureate program or its equivalent). Two-year program applicants must have completed at least one academic semester or its equivalent. Four-year degree program applicants must be in sophomore year or higher at the time of application. Applicants must be full-time students in an educational institution and have at least an overall GPA of 3.0 on a 4.0 scale. **Criteria:** Preference is given to students who are enrolled in a degree program in instrumentation, systems, and automation or other closely related field.

Funds Avail.: No specific amount. **To Apply:** Applicants must submit completed application (with Department Head Signature); two reference letters; original transcript (with raised seal); list of awards and honors; extracurricular activities; employment history; and an essay. Mail the

Awards are arranged alphabetically below their administering organizations

original and ten copies of the complete application with attachments unfolded in an envelope. **Deadline:** February 15. **Contact:** Bill Sneddon at bill.sneddon@qimonda.com.

5239 ■ ISA Section and District Scholarships - Savannah River *(Graduate, Undergraduate/ Scholarship)*

Purpose: To support college or university students who demonstrate outstanding potential for long-range contribution to the fields of automation and control. **Focus:** Automotive technology; Systems engineering. **Qualif.:** Applicants must be currently enrolled in a graduate or undergraduate program in an instrumentation, systems, or automation discipline (2-year program or 4-year baccalaureate program or its equivalent). Two-year program applicants must have completed at least one academic semester or its equivalent. Four-year degree program applicants must be in sophomore year or higher at the time of application. Applicants must be full-time students in an educational institution and have at least an overall GPA of 3.0 on a 4.0 scale. **Criteria:** Preference is given to students who are enrolled in a degree program in instrumentation, systems, and automation or other closely related field.

Funds Avail.: No specific amount. **To Apply:** Applicants must submit completed application (with Department Head Signature); two reference letters; original transcript (with raised seal); list of awards and honors; extracurricular activities; employment history; and an essay. Mail the original and ten copies of the complete application with attachments unfolded in an envelope. **Deadline:** February 15. **Contact:** Lance Brown at ltbrown1@comcast.net.

5240 ■ ISA Section and District Scholarships - Southwestern Wyoming *(Graduate, Undergraduate/ Scholarship)*

Purpose: To promote education in instrumentation, systems, or automation discipline. **Focus:** Automotive technology; Systems engineering. **Qualif.:** Applicant must be currently enrolled in a graduate or undergraduate program in an instrumentation, systems, or automation discipline (2-year program or 4-year baccalaureate program or its equivalent). Two-year program applicants must have completed at least one academic semester or its equivalent. Four-year degree program applicants must be in sophomore year or higher at the time of application. Applicants must be full-time students in an educational institution and have at least an overall GPA of 3.0 on a 4.0 scale. **Criteria:** Preference is given to students who are enrolled in a degree program in instrumentation, systems, and automation or other closely related field.

Funds Avail.: No specific amount. **To Apply:** Applicants must submit completed application (with Department Head Signature); two reference letters; original transcript (with raised seal); list of awards and honors; extracurricular activities; employment history; and an essay. Mail the original and ten copies of the complete application with attachments unfolded in an envelope. **Deadline:** February 15. **Contact:** Tom Kottenstette to swwyoisa@hotmail.com.

5241 ■ ISA Section and District Scholarships - Texas, Louisiana and Mississippi *(Graduate, Undergraduate/Scholarship)*

Purpose: To promote education in instrumentation, systems, or automation discipline. **Focus:** Automotive technology; Systems engineering. **Qualif.:** Applicant must be currently enrolled in a graduate or undergraduate program in an instrumentation, systems, or automation

discipline (2 year program or 4 year baccalaureate program or its equivalent). Two-year program applicants must have completed at least one academic semester or its equivalent. Four-year degree program applicants must be in sophomore year or higher at the time of application. Applicants must be full-time students in an educational institution who have at least an overall GPA of 3.0 on a 4.0 scale. **Criteria:** Preference is given to students who are enrolled in a degree program in instrumentation, systems, and automation or other closely related field.

Funds Avail.: No specific amount. **To Apply:** Applicants must submit a completed application (with Department Head Signature); two reference letters; original transcript (with raised seal); list of awards and honors; extracurricular activities; employment history; and an essay. Mail the original and ten copies of the complete application with attachments unfolded in an envelope. **Deadline:** February 15. **Contact:** Victor Carbajal at viccarba@aol.com.

5242 ■ ISA Section and District Scholarships - Wilmington *(Graduate, Undergraduate/Scholarship)*

Purpose: To promote education in instrumentation, systems, or automation discipline. **Focus:** Automotive technology; Systems engineering. **Qualif.:** Applicant must be currently enrolled in a graduate or undergraduate program in an instrumentation, systems, or automation discipline (2-year program or 4-year baccalaureate program or its equivalent). Two-year program applicants must have completed at least one academic semester or its equivalent. Four-year degree program applicants must be in sophomore year or higher at the time of application. Applicants must be full-time students in an educational institution and have at least an overall GPA of 3.0 on a 4.0 scale. **Criteria:** Preference is given to students who are enrolled in a degree program in instrumentation, systems, and automation or other closely related field.

Funds Avail.: No specific amount. **To Apply:** Applicants must submit completed application (with Department Head Signature); two reference letters; original transcript (with raised seal); list of awards and honors; extracurricular activities; employment history; and an essay. Mail the original and ten copies of the complete application with attachments unfolded in an envelope. **Deadline:** February 15. **Contact:** Bill Balascio at W_Balascio@ CarewAssoc.com; George Bentinck at george.c.bentinck-2@usa.dupont.com.

5243 ■ ISA Technical Division Scholarships - Analysis Division *(Graduate, Undergraduate/ Scholarship)*

Purpose: To support outstanding students pursuing careers in the area pertinent to the Division's activity. **Focus:** Automotive technology; Systems engineering. **Qualif.:** Applicant must be currently enrolled in a graduate or undergraduate program in an instrumentation, systems, or automation discipline (2-year program or 4-year baccalaureate program or its equivalent). Two-year program applicants must have completed at least one academic semester or its equivalent. Four-year degree program applicants must be in sophomore year or higher at the time of application. Applicants must be full-time students in an educational institution who have at least an overall GPA of 3.0 on a 4.0 scale. **Criteria:** Preference is given to students who are enrolled in a degree program in instrumentation, systems, and automation or other closely related field.

Funds Avail.: No specific amount. **To Apply:** Applicants must submit completed application (with Department Head

Awards are arranged alphabetically below their administering organizations

Signature); two reference letters; original transcript (with raised seal); list of awards and honors; extracurricular activities; employment history; and an essay. Mail the original and ten copies of the complete application with attachments unfolded in an envelope. **Deadline:** February 15. **Contact:** Mike Chaney at mwchaney@msn.com; Don Nettles at dnettles@chevron.com.

5244 ■ ISA Technical Division Scholarships - Chemical and Petroleum Industries Division *(Graduate, Undergraduate/Scholarship)*

Purpose: To support outstanding students pursuing careers in the area pertinent to the Division's activity. **Focus:** Automotive technology; Systems engineering. **Qualif.:** Applicant must be currently enrolled in a graduate or undergraduate program in an instrumentation, systems, or automation discipline (2-year program or 4-year baccalaureate program or its equivalent). Two-year program applicants must have completed at least one academic semester or its equivalent. Four-year degree program applicants must be in sophomore year or higher at the time of application. Applicants must be full-time students in an educational institution who have at least an overall GPA of 3.0 on a 4.0 scale. **Criteria:** Preference is given to students who are enrolled in a degree program in instrumentation, systems, and automation or other closely related field.

Funds Avail.: No specific amount. **To Apply:** Applicants must submit completed application (with Department Head Signature); two reference letters; original transcript (with raised seal); list of awards and honors; extracurricular activities; employment history; and an essay. Mail the original and ten copies of the complete application with attachments unfolded in an envelope. **Deadline:** Febuary 15.

5245 ■ ISA Technical Division Scholarships - Food and Pharmaceutical Industries Division *(Graduate, Undergraduate/Scholarship)*

Purpose: To support outstanding students pursuing careers in the area pertinent to the Division's activity. **Focus:** Automotive technology; Systems engineering. **Qualif.:** Applicant must be currently enrolled in a graduate or undergraduate program in an instrumentation, systems, or automation discipline (2-year program or 4-year baccalaureate program or its equivalent). Two-year program applicants must have completed at least one academic semester or 12 semester hours or its equivalent. Four-year degree program applicants must be in sophomore year or higher at the time of application. Applicants must be full-time students in an educational institution and have an at least 3.0 GPA on a 4.0 scale. **Criteria:** Preference is given to students who are enrolled in a degree program in instrumentation, systems, and automation or other closely related field.

Funds Avail.: $5,000. **To Apply:** Applicants must submit completed application (with Department Head Signature); two reference letters; original transcript (with raised seal); list of awards and honors; extracurricular activities; employment history; and an essay. Mail the original and ten copies of the complete application with attachments unfolded in an envelope. **Deadline:** February 15. **Contact:** Rodney Jones at rjones@isa.org.

5246 ■ ISA Technical Division Scholarships - Power Industry Division *(Graduate, Undergraduate/Scholarship)*

Purpose: To support outstanding students pursuing careers in the area pertinent to the Division's activity. **Focus:** Automotive technology; Systems engineering. **Qualif.:** Ap-

plicants must be currently enrolled in a graduate or undergraduate program in an instrumentation, systems, or automation discipline (2-year program or 4-year baccalaureate program or its equivalent). Two-year program applicants must have completed at least one academic semester or 12 semester hours or its equivalent. Four-year degree program applicants must be in sophomore year or higher at the time of application. Applicants must be full-time students in an educational institution who have an overall GPA of 3.0 on a 4.0 scale. **Criteria:** Preference is given to students who are enrolled in a degree program in instrumentation, systems, and automation or other closely related field.

Funds Avail.: No specific amount. **To Apply:** Applicants must submit completed application (with Department Head Signature); two reference letters; original transcript (with raised seal); list of awards and honors; extracurricular activities; employment history; and an essay. Mail the original and ten copies of the complete application with attachments unfolded in an envelope. **Deadline:** February 15. **Contact:** Mike Skoncey at mskoncey@firstenergy.corp.com.

5247 ■ ISA Technical Division Scholarships - Process Measurement and Control Division *(Graduate, Undergraduate/Scholarship)*

Purpose: To support outstanding students pursuing careers in the area pertinent to the Division's activity. **Focus:** Automotive technology; Systems engineering. **Qualif.:** Applicants must be currently enrolled in a graduate or undergraduate program in an instrumentation, systems, or automation discipline (2-year program or 4-year baccalaureate program or its equivalent). Two-year program applicants must have completed at least one academic semester or 12 semester hours or its equivalent. Four-year degree program applicants must be in sophomore year or higher at the time of application. Applicants must be full-time students in an educational institution who have at least an overall GPA of 3.0 on a 4.0 scale. **Criteria:** Preference is given to students who are enrolled in a degree program in instrumentation, systems, and automation or other closely related field.

Funds Avail.: No specific amount. **To Apply:** Applicants must submit completed application (with Department Head Signature); two reference letters; original transcript (with raised seal); ISA membership form (if not a member); list of awards and honors; extracurricular activities; employment history; and an essay. Mail the original and ten copies of the complete application with attachments unfolded in an envelope. **Deadline:** February 15. **Contact:** Murtaza Gandhi at musra.gandi@chevron.com.

5248 ■ ISA Technical Division Scholarships - Pulp and Paper Industry Division *(Graduate, Undergraduate/Scholarship)*

Purpose: To support outstanding students pursuing careers in the area pertinent to the Division's activity. **Focus:** Automotive technology; Systems engineering. **Qualif.:** Applicants must be currently enrolled in a graduate or undergraduate program in an instrumentation, systems, or automation discipline (2-year program or 4-year baccalaureate program or its equivalent). Two-year program applicants must have completed at least one academic semester, or 12 semester hours, or its equivalent. Four-year degree program applicants must be in sophomore year or higher at the time of application. Applicants must be full-time students in an educational institution who have an

Awards are arranged alphabetically below their administering organizations

overall GPA of 3.0 on a 4.0 scale. **Criteria:** Preference is given to students who are enrolled in a degree program in instrumentation, systems, and automation or other closely related field.

Funds Avail.: $2,000. **To Apply:** Applicants must submit completed application (with Department Head Signature); two reference letters; original transcript (with raised seal); list of awards and honors; extracurricular activities; employment history; and an essay. Mail the original and ten copies of the complete application with attachments unfolded in an envelope. **Deadline:** February 15. **Contact:** Brad Carlberg at brad.carlberg@bsc-engineering.com.

5249 ■ ISA Technical Division Scholarships - Test Measurement Division (Graduate, Undergraduate/Scholarship)

Purpose: To support outstanding students pursuing careers in the area pertinent to the Division's activity. **Focus:** Automotive technology; Systems engineering. **Qualif.:** Applicants must be currently enrolled in a graduate or undergraduate program in an instrumentation, systems, or automation discipline (2-year program or 4-year baccalaureate program or its equivalent). Two-year program applicants must have completed at least one academic semester, or 12 semester hours, or its equivalent. Four-year degree program applicants must be in sophomore year or higher at the time of application. Applicants must be full-time students in an educational institution and have at least an overall GPA of 3.0 on a 4.0 scale. **Criteria:** Preference is given to students who are enrolled in a degree program in instrumentation, systems, and automation or other closely related fields.

Funds Avail.: No specific amount. **To Apply:** Applicants must submit completed application (with Department Head Signature); two reference letters; original transcript (with raised seal); list of awards and honors; extracurricular activities; employment history; and an essay. Mail the original and ten copies of the complete application with attachments unfolded in an envelope. **Deadline:** February 15. **Contact:** J. Brandon Jones at joshua.jones@arnold.af.mil.

5250 ■ ISA Technical Division Scholarships - Water and Wastewater Industries Division (Graduate, Undergraduate/Scholarship)

Purpose: To support outstanding students pursuing careers in the area pertinent to the Division's activity. **Focus:** Automotive technology; Systems engineering. **Qualif.:** Applicants must be currently enrolled in a graduate or undergraduate program in an instrumentation, systems, or automation discipline (2-year program or 4-year baccalaureate program or its equivalent). Two-year program applicants must have completed at least one academic semester, or 12 semester hours, or its equivalent. Four-year degree program applicants must be in sophomore year or higher at the time of application. Applicants must be full-time students in an educational institution and have at least an overall GPA of 3.0 on a 4.0 scale. **Criteria:** Preference is given to students who are enrolled in a degree program in instrumentation, systems, and automation or other closely related field.

Funds Avail.: No specific amount. **To Apply:** Applicants must submit completed application (with Department Head Signature); two reference letters; original transcript (with raised seal); list of awards and honors; extracurricular activities; employment history; and an essay. Mail the original and ten copies of the complete application with at-

tachments unfolded in an envelope. **Deadline:** February 15. **Contact:** Mike Fedenyszen at mfedenyszen@vanderweil.com.

5251 ■ Bob and Mary Ives Scholarships (Graduate, Undergraduate/Scholarship)

Purpose: To promote education in an instrumentation, systems, or automation discipline. **Focus:** Automotive technology; Systems engineering. **Qualif.:** Applicant must be currently enrolled in a graduate or undergraduate program in an instrumentation, systems, or automation discipline (2 year program or 4 year baccalaureate program or its equivalent). Two-year program applicants must have completed at least one academic semester or its equivalent. Four-year degree program applicants must be in sophomore year or higher at the time of application. Applicants must be full-time students in an educational institution who have at least an overall GPA of 2.5 on a 4.0 scale. **Criteria:** Preference is given to students who are enrolled in a degree program in instrumentation, systems, and automation or other closely related field.

Funds Avail.: No specific amount. **To Apply:** Applicants must submit a completed application (with Department Head Signature); two reference letters; original transcript (with raised seal); list of awards and honors; extracurricular activities; employment history; and an essay. Mail the original and ten copies of the complete application with attachments unfolded in an envelope. **Deadline:** February 15.

5252 ■ Islamic Scholarship Fund (ISF)

2140 Shattuck Ave., Ste.706
Berkeley, CA 94704
Ph: (650)995-6782
E-mail: contact@islamicscholarshipFund.org
URL: islamicscholarshipfund.org

5253 ■ Islamic Scholarship Fund Scholarships (ISF) (Postgraduate, Undergraduate/Scholarship)

Purpose: To encourage Muslim students to pursue college or post-graduate degrees in humanities, social sciences, liberal arts and law. **Focus:** General studies/Field of study not specified. **Qualif.:** Applicants must be Muslims; must be U.S. citizens or permanent residents; have been accepted to top ranked four-year colleges or universities in the United States for undergraduate and post-graduate studies; have a minimum 3.0 grade point average; be active members of their community; have a college sophomore standing or above. **Criteria:** Selection will be based on academic record; school activities; extracurricular activities especially in the Muslim community; personal interview; and other factors that help in distinguishing the applicant based on the information submitted.

Funds Avail.: $1,000-$10,000. **Duration:** Annual. **To Apply:** Applicant must submit a completed application form; an essay; official college transcripts; two recommendation letters to be sent to the selection committee. **Deadline:** April 14. **Contact:** Islamic Scholarship Fund, at the above address, or Email: contact@islamicscholarshipfund.org.

5254 ■ Islamic Society of North America (ISNA)

6555 S County Road 750 E
Plainfield, IN 46168
Ph: (317)839-8157
E-mail: membership@isna.net

Awards are arranged alphabetically below their administering organizations

URL: www.isna.net

5255 ■ HRH Prince Alwaleed Bin Talal ISNA Fellowships *(Graduate/Fellowship)*

Purpose: To provide support and training in education, philanthropy, and management for Muslim Americans pursuing graduate studies in the United States. **Focus:** Management. **Qualif.:** Applicants must be graduate students or recent graduates from an undergraduate program looking to pursue their Masters degree; must complete all admissions and GRE testing requirements for application to academic program; must be U.S. citizens or have legal permanent residency; able to complete an internship with a U.S. non-profit organization consisting of a minimum of 480 hours; must be available to attend an intensive five-day orientation and training program as well as to assist with work at the ISNA Annual Convention with all expenses paid. **Criteria:** Selection is based on high academic achievement with a preference to applicants with a 3.0 GPA or higher; consistent active participation in public service-oriented activities; evidence of leadership skills and potential for growth; superior analytical and communication skills (oral and written); confirmation of ability to meet program requirements. Based on the application scores, candidates will be interviewed and considered for the funding.

Funds Avail.: $25,000. **Duration:** Annual. **Number Awarded:** 10. **To Apply:** Applicants should submit a completed application form; an essay and two letters of recommendation.

5256 ■ Italian American Lawyers Association (IALA)

PO Box 712057
Los Angeles, CA 90071
E-mail: iala07@yahoo.com
URL: www.iala.info

5257 ■ Italian American Lawyers Association Annual Scholarships *(Undergraduate/Scholarship)*

Purpose: To inspire excellence in the practice of law by rendering financial aid and assistance for individuals intending to pursue legal education. **Focus:** Law. **Qualif.:** Program is open to individuals pursuing legal education. **Criteria:** Award is given based on academic achievement, potential contribution to the Italian-American Community and financial need. The selection will be made based upon the quality of applicants received each year.

Funds Avail.: $3,000. **Duration:** Annual. **To Apply:** Applicants must submit completed application available in the website and must provide a copy of their transcript. In some cases, applicants may also be asked to attend a personal interview. **Deadline:** September 30. **Contact:** Italian American Lawyers Association, c/o J. Sheldon Capeloto, Esq., jcapeloto@capelotolaw.com.

5258 ■ Ivanhoe Foundation

160 S Lomita Ave.
Ojai, CA 93023
Fax: (805)646-8620
E-mail: info@theivanhoefoundation.com
URL: www.theivanhoefoundation.com

5259 ■ Ivanhoe Foundation Fellowships *(Master's/Fellowship)*

Purpose: To support the education of students studying practical Master of Science degree in engineering or science, with an emphasis on water resources. **Focus:** Land management; Waste management; Water resources. **Qualif.:** Applicant must have a Bachelor's degree or equal level certificate; proficient in English; eligible for a research assistantship; and have work experience between degrees or field-related intern experience. **Criteria:** Selection is based on the submitted letter of nomination.

Funds Avail.: $5,000. **Duration:** Annual. **To Apply:** There is no application form. A letter of nomination must be submitted by the student's professor.

5260 ■ Jack and Jill of America Foundation (JJAF)

1930 17th St. NW
Washington, DC 20009
Ph: (202)232-5290
Fax: (202)232-1747
E-mail: administration@jackandjillfoundation.org
URL: www.jackandjillfoundation.org

5261 ■ Jack and Jill of America Scholarship Awards *(Undergraduate/Scholarship)*

Purpose: To provide financial assistance to African American students in preparing them to reach their fullest potential through higher education. **Focus:** General studies/Field of study not specified. **Qualif.:** Applicants must be African American high school seniors with a minimum GPA of 3.0 who will be pursuing a bachelor's degree at any accredited postsecondary institution in the United States. **Criteria:** Applicants will be evaluated based on scholastic performance and active community service.

Funds Avail.: Up to $2,500. **Duration:** Annual. **Number Awarded:** Varies. **To Apply:** Applicants must submit an essay, resume, academic transcript, letters of recommendation and confirmation of 60 hours or more of active community service. **Deadline:** June 1.

5262 ■ Jack Kent Cooke Inc.

44325 Woodridge Pkwy.
Lansdowne, VA 20176
Ph: (703)723-8000
Fax: (703)723-8030
E-mail: events@jkcf.org
URL: www.jkcf.org

5263 ■ Jack Kent Cooke Dissertation Fellowship Award *(Doctorate/Fellowship)*

Purpose: To support advanced doctoral students completing dissertations that further the understanding of the educational pathways and experiences of high-achieving, low-income students. **Focus:** General studies/Field of study not specified. **Qualif.:** Applicants may be U.S. citizens, U.S. permanent residents, or non-U.S. citizens; must be currently studying in an accredited U.S. institution; must be advanced doctoral students who have completed all predissertation requirements; must have successfully defended their dissertation proposal before the application deadline; must not have previously received a scholarship or other funding from the foundation. **Criteria:** The Foundation will select fellows based on the their superior academic ability and achievement; dissertation's significant contribution to exploring; the quality of the proposal with regard to its methodology, scope, theoretical framework, and grounding in the relevant scholarly literature; and the feasibility of the

Awards are arranged alphabetically below their administering organizations

project and the likelihood that the applicant will execute the work within the proposed timeframe.

Funds Avail.: $100,000. **Duration:** Annual. **Number Awarded:** 4. **To Apply:** Interested applicants must provide and submit the following via the electronic site or mail: online application form; cover letter describing the relevance of proposed research with the mission of the Foundation; summary of the proposal, limited to six pages; work plan or timeline for completing dissertation; one letter of support; an official graduate transcript; and curriculum vitae.

5264 ■ Jack Kent Cooke Graduate Arts Awards
(Graduate/Award)

Purpose: To provide funding for higher education to selected students pursuing degree on performing arts, visual arts, and creative writing. **Focus:** Creative writing; Performing arts; Visual arts. **Qualif.:** Candidates must have senior standing or have graduated from an accredited four-year US college or university within the past five years; must have a cumulative undergraduate GPA of 3.20 or better on a scale of 4.0; must demonstrate unmet financial need; must have a bachelor's degree by the start of the fall of the current semester; must have plans to begin their first graduate degree program in the performing arts, visual arts or creative writing at an accredited college or university in the fall of the current year. **Criteria:** Criteria will be based on the applicants academic achievement, artistic or creative merit, financial need, and resilience.

Funds Avail.: $50,000. **Duration:** Annual. **Number Awarded:** 20. **To Apply:** Interested applicants may visit the website for the online application process and other informations.

5265 ■ Jackson Community Foundation (JCF)
1 S Jackson Sq., Ste. 308
Jackson, MI 49201
Ph: (517)787-1321
Fax: (517)787-4333
E-mail: jcf@jacksoncf.org
URL: www.jacksoncf.org

5266 ■ Bernice Barabash Sports Scholarships
(Undergraduate/Scholarship)

Purpose: To support the pursuit of higher education in Jackson County. **Focus:** Sports studies. **Qualif.:** Applicants must be students in grades seven to twelve who hold a minimum of 3.0 GPA; must play hockey during the school year; must be residing in Jackson County or surrounding communities that do not have ice arenas in the area; must plan to attend an accredited college or university program or vocational/technical institute. **Criteria:** Recipients are selected based on lottery draw of qualified applicants.

Funds Avail.: $1,000. **Duration:** Annual. **To Apply:** Applicants must submit a completed application form and a copy of report card or transcript from the 2nd semester. Do not complete the web based application. Instead download the application from the web page, fill out by hand and return to the JCF office. **Deadline:** March 2.

5267 ■ Dennis J. Beck Memorial Scholarships
(Undergraduate/Scholarship)

Purpose: To assist graduating seniors from Jackson County high schools and other Jackson County residents who are attending college. **Focus:** General studies/Field of study not specified. **Qualif.:** Applicants must be Ethnic

minorities pursuing any field of study with special consideration given to those pursuing a degree in Manufacturing. **Criteria:** Recipients are selected based on demonstrated personal responsibility through work, community or family activities.

Funds Avail.: Up to $1,000. **Duration:** Annual. **To Apply:** Applicants must submit a completed application form and must provide a proof of acceptance at an accredited college, university, vocational or technical school. **Deadline:** March 2. **Contact:** Jackson County Community Foundation, at the above address.

5268 ■ Dorothy and Dick Burgess Scholarships
(Undergraduate/Scholarship)

Purpose: To support the pursuit of higher education in Jackson County. **Focus:** Engineering. **Qualif.:** Applicants must have plan to pursue a course of study that leads to a degree in earth science, engineering, premedical or Christian ministry; must have plan to complete a baccalaureate within four consecutive years; must have a cumulative GPA of 3.0 or above; must have demonstrated good citizenship, high moral character and potential for leadership and academic success. **Criteria:** Selection shall be based on the aforementioned qualifications and compliance with the application details.

Funds Avail.: $4,000. **Duration:** Annual. **To Apply:** Applicants must submit a completed application form and must provide a proof of financial need. **Deadline:** March 2.

5269 ■ June Danby and Pat Pearse Education Scholarships *(Undergraduate/Scholarship)*

Purpose: To assist graduating seniors from Jackson County high schools and other Jackson County residents who are attending college. **Focus:** Education; Teaching. **Qualif.:** Applicants must be Jackson High School graduating senior students with cumulative GPA of 3.25 or higher; must be full or part-time students in an accredited college or university majoring in the field of education. **Criteria:** Recipients are selected based on participation in school, community service or volunteer activities, academic performance and financial need.

Funds Avail.: $1,000. **Duration:** Annual. **To Apply:** Applicants must submit a completed application form.

5270 ■ Antonia Dellas Memorial Scholarships
(Undergraduate/Scholarship)

Purpose: To support the pursuit of higher education in Jackson County. **Focus:** Education, Special. **Qualif.:** Applicants must be high school senior students with a minimum of 3.25 or above GPA; must be accepted or attending an accredited Michigan college or university; must intend to enroll or are already enrolled in a school of education. **Criteria:** Recipients are selected based on financial need and participation in school, community or volunteer activity. Preference will be given to those majoring in special education.

Funds Avail.: $2,000. **Duration:** Annual. **To Apply:** Applicants must submit a completed application form and provide a proof of financial need. **Deadline:** March 2.

5271 ■ The Eleonor A. Ernest Scholarships
(Undergraduate/Scholarship)

Purpose: To assist graduating seniors from Jackson County high schools and other Jackson County residents who are attending college. **Focus:** General studies/Field of study not specified. **Qualif.:** Applicants must be valedicto-

Awards are arranged alphabetically below their administering organizations

rian, salutatorian or students with highest GPA from a smaller Jackson County High School; must have a cumulative GPA of 3.0 or higher who participates in school activities and/or sports; must have a good citizenship, leadership and outside activities including work experience. **Criteria:** Recipients are selected based on academic performance.

Funds Avail.: $1,000. **Duration:** Annual. **To Apply:** Applicants must submit a completed application form. **Deadline:** March 2. **Contact:** Jackson County Community Foundation, at the above address.

5272 ■ Melissa Eleanor Ernest Scholarships
(Undergraduate/Scholarship)

Purpose: To support the pursuit of higher education in Jackson County. **Focus:** Cosmetology. **Qualif.:** Applicants must be Jackson County residents; must be adult returning to school, graduating high school senior students already enrolled in an accredited institution of Cosmetology; must be full- or part-time students with a cumulative 2.0 GPA or higher. **Criteria:** Recipients are selected based on financial need.

Funds Avail.: No specific amount. **To Apply:** Applicants must submit a completed application form.

5273 ■ Robert P. Ernest Scholarships
(Undergraduate/Scholarship)

Purpose: To support the pursuit of higher education in Jackson County. **Focus:** General studies/Field of study not specified. **Qualif.:** Applicants must be valedictorian, salutatorian or students with highest GPA from a larger Jackson County High School (with 149 students of more in graduating class); and have a cumulative GPA of 3.0 or higher **Criteria:** Selection shall be based on participation in school activities and/or sports, and having a good citizenship, leadership and outside activities including work experience.

Funds Avail.: Up to $1,000. **Duration:** Annual. **To Apply:** Applicants must submit a completed application form. **Deadline:** March 2.

5274 ■ Martha and Oliver Hansen Memorial Scholarships *(Undergraduate/Scholarship)*

Purpose: To support the pursuit of higher education in Jackson County. **Focus:** Education. **Qualif.:** Applicants must be incoming college junior or senior majoring in Education with the intention of teaching in the classroom; must attend an accredited Michigan college or university who holds 2.5 GPA or above. **Criteria:** Recipients are selected based on financial need.

Funds Avail.: $1,000. **Duration:** Annual. **To Apply:** Applicants must submit a completed application form. **Deadline:** March 2.

5275 ■ Bob and Dawn Hardy Automotive Scholarships *(Undergraduate/Scholarship)*

Purpose: To support the pursuit of higher education in Jackson County. **Focus:** Automotive technology. **Qualif.:** Applicants must be currently enrolled full- or part-time at Jackson Community College in Automotive Service Technology or Ford Maintenance and Light Repair Associate in Applied Science program or Automotive Service Technology; must have 2.0 GPA or higher. **Criteria:** Recipients are selected based on financial need and result of an interview.

Funds Avail.: $3,000. **Duration:** Annual. **To Apply:** Applicants must submit a completed application form. **Deadline:** March 2.

5276 ■ William and Beatrice Kavanaugh Scholarships *(Undergraduate/Scholarship)*

Purpose: To support the pursuit of higher education in Jackson County. **Focus:** General studies/Field of study not specified. **Qualif.:** Applicants must: be graduating students of Grass Lake High school seniors who attended the school for the full academic year; have a cumulative GPA of 2.8 or higher; have plan to be full-time students and carry at least 12 credit hours or equivalent; must be accepted at an accredited college or university and demonstrate a good citizenship qualities in school and/or community. **Criteria:** Selection shall be based on the aforementioned qualifications and compliance with the application details.

Funds Avail.: Up to $1,000. **Duration:** Annual. **To Apply:** Applicants must submit a completed application form. **Deadline:** March 2.

5277 ■ The Otis and Florence Lapham Memorial Scholarships *(Undergraduate/Scholarship)*

Purpose: To support the pursuit of higher education in Jackson County. **Focus:** General studies/Field of study not specified. **Qualif.:** Applicants must be senior graduating students of Hanover-Horton High School who hold a minimum of 2.5 GPA; must demonstrate a good work history and participated in both school and extracurricular activities. **Criteria:** Recipients are selected based on financial need.

Funds Avail.: $1,000. **Duration:** Annual. **To Apply:** Applicants must submit a completed application form. **Deadline:** March 2.

5278 ■ Lucille E. McGee Scholarships
(Undergraduate/Scholarship)

Purpose: To support the pursuit of higher education in Jackson County. **Focus:** General studies/Field of study not specified. **Qualif.:** Applicants must be senior graduating students of Hanover-Horton High School who hold a minimum of 2.5 GPA; must demonstrate a good work history and participated in both school and extracurricular activities. **Criteria:** Recipients are selected based on financial need.

Funds Avail.: No specific amount. **To Apply:** Applicants may contact their school counselor for the application process and other information.

5279 ■ Phillip Guy Richardson Memorial Scholarships *(Undergraduate/Scholarship)*

Purpose: To support the pursuit of higher education in Jackson County. **Focus:** General studies/Field of study not specified. **Qualif.:** Applicants must be Napoleon High school candidates for graduation with a minimum GPA of 3.0 or higher; must participated in school activities and/or sports. **Criteria:** Recipients are selected based on academic performance, leadership and outside activities including work experience.

Funds Avail.: $2,000. **Duration:** Annual. **To Apply:** Applicants must submit a completed application form. **Deadline:** March 2.

5280 ■ Dr. William A. and Marceleine J. Sautter Hanover-Horton High School Youth of Promise Scholarships *(Undergraduate/Scholarship)*

Purpose: To support the pursuit of higher education in Jackson County. **Focus:** General studies/Field of study not specified. **Qualif.:** Applicants must: be graduating Hanover-

Awards are arranged alphabetically below their administering organizations

Horton High School senior students who hold a GPA of 3.0; have attended the school for at least one full academic year and demonstrate good character with focused goals; have the plan to be full-time students and carry a minimum of 12 credit hours or equivalent; and, have plan to attend an accredited Michigan college or university. **Criteria:** Recipients are selected based on academic performance and financial need.

Funds Avail.: Up to $1,000. **Duration:** Annual. **To Apply:** Applicants must submit a completed application form. **Deadline:** March 2.

5281 ■ The Eileen J. Smith, R.N. Memorial Scholarships (Undergraduate/Scholarship)

Purpose: To support the pursuit of higher education in Jackson County. **Focus:** Health care services. **Qualif.:** Applicants must be enrolled in an accredited college or university with a major in a medical profession; either part- or full-time students with cumulative 3.0 GPA or higher. **Criteria:** Recipients are selected based on academic performance and financial need.

Funds Avail.: $1,000. **Duration:** Annual. **To Apply:** Applicants must submit a completed application form. **Deadline:** March 2.

5282 ■ Faith Speckhard Scholarships (Undergraduate/Scholarship)

Purpose: To support the pursuit of higher education in Jackson County. **Focus:** General studies/Field of study not specified. **Qualif.:** Applicants must be Jackson High School graduating seniors that have a minimum of 2.4 GPA and must be full or part-time students in an accredited college or university. **Criteria:** Recipients are selected based on academic performance, financial need and participation in community activities, leadership and service.

Funds Avail.: $5,000. **Duration:** Annual. **To Apply:** Applicants must submit a completed application form and proof of acceptance in an accredited college, university, vocational or technical institute. **Deadline:** March 2.

5283 ■ Paul Tejada Memorial Scholarships (Undergraduate/Scholarship)

Purpose: To assist graduating seniors from Jackson County high schools and other Jackson County residents who are attending college. **Focus:** Health care services; Nursing. **Qualif.:** Applicants must have plans to pursue a course of study leading to a degree in health services administration, nursing or human medicine; must be full or part-time students who maintain a minimum of 12 credit hours with a minimum of 3.0 GPA. **Criteria:** Recipients are selected based on demonstrated good citizenship, high moral character and potential leadership.

Funds Avail.: $1,500. **Duration:** Annual. **To Apply:** Applicants must submit a completed application form. **Deadline:** March 2. **Contact:** Jackson County Community Foundation, at the above address.

5284 ■ Barbara and Howard Thompson Scholarships (Undergraduate/Scholarship)

Purpose: To support the pursuit of higher education in Jackson County. **Focus:** History; Political science. **Qualif.:** Applicants must be Jackson High School graduating seniors or previous recipients who have plan to pursue a degree in history and/or political science; must be accepted at an accredited two or four-year college or university; must have 3.0 GPA. **Criteria:** Recipients are selected based on academic performance, financial need, demonstrated good citizenship, leadership qualities and participation in school and/or sports.

Funds Avail.: $5,000. **Duration:** Annual. **To Apply:** Applicants must submit a completed application form. **Deadline:** March 2.

5285 ■ Sue Walicki Nursing Scholarships (Undergraduate/Scholarship)

Purpose: To assist graduating seniors from Jackson County high schools and other Jackson County residents who are attending college. **Focus:** Nursing. **Qualif.:** Applicants must be Jackson County residents or current employees of a Jackson county health care facility; must be full or part-time students at an accredited Michigan college or university; must have plans to start, continue or advance education in the field of nursing-related field. **Criteria:** Preference will be given to applicants who are currently enrolled in a college nursing program.

Funds Avail.: Up to $5,000. **Duration:** Annual. **To Apply:** Applicants must submit a proof of acceptance in an accredited Nursing Program and proof of financial need. **Deadline:** March 2. **Contact:** Jackson County Community Foundation, at the above address.

5286 ■ Jain Foundation
9725 Third Ave., NE Ste. 204
Seattle, WA 98115
Ph: (425)658-1703
URL: www.jain-foundation.org

5287 ■ Jain Foundation Merit-Based Scholarships (All/Scholarship)

Purpose: To reward students who teach others about LGMD2B/Miyoshi myopathy. **Focus:** Muscular dystrophy. **Qualif.:** Applicants must be current or former high school/college students between the ages of 17 and 30; and enrolled or will be enrolled in some form of higher education at an accredited U.S. institution in the current year. **Criteria:** Winners will be selected based on their academic record, participation in extracurricular activities and leadership experience, proof of spreading diseases awareness to 10-15 individuals and their answers to two short essay (250 words maximum) questions.

Funds Avail.: $1,000 each. **Number Awarded:** 4. **To Apply:** Applicants must teach at least ten people (friends and family 15 years of age or older) about dysferlinopathy using the provided LGMD2B/Miyoshi myopathy learning materials. Signatures, email addresses and phone numbers are required to document the discussions; fill out the online application form which includes questions about academic achievement, extracurricular activities and GPA. The application includes two short essay questions about the students' experience teaching others about LGMD2B/Miyoshi myopathy. **Deadline:** April 30. **Contact:** scholarship@jain-foundation.org.

5288 ■ Jain Foundation Social-Media Scholarships (All/Scholarship)

Purpose: To reward students who teach others about LGMD2B/Miyoshi myopathy. **Focus:** Muscular dystrophy. **Qualif.:** Applicants must be current or former high school/college students between the ages of 17 and 30; and enrolled or will be enrolled in some form of higher education (including 2 year colleges, 4 year colleges/universities

Awards are arranged alphabetically below their administering organizations

and vocational schools) at an accredited U.S. institution in the current year. **Criteria:** Selection will be based on the social media post of applicants with information about LGMD2B/Miyoshi myopathy to spread disease awareness.

Funds Avail.: $1,000 each. **Number Awarded:** 4. **To Apply:** Applicants must: fill-out the online application (then they will receive their scholarship ID numbers by email after filling out the application); visit the Jain Foundation Facebook Scholarship tab to submit a social medi post, including the scholarship ID number; write a post to teach their friends about LGMD2B/Miyoshi myopathy that includes one LGMD2B/Miyoshi myopathy fact of their choice and post such on the scholarship tab. **Deadline:** May 27. **Contact:** scholarship@jain-foundation.org.

5289 ■ Jamaican Canadian Association

995 Arrow Rd.
Toronto, ON, Canada M9M 2Z5
Ph: (416)746-5772
Fax: (416)746-7035
E-mail: info@jcaontario.org
URL: www.jcaontario.org

5290 ■ Brown Dental Scholarships *(Undergraduate/ Scholarship)*

Purpose: To provide financial assistance to students from the Caribbean/ African community who are pursuing post-secondary studies in Ontario universities/colleges. **Focus:** Dental hygiene; Dental laboratory technology; Dentistry. **Qualif.:** Applicants must be Canadian citizens or landed immigrants of Caribbean/African background; must be enrolled as full-time first-year students at an Ontario university/ college or other post-secondary institution; must demonstrate remarkable academic performance or progress in high school; must demonstrate involvement and leadership in campus and/or community activities; must demonstrate financial need. **Criteria:** Selection of recipients will be based on the following: demonstrated scholastic ability; applicants' response to the essay question; involvement and leadership in community/campus activities; significant personal achievements; references demonstrating the applicants accomplishments; and, commitment to career goals.

Funds Avail.: No specific amount. **Duration:** Annual. **To Apply:** Applicants must submit the completed application form; must include an original or copy of the most recent university/college transcript(s) or report card from the last semester of high school verifying academic performance; two-page, double-spaced essay describing the academic and career goals; two letters of recommendation; two passport-size photo; and proof of status in Canada. **Deadline:** July 18.

5291 ■ Mary Anne Chambers Scholarships *(Undergraduate/Scholarship)*

Purpose: To provide financial assistance to students from the Caribbean/ African community who are pursuing post-secondary studies in Ontario universities/colleges. **Focus:** General studies/Field of study not specified. **Qualif.:** Applicant must be a Canadian citizen or landed immigrant of Caribbean/African background; must be enrolled as a full-time first-year student at an Ontario university/ college or other post-secondary institution; must demonstrate a remarkable academic performance or progress in high school; must demonstrate involvement and leadership in campus and/or community activities; must demonstrate

financial need. **Criteria:** Selection of recipients will be based on the following: demonstrated scholastic ability; applicants' response to the essay question; involvement and leadership in community/campus activities; significant personal achievements; references demonstrating the applicants accomplishments; and, commitment to career goals.

Funds Avail.: No specific amount. **Duration:** Annual. **To Apply:** Applicant must submit a completed application form; must include an original or copy of the most recent university/college transcript(s) or report card from the last semester of high school verifying academic performance; two-page, double-spaced essay describing the academic and career goals; two letters of recommendation; two passport-size photo; and proof of status in Canada. **Deadline:** July 18. **Contact:** Jamaican Canadian Association, at the above address.

5292 ■ Marcus Mosiah Garvey Scholarships *(Undergraduate/Scholarship)*

Purpose: To provide financial assistance to students from the Caribbean/ African community who are pursuing post-secondary studies in Ontario universities/colleges. **Focus:** Minorities; Philosophy; Sociology. **Qualif.:** Applicant must be a Canadian citizen or landed immigrant of Caribbean/ African background; must be enrolled as a full-time first-year student at an Ontario university/ college or other post-secondary institution; must demonstrate a remarkable academic performance or progress in high school; must demonstrate involvement and leadership in campus and/or community activities; must demonstrate financial need. **Criteria:** Selection of recipients will be based on the following: demonstrated scholastic ability; applicants' response to the essay question; involvement and leadership in community/campus activities; significant personal achievements; references demonstrating the applicants accomplishments; and, commitment to career goals.

Funds Avail.: No specific amount. **Duration:** Annual. **To Apply:** Applicant must submit a completed application form; must include an original or copy of the most recent university/college transcript(s) or report card from the last semester of high school verifying academic performance; two-page, double-spaced essay describing the academic and career goals; two letters of recommendation; two passport-size photo; and proof of status in Canada. **Deadline:** July 18. **Contact:** Jamaican Canadian Association, at the above address.

5293 ■ Humber College Institute of Technology and Advanced Learning Scholarships *(Undergraduate/ Scholarship)*

Purpose: To provide financial assistance to students from the Caribbean/ African community who are pursuing post-secondary studies in Ontario universities/colleges. **Focus:** Leadership, Institutional and community. **Qualif.:** Applicant must be a Canadian citizen or landed immigrant of Caribbean/African background; must be enrolled as a full-time first-year student at an Ontario university/ college or other post-secondary institution; must demonstrate a remarkable academic performance or progress in high school; must demonstrate involvement and leadership in campus and/or community activities; must demonstrate financial need. **Criteria:** Selection of recipients will be based on the following: demonstrated scholastic ability; applicants' response to the essay question; involvement and leadership in community/campus activities; significant personal achievements; references demonstrating the applicants accomplishments; and, commitment to career goals.

Awards are arranged alphabetically below their administering organizations

Funds Avail.: No specific amount. **Duration:** Annual. **To Apply:** Applicant must submit a completed application form; must include an original or copy of the most recent university/college transcript(s) or report card from the last semester of high school verifying academic performance; two-page, double-spaced essay describing the academic and career goals; two letters of recommendation; two passport-size photo; and proof of status in Canada. **Deadline:** July 18. **Contact:** Jamaican Canadian Association, at the above address.

5294 ■ I Have a Dream Scholarships (Undergraduate/Scholarship)

Purpose: To assist students with significant personal achievements beyond scholastic ability. **Focus:** General studies/Field of study not specified. **Qualif.:** Applicant must be a Canadian citizen or landed immigrant of Caribbean/African background; must be enrolled as a full-time first-year student at an Ontario university/ college or other post-secondary institution; must demonstrate a remarkable academic performance or progress in high school; must demonstrate involvement and leadership in campus and/or community activities; must demonstrate financial need. **Criteria:** Selection of recipient will be based on the following: demonstrated scholastic ability; applicants' response to the essay question; involvement and leadership in community/campus activities; significant personal achievements; references demonstrating the applicants accomplishments; and, commitment to career goals.

Funds Avail.: No specific amount. **Duration:** Annual. **To Apply:** Applicant must submit a completed application form; must include an original or copy of the most recent university/college transcript(s) or report card from the last semester of high school verifying academic performance; two-page, double-spaced essay describing the academic and career goals; two letters of recommendation; two passport-size photo; and proof of status in Canada. **Deadline:** July 18. **Contact:** Jamaican Canadian Association, at the above address.

5295 ■ Dr. Ezra Nesbeth Scholarships (Undergraduate/Scholarship)

Purpose: To provide financial assistance to students from the Caribbean or African community who are pursuing post-secondary studies in Ontario universities/colleges. **Focus:** Business; Computer and information sciences; Health sciences; Technology. **Qualif.:** Applicant must be a Canadian citizen or landed/immigrants of Caribbean African background; college or university students studying business, technology, computer science or health science; should have high academic standing (minimum B average); have completed at least one (1) year of college or university in Canada; and, involved in extracurricular activities within the university, Afro-Canadian community, or wider Canadian community. **Criteria:** Selection of recipients will be based on the following criteria: leadership ability; strong oral and written communication skills; demonstrate economic need; and, have a good understanding of the importance of economic self-sufficiency and entrepreneurship to the success of African Canadians in the Greater Toronto Area, and elsewhere in Canada.

Funds Avail.: No specific amount. **Duration:** Annual. **To Apply:** Applicant must submit a completed application form; must include an original or copy of the most recent university/college transcript(s) or report card from the last semester of high school verifying academic performance; two-page, double-spaced essay describing the academic and career goals; two letters of recommendation; two

passport-size photo; and proof of status in Canada. The scholarship may have additional application form, as provided by the organization. **Deadline:** July 18. **Contact:** Jamaican Canadian Association, at the above address.

5296 ■ Ryerson Scholarships (College, University/Scholarship)

Purpose: To provide financial assistance to students from the Caribbean/ African community who are pursuing post-secondary studies in Ontario universities/colleges. **Focus:** General studies/Field of study not specified. **Qualif.:** Applicant must be a Canadian citizen or landed immigrant of Caribbean/African background; must be enrolled as a full-time first-year student at an Ontario university/ college or other post-secondary institution; must demonstrate a remarkable academic performance or progress in high school; must demonstrate involvement and leadership in campus and/or community activities; must demonstrate financial need. **Criteria:** Selection of applicants will be based on the criteria of the JCA Scholarship Selection Committee: (a) Demonstrated scholastic ability; (b) Applicant's response to the essay questions; (c) Involvement and leadership in community/campus activities; (d) Significant personal achievements beyond scholastic ability; (e) References; (f) Commitment to career goals.

Funds Avail.: No specific amount. **Duration:** Annual. **To Apply:** Applicant must submit a completed application form; must include an original or copy of the most recent university/college transcript(s) or report card from the last semester of high school verifying academic performance; two-page, double-spaced essay describing the academic and career goals; two letters of recommendation; two passport-size photo; and proof of status in Canada. **Deadline:** July 18. **Contact:** Jamaican Canadian Association, at the above address.

5297 ■ Eva Smith Bursary (Undergraduate/Scholarship)

Purpose: To provide support to African-Canadian youth who are pursuing a post-secondary education. **Focus:** General studies/Field of study not specified. **Qualif.:** Applicant must be a Canadian citizen or landed immigrant of Caribbean/African background; must be enrolled as a full-time first-year student at an Ontario university/ college or other post-secondary institution; must demonstrate remarkable academic performance or progress in high school; must demonstrate involvement and leadership in campus and/or community activities; must demonstrate financial need. **Criteria:** Selection of recipients for every scholarship is based on the criteria established JCA Scholarship Selection Committee: demonstrated scholastic ability; applicant's response to the essay question; involvement and leadership in community/campus activities; significant personal achievements; references demonstrating the applicants accomplishments; and, commitment to career goals.

Funds Avail.: No specific amount. **Duration:** Annual. **To Apply:** Applicant must submit a completed application form; must include an original or copy of the most recent university/college transcript(s) or report card from the last semester of high school verifying academic performance; two-page, double-spaced essay describing the academic and career goals; two letters of recommendation; two passport-size photo; and proof of status in Canada. **Deadline:** July 18. **Contact:** Jamaican Canadian Association, at the above address.

Awards are arranged alphabetically below their administering organizations

5298 ■ Barbara Thomas Bursary (Undergraduate/ Scholarship)

Purpose: To provide financial assistance to students from the Caribbean/ African community who are pursuing post-secondary studies in Ontario universities/colleges. **Focus:** General studies/Field of study not specified. **Qualif.:** Applicants must be Canadian citizens or landed immigrants of Caribbean/African background; must be enrolled as full-time first-year students at an Ontario university/ college or other post-secondary institution; must demonstrate remarkable academic performance or progress in high school; must demonstrate involvement and leadership in campus and/or community activities; must demonstrate financial need. **Criteria:** Selection of recipients will be based on the following: demonstrated scholastic ability; applicants' response to the essay question; involvement and leadership in community/campus activities; significant personal achievements; references demonstrating the applicants accomplishments; and, commitment to career goals.

Funds Avail.: No specific amount. **Duration:** Annual. **To Apply:** Applicants must submit the completed application form; must include an original or copy of the most recent university/college transcript(s) or report card from the last semester of high school verifying academic performance; two-page, double-spaced essay describing the academic and career goals; two letters of recommendation; two passport-size photo; and proof of status in Canada. **Deadline:** July 18. **Contact:** Jamaican Canadian Association, at the above address.

5299 ■ York Regional Police Scholarships (Undergraduate/Scholarship)

Purpose: To provide financial assistance to students from the Caribbean/ African community who are pursuing post-secondary studies in Ontario universities/colleges. **Focus:** General studies/Field of study not specified. **Qualif.:** Applicants must be Canadian citizens or landed immigrants of Caribbean/African background; must be enrolled as full-time first-year students at an Ontario university/ college or other post-secondary institution; must demonstrate remarkable academic performance or progress in high school; must demonstrate involvement and leadership in campus and/or community activities; must demonstrate financial need. **Criteria:** Selection of recipients will be based on the following: demonstrated scholastic ability; applicants' response to the essay question; involvement and leadership in community/campus activities; significant personal achievements; references demonstrating the applicants accomplishments; and, commitment to career goals.

Funds Avail.: No specific amount. **Duration:** Annual. **To Apply:** Applicants must submit the completed application form; must include an original or copy of the most recent university/college transcript(s) or report card from the last semester of high school verifying academic performance; two-page, double-spaced essay describing the academic and career goals; two letters of recommendation; two passport-size photo; and proof of status in Canada. **Deadline:** July 18. **Contact:** Jamaican Canadian Association, at the above address.

5300 ■ Youth Affairs Committee Rising Star Scholarships (Undergraduate/Scholarship)

Purpose: To provide financial assistance to students from the Caribbean/ African community who are pursuing post-secondary studies in Ontario universities/colleges. **Focus:** General studies/Field of study not specified. **Qualif.:** Applicant must be a Canadian citizen or landed immigrant of Caribbean/African background; must be enrolled as a full-time first-year student at an Ontario university/ college or other post-secondary institution; must demonstrate a remarkable academic performance or progress in high school; must demonstrate involvement and leadership in campus and/or community activities; must demonstrate financial need. **Criteria:** Selection of applicants will be based on the criteria of the JCA Scholarship Selection Committee: (a) Demonstrated scholastic ability; (b) Applicant's response to the essay questions; (c) Involvement and leadership in community/campus activities; (d) Significant personal achievements beyond scholastic ability; (e) References; (f) Commitment to career goals.

Funds Avail.: No specific amount. **Duration:** Annual. **To Apply:** Applicant must submit a completed application form; must include an original or copy of the most recent university/college transcript(s) or report card from the last semester of high school verifying academic performance; two-page, double-spaced essay describing the academic and career goals; two letters of recommendation; two passport-size photo; and proof of status in Canada.

5301 ■ Jamaican Canadian Association Alberta (JCAA)

PO Box 22264
Bankers Hall
Calgary, AB, Canada T2P 4K1
Ph: (403)280-6704
E-mail: info@jcaalberta.com
URL: www.jcaalberta.com

5302 ■ Jamaican Canadian Association Alberta Scholarship Program (Undergraduate/Scholarship)

Purpose: To foster education for all members of Jamaican Canadian Association Alberta. **Focus:** General studies/ Field of study not specified. **Qualif.:** Applicants must be members of JCAA who are Jamaicans or descendants of Jamaicans. **Criteria:** Recipients will be selected based on submitted materials.

Funds Avail.: Amount not specified. **To Apply:** Applicants must complete the application form available at the website; must write a statement of no more than 100 words indicating the aspirations and the reasons why they deserve the award; and must attach a transcript of records of the school last attended.

5303 ■ Japan-American Society of Hawaii

1600 Kapiolani Blvd.
Honolulu, HI 96806-1412
Ph: (808)524-4450
Fax: (808)524-4451
E-mail: admindir@jashawaii.org
URL: www.jashawaii.org

5304 ■ Crown Prince Akihito Scholarship Foundation (Graduate/Scholarship)

Purpose: To promote understanding between the U.S. and Japan by offering scholarships for study in Hawaii and Japan. **Focus:** General studies/Field of study not specified. **Qualif.:** Applicants must be graduate students in Japan for study at the University of Hawaii at Manoa; American graduate students at the University of Hawaii at Manoa for study in Japan who are pursuing a subject area leading to better understanding between Japan and the U.S.; must have a

Awards are arranged alphabetically below their administering organizations

friendly outgoing personality, a sympathetic interest in the altitude and way of life of the people of a different culture, and the ability to communicate their ideas readily and effectively; must have a good knowledge of the history, culture, geography and current affairs of the U.S. **Criteria:** Selection will be based on applicant's academic qualifications based upon graduate-level GPA and the relevancy of courses taken to area of research or study; ability to do research; a coherent and well-thought out study plan; career goals; recommendations of professors; professional bearing and demeanor.

Funds Avail.: $30,000 for American students plus a $15,000 annual allowance; $25,000 for Japanese students plus a full tuition scholarship. **Duration:** Annual. **Number Awarded:** 2. **To Apply:** Application form can be downloaded from the website. Applicants must provide a brief statement of their previous work experience, if any, giving a brief indication of the nature and length of employment and explaining how this experience will help them reach their long-range objectives. Applicants must also submit the following supplementary documents: medical certificate filled out by a licensed physician; signed recommendations from two professors; official transcripts. **Remarks:** Established in 1959.

5305 ■ Japan Foundation, New York (JFNY)

152 W 57th St., 17th Fl.
New York, NY 10019-3310
Ph: (212)489-0299
Fax: (212)489-0409
E-mail: info@jfny.org
URL: www.jfny.org

5306 ■ Japan Foundation, New York Doctoral Fellowship Program *(Doctorate/Fellowship)*

Purpose: To support outstanding scholars in the field of Japanese Studies by offering the opportunity to conduct research in Japan. **Focus:** Japanese studies. **Qualif.:** Applicants must be doctoral candidates in the humanities or social sciences, and have achieved ABD status by the time the fellowship begins. **Criteria:** Selection of applicants shall be based on the following: project quality; training academic history, academic rank or position, professional reputation, and accomplishments; (3) former Japan Foundation fellows who have been awarded two or more Foundation fellowships will be put under particularly rigorous examination. Higher priority will be given to those who are expected to submit their dissertation thesis shortly after the completion of the fellowship. Preference will normally be given to doctoral candidates under 35 years of age.

Funds Avail.: No specific amount. **Duration:** Annual; 4-12 Months. **To Apply:** Applicants must have completed all academic requirements except the dissertation when they begin the fellowship and are expected to have sufficient proficiency in the Japanese language to pursue their research in Japan. Higher priority will be given to applicants who expect to submit their dissertation shortly after the completion of their fellowship. Three letters of reference; an evaluation of Japanese-language ability; and academic transcripts must accompany all applications. Other guidelines and procedures are available in the JFNY website. **Deadline:** November 3.

5307 ■ Japan Foundation, New York Long-Term Research Fellowship Program *(Professional development/Fellowship)*

Purpose: To support outstanding scholars in the field of Japanese Studies by offering the opportunity to conduct research in Japan. **Focus:** Japanese studies. **Qualif.:** Applicants must be scholars and researchers in the humanities or social sciences and holding Ph.D. or equivalent professional experience. **Criteria:** Priority will be given to relatively junior scholars and researchers and to those with less research experience in Japan.

Funds Avail.: No specific amount. **Duration:** Annual; 2-12 months. **To Apply:** Applicants must submit the two pages application form; three letters of reference; letter of affiliation; Japanese Language Ability Assessment Form; and an official transcript of records. For those who have U.S. citizenship or permanent residency should complete the application materials and submit them to the Japan Foundation New York Office. Applications should be sent directly by mail only. U.S. citizenship holders should use a different form, which is available in the nearest Japan Foundation office or Japanese diplomatic mission. Multiple applications will make all applications invalid. Other guidelines and procedures are available in the website. **Deadline:** November 3.

5308 ■ Japan Foundation, New York Short-Term Fellowship Program *(Professional development/Fellowship)*

Purpose: To support outstanding scholars in the field of Japanese Studies by offering the opportunity to conduct research in Japan. **Focus:** Japanese studies. **Qualif.:** Applicants must be scholars and researchers in the humanities and social sciences who need to conduct intensive research in Japan, and holding Ph.D. or equivalent professional experience. **Criteria:** Recipients will be evaluated based on quality of the project. Priority will be given to relatively experienced scholars and researchers who are expected to publish their research results shortly after the completion of their fellowship.

Funds Avail.: No specific amount. **Duration:** Annual; 21-59 days. **To Apply:** Applicants who have U.S. citizenship or permanent residency should complete the application materials and submit them to the Japan Foundation New York Office. Two-page application form is required; three letters of reference; letter of affiliation; Japanese Language Ability Assessment Form; and an official transcript of grades. Applications and other supporting documents should be sent directly (by mail only) to the JFNY office. Other guidelines and procedures are available in the JFNY website. **Deadline:** November 3.

5309 ■ Japanese American Bar Association (JABA)

PO Box 71961
Los Angeles, CA 90071
E-mail: info@jabaonline.org
URL: www.jabaonline.org

5310 ■ Justice John F. Aiso Scholarships *(Undergraduate/Scholarship)*

Purpose: To support deserving law students and/or recent law school graduates. **Focus:** Law. **Qualif.:** Applicants must be law students who have the following criteria: service in the Asian Pacific American community; financial need; overcoming adversity; academic achievement; desire to practice law in the Southern California area. **Criteria:** Selection will be based on the committee's criteria.

Funds Avail.: $2,000. **Duration:** Annual. **To Apply:** Applicants must visit the website for the online application process. Applicants must also include their most recent of-

Awards are arranged alphabetically below their administering organizations

ficial or unofficial law school transcript, current resume and personal statement of no more than 500 words. Send completed application through email on or before the deadline. **Deadline:** January 18. **Contact:** JABA Scholarships at JEFSCHOLARSHIP@gmail.com.

5311 ■ Japanese American Bar Association Scholarships *(Graduate, Undergraduate/Scholarship)*

Purpose: To encourage pursuits in legal education among law students with ethnic backgrounds. **Focus:** Law. **Qualif.:** Applicants must be law students of various ethnic backgrounds. **Criteria:** Selection will be based on academic achievement, financial need, overcoming adversity, and desire to practice law in the Southern California.

Funds Avail.: $2,000 each. **Number Awarded:** 5. **To Apply:** Applicants must submit completed application along with their most recent law school transcript, current resume and a personal statement of no more than 500 words. **Deadline:** January 18. **Remarks:** Established in 2006. **Contact:** Jeff Maloney and Allyson Sakai, Scholarship, Committee Co-Chairs, at JEFscholarship@gmail.com.

5312 ■ Judge Edward Y. Kakita Memorial Scholarships *(Undergraduate/Scholarship)*

Purpose: To support deserving law students and/or recent law school graduates. **Focus:** Law. **Qualif.:** Applicants must be law students who have the following criteria: service in the Asian Pacific American community; financial need; overcoming adversity; academic achievement; desire to practice law in the Southern California area; desire to practice in the areas of international law, commercial litigation and/or corporate law. **Criteria:** Selection will be based on the committee's criteria.

Funds Avail.: $2,000. **Duration:** Annual. **To Apply:** Applicants must visit the website for the online application process. Applicants must also include their most recent official or unofficial law school transcript, current resume and personal statement of no more than 500 words. Send completed application through email on or before the deadline. **Deadline:** January 18. **Remarks:** Established in 2006. **Contact:** JABA Scholarships at JEFscholarship@gmail.com.

5313 ■ Lim Ruger Foundation Scholarships *(Undergraduate/Scholarship)*

Purpose: To support minority law students who are pursuing of a more equitable society. **Focus:** Law. **Qualif.:** Applicants must be law students who have the following criteria: service in the Asian Pacific American community; financial need; overcoming adversity; academic achievement; desire to practice law in the Southern California area. **Criteria:** Selection will be based on the committee's criteria.

Funds Avail.: $2,000. **Duration:** Annual. **To Apply:** Applicants must visit the website for the online application process. Applicants must also include their most recent official or unofficial law school transcript, current resume and personal statement of no more than 500 words. Send completed application through email on or before the deadline. **Deadline:** January 18. **Remarks:** Established in 2007. **Contact:** JABA Scholarships at JEFscholarship@gmail.com.

5314 ■ Justice Stephen K. Tamura Scholarships *(Undergraduate/Scholarship)*

Purpose: To support deserving law students and/or recent law school graduates. **Focus:** Law. **Qualif.:** Applicants

must be law students who have the following criteria: service in the Asian Pacific American community; financial need; overcoming adversity; academic achievement; desire to practice law in the Southern California area. **Criteria:** Selection will be based on the committee's criteria.

Funds Avail.: $2,000. **Duration:** Annual. **To Apply:** Applicants must visit the website for the online application process. Applicants must also include their most recent official or unofficial law school transcript, current resume and personal statement of no more than 500 words. Send completed application through email on or before the deadline. **Deadline:** January 18. **Contact:** JABA Scholarships at JEFscholarship@gmail.com.

5315 ■ Japanese American Citizens League (JACL)
1765 Sutter St.
San Francisco, CA 94115
Ph: (415)345-1075
E-mail: ncwnp@jacl.org
URL: www.jacl.org

5316 ■ Kyutaro and Yasuo Abiko Memorial Scholarships *(Undergraduate/Scholarship)*

Purpose: To provide financial assistance for qualified individuals. **Focus:** Agriculture, Economic aspects; Journalism. **Qualif.:** Applicants must be active National JACL members at either individual or Student/Youth level; must be planning to attend full-time at a college, university, trade school, business school, or any other institution of higher learning within the United States at the undergraduate or graduate school level. Freshman applicants must be high school seniors. **Criteria:** Preference will be given to a student studying journalism or agriculture.

Funds Avail.: No specific amount. **Duration:** Annual. **To Apply:** Applicants must fill out completely the provided application then submit such together with the following: JACL Membership, Personal Statement, Letter of Recommendation, Official Transcripts including SAT and/or ACT test score verification, Work Experience, and JACL and Community Involvement. **Deadline:** April 1. **Contact:** JACL Membership Department or Membership Coordinator Annie Noguchi: anoguchi@jacl.org.

5317 ■ Grace Andow Memorial Scholarships *(Undergraduate, Graduate/Scholarship)*

Purpose: To support qualified students in pursuing their educational dreams. **Focus:** Law. **Qualif.:** Applicants must be active National JACL members; must be planning to attend full-time college, university, or any other institution of higher learning within the United States at the undergraduate or graduate level. **Criteria:** Selection will be based on the committee's criteria.

Funds Avail.: No specific amount. **To Apply:** Applications can be obtained at the website. The following supporting documents are required to complete the JACL Scholarship Application: JACL Membership; personal statement; letter of recommendation; official transcripts including SAT and/or ACT test score verification; work experience; community involvement. **Deadline:** April 1.

5318 ■ Alice Yuriko Endo Memorial Scholarships *(Undergraduate/Scholarship)*

Purpose: To provide financial assistance for qualified individuals. **Focus:** Public service; Social work. **Qualif.:**

Awards are arranged alphabetically below their administering organizations

Applicants must be active National JACL members at either individual or Student/Youth level; must be planning to attend full-time at a college, university, trade school, business school, or any other institution of higher learning within the United States at the undergraduate or graduate school level. Freshman applicants must be high school seniors. **Criteria:** Preference for this scholarship will be given to a student residing in the Eastern District Council and/or a student with an interest in public and social service.

Funds Avail.: No specific amount. **Duration:** Annual. **To Apply:** Applicants must fill out completely the provided application then submit such together with the following: JACL Membership, Personal Statement, Letter of Recommendation, Official Transcripts including SAT and/or ACT test score verification, Work Experience, and JACL and Community Involvement. **Deadline:** April 1. **Contact:** JACL Membership Department or Membership Coordinator Annie Noguchi at anoguchi@jacl.org.

5319 ■ Thomas T. Hayashi Memorial Scholarships (Graduate/Scholarship)

Purpose: To support individuals who are planning to pursue a legal profession. **Focus:** Law. **Qualif.:** Applicant must be an active National JACL member at either an individual or student/youth level; must be planning to attend full-time at a college, university, trade school, business school or any other institution of higher learning within the United States at the graduate school level. **Criteria:** Recipients will be selected based on their application requirements.

Funds Avail.: No specific amount. **Duration:** Annual. **To Apply:** Applicant must fill out completely the provided application then submit such together with the following: JACL Membership, Personal Statement, Letter of Recommendation, Official Transcripts including SAT and/or ACT test score verification, Work Experience, and JACL and Community Involvement. **Deadline:** April 1. **Contact:** JACL Membership Department or Membership Coordinator Annie Noguchi: anoguchi@jacl.org.

5320 ■ Magoichi and Shizuko Kato Memorial Scholarships (Graduate, Master's, Doctorate/Scholarship)

Purpose: To provide financial assistance for qualified individuals. **Focus:** Medicine. **Qualif.:** Applicants must be active National JACL members at either individual or Student/Youth level; must be planning to attend full-time at a college, university, trade school, business school, or any other institution of higher learning within the United States at the undergraduate or graduate school level. **Criteria:** Preference will be given to a student planning a career in medicine or ministry.

Funds Avail.: No specific amount. **Duration:** Annual. **To Apply:** Applicants must fill out completely the provided application then submit such together with the following: JACL Membership, Personal Statement, Letter of Recommendation, Official Transcripts including SAT and/or ACT test score verification, Work Experience, and JACL and Community Involvement. **Deadline:** April 1. **Contact:** JACL Membership Department or Membership Coordinator Annie Noguchi: anoguchi@jacl.org.

5321 ■ Sam and Florice Kuwahara Memorial Scholarship (Undergraduate/Scholarship)

Purpose: To provide financial support for qualified students intending to pursue their education. **Focus:** Agriculture, Economic aspects. **Qualif.:** Applicants must be active National JACL members at either individual or Student/

Youth level; must be planning to attend full-time at a college, university, trade school, business school, or any other institution of higher learning within the United States at the undergraduate or graduate school level. Freshman applicants must be high school seniors. **Criteria:** Preference for this scholarship will be given to students with an interest in agriculture or related field.

Funds Avail.: No specific amount. **Duration:** Annual. **To Apply:** Applicants must fill out completely the provided application then submit such together with the following: JACL Membership, Personal Statement, Letter of Recommendation, Official Transcripts including SAT and/or ACT test score verification, Work Experience, and JACL and Community Involvement. **Deadline:** March 2. **Remarks:** Established in 2009. **Contact:** JACL Membership Department or Membership Coordinator Annie Noguchi: anoguchi@jacl.org.

5322 ■ Henry and Chiyo Kuwahara Memorial Scholarships (Undergraduate, Graduate/Scholarship)

Purpose: To help qualified students nationwide to achieve their educational dreams with the scholarship. **Focus:** General studies/Field of study not specified. **Qualif.:** Applicants must be active National JACL members; must be planning to attend full-time college, university, trade school, business school or any other institution of higher learning within the United States at the graduate school level. **Criteria:** Selection will be based on the committee's criteria.

Funds Avail.: No specific amount. **To Apply:** The application can be obtained at the website. The following supporting documents are required to complete the JACL Scholarship Application: JACL Membership; personal statement; letter of recommendation; official transcripts including SAT and/or ACT test score verification; work experience; community involvement. **Deadline:** April 1.

5323 ■ Mary Reiko Osaka Memorial Scholarships (Undergraduate, Graduate/Scholarship)

Purpose: To support qualified students in pursuing their educational dreams. **Focus:** Law. **Qualif.:** Applicants must be active National JACL members; must be planning to attend full-time college, university, or any other institution of higher learning within the United States at the undergraduate or graduate level. **Criteria:** Selection will be based on the committee's criteria.

Funds Avail.: No specific amount. **To Apply:** Applications can be obtained at the website. The following supporting documents are required to complete the JACL Scholarship Application: JACL Membership; personal statement; letter of recommendation; official transcripts including SAT and/or ACT test score verification; work experience; community involvement. **Deadline:** April 1.

5324 ■ Railroad and Mine Workers Memorial Scholarships (Graduate/Scholarship)

Purpose: To help qualified students nationwide to achieve their educational dreams with the scholarship. **Focus:** General studies/Field of study not specified. **Qualif.:** Applicants must be active National JACL members; must be planning to attend full-time college, university, trade school, business school or any other institution of higher learning within the United States at the graduate school level. **Criteria:** Selection will be based on the committee's criteria.

Funds Avail.: No specific amount. **To Apply:** Applications can be obtained at the website. The following supporting documents are required to complete the JACL Scholarship

Awards are arranged alphabetically below their administering organizations

Application: JACL Membership; personal statement; letter of recommendation; official transcripts including SAT and/or ACT test score verification; work experience; community involvement. **Deadline:** April 1.

5325 ■ Sho Sato Memorial Scholarships
(Undergraduate, Graduate/Scholarship)

Purpose: To support qualified students in pursuing their educational dreams. **Focus:** Law. **Qualif.:** Applicants must be active National JACL members; must be planning to attend full-time college, university, or any other institution of higher learning within the United States at the undergraduate or graduate level. **Criteria:** Selection will be based on the committee's criteria.

Funds Avail.: No specific amount. **To Apply:** Applications can be obtained at the website. The following supporting documents are required to complete the JACL Scholarship Application: JACL Membership; personal statement; letter of recommendation; official transcripts including SAT and/or ACT test score verification; work experience; community involvement. **Deadline:** April 1.

5326 ■ Chiyoko and Thomas Shimazaki Scholarships *(Graduate/Award)*

Purpose: To help qualified students nationwide to achieve their educational dreams with the scholarship. **Focus:** General studies/Field of study not specified. **Qualif.:** Applicants must be active National JACL members; must be planning to attend full-time college, university, trade school, business school or any other institution of higher learning within the United States at the graduate school level. **Criteria:** Selection will be based on the committee's criteria.

Funds Avail.: No specific amount. **To Apply:** Applications can be obtained at the website. The following supporting documents are required to complete the JACL Scholarship Application: JACL membership; personal statement; letter of recommendation; official transcripts including SAT and/or ACT test score verification; work experience; community involvement. **Deadline:** April 1.

5327 ■ Dr. Kiyoshi Sonoda Memorial Scholarships
(Graduate, Master's, Doctorate/Scholarship)

Purpose: To provide financial assistance for qualified individuals. **Focus:** Dentistry. **Qualif.:** Applicants must be active National JACL members at either individual or Student/Youth level; must be planning to attend full-time at a college, university, trade school, business school, or any other institution of higher learning within the United States at the undergraduate or graduate school level. **Criteria:** Applicants will be selected based on the application requirements.

Funds Avail.: No specific amount. **Duration:** Annual. **To Apply:** Preference will be given to students studying in the field of dentistry. **Deadline:** April 1. **Contact:** JACL Membership Department or Membership Coordinator Annie Noguchi: anoguchi@jacl.org.

5328 ■ Reverend H. John Yamashita Memorial Scholarships *(Graduate/Scholarship)*

Purpose: To help qualified students nationwide to achieve their educational dreams with the scholarship. **Focus:** General studies/Field of study not specified. **Qualif.:** Applicants must be active National JACL members; must be planning to attend full-time college, university, trade school, business school or any other institution of higher learning within the United States at the graduate school level. **Criteria:** Selec-

tion will be based on the committee's criteria.

Funds Avail.: No specific amount. **To Apply:** Applications can be obtained at the website. The following supporting documents are required to complete the JACL Scholarship Application: JACL Membership; personal statement; letter of recommendation; official transcripts including SAT and/or ACT test score verification; work experience; community involvement. **Deadline:** April 1.

5329 ■ Minoru Yasui Memorial Scholarships *(Graduate, Master's, Doctorate/Scholarship)*

Purpose: To provide financial assistance for qualified individuals. **Focus:** Civil rights; Education; Human rights; Law; Sociology. **Qualif.:** Applicant must be an active National JACL member at either an individual or student/youth level; must be planning to attend full-time at a college, university, trade school, business school or any other institution of higher learning within the United States at the graduate school level. **Criteria:** Preference will be given to students with a strong interest in human rights and civil rights.

Funds Avail.: No specific amount. **Duration:** Annual. **To Apply:** Applicant must fill out completely the provided application then submit such together with the following: JACL Membership, Personal Statement, Letter of Recommendation, Official Transcripts including SAT and/or ACT test score verification, Work Experience, and JACL and Community Involvement. **Deadline:** April 1. **Contact:** JACL Membership Department or Membership Coordinator Annie Noguchi: anoguchi@jacl.org.

5330 ■ JCC Association
520 8th Ave.
New York, NY 10018
Ph: (212)532-4949
Fax: (212)481-4174
URL: www.jcca.org

5331 ■ JCC Association Graduate Education Scholarships *(Graduate/Scholarship)*

Purpose: To provide exceptionally talented and highly motivated individuals with a scholarship that enables them to pursue a graduate course of study leading to a career in the JCC Movement. **Focus:** Education, Early childhood; Education, Physical; Health education. **Qualif.:** Applicant must be a full-time student pursuing graduate studies that lead to a professional career in the JCC Movement. **Criteria:** Selection is based on the submitted application materials.

Funds Avail.: $20,000. **Duration:** 2 years. **Number Awarded:** 3. **To Apply:** Applicants must submit a completed application form together with a two-page personal essay, university transcripts, and 5 letters of reference from individuals who have been listed by the applicant.

5332 ■ Jefferson Scholars Foundation
112 Clarke St.
Charlottesville, VA 22903
Ph: (434)243-9029
Fax: (434)243-9081
E-mail: jeffsch@virginia.edu
URL: www.jeffersonscholars.org

5333 ■ Jefferson Graduate Fellowships *(Doctorate, Graduate/Fellowship)*

Purpose: To attract Ph.D. and M.B.A. candidates who demonstrate outstanding achievement and the highest

Awards are arranged alphabetically below their administering organizations

promise as scholars, teachers, public servants, and business leaders in the United States and beyond. **Focus:** General studies/Field of study not specified. **Qualif.:** Candidates must be seeking a PhD, MBA or JD and show outstanding achievement and the highest promise as scholars, teachers, public servants and business leaders in the United States and beyond; and must be admitted to the University of Virginia. **Criteria:** Recipients will be selected based on merit.

Funds Avail.: Varies. **To Apply:** Applicants must check the website for the proper guidelines and required materials. **Remarks:** Established in 2001. **Contact:** Jefferson Scholars Foundation, at the above address.

5334 ■ Jefferson Science Associates L.L.C. (JSA)

1201 New York Ave., Ste. 430
1201 New York Ave., Ste. 430
Washington, DC 20005
Ph: (202)408-2410
E-mail: kubiak@sura.org
URL: www.jsallc.org

5335 ■ JSA/Jefferson Lab Graduate Fellowships
(Doctorate, Graduate/Fellowship)

Purpose: To provide the environment and financial resources for graduate students to work alongside Jefferson Lab researchers as they continue their academic studies and pursue research opportunities in this field of science. **Focus:** Science. **Qualif.:** Applicant must be enrolled full-time in a relevant doctoral program at a SURA member university. **Criteria:** Selection is based on: Merit and quality of proposed research based on applicant's research plan; Utility and relevance of proposed research to the Jefferson Lab, including proposed utilization of Lab resources; Likelihood that proposed research objectives can be accomplished by graduation.

Funds Avail.: $2,000 - $10,000. **Duration:** Annual. **Number Awarded:** 8. **To Apply:** Applicants must submit a completed application form including a completed reference form from three individuals for letters of recommendation. **Remarks:** Established in 1989.

5336 ■ The Jewish Community Foundation of Montreal

1 Qummings Square
Montreal, QC, Canada H3W 1M6
Ph: (514)345-6414
Fax: (514)345-6410
URL: www.jcfmontreal.org/en/home

5337 ■ Evelyn Joy Abramowicz Memorial Scholarships *(Undergraduate/Scholarship)*

Purpose: To support students with disabilities entering CEGEP or enrolled in university programs. **Focus:** Jewish studies. **Qualif.:** Applicants must be students with disability and good academic standing. **Criteria:** Preference will be given to first time applicants.

Funds Avail.: No specific amount. **To Apply:** Applicants must submit the following requirements: letter of acceptance from a university or proof of enrollment; letter of application outlining disability and reasons for request; transcripts of grades; proof of Quebec residency; social insurance number; Montreal address and telephone number; e-mail address. **Deadline:** May 31.

5338 ■ Jenny Panitch Beckow Memorial Scholarships Canada *(Undergraduate, Graduate/Scholarship)*

Purpose: To provide financial assistance for Israeli students. **Focus:** Jewish studies. **Qualif.:** Applicants must be Israeli students of any age who are entering into or who are currently enrolled in a program of graduate studies at a Canadian university with good academic standing. **Criteria:** Selection will be based on the committee's criteria.

Funds Avail.: $18,000. **To Apply:** Applicants must submit the following requirements: letter of application setting forth area of study and proposed post-graduate plans; transcripts; two letters of reference; proof of Israeli citizenship; letter of acceptance to college or university or proof that studies have commenced at that institution; social insurance number or Israeli equivalent; e-mail address.

5339 ■ Jenny Panitch Beckow Memorial Scholarships Israel *(Graduate/Scholarship)*

Purpose: To assist Canadian students in their graduate study or research at an Israeli university. **Focus:** Art; Culture; Literature; Medicine; Music; Science. **Qualif.:** Applicants must be Canadian students who are entering into or are currently enrolled in a program of graduate studies at an Israeli university. **Criteria:** Selection will be based on merit. Preference will be given to first time applicants.

Funds Avail.: 18,000 Canadian Dollars. **To Apply:** Applicants must submit the following requirements: letter of application setting forth area of study and proposed postgraduate plans; transcripts; two letters of reference; proof of Canadian citizenship; letter of acceptance to college or university or proof that studies have commenced at that institution; social insurance number; and email address. Moreover, they must submit progress report within 6 months after commencement of study and a final report within 60 days after completing the academic year. **Deadline:** March 15. **Contact:** Jenny Panitch Beckow Memorial Scholarships, c/o Michael Vineberg, 2600-1501 McGill College 26th Fl., Montreal, Quebec, Canada H3A 3N9.

5340 ■ Therese and David Bohbot Scholarships *(Undergraduate/Scholarship)*

Purpose: To assist needy university students who require additional assistance for living expenses. **Focus:** General studies/Field of study not specified. **Qualif.:** Applicants must be residents of Quebec who are planning to enroll, or currently enrolled, in Montreal University. **Criteria:** Selection will be based on financial need and history of involvement in community work.

Funds Avail.: No specific amount. **To Apply:** Applicants must submit the following requirements: letter explaining goals/reasons for request; proof of Quebec residency; grade transcripts; acceptance letter to University (1st yr. students); two letters of reference; Social Insurance number; and Montreal address and telephone number. **Deadline:** May 31.

5341 ■ Stephen Bronfman Scholarship Funds in Environmental Studies *(Graduate/Scholarship)*

Purpose: To enrich environmental research among graduate level students. **Focus:** Environmental science. **Qualif.:** Applicants must be legal residents of Quebec; must be second year Masters or Ph.D. students in a recognized environmental graduate program anywhere in the world. **Criteria:** Selection will be based on the committee's criteria.

Funds Avail.: 7,500 Canadian Dollars (6,000 of such will be received as first payment; 1,500 will be awarded in the

Awards are arranged alphabetically below their administering organizations

final). **To Apply:** Applicants must submit a maximum two-page letter outlining, in order of importance: how the scholarship will (one or a combination of these): further environmental research and studies; have eventual concrete applications for natural or urban communities; assist in original research; offset travel costs to actively participate in scientific conferences; and, how the scholarship will assist the applicants (financial need) and/or reward their academic excellence and/or exceptional environmental engagement. The letter would need to be completed with the following application requirements: curriculum vitae highlighting personal, academic and professional achievements; official transcript of academic results; social insurance number; email address; two letters of recommendation from professors and/or mentors supervising the students' work that confirms the pertinence of the research being assisted and/or how the scholarship will enrich the student' studies; and proof of full-time status at the time of the request. **Deadline:** May 31.

5342 ■ Bernice and Gordon Brown Scholarships
(Undergraduate/Scholarship)

Purpose: To support Montreal students in their study and participation in the Jewish community. **Focus:** Jewish studies. **Qualif.:** Applicants must be permanent residents of Montreal who have demonstrated academic excellence and agree to return to Montreal and participate in the Jewish community. **Criteria:** Selection will be based on the aforesaid eligibility and compliance with the application process.

Funds Avail.: Up to 5,000 Canadian Dollars. **To Apply:** Applicants must submit the following requirements: completed application form; brief letter outlining reasons for wishing to attend university in Israel and career goals; record of involvement in Jewish community; letter of acceptance from an Israeli university; transcript of grades (CEGEP and/or university) and final midterm marks; minimum of 2 letters of recommendation from professors; Social Insurance Number; Montreal address and telephone number; and email address. **Deadline:** May 30.

5343 ■ Hadar Chemtob Memorial Scholarships
(Undergraduate/Scholarship)

Purpose: To support aspiring students wishing to pursue a career in fashion. **Focus:** Fashion design. **Qualif.:** Applicants must be students pursuing a career in fashion. **Criteria:** Selection will be based on the committee's criteria.

Funds Avail.: No specific amount. **Duration:** Annual. **To Apply:** Applicants must complete the following requirements: letter stating objectives and reasons for request; proof of Quebec residency; letter of acceptance for fashion studies program; transcript of grades; two letters of recommendation from teachers or employers; Social Insurance Number; Montreal address and telephone number; e-mail address. **Deadline:** May 31.

5344 ■ Ruth and Victor David Scholarships
(Undergraduate, Graduate/Scholarship)

Purpose: To provide educational expenses for deserving students. **Focus:** Education. **Qualif.:** Applicants must be students enrolled in undergraduate or graduate studies in Montreal or in Israel with good academic standing. **Criteria:** Selection will be based on the committee's criteria.

Funds Avail.: $3,000. **Duration:** Annual. **To Apply:** Applicants must submit the following requirements: letter stating objectives and reasons for request; proof of Quebec residency; letter of university acceptance; transcript of

grades; community involvement; two letters of recommendation from teachers or employers; Social Insurance Number; Montreal address and telephone number; e-mail address. **Deadline:** May 31.

5345 ■ Harry Feldman Memorial Scholarships
(Undergraduate/Scholarship)

Purpose: To support Quebec students in their education. **Focus:** Business. **Qualif.:** Applicants must be undergraduate students who are majoring in business and attending a university in Montreal or in Israel. **Criteria:** Selection will be based on need and merit.

Funds Avail.: No specific amount. **To Apply:** Applicants must submit the following requirements: letter explaining goals/reasons for request; proof of Quebec residency; grade transcripts; acceptance letter to University (1st yr. students); two letters of reference; Social Insurance number; email address; and Montreal address and telephone number. **Deadline:** May 31.

5346 ■ Jack Gitlitz CA Memorial Scholarships for Study in Israel *(Undergraduate/Scholarship)*

Purpose: To support Montreal students in their study and participation in the Jewish community. **Focus:** Jewish studies. **Qualif.:** Applicants must be permanent residents of Montreal who have demonstrated academic excellence and agree to return to Montreal and participate in the Jewish community. **Criteria:** Selection will be based on the aforesaid eligibility and compliance with the application process.

Funds Avail.: 5,000 Canadian Dollars each. **Number Awarded:** 2. **To Apply:** Applicants must submit the following requirements: completed application form; brief letter outlining reasons for wishing to attend university in Israel and career goals; record of involvement in Jewish community; letter of acceptance from an Israeli university; transcript of grades (CEGEP and/or university) and final midterm marks; minimum of 2 letters of recommendation from professors; Social Insurance Number; email address; and Montreal address and telephone number. **Deadline:** May 30.

5347 ■ Harry Hopmeyer Memorial Scholarships
(Undergraduate/Scholarship)

Purpose: To support Quebec students in their education. **Focus:** General studies/Field of study not specified. **Qualif.:** Applicants must be Quebec students enrolled in undergraduate university studies in Montreal. **Criteria:** Selection will be based on need and merit.

Funds Avail.: No specific amount. **To Apply:** Applicants must submit the following requirements: letter explaining goals/reasons for request; proof of Quebec residency; grade transcripts; acceptance letter to University (1st yr. students); two letters of recommendation from teachers or employers; Social Insurance number; email address; and Montreal address and telephone number. **Deadline:** May 31.

5348 ■ Mitchell Karper Memorial Scholarships
(Undergraduate/Scholarship)

Purpose: To support Montreal students in their study and participation in the Jewish community. **Focus:** Jewish studies. **Qualif.:** Applicants must be permanent residents of Montreal who have demonstrated academic excellence and agree to return to Montreal and participate in the Jewish community. **Criteria:** Selection will be based on the

Awards are arranged alphabetically below their administering organizations

aforesaid eligibility and compliance with the application process.

Funds Avail.: Up to 10,000 Canadian Dollars. **To Apply:** Applicants must submit the following requirements: completed application form; brief letter outlining reasons for wishing to attend university in Israel and career goals; record of involvement in Jewish community; letter of acceptance from an Israeli university; transcript of grades (CEGEP and/or university) and final midterm marks; minimum of 2 letters of recommendation from professors; Social Insurance Number; and Montreal address and telephone number. **Deadline:** May 30.

5349 ■ Joseph Katz Memorial Scholarships
(Undergraduate/Scholarship)

Purpose: To assist Quebec students in their education. **Focus:** General studies/Field of study not specified. **Qualif.:** Applicants must be university students living and studying in Montreal. **Criteria:** Selection will be based on financial need and academic achievement. Preference will be given to first time applicants under 25 years old.

Funds Avail.: No specific amount. **To Apply:** Applicants must submit the following requirements: letter explaining goals/reasons for request; proof of Quebec residency; grade transcripts; acceptance letter to University (if applicable); two letters of recommendation from teachers or employers; Social Insurance number; email address; and Montreal address and telephone number. **Deadline:** May 31.

5350 ■ Micki and Norm Keesal Scholarships
(Undergraduate/Scholarship)

Purpose: To support McGill students in their education. **Focus:** General studies/Field of study not specified. **Qualif.:** Applicants must be McGill undergraduate students. **Criteria:** Selection will be based on demonstrated academic excellence.

Funds Avail.: No specific amount. **To Apply:** Applicants must submit the following requirements: letter stating objectives and reasons for request; proof of Quebec residency; letter of university acceptance; transcript of grades; two letters of recommendation from teachers or employers; Social Insurance Number; and Montreal address, telephone number and email address. **Deadline:** May 31.

5351 ■ Henriette and Marcel Korner Scholarships
(Undergraduate/Scholarship)

Purpose: To support students in their study at Montreal CEGEP. **Focus:** General studies/Field of study not specified. **Qualif.:** Applicants must be permanent residents of Quebec. **Criteria:** Selection will be based on the involvement in the Jewish community.

Funds Avail.: No specific amount. **To Apply:** Applicants must submit the following requirements: letter stating objectives and reasons for request; proof of Quebec residency; letter of university acceptance; transcript of grades; two letters of recommendation from teachers or employers; Social Insurance Number; and Montreal address, telephone number and email address. **Deadline:** May 31.

5352 ■ Liela Klinger Kurztman Memorial Scholarships
(Undergraduate/Scholarship)

Purpose: To support Quebec students in their education. **Focus:** Education. **Qualif.:** Applicants must be students entering, or already in, the Faculty of Education. **Criteria:** Selection will be based on academic merit. Preference will

be given to first time candidates under the age of 25.

Funds Avail.: No specific amount. **To Apply:** Applicants must submit the following requirements: letter of acceptance to graduate or post graduate studies in Montreal; letter of application outlining need and goals; transcripts of grades; proof of Quebec residency; two letters of recommendation from professors; Social Insurance Number; Montreal address, telephone number and email address. **Deadline:** May 31.

5353 ■ Karen E. Latt Memorial Scholarships
(Graduate/Scholarship)

Purpose: To support female graduates entering medical school. **Focus:** Medicine. **Qualif.:** Applicants must be female graduates planning to enter in medical school. **Criteria:** Selection will be based on the committee's criteria.

Funds Avail.: No specific amount. **To Apply:** Applicants must submit the following requirements: letter stating goals; reasons for request; letter of acceptance to medical school for the coming academic year; scholastic performance; two letters of recommendation from professors; involvement in extracurricular activities and athletics; e-mail address. **Deadline:** May 31.

5354 ■ Irene Brand Lieberman Memorial Scholarships
(Graduate, Postgraduate/Scholarship)

Purpose: To support graduate students in their studies related to children. **Focus:** General studies/Field of study not specified. **Qualif.:** Applicants must be legal residents of Quebec; must be university graduate students enrolled in a course of study related to children. **Criteria:** Selection will be based on academic merit. Preference will be given to the applicants' need and community involvement.

Funds Avail.: No specific amount. **To Apply:** Applicants must submit the following requirements: letter of acceptance to graduate or postgraduate studies in Montreal; letter of application outlining need and goals; transcripts of grades; proof of Quebec residency; two letters of recommendation from professors; Social Insurance Number; and Montreal address and telephone number and email address. **Deadline:** May 31.

5355 ■ Musia and Leon Schwartz Scholarships
(Undergraduate, Graduate/Scholarship)

Purpose: To support students involved in the humanities with a focus on tolerance and historical events, such as the Holocaust, and the resulting consequences. **Focus:** Humanities. **Qualif.:** Applicants must be graduate or undergraduate students with good academic standing; must be 35 years old or younger, **Criteria:** Selection will be based on the committee's criteria.

Funds Avail.: No specific amount. **Duration:** Annual. **To Apply:** Applicants must submit the following requirements: letter of application describing project, planned use of funds; proof of Quebec residency; university transcripts; proof of age; Social Insurance number; e-mail address. **Deadline:** May 31.

5356 ■ Jean and Manny Spinner Scholarships
(Undergraduate/Scholarship)

Purpose: To provide support to recent immigrants who require assistance for university, professional or vocational study. **Focus:** General studies/Field of study not specified. **Qualif.:** Applicants must be Canadian citizens or have immigrated to Canada within the last ten years and residing in Quebec; must be students enrolling or already enrolled

Awards are arranged alphabetically below their administering organizations

at the college or university level or in professional/ vocational training programs. **Criteria:** Selection will be based on academic merit.

Funds Avail.: No specific amount. **To Apply:** Applicants must contact the Agence Ometz Scholarship Committee for more information and instructions on the application. **Remarks:** The scholarship is administered by Agence Ometz. **Contact:** Olga Davydova at olga.davydova@ometz.ca.

5357 ■ Bernard Michael Tarshis Memorial Scholarships for Jewish Studies (Undergraduate/Scholarship)

Purpose: To assist students in their Jewish studies at McGill. **Focus:** Jewish studies. **Qualif.:** Applicants must be permanent residents of Quebec. **Criteria:** Selection will be based on the committee's criteria.

Funds Avail.: Up to 4,000 Canadian Dollars. **To Apply:** Applicants may visit the website for further information on the application process.

5358 ■ Dr. Steven S. Zalcman Memorial Scholarships (Graduate, Postgraduate/Scholarship)

Purpose: To support students in their specialization in behavioral neuroscience, neuroimmunology, psychoneuroimmunology, or a related field. **Focus:** Immunology; Neurology; Neuroscience. **Qualif.:** Applicants must be graduate or medical students who demonstrated interest in pursuing research in behavioural neuroscience, neuroimmunology, psychoneuroimmunology, or a related field. **Criteria:** Selection will be based on the committee's criteria.

Funds Avail.: No specific amount. **To Apply:** Applicants must submit the following requirements: letter of application describing research intentions and any past or current research the applicants have undertaken; letters of reference from a research supervisor or a professor; university transcripts; social insurance number; and email address. **Deadline:** May 31.

5359 ■ Jewish Guild for the Blind (JGB)
15 W 65th St.
New York, NY 10023-6601
Ph: (212)769-6200
Fax: (212)769-6266
Free: 800-284-4422
E-mail: info@guildhealth.org
URL: www.guildhealth.org

5360 ■ GuildScholar Awards (Undergraduate/Scholarship)

Purpose: To assist blind high school students to pursue college. **Focus:** General studies/Field of study not specified. **Qualif.:** Applicants must be legally blind high school students and be U.S. citizens. **Criteria:** Scholarship recipients will be selected based on Selection Committee's review of the application materials.

Funds Avail.: $15,000. **Number Awarded:** 12-16. **To Apply:** Applicants must provide (in .tif, .jpeg or .pdf format) proof of legal blindness; proof of U.S. citizenship; documentation of academic achievement; three letters of recommendation and two personal statements. Applicants are required to apply online. **Deadline:** September 15. **Remarks:** Chosen school must be accredited by the Council of Higher Education Accreditation. **Contact:** Gordon Rovins, 212-769-7801 or guildscholar@jgb.org.

5361 ■ Jewish Vocational Service (JVS)
216 W Jackson Blvd., Ste. 700
Chicago, IL 60606
Ph: (312)673-3400
Fax: (312)553-5544
Free: 855-463-6587
E-mail: info@jvschicago.org
URL: www.jvschicago.org

5362 ■ Jewish Federation Academic Scholarships (Graduate, Undergraduate/Scholarship)

Purpose: To support the education of a Jewish college or graduate student. **Focus:** Arts; Education; Law; Medicine; Public health; Social work; Urban affairs/design/planning. **Qualif.:** Applicant must be Jewish; be born or raised in either: Cook County, Chicago metropolitan area, or Northwest Indiana; or have one continuous year of full-time employment in Cook County or Chicago metropolitan area prior to starting professional education; must intend to remain in the Chicago metropolitan area after completing school; must be entering as a full-time student in an accredited professional graduate program or entering as junior or senior undergraduate student at an accredited professional education program; and must be demonstrating career promise in a helping profession. **Criteria:** Award will be given based on need.

Funds Avail.: $1,000 - $8,000. **Duration:** Annual. **To Apply:** Applicant must submit a completed Application Data Form; Career Statement Form; Budget Worksheet; and Academic Budget form as an attachment. In addition, applicants must send by mail a Legal Domicility Form; two letter of reference form; IRS Forms; parents' or spouse's IRS; documentation of tuition cost; Release of Information form; and official transcripts. **Deadline:** February 1. **Contact:** JVS Chicago, at jvsscholarship@jvschicago.org.

5363 ■ Jim Dodson Law
310 Wildwood Way
Clearwater, FL 33756
Ph: (727)446-0840
Free: 888-207-0905
URL: www.jimdodsonlaw.com

5364 ■ Jim Dodson Law Scholarships (Undergraduate/Scholarship)

Purpose: To encourage students in furthering their education through creativity and innovation in road safety. **Focus:** General studies/Field of study not specified. **Qualif.:** Applicants must be Florida residents who may be enrolled in any college in the United States, or currently enrolled in a 4-year college as full- or part-time students; must have a 3.0 GPA; and must be successfully completed 12 credit hours of college courses. **Criteria:** Selection will be based on the committee's criteria. Demonstration of community involvement or volunteer experience is a plus.

Funds Avail.: $1,500. **To Apply:** Applicants are required to submit an innovative and educational video (video guidelines are enumerated at the scholarship website). Video must be 90 seconds or less; should show creativity and have a clear and effective message; must demonstrate their solution to enhanced bicycle, pedestrian and/or motor vehicle safety or any one of three; and must be uploaded to YouTube. **Deadline:** November 10. **Contact:** kati@jimdodsonlaw.com.

Awards are arranged alphabetically below their administering organizations

5365 ■ Johns Hopkins Medicine - Department of Emergency Medicine

1830 East Monument St., Ste. 6-100
Baltimore, MD 21287
Ph: (410)955-8708
Fax: (410)955-0141
URL: www.hopkinsmedicine.org/emergencymedicine

5366 ■ Johns Hopkins Department of Emergency Medicine Administration Fellowships *(Advanced Professional, Professional development/Fellowship)*

Purpose: To educate the next generation of business and operational leaders in Emergency Medicine. **Focus:** Emergency and disaster services; Medicine. **Qualif.:** Candidate must be Board Certified or Prepared in Emergency Medicine. **Criteria:** Selection will be based on the committee's criteria.

Funds Avail.: No specific amount. **Duration:** One year. **To Apply:** Interested applicants must contact the Department for the application process. **Contact:** James Scheulen, PA-C, MBA; Email: scheule@jhmi.edu.

5367 ■ Johns Hopkins Department of Emergency Medicine Critical Care Fellowships *(Advanced Professional, Professional development/Fellowship)*

Purpose: To train board prepared Emergency Medicine physicians to become nationally recognized leaders in critical care and emergency medicine. **Focus:** Emergency and disaster services; Medicine. **Qualif.:** Applicants must be Board Prepared or Certified in Emergency Medicine. **Criteria:** Selection will be based on the committee's criteria.

Funds Avail.: No specific amount. **Duration:** Two years. **To Apply:** Interested applicants must contact the Department for the application process. **Contact:** Julius Pham, MD; Email: jpham3@jhmi.edu.

5368 ■ Johns Hopkins Medicine Disaster Fellowships *(Professional development/Fellowship)*

Purpose: To train academic and management leaders in disaster preparedness, response, and research. **Focus:** Emergency and disaster services. **Qualif.:** Applicants must be Board Certified or Prepared in Emergency Medicine. Other post-graduate physician applicants may be considered. **Criteria:** Selection will be based on the committee's criteria.

Funds Avail.: No specific amount. **Duration:** Annual. **To Apply:** Interested applicants should contact the Fellowship Director for more information and should provide: personal statement and curriculum vitae (CV), and two letters of recommendation.

5369 ■ Johns Hopkins Medicine Emergency Medical Services Fellowship *(Professional development/Fellowship)*

Purpose: To prepare highly qualified and motivated academic emergency physicians for leadership and medical oversight of pre- and out-of-hospital emergency care systems with advanced competencies in EMS system design, administration, and clinical care. **Focus:** Emergency and disaster services; Medicine. **Qualif.:** Applicants must be Board Prepared or Certified in Emergency Medicine. **Criteria:** Selection will be based on the committee's criteria.

Funds Avail.: No specific amount. **Duration:** Annual. **To Apply:** Interested applicants must contact the Department for the application process.

5370 ■ Johns Hopkins Medicine International Emergency and Public Health Fellowships *(Graduate/Fellowship)*

Purpose: To develop an area of expertise in public health and international emergency medicine for physicians interested in pursuing a career in global health research and practice. **Focus:** Emergency and disaster services; Public health. **Qualif.:** Candidate must have graduate training in Emergency Medicine only; must produce at least 1 peer reviewed research manuscript at completion of fellowship program; must successfully complete an MPH degree at the Bloomberg School of Public Health; must successfully complete the two months as teaching attending at JHU over the two years. **Criteria:** Selection will be based on the committee's criteria.

Funds Avail.: No specific amount. **Duration:** Annual. **To Apply:** Application materials may be submitted to the International Emergency Medicine Fellowship consortium website, however in addition a separate application must also be sent via provided email: three letters of recommendation, personal statement, and curriculum vitae. **Deadline:** September 15.

5371 ■ Johns Hopkins Medicine Medical Education Fellowships *(Professional development/Fellowship)*

Purpose: To develop knowledge and expertise in the essential areas of medical education, including administration of Emergency Medicine residency programs and undergraduate medical education programs as well as educational skills and program design. **Focus:** Emergency and disaster services; Medicine. **Qualif.:** Candidates must be Board Prepared or Certified in Emergency Medicine. **Criteria:** Selection will be based on the committee's criteria.

Funds Avail.: No specific amount. **Duration:** Annual. **To Apply:** Interested candidates should contact the fellowship director for more information and should provide: personal statement, curriculum vitae, and two letters of recommendation.

5372 ■ Johns Hopkins Medicine Observation Medicine Fellowships *(Professional development/Fellowship)*

Purpose: To produce innovative academic leaders of Acute Care Medicine. **Focus:** Medicine. **Qualif.:** Applicants must be Board Prepared or Certified in Emergency Medicine. **Criteria:** Selection will be based on the committee's criteria.

Funds Avail.: No specific amount. **Duration:** Annual. **To Apply:** Interested candidates should email the fellowship director for more information and should provide: personal statement, curriculum vitae, and two letters of recommendation.

5373 ■ Johns Hopkins Medicine Research Fellowships *(Professional development/Fellowship)*

Purpose: To train physician scientists to become independent investigators and nationally recognized leaders in emergency medicine research. **Focus:** Emergency and disaster services; Medicine. **Qualif.:** Candidates must be Board Prepared or Certified in Emergency Medicine; must have recommendation from Emergency Medicine researcher. **Criteria:** Selection will be based on the committee's criteria.

Funds Avail.: No specific amount. **Duration:** Annual. **To Apply:** Interested applicants must submit, via email, the following: curriculum vitae and two letters of recommendation to the contact provided.

Awards are arranged alphabetically below their administering organizations

5374 ■ Johns Hopkins Medicine Ultrasound Fellowships *(Professional development/Fellowship)*

Purpose: To train leaders in Emergency Ultrasound with advanced knowledge and skills in ultrasound, and experience in ultrasound education, research, and administration. **Focus:** Emergency and disaster services; Medical laboratory technology. **Qualif.:** Candidates must be Board Prepared or Certified in EM. **Criteria:** Selection will be based on the committee's criteria.

Funds Avail.: No specific amount. **Duration:** Annual. **Number Awarded:** Varies. **To Apply:** Interested applicants must contact the Department for the application process.

5375 ■ Louis August Jonas Foundation (LAJF)

152 Madison Ave., Ste. 2400
New York, NY 10016
Ph: (212)686-1930
Fax: (212)981-3722
E-mail: contact@lajf.org
URL: www.lajf.org

5376 ■ George E. Jonas Scholarships *(Graduate, Undergraduate/Scholarship)*

Purpose: To provide financial assistance to Camp Rising Sun alumni. **Focus:** General studies/Field of study not specified. **Qualif.:** Applicants must be undergraduate or graduate students in a college or university in the United States; must be alumni of the Camp Rising Sun; international alumni as well as American alumni are eligible as long as their university studies will be in the United States; or either high school seniors planning to enter a college are also accepted. **Criteria:** Applicants will be judged based on intellectual ability, character, financial need, evaluation of experience(s) and future promise for fostering the values of Camp Rising Sun.

Funds Avail.: $1,000-$5,000. **Duration:** Annual. **To Apply:** Applicants must submit a completed application form together with the consent form. **Deadline:** May 15.

5377 ■ The Howard and Georgeanna Jones Foundation for Reproductive Medicine

601 Colley Avenue
Norfolk, VA 23507
Ph: (757)446-8932
URL: www.jonesfound.org

5378 ■ Abby and Howard Milstein Innovation Award in Reproductive Medicine *(Advanced Professional, Professional development/Award, Grant)*

Purpose: To support innovative research project dedicated to attempting to identify the human fertilized egg that has pregnancy potential. **Focus:** Biomedical research; Medical research; Medicine. **Qualif.:** Applicants must be working actively in areas related to reproductive medicine at an accredited medical school in the United States, and must also qualify as independent investigators who have completed their training; must have a full-time faculty/research appointment. **Criteria:** Selection will be based on the committee's criteria.

Funds Avail.: $200,000. **Duration:** Annual. **To Apply:** Application documents must include the following: title page including applicants' name, title of proposal and name of sponsoring institution; letter from the applicants that

contains statements asked by the Foundation; curriculum vitae of up to six pages; bibliography listing of peer-reviewed publications; letter of not more than two pages written by the Chair of the Department on behalf of the candidate; two Letters of Recommendation from independent colleagues; 10-12 pages research proposal with formats prescribed by the Foundation; budget justification for the project. Applications must be submitted online at http://www.jonesfound.org. **Deadline:** September 30. **Contact:** Howard and Georgeanna Jones Foundation for Reproductive Medicine, Attn: Mary Davies, at the above address or Email: mary.davies@jonesfound.org.

5379 ■ Abby and Howard Milstein Reproductive Medicine Research Award *(Advanced Professional, Professional development/Award, Grant)*

Purpose: To facilitate investigation into any aspect of reproductive medicine but preference will be given to investigations designed to improve the efficiency of in vitro fertilization. **Focus:** Biomedical research; Medical research; Medicine. **Qualif.:** Applicants must be working actively in areas related to reproductive medicine at an accredited medical school in the United States. **Criteria:** Preference will be given to those under the age of 45 with a rank of instructor or institutional equivalent up through associate professor.

Funds Avail.: $60,000. **Duration:** Annual. **To Apply:** Application documents must include the following: title page including applicant's name, title of proposal and name of sponsoring institution; letter from the applicants that contains statements asked by the Foundation; curriculum vitae of up to two pages; bibliography listing of peer-reviewed publications; letter of not more than two pages written by the Chair of the Department on behalf of the candidate; a written note from a funded mentor within the Institution; research proposal of no more than two pages; and budget justification. **Deadline:** February 28. **Contact:** Howard and Georgeanna Jones Foundation for Reproductive Medicine, Attn: Mary Davies; Email: mary.davies@jonesfound.org.

5380 ■ Young Investigators Achievement Award *(Advanced Professional, Professional development/Award, Grant)*

Purpose: To foster the career development of a young research investigator working in an approved fellowship program of reproductive medicine. **Focus:** Biomedical research; Medical research; Medicine. **Qualif.:** Applicants must be working actively in areas related to reproductive medicine at an accredited medical school in the United States. **Criteria:** Preference will be given to those under the age of 45 with a rank of instructor or institutional equivalent up through associate professor.

Funds Avail.: $60,000. **Duration:** Annual. **To Apply:** Application documents must include the following: title page including applicant's name, title of proposal and name of sponsoring institution; letter from the applicant that contains statements asked by the Foundation; curriculum vitae of up to two pages; bibliography listing of peer-reviewed publications; letter of not more than two pages written by the Chair of the Department on behalf of the candidate; a written note from a funded mentor within the Institution; research proposal of no more than two pages; and budget justification. Applications must be submitted online at http://www.jonesfound.org. **Deadline:** March 15. **Contact:** Howard and Georgeanna Jones Foundation for Reproductive Medicine, Attn: Mary Davies, Email: mary.davies@jonesfound.org.

Awards are arranged alphabetically below their administering organizations

5381 ■ Journalism Association of Community Colleges (JACC)

PO Box 163509
Sacramento, CA 95816
E-mail: jaccpayment@gmail.com
URL: jacconline.org

5382 ■ Warren Mack Scholarship *(Undergraduate/Scholarship)*

Purpose: To support the education of journalism students. **Focus:** Journalism. **Qualif.:** Applicants must be either transfer or continuing journalism students. **Criteria:** Selection will be based on the committee's criteria.

Funds Avail.: $750. **Duration:** Annual. **To Apply:** Applicants must submit the following in one application packet: a coversheet/form; transcript (may be unofficial); letter of recommendation from the applicants' adviser; a maximum of one page personal statement explaining what the applicants have gained from their journalistic experience, their hopes for a future in journalism, and any special circumstances regarding their background or status; a list of journalism-related experiences other than their community college work (dates and brief descriptions of volunteer or paid work): a list of non-journalism activities and involvements (dates and brief descriptions). **Deadline:** March 10.

5383 ■ Art Margosian Scholarship *(Undergraduate/Scholarship)*

Purpose: To support the education of journalism students. **Focus:** Journalism. **Qualif.:** Applicants must be journalism students. **Criteria:** Selection shall be based on the credentials of the applicants and of the applications required.

Funds Avail.: $750. **Duration:** Annual. **Number Awarded:** 2. **To Apply:** Applicants must complete and submit the application form including all required documents. **Deadline:** March 10.

5384 ■ Journalism Education Association (JEA)

Kansas State University
105 Kedzie Hall
Manhattan, KS 66506-1505
Ph: (785)532-5532
Fax: (785)532-5563
Free: 866-532-5532
E-mail: staff@jea.org
URL: www.jea.org

5385 ■ Future Teacher Scholarships *(Undergraduate, Master's/Scholarship)*

Purpose: To support education majors who intend to teach scholastic journalism. **Focus:** Journalism. **Qualif.:** Applicants must be upper-division or master's degree students in a college program designed to prepare them for teaching at the secondary-school level. Current secondary-school journalism teachers who are in a degree program to improve their journalism teaching skills are also eligible. **Criteria:** Selection of recipients shall be based on the applicants' compliance with the submission of prescribed requirements, and other criteria set by the committee of teachers and university personnel involved in journalism teacher education that will make the selection.

Funds Avail.: $1,000. **Duration:** Annual. **Number Awarded:** 5. **To Apply:** Applicants must complete the ap-

plication and include the following: 250-word essay explaining their desire to teach high school journalism; answers to the three questions provided at the bottom of the application form; two recommendation letters, preferably from those who have firsthand knowledge of their work with student journalists; and, college transcript(s) showing academic standing. **Deadline:** July 15.

5386 ■ Sister Rita Jeanne Scholarships *(Undergraduate, High School/Scholarship, Monetary)*

Purpose: To recognize some of the top high school journalists in the country. **Focus:** Journalism. **Qualif.:** Applicants must be graduating high school seniors who plan to study journalism or mass communications in college and pursue a journalism or mass communications career; must have at least a 3.0 GPA on a 4.0 scale with at least two years in high school journalism; must be a student of a JEA member adviser. **Criteria:** Selection is based on skills, variety of journalistic experiences, and quality of work with the school media.

Funds Avail.: $3,000 - 1st place; $850 - runners-up. **Duration:** Annual; One academic year. **Number Awarded:** 7. **To Apply:** Applicants may apply online and must submit a portfolio which includes: an official entry form; a self-analytical evaluation of "journalistic life" using the most creative form; photo of the applicant that shows journalism (for example: interviewing, taking a photograph, etc.); official copy of transcript; 3 or 4 letters of recommendation from an adviser, people who see the applicant's leadership and journalistic abilities, and practitioners that the applicants have worked with. Applicants must also include samples of their work. **Deadline:** March 15.

5387 ■ Journyx Inc.

7600 Burnet Rd., Ste. 300
Austin, TX 78759-7251
Ph: (512)834-8888
Free: 800-755-9878
E-mail: info@journyx.com
URL: www.journyx.com

5388 ■ Journyx Scholarships *(Undergraduate, Graduate/Scholarship)*

Purpose: To improve the philosophy and the technology of project accounting. **Focus:** Accounting. **Qualif.:** Applicant must be over 18 years old; a resident of the United States; currently enrolled as a full-time graduate or undergraduate at a university in the United States. **Criteria:** Award is given based on the submitted essay.

Funds Avail.: $500. **Number Awarded:** 1. **To Apply:** Students must submit their entries (an essay of 600 words or less) describing "How can modern businesses creatively use time management strategies to increase productivity?"; along with an official academic transcript containing the student's spring semester grades for the academic year in progress and a copy of student's resume that includes e-mail address, campus address and phone number, student ID number, permanent address and phone number, major and expected graduation date. Submit materials via e-mail. **Deadline:** July 1. **Contact:** scholarship@journyx.com.

5389 ■ Junior Achievement (JA)

1 Education Way
Colorado Springs, CO 80906

Awards are arranged alphabetically below their administering organizations

Ph: (719)540-8000
Fax: (719)540-6299
E-mail: newmedia@ja.org
URL: www.juniorachievement.org/web/ja-usa/home

5390 ■ Joe Francomano Scholarships
(Undergraduate/Scholarship)

Purpose: To allow educational advancements by providing financial assistance. **Focus:** General studies/Field of study not specified. **Qualif.:** Applicants must be high school seniors graduating before June 30; must have a minimum GPA of 3.0; must have demonstrated leadership and excellent extracurricular and community activities; and must have financial need. **Criteria:** Selection will be based on financial need, demonstrated leadership, extracurricular and community activities.

Funds Avail.: $5,000 per year. **Duration:** Annual; 4 years. **Number Awarded:** 1. **To Apply:** Applicants must submit a completed application form along with other supporting materials. Applications are available online or from your local JA office or by contacting the JA Worldwide Scholarships Coordinator. **Deadline:** February 1. **Contact:** Joe Francomano Scholarship, Junior Achievement USA at the above address.

5391 ■ Johnson and Wales University Scholarships
(Undergraduate/Scholarship)

Purpose: To allow educational advancements by providing financial assistance. **Focus:** Business; Culinary arts; Teaching; Technology. **Qualif.:** Program is open to individuals who are majoring in the field of business, culinary arts, hospitality, technology or teacher education. **Criteria:** Applicants will be chosen based on academic achievements and contributions to Junior Achievement.

Funds Avail.: $1,000 - $7,500. **Duration:** Annual; up to 4 years. **Number Awarded:** Varies. **To Apply:** Applicants must submit a completed application form together with other supporting materials. **Deadline:** February 1.

5392 ■ Junior Service League of LaGrange
PO Box 2195
LaGrange, GA 30241
E-mail: info@jsloflagrange.com
URL: jsloflagrange.com

5393 ■ Mollie Lukken Memorial Scholarships
(Graduate, Other/Scholarship)

Purpose: To help teachers provide a specialized education for students with learning disabilities. **Focus:** Education, Special. **Qualif.:** Applicants must be qualified teachers in Troup County enrolled in a college/university program pursuing graduate studies in the field of special education interrelated education. **Criteria:** Selection will be based on the evaluation of submitted documents and specific criteria.

Funds Avail.: No specific amount. **Duration:** Annual. **To Apply:** Applicants must submit a completed application form; evidence of enrollment in a college/university program pursuing a degree in Special Education; evidence of the cost of the program; three recommendation letters; one-page, typed essay detailing interest, experience and plans in the field of special education - interrelated education. **Remarks:** Established in 1984. **Contact:** Junior Service League, Attention: Mollie Lukken Scholarship Committee, at the above address.

5394 ■ Just Health Shops
11840 W Market Pl., Ste. H
Fulton, MD 20759

Fax: (301)776-0716
Free: 800-998-7750
URL: www.justhealthshops.com

5395 ■ BedwettingStore.com Design a Mascot Scholarships *(Undergraduate, Graduate/Scholarship)*

Purpose: To provide financial assistance to students for their educational expenses. **Focus:** Design. **Qualif.:** Applicants must be freshmen, sophomores, juniors, seniors and graduate students; and must be legal U.S. residents enrolled in an accredited U.S. college, university or technical school. **Criteria:** Selection will be based on how strong the mascot concept is and how good the drawing/design is.

Funds Avail.: $1,000. **To Apply:** Applicants must design or draw a mascot who's friendly and will make the subject of bedwetting or enuresis easier to approach and talk about. Applicants must submit the name and basic concepts of the mascot. Drawings can be created electronically or by hand, for hand drawn designs kindly submit a scanned image file. Email the concept and drawing including the applicants' full name, contact information, school year and college acceptance letter or transcript. If the applicants' transcript contains social security number or other highly confidential information, please black that out before sending it. **Deadline:** December 31. **Contact:** scholarship@bedwettingstore.com.

5396 ■ Dry Defender Protect Your Bed Scholarships
(Undergraduate, Graduate/Scholarship)

Purpose: To provide financial assistance to students with creative minds and artistic talents. **Focus:** Drafting. **Qualif.:** Applicants must be college freshmen, sophomores, juniors, seniors, and graduate students; and must be legal U.S. residents. **Criteria:** Selection will be based on how good the concept for Dry Defender's nemesis is, and for the creativity and effort put into the creative piece submitted.

Funds Avail.: $1,000. **To Apply:** Applicants must make some type of creative piece of Dry Defender and his nemesis facing off (comic, short film, drawing, etc.) and must submit the creative piece including their full name, contact information, school year, college acceptance letter or transcript and brief explanation of which Dry Defender's nemesis is. **Deadline:** June 30. **Remarks:** Administered by Protective Bedding Store. **Contact:** scholarship@drydefender.com.

5397 ■ JustNebulizers.com Respiratory Care Scholarships *(Undergraduate, Graduate/Scholarship)*

Purpose: To assist with the educational expenses of students with respiratory conditions. **Focus:** Respiratory therapy. **Qualif.:** Applicants must be college freshmen, sophomores, juniors, seniors or graduate students; and must be legal residents and have a respiratory condition. Employees or relatives of JustNebulizers.com are not eligible. **Criteria:** Selection will be based on the answers and creativity presenting those answers.

Funds Avail.: $1,000. **To Apply:** Applicants must send a creative video under three minutes long answering the following two questions: "how has living with a respiratory condition molded who you are?" and "what advice would you give to others in your shoes?" Applicants must email the link of their video along with their full name and name of their school. **Deadline:** December 31. **Contact:** scholarship@justnebulizers.com.

Awards are arranged alphabetically below their administering organizations

5398 ■ JustWalkers.com Mobility Scholarships
(Undergraduate, Graduate/Scholarship)

Purpose: To provide financial assistance to students. **Focus:** Disabilities. **Qualif.:** Applicants must be college freshman, sophomores, juniors, seniors and graduate students; must have a minimum 3.0 GPA; must be legal U.S. resident or have valid student visa; and must be using a mobility device such as wheelchair, power scooter, crutches or rollator on a regular basis. **Criteria:** Selection will be based on the committee's criteria.

Funds Avail.: $1,000. **To Apply:** Applicants must write a 600 word maximum essay in response on the following prompt: "describe a time when you faced a major obstacle, what did you do and what did the experience teach you?"; and must email their essay along with full name, contact information, school year, college acceptance letter or transcript and physician's statement of diagnosis. **Deadline:** June 30.

5399 ■ Juvenile Diabetes Research Foundation International (JDRF)
26 Broadway
New York, NY 10004
Fax: (212)785-9595
Free: 800-533-CURE
E-mail: info@jdrf.org
URL: www.jdrf.org

5400 ■ Early-Career Patient-Oriented Diabetes Research Awards *(Professional development/Award)*

Purpose: To provide crucial support to investigators who plan to pursue a career in diabetes-related clinical investigation, **Focus:** Diabetes. **Qualif.:** Applicants must have an MD or MD-PhD, hold an appointment or joint appointment in a subspecialty of clinical medicine and conduct human clinical research. In exceptional circumstances, non-MD candidates will be considered if their work is likely to contribute significantly to a clinical outcome. Applicants must be sponsored by investigators who are affiliated full-time with an accredited institution, who pursue clinical research and agree to supervise the applicants' training. Research may be conducted at foreign or domestic, for-profit or nonprofit, and public or private organizations such as universities, colleges, hospitals, laboratories, units of state and local governments and eligible agencies of the federal government. **Criteria:** Awards will be made to applicants who have demonstrated superior scholarship and show promise for future achievement in clinical research, particularly in those areas that require the unique training of a clinical investigator.

Funds Avail.: $150,000 per year. **Duration:** Five years. **To Apply:** The research plan may not exceed 12 pages, including figures and tables, and should include narrative to the following items: specific aims; background and significance of this work to type 1 diabetes; preliminary studies; research design and methods; literature cited. At the end of the research plan section, the applicants must include a future career plans statement, which is limited to two pages. The applicants must include a statement of career goals and indicate the relevance of these goals to type 1 diabetes-related research. The training plan statement is limited to four pages. The sponsor must provide a biographical sketch, list of previous trainees and a statement of the plan for training the applicants. The training plan statement must outline a detailed training program for the applicants as well as confirm the availability of facilities to conduct the

research project. The sponsor's statement should address plans for supervision, guidance, counseling or other formal or informal training of the applicants. Three recommendation references assessing the scientific abilities and potential of the applicants must be submitted. The recommendation references must be submitted directly to RMS360 by the referee. The applicants' institution must provide detailed evidence that their facilities are adequate for the proposed research and that they have made a tangible commitment to fostering the career-development of clinical investigators conducting patient-oriented research. This departmental head statement must be included as a supporting document and uploaded as a proposal attachment. **Deadline:** August 30.

5401 ■ Innovative Grants-Pilot and Research Tool Grants *(Postdoctorate/Grant)*

Purpose: To support proposals for highly innovative research with significant potential to accelerate the mission of JDRF. **Focus:** Diabetes. **Qualif.:** Applicants must hold an MD, DMD, DVM, PhD or equivalent and have a faculty position or equivalent at a college, university, medical school, or other research facility. To assure continued excellence and diversity among applicants and awardees, JDRF welcomes proposals from all qualified individuals and encourages proposals from persons with disabilities, women and members of minority groups underrepresented in the sciences. **Criteria:** Evaluations will be competitive and performed by an appropriate review panel convened by JDRF. Proposals will be evaluated in accordance with the following criteria: innovation, potential impact and relevance to JDRF goals; feasibility of experimental approach and completing in one year; clarity of proposed objectives; qualifications and research experience of the principal investigators and collaborators; availability of resources and facilities necessary for the project; appropriateness of the proposed budget in relation to the proposed research; for the research tool proposals, demonstrable need for the novel reagents/tools.

Funds Avail.: $110,000. **To Apply:** Applicants must visit the website to create a proposalCENTRAL (pC) account. After creating an account, applicants must select the appropriate application from the list of JDRF funding opportunities and to gain access to the application template. Applicants must complete each of the proposal sections listed in the menu on the left side of the screen and must limit the file size of each uploaded attachment to 3-4 MB.

5402 ■ JDRF Advanced Postdoctoral Fellowships *(Postdoctorate/Fellowship)*

Purpose: To attract qualified, promising scientists to receive full time research training and to assist these promising individuals in transitioning from a fellowship to an independent (faculty-level) position. **Focus:** Diabetes. **Qualif.:** Fellowships are intended for those in a relatively early stage of their career. Ordinarily, their first degree (PhD, MD, DMD, DVM or equivalent) must have been received no more than five years before the fellowship. Applicants must be sponsored by investigators who are affiliated full-time with an accredited institution and who agree to supervise the applicants' training. The sponsor does not necessarily need to have a background in diabetes, but the research project must be type 1 diabetes-related. Fellowship research may be conducted at foreign or domestic, for-profit or non-profit, and public or private organizations such as universities, colleges, hospitals, laboratories, units of state and local governments and eligible agencies of the federal government. **Criteria:** Fellowships will be awarded

Awards are arranged alphabetically below their administering organizations

on the basis of the applicants' previous experience, academic record, the caliber of the proposed research and the quality of the mentor, training program and environment.

Funds Avail.: $90,000 per year. **Duration:** Three years. **To Apply:** Applicants must visit the website to create a proposalCENTRAL (pC) account. After creating an account, applicants must select the appropriate application from the list of JDRF funding opportunities and to gain access to the application template. Applicants must complete each of the proposal sections listed in the menu on the left side of the screen and must limit the file size of each uploaded attachment to 3-4 MB. **Deadline:** July 31.

5403 ■ JDRF Career Development Awards (Professional development, Postdoctorate/Award)

Purpose: To attract qualified and promising scientists early in their faculty careers and to give them the opportunity to establish themselves in areas that reflect the JDRF research emphasis areas. **Focus:** Diabetes. **Qualif.:** Applicants must be in a relatively early stage of their career. Ordinarily, their first degree (MD, PhD, DMD, DVM or equivalent) must have been received at least three, but not more than seven, years before the award. The applicants must hold an academic faculty-level position at the time of the proposal at a university, health science center, or comparable institution with strong, well-established research and training programs for the chosen area of interest. **Criteria:** Awards will be made on the basis of the applicants' perceived ability and potential for a career in type 1 diabetes research, the caliber of the proposed research and the quality and commitment of the institution. The applicants' ability and promise will hold the highest priority in selection and will be assessed on the basis of items such as letters of recommendation, publications, career plans, and prior clinical and research training.

Funds Avail.: $150,000 per year. **Duration:** Five years. **To Apply:** Applicants must visit the website to create a proposalCENTRAL (pC) account. After creating an account, applicants must select the appropriate application from the list of JDRF funding opportunities and to gain access to the application template. Applicants must complete each of the proposal sections listed in the menu on the left side of the screen and must limit the file size of each uploaded attachment to 3-4 MB. The Career Development Award research plan should describe a five-year project. The project should address a specific and substantive question that is relevant to the JDRF mission. The research plan may not exceed 12 pages, including figures and tables and should include a narrative to the following items: specific aims; background and significance of this work to type 1 diabetes; preliminary studies; research design and methods; literature cited. At the end of the research plan section, the applicants must include a future career plans statement, which is limited to two pages. The applicants must include a statement of career goals and indicate the relevance of these goals to type 1 diabetes-related research. Three recommendation references assessing the scientific abilities and potential of the applicants must be submitted. The recommendation references must be submitted directly to RMS360 by the referee. The applicants' institution must, through the departmental supervisor, provide assurance of an academic commitment to the applicants and to the research project. This departmental head statement must be included as a supporting document and uploaded as a proposal attachment. **Deadline:** August 30.

5404 ■ JDRF Postdoctoral Fellowships (Postdoctorate/Fellowship)

Purpose: To support qualified, promising scientists entering their professional career in the T1D research field. **Focus:** Diabetes. **Qualif.:** Applicants must be in a relatively early stage of their career. Ordinarily, their first degree (PhD, MD, DMD, DVM or equivalent) must have been received no more than five years before the fellowship. Applicants must be sponsored by investigators who are affiliated full-time with an accredited institution and who agree to supervise the applicants' training. Fellowship research may be conducted at foreign or domestic, for-profit or non-profit, and public or private organizations such as universities, colleges, hospitals, laboratories, units of state and local government and eligible agencies of the federal government. To assure continued excellence and diversity among applicants and awardees, JDRF welcomes proposals from all qualified individuals and encourages proposals from persons with disabilities, women and members of minority groups underrepresented in the sciences. **Criteria:** Fellowships will be awarded on the basis of the applicants' previous experience, academic record, the caliber of the proposed research and the quality of the mentor, training program and environment.

Funds Avail.: $5,500-$2,000. **Duration:** Three years. **To Apply:** Applicants must visit the website to create a proposalCENTRAL (pC) account. After creating an account, applicants must select the appropriate application from the list of JDRF funding opportunities and to gain access to the application template. Applicants must complete each of the proposal sections listed in the menu on the left side of the screen and must limit the file size of each uploaded attachment to 3-4 MB. **Deadline:** July 31.

5405 ■ JW Surety Bonds
6023A Kellers Church Rd.
Pipersville, PA 18947
E-mail: info@jwsuretybonds.com
URL: www.jwsuretybonds.com

5406 ■ JW Surety Bonds Scholarships (Undergraduate, Graduate/Scholarship)

Purpose: To aid students and prospective students who demonstrate creativity and talent in their respective fields of study. **Focus:** General studies/Field of study not specified. **Qualif.:** Applicants must be college students, or prospective college students, planning to attend an accredited U.S. institution. **Criteria:** Applicants will be selected based on their submitted entries. Entries are judged based on creativity, professionalism, and accuracy.

Funds Avail.: $1,000. **Duration:** Annual. **Number Awarded:** 1. **To Apply:** Applicants must submit their respective entries (in the form of articles, videos, slideshows or infographics) through email. **Deadline:** September 30. **Contact:** scholarship@jwsuretybonds.com.

5407 ■ Kaiser Family Foundation (KFF)
2400 Sand Hill Rd.
Menlo Park, CA 94025
Ph: (650)854-9400
Fax: (650)854-4800
URL: kff.org

Awards are arranged alphabetically below their administering organizations

5408 ■ Kaiser Media Fellowships in Health Reporting *(Advanced Professional, Professional development/ Fellowship)*

Purpose: To encourage print, broadcast and online journalists to pursue an area of interest in U.S. health policy issues. **Focus:** Editors and editing; Health education; Journalism. **Qualif.:** Applicants must: be journalists, editors, or producers specializing in health reporting (or wanting to do so); be U.S. citizens, or must work for an accredited U.S. media organization; and be in the early to mid-career range, with at least five years experience as journalists. **Criteria:** Selection shall be based on applicants' previous and potential work, demonstrated commitment to report on health issues and on the committee's determination of which candidates would benefit most from program.

Funds Avail.: $55,000. **Duration:** Annual. **To Apply:** Applicants must submit a detailed letter on reasons for applying, career goals, a short outline of the project(s) to complete during the fellowship year, and aims to accomplish as a result of the fellowship; a brief description of what the applicant hopes to do with the work beyond the immediate outlet about to use; a budget outline and estimated project timeframe; curriculum vitae or resume; details of previous awards or fellowships; examples of recent work; and one or more letters of support from other journalists, including a letter from current senior editor or news director supporting the application (freelance journalists should send a letter of support from an editor, producer or colleague). **Deadline:** March 3. **Remarks:** Established in 2011. **Contact:** Kaiser Family Foundation, at the above address.

5409 ■ Kaiser Permanente Division of Research

2000 Broadway
Oakland, CA 94612
Ph: (510)891-3400
URL: www.dor.kaiser.org/external/dorexternal/index.aspx

5410 ■ Kaiser Permanente Northern California Delivery Science Fellowships Program *(Postgraduate/Fellowship)*

Purpose: To support the ongoing improvement of the Kaiser Permanente health care system, as well as the US health care system. **Focus:** Health care services. **Qualif.:** Applicants must be outstanding candidates with a health professional doctorate (MD, DO or equivalent) and/or research doctorate degree (PhD, ScD, DrPH or equivalent) in related fields. Women and minority candidates are encouraged to apply. **Criteria:** Selection will be based on the committee's criteria.

Funds Avail.: Amount varies. **Duration:** Annual. **To Apply:** Applicants must submit a completed application form, curriculum vitae, personal statement and three recommendation letters through email. Application forms can be obtained at the website. **Deadline:** September 15. **Contact:** Beth Dameron, MS, Program Coordinator at beth.dameron@kp.org.

5411 ■ Kansas Association of Broadcasters (KAB)

214 SW 6th Ave., No. 300
Topeka, KS 66603
Ph: (785)235-1307
URL: www.kab.net

5412 ■ Kansas Association of Broadcasters Scholarships *(Undergraduate/Scholarship)*

Purpose: To promote a greater understanding of journalistic ethics and societal responsibility of broadcasters. **Focus:** Broadcasting. **Qualif.:** Applicants must be residents enrolled in a college/technical college who are financially needy and academically qualified. **Criteria:** Preference will be given to students who demonstrate an interest in sales and engineering/technology and a commitment to stay in Kansas upon graduation.

Funds Avail.: Up to $16,000. **Duration:** Annual. **To Apply:** Applicants must submit a completed application form. **Deadline:** May 1. **Contact:** Scholarship Committee, Kansas Association of Broadcasters, at the above address.

5413 ■ Kansas Board of Regents (KBOR)

1000 SW Jackson St., Ste. 520
Topeka, KS 66612-1368
Ph: (785)296-3421
Fax: (785)296-0983
URL: www.kansasregents.org

5414 ■ Kansas Optometry Service Scholarships *(Graduate, Undergraduate/Scholarship)*

Purpose: To help pay the difference between resident and non-resident tuition at eligible out-of-state institutions. **Focus:** Optometry. **Qualif.:** Applicants must be selected by a participating school; must be Kansas residents and agree to enroll in the Missouri School of Optometry, University of Missouri-St. Louis and pay the resident fees, Southern College of Optometry, Memphis, TN or the School of Optometry at Northeastern State University, Tahlequah, OK. **Criteria:** Evaluations will be based on academic considerations and Kansas residency.

Funds Avail.: No specific amount. **Duration:** Annual. **To Apply:** Applicants must submit a completed application form. **Deadline:** May 1. **Contact:** Kansas Board of Regents, Kansas Optometry Service Scholarship, at the above address, or Email: loldhamburns@ksbor.org.

5415 ■ Kansas Osteopathic Medical Service Scholarships *(Graduate, Other/Scholarship)*

Purpose: To encourage doctors to establish practices in rural areas of Kansas. **Focus:** Medicine, Osteopathic. **Qualif.:** Applicants must be Kansas residents; must be committed to providing primary medical care in Kansas' underserved areas; must demonstrate financial aid eligibility as measured by the federal formula; and must be admitted in an accredited school of osteopathy in the United States. **Criteria:** Selection will be based on evaluation of residential status; financial need as measured by the federal formula; likelihood of primary care medical practice in underserved Kansas areas which have an emphasis on the applicants' statement outlining past and present commitments to medical care or employment including voluntary or paid health care efforts.

Funds Avail.: $25,000 per year (Up to four years.). **Duration:** Annual; up to four years. **To Apply:** Applicants must submit a completed scholarship application form; one-page statement of purpose; signed copy of Student Aid Report; copy of the most recent federal income tax return. **Deadline:** May 1. **Contact:** Bob Williams, Exec. Dir. at 1260 SW Topeka Blvd., Topeka, KS 66612-1889; Call at 785-234-5563 or e-mail at kansasdo@aol.com.

Awards are arranged alphabetically below their administering organizations

5416 ■ Kansas Health Information Management Association (KHIMA)

301 S Estates
Salina, KS 67401
Ph: (785)825-7340
Fax: (785)825-7340
URL: www.khima.com

5417 ■ KHIMA Graduate Scholarships *(Graduate/ Scholarship)*

Purpose: To provide financial assistance to students pursuing their education as Health Information Management professionals. **Focus:** Health education. **Qualif.:** Applicants must be full or part-time graduate studies students. **Criteria:** Selection of applicants will be based on the following criteria: (a) scholastic achievements; (b) leadership potential via officer or student representative within organizations, honors and awards, presentations and publications; (c) social consciousness via membership in organizations, volunteer activities, etc.; and (d) knowledge of, and commitment to the health information management profession via evaluation of student's completed application, employment in the health information management field and AHIMA membership. Written communication skills will also be evaluated.

Funds Avail.: No specific amount. **Duration:** Annual. **Number Awarded:** 1. **To Apply:** Applicants must complete the application form and must submit the verification of enrollment form and references to the Recognition Committee Chairperson; must have two letters of recommendation submitted by an employer, academic counselor, directed practice supervisor or professional contact. **Deadline:** October 31. **Contact:** Kansas Health Information Management Association, at the above address.

5418 ■ Sue A. Malone Scholarships *(Doctorate, Graduate, Professional development/Scholarship)*

Purpose: To provide scholarship funds for professional enhancement of Health Information Management professionals. **Focus:** Health education; Health sciences. **Qualif.:** Applicants must be full or part-time students within their last year of study at one of the following programs: (1) HIA Program at the University of Kansas in Kansas City, (2) HIT Program at Washburn University in Topeka, (3) HIT Program at Hutchinson Community College in Hutchinson, (4) KHIMA members who are attending an accredited HIM program; must be in higher level of education and limited to RHIT progression students; must be in RHIA for Masters or Doctorate in Public Health, Law School, Business Administration, Public Administration, or any other applicable degrees for HIM profession. **Criteria:** Selection of applicants will be based on the following criteria: (a) scholastic achievements; (b) leadership potential via officer or student representative within organizations, honors and awards, presentations and publications; (c) social consciousness via membership in organizations, volunteer activities, etc.; (d) knowledge of, and commitment to the health information management profession via evaluation of student's completed application, employment in the health information management field and AHIMA membership. Written communication skills will also be evaluated.

Funds Avail.: No specific amount. **Duration:** Annual. **Number Awarded:** 1. **To Apply:** Applicants must complete the application form; must submit the verification of enrollment form and references to the Recognition Committee chairperson; must have two letters of recommendation submitted by an employer, academic counselor, directed practice

supervisor or professional contact. **Deadline:** October 31. **Remarks:** Established in 1995. **Contact:** Kansas Health Information Management Association, at the above address.

5419 ■ Karen Schuvie Scholarships *(Undergraduate/ Scholarship, Loan)*

Purpose: To provide financial assistance to students pursuing their potential as Health Information Management professionals. **Focus:** Health education. **Qualif.:** Applicants must be full or part-time students within their last year of study at one of the following programs: (1) HIA Program at the University of Kansas, (2) HIT Program at Washburn University in Topeka, (3) HIT Program at Hutchinson Community College in Hutchinson, (4) KHIMA members who are attending an accredited HIM program. **Criteria:** Selection of applicants will be based on the following criteria: (a) scholastic achievements; (b) leadership potential via officer or student representative in organizations, honors and awards, presentations and publications; (c) social consciousness via membership in organizations, volunteer activities, etc.; (d) knowledge of, and commitment to, the health information management profession via evaluation of student's completed application, employment in the health information management field and AHIMA membership. Written communication skills will also be evaluated.

Funds Avail.: No specific amount. **Duration:** Annual. **To Apply:** Applicants must complete the application form; must submit the verification of enrollment form and references to the Recognition Committee Chairperson; must have two letters of recommendation submitted by an employer, academic counselor, directed practice supervisor or professional contact. **Deadline:** October 31. **Remarks:** Established in 1986. **Contact:** Kansas Health Information Management Association, at the above address.

5420 ■ Kappa Delta Pi (KDP)

3707 Woodview Trace
Indianapolis, IN 46268-1158
Ph: (317)871-4900
Fax: (317)704-2323
Free: 800-284-3167
E-mail: pubs@kdp.org
URL: www.kdp.org

5421 ■ Louise Berman Fellows Award *(Graduate, Master's, Doctorate/Fellowship, Award)*

Purpose: To advance curriculum, drive creative inquiry into the human condition, collaborate on cross-national education projects and encourage personal growth. **Focus:** Education--Curricula. **Qualif.:** Applicants must be graduate students at the master's and doctorate levels, as well as to practicing educators at all levels. **Criteria:** Selection will be based on the committee's criteria.

Funds Avail.: $1,200 - $1,800. **To Apply:** Applicants must submit a completely answered application form and a proposal containing various documents specified by the bestowing organization.

5422 ■ Harold D. Drummond Scholarships *(Undergraduate, Graduate/Scholarship)*

Purpose: To support and enhance the professional growth and teaching practices of member educators throughout the phases and levels of their teaching careers. **Focus:** Education, Elementary. **Qualif.:** Applicants must be

Awards are arranged alphabetically below their administering organizations

undergraduate or graduate students in Elementary Education. **Criteria:** Preference will be given to students who demonstrate financial needs.

Funds Avail.: $750 each. **Duration:** Annual. **Number Awarded:** Varies. **To Apply:** Applicants must submit an essay of no more than 750 words, 3,800 characters, on the topic: "What life experiences have led you to study education and how will those experiences influence your role as an eleementary educator?" Statement of financial need must also be attached. **Deadline:** May 1.

5423 ■ J. Everett and Louise Light Scholarships
(Undergraduate, Graduate/Scholarship)

Purpose: To support KDP members who have demonstrated financial need. **Focus:** Education, Special. **Qualif.:** Applicants must be undergraduate, graduate or doctoral students in Special Education. **Criteria:** Selection will be based on the committee's criteria.

Funds Avail.: $1,500. **Duration:** Annual. **To Apply:** Applicants must complete and submit their application together with the following documents: essay or research paper covering the specific topic required for the scholarship that the applicants applying for; reference letter from the correct individual required by this scholarship program; transcript; program prospectus or course of study; CV or resume for doctoral members; explanation of scholarship use; statement of financial need; description of service. **Deadline:** May 1.

5424 ■ Stephen J. Fortgang/University of Northern Iowa Chapter Scholarship *(Undergraduate/ Scholarship)*

Purpose: To honor and encourage undergraduate Kadelpians who show signs of mastering pedagogy, but most particularly possess a vital love of knowledge and its centrality to developing educated people and an enlightened democratic citizenry through great teaching. **Focus:** Education; Liberal arts. **Qualif.:** Applicants must be undergraduate students. **Criteria:** Selection will be based on the committee's criteria.Candidates are expected to provide evidence of a strong command of and commitment to academic curriculum.

Funds Avail.: $1,500. **Duration:** Annual. **Number Awarded:** 1. **To Apply:** Applicants must submit an essay of no more than 750 words, 3,800 characters, addressing the importance of coherent content planning to ensure excellent teaching in the particular areas of concentration. **Deadline:** May 1.

5425 ■ Sandra Jo Hornick Scholarships
(Undergraduate/Scholarship)

Purpose: To support students who have demonstrated financial need. **Focus:** General studies/Field of study not specified. **Qualif.:** Applicants must be undergraduate students. One must be a KDP member and one must be a student at Kent State University. **Criteria:** Selection will be based on the committee's criteria.

Funds Avail.: $1,500 each. **Duration:** Annual. **Number Awarded:** 2. **To Apply:** Applicants must write an original essay that reflects their reasons for wanting to be a teacher and indicate what professional challenges they expect to face upong the completion of their degree. Essay must contain no more than 750 words limited to 3800 characters. **Deadline:** May 1.

5426 ■ J. Jay Hostetler Scholarships
(Undergraduate/Scholarship)

Purpose: To support and enhance the professional growth and teaching practices of member educators throughout the phases and levels of their teaching careers. **Focus:** Teaching. **Qualif.:** Applicants must be undergradute student teachers. **Criteria:** Selection will be based on the committee's criteria.

Funds Avail.: $1,000. **Duration:** Annual. **Number Awarded:** 2. **To Apply:** Applicants are required to write an essay that portrays their personal vision as educators and how their student teaching experience influenced their future career goals. Essay must contain no more than 750 words limited to 3800 characters. **Deadline:** May 1.

5427 ■ KDP Huntington Bank Scholarship
(Undergraduate/Scholarship)

Purpose: To support and enhance the professional growth and teaching practices of member educators throughout the phases and levels of their teaching careers. **Focus:** Education. **Qualif.:** Applicants must be undergraduate students in education major with Pre-K to 12 emphasis and be residents of Indiana or Ohio. **Criteria:** Selection will be based on the committee's criteria.

Funds Avail.: $1,200. **Duration:** Annual. **Number Awarded:** 1. **To Apply:** Applicants are required to submit an essay that reflects their reasons for wanting to be a teacher and indicate what professional challenges they expect to face upon the completion of their degree. **Deadline:** May 1.

5428 ■ KDP International Scholarship Program - President Scholarship *(Undergraduate, Graduate, Doctorate/Scholarship)*

Purpose: To support students who demonstrated financial needs. **Focus:** Education; Leadership, Institutional and community. **Qualif.:** Applicants must be undergraduate, graduate, doctoral students or practicing educator dedicated to leadership and service in Kappa Delta Pi. **Criteria:** Selection will be based on the committee's criteria.

Funds Avail.: $1,500. **Duration:** Annual. **To Apply:** Applicants are required to write and submit an essay on the topic "What are your professional and personal reasons in seeking leadership and service opportunities in Kappa Delta Pi; how have your acaemic program and experience prepared you for such an endeavor?" Essay must contain no more than 750 words limited to 3800 characters. **Deadline:** May 1.

5429 ■ KDP MBNA Scholarships *(Undergraduate, Graduate/Scholarship)*

Purpose: To support students who demonstrated financial need. **Focus:** Education, Special. **Qualif.:** Applicants must be undergraduate or graduate students in Special Education. **Criteria:** Selection will be based on the committee's criteria.

Funds Avail.: $1,200. **Duration:** Annual. **To Apply:** Applicants are required to write and submit an essay on the following topic: "What are the challenges facing teachers working with special needs students?" Essay must contain no more than 750 words limited to 3800 characters. **Deadline:** May 1.

5430 ■ Dr. Eva Kleinpeter Scholarship
(Undergraduate/Scholarship)

Purpose: To support and enhance the professional growth and teaching practices of member educators throughout the phases and levels of their teaching careers. **Focus:** Education, Elementary. **Qualif.:** Applicants must be undergraduate students with a focus on Elementary Educa-

Awards are arranged alphabetically below their administering organizations

tion and Common Core Standards. **Criteria:** Preference will be given to students at Louisiana college or university.

Funds Avail.: $750. **Duration:** Annual. **Number Awarded:** 2. **To Apply:** Applicants must submit a briefly discribed essay on how they are prepared to address the philosophy, content, principles, goals, objectives and skills of the Common Core Standards and how they plan to implement the standards using the best practices and technology for addressing the learning styles of each student. **Deadline:** May 1.

5431 ■ Marsh Writing/Research Scholarship Awards
(Undergraduate, Graduate/Scholarship, Award)

Purpose: To support students who demonstrated financial need. **Focus:** Education. **Qualif.:** Applicants must be undergraduate and graduate students who write research papers based on issues that affect teachers and learning. **Criteria:** Papers will be considered on the basis of the following criteria: significant topic; adequacy and appropriateness of methodology; writing clarity; potential contribution to the field.

Funds Avail.: $600 each. **Duration:** Annual. **Number Awarded:** 2. **To Apply:** Applicants must submit a completed research paper as part of an undergraduate or graduate program in a recognized school or college of education. Individuals may nominate their own papers, or nominations may be made by advisers, department chairs, Deans, KDP Chapters Counselors or Chapter Presidents. Each nomination must include a completed application. **Deadline:** May 1.

5432 ■ William B. Martin East Carolina University Scholarships *(Undergraduate/Scholarship)*

Purpose: To support and enhance the professional growth and teaching practices of member educators throughout the phases and levels of their teaching careers. **Focus:** Education, Special. **Qualif.:** Applicants must be undergraduate students enrolled at East Carolina University in Special Education and Middle Grades Education. **Criteria:** Selection will be based on the committee's criteria.

Funds Avail.: $900 each. **Duration:** Annual. **Number Awarded:** 2. **To Apply:** Applicants must submit an essay that reflects their reasons for wanting to be a special education or middle grades teacher, and indicate what professional challenges they expect to face upon the completion of their degree. **Deadline:** May 1.

5433 ■ Vincent McGrath Scholarship *(Undergraduate/Scholarship)*

Purpose: To support and enhance the professional growth and teaching practices of member educators throughout the phases and levels of their teaching careers. **Focus:** Education, Elementary. **Qualif.:** Applicants must be undergraduate students in Elementary Education. **Criteria:** Selection will be based on the committee's criteria.

Funds Avail.: $1,000. **Duration:** Annual. **Number Awarded:** 1. **To Apply:** Applicants are required to submit an essay that reflects their reasons for wanting to be elementary teachers, and indicate what professional challenges they expect to face upon the completion of their degree. **Deadline:** May 1.

5434 ■ Nicholas H. Noyes, Jr. Scholarship *(Undergraduate/Scholarship)*

Purpose: To support and enhace the professional growth and teaching practices of member educators throughout the phases and levels of their teaching careers. **Focus:** Education. **Qualif.:** Applicants must be undergraduate students in Education residing in Marion County, Indiana and attending a college or university in Indiana. **Criteria:** Selection will be based on the committee's criteria.

Funds Avail.: $1,200. **Duration:** Annual. **Number Awarded:** 1. **To Apply:** Applicants must provide an essay that reflects their reasons for wanting to be a teacher and indicate what professional challenges they expect to face upon the completion of their degree. **Deadline:** May 1.

5435 ■ Louisa Anne Oriente Scholarships *(Graduate/Scholarship)*

Purpose: To support students who demonstrated financial need. **Focus:** Education--Curricula; Teaching. **Qualif.:** Applicants must be graduate students in Curriculum and Teaching. **Criteria:** Selection will be based on the committee's criteria.

Funds Avail.: $1,000. **Duration:** Annual. **Number Awarded:** 1. **To Apply:** Applicants are required to write and submit an essay with a topic "What challenging demands and opportunities of the 21st century make a graduate degree program in the practices and policies of curriculum and teaching desirable?" Essay must contain no more than 750 words limited to 3800 characters. **Deadline:** May 1.

5436 ■ Jerry Robbins Scholarship *(Undergraduate/Scholarship)*

Purpose: To support and enhance the professional growth and teaching practices of member educators throughout the phases and levels of their teaching careers. **Focus:** Education, Music. **Qualif.:** Applicants must be students in Instrumental Music Education. **Criteria:** Selection will be based on the committee's criteria.

Funds Avail.: $1,000. **Duration:** Annual. **Number Awarded:** 1. **To Apply:** Applicants must submit an essay that portrays their personal vision as educators and how they intend to make a difference in the musical and general education of children and youth. **Deadline:** May 1.

5437 ■ Jack Rosen Scholarship *(Undergraduate/Scholarship)*

Purpose: To support and enhance the professional growth and teaching practices of member educators throughout the phases and levels of their teaching careers. **Focus:** Education, Elementary; Mathematics and mathematical sciences; Science; Technology. **Qualif.:** Applicants must be undergraduate students major in Elementary Education with a science, math or technology focus. **Criteria:** Selection will be based on the committee's criteria.

Funds Avail.: $1,000. **Duration:** Annual. **Number Awarded:** 1. **To Apply:** Applicants must submit an essay that portrays their personal vision as educators and how they intend to make a difference in the general education of children and youth through science, math or technology. **Deadline:** May 1.

5438 ■ Donna Gail Shaw Scholarship for Chapter Service *(Undergraduate, Graduate, Doctorate/Scholarship)*

Purpose: To support students who demonstrated financial need. **Focus:** Education; Teaching. **Qualif.:** Applicants must be undergraudate, graduate or doctoral students or practicing K-12 educator in the first three years of teaching. **Criteria:** Selection will be based on the committee's criteria.

Awards are arranged alphabetically below their administering organizations

Funds Avail.: $1,800. **Duration:** Annual. **To Apply:** Applicants are required to write and submit an essay on the topic "What is the role of service in becoming a professional educator?" Essay must contain no more than 750 words limited to 3800 characters. Applicants must also provide a description of their service to the chapter, community and profession, and how their service made a difference. **Deadline:** May 1.

5439 ■ Kappa Gamma Pi
7250 Overcliff Rd.
Cincinnati, OH 45233-1038
Ph: (305)525-3744
Fax: (305)718-9362
E-mail: kappagammapi@cinci.rr.com
URL: www.kappagammapi.org

5440 ■ Cornaro Scholarships for Graduate Studies
(Graduate/Scholarship)

Purpose: To provide financial support to individuals as needed for graduate expenses at any accredited college or university. **Focus:** General studies/Field of study not specified. **Qualif.:** Applicant must be a member of the Kappa Gamma Pi. **Criteria:** Applicant must be already accepted into an accredited graduate or professional program.

Funds Avail.: $5,000. **Number Awarded:** One or more. **To Apply:** Applicants must submit the completed application form along with the required supporting documents via e-mail. **Deadline:** April 20. **Contact:** KGP Cornaro Scholarship Committee Chair, 6334 North Lakewood Avenue, Chicago, IL 60660; cornarokgp@yahoo.com.

5441 ■ Kappa Kappa Gamma
530 E Town St.
Columbus, OH 43216
Ph: (614)228-6515
Fax: (614)228-7809
Free: 866-KKG-1870
E-mail: communications@kkg.org
URL: www.kappakappagamma.org

5442 ■ Kappa Kappa Gamma Graduate Scholarships *(Graduate/Scholarship)*

Purpose: To deliver educational and leadership training, preserve the Fraternity's heritage from an historical perspective, and to provide financial assistance to members in need. **Focus:** General studies/Field of study not specified. **Qualif.:** Applicants must be members of Kappa Kappa Fraternity who have a grade average of B or above and who were in good standing as undergraduates. **Criteria:** Scholarship will be evaluated based on the application materials.

Funds Avail.: Varies. **Duration:** Annual. **To Apply:** Applicant must submit a personal essay or letter stating educational and career goals and financial need; must have official transcripts from all colleges or universities attended; two recommendation letters, one academic (professor, adviser, dean) and one chapter (President, Vice President-Standards or Chapter Council Adviser). **Deadline:** February 1.

5443 ■ Kappa Kappa Gamma Undergraduate Scholarships *(Undergraduate/Scholarship)*

Purpose: To deliver educational and leadership training, preserve the Fraternity's heritage from an historical perspective, and to provide financial assistance to members in need. **Focus:** General studies/Field of study not specified. **Qualif.:** Applicant must be a member of Kappa Kappa Gamma Fraternity who has a grade average of B or above (3.0 on 4.0 scale) and is in good standing. **Criteria:** Selection will be based on the submitted application materials.

Funds Avail.: No specific amount. **Duration:** Annual. **To Apply:** Applicant must submit a personal essay or letter stating educational and career goals and financial need; must have official transcripts from all colleges or universities attended; two recommendation letters, one academic (professor, adviser, dean) and one chapter (President, Vice President-Standards or Chapter Council Adviser). **Deadline:** February 1.

5444 ■ Kappa Kappa Gamma Foundation of Canada
2384 Yonge St.
Toronto, ON, Canada M4P 3E5
E-mail: info@kkgfoundationofcanada.org
URL: www.kkgfoundationofcanada.org

5445 ■ Kappa Kappa Gamma Foundation of Canada Graduate Scholarships *(Graduate, Doctorate/ Scholarship)*

Purpose: To support Canadian women in their pursuit of graduate degrees. **Focus:** General studies/Field of study not specified. **Qualif.:** Applicants must be female Canadian citizens who are currently enrolled in or pursuing a Ph.D. program. **Criteria:** Selection will be based on committee's criteria.

Funds Avail.: 2,500 Canadian Dollars. **To Apply:** Applicants must verify the scholarship website and retrieve the provided scholarship application form. Their application must be accompanied by a non-refundable filling fee worth 30 Canadian dollars (can be paid by personal cheque or mail order made payable to the KKG but not by payment card). Additional documents include transcripts and reference letters sealed separately from their application (letters can be separately sent directly by their referees). All packets must be sent to the Scholarship Committee. **Deadline:** March 15. **Contact:** scholarship@kkgfoundationofcanada.org.

5446 ■ Kappa Omicron Nu (KON)
4990 Northwind Dr., Ste. 140
East Lansing, MI 48823-5031
Ph: (517)351-8335
E-mail: info@kon.org
URL: www.kon.org

5447 ■ Hettie Margaret Anthony Fellowship
(Doctorate/Fellowship)

Purpose: To support members who have demonstrated scholarship, research and leadership potential. **Focus:** Science. **Qualif.:** Applicant must be active members of Kappa Omicron Nu. **Criteria:** Selection will be based on the committee's criteria.

Funds Avail.: $2,000. **Duration:** Annual. **To Apply:** Interested applicants may contact the Kappa Omicron Nu for the application process and other information.

5448 ■ Marjorie M. Brown Dissertation Fellowship
(Doctorate/Fellowship)

Purpose: To support research in critical science. **Focus:** Science. **Qualif.:** Applicants must be PhD or D.Ed students

Awards are arranged alphabetically below their administering organizations

seeking doctoral degrees from accredited US institutions of higher education; must be students who are in the process of formulating their dissertation proposals as well as doctoral candidates with approved dissertation proposals. **Criteria:** Fellowship will be awarded on a competitive basis.

Funds Avail.: $10,000. **Duration:** Annual. **Number Awarded:** 4. **To Apply:** Interested appllicants may contact Kappa Omicron Nu for the application process and other information. **Deadline:** January 15.

5449 ■ Kappa Omicron Nu Leadership Undergraduate Scholarships *(Undergraduate/Scholarship)*

Purpose: To provide opportunity for its member to attend The LeaderShape Institute. **Focus:** Leadership, Institutional and community. **Qualif.:** Applicant must be undergraduate student member with at least one more year in the undergraduate program of studies. **Criteria:** Applications are accepted on a first-come first-serve basis.

Funds Avail.: $1,025. **To Apply:** Applicant must submit a short statement of commitment to leadership on campus during the current academic year, and a short description of academic status. **Deadline:** February 1. **Contact:** Dorothy Mitstifer, dmitstifer@kon.org.

5450 ■ Kappa Omicron Nu National Alumni Fellowships *(Graduate/Fellowship)*

Purpose: To support members with studies and research in family and consumer sciences. **Focus:** Home Economics. **Qualif.:** Applicant must be an active Kappa Omicron Nu member; enrolled in a master's program in home economics or one of the specializations. **Criteria:** Selection is based on applicant's potential for professional leadership and relevance of study or research to significant concerns related to home and family.

Funds Avail.: $2000. **Duration:** Biennial. **To Apply:** Applicants must submit five (5) copies of the application form, typed or printed together with three letters of recommendations. **Deadline:** April 1. **Remarks:** Awarded biennially by the National Alumni Chapter.

5451 ■ KON National Alumni Chapter Grant *(Professional development/Grant)*

Purpose: To support the research agenda of Kappa Omicron Nu in the field of human sciences or in other related specializations. **Focus:** Science. **Qualif.:** Applicants must be active members of Kappa Omicron Nu. **Criteria:** Selection will be based on Kappa Omicron Nu's criteria.

Funds Avail.: $1,000. **Duration:** Annual. **To Apply:** Applicants must submit the application form and all supporting documents electronically to Kappa Omicron Nu. The research/project proposal shall be limited to 10 pages including supplementary materials and shall include the following: abstract; cross-specialization and integrative research approach; justification or rationale for project; statement of objective/hypotheses; description of project including methodology or design, subjects or participants, implementation plan, data collection and analysis, and implications; management plan including staff responsibilities/qualifications, and timeline for activities; budget; literature citations; supplementary materials.

5452 ■ KON New Initiatives Grant *(Professional development/Grant)*

Purpose: To support the research agenda of Kappa Omicron Nu in the field of human sciences or in other related specializations. **Focus:** Science. **Qualif.:** Applicants

must be active members of Kappa Omicron Nu. **Criteria:** Selection will be based on Kappa Omicron Nu's criteria.

Funds Avail.: $3,000. **Duration:** Annual. **To Apply:** Applicants must submit the application form and all supporting documents electronically to Kappa Omicron Nu. The research/project proposal shall be limited to 10 pages including supplementary materials and shall include the following: abstract; cross-specialization and integrative research approach; justification or rationale for project; statement of objective/hypotheses; description of project including methodology or design, subjects or participants, implementation plan, data collection and analysis, and implications; management plan including staff responsibilities/qualifications, and timeline for activities; budget; literature citations; supplementary materials.

5453 ■ Eileen C. Maddex Fellowships *(Graduate/ Fellowship)*

Purpose: To support members with studies and research in family and consumer sciences. **Focus:** Home Economics. **Qualif.:** Applicant must be an active Kappa Omicron Nu member; enrolled in a master's program in home economics or one of the specializations. **Criteria:** Selection is based on applicant's potential for professional leadership and relevance of study or research to significant concerns related to home and family.

Funds Avail.: $2000. **Duration:** Annually. **To Apply:** Applicants must submit five (5) copies of the application form, typed or printed together with three letters of recommendations. **Deadline:** April 1.

5454 ■ Kappa Omicron Nu Honor Society
4990 Northwind Dr., Ste. 140
East Lansing, MI 48823-5031
Ph: (517)351-8335
E-mail: info@kon.org
URL: www.kon.org

5455 ■ Hettie M. Anthony Fellowships *(Postdoctorate/Fellowship)*

Purpose: To provide funding support for a study and research in family and consumer sciences or one of its specializations at colleges or universities with strong research programs and supporting disciplines for the chosen major topic. **Focus:** Home Economics; Science. **Qualif.:** Applicants must have demonstrated interest in research; must be enrolled in a doctoral program in home economics or one of the specializations in a university that has a strong research program with supporting disciplines in the area of research interest; and must be current active members of Kappa Omicron Nu. **Criteria:** Recipients are selected based on demonstrated interest in research; relevance of study and/or research to significant concerns related to home and family; potential for professional leadership; demonstrated scholarship; enrollment in a master's program in home economics or one of the specializations in a university that has a strong research program with supporting disciplines in the area of research interest; and current active membership in Kappa Omicron Nu.

Funds Avail.: $2,000. **Duration:** Annual. **To Apply:** Applicants must submit five copies of the application form, type or printed along with three letters of recommendations from persons that can represent the applicants' scholarship, research, and potential for professional leadership. **Deadline:** January 15.

Awards are arranged alphabetically below their administering organizations

5456 ■ Marjorie M. Brown Fellowship Program
(Postdoctorate/Fellowship)

Purpose: To support research projects intending to continue Brown's Philosophical work using critical social theory, demonstrating understanding of Brown's Philosophical Studies and other recent pieces of work and their ongoing significance for the FCS/Human Sciences profession. **Focus:** General studies/Field of study not specified. **Qualif.:** Applicants must be Ph.D. or D.Ed. students seeking doctoral degrees from accredited U.S. institutions of higher education; tenure track professors seeking support for a research agenda using critical social theory; or associate professors or professors seeking support for the design and implementation of a graduate course that teaches a critical science research approach. **Criteria:** Recipients are selected based on the evaluation of the Award Committee.

Funds Avail.: $10,000. **Duration:** Annual. **To Apply:** Applicants must submit a cover page; an abstract of 100 words or less; introduction of the research including background, need for the study, and statement of the objectives; review of literature; method including research design, plan of work, approach to analysis; literature citations and supplementary materials; and applicants' five copies of the application form. **Deadline:** January 15.

5457 ■ KON/GEICO LeaderShape Undergraduate Scholarship *(Undergraduate/Scholarship)*

Purpose: To equip young adults to become extraordinary leaders. **Focus:** General studies/Field of study not specified. **Qualif.:** Applicants must be present undergraduate members who will have at least one more year in the undergraduate program of studies. **Criteria:** Recipients are selected based on the research; service learning including reflection about the impact on professional development; excellence in communication both oral and written; leadership of a campus or unit change project; and overall record of achievement.

Funds Avail.: $1,025. **Duration:** Annual. **Number Awarded:** 2. **To Apply:** Applicants must complete the application form and submit to National Kappa Omicron Nu. **Deadline:** February 15. **Contact:** dmitstifer@kon.org.

5458 ■ Omicron Nu Research Fellowships
(Postdoctorate/Fellowship)

Purpose: To provide funding support for a study and research in family and consumer sciences or one of its specializations at colleges or universities with strong research programs and supporting disciplines for the chosen major topic. **Focus:** Home Economics; Science. **Qualif.:** Applicants must have demonstrated interest in research; must be enrolled in a doctoral program in home economics or one of the specializations in a university that has a strong research program with supporting disciplines in the area of research interest. **Criteria:** Recipients are selected based on the demonstrated interest in research; relevance of study and/or research to significant concerns related to home and family; potential for professional leadership; demonstrated scholarship; enrollment in a master's program in home economics or one of the specializations in a university that has a strong research program with supporting disciplines in the area of research interest; and current active membership in Kappa Omicron Nu.

Funds Avail.: $2,000. **Duration:** Annual. **To Apply:** Applicants must submit five copies of the application form, type or printed along with three letters of recommendations from persons that can represent the applicants' scholar-ship, research, and potential for professional leadership. **Deadline:** January 15.

5459 ■ Kappa Sigma
1610 Scottsville Rd.
Charlottesville, VA 22902-7108
Ph: (434)295-3193
Fax: (434)296-9557
E-mail: help@kappasigma.org
URL: www.kappasigma.org

5460 ■ Scholarship/Leadership Awards
(Undergraduate/Scholarship)

Purpose: To support undergraduate members who excel in academics, campus involvement and fraternity leadership. **Focus:** General studies/Field of study not specified. **Qualif.:** Applicants must be members of Kappa Sigma Fraternity; must be full-time undergraduates who will be returning to college for the spring term; must have a minimum 2.5 cumulative grade-point average (GPA) on a 4.0 scale; must attain a minimum leadership qualification points based on university classification. **Criteria:** Selection will be based on the committee's criteria.

Funds Avail.: No specific amount. **Duration:** Annual. **Number Awarded:** September 30. **To Apply:** Applicants must visit the website for the online application process.

5461 ■ Kappa Tau Alpha (KTA)
University of Missouri
School of Journalism
76 Gannett Hall
Columbia, MO 65211-1200
Ph: (573)882-7685
Fax: (573)884-1720
E-mail: umcjourkta@missouri.edu
URL: www.kappataualpha.org

5462 ■ KTA Chapter Adviser Research Grant Award
(Professional development/Grant)

Purpose: To provide research assistance and to recognize and reward KTA advisers for their good work and to support their academic endeavors. **Focus:** General studies/Field of study not specified. **Qualif.:** Applicants must be current KTA Advisors or co-advisers of active chapters who have served for at least two full years at the time of application. **Criteria:** Selection will be based on the committee's criteria.

Funds Avail.: $1,000 each. **Duration:** Annual. **Number Awarded:** Up to 3. **To Apply:** Applicants must complete and submit the application form available online and must provide a one to three-page prospectus/overview of the project, including a budget with timelines and expected outlets for the research. Applicants must also submit a vita of no more than three pages and department head endorsement letter. Applications must be submitted to the Executive Director in digital form or PDF. **Deadline:** October 1.

5463 ■ Josephine de Karman Fellowship Trust
PO Box 3389
San Dimas, CA 91773
Ph: (909)592-0607
E-mail: info@dekarman.org
URL: www.dekarman.org

Awards are arranged alphabetically below their administering organizations

5464 ■ Josephine de Karman Fellowships *(Graduate, Undergraduate/Fellowship)*

Purpose: To support students with their educational goals. **Focus:** General studies/Field of study not specified. **Qualif.:** Applicants must be currently enrolled at a U.S. university and either be a senior undergraduate student (will receive Bachelor's Degree) or be in the final year of a PhD program (will defend dissertation). **Criteria:** Special consideration will be given to applicants in the Humanities.

Funds Avail.: $22,000 for graduate students and $14,000 for undergraduate students. **Duration:** Annual. **Number Awarded:** Minimum of 8. **To Apply:** Applicants must submit a completed application form together with official transcripts of graduate and undergraduate studies, and two letters of recommendations (in a sealed envelope with the signature of the writer across the outside flap). **Deadline:** January 31. **Remarks:** Established in 1954. **Contact:** Judy McClain at the above address.

5465 ■ Ka'u Chamber of Commerce
PO Box 6710
Ocean View, HI 96737
Ph: (808)939-8449
URL: www.kauchamber.org

5466 ■ Ka'u Chamber of Commerce College Scholarships *(Undergraduate/Scholarship)*

Purpose: To provide educational funding assistance to individuals with progressive ideas for the future of Ka'u to be determined by an essay competition. **Focus:** General studies/Field of study not specified. **Qualif.:** Students must be current high school seniors in good standing who are from the Ka'u District; must attend a two or four-year college program. **Criteria:** Selection will be based on the submitted essay.

Funds Avail.: $250 - $1,000. **Duration:** Annual. **Number Awarded:** 3. **To Apply:** Application form can be obtained from their school counseling office. Applicants must submit completed application form together with two letters of recommendation from someone who is familiar with the student and has known him/her for at least one year; unofficial transcript; essay and personal statements. **Deadline:** May 1.

5467 ■ Keats-Shelley Association of America (KSAA)
476 5th Ave.
New York Public Library, Rm. 226
New York, NY 10018
URL: k-saa.org

5468 ■ Carl H. Pforzheimer, Jr. Research Grants *(Graduate, Other/Grant)*

Purpose: To provide funding for expenses related to research in the field of British Romanticism and literary culture between 1789 and 1832, especially projects involving authors featured in the "Keats-Shelley Journal" bibliography. **Focus:** British studies. **Qualif.:** Applicants must be advanced graduate students, independent scholars and untenured faculty members. **Criteria:** Selection shall be based on the aforementioned qualifications and compliance with the application details. Preference will be given to projects involving authors featured in the bibliography of the "Keats-Shelley Journal", the Association's annual publication.

Funds Avail.: No specific amount. **Duration:** Annual. **To Apply:** Applicants must submit the following: completed application form provided at the program website; curriculum vitae; description of the project (up to 3 pages only); one-page bibliography of publications that treat the topic; and, two letters of reference from people who know the applicants work well and can judge its values. **Deadline:** November 1. **Remarks:** The grants were established to honor the late Carl H. Pforzheimer, Jr., a past President of the Association and among its most vigorous advocates. He also headed The Carl and Lily Pforzheimer Foundation, Inc., long distinguished for funding scholarship centered on early nineteenth-century English literature. Established in 2000. **Contact:** Doucet Fischer, Phone: 212-764-0655.

5469 ■ Donald Keene Center of Japanese Culture
507 Kent Hall, MC 3920
Columbia University
1140 Amsterdam Ave.
New York, NY 10027
Ph: (212)854-5036
Fax: (212)854-4019
URL: www.keenecenter.org

5470 ■ The Shincho Graduate Fellowships for Study in Japan *(Graduate/Fellowship)*

Purpose: To provide financial assistance to cover all expenses of the fellow, including air travel, tuition, research expenses, living expenses, insurance and other kind of expenses. **Focus:** Japanese studies. **Qualif.:** Applicants must be degree candidates in a graduate program at Columbia University in field of Japanese cultural studies; must have been accepted as a research student in a graduate level program at a Japanese public or private university; and must be eligible for an appropriate visa (student or cultural) according to Japanese immigration law. **Criteria:** Applicants will be evaluated under the direction of the Donald Keene Center Selection Committee and the Center Director.

Funds Avail.: No specific amount. **Duration:** Annual; One year. **Number Awarded:** 2. **To Apply:** Applicant must notify the Foundation in writing of his/her address in Japan and report on his/her program of study or research, which must have been approved in advance by the Selection Committee of the Donald Keene Center. Any change in address or program of study must be reported to the Foundation and the Center; must submit a summary report of his/her study in both Japanese and English to the Selection Committee of Donald Keene Center one month before the completion of the fellowship. A Japanese version of that summary must be submitted to the Foundation by the same deadline. Applicants must submit seven sets of the following: (four-page) application form; five-page (approximately 1,200-1,500 words) statement of purpose stating the objectives, methodology, schedule, plans for academic affiliation in Japan which reveals the relevant training and background of the applicant regarding the project; official transcripts; and curriculum vitae. Three letters of recommendation from professors must be sent directly to the DKC by the deadline. **Deadline:** February 27. **Remarks:** Established in 1992. **Contact:** donald-keene-center@columbia.edu.

5471 ■ Kegler, Brown, Hill, and Ritter Company, L.P.A
65 E State St., Ste. 1800
Columbus, OH 43215

Awards are arranged alphabetically below their administering organizations

Ph: (614)462-5400
Fax: (614)464-2634
Free: 800-860-7885
E-mail: jcartmille@keglerbrown.com
URL: www.keglerbrown.com

5472 ■ Kegler Brown Minority Merit Scholarships
(College, University, Graduate/Scholarship)

Purpose: To assist minority students financially with their legal education. **Focus:** Law. **Qualif.:** Applicants must be first year minority students studying law from all schools. **Criteria:** Award is given based on academic performance, accomplishments, activities and potential contributions to the legal community.

Funds Avail.: $5,000. **Duration:** Annual. **Number Awarded:** 2. **To Apply:** Students may contact the office for more information about the scholarship.

5473 ■ Kellogg Community College Foundation
450 N Ave.
Battle Creek, MI 49017
Ph: (269)965-3931
URL: www.kellogg.edu

5474 ■ Foundation Scholarships *(Undergraduate/Scholarship)*

Purpose: To generate and encourage philanthropic giving and manage funds to enhance the quality of education while building stronger communities. **Focus:** General studies/Field of study not specified. **Qualif.:** Applicants must have a cumulative GPA of 2.5 and be working towards their first college degree. **Criteria:** Recipients are selected based on financial need, demonstrated academic achievements, number of credit hours and/or special circumstances.

Funds Avail.: No specific amount. **To Apply:** Applicants must submit a 150 word personal statement detailing their goals and achievements, a copy of transcript of records and three letters of recommendation from high school or college instructors, counselors or employers.

5475 ■ Gold Key Scholarships *(Undergraduate/Scholarship)*

Purpose: To generate and encourage philanthropic giving and manage funds to enhance the quality of education while building stronger communities. **Focus:** General studies/Field of study not specified. **Qualif.:** Applicants must be students within the KCC district; must have completed no more than 24 credit hours of college; must have 3.2 cumulative GPA and ACT of 20 or higher. **Criteria:** Recipients are selected based on leadership experience.

Funds Avail.: $6,000. **Duration:** Two years. **To Apply:** Applicants must submit: a completed application form; an official high school and/or college transcript; three written letters of recommendation; ACT scores; 150 word written essay discussing achievements and future goals; and resume or employment information including activities, leadership, volunteer or school-related positions.

5476 ■ Walter and Lucille Harper Scholarships
(Undergraduate/Scholarship)

Purpose: To generate and encourage philanthropic giving and manage= funds to enhance the quality of education while building stronger communities. **Focus:** General

studies/Field of study not specified. **Qualif.:** Applicants must be second year KCC students graduating with an associate's degree; must have a minimum of 3.0 GPA; must be citizens of the United States. **Criteria:** Recipients are selected based on academic performance and financial need.

Funds Avail.: No specific amount. **To Apply:** Applicants must submit: a completed application form; a copy of transcript of records; 150 word personal statement detailing their future aspirations; and three written letters of recommendation from teachers, counselors and employers. **Deadline:** March 14.

5477 ■ Trustee Scholarships *(Undergraduate/Scholarship)*

Purpose: To generate and encourage philanthropic giving and manage funds to enhance the quality of education while building stronger communities. **Focus:** General studies/Field of study not specified. **Qualif.:** Applicants must be graduating high school seniors within the KCC district; must be in the top 20% of graduating class and have at least a 3.0 GPA. **Criteria:** Recipients are selected based on academic performance and financial need.

Funds Avail.: No specific amount. **To Apply:** Applicants must submit a completed application form; a 150 word essay; copy of high school and college transcripts; private copy of ACT scores; resume; three recommendation letters from teachers, instructors or community members. **Deadline:** March 14.

5478 ■ The Deana Kendrick Foundation (TDKF)
c/o Kay Litchy
PO Box 14146
Springfield, MO 65814
E-mail: info@tdkf.org
URL: www.cfmconline.org

5479 ■ Kendrick Foundation, Inc. Scholarships
(Undergraduate/Scholarship)

Purpose: To support Morgan County residents who are pursuing a career in health field education. **Focus:** Dentistry; Health care services; Medicine; Nursing. **Qualif.:** Applicants must be Morgan County, Indiana residents who have: graduated by the end of June of the current year, with a diploma from an Indiana high school or an equivalent education; and, been accepted into a program at an accredited college, university or other educational institution to complete a course of study in a health care field (including medicine, dentistry, allied health, and nursing) beginning in the fall of the current year. **Criteria:** Selection shall be based on the aforementioned qualifications and compliance with the application details.

Funds Avail.: $15,000 per person. **Duration:** Annual. **Number Awarded:** Varies. **To Apply:** Applicants may visit the website to verify the application process and other pieces of information.

5480 ■ Kennedy Krieger Institute (KKI)
707 N Broadway
Baltimore, MD 21205
Ph: (443)923-9200
Fax: (443)923-9317
Free: 800-873-3377
E-mail: info@kennedykrieger.org

Awards are arranged alphabetically below their administering organizations

URL: www.kennedykrieger.org

5481 ■ Dr. James A. Ferguson Emerging Infectious Diseases Fellowships *(Graduate/Fellowship)*

Purpose: To provide public health research and professional development in the area of infectious diseases and health disparities with a special focus on increasing knowledge and interest in public health careers among students from under-represented populations. **Focus:** Infectious diseases. **Qualif.:** Applicants must be U.S. citizens, U.S. nationals, or permanent residents who are currently enrolled as full-time students in a medical, dental, pharmacy, veterinary, or public health graduate program; must have 3.0 GPA or higher on a 4.0 scale; and must be able to commit to the full length of the fellowship. **Criteria:** Selection will be based on the applicants' eligibility and their compliance with the application process.

Funds Avail.: $4,000. **To Apply:** Applicants may contact the Institute for the online application process. **Deadline:** January 31. **Remarks:** The nine-week fellowship program is funded by the Centers for Disease Control and Prevention (CDC). **Contact:** To apply, please go to http://kennedykrieger.org/Ferguson. For additional program information, please contact Ferguson_Fellowship@kennedykrieger.org.

5482 ■ John F. Kennedy Presidential Library and Museum

Columbia Point
Boston, MA 02125
Ph: (617)514-1600
Fax: (617)514-1652
Free: 866-535-1960
E-mail: kennedy.library@nara.gov
URL: www.jfklibrary.org

5483 ■ Marjorie Kovler Research Fellowships *(Professional development/Fellowship)*

Purpose: To support a student in the production of a substantial work in the area of foreign intelligence and the presidency or a related topic. **Focus:** General studies/Field of study not specified. **Qualif.:** Applicant must be conducting a research in the area of foreign intelligence and the presidency or related field. **Criteria:** Selection is based on the submitted application and supporting materials. Preference is given to projects not supported by large grants from other institutions.

Funds Avail.: Up to $2,500. **To Apply:** Applicants must submit a completed application form along with brief proposal (3-4 pages) in the form of letter describing the planned research, its significance, the intended audience, and expected outcome; two letters of recommendation from academic or other appropriate references; sample of writing; a project budget; and a vita. **Deadline:** August 15.

5484 ■ Arthur M. Schlesinger, Jr. Fellowships *(Professional development/Fellowship)*

Purpose: To support individuals conducting research in Latin American or Western Hemisphere history or policy studies during the Kennedy Administration or the period from the Roosevelt through the Kennedy presidencies. **Focus:** History, American; Latin American studies. **Qualif.:** Applicant must be a scholar in the production of substantial works on the foreign policy of the Kennedy years, especially with regard to the western hemisphere, or on Kennedy

domestic policy, especially with regard to racial justice and to the conservation of natural resources. **Criteria:** Selection is based on the submitted application and supporting materials. Preference is given to projects not supported by large grants from other institutions.

Funds Avail.: Up to $5,000. **Number Awarded:** 1 or 2. **To Apply:** Applicants must submit a completed application form along with brief proposal (3-4 pages) in the form of letter describing the planned research, its significance, the intended audience, and expected outcome; two letters of recommendation from academic or other appropriate references; sample of writing; a project budget; and a vita. **Deadline:** August 15.

5485 ■ Abba P. Schwartz Research Fellowships *(Professional development/Fellowship)*

Purpose: To support a student in the production of a substantial work in the area of immigration, naturalization, or refugee policy. **Focus:** Immigration. **Qualif.:** Applicant must be conducting a research in the area of immigration, naturalization, or refugee policy. **Criteria:** Selection is based on the submitted application and supporting materials. Preference is given to projects not supported by large grants from other institutions.

Funds Avail.: Up to $3,100. **Number Awarded:** 1. **To Apply:** Applicants must submit a completed application form along with brief proposal (3-4 pages) in the form of letter describing the planned research, its significance, the intended audience, and expected outcome; two letters of recommendation from academic or other appropriate references; sample of writing; a project budget; and a vita. **Deadline:** August 15.

5486 ■ Theodore C. Sorensen Research Fellowships *(Professional development/Fellowship)*

Purpose: To support a student in the production of a substantial work in the areas of domestic policy, political journalism, polling, press relations or a related topic. **Focus:** Public affairs. **Qualif.:** Applicant must be conducting research in the areas of domestic policy, political journalism, polling, press relations or a related topic. **Criteria:** Selection is based on the submitted application and supporting materials. Preference is given to projects not supported by large grants from other institutions.

Funds Avail.: Up to $3,600. **Number Awarded:** 1. **To Apply:** Applicants must submit a completed application form along with brief proposal (3-4 pages) in the form of letter describing the planned research, its significance, the intended audience, and expected outcome; two letters of recommendation from academic or other appropriate references; sample of writing; a project budget; and a vita. **Deadline:** August 15.

5487 ■ Kentucky Association of Realtors (KAR)

161 Prosperous Pl., Ste. 100
Lexington, KY 40509
Ph: (859)263-7377
Fax: (859)263-7565
Free: 800-264-2185
E-mail: kar@kar.com
URL: www.kar.com

5488 ■ Graduate Realtor Institute Scholarships *(Graduate/Scholarship)*

Purpose: To provide quality educational services and programs for the real estate industry and the public. **Focus:**

Awards are arranged alphabetically below their administering organizations

Real estate. **Qualif.:** Applicants must be residents of Kentucky; must be members that have been in the business for at least 2 years and in good standing with local, state and national association; must complete all GRI courses in the state of Kentucky within two years of the first course taken. **Criteria:** Recipient will be selected by the KREEF Selection Committee.

Funds Avail.: Up to $1,000. **Duration:** Annual; up to 36 months. **To Apply:** Applicants must complete the application available on the website; must attach a letter of verification of realtor membership from a local board/association and submit the package to Kentucky Real Estate Education Foundation. **Deadline:** June 12. **Contact:** Kentucky Real Estate Education Foundation; Email: bbaxter@kar.com.

5489 ■ Kentucky Paralegal Association (KPA)
PO Box 2675
Louisville, KY 40201-2675
URL: www.kypa.org

5490 ■ Kentucky Paralegal Association Student Scholarships *(Undergraduate/Scholarship)*

Purpose: To provide financial assistance to those students who are in need. **Focus:** Paralegal studies. **Qualif.:** Applicants must be enrolled in a paralegal program within the Commonwealth of Kentucky; must have at least 12 credit hours of paralegal coursework completed with a GPA in those courses of 3.50 or higher and an overall GPA of 3.25 or higher. **Criteria:** Preference will be given to those students who meet the criteria.

Funds Avail.: $1,000. **To Apply:** Applicants must submit the following: application form (typed); 2 letters of recommendation and forms; one writing sample; an essay and official transcript. **Deadline:** May 31. **Contact:** Leslie Smith, KPA Vice President, 63 Windfield Way, Florence, KY 41042.

5491 ■ Kentucky Society of Certified Public Accountants (KyCPA)
1735 Alliant Ave.
Louisville, KY 40299
Ph: (502)266-5272
Fax: (502)261-9512
Free: 800-292-1754
URL: www.kycpa.org

5492 ■ The Educational Foundation of KyCPA Scholarships *(Undergraduate/Scholarship)*

Purpose: To support students aspiring to become a Certified Public Accountant. **Focus:** Accounting. **Qualif.:** Applicants must: be enrolled in a Kentucky-based college or university and be at least a sophomore at the time of application; be U.S. citizens; have an overall grade point average of at least 2.75 and an accounting grade point average of 3.0; have completed Principles of Accounting; have completed or are enrolled in Intermediate Accounting; indicate plans to sit for the CPA exam (applicants who have completed all or parts of the exam are also eligible); intend to stay and work/live in Kentucky upon graduation; and, need to agree to submit an application for student membership for the KyCPA before the scholarship is awarded. **Criteria:** Scholarship awards are based on acceptable academic performance and financial need.

Funds Avail.: $1,000 to $2,500. **Duration:** Annual. **To Apply:** Applicants must complete the online application. After

such, documents below must be uploaded in the following order: college transcript(s) or unofficial transcripts; one page resume (include info on community service, academic organizations and activities); one page essay stating career goals, reasons for choosing accounting, how applicants are financing their education and why they should receive the scholarship; and, two recommendations, one must be from an accounting faculty member. **Deadline:** February 20. **Remarks:** Established in 1988. **Contact:** Vicky Blair at vblair@kycpa.org or call 502-266-5272.

5493 ■ Kevin Kitchnefsky Foundation
109 German Hill Rd.
Tunkhannock, PA 18657
Ph: (570)836-1240
E-mail: kkitch@mymail.emcyber.com
URL: helpkevinwalk.org

5494 ■ Individual K Grants *(All/Grant)*

Purpose: To substantially improve the quality of life for the people affected. **Focus:** Spinal cord injuries and research. **Qualif.:** Applicants must be any residents of Pennsylvania who have suffered a spinal injury. **Criteria:** Selection will be based on the committee's criteria.

Funds Avail.: No specific amount. **To Apply:** Applicants must print and fill out the application, available at the website, as completely as possible. Use additional paper for the essays, and then attach them to the application. It is necessary that they must include a copy of letter from their doctor, certifying and explaining the nature of their injury. When the grant is awarded, the Foundation pays the monies directly to the organization or individual providing the product or service that the applicants requesting. **Contact:** Kevin or Yvonne at 570-836-1240.

5495 ■ Kidney Foundation of Canada (KFOC)
310-5160 Decarie Blvd.
Montreal, QC, Canada H3X 2H9
Ph: (514)369-4806
Fax: (514)369-2472
Free: 800-361-7494
E-mail: info@kidney.ca
URL: www.kidney.ca

5496 ■ KFOC Allied Health Doctoral Fellowship *(Doctorate/Fellowship)*

Purpose: To promote and enhance the development of nephrology/urology allied health investigators in Canada. **Focus:** Health sciences; Nephrology. **Qualif.:** Applicant must serve as a nephrology nurse or technician, social worker, dietician, transplant coordinator or other allied health professional; must have a demonstrated commitment to the area of nephrology or organ donation; must hold Canadian citizenship of landed immigrant status; must be accepted in proposed course of full-time study; and must have the intention to return to Canada (if studies are outside the country). **Criteria:** Preference will be given to applicants with a minimum of two years full-time equivalent experience in the area of nephrology.

Funds Avail.: Up to $31,000/year. **Duration:** up to 2 years. **To Apply:** Applicants must submit one complete original copy of the application package (unstapled) and one PDF copy on CD. Application package includes: the checklist; Allied Health Doctoral Fellowships application; minimum of

Awards are arranged alphabetically below their administering organizations

two sponsors' assessment forms; certified academic transcripts (graduate and undergraduate); permanent resident document (if applicable); proof of acceptance into a full-time studies program; a program description provided by the institution; CV Module for applicant; CV Module(s) for supervisor(s); and up to five peer-review articles. **Deadline:** March 15.

5497 ■ KFOC Allied Health Scholarships *(Graduate/ Scholarship)*

Purpose: To assist students with a demonstrated interest in nephrology/urology who are pursuing education at the masters or doctoral level. **Focus:** Health sciences; Nephrology; Urology. **Qualif.:** Applicant must serve as a nephrology nurse or technician, social worker, dietician, transplant coordinator or other allied health professional; must have a demonstrated commitment to the area of nephrology or organ donation; must hold Canadian citizenship or landed immigrant status; and must be accepted in proposed course of full-time or part-time study. **Criteria:** Preference will be given to applicants with a minimum of two years full-time equivalent experience in the area of nephrology.

Funds Avail.: No specific amount. **Duration:** one year. **To Apply:** Applicants must submit one complete original copy of the application package (unstapled) and one PDF copy on CD. Application package includes: the checklist; Allied Health Scholarship application; permanent resident document (if applicable); letter from academic institution confirming acceptance into a full-time or part-time course of study; program description provided by the institution; two referees' assessment of candidate forms; and certified academic transcripts (post secondary). **Deadline:** March 15.

5498 ■ KFOC Biomedical Fellowships *(Postdoctorate/Fellowship)*

Purpose: To encourage research that may further current knowledge pertaining to the kidney and urinary tract. **Focus:** Biomedical research. **Qualif.:** Applicants must be Canadian citizens or landed immigrants. Eligibility for fellowships will include MDs or postdoctoral PhDs. **Criteria:** Priority will be given to applicants who are at the beginning of their research training and to those planning a career in Canada.

Funds Avail.: $35,000-$45,000 with travel allowance of $1,800/year (for scientific purposes only). **Duration:** Up to three years. **To Apply:** Applicants must submit one complete original copy of the application package (unstapled) and one PDF copy on CD. Application package includes: checklist; Post Doctoral Fellowship Module; letter from proposed supervisor; written proof of offer of permanent position (if applicable); three sponsors' assessment forms; CV Module for Principal applicant; CV Module(s) for supervisor(s); up to five publications from the past five years (relevant to the proposal); and declaration by the applicant and supervisor. **Deadline:** January 15. **Contact:** Wim Wolfs at 514-369-4806 x-225, 514-369-2472 (fax) or wim.wolfs@kidney.ca; Christine Marquis at 514-369-4806 x-232 or chris.marquis@kidney.ca.

5499 ■ KFOC Biomedical Scholarships *(Doctorate/ Scholarship)*

Purpose: To provide salary support of an initial faculty appointment at the rank of assistant professor or its equivalent. **Focus:** Nephrology; Urology. **Qualif.:** Applicants should have an MD and have completed clinical training in

nephrology or urology or a PhD and have been appointed to a medical school. Applicants must have demonstrated interest in nephrology or urology and should have completed at least two years of research training at the time of the award. **Criteria:** Selection is based on the research program outlined in the application.

Funds Avail.: $45,000/year. **Duration:** Up to two years. **To Apply:** Applicants must submit one complete original copy of the application package (unstapled) and one PDF copy on CD. Application package includes: the checklist; Biomedical Scholarship Module; letters of collaboration and/or support; list of operating and other grants applied for, or which are planned to apply for; appropriate ethical form(s); CV Module for principal applicant; and up to ten publications in the past five years (relevant to the proposal). **Deadline:** October 15. **Contact:** Wim Wolfs at 514-369-4806 x-225, 514-369-2472 (fax) or wim.wolfs@kidney.ca; Christine Marquis at 514-369-4806 x-232 or chris.marquis@kidney.ca.

5500 ■ Killingworth Foundation
PO Box 621
Killingworth, CT 06419
E-mail: info@killingworthfoundation.org
URL: www.killingworthfoundation.org

5501 ■ Killingworth Foundation Scholarships *(Undergraduate/Scholarship)*

Purpose: To provide funds for the education of students in Killingworth. **Focus:** General studies/Field of study not specified. **Qualif.:** Applicants must be Killingworth residents currently enrolled as full-time high school students; have a cumulative high school GPA equivalent to a "B" or higher at the time of application; and applying to a post-secondary educational institution. **Criteria:** Selection is based on academic achievement, fullness of character, community service, and both school and community extra-curricular activities or employment.

Funds Avail.: No specific amount. **Duration:** Annual. **To Apply:** Applicants must submit a completed application form together with the hand-written essay. Official transcripts (includes SAT/ACT scores) must be sent directly to the Foundation from the Guidance Department of the applicant's high school. **Deadline:** March 1. **Contact:** Killingworth Foundation, at the above address.

5502 ■ Sidney Kimmel Foundation for Cancer Research
c/o Gary Cohen, Director
Cancer Ctr. at GBMC
6569 N Charles St., Ste. 300
Baltimore, MD 21204
Ph: (443)849-3729
Fax: (443)849-3719
URL: www.kimmel.org

5503 ■ Kimmel Scholars Award *(Doctorate/Grant)*

Purpose: To improve the basic understanding of cancer biology and to develop new methods for the prevention and treatment of cancer. **Focus:** Oncology. **Qualif.:** Applicants must be those researchers who achieved the equivalent rank of Assistant Professor on or after July of the calendar year, and who do not yet have their own R01 funding. Moreover, they must also hold an M.D., Ph.D. or equivalent

Awards are arranged alphabetically below their administering organizations

graduate degree and must perform research in an American not-for-profit institution during the period of Kimmel Foundation support. **Criteria:** Applicants will be judged on the basis of quality of prior work, research proposed and letters of support.

Funds Avail.: $100,000/year. **Duration:** Annual. **Number Awarded:** Up to 10. **To Apply:** Applicants may visit the program website for further information regarding the application details/process. **Deadline:** December 3. **Contact:** kfletche@gbmc.org.

5504 ■ Esther A. and Joseph Klingenstein Fund

125 Park Ave., Ste. 1700
New York, NY 10017-5529
Ph: (212)492-6195
URL: www.klingfund.org

5505 ■ Klingenstein Fellowships in the Neurosciences *(Doctorate, Other/Fellowship)*

Purpose: To support young investigators engaged in basic or clinical research that may lead to a better understanding of epilepsy. **Focus:** Neuroscience. **Qualif.:** Applicant must hold a PhD or M.D. degree; have completed all research training, including post-doctoral training; must be a permanent resident of the U.S.; must be conducting research which will be carried out in a U.S. institution; must be an independent investigator holding a tenure track academic rank (but not yet tenured) in a university or medical school, or the equivalent standing in a research institute or medical center. **Criteria:** Applications will be reviewed and selections will be made by an Advisory Committee of distinguished neuroscientists.

Funds Avail.: $75,000. **Duration:** Annual. **Number Awarded:** 12. **To Apply:** Applicants must submit one original and ten copies of completed application form, and three letters of recommendation.

5506 ■ Klingenstein Third Generation Foundation (KTGF)

125 Park Ave., Ste. 1700
New York, NY 10017-5529
Ph: (212)492-6179
E-mail: info@ktgf.org
URL: www.ktgf.org

5507 ■ Depression and ADHD Fellowships *(Postdoctorate/Fellowship)*

Purpose: To support graduates who have demonstrated outstanding promise and are eager to continue in an academic research career. **Focus:** Child development; Psychiatry. **Qualif.:** Candidates must be post-doctoral investigators with a PhD and/or MD who have completed all critical training; should be planning a career in research related to child and adolescent psychiatry and psychology; and should have demonstrated skills for independent research. **Criteria:** Recipients will be selected based on originality; soundness; contribution to progress within the field; quality of institutional support; mentoring and training program.

Funds Avail.: $30,000. **Duration:** Two years. **To Apply:** Candidates must be nominated by their institutions. **Deadline:** January 10.

5508 ■ Klingon Language Institute (KLI)

PO Box 794
Blue Bell, PA 19422

URL: www.kli.org

5509 ■ Kor Memorial Scholarships *(Undergraduate, Graduate/Scholarship)*

Purpose: To provide financial support to students who are in need. **Focus:** Foreign languages. **Qualif.:** Applicants must be full-time graduate or undergraduate students in a program leading to a degree in a field of language studies and must be nominated by an academic department chair/head and/or dean. **Criteria:** Selection shall be based on the aforementioned applicants' qualifications and compliance with the application details.

Funds Avail.: No specific amount. **Duration:** Annual. **To Apply:** Applicants may visit the scholarship section of the bestowing organization's website for further information regarding the application details.

5510 ■ John W. Kluge Center at the Library of Congress

101 Independence Ave. SE
Washington, DC 20540-4860
Ph: (202)707-3302
Fax: (202)707-3595
E-mail: scholarly@loc.gov
URL: www.loc.gov/loc/kluge

5511 ■ Kislak Fellowships in American Studies *(Graduate, Postdoctorate/Fellowship)*

Purpose: To support research that contributes significantly to a greater understanding of the cultures and history of the Americas. **Focus:** United States studies. **Qualif.:** Applicant may be of any nationality and must possess a PhD degree or equivalent terminal degree by time of the application deadline. **Criteria:** Selection is based on the submitted application materials.

Funds Avail.: $4,200/month. **Duration:** Annual; Up to eight months. **To Apply:** Applicants must submit an application form; a two-page curriculum vitae; a one-paragraph project summary; a bibliography of basic sources; a research proposal of no more than 1,500 words; and three letters of reference (in English) from people who have read the research proposal. **Deadline:** October 15. **Contact:** scholarly@loc.gov.

5512 ■ Kislak Short Term Fellowships Opportunities in American Studies *(Undergraduate, Graduate/Fellowship)*

Purpose: To support research that contributes significantly to a greater understanding of the cultures and history of the Americas. **Focus:** United States studies. **Qualif.:** Applicant may be an independent scholar, undergraduate or graduate student or a college/university faculty in any discipline. There is no degree requirement but relevant educational information should be supplied in the application. **Criteria:** Selection is based on the submitted application materials.

Funds Avail.: $4,200/month. **Duration:** Up to four months. **To Apply:** Applicants must submit a cover letter; curriculum vitae (no more than 600 words); research proposal (no more than 600 words); and two letters of reference. **Contact:** scholarly@loc.gov.

5513 ■ Kluge Fellowships *(Doctorate, Graduate/Fellowship)*

Purpose: To support students who wish to conduct research at the John W. Kluge Center. **Focus:** Architecture;

Awards are arranged alphabetically below their administering organizations

Humanities; Law; Social sciences. **Qualif.:** Applicant must have received a terminal advanced degree within the past seven years in the humanities, social sciences or in a professional field such as architecture or law. **Criteria:** Selection is based on the submitted application materials.

Funds Avail.: $4,200/month. **Duration:** Annual; Up to 11 months. **To Apply:** Applicants must submit an original (signed) and six copies of full applications including the proposal (no longer than three single-spaced pages); bibliography of basic sources; a one paragraph project summary; two-page curriculum vitae; and three letters of reference (in English). **Deadline:** July 15. **Contact:** scholarly@loc.gov.

5514 ■ David B. Larson Fellowships in Health and Spirituality (Doctorate/Fellowship)

Purpose: To support students who wish to conduct research at the John W. Kluge Center. **Focus:** Health education; Religion. **Qualif.:** Applicant must be a U.S. citizen or permanent resident and must possess a doctoral degree (PhD, MD, ScD, DrPH, DSW, PPsy, DST, ThD and JD). **Criteria:** Selection is based on the submitted application materials.

Funds Avail.: $4,200/month. **Duration:** Annual; 6-12 months. **To Apply:** Applicants must submit a complete formal application packet including an application form; two page curriculum vitae; one paragraph project summary; a bibliography of basic sources; research proposal of no more than 1,500 words; and three letters of reference (in English) from people who have read the research proposal. **Deadline:** April 17. **Contact:** scholarly@loc.gov.

5515 ■ Knight-Wallace Fellows at Michigan
University of Michigan
Mike and Mary Wallace House
620 Oxford Road
Ann Arbor, MI 48104
Ph: (734)998-7666
URL: www.kwfellows.org

5516 ■ Knight-Wallace Fellowship (Professional development/Fellowship)

Purpose: To provide a life-changing experience to journalists from US and abroad. **Focus:** Journalism. **Qualif.:** Applicants must be full-time journalists, with a minimum five years professional experience, whose work appears regularly as e1mployees or freelancers. Print, broadcast, photo, documentary and internet journalists are eligible. **Criteria:** Preferences will be given to the best and brightest mid-career professionals, with at least five years of professional experience and solid track records and demonstrated leadership in aspect of journalism.

Funds Avail.: $70,000; stipends for international fellows vary. **Duration:** Annual. **Number Awarded:** 1 U.S. Applicant; up to 6 international Applicants. **To Apply:** Interested applicants may visit the website for the online application process and must provide a resume, essays, work samples and letters of recommendation. **Deadline:** February 1. **Contact:** apply2KWF@umich.edu.

5517 ■ Knights of Columbus
1 Columbus Plz.
New Haven, CT 06510-3326
Ph: (203)752-4000
E-mail: info@kofc.org

URL: www.kofc.org

5518 ■ Bishop Charles P. Greco Graduate Fellowships (Graduate, Master's/Fellowship)

Purpose: To provide financial assistance to students enrolled in a Master's degree program designed for teachers of people with intellectual disabilities. **Focus:** General studies/Field of study not specified. **Qualif.:** Applicants must be enrolled in a full-time master's degree program for teachers of people with intellectual disabilities; must be members in good standing of the Knights of Columbus, or the wife, sons or daughters of such a member or deceased member. **Criteria:** Selection will be based on the evaluation of submitted documents and specific criteria.

Funds Avail.: Up to $2,000. **Duration:** Annual. **To Apply:** Applications may be obtained from the Committee on Fellowships. **Deadline:** May 1. **Remarks:** Established in 1973.

5519 ■ Kobe College Corporation-Japan Education Exchange (KCC-JEE)
540 W Frontage Rd., Ste. 3335
Northfield, IL 60093
Ph: (847)386-7661
Fax: (847)386-7662
E-mail: kccjee@comcast.net
URL: www.kccjee.org

5520 ■ KCC-JEE Graduate Fellowships (Graduate/Fellowship)

Purpose: To support future American educators who teach more effectively about Japan. **Focus:** Aesthetics; Japanese studies; Religion. **Qualif.:** Applicants must be graduate students who have records of teaching effectively about Japan, or who show promise to do so in the future; must be U.S. citizens enrolled, in good standing, in a graduate program at an accredited higher education institution in the United States. Recipients must plan to teach in the United States after completing their degree, either at the secondary or higher education levels and should have good public speaking skills. **Criteria:** Selection will be based on: scholarly excellence of the applicants; quality of the proposal; quality of the preparation to undertake the proposed fellowship plan; plan for teaching upon completion of degree; documented interest in women's education; and feasibility of the project and proposed schedule. Applications will be reviewed by a distinguished panel of scholars and should be prepared accordingly. Preference will be given to applicants who provide a written confirmation of the research or study site in Japan.

Funds Avail.: $30,000. **Duration:** Annual. **Number Awarded:** Varies. **To Apply:** Applicants must contact KCC-JEE for the application information. **Deadline:** December 20. **Remarks:** Established in 1996. **Contact:** KCC Japan Education Exchange; Email: kccjee@comcast.net.

5521 ■ Herb Kohl Educational Foundation
PO Box 877
Sheboygan, WI 53082-0877
Ph: (920)457-1727
E-mail: marggraf@excel.net
URL: www.kohleducation.org

5522 ■ Herb Kohl Educational Foundation Excellence Scholarships (Undergraduate/Scholarship)

Purpose: To help graduating high school students pursue an undergraduate education. **Focus:** General studies/Field

Awards are arranged alphabetically below their administering organizations

of study not specified. **Qualif.:** Applicants must be graduating high school students who intend to enroll in a post-secondary institution, university, college, or vocational/technical college. **Criteria:** Recipients will be chosen for their demonstrated academic potential, outstanding leadership, citizenship, community service and integrity, future, personal, community/society and career goals.

Funds Avail.: $3,000. **Number Awarded:** 100. **To Apply:** Applicants must submit a completed application form.

5523 ■ Herb Kohl Educational Foundation Fellowships *(Professional development/Fellowship)*

Purpose: To recognize the contribution of Wisconsin classroom teachers. **Focus:** General studies/Field of study not specified. **Qualif.:** Applicants must be Pre-K through Grade 12 Wisconsin teachers who intend to continue teaching for at least the year following the receipt of the fellowship; must be nominated by a parent, teacher, student, community member or administrator. **Criteria:** Educators will be chosen for their superior ability to inspire a love of learning in their students and ability to motivate others through leadership and service within and outside the classroom.

Funds Avail.: $3,000. **Number Awarded:** 100. **To Apply:** Applicants must contact Hern Kohl Educational Foundation office for further information.

5524 ■ Herb Kohl Educational Foundation Initiative Scholarships *(High School/Scholarship)*

Purpose: To recognize students who have not yet received other academic-based scholarships. **Focus:** General studies/Field of study not specified. **Qualif.:** Applicants must be graduating high school students. **Criteria:** Recipients will be selected based on demonstrated high level of motivation to achieve, have shown strong promise for achieving success in college and beyond, have overcome significant personal obstacles or adversity.

Funds Avail.: $3,000. **Duration:** Annual. **Number Awarded:** 85. **To Apply:** Applicants must contact Herb Kohl Educational Foundation office for further information.

5525 ■ Susan G. Komen for the Cure

5005 LBJ Freeway, Ste. 250
Dallas, TX 75244
Free: 877-465-6636
URL: ww5.komen.org

5526 ■ Susan G. Komen for the Cure College Scholarship Awards *(Two Year College/Award, Scholarship)*

Purpose: To assist young adults in their academic pursuits. **Focus:** General studies/Field of study not specified. **Qualif.:** Applicants must be U.S. citizens, high school or college graduate students who have lost a parent to breast cancer; planning to attend state-supported college or university in their state where they permanently reside and were never subjected to disciplinary action by any institution; must have 2.8 GPA on a 4.0 scale; and not older than 25 years old. **Criteria:** Applicants will be evaluated based on scholastic achievement, community service, financial need, and demonstrated leadership potential.

Funds Avail.: $5,000. **Duration:** Four years. **To Apply:** Applicants must send an email to Susan G. Komen Breast Cancer Foundation to apply for the application. **Deadline:** October 15. **Contact:** For additional information, contact

ISTS at contactus@applyists.com.

5527 ■ Koniag Education Foundation (KEF)

4241 B St., Ste. 303 B
Anchorage, AK 99503
Ph: (907)562-9093
Fax: (907)562-9023
Free: 888-562-9093
E-mail: kef@koniageducation.org
URL: www.koniageducation.org

5528 ■ Glenn Godfrey Memorial Scholarships *(Undergraduate, Graduate/Scholarship)*

Purpose: To help Alutiiq people pursue self-improvement and positive leadership roles. **Focus:** General studies/Field of study not specified. **Qualif.:** Applicants must be college sophomores, juniors, or seniors in the upcoming school year; be Alaska Native shareholders or descendants (may be adopted) of the Koniag Region; accepted to or enrolled in a nationally, regionally, or municipally accredited vocational school; be graduating high school seniors, or high school or GED graduates, or have successfully completed one or more college, university or graduate school terms; and have and maintain a minimum cumulative GPA of 2.50 or better. **Criteria:** Selection shall be based on the aforementioned applicants' qualifications and compliance with the application details.

Funds Avail.: $5,000. **Duration:** Annual. **Number Awarded:** 1. **To Apply:** Applicants must submit the summary of Application Information; completed student application (pages 3-4, excluding the guidelines); essay; two letters of recommendation; college transcript; and Birth Certificate to prove Descendant status (necessary for descendants only), or a Koniag Descendant Registration or proof of application for descendants (necessary for descendants only). Submit all materials (in order) in one envelope. **Deadline:** June 1. **Remarks:** The scholarship was named in honor of Glenn Godfrey, an Aleut political and social leader who was raised on Kodiak Island. **Contact:** scholarships@koniageducation.org.

5529 ■ KEF Academic Scholarships *(Undergraduate, Graduate/Scholarship)*

Purpose: To seek out and honor students who excel academically and who show the potential to succeed in college studies. **Focus:** General studies/Field of study not specified. **Qualif.:** Applicants must: be Alaska Native shareholder or descendants (may be adopted) of the Koniag Region; accepted or enrolled in a nationally, regionally, or municipally accredited or recognized institution of higher learning or vocational school; be graduating high school seniors, or high school or GED graduates, or have successfully completed one or more college, university or graduate school terms; and, have and maintain a minimum cumulative GPA of 2.00 or equivalent scores. **Criteria:** Selection shall be based on the aforementioned applicants' qualifications and compliance with the application details.

Funds Avail.: Up to $2,500 each. **Duration:** Annual. **Number Awarded:** Varies. **To Apply:** Applicants must submit a completed, signed and dated application form together with a proof of eligibility as Alaska Native shareholder or descendent (may be adopted) of the Koniag Region; essay (300-600 words); transcript; two letters of recommendation (for New students); proof of acceptance (for New students); a recent photo; a resume; and a Koniag Descendant

Awards are arranged alphabetically below their administering organizations

Database form. **Deadline:** March 15 (Summer term); June 1 (Fall term). **Contact:** scholarships@koniageducation.org.

5530 ■ KEF College/University Basic Scholarships
(Undergraduate/Scholarship)

Purpose: To seek out and honor students who show the potential to succeed in college studies. **Focus:** General studies/Field of study not specified. **Qualif.:** Applicants are those who are accepted to or enrolled in an accredited institute and have completed high school or received their GED who maintain a minimum cumulative GPA of 2.00. **Criteria:** Selection shall be based on the aforementioned applicants' qualifications and compliance with the application details.

Funds Avail.: Up to $2,500 each. **Duration:** Annual. **Number Awarded:** Varies. **To Apply:** Applicants must submit a completed, signed and dated application form together with a proof of eligibility as Alaska Native shareholder or descendent (may be adopted) of the Koniag Region; essay (300-600 words); transcript; two letters of recommendation (for New students); proof of acceptance (for New students); a recent photo; a resume; and a Koniag Descendant Database form. **Deadline:** March 15 (Summer term); June 1 (Fall term). **Contact:** scholarships@koniageducation.org.

5531 ■ KEF Vocational Education Scholarship
(Undergraduate/Scholarship)

Purpose: To seek out and honor students who have chosen to further their education through vocational training lasting more than six weeks. **Focus:** General studies/Field of study not specified. **Qualif.:** Applicants are those who accepted to or enrolled in an accredited vocational school and maintain a minimum cumulative GPA of 2.00 as well as demonstrating how the training will assist in gaining employment or advancement. **Criteria:** Selection shall be based on the aforementioned applicants' qualifications and compliance with the application details.

Funds Avail.: Up to $2,500 each. **Duration:** Annual. **Number Awarded:** Varies. **To Apply:** Applicants must submit a completed, signed and dated application form together with a proof of eligibility as Alaska Native shareholder or descendent (may be adopted) of the Koniag Region; essay (300-600 words); transcript; two letters of recommendation (for New students); proof of acceptance (for New students); a recent photo; a resume; and a Koniag Descendant Database form. **Deadline:** March 15 (Summer term); June 1 (Fall term). **Contact:** scholarships@koniageducation.org.

5532 ■ Larry Matfay Scholarships *(Undergraduate, Graduate/Scholarship)*

Purpose: To revitalize and renew heritage and pride of the Alutiiq culture. **Focus:** Anthropology; History; Native American studies. **Qualif.:** Applicants must: be majoring in anthropology, history, Alaskan Native or American Indian Studies, or other disciplines which involves research and learning about Alutiiq culture; be Alaska Native shareholders or descendants (may be adopted) of the Koniag Region; accepted or enrolled in a nationally, regionally, or municipally accredited or recognized institution of higher learning; be graduating high school seniors, or high school or GED graduates, or have successfully completed one or more college, university or graduate school terms; and, have and maintain a minimum cumulative GPA of 2.50 or better and a minimum GPA of 3.0 within their major. **Criteria:** Selection shall be based on the aforementioned applicants' qualifications and compliance with the application details.

Funds Avail.: $1,000. **Duration:** Annual. **Number**

Awarded: 1. **To Apply:** Applicants must submit a completed application form together with a 300-600 word essay; transcript; two letters of recommendation; letter of acceptance; a resume; and a recent photo. **Deadline:** June 1. **Contact:** scholarships@koniageducation.org.

5533 ■ The Korea Society (TKS)
950 3rd Ave., 8th Fl.
New York, NY 10022
Ph: (212)759-7525
Fax: (212)759-7530
URL: www.koreasociety.org

5534 ■ Fall Fellowships in Korean Studies *(Other/ Fellowship)*

Purpose: To provide a general overview of Korea's past and present by covering all the expenses of the participants including round-trip international airfare, accommodations and meals. **Focus:** Korean studies. **Qualif.:** Applicant must be an American educator who is professionally engaged as a textbook writer and editor or an East Asia specialist in higher education who would like to include Korea in his/her teaching, research or writing. **Criteria:** Priority is given to applicants who are planning to author textbooks on world history or Asian history and are intending to contribute articles to reference works and who will be editors of such works.

Funds Avail.: No specific amount. **Duration:** Annual. **To Apply:** Applicant must submit a completed application packet including the application form and supporting documentation. **Deadline:** August 22.

5535 ■ Korean Language Study Awards *(Graduate/ Scholarship)*

Purpose: To provide financial assistance for Korean language study at a university in Korea. **Focus:** Korean studies. **Qualif.:** Applicants must be a U.S. citizen or permanent resident, graduate students, enrolled in degree programs, recent college graduates or young professionals with a clearly defined interest in Korea. **Criteria:** Recipients will be selected based on criteria designed by the Scholarship Committee.

Funds Avail.: No amount mentioned. **Duration:** Annual. **Number Awarded:** 2. **To Apply:** Applicants must submit application form; resume; official college transcripts; and two letters of reference.

5536 ■ Korean American Scholarship Foundation (KASF)
1952 Gallows Rd., Ste. 310
Vienna, VA 22182
E-mail: feedback@kasf.org
URL: www.kasf.org

5537 ■ KASF Chair Scholarships *(Graduate, Undergraduate/Scholarship)*

Purpose: To help meet the financial needs of Korean-American students seeking higher education. **Focus:** General studies/Field of study not specified. **Qualif.:** Applicant must be a Korean-American student currently enrolled in a full-time undergraduate or graduate program. **Criteria:** Recipient is selected based on financial need, academic achievement, school activities and community service.

Funds Avail.: $1,000-$5,000. **Duration:** Annual. **To Ap-**

Awards are arranged alphabetically below their administering organizations

ply: Applicants must submit a completed scholarship application to the respective KASF region (each region is designated by the state where school is located).

5538 ■ KASF Designated Scholarships *(Graduate, Undergraduate/Scholarship)*

Purpose: To help meet the financial needs of the students seeking higher education. **Focus:** General studies/Field of study not specified. **Qualif.:** Applicant must be a Korean-American student currently enrolled in a full-time undergraduate or graduate program in a specific field. **Criteria:** Recipient is selected based on financial need, academic achievement, school activities and community services.

Funds Avail.: $1000. **Duration:** Annual. **To Apply:** Applicant must submit a completed scholarship application to the respective KASF region (each region is designated by the state where school is located).

5539 ■ KASF General Scholarships *(Graduate, Undergraduate/Scholarship)*

Purpose: To provide educational support for the Korean-American students who are seeking higher education. **Focus:** General studies/Field of study not specified. **Qualif.:** Applicants must be Korean-American students currently enrolled in a full-time undergraduate or graduate program in one of various academic fields. **Criteria:** Recipients is selected based on financial need, academic achievement, school activities and community services.

Funds Avail.: $1,000-$5,000 (college/graduate students); $500 (high school students). **To Apply:** Applicants must submit a completed scholarship application to the respective KASF region (each region is designated by the state where school is located). **Deadline:** Varies with the region.

5540 ■ Kosciuszko Foundation (KF)

15 E 65th St.
New York, NY 10065
Ph: (212)734-2130
Fax: (212)628-4552
E-mail: info@thekf.org
URL: www.thekf.org

5541 ■ Kosciuszko Foundation Graduate Study and Research in Poland Scholarships *(Graduate/Scholarship)*

Purpose: To support the graduate level research at universities in Poland by American graduate students and university faculty members. **Focus:** Polish studies. **Qualif.:** Applicants must be U.S. citizens with permanent residency status in the United States who are graduate level students; must possess proficiency in the Polish language. **Criteria:** Selection will be based on academic excellence; motivation and need to pursue research in Poland; and a clear and well-defined research proposal. The host institution must fall under the jurisdiction of the Polish Ministry of Education and Sports.

Funds Avail.: No specific amount. **To Apply:** Applicants must complete the Polish Ministry of National Education application entitled Bureau for Academic Recognition and International Exchange; must provide an abstract of the project proposal; must attach copies of study certificates such as the level of language proficiency; copies of undergraduate and graduate diplomas; must have two letters of recommendation from professor; must submit a letter of invitation from the University/Institute in Poland where

research is conducted; must have two passport-size photos with printed name on the reverse. **Deadline:** January 7.

5542 ■ Kosciuszko Foundation Tuition Scholarships *(Graduate/Scholarship)*

Purpose: To support American students of Polish descent for full-time graduate studies in the United States. **Focus:** Polish studies. **Qualif.:** Applicant must be a United States citizen or permanent resident of Polish descent who is in the beginning of or continuing graduate studies in the academic year; must have a minimum GPA of 3.0; and must be a full-time student. United States citizen of non-Polish descent is considered when his/her area of study is primarily focused on Polish studies. Special funding is allocated for law and engineering studies at DePaul University; Bayonne, NJ residents for studies in nursing, teaching and business; and residents of Amsterdam, NY, Chicopee, MA and New Hampshire. **Criteria:** Selection is based on academic excellence, applicant's academic achievements, interests and motivation, applicant's interest in Polish subjects or involvement in the Polish American community. Financial need is taken into consideration.

Funds Avail.: $1,000 - $7,000. **Duration:** One academic year. **To Apply:** Applicant must complete the Tuition Scholarship application form and Financial Information page (application may be obtained from the Kosciuszko Foundation); must submit a personal statement about their academic goals, career goals, major they are pursuing and area of specialization; must have two passport photos for publication purposes; must have the official transcript; must prepare two confidential letters of academic reference from professors/teachers submitted on letterhead; must provide proof of Polish ancestry. **Deadline:** January 7.

5543 ■ Kosciuszko Foundation Year Abroad Scholarships *(Graduate, Undergraduate/Scholarship)*

Purpose: To support the deserving students to continue their Polish language studies. **Focus:** Polish studies. **Qualif.:** Applicant must be a United States citizen and permanent resident of Polish descent who is an undergraduate sophomore, junior, senior or graduate student; must have a minimum GPA of 3.0. **Criteria:** Selection is based on academic excellence, motivation for pursuing Polish studies, interest in Polish subjects and involvement in the Polish American community.

Funds Avail.: No specific amount. **Duration:** One academic year. **To Apply:** Applicant must complete the Polish Ministry of National Education application entitled Bureau for Academic Recognition and International Exchange; must attach copies of transcript of records; must submit two letters of recommendation from professors and must have two passport size photos with printed name on the reverse. **Deadline:** January 7.

5544 ■ Massachusetts Federation of Polish Women's Clubs Scholarships *(Undergraduate/Scholarship)*

Purpose: To support the qualified residents of Massachusetts to pursue their education. **Focus:** Polish studies. **Qualif.:** Applicant must be a United States citizen of Polish descent or Polish citizens with permanent residency status in the United States residing in Massachusetts who will engage in second, third or fourth year of undergraduate studies during academic year; must have a minimum GPA of 3.0. **Criteria:** Selection will be based on academic excellence, the applicant's academic achievements, interests, motivation, interest in Polish subjects and involvement in

Awards are arranged alphabetically below their administering organizations

the Polish American community. Financial need is taken into consideration.

Funds Avail.: $1,250. **Duration:** One academic year. **Number Awarded:** 3. **To Apply:** Applicant must complete the scholarship application form and financial information page; must submit a personal statement about their academic goals, career goals and specialization; must have a two passport-sized photos for publication purposes; must submit official transcripts; must have two confidential letters of academic reference from professor and teachers; must provide proof of Polish ancestry. **Deadline:** January 7.

5545 ■ Polish American Club of North Jersey Scholarships *(Graduate, Undergraduate/Scholarship)*

Purpose: To provide financial assistance to qualified students in the United States. **Focus:** Polish studies. **Qualif.:** Applicant must be a United States citizen of Polish descent or Polish citizens with permanent residency status in the U.S who are active members of the Polish American Club of North Jersey; must have a minimum GPA of 3.0; must be children or grandchildren of club members. **Criteria:** Selection is based on academic excellence, the applicant's academic achievements, interests, motivation, interest in Polish subjects and involvement in the Polish American community. Financial need is taken into consideration.

Funds Avail.: $500 - $2,000. **Duration:** One academic year. **To Apply:** Applicant must complete the scholarship application form and financial information page; must have a personal statement about their academic goals, career goals and specialization; must have two passport photos for publication purposes; must submit an official transcript; must prepare two confidential letters of academic reference from professor and teachers; must provide proof of Polish ancestry. **Deadline:** January 15.

5546 ■ Polish National Alliance of Brooklyn, USA Scholarships *(Undergraduate/Scholarship)*

Purpose: To provide financial assistance to all qualified students wanting to pursue their studies in the United States. **Focus:** Polish studies. **Qualif.:** Applicants must be United States citizens of Polish descent or Polish citizens with permanent residency status in the U.S. who are members in good standing of the Polish National Alliance of Brooklyn, USA and the Polish National Alliance of the United States of North America; must have a minimum GPA of 3.0. **Criteria:** Selection is based on the academic excellence, the applicants' academic achievements, interests, motivation, interest in Polish subjects and involvement in the Polish American community. Financial need is taken into consideration.

Funds Avail.: $2,000. **Duration:** One academic year. **To Apply:** Applicants must complete the scholarship application form and financial information page; must submit a personal statement about their academic goals, career goals and the major expect to pursue; must have two passport photos for publication purposes; must have two confidential letters of academic reference; must have an official transcript of record; must have two letters of academic reference from professor and teachers; must provide proof of Polish ancestry. **Deadline:** January 7.

5547 ■ Dr. Marie E. Zakrzewski Medical Scholarships *(Doctorate/Scholarship)*

Purpose: To support young women of Polish ancestry in their education. **Focus:** Polish studies. **Qualif.:** Applicant must be a U.S. citizen of Polish descent or Polish citizens

with permanent residency status in United States who are entering first, second or third year of M.D. studies in academic year; must have a minimum GPA of 3.0; must be a female **Criteria:** Selection is based on academic excellence, applicant's academic achievements, interest, motivation, interest in Polish subjects and involvement in the Polish American Community. Financial need is taken into consideration and preference is given to residents of the state of Massachusetts.

Funds Avail.: $3,500. **Duration:** One academic year. **To Apply:** Applicant must submit a personal statement about the academic goals, career goals and area of specialization; must have a two passport sized photos for publication purposes; must have an official transcript and two confidential letters of academic reference from professors and teachers; must provide proof of Polish ancestry. **Deadline:** January 7.

5548 ■ KPMG Foundation
3 Chestnut Ridge Rd.
Montvale, NJ 07645
E-mail: us-kpmgfoundation@kpmg.com
URL: www.kpmgfoundation.org

5549 ■ KPMG Foundation Minority Accounting Doctoral Scholarships *(Graduate, Doctorate/Scholarship)*

Purpose: To provide financial assistance to minority students in order to meet the escalating costs of higher education. **Focus:** Accounting. **Qualif.:** Applicants must be African-American, Hispanic-American or Native American doctoral students; must be US citizens or a permanent resident of the United States; must be enrolled, on campus, in a full time AACSB-accredited, Accounting business doctoral program. **Criteria:** Applicants are evaluated based on financial need.

Funds Avail.: $10,000 each. **Duration:** Annual. **Number Awarded:** Varies. **To Apply:** Applicants must submit a completed copy of the application Form; a brief cover letter explaining the reason for pursuing a PhD in accounting; a copy of most recent resume; undergraduate and graduate transcripts; and proof of matriculation status. **Remarks:** Established in 1993. **Contact:** KMPG Foundation, at the above address.

5550 ■ Krell Institute
1609 Golden Aspen Dr., Ste. 101
Ames, IA 50010
Ph: (515)956-3696
Fax: (515)956-3699
E-mail: shelly@krellinst.org
URL: www.krellinst.org

5551 ■ DOE Computational Science Graduate Fellowships (DOE CSGF) *(Doctorate, Graduate/Fellowship)*

Purpose: To provide outstanding benefits and opportunities to students pursuing a PhD in scientific or engineering disciplines with an emphasis in high-performance computing. **Focus:** Aerospace sciences; Astronomy and astronomical sciences; Biology; Chemistry; Computer and information sciences; Engineering, Biomedical; Engineering, Electrical; Engineering, Mechanical; Engineering, Nuclear; Environmental science; Materials research/science; Math-

Awards are arranged alphabetically below their administering organizations

ematics and mathematical sciences; Oceanography; Physics. **Qualif.:** Applicant must be planning full-time, uninterrupted study toward a PhD degree at a U.S. university; be in the first or second year of graduate study in the physical, engineering, computer, mathematical, or life sciences (exceptional senior undergraduates who can meet all the requirements may apply); and must be either U.S. citizen or permanent resident alien. **Criteria:** Selection is based on the application.

Funds Avail.: Full tuition, a yearly stipend of $36,000, plus a $1,000/year academic allowance. **Duration:** Four years. **To Apply:** Applicants must register and apply online. **Deadline:** January 28. **Contact:** csgf@krellinst.org.

5552 ■ Samuel H. Kress Foundation
174 E 80th St.
New York, NY 10075
Ph: (212)861-4993
Fax: (212)628-3146
E-mail: info@kressfoundation.org
URL: www.kressfoundation.org

5553 ■ Kress Conservation Fellowships (Graduate/Fellowship)

Purpose: To encourage qualified individuals to prepare for careers as conservators in museums of art. **Focus:** Art conservation. **Qualif.:** Applicant must be an individual who has completed an M.A degree in art conservation; must be a U.S citizen. **Criteria:** Selection of applicant will be based on the fellowship criteria.

Funds Avail.: $27,000 as a fellowship stipend and $5,000 toward administrative costs. **Duration:** Annual; One year. **Number Awarded:** 9. **To Apply:** Application must be made by the museum or conservation research facility at which the internship will be based. Applicant must have a brief description of the internship, curriculum vitae of the individual nominated; must have three letters of recommendation; and must provide a self-addressed, stamped postcard. **Deadline:** January 22.

5554 ■ Kress Curatorial Fellowships (Doctorate/Fellowship)

Purpose: To encourage qualified individuals to prepare for careers as curators in museums of art. **Focus:** European studies. **Qualif.:** Applicant must be an individual who has completed a Ph.D. in the history of European art. **Criteria:** Selection of applicant will be based on the fellowship criteria.

Funds Avail.: $25,000 as a fellowship stipend, and $5,000 toward administrative costs, benefits for the Fellow, and other direct costs of the Fellowship. **Duration:** Annual; One year. **To Apply:** Application must be made at which the fellowship will be based. Applicant must have a brief description of the internship, curriculum vitae of the individual nominated; must have three letters of recommendation.

5555 ■ Kress Fellowships in Art History at Foreign Institutions (Doctorate/Fellowship)

Purpose: To assist promising art historians to complete the final phases of their dissertation research. **Focus:** European studies. **Qualif.:** Applicant must be a pre-doctoral candidate in the history of art; must be a U.S. citizen or individual matriculated at an American university; and have a research focusing on European art from antiquity to the early 19th century. **Criteria:** Selection of applicant will be

based on the fellowship criteria.

Funds Avail.: $22,500. **Duration:** Annual; Two years. **Number Awarded:** 4. **To Apply:** Applicant must submit one original and four copies of application form; must include the following: five-page summary of the proposed dissertation research project; a five-page bibliography containing works of primary concerns; five-page description of the proposed research; a one-page description of the work completed on the dissertation; two pages of description of the previous research and travel experience; and the amount needed. Applicant must attach a copy of current curriculum vitae, a transcript from university where MA received, three letters of evaluation, three copies of original letter, and self-addressed, stamped postcard which will be returned in verifying the receipt of the application. **Deadline:** November 30.

5556 ■ Kress Travel Fellowships in the History of Art (Doctorate/Fellowship)

Purpose: To assist promising art historians to complete the final phases of their dissertation research. **Focus:** European studies. **Qualif.:** Applicants must be predoctoral candidates in the history of art; must be U.S citizens or individuals matriculated at an American university. **Criteria:** Selection will be based on the committee's criteria.

Funds Avail.: $3,500 - $10,000. **Duration:** Annual. **Number Awarded:** 15-20. **To Apply:** Applicants must submit one original and four copies of application form; must include the following: five-page summary of the proposed dissertation research project; five-page bibliography containing works of primary concerns; five-page description of the proposed research; one-page description of the work completed on the dissertation; three pages of description of the previous research and travel experience; and the amount needed. **Deadline:** November 30.

5557 ■ La Raza Lawyers Association of Santa Clara County
75 E Santa Clara St.
San Jose, CA 95113
Ph: (408)298-7700
URL: larazalawyers-santaclara.com

5558 ■ Santa Clara La Raza Lawyers Scholarships (Graduate/Scholarship)

Purpose: To support the education of law students. **Focus:** Law. **Qualif.:** Applicants must be currently enrolled La Raza law students (1st, 2nd, 3rd, or 4th) from the Bay area or attending Santa Clara University, Lincoln, UC Berkeley, University of San Francisco, UC Hastings, Stanford, Golden Gate University, UC Davis or McGeorge Schools of Law. **Criteria:** Selection is based on financial need.

Funds Avail.: $3,500. **Duration:** Annual. **To Apply:** Applicants must submit a completed scholarship application form along with a verification of enrollment from the applicant's law school; and letters of recommendation (optional). **Deadline:** October 3. **Contact:** La Raza Lawyers Association of Santa Clara County, at the above address.

5559 ■ LA Tutors 123
9454 Wilshire Blvd., Ste. 600
Beverly Hills, CA 90212
Ph: (424)335-0035
Free: 866-608-8867
URL: www.latutors123.com

Awards are arranged alphabetically below their administering organizations

5560 ■ LA Tutors Innovation in Education Scholarships (All/Scholarship)

Purpose: To commend those outstanding students who have made a difference in the lives of others in some innovative or technological fashion. **Focus:** General studies/Field of study not specified. **Qualif.:** Applicants must be currently enrolled as high school or college/university students within the United States or Canada; have a cumulative GPA of at least 3.0 (or the equivalent); be citizens of, permanent residents of, or hold their own valid student visas in the United States or Canada; and have designed an innovative project that makes a difference in the lives of others (such could be a website, series of blogs, an app, fundraising event, etc.). **Criteria:** Selection will be based on the applicants' winning projects. Those projects will be judged on the basis of creativity, innovation, and user experience.

Funds Avail.: $500. **Duration:** Monthly. **Number Awarded:** 1 per month. **To Apply:** Applicants must submit their respective essays (must be of their original work) describing the goal of the particular project (as mentioned in the qualifications) and provide supporting documentation. All entries must be entered using the official LA Tutors 123 Innovation Scholarship submission form which can be accessed at the scholarship website. All essays must be written in English and must be uploaded in either a Microsoft Word or PDF format. **Deadline:** Every 20th of each month. **Contact:** scholarship@latutors123.com.

5561 ■ Ladah Law Firm, PLLC
5175 3rd St.
Las Vegas, NV 89101
Ph: (705)570-1264
URL: www.ladahlaw.com

5562 ■ Ladah Law Firm, PLLC Injury Scholarships (Undergraduate, Graduate/Scholarship)

Purpose: To provide financial assistance to students who want to pursue their dreams in the legal profession. **Focus:** Law. **Qualif.:** Applicants must be attending college or planning to attend law school but will not yet have graduated from law school; must have a minimum GPA of 3.0. **Criteria:** Selection will be based on the committee's criteria.

Funds Avail.: $2,000. **To Apply:** Applicants must submit the complete online application form together with transcript and recommendation letters and/or resumes to substantiate the application. Applicants will be required to demonstrate both their merit and their need for the scholarship: how an injury or someone close to the applicants' experienced have impacted their lives; how experience with an injury or an accident have contributed the applicants' desire and motivation to become an attorney; and personal commitment to working with, helping or caring for those affected by injuries and accidents. Selected finalist must submit an un-opened copy of official transcripts. **Deadline:** May 31.

5563 ■ The LAGRANT Foundation
600 Wilshire Blvd., Ste. 1520
Los Angeles, CA 90017
Ph: (323)469-8680
Fax: (323)469-8683
URL: www.lagrantfoundation.org

5564 ■ The Lagrant Foundation - Graduate Students Scholarships (Graduate/Scholarship)

Purpose: To provide financial support for the education of graduate students who belong to one of the following ethnic groups: African American, Asian Pacific American, Hispanic or Native American or Alaska Native. **Focus:** Advertising; Marketing and distribution; Public relations. **Qualif.:** Applicants must be U.S. citizens and full-time students at a college or university that is accredited by a regional accrediting association; have a minimum of 3.2 GPA; major in a field of study that has an emphasis in public relations, marketing or advertising; have a minimum of two academic semesters or one-year left to complete his/her master's degree. **Criteria:** Applicants are evaluated based on scholastic performance.

Funds Avail.: $5,000. **To Apply:** Applicants must submit a one- to two-page typewritten essay outlining their career goals and why they feel it is important to increase ethnic representation in the fields of advertising, marketing and public relations; must define the role of an advertising, marketing or public relations practitioner (depending on emphasis), including accomplishments relevant to increasing awareness about diversity in their community; brief paragraph explaining graduate school and/or community activities in which they are involved and describing any honors and awards that they have received; and a letter of reference from a professor or internship advisor; resume which should reflect what they would present to a prospective employer, with the career objective clearly stated; official transcripts from college/university; and proof of acceptance to graduate school (if not currently enrolled). **Contact:** The Lagrant Foundation at the above address.

5565 ■ The Lagrant Foundation - Undergraduate Students Scholarships (Undergraduate/Scholarship)

Purpose: To provide financial support for the education of undergraduate students who belong to ethnic groups: African American, Asian Pacific American, Hispanic or Native American or Alaska Native. **Focus:** Advertising; Marketing and distribution; Public relations. **Qualif.:** Applicants must be U.S. citizens and full-time students at a four-year, accredited institution, carrying a total of 12 units or more per semester/quarter; must have a minimum of 2.75 GPA; and must major in a field of study that has an emphasis on public relations, marketing or advertising or must minor in communications with desire to pursue a career in public relations, marketing or advertising. **Criteria:** Applicants will be evaluated based on academic performance.

Funds Avail.: $2,500. **To Apply:** Applicants must submit a one- to two-page typewritten essay outlining their career goals and what steps they will take to increase the lack of ethnic representation in the fields of advertising, marketing and public relations (must define the role of advertising, marketing or public relations practitioner depending on emphasis); accomplishments relevant to increasing awareness about diversity in their community; brief paragraph describing any honors and awards that they have received (must put the particular dates); a letter of reference from a college professor or internship advisor. **Contact:** The Lagrant Foundation at the above address.

5566 ■ Lake George Scholarship Association
381 Canada St.
Lake George, NY 12845
URL: www.lgscholarship.org

Awards are arranged alphabetically below their administering organizations

5567 ■ Lake George Dollars for Scholars Awards
(Undergraduate/Scholarship)

Purpose: To support students who wish to further their education beyond high school. **Focus:** General studies/ Field of study not specified. **Qualif.:** Applicants must be senior students enrolled in a two or four year education programs. **Criteria:** Recipients will be selected based on merit, financial need and community service.

Funds Avail.: $500. **To Apply:** Applicants must complete an application form. **Contact:** For more information, feel free to contact James Mathis; Phone: 518-668-5851; E-mail: jmathis@nycap.rr.com.

5568 ■ Lakselaget
c/o Kay Romness Shores, Director
506 Pine St. W, Apt. 2
Stillwater, MN 55082
E-mail: president@lakselaget.org
URL: www.lakselaget.org

5569 ■ Lakselaget Foundation Scholarships *(Graduate, Undergraduate/Scholarship)*

Purpose: To promote the international connections between Norway and Minnesota, and learn, teach and share knowledge that will benefit women in their complex roles in today's society. **Focus:** Biology; Mathematics and mathematical sciences; Science. **Qualif.:** Applicants must be women; an American citizens residing in Minnesota, enrolled in undergraduate or graduate studies at an accredited Minnesota college or university or at the University of North Dakota, Grand Forks and wish to study in Norway; or must be Norwegian citizens attending undergraduate or graduate studies at an accredited Norwegian college or university, who wishes to study at a Minnesota college or university or at the University of North Dakota, Grand Forks. Study areas may include, but are not limited to, non-traditional women's studies such as biotechnology, mathematics and the sciences. Applicants must be full-time undergraduates who have completed at least one year or full-time graduate students. American students should have a GPA of 3.0 or better, Norwegians the equivalent. **Criteria:** Award is given to applicant who best exemplifies the organization's motto.

Funds Avail.: $1,000. **To Apply:** Applicant must submit a completed application form with official transcripts, two letters or recommendation, a letter from an individual who can assess the applicant's Norwegian language skills (if an American), and a 1000-word essay. **Deadline:** March 1.

5570 ■ Lalor Foundation
c/o GMA Foundations
77 Summer St., 8th Fl.
Boston, MA 02110-1006
Ph: (617)426-7080
Fax: (617)426-7087
E-mail: shaff@gmafoundations.com
URL: 66.147.244.193/~lalorfou

5571 ■ Lalor Foundation Post-Doctoral Fellowships
(Postdoctorate/Fellowship)

Purpose: To support promising new researchers in establishing scientific and teaching careers. **Focus:** General studies/Field of study not specified. **Qualif.:** U.S. institutions must be exempted from federal income taxes

under Section 501 (c)(3) of the U.S. Internal Revenue Code. The individual nominated by the applicant institution for the postdoctoral fellowship for conduct of the work may be a citizen of any country. The individual should have training and experience at least equal to the PhD or MD level and should have a faculty appointment. e **Criteria:** Recipient will be evaluated based on eligibility and submitted materials.

Funds Avail.: $50,000. **Duration:** Annual. **To Apply:** The applicant institution may make its nomination of a fellow from among its own personnel or elsewhere, but qualifications being equal, candidates from other than the proposing institution itself may carry modest preference. The application must name the institution's nominee for fellowship and include his or her performance record. **Deadline:** January 15. **Contact:** fellowshipmanager@ gmafoundations.com.

5572 ■ LAM Foundation
4015 Executive Park Dr., Ste. 320
Cincinnati, OH 45241-4015
Ph: (513)777-6889
Free: 877-287-3526
E-mail: info@thelamfoundation.org
URL: www.thelamfoundation.org

5573 ■ LAM Pilot Project Awards *(Master's, Postdoctorate/Grant)*

Purpose: To support the initiation of innovative Lymphangioleiomyomatosis (LAM)research projects. **Focus:** Medical research. **Qualif.:** Candidates must have at least two years of experience, an M.D., Ph.D. or equivalent degree, and perform the work in a laboratory with established expertise in smooth muscle biology or the genetics of tuberous sclerosis.

Funds Avail.: $25,000. **Duration:** Annual. **To Apply:** The Proposed Research section of the online grant application for all LAM awards is limited to 10 pages, including references and figures. Proposals should include: hypotheses and specific aims; literature review, preliminary data; research plan and experimental methods;significance, importance. **Deadline:** July 15.

5574 ■ Lamaze International
2025 M St. NW, Ste. 800
Washington, DC 20036-3309
Ph: (202)367-1128
Fax: (202)367-2128
Free: 800-368-4404
E-mail: bookstore@lamaze.com
URL: www.lamaze.org

5575 ■ Childbirth Educator Program Scholarships
(All/Scholarship)

Purpose: To provide financial support to cover the cost of enrolling in a Lamaze Accredited Childbirth Educator Program. **Focus:** Motherhood. **Qualif.:** Applicants must be currently enrolled or planning to enroll in a Lamaze Childbirth Educator Program; current members of Lamaze International, in good standing; in need of financial assistance. **Criteria:** Scholarship recipients are selected by lottery from a pool of applications that meet the eligibility requirements.

Funds Avail.: $500. **To Apply:** Applicants must submit a

Awards are arranged alphabetically below their administering organizations

completed Childbirth Educator Program Scholarship application and must include the following information in the statement: circumstances of need, e.g., employment or self-employment status and anticipated gross yearly income (spouse information needed if they file a joint tax return or the equivalent); special medical, educational or unemployment-related circumstances (including disabilities and worker's compensation claims), include number of dependents, students they support in college, and special needs family members; other sources of income (savings, bonds stocks, scholarships, etc); and how they will finance the remaining fees, lodging, travel, meals and away-from-home expenses, if they receive a scholarship; and a letter describing how they plan to promote the Lamaze International Philosophy of Birth. **Deadline:** January 31 and June 30.

5576 ■ Lambda Iota Tau (LIT)

Ball State University
Dept. of English
200 W University Ave.
Muncie, IN 47306
Ph: (765)285-8370
Fax: (765)285-3765
E-mail: mcupchurch@bsu.edu
URL: achsnatl.org/society.asp?Society=lit

5577 ■ LIT Scholarships *(Undergraduate, Graduate/ Scholarship)*

Purpose: To support student fraternity members in their education. **Focus:** General studies/Field of study not specified. **Qualif.:** Applicants must be members of Lambda Iota Tau who demonstrate the writing of high quality literature (short stories, novels, essays, poems) or the writing of high quality research about literature. **Criteria:** Applicants will be evaluated by the committee based on scholarship, leadership, character, as well as service.

Funds Avail.: $1,000 each. **Duration:** Annual. **Number Awarded:** 2 or more. **To Apply:** Applicants must submit the nomination letter from the sponsor; an essay or piece of creative writing; and another essay of 1000 words or less on career goals and objectives. **Contact:** Lambda Iota Tau, at the above address; or contact Mary Clark-Flynn by email: mcupchurch@bsu.edu, or at 765-285-8370 or 765-285-8456.

5578 ■ Landscape Architecture Foundation (LAF)

1129 20th St. NW, Ste. 202
Washington, DC 20036
Ph: (202)331-7070
Fax: (202)331-7079
E-mail: scholarships@lafoundation.org
URL: lafoundation.org

5579 ■ ASLA Council of Fellows Scholarships *(Undergraduate/Scholarship)*

Purpose: To aid outstanding students who would not otherwise have an opportunity to continue a professional degree program due to unmet financial need, increase the interest and participation of economically disadvantaged and under-represented populations in the study of landscape architecture, and enrich the profession of landscape architecture. **Focus:** Landscape architecture and design. **Qualif.:** Applicants must be permanent U.S. citizens or

permanent resident aliens who are Student ASLA members and third-, fourth-, or fifth-year undergraduates at Landscape Architecture Accreditation Board (LAAB) accredited programs of landscape architecture. Applicants seeking special consideration for the diversity scholarship should indicate and identify their association with a specific ethnic or cultural group. **Criteria:** Selection shall be based on the aforementioned applicants' qualifications and compliance with the application details.

Funds Avail.: $4,000 each. **Duration:** Annual. **Number Awarded:** 3. **To Apply:** Applicants must submit an entry form, a photo (head shot with a plain background; 300 ppi, size 4 x 6 inches in .jpg format) and a personal profile (two page maximum including education, extracurricular activities and financial information); a 300-word essay about how the applicant envisions herself/himself contributing to the profession of landscape architecture; two letters of recommendation addressing the quality of performance as a student of landscape architecture and the promise as a professional. One letter of recommendation must come from a faculty member; the other letter may be sent by a non-academic member of ASLA or another faculty member; a Student Aid Report (SAR) as proof of unmet financial need. All application materials (with the exception of reference letters) must be sent through email as a single document. Each document must be formatted as follows: create one-inch minimum margins; include page number and surname/document name/award name on all pages of all documents prepared by applicant. **Deadline:** February 15. **Remarks:** Established in 2004. **Contact:** Email: scholarships@lafoundation.org.

5580 ■ Steven G. King Play Environments Scholarships *(Undergraduate/Scholarship)*

Purpose: To recognize a student who has a high potential in the design of play environments. **Focus:** Landscape architecture and design. **Qualif.:** Applicants must be landscape architecture students with an interest and aptitude in the design of play environments. They must be enrolled in graduate or the final two years of undergraduate study in LAAB accredited schools. **Criteria:** Recipients shall be selected on the basis of creativity, openness to innovation and a demonstrated interest in park and playground planning.

Funds Avail.: $5,000. **Duration:** Annual. **Number Awarded:** 1. **To Apply:** Applicants must submit an entry form, a photo (head shot with a plain background; 300 ppi, size 4 x 6 inches in extracurricular activities and financial information); a 300 to 500-word essay describing the applicant's views of the significant social and educational value of play and the value of integrating playgrounds into play and recreation environments; a plan and details of a play environment of the applicant's design in either .jpg or PDF format; two letters of recommendation from current professors familiar with the applicant's demonstrated interest in park and playground planning, creativity and openness to innovation. All application materials (with the exception of reference letters) must be sent through email as a single document. Each document must be formatted as follows: create one-inch minimum margins; include page number and surname/document name/award name on all pages of all documents prepared by applicant. **Deadline:** February 15. **Remarks:** The Steven G. King Play Environments Scholarship was created by Steven G. King, FASLA, founder and Chairman of Landscape Structures Inc., and the inventor of the "continuous play" concept. **Contact:** Email: scholarships@lafoundation.org.

Awards are arranged alphabetically below their administering organizations

5581 ■ LAF Landscape Forms Design for People Scholarships (Undergraduate/Scholarship)

Purpose: To assist students in their study of landscape architecture. **Focus:** Landscape architecture and design. **Qualif.:** Applicants must be landscape architecture students who will be starting their final year of full-time undergraduate study in an LAAB-accredited program. **Criteria:** Applicants must show a proven contribution to the design of public spaces that integrates landscape design and the use of amenities to promote social interaction. Recipients shall be selected on the basis of academic accomplishment and creative ability.

Funds Avail.: $3,000. **Duration:** Annual. **Number Awarded:** 1. **To Apply:** Applicants must submit an entry form, a photo (head shot with a plain background; 300 ppi, size 4 x 6 inches in .jpg format) and a personal profile (two-page maximum including education, extracurricular activities and financial information); a 300-word maximum essay describing the qualities essential to the creation of great and successful public spaces; three 8 1/2 x 11 academic or internship work samples in either .jpg or PDF format; two letters of recommendation from current professors and/or internship employers. All application materials (with the exception of reference letters) must be sent through email as a single document. Each document must be formatted as follows: create one-inch minimum margins; include page number and surname/document name/award name on all pages of all documents prepared by applicant. **Deadline:** February 15. **Contact:** Email: scholarships@lafoundation.org.

5582 ■ Courtland P. Paul Scholarships (Undergraduate/Scholarship)

Purpose: To assist students in their study of landscape architecture. **Focus:** Landscape architecture and design. **Qualif.:** Applicants must: be United States citizens who are undergraduate students in the final two years of study in Landscape Architecture Accreditation Board accredited schools; demonstrate financial need; and, have a minimum grade point average of C. **Criteria:** Selection shall be based on the aforementioned applicants' qualifications and compliance with the application details.

Funds Avail.: $5,000. **Duration:** Annual. **To Apply:** Applicants must submit an entry form, a photo (head shot with a plain background; 300 ppi, size 4 x 6 inches in jpg format) and a personal profile (two page maximum including education, extracurricular activities and financial information); 500-word maximum essay describing the applicant's aspirations, ability to surmount obstacles, high level of drive and need for financial assistance; two letters of recommendation from current professors familiar with the applicant's character and goals in pursuing an education in landscape architecture. Letters of recommendation should be written on electronic letterhead with an electronic signature from the recommender and must be sent electronically. Recommenders must request a delivery receipt for the e-mail or provide a copy in case of transmittal problem. All application materials (with the exception of reference letters) must be sent through email as a single document. Each document must be formatted as follows: create one-inch minimum margins; include page number and surname/document name/ award name on all pages of all documents prepared by applicant. **Remarks:** The scholarship is given in honor of Courtland P. Paul. **Contact:** Email: scholarships@lafoundation.org.

5583 ■ Peridian International, Inc./Rae L. Price, FASLA Scholarships (Undergraduate/Scholarship)

Purpose: To bring young creative individuals into the profession who may not otherwise have the financial ability to cover all the costs of their educational program. **Focus:** Landscape architecture and design. **Qualif.:** Applicants must be United States citizens; students in the final two years of study in Landscape Architecture at the University of California at Los Angeles Extension Program, or in the case of UCLA's termination of the program, other California accredited schools of programs in Landscape Architecture. Applicants must also demonstrate financial need and have a minimum grade point average of B. **Criteria:** Selection shall be based on the aforementioned applicants' qualifications and compliance with the application details.

Funds Avail.: $5,000. **Duration:** Annual. **Number Awarded:** 1. **To Apply:** Applicants must submit an entry form, a photo (head shot with a plain background; 300 ppi, size 4 x 6 inches in .jpg format) and a personal profile (two pages including education, extracurricular activities and financial information); a 500-word essay describing the applicant's aspirations, ability to surmount obstacles, high level of drive and need for financial assistance; two letters of recommendation from current professors familiar with the applicant's character and goals in pursuing an education in landscape architecture. All application materials (with the exception of reference letters) must be sent through email as a single document. Each document must be formatted as follows: create one-inch minimum margins; include page number and surname/document name/award name on all pages of all documents prepared by applicant. **Deadline:** February 15. **Remarks:** The use of funds is restricted to tuition, books and program required supplies within the school year of the award. **Contact:** Email: scholarships@lafoundation.org.

5584 ■ Rain Bird Intelligent Use of Water Scholarships (Undergraduate/Scholarship)

Purpose: To recognize an outstanding landscape architecture, horticulture or irrigation science student. **Focus:** Horticulture; Landscape architecture and design. **Qualif.:** Applicants must be students in the final two years of undergraduate study (third-, fourth-, or fifth-year students) who have demonstrated commitment to these professions through participation in extracurricular activities and exemplary scholastic achievements. **Criteria:** Selection shall be based on the aforementioned applicants' qualifications and compliance with the application details.

Funds Avail.: $2,500. **Duration:** Annual. **Number Awarded:** 1. **To Apply:** Applicants must submit an entry form, a photo (head shot with a plain background; 300 ppi, size 4 x 6 inches in extracurricular activities and financial information); a cover letter; a typed, double-spaced 300-word essay stating career goals and explaining how the applicant will contribute to the advancement of the profession of landscape architecture, horticulture or irrigation science. All application materials (with the exception of reference letters) must be sent through email as a single document. Each document must be formatted as follows: create one-inch minimum margins; include page number and name/document name/award name on all pages of all documents prepared by applicant. **Deadline:** February 15. **Contact:** Email: scholarships@lafoundation.org.

5585 ■ Hawaii Chapter/David T. Woolsey Scholarships (Undergraduate, Graduate/Scholarship)

Purpose: To recognize an outstanding architect student. **Focus:** Landscape architecture and design. **Qualif.:** Ap-

Awards are arranged alphabetically below their administering organizations

plicants must be third, fourth, or fifth year undergraduate or graduate students of landscape architecture who are permanent residents of Hawaii. **Criteria:** Recipients are selected based on academic achievement.

Funds Avail.: $2,000. **Duration:** Annual. **Number Awarded:** 1. **To Apply:** Applicants must submit all of the following: online general scholarship form; photo; 150-word maximum bio for LAF website; two-page resume; financial aid form; two letters of recommendation; and, two-page maximum originally written essay in PDF format with specific formats provided. Additional is the proof of Hawaii residency. **Deadline:** February 15. **Contact:** Landscape Architecture Foundation at scholarships@lafoundation.org; Phone: 202-331-7070 x13.

5586 ■ Lane Powell PC
1420 5th Ave., Ste. 4200
Seattle, WA 98111
Ph: (206)223-7000
Fax: (206)223-7107
Free: 800-426-5801
E-mail: info@lanepowell.com
URL: www.lanepowell.com

5587 ■ George V. Powell Diversity Scholarships
(Graduate/Scholarship)

Purpose: To support the education of a minority law student. **Focus:** Law. **Qualif.:** Applicants must be second-year students in good standing at an ABA accredited law school. Students in four-year joint degree programs will be considered after third year. **Criteria:** Award is given to candidates who will contribute meaningfully to the diversity of the legal community, and who have demonstrated desire to work, live and eventually practice law in Seattle or Portland. Candidate's academic achievements, record of leadership abilities, community service and involvement in community issues will be given consideration.

Funds Avail.: $7,500. **Duration:** Annual. **To Apply:** Applicants must submit a cover letter including a statement indicating eligibility to participate in the program; a resume; current copy of law school transcript; legal writing sample; and a list of two or three professional or academic references. **Deadline:** September 1. **Contact:** Len Roden, Manager of Attorney Recruiting, redenl@lanepowell.com.

5588 ■ Lang, Richert & Patch
Fig Garden Financial Center
5200 N Palm Ave., 4th Fl.
Fresno, CA 93704
Ph: (559)228-6700
Fax: (559)228-6727
URL: www.lrplaw.net

5589 ■ Frank H. Lang Merit Scholarships
(Undergraduate/Scholarship)

Purpose: To help students defray their law school tuition. **Focus:** Law. **Qualif.:** Applicants must be incoming law students. Those who have applied to law school and have been accepted but have not yet chosen which school to attend are also eligible to apply. Applicants must also be graduated from high school in one of the following California counties: Kern, Tulare, Fresno, Kings, Madera, Merced, Mariposa, Stanislaus, San Joaquin, Tuolumne or Calaveras. **Criteria:** Scholarship will be awarded based on merit.

Funds Avail.: $1,000. **Duration:** Annual. **To Apply:** Interested applicants should complete the online application form. In addition, candidates will be prompted during the online application process to submit the following documentation as PDF attachments: a resume including law school GPA; a law school transcript or copy of last score if incoming 1L; a college transcript; a 1-2 page personal statement explaining why the applicant has chosen to attend law school and their ties to the Central Valley (12 point Times New Roman font, double space with standard margins); list of three references, including names, email addresses and telephone numbers. **Deadline:** May 1.

5590 ■ Lanier Technical College
2990 Landrum Education Dr.
Oakwood, GA 30566
Ph: (770)531-6300
Fax: (770)531-6328
URL: www.laniertech.edu

5591 ■ Kenneth H. Breeden Scholarships
(Undergraduate/Scholarship)

Purpose: To provide financial support to deserving students who lose HOPE funding prior to the completion of their program of study. **Focus:** General studies/Field of study not specified. **Qualif.:** Applicants must have a previous approved for HOPE grant or HOPE Scholarship funding; must be in good academic standing in accordance with college guidelines. **Criteria:** Awards will be made on a first come, first serve basis. The Lanier Technical College Foundation Scholarship Committee will award the scholarship based upon their normal review procedure, evaluation of the Kenneth H. Breeden Scholarship criteria, and the applicants' academic record if applicable.

Funds Avail.: $500. **Duration:** Quarterly. **To Apply:** Applicants must submit a Kenneth H. Breeden Scholarship application (available online) along with a letter of recommendation from an advisor or instructor. Application documents must be sent to the Financial Aid Office three weeks prior to registration for the quarter aid is requested.

5592 ■ Forsyth County United Way Scholarships
(Undergraduate/Scholarship)

Purpose: To assist the students who are residents of Forsyth County and to support students offset their educational costs, specifically with books and supplies. **Focus:** General studies/Field of study not specified. **Qualif.:** Applicants must be in good academic standing in accordance with college and Financial Aid guidelines and must be residents of Forsyth County. **Criteria:** Awards are given on a first come, first serve basis. The United Way Scholarship Committee will award the scholarship based on the evaluation of the United Way Scholarship criteria which include the applicants' academic record and letters of recommendation.

Funds Avail.: $250. **Duration:** Quarterly. **To Apply:** Applicants must submit a completed United Way Scholarship Application along with a letter of recommendation from an advisor, instructor or a responsible member of the community capable of reporting applicants' work record, leadership and notable skills. Application and other documentations must be submitted to the Financial Aid Office two weeks prior to registration for the quarter aid is requested.

5593 ■ Edna A. Noblin Dawsonville Lions Club Scholarships *(Undergraduate/Scholarship)*

Purpose: To provide financial assistance for deserving students who are residents of Dawson or Lumpkin Coun-

Awards are arranged alphabetically below their administering organizations

ties. **Focus:** General studies/Field of study not specified. **Qualif.:** Applicants must be residents of Dawson County or Lumpkin County. **Criteria:** Awards will be made on a first come, first serve bases.

Funds Avail.: No specific amount. **To Apply:** Applicants must submit a completed scholarship application form; a short letter from applicants explaining the need for financial assistance; a list of specific costs for which the applicants require assistance; and a recommendation letter from faculty member or responsible member of the community capable of reporting applicant's work record, leadership, and notable skills. **Deadline:** Spring December 1; Summer April 1; Fall July 1.

5594 ■ Lapper County Community Foundation (LCCF)
264 Cedar St.
Lapeer, MI 48446
Ph: (810)664-0691
URL: www.lapeercountycommunityfoundation.org

5595 ■ The Clarke B. Adams Memorial Foundation Lapeer County Community Foundation Fund
(Undergraduate/Scholarship)

Purpose: To support the education of Lapeer community students who have lost an immediate family member. **Focus:** General studies/Field of study not specified. **Qualif.:** Applicants must be graduating seniors of Lapeer High School. **Criteria:** Preference will be given to applicants who have lost an immediate family member (please include any pertinent information in the application); however, all students are encouraged to apply.

Funds Avail.: $1,000 each. **Duration:** Annual. **Number Awarded:** 5. **To Apply:** Applicants may visit the website to verify the application process and other pieces of information. **Deadline:** March 31. **Contact:** Ashley White, Exec. Dir., Email: awhite@lapeercountycommunityfoundation.org; Phone: 810-664-0691.

5596 ■ Ross P. Broesamle Educational Scholarship Fund *(Undergraduate/Scholarship)*

Purpose: To support educational assistance to students from Almont Township or the Village of Almont and the Township of Dryden of the Village of Dryden. **Focus:** General studies/Field of study not specified. **Qualif.:** Applicants must be residents of Almont Township, Village of Almont, Dryden Township, or the Village of Dryden. **Criteria:** Awards are based upon financial need and scholastic record.

Funds Avail.: $500. **Duration:** Annual. **To Apply:** Applicants must be prepared to participate in a brief interview; must submit a transcript of records, test scores, photos and federal tax return for self or family. **Deadline:** March 31. **Contact:** Ashley White, Exec. Dir., Email: awhite@lapeercountycommunityfoundation.org; Phone: 810-664-0691.

5597 ■ Irma Gelhausen Scholarship Fund
(Undergraduate/Scholarship)

Purpose: To assist Lapeer community students pursuing a career in education. **Focus:** General studies/Field of study not specified. **Qualif.:** Applicants must be in the third year (or higher) of college/university studies; must have a GPA of 3.0 or higher for post-secondary studies and must be residents of Lapeer County. **Criteria:** Preference will be given to graduates of Lapeer Community Schools and those

pursuing a career in elementary education studies, although applicants pursuing a career in secondary education will be considered as well.

Funds Avail.: $1,000. **Duration:** Annual. **To Apply:** Applicants must submit a completed application form, a "200-word" essay discussing the expectations to achieve as an educator; must attach the most recent transcript of records, verification of current GPA and standardized test scores, IRS federal tax return and current photo to be used for publicity purposes. **Deadline:** April 30. **Remarks:** Established in 2005. **Contact:** Ashley White, Exec. Dir., Email: awhite@lapeercountycommunityfoundation.org; Phone: 810-664-0691.

5598 ■ Wayne Hildebrant Police Scholarship Fund
(Undergraduate/Scholarship)

Purpose: To support education in the law enforcement fields. **Focus:** Law enforcement. **Qualif.:** Applicants must be residents of Lapeer County accepted into an accredited police academy of college/university law enforcement program, have a cumulative GPA of 3.0 or higher, and show financial need. **Criteria:** Selection shall be based on the aforementioned qualifications and compliance with the application details.

Funds Avail.: $500. **Duration:** Annual. **To Apply:** Applicants must be prepared to participate in a brief interview; must submit a transcript of records, test scores, photos and federal tax return for self or family. **Deadline:** March 31. **Remarks:** The scholarship is named in memory of Wayne Hildebrant, long-time Metamora police chief. **Contact:** Ashley White, Exec. Dir., Email: awhite@lapeercountycommunityfoundation.org; Phone: 810-664-0691.

5599 ■ Lapeer County Medical Scholarship Fund
(Undergraduate/Scholarship)

Purpose: To support students pursuing medical education and profession. **Focus:** Education, Medical. **Qualif.:** Applicants must be residents of Lapeer County, at least a second year-enrolled college student in a pre-science medical professional career such as medical, dental, nursing, or physician's assistant program; and maintain a 3.2 GPA. **Criteria:** Preference is given to applicants based on financial need.

Funds Avail.: $500. **Duration:** Annual. **To Apply:** Applicants must be prepared to participate in a brief interview; must submit a transcript of records, test scores, photos and federal tax return for self or family. **Deadline:** March 31. **Contact:** Ashley White, Exec. Dir., Email: awhite@lapeercountycommunityfoundation.org; Phone: 810-664-0691.

5600 ■ Hazel Simms Nursing Scholarships *(Other/Scholarship)*

Purpose: To provide nursing scholarships for residents of Lapeer County. **Focus:** Nursing. **Qualif.:** Applicants must either have completed one year or more of college and have been accepted into a nursing program approved by the Michigan Board of Nursing or may also be certified as registered nurses pursuing a Bachelor of Science degree in nursing. They must also be residents of the following school districts: Almont, Dryden, Imlay City, LakeVille, Lapeer, and North Branch. **Criteria:** Recipients are selected based on financial need, scholastic record of the applicant and recommendations from college faculty and official of the college.

Funds Avail.: $500. **Duration:** Annual. **To Apply:** Ap-

Awards are arranged alphabetically below their administering organizations

plicants must submit a completed application form, statement of applicant, copy of applicant's most recent household federal tax, statement by the Director/Faculty Member of Nursing Program, transcript of courses completed at all colleges and current photo. **Deadline:** April 30. **Contact:** Ashley White, Exec. Dir., Email: awhite@ lapeercountycommunityfoundation.org; Phone: 810-664-0691.

5601 ■ Latham and Watkins L.L.P.
12636 High Bluff Dr., Ste. 400
San Diego, CA 92130
Ph: (858)523-5400
Fax: (858)523-5450
URL: www.lw.com

5602 ■ Latham Diversity Scholars *(Undergraduate/ Scholarship)*

Purpose: To increase the number of diverse attorneys who want to pursue careers in global law firms. **Focus:** Law. **Qualif.:** Applicant must be enrolled in an ABA-accredited law school and who intends to practice law in a major U.S. city and who has successfully completed the first year of a full-time JD program. **Criteria:** Selection is based on academic and leadership achievements, experiences and challenges that shape values, desire to practice at a global law firm and contributions to its diversity objectives.

Funds Avail.: $10,000. **Number Awarded:** 4. **To Apply:** Applicants must submit a completed (signed and dated) application form along with a resume, unofficial or official law school transcript and a personal statement (maximum of 500 words). **Deadline:** September 26. **Remarks:** Established in 2005. **Contact:** Application package must be submitted to Heather Sardinha at the above address; E-mail: heather.sardinha@lw.com. For further information about the scholarship, applicants must contact Elizabeth Krichmar at elizabeth.krichmar@lw.com.

5603 ■ Latin American Educational Foundation (LAEF)
561 Santa Fe Dr.
Denver, CO 80204
Ph: (303)446-0541
Fax: (303)446-0526
E-mail: info@laef.org
URL: www.laef.org

5604 ■ Latin American Educational Foundation Scholarships *(Undergraduate, Vocational/ Occupational/Scholarship)*

Purpose: To award funds to qualified students who have demonstrated a commitment to the Hispanic community. **Focus:** Hispanic American studies. **Qualif.:** Applicants must be Colorado residents with Hispanic heritage and/or are actively involved in the Hispanic community; must be accepted in an accredited college, university or vocational school; must at least have a 3.0 cumulative grade point average. Recipients will be required to fulfill 10 hours of community service during the year of funding. **Criteria:** Award is given based on the following: academic achievement; financial need; community involvement; letters of recommendation; personal essay; and personal interview of finalists.

Funds Avail.: No specific amount. **To Apply:** Applicants

must submit completed application form available in the LAEF website; most recent federal income tax returns; a list of community service and extracurricular activities for the previous 2 years including leadership positions held; a one-page essay to include the applicants' interests and career goals; and how they anticipates achieving their goals and what have motivated them to pursue higher education; two letters of recommendation on official letterhead (the first letter must come from an educator and the other must come from a community service organization, employer, clergy or coach). Letters should discuss the applicants' academic achievements and community service as well as their potential for future success. Qualities such as maturity, motivation, self-confidence, leadership and commitment should be addressed.

5605 ■ Latina Leadership Network (LLN)
PO Box 14557
San Luis Obispo, CA 93406
URL: www.latina-leadership-network.org

5606 ■ LLN Student Scholarships *(Undergraduate/ Scholarship)*

Purpose: To support students who are currently attending California Community Colleges. **Focus:** General studies/ Field of study not specified. **Qualif.:** Applicants must: be of Latino heritage (one parent fully Latino or each parent half Latino); be able to complete 24 units of college work (may include work in-progress); and, have a minimum 2.5 Cumulative GPA. **Criteria:** Selection shall be based on the aforementioned applicants' qualifications and the following: personal essay; academic achievement; community involvement; and compliance with the application details.

Funds Avail.: $500 each. **Duration:** Annual. **Number Awarded:** 4. **To Apply:** Applicants must provide and submit the following application packets: personal essay; completed and signed application provided by the organization; academic transcripts (unofficial transcripts will be accepted); and, two letters of recommendation with completed Recommendation Data Sheet. Mail complete application packets to the contact provided. **Deadline:** March 6. **Contact:** Dolores Cornejo, Fullerton College, 321 E. Chapman Ave. fullerton, California 92832-2095; Email: dconejo.fullcoll.edu.

5607 ■ Law Foundation of British Columbia
1340-605 Robson St.
Vancouver, BC, Canada V6B 5J3
Ph: (604)688-2337
Fax: (604)688-4586
E-mail: info@lawfoundationbc.org
URL: www.lawfoundationbc.org

5608 ■ Law Foundation of British Columbia Graduate Fellowships *(Graduate/Fellowship)*

Purpose: To provide financial assistance to qualified individuals who want to pursue their careers in legal profession. **Focus:** Law. **Qualif.:** Applicants must: be residents of British Columbia; must be graduates of British Columbia law school; be members of the British Columbia Bar; and, devote themselves primarily to full-time graduate studies in law or a law related area. **Criteria:** Recipients will be selected based on academic achievements, leadership qualities, involvement in community activities and proposed course of study.

Awards are arranged alphabetically below their administering organizations

Funds Avail.: 15,000 Canadian Dollars each. **Duration:** Annual. **Number Awarded:** Up to 6. **To Apply:** Applicants must complete the application form available online. They should also submit transcript of records and three letters of reference. **Deadline:** January 7. **Contact:** projects@lawfoundationbc.org.

5609 ■ Law Foundation of Ontario
20 Queen St. W, Ste. 3002
Toronto, ON, Canada M5H 3R3
Ph: (416)598-1550
Fax: (416)598-1526
E-mail: general@lawfoundation.on.ca
URL: www.lawfoundation.on.ca

5610 ■ Law Foundation of Ontario Community Leadership in Justice Fellowships *(Other/Fellowship)*
Purpose: To provide an opportunity for professional development and renewal for a recognized community leader. **Focus:** Law. **Qualif.:** Applicant must be active in public organizations dedicated to law reform, legal advocacy or the justice system. Academic hosts must be either a law school or a department dedicated to legal or justice studies (including but not limited to criminology, sociology, social work, political science, and law and society programs). **Criteria:** Selection of the recipient will be based strictly on merit.

Funds Avail.: 50,000 Canadian Dollars each to cover the fellows' salaries and up to 15,000 Canadian Dollars is available to each academic host. **Number Awarded:** 2. **To Apply:** Applicants must submit a completed CLJF Application Form via email. **Deadline:** April 30. **Remarks:** Established in 2006.

5611 ■ Law Office of John J. Sheehan
44 School St., No. 815
Boston, MA 02108
Ph: (617)973-1593
URL: www.attorneysheehan.com

5612 ■ Vision Zero Auto Accident Prevention Scholarships *(Postgraduate/Scholarship)*
Purpose: To encourage and support students in their pursuit of legal education. **Focus:** Law. **Qualif.:** Applicants must be U.S. citizens who are currently in their first or second year of law school, or entering law school in the fall of the current year and accepted to or currently attending an ABA accredited law school or program within United States. Applicants' academic achievement must be reflected by an undergraduate cumulative minimum 3.0 GPA. **Criteria:** Selection will be based on the applicants' eligibility and compliance with the application process.

Funds Avail.: $1,000. **To Apply:** Applicants must submit the following requirements: proof of Legal Residency in U.S. (i.e. birth certificate, passport, permanent resident card, etc.); a completed scholarship application form; one-page typed essay; an official copy of a law school or undergraduate college transcript; an official copy of a driving record since being eligible to drive; and if entering a law school program or school in the fall of current year, an acceptance letter from an accredited law school. **Deadline:** July 31.

5613 ■ The Law Office of Steven A. Leahy, P.C.
150 N Michigan Ave., No. 1120
Chicago, IL 60601
Ph: (312)664-6649
URL: chicagotaxteam.com

5614 ■ Steven A. Leahy Law Office Marine Service/Law School Scholarships *(Postgraduate/Scholarship)*
Purpose: To support those individuals whose families have served the country, while giving a promising young student the chance to finish law school. **Focus:** Law. **Qualif.:** Applicants must be U.S. citizens at least 18 years old; must be law students attending (or accepted and planning to attend) an accredited law school; and must have a family member in the Marine Corps. **Criteria:** Selection will be based on academic achievement (demonstrated through a cumulative GPA of 3.0 from undergraduate or current law school work), eligibility, and compliance with the application process.

Funds Avail.: $1,000. **Number Awarded:** 1. **To Apply:** Applicants must submit the completed application form and a one to three (1-3) page typed essay describing every applicants' experience and the impact of the Marine service to the family. Such essay will be attached as a separate document. Other documents required to submit are official copy (or copies) of undergraduate and/or law school transcripts with GPA and proof of Marine service. Completed applications and materials should be mailed (or emailed in PDF format) to Steven A. Leahy. **Deadline:** June 30. **Contact:** Steven A. Leahy, at the above address; or email at Scholarship@it-lawyer.com.

5615 ■ Law Offices of Michael A. DeMayo L.L.P.
1211 E Morehead St.
Charlotte, NC 28204
Ph: (704)333-1000
Fax: (704)333-6677
Free: 877-529-1222
E-mail: info@demayolaw.com
URL: www.demayolaw.com

5616 ■ Law Offices of Michael A. DeMayo Scholarships *(Undergraduate/Scholarship)*
Purpose: To fund high school senior students who wish to continue their education. **Focus:** General studies/Field of study not specified. **Qualif.:** Applicants must be students who have applied for acceptance for full-time studies at a four-year college or university. **Criteria:** Selection will be based on the application materials submitted.

Funds Avail.: $2,500 each. **Duration:** Annual. **Number Awarded:** 15. **To Apply:** Students must submit the following items: a typewritten or neatly printed application; a presentation (video/PowerPoint/brochure/website/essay) that encourages fellow teens to abstain from underage drinking and driving and/or highlights the dangers of drinking and driving; a high school transcript; SAT scores (if not included in transcript, a printout from CollegeBoard.com is acceptable); two letters of recommendation (from teachers, athletic coaches, school administrators, club advisors, volunteer work supervisors, employers religious leaders or family friends). Types of acceptable presentations are: Video - Public service announcement (no more than 60 seconds). Must be recorded on DVD. Student's name and school should appear directly on DVD and applicant must provide a copy of the script; Essay - 750-1,000 words. Must be typed and double-spaced; PowerPoint - 15-slide minimum. Applicant must provide a copy of the PowerPoint on CD/DVD, as well a hard copy of full-sized, color slides.

Awards are arranged alphabetically below their administering organizations

Student's name and school should appear directly on the CD/DVD; Brochure/Booklet - 8-page minimum. Provide a copy of the brochure/booklet on DC/DVD, as well as hard copy printed in color. Student's name and school should appear directly on the CD/DVD; Website - 10 page minimum. **Contact:** Josh Madsen, Marketing Director, at 704-343-4644 or jmadsen@demayolaw.com.

5617 ■ The Law Offices of Tad Nelson & Associates

1221 Studewood St., No. 107
Houston, TX 77008
Ph: (713)802-1631
E-mail: tad@thenelsonfirm.com
URL: tadnelsonlaw.com

5618 ■ Tad Nelson Law Firm Scholarships
(Undergraduate/Scholarship)

Purpose: To support students' expenses for their future career in law. **Focus:** Law. **Qualif.:** Applicants must be high school seniors or high school graduates in Texas that seek a future career in law. **Criteria:** Selection will be based on the committee's criteria.

Funds Avail.: $500. **Duration:** Non-renewable. **Number Awarded:** 1. **To Apply:** Applicants must submit the following application materials: student aid report showing income status of their household; have a minimum GPA of 3.0.; and a transcript together with counselor or school representative signature. **Deadline:** May 31.

5619 ■ Law School Admission Council (LSAC)

662 Penn St.
Newtown, PA 18940-2176
Ph: (215)968-1001
Fax: (215)968-1277
E-mail: lsacinfo@lsac.org
URL: www.lsac.org

5620 ■ Diversity Initiatives Grants *(Graduate/Grant)*

Purpose: To encourage underrepresented groups to pursue legal education and to pursue legal education and to increase the enrollment and successful law school completion of minority students. **Focus:** Law. **Qualif.:** Applicants must be from underrepresented groups pursuing legal education. **Criteria:** Selection will be based on the committee's criteria.

Funds Avail.: No specific amount. **Duration:** Annual. **To Apply:** Interested applicants may contact the Administrative Assistant for the application process.

5621 ■ LSAC Research Grant Program *(Professional development/Grant)*

Purpose: To provide funding on significant research on a wide variety of topics related to the mission of LSAC. **Focus:** Law. **Qualif.:** Applicants must be principal investigators from all countries. Principal investigators need not be based in law schools. **Criteria:** Selection will be based on the applicants' eligibility and their research proposals. Proposals will be judged on the importance of the questions addressed, their relevance to the mission of LSAC, the quality of the research designs, and the capacity of the researchers to carry out the project.

Funds Avail.: $200,000. **To Apply:** Applicants are required

to submit a feasible research proposal. The program welcomes proposals for research proceeding from any of a variety of methodologies, a potentially broad range of topics, and varying time frames. Proposals should include the following sections: cover sheet, summary, project description (problem statement, literature review, and research methods), work plan and timetable, dissemination plan, budget, curriculum vitae, and supporting documents. The proposal should be double-spaced and printed in a font not smaller than 12-point. Submit two hard copies plus an electronic copy in PDF format. **Deadline:** August 15. **Contact:** Ann Gallagher at agallagher@LSAC.org.

5622 ■ Law and Society Association (LSA)

423 S Wakara Way, Ste. 205
Salt Lake City, UT 84108-3534
Ph: (801)581-3219
Fax: (888)292-5515
E-mail: lsa@lawandsociety.org
URL: www.lawandsociety.org

5623 ■ John Hope Franklin Prize *(Other/Prize)*

Purpose: To recognize exceptional scholarship in the field of race, racism and the law. **Focus:** Law. **Qualif.:** Candidates must be author of an article published in any scholarly journal, including socio-legal journals, journals in other disciplines, law reviews, or may be a chapter in a book volume. **Criteria:** Selection will be based on the committee's criteria.

Funds Avail.: $500. **Duration:** Annual. **To Apply:** Candidates must submit a sample of an article published. It should be written in English. Article and nomination must be submitted as an attachment in Word or in PDF format. **Deadline:** Mid-January. **Remarks:** Established in 2010. **Contact:** Law and Society Association, at the above address.

5624 ■ Law and Society Association Article Prize
(Other/Prize)

Purpose: To recognize exceptional scholarship in the field of socio-legal studies for an article published in the previous two years. **Focus:** Law. **Qualif.:** Applicants must be authors of an article published in any scholarly journal, including socio-legal journals, journals in other disciplines, law reviews, or edited books. **Criteria:** Selection will be based on the committee's criteria.

Funds Avail.: $500. **Duration:** Annual. **To Apply:** Applicants must submit a sample of a published article. It should be written in English. An article may be nominated by sending a copy by email attachment in Word or PDF format. The nomination message must include full bibliographic citation. Self-nominations are welcome. **Remarks:** Established in 1998.

5625 ■ Law and Society Association Dissertation Prize *(Other/Prize)*

Purpose: To recognize individuals whose dissertation best represents outstanding work in law and society. **Focus:** Law. **Qualif.:** Candidates must be author whose dissertation best represents outstanding work in law and society research. **Criteria:** Selection will be based on the committee's criteria.

Funds Avail.: $500. **Duration:** Annual. **Number Awarded:** 1. **To Apply:** Submissions should be of outstanding work; models of law and society research can be found in Law

Awards are arranged alphabetically below their administering organizations

and Society Review and other leading journals of socio-legal research; dissertation may be based on research about law in any discipline or on interdisciplinary research; a complete nomination includes the following: dissertation, electronic copy in Word or PDF format on CD or flash drive; abstract, copied to a separate file on the same CD/drive; letter of recommendation from Faculty member or Advisor; current address of the dissertator. **Deadline:** Mid-January. **Contact:** Law and Society Association, at the above address.

5626 ■ Law and Society Association International Prize *(Other/Prize)*

Purpose: To recognize individuals who have made contributions toward advancement of knowledge in the field of law and society. **Focus:** Law. **Qualif.:** Candidate must be a resident outside the United States. **Criteria:** Selection will be based on the committee's criteria.

Funds Avail.: $500. **Duration:** Annual. **To Apply:** Nominators must contact the Association for the nomination process. **Deadline:** January 15. **Contact:** Law and Society Association, at the above address.

5627 ■ Law and Society Association Undergraduate Student Paper Prize *(Undergraduate/Prize)*

Purpose: To award students whose nominated papers best represent outstanding law and society research. **Focus:** Law. **Qualif.:** Candidates must be undergraduate matriculated students at any institution of higher education. **Criteria:** Selection will be based on the committee's criteria.

Funds Avail.: $500. **Duration:** Annual. **Number Awarded:** 1. **To Apply:** Candidates must submit a sample of their paper works; nominations can be made by non-student members of the Law and Society Association and through the submission of the recommended paper to the Committee on Student Awards; subject matter of the nominated papers should be in the interdisciplinary tradition of law and society research, and should reflect the style of articles that appear in the Law and Society Review; nominated papers should examine law in culture and society, including interpretative, historical, social scientific and jurisprudential scholarship; all papers entered in the competition must be written by matriculated students at any U.S. or non-U.S. institutions of higher education in the two previous years. **Deadline:** January.

5628 ■ Stan Wheeler Mentorship Awards *(Other/ Award)*

Purpose: To recognize a member of the Law and Society community who is regarded by his or her peers and students as an outstanding mentor for graduate, professional or undergraduate students who are working on issues of law and society. **Focus:** Law. **Qualif.:** Candidates must be members of the Law and Society Association or community who are regarded by their peers and students as outstanding mentors for graduates, professionals or undergraduate students who are working on issues of law and society. **Criteria:** Selection will be based on the committee's criteria.

Funds Avail.: $500. **Duration:** Annual. **Deadline:** January 15. **Remarks:** Established in 2008. **Contact:** Law and Society Association, at the above address.

5629 ■ Law Society of British Columbia
845 Cambie St.
Vancouver, BC, Canada V6B 4Z9

Ph: (604)669-2533
Fax: (604)669-5232
Free: 800-903-5300
E-mail: communications@lsbc.org
URL: www.lawsociety.bc.ca

5630 ■ Law Society of British Columbia Scholarships *(Graduate, Undergraduate/Scholarship)*

Purpose: To provide financial assistance for law graduate students intending to complete a full-time program of studies that will benefit students, the province and legal professions in British Columbia. **Focus:** Law. **Qualif.:** Applicants must be law graduates or graduating students at University of British Columbia or University of Victoria who are able to show a real or substantial connection to BC and who must demonstrate outstanding academics. **Criteria:** Recipients will be selected by the Credentials Committee based on the following considerations: (1) academic standing; (2) social contributions; (3) intention to practice in British Columbia after completing the graduate studies; (4) financial need; and (5) importance or significance of the proposed work.

Funds Avail.: $12,000. **To Apply:** Applicants must submit a letter of application including details of their academic career and proposed plan for a graduate study, official transcript of records of all academic institutions attended, and three letters of recommendation (one from the dean and two from professors of the law school). **Deadline:** March 15.

5631 ■ Law Society of Prince Edward Island (LSPEI)
49 Water St.
Charlottetown, PE, Canada C1A 7K2
Ph: (902)566-1666
Fax: (902)368-7557
E-mail: lawsociety@lspei.pe.ca
URL: www.lspei.pe.ca

5632 ■ Prince Edward Island Law Student Scholarships *(Undergraduate/Scholarship)*

Purpose: To provide scholarship assistance to deserving students who want to pursue their studies. **Focus:** Law. **Qualif.:** Applicants must be students enrolled or accepted for enrollment as a full-time law students at an accredited university law school for the academic year; must be residents of Prince Edward Island; must demonstrate scholastic achievement in their last year of academic study; and must demonstrate financial need. **Criteria:** Recipient will be selected by the Council of Law Society of Prince Edward Island.

Funds Avail.: $2,000. **Duration:** Annual. **Number Awarded:** 3. **To Apply:** Applicant must complete the application form available online; must submit an official transcript of record and curriculum vitae. **Deadline:** July 31.

5633 ■ Lawrence Berkeley National Laboratory
1 Cyclotron Rd.
Berkeley, CA 94720
Ph: (510)486-4000
Fax: (510)486-4845
E-mail: library@lbl.gov
URL: www.lbl.gov

Awards are arranged alphabetically below their administering organizations

5634 ■ Advanced Light Source Postdoctoral Fellowship Program *(Postdoctorate/Fellowship)*

Purpose: To identify outstanding individuals in new and emerging scientific and engineering research fields. **Focus:** Engineering; Science. **Qualif.:** Applicants must be legally eligible to work in the United States, regardless of citizenship and have received a doctoral research degree from an accredited academic institution in an appropriate scientific or engineering discipline within three years of the appointment start date. **Criteria:** Applications will be evaluated based on the qualifications of the applicants, the merits of the proposed collaborative research, and the alignment of the project with ALS strategic priorities.

Funds Avail.: No specific amount. **To Apply:** Applicants must complete and submit the following documents online: an application form; curriculum vitae; publication list; maximum of three pages statement of research to be performed (preferably written in consultation with an ALS Scientific mentor); three references. Applicants must also obtain the commitment of an ALS scientific mentor who will work with them throughout the duration of the proposed fellowship.

5635 ■ Luis W. Alvarez Postdoctoral Fellowships in Computational Science *(Doctorate/Fellowship)*

Purpose: To allow recent graduates with a PhD (or equivalent) to acquire further scientific training at one of the leading facilities for scientific computing and to develop professional maturity for independent research. **Focus:** Clinical laboratory sciences. **Qualif.:** Applicant must be recent graduate with a PhD (or equivalent) within the past three years, and have backgrounds and research interests in any computer and computational science discipline. **Criteria:** Selection is based on the application.

Funds Avail.: No specific amount. **To Apply:** Applicants must apply online and submit in a single attachment the following documents: curriculum vitae; a statement of research interests; and a list of three references.

5636 ■ Lawyers' Committee for Civil Rights Under Law (LCCRUL)
1401 New York Ave. NW, Ste. 400
Washington, DC 20005
Ph: (202)662-8600
Fax: (202)783-0857
Free: 888-299-5227
URL: www.lawyerscommittee.org

5637 ■ George N. Lindsay Civil Rights Legal Fellowships *(Graduate/Fellowship)*

Purpose: To provide an opportunity for recent law school graduates to become familiar with civil rights practice by working with many of the nation's leading civil rights experts. **Focus:** Law. **Qualif.:** Applicant must graduate from law school; must demonstrate a commitment to equal justice and equal opportunity for all; be dedicated to the deployment of innovative strategies (including non-litigation strategies) in addressing entrenched or cutting edge racial, national origin and gender discrimination matters. Attorneys who work in law firms are eligible for the fellowship, including pursuant to a leave of absence or sabbatical program. **Criteria:** Preference will be given to those who have been admitted to the bar or are scheduled to take a bar examination.

Funds Avail.: $42,000. **Duration:** Annual. **To Apply:** Ap-

plicants must submit via e-mail an initial application that includes: a cover letter; a resume; a law school transcript; and the application form. **Deadline:** July 8.

5638 ■ League of United Latin American Citizens (LULAC)
1133 19th St. NW, Ste. 1000
Washington, DC 20036
Ph: (202)833-6130
Fax: (202)833-6135
Free: 877-LUL-AC01
URL: lulac.org

5639 ■ League of Latin American Citizens General Electric Scholarships *(Undergraduate, Vocational/Occupational/Scholarship)*

Purpose: To provide high quality educational opportunities to the Hispanic community; to assist and encourage outstanding minority students in completing their college education in the field of business or engineering. **Focus:** Business; Engineering, Electrical. **Qualif.:** Applicant must be a U.S. citizen or legal resident; must be a minority student pursuing full-time studies leading to a bachelor's degree at a college, university, or graduate School, including two-year colleges, or vocational schools that lead to an associate's degree; must not be related to a scholarship Committee member, the Council President, or an individual contributor to the local funds of the Council; must be a sophomore, junior, or senior student in the field of business or engineering; must have a cumulative GPA of at least 3.25 on a 4.0 scale or the equivalent. **Criteria:** Recipients will be selected based on academic performance; performance in business or engineering-related subjects; likelihood of pursuing a career in business or engineering; writing ability; extracurricular activities; and community involvement.

Funds Avail.: $5,000. **Duration:** One semester. **Number Awarded:** 2. **To Apply:** Applicant must submit a completed application form; college transcript(s); letters of reference from three adults (at least one from professor); and (maximum of 300 words) typed personal statement describing professional and career goals. **Deadline:** August 15.

5640 ■ LULAC GM Scholarships *(Graduate, High School, Undergraduate, Vocational/Occupational/Award)*

Purpose: To provide high quality educational opportunities to the Hispanic community. **Focus:** Hispanic American studies. **Qualif.:** Applicants must be American citizens or legal residents; must have applied to or be enrolled in a college, university, or graduate school, including 2-year colleges, or vocational schools that lead to an associate's degree; must not be related to a scholarship committee member, the Council President, or an individual contributor to the local funds of the Council. **Criteria:** Recipients are chosen through a very rigorous selection process by members of LNESC's scholarship committee.

Funds Avail.: No specific amount. **To Apply:** Applicants should be mailed directly their application to the nearest LULAC Council.

5641 ■ LULAC National Scholarship Fund (LNSF) *(Graduate, High School, Undergraduate, Vocational/Occupational/Scholarship)*

Purpose: To provide high quality educational opportunities to the Hispanic community. **Focus:** Hispanic American stud-

Awards are arranged alphabetically below their administering organizations

ies. **Qualif.:** Applicant must be a US citizen or legal resident; must have applied to or be enrolled in a college, university, or graduate school, including 2-year colleges, or vocational schools that lead to an associate's degree; must not be related to a scholarship committee member, the Council President, or an individual contributor to the local funds of the Council. **Criteria:** Recipients are chosen through a very rigorous selection process by members of LNESC's scholarship committee.

Funds Avail.: No specific amount. **Duration:** Annual. **To Apply:** Applications should be mailed directly to the nearest LULAC Council. **Deadline:** March 31. **Remarks:** Established in 1975.

5642 ■ Leakey Foundation
1003B O'Reilly Ave.
San Francisco, CA 94129-1359
Ph: (415)561-4646
Fax: (415)561-4647
E-mail: info@leakeyfoundation.org
URL: leakeyfoundation.org

5643 ■ Franklin Mosher Baldwin Memorial Fellowships *(Master's, Doctorate/Fellowship)*

Purpose: To support scholars and students who wish to obtain an advanced degree from an institution outside the student's home country. **Focus:** Anthropology. **Qualif.:** Applicants must be enrolled in a MA, PhD or equivalent program related to the study of human evolution. **Criteria:** Recipients will be chosen based on the following categories: 1) affiliation and/or employment with an institution in their home country; 2) provisional acceptance to the host institution; 3) demonstrated financial need; and 4) intention to return and work in the home country upon completion of training.

Funds Avail.: $15,000 per year. **Duration:** Up to two years. **To Apply:** Applicants must submit a completed application form and letters from sponsor. **Deadline:** February 15.

5644 ■ Leakey Foundation Research Grants *(Doctorate/Grant)*

Purpose: To support research related specifically to human origins. **Focus:** Anthropology. **Qualif.:** Applicants must be advanced doctoral students and established scientists. **Criteria:** Recipients will be selected based on submitted research. Priority of funding will be given to applicants whose research project meets the stated purpose of the Foundation.

Funds Avail.: $3,000-$15,000. **To Apply:** Applicants must complete the application form. Application must be written in English and it should be submitted in PDF format. **Deadline:** January 5. **Contact:** Paddy Moore, 415-561-4646, grants@leakeyfoundation.org.

5645 ■ Learning Disabilities Association of Alberta (LDAA)
PO Box 29011
Pleasantview
Edmonton, AB, Canada T6H 5Z6
Ph: (780)448-0360
E-mail: execdir@ldalberta.ca
URL: www.ldalberta.ca

5646 ■ Siobhan Isabella Reid Memorial Scholarships *(Graduate, Undergraduate/Scholarship)*

Purpose: To provide financial assistance to qualified individuals who want to pursue their studies. **Focus:** Dis-

abilities; Education, Special. **Qualif.:** Applicant must be a full-time student attending an Alberta University; must be enrolled in a program which will be able to assist children and individual with learning disabilities; must have complete two full academic years at either a university or at a junior college at which courses are accepted by a university as applicable toward a university degree; must be an undergraduate or post graduate student enrolled in any faculty at a university in Alberta. **Criteria:** Recipient will be selected based on the following criteria: (a) student's contributions to his or her community and to campus life; (b) satisfactory academic record; (c) student's future educational program leading toward assisting children and adults with learning disabilities.

Funds Avail.: $1,000. **Duration:** Annual. **To Apply:** Applicant must submit a completed application form available from the website; and include the following materials: (a) official transcript of his or her academic record for the last university or college year; (b) three letters of reference from non-relative; (c) outline of his or her contributions to the applicants community as well as to campus life; (d) outline of the program the student wishes to undertake during the scholarship year. **Deadline:** May 15. **Remarks:** Established in 1982.

5647 ■ Learning Disabilities Association of Kingston (LDAK)
993 Princess St., No. 116
Kingston, ON, Canada K7L 1H3
Ph: (613)546-8524
E-mail: ldak@ldakingston.com
URL: www.ldakingston.com

5648 ■ Tristin Memorial Scholarships *(Undergraduate, Vocational/Occupational/Scholarship)*

Purpose: To encourage Canadian students with learning disabilities to pursue a college, private vocational school or an undergraduate degree at a Canadian university. **Focus:** General studies/Field of study not specified. **Qualif.:** Applicant must have a documented learning disability; a Canadian citizen or permanent resident who has lived in Canada for at least two years as a permanent resident; an Ontario resident living within the city and boundaries of Kingston, towns of Ernestown, Amherst Island, Richmond, Camden, Kaladar, North and South Fredericksburg, Napanee, Lennox and Addington, Townships of Front/Rear Leeds and Lansdown and Front of Yonge, The Town of Gananoque in the county of Leeds and Grenville; and planning to register in a Canadian college, university or vocational school in the next semester or already enrolled in a program. **Criteria:** Selection is based on the submitted application materials.

Funds Avail.: $500. **Duration:** One academic year. **Number Awarded:** 1. **To Apply:** Applicant must complete a letter with personal details and submit along with a 200-word outline on: description of his/her learning disability, how it impacts his/her daily life, coping skills and strategies used at school and at home to compensate for the learning disability, extracurricular activities, community involvement and/or employment experience, future goals, and how the scholarship funds will assist him/her. In addition, applicants must submit a documentation of the learning disability; two letters of recommendation (one from a secondary school teacher); and proof of enrollment as an active student. **Deadline:** May 15. **Contact:** Phil Perrin, 613-544-6925.

Awards are arranged alphabetically below their administering organizations

---

5649 ■ Learning Disabilities Association of Ontario (LDAO)

365 Evans Ave., Ste. 202
Toronto, ON, Canada M8Z 1K2
Ph: (416)929-4311
Fax: (416)929-3905
E-mail: info@ldao.ca
URL: www.ldao.ca

5650 ■ Roy Cooper Scholarships *(Undergraduate/Scholarship)*

Purpose: To support high school students with learning disabilities pursuing a degree in engineering and/or physical sciences. **Focus:** Engineering; Physical sciences. **Qualif.:** Applicant must be a high school student who has a documented learning disability and will be attending a university or college, majoring in an engineering and/or physical science discipline. **Criteria:** Selection is based on the submitted application materials.

Funds Avail.: $1,000. **Duration:** Annual. **To Apply:** Applicants must contact any of the LDAO's local chapters for the scholarship information and application. **Deadline:** June 17.

5651 ■ Gloria Landis Bursary *(Undergraduate, Vocational/Occupational/Scholarship)*

Purpose: To provide financial assistance to a mature individual with learning disabilities who is in a postsecondary program or accredited vocational institute, and has been absent from full-time education for a period of three years. **Focus:** General studies/Field of study not specified. **Qualif.:** Applicant must be diagnosed with a documented learning disability; be at least 25 years of age; has been absent from full-time education for a period of three years; accepted into a postsecondary or accredited vocational institute program; considered by the educational institution to be a mature student within the institution's rules and regulations; and an Ontario resident. **Criteria:** Selection is based on the submitted application materials.

Funds Avail.: $1,000. **Duration:** Annual; One year. **Number Awarded:** 1. **To Apply:** Applicants must submit a completed application form along with two reference letters; 2-3 page essay (400-600 words); proof of admission from the institution; proof of Ontario residency; and proof of learning disability. **Deadline:** June 15.

5652 ■ LeClairRyan

2318 Mill Rd., Ste. 1100
Alexandria, VA 22314
Ph: (703)684-8007
Fax: (703)684-8075
URL: www.leclairryan.com

5653 ■ LeClairRyan Diversity Scholarships *(Undergraduate/Scholarship)*

Purpose: To support diversity law students who most exemplifies the late Oliver W. Hill's qualities of legal excellence and selfless dedication to the fight for justice. **Focus:** Law. **Qualif.:** Applicants must be enrolled in good standing at an ABA-accredited US law school in any state in which LeClairRyan has an office; have one semester of law school completed; a law school GPA of at least 3.0; identify as a member of one of the racial/ethnic groups as defined by the Equal Employment Opportunity Commission, or identify as LGBT. **Criteria:** Selection will be based on the committee's criteria.

Funds Avail.: $5,000. **To Apply:** Students must submit the completed application along with their resume, law school transcript and two letters of recommendation from a professor or member of the Bar and a maximum of 2,000 words essay on pursuing social justice through the law. **Deadline:** April 20. **Contact:** Danielle H. Roberts, Recruiting Manager, Riverfront Plaza, East Tower, 951 E Byrd St., 8th Fl., Richmond, VA 23219; droberts@leclairryan.com.

5654 ■ Legacy Inc.

4162A Carmichael Ct.
Montgomery, AL 36106
Ph: (334)270-5921
Fax: (334)270-5527
Free: 800-240-5115
E-mail: info@legacyenved.org
URL: legacyenved.org

5655 ■ Legacy Inc. College Undergraduate and Graduate Scholarships *(Graduate, Undergraduate/Scholarship)*

Purpose: To provide financial assistance to Alabama students who are pursuing environmentally related careers. **Focus:** Environmental science. **Qualif.:** Applicants must be Alabama residents who are enrolled in Alabama universities and are planning to pursue environmentally related careers. Students must have at least junior standing by Fall Quarter/Semester of the current year. **Criteria:** Selection will be based on the committee's criteria.

Funds Avail.: Up to $1,500 for undergraduate applicants and up to $2,000 for graduate applicants. **To Apply:** Applicants must submit a complete application form, student-issued copy of transcripts from all colleges attended and three letters of reference (two academic references and one personal reference). **Deadline:** May 7. **Contact:** Questions concerning eligibility, applicants must contact the Legacy office at 800-240-5115.

5656 ■ Legal Aid of North Carolina, Inc. (LANC)

313 W Martin St.
Raleigh, NC 27601
Ph: (919)856-2564
Fax: (919)856-2120
Free: 866-369-6923
URL: www.legalaidnc.org

5657 ■ Judge Samuel J. Ervin, III Fellowships *(Graduate/Fellowship)*

Purpose: To provide free legal assistance in civil matters to low-income persons in Alexander, Burke, Caldwell, Catawba and McDowell Counties of northwest North Carolina. **Focus:** Law. **Qualif.:** Candidates must be licensed to practice law in North Carolina; must have a demonstrated commitment to community service and to be able to relate well to low-income people in a rural setting. **Criteria:** Selection will be based on the committee's criteria.

Funds Avail.: No specific amount. **To Apply:** Interested applicants must send a cover letter expressing interest in the fellowship, resume, a no more than 10 pages writing sample and name/contact information of three references.

5658 ■ Clifton W. Everett, Sr. Community Lawyer Fellowships *(Graduate/Fellowship)*

Purpose: To provide excellent opportunities for new law school graduate to gain litigation experience and provide

Awards are arranged alphabetically below their administering organizations

valuable service to low-income, rural communities. **Focus:** Law. **Qualif.:** Applicants must be recently graduated law students; must be expecting to successfully receive a JD from an ABA accredited law school before the fellowship begins; must demonstrate commitment to community service and be able to relate well to low-income people in a rural setting; must be licensed to practice law in North Carolina when the fellowship begins. **Criteria:** Selection will be based on the applicants' legal abilities and their demonstrated commitment to social justice.

Funds Avail.: No specific amount. **To Apply:** Applicants must send a cover letter expressing interest in the current Everett Fellowship opening(s), resume, a writing sample of no more than 10 pages and names/contact information of three references. **Remarks:** Established in 1992.

5659 ■ Gilder Lehrman Institute of American History

49 W 45th St., 6th Fl.
New York, NY 10036
Ph: (646)366-9666
Fax: (646)366-9669
E-mail: info@gilderlehrman.org
URL: www.gilderlehrman.org

5660 ■ Gilder Lehrman Short-Term Fellowships
(Graduate, Postdoctorate/Fellowship)

Purpose: To support historians in their scholarly, pedagogical and professional endeavors. **Focus:** History. **Qualif.:** Applicants may be the following: post-doctoral scholars at any faculty rank; doctoral candidates who have completed exams and dissertation reading and writing; or journalists or independent scholars. **Criteria:** Selection shall be based on the aforementioned applicants' qualifications and compliance with the application details.

Funds Avail.: $3,000 each. **Duration:** Annual. **To Apply:** Applicants must submit a project proposal including current contact information, a list of primary sources to be consulted, and an anticipated budget; curriculum vitae; and two letters of recommendation from established scholars of American history. **Deadline:** May 15. **Contact:** fellowships@gilderlehrman.org.

5661 ■ Les Dames d'Escoffier New York (LDNY)

c/o Joanne Lamb Hayes, Membership Committee Chair
320 E 25th St., Apt. 8CC
New York, NY 10010
URL: www.ldny.org

5662 ■ Les Dames D'Escoffier New York Scholarships *(Undergraduate/Scholarship)*

Purpose: To provide support for talented women in food and wine-related disciplines; hospitality and table arts. **Focus:** Food service careers; Hotel, institutional, and restaurant management; Nutrition. **Qualif.:** Applicants must be enrolled in a higher education program; must be from the Tri-State area (New York, New Jersey, Connecticut). **Criteria:** Selection will be based on evaluation of submitted documents and specific criteria. The LDNY Scholarship Selection Committee reviews all submissions and selects the winning candidates based on how well they meet or exceed the criteria for consideration.

Funds Avail.: Varies. **Duration:** Annual. **To Apply:** Applicants must submit a completed application form; resume;

official transcript from higher education institution; two professional recommendation letters but not from school affiliations; and an essay of less than 500-words. **Contact:** For further information, please contact ldnyscholarship@gmail.com.

5663 ■ Leukemia Research Foundation (LRF)

3520 Lake Ave., Ste. 202
Wilmette, IL 60091-1064
Ph: (847)424-0600
Fax: (847)424-0606
Free: 888-558-5385
E-mail: info@lrfmail.org
URL: www.leukemia-research.org

5664 ■ Hollis Brownstein Research Grants *(Professional development/Grant)*

Purpose: To allow innovative scientists to act on their ideas and try new procedures and experiments that will lead to significant breakthroughs. **Focus:** Leukemia. **Qualif.:** Applicants must be new investigators beginning to establish their own laboratories that are no longer under the tutelage of a senior scientist mentor. Preference will be given to proposals that focus on leukemia, lymphoma and MDS. New investigators are considered to be within seven years of their first independent position. Years as resident physicians, fellow physicians, or post-doctoral fellows are considered to be training years. Applicants must have a NIH KO8 or K23. **Criteria:** Selection will be based on the committee's criteria.

Funds Avail.: $100,000. **Duration:** Annual. **To Apply:** Applicants must submit an application through email and must use the current application cover sheet form, available online. The cover sheet form must be completely filled out for an application to be accepted and assigned for review. The document format should be single spaced with a 12 point font used throughout. The paper size should be 8 1/2 inches by 11 inches. A concise one paragraph description of the project is to be included in the application as a separate page. This paragraph should be in extreme lay terminology, appropriate for an audience without scientific training. Explain terms which cannot be simplified. The PDF file should not exceed 10 MB in size. Application label should read as follows: LastName, FirstName, MiddleInitial. **Deadline:** February. **Contact:** grants@lrfmail.org.

5665 ■ Lewis-Clark State College Library

500 8th Ave.
Lewiston, ID 83501-2691
Ph: (208)792-5272
Fax: (208)792-2831
Free: 800-933-5272
E-mail: refdesk@lcsc.edu
URL: www.lcsc.edu/library

5666 ■ The "21" Endowed Scholarships
(Undergraduate/Scholarship)

Purpose: To offset the educationally-related expenses of a Lewis-Clark State College student from the Culdesac-Lapwai area. **Focus:** General studies/Field of study not specified. **Qualif.:** Applicants must be entering first year students who have a cumulative GPA of at least 2.5. **Criteria:** Recipients will be selected based on financial need.

Awards are arranged alphabetically below their administering organizations

Funds Avail.: Amount varies. **Duration:** Annual. **To Apply:** Applicants must submit a general application. **Deadline:** March 1.

5667 ■ Mamie Adams Memorial Awards
(Undergraduate/Scholarship)

Purpose: To provide educational assistance for students who demonstrate consistency and improvement in their scholastic records. **Focus:** General studies/Field of study not specified. **Qualif.:** Applicants must be high school seniors who are planning to attend college in the fall or undergraduate college students enrolled at a 2- or 4-year institution with at least a 2.5 GPA. **Criteria:** Preference is given to demonstrated consistency and improvement in academic records.

Funds Avail.: $1,000. **Duration:** Annual. **To Apply:** Applicants must accomplish a general application available at the website. **Deadline:** April 30. **Contact:** 4126 Pocahontas Dr., Baytown, TX 77521; Phone and Fax: 713-421-2915.

5668 ■ American Legion Boys/Girls State Scholarships *(Undergraduate/Scholarship)*

Purpose: To acknowledge outstanding Idaho high school seniors who have participated in The American Legion of Idaho Boys and Girls State competition and who have selected Lewis-Clark State College as their school of choice. **Focus:** General studies/Field of study not specified. **Qualif.:** Applicants must be outstanding senior students of Idaho High School who are currently enrolled in LCSC. **Criteria:** Awards are given based on academic merit.

Funds Avail.: $200. **Duration:** Annual. **Number Awarded:** 4 (two Boys state and two Girls state). **To Apply:** Applicants must accomplish a general application available at the website. **Contact:** American Legion, Boys State, 901 Warren, Boise, ID 83706; Phone: 208-342-7061; or American Legion Auxiliary, Girls State, 905 Warren St., Boise, ID 83706; Phone: 208-342-7066.

5669 ■ Banner Bank Business Scholarships
(Undergraduate/Scholarship)

Purpose: To provide financial assistance for outstanding junior or senior students in the Business Division. **Focus:** Business. **Qualif.:** Applicants must be students pursuing a degree in business and entering their junior or senior year. Applicants must demonstrate financial need as determined by the FAFSA form. **Criteria:** Award is given based on merit.

Funds Avail.: $1,000. **Duration:** Annual. **To Apply:** Applicants must accomplish the required general application available in the website. **Deadline:** March 1.

5670 ■ Diana Brown Endowed Scholarships
(Undergraduate/Scholarship)

Purpose: To support a non-traditional student that is a cancer survivor, is currently battling cancer, or who has had to deal with cancer in their immediate family. **Focus:** General studies/Field of study not specified. **Qualif.:** Applicants must be cancer survivors or are currently battling cancer and are registered degree-seeking, full-time students; must demonstrate a 3.0 cumulative GPA. **Criteria:** Recipients will be selected based on financial need.

Funds Avail.: No specific amount. **Duration:** Annual. **To Apply:** Applicants must submit general application. **Deadline:** March 1.

5671 ■ Glen and Babs Carlson Endowed Scholarships *(Undergraduate/Scholarship)*

Purpose: To offset the educationally-related expenses of Lewis-Clark State College students. **Focus:** General studies/Field of study not specified. **Qualif.:** Applicants must be students at Lewis-Clark State College with a cumulative GPA consistent with the minimum required for admission. **Criteria:** Recipients are evaluated based on financial need.

Funds Avail.: No specific amount. **Duration:** Annual. **To Apply:** Applicants must submit a general application. **Deadline:** March 1.

5672 ■ Walter and Elsie Carr Endowed Scholarships *(Undergraduate/Scholarship)*

Purpose: To provide financial assistance for the graduates of Emmett High School. **Focus:** General studies/Field of study not specified. **Qualif.:** Applicants must be enrolled for at least 12 credits. **Criteria:** Recipients are selected based on financial need.

Funds Avail.: No specific amount. **Duration:** Annual. **To Apply:** Applicants must submit a general application. **Deadline:** March 1.

5673 ■ Coeur d'Alene Alumni Scholarships
(Undergraduate/Scholarship)

Purpose: To inspire educational pursuits among less capable individuals by providing financial assistance. **Focus:** General studies/Field of study not specified. **Qualif.:** Applicants must be attending the LCSC Couer d'Alene campus; must be currently enrolled in a minimum of six semester credits through the Coeur d'Alene program which includes credits from LCSC and NIC; must have completed at least one semester of course work through LCSC; and must have a minimum GPA of 3.0. **Criteria:** Preference will be given to students who demonstrate financial need as determined by the Financial Aid Office.

Funds Avail.: Amount varies. **Duration:** Annual. **To Apply:** Applicants must accomplish a general application available at the website. **Deadline:** March 1.

5674 ■ Rob Copeland Memorial Scholarships
(Undergraduate/Scholarship)

Purpose: To provide financial assistance for individuals intending to pursue educational goals. **Focus:** Automotive technology. **Qualif.:** Applicants must be full-time students who are majoring in Auto Mechanics Technology and must have a minimum of 2.5 GPA. **Criteria:** Preference will be given to students who demonstrate financial need.

Funds Avail.: No specific amount. **Duration:** Annual. **To Apply:** Applicants must accomplish a general application available in the website. **Deadline:** March 1.

5675 ■ Rick Crane Group Real Estate Scholarship Fund *(Undergraduate/Scholarship)*

Purpose: To offset the educationally-related expenses of Lewis-Clark State College students intending to pursue a career in the field of real estate. **Focus:** Business administration; Real estate. **Qualif.:** Applicants must be individuals seeking a Bachelor's degree in Business, or an Associate of Applied Science degree in Business Management; must be serious about becoming a real estate agent or otherwise working in the field of real estate, have a grade point average of at least 3.5 with strong potential for academic achievement, and must be full-time students taking 12 or

Awards are arranged alphabetically below their administering organizations

more credits. **Criteria:** Preference will be given to students who are gainfully employed.

Funds Avail.: $100. **Duration:** Annual. **To Apply:** Applicants must accomplish the required general application available in the website. **Deadline:** March 1.

5676 ■ Laura Moore Cunningham Foundation General Scholarships *(Undergraduate/Scholarship)*

Purpose: To provide financial assistance for the Idaho youth. **Focus:** General studies/Field of study not specified. **Qualif.:** Applicants must be classified as full-time students who are carrying 12 or more credits per semester and who have a minimum cumulative GPA of 3.0. and must also be Idaho residents. **Criteria:** Recipient will be selected based on financial need.

Funds Avail.: Amount varies. **Duration:** Annual. **To Apply:** Applicants must submit a general application. **Deadline:** March 1.

5677 ■ Gretchen Dimico Memorial Scholarships *(Undergraduate/Scholarship)*

Purpose: To inspire educational pursuits among less capable individuals by providing financial assistance. **Focus:** Nursing. **Qualif.:** Applicants must be full or part-time RN to BSN students at the LCSC Coeur d'Alene Center; must have a cumulative GPA of 2.25; must be current or former members of the Professional Nursing Organization; and must demonstrate financial need as determined by the Financial Aid Office. **Criteria:** Recipients will be selected based on academic achievements.

Funds Avail.: Amount varies. **Duration:** Annual. **To Apply:** Applicants must accomplish the general application form available at the website. **Deadline:** March 1.

5678 ■ Fisher-Clark Memorial Endowed Scholarships *(Undergraduate/Scholarship)*

Purpose: To offset the educational expenses of Lewis-Clark State College students. **Focus:** General studies/Field of study not specified. **Qualif.:** Applicants must be female students and must have a cumulative grade point average consistent with the minimum required for admission and for progress toward her major. **Criteria:** Recipient is selected based on financial need.

Funds Avail.: No specific amount. **Duration:** Annual. **To Apply:** Applicants must submit a general application. **Deadline:** March 1.

5679 ■ Dean A. Froehlich Endowed Scholarships *(Undergraduate/Scholarship)*

Purpose: To provide financial assistance for students and single parents who are in need and are intending to pursue higher education. **Focus:** General studies/Field of study not specified. **Qualif.:** Applicants must be enrolled for at least 12 credits and have a minimum 2.5 GPA. **Criteria:** Preference is given to students who demonstrate financial need as determined by the Financial Aid Office and to non-traditional, single parents who are returning to higher education and are planning to stay in Idaho.

Funds Avail.: No specific amount. **Duration:** Annual. **To Apply:** Applicants must submit a general application. **Deadline:** March 1. **Remarks:** Established in 2004.

5680 ■ Irene Carlson Gnaedinger Memorial Scholarships *(Undergraduate/Scholarship)*

Purpose: To provide educational assistance for students from Lapwai High School. **Focus:** General studies/Field of

study not specified. **Qualif.:** Applicants must be graduates of Lapwai High School; must demonstrate a minimum cumulative GPA of 2.5; and are enrolled for a minimum of 12 credits in a baccalaureate degree program. **Criteria:** Recipients will be selected based on financial need.

Funds Avail.: Amount varies. **Duration:** Annual. **To Apply:** Applicants must submit a general application. **Deadline:** March 1.

5681 ■ Jack M. and Mary Lou Gruber Scholarships *(Undergraduate/Scholarship)*

Purpose: To provide financial assistance to people who cannot afford college education. **Focus:** General studies/Field of study not specified. **Qualif.:** Applicants must have a minimum of 3.0 GPA and are enrolled for a minimum of 12 credits. **Criteria:** Recipients will be selected based on financial need and active campus and/or community service. Preference will be given to students from the Lewis-Clark Valley.

Funds Avail.: No specific amount. **Duration:** Annual. **To Apply:** Applicants must submit a general application. **Deadline:** March 1.

5682 ■ Jimmy Guild Memorial Scholarships *(Undergraduate/Scholarship)*

Purpose: To provide educational assistance for students intending to pursue a career in the area of Computer Science. **Focus:** Computer and information sciences; Mathematics and mathematical sciences. **Qualif.:** Applicants must be full-time students who are majoring in mathematics; must have interest in Computer science; and must have a cumulative GPA of 3.0. **Criteria:** Selection is based on merit.

Funds Avail.: No specific amount. **Duration:** Annual. **To Apply:** Preference will be given to graduating students from local high schools who are affiliated with a member of the United Paperworkers International Union. **Deadline:** May 16. **Contact:** Financial Aid Office, LCSC, 500 8th Avenue, Lewiston, ID 83501.

5683 ■ Henderson Memorial Endowed Scholarships *(Undergraduate/Scholarship)*

Purpose: To offset the educationally-related expenses of Lewis-Clark State College students. **Focus:** General studies/Field of study not specified. **Qualif.:** Applicants must have completed at least one semester at LCSC and must have a cumulative GPA of at least 3.0. **Criteria:** Priority will be given to students who are in financial need.

Funds Avail.: Amount varies. **Duration:** Annual. **To Apply:** Applicants must submit a general application. **Deadline:** March 1.

5684 ■ Hinman-Jensen Endowed Scholarships *(Undergraduate/Scholarship)*

Purpose: To provide educational assistance for students pursuing either the Bachelor of Arts in Applied Technology or the Bachelor of Arts in Applied Science. **Focus:** Science; Technology. **Qualif.:** Applicants must be classified as full-time students with a cumulative GPA that is consistent with the minimum required for admission and for progress toward their major. **Criteria:** Priority is given to applicants with financial need.

Funds Avail.: Amount varies. **Duration:** Annual. **To Apply:** Applicants must accomplish a general application available at the website. **Deadline:** March 1.

Awards are arranged alphabetically below their administering organizations

5685 ■ Frank and Gladys Hopkins Endowed Scholarships *(Undergraduate/Scholarship)*

Purpose: To support varsity players who are also good in academics. **Focus:** General studies/Field of study not specified. **Qualif.:** Applicants must be classified as full-time students who are participating on the LCSC baseball team. Applicants must also have a cumulative GPA consistent with the minimum required for admission and for progress toward their selected major. **Criteria:** Selection is based on merit.

Funds Avail.: $1,000. **Duration:** Annual. **To Apply:** Applicants must accomplish the required general application available at the website. **Deadline:** March 1.

5686 ■ Margaret G. Johnson and Marge J. Stout Scholarships *(Undergraduate/Scholarship)*

Purpose: To provide financial assistance to students who are currently enrolled in a vocational program. **Focus:** Business; Education, Vocational-technical. **Qualif.:** Applicants must have completed at least 12 credits; must be residents of Idaho; must be enrolled in a two year vocational-technical program at LCSC; and must demonstrate a minimum GPA of 3.0. **Criteria:** Preference will be given to students who are currently enrolled in the Office and Business Technology Program.

Funds Avail.: Amount varies. **Duration:** Annual. **To Apply:** Applicants must accomplish a general application available at the website. **Deadline:** March 1.

5687 ■ LCSC Welding Club Scholarships *(Undergraduate/Scholarship)*

Purpose: To offset educationally-related expenses of Lewis-Clark State College Welding Technology students. **Focus:** Welding. **Qualif.:** Applicants must have completed at least one semester as full-time students enrolled in the Welding Technology program; must be classified as full-time students with a declared major in Welding Technology; and must have a cumulative GPA of at least 3.0. **Criteria:** Recipients will be selected based on financial need.

Funds Avail.: Amount varies. **Duration:** Annual. **To Apply:** Applicants must accomplish a general application available at the website. **Deadline:** March 1.

5688 ■ Lewis-Clark Coin Club Endowed Scholarships *(Undergraduate/Scholarship)*

Purpose: To offset the educationally-related expenses of Lewis-Clark State College students. **Focus:** General studies/Field of study not specified. **Qualif.:** Applicants must be classified as full-time students carrying 12 or more credits per semester with a minimum cumulative GPA of 2.5. **Criteria:** Priority is given to applicants with demonstrated financial need.

Funds Avail.: No specific amount. **Duration:** Biennial. **To Apply:** Applicants must complete and submit the general application available at the website. **Deadline:** March 1.

5689 ■ Lewis-Clark State College Foundation Scholars Scholarships *(Undergraduate/Scholarship)*

Purpose: To support students who have shown consistency and improvement in their scholastic records. **Focus:** General studies/Field of study not specified. **Qualif.:** Applicants must have exceptional academic achievement, community involvement and leadership ability; must be outstanding Idaho and Asotin County, Washington high school seniors with a cumulative GPA of 3.5. **Criteria:** Awards are given based on academic merit.

Funds Avail.: $3,000. **Duration:** Annual. **To Apply:** Applicants must accomplish a general application available at the website. **Deadline:** March 1. **Remarks:** Established in 1991.

5690 ■ Lewis-Clark State College Governor's Cup Scholarships *(Undergraduate/Scholarship)*

Purpose: To support Idaho high school seniors planning to attend an Idaho college or university. **Focus:** Public service. **Qualif.:** Applicants must be residents of Idaho; must be graduating seniors of an Idaho high school; must be enrolled as full-time students in an academic or technical program at an Idaho college or university; must have a cumulative GPA of 2.8 or above; and must have documentation of volunteer work, leadership and public service. **Criteria:** Recipients are selected based on demonstrated commitment to public service.

Funds Avail.: $3,000. **Duration:** Annual. **Number Awarded:** Approximately 25 awards. **To Apply:** Applicants must accomplish a general application available at the website. **Deadline:** February 15.

5691 ■ Lewis-Clark State College - Military Order of the Purple Heart Scholarships *(Undergraduate/Scholarship)*

Purpose: To provide educational assistance for students intending to pursue a career in Special Education. **Focus:** Education, Special. **Qualif.:** Program is open to students committed to pursue a teaching career in special education; must be accepted to the Teacher Education Program; must be enrolled for 12 credits; and must have a GPA of 3.25. **Criteria:** Recipients will be selected based on academic achievement.

Funds Avail.: No specific amount. **Duration:** Annual. **To Apply:** Applicants must accomplish a general application available at the website. **Deadline:** March 1.

5692 ■ Lewis-Clark State College Non-Traditional Student Scholarships *(Undergraduate/Scholarship)*

Purpose: To assist non-traditional students who have been out of high school for at least 5 years at the time of their initial enrollment at Lewis-Clark State College. **Focus:** General studies/Field of study not specified. **Qualif.:** Program is open to full-time, degree seeking students who meet the non-traditional requirement. **Criteria:** Priority is given to students with financial need.

Funds Avail.: Amount varies. **Duration:** Annual. **To Apply:** Applicants must accomplish a general application available in the website. **Deadline:** March 1.

5693 ■ Lewis-Clark State College Provost Scholarships *(Undergraduate/Scholarship)*

Purpose: To recognize promising Idaho High School seniors by providing educational assistance. **Focus:** General studies/Field of study not specified. **Qualif.:** Applicants must have a cumulative GPA of 3.0-3.49; must maintain a 3.0 semester GPA while completing at least 12 credits each semester; and must be at least tentatively admitted to the college and have their 7th semester high school transcripts on file with the Office of Admission. **Criteria:** Recipients will be selected based on academic merit.

Funds Avail.: $1,000 + $500 annual increase, is an option if additional criteria are met. **Duration:** Annual. **To Apply:** Applicants must accomplish general application available in the website. **Deadline:** March 1. **Contact:** Financial Aid Office, LCSC, 500 8th Avenue, Lewiston, ID 83501; Phone:

Awards are arranged alphabetically below their administering organizations

800-933-5272 or 208-792-2224.

5694 ■ Lewis-Clark State College Transfer Scholarships *(Undergraduate/Scholarship)*

Purpose: To assist transfer students intending to complete a bachelor's degree at Lewis-Clark State College. **Focus:** General studies/Field of study not specified. **Qualif.:** Program is open to students who transfer from the following colleges: North Idaho College, Community Colleges in the Spokane area, College of Southern Idaho, Walla Walla Community College, and Treasure Valley Community College. Students must also be full-time, degree seeking students with a cumulative G.P.A. of 3.0 or higher. **Criteria:** Recipients will be selected based on financial need.

Funds Avail.: No specific amount. **Duration:** Annual. **To Apply:** Applicants must submit a general application. **Deadline:** March 1.

5695 ■ Lewiston Service League Memorial Scholarships *(Undergraduate/Scholarship)*

Purpose: To support a family person returning to school and show academic promise with intent to continue their education to the completion of a degree. **Focus:** General studies/Field of study not specified. **Qualif.:** Applicants must be full-time students with at least 12 credit hours; must show academic promise or ability to satisfactorily complete college work with a minimum grade point average of 3.0. **Criteria:** Recipient will be selected based on financial need.

Funds Avail.: No specific amount. **Duration:** Annual. **To Apply:** Applications are available from the Lewiston Service League or the Financial Aid Office. **Deadline:** April 4. **Contact:** Financial Aid Office, Lewis-Clark State College, 500 8th Avenue, Lewiston, ID 83501.

5696 ■ Kaia Lynn Markwalter Endowed Scholarships *(Undergraduate/Scholarship)*

Purpose: To encourage educational pursuits among individuals who have experienced congenital heart defects. **Focus:** Business. **Qualif.:** Applicants must be students at Lewis-Clark State College who have been directly impacted by congenital heart defects. The applicants must also have a 3.0 cumulative G.P.A. and be enrolled in 12 credits each semester. **Criteria:** Recipients will be selected based on financial need.

Funds Avail.: No specific amount. **Duration:** Annual. **To Apply:** Applicants must submit a general application. **Deadline:** March 1.

5697 ■ Elizabeth McKissick Memorial Scholarships *(Undergraduate/Scholarship)*

Purpose: To provide educational support for young people who, for personal, financial, or other reasons discontinued their education, and for those who are in need of retraining who wish to return to school. **Focus:** General studies/Field of study not specified. **Qualif.:** Applicants must be individuals who have graduated from or who attended Lewiston High School. Recipients of this scholarship must be at least 22 years of age at the time of application and must be classified as at least part-time students (taking 6 or more credits per semester). **Criteria:** Recipients will be selected based on financial need.

Funds Avail.: No specific amount. **Duration:** Annual. **To Apply:** Applicants must accomplish a general application available in the website. **Deadline:** March 1.

5698 ■ Robbie Miller Memorial Scholarships *(Undergraduate/Scholarship)*

Purpose: To support students pursuing a degree in a Professional-Technical Program. **Focus:** General studies/Field of study not specified. **Qualif.:** Applicants must be pursuing a degree in a Professional-Technical Program, have a current standing of sophomore or above, and have a minimum cumulative GPA of 2.5. **Criteria:** Priority is given to students with financial need.

Funds Avail.: No specific amount. **Duration:** Annual. **To Apply:** Applicants must accomplish a general application available in the website. **Deadline:** March 1.

5699 ■ Eugene Northrup Scholarships *(Undergraduate/Scholarship)*

Purpose: To provide financial assistance for individuals intending to pursue their educational goals. **Focus:** General studies/Field of study not specified. **Qualif.:** Program is open to graduating seniors of an area high school and who have a GPA of 3.0. **Criteria:** Recipients will be selected based on financial need.

Funds Avail.: $1,000. **Duration:** Annual. **Number Awarded:** 2. **To Apply:** Applicants must sumit a 500-word essay about Unionism. **Deadline:** April 15. **Contact:** Chairman/U.S.W. Scholarship, 1618 Idaho St. Suite 109, Lewiston, ID 83501; Phone: 208-746-3996.

5700 ■ Odd Fellows Lodge No. 8 Endowed Scholarships *(Undergraduate/Scholarship)*

Purpose: To provide financial assistance for individuals intending to pursue their educational goals. **Focus:** General studies/Field of study not specified. **Qualif.:** Applicants must be full-time students carrying 12 or more credits per semester; must have a minimum cumulative GPA of 3.0. **Criteria:** Recipients will be selected based on financial need.

Funds Avail.: $250. **Duration:** Annual. **To Apply:** Applicants must accomplish a general application available at the website. **Deadline:** March 1.

5701 ■ Laura Ann Peck Memorial Endowed Scholarships *(Undergraduate/Scholarship)*

Purpose: To assist Lewis-Clark State College students who are majoring in mathematics. **Focus:** Natural sciences. **Qualif.:** Applicants must have successfully completed three semesters of calculus; must have at least a 2.5 cumulative GPA; and must be registered as degree-seeking, full-time (12 credits) students. **Criteria:** Awards are given based on academic merit.

Funds Avail.: No specific amount. **Duration:** Annual. **To Apply:** Applicants must submit a general application. **Deadline:** March 1.

5702 ■ Eleanor Perry Memorial Endowed Scholarships *(Undergraduate/Scholarship)*

Purpose: To offset the educationally-related expenses of Lewis-Clark State College students. **Focus:** General studies/Field of study not specified. **Qualif.:** Applicants must be full-time students; must have a minimum cumulative GPA of at least a 3.0. **Criteria:** Recipients will be selected based on financial need.

Funds Avail.: Amount varies. **Duration:** Annual. **To Apply:** Applicants must accomplish a general application available at the website. **Deadline:** March 1.

5703 ■ Presidential Out-of-State Tuition Scholarships *(Undergraduate/Scholarship)*

Purpose: To provide financial assistance for students who have shown improvement in their academic records. **Focus:**

Awards are arranged alphabetically below their administering organizations

General studies/Field of study not specified. **Qualif.:** Applicants must be new non-resident students with a high school or transfer minimum cumulative GPA of 3.5 or a 28 ACT composite/1260 SAT critical reading/verbal and math combined score; or cumulative GPA of 3.0-3.49 or a 20 ACT composite/950 SAT critical reading/verbal and math combined score. **Criteria:** Awards are given based on academic merit.

Funds Avail.: $3,000. **Duration:** Annual. **To Apply:** Applicants may contact the Financial Aid Office of LCSC for the application process and other information. **Deadline:** March 1.

5704 ■ Kenneth Rogers Memorial Scholarships
(Undergraduate/Scholarship)

Purpose: To provide educational assistance for eligible students who are enrolled full-time in the Auto Body Repair Program at LCSC. **Focus:** Automotive technology. **Qualif.:** Applicants must have a GPA consistent with the minimum required for Admission and for progress toward completion of the Associates degree or certificate and must be enrolled full-time in the Auto Body Repair Program at LCSC. **Criteria:** Preference will be given to non-traditional students over the age of 25.

Funds Avail.: Amount varies. **Duration:** Annual. **To Apply:** Applicants must accomplish a general application available at the website. **Deadline:** March 1.

5705 ■ Bill Sawyer Memorial Scholarships
(Undergraduate/Scholarship)

Purpose: To offset the educationally-related expenses of Lewis-Clark State College students. **Focus:** Education, Vocational-technical. **Qualif.:** Applicants must have a cumulative GPA consistent with the minimum required for admission and for progress toward their selected major; must be from Idaho County; and must be enrolled in a professional-technical program. **Criteria:** Applicants will be given preference for their special needs such as physical handicap and learning disability.

Funds Avail.: Amount varies. **Duration:** Annual. **To Apply:** Applicants must accomplish a general application available at the website. **Deadline:** March 1.

5706 ■ Susan P. Schroeder Memorial Scholarships
(Undergraduate/Scholarship)

Purpose: To inspire educational pursuits among less capable individuals by providing financial assistance. **Focus:** English language and literature; Natural sciences. **Qualif.:** Applicants must be graduates of Idaho high school; must be majoring in Natural Sciences or English; and must have a cumulative 3.0 GPA. **Criteria:** Preference will be given to graduates from Nez Perce County.

Funds Avail.: Amount varies. **Duration:** Annual. **To Apply:** Applicants must accomplish the general application form available at the website. **Deadline:** March 1.

5707 ■ Shinn Family Scholarships *(Undergraduate/Scholarship)*

Purpose: To offset the educationally-related expenses of Lewis-Clark State College students. **Focus:** Education, Vocational-technical. **Qualif.:** Applicants must be professional/technical students; must have 12 or more credits per semester; and must have completed at least one full semester at LCSC with a cumulative GPA of at least 2.5. **Criteria:** Recipients will be selected based on financial need as determined by the Financial Aid Office.

Funds Avail.: Amount varies. **Duration:** Annual. **To Apply:** Applicants must accomplish a general application available at the website. **Deadline:** March 1.

5708 ■ John Streiff Memorial Scholarships
(Undergraduate/Scholarship)

Purpose: To provide funding for outstanding students who are majoring in social or political science at LCSC. **Focus:** Political science; Social sciences. **Qualif.:** Applicants must be senior or junior students who have a cumulative GPA of 3.0 and are actively involved in both campus and community. **Criteria:** Preference will be given to individuals from the LC County.

Funds Avail.: Amount varies. **Duration:** Annual. **To Apply:** Applicants must accomplish a general application available at the website. **Deadline:** March 1.

5709 ■ Marvin Lewis Community Fund (MLCF)
Longworth Hall, 3rd Fl., Lobby B
700 W Pete Rose Way Unit No. 37
Cincinnati, OH 45203-1873
Ph: (513)381-5437
Fax: (513)381-5439
URL: marvinlewis.org

5710 ■ Marvin Lewis Scholarships *(Undergraduate/Scholarship)*

Purpose: To provide financial support to student athletes who are pursuing educational career. **Focus:** General studies/Field of study not specified. **Qualif.:** Applicant must be a resident of Greater Cincinnati and attending a college as a full-time student; and must have a minimum GPA of 2.75. **Criteria:** Awards are given based on merit.

Funds Avail.: $20,000. **Duration:** Annual. **To Apply:** Applicants must submit a completed scholarship application form along with a copy of recent transcript; Expected Family Contribution (EFC) from Student Aid Report (SAR) in the FAFSA; a copy of Financial Aid Award Letter from their chosen college; a 1000-word essay; and evidence of a varsity letter. Faxed applications will not be considered. **Deadline:** April 23.

5711 ■ Lexington Community Foundation (LCF)
607 Washington St.
Lexington, NE 68850-0422
Ph: (308)324-6704
E-mail: lexfoundation@windstream.net
URL: www.lexfoundation.org

5712 ■ Lexington Alumni Scholarships
(Undergraduate/Scholarship)

Purpose: To promote community philanthropy by working with individuals, families and organizations to develop tailored giving plans that effectively meet the charitable goals and financial circumstances. **Focus:** General studies/Field of study not specified. **Qualif.:** Applicants must be graduating senior students who rank in the upper 1/2 of their class. **Criteria:** Recipients are selected based on qualities of good character and leadership, academic achievement, financial need and participation in extracurriculars and community service.

Funds Avail.: $750. **Duration:** Annual. **Number Awarded:** 3. **To Apply:** Applicants must submit a completed applica-

Awards are arranged alphabetically below their administering organizations

tion form; must provide three letters of recommendation and must attach a recent photo; copy of official high school transcript; high school activities resume; statement of financial need; career objectives statement in 250 words or less. **Deadline:** April 1.

5713 ■ Lexington Community Foundation Annual Scholarships *(Undergraduate/Scholarship)*

Purpose: To promote community philanthropy by working with individuals, families and organizations to develop tailored giving plans that effectively meet the charitable goals and financial circumstances. **Focus:** General studies/ Field of study not specified. **Qualif.:** Applicants must be graduating senior students who rank in the upper 1/3 of their class. **Criteria:** Recipients are selected based on qualities of good character and leadership, academic achievement, financial need and participation in extracurriculars and community service.

Funds Avail.: $3,000. **Duration:** Annual. **Number Awarded:** 2. **To Apply:** Applicants must submit a completed application form; must provide three letters of recommendation and must attach a recent photo; copy of official high school transcript; high school activities resume; statement of financial need; career objectives statement in 250 words or less. **Deadline:** April 1.

5714 ■ Lexington Community Foundation/CCC Scholarships *(Undergraduate/Scholarship)*

Purpose: To promote community philanthropy by working with individuals, families and organizations to develop tailored giving plans that effectively meet the charitable goals and financial circumstances. **Focus:** General studies/ Field of study not specified. **Qualif.:** Applicants must be graduating senior students who rank in the upper 1/2 of their class. **Criteria:** Recipients are selected based on qualities of good character and leadership, academic achievement, financial need and participation in extracurriculars and community service.

Funds Avail.: $600. **Duration:** Annual. **To Apply:** Applicants must submit a completed application form; must provide three letters of recommendation and must attach a recent photo; copy of official high school transcript; high school activities resume; statement of financial need; career objectives statement in 250 words or less. **Deadline:** April 1.

5715 ■ Edsel Newman Scholarships *(Undergraduate/ Scholarship)*

Purpose: To promote community philanthropy by working with individuals, families and organizations to develop tailored giving plans that effectively meet the charitable goals and financial circumstances. **Focus:** Computer and information sciences; Engineering. **Qualif.:** Applicants must be graduating seniors who are planning to pursue a career in the field of engineering and/or computer science; must have ranked in the upper 1/3 of their class and must be U.S. citizens. **Criteria:** Recipients are selected based on qualities of good character and leadership, academic achievement, financial need and participation in extracurriculars and community service.

Funds Avail.: $2,000. **Duration:** One year. **To Apply:** Applicants must submit a completed application form; must provide three letters of recommendation and must attach a recent photo; statement of financial need; copy of transcript; resume listing of memberships and activities. **Deadline:** April 1.

5716 ■ Norall Scholarship Trust *(Undergraduate/ Scholarship)*

Purpose: To promote community philanthropy by working with individuals, families and organizations to develop tailored giving plans that effectively meet the charitable goals and financial circumstances. **Focus:** General studies/ Field of study not specified. **Qualif.:** Applicants must be past graduates of high school in Dawson who are enrolled in a US. college. **Criteria:** Recipients are selected based on goal commitment, academic success, recommendations, financial need and programs of study.

Funds Avail.: No specific amount. **To Apply:** Applicants must complete the application form, a copy of Dawson County High School transcript for first-time applicant, academic transcript for post-secondary education and three personal references. **Deadline:** February 28. **Contact:** PO Box 422 Lexington, NE 68850.

5717 ■ Francelene Skinner Memorial Scholarships *(Undergraduate/Scholarship)*

Purpose: To promote community philanthropy by working with individuals, families and organizations to develop tailored giving plans that effectively meet the charitable goals and financial circumstances. **Focus:** General studies/ Field of study not specified. **Qualif.:** Applicants must be graduating seniors who rank in the upper 1/3 of their class and must be U.S. citizens. **Criteria:** Recipients are selected based on qualities of good character and leadership, academic achievement, financial need and participation in extracurriculars and community service.

Funds Avail.: $500. **Number Awarded:** 2. **To Apply:** Applicants must submit a completed application form; must provide three letters of recommendation and must attach a recent photo; copy of transcript; resume listing of activities; statement of financial need; career objectives statement in 250 words or less. **Deadline:** April 1.

5718 ■ Mark and Vera Turner Memorial Scholarships *(Undergraduate/Scholarship)*

Purpose: To promote community philanthropy by working with individuals, families and organizations to develop tailored giving plans that effectively meet the charitable goals and financial circumstances. **Focus:** General studies/ Field of study not specified. **Qualif.:** Applicants must be graduating senior students who rank in the upper 1/2 of the class; must be graduating Lexington High School seniors who enroll in a university, college, community college or trade school within the state of Nebraska. **Criteria:** Recipients are selected based on qualities of good character and leadership, academic achievement, financial need and participation in extracurriculars and community service.

Funds Avail.: $500. **Duration:** Annual. **Number Awarded:** 4. **To Apply:** Applicants must submit a completed application form; must provide three letters of recommendation and must attach a recent photo; copy of official high school transcript; high school activities resume; career objectives statement in 250 words or less. **Deadline:** April 1.

5719 ■ Robert & Barbara Wade Scholarships *(Undergraduate/Scholarship)*

Purpose: To promote community philanthropy by working with individuals, families and organizations to develop tailored giving plans that effectively meet the charitable goals and financial circumstances. **Focus:** General studies/ Field of study not specified. **Qualif.:** Applicants must be graduating senior students who rank in the upper 1/2 of the

---

Awards are arranged alphabetically below their administering organizations

class; must be U.S. citizens and must be graduating Lexington High School seniors who enroll in a public university, college, community college or trade school within the state of Nebraska. **Criteria:** Recipients are selected based on qualities of good character and leadership, academic achievement, financial need and participation in extracurriculars and community service.

Funds Avail.: $1,000. **To Apply:** Applicants must submit a completed application form; must provide three letters of recommendation and must attach a recent photo. **Deadline:** April 1.

5720 ■ Library and Information Technology Association (LITA)

50 E Huron St.
Chicago, IL 60611-2795
Fax: (312)280-3257
Free: 800-545-2433
E-mail: lita@ala.org
URL: www.ala.org/lita

5721 ■ Christian Larew Memorial Scholarships
(Graduate/Scholarship)

Purpose: To encourage the entry of qualified persons into the library and information technology field. **Focus:** Information science and technology; Library and archival sciences. **Qualif.:** Candidates must not have earned more than 12 hours towards a Master of Library Science degree from an American Library Association (ALA) Accredited MLS program. **Criteria:** The Christian Larew Scholarship Committee reviews the applications and selects the scholarship winner. When all other criteria are equal, recipients will be selected based on financial need.

Funds Avail.: $3,000. **Duration:** One year. **Number Awarded:** 1. **To Apply:** Application forms and instructions are available at ALA/Divisions Scholarship Program. Applicants must submit an application form; a statement indicating the nature of their library experience; letters of reference; transcripts. **Deadline:** March 1.

5722 ■ LITA and LSSI Minority Scholarships
(Graduate/Scholarship)

Purpose: To encourage the entry of qualified persons into the library and automation field. **Focus:** Library and archival sciences. **Qualif.:** Applicants must be U.S. or Canadian citizens and must be members of the following minority groups: American Indian or Alaskan Native, Asian or Pacific Islander, African-American or Hispanic. Candidates must not have earned more than 12 hours towards a Master of Library Science degree from an American Library Association MLS program. **Criteria:** When all other criteria are equal, recipients will be selected based on financial need.

Funds Avail.: $2,500. **Duration:** One year. **Number Awarded:** 1. **To Apply:** Application forms and instructions are available at ALA/Divisions Scholarship Program. Applicants must submit an application form; a statement indicating the nature of their library experience; letters of reference; transcripts. **Deadline:** March 1. **Remarks:** Established in 1994.

5723 ■ LITA/OCLC Minority Scholarships *(Graduate/Scholarship)*

Purpose: To encourage the entry of qualified persons into the library and automation field. **Focus:** Library and archival sciences. **Qualif.:** Applicants must be U.S. or Canadian

citizens and must be members of the following minority groups: American Indian or Alaskan Native, Asian or Pacific Islander, African-American or Hispanic. Candidates must not have earned more than 12 hours towards a Master of Library Science degree from an American Library Association MLS program. **Criteria:** When all other criteria are equal, recipients will be selected based on financial need.

Funds Avail.: $3,000. **Duration:** One year. **Number Awarded:** 1. **To Apply:** Application forms and instructions are available at ALA/Divisions Scholarship Program. Applicants must submit an application form; a statement indicating the nature of their library experience; letters of reference; transcripts. **Deadline:** March 1.

5724 ■ Dolores Zohrab Liebmann Fund

PO Box 227237
Dallas, TX 75222-7237
URL: foundationcenter.org/grantmaker/liebmann

5725 ■ Dolores Zohrab Liebmann Fund - Graduate School Fellowships *(Graduate/Fellowship)*

Purpose: To financially support students pursuing graduate studies. **Focus:** Architecture; Engineering; Humanities; Law; Medicine; Natural sciences; Social sciences. **Qualif.:** Applicant must be a graduate student; a U.S. citizen attending an accredited and designated institution of higher education within the United States; have an outstanding undergraduate record; and demonstrated financial need. **Criteria:** Selection is based on the application.

Funds Avail.: Covers the cost of tuition and an annual $18,000 stipend for living expenses. **Duration:** Annual. **To Apply:** Applications must be submitted through the dean of the university where the student is pursuing graduate studies. **Deadline:** April 15 and November 15.

5726 ■ Dolores Zohrab Liebmann Fund - Independent Research/Study Grants *(Graduate/Grant)*

Purpose: To financially support graduate students conducting a research. **Focus:** General studies/Field of study not specified. **Qualif.:** Applicant must be based in and conducting research in the United States; have an outstanding undergraduate record; demonstrated financial need; and attending a designated college/university. **Criteria:** Selection is based on the application.

Funds Avail.: Covers the cost of tuition and an annual $18,000 stipend for living expenses. **Duration:** Annual. **To Apply:** Applications must be submitted through the dean of the university where the student is pursuing graduate studies. **Deadline:** April 15 and November 15.

5727 ■ Dolores Zohrab Liebmann Fund - Publication Grants *(Graduate/Grant)*

Purpose: To financially support students pursuing graduate studies. **Focus:** Armenian studies. **Qualif.:** Applicant must have an outstanding undergraduate record, demonstrate financial need and be attending a designated college/university. **Criteria:** Selection is based on the application.

Funds Avail.: Cover the cost of tuition and provide an annual $18,000 stipend for living expenses. **Duration:** Annual. **To Apply:** Applications must be submitted through the dean of the university where the student is pursuing graduate studies. **Deadline:** April 15 and November 15.

5728 ■ Life and Health Insurance Foundation for Education

1655 N Fort Myer Dr., Ste. 610
Arlington, VA 22209

Awards are arranged alphabetically below their administering organizations

Free: 888-543-3777
E-mail: info@lifehappens.org
URL: www.lifehappens.org

5729 ■ LIFE Lessons Scholarship Program
(Undergraduate/Scholarship)

Purpose: To help deserving young people realize their dream of achieving a college education. **Focus:** General studies/Field of study not specified. **Qualif.:** Applicants must be: college students and college-bound high school seniors; legal residents of the fifty United States and the District of Columbia; between 17 and 24 years of age. Applicants must have experienced the death of a parent or legal guardian and be currently enrolled in or accepted to a college, university or trade school within the fifty United States or District of Columbia. A minor should have a parent's or legal guardian's permission to enter. **Criteria:** Selection will be based on criteria.

Funds Avail.: $2,000 - $15,000. **Number Awarded:** 46. **To Apply:** Applicants who qualify must submit essays or videos about how the death of a parent or guardian impacted their lives. **Deadline:** March 3. **Contact:** Life and Health Insurance Foundation for Education at the above address.

5730 ■ Life Sciences Research Foundation (LSRF)
3520 San Martin Dr.
Baltimore, MD 21218
Ph: (410)467-2597
URL: www.lsrf.org

5731 ■ Life Sciences Research Foundation Postdoctoral Fellowship Program *(Graduate, Doctorate/Fellowship)*

Purpose: To provide financial assistance to young scientists towards non-targeted biological research. **Focus:** Biology; Life sciences. **Qualif.:** Applicants must be graduate students in the field of biological sciences holding MD, PhD, DVM or DDS degrees. **Criteria:** Awards will be based solely on the quality of applicant's accomplishment and merit of the proposal.

Funds Avail.: A total of $180,000. **Duration:** Up to three years. **To Apply:** Applicants must submit an abstract, curriculum vitae, research proposal, letter from supervisor and three letters of reference. **Deadline:** October 1.

5732 ■ Lighthouse International
15 W 65th St.
New York, NY 10023-6601
Free: 800-284-4422
E-mail: info@lighthouseguild.org
URL: www.lighthouse.org

5733 ■ Lighthouse International Scholarships - College-bound Awards *(High School, Undergraduate/Scholarship)*

Purpose: To provide support to visually impaired students to continue their education to college. **Focus:** General studies/Field of study not specified. **Qualif.:** Applicant must be a senior or high school graduate; legally blind; a U.S. citizen; not related to any Lighthouse employees and not a previous winner of program. **Criteria:** Awards are given based on academic merit and other achievements.

Funds Avail.: $10,000. **To Apply:** Applicant must send an application form (can be downloaded at the website); an essay; proof of the applicant's visual condition; transcripts; and two letters of recommendation. **Deadline:** March 22. **Contact:** Melissa Shorey at mshorey@lighthouse.org.

5734 ■ Lighthouse International Scholarships - Graduate Awards *(Graduate/Scholarship)*

Purpose: To provide support to visually impaired who wants to pursue a graduate -level program. **Focus:** General studies/Field of study not specified. **Qualif.:** Applicant must be a college senior or college graduate; must be legally blind; a U.S. citizen; not related to any Lighthouse employees and not a previous winner of the program. **Criteria:** Awards are given based on academic merit and other achievements.

Funds Avail.: $10,000. **Number Awarded:** 3. **To Apply:** Applicant must send an application form (can be downloaded at the website); an essay; proof of the applicant's visual condition; transcripts; and two letters of recommendation. **Deadline:** March 13. **Contact:** sca@ligthouse.org.

5735 ■ Lighthouse International Scholarships - Undergraduate Awards *(Undergraduate/Scholarship)*

Purpose: To provide support to visually impaired students to continue their education. **Focus:** General studies/Field of study not specified. **Qualif.:** Applicant must be a college student; legally blind; a U.S. citizen; not related to Lighthouse employees and not a previous winner of the program. **Criteria:** Awards are given based on academic merit and other achievements.

Funds Avail.: $10,000. **To Apply:** Applicant must send an application form (can be downloaded at the website); an essay; proof of the applicant's visual condition; transcripts; and two letters of recommendation. **Deadline:** March 22. **Contact:** Melissa Shorey at mshorey@lighthouse.org.

5736 ■ Lime Connect, Inc.
590 Madison Ave., 21st Fl.
New York, NY 10022
Ph: (212)521-4469
Fax: (212)521-4099
URL: www.limeconnect.com

5737 ■ BMO Capital Markets Lime Connect Equity through Education Scholarships *(Undergraduate, Graduate/Scholarship)*

Purpose: To provide scholarships for students with disabilities to achieve their dreams and to develop themselves through education. **Focus:** Disabilities. **Qualif.:** Applicants must be current undergraduate or graduate students at a four-year university in the United States or Canada pursuing a degree in business/commerce, engineering, math, physics, statistics or a related discipline. Applicants with visible or invisible disabilities are eligible to apply. **Criteria:** Preference will be given to the applicants interested in a career in Financial Services with a focus on Capital Markets.

Funds Avail.: $5,000 and $10,000. **To Apply:** Applicants must submit the following requirements: contact and education information; current copy of resume/CV; copy of current university transcripts; answer to an essay question related to the applicant's career goals and an explanation

Awards are arranged alphabetically below their administering organizations

of the applicant on why he/she deserve to be selected as a BMO Capital Markets Lime Connect Equity through Education Scholar; and one letter of reference from a professor, advisor, supervisor, etc. **Remarks:** In partnership with BMO Capital Markets. Established in 2005.

5738 ■ BMO Financial Group Lime Connect Canada Scholarship Program for Students with Disablilities (Undergraduate, Graduate/Scholarship)

Purpose: To support the education of the students with disabilities. **Focus:** Disabilities. **Qualif.:** Applicants must be current undergraduate or graduate students enrolled at a four-year university or recognized college in Canada with strong interest and passion for pursuing a career in retail banking and must be Canadian residents eligible to legally work in Canada. Applicants with visible or invisible disabilities are eligible to apply. **Criteria:** Selection will be based on the committee's criteria.

Funds Avail.: 2,500 Canadian dollars. **To Apply:** Applicants must submit the following requirements: contact and education information; current resume/CV; copy of current university/college transcripts; answer to an essay question (250 words or less) related to how the applicant overcome adversity or a challenge in his/her life; and one letter of reference from a professor, adviser or supervisor.

5739 ■ Google Lime Scholarships for Students with Disabilities (Undergraduate, Graduate, Doctorate/ Scholarship)

Purpose: To help innovators make the most of their talents by providing scholarships and networking retreats. **Focus:** Disabilities. **Qualif.:** Applicants must be undergraduate, graduate or Ph.D. students currently enrolled at a university in the United States or Canada; must have plan to enroll in or accepted as a full time student at a university in the United States or Canada; must be pursuing a Computer Science or Computer Engineering degree, or a degree in a closely related technical field (such as software engineering or electrical engineering with a heavy computer science course load); must have a strong academic performance; and must exemplify leadership and demonstrate a commitment to and passion for computer science and technology. Applicants with disabilities are eligible to apply. **Criteria:** Selection will be based on the committee's criteria.

Funds Avail.: $5,000 and $10,000. **To Apply:** Applicants must submit the following requirements: contact, education and experience information; current resume and unofficial transcripts; three essays regarding computer science; and two recommendation letters from a professor, adviser or supervisor. **Remarks:** Established in 2008.

5740 ■ Abraham Lincoln Brigade Archives
799 Broadway, Ste. 341
New York, NY 10003
Ph: (212)674-5398
Fax: (212)674-2101
E-mail: info@alba-valb.org
URL: www.alba-valb.org

5741 ■ George Watt Prize (Undergraduate, Graduate/ Prize)

Purpose: To recognize the best essay made by students. **Focus:** Human rights. **Qualif.:** Candidates must be undergraduate or graduate students from the United States and elsewhere. **Criteria:** Selection will be based on the committee's criteria.

Funds Avail.: $250. **Duration:** Annual. **Number Awarded: 2. To Apply:** Interested applicants must submit an essay or thesis chapter about any aspect of the Spanish Civil War, the global political or cultural struggles against fascism in the 1920s and 1930s, or the lifetime histories and contributions of the Americans who fought in support of the Spanish Republic from 1936 to 1938. Submissions must be between 3,500 and 7,500 words; must be in Spanish or English; must have been produced to fulfill an undergraduate or graduate course requirement; must be in MS Word or PDF format. Submit applications by email with the name of the award on the subject line. Entries must include a cover page with name, address, email, and telephone number. **Deadline:** August 1.

5742 ■ Lincoln Forum
c/o Russell H. Weidman, Treasurer
6009 Queenston St.
Springfield, VA 22152-1723
E-mail: admin@thelincolnforum.org
URL: www.thelincolnforum.org

5743 ■ Platt Family Scholarship Prize Essay Contest (Graduate, Undergraduate/Scholarship, Monetary)

Purpose: To enhance the understanding and preserve the memory of Abraham Lincoln and the Civil War. **Focus:** History, American. **Qualif.:** Applicants must be full-time students in an American college/university. **Criteria:** Entries will be judged by the essay committee of The Lincoln Forum.

Funds Avail.: $1,500 (1st Prize); $750 (2nd Prize); $500 (3rd Prize). **Duration:** Annual. **Number Awarded:** Varies. **To Apply:** Applicants must submit an essay on a given topic (1,500-5,000 words). The essay must be typed and include a works cited page or bibliography as well as the name and contact information of the applicant's college/ university. **Deadline:** July 31. **Contact:** Don McCue, Lincoln Memorial Shrine, 125 W Vine St. Redlands, CA 92373, Phone: 909-798-7632, e-mail: archives@akspl.org.

5744 ■ Richard Linn American Inn of Court
c/o Olivia T. Luk, Pres.
353 N Clark St.
Chicago, IL 60654
Ph: (312)840-7210
URL: www.linninn.org

5745 ■ Mark T. Banner Scholarships for Law Students (Graduate, Undergraduate/Scholarship)

Purpose: To foster the development of intellectual property lawyers of high ethics, civility and professionalism, and especially those from diverse backgrounds. **Focus:** Law. **Qualif.:** Applicants must be law students who have entered into a JD program at an ABA-accredited law school in the United States. **Criteria:** Selection will be based on the commitment to the pursuit of a career in IP law; commitment, qualities and actions towards ethics, civility and professionalism; academic merit; written and oral communication skills determined in part through a telephone interview; leadership qualities and community involvement; member of a historically under represented group in IP law; an ability to demonstrate commitment to the pursuit of a career in intellectual property law is an essential requirement.

Funds Avail.: $5,000. **To Apply:** Applicants must complete

Awards are arranged alphabetically below their administering organizations

and submit the application form including the following documents for consideration: resume; academic transcripts; three-page statement describing how ethics, civility and professionalism have been a focus of the candidate, how diversity has impacted the candidate, the commitment to the pursuit of a career in IP law; contact information for three references. **Deadline:** November 12.

5746 ■ Patricia Lloyd Scholarship Concert Association (PLSCA)

1163 E March Ln., Ste. D
Stockton, CA 95210
Ph: (209)474-9224
Fax: (209)952-8682
E-mail: info@plsca.net
URL: www.plsca.net

5747 ■ PLSCA Scholarships *(Undergraduate/ Scholarship)*

Purpose: To provide educational assistance to qualified students who want to pursue their career. **Focus:** General studies/Field of study not specified. **Qualif.:** Applicant must be a high school senior who has been accepted into a four-year college or university; must be 40 or more miles away from home; must be living in the city where the college or university is located; must continue to be enrolled in a four-year college or university; provide proof of matriculation at the attending college or university; must maintain at least 2.0 grades point average. **Criteria:** Priority is given to those who come from single parent households.

Funds Avail.: No specific amount. **Duration:** Annual. **To Apply:** Applicant must provide a copy of their grades at the end of each quarter or semester; must complete the application form available in the website. **Deadline:** April 15.

5748 ■ LocalInternetService.com

5202 W Douglas Corrigan Way Ste. 300
Salt Lake City, UT
Ph: (801)430-6076
URL: www.localinternetservice.com

5749 ■ Local Internet Service Scholarships *(Undergraduate/Scholarship)*

Purpose: To give students the opportunity to earn more money for school. **Focus:** General studies/Field of study not specified. **Qualif.:** Applicants must be students or individuals about to attend a school. **Criteria:** Selection will be based on the committee's criteria.

Funds Avail.: No specific amount. **Number Awarded:** 1. **To Apply:** Applicants must submit a 400 words or less essay response to the question on 'What are the top 5 students can use to stay safe online?'. **Deadline:** June 17.

5750 ■ London Goodenough Association of Canada (LGAC)

PO Box 5896, Sta. A
Toronto, ON, Canada M5W 1P3
E-mail: lgac@lgac.ca
URL: www.lgac.ca

5751 ■ London Goodenough Association of Canada Scholarships *(Graduate/Scholarship)*

Purpose: To support the study of graduate students in London, England. **Focus:** General studies/Field of study

not specified. **Qualif.:** Applicants must be Canadian citizens or permanent residents of Canada; must be enrolled full-time at an accredited graduate program in London, or undertaking a research in London while enrolled elsewhere. Winners will be required to reside at Goodenough College for a full academic year. **Criteria:** Recipients will be selected based on academic excellence and extracurricular contributions at Goodenough College.

Funds Avail.: 5,000 British Pounds. **Duration:** Annual. **Number Awarded:** 6. **To Apply:** Applicants must submit a completed application form; must attach all post-secondary transcripts; and three letters of recommendation. **Deadline:** January 6. **Contact:** For further information, applicants must contact Dr. Andrew Gray at the above address; E-mail: admin@lgac.ca. or apply@lgac.ca.

5752 ■ L'Oreal USA Inc.

575 Fifth Ave.
New York, NY 10017-2422
Ph: (212)818-1500
URL: www.lorealusa.com

5753 ■ L'Oreal USA Fellowships for Women in Science *(Postdoctorate/Fellowship)*

Purpose: To recognize and reward five U.S.-based women researchers for their outstanding contributions in science, technology, engineering and math fields. **Focus:** Science. **Qualif.:** Applicants must have a conferred PhD and have started in a postdoctoral research position by July; must maintain the status of postdoctoral researcher throughout the fellowship year; must be American born, naturalized citizen or permanent resident; must be affiliated with a U.S. based academic or research institution; must plan to conduct their postdoctoral studies and research in the U.S.; must be involved in basic research in the life and physical/ material sciences, engineering and technology, computer science and/or mathematics; cannot be in a faculty position; must commit to at least twenty hours of activity in support of women and girls in science (e.g. mentoring, classroom visits, media, events). **Criteria:** Selection will be based on the exceptional academic records and intellectual merit, clearly articulated research proposals with the potential for scientific advancement and outstanding letters of recommendation from advisers.

Funds Avail.: Up to $60,000. **Duration:** Annual. **Number Awarded:** 5. **To Apply:** Interested applicants must visit the webiste for the application process via AAAS's secure online server.

5754 ■ UNESCO-L'Oreal for Women in Science International Fellowships *(Doctorate, Postdoctorate/ Fellowship)*

Purpose: To raise awareness of the contribution of women to the sciences. **Focus:** Life sciences. **Qualif.:** Applicants must be at their doctoral or postdoctoral level whose promising projects have been accepted by a reputable institution outside their home country. **Criteria:** Selection will be based on the committee's criteria.

Funds Avail.: No specific amount. **Duration:** Annual. **To Apply:** Applicants must submit three letters of recommendation, undergraduate and graduate transcripts.

5755 ■ Los Abogados Hispanic Bar Association

PO Box 813
Phoenix, AZ 85001

Awards are arranged alphabetically below their administering organizations

Fax: (855)999-9329
URL: www.losabogados.org

5756 ■ Valdemar A. Cordova Scholarships
(Undergraduate/Award)

Purpose: To Provide scholarships to students in Arizona law schools with a demonstrated commitment to the Hispanic community. **Focus:** Law. **Qualif.:** Candidates must be students from Sandra Day O'Connor College of Law, James E. Rogers College of Law and the Phoenix School of Law. **Criteria:** Scholarships are awarded based on several criteria, including service, leadership, and support efforts in the Hispanic community.

Funds Avail.: No specific amount. **To Apply:** Applicants must complete and submit the application on or before the deadline. Application forms can be obtained at the website. Applicants must also include a personal statement addressing how they currently serve the Hispanic community and how they intend to serve the Hispanic community in the future. Also include a list of any service or leadership activities benefitting the Hispanic community in which they have participated over the past three years.

5757 ■ Louisiana Agricultural Consultants Association (LACA)
11137 Highway 71 S
Cheneyville, LA 71325
Ph: (337)945-3694
URL: www.laca1.org

5758 ■ Louisiana Agricultural Consultants Association Scholarships *(Graduate, Undergraduate/ Scholarship)*

Purpose: To support students financially who are in the field of agriculture. **Focus:** Agribusiness; Botany; Entomology; Horticulture. **Qualif.:** Applicants must be undergraduates or graduate students at the time of application; must have a GPA of 3.0 or above; must have completed 45 semester hours or its equivalent prior to application; must be in any of the following fields: Entomology, Plant Pathology, Weed Science, Botany, Microbiology, Biology, Agronomy, Plant Science, Horticulture, Agribusiness and Vocational Agriculture. **Criteria:** Selection will be based on application materials. Extracurricular activities will be considered.

Funds Avail.: $2,000 each. **Duration:** Annual. **Number Awarded:** 2. **To Apply:** Applicants must submit a completed application form along with two current letters of recommendation and one-page statement (about 200 words) explaining why they deserve the award. **Deadline:** January 10. **Contact:** Paul Templet, Chairman, LACA Scholarship Committee; Email: tomplay43@gmail.com.

5759 ■ Louisiana Association of Criminal Defense Lawyers (LACDL)
PO Box 82531
Baton Rouge, LA 70884
Ph: (225)767-7640
Fax: (225)767-7648
E-mail: jill@tatmangroup.com
URL: www.lacdl.org

5760 ■ Camille F. Gravel, Jr. Scholarships *(Professional development/Scholarship)*

Purpose: To support students by covering their tuition and housing expenses. **Focus:** Law. **Qualif.:** Applicants must be Louisiana lawyers and preference will be given to those who regularly represent indigent defendants and who have practiced more than two, but less than 15 years. **Criteria:** Selection will be based on submitted application.

Funds Avail.: No specific amount. **Duration:** Annual. **To Apply:** Applicants must complete and submit the application form on or before the deadline. Application forms can be obtained at the website. **Deadline:** March 1.

5761 ■ Louisiana Environmental Health Association (LEHA)
PO Box 2661
Baton Rouge, LA 70821
Ph: (225)342-8917
URL: leha.net

5762 ■ Frank L. Dautriel Memorial Scholarships for Graduates *(Graduate, Master's, Doctorate/Scholarship)*

Purpose: To encourage an outstanding graduate student to pursue their education. **Focus:** Engineering; Environmental science; Environmental technology; Public health. **Qualif.:** Nominee must be enrolled as a full-time student in an environmental health, environmental science, environmental engineering or public health-related degree program; must be a Louisiana resident; must have maintained a GPA of 2.75 or higher on a 4.0 point rating system and have a record of good conduct supported by official transcript; must demonstrate a need for the scholarships. **Criteria:** Application form and requirements will be reviewed by the LEHA Awards Committee.

Funds Avail.: $1,000. **Duration:** Annual. **Number Awarded:** 1. **To Apply:** Application forms are available online and must be sent to Louisiana Environmental Health Association. Nominee must submit two letters of recommendation from a faculty of said accredited college or from any LEHA member in good standing. College transcripts must be submitted with the letters of recommendation. **Deadline:** March 1.

5763 ■ Frank L. Dautriel Memorial Scholarships for Undergraduates *(Undergraduate/Scholarship)*

Purpose: To encourage an outstanding undergraduate student to pursue their education. **Focus:** Engineering; Environmental science; Environmental technology; Public health. **Qualif.:** Nominee must be enrolled as a full-time student in an environmental health, environmental science, environmental engineering or public health-related degree program at an accredited university; must be a Louisiana resident; must have maintained an overall 2.75 or higher on a 4.0 point rating system and have a record of good conduct supported by official transcript; must demonstrate a need for a scholarship. **Criteria:** Selection will be based on the criteria of LEHA awards Committee.

Funds Avail.: $1,000. **Duration:** Annual. **Number Awarded:** 1. **To Apply:** Application forms are available online and must be sent to Louisiana Environmental Health Association. Nominee must submit two letters of recommendation, along with his/her college transcript from, said accredited college, or from any LEHA member in good standing. **Deadline:** March 1.

5764 ■ Louisiana Library Association (LLA)
8550 United Plaza Blvd., Ste. 1001
Baton Rouge, LA 70809
Ph: (225)922-4642

Awards are arranged alphabetically below their administering organizations

Fax: (225)408-4422
Free: 877-550-7890
E-mail: office@llaonline.org
URL: www.llaonline.org

5765 ■ Louisiana Library Association Scholarships (Graduate, Master's/Scholarship)

Purpose: To support Louisiana students during their full-time study toward the Master's Degree in Library Science at Louisiana State University SLIS. **Focus:** Library and archival sciences. **Qualif.:** Applicant must be born in Louisiana; or have lived in Louisiana for at least one year exclusive of any period of full-time enrollment in post-secondary education; or with a parent who has lived in Louisiana for a period of five years exclusive of any period of full-time enrollment in post-secondary education. **Criteria:** Preference will be given to applicants having a composite undergraduate GPA of at least 3.2 or a graduate degree with a grade point average of at least 3.5 from that degree on a four point scale, and a combined score on the verbal and quantitative portions of the G.R.E. of at least 1050.

Funds Avail.: $3,000. **Duration:** Annual; Three years. **To Apply:** Applicants must submit a completed application form along with a letter of recommendation from a librarian, professor, or employer who can speak knowledgeably of the applicant's talents and skills in addition to recommendations required for entry into the Louisiana State University School of Library and Information Science. **Deadline:** May 1.

5766 ■ Mary Moore Mitchell Scholarships (Graduate, Master's/Scholarship)

Purpose: To support Louisiana students during their part-time study toward the Master's Degree in Library Science at Louisiana State University SLIS. **Focus:** Library and archival sciences. **Qualif.:** Applicant must be born in Louisiana; or have lived in Louisiana for at least one year exclusive of any period of full-time enrollment in post-secondary education; or with a parent who has lived in Louisiana for a period of five years exclusive of any period of full-time enrollment in post-secondary education. **Criteria:** Preference will be given to applicants having a composite undergraduate GPA of at least 3.2 or a graduate degree with a grade point average of at least 3.5 from that degree on a four point scale, and a combined score on the verbal and quantitative portions of the G.R.E. of at least 1050.

Funds Avail.: $1,000. **Duration:** Annual; Three years. **To Apply:** Applicants must submit a completed application form along with a letter of recommendation from a librarian, professor, or employer who can speak knowledgeably of the applicant's talents and skills in addition to recommendations required for entry into the Louisiana State University School of Library and Information Science. **Deadline:** May 1.

5767 ■ Louisiana Public Health Association (LPHA)

7575 Jefferson Hwy., No. 161
Baton Rouge, LA 70806
Ph: (225)324-6989
URL: www.lpha.org

5768 ■ LPHA Scholarships (Graduate, Undergraduate/Scholarship)

Purpose: To provide financial assistance to qualified individuals who want to pursue their education. **Focus:** Public health. **Qualif.:** Applicants must be LPHA members or dependents; must have a minimum of 3.0 on a 4.0 point system for graduates and undergraduates; must have a GRE of 1000 or above. **Criteria:** Applicants will be selected by the Scholarship Committee Chair.

Funds Avail.: No specific amount. **Duration:** Annual. **Number Awarded:** 1. **To Apply:** Applicants must complete the application form available on the website; must submit two personal references. **Deadline:** February 15.

5769 ■ Louisiana State Paralegal Association (LSPA)

PO Box 51690
Lafayette, LA 70505
URL: www.la-paralegals.org

5770 ■ Rochelle Scholarship (College/Scholarship)

Purpose: To promote paralegal studies in Louisiana. **Focus:** Paralegal studies. **Qualif.:** Applicants must be paralegal students currently enrolled in an institutionally accredited paralegal program in Louisiana which offers a curriculum of at least sixty (60) semester hours; must have an overall grade point average of at least a 3.0; must be enrolled in a minimum of six hours of paralegal studies; must be planning on a future career as a paralegal. **Criteria:** Selection will be based on the committee's criteria.

Funds Avail.: Up to $500. **Duration:** Annual. **To Apply:** Applicants must complete and submit the application form available at the website together with the following materials: a certified copy of each college transcript, including the current paralegal program; copy of current course schedule; three letters of reference from the paralegal program instructor(s), administrator or employer(s). **Deadline:** March 10.

5771 ■ Louisville Institute

1044 Alta Vista Rd.
Louisville, KY 40205
Ph: (502)992-5432
Fax: (502)894-2286
E-mail: info@louisville-institute.org
URL: www.louisville-institute.org

5772 ■ Louisville Institute Dissertation Fellowships (Doctorate/Fellowship)

Purpose: To support the final year PhD or ThD dissertation for students engaged in research pertaining to North American Christianity. **Focus:** Christian education. **Qualif.:** Applicants must be candidates for the PhD or ThD degree who have fulfilled all pre-dissertation requirements, including approval of the dissertation proposal of the award year and expect to complete the dissertation by the end of the following academic year. **Criteria:** Preference will be given to proposals that attempt to describe the following: 1) how the Christian faith is actually lived by contemporary persons and to bring the resources of the Christian faith into closer relation to their daily lives; 2) help individuals understand the institutional reconfiguration of the American religion; and 3) explore the nature and challenge of pastoral leadership.

Funds Avail.: $22,000. **Duration:** Annual. **To Apply:** Applicants must complete the online Information and Project Summary form; must fill-out the downloadable Dissertation Fellowship Program Additional Information form; must

Awards are arranged alphabetically below their administering organizations

include a dissertation prospectus (five to seven pages); must submit two to three-page, double-spaced selective bibliography; must submit a dissertation adviser's letter of recommendation, faculty letter of recommendation and one official copy of graduate and professional transcripts. **Deadline:** February 1.

5773 ■ Louisville Institute First Book Grants for Minority Scholars *(Doctorate/Grant)*

Purpose: To assist junior, non-tenured religion scholars to complete their major research and book project pertaining to American Christianity. **Focus:** Christian education. **Qualif.:** Applicants must be members of racial/ethnic minority group; must have earned a doctoral degree; must be pre-tenured faculty members in a full-time, tenure-track position at an accredited institution of higher education in North America; be able to negotiate a full academic year free from teaching and committee responsibilities; and be engaged in a scholarly research project leading to the publication of their first book. **Criteria:** Applicants will be evaluated based on submitted materials demonstrating proficiency in the academy and commitment to their faith community; must demonstrate intellectual quality of the research and writing project and its potential contribution to scholarship religion and to the vitality of North American Christianity.

Funds Avail.: $40,000. **Duration:** Annual. **To Apply:** Applicants must complete the Information and Project Summary form; must submit a narrative statement (five to seven pages), selective bibliography (two to three-page, double-spaced), detailed budget and budget narrative, copy of current curriculum vitae or resume, a letter from the dean or chairperson and two letters of recommendation. **Deadline:** January 15.

5774 ■ Louisville Institute Project Grant for Researchers *(Doctorate/Grant)*

Purpose: To support projects that can contribute to enhance understanding of important issues concerning Christian faith and life, pastoral leadership and/or religious institutions. **Focus:** Christian education. **Qualif.:** Applicants must be academic and pastoral leaders; must have earned Ph.D or Th.D degree; must demonstrate a capacity to complete the proposed project in a timely fashion. **Criteria:** Recipients will be selected based on submitted project.

Funds Avail.: $25,000. **Duration:** Annual. **To Apply:** Applicants must include Information and Project Summary form; must submit a narrative statement (five to seven pages), selective bibliography (two to three-page, double-spaced), detailed budget and budget narrative, copy of current curriculum vitae or resume and one letter of recommendation **Deadline:** October 1.

5775 ■ Louisville Institute Sabbatical Grants for Researchers *(Doctorate/Grant)*

Purpose: To support pastoral and religious leaders whose research projects can contribute to enhance understanding of issues concerning Christian faith and life, pastoral leadership and/or religious institutions. **Focus:** Christian education. **Qualif.:** Applicants must be both academic and pastoral leaders who are based in the United States or Canada. **Criteria:** Applicants will be evaluated based on submitted research project.

Funds Avail.: $40,000. **Duration:** Annual. **To Apply:** Applicants must complete the Information and Project Summary form; must submit a narrative statement (5-7 pages), selective bibliography (2-3 pages, double-spaced), detailed budget and budget narrative, copy of current curriculum vitae or resume and one letter of recommendation. **Deadline:** November 1.

5776 ■ Loveland Archaeological Society (LAS)
c/o Jean Steinhoff, Secretary
PO Box 226
Berthoud, CO 80513
E-mail: stoneagefair@gmail.com
URL: www.stoneagefair.com

5777 ■ Dorothy Mountain Memorial Scholarships *(Graduate/Scholarship)*

Purpose: To promote the study of archaeology. **Focus:** Archeology. **Qualif.:** Applicant must be a second semester graduate student in Anthropology, with an emphasis toward Archaeology, at the University of Wyoming or Colorado State University; is expected to make Archaeology a vocation and to contribute constructively to its field; and have maintained a 3.0 GPA in all courses. **Criteria:** Selection is based on the application materials.

Funds Avail.: $250. **Duration:** Annual. **To Apply:** Applicants must submit a completed application form along with a short vita; two letters of recommendation, one of which must be from a professional Anthropologist/ Archaeologist; and a verification of GPA by submitting an unofficial transcript from the University of Wyoming or Colorado State University. **Deadline:** April 30.

5778 ■ Harry Walts Memorial Graduate Scholarships *(Graduate/Scholarship)*

Purpose: To promote the study of archaeology. **Focus:** Archeology. **Qualif.:** Applicant must be a second semester graduate student in Anthropology at the University of Wyoming with an emphasis toward archaeology; is expected to make Archaeology a vocation and to contribute constructively to its field; and have maintained a 3.0 GPA in all courses. **Criteria:** Selection is based on the application materials.

Funds Avail.: $500. **Duration:** Annual. **To Apply:** Applicants must submit a completed application form together with a short vita; two letters of recommendation, one of which must be from a professional Anthropologist/ Archaeologist; and a verification of GPA by submitting an unofficial transcript from the University of Wyoming. **Deadline:** April 30.

5779 ■ Lunenfeld-Tanenbaum Research Institute - Research Training Centre
Mount Sinai Hospital
600 University Ave., Rm. 850-1
Toronto, ON, Canada M5G 1X5
Ph: (416)586-4800
Fax: (416)586-8857
URL: www.mshri.on.ca/RTC

5780 ■ Norm Hollend Fellowships in Oncology *(Postdoctorate/Fellowship)*

Purpose: To provide support for individuals conducting research in the area of cancer. **Focus:** Oncology. **Qualif.:** Applicant must be at the post-PhD or post-health professional degree who is conducting a research at the Samuel Lunenfeld Research Institute in the area of cancer. **Criteria:** Selection is based on the submitted application materials.

Awards are arranged alphabetically below their administering organizations

Funds Avail.: No specific amount. **To Apply:** Applicants must submit an up-to-date CV and a one-page summary of the research project to Dr. Cindy Todoroff. **Contact:** Dr. Cindy Todoroff at the above address.

5781 ■ Gail Posluns Fellowships in Hematology
(Postdoctorate/Fellowship)

Purpose: To provide support for individuals conducting research in the area of hematology. **Focus:** Hemophilia. **Qualif.:** Applicant must be at the post-PhD or post-health professional degree who is conducting a research at the Samuel Lunenfeld Research Institute in the area of hematology. **Criteria:** Selection is based on the submitted application materials.

Funds Avail.: No specific amount. **To Apply:** Applicants must submit an up-to-date CV and a one-page summary of the research project.

5782 ■ Lung Cancer Research Foundation
155 E 55 St., Ste. 6H
New York, NY 10022
Ph: (212)588-1580
Fax: (212)308-0972
E-mail: info@lungfund.org
URL: www.lungcancerresearchfoundation.org

5783 ■ LCRF Grants *(Advanced Professional, Professional development/Grant)*

Purpose: To support projects focused on lung cancer research. **Focus:** Medical research; Oncology. **Qualif.:** Applicants must be U.S.-based and international investigators including: junior investigators (e.g. graduate students, medical students, post-doctoral fellows); senior faculty (e.g. assistant/associate/full professors); physicians; and nurse researchers. Projects must be focused on one or more of the following areas of lung cancer research: basic science; translational research; clinical research; supportive care; and quality of care/outcomes. **Criteria:** Selection will be based on the applicants' qualifications and research projects.

Funds Avail.: Maximum of $75,000. **To Apply:** Application forms and other instructions for applying can be verified at the website. **Deadline:** July 1. **Contact:** Questions should be addressed via email at grants@lungfund.org.

5784 ■ Ann and Robert H. Lurie Children's Hospital of Chicago
225 E Chicago Ave.
Chicago, IL 606110
Ph: (312)227-4000
Free: 800-543-7362
E-mail: webfeedback@luriechildrens.org
URL: www.luriechildrens.org

5785 ■ Children's Memorial Hospital Postgraduate Administrative Fellowships *(Postgraduate/Fellowship)*

Purpose: To provide leadership training and growth, contribute to the organization through specific assignments and responsibilities, and develop a mentoring relationship for future professional development. **Focus:** Health care services. **Qualif.:** Applicant must have an MHA, MPA, MPH or MBA with a concentration in healthcare, or equivalent from an accredited graduate program. **Criteria:** Selection is based on the submitted application materials.

Funds Avail.: No specific amount. **Duration:** one year. **To Apply:** Applicants must submit a resume; cover letter; scanned official graduate transcript; 1-2 page personal statement addressing career goals, decision to pursue a fellowship experience and specific expectations of the Lurie Children's fellowship; three letters of recommendation (submitted directly from the recommender to alennox@luriechildrens.org); official graduate transcript; and in one page or less, a statement addressing current challenges facing the pediatric healthcare market. **Deadline:** September 19. **Contact:** Shanna Kirshenblatt, Administrative Fellow; Email: adminfellowship@luriechildrens.org.

5786 ■ Luso-American Education Foundation (LAEF)
7080 Donlon Way, Ste. 200
Dublin, CA 94568
Ph: (925)828-4884
Fax: (925)828-4554
Free: 877-525-5876
E-mail: education@luso-american.org
URL: lwww.uso-american.org/laef.php

5787 ■ Luso-American Education Foundation C-1 General Scholarships *(Undergraduate/Scholarship)*

Purpose: To support students to further their education. **Focus:** Business. **Qualif.:** Applicant must be a California resident; enrolled in trade business school, junior or four-year college/university; have minimum of 3.5 GPA; a Portuguese descent; or currently taking Portuguese language classes with 3.0 GPA. **Criteria:** Scholarship recipients will be selected based on the jury's review of the application materials.

Funds Avail.: $500-$1,500. **Duration:** One year. **To Apply:** Applicants must submit a completed application form; an official transcript; SAT or ACT scores; and two letters of recommendation.

5788 ■ Luso-American Education Foundation G-1 Grants *(Other/Grant)*

Purpose: To promote the Portuguese language and culture. **Focus:** Portuguese studies. **Qualif.:** Applicants must be California residents. **Criteria:** Recipient will be selected based on the Grant Committee's review of the application materials.

Funds Avail.: $500. **To Apply:** Applicants must submit a statement of background and need; description of the research project (if applicable); official transcripts; and three letters of recommendation.

5789 ■ Luso-American Education Foundation G-2 Grants *(Other/Grant)*

Purpose: To support students who wants to pursue the study of Portuguese language and culture. **Focus:** Portuguese studies. **Qualif.:** Applicants must be California residents; must be of Portuguese descent or working in an educational setting with Portuguese adults or children; enrolled in a college or university not offering Portuguese language or literature. **Criteria:** Recipient will be selected based on the Grant Committee's review of the application materials.

Funds Avail.: $750. **Number Awarded:** 1. **To Apply:** Applicants must submit statement of background and need; an essay (written in English and Portuguese) on Portuguese

Awards are arranged alphabetically below their administering organizations

history or literature or both; official transcript; list of past teaching experiences and three letters of recommendation. **Deadline:** February 15.

5790 ■ Luso-American Education Foundation G-3 Grants (Postgraduate/Grant)

Purpose: To improve the professional career of Portuguese teachers. **Focus:** Portuguese studies. **Qualif.:** Applicants must be California residents; be teachers of Portuguese in grades K-12; have B.A. or higher degree in Portuguese studies. **Criteria:** Recipient will be selected based on the Grant Committee's review of the application materials.

Funds Avail.: $1,500. **Number Awarded:** 1. **To Apply:** Applicants must submit a statement of background and need (written in English and Portuguese); an essay (minimum of 2 pages) about Portuguese history; transcript; list of past teaching experiences and three letters of recommendation.

5791 ■ Luso-American Fraternal Federation B-2 Scholarships (Postgraduate/Scholarship)

Purpose: To provide financial support to students to continue or re-enter a post-graduate program. **Focus:** General studies/Field of study not specified. **Qualif.:** Applicants must be a Luso-American Fraternal Federation Luso-American Insurance Society's 20-30s associate member in good standing; 18-39 years old. **Criteria:** Scholarship recipients will be selected based on the jury's review of the application materials.

Funds Avail.: $800. **Duration:** One year. **Number Awarded:** 1. **To Apply:** Applicants must request for the application form available on the Foundation's office. Submit the completed application form together with an official transcript and three letters of recommendation to the Foundation's office.

5792 ■ Luso-American Fraternal Federation B-3 Scholarships (Professional development/Scholarship)

Purpose: To assist students to attend a vocational school program or specialty job training. **Focus:** General studies/Field of study not specified. **Qualif.:** Applicants must be a Luso-American Fraternal Federation Luso-American Insurance Society's 20-30s associate member in good standing; 18-39 years old; in need of financial assistance to attend a vocational school program or a specialty job training program. **Criteria:** Scholarship recipients will be selected based on the jury's review of the application materials.

Funds Avail.: $500. **Duration:** One year. **Number Awarded:** 1. **To Apply:** Applicants must request for the application form available on the Foundation's office. Submit the completed application form together with an official transcript and three letters of recommendation to the Foundation's office.

5793 ■ Luso-American Fraternal Federation B-4 Scholarships (Professional development/Scholarship)

Purpose: To support individuals to make a career change. **Focus:** General studies/Field of study not specified. **Qualif.:** Applicant must be a Luso-American Fraternal Federation Luso-American Insurance Society's 20-30s associate member in good standing; 18-39 years old. **Criteria:** Scholarship recipients will be selected based on the jury's review of the application materials.

Funds Avail.: $500. **Duration:** One year. **To Apply:** Applicants must request for the application form available at the Foundation's office. Submit the completed application

form together with an official transcript and three letters of recommendation to the Foundation's office.

5794 ■ Antonio Mattos Memorial Scholarships (Undergraduate/Scholarship)

Purpose: To provide financial assistance to qualified students to further their education. **Focus:** General studies/Field of study not specified. **Qualif.:** Applicants must be high school graduating seniors or enrolled in a four-year college or university; must have GPA of 3.5 or higher; Sacramento or East Bay area (CA) resident; and members of the Luso-American Fraternal Federation Luso-American Life Insurance Society and policy holder in good standing for a minimum of two years; excel in a sport during the four high school years; and active in Fraternal Community. **Criteria:** Scholarship recipients will be selected based on the jury's review of the application materials.

Funds Avail.: $1,000. **Duration:** One year. **Number Awarded:** 1. **To Apply:** Applicants must request for the application form available on the Foundation's office. Submit the completed application form together with an official transcript and three letters of recommendation to the Foundation's office.

5795 ■ Joaquin Pereira Memorial Scholarships (Undergraduate/Scholarship)

Purpose: To support students achieve their educational goals. **Focus:** General studies/Field of study not specified. **Qualif.:** Applicants must be high school graduating seniors or enrolled in a four-year college or university; must have a GPA of 3.5 or higher; and be members of the Luso-American Fraternal Federation - Luso-American Life Insurance Society and policy holders in good standing for a minimum of two years. **Criteria:** Scholarship recipients will be selected based on the jury's review of the application materials.

Funds Avail.: $1,000. **Number Awarded:** 1. **To Apply:** Applicants must request the application form available at the Foundation's office. Submit the completed application form together with an official transcript and two letters of recommendation to the Foundation's office.

5796 ■ Ryan "Munchie" Taylor Memorial Scholarships (Undergraduate/Scholarship)

Purpose: To provide financial assistance to qualified students who wish to further their education. **Focus:** General studies/Field of study not specified. **Qualif.:** Applicants must be high school graduating senior or enrolled in a four-year college or university; must have a GPA of 3.5 or higher; must have held local or state youth office; a Stanislaus County (CA) resident; member of the Luso-American Fraternal Federation - Luso-American Life Insurance Society and policy holder in good standing for a minimum of two years; must participated in Fraternal Youth activities for two or more years or performed at State Conventions. **Criteria:** Scholarship recipients will be selected based on the jury's review of the application materials.

Funds Avail.: No specific amount. **Number Awarded:** 1. **To Apply:** Applicants must request for the application form available on the Foundation's office. Submit the completed application form together with an official transcript and three letters of recommendation to the Foundation's office.

5797 ■ Lymphoma Research Foundation (LRF)
115 Broadway, Ste. 1301
New York, NY 10006-1623

Awards are arranged alphabetically below their administering organizations

Ph: (212)349-2910
Fax: (212)349-2886
Free: 800-500-9976
E-mail: lrf@lymphoma.org
URL: www.lymphoma.org

5798 ■ Adolescent/Young Adult Lymphoma Cooperative Groups Correlative Studies Grants
(Advanced Professional/Grant)

Purpose: To support adjunct studies that compliment and synergize with ongoing lymphoma clinical trials within the National Cancer Institute Cancer Cooperative Groups. **Focus:** Hematology; Oncology. **Qualif.:** Applicants must be principal investigators holding an academic faculty appointment at a non-profit organizations, or public or private institutions such as universities, colleges, hospitals, and laboratories. **Criteria:** Selection will be based on the committee's criteria.

Funds Avail.: No specific amount. **Duration:** Two years. **To Apply:** Applicants may visit the website for the instructions regarding application process. **Deadline:** September 3. **Contact:** Email at researchgrants@lymphoma.org. For technical assistance or questions on the application process, contact the proposalCentral helpline (phone: 703-964-5840 or 800-875-2562 (toll-free); email: pcsupport@altum.com).

5799 ■ Chronic Lymphocytic Leukemia Collaborative Grants *(Advanced Professional/Grant)*

Purpose: To fund high quality research studies in Chronic Lymphocytic Leukemia (CLL) including the study of primary CLL patient samples to assure relevance to the human disease. **Focus:** Hematology; Oncology. **Qualif.:** Applicants must be principal investigators holding an academic faculty appointment at a non-profit organizations, or public or private institutions such as universities, colleges, hospitals, and laboratories. Eligible investigators must have a title of assistant, associate, or full professor or its equivalent. **Criteria:** Selection will be based on the committee's criteria.

Funds Avail.: No specific amount. **Duration:** Two years. **To Apply:** Applicants may contact the Foundation for the application process and other information. **Deadline:** February 19. **Contact:** Email at researchgrants@lymphoma.org. For technical assistance or questions on the application process, contact the proposalCentral helpline (phone: 703-964-5840 or 800-875-2562 (toll-free); email: pcsupport@altum.com).

5800 ■ Diffuse Large B-Cell Lymphoma Explorations Grants *(Advanced Professional/Grant)*

Purpose: To fund studies that are clinically relevant to the improvement of outcomes for patients with Diffuse Large B-Cell Lymphoma (DLBCL). **Focus:** Hematology; Oncology. **Qualif.:** Applicants must be principal investigators holding an academic faculty appointment at a non-profit organizations, or public or private institutions such as universities, colleges, hospitals, and laboratories. Eligible investigators must have a title of assistant, associate, or full professor or its equivalent. **Criteria:** Selection will be based on the committee's criteria.

Funds Avail.: No specific amount. **Duration:** Two years. **To Apply:** Applicants may contact the Foundation for the application process and other information. **Deadline:** February 19. **Contact:** Email at researchgrants@lymphoma.org. For technical assistance or questions on the application process, contact the proposalCentral helpline (phone: 703-

964-5840 or 800-875-2562 (toll-free); email: pcsupport@altum.com).

5801 ■ Follicular Lymphoma Research Grants
(Advanced Professional/Grant)

Purpose: To fund follicular lymphoma research that includes the study of primary FL patient samples and incorporates collaborative interactions between/among investigators in different disciplines and/or different institutions. **Focus:** Hematology; Oncology. **Qualif.:** Applicants must be principal investigators holding an academic faculty appointment at a non-profit organizations, or public or private institutions such as universities, colleges, hospitals, and laboratories. Eligible investigators must have a title of assistant, associate, or full professor or its equivalent. **Criteria:** Selection will be based on the committee's criteria.

Funds Avail.: No specific amount. **Duration:** Three years. **To Apply:** Applicants may contact the Foundation for the application process and other information. **Deadline:** September 2. **Contact:** Email at researchgrants@lymphoma.org. For technical assistance or questions on the application process, contact the proposalCentral helpline (phone: 703-964-5840 or 800-875-2562 (toll-free); email: pcsupport@altum.com).

5802 ■ Mantle Cell Lymphoma Research Grants
(Advanced Professional/Grant)

Purpose: To accelerate the pace of research in mantle cell lymphoma (MCL). **Focus:** Hematology; Oncology. **Qualif.:** Applicants must be principal investigators holding an academic faculty appointment at a non-profit organizations, or public or private institutions such as universities, colleges, hospitals, and laboratories. Eligible investigators must have a title of assistant, associate, or full professor or its equivalent. **Criteria:** Selection will be based on the committee's criteria.

Funds Avail.: No specific amount. **To Apply:** Applicants may contact the Foundation for the application process and other information. **Deadline:** February 19. **Contact:** Email at researchgrants@lymphoma.org. For technical assistance or questions on the application process, contact the proposalCentral helpline (phone: 703-964-5840 or 800-875-2562 (toll-free); email: pcsupport@altum.com).

5803 ■ Boyd Lyon Sea Turtle Fund
1320 19th St. NW, 5th Fl.
Washington, DC 20036
Ph: (202)887-8992
E-mail: info@oceanfdn.org
URL: boydlyonseaturtlefund.org

5804 ■ Boyd N. Lyon Scholarships *(Doctorate, Graduate, Master's/Scholarship)*

Purpose: To support field research projects that further knowledge on sea turtle behavior and habitat use in the marine environment as well as promotion of management and conservation in coastal ecosystems. **Focus:** Biology, Marine; Oceanography. **Qualif.:** Applicants must be enrolled in an accredited college or university in the United States or international; must be graduate students who have completed minimum of nine credits in a full-time or part-time status; must demonstrate interest in enhancing the understanding of sea turtle behavior and conservation, habitat needs, abundance, spatial and distribution etc. **Criteria:** Selection will be based on evaluation of the submitted documents and specific criteria.

Awards are arranged alphabetically below their administering organizations

Funds Avail.: $2,500. **Duration:** Annual. **Number Awarded:** 1. **To Apply:** Applicants must submit a completed application form; copy of resume or curriculum vitae; research proposal consisting of project description, personal statement and budget; two reference letters (one from sponsoring faculty member). **Deadline:** February 1. **Contact:** Questions regarding the Boyd N. Lyon Scholarship should be addressed to info@ceanfdn.org.

5805 ■ MacArthur Foundation

140 S Dearborn St.
Chicago, IL 60603-5285
Ph: (312)726-8000
Fax: (312)920-6258
E-mail: 4answers@macfound.org
URL: www.macfound.org

5806 ■ MacArthur Fellows Program *(Professional development/Fellowship)*

Purpose: To award unrestricted fellowships to talented individuals who have shown extraordinary originality and dedication in their creative pursuits and a marked capacity for self-direction. **Focus:** General studies/Field of study not specified. **Qualif.:** Candidates must be writers, scientists, artists, social scientists, humanists, teachers, entrepreneurs, or those in other fields, with or without institutional affiliations. **Criteria:** Selection will be based on creativity, originality, and potential to make important contributions in the future.

Funds Avail.: $500,000. **Duration:** Five years. **To Apply:** Nominators will be invited by the Foundation to nominate individuals who demonstrate exceptional creativity and promise. **Contact:** Pete Boyle at pboyle@lipmanhearne.com or Adam Shapiro at ashapiro@lipmanhearne.com; 202-457-8100.

5807 ■ Robert Mack Scholarship Foundation

c/o Jerry Metcalfe, Treasurer
44403 Fernwood Rd.
Mendocino, CA 95460-9746
Ph: (707)937-4505
E-mail: info@robertmacksf.org
URL: robertmacksf.org

5808 ■ Robert Mack Scholarships *(Graduate, Undergraduate/Scholarship)*

Purpose: To support qualified students who wish to pursue studies in healthcare engineering. **Focus:** Engineering; Health care services. **Qualif.:** Applicant must be a student pursuing undergraduate, graduate or vocational courses in the field of healthcare engineering. **Criteria:** Selection is based on the application materials submitted for review.

Funds Avail.: No specific amount. **To Apply:** Applicant must complete the application form available online together with a grade transcript from the most recent school; S.A.T. reasoning score; community service must be detailed; essays, entitled "What does education mean to me?" and "What are my goals in the field of healthcare engineering?"; references, a minimum of three, one of each must be related to school activities. **Deadline:** February 15. **Remarks:** Established in 1986. **Contact:** The Robert Mack Scholarship Foundation; c/o Jerry Metcalfe at the above address or Email: info@robertmacksf.org.

5809 ■ Mackenzie Municipal Services Agency

5109-51 St.
Berwyn, AB, Canada T0H 0E0

Ph: (780)338-3862
Fax: (780)338-3811
E-mail: info@mmsa.ca
URL: mmsa.ca

5810 ■ Robert E. Walter Memorial Scholarship *(Undergraduate/Scholarship)*

Purpose: To financially assist students from the Mackenzie Region. **Focus:** General studies/Field of study not specified. **Qualif.:** Applicants must be residents of the Mackenzie Region in northern Alberta; must be high school graduates who will be attending a post-secondary education program, or currently in the work force but will be attending a post-secondary education program to upgrade skills; and must agree to retain employment in the Mackenzie Region for one year following graduation. **Criteria:** Preference will be given to students enrolled in studies leading towards working in local government.

Funds Avail.: $500. **Duration:** Annual. **Number Awarded:** 1. **To Apply:** Applicants must provide a cover letter indicating the following: intentions for the R. E. Walter Memorial Scholarship funds, future goals, resume and why they deserve the scholarship funds. Applicants must also include two recommendation letters (one must be from teachers or staff from the school they have attended or employers they currently work for and the other one from a member of the community). A copy of grades and list of academic achievements and community involvement must also be included. **Deadline:** March 31.

5811 ■ Macomb County Bar Foundation (MCBF)

40 N Main St., Ste. 435
Mount Clemens, MI 48043
Ph: (586)468-2940
Fax: (586)468-6926
E-mail: mcbf@macombbar.org
URL: macombcountybarfoundation.weebly.com

5812 ■ Philip F. Greco Memorial Scholarships *(Undergraduate/Scholarship)*

Purpose: To provide financial assistance for second or third year law students enrolled in evening classes at the University of Detroit Mercy Law School. **Focus:** Law. **Qualif.:** Applicants must be enrolled as law degree candidates in evening classes at the University of Detroit Marcy Law School. They must demonstrate a need for financial assistance, good academic standing (2.5 GPA or above), and the ability to achieve success as a lawyer. **Criteria:** Selection will be based on the committee's criteria.

Funds Avail.: $3,000. **To Apply:** Application form can be downloaded online. The application packet must include: completed application form; applicants' most recent law school transcript; resume; three letters of recommendation; a personal statement in which the candidate discusses his/her interest in law, reason for applying for scholarship, career goals and any other pertinent information he/she would like the Scholarship Committee to know. **Deadline:** February 21.

5813 ■ Trustees College Scholarships *(Undergraduate/Scholarship)*

Purpose: To award scholarships for students enrolled in Macomb County Community College who have been affected by Michigan's economic circumstances. **Focus:** Law. **Qualif.:** Applicants for the Macomb County Bar Foundation

Awards are arranged alphabetically below their administering organizations

Trustees Scholarship must be enrolled or accepted for enrollment at Macomb Community College at least part-time (six credit hours). **Criteria:** Preference is given to students who are returning to school due to job loss resulting from downsizing, restructuring, lay-off or corporate buyout. Preference is also given to students who seek to adjust skills by enrolling in a law-related education program.

Funds Avail.: $2,500. **To Apply:** Applicants may download application online. The application packet must include: completed application; brief summary of applicant's educational and career goals; resume; three letters of recommendation; a personal statement in which the candidate discuss their interest in law, reason for applying for scholarship, career goals and any other pertinent information he/she would like the Scholarship Committee to know about. **Deadline:** February 20.

5814 ■ Trustees Law School Scholarships
(Undergraduate/Scholarship)

Purpose: To provide financial assistance to law students who are in need. **Focus:** Law. **Qualif.:** Applicants must be second or third year law students who demonstrate a commitment to serve or contribute to the Macomb County legal community; must demonstrate a need for financial assistance; and must have high scholastic achievement. Applicants must be enrolled as a law degree candidate at one of the following Michigan Law Schools: Thomas M. Cooley, Michigan State University, University of Michigan, University of Detroit Mercy, Wayne State University. **Criteria:** Selection will be based on the committee's criteria.

Funds Avail.: $3,000. **To Apply:** Applicants may download application online. The application packet must include: complete application; candidate's undergraduate college transcript; candidate's most recent law school transcript; resume; three letters of recommendation; a personal statement in which the candidate discusses his/her interest in law, reason for applying for scholarship, career goals and any other pertinent information he/she would like the Scholarship Committee to know about. **Deadline:** February 21.

5815 ■ James Madison Memorial Fellowship Foundation
1613 Duke St.
Alexandria, VA 22314
Free: 800-525-6928
URL: www.jamesmadison.com

5816 ■ James Madison Graduate Fellowships
(Graduate/Fellowship)

Purpose: To support individuals desiring to become outstanding teachers of the American Constitution at the secondary school level. **Focus:** General studies/Field of study not specified. **Qualif.:** Applicants must be graduate students, U.S. citizens or U.S. national. **Criteria:** Selection will be based on the committee's review on the application materials.

Funds Avail.: $24,000. **Duration:** Annual. **Number Awarded:** 1. **To Apply:** Interested applicants must register online and accomplish all required fields with complete and accurate information. Applicants' recommenders will receive their emails with information to complete their recommendations. **Deadline:** March 1.

5817 ■ James Madison Foundation - Junior Fellowships
(Advanced Professional/Fellowship)

Purpose: To support outstanding college seniors and college graduates without teaching experience who intend to become secondary school teachers of American history, American government, or social studies at the secondary level. **Focus:** Education; History, American; Teaching. **Qualif.:** Applicants must: be U.S. citizens or U.S. nationals; have plan to become teachers, of American history, American government, or social studies at the secondary school level (grades 7-12); and students who are about to complete, or have completed, undergraduate course of study and plans to begin graduate work on a full-time basis. **Criteria:** Selection shall be based on demonstrated commitment to a career teaching American history, American government, or social studies at the secondary school level; demonstrated intent to pursue and complete a program of graduate study that emphasizes the Constitution and offers instruction in that subject; demonstrated devotion to civic responsibility; demonstrated capacity for study and performance as classroom teachers and proposed courses of graduate study.

Funds Avail.: $24,000. **Duration:** Annual. **Number Awarded:** Varies. **To Apply:** Applicants are required to apply online. In addition, transcript(s) must be submitted at the Iowa Office. **Deadline:** March 1. **Contact:** James Madison Memorial Fellowship Foundation, at the above address.

5818 ■ James Madison Foundation - Senior Fellowships
(Graduate/Fellowship)

Purpose: To support outstanding current teachers who are required to complete graduate study within 5 calendar years of part-time study. **Focus:** Education; History, American; Teaching. **Qualif.:** Applicants must be U.S. citizens or U.S. nationals and teachers of American history, American government, or social studies at the secondary school level (grades 7-12) who wish to undertake work for a graduate degree on a part-time basis through summer and evening classes. **Criteria:** Selection shall be based on demonstrated commitment to a career teaching American history, American government, or social studies at the secondary school level; demonstrated intent to pursue and complete a program of graduate study that emphasizes the Constitution and offers instruction in that subject; demonstrated devotion to civic responsibility; demonstrated capacity for study and performance as classroom teachers and proposed courses of graduate study.

Funds Avail.: $24,000. **Duration:** Annual. **Number Awarded:** Varies. **To Apply:** Applicants are required to apply online. In addition, transcript(s) must be submitted at the Iowa Office. **Deadline:** March 1. **Contact:** James Madison Memorial Fellowship Foundation, at the above address.

5819 ■ MAES: Latinos in Science and Engineering
2437 Bay Area Blvd., No. 100
Houston, TX 77058
Ph: (281)557-3677
Fax: (281)715-5100
E-mail: questions@mymaes.org
URL: mymaes.org

5820 ■ MAES Founders Scholarships *(Graduate, Undergraduate/Scholarship)*

Purpose: To increase the number of Hispanic students completing their higher education goals. **Focus:** Engineering; Mathematics and mathematical sciences; Science; Technology. **Qualif.:** Applicant must be a MAES student

Awards are arranged alphabetically below their administering organizations

member in the field of science, technology, engineering, and mathematics. **Criteria:** Selection is based on academic achievement, financial need, leadership, community service, personal qualities, and completeness of application.

Funds Avail.: $2,750. **Number Awarded:** 1. **To Apply:** Applicants must submit a complete scholarship application packet. **Deadline:** October. **Contact:** MAES National Office at sales@maes-natl.org.

5821 ■ MAES General Scholarships *(Graduate, Undergraduate/Scholarship)*

Purpose: To increase the number of Hispanic students completing their higher education goals. **Focus:** Engineering; Mathematics and mathematical sciences; Science; Technology. **Qualif.:** Applicant must be a MAES student member in the field of science, technology, engineering, and mathematics. **Criteria:** Selection is based on academic achievement, financial need, leadership, community service, personal qualities, and completeness of application.

Funds Avail.: $1,000 each. **Number Awarded:** Varies. **To Apply:** Applicants must submit a complete scholarship application packet. **Contact:** MAES National Office at sales@maes-natl.org.

5822 ■ MAES Graduate Scholarships *(Graduate/Scholarship)*

Purpose: To increase the number of Hispanic students completing their higher education goals. **Focus:** Engineering; Mathematics and mathematical sciences; Science; Technology. **Qualif.:** Applicant must be a MAES student member in the field of science, technology, engineering, and mathematics. **Criteria:** Selection is based on academic achievement, financial need, leadership, community service, personal qualities, and completeness of application.

Funds Avail.: No specific amount. **To Apply:** Applicants must submit a complete scholarship application packet. **Deadline:** October. **Contact:** MAES National Office at sales@maes-natl.org.

5823 ■ MAES Padrino/Madrina Scholarships *(Graduate, Undergraduate/Scholarship)*

Purpose: To increase the number of Hispanic students completing their higher education goals. **Focus:** Engineering; Mathematics and mathematical sciences; Science; Technology. **Qualif.:** Applicant must be a MAES student member in the field of science, technology, engineering, and mathematics. **Criteria:** Selection is based on academic achievement, financial need, leadership, community service, personal qualities, and completeness of application.

Funds Avail.: $5,000 each. **Number Awarded:** 3. **To Apply:** Applicants must submit a complete scholarship application packet. **Contact:** MAES National Office at sales@maes-natl.org.

5824 ■ MAES Pipeline Scholarships *(Graduate, Undergraduate/Scholarship)*

Purpose: To increase the number of Hispanic students completing their higher education goals. **Focus:** Engineering; Mathematics and mathematical sciences; Science; Technology. **Qualif.:** Applicant must be a MAES student member in the field of science, technology, engineering, and mathematics. **Criteria:** Selection is based on academic

achievement, financial need, leadership, community service, personal qualities, and completeness of application.

Funds Avail.: $2,200. **To Apply:** Applicants must submit a complete scholarship application packet. **Contact:** MAES National Office at sales@maes-natl.org.

5825 ■ MAES Presidential Scholarships *(Graduate, Undergraduate/Scholarship)*

Purpose: To increase the number of Hispanic students completing their higher education goals. **Focus:** Engineering; Mathematics and mathematical sciences; Science; Technology. **Qualif.:** Applicant must be a MAES student member in the field of science, technology, engineering, and mathematics. **Criteria:** Selection is based on academic achievement, financial need, leadership, community service, personal qualities, and completeness of application.

Funds Avail.: No specific amount. **To Apply:** Applicants must submit a complete scholarship application packet. **Deadline:** October. **Contact:** MAES National Office at sales@maes-natl.org.

5826 ■ Brandon Magalassi Memorial Scholarship Foundation

13800 E 106th St. N
Owasso, OK 74055
Ph: (918)272-5731
Fax: (918)272-2451
URL: www.magalassifoundation.org

5827 ■ The Brandon Magalassi Memorial Scholarship Foundation Scholarships *(Undergraduate/Scholarship)*

Purpose: To raise awareness about teen suicide. **Focus:** General studies/Field of study not specified. **Qualif.:** Applicants must be graduating seniors in Owasso High School, Rejoice Christian High School, home schooled from Owasso and of First United Methodist Church of Owasso. **Criteria:** Selection will be based on the submitted essay.

Funds Avail.: $1,000. **Duration:** Annual. **To Apply:** Applicants must write an essay on the topic: Teen Suicide, its effects, risk factors and methods of prevention and intervention. **Contact:** Michele Magalassi at 918-519-2077.

5828 ■ Maine Association of Physician Assistants (MEAPA)

30 Association Dr.
Manchester, ME 04351
Ph: (207)620-7577
Fax: (207)622-3332
E-mail: info@mainepa.com
URL: www.mainepa.com

5829 ■ Susan Vincent Memorial Scholarship *(Undergraduate/Scholarship)*

Purpose: To support a Maine resident with desire to become a physician assistant in Maine. **Focus:** Medical assisting. **Qualif.:** Applicants must be students residing in Maine at the time of acceptance into a PA program and share a desire to work and serve in Maine upon graduation. **Criteria:** Selection will be based on the committee's criteria.

Awards are arranged alphabetically below their administering organizations

Funds Avail.: $1,000. **Duration:** Annual. **To Apply:** Applicants must submit a letter of acceptance from an accredited Physician Assistant Program together with the following requirements: a brief statement detailing why they deserve and need this scholarship (maximum length - 2 single-typed pages). Applicants should exemplify those qualities that Susan Vincent modeled during her life - against the odds, achieving goals set forth educationally and career-wise, while serving their community. **Deadline:** June 1.

5830 ■ Maine Bar Foundation
40 Water St.
Hallowell, ME 04347
Ph: (207)622-3477
Fax: (207)623-4140
E-mail: info@mbf.org
URL: www.mbf.org

5831 ■ Frank M. Coffin Family Law Fellowship
(Graduate/Fellowship)

Purpose: To provide experience and training to young lawyers who wish to work in legal services. **Focus:** Law. **Qualif.:** Young lawyers are all qualified to apply. **Criteria:** Selection is based on the application materials.

Funds Avail.: No specific amount. **Duration:** 2 years. **To Apply:** Applicants must submit a letter of interest, resume, references and a brief writing sample to the Executive Director or via email. **Deadline:** October 9. **Contact:** Ms. Diana Scully, Executive Director, Maine Bar Foundation, at jgilbert@mbf.org.

5832 ■ Maine Chapter of the International Association of Arson Investigators (IAAI)
PO Box 1101
Auburn, ME 04211-1101
URL: www.maineiaai.com

5833 ■ Joseph C. Menezes Scholarship
(Undergraduate/Scholarship)

Purpose: To provide financial support for individuals pursuing studies in the field of Fire Science Degree programs. **Focus:** Fires and fire prevention. **Qualif.:** Applicants must be students enrolled in Fire Science Degree programs and must desire becoming involved in fire investigation. **Criteria:** Selection will be based on merit.

Funds Avail.: No specific amount. **To Apply:** Applicants must submit a completed application form along with the supporting documents. **Contact:** Sr. Inv. Richard Shepard, rshepar1@maine.rr.com.

5834 ■ Maine Community Foundation
245 Main St.
Ellsworth, ME 04605
Ph: (207)667-9735
Fax: (207)667-0447
Free: 877-700-6800
E-mail: info@mainecf.org
URL: www.mainecf.org

5835 ■ Daniel Cardillo Charitable Fund *(All/Scholarship)*

Purpose: To encourage young people to achieve their personal best and reach their goals. **Focus:** General studies/Field of study not specified. **Qualif.:** Applicants must be young people pursuing their artistic, academic, athletic, and vocational or life's passion outside of the traditional school environment. **Criteria:** Selection will be based on the committee's criteria.

Funds Avail.: No specific amount. **Duration:** Annual. **To Apply:** Applicants must clearly demonstrate a need for financial assistance, a commitment to their passion, and compassion for others. **Deadline:** May 1. **Remarks:** Established in 1999.

5836 ■ Churchill Family Scholarships
(Undergraduate/Scholarship)

Purpose: To provide financial assistance to people seeking higher education. **Focus:** Education, Music. **Qualif.:** Applicants must be graduating high school seniors pursuing a college degree in vocal music education or performance. **Criteria:** Selection will be based on the committee's criteria.

Funds Avail.: No specific amount. **To Apply:** Applicants may contact the Musica de Filia for application process. **Contact:** musicgirlchoir@verizon.net.

5837 ■ John S. and Marjoria R. Cunningham Camp Scholarships *(All/Scholarship)*

Purpose: To provide scholarships for week-long residential summer camp experiences. **Focus:** General studies/Field of study not specified. **Qualif.:** Recipients must be Maine residents, ages 10-15, whose financial need would otherwise prevent them from affording such experiences. **Criteria:** Recipients will be chosen from the pool of eligible campers attending each camp.

Funds Avail.: No specific amount. **Duration:** Annual. **To Apply:** There is no application for this award. Campers are advised to contact the Foundation for other details.

5838 ■ Downeast Feline Scholarships *(Graduate/Scholarship)*

Purpose: To provide financial assistance to people seeking higher education. **Focus:** Veterinary science and medicine. **Qualif.:** Applicants must be graduates of Maine high schools who are attending a veterinary school of medicine. **Criteria:** Preference is for students in their third or fourth year.

Funds Avail.: No specific amount. **To Apply:** Applicants may contact the Foundation for application process. **Deadline:** June 15. **Remarks:** Established in 1995.

5839 ■ Guy P. Gannett Scholarships *(Undergraduate/Scholarship)*

Purpose: To provide financial assistance to people seeking higher education. **Focus:** Journalism. **Qualif.:** Applicants must be students majoring in journalism or a field reasonably related, including all forms of print, broadcast, or electronic media; must be graduates of Maine high schools or home-schooled in Maine. **Criteria:** Students will be chosen based on demonstrated interest in journalism, financial need, and academic achievement.

Funds Avail.: No specific amount. **Duration:** Annual. **To Apply:** Applicants may contact their high school guidance offices or the Maine Community Foundation for application process. **Deadline:** May 1. **Remarks:** Established in 2000.

5840 ■ Ronald P. Guerrette Future Farmers of America Scholarship Fund *(Undergraduate/Scholarship)*

Purpose: To provide financial assistance to people seeking higher education. **Focus:** Agricultural sciences. **Qualif.:**

Awards are arranged alphabetically below their administering organizations

Applicants must be students from Caribou High School, Aroostook County, and Maine; must be members of Future Farmers of America. **Criteria:** Preference is for applicants pursuing post-secondary studies in farming or agriculture.

Funds Avail.: No specific amount. **Duration:** Annual. **Number Awarded:** 3. **To Apply:** Applicants may contact their Local FFA advisors or Maine Community Foundation for application process. **Deadline:** March 1. **Remarks:** Established in 1998.

5841 ■ Catharine Wilder Guiles Scholarships
(Graduate/Scholarship)

Purpose: To encourage Maine-based professionals in the mental health field to obtain the best graduate level training possible. **Focus:** Mental health. **Qualif.:** Applicants must be Maine residents with demonstrated financial need who are pursuing graduate education in the mental health field at the University of Maine (Orono) or the University of Southern Maine. **Criteria:** Preference will be given to second-year graduate students with demonstrated commitment and potential; students who plan to work in the public sector rather than the private sector in Maine; and to students participating in classroom setting rather than distance learning.

Funds Avail.: No specific amount. **To Apply:** Applicants may contact the Foundation, UMaine or USM financial aid offices for application process.

5842 ■ Iberdrola USA Scholarships *(Undergraduate/Scholarship)*

Purpose: To provide financial assistance to people seeking higher education. **Focus:** General studies/Field of study not specified. **Qualif.:** Applicants must be dependents of employees or recent retirees of Central Maine Power Company or its subsidiaries who are graduating from a Maine high school, residents of towns within CMP's service area, and enrolled in an accredited two- or four-year undergraduate college or university. **Criteria:** Selection will be based on personal aspirations, academic achievement, financial need, and the student's contribution to school or community activities.

Funds Avail.: No specific amount. **To Apply:** Applicants may contact their high school guidance offices, CMP offices or Maine Community Foundation for application process. **Deadline:** May 1.

5843 ■ Ella R. Ifill Fund *(Undergraduate/Scholarship)*

Purpose: To provide financial assistance to people seeking higher education. **Focus:** General studies/Field of study not specified. **Qualif.:** Applicant must be a member of the International Order of the Rainbow Girls in Maine to pursue post-secondary education. **Criteria:** Selection will be based on the committee's criteria.

Funds Avail.: No specific amount. **Duration:** Annual. **To Apply:** Applicants may contact the International Order of Rainbow Girls in Maine for application process.

5844 ■ Island Institute Scholarship Fund
(Undergraduate/Scholarship)

Purpose: To provide financial assistance to people seeking higher education. **Focus:** General studies/Field of study not specified. **Qualif.:** Applicants must be students from Maine's 15 year-round unbridged island communities who are pursuing post-secondary education at a two- or four-year institution. **Criteria:** Selection will be based on the committee's criteria.

Funds Avail.: No specific amount. **Duration:** Annual. **To Apply:** Applicants may contact their high school guidance offices, Island Institute, or Maine Community Foundation for application process. **Deadline:** April 1.

5845 ■ Edward G. Kaelber Scholarships
(Undergraduate/Scholarship)

Purpose: To provide financial assistance to people seeking higher education. **Focus:** Education; Philanthropy. **Qualif.:** Applicants must be students from Maine who have the potential for bold leadership and who will use their skills and talents to bring about change in their communities. **Criteria:** Selection will be based on the committee's criteria.

Funds Avail.: No specific amount. **Duration:** Annual. **To Apply:** Applicants may contact the College of the Atlantic for application process.

5846 ■ Keepers Preservation Education Fund
(Undergraduate/Award)

Purpose: To provide financial support to aspiring or established preservation professionals in the United States to increase or share their professional knowledge or enhance their career potential in historic preservation-related subjects. **Focus:** General studies/Field of study not specified. **Qualif.:** Applicants must be enrolled full or part-time in institutions of higher learning with majors in historic preservation or allied fields including American studies, anthropology, archeology, architecture, landscape architecture, art history, architectural history, history, planning, law, economics, or building conservation. **Criteria:** Preference will be given to applicants who have not received an award in the past 12 months.

Funds Avail.: No specific amount. **Duration:** Annual. **To Apply:** Individuals must apply through a sponsoring institution or organization, which reviews and forwards the application to the Maine Community Foundation. Applications must include a one-page statement explaining why funds are needed. As part of this statement, please include: your name, address, e-mail address, phone number and social security number on the project summary; an explanation of your relationship to the sponsoring organization; and statement of total funds needed in support of the project/activity. The sponsoring institution must submit a short statement explaining how the application was reviewed and how many individuals participated in the screening or selection process. **Remarks:** Established in 1988. **Contact:** Cherie Galyean, 877-700-6800, ext. 1106 or cgalyean@mainecf.org.

5847 ■ Maine Community Foundation - Rice Scholarships *(Undergraduate/Scholarship)*

Purpose: To provide financial assistance to people seeking higher education. **Focus:** General studies/Field of study not specified. **Qualif.:** Applicants must be students who have resided a substantial part of their formative years (K-8) on an offshore island of Maine in the area from Seguin to Eastport who are attending accredited, degree-granting colleges or vocational training schools. Applicants must have graduated from a non-sectarian high school. **Criteria:** Preference is given for residents of offshore islands. Recipients will be selected based on financial need and their ongoing demonstrated commitment to community service.

Funds Avail.: No specific amount. **To Apply:** Applicants may contact their high school guidance offices or Maine Community Foundation for application process. **Deadline:** May 1. **Remarks:** Established in 1996.

Awards are arranged alphabetically below their administering organizations

5848 ■ Maine Vietnam Veterans Scholarships
(Advanced Professional/Scholarship)

Purpose: To support Maine veterans of the United States Armed Services. **Focus:** General studies/Field of study not specified. **Qualif.:** Applicants must be Maine veterans of the United States Armed Services who served in the Vietnam Theater and their descendants or children of veterans of the United States Armed Services. **Criteria:** Selection will be based on the committee's criteria.

Funds Avail.: No specific amount. **To Apply:** Applicants may contact their high school guidance offices or the Maine Community Foundation for application process. **Deadline:** May 1. **Remarks:** Established in 1985.

5849 ■ Joseph W. Mayo ALS Scholarships
(Undergraduate/Scholarship)

Purpose: To assist men and women who are children, stepchildren, grandchildren, spouses, domestic partners, or primary caregivers of Amyotrophic Lateral Sclerosis patients. **Focus:** General studies/Field of study not specified. **Qualif.:** Applicants must be students attending a post-secondary educational institution, including both four-year colleges and two-year associate programs and must be graduates of a Maine high school or GED program. **Criteria:** Selection will be based on the committee's criteria.

Funds Avail.: No specific amount. **Duration:** Annual; One year. **To Apply:** Applicants may contact the Foundation for application process. **Deadline:** May 1. **Contact:** Joseph Pietroksi, joepietroski@gmail.com.

5850 ■ Gary Merrill Memorial Scholarships
(Undergraduate/Scholarship)

Purpose: To provide financial assistance to people seeking higher education. **Focus:** Government. **Qualif.:** Applicants must be Bowdoin undergraduates demonstrating financial need. **Criteria:** Preference given to Government majors who have distinguished themselves in their studies.

Funds Avail.: No specific amount. **To Apply:** Applicants may contact the Department of Government and Legal Studies at Bowdoin College for application process. **Remarks:** Established in 1990.

5851 ■ Ruth Milan-Altrusa Scholarships
(Undergraduate/Scholarship)

Purpose: To provide scholarship support to students who are pursuing a higher education. **Focus:** Nursing. **Qualif.:** Applicants must be students pursuing a B.S. in nursing and enrolled in the EMMC/Husson University Nursing Program. **Criteria:** Selection will be based on the committee's criteria.

Funds Avail.: No specific amount. **Duration:** Annual. **To Apply:** Applicants may contact the Husson University financial aid office for application process. **Remarks:** Established in 1993.

5852 ■ Hugh and Elizabeth Montgomery Scholarships
(Undergraduate/Scholarship)

Purpose: To provide scholarship assistance to deserving students of Franklin County. **Focus:** General studies/Field of study not specified. **Qualif.:** Applicants must be adult learners from Franklin County who are returning to school to continue their education at the post-secondary level. **Criteria:** Preference is given to students for whom a scholarship would make a significant difference in their ability to attend school. First-time applicants need not be enrolled in a degree-granting program but are encouraged

to make that commitment before applying for renewal consideration.

Funds Avail.: No specific amount. **Duration:** Annual. **To Apply:** Applicants must submit an application form, 500 word personal statement, and letter of recommendation from a teacher, employer or friend. Submit completed applications to Betty Gensel, Franklin County Community College Network, PO Box 2, Farmington, ME 04938. **Deadline:** August 14 and December 18. **Contact:** Betty Gensel, 800-517-2859.

5853 ■ Patriot Education Scholarships
(Undergraduate/Scholarship)

Purpose: To provide financial assistance to people seeking higher education. **Focus:** Business; Insurance and insurance-related fields. **Qualif.:** Applicants must be graduates of Maine high schools pursuing a degree in business/insurance at a college or university in Maine. **Criteria:** Preference will be given to applicants who have a demonstrated interest in the insurance profession.

Funds Avail.: No specific amount. **To Apply:** Applicants may contact the Foundation for application process. **Deadline:** June 1. **Contact:** MaineCF at the above address.

5854 ■ Jerome Peters Family Scholarships
(Undergraduate/Scholarship)

Purpose: To provide financial assistance to people seeking higher education. **Focus:** General studies/Field of study not specified. **Qualif.:** Applicant must be a Maine resident who is a second-, third-, or fourth-year student at Bentley University. **Criteria:** Preference is given to residents of Aroostook County.

Funds Avail.: No specific amount. **To Apply:** Applicants may contact the Bentley University office of financial aid for application process.

5855 ■ Lawrence and Louise Robbins Scholarships
(Undergraduate/Scholarship)

Purpose: To provide financial assistance to people seeking higher education. **Focus:** General studies/Field of study not specified. **Qualif.:** Applicants must be employees or retirees of the Robbins Lumber company of Searsmont, or their children or grandchildren, looking to pursue post-secondary education. **Criteria:** Recipients will be selected on the basis of academic achievement, personal aspirations, and contributions to school and the community.

Funds Avail.: No specific amount. **To Apply:** Applicants may contact the Robbins Lumber Inc. for application process. **Contact:** Catherine Robbins, 207-342-5221.

5856 ■ James and Marilyn Rockefeller Scholarships
(Undergraduate/Scholarship)

Purpose: To provide financial assistance to people seeking higher education. **Focus:** General studies/Field of study not specified. **Qualif.:** Applicants must be residents of Knox, Waldo or Washington Counties over the age of 18 who, by circumstance experiences, are on a "road less traveled" and are seeking traditional educational experiences that will change their life and the lives of people around them. **Criteria:** Selection will be based on the committee's criteria.

Funds Avail.: No specific amount. **Duration:** Annual. **To Apply:** Applicant may contact the Foundation for application process. **Deadline:** May 15.

5857 ■ Henry L.P. Schmelzer College Transitions Scholarships
(Undergraduate/Scholarship)

Purpose: To support the post-secondary aspirations of Maine adults returning to school. **Focus:** General studies/

Awards are arranged alphabetically below their administering organizations

Field of study not specified. **Qualif.:** Applicants must be non-traditional students who have successfully completed the Onward program and have matriculated into the University of Maine, Orono. Consideration may also be given to students who have successfully completed at least one year of the Onward Program but who have yet to matriculate into the University of Maine, Orono. **Criteria:** Preference will be given to residents of Hancock County, Washington County, and statewide.

Funds Avail.: No specific amount. **Duration:** Annual. **To Apply:** There is no application for this scholarship. Recipients will be chosen annually from the pool of eligible Onward Program students.

5858 ■ Maine Graphic Arts Association (MGAA)

PO Box 265
Sanford, ME 04073
E-mail: info@megaa.org
URL: www.megaa.org

5859 ■ Maine Graphic Arts Association Scholarships *(Undergraduate/Scholarship)*

Purpose: To reward deserving students who desire to continue their education in the field of graphic arts printing technology. **Focus:** Graphic art and design. **Qualif.:** Applicants must have completed or will complete their secondary education in Maine with at least a C average. Applicant's high school must be a member of the MGAA; and have been accepted into a post-secondary Graphic Arts program. **Criteria:** Selection will be based on the committee's criteria.

Funds Avail.: No specific amount. **Duration:** Annual. **To Apply:** Applicants must attach a copy of their high school grades and two completed Scholarship Candidate Evaluation Forms to their application. **Deadline:** May 15.

5860 ■ Maine Landscape and Nursery Association (MeLNA)

PO Box 4666
Augusta, ME 04330
Ph: (207)623-6430
Fax: (207)623-6431
E-mail: mngmtplus@aol.com
URL: www.melna.org

5861 ■ MELNA Scholarship *(Undergraduate, Graduate/Scholarship)*

Purpose: To promote the secondary horticultural education. **Focus:** Horticulture. **Qualif.:** Applicants must be members of MELNA. **Criteria:** Selection will be based on the committee's criteria.

Funds Avail.: Amount not specified. **Duration:** Annual. **To Apply:** Interested applicants may contact the Association for the application process and other details.

5862 ■ Maine Nutrition Council (MNC)

PO Box 246
Augusta, ME 04330
E-mail: info@mainenutritioncouncil.org
URL: www.mainenutritioncouncil.org

5863 ■ Maine Nutrition Council Scholarships *(Undergraduate/Scholarship)*

Purpose: To provide financial assistance to the students enrolled at the University of Maine. **Focus:** Food science

and technology; Nutrition. **Qualif.:** Applicants must be full-time, second or third year students enrolled in the Department of Food Science and Human Nutrition Program at the University of Maine, or full-time students in a Maine Community College Culinary Arts Program; must have a GPA of 3.0 or higher. **Criteria:** Selection will be based on the submitted application.

Funds Avail.: $500. **Duration:** Annual. **To Apply:** Applicants must submit one letter of recommendation from a faculty member together with their application form. **Deadline:** February 21. **Contact:** Amber Desrosiers, MNC Member at Large, Eastern Maine Healthcare Systems, the Cianchette Bldg., Ste. 500, 43 Whiting Hill Rd., Brewer, ME 04412; adesrosiers@emh.org; 207-944-4657.

5864 ■ Maine State Employees Association (MSEA)

65 State St.
Augusta, ME 04332-1072
Ph: (207)622-3151
Fax: (207)623-4916
Free: 800-452-8794
E-mail: mseaseiu@mseaseiu.org
URL: www.mseaseiu.org

5865 ■ Norma Arnold Clerical Scholarships *(Undergraduate/Scholarship)*

Purpose: To provide assistance to members of the MSEA SEIU community pursuing higher education. **Focus:** General studies/Field of study not specified. **Qualif.:** Applicants must be MSEA members who are furthering their education either on a part-time basis while employed, or on a full time basis after obtaining an educational leave of absence. **Criteria:** Selection will be based on the committee's criteria.

Funds Avail.: $1,500. **Duration:** Annual. **Number Awarded:** 3. **To Apply:** Applicants must complete and submit the application via mail.

5866 ■ Maine Community College Scholarships *(Undergraduate/Scholarship)*

Purpose: To provide assistance to Maine students who lack financial aid for education. **Focus:** General studies/ Field of study not specified. **Qualif.:** Applicants must be: children of MSEA members; students who are under legal guardianship of MSEA members; grandchildren of MSEA members who resides with the grandparents; students entering full-time at any post-secondary educational or vocational institutions for the first time. Full-time shall be defined as complying with federal standards of twelve (12) credit hours per semester. **Criteria:** Selection will be based on the following criteria: character; leadership; service to others; financial need and scholastic ability.

Funds Avail.: $750. **Duration:** Annual. **Number Awarded:** 1. **To Apply:** The following materials should accompany the application: high school transcript; essay on how the union affected the applicants' family or parents/guardians' financial resources and outstanding oblications; Federal Income Tax Return including all statements and schedules; description of extra curricular activities; scholastic and non-scholastic reference letter.

5867 ■ MSEA/SEIU Part-time Student Members Scholarships *(Undergraduate/Scholarship)*

Purpose: To provide financial assistance to students who want to pursue higher education. **Focus:** General studies/

Awards are arranged alphabetically below their administering organizations

Field of study not specified. **Qualif.:** Applicants must be MSEA members who are furthering their education either on a part-time basis while employed, or on a full time basis after obtaining an educational leave of absence. **Criteria:** Selection will be based on the committee's criteria.

Funds Avail.: $500 each. **Duration:** Annual. **Number Awarded:** 3. **To Apply:** The following materials should accompany the application: high school transcript; essay on how the union affacted the applicants' family or parents/guardians' financial resources and outstanding oblications; Federal Income Tax Return including all statements and schedules; description of extra curricular activities; scholastic and non-scholastic reference letter.

5868 ■ Malayalee Engineers Association (MEA)
8303 SW Fwy., Ste. 335
Houston, TX 77074
Ph: (281)686-5969
E-mail: meahouston@gmail.com
URL: www.meahouston.org

5869 ■ Malayalee Engineers Association Scholarships *(Undergraduate/Fellowship)*

Purpose: To encourage young professionals to pursue their engineering, technology, computer science, or naval architecture studies towards a Bachelor's Degree. **Focus:** Architecture, Naval; Computer and information sciences; Engineering; Technology. **Qualif.:** Applicant must be an Engineering graduate student; must be enrolled in a college in Kerala. **Criteria:** Selection of applicants will be based on financial need and academic performance.

Funds Avail.: $500 per year. **Duration:** Annual; 4 years. **To Apply:** Applicants must complete the application form accompanied by a recommendation letter. Applicants are also required to provide a blank letter of recommendation form. Copies of marked lists and a rank certificate shall be attested by the Principal or Head of the Department of the Engineering College where the student is currently enrolled. **Deadline:** October 15.

5870 ■ Mansfield Soccer Association (MSA)
2363 Hwy. 287 N, Ste. 206
Mansfield, TX 76063
Ph: (817)473-1177
Fax: (817)473-7786
URL: www.mansfieldsoccer.org

5871 ■ Mansfield Soccer Association Scholarships *(Undergraduate/Scholarship)*

Purpose: To help individuals pursue their post-secondary education. **Focus:** General studies/Field of study not specified. **Qualif.:** Applicants must live within the MISD boundaries; must have plans to attend an institution of higher education for the upcoming year; and must have been players, coaches or referees in MSA within the last five years. **Criteria:** Selection will be based on academic record, school and community involvement, financial need, work experience and completeness of the application.

Funds Avail.: $1,000 each. **Number Awarded:** 2. **To Apply:** Applicants must submit an attachment of personal profile, high school transcript and letters of recommendation from these categories: a) teacher, counselor, or school principal; b) employer, principal, or neighbor aged 21 years and above. **Deadline:** May 15. **Contact:** Application form

and supporting documents should be mailed to MSA Scholarship Committee, at the above address.

5872 ■ Manufacturing Jewelers and Association of America (MJSA)
8 Hayward St.
Attleboro, MA 02703-2113
Ph: (508)316-2132
Fax: (508)316-1429
Free: 800-444-6572
URL: www.mjsa.org

5873 ■ MJSA Education Foundation Scholarship Fund *(Undergraduate/Scholarship)*

Purpose: To financially support students enrolled in jewelry-related field. **Focus:** Design. **Qualif.:** Applicant must be a U.S. citizen; must be enrolled in a jewelry program; pursuing a career in the jewelry industry; and with demonstrated financial need. **Criteria:** Applicants are assessed based on the course of study, academics, career plans, recommendations, and industry experience.

Funds Avail.: $500-$3,000. **Duration:** Annual. **To Apply:** Applicant must complete the application form available at the website; must submit a copy of financial aid award letter; official transcript; an essay; and a letter of recommendation. Forward completed application and supporting documents in one envelope. **Deadline:** June 15.

5874 ■ March of Dimes Foundation
1275 Mamaroneck Ave.
White Plains, NY 10605
Ph: (914)997-4488
URL: www.marchofdimes.com

5875 ■ March of Dimes Graduate Nursing Scholarships *(Graduate/Scholarship)*

Purpose: To provide financial assistance to registered nurses in a graduate program. **Focus:** Nursing. **Qualif.:** Applicants must be registered nurses, currently enrolled in a graduate program in maternal-child nursing at the master's or doctoral level; must have at least one academic term to complete after August of the year in which the scholarship is awarded; must be members of at least one of the following professional organizations: Association of Women's Health, Obstetric and Neonatal Nurses, American College of Nurse-Midwives or National Association of Neonatal Nurses. **Criteria:** Selection will be based on submitted documents and specific criteria.

Funds Avail.: $5,000. **Duration:** Annual. **To Apply:** Applicants must submit a completed application form, faculty recommendation and an essay. **Deadline:** January 30.

5876 ■ Stephen T. Marchello Scholarship Foundation
1170 E Long Pl.
Centennial, CO 80122
Ph: (303)886-5018
E-mail: stmfoundation@hotmail.com
URL: www.stmfoundation.org

5877 ■ Stephen T. Marchello Scholarships *(Undergraduate/Scholarship)*

Purpose: To support the education of students who have a history of childhood cancer. **Focus:** General studies/Field

Awards are arranged alphabetically below their administering organizations

of study not specified. **Qualif.:** Applicant must be a high school graduate in the states of CO, and MT; must have survived childhood cancer. **Criteria:** Awards are given based on the application materials.

Funds Avail.: No specific amount. **To Apply:** Applicants must submit a completed scholarship application along with a copy of transcript (with GPA); SAT or ACT test scores; a confirmation of the treatment by the doctor or by the hospital or clinic; and a reference letter (from someone other than a family member). **Deadline:** March 15. **Contact:** Stephen T. Marchello Scholarship Foundation at 303-886-5018.

5878 ■ The Margarian Law Firm

801 N., Brand Blvd., Ste. 210
Glendale, CA 91203
Ph: (818)553-1000
Fax: (818)553-1005
Free: 866-975-3666
E-mail: info@margarianlaw.com
URL: www.lemonlawcourt.com

5879 ■ The Margarian Scholarships *(Undergraduate, Graduate/Scholarship)*

Purpose: To support deserving students for their past, present and future expenses. **Focus:** Law. **Qualif.:** Applicants must be students planning to take up a law study. **Criteria:** Applicants will be selected based on their GPA; economic hardship; and commitment to their heritage, community and society.

Funds Avail.: $1,000 each. **Duration:** Annual. **Number Awarded:** 5. **To Apply:** Applicants must submit a completed application form.

5880 ■ Marine Aquarium Societies of North America (MASNA)

PO Box 105603
Atlanta, GA 30348-5603
E-mail: president@masna.org
URL: masna.org

5881 ■ MASNA Student Scholarships *(Undergraduate, Graduate/Scholarship)*

Purpose: To support those undergraduate and graduate students from the various colleges and universities in U.S. as well as to assist each of the chosen applicants in attending MACNA. **Focus:** Biology, Marine. **Qualif.:** Applicants must be current/entering undergraduate or graduate students at an accredited college or university; have declared a major/focus or have intent to declare a major/focus in one of the marine science disciplines. **Criteria:** Selection will be based upon the students' academic history and the contributions and demonstrated commitment to the marine aquarium hobby.

Funds Avail.: $4,000 each. **Duration:** Annual. **Number Awarded:** 2. **To Apply:** Applicants must provide and submit the following requirements: resume, official transcripts from where the applicants are enrolled (i.e. college/university), and reference (for information verification). **Deadline:** June 19.

5882 ■ Marine Biological Laboratory (MBL)

7 MBL St.
Woods Hole, MA 02543

Ph: (508)548-3705
E-mail: comm@mbl.edu
URL: www.mbl.edu

5883 ■ Bruce and Betty Alberts Endowed Scholarships in Physiology *(Graduate, Master's, Doctorate/Scholarship)*

Purpose: To provide support for Physiology students. **Focus:** Physiology. **Qualif.:** Applicants must be attending a Marine Biological Laboratory summer course. **Criteria:** Recipients will be selected based on academic standing and financial need.

Funds Avail.: No specific amount. **Duration:** Annual. **To Apply:** Students who apply for financial aid to attend MBL courses are automatically considered. See the requirements for Physiology Summer Course program.

5884 ■ John and Elisabeth Buck Endowed Scholarships *(Graduate, Postdoctorate/Scholarship)*

Purpose: To provide support for a graduate or postdoctoral student taking a summer course in fundamental biological science. **Focus:** Biology. **Qualif.:** Applicants must be graduate or postdoctoral students attending a summer course at Marine Biological Laboratory. **Criteria:** Recipients will be selected based on academic standing and financial need.

Funds Avail.: No specific amount. **Duration:** Annual. **To Apply:** Students who apply for financial aid to attend MBL courses are automatically considered. See the requirements for the Summer Course program.

5885 ■ C. Lalor Burdick Scholarships *(Graduate, Master's, Doctorate/Scholarship)*

Purpose: To provide support for students attending the Embryology and Frontiers in Reproduction courses. **Focus:** Biological and clinical sciences; Life sciences. **Qualif.:** Applicants must be attending a summer course at Marine Biological Laboratory. **Criteria:** Recipients will be selected based on academic standing and financial need.

Funds Avail.: No specific amount. **Duration:** Annual. **To Apply:** Students who apply for financial aid to attend MBL courses are automatically considered. See the requirements for Embryology and Frontiers in Reproduction Summer Course programs. **Deadline:** February 5.

5886 ■ Max M. Burger Endowed Scholarships in Embryology *(Graduate, Master's, Doctorate/Scholarship)*

Purpose: To provide support for students attending the Embryology course. **Focus:** Biological and clinical sciences; Life sciences. **Qualif.:** Applicants must be attending a summer course at Marine Biological Laboratory. **Criteria:** Recipients will be selected based on academic standing and financial need.

Funds Avail.: $5,950. **Duration:** Annual. **To Apply:** Students who apply for financial aid to attend MBL courses are automatically considered. See the requirements for Embryology Summer Course program. **Deadline:** February 5.

5887 ■ Thomas B. Grave and Elizabeth F. Grave Scholarships *(Undergraduate, Graduate/Scholarship)*

Purpose: To provide support for students studying in any Marine Biological Laboratory summer courses. **Focus:** Biology, Marine. **Qualif.:** Applicants must be attending a sum-

Awards are arranged alphabetically below their administering organizations

mer course at Marine Biological Laboratory. **Criteria:** Recipients will be selected based on academic standing and financial need.

Funds Avail.: No specific amount. **Duration:** Annual. **To Apply:** Students who apply for financial aid to attend MBL courses are automatically considered. See the requirements for the Summer Course program.

5888 ■ Caswell Grave Scholarships *(Undergraduate, Graduate/Scholarship)*

Purpose: To provide support for students studying in any Marine Biological Laboratory summer courses. **Focus:** Biology, Marine. **Qualif.:** Applicants must be attending a summer course at Marine Biological Laboratory. **Criteria:** Recipients will be selected based on academic standing and financial need.

Funds Avail.: No specific amount. **Duration:** Annual. **To Apply:** Students who apply for financial aid to attend MBL courses are automatically considered. See the requirements for the Summer Course program.

5889 ■ William Randolph Hearst Educational Endowments *(Undergraduate, Graduate/Scholarship)*

Purpose: To provide support for students studying in any Marine Biological Laboratory summer courses. **Focus:** Biology, Marine. **Qualif.:** Applicants must be attending a summer course at Marine Biological Laboratory. **Criteria:** Recipients will be selected based on academic standing and financial need.

Funds Avail.: No specific amount. **Duration:** Annual. **To Apply:** Students who apply for financial aid to attend MBL courses are automatically considered. See the requirements for the Summer Course program.

5890 ■ Benjamin Kaminer Endowed Scholarships in Physiology *(Graduate, Master's, Doctorate/Scholarship)*

Purpose: To provide support for students studying in any Marine Biological Laboratory summer courses in Physiology. **Focus:** Physiology. **Qualif.:** Applicants must be attending a summer course at Marine Biological Laboratory. **Criteria:** Recipients will be selected based on academic standing and financial need.

Funds Avail.: No specific amount. **Duration:** Annual. **To Apply:** Students who apply for financial aid to attend MBL courses are automatically considered. See the requirements for Physiology Summer Course program.

5891 ■ Arthur Klorfein Scholarship and Fellowship Fund *(Undergraduate, Graduate/Scholarship)*

Purpose: To provide support for students in their courses and for research fellows working independently in laboratories. **Focus:** Biology, Marine. **Qualif.:** Applicants must be attending a summer course at Marine Biological Laboratory. **Criteria:** Recipients will be selected based on academic standing and financial need.

Funds Avail.: No specific amount. **Duration:** Annual. **To Apply:** Students who apply for financial aid to attend MBL courses are automatically considered. See the requirements for the Summer Course program.

5892 ■ Frank R. Lillie Fellowships and Scholarships *(Undergraduate, Graduate/Scholarship)*

Purpose: To support students in their courses and for research fellows working independently in laboratories.

Focus: Biology. **Qualif.:** Applicants must be attending a Marine Biological Laboratory summer course. **Criteria:** Recipients will be selected based on academic standing and financial need.

Funds Avail.: No specific amount. **Duration:** Annual. **To Apply:** Students who apply for financial aid to attend MBL courses are automatically considered. See the requirements for the Summer Course program.

5893 ■ Marine Biological Laboratory Pioneers Fund *(Undergraduate, Graduate/Scholarship)*

Purpose: To provide support for students attending a Marine Biological Laboratory. **Focus:** Biology, Marine. **Qualif.:** Applicants must be attending a Marine Biological Laboratory summer course. **Criteria:** Recipients will be selected based on academic standing and financial need.

Funds Avail.: No specific amount. **Duration:** Annual. **To Apply:** Applicants must complete the application form. See the requirements for the Summer Course program.

5894 ■ S.O. Mast Founder's Scholarships *(Undergraduate, Graduate/Scholarship)*

Purpose: To provide support for students attending a Marine Biological Laboratory Summer Courses. **Focus:** Biology, Marine. **Qualif.:** Applicants must be attending a Marine Biological Laboratory summer course. **Criteria:** Recipients will be selected based on academic standing and financial need.

Funds Avail.: No specific amount. **Duration:** Annual. **To Apply:** Students who apply for financial aid to attend MBL Summer Courses are automatically considered.

5895 ■ Frank Morrell Endowed Memorial Scholarships *(Graduate, Master's, Doctorate/Scholarship)*

Purpose: To provide support for students attending a neurobiology course. **Focus:** Biology, Marine. **Qualif.:** Applicants must be attending a Marine Biological Laboratory summer course. **Criteria:** Recipients will be selected based on academic standing and financial need.

Funds Avail.: No specific amount. **Duration:** Annual. **To Apply:** Students who apply for financial aid to attend MBL courses are automatically considered. **Deadline:** February 5.

5896 ■ Mountain Memorial Scholarships *(Graduate, Master's, Doctorate/Scholarship)*

Purpose: To provide support for students who are accepted in the physiology course. **Focus:** Physiology. **Qualif.:** Applicants must be attending a summer course at Marine Biological Laboratory. **Criteria:** Recipients will be selected based on academic standing and financial need.

Funds Avail.: No specific amount. **Duration:** Annual. **To Apply:** Students who apply for financial aid to attend MBL courses are automatically considered. See the requirements for Physiology Summer Course program.

5897 ■ Pfizer Inc. Endowed Scholarships *(Undergraduate, Graduate/Scholarship)*

Purpose: To provide support for students who studying at the Marine Biological Laboratory Summer Course Program. **Focus:** Biology, Marine. **Qualif.:** Applicants must be attending a summer course at Marine Biological Laboratory. **Criteria:** Recipients will be selected based on academic standing and financial need.

Funds Avail.: No specific amount. **Duration:** Annual. **Num-**

Awards are arranged alphabetically below their administering organizations

ber Awarded: 2. **To Apply:** Students who apply for financial aid to attend MBL courses are automatically considered. See the requirements for the Summer Course program.

5898 ■ Herbert W. Rand Fellowships and Scholarships *(Undergraduate, Graduate/Scholarship)*

Purpose: To provide support for students in their courses and for research fellows working independently in laboratories. **Focus:** Biology, Marine. **Qualif.:** Applicants must be attending a summer course at Marine Biological Laboratory. **Criteria:** Recipients will be selected based on academic standing and financial need.

Funds Avail.: No specific amount. **Duration:** Annual. **To Apply:** Students who apply for financial aid to attend MBL courses are automatically considered. See the requirements for the Summer Course program.

5899 ■ Lola Ellis Robertson Scholarships *(Graduate, Master's, Doctorate/Scholarship)*

Purpose: To provide support for students studying at the Marine Biological Laboratory. **Focus:** Biological and clinical sciences; Life sciences. **Qualif.:** Applicants must be attending a summer course at Marine Biological Laboratory. **Criteria:** Recipients will be selected based on academic standing and financial need.

Funds Avail.: No specific amount. **Duration:** Annual. **To Apply:** Students who apply for financial aid to attend MBL courses are automatically considered. See the requirements for Embryology Summer Course program.

5900 ■ Florence C. Rose and S. Meryl Rose Scholarships *(Graduate, Master's, Doctorate/Scholarship)*

Purpose: To provide support for students at the Marine Biological Laboratory Embryology Summer Course Program. **Focus:** Biology; Life sciences. **Qualif.:** Applicants must be attending a summer course at Marine Biological Laboratory. **Criteria:** Recipients will be selected based on academic standing and financial need.

Funds Avail.: $5,950. **Duration:** Annual. **To Apply:** Students who apply for financial aid to attend MBL courses are automatically considered. See the requirements for Embryology Summer Course program. **Deadline:** February 5.

5901 ■ Ruth Sager Scholarships *(Undergraduate, Graduate/Scholarship)*

Purpose: To provide support for women students studying at the Marine Biological Laboratory. **Focus:** Biology, Marine. **Qualif.:** Applicants must be attending a summer course at Marine Biological Laboratory. **Criteria:** Recipients will be selected based on academic standing and financial need.

Funds Avail.: No specific amount. **Duration:** Annual. **To Apply:** Applicants must complete the application form. See the requirements for the Summer Course program.

5902 ■ Milton L. Shifman Endowed Scholarships *(Undergraduate, Graduate/Scholarship)*

Purpose: To provide support for students from Dartmouth College studying at the Marine Biological Laboratory. **Focus:** Biology, Marine. **Qualif.:** Applicants must be attending a summer course at Marine Biological Laboratory. **Criteria:** Recipients will be selected based on academic standing and financial need.

Funds Avail.: No specific amount. **Duration:** Annual. **To Apply:** Students who apply for financial aid to attend MBL courses are automatically considered. See the requirements for the Summer Course program.

5903 ■ Horace W. Stunkard Scholarships *(Undergraduate, Graduate/Scholarship)*

Purpose: To provide support for students studying at the Marine Biological Laboratory. **Focus:** Biology, Marine. **Qualif.:** Applicants must be attending a summer course at Marine Biological Laboratory. **Criteria:** Recipients will be selected based on academic standing and financial need.

Funds Avail.: No specific amount. **Duration:** Annual. **To Apply:** Students who apply for financial aid to attend MBL courses are automatically considered.

5904 ■ J.P. and Madeline Trinkaus Endowed Scholarships in Embryology *(Graduate, Master's, Doctorate/Scholarship)*

Purpose: To provide support for students studying at the Marine Biological Laboratory in the embryology course. **Focus:** Biology; Life sciences. **Qualif.:** Applicants must be attending a summer course at Marine Biological Laboratory. **Criteria:** Recipients will be selected based on academic standing and financial need.

Funds Avail.: $5,950. **Duration:** Annual. **To Apply:** Students who apply for financial aid to attend MBL courses are automatically considered. See the requirements for Embryology Summer Course program. **Deadline:** February 5.

5905 ■ Selman A. Waksman Endowed Scholarships in Microbial Diversity *(Graduate, Master's, Doctorate/Scholarship)*

Purpose: To provide support for students participating in the microbial diversity course. **Focus:** Life sciences; Microbiology. **Qualif.:** Applicants must be attending a summer course at Marine Biological Laboratory. **Criteria:** Recipients will be selected based on academic standing and financial need.

Funds Avail.: No specific amount. **Duration:** Annual. **To Apply:** Students who apply for financial aid to attend MBL courses are automatically considered. See the requirements for Microbial Diversity Summer Course program. **Deadline:** February 5.

5906 ■ Marine Corps Engineer Association (MCEA)
807 Carriage Hills Blvd.
Conroe, TX 77384
Ph: (936)273-4830
URL: www.marcorengasn.org

5907 ■ Marine Corps Engineer Association Assistance Fund *(Undergraduate/Scholarship)*

Purpose: To provide financial assistance for the education of the members of the United States Marine Corp's engineer and explosive ordinance disposal communities and their families or for members of the United States Armed Forces who have served with or been attached to Marine Corps Air Ground Task Force engineer or EOD units. **Focus:** Engineering. **Qualif.:** Program is open to citizens of the United States seeking for financial assistance to further education beyond high school at an accredited college, university or higher technical trade school up to a

Awards are arranged alphabetically below their administering organizations

maximum of four years. They can also be individuals who are already enrolled in a post-secondary curriculum. Neither graduate study request nor applications at the high school or prep school level are acceptable. **Criteria:** Applications will be evaluated by the Scholarship Selection Committee.

Funds Avail.: $8,000. **To Apply:** Applicants must complete and submit the application form and enclose all items requested in the application; name and address; and have the application and attachment notarized. **Deadline:** June 30. **Remarks:** Established in 2006.

5908 ■ Marine Corps League Foundation
PO Box 3070
Merrifield, VA 22116-3070
E-mail: president@mclfoundation.org
URL: www.mclfoundation.org

5909 ■ Marine Corps League National Scholarships
(Undergraduate/Scholarship)

Purpose: To grant scholarship to qualified applicants pursuing full-time undergraduate or technical training at a recognized institution. **Focus:** General studies/Field of study not specified. **Qualif.:** Applicant must be the spouse, child, grandchild, great grandchild or step child of a Marine Corps League or Auxiliary member in good standing; or the child of a Marine who died in the line of duty; or a member of the Marine Corps League or Auxiliary in good standing or honorably discharged Marines in need of rehabilitation training not provided by government programs. Sponsors must be a member in good standing of the Marine Corps League or Auxiliary. **Criteria:** Award is given based on the application materials.

Funds Avail.: No specific amount. **To Apply:** Applicants must submit a completed application form in which the sponsor has completely filled out their section.

5910 ■ Marine Technology Society (MTS)
1100 H St. NW, Ste. LL100
Washington, DC 20005
Ph: (202)717-8705
Fax: (202)347-4302
E-mail: membership@mtsociety.org
URL: www.mtsociety.org

5911 ■ Marine Technology Society ROV Scholarships (MTS ROV) *(Undergraduate, Graduate/ Scholarship)*

Purpose: To help students achieve success. **Focus:** Biology, Marine; Engineering, Marine. **Qualif.:** Applicants must be MTS members and students who are interested in remotely operated vehicles (ROVs) or underwater work that furthers the use of ROVs. Applicants must be graduate, undergraduate or high school students. **Criteria:** Recipients will be selected based on academic standing.

Funds Avail.: Up to $10,000. **Duration:** Annual. **Number Awarded:** Varies. **To Apply:** Applicants must submit a written recommendation from a current teacher or counselor in a marine-related field; a written letter of reference from someone who is not a teacher or counselor; an official sealed transcript. For high school seniors, proof of acceptance to a two-year or four-year academic program must be submitted. Applicants must submit a biographical sketch including academic, personal and professional goals. Applicants must also submit a one-page essay about his/her

interest in ROVs or underwater work that furthers the use of Rovs. **Deadline:** April 20.

5912 ■ MTS Scholarship *(Graduate, Undergraduate, High School/Scholarship)*

Purpose: To provide scholarships to students focused on studying marine technology, marine engineering and marine science. **Focus:** Biology, Marine; Engineering, Marine. **Qualif.:** Applicants must be MTS members who are either high school seniors or full-time college students currently enrolled or have been accepted in a 2-year or 4-year academic program. **Criteria:** Selection will be based on the committee's criteria.

Funds Avail.: Varies. **Duration:** Annual. **To Apply:** Applicants must complete and submit the following requirements: one letter of recommendation from a teacher, counselor or professor in a marine-related field that they have studied with or received advice from within the past two years. For high school seniors, the recommendation must be from a current science teacher or counselor in any field. The letter must be on official letterhead, no colored paper, dated, no more than one page, and state that it is a letter of recommendation, signed and addressed to the scholarship committee; one reference letter from someone they know who is not a teacher or counselor or advisor. This letter is to show the qualities, characteristics and capabilities of the person applying for the scholarship. The letter must be dated, not more than one page, no colored paper, and state that it is a letter of reference, signed and addressed to the scholarship committee. **Deadline:** April 15.

5913 ■ The MTS Student Scholarship for Graduate and Undergraduate Students *(Graduate, Undergraduate/Scholarship)*

Purpose: To help students achieve success. **Focus:** Biology, Marine. **Qualif.:** Applicants must be MTS members who are graduate or undergraduate students, and enrolled full-time in a marine-related field. **Criteria:** Recipients will be selected based on academic standing.

Funds Avail.: $2,000. **Duration:** Annual. **Number Awarded:** Varies. **To Apply:** Applicants must apply online, then print and mail or email the application. Submit also the other required documents prescribed by the organization. **Deadline:** April 20. **Contact:** Suzanne Voelker at suzanne.voelker@mtsociety.org.

5914 ■ The MTS Student Scholarship for Graduating High School Seniors *(Undergraduate/Scholarship)*

Purpose: To help students achieve success. **Focus:** Biology, Marine. **Qualif.:** Applicants must be MTS members and high school seniors who have been accepted to either a 2-year or 4-year academic program. **Criteria:** Recipients will be selected based on academic standing.

Funds Avail.: $2,000. **Duration:** Annual. **Number Awarded:** Varies. **To Apply:** Applicants must apply online, then print and mail or email the application. Submit also the other required documents prescribed by the organization. **Deadline:** April 20. **Contact:** Suzanne Voelker at suzanne.voelker@mtsociety.org.

5915 ■ The MTS Student Scholarship for Two-Year, Technical, Engineering and Community College Students *(Undergraduate/Scholarship)*

Purpose: To help students achieve success. **Focus:** Biology, Marine; Engineering, Marine. **Qualif.:** Applicants must

Awards are arranged alphabetically below their administering organizations

be MTS members who are enrolled in a two-year technical, engineering or community college in a marine-related field. **Criteria:** Recipients will be selected based on academic standing.

Funds Avail.: $2,000. **Duration:** Annual. **Number Awarded:** Varies. **To Apply:** Applicants must apply online, then print and mail or email the application. Submit also the other required documents prescribed by the organization. **Deadline:** April 20. **Contact:** Suzanne Voelker at suzanne.voelker@mtsociety.org.

5916 ■ The Paros-Digiquartz Scholarships (Graduate, Undergraduate/Scholarship)

Purpose: To help students achieve success. **Focus:** Biology, Marine. **Qualif.:** Applicants must be MTS members; high school seniors who have been accepted into a full-time undergraduate program, or graduate studies. Applicants must have interests in marine instrumentation. **Criteria:** Recipients will be selected based on academic standing.

Funds Avail.: $2,000. **Duration:** Annual. **Number Awarded:** Varies. **To Apply:** Applicants must apply online, then print and mail or email the application. Submit also the other required documents prescribed by the organization. **Deadline:** April 20. **Contact:** Suzanne Voelker at suzanne.voelker@mtsociety.org.

5917 ■ Marines Memorial Association (MMA)

Marines Memorial Club and Hotel
609 Sutter St.
San Francisco, CA 94102-1027
Ph: (415)673-6672
Fax: (415)441-3649
E-mail: reservations@marineclub.com
URL: www.marineclub.com

5918 ■ Bechtel Engineering and Science Scholarships (High School/Scholarship)

Purpose: To support and encourage students to pursue a study majoring in Engineering or one of the Sciences. **Focus:** Engineering; Science. **Qualif.:** Applicants must be members, dependents, or grandchildren of members; must have plans to attend an engineering program accredited by the Engineering Accreditation Commission of the Accreditation Board for Engineering and Technology (ABET-EAC); and must be full-time high school students who are attending a qualified institution of higher education. **Criteria:** Selection will be based on the submitted application materials.

Funds Avail.: $5,000. **Duration:** Annual. **Number Awarded:** 5. **To Apply:** Applicants must complete an application form; a copy of most recent transcript; typewritten (250 words) essay; and three letters of reference. High school senior applicants are required to submit a copy of SAT and/or ACT scores.

5919 ■ Marketing EDGE

1120 Avenue of the Americas, 13th Fl.
New York, NY 10036-6700
Ph: (212)768-7277
Fax: (212)790-1561
E-mail: admin@marketingedge.org
URL: www.marketingedge.org

5920 ■ Mike Buoncristiano Memorial Scholarship Fund (Undergraduate/Scholarship)

Purpose: To support students further their education in the area of direct and interactive marketing. **Focus:** Marketing and distribution. **Qualif.:** Applicants must be U.S. citizens or permanent residents; must be enrolled in an accredited four-year undergraduate institution; must have a minimum GPA of 3.0 on a 4.0 scale in major and have 3.0 overall; must show a commitment to pursue a career in direct/interactive marketing. **Criteria:** Selection is based on evaluation of submitted documents and specific criteria.

Funds Avail.: No specific amount. **Duration:** Annual. **To Apply:** Applicants must submit a completed application form; official transcripts and resume. **Deadline:** April 15.

5921 ■ Mark Duda Scholarship Fund (Graduate, Undergraduate/Scholarship)

Purpose: To provide financial assistance to the students who are studying data and targeting strategies in direct and interactive marketing. **Focus:** Marketing and distribution. **Qualif.:** Applicants must be U.S. citizens or permanent residents; must be enrolled in an accredited four-year undergraduate institution or be graduate students; must have a minimum GPA of 3.0 on a 4.0 scale in major and have 3.0 overall; must show a commitment to pursue a career in direct/interactive marketing. **Criteria:** Selection is based on evaluation of submitted documents and specific criteria.

Funds Avail.: No specific amount. **Duration:** Annual. **To Apply:** Applicants should submit a completed application form, official transcripts and resume. **Deadline:** April 15.

5922 ■ Lee Epstein Scholarship Fund (Graduate, Undergraduate/Scholarship)

Purpose: To support students further their education in the area of direct and interactive marketing. **Focus:** Marketing and distribution. **Qualif.:** Applicants must be U.S. citizens or permanent residents; must be enrolled in an accredited four-year undergraduate institution or should be graduate students; must have a minimum GPA of 3.0 on a 4.0 scale in major and have 3.0 overall; must show a commitment to pursue a career in direct/interactive marketing. **Criteria:** Selection is based on evaluation of submitted documents and specific criteria.

Funds Avail.: No specific amount. **Duration:** Annual. **To Apply:** Applicants must submit a completed application form, an official transcript of records and resume. **Deadline:** April 15.

5923 ■ Dave Florence Scholarship Fund (Undergraduate/Scholarship)

Purpose: To support students further their education in the area of direct and interactive marketing. **Focus:** Marketing and distribution. **Qualif.:** Applicants must be U.S. citizens or permanent residents; must be enrolled in an accredited four-year undergraduate institution; must have a minimum GPA of 3.0 on a 4.0 scale in major and have 3.0 overall; must show a commitment to pursue a career in direct/interactive marketing. **Criteria:** Selection is based on evaluation of submitted documents and specific criteria.

Funds Avail.: No specific amount. **Duration:** Annual. **To Apply:** Applicants must submit a completed application form, official transcripts and resume. **Deadline:** April 15.

5924 ■ Don Kuhn Memorial Scholarship Fund (Graduate/Scholarship)

Purpose: To provide financial assistance to those students who have demonstrated commitment to pursue a career in

Awards are arranged alphabetically below their administering organizations

non-profit direct/interactive marketing. **Focus:** Marketing and distribution. **Qualif.:** Applicants must be U.S. citizens or permanent residents; must be graduate students enrolled in an accredited four-year institution; must have a minimum GPA of 3.0 on a 4.0 scale in major and have 3.0 overall; must show commitment to pursue a career in direct/interactive marketing. **Criteria:** Selection is based on evaluation of submitted documents and specific criteria.

Funds Avail.: No specific amount. **Duration:** Annual. **To Apply:** Applicants must submit a completed application form, official transcripts and resume. **Deadline:** April 15. **Remarks:** Established in 2006.

5925 ■ Willa Yeck Memorial Scholarship Fund (Undergraduate/Scholarship)

Purpose: To support students further their education in the area of direct and interactive marketing. **Focus:** Marketing and distribution. **Qualif.:** Applicants must be U.S. citizens or permanent residents; must be enrolled in an accredited four-year undergraduate institution; must have a minimum GPA of 3.0 on a 4.0 scale in major and have 3.0 overall; must show a commitment to pursue a career in direct/interactive marketing. **Criteria:** Selection is based on evaluation of submitted documents and specific criteria.

Funds Avail.: No specific amount. **Duration:** Annual. **To Apply:** Applicants must submit a completed application form, official transcripts and resume. **Deadline:** April 15.

5926 ■ Lorraine Zitone Memorial Scholarship Fund (Undergraduate/Scholarship)

Purpose: To support students further their education in the area of direct and interactive marketing. **Focus:** Marketing and distribution. **Qualif.:** Applicants must be U.S. citizens or permanent residents; must be enrolled in an accredited four-year undergraduate institution; must have a minimum GPA of 3.0 on a 4.0 scale in major and have 3.0 overall; must show a commitment to pursue a career in direct/interactive marketing. **Criteria:** Selection is based on evaluation of submitted documents and specific criteria.

Funds Avail.: No specific amount. **Duration:** Annual. **To Apply:** Applicants must submit a completed application form, official transcripts and resume. **Deadline:** April 15.

5927 ■ Thurgood Marshall College Fund (TMCF)
901 F St. NW, Ste. 300
Washington, DC 20004
Ph: (202)507-4851
Fax: (202)652-2934
E-mail: info@tmcfund.org
URL: www.thurgoodmarshallfund.net

5928 ■ TMCF Scholarships (Undergraduate/Scholarship)

Purpose: To provide students seeking financial assistance to complete their education. **Focus:** General studies/Field of study not specified. **Qualif.:** Applicant must be a full-time U.S. citizen student pursuing a degree in any discipline at one of the 47 TMCF member schools who demonstrates commitment to academic excellence and community service with a high school GPA of not less than 3.0; a combined verbal/math score of 1650 or more on the Scholastic Aptitude Test (SAT) or a score of 25 or higher on the American College Testing (ACT) examination, recommended by his high school as academically exceptional or outstanding in the creative and performing arts, and has

financial need. **Criteria:** Candidates will be evaluated based on their merit and financial need. In addition, the scholarship application process is highly competitive and most awards are limited to students attending TMCF member-schools, which are public Historically Black Colleges and Universities.

Funds Avail.: $3,100. **Duration:** One semester. **To Apply:** Applicants must submit general information form, enrollment/certification of academic standing, acceptance form, financial aid information together with high school transcript (for incoming freshman), undergraduate transcript (for graduate and law school), resume and/or personal information form recommendation letters, essay head shot or personal photograph.

5929 ■ Maryland Association of Certified Public Accountants (MACPA)
Dulaney Center II
901 Dulaney Valley Rd., Ste. 710
Towson, MD 21204
Free: 800-782-2036
E-mail: info@macpa.org
URL: www.macpa.org

5930 ■ MACPA Scholarships (Undergraduate, Graduate/Scholarship)

Purpose: To provide scholarship money to accounting majors at Maryland colleges and universities. **Focus:** Accounting. **Qualif.:** Applicants must: be U.S. citizens and Maryland residents attending a Maryland college/university; have completed at least 60 total credit hours by the time of the award of which at least 6 hours of credit are in accounting courses (including Accounting Principles I and II) at the time of the award AND enroll in or successfully complete Intermediate Accounting; be taking enough undergraduate level courses or graduate level courses during the semester in which the application is submitted to qualify as full-time students; have a cumulative GPA of 3.0 or better on a 4.0 scale and maintain at least a 3.0 GPA; demonstrate financial need; and, demonstrate a commitment to pursuing a career as a CPA by joining Tomorrow's CPA. **Criteria:** Selection shall be based on the aforementioned applicants' qualifications and compliance with the application details.

Funds Avail.: Amount varies. **Duration:** Annual. **To Apply:** Applicants are required to submit the following: complete copy of the four-page Student Aid Report (SAR) which is generated upon completion of the Free Application for Federal Student Aid (FAFSA); official, sealed transcript from the previous semester which shows cumulative GPA, total credit hours completed and hours completed during the previous semester; a completed application form; signed Applicant's Statement; and, paperworks to be submitted, together with the enumerated application requirements to the contact provided. **Deadline:** April 15. **Contact:** For more information, and to apply, please contact Margaret DeRoose at 800-782-2036.

5931 ■ Maryland Poison Center
220 Arch St., Office Level 1
Baltimore, MD 21201
Ph: (410)706-7604
Fax: (410)706-7184
Free: 800-222-1222
E-mail: mpcadmin@rx.umaryland.edu
URL: www.mdpoison.com

Awards are arranged alphabetically below their administering organizations

5932 ■ Maryland Poison Center Clinical Toxicology Fellowships *(Doctorate, Graduate/Fellowship)*

Purpose: To train a Doctor of Pharmacy graduate to function in a professional, administrative and research capacity in a regional poison center, clinical toxicology service and/or academic environment. **Focus:** Pharmacy. **Qualif.:** Applicants must possess a PharmD degree from an accredited School of College of Pharmacy. **Criteria:** Selection is based on the application.

Funds Avail.: No specific amount. **To Apply:** Applicants must submit a letter of application, curriculum vita, transcript and three letters of reference. **Contact:** Clinical Toxicology Fellowship at the Maryland Poison Center, please visit the University of Maryland School of Pharmacy website, or at the above address.

5933 ■ Maryland Speech-Language-Hearing Association (MSHA)
PO Box 31
Manchester, MD 21102
Ph: (410)239-7770
E-mail: office@mdslha.org
URL: www.mdslha.org

5934 ■ Maryland Speech Language Hearing Association Graduate Scholarships *(Graduate/Scholarship)*

Purpose: To financially support qualified graduate students who want to pursue their studies in speech language pathology at a university in the state of Maryland. **Focus:** Speech and language pathology/Audiology. **Qualif.:** Applicants must be full-time graduate students who have completed their first semester of graduate study in speech language pathology; must have earned a 4.0 grade point average in their first semester of graduate study. **Criteria:** Recipients will be selected based on their academic excellence, strong interpersonal skills and dedication to the ideals of the profession.

Funds Avail.: No specific amount. **Duration:** Annual. **To Apply:** Applicants must complete the application form available online; must provide a copy of transcripts from the first semester of graduate study; must have two letters of recommendation from faculty on university letterhead; must have typed goal narrative written by the nominee (minimum of one page and maximum of three double-spaced pages); must submit a resume which includes all current activities, practicum, research, association affiliation, volunteer experience, etc. **Contact:** Lisa Oriolo, Association Manager; Email: office@mdslha.org.

5935 ■ Jorge Mas Canosa Freedom Foundation
c/o Mas Family Scholarships
2147 SW 8th St.
Miami, FL 33135
Ph: (305)592-7768
URL: masscholarships.org

5936 ■ Mas Family Scholarships *(Graduate, Undergraduate/Scholarship)*

Purpose: To further the education of students with leadership potential. **Focus:** Business; Communications; Economics; Engineering; International affairs and relations; Journalism. **Qualif.:** Applicant must be a Cuban-American undergraduate or graduate student in the field of Engineer-ing, Business, International Relations, Economics, Communications or Journalism. **Criteria:** Selection is based on an applicant's academic performance, leadership qualities, potential to contribute to the advancement of a free society and likelihood of succeeding in his/her chosen career.

Funds Avail.: Depends on the recipient's cost of tuition. **Duration:** One year. **To Apply:** Applicants must submit a completed and signed application form (plus two copies) together with an official school transcript; admissions test scores; three evaluation forms; essays (three copies, typed, double-spaced, minimum of 1,000 words); proof of Cuban descent; proof of admission; tuition cost information; and statement of need. **Deadline:** January 17.

5937 ■ Massachusetts Association of Land Surveyors and Civil Engineers (MALSCE)
The Engineering Ctr.
1 Walnut St.
Boston, MA 02108-3616
Ph: (617)227-5551
E-mail: malsce@engineers.org
URL: www.malsce.org

5938 ■ MALSCE Scholarships *(Undergraduate/Scholarship)*

Purpose: To provide educational support to the residents of Massachusetts who are studying surveying, civil engineering or environmental engineering programs. **Focus:** Cartography/Surveying; Engineering, Civil. **Qualif.:** Applicants must be enrolled full-time in a college, university, junior college, technical institute or community college; must be residents of Massachusetts or attending an out-of-state school; and must be majoring in surveying, civil or environmental engineering. **Criteria:** Selection of applicants will be based on the scholarship application criteria.

Funds Avail.: No specific amount. **Duration:** Annual. **To Apply:** Applicants must write/call the chairman for an application; must complete the application form available online; must have a letter of recommendation; and must submit a transcript of grades. **Deadline:** July 31.

5939 ■ Massachusetts Association of Women Lawyers (MAWL)
c/o Jennifer R. Silva, Vice President
160 State St., 6th Fl.
Boston, MA 02109
Ph: (617)723-9900
E-mail: info@mawl.org
URL: www.mawl.org

5940 ■ Carol DiMaiti Scholarship Awards *(Undergraduate/Scholarship)*

Purpose: To award scholarships to law students in Massachusetts. **Focus:** Law. **Qualif.:** Applicants must be entering their second or third year of law school; must be in good academic standing; must have demonstrated high financial need. **Criteria:** Selection of scholars will be based on financial need and academic achievement.

Funds Avail.: $1,000. **Duration:** One year. **To Apply:** Applicants must submit a completed application form and must check the available website for details. **Deadline:** April. **Remarks:** This particular fund is maintained solely through voluntary contributions made throughout the year and fund-

Awards are arranged alphabetically below their administering organizations

raising events. **Contact:** Massachusetts Association of Women Lawyers at the above address.

5941 ■ Massachusetts Bar Foundation (MBF)
20 West St.
Boston, MA 02111
Ph: (617)338-0500
Fax: (617)338-0550
E-mail: foundation@massbar.org
URL: www.massbarfoundation.org

5942 ■ Massachusetts Bar Foundation Legal Intern Fellowship Program (LIFP) *(Undergraduate/Fellowship)*

Purpose: To assist law students in gaining practical experience in the public sector. **Focus:** Law. **Qualif.:** Applicant must have secured a volunteer internship with a qualified nonprofit organization in Massachusetts; currently be enrolled in a United States law school; and must demonstrate a commitment to public interest law, including experience working with low-income clients and/or issues that affect this population. **Criteria:** A committee including trustees from both the Massachusetts Bar Foundation and the Smith Family Fund will select the most competitive applicants to receive stipends.

Funds Avail.: $6,000 each. **Number Awarded:** 3. **To Apply:** Applicants must submit a complete application package which includes: Applicant Information Form; essay; Organization Supporting Statement Form; resume; official law school transcript; and one letter of reference. **Deadline:** March 13. **Remarks:** Established in 1996. **Contact:** MBF Legal Intern Fellowship Program, at foundation@massbar.org.

5943 ■ Massachusetts Chapter of the International Association of Arson Investigators, Inc. (MAIAAI)
PO Box 1874
Lowell, MA 01853
E-mail: webmaster@maiaai.com
URL: www.maiaai.com

5944 ■ Sgt. Michael F. Cherven Memorial Scholarships *(Undergraduate/Scholarship)*

Purpose: To support the relatives of IAAI Massachusetts Chapter members in their education. **Focus:** General studies/Field of study not specified. **Qualif.:** Applicants must be: members, immediate family members or grandchildren of a Massachusetts IAAI Chapter member in good standing; and, graduating high school seniors or entering/currently enrolled at a college/university. **Criteria:** Selection will be based on demonstrated commitment to public service or desire to enter public service.

Funds Avail.: $2,500 each. **Duration:** Annual. **Number Awarded:** 2. **To Apply:** Applicants must submit a completed application form provided at the website, along with the required supporting documents such as: essay as to why they believe they should be awarded the scholarship; three recommendation letters from individuals over 21 years old; and official transcript from their current school. **Deadline:** May 27.

5945 ■ Massachusetts Educational Financing Authority (MEFA)
160 Federal St., 4th Fl.
Boston, MA 02110

Free: 800-449-6332
E-mail: info@mega.org
URL: www.mefa.org

5946 ■ MEFA Graduate Loans *(Graduate/Loan)*

Purpose: To address the needs of graduate students attending Massachusetts college or university. **Focus:** General studies/Field of study not specified. **Qualif.:** Applicants must be students enrolled at least half-time in an accredited degree-granting graduate program at an eligible nonprofit college or university; primary borrower and/or applicants' co-borrower must live in Massachusetts, or the student must live in Massachusetts or attend a Massachusetts college or university; must maintain satisfactory academic progress as defined by their college or university; must be either US citizens or permanent residents. **Criteria:** Selection will be based on MEFA's current credit approval standards.

Funds Avail.: Minimum of $2,000 loan amount. **To Apply:** Applicants must provide the following materials: SSN; date of birth; phone number; email address; current and prior address(es); monthly income; housing costs; employment information. Interested applicants must visit the website to create an account. **Contact:** 800-266-0243.

5947 ■ Massachusetts Historical Society (MHS)
1154 Boylston St.
Boston, MA 02215-3695
Ph: (617)536-1608
Fax: (617)859-0074
E-mail: dfiori@masshist.org
URL: www.masshist.org

5948 ■ African American Studies Fellowships *(Graduate, Doctorate/Fellowship)*

Purpose: To support research at the Massachusetts Historical Society in African American History. **Focus:** African-American studies. **Qualif.:** Applicants must be independent scholars, advanced graduate students and holders of the PhD or the equivalent. Applicants must be US citizens or already hold the J-1 visa or equivalent documents that will allow them to accept the stipend. **Criteria:** Preference will be given to candidates who live fifty or more miles from Boston.

Funds Avail.: $2,000. **Duration:** Up to four weeks. **To Apply:** Applicants must submit the following materials online: a cover letter; current curriculum vitae; a project proposal approximately 1,000 words in length; for the applicants who do not hold a PhD, a letter of recommendation from a faculty member familiar with applicants' work and with the project being proposed. A project proposal should include: a description of the project; a statement explaining the historiographical significance of the project; an indication of the specific MHS collections the applicants wishes to consult. **Deadline:** March 1. **Contact:** fellowships@masshist.org; 617-646-0568.

5949 ■ Cushing Academy Fellowships on Environmental History *(Graduate, Doctorate/Fellowship)*

Purpose: To support research on any aspect of environmental history. **Focus:** Environmental science. **Qualif.:** Applicants must be independent scholars, advanced graduate students and holders of the PhD or the equivalent. Applicants must be US citizens or already hold the J-1 visa or

Awards are arranged alphabetically below their administering organizations

equivalent documents that will allow them to accept the stipend. **Criteria:** Selection will be based on the committee's criteria.

Funds Avail.: $2,500. **Duration:** Annual; up to four weeks of research. **To Apply:** Applicants must submit the following materials online: a cover letter; current curriculum vitae; a project proposal approximately 1,000 words in length; for the applicants who do not hold a PhD, a letter of recommendation from a faculty member familiar with applicants' work and with the project being proposed. A project proposal should include: a description of the project; a statement explaining the historiographical significance of the project; an indication of the specific MHS collections the applicants wishes to consult. **Deadline:** March 1. **Contact:** fellowships@masshist.org; 617-646-0568.

5950 ■ W.B.H. Dowse Fellowships (Graduate, Doctorate/Fellowship)

Purpose: To provide support for scholars studying the history of colonial New England. **Focus:** History. **Qualif.:** Applicants must be independent scholars, advanced graduate students and holders of the PhD or the equivalent. Applicants must be US citizens or already hold the J-1 visa or equivalent documents that will allow them to accept the stipend. **Criteria:** Selection will be based on the committee's criteria.

Funds Avail.: $2,000. **Duration:** Up to four weeks. **Number Awarded:** 2. **To Apply:** Applicants must submit the following materials online: a cover letter; current curriculum vitae; a project proposal approximately 1,000 words in length; for the applicants who do not hold a PhD, a letter of recommendation from a faculty member familiar with applicants' work and with the project being proposed. A project proposal should include: a description of the project; a statement explaining the historiographical significance of the project; an indication of the specific MHS collections the applicants wishes to consult. **Deadline:** March 1. **Contact:** fellowships@masshist.org; 617-646-0568.

5951 ■ Malcolm and Mildred Freidberg Fellowships (Graduate, Doctorate/Fellowship)

Purpose: To support research relating to reading and publishing. **Focus:** Publishing; Reading. **Qualif.:** Applicants must be independent scholars, advanced graduate students and holders of the PhD or the equivalent. Applicants must be US citizens or already hold the J-1 visa or equivalent documents that will allow them to accept the stipend. **Criteria:** Selection will be based on the committee's criteria.

Funds Avail.: $2,000. **Duration:** Up to four weeks. **To Apply:** Applicants must submit the following materials online: a cover letter; current curriculum vitae; a project proposal approximately 1,000 words in length; for the applicants who do not hold a PhD, a letter of recommendation from a faculty member familiar with applicants' work and with the project being proposed. A project proposal should include: a description of the project; a statement explaining the historiographical significance of the project; an indication of the specific MHS collections the applicants wishes to consult. **Deadline:** March 1. **Contact:** fellowships@masshist.org; 617-646-0568.

5952 ■ Marc Friedlaender Fellowships (Graduate, Doctorate/Fellowship)

Purpose: To support documentary editing projects and research on the Adams family. **Focus:** General studies/Field of study not specified. **Qualif.:** Applicants must be independent scholars, advanced graduate students and

holders of the PhD or the equivalent. Applicants must be US citizens or already hold the J-1 visa or equivalent documents that will allow them to accept the stipend. **Criteria:** Selection will be based on the committee's criteria.

Funds Avail.: $2,000. **Duration:** Up to four weeks. **To Apply:** Applicants must submit the following materials online: a cover letter; current curriculum vitae; a project proposal approximately 1,000 words in length; for the applicants who do not hold a PhD, a letter of recommendation from a faculty member familiar with applicants' work and with the project being proposed. A project proposal should include: a description of the project; a statement explaining the historiographical significance of the project; an indication of the specific MHS collections the applicants wishes to consult. **Deadline:** March 1. **Contact:** fellowships@masshist.org; 617-646-0568.

5953 ■ Suzanne and Caleb Loring Research Fellowships (Graduate, Doctorate/Fellowship)

Purpose: To support individuals who will conduct a research on the civil war, its origins and consequences. **Focus:** History. **Qualif.:** Applicants must be independent scholars, advanced graduate students and holders of the PhD or the equivalent. Applicants must be US citizens or already hold the J-1 visa or equivalent documents that will allow them to accept the stipend. **Criteria:** Selection will be based on the committee's criteria.

Funds Avail.: $4,000. **Duration:** Atleast four weeks of research. **Number Awarded:** 1. **To Apply:** Applicants must submit the following materials online: a cover letter; current curriculum vitae; a project proposal approximately 1,000 words in length; for the applicants who do not hold a PhD, a letter of recommendation from a faculty member familiar with applicants' work and with the project being proposed. A project proposal should include: a description of the project; a statement explaining the historiographical significance of the project; an indication of the specific Massachusetts Historical Society and Boston Athenaeum collections the applicants wishes to consult. **Deadline:** February 15. **Contact:** fellowships@masshist.org; 617-646-0568.

5954 ■ Massachusetts Society of the Cincinnati Fellowships (Graduate, Doctorate/Fellowship)

Purpose: To support research projects pertaining to the era of the American Revolution. **Focus:** History, American. **Qualif.:** Applicants must be independent scholars, advanced graduate students and holders of the PhD or the equivalent. Applicants must be US citizens or already hold the J-1 visa or equivalent documents that will allow them to accept the stipend. **Criteria:** Selection will be based on the committee's criteria.

Funds Avail.: $2,000. **Duration:** Up to four weeks. **To Apply:** Applicants must submit the following materials online: a cover letter; current curriculum vitae; a project proposal approximately 1,000 words in length; for the applicants who do not hold a PhD, a letter of recommendation from a faculty member familiar with applicants' work and with the project being proposed. A project proposal should include: a description of the project; a statement explaining the historiographical significance of the project; an indication of the specific MHS collections the applicants wishes to consult. **Deadline:** March 1. **Contact:** fellowships@masshist.org; 617-646-0568.

5955 ■ Andrew W. Mellon Fellowships (Graduate, Doctorate/Fellowship)

Purpose: To support any project for which the Society's collection are appropriate. **Focus:** General studies/Field of

Awards are arranged alphabetically below their administering organizations

study not specified. **Qualif.:** Applicants must be independent scholars, advanced graduate students and holders of the PhD or the equivalent. Applicants must be US citizens or already hold the J-1 visa or equivalent documents that will allow them to accept the stipend. **Criteria:** Selection will be based on the committee's criteria.

Funds Avail.: $2,000. **Duration:** Up to four weeks. **Number Awarded:** 9. **To Apply:** Applicants must submit the following materials online: a cover letter; current curriculum vitae; a project proposal approximately 1,000 words in length; for the applicants who do not hold a PhD, a letter of recommendation from a faculty member familiar with applicants' work and with the project being proposed. A project proposal should include: a description of the project; a statement explaining the historiographical significance of the project; an indication of the specific MHS collections the applicants wishes to consult. **Deadline:** March 1. **Contact:** fellowships@masshist.org; 617-646-0568.

5956 ■ MHS Long-Term Research Fellowships
(Professional development/Fellowship)

Purpose: To support individuals who will conduct a long-term research at the Massachusetts Historical Society. **Focus:** General studies/Field of study not specified. **Qualif.:** Applicants must be US citizens and foreign nationals who have lived in the United States for at least three years; must have completed their professional training, ordinarily including an earned doctorate. **Criteria:** Selection will be based on the quality of proposed projects and to their relationship to the Society's collections.

Funds Avail.: $4,200 per month. **Duration:** 4-12 months. **Number Awarded:** 2. **To Apply:** Applicants must submit the following materials online: a cover letter; current curriculum vitae; a project proposal approximately 1,000 words in length; a Certification for Participants form; two letters of recommendation. A project proposal should include: a description of the project; a statement explaining the historiographical significance of the project; an indication of the specific MHS collections the applicants wishes to consult. Applicants must specify the number of months for which they are applying. **Deadline:** January 15. **Contact:** fellowships@masshist.org; 617-646-0568.

5957 ■ Ruth R. and Alyson R. Miller Fellowships
(Graduate, Doctorate/Fellowship)

Purpose: To encourage research in women's history. **Focus:** Women's studies. **Qualif.:** Applicants must be independent scholars, advanced graduate students and holders of the PhD or the equivalent. Applicants must be US citizens or already hold the J-1 visa or equivalent documents that will allow them to accept the stipend. **Criteria:** Selection will be based on the committee's criteria.

Funds Avail.: $2,000. **Duration:** Up to four weeks. **To Apply:** Applicants must submit the following materials online: a cover letter; current curriculum vitae; a project proposal approximately 1,000 words in length; for the applicants who do not hold a PhD, a letter of recommendation from a faculty member familiar with applicants' work and with the project being proposed. A project proposal should include: a description of the project; a statement explaining the historiographical significance of the project; an indication of the specific MHS collections the applicants wishes to consult. **Deadline:** March 1. **Contact:** fellowships@masshist.org; 617-646-0568.

5958 ■ Andrew Oliver Research Fellowships *(Graduate, Doctorate/Fellowship)*

Purpose: To support research in the Society's collections of portraits, engravings, silhouettes and other graphic materials. **Focus:** Graphic art and design. **Qualif.:** Applicants must be independent scholars, advanced graduate students and holders of the PhD or the equivalent. Applicants must be US citizens or already hold the J-1 visa or equivalent documents that will allow them to accept the stipend. **Criteria:** Selection will be based on the committee's criteria.

Funds Avail.: $2,000. **Duration:** Up to four weeks. **To Apply:** Applicants must submit the following materials online: a cover letter; current curriculum vitae; a project proposal approximately 1,000 words in length; for the applicants who do not hold a PhD, a letter of recommendation from a faculty member familiar with applicants' work and with the project being proposed. A project proposal should include: a description of the project; a statement explaining the historiographical significance of the project; an indication of the specific MHS collections the applicants wishes to consult. **Deadline:** March 1. **Contact:** fellowships@masshist.org; 617-646-0568.

5959 ■ Benjamin F. Stevens Fellowships *(Graduate, Doctorate/Fellowship)*

Purpose: To support research on any aspect of the history of New England. **Focus:** History. **Qualif.:** Applicants must be independent scholars, advanced graduate students and holders of the PhD or the equivalent. Applicants must be US citizens or already hold the J-1 visa or equivalent documents that will allow them to accept the stipend. **Criteria:** Selection will be based on the committee's criteria.

Funds Avail.: $2,000. **Duration:** Up to four weeks. **To Apply:** Applicants must submit the following materials online: a cover letter; current curriculum vitae; a project proposal approximately 1,000 words in length; for the applicants who do not hold a PhD, a letter of recommendation from a faculty member familiar with applicants' work and with the project being proposed. A project proposal should include: a description of the project; a statement explaining the historiographical significance of the project; an indication of the specific MHS collections the applicants wishes to consult. **Deadline:** March 1. **Contact:** fellowships@masshist.org; 617-646-0568.

5960 ■ Swensrud Teacher Fellowships at MHS (Massachusetts Historical Society) *(Professional development/Fellowship)*

Purpose: To support the public and/or parochial school teachers and library media specialists. **Focus:** English language and literature; History, American. **Qualif.:** Applicants must be any K-12 teachers with a serious interest in using the collections at the MHS to prepare primary-source-based curricula, supported by documents and visual aids, in the fields of American history, world history or English/language arts. **Criteria:** Awards will be made on the strength of: project design; the plan for using MHS collections; the creativity of the proposed classroom activities; usability in other classrooms; recommendations.

Funds Avail.: $4,000. **Number Awarded:** 3. **To Apply:** Applicants must provide the following materials: a current resume; a letter of intent (no longer than two pages, single spaced) outlining the topic of interest, as well as the scope and goals of the proposed curriculum project; a list of potential primary source materials to be used; a letter of support from the school principal or department head. **Deadline:** February 28. **Contact:** Kathleen Barker, Assistant Dir. of Education, at 617-646-0557; education@masshist.org.

Awards are arranged alphabetically below their administering organizations

5961 ■ Massachusetts LGBTQ Bar Association (MLGBA)

c/o Boston Bar Assn.
16 Beacon St.
Boston, MA 02108
E-mail: administrator@masslgbtqbar.org
URL: www.masslgbtqbar.org

5962 ■ Alexander G. Gray, Jr. Scholarships
(Graduate/Scholarship)

Purpose: To help law students defray the costs of their legal education. **Focus:** Law. **Qualif.:** Applicant must be a law student who demonstrates a commitment to and involvement in the LGBT community, as well as leadership, maturity and responsibility. **Criteria:** Selection is based on the application.

Funds Avail.: $2,500. **Duration:** Annual. **Number Awarded:** 1. **To Apply:** Applicants may contact Gray Scholarship Committee Chair for the application information. **Deadline:** February 17. **Contact:** Rob Quinan; Email: Robert.Quinan@state.ma.us.

5963 ■ Massachusetts Office of Student Financial Assistance

454 Broadway, Ste. 200
Revere, MA 02151-3050
Ph: (617)391-6070
Fax: (617)727-0667
E-mail: osfa@osfa.mass.edu
URL: www.osfa.mass.edu

5964 ■ Early Childhood Educators Scholarship Program *(Undergraduate/Scholarship)*

Purpose: To provide financial assistance for currently employed early childhood and out of school time educators and providers who enroll in an associate's or bachelor's degree program in Early Childhood Education or related programs. **Focus:** Education, Early childhood; Psychology; Sociology. **Qualif.:** Applicants must be permanent legal residents of Massachusetts; United States citizens or eligible non-citizens; eligible under Title IV Regulations and not in default of a state or federal education loan or grant; enrolled, as matriculated students without a bachelor's degree, in an undergraduate degree program (full- or part-time) in early childhood education or a related field (i.e., elementary education, sociology, psychology); employed as early childhood educators or licensed family child care providers in Massachusetts for at least one year; and must continue employment while enrolled in the required degree program. **Criteria:** Applicants are evaluated based on academic achievement and financial need.

Funds Avail.: Varies. **Duration:** Annual. **Number Awarded:** Varies. **To Apply:** Application process is via online. Visit the program website for further information regarding the online application procedures. **Contact:** Massachusetts Office of Student Financial Assistance at the above address.

5965 ■ Massachusetts State Automobile Dealers Association (MSADA)

1 McKinley Sq., 6th Fl.
Boston, MA 02109
Ph: (617)451-1051
Fax: (617)451-9309

URL: www.msada.org

5966 ■ Automotive Technician Scholarship Program *(Undergraduate/Scholarship)*

Purpose: To enrich the lives of auto tech students through scholarships. **Focus:** Automotive technology. **Qualif.:** Applicants must be retraining for a career change or a recent high school graduate. Applicants must be enrolled in an automotive program at an accredited college. **Criteria:** Recipients will be selected based on academic standing and financial need.

Funds Avail.: $6,000 - $13,000. **Duration:** Annual; 2 years. **Number Awarded:** Varies. **To Apply:** Applicants must complete the provided application form which can be downloaded from the program website. Such must be submitted together with the other prescribed requirements. Other procedures must also be followed and complied with. **Deadline:** May 22. **Remarks:** Established in 2003. **Contact:** Jean Fabrizio at: jfabrizio@msada.org.

5967 ■ Master Brewers Association of the Americas (MBAA)

3340 Pilot Knob Rd.
Saint Paul, MN 55121
Ph: (651)454-7250
Fax: (651)454-0766
E-mail: mbaa@mbaa.com
URL: www.mbaa.com

5968 ■ William A. Hipp Scholarships *(All/Scholarship)*

Purpose: To provide funds for MBAA members who wish to further their education in either MBAA Brewing and Malting Science Course or the MBAA Brewery Packaging Technology Course. **Focus:** Food science and technology. **Qualif.:** Applicants must be members of the MBAA and possess a minimum of five years of service in brewing or malting industry. **Criteria:** Recipients are selected based on the application materials submitted.

Funds Avail.: No specific amount. **To Apply:** Applicants must complete an application form; and obtain the endorsement from two Professional members who will sign the application.

5969 ■ Material Handling Industry (MHI)

8720 Red Oak Blvd., Ste. 201
Charlotte, NC 28217-3996
Ph: (704)676-1190
Fax: (704)676-1199
Free: 800-345-1815
E-mail: jnofsinger@mhia.org
URL: www.mhia.org

5970 ■ Material Handling Education Foundation Scholarships *(Doctorate, Graduate, Undergraduate/Scholarship)*

Purpose: To promote the study of material handling and to expose as many students as possible to the material handling industry, including the vast array of equipment, systems and technologies represented by the industry; the role material handling in a productive enterprise; and career paths available within the supplier, distributor and end-user (applications) sides of the industry. **Focus:** Education,

Awards are arranged alphabetically below their administering organizations

Industrial. **Qualif.:** Applicants must be enrolled, or intending to enroll, in either an undergraduate, four-year baccalaureate program or a post graduate programs leading to masters or Ph.D. degree at a pre-qualified institution. Undergraduates must have completed at least two years of their undergraduate education. Students from junior and community colleges or other two-year post secondary institutions are also encouraged to apply if they have been accepted as transfer students to four-year programs; have maintained "B" overall grade point average and be full-time students; enrolled with courses like civil, electrical, industrial and mechanical engineering (and engineering technology); computer engineering; computer science; and business administration with an emphasis in production management, industrial distribution and/or logistics in an accredited and pre-qualified program of study with the resources and means to support the study of material handling and material handling related subjects either through formal course work, independent study, summer work or coop experience, industry internships or some combination of same. **Criteria:** Candidates will be evaluated based on criteria.

Funds Avail.: No amount mentioned. **To Apply:** Applicants must name a primary faculty contact willing to assist in the preparation and submission of the scholarship application; must submit three letters of recommendation; official transcripts of all academic work completed beyond high school; and completed scholarship application. **Deadline:** March 15. **Contact:** Donna Varner at dvarner@mhi.org or 704-676-1190.

5971 ■ Materials Information Society

ASM International
9639 Kinsman Rd.
Materials Park, OH 44073-0002
Ph: (440)338-5151
Fax: (440)338-4634
Free: 800-336-5152
E-mail: customerservice@asminternational.org
URL: www.asminternational.org

5972 ■ Edward J. Dulis Scholarships
(Undergraduate/Scholarship)

Purpose: To encourage and support capable students with interest and potential in the field of metallurgy/materials engineering and related careers. **Focus:** Metallurgy. **Qualif.:** Applicants must be material advantage members; must have an intended major in metallurgy or material science engineering; and have completed at least one year of college. **Criteria:** Recipients are selected based on academic achievement, interest in the field and personal qualities.

Funds Avail.: $1,500. **Duration:** Annual. **Number Awarded:** 1. **To Apply:** Applicants must complete the application form; must write a personal statement (maximum of two pages); must submit a resume, copy of the current academic transcript, completed undergraduate scholarship recommendation form and must include a photograph for publication. Applicants must complete the personal statement with a financial aid officer contact. **Remarks:** Established in 2003.

5973 ■ John M. Haniak Scholarships
(Undergraduate/Scholarship)

Purpose: To encourage and support capable students with interest and potential in the field of metallurgy/materials engineering and related careers. **Focus:** Metallurgy. **Qua-**

lif.: Applicants must be material advantage members; must have an intended major in metallurgy or material science engineering. Applicants must have completed at least one year of college. **Criteria:** Recipients are selected based on academic achievement, interest in the field and personal qualities.

Funds Avail.: $1,500. **Duration:** Annual. **Number Awarded:** 1. **To Apply:** Applicants must complete the application form; must write a personal statement (maximum of two pages); must submit a resume, copy of the current academic transcript, completed undergraduate scholarship recommendation form and must include a photograph for publication. Applicants must complete the personal statement with a financial aid officer contact. **Remarks:** Established in 2003.

5974 ■ Materials Information Society National Merit Scholarships *(Undergraduate/Scholarship)*

Purpose: To encourage and support capable students with interest and potential in the field of metallurgy/materials engineering and related careers. **Focus:** Metallurgy. **Qualif.:** Applicants must be material advantage members; must have an intended major in metallurgy or material science engineering; and have completed at least one year of college. **Criteria:** Recipients are selected based on academic achievement, interest in the field and personal qualities.

Funds Avail.: $1,000. **Duration:** Annual. **Number Awarded:** 1. **To Apply:** Applicants must complete the application form; must write a maximum of two pages personal statement; must submit a resume, copy of the current academic transcript; a completed undergraduate scholarship recommendation form and must include a photograph for publication. Applicants must complete the personal statement with a financial aid officer contact.

5975 ■ William Park Woodside Founder's Scholarships *(Undergraduate/Scholarship)*

Purpose: To encourage and support capable students with interest and potential in the field of metallurgy/materials engineering and related careers. **Focus:** Metallurgy. **Qualif.:** Applicants must be material advantage members; must have an intended major in metallurgy or material science engineering; and have completed at least one year of college. **Criteria:** Recipients are selected based on academic achievement, interest in the field and personal qualities.

Funds Avail.: Maximum amount of $10,000. **Duration:** 1 year. **To Apply:** Applicants must complete the application form; must write a two-page personal statement; must submit a resume, copy of the current academic transcript, completed undergraduate scholarship recommendation form and must include a photograph for publication. Applicants must complete the personal statement with a financial aid officer contact. **Remarks:** Established in 1996.

5976 ■ George A. Roberts Scholarships
(Undergraduate/Scholarship)

Purpose: To encourage and support capable students with interest and potential in the field of metallurgy/materials engineering and related careers. **Focus:** Metallurgy. **Qualif.:** Applicants must be material advantage members; must have an intended major in metallurgy or material science engineering; and have completed at least one year of college. **Criteria:** Recipients are selected based on academic achievement, interest in the field and personal qualities.

Funds Avail.: $6,000. **Duration:** Annual. **Number Awarded:** 7. **To Apply:** Applicants must complete the ap-

Awards are arranged alphabetically below their administering organizations

plication form; must write a two-page personal statement; must submit a resume, copy of the current academic transcript, completed undergraduate scholarship recommendation form and must include a photograph for publication. Applicants must complete the personal statement with a financial officer contact. **Remarks:** Established in 1995.

5977 ■ Lucille and Charles A. Wert Scholarships
(Undergraduate/Scholarship)

Purpose: To encourage and support capable students with interest and potential in the field of metallurgy/materials engineering and related careers. **Focus:** Metallurgy. **Qualif.:** Applicants must be material advantage members; must have an intended major in metallurgy or material science engineering; and have completed at least one year of college. **Criteria:** Recipients are selected based on academic achievement, interest in the field and personal qualities.

Funds Avail.: $10,000. **Duration:** 1 year. **To Apply:** Applicants must complete the application form; must write a personal statement (maximum of two pages); must submit a resume, copy of the current academic transcript, completed undergraduate scholarship recommendation form and must include a photograph for publication. Applicants must complete the personal statement with a financial aid officer contact. **Remarks:** Established in 2006.

5978 ■ Max Bell Foundation
1201 5th St. SW Ste. 380
Calgary, AB, Canada T2R 0Y6
Ph: (403)215-7310
Fax: (403)215-7319
URL: www.maxbell.org

5979 ■ Max Bell Senior Fellow Grants *(Advanced Professional/Grant)*

Purpose: To add value to debates over critical public policy issues in health and wellness, education and environment. **Focus:** Environmental science; Health education; Public health. **Qualif.:** Candidates must be Canadian residents or eligible for retention in keeping with Canadian charitable law. **Criteria:** Selection of recipients will be based on the application.

Funds Avail.: Amount varies. **Duration:** Annual. **Number Awarded:** 1. **To Apply:** Candidates must follow the application process described on the "Apply For Support" page at the program website and indicate in the project title that they are applying for the Senior Fellow grant. The Foundation will review their Letter of Intent and contact them to follow up. Where warranted, they will be asked to develop a full proposal and will be interviewed in person by a Committee of the Board of Directors.

5980 ■ Edmund F. Maxwell Foundation
PO Box 55548
Seattle, WA 98155-0548
E-mail: admin@maxwell.org
URL: www.maxwell.org

5981 ■ Edmund F. Maxwell Scholarships
(Undergraduate/Scholarship)

Purpose: To provide assistance to those who have demonstrated financial need and have shown ability, aptitude and a promise of useful citizenship. **Focus:** General studies/Field of study not specified. **Qualif.:** Applicant

must be planning to attend an accredited independent college/university as freshman; a resident of Western Washington; and have a combined math and reading SAT score of over 1200. **Criteria:** Award is given based on merit.

Funds Avail.: Up to $5,000. **Duration:** Up to 4 years. **To Apply:** Applicants must submit a completed scholarship application along with the 500-word essay; official, certified high school transcript; certification of SAT/ACT scores; and financial aid worksheet (to be completed by each College/University); applicants must also submit a Free Application for Student Aid form (FAFSA) to the institution that they are planning to attend. **Deadline:** April 30.

5982 ■ Ronald McDonald House Charities (RMHC)
One Kroc Dr.
Oak Brook, IL 60523
Ph: (630)623-7048
Fax: (630)623-7488
E-mail: info@rmhc.org
URL: www.rmhc.org

5983 ■ Ronald McDonald House Charities African American Future Achievers Scholarships
(Undergraduate/Scholarship)

Purpose: To help high school seniors attend college. **Focus:** General studies/Field of study not specified. **Qualif.:** Applicants must be high school seniors; must be younger than 21 years old; must be eligible to attend a two- or four-year college or university with a full course of study; must be legal residents of the United States; must be living in a participating local RMHS Chapter's geographic area; and must have at least one parent of African American or Black Caribbean heritage. **Criteria:** Recipients are selected based on academic performance.

Funds Avail.: No specific amount. **To Apply:** Applicants must complete the application form. **Contact:** International Scholarship and Tuition Services, Inc. (ISTS) via email at RMHC@applyists.com.

5984 ■ Ronald McDonald House Charities of Hispanic Heritage *(Undergraduate/Scholarship)*

Purpose: To help high school seniors to attend college. **Focus:** General studies/Field of study not specified. **Qualif.:** Applicants must be high school seniors; must be younger than 21 years old; must be eligible to attend a two- or four-year college or university with a full course of study; must be legal residents of the United States; must be living in a participating local RMHS Chapter's geographic area; and must have at least one parent of Hispanic heritage. **Criteria:** Recipients are selected based on academic performance.

Funds Avail.: No specific amount. **To Apply:** Applicants must complete the application form. **Contact:** Contact International Scholarship and Tuition Services, Inc. (ISTS) via email at RMHC@applyists.com (Subject Line: RMHC).

5985 ■ Ronald McDonald House Charities Scholarships in Asia *(Undergraduate/Scholarship)*

Purpose: To help high school seniors to attend college. **Focus:** General studies/Field of study not specified. **Qualif.:** Applicants must be high school seniors; must be younger than 21 years old; must be eligible to attend a two- or four-year college or university with a full course of study;

Awards are arranged alphabetically below their administering organizations

must be legal residents of the United States; must be living in a participating local RMHS Chapter's geographic area; and must have at least one parent of Asian/Pacific Islander heritage. **Criteria:** Recipients are selected based on academic performance.

Funds Avail.: No specific amount. **To Apply:** Applicants must complete the application form. **Contact:** International Scholarship and Tuition Services, Inc. (ISTS) via email at RMHC@applyists.com.

5986 ■ Ronald McDonald House Charities Scholarships (Undergraduate/Scholarship)

Purpose: To help high school seniors pursue educational goals. **Focus:** General studies/Field of study not specified. **Qualif.:** Applicants must be high school students. All students can apply regardless of race, color, creed, religion, sexual orientation, gender, disability or national origin. Applicants must be legal US residents and be less than 21 years of age and reside within the geographical boundaries of a participating chapter that offers scholarships. **Criteria:** Recipients are selected based on academic performance.

Funds Avail.: No specific amount. **To Apply:** Applicants must complete the application form. Applicants must also submit their transcript, personal statement, letter of recommendation, parent/guardian IRS Form 1040. **Contact:** International Scholarship and Tuition Services, Inc. (ISTS) via email at RMHC@applyists.com.

5987 ■ McDonald's Corp.
2111 McDonald
Oak Brook, IL 60523
Ph: (630)623-3000
Fax: (630)623-5004
Free: 800-244-6227
E-mail: mcdbod@us.mcd.com
URL: www.mcdonalds.com

5988 ■ McDonald's USA National Employee Scholarship Program (Undergraduate/Scholarship)

Purpose: To recognize and support the McDonald's USA student-employees who are pursuing their education while working. **Focus:** General studies/Field of study not specified. **Qualif.:** Applicants must be student employees of any McDonald's branch. Returning college students who attend school part time are highly encouraged to apply. **Criteria:** Recipients are selected based on documented academic achievement, community involvement and job performance.

Funds Avail.: No specific amount. **Duration:** Annual. **To Apply:** Application details depends on the bestowing organization.

5989 ■ Richard D. McDonough Golf Scholarship Foundation
61 N St.
Manchester, NH 03104
Ph: (603)785-3766
E-mail: mcdonoughapplication@comcast.net
URL: mcdonough.nhgolf.com

5990 ■ Dr. George T. Bottomley Scholarships (Undergraduate/Scholarship)

Purpose: To support outstanding young men and women employed at New Hampshire golf courses in pursuing higher education. **Focus:** General studies/Field of study not specified. **Qualif.:** Applicant must have a minimum of 2 summers of successful work at a NH golf course as a caddie, in the Pro Shop, on the grounds crew, or in the clubhouse; must be a high school graduate at an accredited school; have a minimum GPA of 2.5 on a 4.0 scale; demonstrate promise of academic success; must be from the Seacoast area; and have financial need. **Criteria:** Award is given based on submitted scholarship application.

Funds Avail.: No specific amount. **Duration:** Annual. **To Apply:** Applicants must be recommended by the golf club where they have been employed for a minimum of two seasons. Applicants must submit a completed scholarship application; official copy of high school transcript; a copy of acceptance letter; a copy of FAFSA form. **Deadline:** June 15. **Contact:** McDonoughApplication@comcast.net.

5991 ■ Dr. Robert Elliott Memorial Scholarships (Undergraduate/Scholarship)

Purpose: To support outstanding young men and women employed at New Hampshire golf courses in pursuing higher education. **Focus:** General studies/Field of study not specified. **Qualif.:** Applicant must have a minimum of 2 summers of successful work at a NH golf course as a caddie, in the Pro Shop, on the grounds crew, or in the clubhouse; must be a high school graduate at an accredited school; have a minimum GPA of 2.5 on a 4.0 scale; must be of proven character, integrity, and citizenship. **Criteria:** Award is given to student with the highest cumulative GPA in their college work.

Funds Avail.: No specific amount. **Duration:** Annual. **To Apply:** Applicants must be recommended by the golf club where they have been employed for a minimum of two seasons. Applicants must submit a completed scholarship application; an official copy of high school transcript; a copy of acceptance letter; and a copy of FAFSA form. **Deadline:** June 15. **Contact:** McDonoughApplication@comcast.net.

5992 ■ Pauline Elliott Scholarships (Undergraduate/Scholarship)

Purpose: To support outstanding young men and women employed at New Hampshire golf courses in pursuing higher education. **Focus:** General studies/Field of study not specified. **Qualif.:** Applicants must have a minimum of 2 summers of successful work at a NH golf course as a caddie, in the Pro Shop, on the grounds crew, or in the clubhouse; must be high school graduates from an accredited school; must have a minimum GPA of 2.5 on a 4.0 scale; must be of proven character, integrity, and citizenship. **Criteria:** Award will be given based on the submitted scholarship application.

Funds Avail.: No specific amount. **Duration:** Annual. **To Apply:** Applicants must be recommended by the golf club where they have been employed for a minimum of two seasons. Applicants must submit a completed scholarship application; an official copy of high school transcript; a copy of acceptance letter; a copy of FAFSA form. **Deadline:** June 15. **Contact:** McDonoughApplication@comcast.net.

5993 ■ Robert C. Erb Sr. Scholarships (Undergraduate/Scholarship)

Purpose: To support outstanding young men and women employed at New Hampshire golf courses in pursuing higher education. **Focus:** General studies/Field of study not specified. **Qualif.:** Applicant must have a minimum of 2 summers of successful work at a NH golf course as a caddie, in the Pro Shop, on the grounds crew, or in the

Awards are arranged alphabetically below their administering organizations

clubhouse; must be a high school graduate at an accredited school; have a minimum GPA of 2.5 on a 4.0 scale; demonstrate promise of academic success; and have financial need. **Criteria:** Award is given based on submitted scholarship application.

Funds Avail.: No specific amount. **Duration:** Annual. **To Apply:** Applicant must be recommended by the golf club where they have been employed for a minimum of two seasons. Applicant must submit a completed scholarship application; an official copy of high school transcript; a copy of acceptance letter; and a copy of FAFSA form. **Deadline:** June 15. **Contact:** McDonoughApplication@comcast.net.

5994 ■ Phil Friel Scholarships *(Undergraduate/ Scholarship)*

Purpose: To support outstanding young men and women employed at New Hampshire golf courses in pursuing higher education. **Focus:** General studies/Field of study not specified. **Qualif.:** Applicants must have a minimum of 2 summers of successful work at a NH golf course as a caddie, in the Pro Shop, on the grounds crew, or in the clubhouse; must be high school graduates from an accredited school; must have a minimum GPA of 2.5 on a 4.0 scale; must demonstrate promise of academic success; must be pursuing a career in the golf industry; and have financial need. **Criteria:** Award will be given based on submitted scholarship application.

Funds Avail.: No specific amount. **Duration:** Annual. **To Apply:** Applicants must be recommended by the golf club where they have been employed for a minimum of two seasons. Applicants must submit a completed scholarship application; an official copy of high school transcript; a copy of acceptance letter; and a copy of FAFSA form. **Deadline:** June 15. **Contact:** McDonoughApplication@comcast.net.

5995 ■ Alex Gissler Memorial Scholarships *(Undergraduate/Scholarship)*

Purpose: To support outstanding young men and women employed at 45 New Hampshire golf courses in pursuing higher education. **Focus:** General studies/Field of study not specified. **Qualif.:** Applicant must have a minimum of 2 summers of successful work at a NH golf course as a caddie, in the Pro Shop, on the grounds crew, or in the clubhouse; must be a high school graduate at an accredited school; have a minimum GPA of 2.5 on a 4.0 scale; demonstrate promise of academic success; work at Baker Hill Golf Club; and have financial need. **Criteria:** Award is given based on submitted scholarship application.

Funds Avail.: No specific amount. **Duration:** Annual. **To Apply:** Applicants must be recommended by the golf club where they have been employed for a minimum of two seasons. Applicants must submit a completed scholarship application; an official copy of high school transcript; a copy of acceptance letter; and a copy of FAFSA form. **Deadline:** June 15. **Contact:** McDonoughApplication@comcast.net.

5996 ■ Stan Lencki Scholarships *(Undergraduate/ Scholarship)*

Purpose: To support outstanding young men and women employed at New Hampshire golf courses in pursuing higher education. **Focus:** General studies/Field of study not specified. **Qualif.:** Applicants must have a minimum of 2 summers of successful work at a NH golf course as a caddie, in the Pro Shop, on the grounds crew, or in the clubhouse; must be high school graduates at an accredited school; have a minimum GPA of 2.5 on a 4.0 scale; demonstrate promise of academic success; and have

financial need. **Criteria:** Award is given based on submitted scholarship application.

Funds Avail.: No specific amount. **Duration:** Annual. **To Apply:** Applicants must be recommended by the golf club where they have been employed for a minimum of two seasons. Applicants must submit a completed scholarship application; an official copy of high school transcript; a copy of acceptance letter; and a copy of FAFSA form. **Deadline:** June 15. **Contact:** McDonoughApplication@comcast.net.

5997 ■ Rick Mahoney Scholarships *(Undergraduate/ Scholarship)*

Purpose: To support outstanding young men and women employed at New Hampshire golf courses in pursuing higher education. **Focus:** General studies/Field of study not specified. **Qualif.:** Applicant must have a minimum of 2 summers of successful work at a NH golf course as a caddie, in the Pro Shop, on the grounds crew, or in the clubhouse; must be a high school graduate at an accredited school; have a minimum GPA of 2.5 on a 4.0 scale; demonstrate promise of academic success; be resident of Nashua, NH; and have financial need. **Criteria:** Award is given based on submitted scholarship application.

Funds Avail.: No specific amount. **Duration:** Annual. **To Apply:** Applicants must be recommended by the golf club where they have been employed for a minimum of two seasons. Applicants must submit a completed scholarship application; an official copy of high school transcript; a copy of acceptance letter; and a copy of FAFSA form. **Deadline:** June 15. **Contact:** McDonoughApplication@comcast.net.

5998 ■ NHPGA Apprentice Scholarships *(Undergraduate/Scholarship)*

Purpose: To support outstanding young men and women employed at New Hampshire golf courses in pursuing higher education. **Focus:** General studies/Field of study not specified. **Qualif.:** Applicant must have a minimum of 2 summers of successful work at a NH golf course as a caddie, in the Pro Shop, on the grounds crew, or in the clubhouse; must be a high school graduate at an accredited school; have a minimum GPA of 2.5 on a 4.0 scale; demonstrate promise of academic success; and have financial need. **Criteria:** Award is given based on submitted scholarship application.

Funds Avail.: No specific amount. **Duration:** Annual. **To Apply:** Applicants must be recommended by the golf club where they have been employed for a minimum of two seasons. Applicants must submit a completed scholarship application; an official copy of high school transcript; a copy of acceptance letter; and a copy of FAFSA form. **Deadline:** June 15. **Contact:** McDonoughApplication@comcast.net.

5999 ■ Walter T. Philippy Scholarships *(Undergraduate/Scholarship)*

Purpose: To support outstanding young men and women employed at New Hampshire golf courses in pursuing higher education. **Focus:** General studies/Field of study not specified. **Qualif.:** Applicant must have a minimum of 2 summers of successful work at a NH golf course as a caddie, in the Pro Shop, on the grounds crew, or in the clubhouse; must be a high school graduate at an accredited school; have a minimum GPA of 2.5 on a 4.0 scale; demonstrate promise of academic success; must be employed at Derryfield Country Club or a Manchester, NH, golf course; and must have financial need. **Criteria:** Award is given based on submitted scholarship application.

Funds Avail.: No specific amount. **Duration:** Annual. **To**

Awards are arranged alphabetically below their administering organizations

Apply: Applicants must be recommended by the golf club where they have been employed for a minimum of two seasons. Applicants must submit a completed scholarship application; an official copy of high school transcript; a copy of acceptance letter; and a copy of FAFSA form. **Deadline:** June 15. **Contact:** McDMcDonoughApplication@comcast.net.

6000 ■ David J. Pollini Scholarships (Undergraduate/Scholarship)

Purpose: To support outstanding young men and women employed at New Hampshire golf courses in pursuing higher education. **Focus:** General studies/Field of study not specified. **Qualif.:** Applicant must have a minimum of 2 summers of successful work at a NH golf course as a caddie, in the Pro Shop, on the grounds crew, or in the clubhouse; must be a high school graduate at an accredited school; have a minimum GPA of 2.5 on a 4.0 scale; demonstrate promise of academic success; must be an employee of Kingswood Golf Club or Lakes Region golf course; and have financial need. **Criteria:** Award is given based on submitted scholarship application.

Funds Avail.: No specific amount. **Duration:** Annual. **To Apply:** Applicants must be recommended by the golf club where they have been employed for a minimum of two seasons. Applicants must submit a completed scholarship application; an official copy of high school transcript; a copy of acceptance letter; and a copy of FAFSA form. **Deadline:** June 15. **Contact:** McDonoughApplication@comcast.net.

6001 ■ Pope Scholarship Awards (Undergraduate/Scholarship)

Purpose: To support outstanding young men and women employed at New Hampshire golf courses in pursuing higher education. **Focus:** General studies/Field of study not specified. **Qualif.:** Applicants must have a minimum of 2 summers of successful work at a NH golf course as a caddie, in the Pro Shop, on the grounds crew, or in the clubhouse; must be high school graduates at an accredited school; must have a minimum GPA of 2.5 on a 4.0 scale; must be of proven character, integrity, and citizenship. **Criteria:** Award is given based on the submitted scholarship application.

Funds Avail.: No specific amount. **Duration:** Annual. **To Apply:** Applicants must be recommended by the golf club where they have been employed for a minimum of two seasons. Applicants must submit a completed scholarship application; an official copy of high school transcript; a copy of acceptance letter; and a copy of FAFSA form. **Deadline:** June 15. **Contact:** McDonoughApplication@comcast.net.

6002 ■ Jim Sheerin Scholarships (Undergraduate/Scholarship)

Purpose: To support outstanding young men and women employed at New Hampshire golf courses in pursuing higher education. **Focus:** General studies/Field of study not specified. **Qualif.:** Applicant must have a minimum of 2 summers of successful work at a NH golf course as a caddie, in the Pro Shop, on the grounds crew, or in the clubhouse; must be a high school graduate from an accredited school; have a minimum GPA of 2.5 on a 4.0 scale; demonstrate promise of academic success; must be employed at Abenaqui Country Club or at a Seacoast-area golf course; and have financial need. **Criteria:** Award is given based on submitted scholarship application.

Funds Avail.: No specific amount. **Duration:** Annual. **To Apply:** Applicants must be recommended by the golf club

where they have been employed for a minimum of two seasons. Applicants must submit a completed scholarship application; copy of high school transcript; copy of acceptance; a copy of FAFSA form. **Deadline:** June 15. **Contact:** McDonoughApplication@comcast.net.

6003 ■ William H. McGannon Foundation

c/o Joseph Restoule, President
6093 Signal Ridge Heights SW
Calgary, AB, Canada T3H 2P1
Ph: (403)242-7939
URL: www.mcgannonfoundation.ca

6004 ■ William H. McGannon Foundation Scholarships (Graduate, Undergraduate/Scholarship)

Purpose: To provide financial assistance to students enrolled in risk management or other insurance disciplines. **Focus:** Insurance and insurance-related fields; Risk management. **Qualif.:** Applicant must be a full time student at a university (undergraduate or postgraduate) or college; must be enrolled in a risk management or insurance discipline; must be a Canadian citizen or permanent resident of Canada; must have a GPA of 3.0 or higher. **Criteria:** Recipients will be selected by the following criteria: (1) career objective in risk management; (2) academic achievement; (3) community/volunteer involvement; (4) leadership skills; and (5) work related experience. Scholarship is based on merit and does not discriminate on the basis of race, color, sex, religion, age or handicap.

Funds Avail.: No specific amount. **To Apply:** Applicants must submit a completed scholarship application form. **Deadline:** November 30. **Contact:** Joe Restoule; Email at jrestoule@shaw.ca.

6005 ■ McGill University

James Administration Bldg.
845 Sherbrooke St. W
Montreal, QC, Canada H3A 0G4
Ph: (514)398-4455
E-mail: info.communications@mcgill.ca
URL: www.mcgill.ca

6006 ■ Mackenzie King Open Scholarships (Graduate/Scholarship)

Purpose: To provide support for graduating students to pursue their education. **Focus:** General studies/Field of study not specified. **Qualif.:** Applicant must be a graduate of any Canadian university for full-time postgraduate studies in Canada; must be an undergraduate applicant with first Class Honours Standing (CGPA of 3.7 or higher - 3.5 for Law); and must have "straight A" records. **Criteria:** Awards will be based on high academic achievements; personal qualities; and demonstrated aptitudes. Consideration will also be given to the applicant's proposed program of study.

Funds Avail.: $9,000. **Number Awarded:** 1. **To Apply:** Applicant must complete the application form available in the website at www.mkingscholarships.ca; must have three letters of reference from persons who have an initiate knowledge of the record and ability of the applicant and able to give a critical evaluation of their plans for graduate study; must have the official transcript of records and other academic records from each university they have attended. **Deadline:** February 1. **Contact:** Application forms and

Awards are arranged alphabetically below their administering organizations

other supporting documents should be sent to J. Blom, Curtis Bldg., 1822 E Mall, University of British Columbia, Vancouver, BC V6T 1Z1.

6007 ■ Mackenzie King Travelling Scholarships
(Graduate/Scholarship)

Purpose: To provide support for deserving students intending to pursue their studies in the United States or the United Kingdom in the areas of international relations and industrial relations. **Focus:** Industrial and labor relations; International affairs and relations. **Qualif.:** Applicant must be a graduate of any Canadian university who wants to pursue graduate studies in the United States or the United Kingdom in international or industrial relations. **Criteria:** Awards are based on academic achievement, personal qualities and demonstrated aptitudes, as well as proposed program of study. Consideration will be given to an undergraduate applicant with First Class Honours Standing (CGPA of 3.7 or higher - 3.5 for Law) and graduate applicants with cumulative "straight A" records.

Funds Avail.: $10,500. **Duration:** Annual. **Number Awarded:** 4. **To Apply:** Applicant must complete the application form available in the website at www.mkingscholarships.ca; must have three letters of reference from persons who have an initiate knowledge of the record and ability of the applicant and able to give a critical evaluation of their plans for graduate study; must have the official transcript of records and other academic records from each university they have attended. **Deadline:** February 2. **Contact:** Application form and other supporting documents should be sent to: J. Blom, Curtis Bldg. 1822 E Mall, University of British Columbia, Vancouver, BC V6T 1Z1.

6008 ■ Philip F. Vineberg Travelling Fellowships in the Humanities *(Undergraduate/Scholarship)*

Purpose: To provide financial support to a qualified individual who wants to pursue their education. **Focus:** Art; Education; Education, Religious; Law; Library and archival sciences; Music; Social work. **Qualif.:** Applicant must be a registered student at McGill in a degree program in Arts, Education, Law, Library Science, Music, Religious Studies or Social Work. **Criteria:** Selection of applicant will be based on his/her academic achievements and personal qualities.

Funds Avail.: $14,500. **Duration:** One academic year. **To Apply:** Application forms are available online at www.mkingscholarships.ca. Applicant must have a three letters of reference from persons who have an initiate knowledge of the record and ability of the applicant and able to give a critical evaluation of their plans for graduate study; must have the official transcript of records and other academic records from each university they have attended. **Deadline:** February 1. **Remarks:** Established in 1988.

6009 ■ McKelvey Foundation
PO Box 1195
Greenwich, CT 06830
Ph: (212)847-7236
E-mail: info@mckelveyfoundation.org
URL: www.mckelveyfoundation.org

6010 ■ McKelvey Scholarships *(Undergraduate/Scholarship)*

Purpose: To financially support the education of a student who is first in the family to pursue a college education. **Focus:** General studies/Field of study not specified. **Qua-**

lif.: Applicant must attend a partnering high school in the states of NY, PA or WV; be the first generation to attend college (neither mother nor father went to college); have financial need; show involvement in work and/or extracurricular activities; plan to attend a four-year college within home state; and maintain a 2.5 GPA. **Criteria:** Awards are given based on need.

Funds Avail.: No specific amount. **To Apply:** Applicants must submit a completed online scholarship application.

6011 ■ MCRD Museum Foundation
PO Box 400085
San Diego, CA 92140-0085
Ph: (619)524-4426
Fax: (619)524-0076
E-mail: lstuart@mcrdmhs.org
URL: www.mcrdmuseumhistoricalsociety.org

6012 ■ Colonel Nate Smith Memorial Scholarships
(Graduate, Undergraduate/Scholarship)

Purpose: To provide educational assistance for MCRD San Diego enlisted marines or sailors and their dependents that are enrolled in an accredited graduate or undergraduate college program. **Focus:** Military science and education. **Qualif.:** Applicants must be enlisted active duty marines or sailors currently assigned to MCRD San Diego/Western Recruiting Region or their dependents; must be high school graduates and must provide a proof of enrollment in a postsecondary program, or have previously attended college. **Criteria:** Applicants are evaluated based on academic performance, community and/or extracurricular activities and future potentials.

Funds Avail.: $1,000. **Duration:** Annual. **Number Awarded:** 3. **To Apply:** Applicants must submit letters of recommendation from a high school, college counselor, teacher, community, or church leader and must prepare a narrative statement.

6013 ■ The Medalist Club
PO Box 71996
Tuscaloosa, AL 35407
E-mail: membership@gymtide.com
URL: www.gymtide.com

6014 ■ The Medalist Club Post Graduate Scholarships *(Postgraduate/Scholarship)*

Purpose: To support former student athletes in their educational pursuits. **Focus:** General studies/Field of study not specified. **Qualif.:** Applicants must be former University of Alabama athletes who have contributed to the success of the Alabama gymnastics program; must hold a Bachelor's Degree from the University of Alabama; must be accepted to, or be currently enrolled in, a graduate degree program at the University of Alabama; must have a minimum undergraduate GPA of 3.0. **Criteria:** Scholarship Committee will do the final award decisions via a majority vote.

Funds Avail.: Varies. **To Apply:** Applicants must complete and submit the application form available online together with two letters of recommendation, current resume, copy of letter of acceptance to graduate degree program, and University of Alabama undergraduate transcripts. **Deadline:** March 15; November 1.

6015 ■ Medex Biocare Pharmacy L.L.C.
8024 Stage Hills Blvd., Ste. 107
Bartlett, TN 38133

Awards are arranged alphabetically below their administering organizations

Free: 800-962-6339
URL: www.medexbiocare.com

6016 ■ Education Factor Scholarships *(Graduate, Undergraduate/Scholarship)*

Purpose: To provide financial assistance to students living with hemophilia or other bleeding disorder. **Focus:** General studies/Field of study not specified. **Qualif.:** Applicants must have plan to attend an accredited college, private preparatory, graduate or vo-tech school; applicants must have minimum 2.0 GPA on a 4.0 scale; must be U.S. citizens with hemophilia (Factor VII, VIII or IX) or von Willebrand disease (verified by physician) and their immediate family members; must have verified ACT/SAT score (if available). **Criteria:** Selection will be based on application, essay, reference letters and community service.

Funds Avail.: $500 to $1,500. **Duration:** Annual. **To Apply:** Applicants must submit a completed application form; copy of school records to confirm a cumulative GPA of 2.0 or above on a 4.0 scale; 500-word typed essay on "My Academic Field of Study and Why I Chose It"; explanation of financial need in a maximum 100-word typed amplification separate from the required essay; two recommendation letters from teachers/employer; evidence of ongoing community service. **Deadline:** June 15.

6017 ■ Medford Rogue Rotary Club

PO Box 4002
Medford, OR 97501-0144
E-mail: pat.barry@southvalleybank.com
URL: www.medfordrogue.org

6018 ■ Medford Rogue Rotary Scholarship *(Undergraduate/Scholarship)*

Purpose: To financially support those students who are planning to attend Hillsdale College in Hillsdale, Michigan. **Focus:** General studies/Field of study not specified. **Qualif.:** Applicants must be high school graduating seniors from Phoenix, Medford, Central Point, and Eagle Point, including St. Mary's and Cascade Christian high schools. **Criteria:** Selection will be based on the committee's criteria.

Funds Avail.: $2,000 - $3,000. **Duration:** Annual. **To Apply:** Application information is available at Oregon Student Assistance Commission (OSAC).

6019 ■ Media Action Network for Asian Americans (MANAA)

PO Box 6188
Burbank, CA 91510-6188
Ph: (213)486-4433
E-mail: letters@manaa.org
URL: www.manaa.org

6020 ■ MANAA Media Scholarships *(Graduate, Undergraduate/Scholarship)*

Purpose: To promote education in filmmaking and in television production. **Focus:** Filmmaking; Radio and television. **Qualif.:** Applicants must be graduate or undergraduate students pursuing careers as filmmakers and in television production (not broadcast journalism). **Criteria:** Selected on the basis of their academic and personal merit, with the desire to uplift the image of Asian Americans in film and television.

Funds Avail.: $1000. **Number Awarded:** 1. **To Apply:** Ap-

plicants must submit a copy of all official transcripts; copy of completed financial aid documents; two letters of recommendation; a double-spaced essay (maximum of 1,000 words); and a work sample consisting of a short film or screenplay (optional). **Deadline:** October 30. **Remarks:** The scholarship was formed in 1992. **Contact:** scholarship@manaa.org.

6021 ■ Medical Group Management Association (MGMA)

104 Inverness Terr. E
Englewood, CO 80112-5306
Ph: (303)799-1111
Fax: (303)643-4439
Free: 877-275-6462
E-mail: service@mgma.com
URL: www.mgma.com

6022 ■ ACMPE Scholarship Fund Program *(Graduate, Undergraduate/Scholarship)*

Purpose: To support and promote healthcare leaders' personal and professional growth toward advancement of the profession. **Focus:** Health care services. **Qualif.:** Applicants must be students enrolled in an undergraduate or graduate degree program relevant to medical practice management, including public health, business administration, healthcare administration and other related areas. **Criteria:** Applicants will be evaluated by the ACMPE Scholarship Fund Program Committee.

Funds Avail.: $1,000 - $5,000. **Duration:** Annual. **To Apply:** Applicants must complete the online application and submit a recent unofficial academic transcript; a current resume; two reference letters; and for students recently accepted, documentation indicating acceptance into a graduate or undergraduate college or university. Recipients will be asked to provide a black and white photograph. **Deadline:** May 1. **Contact:** For more information, contact International Scholarship and Tuition Services at 800-310-4053.

6023 ■ Medical Library Association (MLA)

65 E Wacker Pl., Ste. 1900
Chicago, IL 60601-7246
Ph: (312)419-9094
Fax: (312)419-8950
E-mail: info@mlahq.org
URL: www.mlanet.org

6024 ■ HLS/MLA Professional Development Grants *(Other/Grant)*

Purpose: To provide librarians working in hospitals and similar clinical settings with the support needed for educational or research activities. **Focus:** Health sciences; Library and archival sciences. **Qualif.:** Applicant must has been employed as a health sciences librarian within the last year in either a hospital or other clinical care institution; must not have previously received an HLS/MLA Professional Development Award or any MLA grant, scholarship or other award within the past year; must be a member of the Hospital Libraries Sections/MLA. **Criteria:** Selection will be based on the submitted application and supporting documents.

Funds Avail.: No specific amount. **Duration:** Annual. **To Apply:** Applicant must submit an application form and

Awards are arranged alphabetically below their administering organizations

signed statement of terms and condition. Nine copies of the completed application and other documents should be provided. **Deadline:** December 1.

6025 ■ David A. Kronick Travelling Fellowships
(Doctorate/Fellowship)

Purpose: To cover the expenses involved in traveling to three or more medical libraries in the United States or Canada. **Focus:** Health care services; Management. **Qualif.:** Applicant must be a U.S. or Canadian citizen or have permanent residence status; member of the Medical Library Association; must have a graduate degree in library science; must be a practicing health sciences librarian with at least five years of professional experience. **Criteria:** Applicant and proposal will be selected based on merits and quality of materials submitted including originality and relevance.

Funds Avail.: $2,000. **To Apply:** Application forms are available at the website. Applicant must prepare a resume/CV; names of three references not related to the applicant; and a proposal containing: title, goals, objectives, methodology, significance and budget of project. Nine copies of completed application and supporting documents should be provided. **Deadline:** December 1. **Remarks:** Established in 2002.

6026 ■ Donald A.B. Lindberg Research Fellowships
(Doctorate, Graduate/Fellowship)

Purpose: To fund a research aimed at expanding the knowledge base used by librarians in improving health care and advances in biomedical research. **Focus:** Biomedical research; Health care services. **Qualif.:** Applicants must be sponsored by an institution or an organization; must be citizens of the United States or Canada; must have a bachelor's, master's, or doctor's degree or is enrolled in a degree program; must be committed to the health sciences. **Criteria:** Applications will be reviewed based on academic, scientific and technical specifications.

Funds Avail.: $10,000. **Duration:** Annual. **To Apply:** Applicants must submit an application electronically together with a curriculum vitae or biographical sketch; research proposal (5-10 pages) including background and rationale, research aims, budget, research design and methodology, timeline, and plans for disseminating the results; letters of support from the applicant's home institution or from sponsoring institutions or organizations. **Deadline:** November 15. **Remarks:** Established in 2003.

6027 ■ Medical Library Association Scholarships for Minority Students *(Graduate/Scholarship)*

Purpose: To support minority students who are pursuing to enter a Masters program. **Focus:** Health sciences; Library and archival sciences. **Qualif.:** Applicant must be a U.S. or Canadian citizen or have permanent residence status; a member of a minority group (African-American, Hispanic, Asian, Native American or Pacific Islander); entering an ALA-accredited graduate library school; must have completed no more than half of the graduate program. **Criteria:** Preference will be given to those who have not been a recipient of the award and based on their qualifications.

Funds Avail.: $5,000. **Duration:** Annual. **To Apply:** Applicant must submit an application form available at the website; (two-to-three) letters of reference from persons not related to the applicant; and an official transcript (sent directly by the respective institution to the MLA office); and statement of career objective. Nine copies of the completed application form and essay and single copy of all related

documents should be provided. **Deadline:** December 1.

6028 ■ MLA Continuing Education Awards (CE)
(Graduate/Grant)

Purpose: To support students in developing their knowledge of theoretical, administrative, or technical aspects of librarianship. **Focus:** Library and archival sciences. **Qualif.:** Applicant must hold a graduate degree in library science; must be a practicing health science librarian with at least two years of professional experience; a member of the MLA; a U.S. or Canadian citizen or have permanent residence status; must clearly identify a continuing education program within the United States or Canada. **Criteria:** Applicant with library experience and their professional activities are given consideration.

Funds Avail.: $100 to $500. **To Apply:** Application forms are available at the website. Applicant must complete seven copies of the application form and names of three references not related to the applicant.

6029 ■ MLA/NLM Spectrum Scholarship Program
(Undergraduate/Scholarship)

Purpose: To support students in their goals to become health sciences information professionals. **Focus:** Health sciences. **Qualif.:** Applicant must be of African American, Hispanic, Asian, Native American or Pacific Islander heritage attending an ALA-accredited library school. **Criteria:** Recipient is selected based on merit.

Funds Avail.: $6,500. **Duration:** Annual. **To Apply:** Applicants must contact ALA Spectrum program for scholarship information. **Deadline:** March 1.

6030 ■ MLA Research, Development, and Demonstration Project Grants *(Graduate/Grant)*

Purpose: To fund a research or project that promotes excellence in the field of health sciences librarianship. **Focus:** Health sciences; Library and archival sciences. **Qualif.:** Applicant must have a graduate degree in library science; should be a practicing health sciences librarian with at least two years of professional experience; an individual member of the Medical Library Association; a U.S. or Canadian citizen or has permanent residence status. **Criteria:** Recipients of the awards will be evaluated based on applicant's ability to meet the proposal criteria set by the Awards committee.

Funds Avail.: $100 to $1,000. **To Apply:** Applicant must submit a completed application form; names of three references; and project proposal. Proposals must contain title, goals, objectives, methodology, significance and budget. Nine copies of the completed application form and all related documents should be submitted provided. **Deadline:** December 1.

6031 ■ Thomson Reuters/MLA Doctoral Fellowships
(Doctorate/Fellowship)

Purpose: To foster and encourage superior students to conduct doctoral work in health sciences librarianship or information science by providing support to individuals who have been admitted to candidacy. **Focus:** Health sciences; Information science and technology; Library and archival sciences. **Qualif.:** Applicant must be a graduate of an ALA-accredited school of library science; a candidate in a Ph.D. program emphasizing on biomedical and health-related information science; and a U.S. or Canadian citizen of permanent residence status. **Criteria:** Preference is given to those applicants who have completed at least 75 percent

Awards are arranged alphabetically below their administering organizations

of their course work and dissertation prospectus either approved or in the approval process.

Funds Avail.: $2,000. **Duration:** Biennial. **To Apply:** Application form is available at the website. Applicant must prepare two letters of reference (submitted directly to MLA); transcript or proof of enrollment in the graduate program and list of completed courses (mailed directly to MLA); and the name, title, address, phone and email of doctoral advisor; an informative summary; detailed budget; and statement of career objectives. Applicant must submit nine copies of completed application and single copy of other supporting materials. **Deadline:** December 1.

6032 ■ Medieval Academy of America (MAA)
17 Dunster St., Ste. 202
Cambridge, MA 02138
Ph: (617)491-1622
Fax: (617)492-3303
E-mail: inf@themedievalacademy.org
URL: www.medievalacademy.org

6033 ■ Birgit Baldwin Fellowships *(Graduate/Fellowship)*

Purpose: To help defray research and living expenses for the equivalent of an academic year of study. **Focus:** Medieval studies. **Qualif.:** Applicant must be a graduate student in a North American university who is researching and writing a significant dissertation for the PhD on any subject in French medieval history that can be realized only by sustained research in the archives and libraries of France; must be a member of the Medieval Academy. **Criteria:** Selection will be based on the committee's criteria.

Funds Avail.: $20,000. **To Apply:** Application form is available from the Medieval Academy office or from the website. Along with the completed application form, applicants must submit the following: a dissertation proposal that has been approved by the applicant's dissertation committee; a letter of recommendation from the applicant's dissertation director certifying that the applicant has passed the qualifying exams and received approval for the dissertation project and discussing the merits of the project and the applicant's preparation to complete it successfully; a second letter of recommendation from a graduate professor discussing the merits of the dissertation project and the applicant's preparation to complete it successfully. **Deadline:** November 15. **Remarks:** Established in 2004.

6034 ■ Medieval Academy Dissertation Grants *(Graduate/Grant)*

Purpose: To support advanced graduate students who are writing doctoral dissertations on medieval topics. **Focus:** Medieval studies. **Qualif.:** Applicants must be graduate students whose primary research focuses on an aspect of medieval studies. Applicants must have received approval from their dissertation committee for their projects by the application date. **Criteria:** Selection will be based on the following criteria: originality of the dissertation project, the clarity of its methodology, and its likelihood to contribute to medieval studies; the cogency of the writing and organization of the dissertation project description; the dissertation director's statement regarding the excellence of the project and the applicant's preparation to complete the project; the applicant's demonstrated need for the grant to complete the dissertation successfully.

Funds Avail.: $2,000. **Number Awarded:** 8. **To Apply:**

Along with the completed application from, applicants must provide a letter of recommendation from the dissertation director certifying that the applicant has passed the qualifying exams and received an approval for the dissertation project and discussing the merits of the project and the applicant's preparation to complete it successfully. The letter of recommendation should be submitted in a sealed envelope signed on the back across the seal or may be sent directly to the Academy office. **Deadline:** February 15.

6035 ■ Schallek Awards *(Graduate/Award)*

Purpose: To support advanced graduate students who are writing doctoral dissertations on medieval topics. **Focus:** Medieval studies. **Qualif.:** Applicants must be graduate students conducting doctoral research in any relevant discipline dealing with late-medieval Britain (ca. 1350-1500); must be members of the Medieval Academy as of January 15 of the yearin which they apply. **Criteria:** Selection will be based on the committee's criteria.

Funds Avail.: $2,000. **Duration:** Annual. **To Apply:** Along with the completed application form, applicants must provide a letter of recommendation from a graduate program professor discussing the merits of the dissertation project and the applicant's preparation to complete it successfully. The letter of recommendation should be submitted in a sealed envelope signed on the back across the seal or may be sent directly to the Academy office. **Deadline:** February 15.

6036 ■ Schallek Fellowships *(Graduate/Fellowship)*

Purpose: To support graduate student who is writing a PhD dissertation in any relevant discipline. **Focus:** Medieval studies. **Qualif.:** Applicants must be graduate students whose dissertation proposals have been approved by their dissertation committees; applicants must be members of the Medieval Academy as of September 15 of the year in which they apply. **Criteria:** Selection will be based on the committee's criteria.

Funds Avail.: $30,000. **Duration:** Annual. **To Apply:** Along with the completed application form, applicants must submit the following: a dissertation proposal that has been approved by the applicant's dissertation committee; a letter of recommendation from the applicant's dissertation director certifying that the applicant has passed the qualifying exams and received approval for the dissertation project and discussing the merits of the project and the applicant's preparation to complete it successfully; a second letter of recommendation from a graduate professor discussing the merits of the dissertation project and the applicant's preparation to complete it successfully. Completed application consists of six copies of the application form and the dissertation proposal and the two letters of recommendation. The letters of recommendation may be submitted by the applicant in a sealed envelope that has been signed by the authors of the letters on the back across the seal; or the letters may be mailed directly by their authors to the Medieval Academy office. **Deadline:** October 15.

6037 ■ Medina County Retired Teachers Association
c/o Nancy McNeal, Treas.
1044 Brimfield Dr.
Medina, OH 44256
Ph: (330)225-2032
E-mail: greglincrane@roadrunner.com
URL: www.medinacrta.org

Awards are arranged alphabetically below their administering organizations

6038 ■ Medina County Retired Teachers Association Scholarship *(Undergraduate/Scholarship)*

Purpose: To support students who have committed themselves to careers in education. **Focus:** General studies/Field of study not specified. **Qualif.:** Applicant must be a graduate of any Medina County high school; majoring in Education; will be a junior or senior in college. **Criteria:** Selection will be based on the committee's criteria.

Funds Avail.: $500. **Duration:** Annual. **To Apply:** Interested applicant may contact the Medina County Retired Teachers Association for the application process and other informations. **Deadline:** May 1. **Contact:** Kay Rasor; Address: 2235 Osage Trail; Wadsworth, Ohio, 44281-8475; Phone: 330-336-1703; Email: grasor@neo.rr.com.

6039 ■ Meeting Professionals International - Connecticut River Valley Chapter (MPI CRV)
330 Main St., 3rd Fl.
Hartford, CT 06106
Ph: (860)541-6438
Fax: (860)541-6484
E-mail: mpicrv@gmail.com
URL: www.crvmpi.org

6040 ■ MPI CRV Scholarships *(Other/Scholarship)*

Purpose: To promote members' professional development and encourage their active participation in the chapter. **Focus:** General studies/Field of study not specified. **Qualif.:** Applicants must be current MPI CRV members in good standing. **Criteria:** Applications will be chosen on a rolling basis.

Funds Avail.: No specific amount. **Duration:** Annual. **To Apply:** Applicants must submit a completed application form with the required materials to Luke Yost.

6041 ■ Meeting Professionals International - Wisconsin Chapter
2830 Agriculture Dr.
Madison, WI 53718
Ph: (608)204-9816
Fax: (608)204-9818
E-mail: admin@mpiwi.org
URL: www.mpiwi.org

6042 ■ Kristin Bjurstrom Krueger Student Scholarship Program *(Undergraduate/Scholarship)*

Purpose: To provide financial support to students pursuing higher education. **Focus:** General studies/Field of study not specified. **Qualif.:** Applicant must be any person currently enrolled in a course of study in the meetings field at an accredited college; must carry a minimum of six credits per semester and maintain a minimum grade point average of 3.25; this scholarship is available to any student attending a Wisconsin college. **Criteria:** Selection will be based on the committee's criteria.

Funds Avail.: $500. **Duration:** Annual. **To Apply:** Interested applicants must complete the online Student Scholarship Application form; create an essay on the topic "Why I Want to Work in the meetings Industry." The essay must be typed, double-spaced and not exceed 500 words; provide one letter of reference from a teacher or an employer; and a transcript that identifies courses of study and grade point average. **Deadline:** June 2.

6043 ■ The Melissa Institute for Violence Prevention and Treatment
6250 Sunset Dr., Ste. 204
Miami, FL 33143
Ph: (786)662-5210
Fax: (305)668-5211
E-mail: info@melissainstitute.org
URL: www.melissainstitute.org

6044 ■ Belfer-Aptman Dissertation Research Awards *(Doctorate/Grant)*

Purpose: To provide financial assistance to support expenses that are directly related to violence prevention research. **Focus:** Aggression and violence. **Qualif.:** Applicants must be students in an accredited doctoral dissertation program. Candidates may be from any academic discipline; must have their dissertation proposal approved by their dissertation committee prior to their application to the Melissa Institute. **Criteria:** Applicants will be evaluated by the Award Selection Committee.

Funds Avail.: $2,000. **Duration:** Annual. **Number Awarded:** 2. **To Apply:** Applicants must submit their proposed thesis; a brief 300-word abstract of proposed study; letter of recommendation from dissertation advisor; and curriculum vitae, including any scientific publications and presentations with a brief description of career plans. **Deadline:** April 1. **Contact:** The Melissa Institute Belfer-Aptman Scholars Award for Dissertation Research, Attn: Donald Meichenbaum, Ph.D at the above address.

6045 ■ Memorial Foundation for Jewish Culture (MFJC)
50 Broadway, 34th Fl.
New York, NY 10004
Ph: (212)425-6606
Fax: (212)425-6602
E-mail: office@mfjc.org
URL: www.mfjc.org/

6046 ■ International Doctoral Scholarships for Studies Specializing in Jewish Fields *(Doctorate/Scholarship, Award)*

Purpose: To help train qualified individuals for careers in Jewish scholarship and research; to help Jewish educational, religious and communal workers to obtain advanced training for leadership positions. **Focus:** Jewish studies. **Qualif.:** Applicant must be a graduate student specializing in a Jewish field and must be officially enrolled or registered in a doctoral program at a recognized university. **Criteria:** Application and references are evaluated by outside experts and then considered by appropriate committees of the foundation.

Funds Avail.: $10,000. **Duration:** Annual; one academic year. **To Apply:** Applicant must submit a documentation of the university. **Deadline:** October 31.

6047 ■ International Fellowships in Jewish Studies and Jewish Culture *(Professional development/Fellowship)*

Purpose: To assist individuals in carrying out an independent scholarly, literary or art project, in a field of Jewish specialization, which makes a significant contribution to the understanding, preservation, enhancement or transmission of Jewish culture. **Focus:** Jewish studies. **Qualif.:** Ap-

Awards are arranged alphabetically below their administering organizations

plicants must be qualified scholars, researchers or artists who possess the knowledge and experience to formulate and implement a project in a field of Jewish. **Criteria:** Projects are evaluated by outside experts. References are required on the background and ability of the applicants. **Funds Avail.:** Up to $10,000. **To Apply:** Applicants must submit a written request with a brief description of the project either by mail or email. **Deadline:** October 31.

6048 ■ International Scholarship Programs for Community Service (Undergraduate/Scholarship)

Purpose: To assist well-qualified individuals to train for careers in the rabbinate, Jewish education, social work and as religious functionaries. **Focus:** Education, Religious; Jewish studies; Social work. **Qualif.:** Applicants must be undergoing (or planning to undergo) training in a recognized yeshiva, teacher training seminary, school of social work, university or other educational institution. Applicants must commit to serve in a community of need for a minimum of two to three years and must be knowledgeable in the language and culture. **Criteria:** Selection of recipients will be done by outside experts and appropriate committees of the foundation.

Funds Avail.: Amount varies. **Duration:** Annual. **To Apply:** Applications may be obtained through individual written requests with a brief description of the project from the Memorial Foundation for Jewish Culture. **Deadline:** November 30.

6049 ■ MFJC International Fellowships in Jewish Studies (Other/Fellowship)

Purpose: To assist well-qualified individuals in carrying out an independent scholarly, literary or art project, in a field of Jewish specialization, which makes a significant contribution to the understanding, preservation, enhancement or transmission of Jewish culture. **Focus:** Jewish studies. **Qualif.:** Applicants must be qualified scholars, researchers, or artists who possess the knowledge and experience to formulate and implement a project in a field of Jewish specialization. **Criteria:** Proposed projects are evaluated by outside experts. Applications are then considered by appropriate Committees of the foundation.

Funds Avail.: $10,000. **Duration:** Annual. **To Apply:** Application materials can be obtained through individual written requests with a brief description of the project from the Memorial Foundation for Jewish Culture. **Deadline:** October 31.

6050 ■ Mennonite Central Committee Canada (MCCC)

134 Plaza Dr.
Winnipeg, MB, Canada R3T 5K9
Ph: (204)261-6381
Fax: (204)269-9875
Free: 888-622-6337
E-mail: canada@mennonitecc.ca
URL: mcccanada.ca

6051 ■ Canadian Japanese-Mennonite Scholarships (Graduate/Scholarship)

Purpose: To assist the protection of minority and human rights in Canada and to reduce the potential for abuse of cultural minorities. **Focus:** Human rights. **Qualif.:** Applicant must be enrolled in a graduate degree program; must be a Canadian citizen studying at a University in Canada; must

be engaged in research that will assist the protection of minority or human rights in Canada. **Criteria:** Selection of applicants will be based on the scholarship criteria given.

Funds Avail.: $2,000. **Number Awarded:** 1. **To Apply:** Applicants must complete the application form available on the website and include a one page description of how the academic work will contribute to the objectives of the scholarship; must provide a reference letter and information page. **Deadline:** May 1. **Contact:** MCC Canada; Attn: CJM Scholarship; Email: canada@mennonitecc.ca.

6052 ■ Menominee Indian Tribe of Wisconsin (MITW)

W2908 Tribal Office Loop Rd.
Keshena, WI 54135
Ph: (715)799-7000
Free: 877-209-5866
URL: menominee-nsn.gov

6053 ■ Menominee Tribal Scholarships (Undergraduate, Graduate/Scholarship)

Purpose: To provide assistance and support to Menominees and Community Residents who are in need of preparation to advance in the workforce and to pursue higher educational opportunities. **Focus:** General studies/Field of study not specified. **Qualif.:** Applicants must be Menominee tribe members and Wisconsin residents pursuing higher education. **Criteria:** Selection shall be based on the aforementioned applicants' qualifications and compliance with the application details.

Funds Avail.: Amount varies. **Duration:** Annual. **Number Awarded:** Varies. **To Apply:** Applicants must provide and submit the following application packets: letter of acceptance; grade report/transcript; letter of recommendation/support; personal essay; and proof of tribal enrollment. **Deadline:** April 24. **Contact:** Menominee Tribal Scholarship, Tribal Education Office, P.O. Box 910 Keshena, WI 54135; Phone: 715-799-5110 or 715-799-5118.

6054 ■ Mensa Canada

PO Box 1570
Kingston, ON, Canada K7L 5C8
Ph: (613)547-0824
Fax: (613)531-0626
E-mail: mensa@eventsmgt.com
URL: www.mensacanada.org

6055 ■ Edgar Kerstan Memorial Scholarships (College, University/Scholarship)

Purpose: To help students pursue their post-secondary education. **Focus:** General studies/Field of study not specified. **Qualif.:** Applicants must be enrolled full-time in a full-time program at a Canadian post-secondary institution; must be Canadian citizens or landed immigrants; must be 18 years old on January 31 of the current year. **Criteria:** Applicants will be evaluated based on submitted essay.

Funds Avail.: $1,000 to 3,000. **Duration:** Annual. **To Apply:** Applicants must submit a 250-word essay describing plans for achieving their goals. It should be written either in English or French; must provide proof of citizenship and two letters of reference. **Deadline:** January 31. **Remarks:** The scholarship was founded in memory of Edgar Kerstan, former member of Mensa Canada. After his passing in 2009, he left a trust fund to be administered by the Mensa

Awards are arranged alphabetically below their administering organizations

Canada Scholarship Programme. In honour of his commitment to Mensa Canada, a scholarship has been set up in his name. Established in 2011. **Contact:** Mensa Canada Society, at the above address.

6056 ■ Mensa Canada General Scholarships
(Undergraduate/Scholarship)

Purpose: To help students pursue their post-secondary education. **Focus:** General studies/Field of study not specified. **Qualif.:** Applicants must be enrolled full-time in a full-time program at a Canadian post-secondary institution; must be Canadian citizens or landed immigrants; must be 18 years old on January 31 of the current year. **Criteria:** Applicants will be evaluated based on submitted essay.

Funds Avail.: $1,000 - $3,000. **Duration:** Annual. **To Apply:** Applicants must submit a 250-word essay describing plans for achieving their goals. It should be written either in English or French; must provide proof of citizenship and two letters of reference. **Deadline:** January 31. **Contact:** Mensa Canada Society, at the above address.

6057 ■ Frank and Betty Woodhams Memorial Scholarships *(College, University/Scholarship)*

Purpose: To help students pursue their post-secondary education. **Focus:** Computer and information sciences; Mathematics and mathematical sciences. **Qualif.:** Applicants must be enrolled full-time in either a Computer Science or Mathematics program at a Canadian university; must be Canadian citizens or landed immigrants. **Criteria:** Applicants will be evaluated based on submitted essay.

Funds Avail.: $2,700. **Duration:** Annual. **To Apply:** Applicants must submit a 250-word essay describing plans for achieving their goals. It should be written either in English or French; must provide proof of citizenship and two letters of reference. **Deadline:** January 31. **Remarks:** The Frank & Betty Woodhams Scholarship is a memorial to Mr. Woodhams' 20-years with Mensa Canada, and his commitment to providing a stimulating intellectual and social environment for its members. This scholarship is also a recognition of a marriage partnership that allowed two people of modest means to helps students in the two fields that Mr. Woodhams loved: mathematics and computer science. **Contact:** Mensa Canada Society, at the above address.

6058 ■ Mensa Education and Research Foundation
1229 Corporate Dr. W
Arlington, TX 76006-6103
Ph: (817)607-5577
Fax: (817)649-5232
Free: 800-666-3672
E-mail: info@mensafoundation.org
URL: www.mensafoundation.org

6059 ■ Mensa Education and Research Foundation U.S. Scholarships *(Undergraduate/Scholarship)*

Purpose: To support students in their educational pursuits. **Focus:** General studies/Field of study not specified. **Qualif.:** Applicants must be U.S. citizens or permanent residents enrolled in a degree program in an accredited U.S. institution of higher learning during the academic year following the application date. **Criteria:** Selection shall be based on the aforementioned applicants' qualifications and compliance with the application details.

Funds Avail.: No specific amount. **Duration:** Annual. **Num-**

ber **Awarded:** Varies. **To Apply:** Applicants must fill out the application form and send it with an essay explaining their career, vocational or academic goals. Essays must be no less than 550 words and must be submitted to the participating local group where the applicant lives. **Deadline:** January 15. **Contact:** Mensa Education and Research Foundation, at above address.

6060 ■ MetroPCS Communications Inc.
2250 Lakeside Blvd.
Richardson, TX 75082
Ph: (214)570-5800
Fax: (214)570-5859
Free: 888-863-8768
URL: www.metropcs.com

6061 ■ MetroPCS Community Scholars Program
(Undergraduate/Scholarship)

Purpose: To encourage high school students to become involved in volunteer activities that give back to their community and to help young people pay for college education. **Focus:** General studies/Field of study not specified. **Qualif.:** Applicants must be graduating high school seniors who plan to continue their education in college or university programs; must have a minimum cumulative GPA of 3.0 on a standard 4.0 grading scale. **Criteria:** Selection will be based on demonstrated exceptional involvement in volunteerism and community service.

Funds Avail.: $2,500. **Duration:** Annual. **To Apply:** Applicants may download an application form online. Application must be submitted together with completed applicant appraisal and current complete transcript of grades. **Remarks:** Established in 2003.

6062 ■ Metropolitan Museum of Art
1000 5th Ave.
New York, NY 10028-0198
Ph: (212)535-7710
Fax: (212)472-2764
E-mail: customer.service@metmuseum.org
URL: www.metmuseum.org

6063 ■ Chester Dale Fellowships *(Doctorate/ Fellowship)*

Purpose: To provide an opportunity for fellows to present short papers on their work in progress to university colleagues and Museum staff. **Focus:** Art. **Qualif.:** Applicants whose fields of study are related to the fine arts of the Western world and who are preferably American citizens under the age of 40. **Criteria:** Selection will be based on the committee's criteria.

Funds Avail.: No specific amount. **Duration:** Three months to one year. **To Apply:** There are no forms. Applicants need not specify the name of a particular fellowship. Fellowship applications must be submitted in English. Three letters of recommendation are required, none of which may be from current Metropolitan Museum of Art staff. The submission of the required letters of recommendation in English is encouraged. Applicants must submit a typed application in triplicate including the following, in the order listed: Name, home and present address, and telephone number; full resume of education and employment; two-part statement, not to exceed 1,000 words, specifying what the applicant wishes to accomplish during the fellowship period and

Awards are arranged alphabetically below their administering organizations

detailing how the Museum's resources can be utilized to accomplish the applicant's goals; tentative schedule of work to be accomplished during the fellowship period; tentative schedule of travel required during the fellowship period; three letters of recommendation (at least one academic and one professional); list of other applications for fellowships or grants applied for in same period; official undergraduate and graduate transcripts (for pre-doctoral applicants). **Deadline:** November 6.

6064 ■ Douglass Foundation Fellowships in American Art *(Graduate/Fellowship)*

Purpose: To provide an opportunity for fellows to present short papers on their work in progress to university colleagues and Museum staff. **Focus:** Arts. **Qualif.:** Applicants must be enrolled for at least one year in an advanced degree program in the field of American art or culture. **Criteria:** Selection will be based on the committee's criteria.

Funds Avail.: No specific amount. **To Apply:** There are no forms. Applicants need not specify the name of a particular fellowship. Fellowship applications must be submitted in English. Three letters of recommendation are required, none of which may be from current Metropolitan Museum of Art staff. The submission of the required letters of recommendation in English is encouraged. Applicants must submit a typed application in triplicate including the following, in the order listed: Name, home and present address, and telephone number; full resume of education and employment; two-part statement, not to exceed 1,000 words, specifying what the applicant wishes to accomplish during the fellowship period and detailing how the Museum's resources can be utilized to accomplish the applicant's goals; tentative schedule of work to be accomplished during the fellowship period; tentative schedule of travel required during the fellowship period; three letters of recommendation (at least one academic and one professional); list of other applications for fellowships or grants applied for in same period; official undergraduate and graduate transcripts (for pre-doctoral applicants). **Deadline:** November 6.

6065 ■ Annette Kade Fellowships *(Graduate/Fellowship)*

Purpose: To provide an opportunity for fellows to present short papers on their work in progress to university colleagues and Museum staff. **Focus:** Art history. **Qualif.:** Applicants must be French or German pre-doctoral art history students who would not otherwise have the opportunity to study in the United States. **Criteria:** Selection will be based on the committee's criteria.

Funds Avail.: No specific amount. **To Apply:** There are no forms. Applicants need not specify the name of a particular fellowship. Fellowship applications must be submitted in English. Three letters of recommendation are required, none of which may be from current Metropolitan Museum of Art staff. The submission of the required letters of recommendation in English is encouraged. Applicants must submit a typed application in triplicate including the following, in the order listed: Name, home and present address, and telephone number; full resume of education and employment; two-part statement, not to exceed 1,000 words, specifying what the applicant wishes to accomplish during the fellowship period and detailing how the Museum's resources can be utilized to accomplish the applicant's goals; tentative schedule of work to be accomplished during the fellowship period; tentative schedule of travel required during the fellowship period; three letters of recommendation (at least one academic and one professional);

list of other applications for fellowships or grants applied for in same period; official undergraduate and graduate transcripts (for pre-doctoral applicants). **Deadline:** November 6.

6066 ■ Metropolitan Museum of Art Bothmer Fellowship *(Doctorate/Fellowship)*

Purpose: To provide an opportunity for fellows to present short papers on their work in progress to university colleagues and Museum staff. **Focus:** Art history. **Qualif.:** Applicants must be outstanding graduate students who have been admitted to the doctoral program of a university in the United States and who have submitted outlines of their theses dealing with either Greek or Roman art. **Criteria:** Preference will be given to the applicant who, in the opinion of the Grants Committee, will profit most from utilizing the resources of the Department of Greek and Roman Art: its collections, library, and photographic and other archives, and the guidance of its curatorial staff.

Funds Avail.: No specific amount. **To Apply:** There are no forms. Applicants need not specify the name of a particular fellowship. Fellowship applications must be submitted in English. Three letters of recommendation are required, none of which may be from current Metropolitan Museum of Art staff. The submission of the required letters of recommendation in English is encouraged. Applicants must submit a typed application in triplicate including the following, in the order listed: Name, home and present address, and telephone number; full resume of education and employment; two-part statement, not to exceed 1,000 words, specifying what the applicant wishes to accomplish during the fellowship period and detailing how the Museum's resources can be utilized to accomplish the applicant's goals; tentative schedule of work to be accomplished during the fellowship period; tentative schedule of travel required during the fellowship period; three letters of recommendation (at least one academic and one professional); list of other applications for fellowships or grants applied for in same period; official undergraduate and graduate transcripts (for pre-doctoral applicants).

6067 ■ Metropolitan Museum of Art Conservation and Scientific Research Fellowships *(Graduate/Fellowship)*

Purpose: To provide an opportunity for fellows to present short papers on their work in progress to university colleagues and Museum staff. **Focus:** Museum science. **Qualif.:** Applicants must be graduate students at the pre-doctoral level as well as post-doctoral researchers. **Criteria:** Selection will be based on the committee's criteria.

Funds Avail.: 42,000 for senior conservators/scientific researchers and $32,000 for junior plus additional $6,000 for travel. **Duration:** 6 weeks. **To Apply:** There are no forms. Applicants need not specify the name of a particular fellowship. Fellowship applications must be submitted in English. Three letters of recommendation are required, none of which may be from current Metropolitan Museum of Art staff. The submission of the required letters of recommendation in English is encouraged. Applicants must submit a typed application in triplicate including the following, in the order listed: Name, home and present address, and telephone number; full resume of education and employment; two-part statement, not to exceed 1,000 words, specifying what the applicant wishes to accomplish during the fellowship period and detailing how the Museum's resources can be utilized to accomplish the applicant's goals; tentative schedule of work to be accomplished during the fellowship period; tentative schedule of travel

Awards are arranged alphabetically below their administering organizations

required during the fellowship period; three letters of recommendation (at least one academic and one professional); list of other applications for fellowships or grants applied for in same period; official undergraduate and graduate transcripts (for pre-doctoral applicants). **Deadline:** December 4.

6068 ■ Metropolitan Museum of Art Research Scholarship in Photograph Conservation *(Graduate/ Scholarship)*

Purpose: To provide an opportunity for fellows to present short papers on their work in progress to university colleagues and Museum staff. **Focus:** Museum science. **Qualif.:** Applicants must have a graduate degree in conservation or equivalent experience and should be completely committed to the conservation of photographs as their area of specialization. **Criteria:** Selection will be based on the committee's criteria.

Funds Avail.: $42,000 per year, plus a $6,000 travel allowance. **To Apply:** There are no forms. Applicants need not specify the name of a particular fellowship. Fellowship applications must be submitted in English. Three letters of recommendation are required, none of which may be from current Metropolitan Museum of Art staff. The submission of the required letters of recommendation in English is encouraged. Applicants must submit a typed application in triplicate including the following, in the order listed: Name, home and present address, and telephone number; full resume of education and employment; two-part statement, not to exceed 1,000 words, specifying what the applicant wishes to accomplish during the fellowship period and detailing how the Museum's resources can be utilized to accomplish the applicant's goals; tentative schedule of work to be accomplished during the fellowship period; tentative schedule of travel required during the fellowship period; three letters of recommendation (at least one academic and one professional); list of other applications for fellowships or grants applied for in same period; official undergraduate and graduate transcripts (for pre-doctoral applicants). **Deadline:** November 6.

6069 ■ J. Clawson Mills Scholarships *(Doctorate/ Scholarship)*

Purpose: To provide an opportunity for fellows to present short papers on their work in progress to university colleagues and Museum staff. **Focus:** Art. **Qualif.:** Applicants must be conducting research at the Museum or abroad in any branch of fine arts relating to the Metropolitan Museum's collection. **Criteria:** Selection will be based on the committee's criteria.

Funds Avail.: No specific amount. **To Apply:** There are no forms. Applicants need not specify the name of a particular fellowship. Fellowship applications must be submitted in English. Three letters of recommendation are required, none of which may be from current Metropolitan Museum of Art staff. The submission of the required letters of recommendation in English is encouraged. Applicants must submit a typed application in triplicate including the following, in the order listed: Name, home and present address, and telephone number; full resume of education and employment; two-part statement, not to exceed 1,000 words, specifying what the applicant wishes to accomplish during the fellowship period and detailing how the Museum's resources can be utilized to accomplish the applicant's goals; tentative schedule of work to be accomplished during the fellowship period; tentative schedule of travel required during the fellowship period; three letters of recommendation (at least one academic and one professional);

list of other applications for fellowships or grants applied for in same period; official undergraduate and graduate transcripts (for pre-doctoral applicants). **Deadline:** November 6.

6070 ■ Theodore Rousseau Fellowships *(Graduate/ Fellowship)*

Purpose: To provide an opportunity for fellows to present short papers on their work in progress to university colleagues and Museum staff. **Focus:** Painting. **Qualif.:** Applicants must be students whose goal is to enter museums as curators of painting; must be enrolled for at least one year in an advanced degree program in the field of art history. **Criteria:** Selection will be based on the committee's criteria.

Funds Avail.: No specific amount. **To Apply:** There are no forms. Applicants need not specify the name of a particular fellowship. Fellowship applications must be submitted in English. Three letters of recommendation are required, none of which may be from current Metropolitan Museum of Art staff. The submission of the required letters of recommendation in English is encouraged. Applicants must submit a typed application in triplicate including the following, in the order listed: Name, home and present address, and telephone number; full resume of education and employment; two-part statement, not to exceed 1,000 words, specifying what the applicant wishes to accomplish during the fellowship period and detailing how the Museum's resources can be utilized to accomplish the applicant's goals; tentative schedule of work to be accomplished during the fellowship period; tentative schedule of travel required during the fellowship period; three letters of recommendation (at least one academic and one professional); list of other applications for fellowships or grants applied for in same period; official undergraduate and graduate transcripts (for pre-doctoral applicants). **Deadline:** November 6.

6071 ■ Slifka Foundation Interdisciplinary Fellowships *(Doctorate, Master's/Fellowship)*

Purpose: To provide an opportunity for fellows to present short papers on their work in progress to university colleagues and Museum staff. **Focus:** Painting. **Qualif.:** Applicants must be in the PHD level for training in an interdisciplinary approach, or joining art historical research with technical investigation of the Museum's early Netherlandish and German paintings. **Criteria:** Selection will be based on the committee's criteria.

Funds Avail.: No specific amount. **To Apply:** Applicants must contact the Grants Office prior to submitting an application. **Deadline:** November 6.

6072 ■ Hanns Swarzenski and Brigitte Horney Swarzenski Fellowship *(Graduate/Fellowship)*

Purpose: To provide an opportunity for fellows to present short papers on their work in progress to university colleagues and Museum staff. **Focus:** Art history. **Qualif.:** Applicants must be promising young scholars who wish to study and research at the Museum. **Criteria:** Preference will be given to applicants with a proven interest in museum work or those planning to pursue a museum career in the field of Medieval Art.

Funds Avail.: No specific amount. **To Apply:** There are no forms. Applicants need not specify the name of a particular fellowship. Fellowship applications must be submitted in English. Three letters of recommendation are required, none of which may be from current Metropolitan Museum

Awards are arranged alphabetically below their administering organizations

of Art staff. The submission of the required letters of recommendation in English is encouraged. Applicants must submit a typed application in triplicate including the following, in the order listed: Name, home and present address, and telephone number; full resume of education and employment; two-part statement, not to exceed 1,000 words, specifying what the applicant wishes to accomplish during the fellowship period and detailing how the Museum's resources can be utilized to accomplish the applicant's goals; tentative schedule of work to be accomplished during the fellowship period; tentative schedule of travel required during the fellowship period; three letters of recommendation (at least one academic and one professional); list of other applications for fellowships or grants applied for in same period; official undergraduate and graduate transcripts (for pre-doctoral applicants). **Deadline:** November 6.

6073 ■ Polaire Weissman Funds (Graduate/ Fellowship)

Purpose: To provide an opportunity for fellows to present short papers on their work in progress to university colleagues and Museum staff. **Focus:** Architecture; Arts; Design. **Qualif.:** Applicants must be graduate students interested in pursuing an academic or museum career in the history or conservation of dress; must be enrolled for at least one year in an advanced degree program in the field of art, architecture, cultural studies, design, or costume history. **Criteria:** Selection will be based on the committee's criteria.

Funds Avail.: No specific amount. **To Apply:** There are no forms. Applicants need not specify the name of a particular fellowship. Fellowship applications must be submitted in English. Three letters of recommendation are required, none of which may be from current Metropolitan Museum of Art staff. The submission of the required letters of recommendation in English is encouraged. Applicants must submit a typed application in triplicate including the following, in the order listed: Name, home and present address, and telephone number; full resume of education and employment; two-part statement, not to exceed 1,000 words, specifying what the applicant wishes to accomplish during the fellowship period and detailing how the Museum's resources can be utilized to accomplish the applicant's goals; tentative schedule of work to be accomplished during the fellowship period; tentative schedule of travel required during the fellowship period; three letters of recommendation (at least one academic and one professional); list of other applications for fellowships or grants applied for in same period; official undergraduate and graduate transcripts (for pre-doctoral applicants). **Deadline:** November 6.

6074 ■ Jane and Morgan Whitney Fellowships (Graduate/Fellowship)

Purpose: To provide an opportunity for fellows to present short papers on their work in progress to university colleagues and Museum staff. **Focus:** Art. **Qualif.:** Applicants must be students of the fine arts whose fields are related to the Museum's collections. **Criteria:** Preference will be given to students in the decorative arts who are under 40 years of age.

Funds Avail.: No specific amount. **To Apply:** There are no forms. Applicants need not specify the name of a particular fellowship. Fellowship applications must be submitted in English. Three letters of recommendation are required, none of which may be from current Metropolitan Museum of Art staff. The submission of the required letters of recom-

mendation in English is encouraged. Applicants must submit a typed application in triplicate including the following, in the order listed: Name, home and present address, and telephone number; full resume of education and employment; two-part statement, not to exceed 1,000 words, specifying what the applicant wishes to accomplish during the fellowship period and detailing how the Museum's resources can be utilized to accomplish the applicant's goals; tentative schedule of work to be accomplished during the fellowship period; tentative schedule of travel required during the fellowship period; three letters of recommendation (at least one academic and one professional); list of other applications for fellowships or grants applied for in same period; official undergraduate and graduate transcripts (for pre-doctoral applicants). **Deadline:** November 6.

6075 ■ Mexican American Bar Foundation
PO Box 862127
Los Angeles, CA 90086-2127
URL: www.themabf.org

6076 ■ MABF Scholarships (Postgraduate/ Scholarship)

Purpose: To support Latino students in their pursuit of legal education. **Focus:** Law. **Qualif.:** Applicants must be matriculated law students who are of Hispanic/Latino heritage or descent; must be currently attend an ABA-accredited law schools in Los Angeles County (Loyola, Pepperdine, Southwestern, UCLA, and USC), or UC Irvine School of Law; and must be going to enroll during the incoming academic year. **Criteria:** The Foundation's scholarship committee considers the applicants' financial need, academic achievement, community service, leadership experience and any hardship experienced in pursuing an education.

Funds Avail.: Range from $7,500 to $15,000. **Number Awarded:** Varies. **To Apply:** Applicants must fill-up completely the provided scholarship application form. Items that should be attached/included to the form are: transcript (plus letter of good standing if 1st Year law students); personal statement; a copy of completed federal financial aid form (or other financial aid form); certification signature; and commitment signature. **Deadline:** March 13. **Contact:** Mail applications to Patricia Higuera Stout, Scholarship Co-Chair of Mexican American Bar Foundation, c/o DLA Piper Southwestern Law School 550 South Hope St., Ste. 2300, Los Angeles, California 90071-2678; or via email at patricia.stout@dlapiper.com.

6077 ■ Mexican American Catholic College (MACC)
3115 W Ashby Pl.
San Antonio, TX 78228-5104
Ph: (210)732-2156
Fax: (210)732-9072
Free: 866-893-6222
E-mail: macc@maccsa.org
URL: www.maccsa.org

6078 ■ MACC Scholarships (Other/Scholarship)

Purpose: To support an individual's spiritual and educational journey. **Focus:** Education, Religious; Foreign languages. **Qualif.:** Applicant must be a member of any religious community. **Criteria:** Priority will be given to ap-

Awards are arranged alphabetically below their administering organizations

plicants ministering in the United States with possible exceptions based on individual requests and based on applicant's need.

Funds Avail.: No specific amount. **To Apply:** Applicant must have the registration form and fee; must have two letters of recommendation from the applicant's superior, bishop, chancellor, pastor, or supervisor; must have one letter from the organization's executive director; must have 2-3 typed pages of autobiography (pastoral program only); must have a questionnaire and placement (language program only). **Contact:** Complete application must be mailed to: MACC Scholarship Committee, 3115 W Ashby Place, San Antonio, TX 78228.

6079 ■ Mexican American Legal Defense and Educational Fund (MALDEF)

634 S Spring St.
Los Angeles, CA 90014
URL: www.maldef.org

6080 ■ MALDEF Dream Act Student Activist Scholarships *(Undergraduate, Graduate/Scholarship)*

Purpose: To support the nation's college and graduate student leaders who have been outstanding advocates for the DREAM Act and all immigrants rights. **Focus:** Civil rights; Law. **Qualif.:** Applicants must be current college or graduate students. Students seeking to enroll in college or university for the first time are also eligible to apply if they will be enrolled in a college or university before the end of the current year. **Criteria:** Selection will be based on the committee's criteria.

Funds Avail.: $5,000. **Duration:** Annual. **To Apply:** Applicants must submit a completed application form; current resume; a 500-word each essay, responses to: applicants' background and financial need; an activism that the applicants engaged in around the DREAM Act and in support of immigrant rights; and applicants' future plans. **Deadline:** July 2.

6081 ■ Mexican American Legal Defense and Educational Fund Law School Scholarships *(Undergraduate/Scholarship)*

Purpose: To increase the number of Latinos in the legal profession; to provide financial assistance to qualified individuals in pursuit of higher education. **Focus:** Law. **Qualif.:** Applicants must be Latino students enrolled full time in law school; and have demonstrated involvement with commitment to serve the Latino community through their profession. **Criteria:** Scholarship will be awarded to candidates who have outstanding academic record including participation and leadership in extracurricular activities, and financial need.

Funds Avail.: $5,000. **Number Awarded:** 5-10. **To Apply:** Applicants must complete and send the following materials: a completed and signed MALDEF Scholarship form; current resume; a typed personal statement of 750 words or less, double-spaced, detailing professional objectives, plans after school, and describing their past involvement in activities for which they believed would served or benefited the Latino community and how these activities affect their decision to pursue a career in the legal profession; an official undergraduate transcript or photocopy of an official transcript; For law students who have already completed one year or more of law school, please, also provide: an official law school transcript or photocopy of an official transcript; a letter of recommendation describing their

involvement in the Latino community from a person familiar with that involvement; a letter of recommendation from a college, or law school professor; and enclosed statement from the financial aid office of the school currently attending which indicates the financial assistance provided. **Deadline:** January 2.

6082 ■ Miami County Retired Teachers Association

c/o Barbara Miller, Membership Chair
6644 Roberta Dr.
Tipp City, OH 45371
Ph: (937)667-1563
E-mail: yaney@windstream.net
URL: miamicountyrta.blogspot.com

6083 ■ Book Scholarships *(Undergraduate/ Scholarship)*

Purpose: To support students with their studies. **Focus:** General studies/Field of study not specified. **Qualif.:** Applicants must be high school seniors or faculty members. **Criteria:** Selection will be based on the committee's criteria.

Funds Avail.: $250. **Duration:** Annual. **Number Awarded:** 4. **To Apply:** Interested applicant may contact the Scholarship Chair for the application process and other information. **Contact:** Alice Fae Detert, Scholarship Chair; Address: 164 Kiser Drive, Tipp City, OH 45371.

6084 ■ Michael Smith Foundation for Health Research

200 - 1285 W Broadway
Vancouver, BC, Canada V6H 3X8
Ph: (604)730-8322
Free: 866-673-4722
E-mail: info@msfhr.org
URL: www.msfhr.org

6085 ■ MSFHR Scholar Awards *(Advanced Professional, Professional development/Grant)*

Purpose: To support new investigators to launch independent research careers and build strong research programs that could benefit the British Columbia area. **Focus:** Medical research. **Qualif.:** Applicants must be researchers or investigators in British Columbia with less than five years of independent research experience. **Criteria:** Selection will be based on the committee's criteria.

Funds Avail.: No specific amount. **Duration:** Up to five years. **To Apply:** Interested applicants may contact the Program Manager for the application process and other information. **Deadline:** February 28. **Contact:** Rashmita Salvi, Programs Manager; Phone: 604-714-2779 or Email: rsalvi@msfhr.org.

6086 ■ MSFHR Trainee Awards *(Postdoctorate, Professional development/Grant)*

Purpose: To support highly qualified applicants at the post-PhD and post-health professional degree stages to prepare for careers as independent health researchers. **Focus:** Medical research. **Qualif.:** Applicants must be individuals in the postdoctoral (PhD) and post-health professional degree (MD, DDS, DVM or DPharm) stages. **Criteria:** Selection will be based on the committee's criteria.

Funds Avail.: No specific amount. **Number Awarded:** Var-

Awards are arranged alphabetically below their administering organizations

ies. **To Apply:** Interested applicants may contact the Program Manager for the application process and other information. **Deadline:** March 17 (letter of intent); April 20 (full application). **Contact:** Rashmita Salvi, Programs Manager; Phone: 604-714-2779 or Email: rsalvi@msfhr.org.

6087 ■ Michigan Association of Certified Public Accountants (MICPA)

5480 Corporate Dr., Ste. 200
Troy, MI 48098-2642
Ph: (248)267-3700
Fax: (248)267-3737
Free: 888-877-4273
E-mail: micpa@micpa.org
URL: www.micpa.org

6088 ■ Michigan Accountancy Foundation Final Year Accounting Scholarship *(Graduate/Scholarship)*

Purpose: To encourage students to become certified public accountants in Michigan. **Focus:** Accounting. **Qualif.:** Applicants must be accounting students attending Michigan colleges and universities who are entering their final year of the Michigan educational requirement for licensure. **Criteria:** Selection shall be based on the aforementioned applicants' qualifications and compliance with the application details.

Funds Avail.: No specific amount. **Duration:** Annual. **To Apply:** Applicants must provide and submit the following: completed application; official transcripts with university/college seal for all college level courseworks, including all courses completed in the term prior to the fixed application deadline (course grades for fall term just prior to deadline may be submitted separately); two essays (500 words or less); two letters of recommendation, including one from a faculty member. **Deadline:** January 30. **Contact:** MAF Accounting Scholarship Program, at the above address.

6089 ■ Michigan Association of Fire Fighters (MAFF)

667 E Big Beaver Rd., Ste. 109
Troy, MI 48083
Fax: (248)509-7160
Free: 800-509-7176
URL: www.maff.org

6090 ■ Carl Parsell Scholarship Fund *(Undergraduate/Scholarship)*

Purpose: To assist members and their families to pursue a college education. **Focus:** General studies/Field of study not specified. **Qualif.:** Applicants must be residents of Michigan; be members or relatives of one of the following organizations: Michigan Association of Police; Michigan Association of Fire Fighters; or Michigan Association of Public Employees; have not been convicted by any misdemeanors or felonies; and must be enrolled full-time at an accredited educational institution. **Criteria:** Recipients will be selected based on quality and relevance of the written response.

Funds Avail.: $2,500. **Duration:** Annual. **To Apply:** Applicants must submit an original application form. **Deadline:** March 2. **Remarks:** Established in 1991.

6091 ■ Michigan Association of Realtors (MAR)

720 N Washington Ave.
Lansing, MI 48906

Fax: (517)334-5568
Free: 800-454-7842
URL: www.mirealtors.com

6092 ■ Michigan Association of Realtors Scholarship Trust (MARST) *(Graduate, Undergraduate/ Scholarship)*

Purpose: To encourage and support outstanding, highly-motivated students to specialize in the study of real estate. **Focus:** Real estate. **Qualif.:** Applicants must have an average grade point of 2.0 on a 4.0 scale or equivalent of a "C" average and show evidence of academic achievement; must exemplify character, including demonstrated evidence of good citizenship; must agree to take courses which are related to the real estate field; must be full-time students, entering junior or senior year or post-graduate work at a major university or college. **Criteria:** Applicants are selected based on the committee's review of the application materials.

Funds Avail.: $2,000. **Duration:** Annual. **To Apply:** Applicants must complete and submit the application before the deadline. Application form can be downloaded at the Michigan Association of Realtors web site. Applicants must also provide a copy of ACT or SAT test scores and a copy of their college transcript. **Deadline:** July 1. **Contact:** Send application to: Michigan Association of REALTORS® Scholarship Trust, P.O. Box 40725, Lansing, Michigan 48901-7925; Phone: 517-372-8890.

6093 ■ Michigan Auto Law

30101 Northwestern Hwy.
Farmington Hills, MI 48334
Ph: (248)353-7575
Free: 800-777-0028
URL: www.michiganautolaw.com

6094 ■ Law Student Diversity Scholarships *(Undergraduate/Scholarship)*

Purpose: To provide financial support to students who contribute to the diversity of the law school student body as they pursue their legal career. **Focus:** Law. **Qualif.:** Applicants must be students currently in their first or second year of law school; must be member of an ethnic or racial minority or demonstrates a defined commitment to issues of diversity within their academic career; must be Michigan resident accepted to or currently attending an accredited law school within the United States, or a non-Michigan resident attending an accredited Michigan law school; must have a cumulative minimum of 3.0 GPA. **Criteria:** Selection will be based on the committee's criteria.

Funds Avail.: $2,000. **Duration:** Annual. **To Apply:** Applicants must submit the following items: a completed application (available at the website); a current academic transcript; a one page essay describing their efforts to encourage greater racial or ethnic diversity within the student body of their law school and/or undergraduate program. **Deadline:** May 1. **Contact:** Natalie Lombardo at 248-353-4504; scholarships@michiganautolaw.com.

6095 ■ Michigan Competing Band Association (MCBA)

10237 Seymour Rd.
Montrose, MI 48457-9014
Ph: (810)639-2442

Awards are arranged alphabetically below their administering organizations

---

Fax: (810)639-3786
E-mail: mcba@mac.com
URL: www.themcba.org/theMCBA.org/Welcome.html

6096 ■ MCBA Scholarship *(Undergraduate/ Scholarship)*

Purpose: To grant scholarships to deserving students from Michigan high schools that are members of MCBA. **Focus:** Music. **Qualif.:** Applicants must be high school seniors who are members of an MCBA marching band and plan to enter a college or university with a major in music or related field. **Criteria:** Selection will be based on the applicants' GPAs, past honors and awards, previous music training and participation in solo and ensemble venues.

Funds Avail.: $1,500. **Duration:** Annual. **Number Awarded:** 4. **To Apply:** The applicants are asked to write a paragraph stating why they should be considered for the scholarship award.

6097 ■ Michigan Council of Women in Technology (MCWT)

PO Box 214585
Auburn Hills, MI 48321
Ph: (248)218-2578
E-mail: info@mcwt.org
URL: www.mcwt.org

6098 ■ Michigan Council of Women in Technology High School Scholarship Program *(Undergraduate/ Scholarship)*

Purpose: To support those women who are pursuing a career in technology. **Focus:** Technology. **Qualif.:** Applicants must be young women entering college. **Criteria:** Preference will be given to students who meet the criteria.

Funds Avail.: $5,000 per annum. **Duration:** up to four years. **To Apply:** Applicants must check the available website for the required materials.

6099 ■ Michigan Council of Women in Technology Undergraduate Scholarship Program *(Undergraduate/Scholarship)*

Purpose: To provide financial assistance for deserving Michigan-based women pursuing a career in technology. **Focus:** Technology. **Qualif.:** Applicants must be Michigan-based women who are currently or will be enrolled in college or university-level courses; must be U.S. citizens; and must have 2.8 GPA. **Criteria:** Preference will be given to applicants who meet the criteria.

Funds Avail.: $5,000 per annum. **Duration:** up to three years. **To Apply:** Applicants must check the available website for the required materials.

6100 ■ Michigan Education Association (MEA)

1216 Kendale Blvd.
East Lansing, MI 48826-2573
Ph: (517)332-6551
Fax: (517)337-5587
Free: 800-292-1934
E-mail: webmaster@mea.org
URL: www.mea.org

6101 ■ Michigan Education Association Scholarships *(Undergraduate/Scholarship)*

Purpose: To provide education, advancement of quality education and security of the rights of education employees. **Focus:** General studies/Field of study not specified. **Qualif.:** Applicants must be graduates of public schools; must be attending Michigan public community/junior college, four-year degree granting institution, or a certification or license granting institution; or attend one of the approved private institutions. Children of MEA staff are eligible if the other parent is MEA member. **Criteria:** Recipients will be selected based on academic achievement; extra-curricular activities; school and community service. First consideration will be given to children of MEA members and students from lower income households.

Funds Avail.: No specific amount. **Duration:** Annual. **Number Awarded:** Varies. **To Apply:** Applicants must submit completed application form. **Deadline:** February 27. **Contact:** MEA Scholarship Fund, Michigan Education Association, Executive Office at the above address.

6102 ■ Michigan League for Nursing (MLN)

3520 Okemos Rd., Ste. 6-160
Okemos, MI 48864
E-mail: info@michleaguenursing.org
URL: www.michleaguenursing.org

6103 ■ Michigan League for Nursing Scholarships *(Undergraduate/Scholarship)*

Purpose: To provide funds and numerous programs addressing complex issues of nursing education and clinical practice for Michigan nursing students. **Focus:** Nursing. **Qualif.:** Applicants must be enrolled in a program leading to a Licensed Practical Nurse certification, an Associate Degree in Nursing or a Bachelor of Science in Nursing. Applicants must have successfully completed at least one nursing course with a clinical component and must have received a "C" grade or better. **Criteria:** Recipients are selected based on quality of essay, academic performance and financial need.

Funds Avail.: No specific amount. **To Apply:** Applicants must submit an unfolded, completed application form in an 8 1/2 x 11 envelope. Must also submit an unfolded letter of endorsement and essay.

6104 ■ Michigan Nursery and Landscape Association (MNLA)

2149 Commons Pky.
Okemos, MI 48864
Ph: (517)381-0437
Fax: (517)381-0638
Free: 800-879-6652
URL: www.mnla.org

6105 ■ Michigan Nursery and Landscape Association Scholarships *(Undergraduate/Scholarship)*

Purpose: To further the education of those students who are pursuing careers in green industry. **Focus:** Landscape architecture and design. **Qualif.:** Applicants must be students pursuing a degree in the area of landscaping. **Criteria:** Recipients are selected based on academic performance and financial need.

Funds Avail.: No specific amount. **Duration:** Annual. **To Apply:** Applicants must submit a completed application form, a cover letter, resume, two letters of recommendation and photos/information on industry work completed. **Deadline:** November 1.

6106 ■ Michigan Nurses Foundation (MNF)

2310 Jolly Oak Rd.
Okemos, MI 48864

Awards are arranged alphabetically below their administering organizations

Ph: (517)349-5640
URL: www.michigannursesfoundation.org

6107 ■ Conduct and Utilization of Research in Nursing (CURN) Awards *(Professional development/Award)*

Purpose: To provide financial support to professionals who took a nursing career. **Focus:** Nursing. **Qualif.:** Principal investigators must be registered nurses who are licensed to practice in Michigan and living in the state and possess or be working on a master's or doctoral degree; must be members of the Michigan Nurses Association. **Criteria:** Selection will be based on the committee's criteria.

Funds Avail.: $5,000. **To Apply:** Applicants must submit the following materials: four copies of the completed grant application; research support and abstract; detailed budget for proposed research; project narrative, must not exceed 10 single spaced pages, excluding appendices. Recipients will be known as CURN Scholars. All publications and publicity must reflect such title and acknowledge the Michigan Nurses Foundation. CURN Scholars will be asked to present their research at the MNA Convention or to write an article for publication in Michigan Nurse describing their research and its implications for nursing practice. **Deadline:** July 15.

6108 ■ Michigan Nurses Foundation Scholarships *(Undergraduate, Graduate/Scholarship)*

Purpose: To assist deserving nursing students who want to pursue their studies. **Focus:** Nursing. **Qualif.:** Applicant must be a student currently enrolled in a Michigan college/school of nursing that grants a certificate or degree for practicing nursing; must be in good academic standing with demonstrated progress toward degree completion. **Criteria:** Preference will be given to applicants that meet the requirements.

Funds Avail.: $1,000. **Duration:** Annual. **Number Awarded:** 4. **To Apply:** Applicant must complete the application form and application requirements before the deadline. **Deadline:** July 15.

6109 ■ Michigan Parkinson Foundation (MPF)

30400 Telegraph Rd., Ste. 150
Bingham Farms, MI 48025
Ph: (248)433-1011
Fax: (248)433-1150
Free: 800-852-9781
E-mail: info@parkinsonsmi.org
URL: www.parkinsonsmi.org

6110 ■ Raymond B. Bauer Research Award *(Professional development/Grant)*

Purpose: To support individuals who are researching and fostering the study of Parkinson's disease with career interests in neurological disorders. **Focus:** Biological and clinical sciences; Epidemiology; Medical research; Nursing; Psychology; Rehabilitation, Physical/Psychological; Social sciences. **Qualif.:** Recipients must be researchers in Michigan colleges, universities and not-for-profit organizations who work with students and trainees. **Criteria:** Selection will be based on the submitted materials.

Funds Avail.: Up to $20,000. **To Apply:** Applicants must complete and submit the following: a project proposal outlining their topic and relevant background, method of study, collaborative or supervisory arrangements and further plans once the project is completed; a letter of support from a chairman or supervisor; a copy of the Institutional Review Board approval prior to the distribution of funds; a current CV, a budget for their studies and a list of other current financial support (include sponsor, title, dates of support, total direct costs funded and PI). **Deadline:** December 15.

6111 ■ Michigan Society of Fellows

0540 Rackham Bldg.
915 E Washington St.
Ann Arbor, MI 48109-1070
Ph: (734)763-1259
E-mail: society.of.fellows@umich.edu
URL: societyoffellows.umich.edu

6112 ■ Michigan Society of Fellows Three-Year Fellowships *(Postdoctorate/Fellowship)*

Purpose: To financially assist Post-Doctoral students. **Focus:** Life sciences; Physical sciences; Social sciences. **Qualif.:** Applicants must have received their PhD degree at the beginning of their academic careers; must be involved in social, physical, life sciences and in the professional schools. **Criteria:** Recipients will be selected based on submitted materials.

Funds Avail.: $55,000. **Duration:** Annual; up to three years. **Number Awarded:** 4. **To Apply:** Applicants must complete the online application; must submit a curriculum vitae, writing sample and research proposal. **Deadline:** September 30.

6113 ■ Michigan Society of Professional Engineers (MSPE)

PO Box 15276
Lansing, MI 48901-5276
Ph: (517)487-9388
Fax: (517)487-0635
URL: www.michiganspe.org

6114 ■ Michigan Society of Professional Engineers Scholarships *(Undergraduate/Scholarship)*

Purpose: To support high school students who have talent and commitment in pursuing engineering degree. **Focus:** Engineering. **Qualif.:** Applicants must be accepted at a Michigan ABET accredited college or university and enroll in an engineering program; must be high school seniors, residents of Michigan and U.S. citizens at the time of application; must have at least 3.0 GPA based on 4.0 scale for the 10th and 11th grades; and must attain a minimum composite test score of 26 on the American College Testing (ACT Exam). **Criteria:** Recipients are selected based on candidate's high school records, participation in extracurricular activities, evidence of leadership, character and self-reliance and comments from teachers and administrators.

Funds Avail.: No specific amount. **To Apply:** Applicants must submit a completed application form which can be obtained from a guidance counselor, local chapters or the MSPE Headquarters; a list of senior classes being taken; and a documented high school transcript and ACT test scores.

6115 ■ Michigan State Horticultural Society (MSHS)

63806 90th Ave.
Hartford, MI 49057

Awards are arranged alphabetically below their administering organizations

Ph: (269)424-3990
Fax: (269)424-3096
E-mail: mihortsociety@aol.com
URL: www.mihortsociety.org

6116 ■ Fruits and Vegetable Industries Scholarships
(Undergraduate/Scholarship)

Purpose: To encourage among the people a greater love for choice fruit products; to awaken a larger interest in Michigan's horticultural possibilities; to offer practical suggestions along modern cultural and marketing methods; and to encourage the improved methods in the production, harvest, handling, storage, marketing and utilization of fruit and vegetable crops as well as a full farm marketers program. **Focus:** Horticulture. **Qualif.:** Applicants must be students who intend to pursue a career in the Midwest fruit industry or vegetable industry. **Criteria:** Recipients are selected based on financial need and academic performance.

Funds Avail.: $1,000. **To Apply:** Applicants must complete the application form. **Deadline:** September 30.

6117 ■ Jordan B. Tatter Scholarships
(Undergraduate/Scholarship)

Purpose: To encourage among the people a greater love for choice fruit products; to awaken a larger interest in Michigan's horticultural possibilities; to offer practical suggestions along modern cultural and marketing methods; and to encourage the improved methods in the production, harvest, handling, storage, marketing and utilization of fruit and vegetable crops as well as a full farm marketers program. **Focus:** Horticulture. **Qualif.:** Applicants must be graduates or junior undergraduate students who show interest in working in the fruit and/or vegetable industry. **Criteria:** Recipients are selected based on financial need.

Funds Avail.: $1,000. **To Apply:** Applicants must complete the application form. **Deadline:** September 30.

6118 ■ Michigan Stormwater-Floodplain Association (MSFA)
PO Box 14265
Lansing, MI 48901-4265
Ph: (734)794-6430
URL: mi.floods.org

6119 ■ Michigan Stormwater-Floodplain Association Scholarships (Graduate, Undergraduate/Scholarship)

Purpose: To support a full time junior, senior or graduate student studying biosystems, civil or environmental engineering. **Focus:** Water supply industry. **Qualif.:** Applicants must be full-time juniors, seniors, or graduate students in biosystems, civil, or environmental engineering with a specialization related to the mission and goals of the MSFA. **Criteria:** Recipients are selected based on academic performance and financial need.

Funds Avail.: $1,500. **Duration:** Annual. **To Apply:** Applicants must submit a completed application form; a copy of their program of study showing courses remaining and photocopy of their transcript; a current resume that includes a statement of their career objectives and graduation date; a one page, typed essay highlighting their academic achievements, extracurricular activities, past and present work experiences, future occupation and commitment to the mission and goals of the MSFA; must submit a letter of recommendation from a faculty member of their department. **Deadline:** October 31.

6120 ■ Michigan Sugar Co.
2600 S Euclid Ave.
Bay City, MI 48707
Ph: (989)686-0161
Fax: (989)671-3695
E-mail: info@michigansugar.com
URL: www.michigansugar.com

6121 ■ Albert Flegenheimer Memorial Scholarships
(Undergraduate/Scholarship)

Purpose: To provide academic support to high school seniors who have completed a documented Youth Sugarbeet Project. **Focus:** General studies/Field of study not specified. **Qualif.:** Applicants must be residents of a county where sugarbeets are grown; must be high school graduating seniors; must have participated in the Michigan Sugar Youth Sugarbeet Program at one time and have completed a Sugarbeet Project. **Criteria:** Applicants are selected based on the committee's review of the application materials.

Funds Avail.: $2,500. **To Apply:** Applicants must submit a completed application form available at the Michigan Sugar Company web site. **Deadline:** April 18.

6122 ■ Michigan Sugar Company Hotel Restaurant/ Resort Management Scholarships (Undergraduate/ Scholarship)

Purpose: To provide financial support to deserving students enrolled in the Hotel Restaurant/Resort Management program of study. **Focus:** Hotel, institutional, and restaurant management. **Qualif.:** Applicants must be enrolled full-time in the Hotel Restaurant/Resort Management program in any college or university. **Criteria:** Applicants are selected based on the committee's review of the application materials.

Funds Avail.: $1,000. **To Apply:** Interested applicants may contact the Financial Aid Office at Northwood University for the application process and other required materials.

6123 ■ Michigan Sugar Queen Scholarships
(Undergraduate/Scholarship)

Purpose: To provide academic support to Sugar Queen participants. **Focus:** General studies/Field of study not specified. **Qualif.:** Applicants must be women, at least 18 years old and not older than 23; must never have been married and have no minor dependents; must be serving as Michigan Sugar Queen or Court attendant for a full year from crowning; must be friendly, courteous and not use tobacco, alcoholic beverages or drugs when appearing at official functions as Michigan Queen or Court attendant; must be residents of a county where sugarbeets are grown (Arenac, Bay, Clare, Clinton, Genesee, Gladwin, Gratiot, Huron, Ionia, Iosco, Isabella, Lapeer, Macomb, Midland, Montcalm, Ogemaw, Saginaw, Sanilac, Shiawassee, St. Clair and Tuscola). A parent/guardian will be required to attend any overnight events as a chaperone. **Criteria:** Applicants are selected based on the committee's review of the application materials.

Funds Avail.: $1,000-$2,000. **Duration:** Annual. **Number Awarded:** 3. **To Apply:** Interested applicants need to complete an application and send it with a picture. Application form can be downloaded at MSC website. **Deadline:** April 25.

6124 ■ Michigan Turfgrass Foundation (MTF)
c/o Rebecca Schoch, Executive Secretary
PO Box 27156
Lansing, MI 48909-7156

Awards are arranged alphabetically below their administering organizations

Ph: (517)392-5003
Fax: (989)936-5911
E-mail: miturfgrass@gmail.com
URL: www.michiganturfgrass.org

6125 ■ Robert Hancock Memorial Scholarship Awards *(Undergraduate/Scholarship)*

Purpose: To support the ongoing research, education and extension in the area of professional turfgrass management that will benefit all individuals who manage turfgrasses or derive pleasure from the results of such management. **Focus:** Management. **Qualif.:** Applicants must be senior undergraduates in the four-year Turfgrass Management Program; and must have a 3.0 GPA or higher. **Criteria:** Recipients are selected based on GPA.

Funds Avail.: $2,000. **Number Awarded:** 1. **To Apply:** Applicants must complete the application form and submit along with a cover letter, resume, questionnaire answers and letter of recommendation. **Deadline:** November 30.

6126 ■ Norman Kramer Scholarship Awards *(Undergraduate/Scholarship)*

Purpose: To support the ongoing research, education and extension in the area of professional turfgrass management that will benefit all individuals who manage turfgrasses or derive pleasure from the results of such management. **Focus:** General studies/Field of study not specified. **Qualif.:** Applicants must be students with a minimum of 42 credits completed and who have a 3.0 GPA or higher. **Criteria:** Recipients are selected based on GPA.

Funds Avail.: $2,500. **Duration:** Annual. **Number Awarded:** 1. **To Apply:** Applicants must complete the application form and submit along with a cover letter, resume, questionnaire answers, and letter of recommendation. **Deadline:** November 30.

6127 ■ Kenyon T. Payne Outstanding Student Awards *(Undergraduate/Award)*

Purpose: To support the ongoing research, education and extension in the area of professional turfgrass management that will benefit all individuals who manage turfgrasses or derive pleasure from the results of such management. **Focus:** Management. **Qualif.:** Applicants must be second year students in the Turfgrass Management Program who have a 3.0 GPA or higher. **Criteria:** Recipients are selected based on GPA, demonstrated leadership, character and estimated potential for future.

Funds Avail.: $2,000. **Duration:** Annual. **Number Awarded:** 1. **To Apply:** Applicants must complete the application form and submit along with a cover letter, resume, questionnaire answers and letter of recommendation.

6128 ■ Michigan Water Environment Association (MWEA)

5815 E Clark Rd., Ste. G
Bath, MI 48808
Ph: (517)641-7377
Fax: (517)641-7388
E-mail: mwea@mi-wea.org
URL: www.mi-wea.org

6129 ■ Antenore C. "Butch" Davanzo Scholarships *(Graduate, Undergraduate/Scholarship)*

Purpose: To support student Member that has excelled in his or her academic pursuits, at a Michigan college or university. **Focus:** Environmental conservation. **Qualif.:** Applicants must be attending a Michigan college or university; must be part-time students and pursuing a course of study leading to a career in Wastewater Treatment or some aspect of the water environment field; must be entering the second year of a two or four-year program in the year following receipt of the award or be in a graduate level course of study; must have at least a 2.5 GPA on a 4.0 scale; must be organization members at the time of the presentation of the award. **Criteria:** Recipients are selected based on academic performance and adherence to the requirements.

Funds Avail.: $1,000. **Duration:** Annual. **To Apply:** Applicants must submit a paper of between 500 and 600 words reflecting on their career interests and objectives and how they envision using their education to enhance water quality; must submit a current copy of their college or university transcript; resume with all full and part-time employment, education history and extracurricular activities; a letter of recommendation from their academic advisor or other appropriate official attesting to their course of study and other aspects of their application. **Deadline:** March 15.

6130 ■ John P. Hennessey Scholarships *(Graduate, Undergraduate/Scholarship)*

Purpose: To support student Member that has excelled in his or her academic pursuits, at a Michigan college or university. **Focus:** Environmental conservation. **Qualif.:** Applicants must be attending a Michigan college or university; must be full-time students and pursuing a course of study leading to a career in Wastewater Treatment or some aspect of the water environment field; must be entering the second year of a two- or four-year program the year following receipt of the award, or be in a graduate level course of study; must have an at least 2.5 GPA on a 4.0 scale; must be organization members at the time of the presentation of the award. **Criteria:** Recipients are selected based on academic performance and adherence to the requirements.

Funds Avail.: $2,000. **Duration:** Annual. **To Apply:** Applicants must submit a paper of between 500 and 600 words reflecting on their career interests and objectives and how they envision using their education to enhance water quality; must submit a current copy of their college or university transcript; resume with all full and part-time employment, education history and extracurricular activities; a letter of recommendation from their academic advisor or other appropriate official attesting to their course of study and other aspects of their application. **Deadline:** March 15.

6131 ■ Jack H. Wagner Scholarships *(Graduate, Undergraduate/Scholarship)*

Purpose: To support student Member that has excelled in his or her academic pursuits, at a Michigan college or university. **Focus:** Environmental conservation. **Qualif.:** Applicants must be enrolled full-time at any Michigan college or university and pursuing a course of study leading to a career in Wastewater Treatment or some other aspect of the water environment and/or environmental engineering field; must be entering the third or fourth year of their undergraduate program or be in a graduate level course of study. Applicants must have an at least 2.5 GPA on a 4.0 scale; must be organization member at the time of the presentation of the award. **Criteria:** Recipients are selected based on academic performance and adherence to the requirements.

Awards are arranged alphabetically below their administering organizations

Funds Avail.: $2,000. **Duration:** Annual. **To Apply:** Applicants must submit: a paper of between 500 and 600 words reflecting on their career interests and objectives and how they envision using their education to enhance water quality; a current copy of their college or university transcript; a resume with all full and part-time employment, education history and extracurricular activities; letter of recommendation from their academic advisor or other appropriate official attesting to their course of study and other aspects of their application. **Deadline:** March 15.

6132 ■ Microsoft Research

One Microsoft Way
Redmond, WA 98052
Free: 800-642-7676
E-mail: msrsch@microsoft.com
URL: research.microsoft.com/en-us

6133 ■ Microsoft Research Graduate Women's Scholarships *(Graduate/Scholarship)*

Purpose: To support women who are pursuing a PhD. **Focus:** Computer and information sciences; Engineering, Electrical; Mathematics and mathematical sciences. **Qualif.:** Students must be nominated by their universities, and their nominations must be confirmed by the office of the chair of the department; must attend a U.S. or Canadian university and be enrolled as full-time graduate students in the field of Computer Science, Electrical Engineering or Mathematics departments; must be enrolled in as first year in their graduate program. **Criteria:** Selection will be based on the committee's criteria.

Funds Avail.: $15,000. **Duration:** Annual. **To Apply:** Applications must include the following: applicants' curriculum vitae; a copy of the students' undergraduate transcript; three letters of reference from established researchers familiar with the applicants' research. One letter of recommendation should come from the students' graduate advisor, one letter of recommendation should come from the student's undergraduate advisor or another academic familiar with the students' undergraduate work, and one letter should come from another academic within the nominating institution. Applications must be submitted online via the application tool in any of the following formats: word documents, text-only file or PDF. All application materials must be submitted by the person designated as the application contact by the departmental chair's office and must not be the applicants. **Deadline:** October 16. **Contact:** Microsoft Research, at the above address, or Email: msrsch@microsoft.com.

6134 ■ Microsoft Research PhD Fellowships *(Doctorate/Fellowship)*

Purpose: To support men and women who are in their third and fourth years of PhD graduate studies. **Focus:** Computer and information sciences; Engineering, Electrical; Mathematics and mathematical sciences. **Qualif.:** Students must be nominated by their universities, and their nominations must be confirmed by the office of the chair of the department; must attend a U.S. or Canadian university and be enrolled as full-time graduate students in the Computer Science, Electrical Engineering or Mathematics departments; must be starting their second or third year in an eligible PhD program. The nominating university will be asked to confirm the student's PhD program start date. **Criteria:** Selection will be based on the committee's criteria.

Funds Avail.: $28,000. **Duration:** Two years. **To Apply:**

Applications must include: nominee's thesis proposal, nominee's curriculum vitae and three letters of reference from established researchers familiar with the nominee's research. One of these should come from the student's advisor. Applications must be submitted online via the application tool in any of the following formats: word documents, text-only file or PDF. All application materials must be submitted by the person designated as the application contact by the departmental chair's office and must not be the applicant. **Deadline:** October 7. **Contact:** Microsoft Research, at the above address; Email: msrfellow@microsoft.com.

6135 ■ Mid-Ohio District Nurses Association (MODNA)

1520 Old Henderson Rd., Ste. 100
Columbus, OH 43220
Ph: (614)326-1630
Fax: (614)326-1633
E-mail: modna@modna.org
URL: www.modna.org

6136 ■ MODNA Nursing Education Scholarships *(Doctorate, Graduate/Fellowship)*

Purpose: To provide financial assistance to qualified MODNA members who want to pursue their nursing profession. **Focus:** Nursing. **Qualif.:** Applicant must be a member in good standing of the American Nurses Association and Mid-Ohio District; must be enrolled or have plan to enroll in NLN-accredited or temporarily accredited programs leading to a Bachelor's Degree or a higher degree in Nursing or directly related field of doctoral study; must have a minimum of 3.0 GPA. **Criteria:** Applicants will be selected based on the following criteria: (1) applicant's professional contributions to nursing through ANA membership, participation in MODNA activities and other volunteer work; (2) previous work experience in Nursing will be considered; (3) applicant's apparent ability and commitment to complete the educational program; (4) candidate's future plans to use the additional knowledge in Nursing.

Funds Avail.: No specific amount. **Duration:** Annual. **To Apply:** Applicant must complete the application form available online; must attach the proof of acceptance to an educational program or proof showing application has been received and is being processed by the educational program; must submit a tentative plan of course work to complete their degree; must submit a page-long narrative explaining how the education program will help them to achieve their personal career goals and a paragraph describing how they envision impacting the nursing association. **Deadline:** December 1.

6137 ■ Middle East Studies Association of North America (MESA)

University of Arizona
1219 N Santa Rita Ave.
Tucson, AZ 85721
Ph: (520)621-5850
Fax: (520)626-9095
E-mail: secretariat@mesana.org
URL: mesa.arizona.edu

6138 ■ MESA Student Travel Fund *(Undergraduate/Grant)*

Purpose: To help subsidize travel expenses for students who are presenting papers at the MESA Annual Meeting.

Awards are arranged alphabetically below their administering organizations

Focus: General studies/Field of study not specified. Qualif.: Applicants must be current students in a degree-seeking program; must be current MESA members; must travel a minimum of 250 miles to attend the annual meeting; and must not be receiving funding to attend the meeting from any other source. Criteria: Recipients will be selected based on submitted application materials.

Funds Avail.: $250. Number Awarded: 4. To Apply: Applicants must submit a letter of application by e-mail or mail outlining their eligibility and have their academic department chair submit to MESA a letter of confirming that they are not receiving departmental support to attend the meeting.

6139 ■ Midlothian Rotary Club
PO Box 1537
Midlothian, TX 76065-1537
E-mail: contact@midlothianrotary.com
URL: www.midlothianrotary.com

6140 ■ Midlothian Rotary Club "Service Above Self" Scholarship *(Undergraduate/Scholarship)*

Purpose: To encourage and promote community service and leadership among Midlothian students, and reward the achievements of those students who have exemplified these ideals. Focus: General studies/Field of study not specified. Qualif.: Applicants must be Midlothian students. Criteria: Selection will be based on the committee's criteria.

Funds Avail.: No specific amount. Duration: Annual. To Apply: Any questions regarding the scholarship and application process should be directed to the Guidance Center.

6141 ■ Midwest Archives Conference (MAC)
4440 PGA Blvd., Ste. 600
Palm Beach Gardens, FL 33410
E-mail: membership@midwestarchives.org
URL: www.midwestarchives.org

6142 ■ MAC Louisa Bowen Memorial Scholarships for Graduate Students in Archival Administration *(Graduate/Scholarship)*

Purpose: To encourage the study in the field of archival administration. Focus: Library and archival sciences. Qualif.: Applicant must be a resident or full-time student residing in Illinois, Indiana, Iowa, Kansas, Kentucky, Michigan, Minnesota, Missouri, Nebraska, North Dakota, Ohio, South Dakota and Wisconsin who is enrolled or accepted in a graduate, multi-course program in archival administration with a GPA of 3.0 on 4.0 scale. Criteria: Recipient is selected based on his or her merits.

Funds Avail.: $750 and a one-year membership. Number Awarded: 1. To Apply: Applicants must submit a completed application form available on the website; transcript of recent academic program; essay (maximum of 500 words) on the applicant's interests and future goals in archival administration; and two letters of recommendation. Applicants must return completed application and related materials to: Helen Conger. Deadline: March 1. Contact: Helen Conger, Archivist, Case Western Reserve University Archives, 20 University West, 10900 Euclid Avenue, Cleveland, OH 44106-7229; Phone:216-368-6774; Email: hconger@case.edu.

6143 ■ MAC Emeritus Scholarships for First-Time Meeting Attendees *(Professional development/Scholarship)*

Purpose: To assist individuals to attend the MAC meetings. Focus: General studies/Field of study not specified. Qualif.: Applicant must be attending his/her first MAC meeting; must be a member or residing within the 13 state MAC region. Criteria: Recipients are selected based on their statements.

Funds Avail.: One Scholarship of $500 or two scholarships of $250. To Apply: Applicants must submit a completed application form available on the website; an essay (maximum of 500 words) on the importance of the MAC meeting to the applicant and a summary of financial requirements; and a letter of support (optional). Applicants return completed application and related materials to: Lydia Lucas. Deadline: February 1.

6144 ■ Archie Motley Memorial Scholarships for Minority Students *(Graduate/Scholarship)*

Purpose: To promote education and career in archival administration. Focus: Library and archival sciences. Qualif.: Applicant must be an African, American Indian, Asian or Pacific Islander, or Latino student; currently enrolled in a graduate, multi-course program in archival administration or accepted into such a program for the next academic year; have a GPA of at least 3.0 on a 4.0 scale. Criteria: Recipients are selected based on their merits.

Funds Avail.: $750 and one-year membership to MAC. Duration: One year. Number Awarded: 2. To Apply: Applicant must submit a completed application form available on the website; transcript of recent academic program; essay (maximum of 500 words) on the applicant's interests and future goals in archival administration; and two letters of recommendation. Applicant completed applications (in hard-copy) should be sent to: Alison Stankrauff. Deadline: March 1. Contact: Alison Stankrauff, Archivist and Associate Librarian, Franklin D. Schurz Library, Indiana University South Bend, PO Box 7111, South Bend, Indiana 46634; Phone:574-520-4392; Email:astankra@iusb.edu.

6145 ■ Midwest Dairy Association (MDA)
2015 Rice St.
Saint Paul, MN 55113
Free: 800-642-3895
E-mail: info@midwestdairy.com
URL: www.midwestdairy.com

6146 ■ Illinois Division Scholarships *(Undergraduate/Scholarship)*

Purpose: To provide financial assistance to college students within the Chicago Division. Focus: General studies/Field of study not specified. Qualif.: Applicants must be enrolled in an accredited college; must be immediate family members of dairy farmers. Criteria: Preference will be given to those students who meet the criteria.

Funds Avail.: $1,000. Duration: One year. To Apply: Applicants must submit a completed application form; typed or printed essay; current transcript of records; and two or three references. Deadline: March 1. Contact: For more information, contact: Marla Behrends at mbehrends@midwestdairy.com.

6147 ■ Iowa Division Scholarships *(Undergraduate/Scholarship)*

Purpose: To provide financial assistance to Iowa students. Focus: General studies/Field of study not specified. Qualif.: Applicants must be enrolled full-time in an accredited college; and must be immediate family members of dairy farmers. **Criteria:** Recipients will be chosen by the committee.

Funds Avail.: $250 - $1,500. **Duration:** Annual. **Number Awarded:** 23. **To Apply:** Applicants must submit a completed application form; typed or printed essay; transcript of high school and/or college records; and two or three references. **Deadline:** March 1. **Contact:** For more information, contact: Bev Lehs at 800-642-3895 or Direct 515-965-4620.

6148 ■ Kansas City Division Scholarships
(Undergraduate/Scholarship)

Purpose: To provide financial assistance to students who are in need. **Focus:** General studies/Field of study not specified. **Qualif.:** Applicants must be enrolled in an accredited college; must be immediate family members of dairy farmers. **Criteria:** Recipients will be chosen by the committee.

Funds Avail.: $500 - $1,000. **Duration:** Annual. **Number Awarded:** 10. **To Apply:** Applicants must check the available website for the required materials. **Deadline:** March 31. **Contact:** For more information, contact: Ron Grusenmeyer, Industry Relations Manager at 816-873-0351.

6149 ■ Minnesota Division Scholarships
(Undergraduate/Scholarship)

Purpose: To provide financial assistance to students who are in need. **Focus:** General studies/Field of study not specified. **Qualif.:** Applicants must be enrolled students at the University of Minnesota CFANS in St. Paul or in Crookston. **Criteria:** Recipients will be chosen by the University as part of their normal scholarship selection process.

Funds Avail.: $1,200-$3,000. **To Apply:** Applicants must check the available website for the required materials. **Contact:** Midwest Dairy Association at the above address.

6150 ■ North Dakota Division Scholarships
(Undergraduate/Scholarship)

Purpose: To provide financial assistance to deserving students. **Focus:** Education; Nutrition. **Qualif.:** Applicants must be juniors or non-graduating seniors majoring in food nutrition, family and consumer science education or education. **Criteria:** Recipients will be chosen by the University.

Funds Avail.: $1,000. **Duration:** Annual. **Number Awarded:** 3. **To Apply:** Applicants must check the available website for the required materials. **Deadline:** January 31. **Contact:** For more information, contact: Char Heer, Industry Relations Manager at 701-782-4154.

6151 ■ Ozarks Division Scholarships
(Undergraduate/Scholarship)

Purpose: To provide financial support to students who are in need. **Focus:** General studies/Field of study not specified. **Qualif.:** Applicants must be enrolled students in an accredited college and must be immediate family members of dairy farmers. **Criteria:** Recipients will be chosen by the committee.

Funds Avail.: $500. **Duration:** Annual. **Number Awarded:** 4. **To Apply:** Applicants must submit a completed application and newspaper information form; must prepare a list of leadership activities and events; transcript of high school and/or college records; and two or three references. **Deadline:** March 31. **Contact:** For more information, contact: Ron Grusenmeyer at 816-873-0351.

6152 ■ South Dakota Division Scholarships
(Undergraduate/Scholarship)

Purpose: To provide financial support to students who are in need. **Focus:** Dairy science. **Qualif.:** Applicants must be incoming freshmen majoring in Dairy Science who are admitted at Dakota State University in Brookings. **Criteria:** Recipients will be chosen by the SDSU selection committee.

Funds Avail.: $1,000 - $3,000. **Duration:** Annual. **Number Awarded:** 5. **To Apply:** Applicants must check the available website for the required materials. **Contact:** For more information, contact: Roger Scheibe, Industry Relations Manager at 605-692-1775.

6153 ■ Midwest Food Processors Association, Inc. (MWFPA)
4600 American Pkwy., Ste. 210
Madison, WI 53718-8334
Ph: (608)255-9946
Fax: (608)255-9838
E-mail: info@mwfpa.org
URL: www.mwfpa.org

6154 ■ Carleton A. Friday Scholarship
(Undergraduate/Scholarship)

Purpose: To support those who are studying agriculture or food science. **Focus:** Agricultural sciences; Food science and technology. **Qualif.:** Applicants must be undergraduate students who are majoring in agriculture or food science within the University of Wisconsin system (currently Madison, Platteville and River Falls). **Criteria:** Recipients are selected based on financial need.

Funds Avail.: Up to $1,500. **Duration:** Annual. **Number Awarded:** 3. **To Apply:** Applicants must submit completed application form indicating GPA; a letter of recommendation from advisor or other faculty member; a letter of interest; letter of recommendation from past employer; document/s indicating financial need; and contact information. **Deadline:** April 30. **Contact:** brian.elliot@mwfpa.org.

6155 ■ Kenneth G. Weckel Scholarships
(Undergraduate/Scholarship)

Purpose: To support those who are studying agriculture or food science. **Focus:** Agricultural sciences; Food science and technology. **Qualif.:** Applicants must be undergraduate students who are majoring in agriculture or food science within the University of Wisconsin system (currently Madison, Platteville and River Falls). **Criteria:** Recipients are selected based on financial need.

Funds Avail.: $1,500. **Duration:** Annual. **Number Awarded:** 3. **To Apply:** Applicants must submit completed application form indicating GPA; a letter of recommendation from advisor or other faculty member; a letter of interest from students; letter of recommendation from past employer; documents indicating financial need; and contact information. **Deadline:** April 30. **Contact:** brian.elliot@mwfpa.org.

6156 ■ Milbank, Tweed, Hadley & McCloy LLP
One Chase Manhattan Plz.
New York, NY 10005
Ph: (212)530-5000
Fax: (212)530-5219
URL: www.milbank.com/en

Awards are arranged alphabetically below their administering organizations

6157 ■ Milbank Diversity Scholarships
(Undergraduate/Scholarship)

Purpose: To inspire career pursuits and excellence in the field of law by providing educational support for qualified law students. **Focus:** Law. **Qualif.:** Applicants must be members of groups traditionally underrepresented in large law firms; must be in good standing at an ABA accredited law school; must have successfully completed their first year of a full-time JD program; may not be the recipient of a similar scholarship award from another law firm; and must have completed two years of a JD program. **Criteria:** Recipients will be selected based on academic achievement, demonstrated leadership ability, excellent writing and interpersonal skills.

Funds Avail.: $25,000. **To Apply:** Applicants must complete the application form available online and submit along with an essay, official law school transcript and resume. Application form and other supporting documents must be sent to Elizabeth A. Crispino, Manager of Campus Recruiting. **Deadline:** August 15.

6158 ■ Military Intelligence Corps Association (MICA)
PO Box 13020
Fort Huachuca, AZ 85670-3020
E-mail: administrator@micorps.org
URL: www.micastore.com

6159 ■ Military Intelligence Corps Association Scholarships *(Undergraduate, Vocational/Occupational/Scholarship)*

Purpose: To provide scholarships for individuals pursuing undergraduate degrees or technical certifications. **Focus:** General studies/Field of study not specified. **Qualif.:** Applicants must be current MICA members in good standing. They must be pursuing post-secondary education through a college, university, vocational school or technical institution and must be accepted or enrolled in a qualified education program and who agree to complete at least one course or class. **Criteria:** The Scholarship Chairman determines evaluation criteria to be used during the board process. The Scholarship Board will judge the applications solely on documentation provided in the application. Areas of evaluation that the Scholarship Board considers are: educational goals (essay); past performance (transcripts); and potential for future success (letters of recommendation).

Funds Avail.: $500 - $1,000. **Duration:** Annual. **To Apply:** Applications must contain the following documentation: scholarship application checklist; scholarship application signed by the applicant; copy of MICA Membership Card (if copy of membership card is not available, please provide some proof of current membership); three letters of Recommendation (all letters of recommendation must be signed and include full point of contact information); essay (include a one-page essay detailing the applicant's educational goals and program of study); transcripts; and proof of acceptance by an educational institution. **Deadline:** May 31. **Contact:** MICA, Attn: MICA Scholarship Chairman, P.O. Box 13020, Fort Huachuca, Arizona 85670-3020.

6160 ■ Military Officers Association of America (MOAA)
201 N Washington St.
Alexandria, VA 22314-2537

Ph: (703)549-2311
Free: 800-234-6622
E-mail: msc@moaa.org
URL: www.moaa.org

6161 ■ MOAA American Patriot Scholarships
(Undergraduate/Scholarship)

Purpose: To help children of Uniformed Services members who died or were severely disabled while in active service as members of the Regular, Guard or Reserve Forces. **Focus:** General studies/Field of study not specified. **Qualif.:** Applicant must be a child of a member of the Uniformed Services who died while in active service; must be under the age of 24 at the time of application (the maximum age for students who are serving or have served in the Armed Forces before completing college will be increased by the number of years served, for up to five years of service or 29 years of age); must be planning to attend an accredited college/university as a full-time student seeking their first undergraduate degree; and must have a cumulative GPA of 3.0 or higher on a 4.0 scale. **Criteria:** Awards are given based on scholastic ability, activities and financial need.

Funds Avail.: At least $2,500. **Duration:** Annual. **To Apply:** Applicants must apply for the scholarship online. **Deadline:** March 1.

6162 ■ General John Paul Ratay Educational Grants
(Undergraduate/Grant)

Purpose: To help children of Uniformed Services members. **Focus:** General studies/Field of study not specified. **Qualif.:** Applicant must be the child of the surviving spouse of a retired officer. **Criteria:** Applicants must apply for a loan in order to be considered.

Funds Avail.: $5,000. **Duration:** Annual. **To Apply:** Applicants must apply online. **Deadline:** March 1.

6163 ■ Mill Creek Business Association (MCBA)
13300 Bothell-Everett Hwy.
Mill Creek, WA 98012
Ph: (425)673-6200
E-mail: info@millcreekbiz.com
URL: www.millcreekbiz.com

6164 ■ Mill Creek Business Association Scholarships *(Undergraduate/Scholarship)*

Purpose: To encourage and assist local high school students in their pursuit of higher learning in Business or Fine Arts. **Focus:** Art; Business. **Qualif.:** Applicants must live in Mill Creek and/or attend school at Jacksonville High school or Archbishop Murphy High School; must be senior students in good standing at the time of application; must be accepted to attend a full-time accredited college, university or Fine Arts school; must be planning an academic course of study in the field of business/fine arts and/or plan to pursue a career in business or fine arts. **Criteria:** Recipients are selected based on academic performance.

Funds Avail.: $2,000. **Number Awarded:** 5. **To Apply:** Applicants must complete the application form; must submit two letters of reference and recommendation from teachers, advisors, and/or local business people; a copy of the letter of acceptance from their institution; must provide a 200 word, typed essay stating their academic and career plans. **Deadline:** May 1.

6165 ■ Glenn Miller Birthplace Society (GMBS)
122 W Clark St.
Clarinda, IA 51632

Awards are arranged alphabetically below their administering organizations

---

Ph: (712)542-2461
Fax: (712)542-2868
E-mail: gmbs@glennmiller.org
URL: glennmiller.org

6166 ■ Glenn Miller Scholarships (Undergraduate/Scholarship)

Purpose: To seek out and assist promising young talents in any field of applied music who may be musical leaders of tomorrow. **Focus:** Music. **Qualif.:** Applicants must be graduating high school seniors or first year college students intending to make music a central part of their future life and high school seniors, unless they have been previous first place winners. **Criteria:** Recipients will be selected based on questions of eligibility, conformance to the rules and their intent.

Funds Avail.: $1,000; $2,000; $3,000. **Duration:** Annual. **Number Awarded:** 6. **To Apply:** Applicants must submit a clear high-quality audio CD or tape; completed application; and statement of musical intentions. **Deadline:** March 2.

6167 ■ Mineralogical Association of Canada (MAC)

490, rue de la Couronne
Quebec, QC, Canada G1K 9A9
Ph: (418)653-0333
Fax: (418)653-0777
E-mail: office@mineralogicalassociation.ca
URL: www.mineralogicalassociation.ca

6168 ■ Mineralogical Association of Canada Scholarships (Doctorate, Postgraduate/Scholarship)

Purpose: To support graduate students engaged in research in any field currently supported by MAC. **Focus:** Mineralogy. **Qualif.:** Applicants must be students entering their second year of an M.Sc. program or the second or third year of a Ph.D. program at any Canadian university or students who are Canadian citizens attending a university located outside of Canada. **Criteria:** Applications will be assessed by a committee consisting of three members of MAC council chaired by the Chairman of MACF.

Funds Avail.: CDN $5,000. **Duration:** Annual. **Number Awarded:** 2. **To Apply:** Applications must be accompanied by an official academic transcript (undergraduate and graduate). Applicants must provide an outline of their thesis project using two pages of single text. Five copies of the application form and thesis project should be provided. **Deadline:** May 1. **Contact:** Pierrete Tremblay at the above address or e-mail at pierrette_tremblay@ete.inrs.ca; Johanne Caron, jcaron@mineralogicalassociation.ca.

6169 ■ Minneapolis Jewish Federation

13100 Wayzata Blvd., Ste. 200
Minnetonka, MN 55305
Ph: (952)593-2600
E-mail: webmaster@mplsfed.org
URL: jewishminneapolis.org

6170 ■ Minneapolis Jewish Federation Camp Scholarships (Undergraduate/Scholarship)

Purpose: To provide financial assistance to children for Jewish summer day and overnight camp programs. **Focus:** General studies/Field of study not specified. **Qualif.:** Applicants must be Jewish; must be residents of the greater Minneapolis area. **Criteria:** Selection will be based on the committee's criteria.

Funds Avail.: No specific amount. **To Apply:** Applicants must submit a completed application form to the Minneapolis Jewish Federation office. **Deadline:** March.

6171 ■ Minnesota Association of County Probation Officers (MACPO)

c/o Kattie Zarns, Agent
13880 Business Center Dr. NW
Elk River, MN 55330-1692
Ph: (763)765-4564
E-mail: president@macpo.net
URL: www.macpo.net

6172 ■ Minnesota Association County Probation Officers Scholarships (Undergraduate/Scholarship)

Purpose: To promote and attract quality students to consider Corrections as a career. **Focus:** Criminal justice. **Qualif.:** Applicants must be junior or senior students majoring in Corrections, Sociology, Criminal justice, Psychology, Social Work, or other related fields who will be/are currently involved in an internship; must have 2.5 GPA; and must be enrolled at an accredited two-year of four-year college or university. **Criteria:** Recipients are selected based on academic attainment; demonstrated leadership; commitment to a career in Corrections; and community involvement.

Funds Avail.: $750. **To Apply:** Applicants must submit the completed application form; one letter of reference from a faculty member or from an internship supervisor/director; and document that answers questions from the application available on website. All applications should be submitted to: Jill Arbeiter Carver County Corrections located at 604 E 4th St., Chaska, MN 55318, phone: 952-361-1471, or e-mail jarbeite@co.carver.mn.us.

6173 ■ Minnesota Association of Public Accountants (MAPA)

1000 Westgate Dr., Ste. 252
Saint Paul, MN 55114
Ph: (651)290-6289
Fax: (651)290-2266
Free: 800-501-4521
E-mail: admin@mapa-mn.com
URL: www.mapa-mn.com

6174 ■ Minnesota Association of Public Accountant Scholarships (Undergraduate/Scholarship)

Purpose: To further the knowledge of the practitioner and offer a source of current information and interplay of ideas among professionals. **Focus:** Accounting. **Qualif.:** Applicants must be undergraduate students entering their junior year; must be enrolled in a degree program at an accredited four-year college or university majoring in accounting with the intention to practice in the field of public accounting; must have at least 2.5 or better grade point average; must be U.S. citizens attending a U.S. accredited school; and must be Minnesota residents. **Criteria:** Recipients are selected based on academic performance.

Funds Avail.: Generally $750 but the amount varies. **Duration:** Annual. **To Apply:** Applicants must submit a com-

Awards are arranged alphabetically below their administering organizations

pleted application form; official transcript; and letters of recommendation from advisors or professors. **Deadline:** April 15. **Contact:** Minnesota Association of Public Accountants at the above address.

6175 ■ Minnesota Association of Townships (MAT)

PO Box 267
Saint Michael, MN 55376
Ph: (763)497-2330
Fax: (763)228-0296
Free: 800-497-2330
E-mail: info@mntownships.org
URL: www.mntownships.org

6176 ■ Minnesota Association of Township Scholarships *(Undergraduate, Vocational/Occupational/ Scholarship)*

Purpose: To foster efficient, effective and economical town governmental services and to further awareness and education about the township government. **Focus:** Government. **Qualif.:** Applicants must be currently enrolled in the 11th grade and attending a Minnesota public, private, or parochial high school or a home study program and plan to further their education at a college, university, or vocational school. **Criteria:** Recipients are selected based on the written essay; originality; knowledge of the subject matter in relationship to the title; supporting statements; correct spelling and punctuation.

Funds Avail.: $1,000. **Duration:** Annual. **Number Awarded:** Up to 6. **To Apply:** Applicants must complete an application form; a 450-500-word, typed, double-spaced written essay; a current high school transcript; and a letter of recommendation from a high school teacher or counselor. **Deadline:** May 1. **Contact:** Minnesota Association of Townships Scholarship Program at the above address.

6177 ■ Minnesota Health Information Management Association (MHIMA)

PO Box 26
Cromwell, MN 55726-0026
Ph: (218)340-1968
Fax: (218)644-3319
E-mail: executivedirector@mnhima.org
URL: www.mnhima.org

6178 ■ Minnesota Health Information Management Association Scholarships *(Undergraduate/ Scholarship)*

Purpose: To promote high quality health information and benefit the public, healthcare providers and other clinical data users. **Focus:** Health education. **Qualif.:** Applicants must be Minnesota residents enrolled in an in-state or out-of-state program or out-of-state students attending a Minnesota school; must have completed accredited Health Information Technology or Health Information Management program; must be in a graduate program related to HIM College or University and accredited by a nationally recognized accrediting agency that has a coding certificate program or AHIMA Coding Basics Interactive Campus program; must have cumulative GPA of 3.0 out of 4.0; and must be members of AHIMA. **Criteria:** Recipients are selected based on academic achievement.

Funds Avail.: Maximum of $1,500. **Duration:** Annual. **To**

Apply: Applicants must submit an application form; one letter of recommendation from faculty advisor, faculty member or mentor; a verification program; an essay with 500 words; and an official transcript of grades indicating cumulative grades. **Contact:** MHIMA Executive Director; e-mail: executivedirector@mnhima.org.

6179 ■ Minnesota Minority Junior Golf Association (MMJGA)

230 TriTech Ctr.
331 2nd Ave. S
Minneapolis, MN 55401-2240
Ph: (612)702-1406
E-mail: info@mmjga.org
URL: www.mmjga.org

6180 ■ Evans Scholarships *(Undergraduate/ Scholarship)*

Purpose: To provide funds for educational costs and to advance golf lessons if committed to golf as profession. **Focus:** Sports studies. **Qualif.:** Applicants must be caddies and golfers who have completed two full years in the MMJGA Caddie Program; must document at least 40 loops of caddying in the two-year period (with at least 25 loops at a private country club in the two-year period); must be assisting in training new caddies; must achieve "A" level or above caddie status at a country club; must be accepted or enrolled at a post-secondary educational program; and must maintain 2.0 or better grade point average. **Criteria:** Recipients will be selected based on functional equivalence of prior experience.

Funds Avail.: No specific amount. **Duration:** Annual. **To Apply:** Applicants must complete the application form and provide an essay.

6181 ■ Minnesota State Archery Association (MSAA)

c/o Cheri Irlbeck, Secretary
33266 County Hwy. 4
Sanborn, MN 56083
Ph: (507)640-1683
E-mail: president.msaa@mnarchery.org
URL: www.mnarchery.org

6182 ■ Minnesota State Archery Association Scholarships Program *(Undergraduate/Scholarship)*

Purpose: To encourage outstanding students to prepare for worthwhile careers at the college of their choice and to promote the sport of archery. **Focus:** General studies/Field of study not specified. **Qualif.:** Applicants must be graduating high school students who are academically successful and who can also demonstrate a sincere interest in the sport of archery. **Criteria:** Recipients are selected based on financial need and participation in activities.

Funds Avail.: $500. **Duration:** Annual. **Number Awarded:** 2. **To Apply:** Applicants must submit a completed application form and a resume. **Deadline:** June 15. **Remarks:** Established in 1971.

6183 ■ Minority Corporate Counsel Association (MCCA)

1111 Pennsylvania Ave. NW
Washington, DC 20004

Awards are arranged alphabetically below their administering organizations

---

Ph: (202)739-5901
Fax: (202)739-5999
E-mail: membership@mmca.com
URL: www.mcca.com

6184 ■ MCCA Lloyd M. Johnson, Jr. Scholarships
(Graduate, Undergraduate/Scholarship)

Purpose: To provide scholarship support for newly entering first year law students pursuing a Juris Doctor degree. **Focus:** Law. **Qualif.:** Applicants must be US citizens and able to show proof of same, if requested; must be enrolled full-time and show proof of acceptance into an ABA-accredited US law school; must have an interest in corporate law, including an interest in working in a corporate law department and/or law firm; must have an interest in diversity; must be financially disadvantaged; must demonstrate community service and leadership qualities; must have earned an undergraduate cumulative GPA of 3.2 or higher. **Criteria:** Applicants will be scored by the MCCA and UNCF and provide a list of the top forty candidates to the LMJ Scholarship Committee to choose the winners.

Funds Avail.: $10,000. **Duration:** Annual. **To Apply:** Application must be submitted online and must include the following uploaded application materials: undergraduate and graduate transcripts, resume, provision of contract information for two recommenders and response to a two-part essay question. **Deadline:** May 15. **Remarks:** Established in 2004.

6185 ■ Mission Aviation Fellowship of Canada
264 Woodlawn Rd. W
Guelph, ON, Canada N1H 1B6
Ph: (519)821-3914
Fax: (519)823-1650
Free: 877-351-9344
E-mail: info@mafc.org
URL: www.mafc.org

6186 ■ MAF Canada Scholarship Fund
(Undergraduate/Scholarship)

Purpose: To support students preparing for a full-time career in mission aviation who have plans to use their skills overseas. **Focus:** Aviation. **Qualif.:** Applicants must be post-secondary students; must be Canadian citizens or landed immigrants; and must have successfully completed at least one year of Bible school. Applicants must possess either of the following: (Pilot) private license or (AME) all required courses completed. **Criteria:** Preference will be given to applicants who have demonstrated financial need.

Funds Avail.: $3,500. **Duration:** Annual. **To Apply:** Applicants must prepare a minimum two-page essay describing their goals and objectives with regards to a vocation in mission aviation. Essay should include all information required to assess the applicant's Christian life and Ministry. It should be accompanied by a transcript of recent grades, copy of their vocational certification and a reference letter from a pastor or senior church official to whom they reported while participating in church ministry or community outreach. **Deadline:** September 1 and January 31. **Contact:** Mission Aviation Fellowship of Canada, at the above address.

6187 ■ Mississippi Society of Certified Public Accountants (MSCPA)
The Commons, Highland Colony Pkwy.
306 Southampton Row
Ridgeland, MS 39157

Ph: (601)856-4244
Fax: (601)856-8255
Free: 800-772-1099
E-mail: mail@ms-cpa.org
URL: www.ms-cpa.org

6188 ■ MSCPA Undergraduate Scholarships
(Undergraduate/Scholarship)

Purpose: To support undergraduate students majoring in accounting. **Focus:** Accounting. **Qualif.:** Applicant must be majoring in accountancy at a four-year Mississippi college/university; have at least six hours of accountancy courses above the principles or introductory level and must have completed (or be completing) the junior year of college in preparation for the senior year; and be a Mississippi resident. **Criteria:** Selection is based on academic excellence, campus involvement, faculty recommendations, written essay and financial need.

Funds Avail.: $2,000. **Duration:** Annual. **To Apply:** Applicants must submit a completed undergraduate student application (5 pages) signed and dated; a recent photograph, one-page essay and official transcript of all college work to the chair of the accounting department or designee of the applicant's institution. **Deadline:** June 1.

6189 ■ Ross/Nickey Scholarships *(Graduate/Scholarship)*

Purpose: To financially support students enrolled at a graduate accounting program. **Focus:** Accounting. **Qualif.:** Applicant must be enrolled in or admitted to a graduate accounting program in Mississippi; a Mississippi resident; and must demonstrate special merit and exceptional promise in the field of accounting. **Criteria:** Selection is based on academic excellence, campus involvement, faculty recommendations, written essay and financial need.

Funds Avail.: $1,000. **Duration:** Annual. **To Apply:** Applicants must submit a completed graduate student application form (5 pages) signed and dated; a recent photograph; a one-page essay; GMAT score; acceptance letter from the college/university chosen for graduate study; and official transcript of all college undergraduate and graduate work to the chair of the accounting department or designee of the applicant's institution. **Deadline:** June 1.

6190 ■ Missouri Department of Health and Senior Services
912 Wildwood Dr.
Jefferson City, MO 65102
Ph: (573)751-6400
Fax: (573)751-6010
Free: 800-235-5503
E-mail: info@health.mo.gov
URL: health.mo.gov

6191 ■ Health Professional Nursing Student Loans
(Undergraduate, Graduate/Loan)

Purpose: To address the needs of students pursuing a degree in nursing. **Focus:** Nursing. **Qualif.:** Applicants must be Missouri residents attending a Missouri institution. Applicants must have been accepted by or currently attending a nursing program approved by the Missouri State Board of Nursing for participation in the program who in the previous year had at least a 80% pass rate. Previous nursing students must have at least a 2.5 GPA to qualify.

Awards are arranged alphabetically below their administering organizations

Criteria: Selection will be based on the committee's criteria.

Funds Avail.: $2,500 for LPN students; $5,000 for professional nursing students. **Duration:** Annual. **To Apply:** Interested applicants may contact the Missouri Department of Health and Senior Services to request an application or may visit the website to download an application.

6192 ■ Modern Language Association of America (MLA)

26 Broadway, 3rd Fl.
New York, NY 10004-1789
Ph: (646)576-5000
Fax: (646)458-0030
E-mail: execdirector@mla.org
URL: www.mla.org

6193 ■ MLA Financial Assistance *(Graduate, Advanced Professional/Grant)*

Purpose: To provide partial travel assistance to the members of the MLA who shall attend preconvention workshops, sessions in their areas of scholarly interest, meetings with job counselors, or interviews. **Focus:** Modern languages. **Qualif.:** Applicants must be, generally, MLA members. Specifically, MLA members interested to avail the program are the following: graduate students, non-tenure track faculty members and unemployed members; and regular and life members residing outside United States and Canada. **Criteria:** Selection will be based on the committee's criteria.

Funds Avail.: $400. **Duration:** Annual. **Number Awarded:** 3. **To Apply:** Applicants may apply online (through MLA website) or via mail as an alternative. Each letter should include complete contact information and a brief statement by students indicating whether they are receiving external support for travel to the convention. All letters required should be mailed to the Travel Grant Program of MLA. **Deadline:** November 30.. **Contact:** MLA; Phone: 646-576-5141; E-mail: awards@mla.org.

6194 ■ Moline Foundation

817 11th Ave.
Moline, IL 61265
Ph: (309)736-3800
Fax: (309)736-3721
URL: www.molinefoundation.org

6195 ■ Clem T. Hanson Scholarship Fund *(Undergraduate/Scholarship)*

Purpose: To provide grants to health, human services, education, community development, the arts and other charitable organizations which benefit the citizens of Moline Foundations. **Focus:** General studies/Field of study not specified. **Qualif.:** Applicants must be graduating high school seniors or community college students preparing to transfer to four-year colleges; must intend to pursue a bachelor's degree on a full-time basis in any career field; must demonstrate financial need; must have achieved high school scholastic performance in the upper one-third of their class or community college grade performance of 2.5 on a 4.0 scale or equivalent. **Criteria:** Recipients are selected based on financial need. Finalists will be evaluated based on personal interview and letters of reference.

Funds Avail.: Varies. **To Apply:** Applicants must complete the application form. **Deadline:** March 16. **Contact:** Linda

Daily, Moline Foundation; E-mail: ldaily@qconline.com.

6196 ■ Lee Womack Scholarship Fund *(Undergraduate/Scholarship)*

Purpose: To provide grants to health, human services, education, community development, arts and other charitable organizations which benefit the citizens of Moline Foundations. To provide funds to deserving students from Moline High School who plan to obtain a college degree in education. **Focus:** Education. **Qualif.:** Applicants must be graduating high school seniors, or community college students preparing to transfer to four-year colleges; must intend to pursue a bachelor's degree on a full-time basis; must demonstrate financial need; have achieved high school scholastic performance in the upper one-third of their class, or community college grade performance of 2.5 on a 4.0 scale, or equivalent; and must be reside within Moline District No. 40 (which includes Coal Valley, IL). **Criteria:** Recipients are selected based on financial need.

Funds Avail.: No specific amount. **Duration:** Annual. **To Apply:** Applicants must complete the application form. **Deadline:** March 16. **Contact:** Linda Daily, Moline Foundation; E-mail: ldaily@qconline.com.

6197 ■ Monadnock Folklore Society (MFS)

c/o Bruce Myrick, Director
54 Brook St.
Keene, NH 03431-3281
Ph: (603)352-8616
E-mail: info@monadnockfolk.org
URL: www.monadnockfolk.org

6198 ■ Johnny Trombly Scholarships *(Undergraduate/Scholarship)*

Purpose: To provide financial assistance to musicians. **Focus:** Music. **Qualif.:** Applicants must be residents of Cheshire, Sullivan or Hillsborough counties (NH). Upper Connecticut River Valley and Windham county (VT) residents are welcome to apply. **Criteria:** Preference will be given to Monadnock area residents.

Funds Avail.: Up to $500. **Duration:** Annual. **To Apply:** Application must be accompanied by at least one recommendation letter from someone who is knowledgeable about the applicant and music. Selected applicants are required to provide a photo and report describing the prospective benefits to be acquired from the funding. **Deadline:** March 15. **Remarks:** Established in 2001. **Contact:** Bruce Myrick, Director, Monadnock Folklore Society at the above address.

6199 ■ Monsanto Co.

800 N Lindbergh Blvd.
Saint Louis, MO 63167
Ph: (314)694-1000
URL: www.monsanto.com

6200 ■ Monsanto Commitment To Agriculture Scholarships *(Undergraduate/Scholarship)*

Purpose: To support the education of students who have long-term career interest in agriculture. **Focus:** Agricultural sciences. **Qualif.:** Applicants must be high school seniors who come from a farm family, plan to enroll as a full-time student in an agriculture-related academic major in an accredited school and be committed to pursuing a career in

Awards are arranged alphabetically below their administering organizations

agriculture. **Criteria:** Applicants will be evaluated on their academic record, leadership, extracurricular activities and personal essays submitted as a part of the application process.

Funds Avail.: $1,500 each. **Number Awarded:** 100. **To Apply:** Applicants may contact the Program Administrator for the application. **Remarks:** The scholarship is in association with the National Association of Farm Broadcasters (NAFB). Established in 1999.

6201 ■ Montana Broadcasters Association (MBA)
18 Ruby Mountain Rd.
Clancy, MT 59634
Ph: (406)431-2139
URL: www.mtbroadcasters.org

6202 ■ Joe Durso, Jr. Memorial Scholarship
(Undergraduate/Scholarship)

Purpose: To promote the values of local, free over-the-air broadcasting to the business community, governmental bodies and the general public in Montana; and to support the Montana broadcasting industry by providing services, information, continuing education, recruitment and a strong unified voice. **Focus:** Broadcasting. **Qualif.:** Applicants must be students entering their senior year, majoring in Radio-TV or Broadcast Journalism. **Criteria:** Recipients are selected based on academic performance.

Funds Avail.: No specific amount. **Duration:** Annual. **To Apply:** Applicants must complete an application form; must include (one-page) statement summarizing their professional abilities, career goals and extra-curricular activities; and two letters of recommendation from an instructor. **Deadline:** February 28.

6203 ■ Great Falls Broadcasters Association Scholarships *(Undergraduate/Scholarship)*

Purpose: To promote the values of local, free over-the-air broadcasting to the business community, governmental bodies and the general public in Montana; and to support the Montana broadcasting industry by providing services, information, continuing education, recruitment and a strong unified voice. **Focus:** Broadcasting. **Qualif.:** Applicants must be students who have graduated from North-Central Montana High School and are enrolled as at least second-year students in Radio-TV at any public or private Montana college or university. **Criteria:** Recipients are selected based on academic performance.

Funds Avail.: No specific amount. **Duration:** Annual. **To Apply:** Applicants must complete an application form; must include a one-page statement summarizing their professional abilities, career goals and extra-curricular activities; and two letters of recommendation from an instructor. **Deadline:** February 28. **Contact:** Montana Broadcasters Association; e-mail: dbruce@mtbroadcasters.org.

6204 ■ Montana Broadcasters Association Engineers' Scholarships *(Undergraduate/Scholarship)*

Purpose: To promote the values of local, free over-the-air broadcasting to the business community, governmental bodies and the general public in Montana; and to support the Montana broadcasting industry by providing services, information, continuing education, recruitment and a strong unified voice. **Focus:** Broadcasting; Engineering. **Qualif.:** Applicants must be second-year students majoring in Engineering at the UM College of Technology; must be interested in pursuing a career in Broadcast Engineering. **Criteria:** Recipients are selected based on academic performance.

Funds Avail.: No specific amount. **Duration:** Annual. **To Apply:** Applicants must complete an application form; must include a one-page statement summarizing their professional abilities, career goals and extra-curricular activities; and two letters of recommendation from an instructor. **Deadline:** February 28. **Contact:** Montana Broadcasters Association; e-mail: dbruce@mtbroadcasters.org.

6205 ■ Montana Health Care Association (MHCA)
36 S Last Chance Gulch, Ste. A
Helena, MT 59601
Ph: (406)443-2876
Fax: (406)443-4614
URL: www.mthealthcare.org

6206 ■ Donald E. Pizzini Memorial Nurse Scholarships *(Undergraduate, Professional development/ Scholarship)*

Purpose: To provide financial assistance to individuals who are interested in pursuing a career in nursing or advancing in their nursing career with an emphasis in long term care. **Focus:** Nursing. **Qualif.:** Applicants must be U.S. citizens or permanent residents; must be on a full-time or part-time basis in a nursing program relevant to the nursing program; must maintain a 3.0 GPA or better in previous studies; must attend a college accredited in the field of nursing for which the scholarship has been granted, including advance practice nursing if applicable; must pursue a nursing program designed to lead to an appropriate degree or certification; must reside and have plan to work within the state of Montana; must be available for the qualifying interview. **Criteria:** Selection will be based on the evaluation of submitted documents and specific criteria.

Funds Avail.: Up to $1,000. **Duration:** Annual. **To Apply:** Applicants must submit a completed application form; official transcripts from attended educational institutions; statement of nursing career intentions; two recommendations from individuals whom applicants are familiar.

6207 ■ Morgan, Lewis and Bockius L.L.P.
1701 Market St.
Philadelphia, PA 19103-2903
Ph: (215)963-5000
Fax: (215)965-5001
E-mail: info@morganlewis.com
URL: www.morganlewis.com

6208 ■ Diversity Fellowship Program (DFP)
(Undergraduate/Fellowship)

Purpose: To promote diversity in the legal profession and to attract future leaders who are committed to the importance of diversity. **Focus:** Law. **Qualif.:** Applicants must be second year law students who have successfully completed one year of law school; have demonstrated excellence; have outstanding leadership skills; and have a demonstrated interest in promoting diversity. **Criteria:** Selection is based on merit.

Funds Avail.: $15,000. **To Apply:** Applicants must sign up for an on-campus interview at the participating law schools and submit a completed application form along with a resume, transcript, and a brief personal statement. **Dead-**

Awards are arranged alphabetically below their administering organizations

line: September 30. **Contact:** Lindsay Callantine, Firmwide Directory of Attorney Recruiting diversityfellowship@ morganlewis.com.

6209 ■ Morgan Library & Museum

225 Madison Ave., 36th St.
New York, NY 10016-3490
Ph: (212)685-0008
Fax: (212)481-3484
E-mail: visitorservices@themorgan.org
URL: www.themorgan.org

6210 ■ Sherman Fairchild Post Graduate Fellowships in Conservation *(Postgraduate/Fellowship)*

Purpose: To provide a junior professional with the opportunity to apply the principles of paper and book conservation acquired through an accredited graduate program in museum/library conservation or equivalent work/ life experience. **Focus:** Library and archival sciences. **Qualif.:** Applicant must be a graduate of a recognized graduate-level program in conservation or be able to demonstrate the acquisition of equivalent skills and knowledge through life/work work/life experience; should possess strong public speaking oral and written communications skills; and have a demonstrated commitment to the profession of conservation and scholarly advancement. **Criteria:** Selection is based on the application materials.

Funds Avail.: No specific amount. **To Apply:** Applicants must submit a cover letter addressing their interest in the Fellowships, including a statement of career goals and areas of particular interest; curricula vitae; and three letters of recommendation. **Contact:** Morgan Library & Museum, at the above address.

6211 ■ Morris County Bar Association (MCBA)

245 South St.
Morristown, NJ 07960
Ph: (973)267-6089
Fax: (973)605-8325
E-mail: yperez@morriscountybar.com
URL: www.morriscountybar.com

6212 ■ Justice Robert L. Clifford Fellowships
(Undergraduate/Fellowship)

Purpose: To support and mentor a minority law student. **Focus:** Law. **Qualif.:** Applicant must be a minority law school student. **Criteria:** Selection is based on merit.

Funds Avail.: $5,000. **Duration:** 10 weeks. **To Apply:** Applicants may contact the foundation office or the financial aid offices at Seton Hall University School of Law or at New York University School of Law for more information on the fellowship. **Remarks:** Established in 1996.

6213 ■ Justice Stewart G. Pollock Fellowships
(Undergraduate/Fellowship)

Purpose: To support and mentor a minority law student. **Focus:** Law. **Qualif.:** Applicant must be a minority law school student. **Criteria:** Selection is based on merit.

Funds Avail.: $5,000. **Duration:** 10 weeks. **To Apply:** Applicants may contact the foundation office or the financial aid offices at Seton Hall University School of Law or at New York University School of Law for more information on the fellowship. **Remarks:** Established in 2004.

6214 ■ The Morris Law Firm

509 Harrison Ave., Ste., No. 200-A
Panama City, FL 32401
Ph: (850)257-5680
Fax: (850)640-3061
URL: www.dmorrislaw.com

6215 ■ Robby Strong Cancer Survivor Scholarships
(Graduate/Scholarship)

Purpose: To support law students whose life have been affected by cancer. **Focus:** Law. **Qualif.:** Applicants must be students planning to attend law school or not yet graduated from law school but with a minimum GPA of 3.0. **Criteria:** Applicants are judged and awarded based on merit and need.

Funds Avail.: $500. **To Apply:** Applicants must submit a transcript, recommendation letters and resumes. **Deadline:** May 31.

6216 ■ James B. Morris Scholarship Fund

PO Box 12145
Des Moines, IA 50312
Ph: (515)864-0922
Fax: (515)864-0922
URL: www.morrisscholarship.org

6217 ■ James B. Morris Scholarships
(Undergraduate/Scholarship)

Purpose: To provide assistance, motivation and internship opportunities for minority students pursuing post-secondary and graduate degrees. **Focus:** General studies/Field of study not specified. **Qualif.:** All applicants must be: U.S. citizens; of minority ethnic status as defined by the Equal Employment Opportunity Commission and have a minimum 2.5 G.P.A. **Criteria:** Applicants will be selected based on financial need and selection criteria.

Funds Avail.: No specific amount. **Duration:** Annual. **To Apply:** Applicants must submit a copy of official high school transcripts (for graduating high school seniors only), official college transcript (most recent semester only); must provide one or more letters of references (at least one must be from an instructor); must provide a writing sample (an essay about the applicant and why they are applying for the scholarship); must complete the application form available online and must have a recent photograph (head and shoulder shot only). **Deadline:** March 16. **Contact:** James B. Morris Scholarship Fund at the above address.

6218 ■ Mortar Board National College Senior Honor Society

1200 Chambers Rd., Ste. 201
Columbus, OH 43212
Ph: (614)488-4094
Free: 800-989-6266
E-mail: mortarboard@mortarboard.org
URL: www.mortarboard.org

6219 ■ Mortar Board National Foundation Fellowships *(Postdoctorate/Fellowship)*

Purpose: To provide financial support for members who want to pursue a post-graduate education. **Focus:** General studies/Field of study not specified. **Qualif.:** Applicant must be a current or former member of Mortar Board working

Awards are arranged alphabetically below their administering organizations

toward a degree beyond his or her bachelor's. **Criteria:** Candidate will be judged based on their academic record, recommendations, goals and objectives, need and contribution/commitment to Mortar Board.

Funds Avail.: $3,000 - $5,000. **Duration:** Annual. **To Apply:** Applicant must complete online application; must submit one official transcript of all works completed on the college level and two recommendations, completed online. If have been out of school for several years, separate statement addressing the items on the Mortar Board Involvement Questionnaire on behalf but still have two recommenders. **Deadline:** January 31.

6220 ■ Morton Cure Paralysis Fund

5021 Vernon Ave., Ste. 145
Minneapolis, MN 55436
Ph: (612)904-1420
E-mail: info@mcpf.org
URL: www.mcpf.org

6221 ■ Morton Cure Paralysis Fund Research Grants *(Professional development, Postdoctorate/ Grant)*

Purpose: To develop effective therapies for paralysis associated with spinal cord injury and other disorders of the central nervous system. **Focus:** Spinal cord injuries and research. **Qualif.:** Applicants must be American or international investigators located at institutions that have clearly established lines of accountability and fiscal responsibility. Either senior scientists or postdoctoral fellows may serve as principal investigators. **Criteria:** Research proposals are evaluated on relevance to MCPF's priorities and scientific merit.

Funds Avail.: $5,000-$75,000. **Duration:** Annual. **To Apply:** Application can be obtained at the website. Applicants must adhere to priority and submission guidelines using the form supplied. A summary of the curriculum vitae of the PI and key personnel plus key references must also be included. **Deadline:** April 30 and October 31.

6222 ■ John R. Mott Scholarship Foundation

1860 19th St. NW
Washington, DC 20009-5501
E-mail: info@mottscholarship.org
URL: www.mottscholarship.org

6223 ■ John R. Mott Scholarships *(Undergraduate/ Scholarship)*

Purpose: To provide scholarship for higher education to students who are natives of Calabria. **Focus:** General studies/Field of study not specified. **Qualif.:** Applicants must be natives to the region of Calabria, Italy who are enrolled at any university or graduate school in the Fall of current year and seeking an education leading to a degree or professional certificate. **Criteria:** Recipients will be selected based on academic achievement and financial need. Consideration is also given to the candidate's past and intended future contributions to the region.

Funds Avail.: $10,000. **To Apply:** Applicants must complete the application form available online. Other requirements are enumerated at the scholarship web page. **Deadline:** April 15.

6224 ■ Mountain Plains Adult Education Association (MPAEA)

c/o Glenda Sinks, President
Community College of Denver

1111 W Colfax Ave.
Denver, CO 80217
Ph: (303)556-2774
URL: www.mpaea.org

6225 ■ Larry B. Wickham Memorial Scholarship for Graduate Studies *(Graduate/Scholarship, Fellowship)*

Purpose: To provide financial assistance for students' tuition, books and school-related expenses. **Focus:** Adult education. **Qualif.:** Applicant must be a student enrolled in a graduate degree program in an MPAEA member state; must be pursuing a graduate degree in adult education or closely related field; or a graduate student who has not previously received the scholarship; and must be an active member of MPAEA. **Criteria:** Applicant will be evaluated based on financial need.

Funds Avail.: $1,000. **Duration:** Annual. **Number Awarded:** 1. **To Apply:** Applicant must review the criteria for eligibility before applying for the scholarship. They are advised to contact state MPAEA Board member for a copy of the application or download it from the MPAEA website: www.mpaea.org. **Deadline:** February 3. **Contact:** Diane White, MPAEA Scholarship Chair, Adult Education/Family Literacy Coordinator, dwhite@uintaeducation.org.

6226 ■ Mu Alpha Theta

c/o University of Oklahoma
601 Elm Ave., Rm. 1102
Norman, OK 73019
Ph: (405)325-4489
Fax: (405)325-7184
E-mail: matheta@ou.edu
URL: www.mualphatheta.org

6227 ■ Mu Alpha Theta Summer Grants *(Undergraduate, Graduate/Scholarship)*

Purpose: To support students enrolled in a summer program to pay their tuition or fees for a summer math program at, or sponsored by, an accredited school or university. **Focus:** Mathematics and mathematical sciences. **Qualif.:** Applicants must be Mu Alpha Theta members. **Criteria:** Selection will be based on the committee's criteria.

Funds Avail.: Up to $2,000. **Duration:** Annual. **To Apply:** Applicants must submit the application form with sponsor's signature, student essay, resume, description of summer program and acceptance letter, two letters of recommendation, itemized list of funds being requested, official high school transcript.

6228 ■ Multiple Myeloma Research Foundation (MMRF)

383 Main Ave., 5th Fl.
Norwalk, CT 06851
Ph: (203)229-0464
Fax: (203)229-0572
E-mail: info@themmrf.org
URL: www.themmrf.org

6229 ■ MMRF Research Fellow Awards *(Postdoctorate, Professional development/Grant)*

Purpose: To help support young investigators to begin their studies in the field of multiple myeloma while advanc-

---

Awards are arranged alphabetically below their administering organizations

ing the understanding of myeloma disease biology, treatment and drug resistance. **Focus:** Medical research. **Qualif.:** Applicants must be researchers who hold a Ph.D., M.D. or equivalent degree at the post-doctorate, clinical fellow, or junior faculty level. **Criteria:** Research Fellow applications are reviewed by an external group of scientists who have the appropriate area of scientific expertise.

Funds Avail.: $75,000. **Duration:** Annual. **To Apply:** Applications should be submitted online at: https://proposalcentral.altum.com. **Deadline:** April 21.

6230 ■ MMRF Senior Research Awards *(Doctorate, Professional development/Grant)*

Purpose: To accelerate the development of therapeutic approaches for myeloma, including proposals in basic science, validation, or clinical research **Focus:** Medical research. **Qualif.:** Applicants must be investigators who hold a Ph.D., M.D. or equivalent degree who have documented experience in blood cancer research or in research areas that are pertinent to multiple myeloma. **Criteria:** Applications are reviewed by an external group of scientists who have the appropriate area of scientific expertise.

Funds Avail.: Up to $100,000 per year for 2 years. **Duration:** Annual. **To Apply:** Applications should be submitted online at: https://proposalcentral.altum.com. **Deadline:** March 17.

6231 ■ Multiple Sclerosis Society of Canada (MSSC)

250 Dundas St. W, Ste. 500
Toronto, ON, Canada M5T 2Z5
Ph: (416)922-6065
Fax: (416)922-7538
Free: 800-268-7582
E-mail: info@mssociety.ca
URL: beta.mssociety.ca

6232 ■ endMS Doctoral Studentship Awards *(Doctorate/Internship)*

Purpose: To support training students in studies related to Multiple Sclerosis and to provide them the opportunity to gain research experience in the field of MS. **Focus:** Multiple sclerosis. **Qualif.:** Applicants must be Canadian citizens or permanent residents of Canada; must be working towards a Ph.D. or related degree pertaining to research in MS; must be enrolled in graduate training at a Canadian Institution or interested in studying abroad; must hold a degree that is recognized by the Canadian medical regulatory authority. **Criteria:** Selection will be based on the committee's criteria.

Funds Avail.: $22,000. **Duration:** Annual; non-renewable. **To Apply:** Applicants are required to use the website for the completion of their proposal and must submit their studentship applications through online system only. **Deadline:** October 1.

6233 ■ endMS Master's Studentship Awards *(Master's/Internship)*

Purpose: To support training students in studies related to Multiple Sclerosis and to provide them the opportunity to gain research experience in the field of MS. **Focus:** Multiple sclerosis. **Qualif.:** Applicants must be Canadian citizens or permanent residents of Canada; must be working towards a Master's degree pertaining to research in MS; must be enrolled in graduate training at a Canadian Institution or

interested in studying abroad; and must hold a degree that is recognized by the Canadian medical regulatory authority. **Criteria:** Selection will be based on the committee's criteria.

Funds Avail.: $20,000. **Duration:** Biennial; non-renewable. **To Apply:** Applicants are required to use the website for the completion of their proposal and must submit their studentship applications through online system only. **Deadline:** October 1.

6234 ■ endMS Postdoctoral Fellowships *(Postdoctorate/Fellowship)*

Purpose: To support training students in studies related to Multiple Sclerosis and to provide them the opportunity to gain research experience in the field of MS. **Focus:** Multiple sclerosis. **Qualif.:** Applicants must be Canadian citizens or permanent residents of Canada; must be enrolled in a postdoctoral training program at any Canadian Institutions or interested in studying abroad; must hold or candidates for a doctoral degree (Ph.D., M.D., or equivalent) or have completed their doctoral degree in the last three years or less by the time of the completion deadline; and must also hold a postdoctoral fellowship at a recognized institution including hospitals and research institutes. **Criteria:** Selection will be based on the committee's criteria.

Funds Avail.: $41,000-$50,500. **Duration:** Annual; non-renewable. **To Apply:** Applicants are required to use the website for the completion of their proposal and must submit their studentship applications through online system only. **Deadline:** October 1.

6235 ■ Anthony Munoz Foundation

8919 Rossash Rd.
Cincinnati, OH 45236
Ph: (513)772-4900
Fax: (513)772-4911
URL: www.munozfoundation.org

6236 ■ Anthony Munoz Scholarships *(Undergraduate/Scholarship)*

Purpose: To support Tri-State youth in achieving their dreams of attending a local college or university. **Focus:** General studies/Field of study not specified. **Qualif.:** Applicants must be: residents of any of the Tri-State region (Kentucky, Indiana and Ohio); attending a local, Tri-State region, non-proprietary college, university or technical college; graduating high school seniors with at least a 2.5 GPA (or a G.E.D. recipient under the age of 23); of any race but of socio-economic need; must maintain a post-secondary GPA of at least a 2.0. **Criteria:** Recipients will be chosen by the Munoz Family based on the submitted application.

Funds Avail.: $20,000. **Duration:** Annual. **Number Awarded:** Up to 7. **To Apply:** Applicants must submit a completed scholarship application form along with a copy of recent transcript; Expected Family Contribution (EFC) from Student Aid Report (SAR), which comes as a result of filing the FAFSA; and a copy of Financial Aid Award Letter from their chosen college. **Deadline:** April 30. **Contact:** Caleigh Willis at cwillis@munozfoundation.org.

6237 ■ Daniel Murphy Scholarship Fund (DMSF)

309 W Washington, Ste. 1250
Chicago, IL 60606
Ph: (312)455-7800
Fax: (312)455-7801

Awards are arranged alphabetically below their administering organizations

URL: www.dmsf.org

6238 ■ Daniel Murphy Scholarships (High School/ Scholarship)

Purpose: To financially support disadvantaged Chicago students who demonstrate academic potential. **Focus:** General studies/Field of study not specified. **Qualif.:** Applicants must be a student preparing to enter high school. Applicants that demonstrate academic potential, strong character and financial need are eligible. Applicants must live in the city of Chicago or the surrounding areas of Cicero or Berwy. **Criteria:** Awards are given based on merit.

Funds Avail.: No specific amount. **To Apply:** Applicant must submit a completed scholarship application form together with a response to two essay questions; provide financial information; recommendation forms, standardized test result and report cards from teachers, principals and/or counselors; **Contact:** Daniel Murphy Scholarship Fund; Phone: 312-455-7800; Fax: 312-455-7801.

6239 ■ Muscular Dystrophy Association (MDA)

222 S Riverside Plz., Ste. 1500
Chicago, IL 60606
Free: 800-572-1717
URL: www.mda.org

6240 ■ MDA Development Grants (Doctorate/Grant)

Purpose: To support the research outlined in the original application submitted to the Association. **Focus:** Muscular dystrophy. **Qualif.:** Applicants must: hold an MD, PhD, DSc or equivalent degree; be members of a research team at an appropriate institution; be qualified to conduct a program of original research under the supervision of a principal investigator; have an acceptable research plan for a specific disease in MDA's program; have access to institutional resources necessary to conduct the proposed research project; have 18 months of post-doctoral research laboratory training at the time of application; be no more than 60 months from receiving their most recent advanced degree; and, not have been funded under the MDA development grant program in the past. **Criteria:** Selection shall be made on the basis of the aforesaid qualifications and compliance with the application details.

Funds Avail.: Amount varies. **Duration:** Annual. **Number Awarded:** Varies. **To Apply:** Applicants must send a completed pre-proposal form to formally request for an application form. **Deadline:** January 15 for the spring; July 15 for the fall.

6241 ■ MDA Research Grants (Advanced Professional/Grant)

Purpose: To support established investigators to accelerate progress against muscle disease. **Focus:** Muscular dystrophy. **Qualif.:** Applicants must: hold an MD, PhD, DSc or equivalent degree; be professional or faculty members (professors, associate professors or assistant professors) at an appropriate educational, medical or research institution; be qualified to conduct and mentor a program of original research within his or her own laboratory; assume both administrative and financial responsibility for the grant; and, have access to institutional resources necessary to conduct the proposed research project. **Criteria:** Selection shall be based on the aforementioned qualifications and compliance with the application details.

Funds Avail.: Amount varies. **Duration:** Annual. **Number**

Awarded: Varies. **To Apply:** Applicant must send a completed pre-proposal form to formally request for an application form. **Deadline:** January 15 for the spring; July 15 for the fall.

6242 ■ Music Library Association (MLA)

1600 Aspen Commons, Ste. 100
Middleton, WI 53562
Ph: (608)836-5825
Fax: (608)831-8200
E-mail: mla@areditions.com
URL: www.musiclibraryassoc.org

6243 ■ Carol June Bradley Awards (Professional development/Grant)

Purpose: To promote education involving the history of music libraries or special collections. **Focus:** Library and archival sciences; Music. **Qualif.:** Award is open to all interested applicants regardless of age, nationality, profession, or institutional affiliation. **Criteria:** Proposals will be reviewed on the basis of merit.

Funds Avail.: No specific amount. **Duration:** Annual. **To Apply:** Applicants must complete and submit the application form together with the following materials: a project summary, a preliminary budget, a current vita, and three names of references.

6244 ■ Dena Epstein Awards for Archival and Library Research in American Music (Professional development/Grant)

Purpose: To support research in archives or libraries internationally on any aspect of American music. **Focus:** Library and archival sciences; Music. **Qualif.:** Award is open to all applicants regardless of age, nationality, profession, or institutional affiliation. **Criteria:** Proposals will be reviewed based on merit.

Funds Avail.: Varies. **Duration:** Annual. **To Apply:** Applicants must submit a brief research proposal (maximum of 10 pages) which includes description, detailed budget indicating the amount, justification, and additional sources of funding; curriculum vitae; and three letters of support from librarians and/or scholars. Submissions made electronically must be in Microsoft Word or PDF format and sent as e-mail attachments. If submitting by mail, include four copies of all documents. **Deadline:** July 9. **Remarks:** Established in 1995.

6245 ■ Kevin Freeman Travel Grants (Graduate, Other/Grant)

Purpose: To support travel and accommodation expenses for attendees of the MLA annual meeting. **Focus:** Library and archival sciences; Music. **Qualif.:** Applicants must be members of MLA; may either be graduate students in library school pursuing to become a music librarian; or a recent graduates of librarianship. **Criteria:** Applicants are selected based on merits.

Funds Avail.: $750. **Duration:** Annual. **To Apply:** Applicant must submit an application form; a current vita; and two letters of support. **Deadline:** September 30. **Remarks:** Established in 1994.

6246 ■ Walter Gerboth Awards (Other/Award)

Purpose: To assist research-in-progress in music or music librarianship. **Focus:** Library and archival sciences; Music.

Awards are arranged alphabetically below their administering organizations

Qualif.: Applicants must be members of MLA who are in the first five years of their professional library careers. **Criteria:** Applicants will be reviewed based on merits.

Funds Avail.: No specific amount. **Duration:** Annual. **To Apply:** Applicants must submit a project description and statement of significance; a detailed total budget; two recommendation letters (one for the applicant and one for the project); and a curriculum vitae. Completed application should be send to Christopher Mehrens via email. **Deadline:** July 9. **Remarks:** Established in 1984.

6247 ■ Muslim Public Affairs Council (MPAC)

3010 Wilshire Blvd., No. 217
Los Angeles, CA 90010
Ph: (323)258-6722
Fax: (323)258-5879
E-mail: contact@mpac.org
URL: www.mpac.org

6248 ■ MPAC-DC Graduate Policy Fellowships
(Graduate/Fellowship)

Purpose: To identify and develop graduate students in international relations, economics, political science, or public policy to engage in faith-based policy research and advocacy in the heart of the nation's capital. **Focus:** Economics; International affairs and relations; Political science; Public affairs. **Qualif.:** Applicant must be committed to the organizational philosophy and civic approach of the Muslim Public Affairs Council; have completed at least one year (or recently matriculated within one year) of a graduate program in International Relations, Political Science, Economics or Public Policy; and with minimum requirements for overall GPA: 3.0, in specialization coursework: 3.3. **Criteria:** Selection is based on the application materials.

Funds Avail.: No specific amount. **To Apply:** Applicants must submit a resume; cover letter addressing how the applicant believes the Fellowship will advance both his/her career goals as well as MPAC's work on Capitol Hill; list of three references with contact information (at least two must be academic, the third may be professional or academic); unofficial academic transcript from most recently graduated university/college; and a three-page writing sample relevant to the topic of the incoming Fellow's research topic at the DC office (information about the topic can found in the "Graduate Policy Fellowship Research Topic" document). **Deadline:** February 26. **Contact:** Muslim Public Affairs Council, at the above address.

6249 ■ MyApartmentMap

c/o Katie Reardon
190 Locke Rd.
Rye, NH 03870
Ph: (603)319-1712
Fax: (888)246-1064
E-mail: info@myapartmentmap.com
URL: www.myapartmentmap.com

6250 ■ MyApartmentMap Housing Scholarships
(Undergraduate/Scholarship)

Purpose: To support students who wants to pursue their educational career. **Focus:** General studies/Field of study not specified. **Qualif.:** Applicant must be a legal U.S. resident who is 18 years or older and is attending or will at-tend an accredited college, university, or trade school. **Criteria:** A qualified panel of judges will select one potential winner based on the criteria of writing ability, creativity, originality, and overall excellence.

Funds Avail.: $1,000. **Duration:** Semiannual. **Number Awarded:** 1. **To Apply:** Applicants must write an essay of 250 words or less that describes how the MyApartmentMap housing scholarship would make their semester better and send it via email in a Microsoft Word document. **Deadline:** August 1 and December 15.

6251 ■ Myasthenia Gravis Foundation of America (MGFA)

355 Lexington Ave., 15th Fl.
New York, NY 10017
Fax: (212)370-9047
Free: 800-541-5454
URL: www.myasthenia.org

6252 ■ Myasthenia Gravis Foundation of America Nursing Research Fellowships *(Undergraduate/Fellowship)*

Purpose: To provide financial assistance to nurses or nursing students interested in studying problems encountered by patients with myasthenia gravis or related neuromuscular conditions. **Focus:** Myasthenia Gravis. **Qualif.:** Applicants must be professional nurses or nursing students. **Criteria:** Applicants will be evaluated based on criteria designed by the Fellowship Committee.

Funds Avail.: $5,000. **Duration:** Annual. **To Apply:** Applicant must submit four copies of a cover letter and the completed application form to the Chief Executive of the MGFA national office. **Deadline:** October 1.

6253 ■ Myasthenia Gravis Foundation of America Student Research Fellowships *(Graduate, Undergraduate/Fellowship)*

Purpose: To provide financial support to current medical students or graduate students interested in the scientific basis of myasthenia gravis or related neuromuscular conditions, serving both to further scientific inquiries into the nature of these disorders and to encourage more research. **Focus:** Myasthenia Gravis. **Qualif.:** Applicants must be medical or graduate students. **Criteria:** Applicants will be evaluated based on criteria designed by the Fellowship Committee.

Funds Avail.: $5,000. **Duration:** Annual. **To Apply:** Applicants must submit one hardcopy or one PDF file of the letter of interest, summary of the research and its significance to myasthenia gravis or related neuromuscular conditions, proposed budget, curriculum vitae of applicant and sponsoring preceptor and letter of recommendation from preceptor that indicates acceptance of the candidate and outlines the proposed work plan for the research study.

6254 ■ The Myositis Association (TMA)

1737 King St., Ste. 600
Alexandria, VA 22314
Ph: (703)299-4850
Fax: (703)535-6752
Free: 800-821-7356
E-mail: tma@myositis.org
URL: www.myositis.org

Awards are arranged alphabetically below their administering organizations

6255 ■ TMA Research Fellowships (Graduate, Postdoctorate/Grant)

Purpose: To support promising post-doctoral investigators who wish to improve and advance their career in myositis research. **Focus:** Health sciences; Medical assisting. **Qualif.:** Applicants must have completed residency training or have received a PhD within the past five years; must have devoted a major portion of their time to research, but may include some study and clinical experience in allied health. **Criteria:** Applicants will be selected by the TMA Board of Directors based on evaluation and recommendation from its Medical Advisory Board.

Funds Avail.: $50,000. **Duration:** Annual; two years. **To Apply:** Applicants must submit a complete application package which includes: application form; curriculum vitae preferably in NIH format; up to three of the most relevant papers the applicant has published or has in press; outline of the research project (up to three pages); letters of nomination form from their current and past supervisors; information about the facilities available for the clinical and/or basic science research. **Deadline:** June 15. **Contact:** Bob Goldberg, TMA Executive Director, at goldberg@ myositis.org.

6256 ■ Myotonic Dystrophy Foundation (MDF)

431 Burgess Dr., Ste. 200
Menlo Park, CA 94025
Ph: (650)267-5562
Fax: (650)267-5564
Free: 866-968-6642
E-mail: info@myotonic.org
URL: www.myotonic.org

6257 ■ MDF Post-Doctoral Fellowships
(Postdoctorate/Fellowship)

Purpose: To support innovative research on myotonic dystrophy. **Focus:** Muscular dystrophy. **Qualif.:** Applicants must have received a PhD, MD, or DO degree from an accredited domestic or foreign institution. **Criteria:** Applicants will be selected based on submitted proposal.

Funds Avail.: $100,000. **Duration:** Up to two years. **To Apply:** Applicants must submit a project proposal for clinical, basic or applied research in any of the following areas: 1) pathogenesis of myotonic dystrophy; 2) studies of disease progression that are necessary steps toward therapeutic trials; 3) best practices and clinical management of myotonic dystrophy; and 4) therapeutic and diagnostic development. **Deadline:** September 5.

6258 ■ NAACP Legal Defense and Educational Fund (LDF)

40 Rector St., 5th Fl.
New York, NY 10006
Ph: (212)965-2200
URL: www.naacpldf.org

6259 ■ Herbert Lehman Education Scholarships
(Undergraduate/Scholarship)

Purpose: To help transform the promise of racial equality into a social, economic, and political reality for all people by supporting talented undergraduate students who need financial help to stay in school and successfully complete their bachelor's degree. **Focus:** General studies/Field of study not specified. **Qualif.:** Applicants must be African-

American students entering a four-year college as full-time for the first time; be U.S. citizens; be of excellent character with recommendations from teachers, community representatives or employers; and have an exceptional leadership potential with an ability to work well in diverse settings. **Criteria:** Award is given to a candidate with an outstanding potential as evidenced by high school academic records, test scores and personal essays.

Funds Avail.: $2,000. **To Apply:** Applications may be requested by writing to The Herbert Lehman Education Fund; must submit three letters of recommendation, one of which must be from a professor, teacher, principal or school counselor; application materials must be typed or neatly printed in ink and must conform to program guidelines. **Deadline:** May 1.

6260 ■ Earl Warren Civil Rights Training Scholarships (Graduate/Scholarship)

Purpose: To support the careers of law students dedicated to advancing the cause of racial justice. **Focus:** Law. **Qualif.:** Applicant must be a U.S. citizen; must be entering first year of full-time study; and must be a college graduate with good academic records, outstanding community service and strong recommendations. **Criteria:** Preference is given to applicants who have a well-defined interest in civil rights and community service.

Funds Avail.: $10,000. **Duration:** Annual. **To Apply:** Requests for applications should be from the applicant and should include information about the applicant's undergraduate background, expected graduation date, law school plans and career goals. **Deadline:** June 30.

6261 ■ NALS of Arizona (NTSA)

c/o Wendy Carpenter, Pres.
PO Box 1851
Tucson, AZ 85702
Ph: (520)325-2000
URL: www.nalsofarizona.org

6262 ■ Gail Goodell Folsom Memorial Scholarships
(Undergraduate/Award)

Purpose: To enhance the education of NOA members and the legal community. **Focus:** Paralegal studies. **Qualif.:** Applicants must be Arizona students who are currently working in the legal field, or are pursuing or plans to pursue a career as legal support professionals. **Criteria:** Selection will be based on the committee's criteria.

Funds Avail.: $250. **To Apply:** Applicants must submit a completed application and must include the following attachment: autobiographical statement or personal letter; current transcript of grades (if currently attending school); and letter of recommendation. **Deadline:** March 15. **Contact:** wbirk@fclaw.com.

6263 ■ NALS of Michigan

c/o Becky Quimby
Warner Norcross & Judd LLP
111 Lyon St., Ste. 900
Grand Rapids, MI 49503
URL: www.nalsofmichigan.org

6264 ■ NALS of Michigan Scholarships
(Undergraduate/Award)

Purpose: To support individuals pursuing their education in the legal field. **Focus:** Paralegal studies. **Qualif.:** Ap-

Awards are arranged alphabetically below their administering organizations

plicants must be high school seniors or enrolled in a school of advanced education (including the current school year); must be residents of Michigan and be enrolling in a Michigan school of advanced education in the legal field; have at least a B average, or if percentile system is used, not below 90%; be in need of financial assistance. **Criteria:** Scholarship will be awarded on the basis of scholastic or legal career achievements, future career goals, demonstration of financial need and leadership ability.

Funds Avail.: $1,000. **Duration:** Annual. **To Apply:** Applicants must submit the following documentation attached to their application: an official transcript of grades; a one-page letter of recommendation from the applicant's current major teacher or counselor, addressed to NALS of Michigan Scholarship Fund; one additional letter of recommendation from someone other than a member of the applicant's family, such as an employer, teacher, pastor or friend, may be submitted if applicant so desires, but is not required; a one-page autobiographical statement prepared by the applicant, showing the date of birth, school attended, employment, school and outside activities, accomplishments, family background, hobbies, and a brief description of applicant's goals and desires. **Deadline:** January 15.

6265 ■ NAMM, the International Music Products Association

5790 Armada Dr.
Carlsbad, CA 92008
Ph: (760)438-8001
Fax: (760)438-7327
Free: 800-767-6266
URL: www.namm.org

6266 ■ William R. Gard Memorial Scholarships (Undergraduate/Scholarship)

Purpose: To enhance education and careers in the music product industry. **Focus:** Education, Music; Music. **Qualif.:** Applicants must be members of NAMM Member firm; have completed 400 hours of employment at the NAMM Member firm; be enrolled as full-time college students; and have completed at least 400 hours of employment. **Criteria:** Applicants will be evaluated based on career intent; academic record; financial need; honors, awards and community involvement.

Funds Avail.: $7,500. **Duration:** Annual. **Number Awarded:** 2. **To Apply:** Application form is available at the website. Applicants must prepare three reference letters; grade transcripts; employer information sheet; photograph; and SAT or ACT scores (optional). Forward completed application form and other required materials to: NAMM, International Music Products Association, William R. Gard Memorial Scholarship, 5790 Armanda Drive, Carlsbad, CA 92008. **Contact:** grants@namm.org.

6267 ■ NAON Foundation

390 N Main St.
Alpharetta, GA 30009
Ph: (678)341-0809
E-mail: info@naonfoundation.org
URL: www.naonfoundation.org

6268 ■ Bachelor of Science in Nursing Academic Scholarships (Graduate/Scholarship)

Purpose: To provide scholarship assistance to nursing students who want to pursue their baccalaureate degree.

Focus: Nursing. **Qualif.:** Applicant must be a current NAON member; must hold current licensure as a registered nurse; must currently spend at least 50% of his/her time devoted to the specialty of orthopedic nursing; must be enrolled full or part time in a nationally accredited school of nursing baccalaureate program. **Criteria:** Selection of applicants will be based on the application form and materials.

Funds Avail.: $1,000. **Number Awarded:** 3. **To Apply:** Applicants must submit a completed application form available online along with the following requirements: (1) proof of current licensure as a registered nurse, NAON membership, and college BSN enrollment status; (2) statement of chosen NAON contribution; (3) signed scholarship agreement form; (4) narrative of 500 words or less, doubled-spaced, one inch margins in 12 point font addressing the applicant's professional goals (as they pertain to the academic activity and orthopedic nursing) and the impact of a nursing education on the applicant's career in orthopedic nursing; (5) two letters of recommendation, one must be from an orthopedic health care professional; (6) one digital photo, head or head-shoulder shot; (7) one self-addressed, stamped postcard for acknowledging receipt of application if submitted by mail. **Contact:** NAON Foundation, at the above address or Email: info@naonfoundation.org.

6269 ■ Master's Degree with a Major in Nursing Academic Scholarships (Graduate/Scholarship)

Purpose: To provide scholarship assistance to nursing students who want to pursue their Master's degree. **Focus:** Nursing. **Qualif.:** Applicant must be a current NAON member; must hold current licensure as a registered nurse; must currently spend at least 50% of his/her time devoted to the specialty of orthopedic nursing; must be currently enrolled full or part time in a nationally accredited Master's degree program in nursing. **Criteria:** Awards are given based on the application materials.

Funds Avail.: $2,000. **Duration:** Annual. **Number Awarded:** 1. **To Apply:** Applicants must submit a completed application form available online together with proof of current licensure as a registered nurse, NAON membership, and college master's enrollment status; must provide a statement of chosen NAON contribution, signed scholarship agreement form, and narrative of 500 words or less, doubled-spaced, one inch margins in 12 point font addressing the applicant's professional goals (as they pertain to the academic activity and orthopedic nursing) and the impact of a nursing education on the applicant's career in orthopedic nursing; must submit two letters of recommendation, one must be from an orthopedic health care professional; one digital photo (head or head-shoulder shot in professional attire); and one self-addressed (stamped postcard for acknowledging receipt of application if submitted by mail). **Deadline:** August 15. **Contact:** NAON Foundation, at the above address or Email: info@naonfoundation.org.

6270 ■ NARAL Pro-Choice America

1156 15th St. NW, Ste. 700
Washington, DC 20005
Ph: (202)973-3000
Fax: (202)973-3096
E-mail: can@prochoiceamerica.org
URL: www.prochoiceamerica.org

Awards are arranged alphabetically below their administering organizations

6271 ■ NARAL Pro-Choice America Development Internships (Undergraduate, Graduate, Professional development/Internship)

Purpose: To support the training of aspiring interns for the benefit of their career training in development policy. **Focus:** Civil rights. **Qualif.:** Applicants must be currently enrolled in or recently completed an accredited undergraduate or graduate degree program; have demonstrated commitment to protecting a woman's right to choose; have strong interest in the political process; have strong research and analytical skills; have the ability to work in a fast-paced collaborative environment; have excellent attention to detail; and be adept in using a variety of online tools to compile background and capacity information for potential donors. Proficiency in NGP is a plus. **Criteria:** Selection will be based on the committee's criteria.

Funds Avail.: No specific amount. **To Apply:** Applicants must send a one-page letter of interest and current resume. **Contact:** Send applications to developmentintern@ prochoiceamerica.org.

6272 ■ NARAL Pro-Choice America Policy Internships (Professional development/Internship)

Purpose: To support the training of aspiring interns for the benefit of their career development in policy research. **Focus:** Civil rights. **Qualif.:** Applicants must have some college experience; must be professional and polished demeanor; must have an understanding of, and commitment to, NARAL Pro-Choice America's mission and goals; must have excellent writing, editing, and proofreading skills; must have excellent organizational skills; must have the ability to handle multiple projects, take initiative, work well with others, and meet deadlines consistently in a fast-paced environment; and must have commitment to diversity and sensitivity to and appreciation of cultural differences. **Criteria:** Selection will be based on the committee's criteria.

Funds Avail.: No specific amount. **To Apply:** Applicants must send their respective resume and cover letters. **Contact:** Send applications to policyjobs@ prochoiceamerica.org.

6273 ■ NARAL Pro-Choice America Political Internships (Undergraduate, Graduate, Professional development/Internship)

Purpose: To support the training of aspiring interns for the benefit of their career development in political campaigns and related matters. **Focus:** Political science. **Qualif.:** Applicants must be currently enrolled in or recently completed an accredited undergraduate or graduate degree program; have demonstrated commitment to protecting a woman's right to choose; have strong interest in the political process; have strong research and analytical skills; have the ability to work in a fast-paced collaborative environment; have excellent attention to detail; have experience with Microsoft Office and Google Drive; and have general computer proficiency. **Criteria:** Selection will be based on the committee's criteria.

Funds Avail.: No specific amount. **To Apply:** Applicants must submit a one-page letter of interest, resume and 1-2 page writing sample.

6274 ■ Elizabeth Nash Foundation

PO Box 1260
Los Gatos, CA 95031-1260
E-mail: info@elizabethnashfoundation.org
URL: www.elizabethnashfoundation.org

6275 ■ Elizabeth Nash Foundation Scholarships (Undergraduate, Graduate/Scholarship)

Purpose: To assist persons with cystic fibrosis (CF) to pursue undergraduate and graduate degrees. **Focus:** General studies/Field of study not specified. **Qualif.:** Applicants must be individuals with CF who are in-going or current undergraduate or graduate students at an accredited US-based college or university. Given limited resources, the program is currently only open to US citizens. **Criteria:** Selection shall be based on the applicants' scholastic record, character, demonstrated leadership, service to CF-related causes and the broader community, and need for financial assistance.

Funds Avail.: $1,000 to $2,500. **Duration:** Annual. **To Apply:** Applicants must submit a completed scholarship application form (there is a separate application for undergraduate and graduate students), attach a one page essay, letter of recommendation from a teacher, a letter confirming CF diagnosis, an academic transcript, a copy of FAFSA, and the specific details of fees and tuition cost from the academic institution. Applications must be typed, and must not be stapled together. **Deadline:** April 6. **Remarks:** Established in 2005. **Contact:** Any questions should be addressed to: scholarships@elizabethnashfoundation.org.

6276 ■ Nashville Catholic Business Women's League (NCBWL)

PO Box 50994
Nashville, TN 37205-0994
E-mail: info@ncbwl.org
URL: www.ncbwl.org

6277 ■ Aurella Varallo Mariani Scholarship Program (Undergraduate/Scholarship)

Purpose: To provide financial support to those students who are in need. **Focus:** General studies/Field of study not specified. **Qualif.:** Applicants must be young Catholic women in the middle Tennessee area. **Criteria:** Preference will be given to those students who meet the criteria.

Funds Avail.: No specific amount. **To Apply:** Applicants must check the available website for details. **Remarks:** The scholarships are named in memory of Aurelia Varallo Mariani, a faithful and loving NCBWL member who graduated from St. Cecilia Academy in 1951. Her love for her alma mater and for this league continued until her untimely death in 1997. **Contact:** Nashville Catholic Business Women's League at the above address.

6278 ■ NCBWL Scholarships (High School/ Scholarship)

Purpose: To provide scholarship assistance to deserving female students. **Focus:** General studies/Field of study not specified. **Qualif.:** Applicants must be female students; must be enrolled at St. Cecilia Academy, Father Ryan High School or Pope John Paul II High School for their full four years of matriculation. **Criteria:** Preference will be given to those students who meet the criteria.

Funds Avail.: No specific amount. **To Apply:** Applicants must submit a completed application form. **Contact:** Nashville Catholic Business Women's League at the above address.

6279 ■ NASSCO

2470 Longstone Ln., Ste. M
Marriottsville, MD 21104

Awards are arranged alphabetically below their administering organizations

Ph: (410)442-7473
Fax: (410)442-7788
E-mail: info@nassco.org
URL: nassco.org

6280 ■ The NASSCO Jeffrey D. Ralston Memorial Scholarship *(Undergraduate/Scholarship)*

Purpose: To improve the success rate of everyone involved in the pipeline rehabilitation industry through education, technical resources and industry advocacy. **Focus:** General studies/Field of study not specified. **Qualif.:** Applicants must be currently enrolled dependents of an active NASSCO member or an active participant in the sewer service industry. Applicants must have at least a 3.0 GPA. **Criteria:** Recipients are selected based on ethics, high integrity, work experience, community service and leadership.

Funds Avail.: $2,000.00 or more. **Number Awarded:** 1. **To Apply:** Applicants must submit a completed application form. **Deadline:** January 31.

6281 ■ National 4th Infantry Ivy Division Association

PO Box 1914
Saint Peters, MO 63376-0035
Ph: (678)480-4422
URL: www.4thinfantry.org

6282 ■ 4th Infantry Division Association Scholarships *(All/Scholarship)*

Purpose: To provide educational assistance to association members and their blood relatives. **Focus:** General studies/Field of study not specified. **Qualif.:** Applicant must be a blood relative, stepchild or adopted child of a current association member in good standing; must be a U.S. citizen. **Criteria:** Recipient will be chosen by lottery at the National Reunion.

Funds Avail.: $2,000. **Duration:** Annual. **Number Awarded:** 10. **To Apply:** Applicant must submit a complete application package. **Deadline:** June 15. **Remarks:** Established in 1969. **Contact:** Alexander Cooker at the above address.

6283 ■ National Academic Advising Association (NACADA)

Kansas State University
2323 Anderson Ave., Ste. 225
Manhattan, KS 66502-2912
Ph: (785)532-5717
Fax: (785)532-7732
E-mail: nacada@ksu.edu
URL: www.nacada.ksu.edu

6284 ■ Wesley R. Habley NACADA Summer Institute Scholarships *(Other/Scholarship)*

Purpose: To assist selected NACADA members who demonstrate involvement in national, regional, state, and/or local advising organizations and exhibit the potential for national leadership roles. **Focus:** General studies/Field of study not specified. **Qualif.:** Applicant must: be a current NACADA member at the time of scholarship application; demonstrate involvement in NACADA activities through commission, region, task force and/or committee participa-

tion; and, provide a description of goals to be accomplished through participation in the Summer Institute. **Criteria:** Selection shall be based on the aforementioned qualifications and compliance with the application details. The selection committee encourages applications from groups which are under-represented in the association.

Funds Avail.: No specific amount. **Duration:** Annual. **To Apply:** Applicant must submit the following documents: completed Online Application Form; resume/vita (CV); current job position description or list of job responsibilities; professional development summary; summer institute participation description; and, letters of recommendation. **Deadline:** May 5.

6285 ■ NACADA Scholarships *(Graduate/Scholarship)*

Purpose: To support the promotion of professional training of advisors. **Focus:** General studies/Field of study not specified. **Qualif.:** Applicant must be a current member of NACADA and have been a NACADA member for two years, be currently enrolled in either a master's or doctoral program, and must have worked as an academic advisor for two years with a minimum of a half-time appointment. **Criteria:** Selection shall be based on the aforementioned qualifications and compliance with the application details.

Funds Avail.: One $1,000; four $500. **Duration:** Annual. **Number Awarded:** 5. **To Apply:** Applicant must submit the following documents: Online NACADA Scholarship Application Form, including financial assessment; Career Goals Statement; Evaluation/Recommendation by Faculty Form; and Evaluation by Employer Form. **Deadline:** March 10.

6286 ■ The National Academies

500 5th St. NW
Washington, DC 20001
Ph: (202)334-2000
E-mail: research@nas.edu
URL: www.nationalacademies.org

6287 ■ Ford Foundation Dissertation Fellowships *(Graduate, Doctorate/Fellowship)*

Purpose: To increase the diversity of the nation's college and university faculties by increasing their ethnic and racial diversity; to maximize educational benefits of diversity; to increase the number of professors who can and will use diversity as a resource for enriching the education of all students. **Focus:** Area and ethnic studies; Interdisciplinary studies; Peace studies. **Qualif.:** Applicants must be nationals of the United States regardless of race, national origin, gender, age, disability, or sexual orientation; must be individuals which have evidence of superior academic achievement; must be committed to a career in teaching and research at the college or university level; must be Ph.D. or Sc.D degree at a U.S. educational institution; and must have not earned a doctoral degree at any time in any field. **Criteria:** Recipients are selected based on evidence of superior academic achievement; degree of promise of continuing achievement as scholars and teachers; capacity to respond in pedagogically productive ways to the learning needs of students from diverse backgrounds; sustained personal engagement with communities that are under-represented in the academy and an ability to bring this asset to learning, teaching, and scholarship at the college or university level; likelihood of using the diversity of human experience as an educational resource in teaching and scholarship. Recipients are also selected based on

Awards are arranged alphabetically below their administering organizations

academic records, essays, letters of recommendation, the application itself, and other appropriate materials that meet the eligibility requirements and the selection criteria.

Funds Avail.: $25,000. **Duration:** Annual. **Number Awarded:** 30. **To Apply:** Applicants must complete the online application form including personal and contact information; a two-page, double-spaced statement of previous research; essay describing proposed plan of graduate study or research and the applicant's long-range career goals; transcript showing baccalaureate degree or undergraduate work; graduate school transcript; letters of reference; verification of Predoctoral Status form; and GRE General Test Scores. **Deadline:** November 14. **Contact:** Fellowships Office, infofell@nas.edu.

6288 ■ Ford Foundation Diversity Fellowships
(Graduate, Doctorate, Postdoctorate, Postgraduate/ Fellowship)

Purpose: To increase the diversity of the nation's college and university faculties by increasing their ethnic and racial diversity; to maximize educational benefits of diversity; and to increase the number of professors who can and will use diversity as a resource for enriching the education of all students. **Focus:** Area and ethnic studies; Interdisciplinary studies; Peace studies. **Qualif.:** Applicants must be nationals of the United States regardless of race, national origin, gender, age, disability, or sexual orientation; must be individuals which have evidence of superior academic achievement; must be committed to a career in teaching and research at the college or university level; must be enrolled in or planning to enroll in an eligible research-based program leading to a Ph.D. or Sc.D degree at a U.S. educational institution; and must have not earned a doctoral degree at any time in any field. **Criteria:** Recipients are selected based on the evidence of superior academic achievement; degree of promise of continuing achievement as scholars and teachers; capacity to respond in pedagogically productive ways to the learning needs of students from diverse backgrounds; sustained personal engagement with communities that are underrepresented in the academy and an ability to bring this asset to learning, teaching, and scholarship at the college or university level; and likelihood of using the diversity of human experience as an educational resource in teaching and scholarship. Recipients are also selected based on the academic records, essays, letters of recommendation, the application itself, and other appropriate materials that meet the eligibility requirements and the selection criteria.

Funds Avail.: No specific amount. **Duration:** Annual. **Number Awarded:** Varies. **To Apply:** Applicants must complete the online application form including personal and contact information; a two-page, double-spaced statement of previous research; an essay describing proposed plan of graduate study or research and the applicant's long-range career goals; transcript showing baccalaureate degree or undergraduate work; Graduate School Transcript; letters of reference; Verification of Predoctoral Status form; and GRE General Test Scores. **Contact:** Fellowships Office, infofell@nas.edu.

6289 ■ Ford Foundation Postdoctoral Fellowships
(Postdoctorate/Fellowship)

Purpose: To increase the diversity of the nation's college and university faculties by increasing their ethnic and racial diversity; to maximize the educational benefits of diversity; to increase the number of professors who can and will use the diversity as a resource for enriching the education of all students. **Focus:** Area and ethnic studies; Interdisciplinary

studies; Peace studies. **Qualif.:** Applicants must be citizens or nationals of the United States; must be individuals with the evidence of superior academic achievement; must be committed to a career in teaching and research at the college or university level; and must be awarded a Ph.D. or Sc.D degree. **Criteria:** Recipients are selected based on the evidence of superior academic achievement; degree of promise of continuing achievement as scholars and teachers; capacity to respond in pedagogically productive ways to the learning needs of students from diverse backgrounds; sustained personal engagement with the communities that are underrepresented in the academy and an ability to bring this asset to learning, teaching, and scholarship at the college and university level; likelihood of using the diversity of human experience as an educational resource in teaching and scholarship. Recipients are also selected based on academic records, essays, letters of recommendation, indications of competence as a teacher, the application itself and other materials that meet the eligibility requirements.

Funds Avail.: $45,000. **Duration:** Annual. **Number Awarded:** 18. **To Apply:** Applicants must complete the application form including personal and contact information; statement of previous research; Annotated biography; one-page limit abstract of dissertation; abstract of proposed plan of study or research and long-range goal. **Deadline:** November 14. **Contact:** Fellowships Office, infofell@nas.edu.

6290 ■ Ford Foundation Predoctoral Fellowships
(Graduate, Doctorate/Fellowship)

Purpose: To increase the diversity of the nation's college and university faculties by increasing their ethnic and racial diversity; to maximize educational benefits of diversity; to increase the number of professors who can and will use diversity as a resource for enriching the education of all students. **Focus:** Area and ethnic studies; Interdisciplinary studies; Peace studies. **Qualif.:** Applicants must be nationals of the United States regardless of race, national origin, gender, age, disability, or sexual orientation; must be individuals who have evidence of superior academic achievement; must be committed to a career in teaching and research at the college or university level; must be enrolled or planning to enroll in an eligible research-based leading to a Ph.D. or Sc.D degree at a U.S. educational institution; and must have not earned a doctoral degree at any time in any field. **Criteria:** Recipients are selected based on the evidence of superior academic achievement; degree of promise of continuing achievement as scholars and teachers; capacity to respond in pedagogically productive ways to the learning needs of students from diverse backgrounds; sustained personal engagement with communities that are underrepresented in the academy and an ability to bring this asset to learning, teaching, and scholarship at the college or university level; likelihood of using the diversity of human experience as an educational resource in teaching and scholarship. Recipients are also selected based on academic records, essays, letters of recommendation, the application itself, and other appropriate materials that meet the eligibility requirements and the selection criteria.

Funds Avail.: $24,000. **Duration:** 3 years. **Number Awarded:** 60. **To Apply:** Applicants must complete the online application form including personal and contact information; a two-page, double-spaced statement of previous research; essay describing proposed plan of graduate study or research and the applicant's long-range career goals; transcript showing baccalaureate degree or under-

Awards are arranged alphabetically below their administering organizations

graduate work; graduate School Transcript; letters of reference; verification of Predoctoral Status form; and GRE General Test Scores. **Deadline:** November 19. **Contact:** Fellowships Office, infofell@nas.edu.

6291 ■ Christine Mirzayan Science and Technology Policy Graduate Fellowships (Graduate/Fellowship)

Purpose: To engage early career professionals in the analytical processes that informs US science and technology policy. **Focus:** Behavioral sciences; Biological and clinical sciences; Business; Engineering; Law; Physical sciences; Public administration; Social sciences. **Qualif.:** Applicants must be graduate and professional school students; must have completed graduate studies within the last five years. **Criteria:** Selection will be based on the committee's criteria.

Funds Avail.: $8,500. **To Apply:** Applicants must submit a completed application. Two references are required and must pertain to the applicants' academic, professional or other work-related experience. **Deadline:** September 1.

6292 ■ National Academy of Education (NAEd)
500 5th St. NW
Washington, DC 20001
Ph: (202)334-2340
E-mail: info@naeducation.org
URL: www.naeducation.org

6293 ■ NAED/Spencer Dissertation Fellowship Program (Graduate, Doctorate/Fellowship)

Purpose: To encourage a new generation of scholars from a wide range of disciplines and professional fields to undertake research relevant to the improvement of education. **Focus:** Education. **Qualif.:** Applicants need not be U.S. citizens; must be candidates for the doctoral degree at a graduate school within the United States. **Criteria:** Recipients are selected based on academic standing and submitted requirements.

Funds Avail.: $25,000. **Duration:** Annual. **Number Awarded:** 30. **To Apply:** Applicants must complete the application form and submit along with a list of publications/presentations; a dissertation abstract; a personal statement; a narrative discussion of the dissertation; a work plan; two letters of recommendation; and graduate transcript of records. **Deadline:** October 6.

6294 ■ National Active and Retired Federal Employees Association (NARFE)
606 N Washington St.
Alexandria, VA 22314
Ph: (703)838-7760
Fax: (703)838-7785
URL: www.narfe.org/departments/home/index.cfm

6295 ■ NARFE-FEEA Scholarship Awards Program (Undergraduate/Scholarship)

Purpose: To provide financial assistance for the education of children and grandchildren of federal employees. **Focus:** General studies/Field of study not specified. **Qualif.:** Applicant must be a child, grandchild, stepchild or great-grandchild of any NARFE member in good standing currently in high school and has at least a 3.0 grade point average on a 4.0 scale. **Criteria:** Applicant are judged according to the residence of the NARFE member.

Funds Avail.: $1,000. **Duration:** Annual. **Number Awarded:** 60. **To Apply:** Applicant must submit copies of their American College Testing (ACT) or Scholastic Aptitude Testing (SAT) scores or other entrance examination scores as applicable; a written letter of recommendation/character reference from a teacher or counselor; a list and brief description of awards and/or community service activities on a separate page; a typed, double-spaced essay on a specific topic determined in the "Official Scholarship Application"; and two stamped, self-addressed No. 10 business-size envelopes. **Deadline:** April 24.

6296 ■ National Administrative Law Judiciary Foundation (NALJF)
c/o National Association of Administrative Law Judiciary
PO Box 5275
Herndon, VA 20170
Free: 855-756-2255
URL: www.naalj.org

6297 ■ Neil Alexander Scholarships (Undergraduate/Scholarship)

Purpose: To provide scholarship to young NAALJ members who wish to study administrative law. **Focus:** Law. **Qualif.:** Applicant must be a NAAJL member and must demonstrate outstanding academic and other qualifications. **Criteria:** Recipient will be selected based on the following criteria: (1) NAALJ involvement, (2) available support to attend the course (including other NJC financial assistance), (3) benefit of course to recipient, and (4) willingness to contribute a newsletter article.

Funds Avail.: $500. **Duration:** Annual. **Number Awarded:** 2. **To Apply:** Applicants must complete the application form available online and send the forms to NAAJL. **Deadline:** November 16.

6298 ■ National Air Filtration Association (NAFA)
PO Box 68639
Virginia Beach, VA 23471
Ph: (757)313-7400
Fax: (757)313-7401
E-mail: nafa@nafahq.org
URL: www.nafahq.org

6299 ■ NAFA Scholarship Programs (Undergraduate/Scholarship)

Purpose: To honor and aid students who demonstrate outstanding personal and academic characteristics. **Focus:** General studies/Field of study not specified. **Qualif.:** Applicants must be immediate family members of NAFA members in good standing, or family members of employees of NAFA member firms. Grandchildren of NAFA members are also qualified. Incoming freshmen must have a minimum ACT score of 22 or SAT score of 900 and rank in the top 35% of the graduating class. Transfer students must have a cumulative GPA of 2.75 on a 4.0 scale. **Criteria:** Applicants are selected based on the NAFA Past Presidents' review of the application materials.

Funds Avail.: $1,000 each. **Duration:** Annual. **Number Awarded:** 2. **To Apply:** Applicants must submit a recent photo for press release purposes; a written essay of 1-2 typewritten pages that gives a brief biographical sketch of the individual along with reasons why they feel they should receive the scholarship; and two letters of recommenda-

Awards are arranged alphabetically below their administering organizations

tion, one of which must be from a recent teacher. Neither recommendation should be from a family member. Applicants must also submit a recent photo attached to the application for press release purposes. **Deadline:** August 1.

6300 ■ National Aircraft Finance Association (NAFA)

PO Box 1570
Edgewater, MD 21037
Ph: (410)571-1740
E-mail: info@nafa.aero
URL: www.nafa.aero

6301 ■ NAFA Corporate Aviation Business Scholarship *(Undergraduate, Graduate/Scholarship)*

Purpose: To support students seeking a business career in Corporate Aviation and, specifically, within the corporate aircraft Finance, Legal and Insurance community. **Focus:** Accounting; Aviation; Business; Economics; Finance. **Qualif.:** Applicants must be full-time undergraduate or graduate students; must have a 3.0 minimum cumulative GPA on a 4.0 grade scale (High School GPA or equivalent for Freshman applicants); must be U.S. citizens or permanent residents. **Criteria:** Selection will be based on the committee's criteria.

Funds Avail.: $1,000 to $5,000. **Duration:** Annual. **To Apply:** Eligible students should apply through their schools' Financial Aid office. All completed applications must be submitted to NAFA by the Financial Aid office on or before the deadline. **Deadline:** April 1. **Contact:** Karen Griggs, Executive Director, NAFA; Phone: 410-571-1740; E-mail: karengriggs@nafa.aero.

6302 ■ National Alliance of Preservation Commissions (NAPC)

PO Box 1605
Athens, GA 30603
Ph: (706)369-5881
Fax: (706)369-5864
E-mail: napc@uga.edu
URL: napc.uga.edu

6303 ■ National Alliance of Preservation Commission Student Scholarships *(Undergraduate/ Scholarship)*

Purpose: To provide financial assistance to graduating students in historic preservation. **Focus:** Historic preservation. **Qualif.:** Applicants must be graduate students in historic preservation or related fields to participate in the National Commission Forum. **Criteria:** Recipients are selected based on their academic standing.

Funds Avail.: No specific amount. **Duration:** Annual. **To Apply:** Applicants must submit a cover letter with name and contact information; a 500-word statement explaining interest and expectations in attending the Forum; an estimate of the Forum expenses and the anticipated financial contribution. Applicants must also submit a proof of current student status; current resume including two academic and/or professional references. **Deadline:** February 28.

6304 ■ National Alpha Lambda Delta

328 Orange St.
Macon, GA 31201

Fax: (478)744-9924
Free: 800-925-7421
E-mail: ald@nationalald.org
URL: www.nationalald.org

6305 ■ ALD Graduate Fellowships *(Graduate/ Fellowship)*

Purpose: To provide financial support for ALD members pursuing a graduate or professional degree. **Focus:** General studies/Field of study not specified. **Qualif.:** Applicant must be a member of Alpha Lambda Delta who has maintained a GPA of 3.5 on a 4.0 scale or equivalent until graduation. **Criteria:** Candidates will be selected based on academic records, recommendations submitted, the applicant's stated purpose and campus and community activities.

Funds Avail.: $3,000, $5,000 and $7,500. **Number Awarded:** 23. **To Apply:** Applicants must submit typed application, official transcript of all academic work, and list of not more than three persons from whom have requested letters of recommendation. **Deadline:** January 31.

6306 ■ Jo Anne J. Trow Scholarships *(Undergraduate/Scholarship)*

Purpose: To provide financial assistance to qualified members for their education. **Focus:** General studies/Field of study not specified. **Qualif.:** Applicants must be members of Alpha Lambda Delta who have maintained the cumulative grade point average of 3.5 on a 4.0 scale or equivalent. **Criteria:** Candidates will be evaluated by the chapter's scholarship selection committee.

Funds Avail.: $1,000 to $6,000. **Number Awarded:** 35. **To Apply:** Applicants must complete application form, prepare the supplemental materials, and submit original application and two complete photocopies of all application materials to ALD chapter's scholarship selection committee's advisor. **Deadline:** April 1.

6307 ■ National American Arab Nurses Association (NAANA)

615 Griswold St., Ste. 925
Detroit, MI 48226
Ph: (313)680-5049
URL: www.n-aana.org

6308 ■ National American Arab Nurses Association Scholarships *(Undergraduate, Master's/Scholarship)*

Purpose: To provide financial assistance to applicants who are engaged in studying nursing at the associate degree, bachelor's degree, and master's degree or RN-BSN levels. **Focus:** Nursing. **Qualif.:** Applicants must be enrolled in an accredited nursing program at the time of application, and should be pursuing a nursing program during the year for which the award is made. In order to be eligible, applicants must be of Arab heritage, citizens or permanent residents of the United States, and must reside within the US or its territories; further, applicants must be members of NAANA. **Criteria:** Recipients will be evaluated on the basis of demonstrated academic excellence; leadership; academic; professional. Applications will be reviewed by a selection committee comprised of members of the Board of Directors.

Funds Avail.: $500 - $1,000. **Duration:** Annual. **To Apply:** Applicants must submit a copy of the most recent college or university transcript; two letters of recommendation from

Awards are arranged alphabetically below their administering organizations

nursing faculty members that addresses the overall academic performance of the student and leadership activities; a one-page essay by the applicant describing eligibility why he/she is deserving for the award; a typewritten scholarship information sheet; resume/curriculum vita; and, the completed Scholarship Information Sheet. **Deadline:** May 30. **Contact:** National American Arab Nurses Association, at the above address.

6309 ■ National Arab American Medical Association (NAAMA)

2265 Livernois Rd., Ste. 720
Troy, MI 48083
Ph: (248)646-3661
Fax: (248)646-0617
E-mail: naama@naama.com
URL: www.naama.com

6310 ■ NAAMA Scholarships *(Undergraduate/ Scholarship)*

Purpose: To provide financial assistance to Arabic students who are studying in a medical, osteopathic, or dental school. **Focus:** Dentistry; Medicine, Osteopathic. **Qualif.:** Applicants must be Arabic students enrolled in a U.S. or Canadian medical, osteopathic, or dental school. **Criteria:** Awards are given based on academic excellence and financial need.

Funds Avail.: $1,000. **Duration:** Annual. **Number Awarded:** 2. **To Apply:** Applicants must send completed application form together with a brief description on the applicant's education; transcripts; description of financial need; description of involvement in the Arab American community after completing studies; and recent 1040 tax return (with spouse and parents). Application must be submitted in typewritten. **Deadline:** July 1.

6311 ■ National Asian Pacific American Bar Association (NAPABA)

1612 K St. NW, Ste. 1400
Washington, DC 20006
Ph: (202)775-9555
Fax: (202)775-9333
URL: www.napaba.org

6312 ■ Anheuser-Busch NAPABA Law Foundation Presidential Scholarships *(Undergraduate/ Scholarship)*

Purpose: To award law students who demonstrate an outstanding leadership potential to serve the Asian Pacific American community. **Focus:** Law. **Qualif.:** Applicants must be students enrolled as law degree candidates in an accredited law school in the United States at least half time as determined by the school. **Criteria:** Applicants will be selected based on consultation with the president of NAPABA.

Funds Avail.: $7,500. **Duration:** Annual. **Number Awarded:** 2. **To Apply:** Applicants must submit complete application form; official copy of most recent law school transcript; resume; two letters of recommendation; and a copy of application to law school for financial assistance.

6313 ■ Lim, Ruger and Kim Scholarships *(Undergraduate/Scholarship)*

Purpose: To award financial aid for law students who demonstrate a commitment to serve or contribute to the

Asian Pacific American community as future leaders. **Focus:** Law. **Qualif.:** Applicant must be a student enrolled as a law degree candidate in an accredited law school in the US at least half time as determined by the school. **Criteria:** Selection will be based on the committee's criteria.

Funds Avail.: $2,500. **Number Awarded:** 1. **To Apply:** Applicants must submit a completed and signed application form from foundation; official copy of the applicant's most recent law school transcript; resume; letter of recommendation from persons not related to the applicant. **Deadline:** September 1. **Contact:** foundation@napaba.org.

6314 ■ NAPABA Law Foundation Scholarships *(Undergraduate/Scholarship)*

Purpose: To award law students who demonstrate a commitment to serve or contribute to the Asian Pacific American community as future leaders. **Focus:** Law. **Qualif.:** Applicant must be a student enrolled as a law degree candidate in an accredited law school in the United States at least half time as determined by the school. **Criteria:** Selection will be based on the demonstrated financial need.

Funds Avail.: No specific amount. **Duration:** Annual. **To Apply:** Applicants must submit a completed and signed application form from foundation; official copy of the applicant's most recent law school transcript; resume; letter of recommendation from persons not related to the applicant. **Remarks:** Established in 1995.

6315 ■ Prudential 1L Summer Internships *(Postgraduate/Internship)*

Purpose: To provide a summer internship opportunity for a highly-motivated first-year law students. **Focus:** Law. **Qualif.:** Applicants must be members of NAPABA; must be enrolled at an ABA-accredited law school; must have successfully completed the first year of law school with a minimum 3.0 GPA on a 4.0 scales (or equivalent) and be scheduled for graduation; must have financial or business-related experience or interest. **Criteria:** Selection will be based on the committee's criteria.

Funds Avail.: No specific amount. **To Apply:** Applicants must submit a cover letter, resume, list of three references and copy of the transcript.

6316 ■ National Association of Abandoned Mine Land Programs (NAAMLP)

c/o Eric Cavazza, President
PO Box 8461
Harrisburg, PA 17105-8461
Ph: (717)783-2267
E-mail: naamlp@naamlp.net
URL: naamlp.net

6317 ■ National Association of Abandoned Mine Land Programs Scholarships *(Undergraduate/ Scholarship)*

Purpose: To assist students who intend to work as scientists or technicians in the field of mine land reclamation. **Focus:** Mining. **Qualif.:** Applicants must be enrolled in a school within the Midwest, Eastern, or Western part of the United States. **Criteria:** Recipients will be selected based on submitted application.

Funds Avail.: $2,000. **Duration:** Annual. **Number Awarded:** 3. **To Apply:** Applicants must complete an application form; must submit a (one-page) essay addressing the following criteria: 1) commitment to the reclamation and

Awards are arranged alphabetically below their administering organizations

restoration of lands affected by the abandoned mining; 2) statement of intended career; 3) declared area of study; 4) educational history and level of education; 5) coursework, employment, and/or volunteer activities; 6) transcript of last year's course work; 7) statement of intent; and 8) personal statement of financial need. **Deadline:** May 30. **Contact:** Application form and other required documents must be sent to Murray Balk at the above address.

6318 ■ National Association for the Advancement of Colored People (NAACP)

4805 Mt. Hope Dr.
Baltimore, MD 21215
Ph: (410)580-5777
Free: 877-NAACP-98
URL: www.naacp.org

6319 ■ Law Fellows Program *(Undergraduate/ Fellowship)*

Purpose: To develop future generations of civil rights attorneys. **Focus:** Law. **Qualif.:** Applicants must be U.S. citizens and students who have completed at least one year of law school. **Criteria:** Law Fellows will be selected based on a number of factors, including: interest in civil rights law, academic credentials, recommendations, and commitment to public interest law.

Funds Avail.: No specific amount. **Duration:** Annual. **To Apply:** Interested applicants may contact Anson Asaka for the application process and further inquiries. **Contact:** Anson Asaka, at aasaka@naacpnet.org.

6320 ■ National Association of Agricultural Educators (NAAE)

University of Kentucky
300 Garrigus Bldg.
Lexington, KY 40546-0215
Ph: (859)257-2224
Fax: (859)323-3919
Free: 800-509-0204
URL: www.naae.org

6321 ■ NAAE Upper Division Scholarships *(Undergraduate/Scholarship)*

Purpose: To support students who are majoring in agricultural education. **Focus:** Agricultural sciences; Education. **Qualif.:** Applicants must be agricultural education majors who want to be agricultural teachers; and, be members of NAAE. **Criteria:** Awards are given based on academics, character and perseverance to the field of teaching in agricultural education.

Funds Avail.: $750 each. **Duration:** Annual. **Number Awarded:** 15. **To Apply:** Applicants must submit original copy and eight copies of application form; description of applicants' leadership and service activities; (400 words) essay entitled "Why I Want to Teach Agriculture"; a letter of recommendation from an agricultural education teacher in the applicant's college or university or from an agricultural education teacher at the local, state or national level; official transcript; and a photograph in a CD. **Deadline:** May 15. **Remarks:** Sponsored by National Geographic Learning and Delmar Cengage Learning.

6322 ■ National Association of Biology Teachers (NABT)

12100 Sunset Hills Rd., Ste. 130
Reston, VA 20190

Ph: (703)264-9696
Fax: (703)264-7778
Free: 888-501-NABT
E-mail: office@nabt.org
URL: www.nabt.org

6323 ■ National Association of Biology Teachers BioClub Student Awards *(Undergraduate/Scholarship)*

Purpose: To support and recognize exceptional students who are inspired to be even better biology teachers. **Focus:** Biology. **Qualif.:** Applicants must be NABTA BioClub student members who are graduating high school seniors and have been accepted to a two or four year college/ university. **Criteria:** Selection will be based on the committee's criteria.

Funds Avail.: No specific amount. **To Apply:** Applicants can nominate themselves or a colleague for one or more of the following NABT awards by filling out the online nomination form. Nominees can also send a letter stating why the candidate should be selected for an award. The nominee will be sent all the information, application materials and cover sheet that he or she needs to complete to be considered for the award. **Deadline:** March 31.

6324 ■ National Association of Black Accountants (NABA)

7474 Greenway Center Dr., Ste. 1120
Greenbelt, MD 20770
Ph: (301)474-6222
Fax: (301)474-3114
Free: 888-571-2939
E-mail: membership@nabainc.org
URL: www.nabainc.org

6325 ■ NABA National Scholarship Program *(Graduate, Undergraduate/Scholarship)*

Purpose: To support students who are planning to enter a business-related field. **Focus:** Accounting; Business; Finance. **Qualif.:** Applicant must be a member of an ethic minority; an active NABA student member; enrolled full-time in a four-year U.S. college or university; must be a freshman, sophomore, junior or first-year senior undergraduate pursuing a major in accounting, finance or business; or a graduate student in a master's level business program; must meet the minimum requirement of 3.5 major GPA and 3.3 overall GPA or equivalent. **Criteria:** Recipients are selected based on submitted application and other supporting materials.

Funds Avail.: $1,000-$10,000. **Duration:** Annual. **To Apply:** Applicants must submit a completed National Scholarship Application (NSA) available on the website; a current official transcript; a copy of the Student/Permanent Resident Visa (for non-U.S. citizen applicants); a resume; two letters of recommendation; a personal biography (maximum of 500 words) discussing career objectives, leadership skills, community activities and involvement in NABA. **Deadline:** January 31.

6326 ■ National Association of Black Social Workers (NABSW)

2305 Martin Luther King, Jr. Ave. SE
Washington, DC 20020-5813
Ph: (202)678-4570
Fax: (202)678-4572

Awards are arranged alphabetically below their administering organizations

E-mail: nabsw.officedir@verizon.net
URL: nabsw.org

6327 ■ Emma and Meloid Algood Tuition Scholarships *(Graduate, Undergraduate/Scholarship)*

Purpose: To provide financial assistance for African-American students who are active in community service and planning to work in the field of social work. **Focus:** Social work. **Qualif.:** Applicants must be African-American students enrolled fro full-time study at an accredited United States bachelor of social work program in the semester that the award will be granted, and have a GPA of 2.5 on a 4.0 scale. They must also express research interest in the black community. **Criteria:** Applicants are evaluated based on academic achievement; community service; and financial need.

Funds Avail.: $1,000. **Duration:** Annual. **Number Awarded:** 1. **To Apply:** Applicants must submit the completed application form along with the following: statement of purpose letter; two recommendation letters; official school registrar letter; and official academic transcript. **Deadline:** February 15.

6328 ■ Dr. Joyce Beckett Scholarships *(Graduate, Undergraduate/Scholarship)*

Purpose: To help students complete graduate work and develop professional skills and talents to work in the African American community. **Focus:** Social work. **Qualif.:** Applicants must be African-American students enrolled fro full-time study at an accredited United States master of social work program in the semester that the award will be granted, and have a GPA of 2.5 on a 4.0 scale. They must also express research interest in the black community. **Criteria:** Applicants are evaluated based on academic achievement; community service; and financial need.

Funds Avail.: $1,000. **Duration:** Annual. **Number Awarded:** 1. **To Apply:** Applicants must submit the completed application form along with the following: statement of purpose letter; two recommendation letters; official school registrar letter; and official academic transcript. **Deadline:** February 15.

6329 ■ Selena Danette Brown Book Scholarships *(Graduate, Undergraduate/Scholarship)*

Purpose: To provide financial assistance for African-American students who are active in community service. **Focus:** Social work. **Qualif.:** Applicants must be African-American students enrolled fro full-time study at an accredited United States social work program in the semester that the award will be granted, and have a GPA of 2.5 on a 4.0 scale. They must also express research interest in the black community. **Criteria:** Applicants are evaluated based on academic achievement; community service; and financial need.

Funds Avail.: $250 each. **Duration:** Annual. **Number Awarded:** 4. **To Apply:** Applicants must submit the completed application form along with the following: statement of purpose letter; two recommendation letters; official school registrar letter; and official academic transcript. **Deadline:** February 15.

6330 ■ Cenie Jomo Williams Tuition Scholarships *(Graduate, Undergraduate/Scholarship)*

Purpose: To provide financial assistance for African-American students who are active in community service. **Focus:** Social work. **Qualif.:** Applicants must be African-

American students enrolled fro full-time study at an accredited United States social work program in the semester that the award will be granted, and have a GPA of 2.5 on a 4.0 scale. **Criteria:** Applicants are evaluated based on academic achievement; community service; and financial need.

Funds Avail.: $2,500 each. **Duration:** Annual. **Number Awarded:** 2. **To Apply:** Applicants must submit the completed application form along with the following: statement of purpose letter; two recommendation letters; official school registrar letter; and official academic transcript. **Deadline:** February 15.

6331 ■ National Association for Campus Activities (NACA)

13 Harbison Way
Columbia, SC 29212-3401
Ph: (803)732-6222
Fax: (803)749-1047
Free: 800-845-2338
E-mail: info@naca.org
URL: www.naca.org

6332 ■ Tese Caldarelli Memorial Scholarships *(Graduate, Undergraduate/Scholarship)*

Purpose: To support undergraduate or graduate students. **Focus:** General studies/Field of study not specified. **Qualif.:** Applicants must be matriculated undergraduate or graduate students with a cumulative GPA of 3.0 or better at the time of the application. **Criteria:** Recipients are selected based on the following criteria: demonstrate significant leadership skills and abilities; hold significant leadership position on campus; make significant contributions via volunteer involvement, either on or off campus.

Funds Avail.: No specific amount. **Duration:** Annual. **To Apply:** Applicants must submit the following: completed and signed application form; at least two letters of recommendation; resume; official verification of the applicant's current enrollment status and a copy of academic transcripts from the college/university registrar **Deadline:** November 1. **Remarks:** Established in 1999.

6333 ■ Markley Scholarships *(Undergraduate/Scholarship)*

Purpose: To support students who have made significant contributions to the Central region and should be used for educational purposes, such as tuition, fees and books. **Focus:** General studies/Field of study not specified. **Qualif.:** Applicants must have a minimum of a 2.5 cumulative GPA; be juniors, seniors, or graduate students at a four-year school in in the NACA Central region or be sophomores at a two-year school in the NACA Central region; and must be U.S. citizens. **Criteria:** Recipients are selected based on the involvement and contribution to NACA Central; demonstrated potential in the field of student activities; contribution to the field of student activities and/or student activities employment; involvement in and contribution to other organizations.

Funds Avail.: No specific amount. **Duration:** Annual. **Number Awarded:** Up to 2. **To Apply:** Applicants must submit the following: completed and signed application form; current resume that highlights the applicant's activities, abilities and accomplishments; and any supporting materials that may enhance candidacy. **Deadline:** September 1. **Remarks:** Established in 1983.

Awards are arranged alphabetically below their administering organizations

6334 ■ NACA Foundation Graduate Scholarships
(Graduate, Master's, Postdoctorate/Scholarship)

Purpose: To assist students pursuing a career in student activities or a related student services field. **Focus:** General studies/Field of study not specified. **Qualif.:** Applicants must be matriculated in a master's doctorate degree program in student personnel services or a related area. Applicants must have demonstrated experience and involvement in campus activities and be committed to pursue a career as a campus activities professional. Applicants must have graduated from a four- year college or university with a minimum GPA of 2.5. **Criteria:** Recipients are selected based on the demonstrated leadership, academic record, and financial need. All scholarship recipients will be selected by an anonymous Scholarship Committee appointed by the Chair of the Board of Trustees.

Funds Avail.: No specific amount. **Duration:** Annual. **To Apply:** Applicants must submit at least two to four letters of reference from professors, advisors or employers who are familiar with the applicant's experience related to campus activities; one copy of the applicant's undergraduate and graduate academic; a summary of the applicant's volunteer and employment activities related to campus activities or resume; a summary of professional goals the applicant hopes to accomplish in one year, five years and ten years. **Deadline:** May 30.

6335 ■ NACA Mid Atlantic Graduate Student Scholarships *(Graduate, Master's, Doctorate/ Scholarship)*

Purpose: To assist students pursuing a career in student activities or a related student services field. **Focus:** General studies/Field of study not specified. **Qualif.:** Applicants must be matriculated in a master's doctorate degree program in student personnel services or a related area; must have demonstrated experience and involvement in campus activities and be committed to pursue a career as a campus activities professional; and must be U.S. citizens. **Criteria:** Recipients are selected based on the demonstrated leadership, academic record and financial need.

Funds Avail.: No specific amount. **Duration:** Annual. **Number Awarded:** Up to 2. **To Apply:** Applicants must submit at least two to four letters of reference from professors, advisors or employers who are familiar with the applicant's experience related to campus activities; one copy of the applicant's undergraduate and graduate academic; a summary of the applicant's volunteer and employment activities related to campus activities or resume; a summary of professional goals the applicant hopes to accomplish in one year, five years and ten years. **Deadline:** May 30. **Remarks:** Established in 1995.

6336 ■ NACA Mid Atlantic Higher Education Research Scholarships *(Master's/Scholarship)*

Purpose: To assist students pursuing a career in student activities or a related student services field. **Focus:** General studies/Field of study not specified. **Qualif.:** Applicants must show that their research will add to the college student personnel knowledge base, particularly campus activities, or address issues challenging student affairs practitioners or higher education as they relate to campus activities. Applicants must be pursuing a master's degree. **Criteria:** Recipients are selected based on the demonstrated leadership, academic record, and financial need. All scholarship recipients will be selected by an anonymous Scholarship Committee appointed by the Chair of the Board of Trustees.

Funds Avail.: Up to $500. **Duration:** Annual. **To Apply:**

Applicants must submit a completed application form; a written statement from the applicant detailing a statement of the problem, purpose of the project, plan and timeline to address the question, anticipated results, including types of evidence to indicate objectives were achieved, a statement of the project's anticipated contribution to the profession, proposed budget that identifies anticipated income from all sources, qualifications of those conducting research, and plans to evaluate the project. Applicants should submit a letter of support from the applicant's supervisor, major professor, department head or other appropriate individual. **Deadline:** June 15. **Remarks:** Established in 1995.

6337 ■ NACA Mid Atlantic Undergraduate Scholarships for Student Leaders *(Undergraduate/ Scholarship)*

Purpose: To assist students pursuing graduate or undergraduate studies leading to a career in student activities or a related student services field. **Focus:** General studies/Field of study not specified. **Qualif.:** Applicants must be matriculated undergraduates in good standing at the time of their application and during the semester in which the award is received; have a GPA of 2.5 on a 4.0 scale; have demonstrated significant leadership skills and ability; have made significant contributions via volunteer involvement, either on or off campus; be enrolled in a college or university within the NACA Mid Atlantic region. **Criteria:** Recipients will be selected based on demonstrated leadership, academic record, and financial need.

Funds Avail.: No specific amount. **Duration:** Annual. **To Apply:** Applicants must submit at least two letters of recommendation; resume or description of the applicant's leadership activities, skills, and ability, training, and accomplishment; official transcript of the applicant's current enrollment status from the college or university. **Deadline:** March 31. **Remarks:** Established in 1995.

6338 ■ NACA Regional Council Student Leadership Scholarships *(Undergraduate/Scholarship)*

Purpose: To assist students pursuing graduate or undergraduate studies leading to a career in student activities or a related student services field. **Focus:** General studies/Field of study not specified. **Qualif.:** Applicants must be matriculated undergraduate in good standing at the time of their application and during the semester in which the award is received; hold a significant leadership position on campus or in the community; have made significant contributions via volunteer involvement, either on or off the campus. **Criteria:** Recipients are selected based on the demonstrated leadership, academic record, and financial need. All scholarship recipients will be selected by an anonymous Scholarship Committee appointed by the Chair of the Board of Trustees.

Funds Avail.: No specific amount. **Duration:** Annual. **Number Awarded:** 1. **To Apply:** Applicants must submit at least two letters of recommendation; resume or description of the applicant's leadership activities, skills, and ability, training, and accomplishment; and official transcript of the applicant's current enrollment status from the college or university. **Deadline:** January 15. **Remarks:** Established in 1996.

6339 ■ NACA South Student Leadership Scholarships *(Undergraduate/Scholarship)*

Purpose: To support undergraduate student enrolled at colleges and universities in the former NACA Southeast Region. **Focus:** General studies/Field of study not speci-

Awards are arranged alphabetically below their administering organizations

fied. **Qualif.:** Applicants must be matriculated undergraduates in good standing at the time of their application and during the semester in which the award is received; have demonstrated significant leadership skills and ability; hold a significant leadership position on campus or in the community; have made significant contributions via volunteer involvement, either on or off the campus; be enrolled in a college or university within the former NACA Southeast Region. **Criteria:** Recipients are selected based on the demonstrated leadership, academic record, and financial need. All scholarship recipients will be selected by an anonymous Scholarship Committee appointed by the Chair of the Board of Trustees.

Funds Avail.: No specific amount. **Duration:** Annual. **Number Awarded:** Up to 4. **To Apply:** Applicants must submit at least two letters of recommendation; resume or description of the applicant's leadership activities, skills, and ability, training, and accomplishment; and official transcript of the applicant's current enrollment status from the college or university. **Deadline:** March 31. **Remarks:** Established in 1994.

6340 ■ National Association of Campus Activities Multicultural Scholarship Programs (Undergraduate, Graduate/Scholarship)

Purpose: To provide economic assistance to qualified under-represented programmers, allowing the recipients to attend NACA-sponsored training workshops, regional conferences and NACA National Conventions. **Focus:** Minorities. **Qualif.:** Applicants must be matriculated undergraduates in good standing at the time of their application and during the semester in which the award is received; must be a member of the African-American, Latina/Latino, Native American, Asian American, or Pacific Islander ethnic minorities; hold a significant leadership position on campus or in the community; have made significant contributions via volunteer involvement, either on or off the campus. **Criteria:** Recipients are selected based on the demonstrated leadership, academic record, and financial need. All scholarship recipients will be selected by an anonymous Scholarship Committee appointed by the Chair of the Board of Trustees.

Funds Avail.: No specific amount. **Duration:** Annual. **To Apply:** Applicants must submit at least two letters of recommendation; resume or description of the applicant's leadership activities, skills, and ability, training, and accomplishment; official transcript of the applicant's current enrollment status from the college or university. Applicants must submit a 350-600-word statement describing their leadership program and how their participation met their professional development objectives. **Deadline:** May 1. **Remarks:** Established in 1981.

6341 ■ National Association of Campus Activities Scholarships for Student Leaders (Undergraduate/Scholarship)

Purpose: To provide financial assistance to undergraduate student leaders enrolled and new professionals employed in colleges and universities. **Focus:** General studies/Field of study not specified. **Qualif.:** Applicants must be undergraduate students in good standing at the time of the application and during the semester in which the award is received. **Criteria:** Recipients are selected based on the demonstrated leadership skills and abilities and significant contributions to their campus communities. All scholarship recipients will be selected by an anonymous Scholarship Committee appointed by the Chair of the Board of Trustees.

Funds Avail.: No specific amount. **Duration:** Annual. **To Apply:** Applicants must submit the following electronically: completed and signed application form; at least two letters of recommendation from administrators or faculty members who are well acquainted with the applicant as a student leader; resume; verification of the applicant's current enrollment status from the college/university registrar. **Deadline:** November 1. **Remarks:** Established in 1985.

6342 ■ Lori Rhett Memorial Scholarships (Graduate, Undergraduate/Scholarship)

Purpose: To support undergraduate or graduate student leaders enrolled in colleges and universities. **Focus:** General studies/Field of study not specified. **Qualif.:** Applicants must be matriculated undergraduate or graduate students with a cumulative GPA of 2.5 or better at the time of application and during the semester in which the award is received. Applicants must demonstrate significant leadership skills and abilities; hold a significant leadership position on campus. Applicants must have made significant contributions via volunteer involvement, either on or off campus. Applicants must be enrolled in a college or university within the former NACA Pacific Northwest Region. **Criteria:** Recipients are selected based on financial need and academic record. All scholarship recipients will be selected by an anonymous Scholarship Committee appointed by the Chair of the Board of Trustees.

Funds Avail.: No specific amount. **Duration:** Annual. **Number Awarded:** 1. **To Apply:** Applicants must complete the application form; at least two letters of recommendation; a resume; official verification of the applicant's current enrollment status and a copy of academic transcripts from the college or university. **Deadline:** June 30. **Remarks:** Established in 1996.

6343 ■ Ross-Fahey Scholarships (Graduate/Scholarship)

Purpose: To provide financial assistance to graduate student leaders enrolled and new professionals employed in colleges and universities in the NACA Northeast region. **Focus:** General studies/Field of study not specified. **Qualif.:** Applicants must be graduate students and new professionals in the former NACA New England Region. **Criteria:** Recipients will be selected based on enrollment or employment at a member school; demonstrated significant leadership skills and abilities; and significant contributions through volunteer involvement, either on or off campus.

Funds Avail.: No specific amount. **Duration:** Annual. **Number Awarded:** Up to 2. **To Apply:** Applicants must submit the following: completed and signed application form; letter of recommendation from the candidate's current supervisor; description or resume that highlights the applicants' activities, abilities and accomplishments **Deadline:** October 1. **Remarks:** Established in 1999.

6344 ■ Wisconsin Region Student Leadership Scholarships (Graduate, Undergraduate/Scholarship)

Purpose: To assist students pursuing graduate or undergraduate studies leading to a related student services field. **Focus:** General studies/Field of study not specified. **Qualif.:** Applicants must be undergraduate or graduate students in good standing and enrolled in the equivalent of at least six semesters at the time of the application and during the semester in which the award is received; be either currently enrolled in or have received a degree from a college or university within Wisconsin or Upper Peninsula of Michigan; have demonstrated leadership skills and signifi-

Awards are arranged alphabetically below their administering organizations

cant service to his/her campus and/or the community. **Criteria:** Recipients are selected based on the record of academic achievement; involvement in and contribution to NACA Northern Plains by a student from Wisconsin or Upper Peninsula of Michigan; potential success in the field of campus activities.

Funds Avail.: No specific amount. **Duration:** Annual. **To Apply:** Applicants must complete the online application and submit, electronically, the following: resume or description of relevant educational experiences; official transcript of record; and three letters of reference.

6345 ■ Zagunis Student Leader Scholarships
(Graduate, Undergraduate/Scholarship)

Purpose: To provide financial assistance to undergraduate or graduate student leaders enrolled in the former NACA Great Lakes Region. **Focus:** General studies/Field of study not specified. **Qualif.:** Applicants must be undergraduate or graduate students with a minimum cumulative GPA of 3.0 or better at the time of the application; must be U.S. citizens who are enrolled in a college or university within the NACA Mid America and Mid Atlantic regions. **Criteria:** Recipients are selected based on the demonstrated leadership skills and abilities and significant contributions to their campus communities. All scholarship recipients will be selected by an anonymous Scholarship Committee appointed by the Chair of the Board of Trustees.

Funds Avail.: No specific amount. **Duration:** Annual. **To Apply:** Applicants must submit the following: completed and signed application form; at least two letters of recommendation; resume; and official verification of the applicants' current enrollment status and a copy of academic transcripts from the college/university registrar. **Deadline:** November 1. **Remarks:** Established in 1998.

6346 ■ National Association of Chain Drug Stores Foundation
1776 Wilson Blvd., Ste. 200
Arlington, VA 22209
Ph: (703)837-4278
URL: www.nacdsfoundation.org

6347 ■ Pharmacy Partners Student Scholarship Program *(Undergraduate/Scholarship)*

Purpose: To support the development of future leaders in chain community pharmacy. **Focus:** Pharmaceutical sciences; Pharmacy. **Qualif.:** Applicants must be enrolled as full-time pharmacy students in accredited U.S. colleges or schools of pharmacy to obtain a doctor of pharmacy degree; must have completed at least one professional year of pharmacy school to apply; must have experience in chain community pharmacy as well as the desire to pursue a career in chain community pharmacy; must have a minimum "C" GPA. Scholarship recipients are not eligible to apply, however, previous applicants are welcome to apply. **Criteria:** Recipients are selected based on the student's letter on career goals and interest in chain community pharmacy practice; recommendation from their chain pharmacy employer; student's credentials including leadership activities, professional, and community involvement and chain community pharmacy experience.

Funds Avail.: Varies. **Duration:** Annual. **Number Awarded:** Varies. **To Apply:** Applicants must submit the completed application form; current resume or curriculum vitae; cover letter explaining their interest and career goals in chain community pharmacy practice (not more than two

pages, typewritten); letter of recommendation from the current or recent community pharmacy employer that explains why the applicant is deserving of the scholarship and letter from a pharmacy faculty member, pharmacy advisor, dean, or transcript office stating that applicant is in good standing. **Contact:** NACDS Foundation, at the above address.

6348 ■ National Association of Collegiate Directors of Athletics (NACDA)
24651 Detroit Rd.
Westlake, OH 44145-2524
Ph: (847)491-8880
URL: www.nacda.com

6349 ■ John McLendon Memorial Minority Postgraduate Scholarships *(Postdoctorate/ Scholarship)*

Purpose: To support minority students pursuing graduate degrees in athletics administration. **Focus:** Sports studies. **Qualif.:** Applicant must be full-time senior or an undergraduate degree with two years work experience, preferably in athletics administration; have a minimum GPA of 3.0 (on a 4.0 scale); official classification as a minority as defined by federal guidelines; intention to attend graduate school to earn a degree in athletics administration; and involvement on the college/university or community level. **Criteria:** Nominations will be sent to a Review Committee of collegiate athletics administrators and top candidates will be sent to a Blue Ribbon Committee that will choose the final five winners.

Funds Avail.: $10,000. **To Apply:** A completed nomination form must be submitted in order to be considered. Forms must be signed and approved by the student's academic advisor. **Deadline:** April 29. **Contact:** Katie Newman at knewman@nacda.com.

6350 ■ National Association of Container Distributors (NACD)
800 Roosevelt Rd., Bldg. C-312
Glen Ellyn, IL 60137
Ph: (630)942-6585
Fax: (630)790-3095
E-mail: info@nacdmeetings.org
URL: www.nacd.net

6351 ■ Henry Hoffman Memorial Scholarship Fund *(Undergraduate/Scholarship)*

Purpose: To provide higher education assistance to children of employees of NACD member companies. **Focus:** General studies/Field of study not specified. **Qualif.:** Applicants must be students who have completed their junior year in high school and are children of employees of member companies of NACD. Students must have a 3.0 GPA in high school and 2.5 GPA in college. As a prerequisite for eligibility, a NACD member company must employ one of the applicant's parents at the time the application is made. **Criteria:** Scholarship recipients will be selected based on past academic performance, performance on tests designated to measure ability and aptitude for higher education, and the applicant's rank in school. Recommendations by instructors or other persons unrelated to the candidate, extra-curricular activities and leadership contributions will also be considered.

Funds Avail.: $2,500 each. **Duration:** Annual. **Number**

Awards are arranged alphabetically below their administering organizations

Awarded: 4. **To Apply:** Applicants must submit a completed application form, counselor's report and a copy of high school transcript. **Deadline:** February 16. **Contact:** NACD Staff at: info@nacd.net.

6352 ■ National Association for County Community and Economic Development (NACCED)
2025 M St. NW, Ste. 800
Washington, DC 20036-3309
Ph: (202)367-1149
Fax: (202)367-2149
URL: www.nacced.org

6353 ■ NACCED Annual John C. Murphy Scholarships *(Graduate, Undergraduate/Scholarship)*

Purpose: To provide financial assistance for undergraduate and graduate students. **Focus:** Housing. **Qualif.:** Applicants must be currently attending an American college or university with a chosen field of study including course work in the areas of affordable housing and/or community and economic development. Applicants must also exhibit financial need. **Criteria:** Recipients will be selected based on the quality of their personal statement, financial need, grade point average and content of the letter of recommendation.

Funds Avail.: $1,500. **Number Awarded:** 1. **To Apply:** All applicants must be nominated by a NACCED member in good standing. Candidates must submit a completed scholarship application; official school transcript with official grade point average; certification of financial need - with an attached Financial Aide Award letter from the university; collegiate letter of acceptance stating the date of enrollment; personal statement of approximately 500 words introducing the applicant; letter of recommendation from a teacher, faculty or civic leader; support letter from a NACCED member in good standing. **Deadline:** September 5.

6354 ■ National Association of Farm Service Agency County Office Employees (NASCOE)
c/o Mark Van Hoose, President
6155 Nichols Ln.
Johnstown, OH 43031
Ph: (740)670-5340
URL: www.nascoe.org/Pages/default.aspx

6355 ■ NASCOE Scholarships *(Undergraduate/Scholarship)*

Purpose: To provide financial assistance to members who wish to enroll in adult education courses aimed at enhancing their careers with FSA. **Focus:** Adult education. **Qualif.:** Applicants must members who are permanent County Office employees; must be either high school seniors or full-time (minimum of 12 credit hours) college students up to the Bachelor Degree level; must have a minimum of "C" average (using the 4.0 system) in both their junior and senior years of high school or as a college student. **Criteria:** Candidates will be evaluated based on their abilities, incentive assistance and other personal characteristics.

Funds Avail.: $1,500-$2,500. **Number Awarded:** 1. **To Apply:** Applicants must submit an application together with official high school and/or college transcript, recommendation letter and all required signatures. **Deadline:** February 20.

6356 ■ National Association of Fellowships Advisors (NAFA)
c/o Alicia Hayes, Secretary
University of California, Berkeley
5 Durant Hall, No.2940
Berkeley, CA 94720-2940
E-mail: info@nafadvisors.org
URL: www.nafadvisors.org

6357 ■ Gates Cambridge Scholarships *(Graduate, Master's, Doctorate, Postgraduate, Postdoctorate/Scholarship)*

Purpose: To award scholarships on the basis of a person's intellectual ability, leadership capacity and desire to use their knowledge to contribute to society throughout the world by providing service to their communities and applying their talents and knowledge to improve the lives of others. **Focus:** General studies/Field of study not specified. **Qualif.:** Applicants must be citizens of any country outside the United Kingdom who are applying to pursue one of the following full-time residential courses of study at the University of Cambridge: PhD (three year research-only degree); MSc or MLitt (two year research-only degree); or a one year postgraduate course (e.g. MPhil, LLM, MASt, Diploma, MBA and so forth), or already a student at Cambridge and want to apply for a new postgraduate course. **Criteria:** Awards will be given to those who meet the scholarship's criteria: outstanding intellectual ability; leadership capacity; commitment to improving the lives of others; and, having convincing arguments for doing a particular postgraduate degree at Cambridge. Selection is vested to the Trust who conduct four stages in selecting awardees.

Funds Avail.: No specific amount. **Duration:** Annual. **Number Awarded:** 80. **To Apply:** Applicants must check the program website for the gathering of information about application details and process. **Contact:** National Association of Fellowships Advisors at the above address.

6358 ■ Golden Key Graduate Scholar Awards *(Graduate, Master's, Doctorate/Scholarship)*

Purpose: To provide financial support for member students who are in need. **Focus:** General studies/Field of study not specified. **Qualif.:** Applicants must be Golden Key members who are full-time or part-time members in a post-baccalaureate program of study at an accredited institution at the time of application, or full-time or part-time members in an undergraduate program who will be enrolled in a post-baccalaureate program in the academic year immediately following the granting of the award. **Criteria:** Judging criteria include academic merit, campus/community/work commitments and significant in local Golden Key chapter.

Funds Avail.: $10,000. **Duration:** Annual. **Number Awarded:** 12. **To Apply:** Applicants must submit all of the following: personal statement of no more than five pages; 500-word essay answering the question about planning to use the post-baccalaureate degree to impact the world through academics, leadership and service; one recommendation letter; resume or curriculum vitae (CV); and, current and comprehensive transcript. All applications must be uploaded online in PDF format except resume/CV. **Contact:** Golden Key International Honour Society, Scholarships and Awards; email: awards@goldenkey.org.

6359 ■ Hertz Foundation Graduate Fellowships *(Graduate, Master's, Doctorate/Fellowship)*

Purpose: To build America's capacity for innovation by nurturing remarkable applied scientists and engineers who

Awards are arranged alphabetically below their administering organizations

show the most promise to change the world. **Focus:** Engineering; Science. **Qualif.:** Applicants must be students of the applied physical, biological and engineering sciences who are citizens or permanent residents of the United States of America, and who are willing to morally commit to make their skills available to the United States in time of national emergency. **Criteria:** Award is based on merit, not need; the bestowing organization screens the applicants and has the criteria set such as: exceptional creativity ad intelligence, excellent technical education, orientation and commitment, extraordinary accomplishment in technical or related professional studies, features of temperament and character conducive to high attainment as a technical professional, appropriate moral and ethical values, and leverage.

Funds Avail.: No specific amount. **Duration:** Annual. **To Apply:** Application is via online. Applicants must visit the program website for the other application details. **Deadline:** October 31. **Contact:** Hertz Foundation Graduate Fellowships: www.hertzfoundation.org.

6360 ■ George J. Mitchell Postgraduate Scholarships *(Postgraduate/Scholarship)*

Purpose: To introduce and connect generations of future American leaders to the island of Ireland while recognizing and fostering intellectual achievement, leadership, and a commitment to public service and community. **Focus:** General studies/Field of study not specified. **Qualif.:** Applicants must be U.S. citizens ages between 18 and 30 years; have a bachelor's degree from an accredited college or university before beginning study as a Mitchell Scholar; degrees from international accredited universities are acceptable, if all other conditions are met; married applicants or applicants with partners are accepted, no allowance is made for the expenses of an applicant's spouse, partner, or dependents. **Criteria:** Criteria for the selection of awardees are the following: academic excellence, leadership, and commitment to community and public service.

Funds Avail.: No specific amount. **Duration:** Annual. **Number Awarded:** 12. **To Apply:** Applicants must submit: passport-style picture (PDF); all transcripts scanned into a single PDF; 1,000-word personal statement; scan of signature. Informations required are: GPA; contact information for 4 Recommenders including email, mailing address and phone number; contact information for Institutional Endorser (for full time undergraduate students only); complete mailing address of the university; university choice and field of study option; other awards, achievements. All information and supporting documents including recommendations and institutional endorsements must be submitted through the online application on the program website. **Deadline:** October 1.

6361 ■ NAFA International Dissertation Research Fellowships *(Graduate, Doctorate/Fellowship)*

Purpose: To support distinguished graduate students in the humanities and social sciences who are writing their respective dissertations and conducting on-site researches outside the United States. **Focus:** Humanities; Social sciences. **Qualif.:** Applicants must be graduate students in the Humanities and Social Sciences who are enrolled in a doctoral program in the United States and conducting a research outside the country; and must have completed all Ph.D. requirements except on-site dissertation research by the time the fellowship begins. **Criteria:** Prospected awardees shall be selected based on their proposals or on-site researches.

Funds Avail.: No specific amount. **Duration:** Annual; 9 to

12 months. **To Apply:** Applicants must fill up completely the provided application form which can be downloaded from the program's website. Other requirements shall be determined by the bestowing organization. **Deadline:** November. **Contact:** IDRF, idrf@ssrc.org.

6362 ■ National Association of Graduate Admissions Professionals (NAGAP)
18000 W 105th St.
Olathe, KS 66061-7543
Ph: (913)895-4616
Fax: (913)895-4652
E-mail: info@nagap.org
URL: www.nagap.org

6363 ■ NAGAP Graduate Student Enrollment Management Research Grants *(Graduate/Grant)*

Purpose: To encourage emerging knowledge and understanding of the complexities of graduate enrollment management including all aspects of admissions and recruitment, enrollment, retention and graduation in higher education. **Focus:** Management. **Qualif.:** Applicants must be individuals who are enrolled in graduate school and desire to conduct research in any aspect of graduate enrollment management activities and programs. **Criteria:** Selection will be based on demonstrated record and knowledge of research experience relevant to higher education and their respective research proposals.

Funds Avail.: $2,500. **To Apply:** Applicants must submit the following: application; abstract of proposed research project; curriculum vitae or resume; list of graduate coursework; personal statement addressing interest in research topic and future career goals; letters of support from major professor and from a graduate enrollment management office at their institution; proposal (there is no set length. Previous proposals have varied from 5-20 pages); timeline with completion date no later than March 15 of the following year; and any other supporting material deemed appropriate by the applicants. **Deadline:** January 30.

6364 ■ National Association of Health Services Executives (NAHSE)
1050 Connecticut Ave. NW, 10th Fl.
Washington, DC 20036
Ph: (202)772-1030
Fax: (202)772-1072
URL: www.nahse.org

6365 ■ Ellis J. Bonner Scholarships *(Graduate/Scholarship)*

Purpose: To recognize the distinguished leadership and academic achievement among, and assist non-traditional graduate students who are striving to become future leaders in Healthcare Management and NAHSE. **Focus:** Health care services; Health services administration. **Qualif.:** Applicants must be African American graduate students and NAHSE members enrolled in an accredited college or university program, pursuing a Master or Doctorate Degree, and majoring in healthcare administration or a related field. They must also have a minimum grade point average (GPA) of 2.5 for undergraduate and 3.0 for graduate on a scale or four (4.00). **Criteria:** Selection shall be based on academic merit and financial need.

Awards are arranged alphabetically below their administering organizations

Funds Avail.: $2,500. **Duration:** Annual. **To Apply:** Applicants must submit completed application; resume; transcripts (if applicable); three letters of reference; (maximum of three pages, double-spaced) composition; tax returns; membership application and dues; and two (black and white, 3x5) photos. **Deadline:** May 1.

6366 ■ Florence S. Gaynor Scholarships (Graduate/Scholarship)

Purpose: To recognize outstanding achievements among, and support female graduate students who are striving to become future leaders in Healthcare Management and NAHSE. **Focus:** Health care services; Health services administration. **Qualif.:** Applicants must be African American graduate students and NAHSE members enrolled in an accredited college or university program, pursuing a Master or Doctorate Degree, and majoring in healthcare administration or a related field. They must also have a minimum grade point average (GPA) of 2.5 for undergraduate and 3.0 for graduate on a scale or four (4.00). **Criteria:** Selection shall be based on academic merit and financial need.

Funds Avail.: $2,500. **Duration:** Annual. **To Apply:** Applicants must submit completed application; resume; transcripts (if applicable); three letters of reference; (maximum of three pages, double-spaced) composition; tax returns; membership application and dues; and two (black and white, 3x5) photos. **Deadline:** May 1. **Remarks:** The scholarship is established in memory of Mrs. Florence Small Gaynor.

6367 ■ Haynes Rice Scholarships (Graduate/Scholarship)

Purpose: To support and encourage African American students to pursue a career in healthcare management. **Focus:** Health care services; Health services administration. **Qualif.:** Applicants must be African American graduate students and NAHSE members enrolled in an accredited college or university program, pursuing a Master or Doctorate Degree, and majoring in healthcare administration or a related field. They must also have a minimum grade point average (GPA) of 2.5 for undergraduate and 3.0 for graduate on a scale or four (4.00). **Criteria:** Selection shall be based on academic merit and financial need.

Funds Avail.: $2,500. **Duration:** Annual. **To Apply:** Applicants must submit completed application; resume; transcripts (if applicable); three letters of reference; (maximum of three pages, double-spaced) composition; tax returns; membership application and dues; and two (black and white, 3x5) photos. **Deadline:** May 1. **Remarks:** The scholarship is established in memory of Mr. Haynes Rice.

6368 ■ National Association of Hispanic Nurses (NAHN)
10 G St. NE, Ste. 605
Washington, DC 20002
Ph: (501)367-8616
Fax: (501)227-5444
E-mail: info@thehispanicnurses.org
URL: nahnnet.org

6369 ■ United Health Foundation National Association of Hispanic Nurses Scholarships (Graduate, Undergraduate/Scholarship)

Purpose: To provide financial assistance to those Hispanic students who want to pursue their nursing profession. **Fo-**

cus: Nursing. **Qualif.:** Applicants must be NAHN members who are currently enrolled in an accredited school of nursing and be U.S. citizens or legal residents of the United States; must have academic standing and a minimum GPA of 3.0. **Criteria:** Selection of grantees will be based on applicant's merit and other designated criteria.

Funds Avail.: A total of $40,000. **Duration:** Annual. **To Apply:** Applicants must complete the application form available on the website; must provide the following supporting documents: one letter of recommendation from a faculty member outlining the applicant's future professional contribution to the nursing profession and potential to act as a role model for other aspiring nursing students; an essay (300 words or less) written by the student that reflects the qualifications and potential for leadership in nursing in the Hispanic community; a resume which includes earned certificates, awards and special honors; official transcript from applicant's college, university, or nursing program. **Contact:** National Association of Hispanic Nurses, at the above address.

6370 ■ National Association of Junior Auxiliaries (NAJA)
845 S Main St.
Greenville, MS 38701-5871
Ph: (662)332-3000
Fax: (662)332-3076
E-mail: najanet@bellsouth.net
URL: www.najanet.org

6371 ■ NAJA Scholarships (Graduate/Scholarship)

Purpose: To support graduate study in fields which address the special needs of children and youth. **Focus:** Counseling/Guidance; Education, Special; Hearing and deafness; Mental health; Psychology; Speech and language pathology/Audiology. **Qualif.:** Applicant must be working or planning to work directly with children; pursuing graduate level studies for one year in fields which address the special needs of children and youth (Counseling, Psychology, Mental Health, Special Education, Speech Pathology, Exceptional Children, Remedial Skills Development, Hearing Impaired, Gifted and Talented, etc.); a U.S. citizen and a permanent resident of a state with a Junior Auxiliary Chapter (Alabama, Arkansas, Florida, Louisiana, Mississippi, Missouri, Tennessee, and Texas); and planning to attend a U.S. college/university for full-time or part-time study. **Criteria:** Selection shall be based on the aforementioned applicant's qualifications and compliance with the application details.

Funds Avail.: Amount varies. **Duration:** Annual. **Number Awarded:** Varies. **To Apply:** Applicant may either apply online or submit a completed typed application form along with six copies of completed application form; seven copies of expense page from current graduate catalog (attached at the back of each application copy), and a photocopy of current driver's license, state issued ID card, passport or voter registration. In addition, applicant must submit three completed Scholarship recommendation Forms with Letter of Recommendation attached, and certified transcripts of all undergraduate and graduate study (mailed directly by the college to NAJA). Submit applications via mail, faxes will not be accepted. **Deadline:** February 1. **Remarks:** Established in 1962. **Contact:** National Association of Junior Auxiliaries, Inc., at the above address.

Awards are arranged alphabetically below their administering organizations

6372 ■ National Association of Multicultural Engineering Program Advocates (NAMEPA)

PO Box 241486
Los Angeles, CA 90024-9286
Ph: (310)206-7336
Fax: (310)825-3908
E-mail: namepa@namepa.org
URL: www.namepa.org

6373 ■ National Association of Multicultural Engineering Program Advocates Beginning Freshmen Awards (NAMEPA) *(Undergraduate/Scholarship)*

Purpose: To support students who have demonstrated potential and interest in pursuing an undergraduate degree in engineering. **Focus:** Engineering. **Qualif.:** Applicants must be African American, Latino and American Indian students who have been approved for admission as engineering majors. Applicants must also have a minimum cumulative grade point average of 2.70-4.00 and minimum cumulative scores on either the ACT/SAT college entrance examination of 25-1000. Students must attend a NAMEPA member institution. **Criteria:** Applicants will be selected based on the coursework in high school and interest in participating in-campus Multi-Cultural Engineering Programs (MEP) initiatives.

Funds Avail.: No Specific Amount. **To Apply:** Applicants must submit the following: an official copy of high school transcript and test scores; a one-page essay expressing their reasons for choosing engineering, why they think they should be selected and an overview of their future aspirations as an engineer; resume; and a completed recommendation form. The application and recommendation forms are available from the website.

6374 ■ National Association of Multicultural Engineering Program Advocates Transfer Engineering Student Awards (NAMEPA) *(Undergraduate/Scholarship)*

Purpose: To support students who have demonstrated potential and interest in pursuing an undergraduate degree in engineering. **Focus:** Engineering. **Qualif.:** Applicants must be African American, Latino and American Indian students; must be transfer students from either a junior college, community college or three/two dual-degree program; and must have a minimum GPA of 2.70-4.00. **Criteria:** High consideration will be given to applicants who demonstrate genuine interest in participating in-campus Multi-Cultural Engineering Programs (MEP) initiatives.

Funds Avail.: No Specific Amount. **To Apply:** Applicants must submit a complete application package including a completed application and recommendation form available on the website; an official copy of college transcripts; resume; and (one-page) essay expressing their reasons for choosing engineering, why they think they should be selected and an overview of their future aspirations as an engineer.

6375 ■ National Association of Negro Business and Professional Women's Clubs (NANBPWC)

1806 New Hampshire Ave. NW
Washington, DC 20009-3206
Ph: (202)483-4206
Fax: (202)462-7253
E-mail: executivedirector@nanbpwc.org
URL: www.nanbpwc.org

6376 ■ Dr. Julianne Malveaux Scholarships *(Undergraduate/Scholarship)*

Purpose: To provide financial assistance for African-American students pursuing their college education. **Focus:** Creative writing; Economics; Journalism; Public administration. **Qualif.:** Applicants must be United States citizens who are African-American females enrolled as college sophomores or juniors in an accredited college or university. They must be majoring in journalism, economics or related field (public policy, creative writing, etc.) and have a cumulative grade point average (GPA) of 3.0 or above on a 4.0 scale. **Criteria:** Applicants are evaluated based on academic achievement and financial need.

Funds Avail.: No specific amount. **Duration:** Annual. **To Apply:** Applicants must complete the scholarship application online and submit a 1,000-word essay on their career plans and their relevance to the Dr. Julianne Malveaux Program Theme: "Black Women's Hands Can Rock the World." **Deadline:** March 1.

6377 ■ Dr. Blanca Moore-Velez Woman of Substance Scholarships *(Undergraduate/Scholarship)*

Purpose: To provide financial assistance for African American students pursuing their college education. **Focus:** General studies/Field of study not specified. **Qualif.:** Applicants must be African American females age 35 and above; must be residents of the state of North Carolina; must be undergraduate students enrolled in an accredited college or university; and must have a cumulative grade point average (GPA) 3.0 or above on a 4.0 scale. **Criteria:** Applicants are evaluated based on academic achievement and financial need.

Funds Avail.: No specific amount. **Duration:** Annual. **To Apply:** Applicants must complete the scholarship application online and submit a 500-word essay on the topic: "Challenges to the Mature Student and How They'd Overcome Them." **Deadline:** March 1.

6378 ■ NANBPWC National Scholarships *(Undergraduate/Scholarship)*

Purpose: To provide financial assistance for African-American students pursuing their college education. **Focus:** General studies/Field of study not specified. **Qualif.:** Applicants must be graduating African-American high school seniors who have a cumulative grade point average of 3.0 or above on a 4.0 scale by February 1st in the year of graduation. **Criteria:** Applicants are evaluated based on financial need.

Funds Avail.: No specific amount. **Duration:** Annual. **To Apply:** Applicants must complete the scholarship application form online and submit a typed essay of no less than 300 words on the topic: "Why education is important to me." **Deadline:** March 1.

6379 ■ National Association of Oil and Energy Service Professionals (OESP)

c/o Judy Garber, Executive Director
PO Box 67
East Petersburg, PA 17520
Fax: (717)625-3077
Free: 888-552-0900
URL: thinkoesp.org

6380 ■ Dave Nelsen Scholarships *(Undergraduate/Scholarship)*

Purpose: To educate and advance oil heat service professionals; to support students who wish to continue their

Awards are arranged alphabetically below their administering organizations

education. **Focus:** Heating, air conditioning, and refrigeration. **Qualif.:** Applicants must be currently attending or planning to attend a technical college or trade school and must be involved in the Oil Heating industry. **Criteria:** Recipients are selected based on the submitted application form.

Funds Avail.: $5,000. **Duration:** Annual. **Number Awarded:** 6. **To Apply:** Applicants must submit completed application form and a 500-word essay stating their goals towards the heating industry. **Remarks:** Established in 1999.

6381 ■ National Association of Pastoral Musicians (NPM)

962 Wayne Ave., Ste. 210
Silver Spring, MD 20910-4461
Ph: (240)247-3000
Fax: (240)247-3001
E-mail: npmsing@npm.org
URL: www.npm.org

6382 ■ NPM Academic Scholarships *(Graduate, Undergraduate/Scholarship)*

Purpose: To assist with the cost of education formation for pastoral musicians. **Focus:** Music. **Qualif.:** Applicants must be NPM members; part-time or full-time in an undergraduate or graduate degree program of studies related to the field of pastoral music during the 2011-2012 school year; and must intend to work at least two years in the field of pastoral music following graduation/program completion. **Criteria:** Candidates must demonstrate financial need.

Funds Avail.: No specific amount. **Duration:** One year. **Number Awarded:** Varies. **To Apply:** Applicants must submit letter or short essay containing the following information: name and contact information including address, home, work phone and email; definition of the term "pastoral musician"; description of talents; previous experience as pastoral musician; educational background; educational program enrolled; recording (cassette or CD format) demonstrating solo performance skills or those of an ensemble under applicants' direction; two letters of recommendation, including one written by pastor; and completed financial need statement. **Deadline:** March 5.

6383 ■ NPM Program Scholarships *(Undergraduate/Scholarship)*

Purpose: To assist pastoral musicians with limited financial resources in taking advantage of opportunities for continuing formation at NPM conventions and institutes. **Focus:** Music. **Qualif.:** Applicants must be NPM members and should be from economically disadvantaged parishes. **Criteria:** Recipient will be selected based on financial need.

Funds Avail.: No amount mentioned. **To Apply:** Applicants must submit completed NPM Program Scholarship Application and the NPM Program Scholarship Applicant's letter; and parish recommendation completed by applicant's pastor or pastoral administrator. **Deadline:** April 10.

6384 ■ National Association of Pediatric Nurse Practitioners (NAPNAP)

5 Hanover Sq., Ste.1401
New York, NY 10004
Ph: (917)746-8300
Fax: (212)785-1713

Free: 877-662-7627
E-mail: info@napnap.org
URL: www.napnap.org

6385 ■ Reckitt Benckiser Student Scholarships *(Graduate/Scholarship)*

Purpose: To provide financial assistance to Pediatric Nurse Practitioner Student to allow for attendance at the NAPNAP Annual Meeting. **Focus:** Nursing. **Qualif.:** Applicant must be a NAPNAP member, registered nurse and a graduate student who has completed at least 1 semester of graduate studies in a Pediatric Nurse Practitioner Program; enrolled in a recognized program of study (associated with an academic institution authorized to award a master's degree or DNP in nursing), leading to completion of qualifications for education and practice as a PNP (a program defined as one which primarily prepares an individual to deliver child health care services, either in primary care, specialty care or acute care settings). **Criteria:** Recipient will be selected by the NAPNAP Foundation Scholarship Committee.

Funds Avail.: $1,600. **Duration:** Annual. **Number Awarded:** 3. **To Apply:** Applicant must submit original plus four copies (total 5) of the completed application with all the support documents. **Deadline:** November 2.

6386 ■ Elaine Gelman Scholarship Awards *(Undergraduate/Scholarship)*

Purpose: To support the education of nurse practitioner students who are demonstrating their ability to articulate and follow through an innovative solution through clinical competence, academic achievement and involvement in political activism relating to a pediatric health care issue. **Focus:** Nursing. **Qualif.:** Applicants must be full or part-time Nurse Practitioner (NP) students enrolled in an accredited NP program with an expected graduation date of two years or less. **Criteria:** Applicants will be judged based on clinical competence, academic achievement and involvement in political activism relating to health care issues. Preference will be given to those applicants who are in a PNP program or those with interest or experience in health policy or advocacy.

Funds Avail.: $500. **Duration:** Annual. **To Apply:** Applicants must submit completed Elaine Gelman Scholarship Award Application Form; personal statement (200 words or less) describing why the individual is competing for this award and specifically what goals would be accomplished if he/she receives the award; two letters of reference from a faculty member and professional colleague. Applicants must provide four copies each to be submitted. **Deadline:** June 30.

6387 ■ National Association of Pediatric Nurse Practitioners McNeil Annual Scholarships *(Undergraduate/Scholarship)*

Purpose: To provide financial assistance to students enrolled in pediatric nurse practitioner programs. **Focus:** Nursing. **Qualif.:** Applicant must be a registered nursing student who has completed at least two semesters or quarters as defined by the university; enrolled at a recognized PNP program; and has no previous formal pediatric nurse practitioner education; must be a full-time student while enrolled in PNP program; have a GPA of 3.0 or higher. **Criteria:** Applicants will be judged based on academic performance and financial need status.

Funds Avail.: $1,500. **Number Awarded:** 2. **To Apply:** Applicant must submit five copies of the application and ac-

Awards are arranged alphabetically below their administering organizations

companing needed materials to the NAPNAP Foundation. **Deadline:** April 30.

6388 ■ National Association of Pediatric Nurse Practitioners McNeil Rural and Underserved Scholarships *(Graduate/Scholarship)*

Purpose: To provide financial support to PNP students who plan on practicing in a rural or underserved geographical region for the first two years after they complete their PNP education. **Focus:** Medicine, Pediatric; Nursing. **Qualif.:** Applicants must be planning on practicing in a rural or undeserved geographical region for the first two years after PNP education completed; must be registered nurses who have completed at least two semesters or quarters as defined by the university; enrolled at a recognized Master's degree program; have no previous formal pediatric nurse practitioner education; and demonstrated financial need. In addition, applicants must be in full-time status (nine or more credit hours/semester) while in PNP program; have GPA of 3.0 or higher; be members of NAPNAP providing with ongoing accounts regarding students. **Criteria:** Recipients will be selected based on academic performance and financial status.

Funds Avail.: $10,000 - $20,000. **Number Awarded:** 2-4. **To Apply:** Applicants must submit five copies of the completed application form; documentation of RN license; documentation of acceptance into a PNP program signed by Faculty coordinating the program; PNP program brochure with designated plan of study highlighted; documentation of the length of clinical coursework; and documentation of tuition fees. **Deadline:** June 30.

6389 ■ National Association for Pupil Transportation (NAPT)
1840 Western Ave.
Albany, NY 12203-4624
Ph: (518)452-3611
Fax: (518)218-0867
Free: 800-989-NAPT
E-mail: mike.martin@napt.org
URL: naptonline.org

6390 ■ Continuing Education Awards
(Undergraduate/Scholarship, Award)

Purpose: To provide financial support to NAPT members in the field of public transportation. **Focus:** Transportation. **Qualif.:** Applicant must be a NAPT member for three or more consecutive years; and who has not been recipient of the award for the four preceding years. **Criteria:** Recipient will be selected based on merit.

Funds Avail.: Up to $1,000 for pre-approved tuition, travel, lodging, and meal expenses. **Duration:** Annual. **Number Awarded:** 2. **To Apply:** Applicant must mail a completed application form (available at the NAPT website) to NAPT Headquarters. **Deadline:** September 15.

6391 ■ National Association of School Psychologists (NASP)
4340 E West Hwy., Ste. 402
Bethesda, MD 20814
Ph: (301)657-0270
Fax: (301)657-0275
Free: 866-331-NASP
E-mail: publications@naspweb.org

URL: www.nasponline.org

6392 ■ NASP-ERT Minority Scholarships for Graduate Training in School Psychology *(Graduate/Scholarship)*

Purpose: To ease the financial burden of minority graduate students enrolled in a psychology program. **Focus:** Psychology. **Qualif.:** Applicant must be a full-time or part-time minority student; a U.S. citizen; enrolled or accepted for enrollment at a NASP-approved and/or regionally accredited school of psychology program in the U.S., with the aim of becoming a practicing school psychologist; in good academic standing; have a minimum cumulative overall GPA of 3.0; and must be a member of the NASP at the time of designation as a scholarship recipient. **Criteria:** Selection is based on the submitted application materials.

Funds Avail.: $5,000. **Duration:** Annual. **Number Awarded:** Varies. **To Apply:** Applicants must submit a completed application form along with the required materials. **Deadline:** November 3. **Remarks:** Established in 1995. **Contact:** Katie Britton at kbritton@naspweb.org or 301-347-1641.

6393 ■ National Association of School Safety and Law Enforcement Officials (NASSLEO)
c/o Larry D. Johnson, President
1331 Franklin St.
Grand Rapids, MI 49504
Ph: (616)819-2100
Fax: (616)819-2017
E-mail: nassleo@nassleo.org
URL: www.nassleo.org

6394 ■ National Association of School Safety and Law Enforcement Officers Scholarships (NASSLEO) *(Undergraduate/Scholarship)*

Purpose: To provide financial assistance to students who have chosen to further their education and are considering a career in school security and/or law enforcement. **Focus:** Law enforcement. **Qualif.:** Candidate must be senior graduating student from a public high school; must be attending an accredited college or university; has not received a full scholarship; has been outstanding in the area of citizenship and community service. **Criteria:** The committee will select one individual student from each region for the award.

Funds Avail.: No specific amount. **Duration:** Annual. **To Apply:** The faculty member must submit the complete nomination form, which can be downloaded at the NASSLEO website. Faculty member must list the individual's accomplishments in the area of citizenship and community service, what he/she has done to improve safety in the school, the contributions the student has made to his/her school, and any recognition received from his/her peers and/or faculty of the school for personal or academic achievement during this past school year. The narrative report must be limited to a single page.

6395 ■ National Association for the Self-Employed (NASE)
PO Box 241
Annapolis Junction, MD 20701-0241
Free: 800-232-6273
E-mail: advocacy@nase.org

Awards are arranged alphabetically below their administering organizations

URL: www.nase.org

6396 ■ Future Entrepreneur *(Undergraduate/Scholarship)*

Purpose: To promote entrepreneurial philosophy. **Focus:** Business. **Qualif.:** Applicants must be dependents of NASE members. **Criteria:** Applicants who demonstrate the characteristics of a future micro-business owner will be given preference.

Funds Avail.: Up to $10,000. **Duration:** Annual. **Number Awarded:** 1. **To Apply:** Applicants must submit a completed application form and original copies of transcripts and test scores.

6397 ■ National Association for the Self-Employed Scholarships *(Professional development/Scholarship)*

Purpose: To assist members in sending their children to college. **Focus:** General studies/Field of study not specified. **Qualif.:** Applicant must be a legal dependent of a NASE member, aged 16-24; must be a high school student or college undergraduate. **Criteria:** Applicants will be selected based on leadership ability; academic performance; teacher recommendations; career and educational background; and school and community participation.

Funds Avail.: $4,000. **To Apply:** Applicants must submit a completed application form and original copies of transcripts and test scores.

6398 ■ National Association of Social Workers (NASW)

750 1st St. NE, Ste. 700
Washington, DC 20002-4241
Ph: (202)408-8600
Fax: (202)336-8313
Free: 800-742-4089
E-mail: membership@naswdc.org
URL: www.naswdc.org

6399 ■ Jane B. Aron Doctoral Fellowships *(Doctorate/Fellowship)*

Purpose: To provide graduate students a financial assistance who are pursuing research in health care policy and practice. **Focus:** Health education. **Qualif.:** Applicant must be an NASW member and enrolled in an accredited social work/social welfare doctoral program. **Criteria:** Applicant's proposal will be evaluated based on the following criteria: (1) relevance and timeliness of project;(2) need in the field;(3) quality of project design;(4) potential for completion.

Funds Avail.: $15,625. **Duration:** Annual. **Number Awarded:** 1. **To Apply:** Applicants must complete the application form available on the website; must provide a three page proposal summary (including objectives of the project, statement of relevance and significance, project design and methodology, and the expected dissertation completion date); must submit a written statement from the dissertation advisor verifying approval of the dissertation proposal; must submit curriculum vitae. **Deadline:** April 14. **Remarks:** Established in 1987.

6400 ■ Eileen Blackey Doctoral Fellowships *(Doctorate/Fellowship)*

Purpose: To financially assist students who want to pursue their research in welfare policy and practice. **Focus:** Social

work. **Qualif.:** Applicant must be an NASW member and enrolled in an accredited social work/social welfare doctoral program. **Criteria:** Applicant's proposal will be evaluated based on the following criteria: (1) relevance and timeliness of project;(2) need in the field;(3) quality of project design;(4) potential for completion.

Funds Avail.: $10,000. **Duration:** Annual. **Number Awarded:** 1. **To Apply:** Applicants must complete the application form available on the website; must provide a three page proposal summary (including objectives of the project, statement of relevance and significance, project design and methodology, and the expected dissertation completion date); must submit a written statement from the dissertation advisor verifying approval of the dissertation proposal; must submit curriculum vitae. **Deadline:** March 4. **Remarks:** Established in 1987.

6401 ■ Consuelo W. Gosnell Memorial Scholarships *(Graduate/Fellowship)*

Purpose: To provide financial assistance to graduate students who want to pursue their education in social work. **Focus:** Social work. **Qualif.:** Applicant must be a student who has demonstrated a commitment to working with, or who has a special affinity with American Indian/Alaska Native or Hispanic/Latino Populations in the United States; must have demonstrated a commitment to working with public or voluntary nonprofit agencies or with local grassroots groups in the United States; must be an NASW member and have applied to or have been accepted into an accredited MSW program; must have a potential for completing an MSW program and have a GPA of 3.0 or above. **Criteria:** Selection of applicants will be based on the projected annual earnings to the fund and contributions.

Funds Avail.: Up to $4,000 each. **Duration:** Annual. **Number Awarded:** Up to 10. **To Apply:** Applicants must complete the application form available on the website; must provide a biographical essay (two typed, doubled-spaced pages); must provide an optional statement of merit and need for the award; must have two letters of support from professional references; must have an official copy of a transcript from their most recent academic work; must have a letter from the candidate's academic advisor. **Deadline:** March 4. **Contact:** Scholarships & Awards; Email: naswfoundation@naswdc.org.

6402 ■ Verne LaMarr Lyons Memorial Scholarships *(Graduate, Master's/Fellowship)*

Purpose: To provide financial assistance to graduate students who want to pursue their education in social work. **Focus:** Social work. **Qualif.:** Applicant must be a Master of Social Work student who has interest and/or demonstrated ability in health/mental health practice and a commitment to working in African American communities; must be an NASW member and have applied to or have been accepted into an accredited MSW Program; must have potential for completing a MSW Program and have a GPA of 3.0 or above; must be enrolled in a MSW program for more than one year. **Criteria:** Selection of applicants will be based on the projected annual earnings to the fund and contributions.

Funds Avail.: $5,500 each. **Duration:** Annual. **Number Awarded:** 4. **To Apply:** Applicants must complete the application form available on the website; must provide a biographical essay (two typed, doubled-spaced pages); must provide two letters of support from professional references; must submit an official copy of a transcript from

Awards are arranged alphabetically below their administering organizations

their most recent academic work; must have a letter from the candidate's academic advisor. **Deadline:** March 4.

6403 ■ National Association of State Land Reclamationists (NASLR)
47 School St., Ste. 301
Philippi, WV 26416
Ph: (304)940-0271
URL: naslr.org

6404 ■ Mined Land Reclamation Educational Grant Program *(Undergraduate/Grant)*

Purpose: To provide deserving individuals with a financial grant that will cover costs associated with education and research regarding mined land reclamation. **Focus:** Land management. **Qualif.:** Applicants must be enrolled as full-time juniors, seniors or graduate students in an accredited college or university in the United States with course works like special studies, and/or research in the area of mined land reclamation or closely related fields. **Criteria:** Applicants will be evaluated based on college grades; quality and relevance of course work or research; proposed special project or research budget; information obtained from references and other related considerations.

Funds Avail.: $1,500. **Duration:** Annual. **To Apply:** Applicants must submit completed application form and all required materials. **Deadline:** July 1.

6405 ■ National Association of Student Anthropologists (NASA)
American Anthropological Association
2300 Clarendon Blvd., Ste. 1301
Arlington, VA 22201
Ph: (703)528-1902
Fax: (703)528-3546
URL: www.studentanthropologists.org

6406 ■ Carrie Hunter-Tate Award *(Undergraduate, Graduate/Grant)*

Purpose: To recognize individuals who devoted their time and talents to the profession of anthropology. **Focus:** Anthropology. **Qualif.:** Applicants must be anthropology students and members of the National Association of Student Anthropologists. **Criteria:** Selection will be based on the applicants' academic and professional achievements.

Funds Avail.: $500. **Duration:** Annual. **To Apply:** All applicants must be nominated with an official nomination form and must submit together with their completed application. All nominated students will become potential applicants who need to send the following specific materials required for the application: name; Social Security Number (if US applicant); address; school and school year; research interests; geographical area of interest; transcripts of universities attended (unofficial copies are acceptable); one to three page essay explaining significance of anthropology, where the applicants see the direction of the field, and how the applicants feel qualified for the award; curriculum vitae for graduate students.

6407 ■ National Association for Surface Finishing (NASF)
1155 15th St. NW, Ste. 500
Washington, DC 20005

Ph: (202)457-8404
Fax: (202)530-0659
E-mail: passante@nasf.org
URL: www.nasf.org

6408 ■ AESF Foundation Scholarships *(Undergraduate, Graduate/Scholarship)*

Purpose: To enable students to further their studies and future careers in the field of surface finishing. **Focus:** Chemistry; Engineering, Chemical; Engineering, Mechanical; Engineering, Metallurgical; Environmental technology; Materials research/science. **Qualif.:** Applicant must be an undergraduate or graduate student (undergraduate student must be junior standing or above when applying and must be of senior standing for that academic year); studying in mechanical engineering, material science or engineering, metallurgical engineering, chemical engineering, environmental engineering, or chemistry; and be attending an accredited college. **Criteria:** Selection shall be based on academic record, personal statement, working experience and extracurricular activities.

Funds Avail.: $1,500 each. **Duration:** Annual. **Number Awarded:** Varies. **To Apply:** Applicant must submit a completed application form along with a statement on career objective and an intended plan of study and/or research in plating and surface finishing science and engineering (2 pages); resume detailing academic achievements (2 pages); three recommendation letters (one must be from an academic advisor); and an official copy of recent undergraduate or graduate transcript (to be sealed by the academic institution where the applicant attends). **Contact:** AESF Foundation; 1155 Fifteenth St. NW, Suite 500; Washington D.C. 20005.

6409 ■ National Association of Teacher Educators for Family and Consumer Sciences (NATE-FACS)
c/o Carol Werhan, PhD, President
Family and Consumer Sciences Education
Pittsburg State University
Pittsburg, KS 66762
Ph: (620)235-4573
Fax: (765)496-1622
E-mail: wfox@purdue.edu
URL: www.natefacs.org

6410 ■ FACS Graduate Fellowships *(Graduate/Fellowship)*

Purpose: To provide financial support to students for the study of family and consumer sciences. **Focus:** Home Economics. **Qualif.:** Applicant must be a U.S. citizen; and a family and consumer sciences education graduate student. **Criteria:** Applications will be rated in consideration of the likelihood of completing the degree and the contribution to family and consumer science education; academic work; professional association involvement; professional experience and scholarly work; and references.

Funds Avail.: $2,000 - $4,000. **To Apply:** Applicants must submit a completed application form together with all required attachments. **Deadline:** November 8. **Contact:** Send completed application to Dr. Lela G. Goar, 225 CR 207A Burnet, TX 78611; Phone: 512-715-8249; Email: lkgoar@earthlink.net.

Awards are arranged alphabetically below their administering organizations

6411 ■ National Association of Women in Construction (NAWIC)

327 S Adams St.
Fort Worth, TX 76104
Ph: (817)877-5551
Fax: (817)877-0324
Free: 800-552-3506
E-mail: nawic@nawic.org
URL: www.nawic.org

6412 ■ Construction Trades Scholarships
(Undergraduate/Scholarship)

Purpose: To encourage women to pursue and establish careers in the construction industry. **Focus:** Construction. **Qualif.:** Applicants must be currently enrolled in a construction-related training program which is approved by the Bureau of Apprenticeship Training or their home state's Post Secondary Education Commission; must be obtaining training in a construction-related craft or trade. Only students attending school in the United States or Canada will be considered for awards. **Criteria:** Application will be reviewed and selected by the NAWIC Founders' Scholarship Foundation Awards Committee.

Funds Avail.: $1,000 - $2,000. **Duration:** Annual. **To Apply:** Applicants must have the following: Complete and signed application form; extracurricular activities and Employment history. **Deadline:** February 28. **Contact:** Application form and supporting documents must be sent to: Carol Chapman, 3115 Shamrock Dr., Charlotte, NC 28215; Phone: 704-531-8514; E-mail: mobconco@aol.com.

6413 ■ National Association of Women in Construction Founders Undergraduate Scholarships
(Undergraduate/Scholarship)

Purpose: To encourage women to pursue and establish careers in the construction industry. **Focus:** Construction. **Qualif.:** Applicants must be currently enrolled in a construction-related degree program at a school in the United States or Canada; must have at least one term remaining in course of study leading to a degree or an associate degree in a construction-related field; desires a career in a construction related field; must be enrolled full-time; must have current cumulative GPA of 3.0 or higher to be considered for awards. **Criteria:** Applications will be reviewed and selected by the NAWIC Founders' Scholarship Foundation Awards Committee. Preference will be given to the applicant's interest in construction, grades, extracurricular activities, employment experience and financial need.

Funds Avail.: $1,000 - $2,000. **Duration:** Annual. **To Apply:** Applicants must have the following: Complete and signed application form; must have the transcript of grades of three most of the most recent semesters; extracurricular activities and employment history. **Deadline:** February 28.

6414 ■ National Association of Women Judges (NAWJ)

1001 Connecticut Ave. NW, Ste. 1138
Washington, DC 20036
Ph: (202)393-0222
Fax: (202)393-0125
URL: www.nawj.org

6415 ■ NAWJ Equal Access to Justice Scholarships
(Undergraduate/Scholarship)

Purpose: To provide financial assistance for law students who have demonstrated a sustained commitment to diversity and equality in the system of justice. **Focus:** Law. **Qualif.:** Applicants must be enrolled second- or third-year law students in good academic standing who demonstrate a sustained and passionate commitment to the achievement of equality of opportunity and access in the system of justice. **Criteria:** Recipient is selected by the Scholarship Selection Committee.

Funds Avail.: No specific amount. **Duration:** Annual. **To Apply:** Applicants must submit the completed application form and a 500-word personal statement and a resume.

6416 ■ Justice Sandra Day O'Connor Scholarship
(Undergraduate/Scholarship)

Purpose: To recognize the achievements and commitment of a law student. **Focus:** Law. **Qualif.:** Recipients must be enrolled second- or third-year law students in good academic standing who demonstrated a sustained and passionate commitment to the achievement of equality of opportunity and access in the system of justice. **Criteria:** Selection will be based on the committee's criteria.

Funds Avail.: No specific amount. **Duration:** Annual. **To Apply:** Applicants must submit a completed application form, 500-word personal statement and resume. **Remarks:** Established in 2006.

6417 ■ National Ataxia Foundation (NAF)

2600 Fernbrook Ln., No. 119
Minneapolis, MN 55447
Ph: (763)553-0020
Fax: (763)553-0167
E-mail: naf@ataxia.org
URL: www.ataxia.org

6418 ■ National Ataxia Foundation Research Fellowships *(Other/Fellowship)*

Purpose: To support a research on hereditary ataxia. **Focus:** Medicine. **Qualif.:** Applicants must have at least completed one year of post-doctoral training but not more than two at the time of application; and must have commitment to research in the field of ataxia. **Criteria:** Applicants will be selected by a Committee appointed by NAF's Director. Priority will be given to those who have high scores on the relevance of research to ataxia.

Funds Avail.: $35,000. **To Apply:** Applicants must submit a completed applications and letters of support as single PDF file attachment with the last name of the researcher in the subject line of the email. **Deadline:** Pre-submission: August 15; Final deadline: September 16. **Contact:** Completed application must be sent to susan@ataxia.org.

6419 ■ National Ataxia Foundation Research Grants *(Other/Fellowship)*

Purpose: To provide funding for early or pilot phases of studies and ongoing investigations. **Focus:** Medicine. **Qualif.:** Applicants must be National Ataxia Foundation members. **Criteria:** Selection of applicants will be evaluated by a Committee appointed by NAF's Research Director. Consideration will be based on the score of applicant's recommendation.

Funds Avail.: $15,000-$30,000. **Duration:** Annual. **To Apply:** For the pre-submission of application, applicants must always include the last name of the principle investigator as the first word in the subject line of any email. Submit email with applicants' intentions to apply for NAF funding,

Awards are arranged alphabetically below their administering organizations

including a full title and a one-page abstract of a proposal. Complete application must be sent as a single PDF file attachment with the last name of the researcher in the subject line of the email. Electronic signatures will be accepted. **Deadline:** July 15 (Pre-submission); August 17 (Full application). **Contact:** Applications and attachments must be sent to susan@ataxia.org.

6420 ■ National Beta Club

151 Beta Club Way
Spartanburg, SC 29306-3012
Fax: (864)542-9300
Free: 800-845-8281
E-mail: betaclub@betaclub.org
URL: www.betaclub.org

6421 ■ National Beta Club Scholarships
(Undergraduate/Scholarship)

Purpose: To provide financial assistance to Beta Club members in their senior year. **Focus:** General studies/Field of study not specified. **Qualif.:** Applicants must be senior high school students who are active National Beta Club members and are registered with the national headquarters as of June 30; must be nominated by their Beta Club chapters to participate. **Criteria:** Applicants are evaluated based on number of factors with special emphasis placed upon academic excellence, demonstrated leadership, character and school/community service.

Funds Avail.: $1,000 - $15,000. **Duration:** Annual. **To Apply:** Applicants must submit all the required application information.

6422 ■ National Biosafety and Biocontainment Training Program (NBBTP)

c/o Frontline Found.
3 Dunwoody Park, Ste. 103
Atlanta, GA 30338
Ph: (678)781-5241
Fax: (678)781-5242
E-mail: info@nbbtp.org
URL: www.nbbtp.org

6423 ■ National Biosafety and Biocontainment Training Program Fellowships *(Graduate, Postgraduate/Fellowship)*

Purpose: To prepare biosafety and biocontainment professionals of the highest caliber to meet the needs of the biomedical, emerging disease and civilian biodefense research communities. **Focus:** Health sciences; Medicine; Microbiology; Public health. **Qualif.:** Applicant must be a U.S. citizen, permanent resident, or a national of the United States; a graduate or post-graduate with academic degree(s) in microbiology, public health, medicine (human or veterinary), or other allied sciences (industrial hygiene, engineering, etc.); have microbiology and/or research laboratory experience combined with excellent professional performance; have an outstanding personal, professional, and academic recommendations; excellent in written & verbal communication skills; proficient in the English language (for non-native English speakers); meets all requirements established under federal regulations & policies necessary to work with Select Agents; have an excellent employment history; participates in academic, professional and/or civic organizations; and committed to the

mission and vision of the NBBT. **Criteria:** Selection is based on academic history, with specialty or focus in the life sciences; research history and experience (if applicable); employment history; participation in professional, academic, and/or civic associations; oral communication; written communication; and interpersonal and team building skills.

Funds Avail.: No specific amount. **Duration:** Annual. **To Apply:** Applicants must submit a completed application form along with the essay; references; additional materials (should be paper-clipped together and labeled with last name on each piece turned in); and transcripts. **Deadline:** July 6.

6424 ■ National Black Coalition of Federal Aviation Employees (NBCFAE)

PO Box 87216
Atlanta, GA 30337
URL: nbcfae.org

6425 ■ NBCFAE Mamie W. Mallory National Scholarship Program *(Undergraduate/Scholarship)*

Purpose: To support students who want to pursue higher education for prospective college, university, vocational or technical school. **Focus:** Aviation. **Qualif.:** Applicants must be dependents of NBCFAE members; must be high school or returning to college students, and have a 2.5 GPA or higher. **Criteria:** Recipients will be selected based on academic merits.

Funds Avail.: No amount mentioned. **Duration:** Annual. **To Apply:** Applicants must submit completed application with signature, transcript, letter of recommendation, and college acceptance letter (if high school student).

6426 ■ National Black Deaf Advocates (NBDA)

PO Box 502658
Indianapolis, IN 46250
E-mail: info@nbda.org
URL: www.nbda.org

6427 ■ Andrew Foster Scholarships *(Undergraduate/Scholarship)*

Purpose: To strengthen the educational and economic advancement of deaf and hard of hearing African-Americans. **Focus:** General studies/Field of study not specified. **Qualif.:** Applicants must be Black deaf students at Gallaudet University with at least 3.0 GPA. **Criteria:** Selection will be based on financial need and academic performance.

Funds Avail.: No specific amount. **To Apply:** Applicants must complete the scholarship application supplement.

6428 ■ National Black Deaf Advocate Scholarships *(Graduate, Undergraduate/Scholarship)*

Purpose: To strengthen the educational and economic advancement of Black Deaf and hard of hearing people. **Focus:** General studies/Field of study not specified. **Qualif.:** Applicant must be a Black deaf or hard of hearing undergraduate or graduate student who is also a member of NBDA; must have at least 2.5 GPA for undergraduate and 3.0 GPA for graduate student. **Criteria:** Selection will be based on the committee's criteria.

Funds Avail.: No specific amount. **To Apply:** Applicant must complete and submit the application form together

Awards are arranged alphabetically below their administering organizations

with two letters of reference, photocopy of official transcript, and photocopy of a valid student ID.

6429 ■ Youth Empowerment Summit Scholarships
(Undergraduate/Scholarship)

Purpose: To strengthen the educational and economic advancement of deaf and hard of hearing African-Americans. **Focus:** General studies/Field of study not specified. **Qualif.:** Applicants must be former or current Youth Empowerment Summit participants; must be deaf or hard of hearing; must be high school seniors or college students; must be or have been in a leadership position; and must have at least B grade average. **Criteria:** Selection will be based on the committee's criteria.

Funds Avail.: No specific amount. **Duration:** Biennial. **To Apply:** Applicants must fill out an application form and submit together with two letters of recommendation, one from a teacher. **Contact:** Y.E.S.; Email: youth@nbda.org.

6430 ■ National Black Graduate Student Association (NBGSA)
228 Park Ave., No. 76326
New York, NY 10003
Free: 800-471-4102
E-mail: nationaloffice@nbgsa.org
URL: www.nbgsa.org

6431 ■ Willie D. Lawson, Jr. Memorial Scholarships
(Doctorate, Graduate, Other/Scholarship)

Purpose: To financially assist NBGSA members in obtaining a higher education. **Focus:** General studies/Field of study not specified. **Qualif.:** Applicants must be members of NBGSA; must be entering or pursuing Master's, Doctoral or Professional degrees; must give NBGSA permission to use applicants' photos taken at the conference, on website and in publications; must have 3.0 GPA or higher; must attend the National Conference; and must be U.S. citizens. **Criteria:** Selection will be based on NBGSA involvement; university, community contributions, and academic excellence.

Funds Avail.: $500. **Duration:** Annual. **Number Awarded:** 3. **To Apply:** Applicants must submit a completed application form; recommendation letter; official transcripts; one-page essay with the theme: "Transforming Roads Ahead." **Deadline:** February 15. **Contact:** For inquiries, please email at vpadmin@nbgsa.org.

6432 ■ National Black MBA Association (NBM-BAA)
1 E Wacker Ste. 3500
Chicago, IL 60601
Ph: (312)236-2622
Fax: (312)236-0390
E-mail: info@nbmbaa.org
URL: www.nbmbaa.org

6433 ■ NBMBAA Graduate Scholarships Program
(Graduate/Scholarship)

Purpose: To financially assist qualified business students who have the potential to make great contributions in the field of business. **Focus:** Business. **Qualif.:** Applicants must be financially active member of the National Black MBA Association; must be a U.S. citizen and must be a student entering their first year, or continuing in a full or part-time master's program at an accredited college or university in the United States or Canada. **Criteria:** Scholarship recipients will be selected based on demonstrated academic excellence; leadership potential; and community involvement.

Funds Avail.: Up to $10,000. **Duration:** One year. **To Apply:** Applicants must submit their complete resume; complete 500 word typewritten essay on the selected topic; and stamped and sealed transcript of records; recommended by a faculty member or individual familiar with applicant's academic achievements or supervisor in a business workplace.

6434 ■ National Black Nurses Association (NBNA)
8630 Fenton St., Ste. 330
Silver Spring, MD 20910-3803
Ph: (301)589-3200
Fax: (301)589-3223
E-mail: info@nbna.org
URL: www.nbna.org

6435 ■ National Black Nurses Association Scholarships
(Undergraduate/Scholarship)

Purpose: To provide funding for continuing education. **Focus:** Nursing. **Qualif.:** Applicants must be members of NBNA and a local chapter; currently enrolled in a nursing program (B.S.N., A.D., Diploma or L.P.N./L.V.N.); in good scholastic standing at the time of application and must have at least one full year of school remaining. **Criteria:** Applicants will be evaluated by the NBNA Scholarship Committee.

Funds Avail.: $500 to $2,000. **To Apply:** Applicants must submit an official transcript from an accredited school of nursing; a two-page written essay; two letters of recommendation (one from applicant's school of nursing and one from the local chapter, or a nurse in the area if a local chapter does not exist); and additional items that will support the applicants' eligibility and desirability. **Deadline:** April 15.

6436 ■ National Black Police Association (NBPA)
3100 Main St., No. 256
Dallas, TX 75226
Ph: (214)942-2022
Fax: (855)879-6272
Free: 855-879-6272
E-mail: nationaloffice@blackpolice.org
URL: www.blackpolice.org

6437 ■ Alphonso Deal Scholarship Awards
(Undergraduate/Scholarship)

Purpose: To support students financially for them to have higher educational training in the academics of law enforcement or other related areas, for the betterment of the Criminal Justice system. **Focus:** Law enforcement. **Qualif.:** Applicant must be a high school senior and a U.S. citizen with good character. **Criteria:** Recipients will be selected based on adherence to contest/application rules.

Funds Avail.: No specific amount. **To Apply:** Applicants must fill up the application form available at the website. Applicant must prepare a recommendation letter (from principal, counselor or teacher); a current high school

Awards are arranged alphabetically below their administering organizations

transcript with picture; and an acceptance letter from a college/university. **Deadline:** May 16.

6438 ■ National Board of Boiler and Pressure Vessel Inspectors (NBBI)
1055 Crupper Ave.
Columbus, OH 43229-1183
Ph: (614)888-8320
Fax: (614)888-0750
E-mail: information@nationalboard.org
URL: www.nationalboard.org

6439 ■ The National Board Technical Scholarships
(Undergraduate/Scholarship)

Purpose: To provide financial assistance to children, step-children, grandchildren or great-grandchildren of past and present staff and members of the National Board and the past or present Commissioned Inspectors employed by a member jurisdiction. **Focus:** Engineering. **Qualif.:** Applicants must be currently enrolled full-time in an accredited four-year college or university in the United States or Canada; or be enrolled as full-time students for the previous academic year with sufficient college credits to be classified as sophomores, juniors or seniors; must be mechanical, manufacturing, electrical, industrial, welding or chemical engineering, or other closely related engineering major; must possess a cumulative college GPA of 3.0 or higher on a 4.0 scale; must be citizens of the United States or Canada; must be children, step-children, grandchildren or great-grandchildren of a past or present National Board member (living or deceased), of a past or present Commissioned Inspector (living or deceased), employed by a member jurisdiction, or of a past or present National Board employee (living or deceased). In order the applicants to be eligible, the National Board member must have been a member for at least one year, the Commissioned Inspector must have been employed by the member jurisdiction for at least one year, or the National Board employee must have been a full-time employee for at least one year. **Criteria:** Applicants will be evaluated on the strength of their academic performance; proficiencies and demonstrated skills in the areas of interest to the National Board and its members.

Funds Avail.: $12,000. **Duration:** Annual. **Number Awarded:** 2. **To Apply:** Applicants must read the application carefully and complete all sections. Applicants must include a personal statement of 500-750 words expressing: a) how college experiences-academics, extracurricular activities, outside activities and work/internship experiences-are shaping their educational and career goals; b) why they should be considered for this scholarship award; and c) other information that may be of importance to the selection committee in its review of the application. Applicants must also submit the following: two letters of recommendation from appropriate college instructors or other college representatives on official school letterhead; a letter of recommendation from a current National Board member, that is the Chief Boiler inspector in a jurisdiction; a listing of current National Board members, including contact information, is shown on National Board's website; names and contact information of two persons (not family members) that the applicants have known for at least one year, to be used as personal references; an official college transcript including the most recent course work. Applicants must sign the last page of the application. **Deadline:** February 28. **Contact:** Connie Homer; email ad-

dress: chomer@nationalboard.org.

6440 ■ National Business Aviation Association (NBAA)
1200 G St. NW, Ste. 1100
Washington, DC 20005-3830
Ph: (202)783-9000
Fax: (202)331-8364
E-mail: info@nbaa.org
URL: www.nbaa.org

6441 ■ Donald A. Baldwin Sr. Business Aviation Management Scholarships *(Professional development/Scholarship)*

Purpose: To promote professional development and business aviation careers and to benefit individuals seeking to become NBAA Certified Aviation Managers (CAMs). **Focus:** Aviation. **Qualif.:** Applicants must be eligible to take the CAM Exam within two years of the date of the scholarship award; must meet the minimum qualifications to take the CAM Exam; must be U.S. citizens; and must score greater than 100 points on CAM application. **Criteria:** Recipients are selected based on academic performance and financial need.

Funds Avail.: $1,225. **Duration:** Annual. **Number Awarded:** 1. **To Apply:** Applicants must submit a completed application form; an official transcript of record; a 250-word, typed, double-spaced essay describing the applicant's interest in and goals for a career in the business aviation industry; two letters of recommendation from those who can comment on the career aspirations and qualifications of the applicant; and current resume. **Deadline:** November 14. **Remarks:** Established in 2007. **Contact:** NBAA's Tyler Austin; E-mail: info@nbaa.org.

6442 ■ Alan H. Conklin Business Aviation Management Scholarships *(Undergraduate/Scholarship)*

Purpose: To promote professional development and business aviation careers. **Focus:** Aviation. **Qualif.:** Applicants must be full-time undergraduate sophomores, juniors, or senior students; officially enrolled or accepted for enrollment in an aviation management program; U.S. citizens; and must have grade point average of 3.0 or above on a 4.0 scale. **Criteria:** Recipients are selected based on academic performance and financial need.

Funds Avail.: $5,000. **Duration:** Annual. **To Apply:** Applicants must submit completed application form; an official transcript of record; a 500-word, typed, double-spaced essay describing the applicant's interest in and goals for a career in business aviation; two letters of recommendation from those qualified to comment on the career aspirations and qualifications of the applicant especially as they relate to business aviation; and current resume. **Deadline:** July 31. **Remarks:** Established in 2007. **Contact:** NBAA's Tyler Austin; E-mail: info@nbaa.org.

6443 ■ William M. Fanning Maintenance Scholarships *(Undergraduate/Scholarship)*

Purpose: To promote professional development and business aviation careers. **Focus:** Aviation. **Qualif.:** Applicants must be students who are currently enrolled in an accredited airframe and powerplant program at an approved FAR Part 147 school or an individual who is not currently enrolled but has been accepted for enrollment in an A&P program; must be U.S. citizens; and must have a grade

Awards are arranged alphabetically below their administering organizations

point average of 3.0 or above on a 4.0 scale. **Criteria:** Recipients are selected based on academic performance and financial need.

Funds Avail.: $2,500. **Duration:** Annual. **Number Awarded:** 2. **To Apply:** Applicants must submit a complete application form; an official transcript of record; a 250-word, typed, double-spaced essay describing the applicant's interest in and goals for a career in the aviation maintenance field; two letters of recommendation from a member or other individual who is familiar with the applicant's capabilities; and current resume. Any e-mailed materials must be signed and provided in a PDF format. **Deadline:** July 31. **Contact:** NBAA's Tyler Austin; E-mail: info@nbaa.org.

6444 ■ Flight Attendants/Flight Technician Scholarships (Other/Scholarship)

Purpose: To promote education and training as a means for business aviation flight attendants and flight technicians to enhance their professional careers. **Focus:** Aviation. **Qualif.:** Applicants must be flight attendants or flight technicians. **Criteria:** Recipients are selected based on academic performance and financial need.

Funds Avail.: No specific amount. **Duration:** Annual. **Number Awarded:** 1. **To Apply:** Applicants must submit a completed application form; one signed aviation or leadership-related letter of recommendation, dated within the last two years; a typed, 100-word essay answering the required question; and current (one-page) resume. **Deadline:** March 16. **Contact:** National Business Aviation Association; E-mail: info@nbaa.org.

6445 ■ Lawrence Ginocchio Aviation Scholarships (Undergraduate/Scholarship)

Purpose: To support students who have demonstrated honesty, integrity, and selflessness in their dealings with others. **Focus:** Aviation. **Qualif.:** Applicants must be full-time undergraduate sophomores, juniors, or senior students officially enrolled or accepted for enrollment in an aviation related two-year, four-year or postgraduate degree program; must be U.S. citizens; and must have grade point average of 3.0 or above on a 4.0 scale. **Criteria:** Recipients are selected based on academic performance and financial need.

Funds Avail.: $4,500. **Duration:** Annual. **Number Awarded:** 5. **To Apply:** Applicants must submit a complete application form; must submit an official transcript of records; a 500 to 1,000-word, typed, double-spaced essay describing the applicant's interest in and goals for a career in the business aviation industry and demonstrating the applicant's strength of character; two letters of recommendation from those qualified to comment on the career aspirations and qualifications of the applicant especially as they relate to business aviation; and current resume. Any e-mailed materials must be signed and provided in a PDF format. **Deadline:** July 31. **Remarks:** Established in 2001. **Contact:** National Business Aviation Association; E-mail: info@nbaa.org.

6446 ■ NORDAM Dee Howard/Etienne Fage Scholarships (Undergraduate/Scholarship)

Purpose: To promote professional development and business aviation careers. **Focus:** Aeronautics; Aviation. **Qualif.:** Applicants must be full-time undergraduate sophomores, juniors, or senior students enrolled in the aerospace engineering or aeronautical systems maintenance engineering major at Embry-Riddle Aeronautical University; must be U.S. citizens; and must have grade point average of 3.0 or

above on a 4.0 scale. **Criteria:** Recipients are selected based on academic performance and financial need.

Funds Avail.: $2,500. **Duration:** Annual. **To Apply:** Applicants must submit a completed application form; an official transcript of record; a 250-word, typed, double-spaced essay describing the applicant's interest in and goals for a career in the business aviation industry; two letters of recommendation from an Embry-Riddle faculty member who is familiar with the applicant's capabilities; and current resume. **Deadline:** July 31. **Contact:** NBAA's Tyler Austin; E-mail: info@nbaa.org.

6447 ■ International Operators Scholarship (Professional development/Scholarship)

Purpose: To promote education and training of individuals to increase the safety and professionalism of their positions. **Focus:** Aviation. **Qualif.:** Applicants must be aviation professionals engaged in international operations. **Criteria:** Recipients are selected based on academic performance and financial need.

Funds Avail.: Up to $5,000. **Duration:** Annual. **To Apply:** Applicants must submit completed application form; a 500-word or less, typed, double-spaced essay that clearly explains how the scholarship will help the applicants achieve their international aviation career goals and necessary funds to achieve these goals; and at least one professional letter of recommendation preferably from an NBAA Member Company Representative. **Deadline:** November 28. **Contact:** NBAA's Tyler Austin; E-mail: info@nbaa.org.

6448 ■ Leadership Conference Scholarship (Other/Scholarship)

Purpose: To promote professional development and business aviation careers and to benefit individuals seeking to become NBAA Certified Aviation Managers (CAMs). **Focus:** Aviation. **Qualif.:** Applicants must be currently working in the business aviation industry or attending a university-level aviation program; and must be U.S. citizens. **Criteria:** Recipients are selected based on academic performance, financial need, career planning and progress of the individual toward a career in business aviation.

Funds Avail.: Up to $800. **Duration:** Annual. **To Apply:** Applicants must submit a completed application form; an official transcript of records; a 250-word, typed, double-spaced essay describing the applicant's interest in and goals for a career in the business aviation industry; two letters of recommendation from either an employee of an NBAA Member Company flight department or a professor at the university where the applicant currently is enrolled; and a current resume. Any e-mailed materials must be signed and provided in a PDF format. **Deadline:** November 30. **Contact:** NBAA's Tyler Austin; E-mail: info@nbaa.org.

6449 ■ Maintenance Technical Reward and Career Scholarships (Undergraduate/Scholarship)

Purpose: To promote technical education and professional development as a means for business aviation maintenance technicians to enhance their careers. **Focus:** Aviation. **Qualif.:** Applicants must be current holder of an airframe and powerplant certificate; currently employed in general aviation; must either be currently enrolled in either an accredited A&P program or an approved FAR Part 147 school; and must complete all professional and educational training within one year from the date of announcement. **Criteria:** Recipients are selected based on academic performance and financial need.

Funds Avail.: No specific amount. **Duration:** Annual. **To**

Awards are arranged alphabetically below their administering organizations

Apply: Applicants must submit completed application form; a 250-word, typed, double-spaced essay describing the applicant's interest in and goals for a career in business aviation maintenance field; current resume; and a letter of recommendation from either a supervisor, faculty member or other individual who is familiar with the applicant's capabilities. **Deadline:** February 20. **Contact:** National Business Aviation Association; E-mail: info@nbaa.org.

6450 ■ Scheduler and Dispatchers Scholarships
(Other/Scholarship)

Purpose: To promote education and training of individuals to increase the safety and professionalism of their positions. **Focus:** Aviation. **Qualif.:** Applicants must have completed all professional/educational training. **Criteria:** Recipients are selected based on academic performance and financial need.

Funds Avail.: Up to $10,000. **To Apply:** Applicants must submit completed application form; a typed essay of 500-words or less; two professional letters of recommendation; and a current resume. **Deadline:** September 26. **Contact:** NBAA's Tyler Austin; e-mail: info@nbaa.org.

6451 ■ UAA Janice K. Barden Aviation Scholarships
(Undergraduate/Scholarship)

Purpose: To promote professional development and business aviation careers. **Focus:** Aviation. **Qualif.:** Applicants must be undergraduate sophomores, juniors, or seniors enrolled in an aviation-related two-year, four-year, or postgraduate degree program; must have GPA of at least 3.0 on a 4.0 scale; must be U.S. citizens; must be officially enrolled at NBAA and University Aviation Association member institutions. **Criteria:** Recipients are selected based on academic performance and financial need.

Funds Avail.: $1,000 each. **Duration:** Annual. **Number Awarded:** 5. **To Apply:** Applicants must submit completed application form; a typed, double-spaced essay of 250 words describing the applicant's interest in and goals for a career in the business aviation industry; a letter of recommendation from a member of the aviation department faculty at the institution in which the applicant is currently enrolled; two professional letters of recommendation; and a current resume. If an applicant is a transfer student, previous college transcript of records is recommended. Mail completed applications to Dr. RoyceAnn Martin, Bowling Green State University, Aerotechnology Annex, East Poe Rd., Bowling Green, OH 43403. **Deadline:** October 30. **Contact:** NBAA's Tyler Austin; e-mail: info@nbaa.org.

6452 ■ U.S. Aircraft Insurance Group Professional Development Program (USAIG PDP) Scholarships
(Undergraduate/Scholarship)

Purpose: To promote professional development and business aviation careers. **Focus:** Aviation. **Qualif.:** Applicants must be full-time undergraduate sophomores, juniors, or senior students in academic year enrolled in an aviation-related two-year, four-year, or postgraduate degree program that incorporates the NBAA PDP; must be U.S. citizens; and must have a grade point average of 3.0 or above on a 4.0 scale. **Criteria:** Recipients are selected based on academic performance and financial need.

Funds Avail.: No specific amount. **To Apply:** Applicants must submit a completed application form; an official transcript of record; a 250-word, typed, double-spaced essay describing the applicant's interest in and goals for a career in business aviation flight department; two letters of recommendation from a member of aviation department

faculty at the institution where the applicant is currently enrolled; and current resume. **Contact:** National Business Aviation Association; E-mail: info@nbaa.org.

6453 ■ National Cattlemen's Foundation (NCF)
9110 E Nichols Ave., Ste. 300
Centennial, CO 80112
Ph: (303)694-0305
E-mail: ncf@beef.org
URL: www.nationalcattlemensfoundation.org

6454 ■ CME Beef Industry Scholarships
(Undergraduate/Scholarship)

Purpose: To identify and encourage talented and thoughtful students who will emerge as industry leaders. **Focus:** Agricultural sciences. **Qualif.:** Applicant must be a graduating high school senior or full-time undergraduate student enrolled at a two or four-year institution and have demonstrated commitment to a career in the beef industry through classes, internships or life experiences. **Criteria:** Awards are given based on the essay, which is judged based on originality, grammar, clarity of expression, accuracy, relevance of topic and the solutions offered.

Funds Avail.: No specific amount. **Duration:** Annual. **To Apply:** Applicants must submit proof of enrollment (as a full-time student); a one page letter of career goals; the essay (maximum of 750 words); and two letters of reference.

6455 ■ W.D. Farr Scholarships *(Graduate/Scholarship)*

Purpose: To promote education in the animal industry. **Focus:** Animal science and behavior. **Qualif.:** Applicant must be a graduate student pursuing degrees in animal science, environmental science (water) or agriculture. **Criteria:** Awards are given based on the application.

Funds Avail.: $12,000. **Duration:** Annual. **Number Awarded:** 2. **To Apply:** Applicants must submit their curriculum vitae, cover letter, and three letters of recommendation (at least one letter must be from a person within the applicant's department, college or university).

6456 ■ National Center for American Indian Enterprise Development (NCAIED)
953 E Juanita Ave.
Mesa, AZ 85204
Ph: (480)545-1298
E-mail: eric.trevan@ncaied.org
URL: www.ncaied.org

6457 ■ American Indian Fellowship in Business Scholarships *(Graduate, Master's, Undergraduate/Scholarship)*

Purpose: To financially support American Indian college or graduate students majoring in business. **Focus:** Business. **Qualif.:** Applicant must be a Business Major; enrolled full time during entire school term; in Junior, Senior or Master level of study; and an enrolled member of American Indian tribe or Alaskan Native. **Criteria:** Selection is based on grades, community involvement, personal challenges, business experiences and on the essay.

Funds Avail.: No specific amount. **Number Awarded:** 5. **To Apply:** Applicants must submit a completed application form together with a letter (stating: Reasons for pursuing

Awards are arranged alphabetically below their administering organizations

higher education; plans following completion of degree program; activities and commitment to community they wish to have considered); essays on community involvement, personal challenges, business experience (250-word each); transcript; letter of Admission/Enrollment; and documentation of Tribal Enrollment. **Deadline:** August 2. **Contact:** Application should be sent at The National Center for American Indian Enterprise Development; Attn: 2013 Scholarship Committee, 953 East Juanita Avenue, Mesa, AZ 85204; Phone: 800-462-2433; Fax: 480-545-4208; Email: scholarships@ncaied.org.

6458 ■ National Center for Farmworker Health (NCFH)
1770 FM 967
Buda, TX 78610
Ph: (512)312-2700
Fax: (512)312-2600
Free: 800-531-5120
E-mail: info@ncfh.org
URL: www.ncfh.org

6459 ■ Migrant Health Scholarships *(Other/Scholarship)*
Purpose: To assist the recipients in pursuing their educational and professional goals. **Focus:** Health education. **Qualif.:** Applicants must be interested in pursuing or continuing a career in the migrant health field, and must be employees at a community/migrant health center. **Criteria:** Awards are given based on demonstrated commitment to working in migrant health, choice of career path, and personal experience, with special recognition of those who have a family history as farmworkers.

Funds Avail.: $1,000. **To Apply:** Application forms are available from the website. Applicants must send an application form; resume; one-page personal statement; letter of reference. **Remarks:** Established in 1984. **Contact:** Janie Favre, favre@ncfh.org.

6460 ■ National Center for Law and Economic Justice (NCLEJ)
275 7th Ave., Ste. 1506
New York, NY 10001-6708
Ph: (212)633-6967
Fax: (212)633-6371
E-mail: info@nclej.org
URL: www.nclej.org

6461 ■ NCLEJ Law School Graduate Fellows and Volunteers *(Graduate/Fellowship)*
Purpose: To provide opportunities for students who would like to participate in various aspects of federal and state court litigation, ranging from case planning, pleading or motion drafting and discovery of trial. **Focus:** Law. **Qualif.:** Applicants must be recent law graduates. **Criteria:** Applications are considered on a rolling basis.

Funds Avail.: No specific amount. **To Apply:** Applicants must provide a cover letter describing their interests; resume; writing sample; and three references. **Contact:** National Center for Law and Economic Justice, at the above address.

6462 ■ National Center for Learning Disabilities (NCLD)
32 Laight St., 2nd Fl.
New York, NY 10013

URL: www.ncld.org

6463 ■ Anne Ford Scholarships *(Undergraduate/Scholarship)*
Purpose: To assist students who are facing the challenges of living with a learning disability. **Focus:** General studies/Field of study not specified. **Qualif.:** Applicant must have a GPA of 3.0 or higher; demonstrated financial assistance; a U.S. citizen; enrolled as a high school senior and pursuing a four-year undergraduate degree. **Criteria:** Selection will be based on the committee's criteria.

Funds Avail.: $10,000. **Duration:** Annual; Four years. **Number Awarded:** 1. **To Apply:** Applicant must submit a completed application form; a personal statement; a high school transcript; three letters of recommendation; a financial statement; copies of SAT/ACT scores; and a current documentation of a learning disability that includes evaluation reports. **Deadline:** December 31. **Contact:** For further information, applicants may send an e-mail at afscholarship@ncld.org.

6464 ■ National Chapter of Canada IODE
40 Orchard View Blvd., Ste. 219
Toronto, ON, Canada M4R 1B9
Ph: (416)487-4416
Free: 866-827-7428
E-mail: iodecanada@bellnet.ca
URL: www.iode.ca

6465 ■ War Memorial Doctoral Scholarships *(Postgraduate/Scholarship)*
Purpose: To provide bursaries for university studies in Canada to children of men killed or permanently disabled in the Great War. **Focus:** General studies/Field of study not specified. **Qualif.:** Applicants must be Canadian citizens and at least in the second year of their doctoral program; must be graduates of Canadian university and must have done or be doing post-graduate work. **Criteria:** Applications will be evaluated by the National Selection Committee. Selection of applicants will be based on their academic attainments; commitment; personal character; and career goals.

Funds Avail.: $15,000. **Number Awarded:** 5. **To Apply:** Applicants must submit certified copy of academic transcripts; three letters of reference; copy of birth or baptismal certificate; and proof of Canadian citizenship if not born in Canada. Applicants must also provide an original and seven photocopies of the following: completed signed application form; (maximum of 250 words) statement of research topic, reasons of choosing the school including graduate work completed, plans and career goals; list of secondary awards received; bibliographic list of publications or research; involvement in activities; and list of scholarships that have been applied for. **Deadline:** December 1.

6466 ■ National Child Support Enforcement Association (NCSEA)
7918 Jones Branch Dr., Ste. 300
McLean, VA 22102
Ph: (703)506-2880
Fax: (703)506-3266
E-mail: Customerservice@ncsea.org
URL: www.ncsea.org

Awards are arranged alphabetically below their administering organizations

6467 ■ NCSEA Judge Ross Leadership Scholarships (Professional development/Scholarship)

Purpose: To assist those who are able to demonstrate outstanding potential in improving their team's performance in child support. **Focus:** Leadership, Institutional and community. **Qualif.:** Applicants must have been managers within the state of Wisconsin for two years or less and demonstrating outstanding potential to improve their team's performance. **Criteria:** Selection will be based on the applicants' eligibility and compliance with the application process.

Funds Avail.: No specific amount. **To Apply:** Applicants must provide a brief statement (150 words) on how they will utilize information and networking gained in the course of attending the Leadership Symposium and how they would then share that information upon return to the agency. In addition to the statement, the applicants' respective managers need to submit a letter of recommendation as well as a statement that if chosen, the applicants will be able to travel to the Leadership Symposium. **Deadline:** June 26. **Contact:** Colleen Eubanks at colleeneubanks@ncsea.org.

6468 ■ NCSEA New Leader Scholarships (Professional development/Scholarship)

Purpose: To assist those who are able to demonstrate outstanding potential in improving their team's performance in child support. **Focus:** Leadership, Institutional and community. **Qualif.:** Applicants must have been managers outside the state of Wisconsin for two years or less and demonstrating outstanding potential to improve their team's performance. **Criteria:** Selection will be based on the applicants' eligibility and compliance with the application process.

Funds Avail.: $500. **To Apply:** Applicants must provide a brief statement (150 words) on how they will utilize information and networking gained in the course of attending the Leadership Symposium and how they would then share that information upon return to the agency. In addition to the statement, the applicants' respective managers need to submit a letter of recommendation as well as a statement that if chosen, the applicants will be able to travel to the Leadership Symposium. **Deadline:** June 26. **Contact:** Colleen Eubanks at colleeneubanks@ncsea.org.

6469 ■ National Collegiate Athletic Association (NCAA)

700 W Washington St.
Indianapolis, IN 46206
Ph: (317)917-6222
Fax: (317)917-6888
URL: www.ncaa.org

6470 ■ Walter Byers Postgraduate Scholarships (Graduate, Postgraduate/Scholarship)

Purpose: To promote and encourage postgraduate education for student-athletes. **Focus:** Sports studies. **Qualif.:** Student-athletes must have overall undergraduate cumulative GPA of 3.50 or better (based on a maximum 4.0), or the equivalent; have competed in intercollegiate athletics as a member of a varsity team at an NCAA member institution; be graduating seniors or enrolled in graduate studies at an NCAA member institution; have intentions of applying for admission into a graduate degree program at a properly accredited, nonprofit educational institution or into a post baccalaureate professional degree program at a professionally accredited law school, medical school, or the equivalent, without restriction as to the national site of the institution; committed to work on a full-time basis toward a graduate degree or toward a post baccalaureate professional degree; have evidenced superior character and leadership; have demonstrated that participation in athletics has been a positive influence in personal and intellectual development; and enrolled in a graduate degree program within five years of being named a Byer's Scholar. **Criteria:** Recipients will be selected based on financial need.

Funds Avail.: $24,000. **Duration:** One academic year. **Number Awarded:** One male and one female. **To Apply:** Student-athletes must be nominated by the Institution's Faculty Athletics Representative (FAR) or a FAR designee (an individual in academics); must complete the application form; must submit personal essay outlining the nominees long and short-term goals; separate factual lists of: (1) principal activities while in college; (2) honors received; and (3) principal involvement in community activities; four recommendation letters; and official transcript of records. **Deadline:** January 27. **Contact:** Contact Lori Thomas at the NCAA national office at 317/917-6222 or by e-mail at lthomas@ncaa.org.

6471 ■ Ethnic Minority and Women's Enhancement Postgraduate Scholarships (Graduate/Scholarship)

Purpose: To increase the pool of opportunities for qualified minority and female candidates in intercollegiate athletics. **Focus:** Sports studies. **Qualif.:** Applicant must be seeking admission or have been accepted into a sports administration or sports-related program that will assist in obtaining a career in intercollegiate athletics (athletics administrator, coach, athletic trainer or other careers that provide a direct service to intercollegiate athletics); has not yet begun any initial postgraduate studies; U.S. citizen; and have performed with distinction as a student body member at their respective undergraduate institution. **Criteria:** A subcommittee from the NCAA Committee on Women's Athletics will select 13 award recipients, and a subcommittee from the NCAA Minorities Opportunities and Interests Committee will select 13 award recipients.

Funds Avail.: $6000. **Duration:** One academic year. **Number Awarded:** 26. **To Apply:** Applicants should submit their application using the online submission system. **Deadline:** December 6. **Contact:** Teaera Strum at tstrum@ncaa.org.

6472 ■ National Collegiate Athletic Association Postgraduate Scholarships (Postgraduate/Scholarship)

Purpose: To promote and encourage postgraduate education for student-athletes. **Focus:** General studies/Field of study not specified. **Qualif.:** Applicant must be a student-athlete at an active NCAA member institution and in the final season of NCAA athletics eligibility or will not be using any remaining athletics eligibility; have an overall undergraduate minimum cumulative GPA of 3.200 (based on a 4.000 scale) or its equivalent; have performed with distinction as a member of the varsity team in the sport in which the student-athlete is being nominated; intend to continue academic work beyond the baccalaureate degree and enroll in a graduate degree program on a part- or full-time basis at an accredited graduate or degree-granting professional school; and an outstanding citizen and excellent role model for the institution and intercollegiate athletics as a whole; must be in his/her final year of intercollegiate athletics competition. **Criteria:** Nominations are initially reviewed by seven regional selection committees.

Awards are arranged alphabetically below their administering organizations

Funds Avail.: $7,500. **Number Awarded:** 87 men; 87 women. **To Apply:** Student-athletes must be nominated by the institution's Faculty Athletics Representative (FAR) or a FAR designee (an individual in academics).

6473 ■ National Collegiate Cancer Foundation (NCCF)
4858 Battery Ln., No. 216
Bethesda, MD 20814
Ph: (240)515-6262
E-mail: info@collegiatecancer.org
URL: collegiatecancer.org

6474 ■ National Collegiate Cancer Foundation Scholarships (Undergraduate/Scholarship)

Purpose: To provide financial support for college students who have a personal diagnosis with cancer and are seeking to continue their higher education. **Focus:** General studies/Field of study not specified. **Qualif.:** Applicants must be college students who have been diagnosed with cancer and are seeking to continue their higher education; must be between the ages of 18-35. **Criteria:** Awards will be based on four criteria: financial need, quality of essay and recommendations, displaying a "Will Win" attitude, overall story of cancer survivorship, and displaying a "Will Win" attitude with respect to his or her cancer experience.

Funds Avail.: $1,000. **To Apply:** Applicants must check the available website for the required materials. **Contact:** National Collegiate Cancer Foundation, 4858 Battery Ln., No. 216, Bethesda, MD 20814; Phone: 240-515-6262; Email: contact@collegiatecancer.org.

6475 ■ National Community Pharmacists Association (NCPA)
100 Daingerfield Rd.
Alexandria, VA 22314
Ph: (703)683-8200
Fax: (703)683-3619
Free: 800-544-7447
E-mail: info@ncpanet.org
URL: www.ncpanet.org

6476 ■ J.C. and Rheba Cobb Memorial Scholarships (Undergraduate/Scholarship)

Purpose: To promote the continuing growth and prosperity of independent community pharmacy in the United States. **Focus:** Pharmacy. **Qualif.:** Applicants must be full-time pharmacy students in an accredited United States college of pharmacy and must be student members of NCPA. **Criteria:** Recipients are selected based on leadership qualities, academic achievement and demonstrated interest in government affairs.

Funds Avail.: No specific amount. **To Apply:** Applicants must submit a copy of the most recent official transcript of record. Applicants must submit a letter from school official familiar with the students activities; a letter from a pharmacy owner or manager, preferably an NCPA member; a letter from the applicants to the NCPA Foundation Scholarships Award Committee outlining his or her school and civic accomplishments and objectives for the future; a resume or curriculum vitae describing the student's work and professional experience. **Contact:** NCPA Foundation Scholarship Committee, at the above address.

6477 ■ National Community Pharmacists Association Presidential Scholarships (Undergraduate/Scholarship)

Purpose: To promote the continuing growth and prosperity of independent community pharmacy in the United States. **Focus:** Pharmacy. **Qualif.:** Applicants must be full-time pharmacy students at an accredited college of pharmacy. **Criteria:** Recipients are selected based on leadership qualities and academic achievement.

Funds Avail.: $3,700 each. **To Apply:** Applicants must submit a copy of the most recent official transcript of record. Applicants must submit a letter from a school official familiar with the students activities; a letter from a pharmacy owner or manager, preferably an NCPA member; a letter from the applicant to the NCPA Foundation Scholarships Award Committee outlining his or her school and civic accomplishments and objectives for the future; a resume or curriculum vitae describing the student's work and professional experience. **Deadline:** July 15. **Contact:** NCPA Foundation Scholarship Committee, at the above address.

6478 ■ National Community Pharmacists Association Summer Internship Programs (Undergraduate/Internship)

Purpose: To provide undergraduate pharmacy students with an opportunity to become more aware of the vast opportunities that exist in independent pharmacy practice. To provide an experience that demonstrates the importance of a national pharmacy association to the profession. **Focus:** Pharmacy. **Qualif.:** Applicants must be enrolled in a full-time pharmacy program in pursuit of their first professional pharmacy degree; applicants must have a minimum of 2.50 cumulative GPA at an accredited U.S. college of pharmacy; a demonstrated interest in independent pharmacy practice through school activities and work experience; exhibit an interest in organizational involvement through participation in student organizations in college and/or community organizations. **Criteria:** Recipients are selected based on academic standing.

Funds Avail.: No specific amount. **To Apply:** Applicants must submit a letter of recommendation explaining their interest in the internship, career goals and how the internship will help meet the goals; a resume or curriculum vitae; a school transcript to verify a cumulative GPA of at least 2.5; two letters of recommendation, one from pharmacy school dean and one from the state pharmacy association executive, recent employer or NCPA Faculty Liaison. **Deadline:** January 15. **Contact:** NCPA Student Affairs, at studentaffairs@ncpanet.org.

6479 ■ Neil Pruitt, Sr. Memorial Scholarships (Undergraduate/Scholarship)

Purpose: To promote the continuing growth and prosperity of independent community pharmacy in the United States. **Focus:** Pharmacy. **Qualif.:** Applicants must be full-time pharmacy students at an accredited U.S. college of pharmacy and members of NCPA. **Criteria:** Recipients are selected based on leadership qualities, academic achievement and demonstrated interest in entrepreneurism.

Funds Avail.: $2,500. **Number Awarded:** 1. **To Apply:** Applicants must submit a copy of the most recent official transcript of records; a letter from a school official familiar with the students activities; a letter from a pharmacy owner or manager, preferably an NCPA member; a letter from the applicant to the NCPA Foundation Scholarships Award Committee outlining his or her school and civic accomplish-

Awards are arranged alphabetically below their administering organizations

ments and objectives for the future; a resume or curriculum vitae describing the students work and professional experience. **Deadline:** March 15. **Contact:** NCPA Foundation Scholarship Committee, at the above address.

6480 ■ Willard B. Simmons Sr. Memorial Scholarships (Undergraduate/Scholarship)

Purpose: To promote the continuing growth and prosperity of independent community pharmacy in the United States. **Focus:** Pharmacy. **Qualif.:** Applicants must be full-time pharmacy students at an accredited United States college of pharmacy and must be student members of NCPA. **Criteria:** Recipients are selected based on leadership qualities, academic achievement and demonstrated interest in independent pharmacy management.

Funds Avail.: $2,500. **Number Awarded:** 1. **To Apply:** Applicants must submit a copy of the most recent official transcript of record. Applicants must submit a letter from school official familiar with the students activities; a letter from a pharmacy owner or manager, preferably an NCPA member; a letter from the applicants to the NCPA Foundation Scholarships Award Committee outlining his or her school and civic accomplishments and objectives for the future; a resume or curriculum vitae describing the student's work and professional experience. **Deadline:** March 15. **Contact:** NCPA Foundation Scholarship Committee, at the above address.

6481 ■ National Conference of Bar Examiners (NCBE)

302 S Bedford St.
Madison, WI 53703-3622
Ph: (608)280-8550
Fax: (608)280-8552
E-mail: contact@ncbex.org
URL: www.ncbex.org

6482 ■ The Joe E. Covington Awards for Research on Bar Admissions Testing (Doctorate, Graduate/Award)

Purpose: To provide support for graduate students in any discipline doing research germane to bar admissions. **Focus:** General studies/Field of study not specified. **Qualif.:** Applicant must be a student conducting a research and is enrolled in a doctoral program and has completed a minimum of one year of study towards a Ph.D. degree or just completing a Ph.D degree. **Criteria:** Recipient will be selected by the Award Committee.

Funds Avail.: $6,000; $1,000 for the advisor. **Duration:** Annual. **To Apply:** Applicant must submit an application which includes a) a curriculum vitae; b) a letter of intent from the student's project advisor; c) a brief research proposal of up to four pages; d) a cover letter to Dr. Mark Albanese. **Deadline:** November 8. **Contact:** Application form and other supporting documents should be sent to Dr. Mark A. Albanese, Dir. of Research, Phone: 608-316-3051; Fax: 608-442-7974; E-mail: malbanese@ncbex.org.

6483 ■ National Conservation District Employees Association (NCDEA)

509 Capitol Ct. NE
Washington, DC 20002-4937
Ph: (202)547-6223
Fax: (202)547-6450

E-mail: myncdea@gmail.com
URL: sites.google.com/site/myncdea/home

6484 ■ Don Aron Scholarships (Undergraduate/Scholarship)

Purpose: To provide financial support to a district employee or member of their immediate family who is participating in a resource conservation curriculum while enrolled in an accredited college or university. **Focus:** Agriculture, Economic aspects. **Qualif.:** Applicant must be currently employed for a period of one year by a conservation district of the United States. Applicant must demonstrate integrity, ability, and competence in their work and possess skills gained through training or experience; or applicant must be an immediate family member of a conservation district employee. He/she must demonstrate an interest in soil and water conservation and have the intent to pursue a course in natural resource conservation. **Criteria:** Recipients are selected based on the academics; demonstrated leadership; financial need; letters of recommendation; quality of application.

Funds Avail.: $1,000. **Duration:** Not stated. **To Apply:** Applicant must fill out the application form and provide proof that he/she is currently enrolled. **Deadline:** May 1. **Contact:** Rich Duesterhaus at 509 Capitol Court, NE Washington, DC 20002; 202-547-6223.

6485 ■ National Costumers Association (NCA)

6000 E Evans Ave., No. 3-205
Denver, CO 80222
Ph: (303)758-9611
Fax: (303)758-9616
Free: 800-NCA-1321
E-mail: office@costumers.org
URL: www.costumers.org

6486 ■ National Costumers Association Scholarships (Undergraduate/Scholarship)

Purpose: To promote the costume industry through education. **Focus:** General studies/Field of study not specified. **Qualif.:** Applicants must be 17 years old and above, with a GPA of 2.75 or higher and enrolled in an accredited university or school. **Criteria:** Awards are given based on academic merit.

Funds Avail.: No specific amount. **Number Awarded:** 3. **To Apply:** Applicants must submit a completed and signed application form; proof of GPA; copy of online transcript; and one photo - preferably a headshot. Candidates must also submit a 100-word (max) biography and a 500-word (min) essay of the candidate's field of study and how it applies to the costume industry. **Deadline:** April 1. **Contact:** Dorothy Shadrick, office@costumers.org; Phone: 800-NCA-1321.

6487 ■ National Council on Education for the Ceramic Arts (NCECA)

4845 Pearl East Cir., Ste. 101
Boulder, CO 80301
Ph: (303)828-2811
Fax: (303)828-0911
Free: 866-266-2322
URL: nceca.net

6488 ■ Regina Brown Undergraduate Student Fellowships (Undergraduate/Fellowship)

Purpose: To promote and improve the ceramic arts through education, research and creative practice. **Focus:** Arts.

Awards are arranged alphabetically below their administering organizations

Qualif.: Applicant must be a NCECA member; a full-time undergraduate student matriculated in a degree program at an accredited college, university or art institute in the U.S.; and must have attained the classification of at least a junior or its equivalent. **Criteria:** Selection is based on the application.

Funds Avail.: $1,800. **Number Awarded:** 3. **To Apply:** Applications should be supported by two letters of recommendation written by a ceramics teacher who has taught the student, along with one additional letter of support. **Deadline:** October 21. **Contact:** Patsy Cox, Nominations Committee Chair; Email: patsycoxnceca.@gmail.com; For technical assistance contact kate@nceca.net or candice@nceca.net.

6489 ■ NCECA Graduate Student Fellowships
(Graduate/Fellowship)

Purpose: To promote and improve the ceramic arts through education, research and creative practice. **Focus:** Arts. **Qualif.:** Applicant must be a NCECA member, and a full-time graduate student matriculated in a degree program at an accredited college, university or art institute in the U.S. **Criteria:** Selection is based on the application.

Funds Avail.: $2,000. **Duration:** Annual. **Number Awarded:** 3. **To Apply:** Applications should be supported by two letters of recommendation written by a ceramics teacher who has taught the student, along with one additional letter of support. All materials must be submitted electronically. **Deadline:** October 21. **Remarks:** Established in 2005. **Contact:** Patsy Cox, Nominations Committee Chair; Email: patsycoxnceca.@gmail.com or for Technical Assistance contact kate@nceca.net or candice@nceca.net.

6490 ■ National Council on Public History (NCPH)
127 Cavanaugh Hall
425 University Blvd.
Indianapolis, IN 46202
Ph: (317)274-2716
E-mail: ncph@iupui.edu
URL: ncph.org

6491 ■ National Council on Public History Graduate Student Travel Awards *(Doctorate, Graduate/Grant)*

Purpose: To provide assistance with conference travel costs for graduate student members who have a paper, poster, or other presentation accepted for inclusion in the program of the NCPH annual meeting. **Focus:** History. **Qualif.:** Applicants must be currently enrolled MA or PhD students doing research and/or practice that is recognizably public history; must have had a paper, poster or other presentation accepted for inclusion in the program of the NCPH annual meeting for which they seek a travel award. **Criteria:** Selection will be based primarily on the merit of the planned presentation.

Funds Avail.: $300 each. **Duration:** Annual. **Number Awarded:** 5. **To Apply:** Applicants must submit a completed application. The paper, poster or presentation abstract must be of exceptional quality. Completed application consists of: signed and completed application form; copy of the abstract submitted for the annual meeting regular session or poster session; copy of applicant's resume including the their education, honors/awards, publications and public history research and/or experience. **Deadline:** December 1.

6492 ■ National Council on Public History Student Project Awards *(Undergraduate/Grant)*

Purpose: To support and recognize students who have the most outstanding work to the field of public history. **Focus:** History. **Qualif.:** Applicants must meet the following criteria: the project must be the work of one or more students in a public history program, and have been completed within the two academic years preceding the date of submission; the project must have been initiated as academic coursework, then subsequently recognized beyond the classroom as a contribution to public history; and, the sponsoring faculty members or academic institutions must be members of NCPH. **Criteria:** Selection will be based on the committee's criteria.

Funds Avail.: $500 travel grant. **Duration:** Annual. **To Apply:** Applicants must submit a cover sheet and a two-page written description of the project explaining its methods, conclusions and significance to public history. Include appropriate supporting materials such as written text, graphics, photographs, audio/video tapes and printed materials. Endorsements must include the following: a letter from the project's faculty sponsor explaining the relationship of the project to the coursework, evaluating the project as a contribution to public history and verifying the applicant's status as a full-time student at the time the project was undertaken; a letter from the institution which accepted the project, explaining the relationship between the institution and the student(s) and how the project helped advance the institution's public history mission. Send endorsement letters directly to the NCPH Executive Offices, marked: "Student Project Award". **Deadline:** December 1.

6493 ■ National Council of Teachers of English (NCTE)
1111 W Kenyon Rd.
Urbana, IL 61801-1096
Ph: (217)328-3870
Fax: (217)328-9645
Free: 877-369-6283
E-mail: public_info@ncte.org
URL: www.ncte.org

6494 ■ NCTE Research Foundation Grants *(Other/Grant)*

Purpose: To support research projects about the teaching and learning of language and literacies. **Focus:** English language and literature. **Qualif.:** Applicants must be member of NCTE in good standing conducting a research related to teaching and learning of language and literacies. **Criteria:** Preference will be given to an applicant who will best meet the requirements.

Funds Avail.: Up to $5,000. **Duration:** One year. **To Apply:** Applicants may download the Research Foundation Grant Application Cover Sheet and guidelines from the website www.ncte.org/groups/cee. Applicants must also submit a (150-word and double-spaced) abstract which discusses the research; an itemized budget; and appendices. **Deadline:** June 15.

6495 ■ Edwyna Wheadon Postgraduate Training Scholarship Fund *(Postgraduate/Scholarship)*

Purpose: To support postgraduate training to enhance teaching skills. **Focus:** English language and literature; Teaching. **Qualif.:** Applicants must be teachers of English/Language Arts in a publicly funded institution. **Criteria:**

Awards are arranged alphabetically below their administering organizations

Recipients are selected based on submitted requirements.

Funds Avail.: $500. **Duration:** Annual. **To Apply:** Applicants must complete the application form. Applicant must also indicate the professional development experience for which he/she seeks support (separate piece of paper, less than 500 words). **Deadline:** January 31.

6496 ■ National Council of Teachers of Mathematics (NCTM)

1906 Association Dr.
Reston, VA 20191-1502
Ph: (703)620-9840
Fax: (703)476-2970
Free: 800-235-7566
E-mail: nctm@nctm.org
URL: www.nctm.org

6497 ■ Future Leader Initial NCTM Annual Meeting Attendance Awards (Advanced Professional/Award)

Purpose: To provide financial assistance to a first-time attendee at an NCTM annual meeting and exposition. **Focus:** Mathematics and mathematical sciences; Teaching. **Qualif.:** Applicants must: have full-time teaching position for the current school year; secondary school teachers must be teaching mathematics for at least 50 percent of their schedule in the school year; have earned at least a bachelor's degree; and, be teaching at the time of the application and anticipate teaching during the following school year. **Criteria:** Selection shall be based on the credentials of the qualified applicants. Special consideration will be given to a teacher of underserved and rural students.

Funds Avail.: Up to $1,200. **Duration:** Annual. **Number Awarded:** Varies. **To Apply:** Applicants must submit a proposal. Formats and other instructions for the application is provided at the program website. **Deadline:** October 15.

6498 ■ NCTM Emerging Teacher-Leaders in Elementary School Mathematics Grants for Grades K-5 Teachers (Other/Grant)

Purpose: To increase the breadth and depth of the mathematics content knowledge of one elementary school teacher who has a demonstrated commitment to mathematics teaching and learning. **Focus:** Mathematics and mathematical sciences. **Qualif.:** Applicants must: have the support of the school principal in becoming mathematics teacher-leaders within their respective schools or districts; be current full individuals or E-Members of NCTM; and, be full-time elementary school teachers with at least three years of experience; having mathematics as their regular teaching responsibility. **Criteria:** Selection shall be based on the aforementioned qualifications and compliance with the application details.

Funds Avail.: $6,000. **Duration:** Annual. **To Apply:** Interested teachers are invited to submit a proposal. The MET Proposal Cover Form must be completed and serve as the top page of each copy of the proposal. The proposal must be typewritten, double-spaced and single-sided (please organize as outlined below), with margins of at least one inch on 8.5″ x 11″ paper. Font size must be no smaller than 10-point, and width between characters should be normal (100%). Five copies (one original and four copies) of the proposal should be included in a single packet addressed to the Mathematics Education Trust. Additional document is the Principal's letter of support. **Deadline:** November 6.

6499 ■ NCTM Prospective 7-12 Secondary Teacher Course Work Scholarships (Professional development/Scholarship)

Purpose: To provide financial support to college students preparing for teaching secondary school mathematics. **Focus:** Mathematics and mathematical sciences. **Qualif.:** Applicants must be persons currently completing their sophomore year of college, scheduling for full-time study at a four- or five-year college or university in the next academic year, and pursuing a career goal of becoming a certified teacher of secondary school mathematics. **Criteria:** Preference will be given to applicants with definitive career objectives and present evidence of exceptional university and community service.

Funds Avail.: $10,000. **Duration:** Annual. **Number Awarded:** 1. **To Apply:** Interested applicants are invited to submit a proposal. The MET Proposal Cover Form must be completed and serve as the top page of each copy of the proposal. The proposal must be typewritten, double-spaced and single-sided (please organize as outlined below), with margins of at least one inch on 8.5″ x 11″ paper. Font size must be no smaller than 10-point, and width between characters should be normal (100%). Five copies (one original and four copies) of the proposal should be included in a single packet addressed to the Mathematics Education Trust. Additional document is the Principal's letter of support. **Deadline:** May 4.

6500 ■ NCTM School In-Service Training Grants for Grades 6-8 Teachers (Undergraduate/Grant)

Purpose: To provide financial assistance to middle schools for in-service education in mathematics. **Focus:** Mathematics and mathematical sciences. **Qualif.:** Eligible are schools with a current NCTM K-8 school membership. **Criteria:** Preference will be given to schools with the most financial need.

Funds Avail.: $4,000. **Duration:** Annual. **To Apply:** Interested teachers are invited to submit a proposal. The MET Proposal Cover Form must be completed and serve as the top page of each copy of the proposal. The proposal must be typewritten, double-spaced and single-sided (please organize as outlined below), with margins of at least one inch on 8.5″ x 11″ paper. Font size must be no smaller than 10-point, and width between characters should be normal (100%). Five copies (one original and four copies) of the proposal should be included in a single packet addressed to the Mathematics Education Trust. Additional document is the Principal's letter of support. **Deadline:** May 4.

6501 ■ NCTM School In-Service Training Grants for Grades 9-12 Teachers (Undergraduate/Grant)

Purpose: To provide financial assistance to secondary schools for in-service education in mathematics. **Focus:** Mathematics and mathematical sciences. **Qualif.:** Eligible are secondary schools. **Criteria:** Preference will be given to schools with the most financial need.

Funds Avail.: $4,000. **Duration:** Annual. **To Apply:** Interested teachers are invited to submit a proposal. The MET Proposal Cover Form must be completed and serve as the top page of each copy of the proposal. The proposal must be typewritten, double-spaced and single-sided (please organize as outlined below), with margins of at least one inch on 8.5″ x 11″ paper. Font size must be no smaller than 10-point, and width between characters should be normal (100%). Five copies (one original and four copies) of the proposal should be included in a single packet addressed to the Mathematics Education Trust. Additional document is

Awards are arranged alphabetically below their administering organizations

the Principal's letter of support. **Deadline:** May 4.

6502 ■ NCTM School In-Service Training Grants for Grades K-5 Teachers *(Undergraduate/Grant)*

Purpose: To provide financial assistance to elementary schools for in-service education in mathematics. **Focus:** Mathematics and mathematical sciences. **Qualif.:** Schools with a current NCTM K-8 school membership are eligible. **Criteria:** Preference will be given to schools with the most financial need.

Funds Avail.: $4,000. **Duration:** Annual. **To Apply:** Interested teachers are invited to submit a proposal. The MET Proposal Cover Form must be completed and serve as the top page of each copy of the proposal. The proposal must be typewritten, double-spaced and single-sided (please organize as outlined below), with margins of at least one inch on 8.5" x 11" paper. Font size must be no smaller than 10-point, and width between characters should be normal (100%). Five copies (one original and four copies) of the proposal should be included in a single packet addressed to the Mathematics Education Trust. Additional document is the Principal's letter of support. **Deadline:** May 4.

6503 ■ National Council on U.S.-Arab Relations (NCUSAR)

1730 M St. NW, Ste. 503
Washington, DC 20036
Ph: (202)293-6466
Fax: (202)293-7770
URL: www.ncusar.org

6504 ■ Joseph J. Malone Fellowships in Arab and Islamic Studies *(Professional development/Fellowship)*

Purpose: To provide first-hand exposure to the region's considerable cultural, economic, political, and social diversity pursuant to increased knowledge and understanding. **Focus:** General studies/Field of study not specified. **Qualif.:** Applicants must be American professionals in academia, government and business. Applicants must be US citizens. **Criteria:** Selection will be based on the committee's criteria.

Funds Avail.: No specific amount. **To Apply:** Applicants must contact the Council for the application process.

6505 ■ National Court Reporters Association (NCRA)

8224 Old Courthouse Rd.
Vienna, VA 22182-3808
Ph: (703)556-6272
Fax: (703)556-6291
Free: 800-272-6272
E-mail: president@ncrahq.org
URL: www.ncra.org

6506 ■ National Court Reporters Association Student Intern Scholarship *(Undergraduate/Scholarship)*

Purpose: To provide scholarships to NCRA students. **Focus:** General studies/Field of study not specified. **Qualif.:** The nominee must be a current NCRA student member and must be an intern in any of the three career paths: judicial, CART, and captioning. The nominee must also be enrolled in an NCRA-certified Court Reporter Training

Program. The nominee in a judicial court reporting program must have passed at least one of the program's Q and A tests at a minimum of 190 words per minute. The nominee in a CART or captioning program must have passed at least one of the program's literary tests at a minimum of 160 words per minute. Nominee must have a GPA of at least 3.5 overall, based on a 4.0 standard or equivalent. **Criteria:** Selection will be based on the committee's criteria.

Funds Avail.: $1,000. **Duration:** Annual. **Number Awarded:** 2. **To Apply:** Nominator may download a nomination form via NCRA web site. **Contact:** B.J. Shorak, NCRF's Deputy Executive Director; email at bjshorak@ncra.org.

6507 ■ New Professional Reporter Grant *(Other/Grant)*

Purpose: To support new employees in their first year out of school. **Focus:** General studies/Field of study not specified. **Qualif.:** The nominee must be a current NCRA student member and must be enrolled in an NCRA-certified court reporting program. The nominee must have passed at least one of the court reporting program's Q and A tests at a minimum of 200 words per minute; must have a GPA of at least 3.5 overall, based on a 4.0 standard; must have a demonstrated a need for financial assistance. The nominee must also possess all the qualities exemplified by a professional court reporter, including professional attitude, demeanor, dress and motivation. All criteria must be confirmed and verified by the submitting court reporting program. **Criteria:** The winner will be selected by random drawing of all qualified nominees and will be publicized in the JCR, Newsflash, Caselines, and online, and will be formally announced at the NCRA's annual convention.

Funds Avail.: $2,000. **Duration:** Annual. **To Apply:** Applicant must submit his/her name to NCRA's New Professionals Community of Interest within one month of receiving the grant. **Deadline:** March 27. **Contact:** B.J. Shorak, NCRF's Deputy Executive Director; email at bjshorak@ncra.org.

6508 ■ Frank Sarli Memorial Scholarship *(Undergraduate/Scholarship)*

Purpose: To provide scholarships to NCRA students. **Focus:** General studies/Field of study not specified. **Qualif.:** The nominee must be a current NCRA student member and must be enrolled in an NCRA-certified court reporting program. The nominee must have also passed at least one of the court reporting program's Q and A tests at a minimum of 200 words per minute; must have a grade point average of at least a 3.5 overall, based on a 4.0 standard; must have a demonstrated need for financial assistance; must possess all the qualities exemplified by a professional court reporter, including professional attitude, demeanor, dress and motivation. All criteria must be confirmed and verified by the submitting court reporting program. **Criteria:** Scholarship is given based on the committee's criteria.

Funds Avail.: No specific amount. **Duration:** Annual. **To Apply:** Nominator may nominate a student who meets the criteria for the scholarship. **Contact:** B.J. Shorak, NCRF's Deputy Executive Director; email at bjshorak@ncra.org.

6509 ■ National Cowboy and Western Heritage Museum

1700 NE 63rd St.
Oklahoma City, OK 73111
Ph: (405)478-2250

Awards are arranged alphabetically below their administering organizations

Fax: (405)478-4714
E-mail: mmyers@nationalcowboymuseum.org
URL: www.nationalcowboymuseum.org

6510 ■ John F. and Anna Lee Stacey Scholarships
(All/Scholarship)

Purpose: To support the education of young men and women who aim to make art their profession. **Focus:** Art. **Qualif.:** Applicants must be U.S. citizens and be 18 to 35 years old. **Criteria:** Selection is based on the applications and the submitted work examples.

Funds Avail.: $5,000 each. **Duration:** Annual. **Number Awarded:** Varies. **To Apply:** Applicants must complete the scholarship application form and prepare digital images on a disk (not more than 10 images), preferably 150 dpi with maximum width or height set to 16 inches as a work example (print the applicant's name, the title, dimensions, medium, and date of the execution of the work on the disk). Completed application forms must be sent with a recent photo; a letter of ambitions, plans, and objectives; letters of reference; and the images in one package by U.S. mail or air express. **Deadline:** February 1. **Contact:** Mike Leslie at mleslie@nationalcowboymuseum.org.

6511 ■ National Dairy Herd Information Association (NDHIA)
421 S Nine Mound Rd.
Verona, WI 53593
Ph: (608)848-6455
Fax: (608)848-7675
URL: www.dhia.org

6512 ■ National Dairy Herd Information Association Scholarship Program (Undergraduate/Scholarship)

Purpose: To provide financial assistance for the education of incoming and continuing students at technical and two-year and four-year institutions. **Focus:** Education, Vocational-technical. **Qualif.:** Applicants must be family members or employees of a herd on DHIA testing, or family members of an employee or employees of a DHIA affiliate. **Criteria:** Recipients will be selected based on scholastic achievements and leadership in school and community activities.

Funds Avail.: $750. **Duration:** Annual. **Number Awarded:** 20. **To Apply:** Applicants must submit all the required application information. **Deadline:** October 15. **Contact:** Holly Thompson, National DHIA scholarship committee chair; E-mail: lilvaledairy@aol.com, or JoDee Sattler, National DHIA communications and events manager; E-mail: jdsattler@dhia.org.

6513 ■ National Dairy Shrine (NDS)
PO Box 725
Denmark, WI 54208
Ph: (920)863-6333
Fax: (920)863-6333
E-mail: info@dairyshrine.org
URL: www.dairyshrine.org

6514 ■ Progressive Dairy Producer Awards (All/Grant)

Purpose: To provide funds for educational travel. **Focus:** Agribusiness; Agricultural sciences; Business; Dairy sci-

ence. **Qualif.:** Candidate must be an individual, couple, family or multiple partner operation dairy producer between 21-45 years of age at the time of the application due date. **Criteria:** Priority will be given to nominees who own or manage operations.

Funds Avail.: $2,000. **Duration:** One year. **Number Awarded:** 2. **To Apply:** Applicant must submit the following: two letters of support; Six copies of nomination and supporting information; two letters of reference. Applicant's references must submit their letters directly to National Dairy Shrine. **Deadline:** March 15.

6515 ■ National Defense Industrial Association - Iowa-Illinois Chapter
c/o John W. Masengarb
15820 - 107th Ave.
Davenport, IA 52804-9123
Ph: (563)650-3252
E-mail: admin@ndia-ia-il.org
URL: www.ndia-ia-il.org

6516 ■ Sergeant Paul Fisher Scholarships
(Undergraduate/Scholarship)

Purpose: To provide opportunities for higher education for students who are interested in achieving a place of leadership in their chosen fields. **Focus:** General studies/Field of study not specified. **Qualif.:** Applicants must: be children of active military, reserve, National Guard, or veteran in zip codes 61200-61699 in Illinois and 50000-52899 in Iowa; be senior students currently enrolled in an Iowa or Illinois high school with a cumulative GPA between 2.60 and 4.0 on a 4.0 scale computed at the end of the junior year in high school; and, have shown a growing interest in college preparatory studies and have been active within the school community. **Criteria:** Selection shall be based on the aforesaid applicants' qualifications and compliance with the application details.

Funds Avail.: $2,000 each. **Duration:** Annual. **Number Awarded:** 2. **To Apply:** Applicants must complete the Scholastic application and submit it to the counselor no later than April. Students must then take ACT or SAT of the College Entrance Examination Board no later than December. Applicants must prepare a 500-word essay and two letters of recommendation. Submit completed Confidential Scholastic and Personal Data Form in a package and a copy of high school transcripts along with the Scholastic application. **Deadline:** March 31. **Remarks:** Established in 2005.

6517 ■ National Defense Industrial Association - Picatinny Chapter
PO Box 528
Wharton, NJ 07885
Ph: (973)442-8200
URL: www.ndiapicatinny.com

6518 ■ NDIA Picatinny Chapter Scholarships
(Undergraduate/Scholarship)

Purpose: To provide financial assistance to students in pursuit of higher technology educational programs. **Focus:** Technology. **Qualif.:** Applicants must be graduating high school seniors. **Criteria:** Selection shall be based on ability as demonstrated in the transcripts, class rank and SAT scores; participation in extracurricular activities and awards

Awards are arranged alphabetically below their administering organizations

received; counselor and one teacher recommendation; career objectives; completion of the essay; immediate family member working in the Picatinny community and/or NDIA membership; and financial need.

Funds Avail.: $3,000 each. **Duration:** Annual. **Number Awarded:** 3. **To Apply:** Applicants must submit a completed scholarship application form provided at the scholarship website. **Deadline:** May 8. **Contact:** NDIA, Scholarship Fund Corporation, P.O. Box 528, Wharton, NJ 07885; Questions to: NDIA, Henry Rand randy.rand@us.army.mil.

6519 ■ National Defense Science and Engineering Graduate Fellowship (NDSEG)

c/o American Society for Engineering Education (ASEE)
1818 N St. NW, Ste. 600
Washington, DC 20036
Ph: (202)649-3831
Fax: (202)265-8504
E-mail: ndseg@asee.org
URL: ndseg.asee.org

6520 ■ NDSEG Fellowships *(Graduate/Fellowship)*

Purpose: To increase the number and quality of scientists and engineers. **Focus:** Architecture, Naval; Behavioral sciences; Biology; Chemistry; Computer and information sciences; Engineering, Aerospace/Aeronautical/Astronautical; Engineering, Chemical; Engineering, Civil; Engineering, Electrical; Engineering, Materials; Engineering, Ocean; Geosciences; Oceanography; Physics. **Qualif.:** Applicants must be: citizens or nationals of the U.S. who have received or be on track to receive a bachelor's degree; and, at or near the beginning of doctoral studies in science or engineering. **Criteria:** Selection shall be based on the aforementioned applicants' qualifications and compliance with the application details.

Funds Avail.: $1,000 medical insurance (excluding dental and vision insurance). **Duration:** Annual; up to three years. **To Apply:** Applicants are required to register and apply online. **Contact:** National Defense Science and Engineering Graduate Fellowship, at the above address.

6521 ■ National Defense Transportation Association (NDTA)

50 S Pickett St., Ste. 220
Alexandria, VA 22304-7296
Ph: (703)751-5011
Fax: (703)823-8761
URL: www.ndtahq.com

6522 ■ NDTA Academic Scholarship Program A
(Undergraduate/Scholarship)

Purpose: To encourage good college students to study the fields of logistics, transportation, supply chain, physical distribution, and passenger travel services. **Focus:** Logistics; Transportation. **Qualif.:** Applicants must be members of NDTA or dependents of an NDTA member in good standing. **Criteria:** The Forum, Education and Professional Development Committee will select scholarship recipients based upon the merit of each applicant as attested to by academic performance and extracurricular involvement in school and community life. Scholarships are limited to those seeking an undergraduate degree.

Funds Avail.: No specific amount. **Duration:** Annual. **To**

Apply: Applicants must note that at the time of filing their application, the students must have satisfactorily completed 45 semester hours of work at regionally accredited colleges or universities. The regionally accredited college/university, which the applicants plans to attend must offer a minimum of 15 semester hours in transportation, supply chain management, or logistics or some combination of the above. The applicants must indicate on their application the transportation/physical distribution, logistics or information technology courses they plan to incorporate into their degree program. These courses must comprise at least 15 semester hours of the students' required hours for a degree. Applicants must attach a brief statement from a responsible administrator stating that the proposed courses will constitute acceptable work toward a degree. The NDTA member may obtain a blank application forms to the following: The forum, Education and Professional Development Committee; NDTA Headquarters; or their local Chapter. Applicants must submit a completed application to the Forum, Education and Professional Development Committee. **Deadline:** April 16.

6523 ■ NDTA Academic Scholarship Program B
(Undergraduate/Scholarship)

Purpose: To assist high school graduates achieve their academic goals in the fields of business/ management, logistics, transportation, supply chain, physical distribution, and passenger travel services. **Focus:** Logistics; Transportation. **Qualif.:** Applicants must be NDTA members or financial dependents under the IRS code of an NDTA member. **Criteria:** Selection will be based upon the merit of each applicant as attested to by academic performance and extracurricular involvement in school and community life.

Funds Avail.: No specific amount. **To Apply:** Blank application forms may be obtained by the NDTA member from: The forum, Education and Professional Development Committee; NDTA Headquarters; or his/her local Chapter. Completed applications must be submitted to the Forum, Education and Professional Development Committee. **Deadline:** April 16.

6524 ■ National Dental Hygienists' Association (NDHA)

c/o LaVerna Wilson, Treasurer
366 E Gorgas Ln.
Philadelphia, PA 19119
URL: ndhaonline.org

6525 ■ National Dental Hygienists' Association Scholarships *(Undergraduate/Scholarship)*

Purpose: To increase interest in dental hygiene particularly among African American students by providing financial assistance. **Focus:** Dental hygiene. **Qualif.:** Applicant must be a current member of the NDHA; must be a U.S. citizen particularly African American; must have minimum of 2.5 GPA or greater. **Criteria:** Awards are given based on merit.

Funds Avail.: No specific amount. **To Apply:** Applicant must send completed application form (downloadable from the website); NDHA student membership of $35; a copy of official sealed transcript; a print verification of enrollment form signed by Registrar/Office of Dean of Students; a passport type photo; two recommendation letters (one from a dental hygiene director and the other one from dental hygiene teacher or employer); proof of financial need; statement of leadership skills; and stated ideas on how to

Awards are arranged alphabetically below their administering organizations

promote the profession of dental hygiene and the NDHA Organization. **Deadline:** March 15. **Contact:** Applications should be submitted to Linda Hart Lewis, Scholarship Committee Chair, 1613 W Ormsby Ave., Louisville, KY 40210.

6526 ■ National Eagle Scout Association (NESA)
Boy Scouts of America
1325 W Walnut Hill Ln.
Irving, TX 75015-2079
Ph: (972)580-2000
E-mail: nesa@scouting.org
URL: www.nesa.org

6527 ■ American Legion Eagle Scout of the Year Scholarships *(High School/Scholarship)*

Purpose: To support the education of a student active in Boy Scouting, Varsity Scouting, or Venturing. **Focus:** General studies/Field of study not specified. **Qualif.:** Applicant must have received the Eagle Scout Award and the religious emblem awarded by his religious institution; have demonstrated practical citizenship in church, school, Scouting, and the community; son or grandson of an American Legion or American Legion Auxiliary member; or must be a member of a Scouting unit chartered to a Legion post, an Auxiliary unit, or a Sons of the American Legion squadron. **Criteria:** Selection is based on the committee's review on the applications.

Funds Avail.: $2,500 up to $10,000. **To Apply:** Applicant must complete and file the nomination form. **Deadline:** March 1. **Contact:** Contact the American Legion department in their state.

6528 ■ Rick Arkans Eagle Scout Scholarships *(High School/Scholarship)*

Purpose: To support the education of a student active in Boy Scouting, Varsity Scouting, or Venturing. **Focus:** General studies/Field of study not specified. **Qualif.:** Applicant must be currently registered and active in Boy Scouting, Varsity Scouting, or Venturing; have earned the Eagle Scout Award; have earned the Ner Tamid or Etz Chaim religious emblem; active in a synagogue; have demonstrated practical citizenship in the synagogue, school, Scouting unit, and community; have demonstrate financial need; and be enrolled in an accredited high school and in his final year. **Criteria:** Selection is based on the committee's review on the applications.

Funds Avail.: $1,000. **Number Awarded:** 1. **To Apply:** Applicants must submit a complete application. **Deadline:** February 28.

6529 ■ Birmingham-Southern College Eagle Scout Scholarships *(Undergraduate/Scholarship)*

Purpose: To assist the education of an Eagle scout student. **Focus:** General studies/Field of study not specified. **Qualif.:** Applicant must be an incoming freshmen at the Birmingham Southern College; and an Eagle Scout. **Criteria:** Selection will be based on the committee's criteria.

Funds Avail.: No specific amount. **Number Awarded:** Varies. **To Apply:** Applicant must submit a completed application form; a letter of recommendation; an essay on the applicant's project with description and purpose (250-500 words); a copy of the Eagle Scout or Gold Award Certificate; photographs and documentation related to the project (optional). **Deadline:** January 15. **Contact:** Admission Office, Birmingham-Southern College Box 549008 Birming-

ham, AL 35254, at 800-523-5793.

6530 ■ Emmett J. Doerr Memorial Distinguished Scout Scholarships *(High School/Scholarship)*

Purpose: To support the education of high school seniors who are currently registered and active in Boy Scouting, Varsity Scouting, or Venturing. **Focus:** General studies/ Field of study not specified. **Qualif.:** Applicants must be outstanding Catholic high-school seniors currently registered and active in Boy Scouting, Varsity Scouting, or Venturing; have earned the Eagle Scout Award or the Silver Award; have earned the Ad Altare Dei or Pope Pius XII religious emblem; have held a Scouting leadership position; and have served in parish. **Criteria:** Selection is based on the committee's review on the applications.

Funds Avail.: $2,000. **Duration:** Annual; One year. **Number Awarded:** 5. **To Apply:** Applicants must submit a complete application. **Deadline:** March 1. **Contact:** National Catholic Committee on Scouting, 1325 West Walnut Hill Lane, Irving, TX 75015-2079, nccs@netbsa.org.

6531 ■ Dofflemyer Scholarships *(Undergraduate/ Scholarship)*

Purpose: To support the education of an Eagle Scout student. **Focus:** General studies/Field of study not specified. **Qualif.:** Applicant must be an Eagle Scout entering Stanford University. **Criteria:** Selection is based on a family's demonstrated need.

Funds Avail.: Varies. **To Apply:** Applicant must follow the university's standard application process. **Deadline:** February 1. **Contact:** Financial Aid Office, Stanford University, Montag Hall 355 Galvez St. Stanford, CA 94305-6106, at 888-326-3773, or financialaid@stanford.edu.

6532 ■ Eastern Orthodox Scouting Scholarships *(High School/Scholarship)*

Purpose: To support the education of a student active in Scouting, Varsity Scouting, or Venturing. **Focus:** General studies/Field of study not specified. **Qualif.:** Applicant must be registered and active in Boy Scouting or Girl Scouting; must have earned the Eagle Scout Award (Boy Scouts) or the Gold Award (Girl Scouts); active in an Eastern Orthodox church; and have earned the Alpha Omega religious emblem. **Criteria:** Selection is based on merit.

Funds Avail.: $500 - $1,000. **Duration:** Annual. **To Apply:** Applicants must submit four letters of recommendation with the application. **Deadline:** May 1. **Contact:** George N. Boulukos, 862 Guy Lombardo Ave. Freeport, New York 11520, at 516-868-4050.

6533 ■ Epsilon Tau Pi's Soaring Eagle Scholarships *(Undergraduate/Scholarship)*

Purpose: To assist the education of an Eagle Scout student. **Focus:** General studies/Field of study not specified. **Qualif.:** Applicant must be an Eagle Scout entering as freshman at the University of Dayton; have demonstrated leadership ability in Scouting, and has a strong record of community participation beyond Scouting; have a SAT score of at least 1600 or an ACT score of at least 25. **Criteria:** Selection is based on the committee's review on the applications.

Funds Avail.: $500. **Duration:** Annual. **To Apply:** Applicants must visit the Epsilon Tau Pi Alpha Chapter's website for the application process and other details. **Deadline:** August 15. **Contact:** Soaring Eagle Scholarship, Epsilon Tau Pi, 1915 Trinity Ave. Dayton, OH 45409.

Awards are arranged alphabetically below their administering organizations

6534 ■ Gaebe Eagle Scout Awards *(Undergraduate/Scholarship)*

Purpose: To assist the education of an Eagle Scout student. **Focus:** General studies/Field of study not specified. **Qualif.:** Applicant must be entering as freshman at Johnson and Wales University and must be an Eagle Scout. **Criteria:** Selection will be based on the submitted application.

Funds Avail.: $1,000. **To Apply:** Applications are available at JWU's NSO Office; submit application and a transcript of grades to the NSO Office. **Deadline:** February 1. **Contact:** National Student Organizations, Johnson and Wales University, 8 Abbott Park Place Providence, RI 02903, at 800-342-5598, x-2345.

6535 ■ Gold Award/Eagle Scout Scholarships *(Undergraduate/Scholarship)*

Purpose: To assist the education of a boy and girl scout student. **Focus:** General studies/Field of study not specified. **Qualif.:** Applicant must have a high-school core GPA of at least 2.5 as calculated by Mississippi State University, or at least 48 hours of transferable community college course credit with a minimum cumulative GPA of 2.5; a Mississippi resident or have received the Eagle Scout Award or Gold Award in a Mississippi-based Scouting council. **Criteria:** Selection is based on the committee's review of the applications.

Funds Avail.: $1,000 ($500 per semester). **To Apply:** Applicant must follow the university's standard application process. **Deadline:** February 1. **Contact:** Office of Admissions and Scholarships, Mississippi State University P.O. Box 6334 Mississippi State, MS 39762-6334, at 662-325-2224, or admit@msstate.edu.

6536 ■ Zenon C.R. Hansen Leadership Scholarships *(Undergraduate/Scholarship)*

Purpose: To assist the education of an Eagle Scout student. **Focus:** General studies/Field of study not specified. **Qualif.:** Applicant must be a full-time Doane College student who is an Eagle Scout; active in the Boy Scouts of America, and planning to remain active in Scouting and leadership activities. **Criteria:** Selection is based on the committee's review on the applications.

Funds Avail.: Varies. **Duration:** Annual; One year. **To Apply:** Applicants must visit the Doane College website for the details of application. **Deadline:** March 10. **Contact:** Financial Aid Office, Doane College 1014 Boswell Avenue Crete, NE 68333, at 800-333-6263.

6537 ■ Arthur M. and Berdena King Eagle Scout Scholarships *(High School/Scholarship)*

Purpose: To support the education of Eagle Scouts. **Focus:** General studies/Field of study not specified. **Qualif.:** Applicant must be Eagle Scouts currently registered in Scouting and have not reached their 19th birthday. **Criteria:** Selection is based on the application.

Funds Avail.: $2,000 - $8,000. **Number Awarded:** 3. **To Apply:** Applicants must submit a completed application form together with the Four Generation ancestor chart, and the 500-word essay. **Deadline:** Varies by state and chapter. **Contact:** Contact the SAR department in their state.

6538 ■ Lamar University College of Engineering Scholarships *(Undergraduate/Scholarship)*

Purpose: To assist the education of an Eagle Scout student. **Focus:** Engineering. **Qualif.:** Applicant must be a Lamar University undergraduate student, including entering freshmen, majoring in chemical, civil, electrical, industrial, or mechanical engineering; must score at least 1200 on the verbal and math portions of the SAT. **Criteria:** Recipients will be selected based on displayed leadership abilities and extracurricular activities. Preference is given to an Eagle Scout student.

Funds Avail.: $5,000 per year. **Duration:** Annual. **To Apply:** Applicant must submit a completed Scholarship application form. **Deadline:** February 1. **Contact:** Ron Peevy, Director of Recruiting and Cooperative Education, Lamar University College of Engineering P.O. Box 10057 Beaumont, TX 77710, at 409-880-7870, or ronald.peevy@lamar.edu.

6539 ■ Lindenwood University Scouting Scholarships *(Undergraduate/Scholarship)*

Purpose: To assist the education of an Eagle Scout student. **Focus:** General studies/Field of study not specified. **Qualif.:** Applicants must be undergraduate residential students who have been Boy Scouts. **Criteria:** Selection is based on the committee's review of the applications.

Funds Avail.: $6,000 - $12,000 per year. **Number Awarded:** 2. **To Apply:** Applicants must visit the Lindenwood University website for the details of application. **Contact:** Office of Undergraduate Admissions, Lindenwood University 209 South Kings Highway St. Charles, MO 63301-1695, at 636-949-4949, or admissions@lindenwood.edu.

6540 ■ McDaniel College Eagle Scout Scholarships *(Undergraduate/Scholarship)*

Purpose: To assist the education of an Eagle Scout student. **Focus:** General studies/Field of study not specified. **Qualif.:** Applicant must be enrolled full-time and have a minimum 2.50 cumulative GPA and a minimum SAT-I combined score of 1000. **Criteria:** Selection is based on the Committee's review on the applications.

Funds Avail.: $2,000. **To Apply:** Applicant must visit the McDaniel College website for the details of application. **Deadline:** February 1. **Contact:** McDaniel College, 2 College Hill Westminster, MD 21157, at 410-848-7000.

6541 ■ Newman University Scouting Scholarships *(Undergraduate/Scholarship)*

Purpose: To assist the education of a boy and a girl scout student. **Focus:** General studies/Field of study not specified. **Qualif.:** Applicant must be an Eagle Scout or a Girl Scout (Gold Award winners) with a high school GPA of 2.5 or higher on a 4.0 scale; a first-time freshman at Newman University; full-time student and maintains a cumulative GPA of at least 2.25; and active in one or more campus organization each year. **Criteria:** Selection is based on the Committee's review of the applications.

Funds Avail.: $1,500 per year. **To Apply:** Applicant must visit the Newman University website for the details of application. **Contact:** Newman University, 3100 McCormick Ave. Wichita, KS 67213, or call 877-639-6268.

6542 ■ Saint Vincent College Eagle Scout Scholarships *(Undergraduate/Scholarship)*

Purpose: To assist the education of an Eagle Scout student. **Focus:** General studies/Field of study not specified. **Qualif.:** Applicant must be an Eagle Scout student admitted at Saint Vincent College. **Criteria:** All Eagle Scout student will be qualified.

Awards are arranged alphabetically below their administering organizations

Funds Avail.: $500. **Duration:** Annual. **To Apply:** Applicant must submit a documentation to the admission counselor as part of the admission process. **Contact:** Saint Vincent College, 300 Fraser Purchase Road Latrobe, PA 15650, at 800-782-5549.

6543 ■ University of Louisville Eagle Scout Scholarships *(Undergraduate/Scholarship)*

Purpose: To assist the education of an Eagle Scout student. **Focus:** General studies/Field of study not specified. **Qualif.:** Applicant must be an incoming freshman; a resident of Kentucky or Indiana; achieved the rank of Eagle Scout in the Lincoln Heritage Council, Blue Grass Council, Shawnee Trails Council, Dan Beard Council, or Tri-State Area Council; have a minimum high-school GPA of 3.35 on a 4.0 scale and a minimum score of 24 on the ACT or 1090 on the SAT-I. **Criteria:** Selection is based on the committee's review on the applications.

Funds Avail.: $2,000 to full in-state tuition. **To Apply:** Applicant must visit the University of Louisville website for the details of application. **Deadline:** January 15. **Contact:** Student Financial Aid Office, University of Louisville, Louisville, KY 40292, at 502-852-5511, or finaid@louisville.edu.

6544 ■ Chester M. Vernon Memorial Eagle Scout Scholarships *(High School/Scholarship)*

Purpose: To support the education of a student active in Boy Scouting, Varsity Scouting, or Venturing. **Focus:** General studies/Field of study not specified. **Qualif.:** Applicant must be currently registered and active in Boy Scouting, Varsity Scouting, or Venturing; have earned the Eagle Scout Award; have earned the Ner Tamid or Etz Chaim religious emblem; active in a synagogue; have demonstrated practical citizenship in the synagogue, school, Scouting unit, and community; have demonstrated financial need; and be enrolled in an accredited high school and in his final year. **Criteria:** Selection is based on the committee's review on the applications.

Funds Avail.: $1,000 per year. **Duration:** Four years. **Number Awarded:** 1. **To Apply:** Applicant must submit a completed application and other required materials. **Deadline:** February 28.

6545 ■ Veterans of Foreign Wars Scout of the Year *(High School/Scholarship)*

Purpose: To support the education of a student active in Boy or Girl Scouting, Sea Scouting, or Venturing. **Focus:** General studies/Field of study not specified. **Qualif.:** Applicant must be an active members of a Boy or Girl Scout Troop, Venturing Crew, or Sea Scout Ship who received the Eagle Scout Award, Girl Scout Gold Award, Venture Summit Award or Sea Scout Quartermaster Award; 15 years of age or a high school student who reached their 18th birthday during the nomination year; have demonstrated practical citizenship in school, scouting, and the community; must be enrolled in highschool at the time of selection. **Criteria:** Selection is based on the committee's review on the applications.

Funds Avail.: First Place - $5,000; Second Place - $3,000; and Third Place - $1,000. **Number Awarded:** 3. **To Apply:** Applicant must submit the completed VFW Scouting Scholarship form, resume of high school activities, scouting record, community service record and letters of recommendation to a local VFW Post. **Deadline:** March 1. **Contact:** Veterans of Foreign Wars, 406 W. 34th St. Kansas City, Missouri 64111 816-756-3390, info@vfw.org.

6546 ■ Frank L. Weil Memorial Eagle Scout Scholarships *(Undergraduate/Scholarship)*

Purpose: To support the education of a student active in Boy Scouting, Varsity Scouting, or Venturing. **Focus:** General studies/Field of study not specified. **Qualif.:** Applicant must be currently registered and active in Boy Scouting, Varsity Scouting, or Venturing; have earned the Eagle Scout Award; have earned the Ner Tamid or Etz Chaim religious emblem; active in a synagogue; have demonstrated practical citizenship in the synagogue, school, Scouting unit, and community; and be enrolled in an accredited high school and in his final year. **Criteria:** Selection is based on the committee's review on the applications.

Funds Avail.: $500 - $1,000. **Number Awarded:** 1 winner and 2 runners-up. **To Apply:** Applicants must submit a completed application. **Deadline:** February 28.

6547 ■ National Electrical Manufacturers Representatives Association (NEMRA)
28 Deer St., Ste. 302
Portsmouth, NH 03801
Ph: (914)524-8650
Fax: (914)524-8655
Free: 800-446-3672
E-mail: nemra@nemra.org
URL: www.nemra.org

6548 ■ NEMRA Educational Scholarship Foundation *(Undergraduate, Vocational/Occupational/Scholarship)*

Purpose: To reward the academic excellence of the sons and daughters of NEMRA members and their employees. **Focus:** General studies/Field of study not specified. **Qualif.:** Applicants must be children of members of NEMRA (or their employees) who are in good standing as of December 31, and attend, or plan to attend (full-time) an accredited college, university or vocational-technical school. **Criteria:** Scholarships are awarded based on academic record, as well as participation in school and community activities, work experience, and unusual personal or family circumstances with preference given to applicants demonstrating interest in club membership or majoring in Business administration, marketing and sales or electrical engineering-related fields.

Funds Avail.: No specific amount. **Number Awarded:** 14. **To Apply:** Applicants must submit a completed and signed application form; a current official transcript; a recommendation from an individual who can give an honest assessment of the applicant's academic and personal abilities such as a teacher, pastor or college advisor. Application materials must be placed in a stamped No. 10 business size envelope. Two first class stamps are required. **Deadline:** December 31. **Remarks:** Established in 1985.

6549 ■ National Environmental Health Association (NEHA)
720 S Colorado Blvd., Ste. 1000-N
Denver, CO 80246
Ph: (303)756-9090
Fax: (303)691-9490
Free: 866-956-2258
E-mail: staff@neha.org
URL: www.neha.org

6550 ■ NEHA/AAS Scholarship *(Graduate, Undergraduate/Scholarship)*

Purpose: To encourage and support early commitment by students to a career in environmental health. **Focus:** Envi-

Awards are arranged alphabetically below their administering organizations

ronmental science. **Qualif.:** Applicants must be enrolled in an undergraduate or graduate program of studies in environmental health sciences and/or public health. **Criteria:** Applicants are selected based on the committee's review of the application materials.

Funds Avail.: No specific amount. **Duration:** Annual. **To Apply:** Applicants must complete the official application form (no faxes, copies or email submissions will be accepted); must provide an official copy of academic transcript; submit two faculty letters of recommendation from the school in which they are currently enrolled; and submit a letter of recommendation from an active NEHA member (three letters of recommendation must be received for an application to be considered). **Deadline:** February 1. **Contact:** NEHA/AAS Scholarship, Cindy Dimmitt, Scholarship Liaison; Address: 720 S. Colorado Blvd., Ste. 1000-N, Denver, CO 80246-1926; Phone: (303) 756-9090, ext. 0; Email: cdimmitt@neha.org.

6551 ■ National Estuarine Research Reserve System (NERRS)
Estuarine Reserves Division, N/ORM5
Office of Ocean and Coastal Resource Management
NOAA Ocean Service
1305 E W Hwy.
Silver Spring, MD 20910
Ph: (301)713-3155
Fax: (301)713-4367
URL: www.nerrs.noaa.gov

6552 ■ NERRS Graduate Research Fellowships (GRF) *(Graduate/Fellowship)*
Purpose: To support management-related research projects that will enhance scientific understanding of the reserve ecosystem, provide information needed by reserve management and coastal management decision-makers and improve public awareness and understanding of estuarine ecosystems and estuarine management issues. **Focus:** Ecology. **Qualif.:** Applicants must be admitted to or enrolled in a full-time master's or doctoral program at a U.S. accredited university; have completed a majority of the graduate course work at the beginning of the fellowship; and have an approved thesis research program. **Criteria:** Selection is based on the application materials submitted for review.

Funds Avail.: $20,000/year stipend. **Duration:** Up to three years. **Number Awarded:** Varies. **To Apply:** Applicants must submit Federal application forms (SF424. SF424A(s), SF424B and CD511) along with academic resume or a curriculum vitae; a cover letter (indicating current academic status, research interests, career goals, and how the proposed research fits into the degree program); unofficial copy of all undergraduate and graduate transcripts; signed letter of support and recommendation from the applicant's graduate advisor; two signed letters of recommendation; research proposal (Title page, Abstract, Project Description; Milestone schedule, Personnel and Project Management, Literature Cited); a proposed budget; a copy of applicable local, state or federal permit; and other supporting documentation attached as appendices. **Deadline:** November 1. **Contact:** Alison Krepp at 301-713-3155 ext. 105 or email at Alison.Krepp@noaa.gov.

6553 ■ National Federation of the Blind (NFB)
200 E Wells St.
Baltimore, MD 21230-4850

Ph: (410)659-9314
Fax: (410)685-5653
URL: nfb.org

6554 ■ Kenneth Jernigan Scholarships *(Undergraduate/Scholarship)*
Purpose: To support and create opportunities to all blind people. **Focus:** General studies/Field of study not specified. **Qualif.:** All applicants must be legally blind in both eyes; must be pursuing or planning to pursue a full-time, postsecondary course of study in a Degree Program at a United States institution; must be participants in NFB national convention and in all scheduled scholarship program activities. **Criteria:** Committee of Scholarship Program will evaluate the application based on the academic excellence, community service, and financial need.

Funds Avail.: $12,000. **Duration:** Annual. **Number Awarded:** 1. **To Apply:** Applicants must fill out the application form; must submit two letters of recommendation from individuals that can describe the academic ability, leadership skills, and/or community involvement; copies of transcript of record and a photocopy of score reports for all standardized tests taken for college admission (ACT, SAT or other); applicant must provide a letter of proof of legal blindness from a qualified professional; and an affiliate President's letter. **Deadline:** March 31.

6555 ■ Charles and Melva T. Owen Memorial Scholarships *(Undergraduate/Scholarship)*
Purpose: To support and create opportunities to all blind people. **Focus:** General studies/Field of study not specified. **Qualif.:** All applicants must be legally blind; must be pursuing or planning to pursue a full-time, postsecondary course of study in a degree program at a United States institution; must be participants in the NFB national convention and in all scheduled scholarship program activities. **Criteria:** Committee of Scholarship Program will evaluate the application based on academic excellence, community service, and financial need.

Funds Avail.: $3,000; $10,000. **To Apply:** Applicants must fill out the application form available online and the following materials: two letters of recommendation from individuals that can describe the academic ability, leadership skills, and/or community involvement; copies of transcript of record and a photocopy of score reports for all standardized tests taken for college admission (ACT, SAT or other); letter of proof of legal blindness from a qualified professional; and an affiliate President's letter. **Deadline:** March 31.

6556 ■ E.U. and Gene Parker Scholarships *(Undergraduate/Scholarship)*
Purpose: To support and create opportunities to all blind people. **Focus:** General studies/Field of study not specified. **Qualif.:** All applicants must be legally blind; must be pursuing or planning to pursue a full-time, postsecondary course of study in a degree program at a United States institution; must be participants in the NFB national convention and in all scheduled scholarship program activities. **Criteria:** Committee of Scholarship Program will evaluate the application based on the academic excellence, community service, and financial need.

Funds Avail.: $3,000. **To Apply:** Applicants must fill out the application form available at the website and must submit the following materials: two letters of recommenda-

Awards are arranged alphabetically below their administering organizations

tion from individuals that can describe the academic ability, leadership skills, and/or community involvement; copies of transcript of record and a photocopy of score reports for all standardized tests taken for college admission (ACT, SAT or other); letter of proof of legal blindness from a qualified professional; and an affiliate President's letter. **Deadline:** March 31.

6557 ■ National Federation of Paralegal Associations (NFPA)

23607 Hwy. 99 Ste. 2-C
Edmonds, WA 98026
Ph: (425)967-0045
Fax: (425)771-9588
E-mail: info@paralegals.org
URL: www.paralegals.org

6558 ■ NFPA/PACE Scholarships *(Other/Scholarship)*

Purpose: To promote a global presence for the paralegal profession and leadership in the community. **Focus:** Paralegal studies. **Qualif.:** Applicants must be NFPA members; must be eligible to take the PACE exam. **Criteria:** Recipients are selected based on the quality of the essay and financial needs.

Funds Avail.: No specific amount. **To Apply:** Applicants must complete the application form; must sign the affidavit; write an essay of no more than four-pages responding to the question, "Why is it important to become a PACE Registered Paralegal?" **Deadline:** July 1. **Contact:** National Federation of Paralegal Associations at the above address.

6559 ■ PCCE Scholarship *(Undergraduate/ Scholarship)*

Purpose: To support students of paralegal studies who are members of NFPA. **Focus:** Paralegal studies. **Qualif.:** Applicants must be NFPA member and eligible to take the PCC Exam. **Criteria:** Selection will be based on the committee's criteria.

Funds Avail.: No specific amount. **Duration:** Annual. **To Apply:** Applicants must: complete the application and the affidavit; must answer all the questions in the application form; must write four-page essay responding to the question: "Why are you seeking a professional credential? How will you use the CRP credential to promote or advance your career?" Essay not intended to be a research paper, nor is it simply repeat wording from the PCCE pages of the NFPA website. Applicants must submit original plus three copies of application, signed affidavit, answers to the questions and essay and accompanying documentation to NFPA via delivery method. **Deadline:** July 1.

6560 ■ National Federation of Republican Women (NFRW)

124 N Alfred St.
Alexandria, VA 22314
Ph: (703)548-9688
Fax: (703)548-9836
E-mail: mail@nfrw.org
URL: www.nfrw.org

6561 ■ National Pathfinder Scholarships *(Graduate, Master's, Undergraduate/Scholarship)*

Purpose: To support students with their education. **Focus:** General studies/Field of study not specified. **Qualif.:** Ap-

plicant must be a college undergraduate sophomore, junior or senior, or student enrolled in a master's degree program must be a U.S. citizen. **Criteria:** Applications must be received by applicant's State Federation President and will choose to be submitted to NFRW. Only completed applications will be considered.

Funds Avail.: $2,500. **Duration:** Annual. **Number Awarded:** 3. **To Apply:** Applicants must submit a completed application form together with three letters of recommendation (include contact numbers of the authors); an official copy of recent college transcript; a (one-page, typed) essay stating why the applicant deserves the scholarship; another (one-page, typed) essay on career goals; a photograph (optional); and State Federation President Certification. **Deadline:** June 1. **Remarks:** Founded in honor of First Lady Nancy Reagan. Established in 1985.

6562 ■ Betty Rendel Scholarships *(Undergraduate/ Scholarship)*

Purpose: To support students with their education. **Focus:** Economics; Government; Political science. **Qualif.:** Applicant must be a college undergraduate student majoring in political science, government or economics; and have completed at least two years of college coursework. **Criteria:** Applications must be received by applicant's State Federation President who will choose an application to submit to NFRW.

Funds Avail.: $1,000. **Duration:** Annual. **Number Awarded:** 3. **To Apply:** Applicants must submit a completed application form together with three letters of recommendation (include contact numbers of the authors); an official copy of recent college transcript; a 1-page typed essay stating why the applicant deserves the scholarship; another 1-page typed essay on career goals; a photograph (optional); and State Federation President Certification. **Deadline:** June 1. **Remarks:** Founded in honor of NFRW Past President Betty Rendel's extraordinary leadership skills and dedication to the Republican Party in her home state of Indiana. Established in 1995.

6563 ■ National Forum for Black Public Administrators (NFBPA)

777 N Capitol St. NE, Ste. 807
Washington, DC 20002
Ph: (202)408-9300
Fax: (202)408-8558
URL: www.nfbpa.org

6564 ■ CIGNA Healthcare Graduate Scholarships *(Graduate/Scholarship)*

Purpose: To support the education and development of African-American students and prepare them for careers in public administration. **Focus:** Political science; Public administration; Urban affairs/design/planning. **Qualif.:** Applicants must be full-time students, working towards a graduate degree in public administration, political science, urban affairs, public policy, or a related field preferably at an HBCU with excellent interpersonal and analytical abilities, strong oral and written communication skills and a 3.0 or better GPA for at least 1 remaining full-time semester. **Criteria:** Applicants will be evaluated based on some criteria designed by the Scholarship Selection Committee.

Funds Avail.: $5,000. **Duration:** Annual. **Number Awarded:** 2. **To Apply:** Applicants must submit cover letter describing status as a student and other relevant informa-

Awards are arranged alphabetically below their administering organizations

tion that might be used in evaluating application (extra-curricular activities, volunteer activities, etc.); official copies of all graduate (if applicable) and undergraduate transcripts; two reference letters, at least one of which should be from a faculty member; three-page essay, detailing autobiography and career goals and objectives; and a current resume. **Deadline:** March 22.

6565 ■ CIGNA Healthcare Undergraduate Scholarships (Undergraduate/Scholarship)

Purpose: To support the education and development of African-American students and prepare them for careers in public administration. **Focus:** Political science; Public administration; Urban affairs/design/planning. **Qualif.:** Applicants must be full-time students, working towards an undergraduate degree in public administration, political science, urban affairs, public policy, or a related field preferably at an HBCU with excellent interpersonal and analytical abilities, strong oral and written communication skills and a 3.5 or better grade point average for completed 1 full-time college semester and at least 1 full-time academic year. **Criteria:** Recipient will be selected based on financial need.

Funds Avail.: $10,000. **Duration:** Annual. **Number Awarded:** 1. **To Apply:** Applicants must submit a cover letter describing their current student status and other relevant information to support in evaluating the application. Applicants must also submit the following materials: official copies of all graduate and undergraduate transcripts; two reference letters (at least one of which should be from a faculty member); three-page essay detailing autobiography and career goals and objectives; a current resume; three-page essay answering the question, "In your opinion, what are the five most critical skills public administrators ought to possess, and why?". **Deadline:** March 22.

6566 ■ Johnnie L. Cochran, Jr./MWH Scholarships (Graduate, Undergraduate/Scholarship)

Purpose: To help NFBPA further achieve its mission of attracting the best and brightest African Americans to careers in public service. **Focus:** Public service. **Qualif.:** Applicants must be full-time students working towards an undergraduate or graduate degree in public administration, political science, urban affairs, public policy, or a related field who have excellent interpersonal and analytical abilities, strong oral and written communication skills and have 3.0 or better GPA for at least 1 full time semester remaining. **Criteria:** Applicants will be evaluated based on the criteria designed by the Scholarship Committee.

Funds Avail.: $5,000. **Duration:** Annual. **To Apply:** Applicants must submit a cover letter describing their current student status and other relevant information to support in evaluating the application. Applicants must also submit the following materials: official copies of all graduate and undergraduate transcripts; two reference letters (at least one of which should be from a faculty member); three-page essay detailing autobiography and career goals and objectives; and current resume.

6567 ■ CH2M Hill - Willie T. Loud Scholarships (Undergraduate, Graduate/Scholarship)

Purpose: To assist NFBPA to further achieve its mission of grooming the next generation of African Americans for careers in public service. **Focus:** Public service. **Qualif.:** Applicants must be full-time students with 3.0 or better GPA who are at least 1 full-time semester remaining or working towards a Bachelor's or Master's degree in Public Administration or a related field and should have strong

interpersonal skills, excellent writing, analytical, and oral communication abilities. **Criteria:** Applicants will be evaluated based on criteria designed by the Scholarship Committee.

Funds Avail.: $5,000. **Duration:** Annual. **To Apply:** Applicant must submit a cover letter describing current student status and other relevant information that might be used in evaluating application; official copies of all graduate and undergraduate transcripts; two reference letters (at least one of which should be from a faculty member); three-page essay detailing his/her autobiography and career goals and objectives; and current resume. **Deadline:** March 22.

6568 ■ NFBPA Future Colleagues Scholarships (Undergraduate/Scholarship)

Purpose: To provide financial assistance for the education of undergraduate students pursuing a career in public service. **Focus:** Public service. **Qualif.:** Applicants must be full-time undergraduate students with average academic credentials (2.5 to 3.0) and strong written, oral and analytical abilities, and have at least 1 full-time semester remaining. **Criteria:** Applicants will be evaluated based on the criteria designed by the Scholarship Selection Committee.

Funds Avail.: $1,000. **Duration:** Annual. **To Apply:** Applicants must submit a cover letter describing the current student status and other relevant information that might be used in evaluating the application (extra-curricular activities, volunteer activities, etc); a 500-word essay which provides an example of prior public or community service involvement and how it has influenced their future aspirations in public administration; official copies of all undergraduate transcripts; two (2) reference letters (at least one of which should be from a faculty member); and a current resume.

6569 ■ NFBPA Land-Use Planning Scholarships (Master's, Doctorate/Scholarship)

Purpose: To support the education and development of post-secondary African American students. **Focus:** Public service. **Qualif.:** Applicants must be full-time students working towards a graduate degree (master's or doctoral) in urban planning or a related field (such as transportation engineering, landscape architecture, environmental planning, etc.); must be enrolled in an accredited college or university and either have a home domicile in the state of Maryland or attend a college or university located in Maryland; should have excellent interpersonal and analytical abilities, strong oral and written communication skills; should have a 3.0 or better grade point average and at least 1 full-time semester remaining. **Criteria:** Applicants will be evaluated by the Scholarship Selection Committee.

Funds Avail.: $3,000. **Duration:** Annual. **To Apply:** Applicants must submit a cover letter describing their current student status and other relevant information to support in evaluating the application. Applicants must also submit the following materials: official copies of all graduate and undergraduate transcripts; two reference letters (at least one of which should be from a faculty member); three-page essay detailing autobiography and career goals and objectives; and current resume.

6570 ■ RA Consulting Service/Maria Riley Scholarships (Graduate, Undergraduate/Scholarship)

Purpose: To provide financial assistance for the education and development of public administrators serving in the engineering and information technology field. **Focus:** Engineering. **Qualif.:** Applicants must be full-time students,

Awards are arranged alphabetically below their administering organizations

working towards an undergraduate or graduate degree in engineering or information technology with excellent interpersonal and analytical abilities, strong oral and written communication skills and a 3.0 or better grade point average for at least 1 remaining full-time semester. **Criteria:** Applicants will be evaluated by the Scholarship Selection Committee.

Funds Avail.: $2,500. **Duration:** Annual. **To Apply:** Applicants must submit a cover letter describing their current student status and other relevant information to support in evaluating the application. Applicants must also submit the following materials: official copies of all graduate and undergraduate transcripts; two reference letters (at least one of which should be from a faculty member); three-page essay detailing autobiography and career goals and objectives; and current resume.

6571 ■ National Foster Parent Association (NFPA)

1202 Westrac Dr., Ste. 400
Fargo, ND 58103
Fax: (888)925-5634
Free: 800-557-5238
E-mail: info@nfpaonline.org
URL: nfpaonline.org

6572 ■ NFPA Youth Scholarships *(Undergraduate, Vocational/Occupational/Scholarship)*

Purpose: To support foster parents in achieving safety, permanence and well-being for the children and youth in their care. **Focus:** General studies/Field of study not specified. **Qualif.:** Applicant must be a foster youth, adopted youth, or biological youth of currently licensed foster parents, who wish to further education beyond high school, including college or university studies, vocational or technical school or junior college; Must also be at least 17 years old or must be in their senior year of high school. **Criteria:** Scholarships are awarded based on the academic performance.

Funds Avail.: $500. **Number Awarded:** 5. **To Apply:** Applicants must submit a completed online application form; have a parent or adult that is a member of NFPA; a minimum of two (2) letters of recommendation from: foster parents, social workers, residential center, principal/teacher/guidance counselor, employer, etc.; and an essay in 300-500 words on "How my foster care experience has shaped my future goals". Applicants must also provide a copy of high school transcript (planning to attend College or University); return unused portion or appropriate percentage if withdrawing from college/university or course/program or unable to maintain grade point average required by the college/university or course/program. **Deadline:** March 14.

6573 ■ National Foundation for Infectious Diseases (NFID)

7201 Wisconsin Ave., Ste. 750
Bethesda, MD 20814-5278
Ph: (301)656-0003
Fax: (301)907-0878
E-mail: info@nfid.org
URL: www.nfid.org

6574 ■ NFID Advanced Vaccinology Course Travel Grants *(Postdoctorate/Grant)*

Purpose: To support researches dedicated to the study of infectious diseases. **Focus:** Medical research. **Qualif.:** Ap-

plicant must be a recent postdoctoral graduate with a demonstrated interest in a career in vaccinology; must be a citizen and resident of the United States at the time of the course; must be conducting research or working in a recognized and accredited US institution of higher learning or in a governmental agency. **Criteria:** Priority is given to applicants with demonstrated financial need.

Funds Avail.: 4,000. **Duration:** Annual. **Number Awarded:** 2. **To Apply:** Application package must include a letter from the applicant (not exceeding two pages) stating the applicant's long term interest in vaccinology, proposed research or work in vaccinology for the next 2-3 years, location of the proposed research or work and department or division chairman, and financial need; a letter of support from the department or division chairman (not exceeding one page) reiterating the applicant's research or work in vaccinology; applicant's curriculum vitae; and a copy of the applicant's application to the advanced vaccinology course. **Deadline:** December 31.

6575 ■ National Gallery of Art

2000B S Club Dr.
Landover, MD 20785
Ph: (202)737-4215
Fax: (202)789-3068
E-mail: dcl@nga.gov
URL: www.nga.gov

6576 ■ Conservation Fellowships *(Graduate/Fellowship)*

Purpose: To enable graduates of conservation program to participate in the Gallery's mission to care for the collections. **Focus:** Art conservation. **Qualif.:** Candidates should be graduates of a recognized training program or have equivalent training; should have no more than five years of work experience and a proven record of research and writing ability; and must possess English-language skills. **Criteria:** Selection will be based on the committee's criteria.

Funds Avail.: Amount not specified. **Duration:** 3/year. **To Apply:** Interested candidates must prepare the following: transcripts of both undergraduate and graduate courses of academic study; a curriculum vitae with basic biographical information; current addresses and telephone numbers; a brief statement of interest and intent for the fellowship; offprints of any publications or lectures; two supporting letters of recommendation; and one letter of personal reference.

6577 ■ National Garden Clubs

4401 Magnolia Ave.
Saint Louis, MO 63110-3406
Ph: (314)776-7574
Fax: (314)776-5108
E-mail: headquarters@gardenclub.org
URL: www.gardenclub.org

6578 ■ NGC College Scholarships *(Graduate, Undergraduate/Scholarship)*

Purpose: To promote the study of Agriculture. **Focus:** Agricultural sciences; Biology; Botany; Ecology; Economics; Environmental conservation; Floriculture; Forestry; Horticulture; Land management; Landscape architecture and design; Wildlife conservation, management, and science. **Qualif.:** Applicants must: be legal residents of the

Awards are arranged alphabetically below their administering organizations

U.S. attending a college or university in the U.S.; have at least 3.25 GPA on a 4.00 scale; be full-time students enrolled for a minimum of 9 graded hours of classes (graduate) or 12 graded hours (undergraduate). **Criteria:** Recipients are selected based on academic record, applicant's letter, listings of honors/extracurricular activities/work experiences, financial need, and recommendations.

Funds Avail.: $3,500 each. **Duration:** Annual. **Number Awarded:** 35. **To Apply:** Applicants must submit a completed application form together with official academic transcript(s); a letter discussing goals, background, financial need and commitment to chosen field of study (limited to 2 typed pages); a list of extracurricular activities, honors and recognitions received; signed Financial Aid Form; and three letters of recommendation (each limited to 1 typed page). **Deadline:** February 1 (student applications due to State Chairman); March 1 (State Chairmen's submissions due to NGC Scholarship Chairman and Committee). **Contact:** National Garden Clubs, at the above address.

6579 ■ National GEM Consortium
1430 Duke St.
Alexandria, VA 22314-3403
Ph: (703)562-3646
Fax: (202)207-3518
E-mail: info@gemfellowship.org
URL: www.gemfellowship.org

6580 ■ National GEM Consortium - MS Engineering Fellowships *(Graduate/Fellowship)*

Purpose: To support highly qualified but underrepresented students who wish to pursue graduate studies in engineering or science. **Focus:** Engineering; Science. **Qualif.:** Applicant must be a member of an underrepresented group (American Indian/Native, African American/Black, Hispanic American/Latino); a U.S. citizen at the time of application; must sign up to take the GRE at the time of application; be admitted into a GEM member university graduate program before the Fellowship is awarded; a junior, senior or graduate of an engineering or computer science program accredited by the Accreditation Board for Engineering and Technology (ABET); have a minimum cumulative GPA of 2.8/4.0; and must contractually agree to intern with sponsoring a GEM Employer until completion of graduate school. **Criteria:** Selection is based on the application materials submitted.

Funds Avail.: Full tuition and fees, and $16,000 stipend. **Duration:** 3 semesters or 4 quarters. **To Apply:** Applicants must complete the application form online. In addition, applicants must submit official transcript(s); statement of purpose (1 page); copy of official GRE scores; and three letters of recommendation (recommenders must submit recommendations on-line). **Deadline:** November 15.

6581 ■ National GEM Consortium - PhD Engineering Fellowships *(Doctorate, Graduate/Fellowship)*

Purpose: To offer funding to underrepresented minority students who have either completed or are currently enrolled in a master's in engineering program. **Focus:** Engineering. **Qualif.:** Applicant must be a member of an underrepresented group (American Indian/Native, African American/Black, Hispanic American/Latino); a U.S. citizen at the time of application; must sign up to take the GRE at the time of application; be admitted into a GEM member university graduate program before the Fellowship is awarded; a senior, masters student or graduate of an

engineering or applied science program accredited by the Accreditation Board for Engineering and Technology (ABET) at the time of application; have a cumulative GPA of 3.0/4.0; and must contractually agree to intern with a GEM employer member at least once early on or before the start of the PhD program. **Criteria:** Selection is based on the application materials submitted.

Funds Avail.: $16,000. **Duration:** Five years. **To Apply:** Applicants must complete the application form online. In addition, applicants must submit official transcript(s); statement of purpose (1 page); copy of official GRE scores; and three letters of recommendation (recommenders must submit recommendations on-line). **Deadline:** November 15.

6582 ■ National GEM Consortium - PhD Science Fellowships *(Doctorate, Graduate/Fellowship)*

Purpose: To increase the number of minority students who pursue doctoral degrees in the natural science disciplines. **Focus:** Biological and clinical sciences; Chemistry; Computer and information sciences; Earth sciences; Mathematics and mathematical sciences; Physics. **Qualif.:** Applicant must be a member of an underrepresented group (American Indian/Native, African American/Black, Hispanic American/Latino); a U.S. citizen at the time of application; must sign up to take the GRE at the time of application; be admitted into a GEM member university graduate program before the Fellowship is awarded; a senior, masters student, or graduate of an engineering or applied science program accredited by the Accreditation Board for Engineering and Technology (ABET) at the time of application; have a cumulative GPA of 3.0/4.0; and must contractually agree to intern with a GEM employer member at least once early on or before the start of the PhD program. **Criteria:** Selection is based on the application materials submitted.

Funds Avail.: Full tuition and fees, and minimum $16,000 academic year stipend for year 1. **Duration:** Five years. **To Apply:** Applicants must complete the application form online. In addition, applicants must submit official transcript(s); statement of purpose (1 page); copy of official GRE scores; and three letters of recommendation (recommenders must submit recommendations on-line). **Deadline:** November 15.

6583 ■ National Geographic Society
1145 17th St. NW
Washington, DC 20036-4688
Ph: (813)979-6845
Free: 800-647-5463
E-mail: askngs@nationalgeographic.com
URL: www.nationalgeographic.com

6584 ■ National Geographic Conservation Trust Grants *(Doctorate, Advanced Professional/Grant)*

Purpose: To support conservation activities around the world as they fit within the mission of the National Geographic Society. **Focus:** Environmental conservation. **Qualif.:** Applicants are not expected to have a PhD or other advanced degrees. However, applicants must provide a record of prior research or conservation action as it pertains to the proposed project. **Criteria:** Selection will be based on the committee's criteria.

Funds Avail.: $15,000 to $20,000. **Duration:** Annual. **To Apply:** Application forms can be obtained at the website. Each principal investigator must submit a preapplication

Awards are arranged alphabetically below their administering organizations

form online. Applicants will be asked to upload an electronic copy of their curriculum vitae while completing the form. Preapplications must be submitted at least eight months prior to anticipated field dates. **Contact:** conservationtrust@ngs.org.

6585 ■ National Geographic Expedition Council Grants *(Advanced Professional/Grant)*

Purpose: To support exploration and adventure worldwide. **Focus:** Environmental conservation. **Qualif.:** Applicants are expected to have qualifications and experience pertinent to the expedition or project they propose. Advanced academic degrees may be required, depending on the nature of the project. International applicants are encouraged. **Criteria:** Selection will be based on the committee's criteria.

Funds Avail.: $15,000 to $35,000. **Duration:** Annual. **To Apply:** Before receiving an application form, the team leader must submit a preapplication form online. Applicants must go to the website to create an account. Preapplication forms can be completed in multiple sessions. Applicants will be asked to upload their curriculum vitae while completing the form. **Contact:** ecouncil@ngs.org.

6586 ■ National Geographic Society/Waitt Grants *(Advanced Professional/Grant)*

Purpose: To fund projects that require venture capital, supporting exceptional projects while foregoing a time-consuming peer-review process. **Focus:** Environmental conservation. **Qualif.:** Applicants are not required to have advanced degrees to be eligible for funding, though they will be required to show a commensurate level of expertise and experience. Applicants must have an affiliation with an educational organization or other institution. **Criteria:** Selection will be based on scientific merit.

Funds Avail.: $5,000 to $15,000. **Duration:** Annual. **To Apply:** Applicants may visit the website for the online application process. The application form can be completed in multiple sessions. Applicants will be allowed to save their work to an online account and complete it at another time. Applicants must upload electronic copies of their curriculum vitae, publication record, maps, images and alternative budgets before submitting their application. In order to ensure quick turnaround, applicants should encourage their recommended reviewers to submit their reviews/letter of reference in a timely fashion. **Contact:** waitt@ngs.org.

6587 ■ National Geographic Young Explorers Grants *(Advanced Professional/Grant)*

Purpose: To offer opportunities to individuals to pursue research, conservation, and exploration-related projects consistent with National Geographic's existing grant programs, including: the Committee for Research and Exploration (CRE), the Expeditions Council (EC), and the Conservation Trust (CT). **Focus:** Conservation of natural resources; Environmental conservation. **Qualif.:** Applicants must be US citizens or foreign nationals. Researchers planning to work in countries abroad should make great effort to include at least one local collaborator as part of their team. Applicants are not required to have advanced degrees. However, a record of prior experience in the fields of research, conservation, or exploration should be submitted as it pertains to the proposed project. **Criteria:** Selection will be based on the submitted application.

Funds Avail.: $2,000 to $5,000. **Duration:** Annual. **To Apply:** Applicants must submit a preapplication form online. If the preapplication is approved, applicants will be sent an email with a link and a password giving them access to the full application online. Applicants will be asked to upload an electronic copy of their curriculum vitae while completing the preapplication form. **Contact:** cre@ngs.org; conservationtrust@ngs.org; council@ngs.org.

6588 ■ National Ground Water Association (NGWA)
601 Dempsey Rd.
Westerville, OH 43081
Ph: (614)898-7791
Fax: (614)898-7786
Free: 800-551-7379
E-mail: ngwa@ngwa.org
URL: www.ngwa.org

6589 ■ Len Assante Scholarship Fund *(Undergraduate/Scholarship)*

Purpose: To assist those studying groundwater-related fields. **Focus:** Water supply industry. **Qualif.:** Applicants must be high school or full-time undergraduate students enrolled in a four-year college program or two-year drilling associate degree program; entering the field of study that serves, supports, or promotes the ground water industry; must maintain 2.5 GPA. **Criteria:** Recipients are selected based on academic performance and financial need. Incomplete applications will not be evaluated. An independent panel decides how to distribute the funds and the number of scholarships to be awarded from the pool of scholarship applicants.

Funds Avail.: Up to $5,000. **Duration:** Annual. **Number Awarded:** Varies. **To Apply:** Applicants must complete the application form. **Deadline:** January 15. **Contact:** Rachel Geddes, Foundation Administrator, at rgeddes@ngwa.org.

6590 ■ National Guard Association of Rhode Island
645 New London Ave.
Cranston, RI 02920-3003
E-mail: ngarinews@gmail.com
URL: www.ngari.org

6591 ■ National Guard Association of Rhode Island Scholarship *(Undergraduate/Scholarship)*

Purpose: To support members and their families by providing them with a scholarship. **Focus:** General studies/Field of study not specified. **Qualif.:** Applicants must be NGARI members or retired members and their families; must be high school seniors, high school graduates or higher education undergraduates; must be accepted to any accredited colleges, universities, or vocational/technical schools beyond high school. **Criteria:** Selection will be based on the committee's criteria.

Funds Avail.: No specific amount. **Duration:** Annual. **To Apply:** Applicants must furnish copies of College Board exam scores (PSAT, SAT, etc) and high school or college transcripts with fully completed application. Applicants are strongly encouraged to provide any additional information that may be helpful to the selection committee. **Deadline:** May 31.

6592 ■ National Guard Association of Texas (NGAT)
3706 Crawford Ave.
Austin, TX 78731-6308

Awards are arranged alphabetically below their administering organizations

Ph: (512)454-7300
Fax: (512)467-6803
Free: 800-252-6428
URL: www.ngat.org

6593 ■ NGAT Educational Scholarships *(Graduate, Undergraduate/Scholarship)*

Purpose: To provide educational assistance for deserving students and dependents of the Texas Military Forces who want to pursue their education. **Focus:** General studies/ Field of study not specified. **Qualif.:** Applicants must be current annual or life member of NGAT or the spouse or dependent son or daughter of a current annual or life member. **Criteria:** Applicants will be selected based on the criteria of the scholarship committee.

Funds Avail.: $500 - $5,000. **To Apply:** Applicants must submit a completed application form available online along with an essay stating their specific facts about their desire to continue their education. For high school applicants: have a recent educational transcript and should reflect class rank; must include the first semester of the 12th grade transcript. For college freshmen: must include their high school transcript with their application. For undergraduate and graduate: must have a copy of their latest college transcript; must have a letter of recommendation from commanders, teachers, ministers, or others not related to applicant. **Deadline:** February 13. **Contact:** Ray Lindner; email rlindner@ngat.org.

6594 ■ National Hartford Centers of Gerontological Nursing Excellence

Coordinating Ctr.
1220 L St. NW, Ste. 901
Washington, DC 20005
Ph: (202)842-1275
E-mail: nhcgne@geron.org
URL: www.geriatricnursing.org

6595 ■ NHCGNE Patricia G. Archbold Predoctoral Scholar Award *(Doctorate/Scholarship)*

Purpose: To support doctoral work for nurses committed to careers in academic gerontological nursing. **Focus:** Medicine, Geriatric. **Qualif.:** Applicants must: be registered nurses holding degree(s) in nursing; be enrolled or accepted in a doctoral nursing degree program (not including DNP) at an institution that is a member of NHCGNE; be U.S. citizens or permanent U.S. residents; plan an academic and research career; and demonstrate potential for long-term contributions to geriatric nursing. **Criteria:** Selection shall be based on the aforementioned applicants' qualifications and compliance with the application details.

Funds Avail.: $100,000 ($50,000 per annum). **Duration:** Annual; up to two years. **To Apply:** Applicants must be able to submit the three major components: first is the application to be uploaded in the Dropbox on the Filesany-where website as a single PDF document; second is the three (3) references from individuals who can speak to the each of the applicant's potential to succeed in the award program and offer specific evidence of the candidate's potential for academic and professional leadership in the field; last component is the official transcripts from baccalaureate program as well as any postbaccalaureate and graduate nursing degree program. Other details regarding application checklist can be verified at the program website. **Deadline:** January 16. **Contact:** NHCGNE Coordinating

Center at proberts@geron.org.

6596 ■ Claire M. Fagin Fellow Award *(Doctorate/ Fellowship)*

Purpose: To assist doctorally prepared nurses committed to academic careers in gerontological nursing. **Focus:** Medicine, Geriatric. **Qualif.:** Applicants must: be doctorally-prepared registered nurses (not including DNP); hold degree(s) in nursing; be U.S. citizens or permanent U.S. residents; have potential to develop into independent investigators; and demonstrate potential for long-term contributions to geriatric nursing. **Criteria:** Selection shall be based on the aforementioned applicants' qualifications and compliance with the application details.

Funds Avail.: $120,000 each ($60,000 per annum). **Duration:** Annual; up to two years. **To Apply:** Applicants must be able to submit the three major components: first is the application to be uploaded in the Dropbox on the Filesany-where website as a single PDF document; second is the three (3) references from individuals who can speak to the each of the applicant's potential to succeed in the award program and offer specific evidence of the candidate's potential for academic and professional leadership in the field; last component is the official transcripts from baccalaureate program as well as any postbaccalaureate and graduate nursing degree program. Other details regarding application checklist can be verified at the program website. **Deadline:** January 16. **Contact:** NHCGNE Coordinating Center at proberts@geron.org.

6597 ■ National Heart, Lung, and Blood Institute (NHLBI)

NIH Bldg. 31, Rm. 5A48, MSC 2486
31 Center Dr.
Bethesda, MD 20892
Ph: (301)592-8573
Fax: (301)592-8563
E-mail: nhlbiinfo@nhlbi.nih.gov
URL: www.nhlbi.nih.gov

6598 ■ Ruth L. Kirschstein NRSA Individual Pre-Doctoral Fellowships *(Doctorate/Fellowship)*

Purpose: To provide financial assistance to students from underrepresented racial and ethnic groups pursuing biomedical and behavioral sciences. **Focus:** Behavioral sciences; Biomedical sciences. **Qualif.:** Applicants must be U.S. citizens or permanent residents; must have a baccalaureate degree and currently enrolled in an eligible doctoral program; must be individuals with disabilities or from underrepresented racial and ethnic groups or from disadvantaged backgrounds pursuing advanced degrees in biomedical and behavioral sciences. **Criteria:** Selection will be based on evaluation of submitted documents and specific criteria.

Funds Avail.: No specific amount. **To Apply:** Applicants must submit the application materials electronically using the SF 424 Research and Related (R&R) forms and the SF 424 (R&R) Individual Fellowship Application Guide. **Deadline:** April 13, August 13, December 13. **Contact:** Xenia J. Tigno, PhD, Program Director; Phone: 301-435-0202; Email: tignoxt@mail.nih.gov.

6599 ■ National Hemophilia Foundation (NHF)

116 W 32nd St., 11th Fl.
New York, NY 10001

Awards are arranged alphabetically below their administering organizations

---

Ph: (212)328-3700
Fax: (212)328-3777
E-mail: handi@hemophilia.org
URL: www.hemophilia.org

6600 ■ BioRx/Hemophilia of North Carolina Educational Scholarships *(Undergraduate/Scholarship)*

Purpose: To provide financial assistance to those students who are pursuing higher educational goal. **Focus:** General studies/Field of study not specified. **Qualif.:** Applicant must be caregivers of children affected with bleeding disorders, a person who has been diagnosed with hemophilia, or a sibling of a person diagnosed with hemophilia. **Criteria:** Priority is given to a hemophilia community member, parent and family members seeking healthcare related education from an accredited college or university or certified training program.

Funds Avail.: $500 to $2,000. **Number Awarded:** 4. **To Apply:** Applicants may call or write for application; program instructions are available at the website. **Deadline:** May 1.

6601 ■ Beth Carew Memorial Scholarships *(Undergraduate/Scholarship)*

Purpose: To provide assistance and support to individual and families affected by chronic illness and help these students obtain higher education degree. **Focus:** General studies/Field of study not specified. **Qualif.:** Any student with hemophilia, von Willebrand disease, or a related inherited bleeding disorder is eligible to apply for this Scholarship; high school seniors who have been accepted to an accredited college or university may apply; College freshmen, sophomores, and juniors may also apply. **Criteria:** Recipient is chosen based on merit.

Funds Avail.: $4,000. **Duration:** Annual. **To Apply:** Applicants must call, write, or e-mail for application or download application from the website. **Deadline:** April 15.

6602 ■ Kevin Child Scholarships *(Undergraduate/Scholarship)*

Purpose: To encourage aspirations of higher education among individuals with bleeding disorders by supporting their education. **Focus:** General studies/Field of study not specified. **Qualif.:** Applicants must be individuals diagnosed with hemophilia A or B and either: (1) high school seniors with aspirations of attending a US college, university or vocational-technical school, or (2) college students already pursuing a post-secondary education, or (3) students in a graduate-level program. **Criteria:** Recipients will be selected based on academic performance, participation in school or community activities and an essay detailing educational and career goals.

Funds Avail.: $1,000. **Duration:** Annual. **Number Awarded:** 1. **To Apply:** Applicants must send a complete copy of the application (available from the website) along with a current official transcript of grades and one recommendation from an individual not related to the applicants. **Deadline:** June 3.

6603 ■ Pfizer Soozie Courter Hemophilia Scholarship Program *(Undergraduate/Scholarship)*

Purpose: To provide educational assistance to people with hemophilia and their families. **Focus:** General studies/Field of study not specified. **Qualif.:** Applicants must: have been diagnosed with hemophilia A or B; be U.S. residents attending a school in the U.S. and meet one of the following educational criteria: high school seniors or graduates, or have completed high school or an equivalent, or currently accepted to (or enrolled in) a junior college, college (undergraduate or graduate), or vocational school. **Criteria:** Recipients are selected based on the best combination of a creative and persuasive essay, excellent recommendations, and superior academic standing.

Funds Avail.: $4,000 each (graduates); $2,500 each (undergraduates). **Duration:** Annual. **Number Awarded:** 5 graduates; 10 undergraduates. **To Apply:** Applicants may visit the website for necessary forms and further instructions. **Deadline:** May 20. **Contact:** Hemophilia Scholarship Program, 7 World Trade Center, 250 Greenwich St., 36th Floor, New York, New York 10007.

6604 ■ "Education is Power" Scholarships *(Undergraduate/Scholarship)*

Purpose: To inspire attainment of higher education among individuals with hemophilia and von Willebrand Disease by providing educational funds. **Focus:** General studies/Field of study not specified. **Qualif.:** Applicants must be U.S. residents living with hemophilia or von Willebrand disease and attending a community college, junior college, four-year college, university, or vocational school. **Criteria:** Selection shall be based on the aforementioned qualifications and compliance with the application details.

Funds Avail.: $500 to 2,500. **Duration:** Annual. **Number Awarded:** 20. **To Apply:** Applicants must submit the completed application form available from the website (www.medprorx.com); documentation from a physician/nurse of the applicant's bleeding disorder; copy of diploma or graduate equivalency diploma (GED); most recent transcript; proof of admission to the school; proof of school tuition; a separate document outlining the applicant's community involvement and/or volunteer work; an essay (no less than 250 words); and one letter of recommendation or character reference. **Deadline:** May 1. **Contact:** MedPro Rx, Inc., 140 Northway Court, Raleigh, North Carolina 27615-4916; Att'n: Kathy Robinette-Stoneberg, Scholarship Coordinator; Phone: 866-528-4963; Email: educationispower@medprorx.com.

6605 ■ Joshua Gomes Memorial Scholarship Fund *(Undergraduate, Graduate/Scholarship)*

Purpose: To provide academic scholarships for young adults with HIV/AIDS. **Focus:** General studies/Field of study not specified. **Qualif.:** Applicants must be individuals living with HIV/AIDS accepted or enrolled in a college in the U.S. **Criteria:** Selection shall be based on the aforementioned qualifications and compliance with the application details.

Funds Avail.: $1,000. **Duration:** Annual. **Number Awarded:** 1. **To Apply:** Applicants must submit the completed application form available from the website; letter from a doctor certifying that the applicant is HIV positive or has AIDS; official transcripts from high school showing the applicant's cumulative GPA; letter of acceptance from a U.S. college or university; three letters of recommendation; and an attached 500-word essay. **Deadline:** July 15. **Contact:** Joshua Gomes Memorial Scholarship Fund, 45767 McKenzie Highway, Vida, Oregon 97488; Phone: 541-896-3023.

6606 ■ Professor Ulla Hedner Scholarships *(Undergraduate/Scholarship)*

Purpose: To provide educational assistance to members of the bleeding disorders community. **Focus:** General studies/

Awards are arranged alphabetically below their administering organizations

Field of study not specified. **Qualif.:** Applicants must be high school seniors and college or vocational students. **Criteria:** Scholarship is awarded on a competitive basis.

Funds Avail.: $7,000. **Duration:** Annual. **Number Awarded:** 1. **To Apply:** Applicants must submit a completed application form to Novo Nordisk. **Deadline:** May 6. **Contact:** Scholarship Managers, Inc., SevenSECURE, Novo Nordisk, Inc.; Phone: 877-668-6777.

6607 ■ Lawrence Madeiros Scholarships
(Undergraduate/Scholarship)

Purpose: To inspire educational pursuits among individuals with bleeding disorders by providing financial aid. **Focus:** General studies/Field of study not specified. **Qualif.:** Applicants must be students with inherited bleeding disorder or other chronic disorder attending an accredited college or university. **Criteria:** Recipients are chosen based on combined merit and need.

Funds Avail.: $1,000. **Duration:** Annual. **Number Awarded:** 1. **To Apply:** Applicants must submit the completed application form available from the website along with a copy of current transcript and a statement of recommendation. **Deadline:** May 1. **Contact:** The Lawrence Madeiros Scholarship, P.O. Box 11 Mayfield, New York 12117; Phone: 518-863-8998.

6608 ■ Doreen McMullan McCarthy Memorial Academic Scholarship for Women with Bleeding Disorders *(Undergraduate/Scholarship)*

Purpose: To assist women with bleeding disorders in their pursuit of post high school studies. **Focus:** Hemophilia. **Qualif.:** Applicants must be female residents of the U.S. and have a bleeding or clotting disorder diagnosed by a hematologist, including those with a diagnosis of von Willebrand disease, hemophilia, platelet disorder, or other factor deficiency, carrier status or clotting disorder. **Criteria:** Applications will be evaluated by a review committee. The scholarship will be awarded based on a complete application, essay, achievements, and community service to the bleeding disorders community.

Funds Avail.: $2,500. **Duration:** Annual. **Number Awarded:** 1. **To Apply:** Applicants must submit the following: application form; essay; and, personal reference. **Deadline:** June 6. **Contact:** Sudha Sarode at ssarode@hemophilia.org; Fax: 212-328-3777.

6609 ■ Christopher Mark Pitkin Memorial Scholarships *(Undergraduate/Scholarship)*

Purpose: To expand opportunities for members of the hemophilia community by providing funds for their educational pursuits. **Focus:** General studies/Field of study not specified. **Qualif.:** Applicants must be pursuing a post-high school or college or technical/trade school education. All members of the hemophilia and bleeding disorders community, including spouses, siblings and children. In particular, persons living with hemophilia and HIV, and their family members are encouraged to apply. **Criteria:** Recipients will be selected based on goal orientation, drive and motivation.

Funds Avail.: $500 to $1,000. **Duration:** Annual. **Number Awarded:** 1. **To Apply:** Applicants must complete application packages which include an application form available from the website; two letters of recommendation from someone who can assess the applicants' academic potentials and knows the applicant in general terms (doctor, nurse, social worker, friend, relative, or community

leader). Finalists will be asked to submit transcripts and evidence of enrollment in an educational or vocational institution. **Deadline:** July 24. **Contact:** Hemophilia Foundation of Southern California; 6720 Melrose Ave., Hollywood, CA 90038, Phone: 323-525-0440; Email: ofcmgr@hemosocal.org.

6610 ■ National Hispanic Coalition of Federal Aviation Employees (NHCFAE)
PO Box 23276
Washington, DC 20026-3276
E-mail: dopa@nhcfae.org
URL: nhcfae.org

6611 ■ Rene Matos Memorial Scholarships
(Undergraduate, Vocational/Occupational/Scholarship)

Purpose: To assist dependents of NHCFAE members, students of minority and women complete their higher education efforts by recognizing and rewarding academically superior performance and achievements, leadership and community involvement. **Focus:** General studies/Field of study not specified. **Qualif.:** Applicants must be accepted to or attending an accredited college, university, or vocational/ trade school at the time the scholarship is awarded. Must be a US Citizen or residing in the United states or Puerto Rico. **Criteria:** Selection of scholars will be based on the following criteria: (1) financial need; (2) academic achievement; (3) student activities; (4) honors/awards received; (5) community involvement (6) leadership (7) personal qualities and strengths.

Funds Avail.: No specific amount. **To Apply:** Applicants must submit the following: completed application form; financial need statement; official transcript; letter of recommendation; and a recent photograph. Faxed applications will not be accepted. **Deadline:** May 1. **Contact:** NHCFAE Scholarship Selection Committee at the above address.

6612 ■ National Hispanic Foundation for the Arts (NHFA)
1010 Wisconsin Ave. NW, Ste. 650
Washington, DC 20007
Ph: (202)293-8330
Fax: (202)965-5252
E-mail: info@hispanicarts.org
URL: www.hispanicarts.org

6613 ■ NHFA Scholarships *(Graduate/Scholarship)*

Purpose: To support the education of Hispanic youth in the media, arts, and communications industry. **Focus:** Arts; Communications; Media arts. **Qualif.:** Applicants must be: of Hispanic heritage (one parent fully Hispanic or each parent half Hispanic); U.S. citizens or legal permanent residents with permanent resident cards or passports stamped I-551 (current); graduate students enrolled full-time at one of the selected universities (Yale, Harvard, Columbia, NYU, Northwestern, UCLA, USC, and UT Austin); and, pursuing a degree in one of the following areas: Drama/Theater, Set Design/Costume Design, Lighting Design, Film (writing/directing/production), Broadcast Communications, Entertainment Law, or Business Administration with an emphasis on entertainment management. They must also have a minimum cumulative GPA of 3.0 on a 4.0 scale. **Criteria:** Selection shall be based on academic record, academic plans and career goals, financial need

Awards are arranged alphabetically below their administering organizations

(for educational purposes), community service, compelling essay responses, letter of recommendation, and portfolio submission.

Funds Avail.: No specific amount. **Duration:** Annual. **To Apply:** Applicants must complete the scholarship application online. **Deadline:** July 31. **Remarks:** Established in 1997. **Contact:** National Hispanic Foundation for the Arts, at the above address.

6614 ■ National Honor Society (NHS)

1904 Association Dr.
Reston, VA 20191-1537
Ph: (703)860-0200
Fax: (703)476-5432
Free: 866-647-7253
E-mail: nhs@nhs.us
URL: www.nhs.us

6615 ■ NHS National Scholarships (Undergraduate/ Scholarship)

Purpose: To provide educational assistance to NHS members. **Focus:** General studies/Field of study not specified. **Qualif.:** Candidate must be a senior student member nominated by an active NHS chapter. **Criteria:** Selection is based on the outstanding scholarship, leadership, service and character.

Funds Avail.: State Finalist - $1,000; State Winner - $500; Regional Winner - $1,500; National Winner - $10,000. **Number Awarded:** 4. **To Apply:** Interested applicants may contact the Society for the application process and other details. **Remarks:** From among the nine Regional Winners, one National Winner will be identified to receive an additional $10,000 in college scholarship funding. Established in 1946. **Contact:** Membership Department, 800-253-7746 x-214, or email at membership@nhs.us.

6616 ■ National Housing Endowment

1201 15th St. NW
Washington, DC 20005
Fax: (202)266-8177
Free: 800-368-5242
E-mail: nhe@nahb.org
URL: www.nationalhousingendowment.org

6617 ■ Lee S. Evans/National Housing Endowment Scholarships (Undergraduate, Graduate/Scholarship)

Purpose: To address the pressing need for educating and training construction managers in the residential building industry. **Focus:** Construction. **Qualif.:** Applicants must: be registered as full-time undergraduate or graduate students; have at least one full academic year of course work remaining after the scholarship is awarded; and, demonstrate interest in obtaining employment in the residential construction industry upon graduation. **Criteria:** Selection criteria include financial need, career goals, academic achievement, employment history, extracurricular activities and recommendations. Preference will be given to students who are current members (or will be members in the upcoming semester) of a student chapter of the National Association of Home Builders and to students enrolled in a four-year programs emphasizing construction.

Funds Avail.: No specific amount. **Duration:** Annual. **To Apply:** Applicants must submit the completed application

form available at the website; transcript(s) and course requirements; essay; and two letters of recommendation. **Deadline:** March 17. **Remarks:** Established in 1990. **Contact:** For more information, please contact NHE Scholarship Info. at 202-266-8069 or via email at Scholarships@ nahb.org.

6618 ■ Herman J. Smith Scholarships (Undergraduate, Graduate/Scholarship)

Purpose: To address the pressing need for educating and training construction managers in the residential building industry. **Focus:** Construction. **Qualif.:** Applicants must: be registered as full-time undergraduate or graduate students; have at least one full academic year of course work remaining after the scholarship is awarded; be majoring in construction management, mortgage finance, or a construction related field in an accredited four-year institution; and, demonstrate an interest in obtaining employment in the construction industry, mortgage finance, or a construction related field upon graduation. **Criteria:** Selection criteria include financial need, career goals, academic achievement, employment history, extracurricular activities and recommendations. Preference will be given to applicants who are legal residents of Texas, or juniors or seniors who attend an institution in Texas.

Funds Avail.: No specific amount. **Duration:** Annual. **To Apply:** Application package includes application form, transcript; three letters of recommendation; and an essay. **Deadline:** March 15. **Contact:** For more information, please contact NHE Scholarship Info. at 202-266-8069 or via email at Scholarships@nahb.org.

6619 ■ National Huguenot Society (NHS)

7340 Blanco Rd., Ste. 104
San Antonio, TX 78216
Ph: (210)366-9995
URL: huguenot.netnation.com/general

6620 ■ National Huguenot Society Scholarships (Undergraduate/Scholarship)

Purpose: To provide financial aid for higher education of students who are members of the National Huguenot Society. **Focus:** General studies/Field of study not specified. **Qualif.:** Applicants must be regular members of the National Huguenot Society; must be students at an accredited college or graduate school with at least two semesters of history which include at least in part a history of religion; applicants must have completed at least two years of college with a 3.0 GPA on a 4.0 scale. **Criteria:** Recipients are selected based on academic standing and financial need.

Funds Avail.: $5,000. **Duration:** Annual. **To Apply:** Applicants must complete the application form; attach proof of enrollment at an accredited college or graduate school; attach a transcript of college grades for last two years showing a 3.0 or better GPA; attach proof of membership in the National Huguenot Society. **Contact:** Neoma O. O'Brien, Chairman, Huguenot Scholarship Awards, 812 Braeburn Drive, Fort Washington, MD 20744-3021; email: scholarship@huguenot.netnation.com.

6621 ■ National Humanities Center (NHC)

7 TW Alexander Dr.
Research Triangle Park, NC 27709
Ph: (919)549-0661

Awards are arranged alphabetically below their administering organizations

Fax: (919)990-8535
URL: nationalhumanitiescenter.org

6622 ■ National Humanities Center Fellowships
(Doctorate, Postdoctorate/Fellowship)

Purpose: To promote and encourage advanced study and research on humanities. **Focus:** Humanities. **Qualif.:** Applicants must have doctorate or equivalent scholarly credentials. Young scholars as well as senior scholars are encouraged to apply, but they must have a record of publication, and new Ph.D.s should be aware that the Center does not normally support the revision of a doctoral dissertation. **Criteria:** Selection shall be based on the aforementioned applicants' qualifications and compliance with the application details.

Funds Avail.: No specific amount. **Duration:** Annual. **Number Awarded:** Up to 40. **To Apply:** Applicants must submit the completed application form together with a curriculum vitae (maximum of 4 pages); a project description (1,000-word); a one-page tentative outline of chapters; and a short bibliography. Submit application materials in five copies via regular mail (materials must not be stapled). **Deadline:** October 15. **Contact:** nhc@nationalhumanitiescenter.org.

6623 ■ National Industrial Belting Association (NIBA)
6737 W Washington St., Ste. 1300
Milwaukee, WI 53214
Ph: (414)389-8606
Fax: (414)276-7704
E-mail: staff@niba.org
URL: www.niba.org

6624 ■ NIBA Presidential Scholarships
(Undergraduate/Scholarship)

Purpose: To provide financial assistance to an individual pursuing a minimum two-year course at an accredited college, university or technical school. **Focus:** General studies/Field of study not specified. **Qualif.:** Applicants must be children of NIBA Distributor/ Fabricator Member Company employees and must attend a two-year or more accredited college, university or technical school. **Criteria:** Candidates will be evaluated based on academic achievement, community service/activities, demonstration of leadership and written thesis.

Funds Avail.: $4,000. **Duration:** Annual. **Number Awarded:** 6. **To Apply:** Applicants must submit resume including: contact information, work experience, leadership roles, community and volunteer activities; and (one-page) thesis explaining: goals, objectives and personal influences. **Deadline:** May 1.

6625 ■ National Institute of Justice (NIJ)
810 Seventh St. NW
Washington, DC 20531
Ph: (202)307-2942
Free: 800-851-3420
E-mail: info@oip.usdoj.gov
URL: www.ojp.usdoj.gov

6626 ■ W.E.B. Du Bois Fellowships *(Doctorate/ Fellowship)*

Purpose: To provide talented researchers with an opportunity, early in their career, to elevate independently generated research and ideas to the level of national discussion. **Focus:** Criminal justice. **Qualif.:** Applicants must have a terminal degree in any academic discipline and not yet have been awarded tenure. **Criteria:** Selection will be based on the committee's criteria.

Funds Avail.: Up to $100,000. **Duration:** Annual. **To Apply:** Applicants must visit the website for the application or may contact the Institute for other application information. **Contact:** W.E.B. Du Bois Fellowships: Nadine Frederique; E-mail: Nadine.Frederique@usdoj.gov.

6627 ■ NIJ Visiting Fellowships *(Other/Fellowship)*

Purpose: To encourage researchers from a broad range of disciplines related to crime and justice. **Focus:** Criminal justice. **Qualif.:** Applicants must be researchers in all areas of criminal justice scholarship pertinent to NIJ's broad research mission - including the social sciences, forensic sciences and criminal justice technology. **Criteria:** Selection will be based on the committee's criteria.

Funds Avail.: No specific amount. **Duration:** Annual. **To Apply:** Applicants must visit the website for the application or may contact the Institute for other application information. **Contact:** Visiting Fellowships: Thomas Feucht; E-mail: Thomas.Feucht@usdoj.gov.

6628 ■ National Institutes of Health (NIH)
9000 Rockville Pke.
Bethesda, MD 20892
Ph: (301)496-4000
URL: www.nih.gov

6629 ■ National Institute of Health Undergraduate Scholarship Program (NIH UGSP) *(Undergraduate/ Scholarship)*

Purpose: To aid students from disadvantaged backgrounds who are committed to careers in biomedical, behavioral, and social science health-related research. **Focus:** Behavioral sciences; Biomedical research; Social sciences. **Qualif.:** Applicants must be U.S. citizens or permanent residents enrolled or accepted for enrollment as full-time students at an accredited four-year undergraduate institution in the United States. They must also have an undergraduate GPA of 3.3 or higher on a 4.0 scale or be within the top five of their class. **Criteria:** Selection will be based on students' commitment in pursuing a career in biomedical, behavioral or social science health-related research, as well as exceptional financial need.

Funds Avail.: $20,000. **Duration:** Annual; up to four years. **To Apply:** Applicants may apply online at ugsp.nih.gov; and must provide the following forms: 1) application checklist; 2) application form; 3) undergraduate institution certification form; and 4) four copies of recommendation forms. **Deadline:** March 9.

6630 ■ National Investment Company Service Association (NICSA)
8400 Westpark Dr., 2nd Fl.
McLean, VA 22102
Ph: (508)485-1500
Fax: (508)485-1560
E-mail: info@nicsa.org
URL: www.nicsa.org

6631 ■ William T. Blackwell Scholarship Fund
(Undergraduate/Scholarship)

Purpose: To financially support dependents of NICSA member company employees in their education. **Focus:**

Awards are arranged alphabetically below their administering organizations

General studies/Field of study not specified. **Qualif.:** Applicants must be dependents of full-time employees of NICSA member companies; be enrolled or planning to enroll in a full-time degree seeking course at an accredited four-year college or university. **Criteria:** Recipients are selected based on academic record; leadership; and participation in school and community activities, honors, work experience, statement of goals and aspirations, unusual personal or family circumstances and an outside appraisal.

Funds Avail.: $3,000-$5,000. **Duration:** One year. **To Apply:** Application form is available from the website. Applicants must prepare a current transcript of grades and an appraisal provided by the school (sent in a sealed envelope). **Deadline:** December 13. **Remarks:** The program is administered by Scholarship America. **Contact:** Scholarship Management Services, One Scholarship Way PO Box 297, St. Peter, MN 56082; Phone: 507-931-1682.

6632 ■ National Iranian American Council (NIAC)

1411 K St. NW, Ste. 250
Washington, DC 20005
Ph: (202)386-6325
URL: www.niacouncil.org/site/
PageServer?pagename=NIAC_index

6633 ■ Evolving Perceptions Scholarships
(Undergraduate/Scholarship)

Purpose: To support young Iranian-American artists. **Focus:** Art. **Qualif.:** Applicants must be Iranian or Iranian-American artists living and studying fine arts in the United States. Applicants must be between the ages of 18 and 30. **Criteria:** Selection is based on eligibility and merit.

Funds Avail.: No specific amount. **To Apply:** Applicants may visit the scholarship website (www.evolvingperceptions.com/scholarship.html) for application process.

6634 ■ The Iranian-American Scholarship Fund
(Graduate, Undergraduate/Scholarship)

Purpose: To provide scholarships to students of Iranian descent. **Focus:** General studies/Field of study not specified. **Qualif.:** Applicants must be of Iranian heritage; Undergraduates (sophomores or above); Graduates (Masters Program or equivalent); and must have GPA 3.5 or above. **Criteria:** Recipients will be selected based on financial need and demonstrated commitment to community service.

Funds Avail.: No specific amount. **Duration:** Annual. **Number Awarded:** Varies. **To Apply:** Applicants must submit the completed application form; must submit Student Aid Report (SAR); two essays; two letters of recommendation and two Standard Recommendation Forms; official transcript; and GPA certification form for non-GPA schools (only required for applicants whose transcripts are unable to display GPA on a 4.0 scale). **Remarks:** Established in 1998.

6635 ■ Momeni Foundation Scholarships
(Undergraduate/Scholarship)

Purpose: To provide scholarships to students of Iranian descent. **Focus:** General studies/Field of study not specified. **Qualif.:** Applicants must be college students and graduating high school seniors of Iranian descent of any citizenry, anywhere in the world; must have a cumulative GPA of 3.5 (Scholastic Achievement) or 3.0 (Financial As-

sistance); must be enrolling or enrolled in an accredited college. **Criteria:** Selection will be based on merit.

Funds Avail.: $500-$1,000. **Duration:** Annual. **Number Awarded:** 13. **To Apply:** Applicants must submit a resume or list of extra curricular activities, community leadership or voluntarism, membership in clubs or organizations and any other evidence of outstanding achievement; must submit a short narrative describing goals and plans and motivation towards such; must also submit a copy of document indicating the acceptance to college. **Deadline:** June 30. **Remarks:** Established in 2001. **Contact:** Momeni Foundation at the above address.

6636 ■ National Iranian American Council Fellowships *(Graduate, Undergraduate/Fellowship)*

Purpose: To provide outstanding Iranian-American college students with internships in political and media organizations. **Focus:** Economics; International affairs and relations; Journalism; Political science. **Qualif.:** Applicants must be college junior, senior and graduate students who are U.S. citizens or a legal permanent residents of Iranian descent. A background in public policy, political science, economics, international affairs, or journalism is preferred. **Criteria:** Selection process is highly competitive. Applicants are judged on the basis of their academic credentials; demonstrated interest in community and public service; and the ability to fulfill the needs and expectations of the congressional office they will be placed in.

Funds Avail.: Varies. **Duration:** Annual. **To Apply:** Applicants must submit the following requirements: a completed application form; three letters of recommendation (two academic and one from an employment supervisor); resume; current college transcript; a 500-word essay answering the question: "How has being Iranian-American influenced your decision to pursue a career in public service or journalism?" **Deadline:** Varies.

6637 ■ National Italian American Bar Association (NIABA)

2020 Pennsylvania Ave. NW
Washington, DC 20006-1846
Ph: (414)750-4404
Fax: (414)255-3615
E-mail: dana@barefoot-marketing.com
URL: www.niaba.org

6638 ■ NIABA/NIAF Scholarships *(Graduate/Scholarship)*

Purpose: To assist deserving and qualified students who wish to further their legal education at a law school. **Focus:** Law. **Qualif.:** Applicants must be enrolled at a Law School member of the National Italian American Bar Association. **Criteria:** Major criteria for selection are financial need, but academic and leadership potential are also important considerations.

Funds Avail.: Amount varies. **Duration:** Annual. **Number Awarded:** Varies. **To Apply:** Applicants must submit an official law school grade transcript for the most recent academic year; (two-page, double-spaced) personal letter in support of the application; and two letters of reference. **Deadline:** February 28.

6639 ■ National Italian American Foundation (NIAF)

1860 19th St. NW
Washington, DC 20009

Awards are arranged alphabetically below their administering organizations

Ph: (202)387-0600
Fax: (202)387-0800
E-mail: information@niaf.org
URL: www.niaf.org

6640 ■ NIAF Scholarships - General Category I
(Undergraduate, Graduate, Postgraduate/Scholarship)

Purpose: To financially support the education of Italian American students. **Focus:** General studies/Field of study not specified. **Qualif.:** Applicant must be enrolled in a U.S. accredited institution of higher education for the fall; must have a GPA of at least 3.5 out of 4.0 (or the equivalent); must be a U.S. citizen or a permanent resident alien; and must be an Italian American student who demonstrates outstanding potential and high academic achievements. **Criteria:** Awards are given based on academic performance, field of study, career objectives, and the potential, commitment, and abilities applicants have demonstrated that would enable them to make significant contributions to their chosen field of study.

Funds Avail.: $2,000-$12,000. **Duration:** Annual. **To Apply:** Applicants must submit completed student application and Teacher Evaluation Form online, official school transcript and FAFSA Financial Aid Form (optional), submitted by mail. **Deadline:** April 30.

6641 ■ NIAF Scholarships - General Category II
(Undergraduate, Graduate, Postgraduate/Scholarship)

Purpose: To promote the study of Italian American studies or a related field. **Focus:** Italian studies. **Qualif.:** Applicant must be enrolled in an U.S. accredited institution of higher education for the fall; must have a GPA of at least 3.5 out of 4.0 (or the equivalent); must be a U.S. citizen or a permanent resident alien; and must be from any ethnic background majoring or minoring in Italian language, Italian studies, Italian American studies or a related field who demonstrate outstanding potential and high academic achievements. **Criteria:** Awards are given based on academic performance, field of study, career objectives and the potential, commitment, and abilities of applicants have demonstrated that would enable them to make significant contributions to their chosen field of study.

Funds Avail.: $2,000-$12,000. **Duration:** Annual. **To Apply:** Applicants must submit completed student application and Teacher Evaluation Form online; and submit official school transcript and FAFSA Financial Aid Form (optional) by mail. **Deadline:** April 30.

6642 ■ National Judges Association (NJA)
222 Gilbert Ave.
Glendale, OR 97442
Fax: (541)832-2647
E-mail: njaoffice@yahoo.com
URL: www.nationaljudgesassociation.org

6643 ■ National Judges Association Scholarships
(Other/Scholarship)

Purpose: To engage in education and research concerning the procedures, powers and practices of non-attorneys. **Focus:** Law. **Qualif.:** Applicants must be non-attorney judges and must be members of National Judges Association (NJA). **Criteria:** Recipients are selected based on financial need.

Funds Avail.: No specific amount. **Duration:** Annual. **To Apply:** Applicants must complete the application form and

must provide evidence that they are members of the American judiciary.

6644 ■ National Junior Angus Association (NJAA)
3201 Frederick Ave.
Saint Joseph, MO 64506
Ph: (816)383-5100
Fax: (816)233-9703
E-mail: info@njaa.info
URL: www.angus.org/njaa

6645 ■ Angus Foundation Scholarships
(Undergraduate/Scholarship)

Purpose: To support education, youth and research by giving scholarship to young men and women who are active in the Angus breed pursuing higher education. **Focus:** General studies/Field of study not specified. **Qualif.:** Applicants must be National Junior Angus Association members, regular or life members of American Angus Association graduating high school seniors or must be enrolled in junior college, four-year college/university or other accredited institution of higher education for the fall term, and must have a minimum 2.0 GPA. Applicants must also be below 25 years old prior to Jan. 1 of the year of application. **Criteria:** Candidates will be evaluated by the Angus Foundation's Scholarship Selection Committee. Emphasis will be placed on an applicants' current and/or past involvement in Junior Angus activities at the local, state and national levels.

Funds Avail.: $1,000 - $5,000. **Duration:** Annual. **Number Awarded:** Varies. **To Apply:** Applicants must seek the latest application forms available at www.angusfoundation.org. Applicants must include a copy of high school transcript (for freshmen) or college/university transcript and three (3) letters of recommendation which should be mailed to the Angus Foundation, postmarked by the U.S. Postal Service by May 1 of the application year. **Deadline:** May 1.

6646 ■ National Junior Horticultural Association (NJHA)
c/o Carole Carney, Executive Secretary
15 Railroad Ave.
Homer City, PA 15748-1378
URL: www.njha.org

6647 ■ National Junior Horticultural Association Alumni Scholarships *(Undergraduate/Scholarship)*

Purpose: To help young people develop their skills and obtain an understanding of horticulture. **Focus:** Horticulture. **Qualif.:** Program is open to any youth intending to return to the NJHA convention to expand their knowledge within NJHA. **Criteria:** Recipients are selected based on demonstrated interest in the field of horticulture and financial need.

Funds Avail.: No specific amount. **Number Awarded:** 2. **To Apply:** Applicants must submit a resume which must include a one paragraph statement about self, one paragraph about NJHA involvement, one paragraph about non-NJHA involvement, one paragraph about financial need, and a letter of recommendation from an NJHA leader. **Deadline:** September 1. **Contact:** For further information, applicants are advised to contact Ted Beebe, 41 Hathorn Blvd, Saratoga Springs. NY 12866; Phone: 518 587-6573 Cell Phone 518 588-7140; Email: tbeebe02@nycap.rr.com.

Awards are arranged alphabetically below their administering organizations

6648 ■ National Junior Swine Association (NJSA)

2639 Yeager Rd.
West Lafayette, IN 47906
Ph: (765)463-3594
Fax: (765)497-2959
E-mail: nsr@nationalswine.com
URL: www.nationalswine.com/NJSA.html

6649 ■ Gregory D. Johnson Memorial Scholarships
(Doctorate, Graduate, Master's/Scholarship)

Purpose: To provide a network uniting purebred swine enthusiast through a youth organization. **Focus:** Agriculture, Economic aspects. **Qualif.:** Applicants must be spring college graduates with a bachelor's degree in an agricultural field or current graduate students pursuing a master's or doctorate degree in swine genetics, swine reproduction or swine nutrition. **Criteria:** Applications will be scored by a committee that will independently review and score each application received and select the recipient(s) based on the their criteria.

Funds Avail.: $1,000. **Number Awarded:** 1. **To Apply:** Applicants must enclose one letter of recommendation from a college advisor who can verify participants' graduate school acceptance or enrollment, in addition to their college activities and involvement. Applicants must submit a graduate school acceptance letter or proof of graduate school enrollment. **Deadline:** March 1.

6650 ■ The Maschhoffs Pork Production Scholarships *(Undergraduate/Scholarship)*

Purpose: To provide a network uniting purebred swine enthusiasts through a youth organization. **Focus:** Agriculture, Economic aspects. **Qualif.:** Applicants must be members of the National Junior Swine Association (NJSA). Applicants must be 18-21 years old and enrolled in an agricultural program at a recognized college/ university. **Criteria:** Application will be scored by a committee selected by the NSR Chief Executive Officer and the NSR Director of Junior Activities. The judging committee will determine the winners of the essay contest. Essays will be judged on overall thought process and merit.

Funds Avail.: $1,000. **Number Awarded:** 5. **To Apply:** Applicants may download an application form online. **Deadline:** May 15.

6651 ■ National Junior Swine Association Outstanding Member Scholarships *(Graduate/Scholarship)*

Purpose: To provide a network uniting purebred swine enthusiasts through a youth organization. **Focus:** Agriculture, Economic aspects. **Qualif.:** Applicants must be members of the National Junior Swine Association. **Criteria:** Applications will be scored by a committee selected by the NSR Chief Executive Officer and the NSR Director of Junior Activities. One NJSA scholarship will be awarded to a student in each of the following age divisions: Intermediate (13-16), Junior (9-12), and Novice (8 and under). Two NJSA scholarships will be awarded to a student in the Senior division (17-21).

Funds Avail.: $200 for novice; $300 junior; $500 intermediate; $1,000 senior. **Number Awarded:** 5. **To Apply:** Applicants may submit their application to the office together with the other requirements. **Deadline:** March 1.

6652 ■ NJSA Visionary Leader Scholarships *(Graduate/Scholarship)*

Purpose: To provide a network uniting purebred swine enthusiasts through a youth organization. **Focus:** Agriculture, Economic aspects. **Qualif.:** Applicants must be members of the NJSA Board of Directors. **Criteria:** Application will be scored by a committee that will independently review and score each application received.

Funds Avail.: $500. **Number Awarded:** 1. **To Apply:** Applications should be typed. Extra pages may be used as necessary. Applications must be signed by a parent or guardian who has knowledge of the applicants' involvement in the NJSA. **Deadline:** March 1.

6653 ■ Claude Robinson Scholarships *(Undergraduate/Scholarship)*

Purpose: To provide a network uniting purebred swine enthusiasts through a youth organization. **Focus:** Agriculture, Economic aspects. **Qualif.:** Scholarship applicants must be sophomores, juniors or seniors enrolled in a collegiate. **Criteria:** Selection will be based on demonstrated leadership activities, livestock judging experience, livestock industry interest and community service.

Funds Avail.: $1,000. **Number Awarded:** 1. **To Apply:** Applicants must send two letters of reference. One letter should be written by their college coach, and the second letter should be written by a non-family member who has knowledge of the applicants' involvement in the livestock industry. **Deadline:** March 1.

6654 ■ Jason Shipley Memorial Scholarships *(Undergraduate/Scholarship)*

Purpose: To provide a network uniting purebred swine enthusiasts through a youth organization. **Focus:** Agriculture, Economic aspects. **Qualif.:** Applicants must be incoming freshmen, sophomores or juniors enrolled in an agriculturally related field. **Criteria:** The selection committee member shall independently review and score each application received and select the recipient(s) based on the criteria.

Funds Avail.: $1,000. **Number Awarded:** 1. **To Apply:** Applicants must send two letters of reference. One letter should be written by an athletic coach, and the second letter should be written by a non-family member who has knowledge of the applicants' involvement in the swine industry. **Deadline:** March 1.

6655 ■ National Kindergarten Alliance (NKA)

c/o Penny Pillack, President
PO Box 309
Agua Dulce, TX 78330
Fax: (361)998-2333
URL: www.nkateach.org

6656 ■ NKA Dr. Violet B. Robinson Memorial Graduate Scholarship *(Advanced Professional/Scholarship)*

Purpose: To assist a classroom teacher pursuing an advanced degree in Early Childhood Education or a closely related field. **Focus:** Education, Early childhood. **Qualif.:** Applicants must be NKA members in good standing for at least one year and be classroom teachers pursuing an advanced degree in Early Childhood Education or related field. **Criteria:** Selection shall be based on the aforementioned qualifications and compliance with the application details.

Funds Avail.: $250. **Duration:** Annual. **To Apply:** Applicants must submit a completed application form; a narrative (two or three pages) of professional work experience, extracurricular activities responsibilities, leadership, citizen-

Awards are arranged alphabetically below their administering organizations

ship activities, and awards and honors; reasons for choosing Early Childhood Education as a career; post graduation plans; a copy of transcripts; and two professional letters of recommendation. **Deadline:** March 1.

6657 ■ National Law Enforcement and Firefighters Children's Foundation (NLEAFCF)

928 Broadway, Ste. 703
New York, NY 10010
Ph: (646)822-4236
E-mail: nleafcf@nleafcf.org
URL: nleafcf.org

6658 ■ Victoria Ovis Memorial Scholarships
(Undergraduate/Scholarship)

Purpose: To provide financial assistance for qualified individuals. **Focus:** General studies/Field of study not specified. **Qualif.:** Applicants must be college-bound, undergraduate or graduate students who are children of law enforcement officers or firefighters who died in the line of duty; must have grown up or currently reside and attend school preferably in the metro New York area or New York State; must show evidence of enrollment or acceptance in an appropriate degree or certificate program for the current or following academic year before receiving the award; must show evidence that he/she is the child of a law enforcement officer or firefighter killed in the line of duty. **Criteria:** Selection will be based on scholastic and other achievements.

Funds Avail.: No specific amount. **Duration:** Annual. **Number Awarded:** 1. **To Apply:** Applicants must submit a completed application form; personal essay not exceeding 500 words that summarizes their personal accomplishments, chosen course of study and personal and professional goals; documentation verifying connection to law enforcement and firefighter decent (the statement may come from an agency representative); copy of tuition bill or statement from school or degree program; proof of US citizenship (birth certificate, naturalization papers or US passport); documentation of academic record and current school status. Include the most recent transcripts and letter of acceptance into chosen school and study program; letters of recommendation from two individuals other than family members, including one academic and one personal reference. **Deadline:** July 1. **Contact:** Sarahbeth Grossman, at nleafcf@nleafcf.org.

6659 ■ National Legal Aid and Defender Association (NLADA)

1901 Pennsylvania Ave. NW, Ste. 500
Washington, DC 20006
Ph: (202)452-0620
Fax: (202)872-1031
E-mail: info@nlada.org
URL: www.nlada100years.org

6660 ■ The C. Lyons Fellowship Program *(Advanced Professional/Fellowship)*

Purpose: To support emerging leaders in the equal justice community. **Focus:** Law. **Qualif.:** Applicants must be members of the NLADA. **Criteria:** Applicants will be evaluated based on demonstrated commitment to the delivery of legal services to the poor; a clearly-defined project or interest that is national in scope and that would be mutually

beneficial to NLADA and the program from which the fellow represents; and the desire to learn about and explore national advocacy and public policy issues.

Funds Avail.: No specific amount. **Duration:** Annual. **Number Awarded:** 1. **To Apply:** Applicants must check the website of the National Legal Aid and Defender Association for more detailed information about the fellowship. **Contact:** Deborah Dubois, Vice President of Marketing, Communications & Development, at the above address.

6661 ■ National Lesbian and Gay Journalists Association (NLGJA)

2120 L St. NW, Ste. 850
Washington, DC 20037
Ph: (202)588-9888
E-mail: info@nlgja.org
URL: www.nlgja.org

6662 ■ Leroy F. Aarons Scholarships *(Graduate, Undergraduate/Scholarship)*

Purpose: To support LGBT students who plan to have a career in journalism. **Focus:** Journalism. **Qualif.:** Applicant must be a high school senior accepted to attend a U.S. community college or four-year university, or who can show proof of application to a community college or four-year university and will attend full-time; an undergraduate student who will attend a U.S. community college or four-year university; or an undergraduate student accepted for the first year at a U.S. graduate school and has submitted a tuition deposit for the academic year (graduate students must be enrolled in a journalism program). Applicant must be planning to pursue a career in journalism and be able to demonstrate passion and commitment to the profession. Must also be a U.S. citizen or permanent resident. **Criteria:** Selection is based on an applicant's journalistic and scholastic ability.

Funds Avail.: $3,000. **Duration:** One academic year. **To Apply:** Applicants must submit a completed application form along with a one page resume; five work samples; official transcript provided in a sealed envelope; a copy of a letter of acceptance to a community college or four-year university (high school seniors); three letters of recommendation (from a teacher or professor - high school students may obtain letters from counselors and/or the principal); and an autobiography in the third person and written as a news story, describing the applicant's commitment and passion for journalism and career goals (maximum of 1,000 words in 11-point typed and double spaced). **Deadline:** May 15. **Remarks:** Established in 2005. **Contact:** aarons@nlgja.org.

6663 ■ Kay Longcope Scholarships *(Graduate, Undergraduate/Scholarship)*

Purpose: To support LGBT students of color who plan to have a career in journalism. **Focus:** Journalism. **Qualif.:** Applicant must be an LGBT student of color pursuing a career in journalism; a high school senior accepted to attend a U.S. community college or four-year university, or who can show proof of application to a community college or four-year university and will attend full-time; an undergraduate student who will attend a U.S. community college or four-year university; or an undergraduate student accepted for the first year of a U.S. graduate school and has submitted a tuition deposit for the academic year (graduate students must be enrolled in a journalism program). **Criteria:** Selection is based on an applicant's

Awards are arranged alphabetically below their administering organizations

journalistic and scholastic ability.

Funds Avail.: $3,000. **Duration:** One academic year. **To Apply:** Applicants must submit a completed application form along with a one page resume; five work samples; official transcript provided in a sealed envelope; a copy of a letter of acceptance to a community college or four-year university (high school seniors); three letters of recommendation (from a teacher or professor - high school students may obtain letters from counselors and/or the principal); and an autobiography in the third person and written as a news story, describing the applicant's commitment and passion for journalism and career goals (maximum of 1,000 words in 11-point type and double spaced). **Deadline:** May 15. **Remarks:** Established in 2008.

6664 ■ National LGBT Bar Association (NLGLA)

1875 I Street NW, Ste. 1100
Washington, DC 20006
Ph: (202)637-7661
E-mail: info@lgbtbar.org
URL: lgbtbar.org

6665 ■ Michael Greenberg Student Writing Competition (Graduate/Monetary, Scholarship)

Purpose: To encourage and recognize outstanding law student scholarship on the legal issues affecting lesbian, gay, bisexual and transgender (LGBT) persons. **Focus:** Law. **Qualif.:** Applicants must be students enrolled in an ABA-accredited law school during the given academic year. **Criteria:** Selection shall be based on the essays submitted.

Funds Avail.: $1,500, as well as $250 each for honorable mentions. **Duration:** Annual. **Number Awarded:** Varies. **To Apply:** Applicants may visit the website to verify the application process and other pieces of information. **Deadline:** May 15. **Contact:** judgescompetition@lgbtbar.org.

6666 ■ National Little Britches Rodeo Association (NLBRA)

5050 Edison Ave., Ste. 105
Colorado Springs, CO 80915
Ph: (719)389-0333
Fax: (719)578-1367
Free: 800-763-3694
URL: nlbra.com

6667 ■ NLBRA/Wrangler Academic Scholarships (Undergraduate/Scholarship)

Purpose: To support student members in their education. **Focus:** General studies/Field of study not specified. **Qualif.:** Applicants must be high school seniors; a competing NLBRA member for the previous three years; and will complete their last year of high school prior to the 2014 National Little Britches Finals Rodeo. **Criteria:** Selection is based on academics.

Funds Avail.: No specific amount. **Duration:** Two years; extension of scholarship can be provided with approval of the NLBRA Scholarship Committee. **To Apply:** Applicants must submit a completed application form (available at their website or at the NLBRA National office) along with a photo and a certified copy of high school transcripts. **Deadline:** June 30.

6668 ■ National Medical Fellowships (NMF)

347 5th Ave., Ste. 510
New York, NY 10016-5007

Ph: (212)483-8880
Fax: (212)483-8897
E-mail: info@nmfonline.org
URL: www.nmfonline.org

6669 ■ National Medical Fellowships Need-Based Scholarships (Undergraduate/Scholarship)

Purpose: To support medical students in educational pursuits. **Focus:** Medicine. **Qualif.:** Applicants must be first or second year medical students; must be African-American, Mexican-American, Native American, Alaska Native, Native Hawaiian, or mainland Puerto Ricans who permanently reside within the 50 U.S. states; must be accepted to AAMC or AOA-accredited U.S. medical schools for study leading to M.D. or D.O. degrees. **Criteria:** Selection is based on financial need.

Funds Avail.: No specific amount. **Number Awarded:** Varies. **To Apply:** Applicants born outside of the U.S. must submit a proof of citizenship. Applicants must also submit the following: student aid report (SAR), financial aid transcript, official letter of financial aid award offer, documentation of loan history, curriculum vitae, current medical school transcript, a brief biosketch (200 words), Two (2) personal statements discussing personal and professional motivation, experiences and goals for a medical career; and experiences, challenges and skills you bring on working for an underserved community, (500-1,000 words) and two (2) recommendation letters.

6670 ■ National Merit Scholarship Corporation (NMSC)

1560 Sherman Ave., Ste. 200
Evanston, IL 60201-4897
Ph: (847)866-5100
Fax: (847)866-5115
URL: www.nationalmerit.org

6671 ■ National Merit Scholarship Program (Undergraduate/Scholarship)

Purpose: To support the education of undergraduate students. **Focus:** General studies/Field of study not specified. **Qualif.:** Applicants must be high school students; have taken the Preliminary SAT/National Merit Scholarship Qualifying Test (PSAT/NMSQT); and must be U.S. citizens or have applied for permanent residence. To be included as semifinalists, applicants must have consistent high academic records. **Criteria:** Recipients will be selected based on abilities, skills and accomplishments.

Funds Avail.: $2,500. **Duration:** Annual. **To Apply:** Applicants must send their application forms to their school principal. To be considered as finalists, applicants must request an official transcript right after the current term ends. **Remarks:** Established in 1955.

6672 ■ NMSC College and University Sponsorship of Merit Scholarship Awards (Undergraduate/Scholarship)

Purpose: To support the education of undergraduate students. **Focus:** General studies/Field of study not specified. **Qualif.:** Applicants must be U.S. citizens or have applied for permanent residence; have taken the Preliminary SAT/National Merit Scholarship Qualifying Test (PSAT/NMSQT); must have been admitted to a college or university. **Criteria:** Recipients will be selected based on abilities, skills and accomplishments.

Awards are arranged alphabetically below their administering organizations

Funds Avail.: $500 - $2,000. **Duration:** Annual; renewable up to four years. **To Apply:** Applicants must complete the NMSC application form; must submit a copy of their Permanent Resident Card (Green Card); or a copy of Form I-797 receipt from U.S. Citizenship and Immigration Services (CIS). Applicants must send their SAT scores to NMSC. **Contact:** Sara R. Burson, Sponsor Services Manager at the above address.

6673 ■ NMSC Corporate-Sponsored Achievement Scholarship Awards (Undergraduate/Scholarship)

Purpose: To financially assist students who have plans to pursue a college education. **Focus:** General studies/Field of study not specified. **Qualif.:** Applicants must be children of NMSC employees or residents of an area served by the National Merit Scholarship Corporation. **Criteria:** Recipients will be selected based on abilities, skills and accomplishments.

Funds Avail.: $2,500. **Duration:** Annual; renewable up to four years. **Number Awarded:** 1 - 100. **To Apply:** Applicants must submit a filled-out application form. **Contact:** Nancy A. Bogart, Director of Sponsor Services, at the above address.

6674 ■ NMSC National Achievement Scholarship Program (Undergraduate/Scholarship)

Purpose: To support the education of undergraduate students. **Focus:** General studies/Field of study not specified. **Qualif.:** Applicants must be high school students; have taken the Preliminary SAT/National Merit Scholarship Qualifying Test (PSAT/NMSQT); and must be U.S. citizens or have applied for permanent residence. To be included as semifinalists, applicants must have consistent high academic records. **Criteria:** Recipients will be selected based on abilities, skills and accomplishments.

Funds Avail.: $2,500. **Duration:** Annual. **To Apply:** Applicants must submit a filled-out application form. **Remarks:** Established in 1964. **Contact:** Nancy A. Bogart, Director of Sponsor Services at the above address.

6675 ■ NMSC Special Scholarships (Undergraduate/Scholarship)

Purpose: To support the education of undergraduate students. **Focus:** General studies/Field of study not specified. **Qualif.:** Applicants who are outstanding but not finalists are eligible to apply. Interested individuals must meet the sponsor's criteria and entry requirements of the National Merit Scholarship Program. **Criteria:** A Scholarship Committee evaluates each candidate based on abilities, skills and accomplishments.

Funds Avail.: No specific amount. **Duration:** Annual; renewable up to four years. **To Apply:** Applicants must submit an entry form to the sponsor organization and a detailed scholarship application.

6676 ■ National Military Family Association (NMFA)

3601 Eisenhower Ave., Ste. 425
Alexandria, VA 22304-6460
Ph: (703)931-6632
Fax: (703)931-4600
E-mail: info@militaryfamily.org
URL: www.militaryfamily.org

6677 ■ Joanne Holbrook Patton Military Spouse Scholarships (Graduate, Undergraduate/Scholarship)

Purpose: To support the spouses of Uniformed Services members to obtain professional certification or to attend post secondary or graduate school. **Focus:** General studies/Field of study not specified. **Qualif.:** Applicant must be a military ID-carrying Uniformed Services' spouse (active duty, retiree, Reserve, National Guard and/or survivor). **Criteria:** Selection is based on the application materials submitted.

Funds Avail.: $1,000. **Duration:** Annual. **To Apply:** Applicants must complete the application online. **Deadline:** December 1. **Contact:** scholarships@militaryfamily.org.

6678 ■ National Military Intelligence Association (NMIA)

PO Box 354
Charlotte Court House, VA 23923-0354
Ph: (703)738-7487
URL: www.nmia.org

6679 ■ NMIA Scholarship Program (Undergraduate, Graduate/Scholarship)

Purpose: To support the growth of professional studies in the field of military intelligence and to recognize and reward excellence in the development and transfer of knowledge about military and associated intelligence disciplines. **Focus:** Military science and education. **Qualif.:** Applicants must be dependents of NMIA active members, mobilized reserve and national guard personnel, and other reserve or National Guard members. **Criteria:** Recipient will be selected based on academic achievement, SAT or ACT scores, extra-curricular activities, and career objectives.

Funds Avail.: $3,000 and $5,000. **Number Awarded:** 4. **To Apply:** Applicants must submit the application form, supporting transcripts and SAT or ACT scores. **Contact:** Ms. Debra Davis, nmiassoc@comcast.net.

6680 ■ National Milk Producers Federation (NMPF)

2101 Wilson Blvd., Ste. 400
Arlington, VA 22201-3062
Ph: (703)243-6111
Fax: (703)841-9328
E-mail: info@nmpf.org
URL: www.nmpf.org

6681 ■ NMPF National Dairy Leadership Scholarships (Graduate, Master's, Doctorate/Scholarship)

Purpose: To support graduate students of dairy-related fields in their education. **Focus:** Agriculture, Economic aspects; Dairy science; Economics; Environmental science; Food science and technology; Nutrition. **Qualif.:** Applicants must be qualified graduate students (enrolled in Master's or Ph.D. programs) who are actively pursuing dairy-related fields of research that are of immediate interest to NMPF member cooperatives. **Criteria:** Selection will be based on the committee's criteria.

Funds Avail.: No specific amount. **Number Awarded:** Varies. **To Apply:** Applicants must be able to provide the application package, which consists of the following three items submitted as a single pdf file (the attached, completed, information form; research summary; current resume); and two letters of recommendation (should come directly from the reference). Details about research summary can be verified at the website. **Deadline:** March 27. **Contact:** Beth Briczinski at bbriczinski@nmpf.org.

Awards are arranged alphabetically below their administering organizations

6682 ■ National Multiple Sclerosis Society - New Jersey Metro Chapter

1480 US Highway 9-N, Ste. 301
Woodbridge, NJ 07095
Ph: (732)660-1005
Fax: (732)855-6984
Free: 800-344-4867
E-mail: njminfo@nmss.org
URL: www.nationalmssociety.org/Chapters/NJM

6683 ■ National MS Society New Jersey Metro Chapter Scholarship Program *(College, Undergraduate/Scholarship)*

Purpose: To assist students who are affected by multiple sclerosis, either by having MS themselves or having a parent with MS. **Focus:** General studies/Field of study not specified. **Qualif.:** Applicants must be: individuals who live with multiple sclerosis, or have a parent with multiple sclerosis, and will be attending an accredited postsecondary school; must be enrolled in at least six credit hours per semester in course work leading to a degree, license, or certificate; must be United States citizens or legal residents living in the U.S., Puerto Rico, U.S. Virgin Islands, Guam or any other U.S. territory and plan to enroll in an undergraduate course of study at an accredited two-or four-year college, university, or vocational-technical school located in the U.S., Puerto Rico, Virgin Islands, Guam or any other U.S. territory. **Criteria:** Finalists will be selected on the basis of demonstrated financial need, academic record, leadership and participation in school or community activities, work experience, an outside appraisal, goals and aspirations special circumstances, and an essay (written by the applicant) regarding the impact of multiple sclerosis on their life.

Funds Avail.: $1,000 to $3,000. **Duration:** Annual. **To Apply:** Applicants must fully complete the online application and mail supporting documents on or before the deadline. **Deadline:** January 13.

6684 ■ National Oceanic and Atmospheric Administration - NOAA Center for Atmospheric Sciences (NCAS)

Howard University Research Bldg.
1840 7th St., NW Rm. 305
Washington, DC 20001
Ph: (202)865-8678
Fax: (202)865-8294
E-mail: noaa-cas@howard.edu
URL: ncas.howard.edu

6685 ■ Dr. Nancy Foster Scholarship Program *(Postgraduate, Graduate/Scholarship)*

Purpose: To provide support for independent graduate-level studies in oceanography, marine biology, or maritime archeology. **Focus:** Biology, Marine; Maritime studies; Oceanography. **Qualif.:** Applicants must be U.S. citizens, pursuing or intend to pursue a masters or doctoral level degree in oceanography, maritime archaeology or marine biology; must have maintain a minimum cumulative and term grade point average of 3.3 or higher; must maintain full-time student status for the duration of the scholarship award. **Criteria:** Selection criteria will be based on the academic record and statement of intent describing goals and objectives of scholarship need; the quality of project

and applicability to program priorities; evaluation of recommendations and/or endorsement letters; additional relevant experience related to diversity of education; and the financial need of the student.

Funds Avail.: $52,000. **Duration:** Annual. **To Apply:** Interested applicants may reach NOAA for the application process and other details.

6686 ■ National Organization for Human Services (NOHS)

1600 Sarno Rd., Ste. 16
Melbourne, FL 32935-4993
Free: 800-597-2306
E-mail: admin@nationalhumanservices.org
URL: www.nationalhumanservices.org

6687 ■ David C. Maloney Scholarships *(Undergraduate/Scholarship)*

Purpose: To support the education of a student in a human service program. **Focus:** Human relations; Humanities. **Qualif.:** Applicants must be Associate, Baccalaureate, or Master's students who are members of NOHS; have a GPA of 3.2 and above on a 4.0 scale; and be enrolled in a Human Services studies program. **Criteria:** Consideration will be given to applicants with special established needs or minority status.

Funds Avail.: No specific amount. **Duration:** Annual. **Number Awarded:** 1. **To Apply:** Applicants must submit an official transcript (sent by the university in a sealed envelope); a resume; an essay (500 words) about the applicant's commitment to the field of helping and quality of Human Service Education; copy of current NOHS membership card; and two reference letters. Send applications as email attachments to Dr. Tammi Milliken. **Deadline:** May 1. **Contact:** Dr. Tammi Milliken at scholar@nationalhumanservices.org.

6688 ■ National Organization of Industrial Trade Unions (NOITU)

148-06 Hillside Ave.
Jamaica, NY 11435
Ph: (718)291-3434
URL: www.noitu.org

6689 ■ Daniel Lasky Scholarship Fund *(Undergraduate/Scholarship)*

Purpose: To provide financial assistance to sons and daughters of the Union. **Focus:** Education, Industrial. **Qualif.:** Applicants must be sons or daughters of a NOITU member who will graduate from high school this year and planning to attend an accredited college in the coming fall term. **Criteria:** Candidates will be judged by the Scholarship Committee.

Funds Avail.: No amount mentioned. **To Apply:** Applicants must submit the following requirements: a) Scholastic Aptitude Test (SAT I) scores; b) verification of acceptance by a college or university approved by the Federation of Regional Accrediting commission of Higher Education; c) letters of recommendation from (2) faculty members in the high school you are attending; high school transcript (showing final grades of the graduating year); and the name and address of the college applicants will be attending.

6690 ■ National Organization of Italian-American Women (NOIAW)

25 W 43rd St., 10th Fl.
New York, NY 10036-7406

Awards are arranged alphabetically below their administering organizations

Ph: (212)642-2003
Fax: (212)642-2006
E-mail: noiaw@noiaw.org
URL: www.noiaw.org

6691 ■ National Organization of Italian-American Women Scholarships *(Undergraduate, Graduate/Scholarship)*

Purpose: To provide financial support for Italian-American women in need of additional support for the education of their choice. **Focus:** General studies/Field of study not specified. **Qualif.:** Applicants must be female students, matriculating full-time and have at least one parent of Italian American descent. **Criteria:** Candidates will be evaluated based on minimum cumulative 3.5 GPA and financial need. Preferential consideration is given to applicants who have demonstrated excellence in fields of study of Italian language and/or culture.

Funds Avail.: No specific amount. **Duration:** Annual. **Number Awarded:** 5. **To Apply:** Applicants must submit completed application form; official college transcript; student aid report; curriculum vitae or resume; two (2) letters of recommendation (academic and professional); a $25 non-refundable processing fee and a two-page essay (double spaced) that addresses the question: "How has being an Italian American impacted you, personally and professionally?" **Deadline:** March 31. **Remarks:** Established in 1980. **Contact:** Donna de Matteo, Chair, Scholarship Committee at 25 W 43rd St., Ste. 1005, New York, NY 10036.

6692 ■ National Organization for the Professional Advancement of Black Chemists and Chemical Engineers (NOBCChE)

PO Box 77040
Washington, DC 20013
Free: 866-599-0253
E-mail: webmaster@nobcche.org
URL: www.nobcche.org

6693 ■ Dow Chemical Company Fellowships *(Graduate/Fellowship)*

Purpose: To support outstanding minority graduate students who have made significant contributions to science and/or engineering research. **Focus:** Biology; Chemistry; Engineering, Chemical; Life sciences. **Qualif.:** Applicant must be a candidate in a PhD program for Chemistry, Chemical Engineering, Biology, or Life Sciences; be in at least second year of graduate study; and be enrolled in the PhD program for the Fall/Spring academic year. **Criteria:** Selection is based on the application.

Funds Avail.: No specific amount. **Duration:** Annual. **To Apply:** Applicant must submit a completed application with official transcripts from undergraduate and graduate schools; a resume; research description (one page); career objective (one page); Title and Abstract for presentation at the meeting; and two completed recommendation forms (at least 1 must be from thesis advisor). Application materials must be submitted electronically.

6694 ■ E.I. DuPont Graduate Fellowship *(Graduate/Fellowship)*

Purpose: To support outstanding minority graduate students who have made significant contributions to science and/or engineering research. **Focus:** Biology;

Chemistry; Engineering, Chemical; Life sciences. **Qualif.:** Applicant must be a candidate in a PhD program for Chemistry, Chemical Engineering, Biology, or Life Sciences; be in at least second year of graduate study; and be enrolled in the PhD program for the Fall/Spring academic year. **Criteria:** Selection is based on the application.

Funds Avail.: No specific amount. **Duration:** Annual. **To Apply:** Applicant must submit a completed application with official transcripts from undergraduate and graduate schools; a resume; research description (one page); career objective (one page); Title and Abstract for presentation at the meeting; and two completed recommendation forms (at least 1 must be from thesis advisor). Application materials must be submitted electronically. **Deadline:** June 30.

6695 ■ Dolphus E. Milligan Graduate Fellowships *(Graduate/Fellowship)*

Purpose: To support outstanding minority graduate students who have made significant contributions to science and/or engineering research. **Focus:** Biology; Chemistry; Engineering, Chemical; Life sciences. **Qualif.:** Applicant must be a U.S. citizen and will have completed undergraduate degrees in chemistry, chemical engineering, or a related discipline. **Criteria:** Fellowship winner will be selected after consideration of the finalists' records and presentations.

Funds Avail.: No specific amount. **Duration:** Annual. **To Apply:** Applicants must send an email communication to the NOBCChE Awards Committee Chair expressing an intention to apply for a Milligan Fellowship. Include as an attachment a written description of research (up to 3 pages, extended abstract format okay) conducted by the applicant prior to obtaining a degree from an undergraduate program of study. All email contacts should have NOBCChE Fellowship and the applicant's surname on the subject line and should be submitted to nobccheawards@gmail.com. Submit a complete application for admission to the graduate program of the Department of Chemistry and Biochemistry, University of Maryland, College Park via the following on-line application link: www.chem.umd.edu/GraduateProgram/application.php. **Deadline:** November 2.

6696 ■ NOBCChE Procter and Gamble Fellowships *(Graduate/Fellowship)*

Purpose: To support outstanding minority graduate students who have made significant contributions to science and/or engineering research. **Focus:** Biology; Chemistry; Engineering, Chemical; Life sciences. **Qualif.:** Applicant must be a candidate in a PhD program for Chemistry, Chemical Engineering, Biology, or Life Sciences; be in at least second year of graduate study; and be enrolled in the PhD program for the Fall/Spring academic year. **Criteria:** Selection is based on the application.

Funds Avail.: No specific amount. **To Apply:** Applicant must submit a completed application with official transcripts from undergraduate and graduate schools; a resume; research description (one page); career objective (one page); Title and Abstract for presentation at the meeting; and two completed recommendation forms (at least 1 must be from thesis advisor). Application materials must be submitted electronically. **Deadline:** November 2.

6697 ■ Lendon N. Pridgen, GlaxoSmithKline - NOBCChE Fellowships *(Graduate/Fellowship)*

Purpose: To support outstanding minority graduate students who have made significant contributions to science and/or engineering research. **Focus:** Chemistry. **Qua-**

Awards are arranged alphabetically below their administering organizations

lif.: Applicant must be in the third or fourth year of graduate study and majoring in Synthetic Organic Chemistry. **Criteria:** Selection is based on the application.

Funds Avail.: No specific amount. **Duration:** Annual. **To Apply:** Applicant must submit a completed application with official transcripts from undergraduate and graduate schools; a resume; research description (one page); career objective (one page); Title and Abstract for presentation at the meeting; and two completed recommendation forms (at least 1 must be from thesis advisor). Application materials must be submitted electronically.

6698 ■ Eastman Kodak Dr. Theophilus Sorrell Fellowships *(Graduate/Fellowship)*

Purpose: To support outstanding minority graduate students who have made significant contributions to science and/or engineering research. **Focus:** Biology; Chemistry; Engineering, Chemical; Life sciences. **Qualif.:** Applicant must be a candidate in a PhD program for Chemistry, Chemical Engineering, Biology, or Life Sciences; be in at least second year of graduate study; and be enrolled in the PhD program for the Fall/Spring academic year. **Criteria:** Selection is based on the application.

Funds Avail.: No specific amount. **Duration:** Annual. **To Apply:** Applicant must submit a completed application with official transcripts from undergraduate and graduate schools; a resume; research description (one page); career objective (one page); Title and Abstract for presentation at the meeting; and two completed recommendation forms (at least 1 must be from thesis advisor). Application materials must be submitted electronically.

6699 ■ National Orientation Directors Association (NODA)

2829 University Ave., Ste. 415
Minneapolis, MN 55414
Ph: (612)301-6632
Fax: (612)627-0153
Free: 866-521-6632
E-mail: noda@umn.edu
URL: www.nodaweb.org

6700 ■ Norman K. Russell Scholarships *(Graduate/Scholarship)*

Purpose: To recognize and assist graduate or doctoral students who have demonstrated a strong commitment to orientation, retention and transition, who will contribute to the enhancement of the orientation field, and who are currently enrolled as graduate students in orientation-related fields. **Focus:** General studies/Field of study not specified. **Qualif.:** Applicants must be enrolled in a graduate program in orientation-related fields. **Criteria:** Selection shall be based on the aforementioned qualifications and compliance with the application details.

Funds Avail.: $1,000 each. **Duration:** Annual. **Number Awarded:** 3. **To Apply:** Applicants must submit a Norman K. Russell Scholarship application form; a statement (double-spaced, three pages); a resume; an official transcript (must state enrollment in a graduate program, or graduation from a graduate program); official verification of present enrollment; and two letters of recommendations **Deadline:** September 15.

6701 ■ National Parking Association (NPA)

1112 16th St. NW, Ste. 840
Washington, DC 20036

Ph: (202)296-4336
Fax: (202)296-3102
Free: 800-647-7275
E-mail: info@npapark.org
URL: www.npapark.org

6702 ■ Parking Industry Institute Scholarship Program *(Undergraduate/Scholarship)*

Purpose: To provide financial aid to support the association's commitment to advance educational opportunities. **Focus:** General studies/Field of study not specified. **Qualif.:** Applicants must be undergraduate students enrolled at an accredited two or four year college/university; a child or spouse of a full-time employee of a firm which is a member of the National Parking Association; a full-time or part-time employee of a firm which is a member of the National Parking Association. **Criteria:** Applicants will be selected on the basis of merits as well as scholastic and extracurricular achievement.

Funds Avail.: $500-$3,000. **Duration:** One year. **To Apply:** Applicants must submit (four pages) application form; statement outlining goals, accomplishments and community involvement; official transcripts; and three letters of recommendation. Copy of acceptance letter is required for those freshmen and transferee applicants. **Deadline:** April 1.

6703 ■ National Pest Management Association (NPMA)

10460 North St.
Fairfax, VA 22030
Ph: (703)352-6762
Fax: (703)352-3031
Free: 800-678-6722
URL: www.npmapestworld.org

6704 ■ Professional Women in Pest Management Scholarships *(Graduate, Other/Scholarship)*

Purpose: To support a female interested in advancing or securing a career in the pest management industry. **Focus:** Pesticide science. **Qualif.:** Applicants must be women who are currently employed in the pest management industry; and have a minimum of two years experience in the industry. **Criteria:** Selection shall be based on the aforementioned applicants' qualifications and compliance with the application details.

Funds Avail.: Minimum of $1,000 plus $500 travel expenses. **Duration:** Annual. **Number Awarded:** 1. **To Apply:** Applicants must submit a resume with work experience; essay (500-1,000 words maximum of 2 pages); and two letters of recommendation. **Deadline:** June 15. **Contact:** Dominique Stumpf, CMP, Professional Women in Pest Management, c/o NPMA, 10460 North Street, Fairfax, VA 22030.

6705 ■ National Physical Science Consortium (NPSC)

3716 S Hope St., Ste. 348
Los Angeles, CA 90007-4344
Ph: (213)743-2409
Fax: (213)821-6329
Free: 800-854-NPSC
E-mail: npsc@npsc.org
URL: www.npsc.org

Awards are arranged alphabetically below their administering organizations

6706 ■ NPSC Fellowships (Graduate/Fellowship)

Purpose: To increase the number of American citizens with graduate degrees in the physical sciences and related engineering fields, emphasizing recruitment of a diverse applicant pool. **Focus:** Astronomy and astronomical sciences; Chemistry; Computer and information sciences; Engineering, Chemical; Engineering, Electrical; Engineering, Mechanical; Geology; Materials research/science; Physics. **Qualif.:** Applicants must be qualified U.S. citizens who have the ability to pursue graduate work at an NPSC member institution. Applicants at any stage of their graduate program may apply, as long as they will be available to accept two summers of paid internship. **Criteria:** Selection shall be based on academic standing (GPA), undergraduate and graduate course work and grades, research experience at a university or the industry, letters of recommendation, and GRE general tests.

Funds Avail.: $26,000 per annum. **Duration:** Annual; up to 6 years. **Number Awarded:** Varies. **To Apply:** Applicants must complete the online application. **Deadline:** November 30. **Remarks:** Established in 1989. **Contact:** National Physical Science Consortium, at the above address.

6707 ■ National Potato Council (NPC)

1300 L St. NW, Ste. 910
Washington, DC 20005
Ph: (202)682-9456
Fax: (202)682-0333
E-mail: spudinfo@nationalpotatocouncil.org
URL: nationalpotatocouncil.org

6708 ■ NPC Scholarships (Graduate/Scholarship)

Purpose: To assist a student conducting research for the benefit of the potato industry. **Focus:** Agribusiness; Engineering, Agricultural. **Qualif.:** Applicants must be graduate students pursuing advanced studies in Agribusiness that supports of the potato industry. **Criteria:** Selection is based on academic achievement, leadership abilities and potato-related areas of graduate study.

Funds Avail.: $10,000. **Duration:** Annual. **Number Awarded:** 1. **To Apply:** Applicants must submit a completed scholarship application form along with an essay (maximum of 200 words), undergraduate and graduate transcripts with cumulative GPA; resume; a list of activities (if applicable), and a list of names and contact information for the references. **Deadline:** June 30. **Contact:** National Potato Council, at the above address.

6709 ■ National Poultry and Food Distributors Association (NPFDA)

2014 Osborne Rd.
Saint Marys, GA 31558
Ph: (678)850-9311
Fax: (770)535-7385
E-mail: kkm@npfda.org
URL: www.npfda.org

6710 ■ National Poultry and Food Distributors Association Scholarships (Undergraduate/Scholarship)

Purpose: To help build "people resources" for the poultry and food industries. **Focus:** Agribusiness; Agricultural sciences; Agriculture, Economic aspects; Food science and technology; Poultry science. **Qualif.:** Applicant must be a full time junior or senior at a U.S. institution for the upcoming award year, and must be pursuing a poultry or related agricultural degree. **Criteria:** Recipients are selected based on the committee's review of their application.

Funds Avail.: $2,000. **Duration:** Entire length of study. **To Apply:** Applicant must submit an application form; official transcript; letter of recommendation from his/her Dean; and a one-page letter describing his/her goals and aspirations. **Deadline:** May 31. **Remarks:** Established in 1979. **Contact:** Application form and supporting documents must be submitted to NPFDA Scholarship Foundation Inc., 2014 Osborne Rd., Saint Marys, GA 31558.

6711 ■ National Preservation Institute (NPI)

PO Box 1702
Alexandria, VA 22313
Ph: (703)765-0100
E-mail: info@npi.org
URL: www.npi.org

6712 ■ National Preservation Institute Scholarships (Professional development/Scholarship)

Purpose: To provide financial assistance to individuals who wish to attend the NPI seminars. **Focus:** General studies/Field of study not specified. **Qualif.:** Applicants must work at least 20 hours a week (paid or volunteer) at the organization that they will represent; must be full-time students. **Criteria:** Recipient will be selected based on the eligibility criteria. Preference will be given to applicants from nonprofit institutions or from diverse ethnic or racial backgrounds or representing ethnic-specific institutions, or to full-time students.

Funds Avail.: No specific amount. **Duration:** Annual. **To Apply:** Interested applicants are advised to visit the website to obtain an application form.

6713 ■ National Press Photographers Association (NPPA)

3200 Croasdaile Dr., Ste. 306
Durham, NC 27705-2588
Ph: (919)383-7246
Fax: (919)383-7261
E-mail: info@nppa.org
URL: nppa.org

6714 ■ Bob Baxter Scholarships (Graduate, Undergraduate/Scholarship)

Purpose: To support students' educational goals. **Focus:** Journalism; Photography. **Qualif.:** Applicants must be full-time students at a school in the United States and intend to pursue a career in photojournalism. **Criteria:** Recipients are selected based on academic standing and financial need.

Funds Avail.: $2,000. **To Apply:** Applicants must submit a cover letter with contact information and list of school(s) attended; references; and portfolio with six or more photos. Picture editors must send three tearsheets. Video journalists must submit tape of three short but complete stories. **Deadline:** March 2.

6715 ■ Reid Blackburn Scholarships (Undergraduate/Scholarship)

Purpose: To support students' educational goals. **Focus:** Journalism; Photography. **Qualif.:** Applicants must be cur-

Awards are arranged alphabetically below their administering organizations

rently enrolled full-time in an accredited four-year college or university in the US or Canada or have been accepted at a four-year institution to complete suspended studies; must be continuing in a program leading to bachelor's degree; and have at least one half year of undergraduate schooling remaining at time of award. **Criteria:** Recipients will be selected based on philosophy and goal statements.

Funds Avail.: $2,000. **To Apply:** Applicants must submit a portfolio with six or more photos. Picture editors must send three tearsheets. Video journalists must submit tape of three short but complete stories. Applicants must submit an essay stating the philosophy and goals of their work. **Deadline:** March 2.

6716 ■ Bob East Scholarships *(Graduate, Undergraduate/Scholarship)*

Purpose: To support students' educational goals. **Focus:** Journalism; Photography. **Qualif.:** Applicants must either be undergraduates in the first three-and-a-half years of college or planning to pursue postgraduate work; and must able to offer some indication of acceptance in such program. **Criteria:** Recipients will be chosen primarily on quality of their portfolio.

Funds Avail.: $2,000. **To Apply:** Applicants must submit five-single-image portfolio with six or more photos. Picture editors must send three tearsheets. Video journalists must submit tape of three short but complete stories. **Deadline:** March 2.

6717 ■ Kit C. King Graduate Scholarships *(Graduate/Scholarship)*

Purpose: To support students' educational goals. **Focus:** Journalism; Photography. **Qualif.:** Applicants must be pursuing an advanced degree in journalism with an emphasis in photojournalism; must have some indication of acceptance to such accredited graduate programs in photojournalism. **Criteria:** Recipients are selected based on the academic standing, financial need and quality of the portfolio.

Funds Avail.: $2,000. **To Apply:** Applicants must submit portfolio with six or more photos stating their goals and philosophy relating to documentary photojournalism. Picture editors must send three tearsheets. For picture portfolios, slide duplicates are preferred. Video journalists must submit tape of three short but complete stories. **Deadline:** March 2.

6718 ■ NPPF Still and Multimedia Scholarships *(Undergraduate/Scholarship)*

Purpose: To promote the study of press photography and research and support students educational goals. **Focus:** Journalism; Photography. **Qualif.:** Applicants must have completed a one year study in photojournalism at a recognized four-year college or university; must be continuing in a program leading to a bachelor's degree; and have at least one half of undergraduate schooling remaining at the time of award. **Criteria:** Recipients are selected based on academic standing, financial need and quality of the portfolio.

Funds Avail.: $2,000. **To Apply:** Applicants must submit a portfolio with six or more photos and state their goals and philosophy relating to documentary photojournalism. Picture editors must send three tearsheets. Video journalists must submit tape of three short but complete stories. **Deadline:** March 2.

6719 ■ NPPF TV News Scholarships *(Undergraduate/Scholarship)*

Purpose: To support students' educational goals. **Focus:** Journalism; Photography. **Qualif.:** Applicants must be enrolled in a recognized four-year college or university with courses in TV news photojournalism; must be continuing in a program leading to a bachelor's degree; and must be in their junior or senior year at the time award is given. **Criteria:** Recipients are selected based on academic standing, financial need and quality of the portfolio.

Funds Avail.: $2,000. **To Apply:** Applicants must submit a portfolio with six or more photos. Picture editors must send three tearsheets. Video journalists must submit a tape of three short but complete stories. Applicants must complete the entry form and submit it along with a videotape containing examples of his or her work; and include (one-page) biographical sketch including a personal statement addressing their professional goals. **Deadline:** March 2.

6720 ■ National Private Truck Council (NPTC)
950 N Glebe Rd., Ste. 2300
Arlington, VA 22203-4183
Ph: (703)683-1300
Fax: (703)683-1217
URL: www.nptc.org

6721 ■ CTP Scholarship Program *(Other/Scholarship)*

Purpose: To promote continuous learning and professional development by providing financial aid for individuals lacking the necessary corporate funding to pursue the CTP designation. **Focus:** Management; Transportation. **Qualif.:** Applicants must: be members in good standing of the National Private Truck Council; be currently employed in a fleet management position; have at least five years of fleet management experience; and, be able to fully participate in all offerings included in the CTP Scholarship. **Criteria:** Recipients who will get the highest score on the following: letters of recommendation; community involvement; work and professional activities; and originality of essay will be selected.

Funds Avail.: Amount varies. **Duration:** Annual. **To Apply:** Applicants must submit a resume which indicates the candidate's history of accomplishments, active participation in transportation/logistics organizations, a continuing pursuit of knowledge and learning and participation in community service or volunteer organizations; two letters of recommendation from a member of the NPTC or from a management personnel within the candidate's company who is familiar with the candidate's job performance; an original essay (not less than 300 words) on "Why I Want a Certified Transportation Professional (CTP) Scholarship." **Deadline:** September 1. **Contact:** Mail complete application to: Institute for Truck Transportation Management, 2200 Mill Rd., Ste. 350, Alexandria, VA 22314.

6722 ■ National Public Employer Labor Relations Association (NPELRA)
1012 S Coast Hwy., Ste. M
Oceanside, CA 92054-5063
Ph: (760)433-1686
Fax: (760)433-1687
Free: 877-673-5721
E-mail: info@npelra.org
URL: www.npelra.org

Awards are arranged alphabetically below their administering organizations

6723 ■ The Anthony C. Russo Scholarships
(Graduate/Scholarship)

Purpose: To provide financial assistance to deserving graduate students studying labor and employee relations or a closely related field. **Focus:** Industrial and labor relations. **Qualif.:** Applicants must be U.S. citizens who are graduate students currently enrolled and seeking a graduate degree in human resources, labor and industrial relations, public administration or political science, with a strong and documented interest in the public sector. **Criteria:** Recipients will be selected based on financial need.

Funds Avail.: No specific amount. **To Apply:** Applicants must submit application form with neatly typed information; resume; recommendations from at least two faculty members; and final undergraduate transcript and most recent graduate school transcript. **Remarks:** Established in 1996.

6724 ■ NPELRA Foundation - Anthony C. Russo Scholarships *(Graduate/Scholarship)*

Purpose: To provide worthy graduate students interested in a career in public sector labor and employee relations with financial assistance. **Focus:** Industrial and labor relations; Personnel administration/human resources; Political science; Public administration. **Qualif.:** Applicants must be students currently enrolled in graduate studies in human resources, labor and industrial relations, public administration or political science with strong documented interest in the public sector. **Criteria:** Recipients will be selected on an objective and nondiscriminatory basis.

Funds Avail.: $3,000. **To Apply:** Applicants must submit a completed application form and other required information and materials for the award. **Deadline:** September 30.

6725 ■ National Recreation and Park Association (NRPA)
22377 Belmont Ridge Rd.
Ashburn, VA 20148-4501
Ph: (703)858-0784
Free: 800-262-6772
E-mail: customerservice@nrpa.org
URL: www.nrpa.org

6726 ■ National Recreation and Park Association Diversity Scholarships *(Undergraduate/Scholarship)*

Purpose: To support individuals from historically underrepresented groups in the parks as well as those that demonstrate outstanding contributions serving diverse communities with hopes of engaging their interest in future leadership roles. **Focus:** Parks and recreation. **Qualif.:** Applicants must be ethnic minorities; be professional, citizen or student members of NRPA at the time of application; be currently employed as professionals in parks and recreation agency or students currently enrolled in a park and recreation degree program. **Criteria:** Recipients are selected based on their compliance with basic eligibility requirements set by the National Recreation and Park Association.

Funds Avail.: $1,000. **Duration:** Annual. **Number Awarded:** 2. **To Apply:** Applicants must submit an application form; two references; and letters of recommendation directly to the National Recreation and Park Association. **Deadline:** May 11.

6727 ■ National Restaurant Association Educational Foundation (NRAEF)
2055 L St. NW
Washington, DC 20036
Free: 800-424-5156
E-mail: scholars@nraef.org
URL: www.nraef.org

6728 ■ Al Schuman Ecolab Undergraduate Entrepreneurial Scholarships *(Undergraduate/Scholarship)*

Purpose: To support students pursuing an education in a restaurant, foodservice, or hospitality related major. **Focus:** Food service careers. **Qualif.:** Applicants must be: citizens or permanent residents of the United States of America planning to attend full-time or substantial part-time in a foodservice related program; and, accepted or enrolled in the following schools: California State Polytechnic University Pomona, Cornell University, Culinary Institute of America, Johnson and Wales University, Kendall College, Lynn University, Michigan State University, New York University, Pennsylvania State University, Purdue University, University of Denver, University of Houston, University of Nevada (Las Vegas) or University of Massachusetts-Amherst. They must also have a minimum grade point average of 3.0. **Criteria:** Recipients are selected based on judges' review of application focusing on presentation, quality of essay, industry related work experience and strength of the recommendation letter(s).

Funds Avail.: One $5,500; One $3,500; Two $3,000. **Duration:** Annual. **Number Awarded:** Varies. **To Apply:** Applicants must submit an application packet which includes completed online application, an entrepreneurial project as described in the application, a copy of college curriculum with the number of credit hours detailed, transcript from current school or a copy of the GED certificate and three letters of recommendation from current or previous employer(s) in the restaurant and/or food service industries, current teachers/professors or personal references. **Deadline:** April 29. **Contact:** Call 800-765-2122 ext. 6744 or email at scholars@nraef.org.

6729 ■ National Roofing Contractors Association (NRCA)
10255 W Higgins Rd., Ste. 600
Rosemont, IL 60018-5607
Ph: (847)299-9070
Fax: (847)299-1183
URL: www.nrca.net

6730 ■ Melvin Kruger Endowed Scholarship Program *(Undergraduate, Vocational/Occupational/Scholarship)*

Purpose: To assist employees, immediate family of employees or immediate family of NRCA contractor members, who plan to pursue post-secondary education in college and vocational programs. **Focus:** General studies/Field of study not specified. **Qualif.:** Applicants must be full-time employees, dependent children or spouse of NRCA contractor or supplier member of the company who have a minimum of one year of employment with their company as of the application deadline date. Applicants must be high school seniors or graduates who plan to enroll or students who are already enrolled in a full-time undergraduate course of study at an accredited two or four year

Awards are arranged alphabetically below their administering organizations

college, university or vocational technical school. **Criteria:** Scholarship recipients are selected based on academic record, potential to succeed, leadership and participation in school and community activities, honors, work experience, a statement of educational and career goals, and an outside appraisal. Financial need is not considered. Final selection of recipients is made by the Alliance board of trustees.

Funds Avail.: $5,000. **Duration:** Four years. **To Apply:** Applicants must complete the application form on the website and mail it along with a current complete official transcript of grades to Scholarship Management Services. **Deadline:** January 31. **Contact:** Scholarship America, One Scholarship Way, PO Box 297, Saint Peter, MN, 56082.

6731 ■ National Science Foundation (NSF)
4201 Wilson Blvd.
Arlington, VA 22230
Ph: (703)292-5111
Free: 800-877-8339
E-mail: info@nsf.gov
URL: www.nsf.gov

6732 ■ EAPSI Fellowships *(Doctorate, Graduate/ Fellowship)*

Purpose: To provide educational opportunities for graduate students in science, education, and engineering. **Focus:** Behavioral sciences; Biological and clinical sciences; Computer and information sciences; Education; Engineering; Geosciences; Mathematics and mathematical sciences; Social sciences. **Qualif.:** Applicants must be U.S. citizens or permanent residents enrolled in a research-oriented master's PhD degree program at a U.S. institution; and pursuing studies in fields of sciences and engineering research and education supported by the NSF. **Criteria:** Selection shall be based on the aforementioned applicants' qualifications and compliance with the application details.

Funds Avail.: Amount varies. **Duration:** Annual. **Number Awarded:** Varies. **To Apply:** Applicants are required to register and apply online. All proposal materials must be submitted electronically via FastLane. **Deadline:** November 13. **Contact:** National Science Foundation, at the above address.

6733 ■ National Science Foundation Graduate Research Fellowship Program (NSF-GRFP) *(Graduate/Fellowship)*

Purpose: To help ensure the vitality and diversity of the scientific and engineering workforce of the United States; and to support also the graduate level students pursuing their own degrees. **Focus:** Engineering; Science; Technology. **Qualif.:** Applicants must be Graduate level students. **Criteria:** Selection will be based on the committee's criteria.

Duration: Annual. **To Apply:** Interested applicants may visit the website to obtain an application form and other related information. **Remarks:** Established in 1952. **Contact:** GRF Operations Center; Email: info@nsfgrfp.org.

6734 ■ National Science Foundation - Directorate for Social, Behavioral, and Economic Sciences - Division of Social and Economic Sciences - Political Science Program
4201 Wilson Blvd., Rm. 995N
Arlington, VA 22230
Ph: (703)292-7284

Fax: (703)292-9195
URL: www.nsf.gov/funding/pgm_summ.jsp?pims_id=5418

6735 ■ Doctoral Dissertation Research Improvement Grants Solicitation *(Doctorate/Grant)*

Purpose: To support research projects on various issues or topics related to the field of political science or politics itself such as campaigns and elections, electoral choice, and electoral systems; citizen support in emerging and established democracies; democratization, political change and anything else. **Focus:** Political science. **Qualif.:** Applicants must be doctoral students. **Criteria:** Proposals will be judged based on their scientific merit, including the theoretical importance of the research question and the appropriateness of the proposed data and methodology to be used in addressing the question.

Duration: Annual. **To Apply:** Interested applicants may contact the Foundation for the application process and other information, **Deadline:** August 15.

6736 ■ National Sculpture Society (NSS)
75 Varick St., 11th Fl.
New York, NY 10013
Ph: (212)764-5645
Fax: (212)764-5651
URL: www.nationalsculpture.org

6737 ■ Alex J. Ettl Grants *(Other/Grant)*

Purpose: To honor sculptors who demonstrate commitment and exceptional ability in their work. **Focus:** Sculpture. **Qualif.:** Applicants must be U.S. citizens; and must be figurative or realist sculptors who are not elected members of the National Sculpture Society (NSA). **Criteria:** Awards are given based on quality of the materials submitted.

Funds Avail.: $5,000. **Duration:** One year. **To Apply:** Applicants must submit at least 12 images of their work (at least ten different works). These images should be submitted in a CD in JPEG format, 72 dpi resolution and approximately 1500 pixels long; a list stating the title, medium and dimensions of the works and a brief biographical sketch or resume. Applicants must also obtain a biography, resume and any other pertinent information. These can be in the form of a Word or PDF file in the CD. **Deadline:** October 1.

6738 ■ National Sculpture Society Scholarships *(Undergraduate/Scholarship)*

Purpose: To provide financial assistance to individuals studying figurative or representational sculpture. **Focus:** Sculpture. **Qualif.:** Applicant must be enrolled in a sculpture school. **Criteria:** Awards are given based on quality of the materials submitted.

Funds Avail.: $150. **Number Awarded:** 10. **To Apply:** Applicants must submit a letter of application including a brief biography and background in sculpture; two letters of recommendation; 10 to 18 images of work on CD with at least five works shown; and a proof of financial need. **Deadline:** April 1.

6739 ■ National Sheriffs' Association (NSA)
1450 Duke St.
Alexandria, VA 22314-3490
Ph: (703)836-7827
Fax: (703)838-5349
Free: 800-424-7827

Awards are arranged alphabetically below their administering organizations

E-mail: nsamail@sheriffs.org
URL: www.sheriffs.org

6740 ■ National Sheriffs' Association Scholarship Program *(Graduate, Undergraduate/Scholarship)*

Purpose: To provide educational assistance to employees of a sheriff's office or their dependents. **Focus:** Criminal justice; Law. **Qualif.:** Applicant must be applying or enrolled in an undergraduate or graduate college program majoring in a criminal justice-related subject area; must be employed by a sheriff's office or a dependent of an individual employed by a sheriff's office; and must not be a previous recipient of the NSA scholarship. **Criteria:** Scholarship is granted to applicants with complete requirements as reviewed by the NSA Awards and Scholarship Committee.

Funds Avail.: No specific amount. **Duration:** Two years. **To Apply:** Applicants must provide a completed Official NSA scholarship application form available at the website; a transcript from high school or college (if already attending college); two letters of recommendation (one must be from a principal, teacher, guidance counselor, or advisor); endorsement letter from the sheriff of applicant's county; statement of financial need; and an essay (minimum of 500 words) stating why does an applicant deserves the scholarship and describing the greatest challenge does sheriffs faces today. Required materials must be photocopied and forwarded to the NSA Awards and Scholarship Committee together with the application form. **Deadline:** March 14. **Contact:** Submissions and questions should be directed to Susan Crow; Phone: 703-838-5335; E-mail: scrow@sheriffs.org.

6741 ■ National Slovak Society of the United States of America (NSS)

351 Valley Brook Rd.
McMurray, PA 15317-3337
Ph: (724)731-0094
Fax: (724)731-0145
Free: 800-488-1890
E-mail: info@nsslife.org
URL: nsslife.org

6742 ■ National Slovak Society Senior Scholarships *(Undergraduate, Vocational/Occupational/Scholarship)*

Purpose: To encourage older members to continue their education and to make fuller use of their leisure time. **Focus:** Education, Vocational-technical; Nursing. **Qualif.:** Applicants must be members of the National Slovak Society; must be 55 years and above; must be enrolled and successfully completed a continuing education or adult education course. Continuing education classes for the attainment or maintenance of a degree or certification are not qualified. **Criteria:** Applications are reviewed by the National Officer.

Funds Avail.: One-half reimbursement of the tuition, limited up to $200. **Duration:** Annual; up to four years. **Number Awarded:** Varies. **To Apply:** Applicants must enroll and pay for the course of their choice, after the applicants have finished the class, they must submit an application, along with the verification that the class was successfully completed. **Deadline:** May 1. **Remarks:** Established in 1966. **Contact:** NSS Home Office at 800-488-1890.

6743 ■ National Society of Accountants (NSA)

1010 N Fairfax St.
Alexandria, VA 22314

Ph: (703)549-6400
Fax: (703)549-2984
Free: 800-966-6679
E-mail: members@nsacct.org
URL: www.nsacct.org

6744 ■ National Society of Accountants Scholarship Program *(Undergraduate/Scholarship)*

Purpose: To assist college students pursuing an accounting major. **Focus:** Accounting. **Qualif.:** Applicant must be a full-time or part-time undergraduate student majoring in accounting at any U.S. accredited institution; must have a "B" (3.0 on a 4.0 scale) or better GPA; and must be a U.S. or Canadian citizen. **Criteria:** Recipients are selected on the basis of academic record, demonstrated leadership and participation in school and community activities, honors, work experience, statement of goals and aspirations, unusual personal or family circumstances and an outside appraisal. Financial need is also considered.

Funds Avail.: $2,000. **Duration:** Annual. **To Apply:** Applicants must complete the application form (available on the website) and mail it along transcript of records.

6745 ■ The Stanley H. Stearman Awards *(Undergraduate/Scholarship)*

Purpose: To provide financial assistance for students majoring in accounting. **Focus:** Accounting. **Qualif.:** Applicant must be a dependent or spouse, niece, nephew, son- or daughter-in-law of an active/retired, living or deceased NSA member. **Criteria:** Recipients are selected based on submitted application; academic record; demonstrated leadership; participation in school and community activities; honors; work experience; statements of goals and aspirations; personal or family circumstances; outside appraisal and financial need.

Funds Avail.: $2,000. **Duration:** Annual. **To Apply:** Applicants must complete the application form (available on the website) and mail it with a transcript of records. **Deadline:** January 1.

6746 ■ National Society of Black Physicists (NSBP)

3303 Wilson Blvd., Ste. 700
Arlington, VA 22201
Ph: (703)617-4176
Fax: (703)536-4203
E-mail: headquarters@nsbp.org
URL: www.nsbp.org

6747 ■ Michael P. Anderson Scholarships in Space Science *(Undergraduate/Scholarship)*

Purpose: To support interest in physics by providing educational assistance for skilled physics majors. **Focus:** Physics. **Qualif.:** Applicants must be physics majors in their junior or senior year. **Criteria:** Recipient is selected based on merit and evaluation of the applicant's scientific abilities and potential which includes versatility, ability to make sound judgments, major academic strengths and weaknesses (if any) and performance in an independent study (if any) as manifested through documents submitted.

Funds Avail.: $1,000. **Number Awarded:** 1. **To Apply:** Applicant must send the complete application package along with official transcripts and a stamped envelope. **Deadline:** December 1.

Awards are arranged alphabetically below their administering organizations

6748 ■ APS Scholarships for Minority Undergraduate Physics Majors *(Undergraduate/Scholarship)*

Purpose: To inspire pursuits in physics education specifically among minority undergraduates. **Focus:** Physics. **Qualif.:** Any African-American, Hispanic American, or Native American U.S. citizen or permanent resident who is majoring or planning to major in physics; a high school senior, college freshman, or sophomore is eligible to apply for the scholarship. **Criteria:** Recipient is selected based on the committee's review of their academic eligibility.

Funds Avail.: $2,000 (for new minority scholars); $3,000 (for renewal students) to be used for tuition, room & board and educational materials. **Duration:** Annual. **To Apply:** Applicants may download application materials in the website. **Remarks:** Established in 1980.

6749 ■ Harvey Washington Banks Scholarships in Astronomy *(Undergraduate/Scholarship)*

Purpose: To support interest in physics by providing educational assistance for skilled physics majors. **Focus:** Physics. **Qualif.:** Applicants must be physics majors in their junior or senior year. **Criteria:** Recipient is selected based on merit and evaluation of the applicant's scientific abilities and potential which includes versatility, ability to make sound judgments, major academic strengths and weaknesses (if any) and performance in an independent study (if any) as manifested through documents submitted.

Funds Avail.: $1,000. **To Apply:** Applicant must send the complete application package along with official transcripts and a stamped envelope. **Deadline:** December 1.

6750 ■ Charles S. Brown Scholarships in Physics *(Graduate, Undergraduate/Scholarship)*

Purpose: To inspire the next generation of physicians by providing financial assistance for individuals pursuing further studies in the field of physics. **Focus:** Physics. **Qualif.:** Graduate students and undergraduate students with a declared major in physics are eligible for this scholarship. **Criteria:** Recipient is selected based on merit and evaluation of the applicant's scientific abilities and potential which includes versatility, ability to make sound judgments, major academic strengths and weaknesses (if any) and performance in an independent study (if any) as manifested through documents submitted.

Funds Avail.: Not specific amount. **To Apply:** Applicant must send complete application package available in the website with official transcript and supply a stamped envelope. **Deadline:** December 1.

6751 ■ Robert A. Ellis Scholarships in Physics *(Undergraduate/Scholarship)*

Purpose: To support interest in physics by providing educational assistance for skilled physics majors. **Focus:** Physics. **Qualif.:** Applicants must be physics majors in their junior or senior year. **Criteria:** Recipient is selected based on merit and evaluation of the applicant's scientific abilities and potential which includes versatility, ability to make sound judgments, major academic strengths and weaknesses (if any) and performance in an independent study (if any) as manifested through documents submitted.

Funds Avail.: No specific amount. **To Apply:** Applicant must send the complete application package along with official transcripts and a stamped envelope. **Deadline:** December 1.

6752 ■ Elmer S. Imes Scholarships in Physics *(Undergraduate/Scholarship)*

Purpose: To support interest in physics by providing educational assistance for skilled physics majors. **Focus:** Physics. **Qualif.:** Applicants must be physics majors in their junior or senior year. **Criteria:** Recipient is selected based on merit and evaluation of the applicant's scientific abilities and potential which includes versatility, ability to make sound judgments, major academic strengths and weaknesses (if any) and performance in an independent study (if any) as manifested through documents submitted.

Funds Avail.: No specific amount. **To Apply:** Applicant must send the complete application package along with official transcripts and a stamped envelope. **Deadline:** December 1.

6753 ■ Walter Samuel McAfee Scholarships in Space Physics *(Undergraduate/Scholarship)*

Purpose: To support interest in physics by providing educational assistance for skilled physics majors. **Focus:** Physics. **Qualif.:** Applicants must be physics majors in their junior or senior year. **Criteria:** Recipient is selected based on merit and evaluation of the applicant's scientific abilities and potential which includes versatility, ability to make sound judgments, major academic strengths and weaknesses (if any) and performance in an independent study (if any) as manifested through documents submitted.

Funds Avail.: $1,000. **To Apply:** Applicant must send the complete application package along with official transcripts and a stamped envelope. **Deadline:** December 1.

6754 ■ Ronald E. McNair Scholarships in Space and Optical Physics *(Undergraduate/Scholarship)*

Purpose: To support interest in physics by providing educational assistance for skilled physics majors. **Focus:** Physics. **Qualif.:** Applicants must be physics majors in their junior or senior year. **Criteria:** Recipient is selected based on merit and evaluation of the applicant's scientific abilities and potential which includes versatility, ability to make sound judgments, major academic strengths and weaknesses (if any) and performance in an independent study (if any) as manifested through documents submitted.

Funds Avail.: $1,000. **To Apply:** Applicant must send the complete application package along with official transcripts and a stamped envelope. **Deadline:** December 1.

6755 ■ Willie Hobbs Moore Scholarships *(Undergraduate/Scholarship)*

Purpose: To support interest in physics by providing educational assistance for skilled physics majors. **Focus:** Physics. **Qualif.:** Applicants must be physics majors in their junior or senior year. **Criteria:** Recipient is selected based on merit and evaluation of the applicant's scientific abilities and potential which includes versatility, ability to make sound judgments, major academic strengths and weaknesses (if any) and performance in an independent study (if any) as manifested through documents submitted.

Funds Avail.: $1,000. **Number Awarded:** 1. **To Apply:** Applicant must send the complete application package along with official transcripts and a stamped envelope. **Deadline:** December 1.

6756 ■ Harry L. Morrison Scholarships *(Undergraduate/Scholarship)*

Purpose: To support interest in physics by providing educational assistance for skilled physics majors. **Focus:** Physics. **Qualif.:** Applicants must be physics majors in their junior or senior year. **Criteria:** Recipient is selected based on merit and evaluation of the applicant's scientific abilities and potential which includes versatility, ability to

Awards are arranged alphabetically below their administering organizations

make sound judgments, major academic strengths and weaknesses (if any) and performance in an independent study (if any) as manifested through documents submitted. **Funds Avail.:** $1,000. **To Apply:** Applicant must send the complete application package along with official transcripts and a stamped envelope. **Deadline:** December 1.

6757 ■ Arthur BC Walker Scholarships
(Undergraduate/Scholarship)

Purpose: To support interest in physics by providing educational assistance for skilled physics majors. **Focus:** Physics. **Qualif.:** Applicants must be physics majors in their junior or senior year. **Criteria:** Recipient is selected based on merit and evaluation of the applicant's scientific abilities and potential which includes versatility, ability to make sound judgments, major academic strengths and weaknesses (if any) and performance in an independent study (if any) as manifested through documents submitted. **Funds Avail.:** $1,000. **To Apply:** Applicant must send the complete application package along with official transcripts and a stamped envelope. **Deadline:** December 1.

6758 ■ National Society, Daughters of the American Revolution (DAR)
1776 D St. NW
Washington, DC 20006
Ph: (202)628-1776
E-mail: searchservice@dar.org
URL: www.dar.org/natsociety

6759 ■ Arthur Lockwood Beneventi Law Scholarships *(Undergraduate/Scholarship)*

Purpose: To award scholarship to students showing dedication to the pursuit of degrees in diverse disciplines including law. **Focus:** Law. **Qualif.:** Applicants must be students who are either enrolled in or attend an accredited law school and have a minimum GPA of 3.25. **Criteria:** Selection will be based on the committee's criteria.

Funds Avail.: $2,000. **To Apply:** Applications must complete and arranged the following in order: scholarship application; statement of 1,000 words or less setting forth career objectives; original transcript of high school or college grades. Major must be indicated on original transcript where specific major is required. Home schooled students must include transcripts for grade 9 through the current year; at least two but not to exceed four letters of recommendation from high school or college they are currently attending. Letter should cover applicant's ability, work habits, integrity, character, potential and volunteer activities. A letter from a sponsoring chapter is optional; list of extra-curricular activities, honors received and scholastic achievements; photocopy of United States citizenship, such as birth certificate, naturalization papers or information page of US Passport. Cover the applicant's photograph if they are submitting a copy of naturalization or passport pages; typed or computer generated financial needs form; self-addressed, stamped postcard. **Deadline:** February 15.

6760 ■ DAR Centennial Scholarship *(Undergraduate/Scholarship)*

Purpose: To support outstanding students pursuing a course of graduate study in the field of historic preservation at a college or university in the United States. **Focus:** Historic preservation. **Qualif.:** Applicants must be students who plan to pursue their course of graduate study in the

field of historic preservation. **Criteria:** Selection shall be based on the aforementioned qualifications and compliance with the application details.

Funds Avail.: $2,000. **Duration:** Annual. **To Apply:** Applicants must obtain a letter of sponsorship from their local DAR chapter. Application forms and other supporting documents must be completed correctly and submitted in one package. **Deadline:** February 15. **Remarks:** The scholarship was established from a portion of the proceeds from the sale of the Centennial Pin. **Contact:** National Vice Chair, DAR Centennial Scholarship, 10837 SW 80th CT Ocala, Florida 34481.

6761 ■ William Robert Findley Graduate Chemistry Scholarship *(Graduate/Scholarship)*

Purpose: To support students attending graduate school full time in any accredited college or university and majoring in chemistry. **Focus:** Chemistry. **Qualif.:** Applicants must be U.S. citizens; must be students attending graduate school full time in any accredited college or university and majoring in chemistry; must have a minimum GPA of 3.25. **Criteria:** Selection will be based on the committee's criteria.

Funds Avail.: $2,000. **Duration:** Annual. **Number Awarded:** 1. **To Apply:** Applicants must fill-up completely both DAR Scholarship Application Form and the Financial Need Form available at the website. The application packet must be completed and arranged in the following order: application form; statement of 1,000 words or less setting forth their career objectives; original transcript of high school (must indicate class rank, size and test scores) or college grades; all scholarships with a minimum GPA are based on a 4.0 scale or the equivalent GPA on the scale used by the applicable educational institution; letters of recommendation; list of extra-curricular activities, honors received and scholastic achievements; photocopy of US citizenship (birth certificate, naturalization papers or information page of US passport); financial need form; self-address, stamped postcard. **Deadline:** February 15. **Contact:** Submission of completed scholarship application form to: National Vice Chair William Robert Findley Graduate Chemistry Scholarship, 55 Longfellow Rd., Worcester, Massachusetts 01602.

6762 ■ Enid Hall Griswold Memorial Scholarships *(Undergraduate/Scholarship)*

Purpose: To encourage students to pursue an undergraduate degree. **Focus:** Economics; Government; History; Political science. **Qualif.:** Applicants must be juniors or seniors enrolled in an accredited college or university in the United States pursuing a major in political science, history, government, or economics. **Criteria:** Selection shall be based on the aforementioned qualifications and compliance with the application details.

Funds Avail.: $1,000. **Duration:** Annual. **Number Awarded:** 1. **To Apply:** Applicants must obtain a letter of sponsorship from their local DAR chapter. Application forms and other supporting documents must be completed correctly and submitted in one package. **Deadline:** February 15. **Contact:** National Vice Chair, Enid Hall Griswold Memorial Scholarship, 4242 Greentree Way Sand Springs, Oklahoma 74063.

6763 ■ Mary Elizabeth Lockwood Beneventi MBA Scholarship *(Graduate/Scholarship)*

Purpose: To support students attending graduate school in any accredited college or university. **Focus:** Business administration. **Qualif.:** Applicants must be U.S. citizens;

Awards are arranged alphabetically below their administering organizations

must be full-time students attending graduate school in any accredited college or university and majoring in business administration; must have a minimum GPA of 3.25. **Criteria:** Selection will be based on the committee's criteria.

Funds Avail.: $2,000. **Duration:** Annual. **Number Awarded:** 1. **To Apply:** Applicants must fill-up completely both DAR Scholarship Application Form and the Financial Need Form available at the website. The application packet must be completed and arranged in the following order: application form; statement of 1,000 words or less setting forth their career objectives; original transcript of high school (must indicate class rank, size and test scores) or college grades; all scholarships with a minimum GPA are based on a 4.0 scale or the equivalent GPA on the scale used by the applicable educational institution; letters of recommendation; list of extra-curricular activities, honors received and scholastic achievements; photocopy of US citizenship (birth certificate, naturalization papers or information page of US passport); financial need form; self-address, stamped postcard. **Deadline:** February 15. **Contact:** National Vice Chair Mary Elizabeth Lockwood Beneventi MBA Scholarship, at the above address.

6764 ■ Dr. Aura-Lee A. and James Hobbs Pittenger American History Scholarships (Undergraduate/Scholarship)

Purpose: To promote the study of American history among students. **Focus:** History, American. **Qualif.:** Applicants must be graduating high school students who will pursue an undergraduate degree with a concentrated study of a minimum of 24 credit hours in American History and American Government. **Criteria:** Selection shall be based on the aforementioned qualifications and compliance with the application details.

Funds Avail.: $2,000 per year. **Duration:** Annual; up to four years. **To Apply:** Applicants must obtain a letter of sponsorship from their local DAR chapter. Application forms and other supporting documents must be completed correctly and submitted in one package. **Deadline:** February 15. **Contact:** National Vice Chair, Dr. Aura-Lee A. and James Hobbs Pittenger American History Scholarship, 5134 29th Ave N Saint Petersburg, Florida 33710.

6765 ■ National Society of Genetic Counselors (NSGC)

330 N Wabash Ave., Ste. 2000
Chicago, IL 60611
Ph: (312)321-6834
Fax: (312)673-6972
E-mail: nsgc@nsgc.org
URL: www.nsgc.org

6766 ■ Jane Engelberg Memorial Fellowship (Professional development/Fellowship)

Purpose: To encourage and fund initiatives by board-certified genetic counselors who are members in good standing of the National Society of Genetic Counselors (NSGC) and by genetic counseling students enrolled in ACGC accredited training programs. **Focus:** Counseling/Guidance; Genetics. **Qualif.:** The principal investigator of a JEMF proposal must be a genetic counselor who is a full member in good standing of the NSGC and is certified in genetic counseling by the American Board of Medical Genetics or the American Board of Genetic Counseling; individuals who have been granted active-candidate status by the American Board of Genetic Counseling also are

eligible to apply for the JEMF.

Funds Avail.: $60,000. **Duration:** Annual. **Remarks:** Established in 1991.

6767 ■ National Society of High School Scholars (NSHSS)

1936 N Druid Hills Rd.
Atlanta, GA 30319
Ph: (404)235-5500
Fax: (404)235-5510
Free: 866-343-1800
URL: www.nshss.org

6768 ■ Abercrombie and Fitch Global Diversity Scholar Awards (High School/Scholarship)

Purpose: To support members to attain higher education. **Focus:** General studies/Field of study not specified. **Qualif.:** Applicants must be high school seniors and members of the NSHSS. **Criteria:** Selection is based on the submitted essay, and will be judged on ingenuity and quality; exploring their perspectives on the theme of diversity and inclusion.

Funds Avail.: $1,000. **Duration:** Annual. **Number Awarded:** 10. **To Apply:** Applicants must submit a completed application form and required materials. **Deadline:** May 16. **Contact:** Dr. Susan Thurman at 866-343-1800 or susan.thurman@nshss.org.

6769 ■ Claes Nobel Academic Scholarships for Members (High School/Scholarship)

Purpose: To support the education of student members. **Focus:** General studies/Field of study not specified. **Qualif.:** Applicants must be high school junior and senior student members. Applicants must submit a personal statement; resume of honors, awards, leadership activities, extracurricular activities, and community service; educator recommendation; transcript, and photo. **Criteria:** Selection is based on academic performance; demonstrated leadership; school and extracurricular activities; and community service.

Funds Avail.: $5,000 and $1,000. **Duration:** Annual. **Number Awarded:** 85. **To Apply:** Apply online by going to the member log in page. **Deadline:** March 15.

6770 ■ NSHSS Academic Paper Awards (High School/Scholarship)

Purpose: To support the education of student members. **Focus:** General studies/Field of study not specified. **Qualif.:** Applicant must be a NSHSS member. **Criteria:** Selection is based on the submitted materials such as a research paper, an original essay, or an analytical paper.

Funds Avail.: $250. **Duration:** One year. **Number Awarded:** 25. **To Apply:** Applicants must submit their written high school academic paper (research paper, original essay or analytical paper) accompanied by the Academic Paper Awards entry form. **Deadline:** May 2. **Remarks:** Applicants may submit one paper per year.

6771 ■ NSHSS National Scholar Awards (High School/Scholarship)

Purpose: To support the education of student members. **Focus:** General studies/Field of study not specified. **Qualif.:** Applicant must be a high school junior and senior student member. **Criteria:** Selection is based on academic

Awards are arranged alphabetically below their administering organizations

performance; demonstrated leadership; school and extra-curricular activities; and community service.

Funds Avail.: $1,000. **Duration:** Annually. **To Apply:** Apply online by going to the member log in page. **Deadline:** March 15. **Remarks:** Award will be given to selected finalist for the Class Nobel Academic Scholarships.

6772 ■ Robert P. Sheppard Leadership Awards
(High School/Scholarship)

Purpose: To support the education of student members. **Focus:** General studies/Field of study not specified. **Qualif.:** Applicant must be a high school student member. **Criteria:** Awards are given to the applicant who demonstrated outstanding commitment to community service and initiative in volunteer activities.

Funds Avail.: $2,500 for the winner; $1,000 for the top 4 finalists. **Duration:** Annual. **Number Awarded:** 5. **To Apply:** Applicants must submit a completed application form together with a personal statement; resume of honors, awards, leadership activities, extracurricular activities, and community service; educator recommendation; transcript, and photo. **Deadline:** March 1.

6773 ■ National Society of Hispanic MBAs (NSH-MBA)

450 E John Carpenter Fwy., Ste. 200
Irving, TX 75062
Ph: (214)596-9338
Fax: (214)596-9325
Free: 877-467-4622
URL: www.nshmba.org

6774 ■ NSHMBA Scholarships *(Graduate/Scholarship)*

Purpose: To assist qualified Hispanics to pursue MBAs. **Focus:** Business. **Qualif.:** Applicant must be a United States Citizen or Legal Permanent Resident; be of Hispanic heritage; have a minimum GPA of 3.0 on a 4.0 scale (or equivalent) from either a bachelor's degree or master's degree OR have a minimum GPA of 2.75 on a 4.0 scale (or equivalent) from a bachelor's degree in combination with two years of full-time work experience; a current NSHMBA member (Applicants who are not currently a NSHMBA member may apply); and be enrolled in a graduate business program in a college/university in the United States or Puerto Rico, accredited by the AACSB (AACSB International) at the time of award. **Criteria:** Selection is based on academic achievement, work experience, financial need, personal statement of goals and aspirations, community service, letters of recommendation, and NSHMBA ambassadorship.

Funds Avail.: $2,500 - $10,000. **To Apply:** Applicants must submit a completed online application and then mail all supporting documentation (undergraduate and graduate) official transcripts, and two letters of recommendation. **Deadline:** April 30. **Contact:** Julie Farlinger at the above address.

6775 ■ National Society for HistoTechnology (NSH)

8850 Stanford Blvd., Ste. 2900
Columbia, MD 21045
Ph: (443)535-4060
Fax: (443)535-4055

E-mail: histo@nsh.org
URL: www.nsh.org

6776 ■ Robert A. Clark Memorial Educational Scholarships *(Professional development/Scholarship)*

Purpose: To promote the study of histotechnology. **Focus:** Histology. **Qualif.:** Applicants must be pursuing advanced education and knowledge within the profession of histotechnology. **Criteria:** Recipients will be selected based on their sincere efforts and not necessarily upon academic merit.

Funds Avail.: $1,000. **Duration:** Annual. **To Apply:** Applicants must complete the online application and submit plans for utilization of a scholarship, up-to-date curriculum vitae and written evaluation of the applicant's supervisor, pathologist or director for the suitability of the candidates. **Deadline:** June 1.

6777 ■ Sakura Finetek Student Scholarships *(Undergraduate/Scholarship)*

Purpose: To promote the study of histotechnology. **Focus:** General studies/Field of study not specified. **Qualif.:** Applicants must be students from approved histotechnology schools. **Criteria:** Applicants will be selected according to their academic ability and financial need.

Funds Avail.: $500. **Duration:** Annual. **To Apply:** Applicants must complete online application and submit with supporting documentation. **Deadline:** February 26.

6778 ■ Irwin S. Lerner Student Scholarships *(Undergraduate/Scholarship)*

Purpose: To promote the study of histotechnology. **Focus:** General studies/Field of study not specified. **Qualif.:** Applicants must be students from approved histotechnology schools. **Criteria:** Applicants will be selected according to their academic ability and financial need.

Funds Avail.: $500. **Duration:** Annual. **To Apply:** Applicants must complete online application and submit with supporting documentation. **Deadline:** February 26.

6779 ■ Newcomer Supply Student Scholarships *(Undergraduate/Scholarship)*

Purpose: To promote the study of histotechnology. **Focus:** General studies/Field of study not specified. **Qualif.:** Applicants must be first time attendees or returning attendees that have not attended a meeting within the past five years; must be members in good standing of NSH. **Criteria:** Applicants will be selected according to their academic ability and financial need.

Funds Avail.: $500. **Duration:** Annual. **Number Awarded:** 1. **To Apply:** Applicants must complete online application and submit with supporting documentation. **Deadline:** April 1.

6780 ■ Leonard Noble Educational Scholarships *(Professional development/Scholarship)*

Purpose: To promote the study of histotechnology. **Focus:** Histology. **Qualif.:** Applicants must be pursuing advanced education and knowledge within the profession of histotechnology. **Criteria:** Recipients will be selected based on their sincere efforts and not necessarily upon academic merit.

Funds Avail.: $1,000. **Duration:** Annual. **Number Awarded:** 1. **To Apply:** Applicants must complete the online application and submit plans for utilization of a

Awards are arranged alphabetically below their administering organizations

scholarship, up-to-date curriculum vitae and written evaluation of the applicant's supervisor, pathologist or director for the suitability of the candidates. **Deadline:** June 1.

6781 ■ Sigma Diagnostics Student Scholarships
(Undergraduate/Scholarship)

Purpose: To provide educational scholarships and student scholarships for recipients on a reimbursement basis. **Focus:** General studies/Field of study not specified. **Qualif.:** The applicants must be students from approved histotechnology schools. **Criteria:** Recipients will be selected according to their academic ability and financial need.

Funds Avail.: No specific amount. **Duration:** Annual. **To Apply:** Applicants must complete online application and submit together with supporting documentation.

6782 ■ Thermo Scientific Educational Scholarships
(Professional development/Scholarship)

Purpose: To promote the study of histotechnology. **Focus:** Histology. **Qualif.:** Applicants must be pursuing advanced education and knowledge within the profession of histotechnology. **Criteria:** Recipients will be selected based on their sincere efforts and not necessarily upon academic merit.

Funds Avail.: $1,000. **Duration:** Annual. **Number Awarded:** 1. **To Apply:** Applicants must complete the online application and submit plans for utilization of a scholarship, up-to-date curriculum vitae and written evaluation of the applicant's supervisor, pathologist or director for the suitability of the candidates. **Deadline:** June 1.

6783 ■ Ventana Medical Systems In Situ Hybridization Awards *(Other/Award)*

Purpose: To provide educational scholarships on a reimbursement basis. **Focus:** Histology. **Qualif.:** Applicants must be pursuing an advanced education within the profession of histotechnology. **Criteria:** Recipient will be selected based on working achievement and/or academic merit.

Funds Avail.: $3,000. **Duration:** Annual. **To Apply:** Applicants must submit a proof of required certification for at least two members of the laboratory staff; up-to-date curriculum vitae for the same members; written evaluation by the laboratory director and/or pathologist as to the laboratory's suitability as the recipient of this award and educational value to the institution; and plans for the utilization which includes identification of educational event. Plans must be utilized within two years after the award is presented. **Deadline:** June 1.

6784 ■ National Society of Professional Surveyors (NSPS)
5119 Pegasus Ct., Ste. Q
Frederick, MD 21704
Ph: (240)439-4615
Fax: (240)439-4952
URL: www.nsps.us.com

6785 ■ NSPS Scholarships *(Undergraduate/Scholarship)*

Purpose: To support students for their college education in geospatial sciences. **Focus:** Cartography/Surveying. **Qualif.:** Applicants must be students enrolled full-time in undergraduate surveying programs. **Criteria:** Recipients will be selected based on their academic record, statement, letters of recommendation and professional activities.

Funds Avail.: $2,000. **Duration:** Annual. **Number Awarded:** Varies. **To Apply:** Applicants must complete the application form and must provide the following: proof of membership in NSPS or AAGS; a brief yet complete statement indicating educational objectives, future plans of study or research, professional activities and financial need; at least three letters of recommendation (minimum of two from faculty members familiar with the student's work); a complete original official transcript through year prior to when the award will be presented. **Deadline:** February 1. **Contact:** trisha.milburn@nsps.us.com.

6786 ■ National Space Biomedical Research Institute (NSBRI)
6500 Main St., Ste. 910
Houston, TX 77030-1402
Ph: (713)798-7412
Fax: (713)798-7413
E-mail: info@nsbri.org
URL: www.nsbri.org

6787 ■ National Space Biomedical Research Institute Postdoctoral Fellowships *(Postdoctorate/Fellowship)*

Purpose: To support talented scientists in conducting space-related biomedical or biotechnological research. **Focus:** Biomedical research. **Qualif.:** Applicants must be U.S. citizens, permanent residents or with pre-existing visas obtained through their sponsoring institutions that permit postdoctoral training for the project's duration. **Criteria:** Selection will be based on merit, need and includes allocation for health insurance.

Funds Avail.: No specific amount. **Duration:** Annual; two years. **To Apply:** Applicants must prepare a proposal with the support of a mentor. **Contact:** NSBRI's Postdoctoral Fellowship Program, at the above address.

6788 ■ National Space Club (NSC)
204 E St. NE
Washington, DC 20002
Ph: (202)547-0060
E-mail: info@spaceclub.org
URL: www.spaceclub.org

6789 ■ Dr. Robert H. Goddard Memorial Scholarships *(Graduate, Undergraduate/Scholarship)*

Purpose: To stimulate the interest of students in the opportunity to advance scientific knowledge through space research and exploration. **Focus:** Engineering; Science. **Qualif.:** Applicants must be U.S. citizens, at least junior years of an accredited university, and have the intention of pursuing undergraduate or graduate studies in science or engineering during the interval of the scholarship. **Criteria:** Recipients will be selected based on the NSC Committee on Scholarships' review of the application materials. Personal need is considered, but not the primary basis.

Funds Avail.: $10,000. **Duration:** Annual. **To Apply:** Applicants must submit an official transcript of college records; letters of recommendation from faculty; accomplishments demonstrating personal qualities of creativity and leadership; scholastic plans that would lead to future participation in some phase of the aerospace sciences and technology; and past research and participation in space-related science and engineering.

Awards are arranged alphabetically below their administering organizations

6790 ■ National Speleological Society (NSS)
6001 Pulaski Pike
Huntsville, AL 35810-1122
Ph: (256)852-1300
E-mail: nss@caves.org
URL: www.caves.org

6791 ■ NSS Sara Corrie Memorial Grants *(Professional development/Grant)*

Purpose: To support cave exploration in the U.S territories. **Focus:** Cave studies. **Qualif.:** Applicants must be NSS members at the time of application. **Criteria:** Selection shall be based on the aforementioned qualifications and compliance with the application details.

Funds Avail.: $250 each. **Duration:** Annual. **Number Awarded:** 6. **To Apply:** Applicants must send a letter to the Chairman of the U.S Exploration Committee explaining the importance and usage of the grant as well as the amount needed. **Contact:** Thomas Shifflett, Committee Chairman, 224 Barker Ln., Bluemont, VA 20135; Phone: 703-404-6323 (W); 540-535-8389 (C); E-mail: tommy.shifflett@toast.net.

6792 ■ NSS Conservation Grants *(Advanced Professional/Grant)*

Purpose: To support a cave conservation-linked research. **Focus:** Cave studies. **Qualif.:** Applicants must be individuals conducting a cave conservation-linked research, including student projects. **Criteria:** Selection is based on merit, impact of research and the qualifications of the applicant.

Funds Avail.: Up to $5,000. **Duration:** Annual. **To Apply:** Applicants are advised to visit the website to obtain an application process and other information. **Contact:** Val Hildreth-Werker, P.O. Box 207, Hillsboro, New Mexico 88042; Phone: 575-895-5050; E-mail: werks@cunacueva.com.

6793 ■ NSS Education Grants *(Undergraduate/Grant)*

Purpose: To promote cave and karst education programs for primary and secondary students. **Focus:** Cave studies. **Qualif.:** Applicants must be individuals or from private organizations. **Criteria:** Awards are given based on merit.

Funds Avail.: No specific amount. **Duration:** Semiannual. **To Apply:** Application form is available at the website. Applicants must submit the completed application form and send it electronically in MS Word or PDF file. **Deadline:** March and September. **Contact:** Education Division Chief, Pam Tegelman Malabad, 231 Price St., Blacksburg, VA 24060; Email: pam.teg.mal@gmail.com.

6794 ■ Ralph W. Stone Graduate Fellowships *(Graduate/Fellowship, Grant)*

Purpose: To support cave-related thesis research. **Focus:** Cave studies. **Qualif.:** Applicants must be NSS members currently pursuing graduate studies. **Criteria:** Recipients are selected based on the committee's review of submitted proposals.

Funds Avail.: $2,000. **Duration:** One year. **Number Awarded:** Two. **To Apply:** Applicants must send a proposal which includes a project description; a resume with NSS number; a transcript; two letters of recommendation (one from the thesis advisor); a budget and its justification. All materials must be attached into a single file (except letters of recommendation) using Word or Adobe Acrobat. **Deadline:** March 15. **Contact:** Dr. Donald A. McFarlane, NSS Research Advisory Committee Chm., e-mail: dmcfarla@jsd.claremont.edu.

6795 ■ National Sporting Clays Association (NSCA)
5931 Roft Rd.
San Antonio, TX 78253
Ph: (210)688-3371
Fax: (210)688-3014
Free: 800-877-5338
URL: www.nssa-nsca.org

6796 ■ NSSA/NSCA Collegiate Scholarships *(Undergraduate/Scholarship)*

Purpose: To support the education of a student active in sporting clays. **Focus:** General studies/Field of study not specified. **Qualif.:** Applicants must be: graduating high school seniors; NSCA/NSSA members; pursuing a 4-year degree program; and active NSCA registered sporting clays participants. **Criteria:** Selection is based on scholarship, citizenship and participation in NSCA activities.

Funds Avail.: $5,000. **Duration:** Four years. **Number Awarded:** 2. **To Apply:** Applicants must submit a completed Scholarship Application; an essay (100 words or less) explaining need of financial assistance; a letter of personal recommendation; copy of class rank/high school grades from the school registrar; and a copy of past shooting history and accomplishments. **Deadline:** May 31. **Contact:** Glynne Moseley.

6797 ■ National Stone, Sand and Gravel Association (NSSGA)
1605 King St.
Alexandria, VA 22314
Ph: (703)525-8788
Fax: (703)525-7742
URL: www.nssga.org

6798 ■ Jennifer Curtis Byler Scholarships *(Undergraduate/Scholarship)*

Purpose: To support a child of an aggregates industry employee who wishes to pursue collegiate studies in public policy, government affairs or related fields. **Focus:** Public affairs. **Qualif.:** Applicants must be graduating high school seniors or students already majoring in public policy, government affairs or related fields in college who are sons or daughters of an aggregates company employee may apply for the scholarship. **Criteria:** Scholarship applications will be reviewed and judged by a panel including the current NSSGA chairman of the Government Affairs Committee, a representative of the industry trade press and a senior NSSGA staff member.

Funds Avail.: $5,000. **Duration:** Annual. **To Apply:** To apply for the Jennifer Curtis Byler Scholarship, please complete the application form at the program website and include a letter of recommendation from the faculty advisor. If applicants do have work experience as summer employees, interns or through a cooperative work program, please include a letter of recommendation from the employer(s).

6799 ■ National Student Nurses' Association (NSNA)
45 Main St., Ste. 606
Brooklyn, NY 11201

Awards are arranged alphabetically below their administering organizations

Ph: (718)210-0705
Fax: (718)797-1186
E-mail: nsna@nsna.org
URL: www.nsna.org

6800 ■ The Foundation of the National Student Nurses' Association Scholarships (Graduate, Undergraduate/Scholarship)

Purpose: To promote education in nursing. **Focus:** Nursing. **Qualif.:** Applicant must be U.S. citizen enrolled in a State-approved school of nursing or pre-nursing in associate degree, baccalaureate, diploma, generic doctorate and generic master's programs; attending classes and taking no less than six credits per semester. **Criteria:** Selection is based on academic achievement; financial need; and involvement in nursing student organizations and community activities related to healthcare. A committee of faculty and students is appointed by the NSNA Foundation to select recipients.

Funds Avail.: $1,000-$2,500. **To Apply:** Applicant must submit a copy of recent nursing school and college transcripts; proof of membership (for NSNA members); and a copy of RN license (if applicable). Completed applications must be accompanied by $10 processing fee. **Deadline:** January 16. **Remarks:** In Memory of Frances Tompkins. **Contact:** FNSNA at 718-210-0705.

6801 ■ National Swimming Pool Foundation (NSPF)

4775 Granby Cir.
Colorado Springs, CO 80919
Ph: (719)540-9119
Fax: (719)540-2787
E-mail: info@nspf.org
URL: www.nspf.org

6802 ■ NSPF Ray B. Essick Scholarship Awards (Other/Scholarship)

Purpose: To encourage healthier living through aquatic education and research. **Focus:** Health education. **Qualif.:** Applicant must be a Certified Pool/Spa Operator; a Certified Pool/Spa Operator Instructor; or have an immediate family member possessing CPO certification. **Criteria:** Selection is based on the applications and supporting materials.

Funds Avail.: $2,000. **Duration:** Annual. **Number Awarded:** 1. **To Apply:** Application form is available at the website. Applicant must prepare a biographical sketch (maximum of 300 words); a resume; a 2″ x 3″ photograph; an essay of no more than five double-spaced, 12 font size, type-written pages; official academic transcripts; a copy of recent SAT or ACT scores; and two letters of recommendation from teachers or college professors. **Deadline:** June 1.

6803 ■ National Swimming Pool Foundation Scholarship Awards (Other/Scholarship)

Purpose: To encourage healthier living through aquatic education and research. **Focus:** Health education. **Qualif.:** Applicants must be Certified Pool/Spa Operators; be Certified Pool/Spa Operator Instructors; or have an immediate family member possessing CPO certification. **Criteria:** Selection shall be based on the aforementioned qualifications and compliance with the application details.

Funds Avail.: $1,000 each. **Duration:** Annual. **Number**

Awarded: 12. **To Apply:** Application form is available at the website. Applicant must prepare a biographical sketch (maximum of 300 words); a resume; a 2″ x 3″ photograph; an essay of no more than five double-spaced, 12 font size, type-written pages; official academic transcripts; a copy of recent SAT or ACT scores; two letters of recommendation from teachers or college professors. **Deadline:** June 1.

6804 ■ National Taxidermists Association (NTA)

PO Box 549
Green Forest, AR 72638
Ph: (855)772-8543
Fax: (870)438-4218
E-mail: info@nationaltaxidermists.com
URL: www.nationaltaxidermists.com

6805 ■ Charlie Fleming Education Fund Scholarships (Undergraduate/Scholarship)

Purpose: To provide cash scholarships for qualified NTA members or their dependents to further their education in Taxidermy; to attain higher education. **Focus:** Taxonomy. **Qualif.:** Applicants must be NTA members and/or their children; member must be in the third year of continuous NTA membership. **Criteria:** Recipients are selected based on the scholarship committee's review of all applications.

Funds Avail.: No specific amount. **To Apply:** Applicants must complete application form and file a statement outlining the reasons for furthering their education, as well as an explanation of how this education will benefit their future in the field of taxidermy.

6806 ■ National Technical Honor Society (NTHS)

PO Box 1336
Flat Rock, NC 28731
Ph: (828)698-8011
Fax: (828)698-8564
URL: www.nths.org

6807 ■ NTHS/HOSA Scholarships (Undergraduate/Scholarship)

Purpose: To promote career opportunities in health care; to enhance the delivery of quality healthcare to all people. **Focus:** Health care services. **Qualif.:** Applicants must be HOSA members who are also NTHS members in good standing. **Criteria:** Scholarship committee will evaluate the application based on the enrolled education; documents such as proof of acceptance into a program of health occupation/health science education for the following academic year, leadership activities and recognition, community involvement, references and personal statement.

Funds Avail.: $1,000. **Duration:** Annual. **Number Awarded:** 6. **To Apply:** Applicants may visit the Health Occupational Students of America website (www.hosa.org) for application process.

6808 ■ National Trust for Historic Preservation

2600 Virginia Ave., Ste. 1000
Washington, DC 20037
Ph: (202)588-6000
Free: 800-944-6847
E-mail: info@savingplaces.org
URL: www.preservationnation.org

Awards are arranged alphabetically below their administering organizations

6809 ■ Mildred Colodny Diversity Scholarships for Graduate Study in Historic Preservation (Graduate/Scholarship)

Purpose: To provide financial assistance to those students who are pursuing degrees in historic preservation. **Focus:** Historic preservation. **Qualif.:** Applicants must be in their final year of undergraduate study intending to enroll in a graduate program in historic preservation or must be graduate students enrolled in or intending to enroll in historic preservation programs; program of study must be at a U.S. university, college or institution; must be eligible to work in the United States. **Criteria:** Selection will be based partly on financial need; partly on application materials; academic performance; promise shown for future achievement; commitment to working in preservation in the United States following graduation; potential to help increase diversity within the preservation movement.

Funds Avail.: Up to $15,000. **Duration:** Annual. **To Apply:** Applicants must submit a completed application form; resume; two recommendation letters; appropriate academic transcripts. **Deadline:** February 28. **Contact:** David Field, Colodny Scholarship Coordinator at the above address; or via email at dfield@savingplaces.org.

6810 ■ National Union of Public and General Employees (NUPGE)
15 Auriga Dr.
Nepean, ON, Canada K2E 1B7
Ph: (613)228-9800
Fax: (613)228-9801
URL: www.nupge.ca

6811 ■ Aboriginal Canadians Scholarship
(Undergraduate/Scholarship)

Purpose: To support students who are planning to enter the first year of a Canadian public post-secondary education. **Focus:** General studies/Field of study not specified. **Qualif.:** Applicants must be Aboriginal Canadian citizens who plan to enter as full-time first-year students at any Canadian public post-secondary educational institutions; must be children, grandchildren or foster children of a NUPGE member.

Funds Avail.: 1,500 Canadian Dollars. **Duration:** Annual. **Deadline:** June 6.

6812 ■ Tommy Douglas Memorial Scholarship
(Undergraduate/Scholarship)

Purpose: To support students who plan to enter the first year of a Canadian public post-secondary education. **Focus:** General studies/Field of study not specified. **Qualif.:** Applicants must be Canadian citizens who plan to enter as full-time first-year students at any Canadian public post-secondary educational institutions; must be children, grandchildren or foster children of a NUPGE member.

Funds Avail.: 1,500 Canadian Dollars. **Duration:** Annual. **Deadline:** July 6.

6813 ■ Terry Fox Memorial Scholarship
(Undergraduate/Scholarship)

Purpose: To enhance the quality of life of people with disabilities. **Focus:** General studies/Field of study not specified. **Qualif.:** Applicants must be Canadian citizens with disabilities who plan to enter as full-time first-year students at any Canadian public post-secondary educational institutions; must be children, grandchildren or foster children of a NUPGE member.

Funds Avail.: 1,500 Canadian Dollars. **Duration:** Annual. **Deadline:** July 6.

6814 ■ Visible Minorities Scholarship
(Undergraduate/Scholarship)

Purpose: To support visible minority students who plan to enter the first year of a Canadian public post-secondary education. **Focus:** General studies/Field of study not specified. **Qualif.:** Applicants must be minority Canadian citizens who plan to enter as full-time first-year students at any Canadian public post-secondary educational institutions; must be children, grandchildren or foster children of a NUPGE member.

Funds Avail.: $1,500. **Duration:** Annual. **Deadline:** July 6.

6815 ■ National Urban Fellows (NUF)
1120 Avenue of the Americas, 4th Fl.
New York, NY 10036
Ph: (212)730-1700
Fax: (212)730-1823
E-mail: info@nuf.org
URL: www.nuf.org

6816 ■ NUF Fellowships (Graduate, Postgraduate, Other/Fellowship)

Purpose: To counter the under-representation of people of color and women in leadership positions. **Focus:** Public service. **Qualif.:** Applicant must be a U.S. citizen; have a bachelor's degree; have a minimum of 5 -7 years administrative or managerial employment; must meet the admission requirements of Baruch College; possess self-discipline and interpersonal and problem-solving skills; have a high standard of integrity and work ethic; and be committed to the solution of urban problems. **Criteria:** Selection is based on a combination of criteria including strong personal character, the highest standard of work ethic and integrity, self-discipline, and a positive attitude with a passion for equity and social justice.

Funds Avail.: $25,000. **Duration:** 14 months. **Number Awarded:** 40-50. **To Apply:** Applicants must submit a completed scholarship application form together with an updated resume and bio; career goal statements; official transcripts; and a non-refundable $150 application fee. Applicants must request three letters from academic and professional evaluators (typewritten on company or personal letterhead).

6817 ■ National Volunteer Fire Council (NVFC)
7852 Walker Dr., Ste. 375
Greenbelt, MD 20770
Ph: (202)887-5700
Fax: (202)887-5291
Free: 888-275-6832
E-mail: nvfcoffice@nvfc.org
URL: www.nvfc.org

6818 ■ Junior Firefighter Scholarships
(Undergraduate/Scholarship)

Purpose: To provide resources on how to establish a program, a network for connecting with other programs and to increase recruitment and retention to junior firefighters.

Awards are arranged alphabetically below their administering organizations

Focus: Fires and fire prevention. **Qualif.:** Applicant must be a high school senior, or a high school graduate within the past three years who is enrolled or will be enrolled in the following school year at an accredited two- or four-year institution of higher learning, a trade school or a certification program; be a past or current junior firefighter in a department that is registered with the NVFC National Junior Firefighter Program; had proven to be an active and vital member of a junior firefighter program for at least one year and currently be active either as a junior firefighter or in some other capacity; must have demonstrated intent to pursue emergency services. **Criteria:** Selection will be based on the objective judgment of the scholarship committee as to which candidates demonstrate the greatest potential for future involvement in emergency services as exhibited by their past emergency service record.

Funds Avail.: $5,000. **Duration:** Annual. **Number Awarded:** 10. **To Apply:** Applicant must complete the scholarship application form; must submit an official transcript from the institution most recently attended; complete a 250-word essay outlining how being a junior firefighter has impacted the applicant's life, how the scholarship will further field of study and plans for the future involvement in emergency services; must submit two letters of recommendation; recent photo to be used for NVFC newsletter, website if selected; fire department must submit a 250-word essay outlining its current junior firefighter program and how a $5,000 grant would benefit the department.

6819 ■ National Water Research Institute (NWRI)
18700 Ward St.
Fountain Valley, CA 92728-8096
Ph: (714)378-3278
Fax: (714)378-3375
URL: www.nwri-usa.org

6820 ■ Ronald B. Linsky Fellowships for Outstanding Water Research *(Graduate, Master's, Doctorate/Fellowship)*

Purpose: To support and encourage graduate students to investigate and develop the innovative procedures, technologies, and policies crucial to resolving these critical water needs. **Focus:** Water resources. **Qualif.:** Applicants must be master's or doctoral graduate students in a US university whose research pertains to water, including water supply, water resources, water quality, and technologies and treatment. **Criteria:** Selection will be based on the committee's criteria.

Funds Avail.: $10,000 per year. **Duration:** Two years. **To Apply:** Applicants must prepare an application package, available at the website, following the NWRI's fellowship application procedures. As part of the application process, applicants are asked to prepare a 1-page, single-spaced essay detailing why they should receive the fellowship. The essay must address their technical capabilities, their interest in other fields beside the one they are studying, their career goals, and where they hope to take their technical expertise and vision in the future. Applicants' research must pertain to NWRI's mission statement, which is to create new sources of water through research and technology and to protect the freshwater and marine environments. NWRI' specific research interests include, but are not limited to: water treatment technologies; water quality; water environmental chemistry; water policy and economics; public health and risk assessment; water resources management.

6821 ■ NWRI Fellowships *(Graduate, Master's, Doctorate/Fellowship)*

Purpose: To support graduate students conducting water-related research. **Focus:** Water resources. **Qualif.:** Applicants must be students at US universities who are currently enrolled fulltime in a master's or doctoral graduate program in the area of water resources and treatment. **Criteria:** Selection will be based on the committee's criteria.

Funds Avail.: $2,000-$15,000. **To Apply:** Interested students may contact the fellowship coordinator for the application process. The fellowship application cover sheet can be downloaded from NWRI's website. Applicants must also submit an original research proposal. **Contact:** fellow@nwri-usa.org.

6822 ■ National Wildlife Federation (NWF)
11100 Wildlife Center Dr.
Reston, VA 20190
Ph: (703)438-6000
Free: 800-822-9919
URL: www.nwf.org

6823 ■ NWF Campus Ecology Fellowships *(Graduate, Undergraduate/Fellowship)*

Purpose: To assist students who are working on projects ranging from campus-wide energy audits to implementing sustainable forestry practices. **Focus:** Earth sciences. **Qualif.:** Applicants must be undergraduate or graduate students working with other members of the faculty, staff, or administration on projects designed to help reverse global warming on campus and beyond. **Criteria:** Project proposals will be evaluated based on: how prospect will measurably contribute to campus climate leadership; demonstrated interest in and experience working within or with diverse constituencies; engagement with students, faculty, community organizations, and businesses; plans for outreach to local and campus newspapers; innovative approaches or models for the national climate action movement; arrangement of academic credit for successful completion of the project, as an independent study or integration of the fellowship project into course curricula; matching funds or other financial support from the campus or another source; securing appropriate project advisor and verifier; nomination of the applicant by a formal environmental or sustainability group or committee on campus; and host campus that is currently enrolled with NWF's Campus Ecology Program and especially those that have applied to earn the designation of NWF Climate Champion.

Funds Avail.: $3,000 each. **Duration:** Annual. **Number Awarded:** Minimum of 2. **To Apply:** Applicants must submit a proposal. Proposals must be 3-5 pages and must include: date, header, summary, purpose, short-term results, long-term results, participation and support, nomination process, education and documentation, timeline, evaluation, qualifications and interests, project budget, and a confirmation of the applicant's availability in attending and to participate in the fellowship meeting (refer to the fellowship guidelines for the format). **Deadline:** March 8. **Remarks:** Established in 2000. **Contact:** National Wildlife Federation, at the above address.

6824 ■ National Women's Studies Association (NWSA)
11 E Mount Royal Ave., Ste. 100
Baltimore, MD 21202-5504

Awards are arranged alphabetically below their administering organizations

Ph: (410)528-0355
Fax: (410)528-0357
E-mail: nwsaoffice@nwsa.org
URL: www.nwsa.org

6825 ■ National Women's Studies Association Lesbian Caucus Award *(Master's, Doctorate/Award)*

Purpose: To recognize a Master's Thesis or Doctoral Dissertation research project in areas of Lesbian, Queer, and LGBT Studies that resonates with the mission of NWSA. **Focus:** General studies/Field of study not specified. **Qualif.:** Applicants must be master's and/or doctoral students who are members of NWSA. **Criteria:** Applications will be evaluated on the basis of: clarity of project description; relevance to mission of NWSA, goals of Lesbian Caucus, and field of Women's and Genter studies; engagement of feminist analytical frameworks/methodologies; potential impact on the fields of lesbian/sexuality studies.

Funds Avail.: $500. **Duration:** Annual. **To Apply:** Applicants must complete and online application and must provide letters of recommendation. **Deadline:** May 15.

6826 ■ NWSA Graduate Scholarships *(Graduate/ Scholarship)*

Purpose: To encourage the participation in NWSA of individuals whose presence enrich the diversity of and increase participation by underrepresented constituencies in the NWSA. **Focus:** General studies/Field of study not specified. **Qualif.:** Program is open to members of NWSA who, in the fall of the year of the award, will be engaged in the research or writing stages of a Master's Thesis or PhD Dissertation in the interdisciplinary field of women's studies. The research project must be on women and must enhance the NWSA mission. **Criteria:** Recipients are selected based on the brief statement of financial need; feminist or community activities; and relevance of the research to NWSA goals.

Funds Avail.: $1,000. **To Apply:** Applicants must complete the application form including name and contact information; dissertation/thesis title; two-to-three page of abstract of the work; and two letters of recommendation. **Deadline:** May 1.

6827 ■ Native Women's Association of Canada (NWAC)

155 International Rd., Unit 4
Akwesasne, ON, Canada K6H 5R7
Ph: (613)722-3033
Fax: (613)722-7687
Free: 800-461-4043
URL: www.nwac.ca

6828 ■ Helen Bassett Commemorative Student Award *(Undergraduate, Graduate/Scholarship)*

Purpose: To provide financial support for students intending to pursue their law careers. **Focus:** Law. **Qualif.:** Applicants must be post-secondary students, specifically Aboriginal females, pursuing a law career; must be under 30 years old; must demonstrate financial need; and must demonstrate commitment to improving the situation of Aboriginal women and youth in Canada politically, culturally, economically or otherwise. **Criteria:** Applicants will be selected based on financial need and academic standing. Priority is given to those studying in law or justice related fields.

Funds Avail.: $1,000 each. **Duration:** Annual. **Number Awarded:** 4. **To Apply:** Applicants must submit application form, proof of age, and proof of Aboriginal descent; must have a proof of attending post-secondary studies: acceptance letter from a post-secondary institution; must have the most recent official transcript, proof of community involvement/interest and dedication in working on Aboriginal women's issues; one reference letter of support from a local community organization, or school, or any relevant organization/person; must provide a short 1-2-page essay and statement of financial need in a letter, plus monthly or yearly budget and a list of other funding sources and scholarships. **Deadline:** July 10.

6829 ■ Natural Sciences and Engineering Research Council of Canada (NSERC)

350 Albert St., 16th Fl.
Ottawa, ON, Canada K1A 1H5
Ph: (613)995-4273
Fax: (613)992-5337
Free: 855-275-2861
E-mail: exec@nserc-crsng.gc.ca
URL: www.nserc-crsng.gc.ca

6830 ■ Banting Postdoctoral Fellowships *(Postdoctorate/Fellowship)*

Purpose: To provide financial assistance to postdoctoral applicants and to develop their careers. **Focus:** General studies/Field of study not specified. **Qualif.:** Applicants must fulfill or have fulfilled all degree requirements for a PhD, PhD equivalent or health professional degree with proposed host institution. Canadian citizens, permanent residents of Canada and foreign citizens are all eligible to apply with the following conditions: applicants who are not Canadian citizens or permanent residents of Canada may only hold their Banting Postdoctoral Fellowship at a Canadian institution; applicants who are Canadian citizens or permanent residents of Canada and who obtained their PhD, PhD-equivalent or health professional degree from a foreign university may only hold their Banting Postdoctoral Fellowship at a Canadian institution; and applicants who are Canadian citizens or permanent residents of Canada and who obtained their PhD, PhD-equivalent or health professional degree from a Canadian university may hold their Banting Postdoctoral Fellowship at either a Canadian institution or an institution outside of Canada. In choosing the right host institutions, applicants must consider one of the following: Canadian and foreign universities; affiliated research hospitals; colleges; and not-for-profit organizations with a strong research mandate. **Criteria:** Applicants will be selected based on qualifications and submitted materials.

Funds Avail.: $70,000. **Duration:** Biennial; non-renewable. **To Apply:** Applicants must submit the completed application in either French or English language including all host institution documents and referee assessments. **Deadline:** September 23.

6831 ■ Alexander Graham Bell Canada Graduate Scholarship Program *(Doctorate, Master's/ Scholarship)*

Purpose: To provide financial support for outstanding eligible students pursuing master's or doctoral studies in a Canadian university. **Focus:** Natural sciences; Pre-Columbian studies. **Qualif.:** Applicant must be a Canadian citizen or a permanent resident of Canada; must hold, or

Awards are arranged alphabetically below their administering organizations

expect to hold (at the time award is taken) a degree in science or engineering from a university whose standing is acceptable to NSERC (if you have a degree in a field other than science or engineering, NSERC may accept your application at its discretion); must intend to pursue, in the following year, full-time graduate studies and research at the master's or doctoral level in an eligible program in one of the areas of the natural sciences and engineering supported by NSERC; and must have obtained a first-class average (a grade of "A-") in each of the last two completed years of study. **Criteria:** Selection of recipients is based on merit.

Funds Avail.: $35,000 a year. **Duration:** maximum of four years. **To Apply:** Applicants must complete the online Form 201 (available on-line) and submit with other supporting materials. **Deadline:** October 15. **Contact:** For further information, applicants may send an email to schol@nserc-crsng.gc.ca.

6832 ■ Industrial R&D Fellowships *(Postdoctorate/Fellowship)*

Purpose: To provide financial support and to enable recent doctoral graduates to engage in research and development in the private sector. **Focus:** Engineering. **Qualif.:** Applicants must be Canadian citizens or permanent resident of Canada or foreign nationals with Ph.D. and graduated from a Canadian postsecondary institution; must hold a doctoral degree in a discipline of science or engineering that NSERC supports; must have completed a doctoral degree within the last five years; must not have been employed for more than six months in an R&D position in the Canadian private sector after receipt of his or her doctoral degree; and must not have received an offer of employment from the nominating company except an offer of this fellowship, conditional upon NSERC approval, or short-term employment of up to six months while awaiting a decision on the fellowship. **Criteria:** Two members of the NSERC IRDF College of Reviewers, composed of federal government employees from departments and agencies with an interest in research and development, and academic researchers who have experience with industrial research collaborations will review each nomination. The members evaluate applicants based on the following criteria: research ability or potential; and communication, interpersonal and leadership abilities. The reviewers evaluate the research proposal based on the following criteria: the research and development environment/opportunity for an industrial R&D experience; the scientific and technical merit of the proposed R&D activities; the significance and feasibility of the proposed R&D activities; incrementality; and the company's overall commitment, including its financial commitment, to the fellow and the project.

Funds Avail.: No specific amount. **Duration:** Annual. **To Apply:** Applicants must first contact a company that is willing to support their nomination. The candidates and the company must negotiate the details of the research project(s) and position. The company will submit the nomination to NSERC. The nomination must include and submit the original of each of the following: Form 200 (Application for an Industrial Postgraduate Scholarship, Industrial R&D Fellowship or Visiting Fellowship in Canadian Government Laboratories), to be completed by the candidate; attach Contributions and statements; Proof of completion of Ph.D. (if completed at time of nomination); Proof of Canadian citizenship, permanent residency or post-graduation work permit; report on the applicant of Form 200, two reports to be completed by persons very familiar with the candidate's previous work; nomination for an Industrial R&D Fellowship (Form 183C); company's official letter/contract offering employment to, and co-signed by, the candidate; letter from the collaborating company(s) outlining the nature of its/their participation and contributions (if applicable); terms and Conditions of Applying Form to be completed by the nominee; and terms and Conditions of Applying Form to be completed by the authorized organization representative.

6833 ■ Natural Sciences and Engineering Research Council Postgraduate Scholarships *(Doctorate/Scholarship)*

Purpose: To provide financial support for outstanding eligible students pursuing master's or doctoral studies in a Canadian university. **Focus:** Natural sciences; Pre-Columbian studies. **Qualif.:** Applicant must be a Canadian citizen or a permanent resident of Canada; must hold, or expect to hold (at the time award is taken) a degree in science or engineering from a university whose standing is acceptable to NSERC (if you have a degree in a field other than science or engineering, NSERC may accept your application at its discretion); must intend to pursue, in the following year, full-time or part-time graduate studies and research at the master's or doctoral level in an eligible program in one of the areas of the natural sciences and engineering supported by NSERC; and must have obtained a first-class average (a grade of "A-") in each of the last two completed years of study. Foreign candidates are also eligible to apply. **Criteria:** Selection of recipients is based on merit.

Funds Avail.: $21,000. **Duration:** up to three years. **To Apply:** Applicants must complete the Form 200 (available on-line) and submit with other supporting materials. **Contact:** For further information, applicants may send an email to schol@nserc-crsng.gc.ca.

6834 ■ Vanier Canada Graduate Scholarships *(Graduate/Scholarship)*

Purpose: To support students who demonstrate a high standard of scholarly achievement in graduate studies in the social sciences and humanities, natural sciences and engineering, and health and to those who demonstrate leadership skills. **Focus:** Health sciences; Humanities; Natural sciences; Social sciences. **Qualif.:** Program is open to both Canadian and international students who must be nominated for a Vanier Canada Graduate Scholarship. **Criteria:** Selection will be based on the committee's criteria.

Funds Avail.: $50,000 per year. **Duration:** three years. **To Apply:** Applicants must visit the Vanier CGS website for further instructions and application procedures. **Contact:** For additional information, applicants may email at vanier@cihr-irsc.gc.ca.

6835 ■ Naval Helicopter Association Scholarship Fund
PO Box 180578
Coronado, CA 92178-0578
Ph: (619)435-7139
URL: www.nhascholarshipfund.org

6836 ■ Naval Helicopter Association Scholarships *(Undergraduate, Graduate/Scholarship)*

Purpose: To assist persons who desire to pursue their educational goals and expand their knowledge. **Focus:** General studies/Field of study not specified. **Qualif.:** Applicants must be prospective or current high school gradu-

Awards are arranged alphabetically below their administering organizations

ates, high school equivalents, or college undergraduate/graduate students, and the following: natural/step/adopted sons or daughters, or grandchildren of active duty, former, or retired Navy, Marine Corps, or Coast Guard rotary-wing aviators, aircrewmen or maintenance/support personnel, or spouses of active duty or former Navy, Marine Corps or Coast Guard rotary wing aviators, aircrewmen or maintenance/support personnel, or active duty or former Navy, Marine Corps or Coast Guard rotary wing aviators, aircrewmen or maintenance/support personnel. **Criteria:** Selection shall be based on the aforementioned applicants' qualifications and compliance with the application details.

Funds Avail.: Amount varies. **Duration:** Annual. **Number Awarded:** Varies. **To Apply:** Application must include four parts: online form submission; teacher/counselor recommendation (minimum one recommendation per application) in which for active duty applicants, a letter of recommendation from their commanding officer; high school and/or undergraduate/graduate transcript; and, documents to establishing eligibility (i.e. any correspondence that shows connection with the naval helicopter community: DD-214, awards, certifications, history of assignment, etc.) All applications (including transcripts/letters of recommendations) must be submitted or postmarked by date identified under Selection Process. **Deadline:** January 31. **Contact:** NHA Scholarship Application, P.O. Box 180578, Coronado, California 92178-0578; Business No.: 619-435-7139.

6837 ■ Naval Research Laboratory (NRL)

4555 Overlook Ave. SW
Washington, DC 20375
Ph: (202)767-3200
Fax: (202)265-8504
E-mail: webmaster@nrl.navy.mil
URL: www.nrl.navy.mil

6838 ■ NRL-ASEE Postdoctoral Fellowships
(Postdoctorate/Fellowship)

Purpose: To increase the involvement of scientists and engineers from academia and industry to scientific and technical areas of interest and relevance to the Navy. **Focus:** Architecture, Naval; Naval art and science. **Qualif.:** Applicants must be U.S. citizens or legal permanent residents and have received the PhD, ScD, or other research doctoral degree recognized in U.S. academic circles as equivalent to the PhD within seven years of the date of application. **Criteria:** Selection is based on the technical quality and relevance of the proposed research, recommendations by the Navy laboratories or centers, academic qualifications, reference reports, and availability of funds.

Funds Avail.: $74,872. **Duration:** Annual. **Number Awarded:** Varies. **To Apply:** Applicants are required to register online to apply. Applicants must prepare a 5-10 page research proposal suitable for the research facility. Official transcripts for each level (undergraduate, graduate, doctoral) must be sent to ASEE projects office.

6839 ■ Naval Weather Service Association (NWSA)

515 Ashley Rd.
Cantonment, FL 32533-5610
Ph: (850)968-0552
E-mail: nwsasectrea@navalweather.org
URL: www.navalweather.org

6840 ■ Naval Weather Service Association Scholarships
(Undergraduate/Scholarship)

Purpose: To assist students who have plan in the field of Meteorology, Oceanography, or Space Engineering. **Focus:** Meteorology; Oceanography. **Qualif.:** Applicants must be U.S. citizens or hold a permanent status; be entering college or currently enrolled prior the year of application; have plan to pursue a degree in the atmospheric, oceanic, aerospace engineering, or any related fields; and must be enrolled as full-time students. **Criteria:** Selection of applicants will be based on scholastic ability and financial need.

Funds Avail.: $5,000. **Duration:** Annual. **To Apply:** Applicants must submit a completed and signed application form; most recent transcript; copies of standardized test scores such as ACT or SAT for graduating high school; and letter of recommendation from a high school teacher or counselor. Undergraduate students need not to submit a recommendation letter however, college transcript is required. Applicants are encouraged to have comments on the following areas: 1) commitment to a career in Meteorology or Aerospace Engineering; 2) academic records; 3) leadership skills; 4) diverse interests and community involvement; and 4) financial need. Applicants are encouraged to contact the nearest NWSA chapter to learn more about the application process. **Deadline:** February 6. **Contact:** Mail original application and required documents to Libby O'Brien at the above address; E-mail: nwsasectreas@panhandle.rr.com.

6841 ■ Navy League of the United States (NLUS)

2300 Wilson Blvd., Ste. 200
Arlington, VA 22201-5424
Ph: (703)528-1775
Fax: (703)528-2333
Free: 800-356-5760
URL: navyleague.org

6842 ■ John G. Brokaw Scholarships
(Undergraduate/Scholarship)

Purpose: To assist in the college/university expenses of the dependents of sea service personnel. **Focus:** General studies/Field of study not specified. **Qualif.:** Applicant must be a U.S. citizen; a dependent or direct descendant of an active, reserve, retired or honorably discharged member of the US Navy, Coast Guard, US-Flag Merchant Marine, Marine Corps or US Naval Sea Cadet Corps; completing the final year of high school; and will be entering an accredited college/university. **Criteria:** Recipients will be selected based on the application materials submitted and other supporting documents.

Funds Avail.: No specific amount. **Duration:** Annual. **To Apply:** Applicants must prepare a copy of all applicable transcripts (grade 9-present); two letters of recommendation; copy of SAT/ACT scores; FAFSA information; proof of qualifying sea service duty; a personal statement (one page) on the reasons to be considered for the program; and a list of extracurricular/scholastic activities (maximum of two pages).

6843 ■ Wesley C. Cameron Scholarships
(Undergraduate/Scholarship)

Purpose: To assist in the college/university expenses of the dependents of sea service personnel. **Focus:** General studies/Field of study not specified. **Qualif.:** Applicant must

Awards are arranged alphabetically below their administering organizations

be a U.S. citizen; a dependent or direct descendant of an active, reserve, retired or honorably discharged member of the US Navy, Coast Guard, US-Flag Merchant Marine, Marine Corps or US Naval Sea Cadet Corps; completing the final year of high school; will be entering an accredited college/university; must be under the age of 25; and have at least 3.0 GPA on a 4.0 scale. **Criteria:** Recipients will be selected based on the application materials submitted and other supporting documents. Preference will be given to those applicants who have demonstrated an interest to continue their education in mathematics or sciences.

Funds Avail.: No specific amount. **Duration:** Annual. **To Apply:** Applicants must prepare a copy of all applicable transcripts (grade 9-present); two letters of recommendation; copy of SAT/ACT scores; FAFSA information; proof of qualifying sea service duty; a personal statement (one page) on the reasons to be considered for the program; and a list of extracurricular/scholastic activities (maximum of two pages).

6844 ■ Captain Winifred Quick Collins Scholarships (*Undergraduate/Scholarship*)

Purpose: To assist in the college/university expenses of the dependents of sea service personnel. **Focus:** General studies/Field of study not specified. **Qualif.:** Applicant must be a U.S. citizen; a dependent or direct descendant of an active, reserve, retired or honorably discharged member of the US Navy, Coast Guard, US-Flag Merchant Marine, Marine Corps or US Naval Sea Cadet Corps; completing the final year of high school; and will be entering an accredited college/university. **Criteria:** Recipients will be selected based on the application materials submitted and other supporting documents.

Funds Avail.: No specific amount. **Duration:** Annual. **To Apply:** Applicants must prepare a copy of all applicable transcripts (grade 9-present); two letters of recommendation; copy of SAT/ACT scores; FAFSA information; proof of qualifying sea service duty; a personal statement (one page) stating the reasons to be considered for the program; and a list of extracurricular/scholastic activities (maximum of two pages).

6845 ■ Gladys Ann Smith Greater Los Angeles Women's Council Scholarships (*Undergraduate/ Scholarship*)

Purpose: To financially assist the dependents of sea service personnel for college/university expenses. **Focus:** General studies/Field of study not specified. **Qualif.:** Applicant must be a U.S. citizen; currently residing in the state of California; a dependent or direct descendant of an active, reserve, retired or honorably discharged member of the US Navy, Coast Guard, US-Flag Merchant Marine, Marine Corps or US Naval Sea Cadet Corps; completing his/her final year of high school and will be entering an accredited college/university. **Criteria:** Preference is given to applicants residing in California.

Funds Avail.: No specific amount. **Duration:** Annual. **To Apply:** Applicants must prepare a copy of all applicable transcripts (grade 9-present); two letters of recommendation; copy of SAT/ACT scores; FAFSA information; proof of qualifying sea service duty; a personal statement (one page) on the reasons to be considered for the program; and a list of extracurricular/scholastic activities (maximum of two pages).

6846 ■ Subic Bay-Cubi Point Scholarships (*Undergraduate/Scholarship*)

Purpose: To assist in the college/university expenses of the dependents of sea service personnel. **Focus:** General

studies/Field of study not specified. **Qualif.:** Applicant must be a U.S. citizen; a dependent or direct descendant of an active, reserve, retired or honorably discharged member of the US Navy, Coast Guard, US-Flag Merchant Marine, Marine Corps or US Naval Sea Cadet Corps; completing the final year of high school; will be entering an accredited college/university; have at least a 3.0 GPA on a 4.0 grade scale (equivalent to a B average); and must demonstrate financial need. **Criteria:** Preference is given to applicants who are dependents or descendants of personnel who were stationed in the Philippines.

Funds Avail.: No specific amount. **Duration:** Annual. **To Apply:** Applicants must prepare a copy of all applicable transcripts (grade 9-present); two letters of recommendation; copy of SAT/ACT scores; FAFSA information; proof of qualifying sea service duty; a personal statement (one page) on the reasons to be considered for the program; and a list of extracurricular/scholastic activities (maximum of two pages).

6847 ■ William A. Sullivan Scholarships (*Undergraduate/Scholarship*)

Purpose: To assist in the college/university expenses of the dependents of sea service personnel. **Focus:** General studies/Field of study not specified. **Qualif.:** Applicant must be a U.S. citizen; a dependent or direct descendant of an active, reserve, retired or honorably discharged member of the US Navy, Coast Guard, US-Flag Merchant Marine, Marine Corps or US Naval Sea Cadet Corps; completing the final year of high school; will be entering an accredited college/university; have at least a 3.0 GPA on a 4.0 grade scale (equivalent to a B average); and must demonstrate financial need. **Criteria:** Preference will be given to residents of San Diego, California.

Funds Avail.: No specific amount. **Duration:** Annual. **To Apply:** Applicants must prepare a copy of all applicable transcripts (grade 9-present); one letter of recommendation; copy of SAT/ACT scores; FAFSA information; proof of qualifying sea service duty; a personal statement (one page) on the reasons to be considered for the program; and a list of extracurricular/scholastic activities (maximum of two pages).

6848 ■ Navy-Marine Corps Relief Society (NM-CRS)

875 N Randolph St., Ste. 225
Arlington, VA 22203-1767
Free: 800-654-8364
URL: www.nmcrs.org

6849 ■ Admiral Mike Boorda Loans Program (*Undergraduate/Loan*)

Purpose: To help eligible Navy and Marine Corps families pursue their academic goals by providing education grants and interest-free loans. **Focus:** General studies/Field of study not specified. **Qualif.:** Applicants must be Sailor or Marine service members participating in one of the following: Marine Enlisted Commissioning Education Program (MECEP), or Medical Enlisted Commissioning Program (MECP). Generally, applicants must be full-time students, enrolled for the entire academic year, and pursuing a first undergraduate degree at a qualifying school and also maintain 2.0 or better GPA on a 4.0 grade scale. **Criteria:** Selection shall be based on the demonstrated financial need for assistance.

Funds Avail.: $500 to $3,000. **Duration:** Annual. **Number**

Awards are arranged alphabetically below their administering organizations

Awarded: Varies. **To Apply:** Applicants must submit the following: completed application form (PDF); official high school or current college transcript; copy of transfer orders to the MECEP or MECP program; and, Student Aid Report (SAR) from completed FAFSA. **Deadline:** June 1.

6850 ■ NMCRS Gold Star Scholarship Program
(Undergraduate/Scholarship)

Purpose: To provide educational assistance to spouses and children of members of the Society. **Focus:** General studies/Field of study not specified. **Qualif.:** Applicants must be either of the following: children (under age 23) of Sailors or Marines who died while serving on active duty or after retirement, or unmarried spouses of Navy or Marine Corps service members who died as a result of the attack on the USS STARK or the Pentagon, or during service in Operation Iraqi Freedom (OIF), Operation Enduring Freedom (OEF), or Operation New Dawn (OND). Generally, applicants must be full-time students, enrolled for the entire academic year, and pursuing a first undergraduate degree at a qualifying school and must also maintain 2.0 or better GPA on a 4.0 grade scale. **Criteria:** Selection shall be based on the demonstrated financial need for assistance.

Funds Avail.: $500 to $2,500. **Duration:** Annual. **Number Awarded:** Varies. **To Apply:** Applicants must submit the following: completed application form (PDF); official high school or current college transcript; copy of DD 1300 or a death certificate; and, Student Aid Report (SAR) from completed FAFSA. **Deadline:** May 1. **Contact:** NMCRS Education Division, Phone: 703-696-4960; Email: education@nmcrs.org.

6851 ■ Spouse Tuition Aid Loan Program (STAP)
(Undergraduate, Graduate/Loan)

Purpose: To help eligible Navy and Marine Corps families pursue their academic goals by providing education grants and interest-free loans. **Focus:** General studies/Field of study not specified. **Qualif.:** Applicants must: be spouses of active duty Navy or Marine Corps service members stationed outside the 50 United States; be part-time or full-time undergraduate or graduate students; and be enrolled at an institution accredited by a regional/national accrediting agency recognized by the U.S. Secretary of Education. **Criteria:** Selection shall be based on the aforementioned qualifications and compliance with the application details.

Funds Avail.: No specific amount. **Duration:** Annual. **To Apply:** Application forms and instructions are available from the website.

6852 ■ Nazareth Association
PO Box 224
Nazareth, MI 49074
Ph: (269)342-1191
E-mail: office@nazarethassociation.org
URL: www.nazarethassociation.org

6853 ■ The Nazareth Scholarships *(Undergraduate/Scholarship)*

Purpose: To provide financial support to students wishing to complete their degree at approved Catholic colleges in Michigan. **Focus:** General studies/Field of study not specified. **Qualif.:** Applicants must be currently enrolled at an approved Catholic college/university; must be undergraduate junior or senior students; and must have cumulative GPA of 3.0 or better on a 4.0 scale at the conclusion of the present year and be in good standing with their academic institution. **Criteria:** Recipients are selected based on demonstration of academic performance, extracurricular volunteer activities and/or community services.

Funds Avail.: Varies. **To Apply:** Applicants must complete the application form and submit along with transcript of records, a 500-word essay and three letters of recommendation. Scholarship applications can be obtained by contacting the Nazareth Association Office. **Deadline:** March 15. **Remarks:** Established in 1994.

6854 ■ Nebraska Farm Bureau
PO Box 80299
Lincoln, NE 68501-0299
Ph: (402)421-4400
Fax: (402)421-4439
Free: 800-742-4016
URL: www.nefb.org

6855 ■ Nebraska Farm Bureau Greater Horizon Scholarships *(Undergraduate/Scholarship)*

Purpose: To encourage and assist young people between the ages of 18 and 35 to meet their personal goals of higher education. **Focus:** Agricultural sciences; Agriculture, Economic aspects. **Qualif.:** Applicants must be members or family of members of the County Farm Bureau in Nebraska; must be residents of Nebraska; must have intention of enrolling full-time in a college or university's agricultural field of studies; must demonstrate leadership potential through extracurricular activities and work experiences. **Criteria:** Applicants are evaluated based on the criteria designed by the Selection Committee, comprised of three YF&R committee members, associate director/member services and assistant treasurer.

Funds Avail.: $1,000 each. **Duration:** Annual. **Number Awarded:** 2. **To Apply:** Applicants must submit the completed application form; three letters of reference; and copy of most recent transcript.

6856 ■ Nebraska High School Rodeo Association
PO Box 10
Arnold, NE 69120
Ph: (308)539-6543
Fax: (308)848-2544
URL: www.hsrodeo-nebraska.com

6857 ■ Tom Boots Memorial Scholarships
(Undergraduate/Scholarship)

Purpose: To provide assistance to students who are participating in the Nebraska State High School Rodeo Association. **Focus:** General studies/Field of study not specified. **Qualif.:** Applicants must be graduating seniors of Nebraska High School. **Criteria:** Recipients are selected based on academic performance.

Funds Avail.: $500. **To Apply:** Applicants must submit a completed application form. **Deadline:** June 10.

6858 ■ Sharon Kreikemeier Memorial Scholarships
(Undergraduate/Scholarship)

Purpose: To provide financial assistance to students in continuing their education. **Focus:** General studies/Field of study not specified. **Qualif.:** Applicants must be enrolled in Nebraska High School. **Criteria:** Recipients are selected

Awards are arranged alphabetically below their administering organizations

based on academic performance.

Funds Avail.: $500. **To Apply:** Applicants must complete the application form. **Deadline:** June 15.

6859 ■ Swede Swanson Memorial Scholarships (Undergraduate/Scholarship)

Purpose: To assist a graduating student who participates in Steer Wrestling at Nebraska High School. **Focus:** Medicine, Sports. **Qualif.:** Applicants must be graduating senior boys who participate in the Steer Wrestling event in the Nebraska High School Rodeo Association. **Criteria:** Recipients are selected based on academic performance.

Funds Avail.: $500. **To Apply:** Applicants must submit a cover sheet including name, address and GPA; must submit at least one page essay stating their career goals, one letter of recommendation and a copy of their grade transcripts. **Deadline:** June 1.

6860 ■ Nebraska Library Association (NLA)

c/o Michael Straatmann, Executive Director
PO Box 21756
Lincoln, NE 68542-1756
Ph: (402)216-0727
E-mail: nebraskalibraries@gmail.com
URL: www.nebraskalibraries.org

6861 ■ Louise A. Nixon Scholarships (Graduate/Scholarship)

Purpose: To support students who pursue graduate level library education. **Focus:** Library and archival sciences. **Qualif.:** Applicants must be accepted by an ALA-accredited graduate school of library/information science; or must be accepted by a graduate media program that meets the ALA/AASL curriculum guidelines within a unit accredited by the National Council for the Accreditation of Teacher Education. Student must also be residents of Nebraska for at least one year; or members of NLA for at least one year; or employees, past or present, of a Nebraska library for at least one year. **Criteria:** Preference will be given to applicants who can demonstrate the best potential for employment in Nebraska libraries after graduation.

Funds Avail.: No specific amount. **Duration:** Annual. **Number Awarded:** 1. **To Apply:** Applicants must submit a completed application form along with an official copy of college transcript; two letters of recommendation; a personal statement explaining employment history, employment expectations after graduation, and expected graduation date; estimated education expenses; and proof of acceptance or current enrollment in a graduate program. **Deadline:** April 15. **Contact:** Nebraska Library Association, at the above address.

6862 ■ Nebraska Paralegal Association (NePA)

PO Box 24943
Omaha, NE 68124
Ph: (402)392-1500
Fax: (402)392-8101
E-mail: info@nebraskaparalegal.org
URL: www.nebraskaparalegal.org

6863 ■ Nebraska Paralegal Association Student Scholarships (Undergraduate/Scholarship)

Purpose: To support students who are in pursuit of training for careers as legal assistants. **Focus:** Law. **Qualif.:** Ap-

plicants must be Nebraska residents or a member of NePA admitted to an accredited paralegal program at a University, College, Community College or Business College; must be in good standing with at least 3.0 GPA at the time of application. **Criteria:** Recipients are selected based on academic performance.

Funds Avail.: $500. **To Apply:** Applicants must submit a completed application form, resume, one letter of recommendation from instructors, employers or community leaders, a copy of a letter of acceptance to a Nebraska legal assistant program, a statement of good academic standing for the most recent college term; recipients must pass the interview. Applicants must also attach their recent high school transcript and, if applicable, most recent college transcript. **Deadline:** March 1.

6864 ■ Nebraska Section American Water Works Association

PO Box 94791
Lincoln, NE 68509-4791
Ph: (402)957-2482
URL: www.awwaneb.org

6865 ■ Colonel Theodore A. Leisen Memorial and Training Endowment Funds (Graduate, Professional development/Grant, Scholarship)

Purpose: To encourage water industry professionals to obtain additional training and encourage graduate students to choose the water industry as their field of work. **Focus:** Water resources; Water supply industry. **Qualif.:** Applicants must be graduate students and water industry professionals seeking additional training and knowledge in the said field. **Criteria:** Selection will be based on the committee's criteria.

Funds Avail.: $500 each. **Number Awarded:** 3. **To Apply:** Interested applicants may contact the AWWA Nebraska Section for the application process and other information. **Deadline:** September 1. **Contact:** Jon Zellars, Committee Chair, at jon_zellars@mudnebr.com.

6866 ■ Nebraska Society of Certified Public Accountants (NSCPA)

635 S 14th St., Ste. 330
Lincoln, NE 68508
Ph: (402)476-8482
Fax: (402)476-8731
Free: 800-642-6178
E-mail: society@nescpa.org
URL: www.nescpa.org

6867 ■ NESCPA Fifth-Year Scholarships (Graduate/Scholarship)

Purpose: To financially support accounting students. **Focus:** Accounting. **Qualif.:** Applicant must be an accounting major who has completed his/her junior year and has enrolled in a fifth-year (150-hour) program at a Nebraska college/university; planning to sit for the CPA exam; and has an interest and is capable of becoming a successful accountant and is considering an accounting career in Nebraska. **Criteria:** Selection is based on the applicant's personality, leadership and character.

Funds Avail.: No specific amount. **To Apply:** Nominations are to be made by the Accounting Department faculty

Awards are arranged alphabetically below their administering organizations

members and approved by an Accounting Department Committee (or equivalent). Scholarship criteria and applications are available upon request, students may contact NESCPA. **Deadline:** April 1. **Contact:** Sheila Burroughs at the above address.

6868 ■ NESCPA General Scholarships *(Graduate, Undergraduate/Scholarship)*

Purpose: To financially support accounting students. **Focus:** Accounting. **Qualif.:** Applicant must be an accounting major who has completed his/her junior year; planning to sit for the CPA exam; and who has an interest and is capable of becoming a successful accountant and is considering an accounting career in Nebraska. **Criteria:** Selection is based on an applicant's personality, leadership and character.

Funds Avail.: No specific amount. **To Apply:** Nominations are to be made by the Accounting Department faculty members and approved by an Accounting Department Committee (or equivalent). Scholarship criteria and applications are available upon request, students may contact NESCPA. **Deadline:** August 1. **Contact:** Sheila Burroughs at the above address.

6869 ■ Craig H. Neilsen Foundation
16830 Ventura Blvd., Ste. 352
Encino, CA 91436
Ph: (818)925-1245
E-mail: contact@chnfoundation.org
URL: www.chnfoundation.org

6870 ■ Neilsen Psychosocial Research Grants - Pilot Psychosocial Research Grants *(Professional development/Grant)*

Purpose: To support new research projects that are in the early exploratory or developmental stages and have the potential to lead to advances in the understanding of psychosocial factors and SCI. **Focus:** Spinal cord injuries and research. **Qualif.:** Applicants must be investigators beyond the postdoctoral level. **Criteria:** Selection will be based on the scientific review board's criteria.

Funds Avail.: No specific amount. **Duration:** One year. **To Apply:** Applicants must go to proposalCENTRAL website at https://proposalcentral.altum.com to register and to submit a letter of intent and application. All applications will be reviewed by the Foundation's scientific review board. **Contact:** Kim Cerise; Phone: 208-320-1423; E-mail: kim@chnfoundation.org.

6871 ■ Neilsen Psychosocial Research Grants - Postdoctoral Psychosocial Fellowships *(Postdoctorate/Fellowship)*

Purpose: To increase professional interest in the SCI field and to specifically encourage researcher from related health disciplines, to undertake training in psychosocial research to benefit the SCI field. **Focus:** Spinal cord injuries and research. **Qualif.:** Applicants must be individuals with a PhD, MD, DVM or a comparable research degree. **Criteria:** Selection will be based on the scientific review board's criteria.

Funds Avail.: No specific amount. **Duration:** Two years. **To Apply:** Applicants must go to proposalCENTRAL website at https://proposalcentral.altum.com to register and to submit a letter of intent and application. All applications will be reviewed by the Foundation's scientific review board.

Contact: Kim Cerise; Phone: 208-320-1423; E-mail: kim@chnfoundation.org.

6872 ■ Neilsen Psychosocial Research Grants - Proof of Concept Research Grants *(Professional development/Grant)*

Purpose: To encourage critical and/or innovative research on psychosocial interventions or related research topics that will lead to improved outcomes for people living with SCI. **Focus:** Spinal cord injuries and research. **Qualif.:** Applicants must be established investigators. **Criteria:** Selection will be based on the scientific review board's criteria.

Funds Avail.: No specific amount. **Duration:** Two years. **To Apply:** Applicants must go to proposalCENTRAL website at https://proposalcentral.altum.com to register and to submit a letter of intent and application. All applications will be reviewed by the Foundation's scientific review board. **Contact:** Kim Cerise; Phone: 208-320-1423; E-mail: kim@chnfoundation.org.

6873 ■ SCIRTS (Spinal Cord Injury Research on the Translational Spectrum) Pilot Research Grants *(Professional development/Grant)*

Purpose: To support basic and clinical research aimed at developing a cure for spinal cord injury. **Focus:** Spinal cord injuries and research. **Qualif.:** Applicants must be scientists whose basic and clinical research is aimed at developing a cure for spinal cord injuries. **Criteria:** Selection will be based on the scientific review board's criteria.

Funds Avail.: No specific amount. **Duration:** Two years. **To Apply:** Applicants must go to proposalCENTRAL website at https://proposalcentral.altum.com to register and to submit a letter of intent and application. All applications will be reviewed by the Foundation's scientific review board. **Contact:** Kim Cerise; Phone: 208-320-1423; E-mail: kim@chnfoundation.org.

6874 ■ SCIRTS (Spinal Cord Injury Research on the Translational Spectrum) Postdoctoral Fellowships *(Postdoctorate/Fellowship)*

Purpose: To support scientist who are wishing to specialize or train in the field of spinal cord injury research. **Focus:** Spinal cord injuries and research. **Qualif.:** Applicants must be postdoctoral scientists who wish to specialize or train in the field of spinal cord injury research. **Criteria:** Selection will be based on the scientific review board's criteria.

Funds Avail.: No specific amount. **Duration:** Two years. **To Apply:** Applicants must go to proposalCENTRAL website at https://proposalcentral.altum.com to register and to submit a letter of intent and application. All applications will be reviewed by the Foundation's scientific review board. **Contact:** Kim Cerise; Phone: 208-320-1423; E-mail: kim@chnfoundation.org.

6875 ■ SCIRTS (Spinal Cord Injury Research on the Translational Spectrum) Senior Research Grants *(Professional development/Grant)*

Purpose: To support spinal cord injury research and rehabilitation. **Focus:** Spinal cord injuries and research. **Qualif.:** Applicants must be senior level independent investigators focused on basic science, translational-preclinical or clinical research projects. **Criteria:** Selection will be based on the scientific review board's criteria.

Funds Avail.: No specific amount. **Duration:** Up to 3 years. **To Apply:** Applicants must go to proposalCENTRAL website at https://proposalcentral.altum.com to register and

Awards are arranged alphabetically below their administering organizations

to submit a letter of intent and application. All applications will be reviewed by the Foundation's scientific review board. **Contact:** Kim Cerise; Phone: 208-320-1423; E-mail: kim@chnfoundation.org.

6876 ■ Nemetschek Vectorworks Inc.

7150 Riverwood Dr.
Columbia, MD 21046-1295
Ph: (410)290-5114
Fax: (410)290-8050
Free: 888-646-4223
E-mail: academicteam@vectorworks.net
URL: www.vectorworks.net

6877 ■ Vectorworks Design Scholarships
(Undergraduate, Graduate/Scholarship, Prize)

Purpose: To support the next generation of creative potential by providing resources and scholarships to those with great designs. **Focus:** Architecture; Construction; Design; Engineering; Environmental design; Graphic art and design; Industrial design; Interior design; Landscape architecture and design; Urban affairs/design/planning. **Qualif.:** Applicants must be enrolled or accepted for enrollment in undergraduate or graduate studies for six or more credits at an accredited university or college; must be pursuing any design-oriented degree. **Criteria:** Selection will be based on the submitted designs of the applicants. Criteria include: design (20%); technology (20%); concept and originality (20%); presentation (20%); and writing (20%).

Funds Avail.: $10,000 for grand winner; $3,000 for finalists. **Duration:** Annual. **Number Awarded:** 1 grand winner; 10-17 finalists. **To Apply:** Applicants must submit their best design and answer three short questions online. **Deadline:** August 31. **Remarks:** Submissions can be created in any software, and can even be a project previously completed for school. Individual and group work is allowed. Additionally, winners' schools will receive free Vectorworks design software, as well as free in-person or virtual training for faculty and students.

6878 ■ Nevada Chapter American Public Works Association

c/o Garth Oksol, President
1105 Terminal Way, Ste. 108
Reno, NV 89502
Ph: (775)332-2137
URL: nevada.apwa.net

6879 ■ Michael Koizumi APWA Scholarships
(Undergraduate/Scholarship, Internship)

Purpose: To promote education in the field of public works, public administration or related field. **Focus:** Public administration. **Qualif.:** Applicants must be Nevada residents; must plan to enroll in a course of study leading to a career in the field of public works, public administration or a related private enterprise (e.g. business, architecture, science, engineering, etc.); and must be an entering their freshman year or currently enrolled in college. **Criteria:** Awards will be given based on nominations by APWA members; financial need-income, family size; desire; achievements; grades. Preference will be given to students attending a Nevada school.

Funds Avail.: $1,500. **Duration:** Annual. **Number**

Awarded: 4. **To Apply:** Applicants must submit completed application form together with copy of transcripts, reference, list of experience, a written statement on financial status, and career objectives. **Deadline:** April 15.

6880 ■ Nevada Organization of Nurse Leaders (NONL)

8920 Mountain Gate Dr.
Las Vegas, NV 89134
Ph: (702)749-3992
URL: www.nonl.org

6881 ■ Dan Mordecai Educational Scholarships
(Graduate, Undergraduate/Scholarship)

Purpose: To provide financial assistance to students taking up nursing education. **Focus:** Nursing. **Qualif.:** Applicant must be enrolled in an undergraduate nursing or graduate program. **Criteria:** Selection will be based on submitted documents.

Funds Avail.: $1,000. **Number Awarded:** 3. **To Apply:** Applicants must submit an completed application form together with a typed essay and letter of recommendation from a supervisor or faculty member. **Deadline:** October 18.

6882 ■ New England Club Managers Association (NECMA)

William F. Connell Golf House and Museum
300 Arnold Palmer Blvd., Ste. 227
Norton, MA 02766-1365
Ph: (774)430-9050
Fax: (774)430-9051
E-mail: necma@necma.org
URL: www.necma.org

6883 ■ Hospitality Food Service Scholarships
(Undergraduate/Scholarship)

Purpose: To support students of hospitality studies and those interested in the club management profession. **Focus:** Food service careers. **Qualif.:** Applicants must be full-time students in a degree program with a minimum 3.0 GPA; must be currently working in the club industry (atleast one season) and demonstrate an interest in continuing to work in the field. **Criteria:** Recipients are selected based on achievement. Preference will be given to those applicants working in the Club Industry who demonstrate an interest in continuing to work in the field.

Funds Avail.: No specific amount. **To Apply:** Applicants must submit a completed and neat application form; a transcript; two references; and an essay. **Deadline:** October 1.

6884 ■ David Meador Foundation Student Scholarships
(Undergraduate/Scholarship)

Purpose: To support students of hospitality studies and those interested in the club management profession. **Focus:** General studies/Field of study not specified. **Qualif.:** Applicants must be full-time students currently working within the club industry while studying; and must be members of an affiliated Student Chapter of CMAA seeking Private Club Management as a career with major or minor in Hospitality. **Criteria:** Applications are reviewed and rated by the Scholarship Committee. Recipients are selected

Awards are arranged alphabetically below their administering organizations

based on achievement. Only single and completed applications will be considered.

Funds Avail.: No specific amount. **Duration:** Annual. **Number Awarded:** 4. **To Apply:** Applicants must submit a completed and neat application form; a transcript; two (2) references; and an essay. **Deadline:** October 1. **Contact:** New England Club Managers Association Attn: Scholarship Chairman at the above address.

6885 ■ New England Library Association (NELA)
55 N Main St., Unit 49
Belchertown, MA 01007
Ph: (413)813-5254
E-mail: rscheier@gmail.com
URL: www.nelib.org

6886 ■ NELA Conference Scholarships *(All/Scholarship)*

Purpose: To provide financial assistance to attend the annual conference of NELA. **Focus:** Library and archival sciences. **Qualif.:** Applicants must be New England residents who would be likely to stay and work in the region; full or part-time students attending an ALA-accredited library school in New England or New York or an ALA-accredited program offered in the New England states, and pursuing a Master's Degree in Library Science; and have demonstrated need for financial assistance. **Criteria:** Selection shall be based on the aforementioned applicants' qualifications and compliance with the application details.

Funds Avail.: $150 each (in check). **Duration:** Annual. **Number Awarded:** Up to 6. **To Apply:** Applicants may visit the scholarship section of the bestowing organization's website for further information regarding the application details. **Contact:** New England Library Association, at the above address.

6887 ■ New Hampshire Association of Educational Office Professionals (NHAEOP)
150 Wakefield St., Ste. 8
Rochester, NH 03867
E-mail: info@nhaeop.org
URL: www.nhaeop.org

6888 ■ NHAEOP Member Scholarships *(Undergraduate/Scholarship)*

Purpose: To help defray the expenses of NHAEOP student members. **Focus:** General studies/Field of study not specified. **Qualif.:** Applicants must be NHAEOP members who are taking college credits. **Criteria:** Award will be given to students who are dues-paying members and who are in financial need.

Funds Avail.: $500. **Duration:** Annual. **To Apply:** Applicants must submit an application form and proof of registration for the desired course. **Deadline:** April 18. **Contact:** Pam Patnode, NHAEOP President, Charlestown Middle School, at ppatnode@sau60.org.

6889 ■ Julia T. Pingree Student Scholarship *(Undergraduate/Scholarship)*

Purpose: To help students further their education. **Focus:** Business. **Qualif.:** Applicants must be graduating high school senior students; must have plans to further their education in a business related program; and must have completed four or more of the following courses: a) computer classes; b) keyboarding/typing; c) shorthand/speedwriting; d) accounting or bookkeeping; e) marketing; f) office practices and procedures; g) business law; and h) business communication. **Criteria:** Recipients will be selected based on submitted application materials.

Funds Avail.: No specific amount. **To Apply:** Applicants must submit a filled-out application form, biographical information, essay and an official transcript of records. Applicants must provide one original and two copies of the application packet in order (no folders, binders, etc.). **Deadline:** March 27. **Contact:** Nancy Morrison, NHAEOP Scholarship Committee; Email:morrisonn@nashua.edu.

6890 ■ New Hampshire Automotive Dealers Association (NHADA)
507 S St.
Concord, NH 03302-2337
Fax: (603)225-4895
Free: 800-852-3372
URL: www.nhada.com

6891 ■ The Medallion Fund Scholarships *(Undergraduate/Scholarship)*

Purpose: To assist individuals who are interested in attending accredited vocational or technical programs; to improve the workforce skills, especially in areas of need, in the state of New Hampshire. **Focus:** Automotive technology. **Qualif.:** Applicants must be legal residents of New Hampshire; must have a keen desire to work in a vocational/technical career. **Criteria:** Recipients are selected based on demonstrated clear vision for how their education will help them achieve or improve their employment goals and on commitment to their educational program, both financially and otherwise.

Funds Avail.: $250-$1,000. **To Apply:** Applicants must submit a completed application form, high school or college transcript, a signed letter of recommendation from an Automotive Technology or other technical instructor and a signed letter of recommendation from a high school math, science or English teacher, verifying applicants' ability to do satisfactory academic work at the postsecondary level.

6892 ■ New Hampshire Charitable Foundation (NHCF)
37 Pleasant St.
Concord, NH 03301
Ph: (603)225-6641
Fax: (603)225-1700
E-mail: info@nhcf.org
URL: www.nhcf.org

6893 ■ Caroline L. Gross Fellowships *(Professional development/Fellowship)*

Purpose: To honor individuals for their extraordinary work in public service. **Focus:** Public service. **Qualif.:** Applicants must hold an elected or appointed position in a state, country, or municipal government within New Hampshire and also demonstrate the highest standards of performance in public service will be considered for this fellowship. **Criteria:** The selection committee looks for candidates who meet the following requirements: experience in public service; capacity to benefit from the program; desire to enhance and improve the public decision-making process in New Hampshire.

Awards are arranged alphabetically below their administering organizations

Funds Avail.: No specific amount. **Duration:** Annual. **To Apply:** Nominators are asked to download a nomination form and fill it out; if there are others who support the nomination, their comments and contact information may be sent along with the primary nomination form. Once nominated, candidates are notified and sent an application. Nomination and application forms must be sent via email, fax, or mail. **Deadline:** February 6.

6894 ■ Piscataqua Region Artist Advancement Grants *(Professional development/Grant)*

Purpose: To provide financial support to individual visual artists and craftspeople in the Piscataqua Region to promote their artistic growth. **Focus:** Crafts; Visual arts. **Qualif.:** Applicants must be over 18 years of age at the time of application; must be visual artists and craftspeople whose resume and body of work demonstrate a strong commitment to an artistic discipline. Collaborating visual artists and craftspeople are also eligible. Eligible art disciplines include: Crafts, which includes work in clay, leather, plastic, fiber, metal, wood, glass, paper and mixed media; 2-Dimensional work, which includes drawing, painting, works on paper, printmaking, book arts, collage, assemblage, mixed media; 3-Dimensional work, which includes sculpture, installation art; experimental visual arts, which includes conceptual, new media; photography. Applicants must have been permanent residents within New Hampshire Charitable Foundation's Piscataqua Region for at least two full years prior to applying and must plan to maintain permanent residence in the region during the entire grant period. **Criteria:** Selection will be based on the following criteria: the artists' body of work, as evidenced by work samples, shows high artistic quality and a strong artistic vision; the artists' body of work and resume demonstrate perseverance and a commitment to their artistic career; the artists' proposed advancement plan is clear and well-reasoned and is likely to make a significant impact on the artists' work and future direction; the proposed amount and use of funds supports the advancement plan and will make a significant impact on the artists' development and that impact will be sustained beyond the grant period.

Funds Avail.: $25,000. **Duration:** Annual. **To Apply:** Applicants must go to www.nhcf.slideroom.com to create an account and must submit the following: resume/CV. Applicants must list their accomplishments and endeavors that have been most important to them and to their work; a timeline of applicants' artistic development; an advancement plan, maximum of two pages, describing how this grant would advance their artistic growth in the short term and the long term. Applicants must include the direction they plan to pursue and/or any activities they intend to undertake during the grant period; budget describing specifically how the applicants plan to use the grant funds and discuss how the use of the grant funds are related to their advancement plan; five digital images of work samples and additional five images to show details of 3-D work. **Deadline:** April 30.

6895 ■ Louise Tillotson Teaching Fellowships *(Professional development/Fellowship)*

Purpose: To raise public awareness about the value of excellence in education and to retain good teachers in the North Country schools of New Hampshire. **Focus:** General studies/Field of study not specified. **Qualif.:** Candidates must be kindergarten through twelfth-grade public school teachers who work in New Hampshire's North Country region. Teachers in Coos County public schools are given

preference. **Criteria:** Selection will be based on the following criteria: The applicants' commitment to serve public education in their school and community; the extent and nature of the applicants' past and present public education service and commitment to continued professional learning; applicants' ability to implement a creative and imaginative educational atmosphere for North Country students; applicants' ability to bring ideas and inspire proactive solutions to resolve educational challenges; applicants' ability to articulate their educational vision, knowledge of content, and teaching methodology with passion; applicants' ability to inspire and challenge the current and next generation of educators and students in the North Country.

Funds Avail.: $10,000-$15,000. **Duration:** Annual. **To Apply:** Nominators are asked to download a nomination form and fill it out, including all contact information for the nominators and candidates. A complete application must include the following: nomination form; two letters of support, each from a different person, in favor of the candidate; copy of a recent resume, curriculum vitae, or biography of the candidates. If there are others who support the nomination, their comments and contact information may be sent along with the nomination form. Completed applications must be submitted via email to jc@nhcf.org or via mail. **Deadline:** April 17. **Remarks:** Established in 2006.

6896 ■ Louise Tillotson Teaching Professional Development Scholarships *(Professional development/Scholarship)*

Purpose: To support individuals who wants to continue their education. **Focus:** General studies/Field of study not specified. **Qualif.:** Candidates must be kindergarten through twelfth-grade public school teachers who work in New Hampshire's North Country region. Teachers in Coos County public schools are given preference. **Criteria:** Selection will be based on the following criteria: The applicants' commitment to serve public education in their school and community; the extent and nature of the applicants past and present public education service and commitment to continued professional learning; applicants' ability to implement a creative and imaginative educational atmosphere for North Country students; applicants ability to bring ideas and inspire proactive solutions to resolve educational challenges; applicants' ability to articulate their educational vision, knowledge of content, and teaching methodology with passion; applicants' ability to inspire and challenge the current and next generation of educators and students in the North Country.

Funds Avail.: $1,000. **To Apply:** Applicants are asked to download an application form and fill it out, including all contact information for the applicants. Completed applications must be submitted via email to jean.clarke@nhcf.org or via mail. **Deadline:** April 17.

6897 ■ New Hampshire Sheep and Wool Growers Association (NHSWGA)
PMB 223
220 Loudon Rd.
Concord, NH 03301
E-mail: president@nhswga.org
URL: www.nhswga.com

6898 ■ Bruce Clement Post-Secondary Education Scholarships *(Undergraduate/Scholarship)*

Purpose: To financially assist students who are pursuing an education related to the sheep industry. **Focus:** Industry

Awards are arranged alphabetically below their administering organizations

and trade. **Qualif.:** Applicants must be NH residents who have completed at least one year at a post-secondary institution; and must be majoring in a field that will benefit the sheep industry. **Criteria:** Recipients will be selected based on past involvement and/or future plans in the sheep industry; volunteer services including youth involvement in agricultural programs; and review of transcript and letters of recommendation.

Funds Avail.: No specific amount. **To Apply:** Applicants must submit a filled-out application form, transcript of records and three letters of recommendation. **Deadline:** June 1. **Contact:** The New Hampshire Sheep & Wool Growers Association Scholarship, at the above address.

6899 ■ New Hampshire Snowmobile Association (NHSA)
614 Laconia Rd., Unit 4
Tilton, NH 03276
Ph: (603)273-0220
Fax: (603)273-0218
E-mail: nhsaoffice@nhsa.com
URL: www.nhsa.com

6900 ■ New Hampshire Snowmobile Association Scholarships *(Undergraduate, Vocational/Occupational/Scholarship)*
Purpose: To assist the education of a dependent of a NHSA member. **Focus:** General studies/Field of study not specified. **Qualif.:** Applicant must be a graduating high school senior, accepted at a college, junior college, or vocational school; or a college student already enrolled. **Criteria:** The scholarship committee will review applications and will select based on academic achievement, extracurricular involvement, community service and the quality of the original essay.

Funds Avail.: $1,000; $500; $250. **Duration:** Annual. **To Apply:** Applicant must submit a completed application form along with letter of acceptance; transcript of grades at high school or grade record of the college; essay; recommendations; and list of extra-curricular activities. **Deadline:** April 10.

6901 ■ New Jersey Association of Osteopathic Physicians and Surgeons (NJAOPS)
1 Distribution Way, Ste. 201
Monmouth Junction, NJ 08852
Ph: (732)940-9000
Fax: (732)940-8899
E-mail: info@njosteo.com
URL: www.njosteo.com

6902 ■ New Jersey Association of Osteopathic Physicians and Surgeons Scholarships *(Undergraduate/Scholarship)*
Purpose: To promote public health, unite professionals for the maintenance of high standards of practice and osteopathic education; to promote scientific research. **Focus:** Medicine, Osteopathic. **Qualif.:** Applicants must be students entering their first year in an osteopathic college; must be residents of New Jersey and have completed four years of pre-medical education; must have a B average or a 3.0 GPA on a 4.0 grading system and be in the upper 25% in class standing. **Criteria:** Recipients are selected based on undergraduate academic achievement, financial

need, motivation and professional promise.

Funds Avail.: No specific amount. **To Apply:** Applicants must submit a completed application form, four completed reference evaluation forms, MCAT scores, pre-med college transcript and an essay stating their reasons for becoming an osteopathic physician. **Deadline:** May 31. **Remarks:** Established in 1969.

6903 ■ New Jersey Broadcasters Association (NJBA)
348 Applegarth Rd.
Monroe Township, NJ 08831
Free: 888-657-2346
E-mail: njba@njba.com
URL: www.njba.com

6904 ■ Howard L. Green Scholarships *(Undergraduate/Scholarship)*
Purpose: To support students enrolled full-time at any colleges or universities in New Jersey. **Focus:** Broadcasting; Communications; Journalism. **Qualif.:** Applicants must be undergraduate students studying broadcasting, journalism or communications at any colleges or universities in New Jersey. **Criteria:** Selection will be based on the committee's criteria.

Funds Avail.: $1,000. **Duration:** Annual. **To Apply:** Applicants must complete and submit the application form available online together with the following materials: a brief statement explaining their interest in broadcasting, how they expect to develop this interest and experience that have had so far in this field in high school, college or professionally; a brief biography; a letter of recommendation from a person qualified to judge their performance and/or aptitude for a career in broadcasting; a short note from their instructor or advisor evaluating their overall academic ability; some representative sample of their work in the field for evaluation by the judges. **Deadline:** April 30.

6905 ■ New Jersey Commission on Brain Injury Research (NJCBIR)
225 E State St., 2nd Fl. W
Trenton, NJ 08625
Ph: (609)633-6465
Fax: (609)943-4213
E-mail: njcbir@doh.state.nj.us
URL: www.state.nj.us/health/njcbir

6906 ■ NJCBIR Individual Research Grants *(Other/Grant)*
Purpose: To encourage investigators to undertake research on neural protection, repair and regeneration after traumatic brain injury; to encourage individuals to undertake research on the effectiveness of clinical interventions for traumatic brain injury; and to enable researchers with novel scientific and clinical ideas to test them and develop pilot data needed to develop a programmatic area of research that can be supported by additional funding from the National Institutes of Health and other funding sources. **Focus:** Neurology. **Qualif.:** Applicants must be affiliated with a New Jersey State academic institution, research organization, public or private agency or other entity with demonstrated capability to conduct research responsibility; any nationality or citizenship status may apply, provided they are employed by or affiliated with a qualified New Jersey State

Awards are arranged alphabetically below their administering organizations

organization/institution. **Criteria:** Selection will be based on the committee's criteria.

Funds Avail.: Up to $150,000 per year. **Duration:** One to three years. **To Apply:** Applicants must comply with the following requirements: terms and conditions for the administration of grants; general and specific grant compliance requirements issued by the granting agency; applicable federal cost principles relating to the applicant. Applications and NJCBIR Research Guidelines governing grants are available for review and submission on the website at www.sage.nj.gov. A letter of intent must also be filed with the NJCBIR office. **Deadline:** August 1 for the Letter of Intent; October 3 for the applications.

6907 ■ NJCBIR Pilot Research Grants *(Other/Grant)*

Purpose: To encourage investigators to undertake research on neural protection, repair and regeneration after traumatic brain injury; to encourage individuals to undertake research on the effectiveness of clinical interventions for traumatic brain injury; and to enable researchers with novel scientific and clinical ideas to test them and develop pilot data needed to develop a programmatic area of research that can be supported by additional funding from the National Institutes of Health and other funding sources. **Focus:** Neurology. **Qualif.:** Applicants must be affiliated with a New Jersey State academic institution, research organization, public or private agency or other entity with demonstrated capability to conduct research responsibility; any nationality or citizenship status may apply, provided they are employed by or affiliated with a qualified New Jersey State organization/institution. **Criteria:** Selection will be based on the committee's criteria.

Funds Avail.: $75,000 per year. **Duration:** One to two years. **To Apply:** Eligible applicants must comply with the following requirements: terms and conditions for the administration of grants; general and specific grant compliance requirements issued by the granting agency; applicable federal cost principles relating to the applicant. Applications and NJCBIR Research Guidelines governing grants are available for review and submission on the website. A letter of intent must also be filed with the NJCBIR office.

6908 ■ NJCBIR Postdoctoral and Graduate Student Fellowships *(Graduate, Postdoctorate/Fellowship)*

Purpose: To encourage investigators to undertake research on neural protection, repair and regeneration after traumatic brain injury; to encourage individuals to undertake research on the effectiveness of clinical interventions for traumatic brain injury; and to enable researchers with novel scientific and clinical ideas to test them and develop pilot data needed to develop a programmatic area of research that can be supported by additional funding from the National Institutes of Health and other funding sources. **Focus:** Neurology. **Qualif.:** Applicants must hold a PhD, MD or equivalent graduate degree. Appropriate degrees must be awarded prior to the activation of award. Candidates must be accepted for postdoctoral training under the supervision of an appropriate mentor at a qualifying academic research institution in New Jersey; must be full-time graduate students in residence in a proposed course of study directly related to regeneration and repair of the damaged brain. Students must begin their study in the semester following activation unless special permission is received prior to activation date. **Criteria:** Selection will based on the committee's criteria.

Funds Avail.: $40,000-$44,000 for the postdoctoral;

$27,500 for the graduate students. **Duration:** Annual. **To Apply:** Applicants must comply with the following requirements: terms and conditions for the administration of grants; general and specific grant compliance requirements issued by the granting agency; applicable federal cost principles relating to the applicant. Applications and NJCBIR Research Guidelines governing grants are available for review and submission on the website. A letter of intent must also be filed with the NJCBIR office. **Deadline:** October 3.

6909 ■ NJCBIR Programmatic Multi-Investigator Project Grants *(Other/Grant)*

Purpose: To enhance in-depth mechanistic analysis and promote translational research. **Focus:** Neurology. **Qualif.:** Applicants must be affiliated with a New Jersey State academic institution, research organization, public or private agency or other entity with demonstrated capability to conduct research responsibility; any nationality or citizenship status may apply, provided they are employed by or affiliated with a qualified New Jersey State organization/institution; must be residents or located within a qualifying institution in the State of New Jersey. **Criteria:** Selection will be based on the committee's criteria.

Funds Avail.: $600,000 per year. **Duration:** One to three years. **To Apply:** Eligible applicants must comply with the following requirements: terms and conditions for the administration of grants; general and specific grant compliance requirements issued by the granting agency; applicable federal cost principles relating to the applicant. Applications and NJCBIR Research Guidelines governing grants are available for review and submission on the website at www.sage.nj.gov. A letter of intent must also be filed with the NJCBIR office. **Deadline:** August 1 for the Letter of Intent; October 3 for the applications.

6910 ■ New Jersey Hospital Association (NJHA)
760 Alexander Rd.
Princeton, NJ 08540-6305
Ph: (609)275-4000
URL: www.njha.com

6911 ■ HRET Health Career Scholarships *(Postgraduate, Undergraduate/Scholarship)*

Purpose: To encourage and enable New Jersey residents to pursue health careers. **Focus:** Health care services; Health sciences; Nursing. **Qualif.:** Applicant must be a New Jersey resident; accepted into a graduate or undergraduate (junior and seniors only) program in hospital or healthcare administration or a graduate or undergraduate (junior or senior only) program in Nursing or Allied Health Profession; have maintained a GPA of at least 3.0 (on a 4 point system or equivalent); demonstrated financial need with a FAFSA document and financial aid application and/or federal tax return from the previous year. **Criteria:** Selection is based on the application.

Funds Avail.: $2,000. **Duration:** Annual. **To Apply:** Applicants must provide a two-page essay letter detailing academic plans for the future and substantiating that the eligibility requirements have been met (essays will be 50% of the judging criteria); one letter of recommendation from the head of the program in which the student is enrolled or from a current supervisor; official transcript (online transcript copies are not accepted); FAFSA, Financial aid application and/or federal tax return from the previous year; and provide a current address, phone number and e-mail address. **Deadline:** July 1. **Contact:** NJHA Communications; Email: press@njha.com.

Awards are arranged alphabetically below their administering organizations

6912 ■ New Jersey Library Association (NJLA)

PO Box 1534
Trenton, NJ 08607
Ph: (609)394-8032
Fax: (609)394-8164
E-mail: ptumulty@njla.org
URL: www.njla.org

6913 ■ NJLA Scholarships *(Graduate, Postgraduate/ Scholarship)*

Purpose: To provide support to students for study leading to a graduate or postgraduate degree in librarianship. **Focus:** Library and archival sciences. **Qualif.:** Applicants must be New Jersey residents and students pursuing graduate or postgraduate degree in librarianship. **Criteria:** Selection shall be based on the aforementioned applicants' qualifications and compliance with the application details.

Funds Avail.: No specific amount. **Duration:** Annual. **To Apply:** Applicants must provide and submit completed application form, essay, resume or CV, sealed official transcripts, and sealed letters of recommendation. **Deadline:** February 18. **Contact:** Kassundra Miller, NJLA Scholarship Committee Co-Chair, Wood-Ridge Memorial Library, 231 Hackensack Street, Wood-Ridge, NJ 07075.

6914 ■ New Jersey Performing Arts Center (NJ-PAC)

1 Center St.
Newark, NJ 07102
Ph: (973)642-8989
Free: 888-466-5722
URL: www.njpac.org

6915 ■ Jeffrey Carollo Music Scholarships *(Undergraduate/Scholarship)*

Purpose: To provide financial assistance to advanced students who study classical vocal and instrumental music. **Focus:** Music. **Qualif.:** Applicants must be enrolled in the music program at the Newark Community School of the Arts and must be 18 years old and below. **Criteria:** Recipients are selected based on demonstrated interest in the field of music.

Funds Avail.: No specific amount. **To Apply:** Applicants must submit a completed application form.

6916 ■ Star-Ledger Scholarships for the Performing Arts *(Undergraduate/Scholarship)*

Purpose: To provide higher education opportunities for the young people of Newark; to provide an opportunity to gain practical experience at the New Jersey Performing Arts Center through internships. **Focus:** Performing arts. **Qualif.:** Applicants must be seniors who attend a Newark high school and have permanent residence in Newark, New Jersey. Applicants must also have an overall academic GPA of 2.5 or higher, however, extremely talented individuals with a GPA of less than 2.5 may be considered. **Criteria:** Recipients are selected based on merit and demonstrated potential to become leading arts professionals.

Funds Avail.: $750 or $40,000. **To Apply:** Applicants must submit a completed application form; high school transcript; three letters of recommendation: one from an arts teacher, one from a non-arts teacher, and one from a principal or guidance counselor; SAT scores; personal essay describing how this scholarship will help them achieve their goals;

resume; list of pieces that will be performed for the audition.

6917 ■ New Jersey Press Foundation (NJPF)

c/o John J. O'Brien, Director
810 Bear Tavern Rd., Ste. 307
West Trenton, NJ 08628-1022
Ph: (609)406-0600
Fax: (609)406-0300
URL: www.njpa.org/foundation

6918 ■ Richard Drukker Memorial Scholarships *(Undergraduate/Scholarship)*

Purpose: To promote journalism careers and newspaper readership among New Jersey residents. **Focus:** Journalism. **Qualif.:** Applicants must be journalism minors and staff members of the Montclarion. **Criteria:** Recipients are selected based on academic standing and financial need.

Funds Avail.: $2,000. **Duration:** Annual. **To Apply:** Applicants must complete the application form and submit an academic transcript for all college work completed; three samples of journalistic writing that has appeared in any newspaper or was done for class assignments; a statement of interest in a newspaper career, written as an autobiographical sketch describing their journalistic skills and achievements (no more than 500 words); and statement of financial or family circumstances. **Deadline:** April 3.

6919 ■ Bernard Kilgore Memorial Scholarships *(Undergraduate/Scholarship)*

Purpose: To promote journalism career and newspaper readership among New Jersey residents. **Focus:** Journalism. **Qualif.:** Applicants must be graduating high school seniors; must be planning to study journalism in college and to pursue a journalism career; must have at least a 3.0 GPA on a 4.0 scale and have participated in high school journalism for at least two years. **Criteria:** Recipients are selected based on academic record and financial need.

Funds Avail.: $5,000. **Duration:** Annual. **To Apply:** Applicants must submit an official entry form; a self-analytical evaluation of the journalistic life using a creative form; and one action photo of themselves in a journalistic role; and an official copy of their transcript. Applicants should secure three to four letters of recommendation from advisers, teachers familiar with their leadership and journalistic abilities or practitioners with whom they have worked. **Deadline:** February 13. **Contact:** Kilgore Scholarship Committee, New Jersey Press Foundation; at the above address.

6920 ■ New Jersey Psychological Association (NJPA)

414 Eagle Rock Ave., Ste. 211
West Orange, NJ 07052
Ph: (973)243-9800
Fax: (973)243-9818
E-mail: njpa@psychologynj.org
URL: www.psychologynj.org

6921 ■ NJPA Foundation Scholarship for Research on Diversity Issues *(Graduate/Scholarship)*

Purpose: To support the needs of underserved communities through research or service. **Focus:** Psychology. **Qualif.:** Applicants must be graduate students enrolled at a

Awards are arranged alphabetically below their administering organizations

New Jersey university or college at the master's or doctoral level of study, or an intern at a New Jersey facility; must be minority group members as defined by federal guidelines; must be students in good standing at their college or university. **Criteria:** Recipients are selected based on social significance of the study, scientific rigor of the study, originality of the study, feasibility and clarity of written expression.

Funds Avail.: $2,000. **Duration:** Annual. **To Apply:** Applicants must submit four copies of a 100-150 word project proposal to the NJPA Foundation; must submit a completed application form; must substantiate his/her claim to minority status according to federal guidelines. **Deadline:** July 11.

6922 ■ New Jersey Society of Certified Public Accountants (NJCPA)

425 Eagle Rock Ave., Ste. 100
Roseland, NJ 07068-1723
Ph: (973)226-4494
Fax: (973)226-7425
E-mail: njcpa@njcpa.org
URL: www.njscpa.org

6923 ■ NJSCPA College Scholarships (Graduate, Undergraduate/Scholarship)

Purpose: To support college students currently in junior year or seniors who will be entering an accounting-related graduate program. **Focus:** Accounting. **Qualif.:** Applicant must be a resident of New Jersey attending a New Jersey college/university; an accounting major or with a concentration in accounting with at least 12 credits in accounting completed; currently at junior-year status or above in an undergraduate program or enrolled in, or entering, an accounting related program. **Criteria:** Selection is based on the application materials submitted.

Funds Avail.: $4,000. **To Apply:** Applicants must submit a completed application together with a letter of recommendation from an accounting professor; an official transcript showing a minimum overall GPA of 3.2; and a resume. **Deadline:** January 9. **Contact:** Mindy Ripp, mripp@njscpa.org or 973-226-4494 x 241.

6924 ■ NJSCPA High School Scholarships (Undergraduate/Scholarship)

Purpose: To support New Jersey high school seniors who plan to major in accounting. **Focus:** Accounting. **Qualif.:** Applicant must intend to begin the study of accounting as a major; a U.S. citizen or lawfully admitted for permanent residence; a New Jersey resident attending, or just recently graduated from, a New Jersey high school; a high school senior planning to enter college; majoring or has a concentration in accounting in college; and has a GPA of 3.0 or above, or a minimum combined verbal, math and essay SAT score of 1500, or minimum average ACT score of 23. **Criteria:** Selection is based on academic performance, an essay and a personal interview.

Funds Avail.: $6,500 - $10,000. **Duration:** Four years. **To Apply:** Applicants must submit a completed application form along with an essay, and a guidance copy of standardized test score, GPA and class rank (if available). **Deadline:** December 20. **Contact:** Janice Amatucci at jamatucci@njscpa.org or 973-226-4494 x-209.

6925 ■ New Jersey State Bar Foundation (NJSBF)

1 Constitution Sq.
New Brunswick, NJ 08901

Ph: (732)249-5000
Fax: (732)828-0034
URL: www.njsbf.org

6926 ■ Abram D. and Maxine H. Londa Scholarships (Undergraduate/Scholarship)

Purpose: To support students who are pursuing legal education. **Focus:** Law. **Qualif.:** Applicants must be students entering their second or third year at a New Jersey law school. **Criteria:** Preference will be given to students from Union County.

Funds Avail.: No specific amount. **Duration:** Annual. **To Apply:** Scholarship applications are available at the beginning of the second semester at the financial aid offices of the New Jersey law schools. **Contact:** Florence Nathan, NJSBF Director of Special Programs, at fnathan@njsbf.org.

6927 ■ Sonia Morgan Scholarships (Undergraduate/Scholarship)

Purpose: To support female students who are pursuing legal education. **Focus:** Law. **Qualif.:** Applicants must be female students entering their second or third year at a New Jersey law school. **Criteria:** The criteria for the selection of candidates include academic excellence (GPA and class standing), participation in extracurricular activities, financial need and community service.

Funds Avail.: No specific amount. **Duration:** Annual. **To Apply:** Scholarship applications are available at the beginning of the second semester at the financial aid offices of the New Jersey law schools. **Contact:** Florence Nathan, NJSBF Director of Special Programs, at fnathan@njsbf.org.

6928 ■ NJSBF Labor Law Scholarships (Undergraduate/Scholarship)

Purpose: To support students who are pursuing legal education. **Focus:** Law. **Qualif.:** Applicants must be students wishing to enter the field of labor law, and are in the second or third year at a New Jersey law school. **Criteria:** Particular attention will be given to academic achievement in the area of labor law.

Funds Avail.: No specific amount. **Duration:** Annual. **To Apply:** Scholarship applications are available at the beginning of the second semester at the financial aid offices of the New Jersey law schools. **Contact:** Florence Nathan, NJSBF Director of Special Programs, at fnathan@njsbf.org.

6929 ■ Wallace Vail Scholarships (Undergraduate/Scholarship)

Purpose: To support students who are pursuing of legal education. **Focus:** Law. **Qualif.:** Applicants must be students entering their second or third year at a New Jersey law school. **Criteria:** Selection will be based on the academic performance of the applicants among the three law schools in New Jersey (Rutgers University School of Law - Newark; Rutgers University School of Law - Camden; and Seton Hall University School of Law).

Funds Avail.: No specific amount. **Duration:** Annual. **To Apply:** Scholarship applications are available at the beginning of the second semester at the financial aid offices of the New Jersey law schools. **Contact:** Florence Nathan, NJSBF Director of Special Programs, at fnathan@njsbf.org.

6930 ■ New Mexico Association for Bilingual Education (NMABE)

PO Box 5190
Clovis, NM 88102-5190

Awards are arranged alphabetically below their administering organizations

Ph: (505)238-6812
Fax: (575)769-0742
E-mail: nmabe@suddenlink.net
URL: www.nmabe.net

6931 ■ New Mexico Association for Bilingual Education Scholarships *(Undergraduate/Scholarship)*

Purpose: To provide financial support for deserving students intending to pursue studies in the area of bilingual education. **Focus:** Education, Bilingual and cross-cultural. **Qualif.:** Applicants must be juniors or seniors in a New Mexico university bilingual education teacher preparation program. Applicants must have a GPA of 3.0 or better for initial consideration and for renewals. They must reapply by the appropriate deadline for consideration each semester. **Criteria:** Preference will be given to those students who meet the criteria.

Funds Avail.: No specific amount. **Duration:** Annual. **To Apply:** Applicants must submit the completed application form; two letters of recommendation; a written essay in Spanish or a Native American language outlining their reasons for entering the field of Bilingual Education; and current university transcripts. **Deadline:** May 1; July 1; October 1.

6932 ■ New York City Bar Association (NYCB)

42 W 44th St.
New York, NY 10036
Ph: (212)382-6600
E-mail: cdunne@nycbar.org
URL: www.nycbar.org

6933 ■ City Bar Diversity Fellowships Program *(Undergraduate/Fellowship)*

Purpose: To offer first-year students from underrepresented populations a unique summer employment opportunity in outstanding law firms and corporate law departments. **Focus:** Law. **Qualif.:** Candidates must be first year students from underrepresented populations. **Criteria:** Selection will be based on the committee's criteria.

Funds Avail.: No specific amount. **To Apply:** Interested applicants may visit the website for the application process and other information. The Committee accordingly invites New York City area law schools to participate in the Fellowship Program.

6934 ■ Thurgood Marshall Fellowships Program *(Undergraduate/Fellowship)*

Purpose: To provide internship experience in public service or civil rights to talented minority law students. **Focus:** Law. **Qualif.:** Applicants must be minority law students. **Criteria:** Selection will be based on the committee's criteria.

Funds Avail.: No specific amount. **To Apply:** Interested applicants may contact the Association for the application process and other information.

6935 ■ C. Bainbridge Smith Scholarships *(Undergraduate/Scholarship)*

Purpose: To award scholarship opportunities to the law students. **Focus:** Law. **Qualif.:** Applicants must be second or third year inner-city law students who have spent a significant portion of their lives in New York City and demonstrate character, intelligence and promising aptitude for the law and face special economic disadvantages. **Cri-**

teria: Selection will be based on the committee's criteria.

Funds Avail.: No specific amount. **To Apply:** Interested applicants may contact the Association for the application process and other information.

6936 ■ The New York Community Trust

909 3rd Ave., 22nd Flr.
New York, NY 10022
Ph: (212)686-0010
Fax: (212)532-8528
URL: www.nycommunitytrust.org

6937 ■ Fahs-Beck Fund for Research and Experimentation - Doctoral Dissertation Grants *(Doctorate/Grant)*

Purpose: To help support dissertation expenses of doctoral students in the United States and Canada whose studies have the potential for adding significantly to knowledge about problems in the functioning or well being of children, adults, couples, families, or communities, or about interventions designed to prevent or alleviate such problems. **Focus:** Public health. **Qualif.:** Applicants must be enrolled in an accredited doctoral program in the United States or Canada; must have a sponsoring organization in which such must agree to accept administrative responsibility for the project and submit required financial forms and reports to the Fund. **Criteria:** Selection will be based on the applicants' research proposals. The committee considers four criteria in evaluating proposals: the compatibility of the proposed work with the areas of funding supported by the Fund; the significance, impact, and expected benefit of the study; conceptual and technical merit of the proposed study; and the likelihood of successful and timely completion of the proposed work.

Funds Avail.: Up to $5,000. **Duration:** Semiannual. **To Apply:** Applicants must submit the following requirements: research proposals (to be submitted electronically as a PDF format with the applicants' name in the subject line); two copies of the completed application form); ten (10) copies of a Project Summary Statement with a completed Project Summary Cover Sheet stapled to the top of each (Cover Sheet is page 4 of the application form); evidences that the dissertation proposals have received official faculty approval; evidences that the dissertation proposals have received official final approval from the IRB of the sponsoring institution; curriculum vitae; a time schedule showing probable dates for completion of data collection, data analysis, and the dissertation; proposed budget; letter of agreement from the applicants (stating that they will: make all reasonable efforts to complete the dissertation on a timely basis; send to the Fahs-Beck Fund a brief progress report and an interim accounting of expenditures from the Fund one year after the awarding of the grant; notify the Fund of the date of acceptance of the dissertation by the sponsoring institution and submit at that time an abstract of the final dissertation (not the complete dissertation); and, submit a final financial report to the Fund on all expenditures from the grant award and return any unused portion of the grant to the Fund); letter from sponsoring organization indicating whether or not charges (maximum 10%) will be assessed for administering the grant; letter from sponsoring organization affirming tax-exempt status, relevant accreditation or certification; and a confidential letter from the applicants' primary faculty dissertation sponsors. The letter should include the faculty sponsors judgment of the competence of the applicants to produce a quality product,

Awards are arranged alphabetically below their administering organizations

the likelihood that the students will complete the dissertation in a timely manner, and the potential contribution of the dissertation. The letter must be written on official letterhead and have an original signature., **Deadline:** April 1; November 1. **Contact:** Email dissertations at dissertation@fahsbeckfund.org.

6938 ■ Fahs-Beck Fund for Research and Experimentation - Postdoctoral Grants
(Postdoctorate/Grant)

Purpose: To help support the research of faculty members or post-doctoral researchers affiliated with non-profit human service organizations in the United States and Canada. **Focus:** Public health. **Qualif.:** Applicants must be faculty members of accredited colleges or universities or individuals affiliated with accredited non-profit human service organizations in the United States or Canada. **Criteria:** Selection will be based on the applicants' project proposals. The committee considers four criteria in evaluating proposals: the compatibility of the proposed work with the areas of funding supported by the Fund; the significance, impact, and expected benefit of the study; conceptual and technical merit of the proposed study; and the likelihood of successful and timely completion of the proposed work.

Funds Avail.: $20,000. **Duration:** Two years. **To Apply:** Applicants must submit the following requirements: 10-page project description (to be sent as PDF formats using the name of the primary investigators in the subject line); two copies of the completed application form with original signatures; printed copy of the project description (no longer than 10 pages, typed in 11-point Tahoma typeface, double spaced including the following: statement of the problem/purpose of the study; brief review of literature; description of intervention and setting, if applicable; description of the research plan, including measures to be used; and the significance, expected benefits); copies of measures to be used; ten (10) copies of a Project Summary Statement with a Project Summary Cover Sheet stapled to the top of each (the Cover Sheet is p. 5 of the application form); evidence of official and final IRB approval; letters of agreement from organizations that will be providing services that are part of the study or access to subjects; curriculum vitae of the principal investigators and other relevant personnel on the project; a chart of the tasks and subtasks necessary for the conduct of the study, indication of the responsible parties, and time line for accomplishment; a proposed budget listing the individual items for which funding is requested, the amount requested for each item, and a budget narrative justifying each item; letter from sponsoring organization indicating whether or not administrative charges (maximum 10%) will be assessed for administering the grant; and, letter from sponsoring organization affirming tax-exempt status, relevant accreditation or certification. **Deadline:** April 1; November 1. **Contact:** Email project proposals at postdoc@fahsbeckfund.org.

6939 ■ NYCT Paid Graduate Student Philanthropy Fellowships - Arts and Historic Preservation
(Graduate/Fellowship)

Purpose: To promote diversity in the arts, as well as to support preservation in low-income and minority communities and the boroughs outside of Manhattan. **Focus:** Arts; Historic preservation. **Qualif.:** Applicants must be students who are entering their last year of a full-time graduate program; and must be able to commit to the entire period of the fellowship. **Criteria:** Selection will be based on the Trust's criteria.

Funds Avail.: $21 per hour. **To Apply:** Applicants should email in PDF format their resume, cover letter, and short (up to 2 pages) writing sample. Please write in the subject line: first name, last name, and which of the four fellowships the applicants are applying for (in this case, Arts). **Deadline:** February 13. **Contact:** Email Janet Morgan at jem@nyct-cfi.org.

6940 ■ NYCT Paid Graduate Student Philanthropy Fellowships - Children, Youth, Families, Education, Human Justice and Workforce
(Graduate/Fellowship)

Purpose: To support individuals in improving the sectors of children, youth, families, education, human justice and workforce. **Focus:** Education; Family planning; Human rights; Youth. **Qualif.:** Applicants must be students who are entering their last year of a full-time graduate program; and must be able to commit to the entire period of the fellowship. **Criteria:** Selection will be based on the Trust's criteria.

Funds Avail.: $21 per hour. **To Apply:** Applicants should email in PDF format their resume, cover letter, and short (up to 2 pages) writing sample. Please write in the subject line: first name, last name, and which of the four fellowships the applicants are applying for (in this case, Children, Youth, Families, Education, Human Justice and Workforce). **Deadline:** March 13 (resume). **Contact:** Email Beth Mirarchi at em@nyct-cfi.org.

6941 ■ NYCT Paid Graduate Student Philanthropy Fellowships - Community Development and the Environment
(Graduate/Fellowship)

Purpose: To promote the community development and protect the environment in the New York community. **Focus:** Environmental conservation; Social work. **Qualif.:** Applicants must be students who are entering their last year of a full-time graduate program; and must be able to commit to the entire period of the fellowship. **Criteria:** Selection will be based on the Trust's criteria.

Funds Avail.: $21 per hour. **To Apply:** Applicants should email in PDF format their resume, cover letter, and short (up to 2 pages) writing sample. Please write in the subject line: first name, last name, and which of the four fellowships the applicants are applying for (in this case, Community Development and the Environment). **Deadline:** March 13 (resume). **Contact:** Email Phoebe Scarborough at ps@nyct-cfi.org.

6942 ■ NYCT Paid Graduate Student Philanthropy Fellowships - Health and People with Special Needs
(Graduate/Fellowship)

Purpose: To support individuals in improving services for children and youth with disabilities, the elderly, and for people with AIDS, mental illness and mental retardation, and/or visual disabilities. **Focus:** AIDS; Disabilities; Health care services; Mental retardation. **Qualif.:** Applicants must be students who are entering their last year of a full-time graduate program; and must be able to commit to the entire period of the fellowship. **Criteria:** Selection will be based on the Trust's criteria.

Funds Avail.: $21 per hour. **To Apply:** Applicants should email in PDF format their resume, cover letter, and short (up to 2 pages) writing sample. Please write in the subject line: first name, last name, and which of the four fellowships the applicants are applying for (in this case, Health and People with Special Needs). **Deadline:** March 13 (resume). **Contact:** Email Phoebe Scarborough at ps@nyct-cfi.org.

Awards are arranged alphabetically below their administering organizations

6943 ■ New York Financial Writers' Association (NYFWA)

PO Box 338
Ridgewood, NJ 07451-0338
Ph: (201)612-0100
Fax: (201)256-4115
E-mail: contact@nyfwa.org
URL: www.nyfwa.org

6944 ■ New York Financial Writers' Associations Scholarships *(Graduate, Undergraduate/Scholarship)*

Purpose: To provide financial assistance to those studying business, finance, and journalism. **Focus:** Business; Finance; Journalism. **Qualif.:** Undergraduate or graduate journalism students in the Metropolitan New York area who are seriously interested in pursuing a career in business and financial journalism. **Criteria:** Recipients are chosen based on the application materials submitted.

Funds Avail.: No specific amount. **To Apply:** Applicants must send an application form together with an essay explaining why the applicant is pursuing a career in business and financial journalism, current resume, list of other scholarships received and samples of financial writings and clippings created. If an application form is unavailable, applicants may submit a cover letter with the requirements listed. **Deadline:** April 15. **Contact:** NYFWS Scholarship Committee at the above address.

6945 ■ NYFWA Scholarships *(Undergraduate, Graduate/Scholarship)*

Purpose: To support students who are seriously interested in pursuing a career in business and financial journalism. **Focus:** Business; Finance; Journalism. **Qualif.:** Applicants must be undergraduate or graduate journalism students in the tri-state New York area. **Criteria:** Selection will be based on the committee's criteria.

Funds Avail.: $3,000. **Duration:** Annual. **Number Awarded:** Varies. **To Apply:** Applicants must submit the following requirements: school, division, major and expected graduation date; present address and permanent home address (if different), telephone number; any other relevant personal information; essay explaining why the applicants are pursuing career in business and financial journalism; current resume, including other scholarships received; samples of financial writing (3 to 5 pieces) including links to online work and print clippings in PDF format. **Deadline:** April 15. **Contact:** Applications should be sent to scholarships@nyfwa.org.

6946 ■ New York Library Association (NYLA)

6021 State Farm Rd.
Guilderland, NY 12084
Ph: (518)432-6952
Fax: (518)427-1697
E-mail: info@nyla.org
URL: www.nyla.org

6947 ■ NYLA-Dewey Scholarship *(Master's, Undergraduate/Scholarship)*

Purpose: To provide financial assistance to deserving student to pursue a Masters Degree in Library Science at an ALA-accredited library school in New York State. **Focus:** Library and archival sciences. **Qualif.:** Applicants must be full- or part-time students; must have maintained at least a B average during the semester. Both the students and the library school must be members of the New York Library Association. The successful candidates are expected to work in a library or library system in New York State for at least two years upon graduation. **Criteria:** Selection will be based on the following criteria: evidence of a commitment to a career in librarianship; demonstrated leadership ability, and scholarly excellence.

Funds Avail.: $1,000. **Duration:** Annual. **To Apply:** Application form can be downloaded online and must be submitted to the Dean of the Library School or Information Sciences at the ALA accredited institution. **Deadline:** September 30.

6948 ■ New York School Nutrition Association (NYSNA)

125 Wolf Rd., Ste. 312
Albany, NY 12205
Ph: (518)446-9061
Fax: (518)446-0113
Free: 800-697-7372
URL: www.nyschoolnutrition.org

6949 ■ Jeff Siegel Scholarships *(Undergraduate/Scholarship)*

Purpose: To help defray the cost of food service education for students; to provide means of recognition for the school food service department. **Focus:** Food service careers. **Qualif.:** Applicants must be recommended by a NYSNA member who has been an active member for at least one year; must be high school graduating students in the year the scholarship is awarded, from the school where the Director is employed; must have been accepted at a college with a program in food service and intend to pursue a career in the food service industry. **Criteria:** Recipients are selected based on the required documents and academic performance.

Funds Avail.: $1,000. **To Apply:** Applicants must attach a letter of recommendation from the NYSNA member who submitted their name for the award; must attach a 200 word essay on how/why they chose food service as their future career; must attach a letter of recommendation from a school official, guidance counselor, principal etc.; must attach a copy of letter of acceptance from college; must submit a copy of high school transcript, including first semester of the senior year; must attach any additional comments or information that will be helpful. **Deadline:** May 1. **Remarks:** Established in 2003.

6950 ■ New York State Association of Agricultural Fairs (NYSAAF)

67 Verbeck Ave.
Schaghticoke, NY 12154
Ph: (518)753-4956
Fax: (518)753-0208
URL: www.nyfairs.org

6951 ■ New York State Association of Agricultural Fairs Scholarships *(Undergraduate/Scholarship)*

Purpose: To provide financial assistance to those high school and college students who have been active in their local fairs and who intend to pursue higher education in an agricultural or fair management related field. **Focus:** Agriculture, Economic aspects. **Qualif.:** Applicants must be in

Awards are arranged alphabetically below their administering organizations

their senior year of high school in New York State or New York residents planning to pursue or already attending college in an agricultural or fair management-related field at an accredited institution of higher education. **Criteria:** Recipients are selected based on quality of the essay, citizenship and leadership, fair participation, field of study, presentation of application and academic achievements.

Funds Avail.: $1,000. **Duration:** Annual. **Number Awarded:** Up to 10. **To Apply:** Applicants must submit a completed application form along with two letters of recommendation and transcript. **Deadline:** Second Friday in April. **Contact:** Renée St. Jacques; Phone: 518-812-5351; E-mail: st.jacques.r@gmail.com.

6952 ■ New York State Government Finance Officers' Association
126 State St., 5th Fl.
Albany, NY 12207
Ph: (518)465-1512
Fax: (518)434-4640
E-mail: info@nysgfoa.org
URL: www.nysgfoa.org

6953 ■ Stanley M. Schoenfeld Memorial Scholarship
(Postgraduate/Scholarship)

Purpose: To provide scholarships to outstanding students who have demonstrated a commitment to public service. **Focus:** Management; Public affairs. **Qualif.:** Applicants must be in a postgraduate program in public affairs/management at an accredited college or university in New York State and members of the National Association of Schools of Public Affairs and Administration. **Criteria:** Selection of applicants will be based on academic records, demonstrated promise of completing a graduate level program at a high level performance and evidence of intention to enter the field of public administration.

Funds Avail.: $3,000 each. **Duration:** Annual. **Number Awarded:** 2. **To Apply:** Applicants must complete the application form available on the website; must provide a letter of recommendation from either their undergraduate program Dean or a professor from the program, a mentor/supervisor they worked for/within the field of public affairs/management and/or the Dean of the graduate program; must provide a statement of proposed plan of graduate study and their career plans; must include an undergraduate grade transcript, GRE scores and resume. **Deadline:** March 21. **Contact:** New York State Government Finance Officers' Association, Inc., Stanley M. Schoenfeld Memorial Scholarship Committee, at the above address.

6954 ■ New York State Higher Education Services Corp.
99 Washington Ave.
Albany, NY 12255
Ph: (518)402-1448
Fax: (518)474-5593
E-mail: customerservice@firstmarkservices.com
URL: www.hesc.ny.gov

6955 ■ Senator Patricia K. McGee Nursing Faculty Scholarships *(Doctorate, Graduate/Scholarship)*
Purpose: To provide financial assistance to faculty nurses providing clinical nursing education in New York state. **Focus:** Nursing. **Qualif.:** Applicants must be legal residents of the United States for at least one year; must be U.S. citizens or eligible non-citizens; be registered nurses professionally licensed to work in New York state; must be enrolled in a master's program in nursing or a doctoral degree program that will qualify them as nursing faculty or adjunct clinical faculty at an accredited school in New York; must complete and return a service agreement in which they agree to practice as nursing faculty for four years. **Criteria:** Evaluation will be made based on submitted documents and specific criteria.

Funds Avail.: Up to $20,000. **Duration:** Annual; up to three years. **To Apply:** Applicants must submit a completed Web Supplement confirmation along with the required documentation according to the instructions. **Deadline:** June 15. **Contact:** New York State Higher Education Services Corp., at the above address.

6956 ■ New York State Senate
Washington Ave.
Albany, NY 12230
URL: www.nysenate.gov

6957 ■ James L. Biggane Fellowships in Finance
(Graduate/Fellowship)

Purpose: To give students the opportunity to experience fields of communications, journalism, and/or public relations. **Focus:** General studies/Field of study not specified. **Qualif.:** Applicant must be a full-time matriculated graduate student in an accredited university during the immediately previous spring and fall semesters. **Criteria:** Selection is based on the application.

Funds Avail.: $33,000. **Duration:** Annual. **Number Awarded:** 1. **To Apply:** Applicants must submit a complete application including course work-in-progress list signed by campus official (if not on transcript); Policy Proposal; Rebuttal of Policy Proposal; Statement of Purpose; resume or CV; all official transcripts (graduate and undergraduate, to be mailed directly to the Office of Student Programs); and three letters of reference from persons familiar with the applicant's character, academic and/or professional abilities (at least two from faculty members). **Deadline:** April 28.

6958 ■ New York State Senate - Legislative Fellowships *(Graduate, Postgraduate/Fellowship)*

Purpose: To provide talented and skilled graduate/postgraduate students with intimate knowledge of New York State government, fostering an understanding of our governmental system, and to attract those able students to public service careers from a variety of academic disciplines. **Focus:** General studies/Field of study not specified. **Qualif.:** Applicant must be a full-time matriculated graduate student in an accredited university during the immediately previous spring and fall semesters. **Criteria:** Selection is based on the application.

Funds Avail.: No specific amount. **Duration:** Annual. **Number Awarded:** 13. **To Apply:** Applicants must submit a complete application including course work-in-progress list signed by campus official (if not on transcript); Policy Proposal; Rebuttal of Policy Proposal; Statement of Purpose; resume or CV; all official transcripts (graduate and undergraduate, to be mailed directly to the Office of Student Programs); and three letters of reference from persons familiar with the applicant's character, academic and/or professional abilities (at least two from faculty members). **Deadline:** April 28. **Contact:** Nicholas J. Parrella, Director, Office of Student Programs, at the above address.

Awards are arranged alphabetically below their administering organizations

6959 ■ Richard J. Roth Journalism Fellowships
(Graduate/Fellowship)

Purpose: To give students the opportunity to experience fields of communications, journalism, and/or public relations. **Focus:** Communications; Journalism; Public relations. **Qualif.:** Applicant must be a full-time matriculated graduate student in an accredited university during the immediately previous spring and fall semesters. **Criteria:** Selection is based on the application.

Funds Avail.: $33,000. **Duration:** Annual. **Number Awarded:** 1. **To Apply:** Applicants must submit a complete application including course work-in-progress list signed by campus official (if not on transcript); Policy Proposal; Rebuttal of Policy Proposal; Statement of Purpose; resume or CV; all official transcripts (graduate and undergraduate, to be mailed directly to the Office of Student Programs); and three letters of reference from persons familiar with the applicant's character, academic and/or professional abilities (at least two from faculty members). **Deadline:** April 28.

6960 ■ Undergraduate Session Assistants Program
(Undergraduate/Other)

Purpose: To provide talented students with firsthand experience in New York State government at the legislative level. **Focus:** Public service. **Qualif.:** Applicant must be enrolled as a full time matriculating undergraduate student in an accredited program; pursuing a career in public service; a United States citizen; maintaining a 3.0 GPA and will have been enrolled full time in the immediately previous spring and current fall semester, or previous two trimesters; and have respectable research and strong communication skills. **Criteria:** Selection is based on the application.

Funds Avail.: $4,140. **Duration:** 4 months. **Number Awarded:** 30. **To Apply:** Applicants must submit a completed application form along with official transcripts of all collegiate work; special areas of skill or honors; a resume (1 page); preferred area of policy interest; three confidential letters of reference from persons familiar with the applicant's academic abilities and professional aptitude; one longer essay (1,200 words) and two policy memoranda; a statement of purpose; a certification by the CLO or other authorized campus official for each applicant stating that the applicant has been interviewed and/or the individual academic record reviewed to ensure applicant is eligible and meets all program and institutional requirements; certification of the applicant's present coursework-in-progress; and a signed Student Statement. **Deadline:** October 31. **Contact:** Nicholas J. Parrella, M.A., Director, NYS Senate Office of Student Programs; E-mail: students@nysenate.gov.

6961 ■ Richard A. Wiebe Public Service Fellowships
(Graduate/Fellowship)

Purpose: To give students the opportunity to experience fields of communications, journalism, and/or public relations. **Focus:** Public service. **Qualif.:** Applicant must be a full-time matriculated graduate student in an accredited university during the immediately previous spring and fall semesters. **Criteria:** Selection is based on legal training and a variety of other backgrounds.

Funds Avail.: $33,000. **Duration:** Annual. **Number Awarded:** 1. **To Apply:** Applicants must submit a complete application including course work-in-progress list signed by campus official (if not on transcript); Policy Proposal; Rebuttal of Policy Proposal; Statement of Purpose; resume or CV; all official transcripts (graduate and undergraduate, to be mailed directly to the Office of Student Programs); and

three letters of reference from persons familiar with the applicant's character, academic and/or professional abilities (at least two from faculty members). **Deadline:** April 28.

6962 ■ New York State Society of Certified Public Accountants (NYSSCPA)
14 Wall St., 19th Fl.
New York, NY 10005
Ph: (212)719-8300
Fax: (212)719-3364
Free: 800-633-6320
E-mail: jbarry@nysscpa.org
URL: www.nysscpa.org

6963 ■ David J. Moynihan Scholarships
(Undergraduate/Scholarship)

Purpose: To provide financial assistance to encourage and aid deserving candidates to enter the accounting profession. **Focus:** Accounting. **Qualif.:** Applicants must have declared and accepted to major in accounting; and, be residents of New York State and either U.S. citizens or permanent residents. **Criteria:** Selection shall be based on the aforementioned applicants' qualifications and compliance with the application details.

Funds Avail.: Amount varies. **Duration:** Annual. **Number Awarded:** Varies. **To Apply:** Applicants must contact their FAE campus ambassador or department chair for the application details. **Deadline:** April 23. **Contact:** New York State Society of Certified Public Accountants, at the above address; or contact Diane Abela by e-mail at dabela@nysscpa.org.

6964 ■ The New York Times Co.
620 8th Ave.
New York, NY 10018
Ph: (212)204-4000
Fax: (212)204-1727
Free: 888-698-6397
E-mail: national@nytimes.com
URL: www.nytco.com

6965 ■ The New York Times College Scholarships
(Undergraduate/Scholarship, Internship)

Purpose: To support high achieving yet financially underprivileged high school students from the greater New York City community. **Focus:** General studies/Field of study not specified. **Qualif.:** Applicants must be high school seniors attending public, parochial or private high schools in New York City; must have demonstrated academic achievement, commitment to learning-especially in the face of financial and other obstacles and community service; and must be citizens or permanent residents of the United States. **Criteria:** Awards are given based on merit and need. Preference will be given to students whose parents have not graduated from accredited American four-year colleges or universities.

Funds Avail.: No specific amount. **Duration:** Annual. **To Apply:** Applicants must complete an online application form; must attach a page listing the most important activities and achievements including the following: (1) academic honors; (2) community service; (3) work experience; and (4) extracurricular activities. Please include dates, place and duration of activities; must attach a brief essay (typed

Awards are arranged alphabetically below their administering organizations

and not more than two pages) describing the significant challenges and obstacles they need to overcome in achieving academic issues; and must also include a one-page chronological account of the most important events in their life (optional). **Remarks:** Established in 1999.

6966 ■ New York University School of Law - Center for Human Rights and Global Justice (CHRGJ)

139 MacDougal St., 5th Fl.
New York, NY 10012
URL: chrgj.org

6967 ■ CHRGJ Emerging Human Rights Scholarship Conference *(Graduate/Scholarship)*

Purpose: To encourage the development of human rights research and scholarship by giving students an opportunity to present papers and works-in-progress in a constructive and collaborative environment. **Focus:** Human rights; Law. **Qualif.:** Applicants must be current NYU School of Law JD, LLM, and JSD students. **Criteria:** Selection shall be based on the submitted papers of the applicants.

Funds Avail.: No specific amount. **Duration:** Annual. **To Apply:** Interested applicants must submit their papers or works-in-progress in all areas of international law and/or human rights. Although there is no strict page limit for submissions, selected papers should ideally not exceed 30 double-spaced pages. **Contact:** Angelina Fisher, at: fishera@exchange.law.nyu.edu.

6968 ■ CHRGJ International Human Rights Fellowships *(Doctorate, Professional development/ Fellowship, Internship)*

Purpose: To provide opportunity to complete a specialized training program in international law, undertake a summer internship at an elite institution, and complete a substantial research paper growing out of that work experience. **Focus:** Human rights; Law. **Qualif.:** Eligible applicants for the Fellowship are persons who are at the time of application full-time first-year JD, second-year JD, LLM and JSD students at NYU School of Law. **Criteria:** Selection shall be based on the interview conducted for assessing the applicants, as well as the aforesaid qualifications.

Funds Avail.: Amount varies. **Duration:** Annual. **Number Awarded:** Varies. **To Apply:** Applications can be obtained at the website. Applicants must complete and submit one copy of the application package by email and in a single document as a PDF file. The application package must include the following: completed cover sheet; resume or CV; undergraduate and graduate transcripts; NYU law school courses; statement of interest for each requested internship placement explaining why the applicants applying for the fellowship, why they are seeking a particular internship placement and what they will bring to such an internship. Applicants may also include the following: applicants' reasons for applying for the Fellowship; significant academic and professional accomplishments relevant to a requested internship; experience that may be relevant to the work of an internship organization, including study or work abroad or work in the United States involving international issues; undergraduate or graduate courses of study in areas involving international law; foreign language abilities; goals for the fellowship. Each statement of interest should not exceed 500 words and should be on one side of one page. **Deadline:** November 12. **Remarks:** Established in 2002. **Contact:** Tish Armstrong, Fellowship Coordinator,

Center for Human Rights and Global Justice; E-mail: tish.armstrong@nyu.edu.

6969 ■ CHRGJ Students Human Rights Scholars Program *(Graduate, Advanced Professional, Professional development/Scholarship)*

Purpose: To encourage and facilitate independent student academic research, writing and publications related to the Center's theme. **Focus:** Human rights; Law. **Qualif.:** Applicants must be current NYU law students who are interested in developing writing in the human rights field for publication. The Center particularly encourages former Global Justice Clinic or International Human Rights Clinic students and former Center Summer Fellowship recipients who wish to develop academic writing about their clinic or fellowship human rights work. **Criteria:** Selection shall be based on applicants' proven academic merit, commitment to human rights practice and to furthering human rights scholarship, and demonstrated potential for engaged and rigorous scholarship.

Funds Avail.: No specific amount. **Duration:** Annual. **To Apply:** Interested applicants must submit a current CV and statement of interest specifying their research/scholarship goals, the timeframe of their commitment and applicants' general interest in being a CHRGJ Human Rights Scholar. **Contact:** Stacy Cammarano, Managing Director. Email: sc4695@nyu.edu.

6970 ■ Arthur Helton Fellowships *(Graduate/ Fellowship)*

Purpose: To support students who have demonstrated a commitment to pursuing careers in international human rights law. **Focus:** Human rights; Law. **Qualif.:** Applicants must be graduate students of NYU School of Law who have demonstrated a commitment to pursuing a career in international human rights law and who have designed sound proposals for work at a host organization that they have chosen. **Criteria:** Selection will be based on the following criteria: applicants' commitment to human rights as demonstrated by relevant internships and professional experience, coursework and extra-curricular activities; qualifications of the applicants to implement the project; quality of the proposal and the relevance and potential impact of the proposed project; relevance of the project to the applicants' career goals.

Funds Avail.: Around $30,000. **Duration:** Annual. **To Apply:** Applications should be submitted as one PDF file containing the following materials: summary page with name and contact information, one-paragraph description of the project, one-paragraph description of host organization and total project budget amount; 1,000-3,000 words proposal outlining the project, including the human rights problems to be addressed, overview of project strategy, description of host organization and support that host will provide, practical issues including necessary visas and permits, skills that the applicants would bring to the project including language skills, explanation of any challenges anticipated including security constraints and how applicants would address those; substantive letter of support from a senior staff member at host organization detailing why the addition of this particular applicant and project would be beneficial; the support, supervision and training they would provide the fellow; relevant information regarding the history and current programs of the organization; project budget detailing all costs including travel to project location, living expenses, health insurance, telecommunications, travel within the country and other relevant expenses; at least one letter of recommendation from a professor at

Awards are arranged alphabetically below their administering organizations

NYU School of Law or a former employer; personal statement setting forth the applicants' commitment to human rights, relevant experience and how the fellowship will contribute to the applicants' career goals; applicants' resume and unofficial law school transcript; supporting documentation such as additional letters, news articles, etc. **Deadline:** February 18. **Remarks:** Established in 2008. **Contact:** pilc.info@nyu.edu.

6971 ■ New York Water Environment Association, Inc. (NYWEA)

525 Plum St., Ste. 102
Syracuse, NY 13204
Ph: (315)422-7811
Fax: (315)422-3851
Free: 877-556-9932
URL: nywea.org

6972 ■ N.G. Kaul Memorial Scholarships *(Doctorate, Graduate/Scholarship)*

Purpose: To support students pursuing graduate or doctoral degrees in environmental/civil engineering or environmental science concentrating on water quality who show a commitment to government service. **Focus:** Environmental science. **Qualif.:** Applicants must be students pursuing graduate or doctoral degrees in environmental/civil engineering or environmental science, concentrating on water quality; must show commitment to government service. **Criteria:** Recipients are selected based on demonstrated interest in or commitment to pursue government service, relevance of career objective to the environmental field related to water quality, academic potential, character and other activities.

Funds Avail.: Up to $5,000. **Duration:** Annual. **To Apply:** Applicants must complete the application form; must provide letter verifying enrollment or acceptance in a college environmental program on college stationary; must attach transcripts, and two requested essays. **Deadline:** February 29.

6973 ■ New York Water Environment Association Scholarships *(Undergraduate/Scholarship)*

Purpose: To help lead the way toward existing state and national clean water programs. **Focus:** Environmental science. **Qualif.:** Applicants must be students enrolled at a college or university where there is a NYWEA student chapter or high school students who will be enrolled in an environmentally related program in a four year college or university. **Criteria:** Recipients are selected based on academic performance.

Funds Avail.: $2,000. **Number Awarded:** 6. **To Apply:** Applicants must complete the application form; must submit a requested essay; official school transcript; and a minimum of two letters of recommendation, from which one must come from a teacher and the other from someone not related to the applicant. **Deadline:** February 10.

6974 ■ New York Women in Communications Foundation (NYWICIF)

355 Lexington Ave., 15th Fl.
New York, NY 10017-6603
Ph: (212)297-2133
Fax: (212)370-9047
URL: www.nywici.org/foundation

6975 ■ New York Women in Communications, Inc. Foundation Scholarships *(Graduate, Undergraduate/Scholarship)*

Purpose: To provide financial assistance for the education of the residents of New York, New Jersey, Connecticut, or Pennsylvania. **Focus:** Advertising; Broadcasting; Communications; Journalism; Marketing and distribution; Media arts; Public relations. **Qualif.:** Applicants must be high school seniors or college undergraduate or graduate students who are permanent residents of NY, NJ, CT or PA majoring or declaring a major in a communications-related field, including but not limited to advertising, broadcasting, communications, English, film, journalism, marketing, new media or public relations. Applicants must have an overall GPA of 3.2 or better (or the high school equivalent). **Criteria:** Recipients are selected based on academic achievement, financial need and involvement in the field of communications.

Funds Avail.: $2,500, $5,000 and $10,000. **Duration:** Annual. **Number Awarded:** 15-20. **To Apply:** Applicants must submit completed application form; resume including extra curricular activities, significant achievements, academic awards, community service work; 300-500 word essay; two recommendation letters; official high school or college transcripts; other supporting documents.

6976 ■ Newberry Library

60 W Walton St.
Chicago, IL 60610
Ph: (312)943-9090
E-mail: spadaforad@newberry.org
URL: www.newberry.org

6977 ■ Frances C. Allen Fellowships *(Graduate/Fellowship)*

Purpose: To encourage American Indian women in their studies of any field related to the Newberry Library's collections. **Focus:** General studies/Field of study not specified. **Qualif.:** Applicants must be women of American Indian heritage; may be working in any graduate or pre-professional field. **Criteria:** Selection will be based on the committee's criteria.

Funds Avail.: $2,500 per month. **Duration:** Monthly; one month to one year. **To Apply:** Applicants of the Allen Fellowship must fill out a supplementary form in addition to the cover sheet for special awards and fellowships. **Deadline:** January 15.

6978 ■ Herzog August Bibliothek Wolfenbüttel Fellowships *(Postdoctorate/Fellowship)*

Purpose: To provide assistance to researchers who wish to use the Newberry Library's collections. **Focus:** General studies/Field of study not specified. **Qualif.:** Applicants for long and short-term fellowships at the Newberry may also ask to be considered for this joint fellowship providing an additional two-month fellowship in Wolfenbuttel, Germany. The proposed project should link the collections of both libraries. Applicants should plan to hold both fellowships sequentially to ensure continuity of research. **Criteria:** Selection will be based on the committee's Criteria.

Funds Avail.: 1,050 Euros plus up to 600 Euros for travel expenses. **To Apply:** Applicants must submit the following: Cover Sheet; Project Abstract of no more than 300 words; Project Description of no more than 1500 words; Curriculum Vitae; Three letters of reference. Applicants should compile

Awards are arranged alphabetically below their administering organizations

their applications electronically and submit them as email attachments not larger than 10 MB. Applicants may download an application form online. **Deadline:** December 1 for linked long-term; January 15 for linked short-term.

6979 ■ Lester J. Cappon Fellowships in Documentary Editing (Postdoctorate/Fellowship)

Purpose: To support post doctoral scholars in historical editing projects based on Newberry sources, and to support residential research in the Newberry's collections in preparation of the edition, and helps defray other costs related to its preparation. **Focus:** General studies/Field of study not specified. **Qualif.:** Applicants must be post-doctoral scholars. **Criteria:** Selection will be based on the committee's criteria.

Funds Avail.: No specific amount. **To Apply:** Applicants must send an application letter to the Committee on Awards with an attached budget listing anticipated expenses by category and supporting documentation as relevant. **Deadline:** January 15.

6980 ■ Arthur and Janet Holzheimer Fellowship in the History of Cartography (Postdoctorate, Doctorate/Fellowship)

Purpose: To support work in residence at the Newberry on projects related to the history of cartography which focus on cartographic materials in the Library's collection. **Focus:** Cartography/Surveying. **Qualif.:** Applicants must be PhD candidates or post-doctoral scholars. **Criteria:** Selection will be based on the committee's criteria.

Funds Avail.: No specific amount. **To Apply:** Applicants must submit the following: Cover Sheet; Project Abstract of no more than 300 words; Project Description of no more than 1500 words; Curriculum Vitae; Three letters of reference. Applicants should compile their applications electronically and submit them as email attachments not larger than 10 MB. Applicants may download an application form online. **Deadline:** January 15.

6981 ■ Institute for the International Education of Students Faculty Fellowships (Other/Fellowship)

Purpose: To provide assistance to researchers who wish to use the Newberry Library's collections. **Focus:** General studies/Field of study not specified. **Qualif.:** Applicants must be faculty members from any IES Center. **Criteria:** Selection will be based on the committee's criteria.

Funds Avail.: $1,200 each. **Duration:** Annual; up to 1 month. **Number Awarded:** 2. **To Apply:** Applicants must submit the following: Cover Sheet; Project Abstract of no more than 300 words; Project Description of no more than 1500 words; Curriculum Vitae; Three letters of reference. Applicants should compile their applications electronically and submit them as email attachments not larger than 10 MB. Applicants may download an application form online. **Deadline:** January 15.

6982 ■ Lloyd Lewis Fellowships in American History (Postdoctorate/Fellowship)

Purpose: To provide assistance to researchers who wish to use the Newberry Library's collections. **Focus:** History, American. **Qualif.:** Applicants must be post-doctoral scholars pursuing projects in any area of American history appropriate to the Newberry's collection. **Criteria:** Selection will be based on the committee's criteria.

Funds Avail.: No specific amount. **To Apply:** Applicants must submit the following: Cover Sheet; Project Abstract of

no more than 300 words; Project Description of no more than 1500 words; Curriculum Vitae; Three letters of reference. Applicants should compile their applications electronically and submit them as email attachments not larger than 10 MB. Applicants may download an application form online. **Contact:** Newberry Library, at the above address.

6983 ■ Lawrence Lipking Fellowships at the Newberry Library (Graduate/Fellowship)

Purpose: To provide assistance to researchers who wish to use the Newberry Library's collections. **Focus:** General studies/Field of study not specified. **Qualif.:** Applicants must be Northwestern graduate students in English. **Criteria:** Selection will be based on the committee's criteria.

Funds Avail.: $5,748. **To Apply:** Applicants should supply a Newberry Library Short-Term and Special Awards Cover Sheet, Curriculum Vitae, a letter of recommendation, and a description (no more than 500 words) of the research they plan to carry out and its relation to Newberry resources. Applications should be submitted as email attachments. **Deadline:** January 15.

6984 ■ Audrey Lumsden-Kouvel Fellowships (Postdoctorate/Fellowship)

Purpose: To provide assistance to researchers who wish to use the Newberry Library's collections. **Focus:** Culture. **Qualif.:** Applicants must be post-doctoral scholars who wish to use the Newberry's extensive holdings in late medieval and early modern history and literature. **Criteria:** Preference will be given to projects focusing on Romance cultures, including work that draws on sources from the colonial Americas.

Funds Avail.: No specific amount. **To Apply:** Applicants must submit the following: Cover Sheet; Project Abstract of no more than 300 words; Project Description of no more than 1500 words; Curriculum Vitae; Three letters of reference. Applicants should compile their applications electronically and submit them as email attachments not larger than 10 MB. Applicants may download an application form online. **Contact:** Newberry Library, at the above address.

6985 ■ Midwest Modern Language Association Fellowships (Doctorate, Postdoctorate/Fellowship)

Purpose: To provide assistance to researchers who wish to use the Newberry Library's collections. **Focus:** General studies/Field of study not specified. **Qualif.:** Applicants must be PhD candidates or post-doctoral scholars. **Criteria:** Selection will be based on the committee's criteria.

Funds Avail.: No specific amount. **To Apply:** Applicants must submit the following: Cover Sheet; Project Abstract of no more than 300 words; Project Description of no more than 1500 words; Curriculum Vitae; Three letters of reference. Applicants should compile their applications electronically and submit them as email attachments not larger than 10 MB. Applicants may download an application form online. **Deadline:** April 15.

6986 ■ Newberry Consortium on American Indian Studies Faculty Fellowships (Other/Fellowship)

Purpose: To provide assistance to researchers who wish to use the Newberry Library's collections. **Focus:** Native American studies. **Qualif.:** Applicants must be faculty members at institutions participating in the consortium. **Criteria:** Preference is given to scholars at an early career stage.

Funds Avail.: No specific amount. **To Apply:** Applicants

Awards are arranged alphabetically below their administering organizations

should apply directly to the Newberry's D'Arcy McNickle Center for American Indian History. **Contact:** Newberry Library, at the above address.

6987 ■ Newberry Consortium on American Indian Studies Graduate Student Fellowships *(Doctorate/ Fellowship)*

Purpose: To provide assistance to researchers who wish to use the Newberry Library's collections. **Focus:** General studies/Field of study not specified. **Qualif.:** Applicants must be doctoral candidates at institutions participating in the consortium. **Criteria:** Selection will be based on the committee's criteria.

Funds Avail.: $2,500. **Duration:** Monthly; up to 2 months. **To Apply:** Applicants should apply directly to the Newberry's D'Arcy McNickle Center for American Indian History. **Deadline:** January 15. **Contact:** Office of Research and Academic Programs, Newberry Library; Email: research@ newberry.org.

6988 ■ Newberry Library ACM/GLCA Faculty Fellowships *(Other/Fellowship)*

Purpose: To provide assistance to researchers who wish to use the Newberry Library's collections. **Focus:** General studies/Field of study not specified. **Qualif.:** Applicants must be faculty from the colleges of the Associated Colleges of the Midwest and the Great Lakes Colleges Association, Inc.; must be Fellows who teach a small group of selected undergraduate students in an advanced research seminar; must come from any of the colleges in ACM or GLCA, in any discipline. **Criteria:** Selection will be based on the committee's criteria.

Funds Avail.: No specific amount. **To Apply:** For more information, visit the Associated Colleges of the Midwest call for proposals. **Contact:** Joan Gillespie at the ACM or jgillespie@acm.edu.

6989 ■ Newberry Library/Ecole Nationale des Chartes Exchange Fellowships *(Graduate/Fellowship)*

Purpose: To provide assistance to researchers who wish to use the Newberry Library's collections. **Focus:** General studies/Field of study not specified. **Qualif.:** Applicants must be American or Canadian graduate students who plan to study at the Ecole Nationale des Chartes in Paris. Students who are in the early stages of preparing their dissertations are especially encouraged. **Criteria:** Preference will be given to students attending institutions that are members of the Center for Renaissance Studies Consortium.

Funds Avail.: No specific amount. **Duration:** 3 months. **To Apply:** Applicants must submit the following: Cover Sheet; Project Abstract of no more than 300 words; Project Description of no more than 1500 words; Curriculum Vitae; Three letters of reference. Applicants should compile their applications electronically and submit them as email attachments not larger than 10 MB. Applicants may download an application form online. **Deadline:** January 10. **Contact:** Newberry Library; Email: research@newberry.org.

6990 ■ Newberry Library National Endowment for the Humanities Fellowships *(Postdoctorate/ Fellowship)*

Purpose: To support postdoctoral scholars in any field appropriate to Newberry's collection. **Focus:** Humanities. **Qualif.:** Applicants must be post-doctoral scholars; must be U.S. citizens or foreign nationals with three continuous

years' residence. **Criteria:** Preference will be given to applicants who have not held major fellowships for three years preceding the proposed period of residency.

Funds Avail.: No specific amount. **Duration:** Annual; from 4 to 12 months. **To Apply:** Applicants must submit the following: Cover Sheet; Project Abstract of no more than 300 words; Project Description of no more than 1500 words; Curriculum Vitae; Three letters of reference. Applicants should compile their applications electronically and submit them as email attachments not larger than 10 MB. Applicants may download an application form online. **Deadline:** December 1.

6991 ■ Newberry Library Short-Term Resident Fellowships for Individual Research *(Postdoctorate, Doctorate/Fellowship)*

Purpose: To provide assistance to researchers who wish to use the Newberry Library's collections. **Focus:** General studies/Field of study not specified. **Qualif.:** Applicants must be post-doctoral scholars who live and work outside the Chicago area. **Criteria:** Selection will be based on the committee's criteria.

Funds Avail.: No specific amount. **To Apply:** Applicants must submit the following: Cover Sheet; Project Abstract of no more than 300 words; Project Description of no more than 1500 words; Curriculum Vitae; Three letters of reference. Applicants should compile their applications electronically and submit them as email attachments not larger than 10 MB. Applicants may download an application form online.

6992 ■ Susan Kelly Power and Helen Hornbeck Tanner Fellowships *(Doctorate, Postdoctorate/Fellowship)*

Purpose: To provide assistance to researchers who wish to use the Newberry Library's collections. **Focus:** General studies/Field of study not specified. **Qualif.:** Applicants must be PhD candidates and post-doctoral scholars of American Indian heritage. **Criteria:** Selection will be based on the committee's criteria.

Funds Avail.: No specific amount. **To Apply:** Applicants must submit the following: Cover Sheet; Project Abstract of no more than 300 words; Project Description of no more than 1500 words; Curriculum Vitae; Three letters of reference. Applicants should compile their applications electronically and submit them as email attachments not larger than 10 MB. Applicants may download an application form online. **Remarks:** Established in 2002. **Contact:** Newberry Library, at the above address.

6993 ■ South Central Modern Language Association Fellowships *(Doctorate, Postdoctorate/Fellowship)*

Purpose: To provide assistance to researchers who wish to use the Newberry Library's collections. **Focus:** General studies/Field of study not specified. **Qualif.:** Applicants must be PhD candidates or post-doctoral scholars who are members of the South Central Modern Language Association.. **Criteria:** Selection will be based on the committee's criteria.

Funds Avail.: No specific amount. **To Apply:** Applicants must submit the following: Cover Sheet; Project Abstract of no more than 300 words; Project Description of no more than 1500 words; Curriculum Vitae; Three letters of reference. Applicants should compile their applications electronically and submit them as email attachments not larger than 10 MB. Applicants may download an application form online. **Contact:** Newberry Library, at the above address.

Awards are arranged alphabetically below their administering organizations

6994 ■ Arthur and Lila Weinberg Fellowship for Independent Scholars and Researchers (Other/Fellowship)

Purpose: To provide assistance to researchers who wish to use the Newberry Library's collections. **Focus:** General studies/Field of study not specified. **Qualif.:** Applicants must be scholars, writers, filmmakers, and other humanists with careers primarily outside the academy, who wish to use the Library's collections in the creation of a publication or comparable product. **Criteria:** Preference will be given to scholars working on historical issues related to social justice or reform.

Funds Avail.: $2,500. **To Apply:** Applicants must submit the following: Cover Sheet; Project Abstract of no more than 300 words; Project Description of no more than 1500 words; Curriculum Vitae; Three letters of reference. Applicants should compile their applications electronically and submit them as email attachments not larger than 10 MB. Applicants may download an application form online. **Deadline:** January 15.

6995 ■ Newkirk Center for Science and Society

University of California, Irvine
5542 Social and Behavioral Sciences Gateway
Irvine, CA 92697-7090
Ph: (949)824-3119
Fax: (949)824-9420
E-mail: newkirk@uci.edu
URL: www.newkirkcenter.uci.edu

6996 ■ Newkirk Center for Science and Society Graduate Student Fellowships (Doctorate, Graduate/Fellowship)

Purpose: To promote effective uses of research in natural and social sciences fields and to financially assist graduate students. **Focus:** Natural sciences; Social sciences. **Qualif.:** Applicants must be UCI doctoral students. **Criteria:** Applications will be evaluated based on the following category: 1) determine the practical uses of results of basic research; 2) increase the knowledge of relevant communities and policymakers about specific scientific results and implications of those results; 3) theory in design of applied research that has potentially important social consequences; 4) determine effective methods to educate policymakers and the general public in the realm of scientific findings; and 5) establish collaborative relationships between scientists and potential end-users of scientific results.

Funds Avail.: $8,000. **Duration:** Annual. **To Apply:** Applicants must submit a project proposal addressing scientific research issues; must also submit a detailed budget and letter of support from a faculty. **Deadline:** May 2.

6997 ■ Newswomen's Club of New York (NCNY)

15 Gramercy Park S
New York, NY 10003-1705
Ph: (212)777-1610
E-mail: newswomensclub@verizon.net
URL: www.newswomensclubnewyork.com

6998 ■ Anne O'Hare McCormick Scholarship Fund (Graduate/Scholarship)

Purpose: To provide financial assistance to aspiring journalists to pursue their careers. **Focus:** Journalism. **Qua-**

lif.: Applicants must be women journalists attending Columbia University's Graduate School of Journalism; must be citizens of the United States; have financial needs and shows evidence of talent. **Criteria:** Selections are based on Trustee's estimate of each candidate's ability, determination to succeed and potential for a career in journalism.

Funds Avail.: No specific amount. **Duration:** Annual. **Number Awarded:** Varies. **To Apply:** Application form must be printed or typed clearly. Applicants must submit the list of job-related experiences, with dates of employment; must have a brief statement of financial resources, including needs for tuition and living expenses during the academic year; must have two letters of recommendation that focus on the applicants' qualifications in the field of journalism; must prepare a maximum of 1,000 words autobiographical essay mentioning family, educational background, journalistic experience and goals; and one or two examples of the applicant's writing. Applicants (broadcast students) must include links to Youtube or Vimeo videos of your work (may include scripts used). **Deadline:** May 22.

6999 ■ Nigerian Women Association of Georgia (NWAG)

PO Box 14532
Atlanta, GA 30324
Ph: (770)496-4380
URL: www.nwag.org

7000 ■ NWAG Georgia, USA Scholarships (Undergraduate/Scholarship)

Purpose: To financially assist Nigerian male/female students in Georgia high school. **Focus:** General studies/Field of study not specified. **Qualif.:** Applicants must be of Nigerian descent; must be high school seniors and be residents of Georgia; must have cumulative GPA of 3.0 or higher on a 4.0 scale. **Criteria:** Recipients will be selected based on submitted materials.

Funds Avail.: $500. **Number Awarded:** 2. **To Apply:** Applicants must complete the application form; must provide a proof of admission to college or university (photocopy of letter of acceptance); must submit one letter of recommendation from any of the following personnel in school currently attending, one letter of recommendation from a community leader, pastor/imam, director of a non-profit organization or facility; must show evidence of 50 hours community service involvement; must submit a photocopy of current student identification card; and must provide an essay on the topic given by the scholarship committee. All electronic submissions must be in PDF format. **Deadline:** May 15. **Contact:** nwagscholarship@yahoo.com.

7001 ■ NWAG Nigeria Scholarships (Undergraduate/Scholarship)

Purpose: To help Nigerian female students pursue their education. **Focus:** General studies/Field of study not specified. **Qualif.:** Applicants must be Nigerian female, undergraduate students in a Nigerian university. **Criteria:** Recipients will be chosen based on submitted materials.

Funds Avail.: 50,000 Nigerian Naira. **Number Awarded:** 37. **To Apply:** Applicants must complete the application form; must submit a proof of state of origin, two letters of recommendation from any two of the following: Pastor/Imam, village head, local government chairperson or one of the lecturers; must also submit one letter of recommendation from either the Dean of the Faculty or Head of the

Awards are arranged alphabetically below their administering organizations

Department, photocopy of current university student identification card, a current photo; must provide an explanation on why applicant deserves the award and an essay on the topic given by the scholarship committee. **Deadline:** May 30.

7002 ■ Ninety Nines, International Organization of Women Pilots

4300 Amelia Earhart Dr., Ste. A
Oklahoma City, OK 73159
Ph: (405)685-7969
Fax: (405)685-7985
Free: 800-994-1929
E-mail: 99s@ninety-nines.org
URL: www.ninety-nines.org

7003 ■ AE Flight Training Scholarships *(Other/Scholarship)*

Purpose: To assist licensed pilot members who wish to complete an additional pilot certificate and pilot training course. **Focus:** Aviation. **Qualif.:** Applicant must be a woman pilot and a member of The Ninety-Nines Inc.; a current pilot with appropriate medical certificate; must have sufficient flight time experience to meet or exceed the flight time requirement for the certificate; must demonstrate financial need; must be qualified as a pilot. **Criteria:** Awards are given based on credentials and financial need.

Funds Avail.: No specific amount. **To Apply:** Applicant must complete the application form (please visit website) on an 8 1/2x11 paper (clipped or stapled) and submit it to the Section AE Scholarship Chairman or to Section Governor.

7004 ■ AE Jet Type Rating Scholarships *(Other/Scholarship)*

Purpose: To assist licensed pilot members who wish to complete type rating certification in any jet aircraft. **Focus:** Aviation. **Qualif.:** Applicant must be a woman pilot and a member of The Ninety-Nines Inc.; a current Airline Transport Pilot with first-class medical certificate; must have a minimum of 100 hours multi-engine flight time or combined multi-engine and turbine time. **Criteria:** Awards are given based on credentials and financial need.

Funds Avail.: No specific amount. **To Apply:** Applicant must complete the application form (please visit website) on an 8 1/2x11 paper (clipped or stapled) and submit it to the Section AE Scholarship Chairman or to Section Governor. **Deadline:** December 20.

7005 ■ AE Technical Training Scholarships *(Other/Scholarship)*

Purpose: To assist licensed pilot members to complete an aerospace technical training or certification course. **Focus:** Aviation. **Qualif.:** Applicant must be a woman pilot and a member of The Ninety-Nines Inc.; must have a specific goal for advancement in aviation or aerospace; must demonstrate financial need. **Criteria:** Awards are given based on credentials and financial need.

Funds Avail.: No specific amount. **To Apply:** Applicant must complete the application form (please visit website) on an 8 1/2x11 paper (clipped or stapled) and submit it to the Section AE Scholarship Chairman or to Section Governor. **Deadline:** December 20.

7006 ■ Amelia Earhart Memorial Academic Scholarships *(Professional development/Scholarship)*

Purpose: To assist licensed pilot members who wish to complete type rating certification in any jet aircraft. **Focus:** Aviation. **Qualif.:** Applicant must be a woman pilot; currently enrolled in a degree-seeking institution in the field of aerospace and aviation; must be a member of The Ninety-Nines Inc. Associates and bachelor degree students must have a cumulative GPA of 3.0 or better on a 4.0 scale, or equivalent; and must demonstrate financial need. **Criteria:** Awards are given based on credentials and financial need.

Funds Avail.: No specific amount. **Duration:** Annual. **To Apply:** Applicant must complete the application form (please visit website) on an 8 1/2x11 paper (clipped or stapled) and submit it to Section AE Scholarship Chairman or to Section Governor. **Deadline:** December 20.

7007 ■ Non Commissioned Officers Association of the United States of America (NCOA)

9330 Corporate Dr., Ste. 701
Selma, TX 78154-1257
Ph: (210)653-6161
Fax: (210)637-3337
Free: 800-662-2620
URL: www.ncoausa.org

7008 ■ Non Commissioned Officers Association Scholarships *(Undergraduate/Scholarship)*

Purpose: To assist the children and spouses of NCOA members who wish to pursue their education. **Focus:** General studies/Field of study not specified. **Qualif.:** Applicant must be a spouse or child of a NCOA member and must be 25 years old and below (for children of members). Any spouse who will be awarded must apply among these membership categories: Regular; Associate; Veteran; Auxiliary or Apprentice. **Criteria:** Recipients will be selected by the committee of educators.

Funds Avail.: No specific amount. **To Apply:** Children of NCOA members must submit a completed application form; two letters of recommendation; a handwritten autobiography; personal letter of recommendation; transcripts; copy of ACT/SAT scores; and a composition (maximum of 200 words) about Americanism. Spouses of NCOA members must submit a completed application form; a copy of high school diploma or GED; transcript of completed college courses (if any); a certificate of completion for other training courses; a brief biography; and a letter of intent on: degree course of study, plans for completion of a degree program, and a paragraph about, "What a College Degree Means to Me." Mail all documents in one complete package. **Deadline:** March 31. **Remarks:** Students must maintain a B average to be considered for renewal. Established in 1970.

7009 ■ North American Conference on British Studies (NACBS)

c/o Keith Wrightson, President
PO Box 208324
New Haven, CT 06520-8324
Ph: (203)432-7248
URL: www.nacbs.org

7010 ■ North American Conference on British Studies Dissertation Year Fellowships *(Doctorate, Postdoctorate/Fellowship)*

Purpose: To support dissertation research in the British Isles on any topic of British history or British studies. **Focus:** History. **Qualif.:** Applicant must be a citizen or permanent

Awards are arranged alphabetically below their administering organizations

resident of the United States or Canada; enrolled in a PhD program in a U.S. or Canadian institution; has completed all degree requirements for dissertation; must be nominated by a dissertation advisor; must need to travel to the British Isles for the purpose of dissertation research and must conduct full-time research in the British Isles for a period of at least six months. **Criteria:** Selection is based on merit and importance of research.

Funds Avail.: $10,000; $5,000 for runner-up. **Duration:** Annual. **Number Awarded:** 1. **To Apply:** Nomination must be supported by a letter of recommendation; application consists of the two letters of nomination and recommendation, (one-page) curriculum vitae, a (1000-word) research proposal which should explain the importance of the topic to the field of British history. **Deadline:** April 1. **Contact:** Application form and supporting documents must be sent to: Dr. Robert Ingram, Ohio University, Department of History, Bentley Annex 415, Athens, NY 45701; E-mail: ingramr@ohio.edu.

7011 ■ North American Conference on British Studies-Huntington Library Fellowships (Doctorate, Postdoctorate/Fellowship)

Purpose: To aid in dissertation research in British studies using the collections of the library. **Focus:** History. **Qualif.:** Applicants must be U.S. or Canadian citizens or permanent residents; must be enrolled in a PhD program in a U.S. or Canadian institution; the time of fellowship tenure must be spent in residence at the Huntington Library. **Criteria:** Selection is based on merit and importance of research.

Funds Avail.: $3,000. **Duration:** Annually. **To Apply:** Applications should consist of a curriculum vitae; two supporting letters (one from applicant's dissertation advisor); and a description of the research project. A copy of the application package must be sent to each member of the Huntington Library Fellowship Committee. Letters should be placed in sealed envelopes with signature across the flap. **Deadline:** November 15. **Contact:** Mail application and supporting documents to: Dr. Steve Hindle, The Huntington Library, 1151 Oxford Road, San Marino, Ca, 9108; Email: shindle@huntington.org.

7012 ■ North American Serials Interest Group (NASIG)
1902 Ridge Rd.
PMB 305
West Seneca, NY 14224-3312
E-mail: info@nasig.org
URL: www.nasig.org

7013 ■ John Riddick Student Grants (Graduate/Grant)

Purpose: To encourage participation in the serials information chain. **Focus:** Computer and information sciences. **Qualif.:** Applicants must be full or part-time students who are currently enrolled at the graduate level at an ALA-accredited library school. Applicants must also not have attended a previous NASIG conference, but may have participated in a NASIG conference as a local volunteer. **Criteria:** Selection shall be based on the aforementioned qualifications and compliance with the application details.

Funds Avail.: Amount varies. **Duration:** Annual. **To Apply:** Applicants must submit a completed application form and a reference questionnaire. **Deadline:** February 10. **Remarks:** Established in 1988. **Contact:** Dana Whitmire, Chair,

NASIG Awards & Recognition Committee, UT Health Science Center San Antonio, Texas; Email: whitmired@uthscsa.edu; Phone: 210-567-2464.

7014 ■ Fritz Schwartz Serials Education Scholarships (Graduate, Other/Scholarship)

Purpose: To advance the serials profession by providing educational opportunities for students with prior serials experience. **Focus:** Information science and technology; Library and archival sciences. **Qualif.:** Applicants must be students in any NASIG member country (defined for this purpose as the United States, Canada, Mexico, and Greenland); must be entering an ALA-accredited graduate library program (or Mexican equivalent); must have completed no more than 12 hours of academic requirements towards the graduate degree at the time of enrollment. **Criteria:** Priority is given to applicants with serials-related work experience and a desire to pursue a professional serials career after earning the graduate library degree.

Funds Avail.: $3,000. **To Apply:** Applicants must submit a completed application form along with the Reference Questionnaire from two information professionals; a current resume; a personal statement; and a copy of current Library/Information Science Graduate transcript or proof of admission. **Deadline:** January 27. **Remarks:** Established in 1985. **Contact:** Sandy Folsom; email: sandy.l.folsom@cmich.edu; phone: 989-774-2166; fax: 989-774-2145.

7015 ■ North American Van Lines Inc.
5001 U.S. Hwy 30 W., POB 988
Fort Wayne, IN 46818
Ph: 429-2511
Fax: 972-2405
E-mail: customer_service@navimail.com
URL: www.navl.com

7016 ■ North American Van Lines Military Scholarship Competition (Undergraduate/Scholarship)

Purpose: To support the education of those in the military services, as well as their relatives. **Focus:** Business; Logistics; Management. **Qualif.:** Applicants must be either U.S. citizens or permanent residents who are enrolled, or planning to enroll, as full time students at an accredited college/university within the United States for completion of an undergraduate degree in Logistics or equivalent field; or honorably discharged veterans or current members of the active military (including National Guard and Reserves); or spouses of current military service members or honorably discharged veterans; or children (under the age of 21 or full-time students under age 23) of current military service members or honorably discharged veterans. **Criteria:** Selection will be based on the committee's criteria.

Funds Avail.: $1,000 each. **Number Awarded:** 2. **To Apply:** Applicants must submit a brief essay of between 400 and 800 words, detailing why a career in logistics/supply chain management is their college major of choice. Personalized tones, referencing sincere firsthand experiences and sentiments, are best and no need to be too formal. Additional requirements include current transcript and verification of enrollment. **Deadline:** September 1. **Contact:** Call Ryan Cox via phone at 630-570-3612.

7017 ■ North Carolina Adult Education Association (NCAEA)
c/o Melita Pope Mitchell
9201 University City Blvd.

Awards are arranged alphabetically below their administering organizations

Colard 1017
Charlotte, NC 28223
E-mail: info@ncadulteducation.org
URL: ncadulteducation.org

7018 ■ NCAEA Scholarships *(Graduate/Scholarship)*

Purpose: To support graduate students pursue advanced learning in Adult Education study. **Focus:** Adult education. **Qualif.:** Applicants must be either accepted into an accredited graduate program at the time of application or be enrolled in an accredited graduate program for a minimum of six credit hours; must have a cumulative grade point average of 3.25; must be recommended by a current member of NCAEA; and must be at least 22 years of age. **Criteria:** Applicants will be selected based on financial need and eligibility.

Funds Avail.: $500. **Duration:** Annual. **To Apply:** Applicants must submit a completed application form available online and supporting materials; must submit a personal statement of their education and career goals, and college transcripts of all educational institutions attended. **Deadline:** March 25. **Contact:** Dr. Phyllis Broughton at broughtonp@ecu.edu.

7019 ■ North Carolina Association of Certified Public Accountants (NCACPA)

3100 Gateway Centre Blvd.
Morrisville, NC 27560
Ph: (919)469-1040
Fax: (919)378-2000
Free: 800-722-2836
URL: www.ncacpa.org

7020 ■ North Carolina CPA Foundation Scholarships *(Undergraduate/Scholarship)*

Purpose: To further the development of accounting education and the accounting profession in North Carolina. **Focus:** Accounting. **Qualif.:** Applicant must be a North Carolina resident and enrolled in a North Carolina college/university; must have completed at least one college/university-level accounting course; must have completed at least 36 semester hours (or equivalent) by the start of the spring semester of the year of application; must be enrolled in an academic program leading to a degree in accounting or its equivalent, either currently or during the first semester following the awarding of the scholarship. **Criteria:** Selection is based on the essay content and grammar as well as the applicant's extra curricular/work activities.

Funds Avail.: $1,000 - $5,000. **Duration:** Annual; Three years. **To Apply:** Applicants are required to complete the application and essay online. In addition, applicants must send the transcripts of all course work completed (sent directly from the Registrar's Office to the NC CPA Foundation). **Deadline:** February 13.

7021 ■ Outstanding Minority Accounting Student Scholarships *(Undergraduate/Scholarship)*

Purpose: To further the development of accounting education and the accounting profession in North Carolina. **Focus:** Accounting. **Qualif.:** Applicant must be enrolled full time in an accredited North Carolina college/university and have had a legal residence in North Carolina for the last year; must have completed at least four college/university level accounting courses; must have completed at least 36 semester hours (or equivalent); and enrolled in an academic program leading to a degree in accounting or its equivalent, either currently or during the first semester following the awarding of the scholarship. **Criteria:** Selection is based on the essay content, essay grammar, GPA and extracurricular activities.

Funds Avail.: $1,000 - $2,000. **Duration:** Annual. **To Apply:** Applicants must submit a completed application form together with the essay (maximum of 500 words) and transcript of all course work completed (official, sealed and may be sent directly from the Registrar's office to the NC CPA Foundation). **Deadline:** February 28.

7022 ■ North Carolina Association of Health Care Recruiters (NCAHCR)

c/o JoEllen M. Liles, President
Hedrick Bldg., Ste. 1030
211 Friday Center Dr.
Chapel Hill, NC 27517
URL: www.ncahcr.org

7023 ■ North Carolina Association of Health Care Recruiters Scholarships *(Undergraduate/Scholarship)*

Purpose: To assist, encourage and enable deserving students currently enrolled in an accredited program for health professions. **Focus:** Health care services. **Qualif.:** Applicants must be full-time students in North Carolina who have been accepted into an accredited ADN, BSN or allied health program. **Criteria:** Recipients are selected based on academic performance.

Funds Avail.: $500. **To Apply:** Applicants may secure a Scholarship Program Application, Recommendation Forms and a copy of the Program Guidelines from the president-elect.

7024 ■ North Carolina Commercial Flower Growers Association (NCCFGA)

PO Box 58220
Raleigh, NC 27658
Ph: (919)782-3058
Fax: (919)882-8533
URL: www.nccfga.org

7025 ■ North Carolina Commercial Flower Growers Association Floriculture Scholarships *(Graduate, Undergraduate/Scholarship)*

Purpose: To support research on biological control of sweet potato and other integrated pest management approaches for greenhouse insect control. **Focus:** Entomology; Horticulture. **Qualif.:** Applicants must be full-time horticulture, entomology, or plant pathology students with an emphasis in greenhouse floriculture production; must be in their final year at a two-year, four-year or graduate institution. **Criteria:** Recipients are selected based on academic performance.

Funds Avail.: $500. **Duration:** Annual. **Number Awarded:** 2. **To Apply:** Applicants must submit a completed application form.

7026 ■ North Carolina Council of Epsilon Sigma Alpha

904 Parkway Ave.
Madison, NC 27025
URL: northcarolinaesa.wix.com/ncesa

Awards are arranged alphabetically below their administering organizations

7027 ■ North Carolina Council of Epsilon Sigma Alpha Scholarships *(Graduate, Other, Undergraduate/ Scholarship)*

Purpose: To support individuals training for work with exceptional children. **Focus:** Teaching. **Qualif.:** Applicant must be a student enrolled in an accredited college/ university either as an undergraduate student or as a current NC teacher seeking additional training; training to work specifically with special needs persons up to age 21, excluding the academically gifted, in any educational setting; and must agree to teach in a North Carolina Public School system for one year after graduation as a teacher of exceptional children. **Criteria:** Selection is based on need, desire and academics.

Funds Avail.: $500 - $2,500. **Duration:** Annual. **To Apply:** Applicants must submit a completed application form together with a letter of recommendation, brief essay and financial aid statement filled out by the college Financial Aid Director. **Deadline:** April 1. **Contact:** scholarship-chair@esa-nc.org.

7028 ■ North Carolina Economic Developers Association (NCEDA)

1201 Edwards Mill Rd., 1st Fl.
Raleigh, NC 27607
Ph: (919)882-1961
Fax: (919)882-1902
Free: 888-246-2332
E-mail: nceda@capstrat.com
URL: www.nceda.org

7029 ■ Jack Ervin EDI Scholarships *(Other/ Scholarship)*

Purpose: To recognize and support the advancement of outstanding practitioners; to offer an advanced level of training on a broad range of subjects and skills required to carry out an effective economic development program; to prepare participants for professional certification eligibility; and to provide graduates the necessary level of education. **Focus:** Economics. **Qualif.:** Applicants must be residing and working in North Carolina; must be members of NCEDA for duration of the program; and must have completed two years of economic development work. Additionally, applicants must show completion of or plans to complete the Basic Course, a prerequisite to the Economic Development Institute. **Criteria:** Recipients are selected based on financial need and professional development.

Funds Avail.: $650. **Duration:** Annual. **To Apply:** Application package must include documents demonstrating need for financial assistance as well as documents demonstrating planned career path in the profession (past, present and future) and how the program fits into those plans; letters of recommendation are suggested. Four (4) original copies of all documents must be submitted.

7030 ■ Governor James E. Holshouser Professional Development Scholarships *(Other/Scholarship)*

Purpose: To recognize and support the advancement of outstanding practitioners. **Focus:** Economics. **Qualif.:** Applicants must be residing and working in North Carolina; must be members of NCEDA for duration of the program; and must have demonstrated financial need. Additionally, applicants must show completion of or plans to complete the Basic Course, a prerequisite to the Economic Development Institute. **Criteria:** Recipients are selected based on financial need.

Funds Avail.: $1,000 per year for two years. **Duration:** Annual. **To Apply:** Application package must include documents demonstrating need for financial assistance as well as documents demonstrating planned career path in the profession (past, present and future) and how the program fits into those plans; letters of recommendation are suggested. Four (4) original copies of all documents must be submitted.

7031 ■ Dan Stewart Scholarships *(Other/Scholarship)*

Purpose: To recognize and support the advancement of outstanding practitioners by paying tuition to the one-week basic economic development course at UNC-Chapel Hill. **Focus:** Economics. **Qualif.:** Applicants must be: residing and working in North Carolina; members of NCEDA for the duration of the program; and willing to complete all coursework. **Criteria:** Recipients are selected based primarily on financial need, followed by demonstrated professional development and presentation of the application itself.

Funds Avail.: $575. **Duration:** Annual. **To Apply:** Application package must include documents demonstrating need for financial assistance as well as documents demonstrating chosen career path in the profession (past, present and future) and how the program fits into those plans; letters of recommendation are suggested. Four (4) original copies of all documents must be submitted.

7032 ■ North Carolina Federation of Republican Women (NCFRW)

2941 St. Claire Rd.
Winston Salem, NC 27106
Ph: (336)659-9254
URL: www.ncfederationofrepublicanwomen.org

7033 ■ Dottie Martin Teacher Scholarships *(Graduate, Undergraduate/Scholarship)*

Purpose: To assist aspiring teachers who are interested in child guidance and counseling and who want to make a difference in the lives of North Carolina's children. **Focus:** Counseling/Guidance; Education. **Qualif.:** Applicant must be enrolled and studying in the field of education. **Criteria:** Selection is based on the applicant's submitted application.

Funds Avail.: $500. **Duration:** Annual. **To Apply:** Applicants must submit a completed application form along with three letters of recommendation (including telephone number of authors); most recent copy of college or university transcript; and a typed essay. **Deadline:** June 1. **Remarks:** Established in 1991. **Contact:** Applications must be mailed to Dottie W. Salerno, 5 Bearkling Place, Greensboro, NC 27407; Phone: 336-852-4799.

7034 ■ North Carolina Heroes Fund

PO Box 652
Pineville, NC 28134
Ph: (828)284-2858
Fax: (980)225-0395
E-mail: info@ncheroes.org
URL: www.ncheroes.org

7035 ■ North Carolina Heroes Financial Hardship Grant *(All/Grant)*

Purpose: To provide financial assistance to military men and women who were returning from active duty and facing

Awards are arranged alphabetically below their administering organizations

very difficult transitions as well as financial hardships. **Focus:** General studies/Field of study not specified. **Qualif.:** Applicants must be Military Servicemen or Servicewomen (or the immediate family members); native of North Carolina; currently permanent residents of North Carolina; currently or was recently stationed at a base or facility in North Carolina. **Criteria:** Selection shall be based on the aforementioned applicants' qualifications and compliance with the application details.

Funds Avail.: No specific amount. **Duration:** Annual. **To Apply:** Applicants may visit the program website for further information regarding the application details. **Contact:** North Carolina Heroes Fund, at the above address.

7036 ■ North Carolina Nursery and Landscape Association Inc. (NCNLA)
968 Trinity Rd.
Raleigh, NC 27607
Ph: (919)816-9119
Fax: (919)816-9118
E-mail: info@ncnla.com
URL: www.ncnla.memberclicks.net

7037 ■ North Carolina Nursery and Landscape Association Horticulture Scholarships *(Undergraduate/ Scholarship)*

Purpose: To identify and reward horticulture students who exemplify scholastic aptitude, positive attitude and industry potential. **Focus:** Horticulture. **Qualif.:** Applicants must be full-time students who are enrolled in a two-to-four year ornamental horticulture or landscape program in North Carolina. **Criteria:** Recipients are selected based on academic performance, attitude and leadership potential.

Funds Avail.: $1,000. **To Apply:** Applicants must complete the application form; must submit a resume, transcripts and a wallet size black and white photograph. **Deadline:** May 15.

7038 ■ North Carolina Restaurant and Lodging Association (NCRLA)
6036 Six Forks Rd.
Raleigh, NC 27609
Ph: (919)844-0098
Fax: (919)844-0190
Free: 800-582-8750
E-mail: info@ncrla.org
URL: ncrla.org

7039 ■ William F. Carl Scholarships *(Undergraduate, Vocational/Occupational/Scholarship)*

Purpose: To support the education of children of hourly employees in the restaurant industry. **Focus:** General studies/Field of study not specified. **Qualif.:** Applicant must be a high school senior, high school graduate or current undergraduate college student aged 24 and under who is a legal U.S. resident; a child of a restaurant employee; must enroll in a full-time undergraduate course of study at an accredited two- or four-year college, university or vocational-technical school in the U.S. **Criteria:** Selection is based on the applicant's academic success, community involvement and recommendations. Preference will be given to students majoring in a hospitality related field.

Funds Avail.: $500 - $5,000. **Duration:** Annual. **To Apply:**

Applicants must submit a completed application form together with the letters of recommendation and transcripts. **Deadline:** February 8.

7040 ■ Vickie Clark-Flaherty Scholarships *(Undergraduate, Vocational/Occupational/Scholarship)*

Purpose: To support female students who wish to continue their education in the restaurant industry. **Focus:** Culinary arts; Hotel, institutional, and restaurant management. **Qualif.:** Applicant must be a female high school senior, high school graduate or current undergraduate college student enrolled in a full-time undergraduate course of study at an accredited two- or four-year college, university or vocational-technical school in the U.S. **Criteria:** Preference will be given to students majoring in a hospitality related field.

Funds Avail.: $1,500 - $2,500. **Duration:** Annual. **To Apply:** Applicants must submit a completed application form along with letters of recommendation. **Deadline:** February 8. **Contact:** Alyssa Barkley at abarkley@ncrla.org.

7041 ■ Golden Corral Scholarships *(Undergraduate/ Scholarship)*

Purpose: To support a college junior student enrolled in a four-year culinary or hospitality program in North Carolina. **Focus:** Culinary arts; Hotel, institutional, and restaurant management. **Qualif.:** Applicant must be a permanent North Carolina resident and a college junior enrolled in a four-year culinary or hospitality program in North Carolina. **Criteria:** Selection is based on the submitted application materials.

Funds Avail.: $4,000. **Number Awarded:** 1. **To Apply:** Applicants must submit a completed application form together with a current complete official transcript of grades. All materials must be sent to NC Hospitality Education Foundation Scholarships.

7042 ■ K & W Cafeterias Scholarships *(Undergraduate/Scholarship)*

Purpose: To support a college junior student enrolled in a four-year culinary or hospitality program in North Carolina. **Focus:** Culinary arts; Hotel, institutional, and restaurant management. **Qualif.:** Applicant must be a permanent North Carolina resident and a college junior enrolled in a four-year culinary or hospital program in North Carolina. **Criteria:** Selection is based on the submitted application materials.

Funds Avail.: $3,000. **Number Awarded:** 1. **To Apply:** Applicants must submit a completed application form together with a current complete official transcript of grades. All materials must be sent to NC Hospitality Education Foundation Scholarships.

7043 ■ NC Hospitality Education Foundation Scholarships - Four Year College or University *(Undergraduate/Scholarship)*

Purpose: To support students pursuing a career in culinary arts, hospitality management or tourism. **Focus:** Culinary arts; Hotel, institutional, and restaurant management; Travel and tourism. **Qualif.:** Applicant must be a student enrolled in a full-time undergraduate course of study at an accredited four-year college, university or culinary program in NC; pursing a degree in culinary arts, hospitality management or tourism; and a permanent NC resident. **Criteria:** Selection is based on the submitted application materials.

Funds Avail.: $1,500. **Duration:** Annual. **Number**

Awards are arranged alphabetically below their administering organizations

Awarded: 10. **To Apply:** Applicants must submit a completed application form together with current complete official transcript(s) of grades. All materials must be mailed to NC Hospitality Education Foundation Scholarships. **Deadline:** February 8. **Contact:** Alyssa Barkley at abarkley@ncrla.org.

7044 ■ NC Hospitality Education Foundation Scholarships - Graduate *(Graduate/Scholarship)*

Purpose: To support graduate students pursuing a graduate course in a hospitality related field, or MBA, in NC. **Focus:** Culinary arts; Hotel, institutional, and restaurant management. **Qualif.:** Applicant must be a graduate of a four-year program with a hospitality or culinary degree; planning to enroll (or is already enrolled) in a full-time graduate course of study in a hospitality related field, or MBA, in NC; and a permanent NC resident. **Criteria:** Selection is based on the submitted application materials.

Funds Avail.: $1,500. **Duration:** Annual. **Number Awarded:** 10. **To Apply:** Applicants must submit a completed application form together with current complete official transcript(s) of grades. All materials must be mailed to NC Hospitality Education Foundation Scholarships. **Contact:** Alyssa Barkley at abarkley@ncrla.org.

7045 ■ NC Hospitality Education Foundation Scholarships - High School *(Undergraduate, Vocational/Occupational/Scholarship)*

Purpose: To support students pursuing a career in culinary arts, hospitality management or tourism. **Focus:** Culinary arts; Hotel, institutional, and restaurant management; Travel and tourism. **Qualif.:** Applicant must be a high school senior planning to enroll (or is already enrolled) in a full-time undergraduate course of study at an accredited two- or four-year college, university or vocational/technical school in North Carolina; pursuing culinary arts, hospitality management or tourism; and a permanent NC resident. **Criteria:** Selection is based on the submitted application materials.

Funds Avail.: $750 - $1,500. **Duration:** Annual. **Number Awarded:** 10. **To Apply:** Applicants must submit a completed application form together with current complete official transcript(s) of grades. All materials must be mailed to NC Hospitality Education Foundation Scholarships. **Contact:** Alyssa Barkley at abarkley@ncrla.org.

7046 ■ NC Hospitality Education Foundation Scholarships - Two Year Community or Junior College *(Undergraduate/Scholarship)*

Purpose: To support students pursuing a career in culinary arts, hospitality management or tourism. **Focus:** Culinary arts; Hotel, institutional, and restaurant management; Travel and tourism. **Qualif.:** Applicant must be a student enrolled in a full-time undergraduate course of study at an accredited two-year college or culinary program in NC; pursuing a degree in culinary arts, hospitality management or tourism; and a permanent NC resident. **Criteria:** Selection is based on the submitted application materials.

Funds Avail.: $750. **Duration:** Annual. **Number Awarded:** 10. **To Apply:** Applicants must submit a completed application form together with current complete official transcript(s) of grades. All materials must be mailed to NC Hospitality Education Foundation Scholarships. **Deadline:** February 8. **Contact:** Alyssa Barkley at abarkley@ncrla.org.

Awards are arranged alphabetically below their administering organizations

7047 ■ North Carolina Section of the American Water Works Association (NC AWWA)
3725 National Dr., Ste. 217
Raleigh, NC 27612
Ph: (919)784-9030
Fax: (919)784-9032
URL: www.ncsafewater.org

7048 ■ Carol Bond Community College Scholarships *(Undergraduate/Scholarship)*

Purpose: To encourage interest in environmental education. **Focus:** Environmental science. **Qualif.:** Applicants must be future or current community college students; must be either high school seniors accepted for enrollment or current community college students enrolled at a North Carolina community college; must be pursuing a degree in Environmental Sciences or Water Resources Management concentrations; must be U.S. citizens. **Criteria:** Recipients are selected based on potential to provide leadership in the environmental sciences and environmental engineering fields and potential to positively impact the fields.

Funds Avail.: $1,000. **To Apply:** Applicants must submit: an official application form; one copy of an official, sealed transcript of all university education; two letters of recommendation from professors, employers, or academic advisors; a 500-750 word typed or legibly written essay that discusses why they should be a scholarship recipient; proof of U.S. citizenship. **Deadline:** February 28.

7049 ■ Carol Bond University Scholarships *(Undergraduate/Scholarship)*

Purpose: To encourage interest in environmental education. **Focus:** Environmental science. **Qualif.:** Program is open to four-year university students pursuing a bachelor's degree in either Environmental Sciences or Environmental Engineering. Applicants must have a minimum overall 2.75 GPA and must be U.S. citizens. **Criteria:** Recipients are selected based on academic records and potential to provide leadership in the environmental sciences and environmental engineering fields.

Funds Avail.: $1,000. **To Apply:** Applicants must submit: an official application form; a copy of an official, sealed transcript of all university education; two letters of recommendation from professors, employers, or academic advisors; a 500-750 word typed or legibly written essay that discusses why they should be a scholarship recipient; proof of U.S. citizenship. **Deadline:** February 28.

7050 ■ North Carolina Simmental Association (NCSA)
1341 US 21 Highway
Hamptonville, NC 27020
Ph: (336)468-1679
Fax: (336)468-1686
E-mail: ncsa@yadtel.net
URL: www.ncsimmental.com

7051 ■ Jim Graham Scholarships *(Undergraduate/Scholarship)*

Purpose: To provide educational support to students planning to pursue a career in an agricultural-related field of study. **Focus:** Agricultural sciences. **Qualif.:** Applicants must be high school or college students planning to pursue or pursuing a career in an agricultural-related field of study;

must maintain a 2.0 GPA. **Criteria:** Recipients are selected based on the need for financial assistance, satisfactory scholastic record, leadership potential and character.

Funds Avail.: $500. **To Apply:** Applicants must complete the application form; attach a photo; submit a transcript of high school grades or college grades with SAT scores. **Deadline:** July 15.

7052 ■ North Dakota Farmers Union (NDFU)
1415 12th Ave. SE
Jamestown, ND 58401
Ph: (701)252-2341
Fax: (701)252-6584
Free: 800-366-8331
URL: www.ndfu.org

7053 ■ Bergman Scholarships *(Undergraduate/ Scholarship)*

Purpose: To provide scholarship to Farmers Union Torchbearers. **Focus:** General studies/Field of study not specified. **Qualif.:** Applicants must be receiving Torchbearer award at the upcoming Farmers Union State Convention and have at least 2.50 grade point average. **Criteria:** Applications will be evaluated based on applicants' response to several essay questions relating to farmer's union, rural issues and personal leadership.

Funds Avail.: No specific amount. **Duration:** Annual. **To Apply:** Applicants must submit all the required application information. **Deadline:** November 6.

7054 ■ Farmers Union Industries Foundation Stanley Moore Scholarships *(Undergraduate/ Scholarship)*

Purpose: To provide financial assistance for deserving students to further their college education. **Focus:** General studies/Field of study not specified. **Qualif.:** Applicants must be Farmers Union members and their children in Minnesota, Montana, North Dakota and Wisconsin; and high school seniors, college students or non-traditional students seeking funding to attend either a two or four-year accredited college, university or technical school for any area of study. **Criteria:** Applicants are evaluated based on academic record; social and community activities; essay or oral speech (video); and, final interview.

Funds Avail.: $1,500 each. **Duration:** Annual. **Number Awarded:** Varies. **To Apply:** Applicants must submit a completed application form; copy of high school/college transcripts; letters of recommendation from a Farmer Union leader and from a teacher or professor; a three-page written essay. **Deadline:** April 21. **Contact:** Dave G. Velde, FUMP Foundation, 1118 Broadway, Alexandria MN 56308; Phone: 320-763-6561.

7055 ■ NFU Foundation Stanley Moore Scholarships *(Undergraduate/Scholarship)*

Purpose: To provide financial assistance for students who deserve to pursue college but financially constrained. **Focus:** General studies/Field of study not specified. **Qualif.:** Applicants must be Farmers Union members, high school seniors, college students or nontraditional students seeking funding to attend a two- or four-year accredited college, university or technical school for any area of study. **Criteria:** Recipients are selected based on academic achievement; social and community involvement; an essay; and phone interview.

Funds Avail.: $1,000 each. **Duration:** Annual. **Number Awarded:** Varies. **To Apply:** Applicants must submit completed application; essay; grade transcripts and letters of recommendation. **Deadline:** April 15. **Contact:** Sue Arends, NFU Education Assistant, 4945 E 109th Court Thornton, CO 80233.

7056 ■ North Dakota Farmers Union Co-op House Scholarships *(Undergraduate/Scholarship)*

Purpose: To support students who are financially in need for their education. **Focus:** General studies/Field of study not specified. **Qualif.:** Applicants must: plan to enroll as freshmen at North Dakota State University; be either Farmers Union members, relatives of past Co-op House members or members of a cooperative; and, have at least 2.50 grade point average during the last three years of high school. **Criteria:** Applicants are evaluated based on academic performance and financial need.

Funds Avail.: No specific amount. **Duration:** Annual. **To Apply:** Applicants must submit a completed application form along with transcripts and ACT scores. **Deadline:** March 15.

7057 ■ North Dakota Farmers Union Scholarships *(Undergraduate/Scholarship)*

Purpose: To support first-year or undergraduate students enrolled in a secondary educational facility. **Focus:** Agribusiness; Agricultural sciences; Agriculture, Economic aspects. **Qualif.:** Applicants must be first year or undergraduate students enrolled in a secondary educational facility. They must be pursuing a career important to rural America, but not limited to agribusiness, farm operation or production agriculture, and have at least 2.5 GPA during the last three years of schooling. **Criteria:** Applicants are evaluated based on academic merit and financial need.

Funds Avail.: No specific amount. **Duration:** Annual. **To Apply:** Applicants must submit a completed application; financial information; letters of recommendation; and grade transcript. **Deadline:** January 31.

7058 ■ Hubert K. and JoAnn Seymour Scholarships *(Undergraduate/Scholarship)*

Purpose: To provide financial assistance for students who deserve to pursue college but are financially constrained. **Focus:** General studies/Field of study not specified. **Qualif.:** Applicants must be Farmers' Union members, graduating high school seniors enrolled in an accredited two- or four-year college or university. **Criteria:** Applicants are evaluated based on academic record; social and community activities; written essay; and final phone interview.

Funds Avail.: $1,000 to $2,000. **Duration:** Annual. **Number Awarded:** 1 or 2. **To Apply:** Applicants must submit a completed application form; copy of high school transcript; two letters of recommendation - one from a Farmers Union leader and one from a school counselor or teacher; an essay, identifying and discussing the significance of rural values in America and on their life. **Deadline:** March 5.

7059 ■ North Dakota Veterinary Medical Association (NDVMA)
921 S 9th St., Ste. 120
Bismarck, ND 58504
Ph: (701)221-7740
Fax: (701)258-9005
E-mail: ndvma@btinet.net
URL: www.ndvma.com

Awards are arranged alphabetically below their administering organizations

7060 ■ Dr. Roger E. Meisner Veterinary Medicine Educational Scholarship Fund *(Undergraduate/ Scholarship)*

Purpose: To promote veterinary medicine and quality animal care through communication, fellowship and professional growth. **Focus:** Veterinary science and medicine. **Qualif.:** Applicants must be students who have graduated from North Dakota High School and have been accepted in a college of veterinary medicine in North America. **Criteria:** Recipients are selected based on need and motivation.

Funds Avail.: No specific amount. **To Apply:** Applicants must submit a completed application form and a statement of less than one page of their reasons for choosing veterinary medicine as a career, plans and extracurricular activities. **Deadline:** June 15.

7061 ■ North Dakota Veterinary Medical Association Scholarships *(Undergraduate/Scholarship)*

Purpose: To promote veterinary medicine and quality animal care through communication, fellowship and professional growth. **Focus:** Veterinary science and medicine. **Qualif.:** Applicants must be students pursuing a career in veterinary medicine who graduated from North Dakota High School; must be residents of North Dakota for two years prior to application; must be enrolled in the professional school of any accredited college of veterinary medicine in North America. **Criteria:** Recipients are selected based on financial need and an expressed interest in returning to North Dakota to practice veterinary medicine.

Funds Avail.: No specific amount. **To Apply:** Applicants must submit a completed application form; autobiography; college transcripts; verification of graduation from North Dakota High School or proof of two years residency; verification of acceptance to veterinary school; and must send references and residency verification for those applicants who have not applied before for the NDVMA scholarship. **Deadline:** May 15. **Contact:** ndvma@btinet.net.

7062 ■ Dr. William "Tim" Whalen Memorial Scholarships *(Undergraduate/Scholarship)*

Purpose: To promote veterinary medicine and quality animal care through communication, fellowship and professional growth. **Focus:** Veterinary science and medicine. **Qualif.:** Applicants must be residents of North Dakota or Clay County for at least one year prior to scholarship application; must be accepted in the professional school of any AVMA accredited college of veterinary medicine in North America. **Criteria:** Recipients are selected based on financial need.

Funds Avail.: $5,000. **To Apply:** Applicants must submit: completed application form; a typed and short autobiography including educational objectives, veterinary-related work experiences, career plans and other activities, awards, honors and special interests; college transcript; three references; verification of one year residency; and verification of acceptance to veterinary school. **Deadline:** May 15. **Contact:** Application form and other supporting documents should be sent to 2802 1st S. N Fargo, ND 58102.

7063 ■ North Texas Relocation Professionals (NTRP)
5600 W Lovers Ln., Ste. 116
Dallas, TX 75209-4330
URL: www.northtexasrelocationprofessionals.org

7064 ■ North Texas Relocation Professionals Scholarships *(Undergraduate, High School/ Scholarship)*

Purpose: To support students enrolled in a Dallas/Fort Worth area accredited high school. **Focus:** General studies/ Field of study not specified. **Qualif.:** Applicants must be members of NTRP; must currently be seniors who are in good standing in a Dallas/Fort Worth area accredited high school; must be relocated between grades 9 and 12; must be relocated more than 50 miles and changed schools due to their family's relocation; currently have a cumulative grade point average of 3.0 on a scale of 4.0 (or equivalent achievement on a different scale). **Criteria:** Selection will be based on the submitted application.

Funds Avail.: $1,500. **Duration:** Annual. **Number Awarded:** 2 in 2014. **To Apply:** Applicants must submit a list of all extra-curricular activities and work experience during high school along with their completed application to their Guidance Department. Applicants must also submit an essay addressing the following: their experiences associated with relocation into the Dallas area; family background, challenges encountered with the relocation as well as successful achievements; and advice to other teenagers who are also preparing to relocate. An essay should be between 1,000 to 1,500 words and must be e-mailed in a Word document format. **Deadline:** March 2. **Contact:** Bruce Waller; Phone: 972-389-5673; bwaller@goarmstrong.com.

7065 ■ Northampton County Medical Society Alliance (NCMSA)
PO Box 21012
Lehigh Valley, PA 18002
E-mail: medsocietyalliance@gmail.com
URL: www.ncmsa.org

7066 ■ Northampton County Medical Society Alliance Scholarships *(Undergraduate/Scholarship)*

Purpose: To provide financial assistance to eligible medical, nursing and physician assistant students. **Focus:** Medical assisting; Nursing; Physics. **Qualif.:** Applicant must be a U.S. citizen residing in Northampton County, Pennsylvania, or has a Bethlehem mailing address; and must be accepted or enrolled in a fully accredited institute of medicine. **Criteria:** Selection is based on academic; financial and community service criteria.

Funds Avail.: $1,000. **Duration:** Annual. **To Apply:** Applicant must complete the application form along with the following: demographic and financial forms; written recommendation letter; one-page personal statement; and a current transcript of records. Entering students must include a letter of acceptance from medical, nursing, or physician assistant program. **Deadline:** March 15.

7067 ■ Northeast Conference on the Teaching of Foreign Languages (NECTFL)
Dickinson College
PO Box 1773
Carlisle, PA 17013-2896
Ph: (717)245-1977
Fax: (717)245-1976
E-mail: nectfl@dickinson.edu
URL: www.nectfl.org

7068 ■ SANS Inc./Mead Leadership Fellows Program *(Professional development/Fellowship)*

Purpose: To support an individual in the development of a project that contributes to the foreign language teaching

Awards are arranged alphabetically below their administering organizations

profession and advances quality language instruction. **Focus:** Education, Bilingual and cross-cultural; Foreign languages. **Qualif.:** Candidates must be foreign language teachers who demonstrate leadership potential at their schools, colleges or universities. **Criteria:** Selection is based on work experience and merits.

Funds Avail.: No amount specified. **Duration:** Annual. **To Apply:** Candidates must submit a completed application from; a resume or curriculum vitae (maximum of two pages); a letter of nomination (maximum of two pages) from the nominating body declaring the leadership potential of the candidate; and a written commitment containing a draft of specific plan of action. **Deadline:** January 31.

7069 ■ Northeast Modern Language Association (NeMLA)

University at Buffalo
Dept. of English
306 Clemens Hall
Buffalo, NY 14260-4610
Ph: (716)645-6342
Fax: (716)645-5980
E-mail: support@nemla.org
URL: www.nemla.org

7070 ■ NEMLA Summer Fellowships *(Graduate, Other/Fellowship)*

Purpose: To defray the cost of traveling incurred by researchers who are pursuing their work-in-progress over the summer. **Focus:** General studies/Field of study not specified. **Qualif.:** Applicants must be untenured junior faculties, graduate students and independent scholars; must be NEMLA members. **Criteria:** Recipients will be selected based on submitted research.

Funds Avail.: Up to $1,500. **Duration:** Annual. **To Apply:** Applicants must submit a two-page application that describes the summer project and includes a timeline; an itemized budget; two letters from colleagues in the field supporting the proposed project. For electronic submission, letters must be on university letterhead which includes the e-mail account's electronic signature. For hard copy submissions, letters should be included in sealed and signed envelope. Applications should have a subject line "NEMLA Summer Fellowship". **Deadline:** February 6.

7071 ■ Northeast Spa and Pool Association (NE-SPA)

6B S Gold Dr.
Hamilton, NJ 08691
Ph: (609)689-9111
Fax: (609)689-9110
E-mail: info@nespapool.org
URL: www.nespapool.org

7072 ■ H.J. "Duke" Ellington Memorial Scholarship Award *(Undergraduate/Scholarship)*

Purpose: To provide support to students who selflessly perform acts of service for the good of others. **Focus:** General studies/Field of study not specified. **Qualif.:** Candidates must be graduating high school seniors or matriculated college students who permanently reside within the NESPA region area. **Criteria:** Selection will be based on the performance of good deeds or community service.

Funds Avail.: No specific amount. **Duration:** Annual. **To Apply:** The individual must be nominated by an owner or employee of an NESPA member firm. Candidates must provide a written statement explaining the good deed or public/community service for which they are being nominated. Also include all types of volunteer and community service activities. Candidates must enclose verification of student's current school enrollment and current grade average. For graduating high school seniors, please add verification of college acceptance. **Remarks:** Established in 1985.

7073 ■ Anthony Rizzo Scholarship Award *(Professional development/Scholarship)*

Purpose: To enable employees to take advantage of education programs being offered in PTI and to assist members in reaching a higher level of performance. **Focus:** General studies/Field of study not specified. **Qualif.:** Eligibility will be based on employees and/or company's financial needs. The company must be a current NESPA member in good standing and have held membership at least one year (eligibility limited to Region I members only); employees must be employed on a full time basis in a position directly related to the pool and spa business; scholarships are limited to one employee per company per year. **Criteria:** All scholarships are awarded on a first come, first served basis. But all applications must be submitted prior to course selections.

Funds Avail.: No specific amount. **Duration:** Annual. **To Apply:** Employees must submit a completed application with company's sign off.

7074 ■ The Northern Arizona Native-American Foundation (TNANAF)

PO Box 682
Page, AZ 86040
URL: www.tnanaf.org

7075 ■ Northern Arizona Native-American Foundation Scholarships *(Undergraduate, Vocational/Occupational/Scholarship)*

Purpose: To assist high school seniors who are matriculating to college with scholarships. **Focus:** General studies/Field of study not specified. **Qualif.:** Applicants must be freshmen, sophomores, or juniors in high school who are interested in attending a four-year college, community college, art school, or vocational school. **Criteria:** Applicants are evaluated based on merit and financial need.

Funds Avail.: $250; $500; $2,000. **To Apply:** Applicants must answer the questions (at website) in a Word Document and return with printed responses, along with a copy of high school transcript, letter of acceptance from the college/university or summer program, and one recommendation letter from a high school teacher. **Deadline:** May 1.

7076 ■ Northern Illinois University - Center for Southeast Asian Studies

520 College View Ct.
DeKalb, IL 60115
Ph: (815)753-1771
Fax: (815)753-1776
E-mail: tjacobsen1@niu.edu
URL: www.cseas.niu.edu/cseas/index.shtml

Awards are arranged alphabetically below their administering organizations

---

7077 ■ NIU-CSEAS Foreign Language and Area Studies (FLAS) Fellowships *(Undergraduate, Graduate/Fellowship)*

Purpose: To assist students with the study of Southeast Asian languages at any educational institution. **Focus:** Linguistics; South Asian studies. **Qualif.:** Applicants must be undergraduate or graduate students from any accredited US higher education institution. **Criteria:** Preference will be given to students planning to study a language in a Southeast Asian country.

Funds Avail.: $2,000 stpend; up to $4,000 tuition. **Number Awarded:** 2. **To Apply:** The Language Reference Form can be downloaded at the website. **Deadline:** January 1 - Summer; February 1 - Academic year.

7078 ■ Northern Indiana Community Foundation (NICF)

715 Main St.
Rochester, IN 46975
Ph: (574)223-2227
Fax: (574)224-3709
Free: 877-432-6423
URL: www.nicf.org

7079 ■ Frederick Rakestraw Law Scholarships *(Graduate/Scholarship)*

Purpose: To provide scholarships for qualified college graduates pursuing a degree in law. **Focus:** Law. **Qualif.:** Applicants must be residents of Fulton County Indiana for at least three years during their high school career; must be graduate students pursuing a Degree in Law enrolled in any school in United States. **Criteria:** Selection of recipients is based on merit.

Funds Avail.: $1,000. **Duration:** Annual. **To Apply:** Applicants must submit a completed scholarship form; an acceptance letter or other proof of enrollment in any school of law in the US; a current transcript; and three letters of recommendation. **Deadline:** July 1. **Contact:** corinne@nicf.org.

7080 ■ Northern Ohio Chapter of Healthcare Information Management Systems Society (NO-HIMSS)

c/o Dr. Christine Hudak
Case Western Reserve University
10900 Euclid Ave.
Cleveland, OH 44106
E-mail: cahudak@gmail.com
URL: www.nohimss.org

7081 ■ NOHIMSS Student Scholarship Program *(Undergraduate, Master's, Doctorate/Scholarship)*

Purpose: To financially assist HIMSS student members who exhibit excellence and future leadership potential in healthcare information and management systems industry and whose intention is to practice in the North Eastern Ohio area. **Focus:** Health care services. **Qualif.:** Applicants must be Baccalaureate, Master's or PhD students enrolled in an accredited academic program related to healthcare information and management systems; must be members in good standing of both HIMSS and NOHIMSS; must be attending an accredited educational program in Ohio at least half-time as determined by the educational institution.

Undergraduate applicants must be first time juniors when the scholarship is awarded. **Criteria:** Preference will be given to applicants whose program includes a strong research component.

Funds Avail.: No specific amount. **To Apply:** Applicants must submit a personal statement each relating to healthcare information management, involvement to date in HIMSS and NOHIMSS, professional achievement and academic society activity; must include three letters of recommendation, an official transcript of records; and must attach a technical paper or essay (no more than eight pages) relating to healthcare information management.

7082 ■ Northern Tier Hardwood Association (NTHA)

200 Lake Rd., Ste. C
Towanda, PA 18848
Ph: (570)265-7753
URL: www.nthardwoods.org

7083 ■ NTHA Forest Resources Scholarships for College Students *(Undergraduate/Scholarship)*

Purpose: To help students pursue their education in forest management, forest products or closely related field. **Focus:** Forestry. **Qualif.:** Applicants should be current students at a two or four year college or university majoring in forest management, forest products, or a closely related field. They also need to have graduated from a high school or lived in one of the following counties in Pennsylvania: Bradford, Sullivan, Susquehanna, Tioga, Wyoming, Pike, Wayne, Lackawanna, and Luzerne. **Criteria:** Selection shall be based on the aforementioned qualifications and compliance with the application details.

Funds Avail.: $500 each. **Duration:** Annual. **Number Awarded:** 2. **To Apply:** Applicants may verify the application process through the program website. **Deadline:** June 1.

7084 ■ Northwest-Shoals Community College (NW-SCC)

800 George Wallace Blvd.
Muscle Shoals, AL 35661
Ph: (256)331-5200
Fax: (256)331-5222
Free: 800-645-8967
URL: www.nwscc.edu

7085 ■ Alabama Power Scholarships *(Undergraduate/Scholarship)*

Purpose: To support NW-SCC students with their educational pursuit. **Focus:** General studies/Field of study not specified. **Qualif.:** Applicants must be high school students entering Northwest-Shoals Community College. **Criteria:** Students will be selected by high school counselors or by the NW-SCC Foundation Scholarship Committee.

Funds Avail.: No specific amount. **Duration:** Annual. **To Apply:** Applicants must submit a completed application form together with the required materials and information. **Deadline:** March 1.

7086 ■ Billy Bowling Memorial Scholarship *(Undergraduate/Scholarship)*

Purpose: To support NW-SCC students with their educational pursuit. **Focus:** General studies/Field of study not

Awards are arranged alphabetically below their administering organizations

specified. **Qualif.:** Applicants must be high school students entering Northwest-Shoals Community College. **Criteria:** Students will be selected by high school counselors or by the NW-SCC Foundation Scholarship Committee.

Funds Avail.: No specific amount. **Duration:** Annual. **To Apply:** Applicants must submit a completed application form together with the required materials and information. **Deadline:** March 1.

7087 ■ Cecil Earl Clapp, Sr. Memorial Scholarship (Undergraduate/Scholarship)

Purpose: To support NW-SCC students with their educational pursuit. **Focus:** Forestry. **Qualif.:** Applicants must be high school students entering Northwest-Shoals Community College. **Criteria:** Students will be selected by high school counselors or by the NW-SCC Foundation Scholarship Committee.

Funds Avail.: No specific amount. **Duration:** Annual. **To Apply:** Applicants must submit a completed application form together with the required materials and information. **Deadline:** March 1.

7088 ■ Marvin E. Daly Memorial Scholarship (Undergraduate/Scholarship)

Purpose: To support NW-SCC students with their educational pursuit. **Focus:** General studies/Field of study not specified. **Qualif.:** Applicants must be Lauderdale County senior students entering Northwest-Shoals Community College. **Criteria:** Students must be selected by high school counselors or by the NW-SCC Foundation Scholarship Committee.

Funds Avail.: No specific amount. **Duration:** Annual. **To Apply:** Applicants must submit a completed application form together with the required materials and information. **Deadline:** March 1.

7089 ■ Michael Denton Scholarship (Undergraduate/ Scholarship)

Purpose: To support NW-SCC students with their educational pursuit. **Focus:** General studies/Field of study not specified. **Qualif.:** Applicant must be a Colbert Heights High School senior student entering Northwest-Shoals Community College. **Criteria:** Students must be selected by high school counselors or by the NW-SCC Foundation Scholarship Committee.

Funds Avail.: No specific amount. **Duration:** Annual. **To Apply:** Applicants must submit a completed application form together with the required materials and information. **Deadline:** March 1.

7090 ■ Homajean Grisham Memorial Scholarship (Undergraduate/Scholarship)

Purpose: To support NW-SCC students with their educational pursuit. **Focus:** General studies/Field of study not specified. **Qualif.:** Applicants must be Cherokee High School Senior students entering Northwest-Shoals Community College **Criteria:** Students will be selected by high school counselors or by the NW-SCC Foundation Scholarship Committee.

Funds Avail.: No specific amount. **Duration:** Annual. **To Apply:** Applicants must submit a completed application form together with the required materials and information. **Deadline:** March 1.

7091 ■ Howell Heflin Memorial Scholarship (Undergraduate/Scholarship)

Purpose: To support NW-SCC students with their educational pursuit. **Focus:** General studies/Field of study not

specified. **Qualif.:** Applicants must be high school students entering Northwest-Shoals Community College. **Criteria:** Students will be selected by high school counselors or by the NW-SCC Foundation Scholarship Committee.

Funds Avail.: No specific amount. **Duration:** Annual. **To Apply:** Applicants must submit a completed application form together with the required materials and information. **Deadline:** March 1.

7092 ■ Broughton Isom Memorial Scholarship (Undergraduate/Scholarship)

Purpose: To support NW-SCC students with their educational pursuit. **Focus:** General studies/Field of study not specified. **Qualif.:** Applicants must be Phil Campbell High School senior students entering Northwest-Shoals Community College. **Criteria:** Students will be selected by high school counselors or by the NW-SCC Foundation Scholarship Committee.

Funds Avail.: No specific amount. **Duration:** Annual. **To Apply:** Applicants must submit a completed application form together with the required materials and information. **Deadline:** March 1.

7093 ■ Franklin A. Lenfesty Memorial Scholarship (Undergraduate/Scholarship)

Purpose: To support NW-SCC students with their educational pursuit. **Focus:** General studies/Field of study not specified. **Qualif.:** Applicants must be high school students entering Northwest-Shoals Community College. **Criteria:** Students will be selected by high school counselors or by the NW-SCC Foundation Scholarship Committee.

Funds Avail.: No specific amount. **Duration:** Annual. **To Apply:** Applicants must submit a completed application form together with the required materials and information. **Deadline:** March 1.

7094 ■ Muscle Shoals Kiwanis/Wal-Mart Scholarship (Undergraduate/Scholarship)

Purpose: To support NW-SCC students with their educational pursuit. **Focus:** General studies/Field of study not specified. **Qualif.:** Applicants must be Muscle Shoals High School Senior students entering Northwest-Shoals Community College. **Criteria:** Students will be selected by high school counselors or by the NW-SCC Foundation Scholarship Committee.

Funds Avail.: No specific amount. **Duration:** Annual. **To Apply:** Applicants must submit a completed application form together with the required materials and information. **Deadline:** March 1.

7095 ■ Northwest-Shoals Community College Academic Scholarships (Undergraduate/Scholarship)

Purpose: To support students in their educational pursuit. **Focus:** General studies/Field of study not specified. **Qualif.:** Applicant must be currently enrolled at Northwest-Shoals Community College with at least 3.0 overall GPA; have completed at least 16 credit hours; have enrolled 12 or more hours each; valid for fall and spring semesters only. **Criteria:** Consideration is given to student with the highest GPA and the greatest potential for success at NW-SCC.

Funds Avail.: No specific amount. **To Apply:** Applicant must submit a completed application form along with the required materials and information; must attach a copy of his/her high school and/or college transcript; and must provide a portfolio. **Deadline:** March 2. **Contact:** Financial

Awards are arranged alphabetically below their administering organizations

Aid Office at 256-331-5417, 256-331-6232 or contact the Foundation at 256-331-5215.

7096 ■ Northwest-Shoals Community College Applied Technology Scholarships (Undergraduate, Vocational/Occupational/Scholarship)

Purpose: To support students with their educational pursuit. **Focus:** Education, Vocational-technical. **Qualif.:** Applicants must be entering freshmen and enrolled full-time in technical or occupational program; must have an overall GPA of 3.0. **Criteria:** Selection is based on merit.

Funds Avail.: No specific amount. **Duration:** Annual. **To Apply:** Interested students must file a Northwest-Shoals Community College Application for Admission; and must submit a completed scholarship application form together with the required materials and information. **Deadline:** March 1.

7097 ■ Northwest-Shoals Community College Athletic Scholarships (Undergraduate/Scholarship)

Purpose: To support NW-SCC students with their educational pursuit. **Focus:** Athletics; General studies/Field of study not specified. **Qualif.:** Applicant must be an entering full-time freshman or a currently enrolled full-time student; must have an overall GPA of 2.0; in basketball, baseball, softball, volleyball, cheerleaders or managers. **Criteria:** Selection is based on the result of the tryouts.

Funds Avail.: No specific amount. **To Apply:** Applicant must file a Northwest-Shoals Community College Application for Admission; must submit a high school or previous college transcript; and portfolio. **Deadline:** March 2.

7098 ■ Northwest-Shoals Community College Bank Independent Scholarships (Undergraduate/ Scholarship)

Purpose: To support NW-SCC students in their educational pursuit. **Focus:** General studies/Field of study not specified. **Qualif.:** Applicant must be a high school student entering Northwest-Shoals Community College. **Criteria:** Students must be selected by high school counselors or by the NW-SCC Foundation Scholarship Committee.

Funds Avail.: No specific amount. **To Apply:** Applicants must submit a completed application form together with the required materials and information.

7099 ■ Northwest-Shoals Community College Fine Arts Scholarships - Art (Undergraduate/Scholarship)

Purpose: To support NW-SCC students with their educational pursuit. **Focus:** Art. **Qualif.:** Applicants must be entering full-time college freshmen or currently enrolled full-time students; and have an overall GPA of 2.25. **Criteria:** Selection will be based on the submitted portfolio and other requirements.

Funds Avail.: $750 per semester. **Duration:** Annual. **Number Awarded:** 1. **To Apply:** To qualify, students must file a Northwest-Shoals Community College Application for Admission; and must submit a completed scholarship application form together with the portfolio. **Deadline:** March 5. **Contact:** Art Scholarships: Jan Frederick, jfrederick@nwscc.edu.

7100 ■ Northwest-Shoals Community College Fine Arts Scholarships - Drama (Undergraduate/ Scholarship)

Purpose: To support NW-SCC students with their educational pursuit. **Focus:** Criticism (Art, Drama, Literary). **Qua-lif.:** Applicants must be entering full-time freshmen or currently enrolled full-time students; and have an overall GPA of 2.5. **Criteria:** Selection will be based on the result of the audition.

Funds Avail.: No specific amount. **Number Awarded:** 1. **To Apply:** To qualify, students must file a Northwest-Shoals Community College Application for Admission. Applicants must submit a completed scholarship application form along with the required materials. **Deadline:** March 2.

7101 ■ Northwest-Shoals Community College Fine Arts Scholarships - Music (Undergraduate/ Scholarship)

Purpose: To support NW-SCC students with their educational pursuit. **Focus:** Music. **Qualif.:** Applicants must be entering full-time college freshman or currently enrolled full-time students; and have an overall GPA of 2.0. **Criteria:** Selection will be based on the results of the auditions.

Funds Avail.: No specific amount. **Duration:** Annual. **To Apply:** To qualify, students must file a Northwest-Shoals Community College Application for Admission; and must submit a completed scholarship application form together with the required materials. **Deadline:** March 5. **Contact:** Music Scholarships: Phil Campbell Campus, Jeff McAlister, j.mcalister@nwscc.edu.

7102 ■ Northwest-Shoals Community College High School Academic Scholarships (Undergraduate/ Scholarship)

Purpose: To support students with their educational pursuit. **Focus:** General studies/Field of study not specified. **Qualif.:** Applicant must be a graduating high school senior; have an overall GPA of 3.25; and enrolled full-time. **Criteria:** Selection is based on merit.

Funds Avail.: $750. **To Apply:** To qualify, students must file a Northwest-Shoals Community College Application for Admission; and must submit a completed scholarship application form together with the required materials and information. **Deadline:** March 2.

7103 ■ Northwest-Shoals Community College Independent Computer Scholarships (Undergraduate/Scholarship)

Purpose: To support NW-SCC students in their educational pursuit. **Focus:** General studies/Field of study not specified. **Qualif.:** Applicant must be a high school student entering Northwest-Shoals Community College. **Criteria:** Students must be selected by high school counselors or by the NW-SCC Foundation Scholarship Committee.

Funds Avail.: No specific amount. **To Apply:** Applicants must submit a completed application form together with the required materials and information.

7104 ■ Northwest-Shoals Community College Student Activities Scholarships (Undergraduate/ Scholarship)

Purpose: To support NW-SCC students with their educational pursuit. **Focus:** General studies/Field of study not specified. **Qualif.:** Applicants must be entering full-time freshmen or currently enrolled full-time students; have an overall GPA of 2.5; and have successfully completed tryouts, interviews, or have been elected/appointed to positions (SGA President, Vice President or Secretary/Treasurer; Ambassadors; College Bowl). **Criteria:** Selection will be based on merit.

Awards are arranged alphabetically below their administering organizations

Funds Avail.: No specific amount. **Duration:** Annual. **To Apply:** Interested students must file a Northwest-Shoals Community College Application for Admission; and must submit a completed scholarship application form together with the required materials and information. **Deadline:** March 1.

7105 ■ D. Mitchell Self Memorial Scholarship
(Undergraduate/Scholarship)

Purpose: To support NW-SCC students with their educational pursuit. **Focus:** General studies/Field of study not specified. **Qualif.:** Applicants must be high school students entering Northwest-Shoals Community College. **Criteria:** Students will be selected by high school counselors or by the NW-SCC Foundation Scholarship Committee.

Funds Avail.: No specific amount. **Duration:** Annual. **To Apply:** Applicants must submit a completed application form together with the required materials and information. **Deadline:** March 1.

7106 ■ Aaron B. Singleton Memorial Scholarship
(Undergraduate/Scholarship)

Purpose: To support NW-SCC students with their educational pursuit. **Focus:** General studies/Field of study not specified. **Qualif.:** Applicants must be Muscle Shoals High School senior students entering Northwest-Shoals Community College. **Criteria:** Students will be selected by high school counselors or by the NW-SCC Foundation Scholarship Committee.

Funds Avail.: No specific amount. **Duration:** Annual. **To Apply:** Applicants must submit a completed application form together with the required materials and information. **Deadline:** March 1.

7107 ■ Tuscumbia Kiwanis Scholarship
(Undergraduate/Scholarship)

Purpose: To support NW-SCC students with their educational pursuit. **Focus:** General studies/Field of study not specified. **Qualif.:** Applicants must be Deshler High School Senior students entering Northwest-Shoals Community College. **Criteria:** Students must be selected by high school counselors or by the NW-SCC Foundation Scholarship Committee.

Funds Avail.: No specific amount. **Duration:** Annual. **To Apply:** Applicants must submit a completed application form together with the required materials and information. **Deadline:** March 1.

7108 ■ Wayne County Bank Scholarships
(Undergraduate/Scholarship)

Purpose: To support NW-SCC students with their educational pursuit. **Focus:** General studies/Field of study not specified. **Qualif.:** Applicants must be Wayne County High School Senior students entering Northwest-Shoals Community College. **Criteria:** Students will be selected by high school counselors or by the NW-SCC Foundation Scholarship Committee.

Funds Avail.: $1,000. **Duration:** Annual. **To Apply:** Applicants must submit a completed application form together with the required materials and information. **Deadline:** March 1.

7109 ■ Nova Scotia Salmon Association (NSSA)
PO Box 396
Chester, NS, Canada B0J 1J0
Ph: (902)275-3407

Fax: (902)275-3407
E-mail: info@nssalmon.ca
URL: www.nssalmon.ca

7110 ■ Nova Scotia Salmon Association Scholarships *(Undergraduate/Scholarship)*

Purpose: To financially support students in their academic and in-river pursuits. **Focus:** Aquaculture. **Qualif.:** Applicants must have undertaken or be in the process of undertaking a scholarly pursuit related to the enhancement or conservation of the Atlantic salmon and/or trout; must propose to publish or have published an article or scientific paper in any field which features the enhancement of the Atlantic salmon and/or trout; must promote the cause of the Atlantic salmon and trout by outstanding leadership or participation; be engaged in endeavors of an association which results to the conservation of the Atlantic salmon and trout. **Criteria:** Applicants will be evaluated based on the criteria designed by the NSSA Scholarship Committee.

Funds Avail.: $500. **Duration:** Annual. **To Apply:** Applicants must complete all the needed information in the application form; must attach a (maximum limit 500 words) statement explaining the following: (1) general interests and activities; (2) proposed course of study and present intention for future career development; and (3) summary of the applicant's endeavors in conserving the Atlantic Salmon and/or Trout in Nova Scotia; and must include two references that will provide information regarding the applicant's qualifications.

7111 ■ Nuffield Canada
35011 Range Road 13
Red Deer County, AB, Canada T4G 0J1
Ph: (403)224-2633
Fax: (403)227-7200
E-mail: secretary@nuffield.ca
URL: www.nuffield.ca

7112 ■ Nuffield Canada Farming Scholarships
(Undergraduate/Scholarship)

Purpose: To help students develop their leadership within Canada's rural industries, communities and practices of agriculture. **Focus:** Agriculture, Economic aspects. **Qualif.:** Applicants must be Canadian citizens between ages 25 to 45 who are working in the field of agriculture. **Criteria:** Applicants will be selected based on contributions and innovations within their respective fields of study upon return to Canada.

Funds Avail.: $15,000. **Duration:** Annual. **Number Awarded:** 3. **To Apply:** Applicants must submit a filled-out application form with attached resume. **Deadline:** April 30. **Contact:** Nuffield Canada, at the above address.

7113 ■ Nurses Organization of Veterans Affairs (NOVA)
47595 Watkins Island Sq.
Sterling, VA 20165
Ph: (703)444-5587
Fax: (703)444-5597
E-mail: nova@vanurse.org
URL: www.vanurse.org

7114 ■ NOVA Foundation Scholarships *(Doctorate, Graduate, Master's/Scholarship)*

Purpose: To help students further their education in a graduate degree program. **Focus:** Nursing. **Qualif.:** Ap-

Awards are arranged alphabetically below their administering organizations

plicants must be a VA employee; must be a U.S. citizen; must be enrolled or accepted for enrollment in a baccalaureate, masters, post-masters or doctoral program; must have a positive recommendations from Academic Program Director/Dean and VA Nurse Executive. **Criteria:** Applicants will be selected based on the following criteria: (1) career goals, (2) professional and civic activities, (3) academic performance, (4) recommendation of the Academic Program Director/Dean and VA Nurse Executive.

Funds Avail.: $1,500 each. **Number Awarded:** 11. **To Apply:** Applicants must submit an official transcript record, letter of acceptance to academic program for which the scholarship is to be used, and recommendation of the Academic Program Director/Dean and VA Nurse Executive. **Deadline:** June 1. **Contact:** NOVA at the above address or Email: nova@vanurse.org.

7115 ■ Nuts, Bolts and Thingamajigs
833 Featherstone Rd.
Rockford, IL 61107-6302
Ph: (815)399-8700
Free: 888-394-4362
E-mail: foundation@fmanet.org
URL: www.nutsandboltsfoundation.org

7116 ■ Nuts, Bolts and Thingamajigs Scholarships
(Undergraduate, Vocational/Occupational/Scholarship)

Purpose: To provide financial support to students in courses of study that may lead to careers in manufacturing. **Focus:** Engineering; Manufacturing. **Qualif.:** Applicants must be full-time students with a minimum 3.0 GPA (for a college scholarship) or a 2.5 GPA (for a trade/technical school scholarship), enrolled in an engineering or manufacturing-related course of study, or a trade or technical program, that may lead to a career in manufacturing; or a member of FMA, TPA or OPC the employee of a member company; or the child of a member; or the child of a member company's employee. **Criteria:** Applicants are evaluated based on academic achievement.

Funds Avail.: Varies. **Duration:** Semiannual. **To Apply:** Applicants must submit completed online application form and other materials by the application deadline. **Deadline:** March 31 and September 30.

7117 ■ NVIDIA Corp.
2701 San Tomas Expy.
Santa Clara, CA 95050
Ph: (408)486-2000
Fax: (408)486-2200
Free: 877-768-4342
URL: www.nvidia.com

7118 ■ NVIDIA Graduate Fellowships *(Graduate/Fellowship)*

Purpose: To provide funding to PhD students who are researching topics that will lead to major advances in the graphics and high-performance computing industries. **Focus:** Computer and information sciences; Engineering, Computer; Engineering, Electrical. **Qualif.:** Applicant must have already completed the first year of PhD level; majoring in Computer Science, Computer Engineering, System Architecture, Electrical Engineering, or a related area; hold a current membership on an active research team; and enrolled as a full time PhD student during the academic

year of the award. **Criteria:** Applicants will be reviewed competitively in several review sessions.

Funds Avail.: $25,000. **Number Awarded:** Up to 10. **To Apply:** Applicants must complete the application online. In addition, applicants must provide 1-2 page research summary/thesis proposals; resume including contact information; and Professor Nomination Form including nomination letter. **Deadline:** January 15.

7119 ■ The O'Brien Foundation
600 Deerwood Dr., Sta. A
Fredericton, NB, Canada E3B 4Z9
Ph: (506)454-6590
E-mail: information@obrienfoundation.ca
URL: www.obrienfoundation.ca/

7120 ■ O'Brien Foundation Fellowships *(Postgraduate, Master's, Doctorate/Fellowship)*

Purpose: To pursue advanced study or research in any academic, artistic, or professional field at any recognized university or research establishment. **Focus:** Education. **Qualif.:** Applicants must have a degree or training equivalent to a degree; must be residents of the Province of New Brunswick. **Criteria:** Applicants will be selected based on their application requirements.

Funds Avail.: $15,000. **Duration:** Annual. **Number Awarded:** 10. **To Apply:** Applicants must complete the online application form and submit three letters of support and official transcripts. **Deadline:** November 1.

7121 ■ Oceanic Research Group (ORG)
PO Box 94
North Reading, MA 01864
Ph: (978)664-9091
E-mail: info@oceanicresearch.org
URL: www.oceanicresearch.org

7122 ■ Oceanic Research Group Scholarships
(Graduate, Undergraduate/Scholarship)

Purpose: To provide assistance to deserving students pursuing marine-related undergraduate or graduate studies. **Focus:** Biology, Marine. **Qualif.:** Applicants must be undergraduates entering the junior or senior year or graduate students enrolled in an accredited U.S. college or university with an overall GPA of at least 3.0 on a 4.0 scale; must be pursuing a marine-related career; must provide information regarding financial need; must be U.S. citizens. **Criteria:** Selection will be based on submitted documents and demonstrated financial need.

Funds Avail.: $1,000. **Duration:** Annual. **To Apply:** Applicants should submit a completed application form and transcript for each college or university attended. **Deadline:** October 1. **Contact:** Oceanic Research Group, at the above address, or E-mail at scholarship@oceanicresearch.org.

7123 ■ Ohio Association of Broadcasters (OAB)
17 S High St., Ste. 1010
Columbus, OH 43215
Ph: (614)228-4052
Fax: (614)228-8133
Free: 866-OAB-5794
E-mail: oab@oab.org

Awards are arranged alphabetically below their administering organizations

URL: www.oab.org

7124 ■ Ohio Association of Broadcaster's Kids Scholarships *(Undergraduate/Scholarship)*

Purpose: To encourage high standards of professionalism in the industry; to foster a stronger relationship between higher education and the profession; to promote a greater understanding of the ethics and societal responsibility of broadcasters; to support potential and commitment in promising future broadcasters; to advance a continuing commitment to diversity in the industry. **Focus:** Broadcasting. **Qualif.:** Applicants must be high school seniors who are children of a full-time employee of an OAB member station; must plan to enroll in a postsecondary institution. **Criteria:** Recipients are selected based on academic performance.

Funds Avail.: $1,500. **Number Awarded:** 1. **To Apply:** Applicants must submit a completed application form; a two page essay; a copy of high school transcript and one letter of recommendation. **Remarks:** Established in 2004.

7125 ■ Ohio Association of Broadcasters Scholarships *(Undergraduate/Scholarship)*

Purpose: To support students who are pursuing career in broadcasting. **Focus:** Broadcasting; Communications. **Qualif.:** Applicants must be college students interested in pursuing a career in broadcasting; must be residents of Ohio; must be working toward a major or minor in their school's radio or television broadcasting or communications program; must have a minimum of 2.75 on a 4.0 scale, or the equivalent. **Criteria:** Recipients are selected based on academic performance.

Funds Avail.: $3,000. **Number Awarded:** 2. **To Apply:** Applicants must submit their completed the application form, transcripts, three-page essay and two letters of recommendation.

7126 ■ Ohio Farm Bureau Federation (OFBF)

280 N High St., 6th Fl.
Columbus, OH 43215
Ph: (614)249-2400
Fax: (614)249-2200
URL: ofbf.org

7127 ■ Women's Leadership in Agriculture Scholarship Program *(Undergraduate/Scholarship)*

Purpose: To provide financial support to deserving women. **Focus:** Agricultural sciences. **Qualif.:** Applicants must be enrolled in an accredited college or university. **Criteria:** Selection will be based on community involvement.

Funds Avail.: $1,500. **Duration:** Annual. **To Apply:** Applicants must submit a completed application form. **Deadline:** February 28. **Contact:** Ohio Farm Bureau Federation at the above address.

7128 ■ Ohio Newspaper Association (ONA)

1335 Dublin Rd., Ste. 216B
Columbus, OH 43215
Ph: (614)486-6677
Fax: (614)486-4940
URL: www.ohionews.org/aws/ONA/pt/sp/home_page

7129 ■ Harold K. Douthit Regional Scholarships *(Undergraduate/Scholarship)*

Purpose: To provide educational assistance for students from Northern Ohio. **Focus:** Advertising; Communications; Journalism; Marketing and distribution. **Qualif.:** Applicants must: have graduated from a high school in Cuyahoga, Lorain, Huron, Erie, Wood, Geauga, Sandusky, Ottawa or Lucas county; be enrolled as sophomores, juniors or seniors at any Ohio college or university; and, have a minimum grade point average of 3.0 (B); and must clearly demonstrate ability to write. **Criteria:** Selection will be based on the committee's criteria.

Funds Avail.: $1,500. **Duration:** Annual. **To Apply:** Applicants must submit a completed, typed or printed legibly, application form; official university or college transcript; an autobiography of 750 to 1,000 words describing academic and career interests, awards, extracurricular activities and any journalism-related activities; and two letters of recommendation from college or university faculty members familiar with the student's work and career interests, with special emphasis on the student's financial need. Students are encouraged to provide writing samples or articles that have been published. **Deadline:** March 31. **Contact:** Ann Riggs, ONA receptionist and secretary, at ariggs@ohionews.org.

7130 ■ Ohio Newspaper Association Minority Scholarships *(Undergraduate/Scholarship)*

Purpose: To provide educational assistance for minority high school seniors in Ohio intending to pursue a newspaper journalism career. **Focus:** Advertising; Communications; Journalism; Marketing and distribution. **Qualif.:** Applicants must: be graduating seniors at any Ohio high school; must be enrolled as college freshmen at any Ohio college or university; must have a minimum high school GPA of 2.5 (C+); must clearly demonstrate the ability to read and write; and, be African American, Hispanic, Asian American or American Indian. **Criteria:** Selection will be based on the committee's criteria.

Funds Avail.: $1,500. **Duration:** Annual. **To Apply:** Applicants must submit completed application form typed or printed legibly by the applicant; an autobiography of 750 to 1,000 words describing academic and career interest, awards, extracurricular activities and any journalism-related activities; and two letters of recommendation from high school faculty members familiar with the student's work and career interests. Students may provide additional information such as samples or articles that have been published. **Deadline:** March 31. **Contact:** Ann Riggs, ONA receptionist and secretary, at ariggs@ohionews.org.

7131 ■ Ohio Newspaper Association University Journalism Scholarships *(Undergraduate/Scholarship)*

Purpose: To provide educational assistance for students demonstrating a career commitment to newspaper journalism. **Focus:** Journalism. **Qualif.:** Applicants must be enrolled as sophomores, juniors or seniors at an Ohio college or university; must have a minimum grade point average of 2.5 (C+); and must clearly demonstrate ability to write. **Criteria:** Preference will be given to students demonstrating a career commitment to newspaper journalism.

Funds Avail.: $1,500 each. **Duration:** Annual. **Number Awarded:** 3. **To Apply:** Applicants must submit a completed, typed or printed legibly, application form; official college or university transcript; an autobiography of 750 to 1,000 words describing academic and career interests, awards, extracurricular activities and any journalism-related activities (emphasis should be given to newspaper or print journalism); two letters of recommendation from college or

Awards are arranged alphabetically below their administering organizations

university faculty members familiar with the students' work and career interests; and writing samples or articles that have been published. **Deadline:** March 31. **Remarks:** Established in 2014. **Contact:** Ann Riggs, ONA receptionist and secretary, at: ariggs@ohionews.org.

7132 ■ Ohio Newspaper Association Women's Scholarships *(College, University/Scholarship)*

Purpose: To provide educational assistance for students in an Ohio college or university. **Focus:** Advertising; Communications; Journalism; Marketing and distribution. **Qualif.:** Applicants must be students currently enrolled as juniors or seniors at an Ohio college or university and majoring in a field relevant to the industry, particularly journalism, advertising, marketing or communications degree program. **Criteria:** Selection will be based on the committee's criteria.

Funds Avail.: $1,500. **Duration:** Annual. **To Apply:** Applicants must submit a completed application form together with official college or university transcript, two letters of recommendation, three to four news clippings, and statements answering the following questions: Who or what was your inspiration to get involved in the field of journalism, adverstising, marketing or communications and why did you select your chosen field as your area of interest?; Why do you need a scholarship? What do you think qualifies you for a scholarship?; What do you hope to accomplish during your career as a newspaper industry professional? **Deadline:** March 31. **Contact:** Ann Riggs, ONA receptionist and secretary, at ariggs@ohionews.org.

7133 ■ Ohio Nursery and Landscape Association (ONLA)

72 Dorchester Sq.
Westerville, OH 43081
Ph: (614)899-1195
Fax: (614)899-9489
Free: 800-825-5062
E-mail: info@onla.org
URL: www.onla.org

7134 ■ The Artist in Landscape Design Scholarship by Fullmer's Landscaping *(Undergraduate/Scholarship)*

Purpose: To provide financial support to students who aim to achieve higher education in horticultural field. **Focus:** Horticulture. **Qualif.:** Applicants must be students studying in the horticultural field and attending school in the Tri-State area of Ohio, Indiana, or Kentucky. **Criteria:** Selection will be based on the committee's criteria.

Funds Avail.: $2,000. **Duration:** Every two years. **Number Awarded:** 1. **To Apply:** Applicants must submit a completed application form along with their statement of purpose, college transcripts, recommendation letter on school letterhead, and a resume. To be submitted by the student directly to the ONLA office.

7135 ■ Bryan A. Champion Memorial Scholarship *(Undergraduate/Scholarship)*

Purpose: To provide financial support to students who aim to achieve higher education in horticulture and related fields. **Focus:** Horticulture. **Qualif.:** Applicants must be horticulture students enrolled full- or part-time in programs at the following schools only: The Ohio State University, The Ohio State University Agricultural Technical Institute,

Kent State Univer-sity-Salem, Clark State Community College, Owens Community College, Columbus State Community College, Cuyahoga Community College, Cincinnati State Technical & Community College, and the University of Cincinnati. **Criteria:** Selection will be based on the committee's criteria.

Funds Avail.: Amount not specified. **Duration:** Annual. **Number Awarded:** 1. **To Apply:** Applicants must submit a completed application form along with their statement of purpose, college transcripts, recommendation letter on school letterhead, and a resume. To be submitted by the student directly to the ONLA office.

7136 ■ FFA Scholarship *(Undergraduate/Scholarship)*

Purpose: To provide financial support to students who aim to achieve higher education on horticulture and related fields. **Focus:** Horticulture. **Qualif.:** Applicants must be horticulture students enrolled full- or part-time in programs at the following schools only: The Ohio State University, The Ohio State University Agricultural Technical Institute, Kent State Univer-sity-Salem, Clark State Community College, Owens Community College, Columbus State Community College, Cuyahoga Community College, Cincinnati State Technical & Community College, and the University of Cincinnati. **Criteria:** Selection will be based on the committee's criteria.

Funds Avail.: $500. **Duration:** Annual. **To Apply:** Applicants must submit completed application forms along with their statement of purpose, college transcripts, recommendation letter on school letterhead, and a resume. To be submitted by the student directly to the ONLA office.

7137 ■ Southwest Ohio Environmental Horticulture Association (SOEHA) Lloyd W. Kennedy Scholarship *(Undergraduate/Scholarship)*

Purpose: To provide financial support to students who aim to achieve higher education in horticulture and related fields. **Focus:** General studies/Field of study not specified. **Qualif.:** Applicants must be enrolled full- or part-time in programs at the following schools: The Ohio State University, The Ohio State University Agricultural Technical Institute, Kent State Univer-sity-Salem, Clark State Community College, Owens Community College, Columbus State Community College, Cuyahoga Community College, Cincinnati State Technical & Community College, and the University of Cincinnati. **Criteria:** Selection will be based on the committee's criteria.

Funds Avail.: $500.00. **Duration:** Annual. **Number Awarded:** 1. **To Apply:** Applicants must submit a completed application form along with their statement of purpose, college transcripts, recommendation letter on school letterhead, and a resume. To be submitted by the student directly to the ONLA office.

7138 ■ ONLA Phil Kozel Memorial Scholarship *(Undergraduate/Scholarship)*

Purpose: To provide financial support to students who aim to achieve higher education in horticulture. **Focus:** Horticulture. **Qualif.:** Applicants must be horticulture students enrolled full- or part-time in programs at the following schools: The Ohio State University, The Ohio State University Agricultural Technical Institute, Kent State University-Salem, Clark State Community College, Owens Community College, Columbus State Community College, Cuyahoga Community College, Cincinnati State Technical & Community College, and the University of Cincinnati. **Criteria:** Selection will be based on the committee's criteria.

Awards are arranged alphabetically below their administering organizations

Funds Avail.: Amount not specified. **Duration:** Annual. **Number Awarded:** 1. **To Apply:** Applicants must submit a completed application form along with their statement of purpose, college transcripts, recommendation letter on school letterhead, and a resume. To be submitted by the student directly to the ONLA office.

7139 ■ ONLA President's Scholarship
(Undergraduate/Scholarship)

Purpose: To provide financial support to students who aim to achieve higher education in horticulture and related fields. **Focus:** General studies/Field of study not specified. **Qualif.:** Applicants must be horticulture students enrolled full- or part-time in programs at the following schools: The Ohio State University, The Ohio State University Agricultural Technical Institute, Kent State Univer-sity-Salem, Clark State Community College, Owens Community College, Columbus State Community College, Cuyahoga Community College, Cincinnati State Technical & Community College, and the University of Cincinnati. **Criteria:** Selection will be based on the committee's criteria.

Funds Avail.: $300,000. **Duration:** Annual. **Number Awarded:** 1. **To Apply:** Applicants must submit a completed application form along with their statement of purpose, college transcripts, recommendation letter on school letterhead, and a resume. To be submitted by the student directly to the ONLA office.

7140 ■ Ohio Rural Electric Cooperatives Inc.
6677 Busch Blvd.
Columbus, OH 43226-0036
Ph: (614)846-5757
E-mail: dmingyar@buckeyepower.com
URL: www.buckeyepower.com

7141 ■ Touchstone Special Achievement Scholarships *(Undergraduate/Scholarship)*

Purpose: To support high school seniors who are pursuing their education at a college, vocational or technical school. **Focus:** General studies/Field of study not specified. **Qualif.:** Applicants must be graduating high school senior students whose parents or guardians are electric members of an Ohio rural electric cooperative. **Criteria:** Applicants will be judged on how well their activities reflect the Touchstone Energy core values of accountability, integrity, innovation and commitment to community, as well as their drive and dedication to achieving a college education despite personal obstacles or challenges.

Funds Avail.: $2,000 each. **Duration:** Annual. **Number Awarded:** 6. **To Apply:** Applicants must submit a completed scholarship application to Ohio Rural Electric Cooperative (OREC).

7142 ■ Ohio School Counselor Association (OSCA)
PO Box 1445
Dublin, OH 43017-6445
Free: 866-230-1042
E-mail: osca@ohioschoolcounselor.org
URL: www.ohioschoolcounselor.org

7143 ■ OSCA Graduate Student Scholarship Program *(Graduate/Scholarship)*

Purpose: To help quality school counseling graduate students fulfill their educational goals. **Focus:** Counseling/

Guidance. **Qualif.:** Applicants must be currently enrolled in a master's school counselor program in the state of Ohio (students enrolled in online programs are not eligible to apply); have completed at least six semester hours of graduate work (students enrolled in the final semester of study and preparing to graduate are not eligible to apply); and must maintain an active membership with OSCA. **Criteria:** Selection will be based on application.

Funds Avail.: $1,000 each. **Duration:** Annual. **Number Awarded:** 2. **To Apply:** Applicants must submit four complete copies of: completed scholarship application form; a typewritten essay of no more than one double-spaced page; copy of official graduate school transcripts showing a minimum of six completed credit hours (may submit one original and three photocopies); professional letter of support written by a current academic adviser or professor. **Deadline:** April 30. **Contact:** Ohio School Counselor Association, at the above address; Email: grantsawards@ohioschoolcounselor.org.

7144 ■ Ohio Space Grant Consortium (OSGC)
22800 Cedar Point Rd.
Cleveland, OH 44142
Ph: (937)775-3575
Fax: (937)775-5009
URL: www.osgc.org

7145 ■ Ohio Space Grant Consortium Graduate Fellowships *(Graduate, Doctorate, Master's/Fellowship)*

Purpose: To provide financial support through competitively awarded fellowships to Master's and Doctoral students. **Focus:** Engineering; Mathematics and mathematical sciences; Science; Technology. **Qualif.:** Applicants must be Master's and Doctoral students pursuing degrees in one of the STEM disciplines (science, technology, engineering, or mathematics) at OSGC universities. **Criteria:** Selection will be based on the committee's criteria.

Funds Avail.: $16,000. **To Apply:** Applicants must submit a completed application form (available from the website); a resume (maximum of two pages); undergraduate and previous graduate official transcript(s); two completed recommendation forms (in sealed envelopes). Completed application form must be sent or delivered to the Ohio Space Grant Consortium Campus Representative at the member university where you intend to pursue your studies. **Deadline:** February 1. **Contact:** Ohio Space Grant Consortium, at the above address.

7146 ■ Ohio Space Grant Consortium Special Minority Fellowships *(Doctorate, Graduate, Master's/Fellowship)*

Purpose: To provide financial support through competitively awarded fellowships to Master's and Doctoral students. **Focus:** Engineering; Mathematics and mathematical sciences; Science; Technology. **Qualif.:** Applicants must be underrepresented-underserved minority seniors who are holders of undergraduate OSGC scholarships at any of the OSGC universities. **Criteria:** Selection will be based on the committee's criteria.

Funds Avail.: No specific amount. **Duration:** Annual. **Number Awarded:** 1. **To Apply:** Applicants must submit a completed application form (available from the website); a resume (maximum of two pages); undergraduate and previous graduate official transcript(s); two completed recommendation forms (in sealed envelopes). Completed ap-

Awards are arranged alphabetically below their administering organizations

plication form must be sent or delivered to the Ohio Space Grant Consortium Campus Representative at the member university where you intend to pursue your studies. **Deadline:** February 1.

7147 ■ Ohio State University - Kiplinger Program in Public Affairs Journalism
21 E 11th Avenue
South Campus Gateway
Columbus, OH 43201-2126
Ph: (614)688-0955
E-mail: haddix.12@osu.edu

7148 ■ Kiplinger Fellowship *(Professional development/Fellowship)*
Purpose: To help journalists in maximizing the use of new online tools and channels on the online digital revolution. **Focus:** Journalism. **Qualif.:** Applicants must be journalists with five or more years of experience at a news organization. **Criteria:** Selection criteria will be determined by the committee.

Funds Avail.: Amount not specified. **Duration:** Annual. **To Apply:** Interested applicants may contact the Kiplinger Program for the application process and other informations.

7149 ■ Oklahoma City University School of Law
800 N Harvey
Oklahoma City, OK 73102
Ph: (405)208-5337
E-mail: lawquestions@okcu.edu
URL: www.okcu.edu/law

7150 ■ Oklahoma City University Merit Scholarships *(Undergraduate/Scholarship)*
Purpose: To provide financial assistance to incoming law students enrolled in the full-time and part-time program who have demonstrated academic excellence at the undergraduate level, and who have a strong performance on the LSAT. **Focus:** Law. **Qualif.:** Applicants must have high GPA (generally 2.0 or above) and high LSAT (generally at the 80th percentile or above). **Criteria:** Selection is based on LSAT and GPA average.

Funds Avail.: No specific amount. **Duration:** Annual. **To Apply:** No application needed, all admitted students are considered. **Deadline:** March 2.

7151 ■ Hatton W. Sumners Scholarships *(Undergraduate/Scholarship)*
Purpose: To provide financial assistance for qualified law students intending to pursue their studies. **Focus:** Law. **Qualif.:** Applicants must be U.S. citizens; must rank in the top quarter of their class; must be residents of or students/graduates of colleges or universities in Oklahoma, Arkansas, Kansas, Missouri, Texas, Louisiana, Nebraska, or New Mexico; and must be admitted to the school of law. **Criteria:** Selection is based on academic proficiency, extra-curricular achievement and demonstrated capacity for public service.

Funds Avail.: No specific amount. **Duration:** Annual. **To Apply:** Applicants must complete the application form available online must also submit their undergraduate transcript and letters of recommendation. **Deadline:** February 15. **Contact:** Hatton W. Sumners Scholarship Committee, OCU Law; Address: PO Box 61310, Oklahoma City, OK 73146-1310.

7152 ■ Oklahoma Restaurant Association (ORA)
3800 N Portland Ave.
Oklahoma City, OK 73112
Ph: (405)942-8181
Fax: (405)942-0541
Free: 800-375-8181
URL: www.okrestaurants.com

7153 ■ Oklahoma Restaurant Association Scholarships *(Graduate, Undergraduate/Scholarship)*
Purpose: To help students pursue their undergraduate, master's degree, or continuing education at a post-secondary program. **Focus:** Culinary arts; Food service careers; Hotel, institutional, and restaurant management. **Qualif.:** Applicants must be enrolled in one of the following college hospitality industry programs: Hospitality Management, Hotel and Restaurant Management and Culinary Arts Education in the state of Oklahoma. **Criteria:** The Board of Directors of the Oklahoma Restaurant Association Education Committee and the Oklahoma Hospitality Foundation will select applicants based on their academic achievement, scholastic aptitude, enthusiasm, creativity and future promise in the food service/hospitality industry.

Funds Avail.: No specific amount. **To Apply:** Applicants must submit a signed, hard copy of application. Guardians must sign the application if applicants are below 18; copies of paycheck stubs from an employer indicating the completion of 250 hours food service related work; two letters of recommendation from a faculty member and industry employer; a copy of high school or college transcript; and (maximum of 500 words, double-spaced) essay explaining the reasons of applying the scholarship, plans and career goals. **Deadline:** February 3 and April 24.

7154 ■ Oklahoma Speech-Language-Hearing Association (OSHA)
1741 S Cleveland Ave., Ste. 199
Sioux Falls, SD 57103
Ph: (405)802-1630
Fax: (405)509-7102
E-mail: office@oslha.org
URL: www.oslha.org

7155 ■ OSHA Graduate Scholarships *(Graduate/Scholarship)*
Purpose: To provide financial assistance to students majoring in speech-language pathology or audiology. **Focus:** Speech and language pathology/Audiology. **Qualif.:** Applicants must be full-time graduate or clinical doctorate students in a CAA accredited program of study in speech-language pathology or audiology. **Criteria:** Selection will be based on the evaluation of submitted documents and specific criteria.

Funds Avail.: $1,000. **Duration:** Annual. **To Apply:** Applicants must submit a completed application form; transcripts; cumulative undergraduate and graduate GPA; description of undergraduate and graduate involvement in pre-professional and volunteer organizations; statement of career objectives and professional interests (not exceeding 500 words); two recommendation letters; brief statement of financial need. Letters of reference should be included in the packet in a sealed envelope with the writer's signature on the outside of the seal. If applicants are incoming first year graduate students, they must submit a copy of acceptance letter into one of the graduate programs in the state.

Awards are arranged alphabetically below their administering organizations

7156 ■ Olympia Tumwater Foundation (OTF)

110 Deschutes Pkwy. SW
Tumwater, WA 98501
Ph: (360)943-2550
Fax: (360)943-6755
E-mail: otf@olytumfoundation.org
URL: www.olytumfoundation.org

7157 ■ Olympia Tumwater Foundation Traditional Scholarships *(Undergraduate/Scholarship)*

Purpose: To provide support for qualified students. **Focus:** General studies/Field of study not specified. **Qualif.:** Applicant must be graduating from a Thurston County high school; must be a Thurston County resident; must be planning to attend a public or private school in Washington State; must have a GPA of 3.0 or better; must show a need for financial aid and academic promise; and must have a strong work ethic and be involved in the community. **Criteria:** Recipient will be selected based on academic records, work ethic, community involvement, and financial need.

Funds Avail.: $5,000-$10,000. **To Apply:** Applicants must submit an application form and following: 1) Student Aid Report; 2) School Financial Aid Offers; 3) transcript of records; 4) SAT scores; 5) separate sheet for honors or awards, list of community involvement, essay explaining the reasons for application and describing influential person; 6) letter of recommendation; and 7) applicant's and counselor's signature.

7158 ■ Olympia Tumwater Foundation Transitional (non-traditional) Scholarships *(Undergraduate/ Scholarship)*

Purpose: To provide educational assistance for non-traditional students at South Puget Sound Community College, The Evergreen State College and Saint Martin's University. **Focus:** General studies/Field of study not specified. **Qualif.:** Applicant must be a resident of Thurston County; must have completed at least 50% of his/her degree or certificate program and have an established plan for completion of the program; and must be in good academic standing. **Criteria:** Recipients will be selected based on the criteria set by the Scholarship Selection Committee.

Funds Avail.: No specific amount. **To Apply:** Application forms are available at the financial aid offices of St. Martins University, Sound Puget Community College, and the Evergreen State College.

7159 ■ Omicron Delta Kappa

224 McLaughlin St.
Lexington, VA 24450-2002
Free: 877-635-6437
E-mail: odknhdq@odk.org
URL: www.odk.org

7160 ■ Omicron Delta Kappa Foundation Scholarships *(Graduate/Scholarship)*

Purpose: To support students with their educational pursuit. **Focus:** General studies/Field of study not specified. **Qualif.:** Applicant must be a voting member of Omicron Delta Kappa as defined in the manual; be a senior at the time of the application or have graduated within the past five years (Students who are classified as juniors during the semester/quarter and attain senior standing upon completion of the semester/quarter are not eligible to ap-

ply); expected to enroll in an accredited graduate or professional school in the United States or a foreign country within three years of the semester following the award of the scholarship (Students deferring entrance into a graduate school must indicate in the application); and must have earned a cumulative GPA of 3.5 (on a 4.0 scale), or higher, on all academic work attempted for the bachelor's degree. **Criteria:** Selection is based on the application.

Funds Avail.: No specific amount. **Duration:** Annual. **To Apply:** Applications can be submitted using the online application. Applicants must upload the supporting documents (.doc, .pdf, or picture files): a cover letter or personal statement reflecting vocational objectives; a 1-2 page resume or vitae that includes a list of involvement in Honor Societies, Student Organizations, and Community Involvement; no more than three letters of recommendation (at least one (1) academic reference and (1) leadership reference); a copy of Final Transcripts; and a formal picture. **Deadline:** April 1. **Contact:** Frank Krimowski; Email: frank@odk.org.

7161 ■ Omohundro Institute of Early American History and Culture (OIEAHC)

PO Box 8781
Williamsburg, VA 23187-8781
Ph: (757)221-1114
Fax: (757)221-1047
URL: oieahc.wm.edu

7162 ■ Institute-NEH Postdoctoral Fellowships *(Doctorate, Other/Fellowship)*

Purpose: To promote study in any area of early American studies. **Focus:** United States studies. **Qualif.:** Applicant must have completed the Ph.D. by the date the fellowship begins; must be a U.S. citizen or have lived in the United States for the three years preceding the fellowship award (required for NEH funding); have not previously published a scholarly book or have entered into a contract for the publication of a scholarly monograph; proposed fellowship project must not be under contract with another publisher. **Criteria:** A principal criterion for selection is that the candidate's dissertation or other manuscript has significant potential as a distinguished, book-length contribution to scholarship.

Funds Avail.: No specific amount. **To Apply:** Applicant must submit a completed application form; curriculum vitae; abstract of the project; Statement of Proposed Work; Manuscript (written a substantial portion of the dissertation or proposed book project, at least 100 pages); table of contents (list of the chapters in the manuscript); and three references sent directly to the Director, Omohundro Institute of Early American History and Culture. **Contact:** ieahc1@wm.edu.

7163 ■ Institute Andrew W. Mellon Postdoctoral Research Fellowships *(Doctorate/Fellowship)*

Purpose: To promote study in any area of early American studies. **Focus:** United States studies. **Qualif.:** Applicants must have received their Ph.D. at least 12 months prior to the fellowship; have not previously published a book or have entered into a contract for the publication of a scholarly monograph; proposed fellowship project must not be under contract with another publisher. **Criteria:** The principal criterion for selection is that the manuscript has significant potential for publication as a distinguished, book-length contribution to scholarship.

Funds Avail.: 55,000. **Duration:** One year. **To Apply:** Ap-

Awards are arranged alphabetically below their administering organizations

plicants must submit one copy of a completed dissertation or book manuscript; completed application form (four copies); curriculum vitae (four copies); samples of work; statement of proposed work; abstract (four copies); and three references sent directly to Beverly Smith, Manager, Institute Administration, Mellon Fellowship. **Deadline:** November 1. **Contact:** ieahc1@wm.edu.

7164 ■ Oncology Nursing Society Foundation

125 Enterprise Dr.
Pittsburgh, PA 15275-1214
Ph: (412)859-6228
Fax: (412)859-6163
Free: 866-257-4667
E-mail: info@onsfoundation.org
URL: www.onsfoundation.org

7165 ■ Clinical Project Funding for Advanced Practice Oncology Nurses (Advanced Professional, Professional development/Grant)

Purpose: To provide support for a clinical project for the purpose of facilitating innovative solutions to the challenges of delivering patient-centered, evidenced based and accessible care. **Focus:** Nursing, Oncological. **Qualif.:** Applicants must be graduates of any of the following: Master of Nursing (MN), Master of Science in Nursing (MSN), or Doctor of Nursing Practice (DNP) programs; and must be currently practicing in an Advanced Practice Nurses (APN) role. **Criteria:** Selection will be based on the committee's criteria.

Funds Avail.: Up to $5,000 per year. **Duration:** Two years. **To Apply:** Applicants may contact the Foundation for the application process and other information. **Deadline:** June 15. **Contact:** ONS Research Department at research@onsfoundation.org.

7166 ■ Leadership Development Online Course Scholarships (Professional development/Scholarship)

Purpose: To help increase the leadership skills of oncology nurses. **Focus:** Nursing, Oncological. **Qualif.:** Applicants must be registered nurses involved in cancer nursing; must be registered for the ONS Leadership Online Course; and must be willing to participate in a follow-up evaluation and share their pre and post course assessments. **Criteria:** Selection will be based on the Foundation's criteria.

Funds Avail.: $199. **To Apply:** Applicants must read the "how-to" instructions before accessing the online application; must register by creating a username and password on the Closerware Grantmaker site; and must access the online application. **Deadline:** September 8.

7167 ■ Pearl Moore Career Development Awards (Professional development/Grant)

Purpose: To support staff nurses by providing financial assistance to attend a continuing education program(s) that will further the nurses' professional goals. **Focus:** Nursing, Oncological. **Qualif.:** Applicants must be currently employed as staff nurses with a minimum of 75% time devoted to direct patient care with an oncology population and with two or more years in oncology nursing practice by application due date; and must be in pursuit of a BSN or an MSN. **Criteria:** Selection will be based on the Foundation's criteria.

Funds Avail.: Up to $3,000. **To Apply:** Application is via online. Applicants who are first-time users must follow the steps: read the "how-to" instructions before accessing the

online application; register by creating a username and password on the Closerware Grantmaker site; and access the online application.

7168 ■ Oncology Nursing Society Foundation - Bachelor's Scholarships (Undergraduate/Scholarship)

Purpose: To provide funding to individuals interested in and committed to oncology nursing and pursuing a baccalaureate degree in nursing. **Focus:** Nursing, Oncological. **Qualif.:** Applicants must be currently enrolled for their senior year of a bachelor of nursing degree program at an NLN or CCNE accredited School of Nursing in the given academic year. **Criteria:** Selection shall be based on the aforementioned applicants' qualifications and compliance with the application details.

Funds Avail.: $3,000 to $5,000 each. **Duration:** Annual. **Number Awarded:** Varies. **To Apply:** Applicants must submit a completed application form (Part A question 1-9 and Part B) along with a transcript, to date, of current nursing program and nursing diploma or ADN program transcript, and a $5.00 application fee made payable to the ONS Foundation. Submit original and five copies of the entire application to ONS Foundation. **Deadline:** February 1. **Contact:** Oncology Nursing Society Foundation, at the above address.

7169 ■ Oncology Nursing Society Foundation - Doctoral Scholarships (Doctorate/Scholarship)

Purpose: To provide funding to registered nurses interested in and committed to oncology nursing to continue their education by pursuing a doctoral degree. **Focus:** Nursing, Oncological. **Qualif.:** Applicants must: be currently enrolled in (or applying to) a doctoral nursing degree or related program; have their current licenses to practice as registered nurses; and, have an interest in and commitment to oncology nursing. Applicants entering a doctoral program without master's degree must have completed the first two years of the doctoral program curriculum. **Criteria:** Selection shall be based on the aforementioned applicants' qualifications and compliance with the application details.

Funds Avail.: $5,000 and $7,000. **Duration:** Annual. **Number Awarded:** Varies. **To Apply:** Applicants must submit a completed application form together with transcripts (one copy of the transcripts from each nursing degree earned and current doctoral program transcript); two support letters; and a $5.00 application fee payable to ONS Foundation. Submit original and five copies of the application and support letters to ONS Foundation (Faxed materials will not be accepted). **Deadline:** February 1. **Contact:** Oncology Nursing Society Foundation, at the above address.

7170 ■ Oncology Nursing Society Foundation - Master's Scholarships (Graduate, Master's/ Scholarship)

Purpose: To provide scholarships to registered nurses who are interested in and committed to oncology nursing to continue their education by pursuing a master's degree in nursing. **Focus:** Nursing, Oncological. **Qualif.:** Applicants must: be currently enrolled in (or applying to) a master's nursing degree at an NLN or CCNE accredited School of Nursing; have their current licenses to practice as registered nurses; and, have an interest in and commitment to oncology nursing. **Criteria:** Selection shall be based on the aforementioned applicants' qualifications and compliance with the application details.

Funds Avail.: $5,000 each. **Duration:** Annual. **Number Awarded:** Varies. **To Apply:** Applicants must submit a

Awards are arranged alphabetically below their administering organizations

completed application form along with transcripts (bachelors and masters), and a $5.00 application fee made payable to ONS Foundation. Submit original and five copies of the application to ONS Foundation (Faxed materials will not be accepted). **Deadline:** February 1. **Contact:** Oncology Nursing Society Foundation, at the above address.

7171 ■ ONS Foundation Congress Scholarships
(Professional development/Scholarship)

Purpose: To support registered nurses interested in improving cancer care by developing their personal knowledge as a result of attending the ONS Congress and sharing this new knowledge with others. **Focus:** Nursing, Oncological. **Qualif.:** Applicants must be registered nurses living or working within a 50 mile radius of the conference location. **Criteria:** Selection will be based on the Foundation's criteria.

Funds Avail.: $1,200. **To Apply:** Applicants may visit the website for more information. **Deadline:** December 1.

7172 ■ ONS Foundation Dissertation Research Grants *(Doctorate, Professional development/Grant)*

Purpose: To support oncology nursing research for doctoral (PhD) dissertations. **Focus:** Nursing, Oncological. **Qualif.:** Applicants must be principal investigators who are registered nurses (RN) or PhD students and actively pursuing a career in some aspect of cancer patient care, education, or research. **Criteria:** Selection will be based on the Foundation's criteria. Funding preference will be given to projects that promote theoretically based oncology practice.

Funds Avail.: $5,000 per year. **Duration:** Two years. **To Apply:** Applicants may visit the Foundation's website (particularly the RE03 page) to obtain a copy of the required materials and for the application submission process. **Deadline:** August 15 (letters of intent); September 15 (applications). **Contact:** ONS Research Department at research@onsfoundation.org.

7173 ■ ONS Foundation Research Grants *(Advanced Professional/Grant)*

Purpose: To support oncology nursing research. **Focus:** Nursing, Oncological. **Qualif.:** Applicants must be principal investigators who are actively involved in some aspect of cancer patient care, education, or research; and must be PhD- or DNSc-prepared. **Criteria:** Selection will be based on the Foundation's criteria. Funding preference will be given to projects that involve nurses in the design and conduct of the research activity and that promote theoretically based oncology practice.

Funds Avail.: $25,000 each. **Duration:** Two years. **To Apply:** Applicants may visit the Foundation's website (particularly the RE01 page) to obtain a copy of the required materials and for the application submission process. **Deadline:** August 15 (letters of intent); September 15 (applications). **Contact:** ONS Research Department at research@onsfoundation.org.

7174 ■ Research Career Development Awards
(Professional development/Fellowship, Grant)

Purpose: To support short-term oncology research training and mentorship. **Focus:** Nursing, Oncological. **Qualif.:** Applicants must be registered nurses with an interest in oncology and with a completed PhD degree in nursing or a related discipline. **Criteria:** Selection will be based on the Foundation's criteria.

Funds Avail.: $20,000 ($18,000 for the fellows; $2,000 for

the mentor or mentor's institution). **To Apply:** Applicants may visit the Foundation's website (particularly the RCDA page) to obtain a copy of the required materials and for the application submission process. **Remarks:** The Research Career Development Award is funded by the ONS Foundation through an unrestricted grant from Genentech BioOncology. **Contact:** ONS Research Department at research@onsfoundation.org.

7175 ■ Ontario Centres of Excellence (OCE)
156 Front St. W, Ste. 200
Toronto, ON, Canada M5J 2L6
Ph: (416)861-1092
Fax: (416)971-7164
Free: 866-759-6014
URL: www.oce-ontario.org

7176 ■ Martin Walmsley Fellowships for Technological Entrepreneurship *(Graduate/Fellowship)*

Purpose: To support a researcher committed to founding in Ontario a new technologically innovative business (TIB) venture. **Focus:** Business. **Qualif.:** Applicant must be a Canadian citizen or permanent resident committed to founding in Ontario a new TIB venture; must be a researcher (faculty member, graduate student, or postdoctoral fellow); and must demonstrate the requisite motivation and skills to extract the proposed technology nugget from the research in which he/she have been engaged. Selected candidates must have the Intellectual Property through an OCE-sponsored research program. **Criteria:** Selection is based on submitted proposals.

Funds Avail.: $50,000 per year. **Duration:** 2 years. **To Apply:** Applicants must submit the required application materials. **Contact:** For further information, applicants must contact Binny Arora, Program Manager; Phone: 416-861-1092 x1037; Email: binny.arora@oce-ontario.org; Linda Wong, Program Coordinator; Phone: 613-726-3430 x4279; Email: linda.wong@oce-ontario.org.

7177 ■ Ontario English Catholic Teachers Association
65 St. Claire Ave., E Ste. 400
Toronto, ON, Canada M4T 2Y8
Ph: (416)925-2493
Fax: (416)925-7764
Free: 800-268-7230
URL: www.oecta.on.ca

7178 ■ Mary Babcock Fellowships for Labour Studies Application *(Graduate/Fellowship)*

Purpose: To support members seeking full-time study in labour studies. **Focus:** Industrial and labor relations. **Qualif.:** Applicants must be OECTA members. **Criteria:** Selection will be based on committee's criteria.

Funds Avail.: 10,000 Canadian Dollars. **Duration:** Annual. **To Apply:** Applicants may write to the provincial office for further information. **Deadline:** April 1.

7179 ■ Doreen Brady Memorial Scholarships
(Postgraduate/Scholarship)

Purpose: To financially assist members with their full-time post-graduate study. **Focus:** General studies/Field of study not specified. **Qualif.:** Applicants must be OECTA members.

Awards are arranged alphabetically below their administering organizations

Criteria: Selection will be based on committee's criteria.

Funds Avail.: 10,000 Canadian Dollars. **Duration:** Annual. **To Apply:** Applicants may write to the provincial office for further information. **Deadline:** April 1.

7180 ■ Rose Cassin Memorial Scholarships
(Postgraduate/Scholarship)

Purpose: To financially assist members with their full-time post-graduate study. **Focus:** General studies/Field of study not specified. **Qualif.:** Applicants must be OECTA members. **Criteria:** Selection will be based on committee's criteria.

Funds Avail.: 10,000 Canadian Dollars. **Duration:** Annual. **To Apply:** Applicants may write to the provincial office for further information. **Deadline:** April 1.

7181 ■ Father J. Harold Conway Memorial Scholarships *(Postgraduate/Fellowship)*

Purpose: To financially assist members with their full-time post-graduate study. **Focus:** General studies/Field of study not specified. **Qualif.:** Applicants must be OECTA members. **Criteria:** Selection will be based on committee's criteria.

Funds Avail.: 10,000 Canadian Dollars. **Duration:** Annual. **To Apply:** Applicants may write to the provincial office for further information. **Deadline:** April 1.

7182 ■ Joan Kamps Memorial Bursaries
(Undergraduate, Graduate, Postgraduate, Professional development/Scholarship)

Purpose: To financially assist members with their continuing education. **Focus:** General studies/Field of study not specified. **Qualif.:** Applicants must be OECTA members. **Criteria:** Selection will be based on committee's criteria. Members in pre-degree categories taking undergraduate courses are given priority, but those who want to pursue post-graduate studies or professional development activities are also eligible.

Funds Avail.: 1,000 Canadian Dollars. **Duration:** Annual. **To Apply:** Applicants may write to the provincial office for further information. **Deadline:** May 15.

7183 ■ Margaret Lynch Religious Study Fellowships
(Graduate/Scholarship)

Purpose: To support members seeking full-time study in religious education. **Focus:** Education, Religious. **Qualif.:** Applicants must be OECTA members. **Criteria:** Selection will be based on committee's criteria.

Funds Avail.: 10,000 Canadian Dollars. **Duration:** Annual. **To Apply:** Applicants may write to the provincial office for further information. **Deadline:** April 1.

7184 ■ Cecilia Rowan Religious Study Fellowships
(Graduate/Fellowship)

Purpose: To support members seeking full-time study in religious education. **Focus:** Education, Religious. **Qualif.:** Applicants must be OECTA members. **Criteria:** Selection will be based on committee's criteria.

Funds Avail.: 10,000 Canadian Dollars. **Duration:** Annual. **To Apply:** Applicants may write to the provincial office for further information. **Deadline:** April 1.

7185 ■ Ontario HIV Treatment Network (OHTN)
1300 Yonge St., Ste. 600
Toronto, ON, Canada M4T 1X3
Ph: (416)642-6486
Fax: (416)640-4245

Free: 877-743-6486
E-mail: info@ohtn.on.ca
URL: www.ohtn.on.ca

7186 ■ OHTN Postdoctoral Fellowships *(Doctorate/Fellowship)*

Purpose: To enable candidates to develop a line of research and to consolidate a research career. **Focus:** Acquired immune deficiency syndrome; Biological and clinical sciences; Epidemiology. **Qualif.:** Applicant must hold a PhD or a health professional degree or equivalent (medicine, dentistry, pharmacy, optometry or nursing) who holds licensure in Canada or who must be enrolled in a program leading to licensure in Canada or hold an educational license at the time of the award. Consideration will be given to candidates who wish to spend some or all of the award period at an institution outside Ontario. **Criteria:** Recipients will be selected based on research project and applicant's productivity, experience and training.

Funds Avail.: $50,000/year plus research allowance of $5,000/year. **Duration:** up to five years. **To Apply:** Applicants must submit a complete application both online and on hard copy; must include the required attachments: 1) cover letter; 2) research project description; 3) previous reviews (resubmissions only); 4) letter from Department Head; 5) Supervisor's curriculum vitae; 6) transcript of records. If available, must upload the optional attachments: appendices, support letters, research ethics and animal care approval, consent form(s) and laboratory/Bio-Safety approval. **Deadline:** April 20. **Contact:** Jennifer Major at 416-642-6486 x-2249 or jmajor@ohtn.on.ca; Stephanie Lemelin-Bazinet at 416-642-6486 x-2244 or sbazinet@ohtn.on.ca.

7187 ■ Ontario Mental Health Foundation (OMHF)
180 Bloor St. W
UC 101
Toronto, ON, Canada M5S 2V6
Ph: (416)920-7721
Fax: (416)920-0026
E-mail: grants@omhf.on.ca
URL: www.omhf.on.ca

7188 ■ OMHF Postdoctoral Fellowships
(Postdoctorate/Fellowship)

Purpose: To provide an opportunity for a person with a PhD to obtain further training. **Focus:** Mental health. **Qualif.:** Applicant must hold a professional qualification in a field relevant to mental health. **Criteria:** Preference will be given to applicants who have not yet previously held a postdoctoral position.

Funds Avail.: $450/year. **Duration:** 2-3 years. **To Apply:** Applicants must submit a complete application consisting of: applicant's letter (plans for a long-term career and details of any support anticipated or sought from other sources); factsheet (page A); resubmission sheet (page B); project summary sheet (page C); administration of funds (page G); plain language statement; project description (background, hypothesis/research question, methods, originality, timetable, references); consent forms; curriculum vitae and recent publications; department head's acceptance letter; supervisor's letter; transcripts; and references (in signed, sealed envelopes). Applicants are required to submit applications both online and in a paper format. **Deadline:** October 31.

Awards are arranged alphabetically below their administering organizations

7189 ■ Ontario Ministry of Children and Youth Services

900 Bay St.
Toronto, ON, Canada M7A 1N3
Fax: (416)212-1977
Free: 866-821-7770
E-mail: mcsinfo@mcys.gov.on.ca
URL: www.children.gov.on.ca

7190 ■ Grant Assistance Program for Autism Professionals - College Programs *(Undergraduate/ Grant)*

Purpose: To support qualified staff in their college level study. **Focus:** Mental health; Psychology. **Qualif.:** Applicants must be full-time or part-time employees working in MCYS funded Autism Intervention Program or Applied Behaviour Analysis (ABA)-based services and support for at least one year continuously at the time of application and employed as members of the program's team involved directly in the provision of IBI and/or ABA-based interventions; legally entitled to live and work in Canada; and enrolled in or accepted to The Ontario College Graduate Certificate in Autism and Behavioural Science, or any advanced diploma or applied degree in behavioural science or behavioural psychology. **Criteria:** Applicants are selected based on eligibility and compliance with the application process.

Funds Avail.: Up to 5,000 Canadian Dollars. **Duration:** Quarterly. **To Apply:** Applicants must submit a completed application in addition to the following supporting documents: letter of employment from the regional Autism Intervention Program provider or the ABA-based services and supports provider; documented proof of enrolment in or acceptance to a qualifying academic program; and copy of tuition receipts for courses completed to date. **Contact:** Applications must be sent to the Grant Assistance Program Administrator, North Bay Regional Health Centre, 680 Kirkwood Drive, Sudbury, ON P3E 1X3; Phone: 705-675-9193 ext. 8411; Email: info@autismgrantprogram.on.ca.

7191 ■ Grant Assistance Program for Autism Professionals - Doctoral Programs *(Doctorate/Grant)*

Purpose: To support qualified staff in their pursuit of a doctoral degree in clinical or behavioral psychology with a focus on autism or behavior analysis. **Focus:** Mental health; Psychology. **Qualif.:** Applicants must be full-time or part-time employees working in MCYS funded Autism Intervention Program or Applied Behaviour Analysis (ABA)-based services and support for at least one year continuously at the time of application and employed as members of the program's team involved directly in the provision of IBI and/or ABA-based interventions; legally entitled to live and work in Canada; and enrolled in or accepted to any doctoral program in clinical or behavioural psychology with a focus on autism or behaviour analysis. **Criteria:** Applicants are selected based on eligibility and compliance with the application process.

Funds Avail.: 24,000 Canadian Dollars. **Duration:** Quarterly. **To Apply:** Applicants must submit a completed application in addition to the following supporting documents: letter of employment from the regional Autism Intervention Program provider or the ABA-based services and supports provider; documented proof of enrolment in or acceptance to a qualifying academic program; and copy of tuition receipts for courses completed to date. **Contact:** Applications must be sent to the Grant Assistance Program

Administrator, North Bay Regional Health Centre, 680 Kirkwood Drive, Sudbury, ON P3E 1X3; Phone: 705-675-9193 ext. 8411; Email: info@autismgrantprogram.on.ca.

7192 ■ Grant Assistance Program for Autism Professionals - Institutional Standards *(Undergraduate, Graduate/Grant)*

Purpose: To support qualified staff in obtaining their degree in clinical or behavioral psychology. **Focus:** Mental health; Psychology. **Qualif.:** Applicants must be full-time or part-time employees working in MCYS funded Autism Intervention Program or Applied Behaviour Analysis (ABA)-based services and support for at least one year continuously at the time of application (or cumulatively in the case of applicants from isolated communities) and employed as members of the program's team involved directly in the provision of IBI and/or ABA-based interventions; legally entitled to live and work in Canada; and enrolled in or accepted to the following: any college diploma or applied degree (toward professional certification) offered by an accredited Ontario college of applied arts and technology or by a college or diploma-granting institution in another jurisdiction operating in conformity with the applicable laws of that jurisdiction; or, any undergraduate, Master's or doctoral degree (toward professional certification) offered by a duly established university or degree-granting institution in Canada or by a university or degree-granting institution in another jurisdiction operating in conformity with the laws of that jurisdiction where available, accredited by a recognized institutional accrediting agency or association. **Criteria:** Applicants are selected based on eligibility and compliance with the application process.

Funds Avail.: Up to 12,000 Canadian Dollars. **Duration:** Quarterly; up to two or more years. **To Apply:** Applicants must submit a completed application in addition to the following supporting documents: letter of employment from the regional Autism Intervention Program provider or the ABA-based services and supports provider; documented proof of enrolment in or acceptance to a qualifying academic program; and copy of tuition receipts for courses completed to date. **Contact:** Applications must be sent to the Grant Assistance Program Administrator, North Bay Regional Health Centre, 680 Kirkwood Drive, Sudbury, ON P3E 1X3; Phone: 705-675-9193 ext. 8411; Email: info@autismgrantprogram.on.ca.

7193 ■ Grant Assistance Program for Autism Professionals - Masters Programs *(Master's/Grant)*

Purpose: To support qualified staff in their graduate level study. **Focus:** Mental health; Psychology. **Qualif.:** Applicants must be full-time or part-time employees working in MCYS funded Autism Intervention Program or Applied Behaviour Analysis (ABA)-based services and support for at least one year continuously at the time of application and employed as members of the program's team involved directly in the provision of IBI and/or ABA-based interventions; legally entitled to live and work in Canada; and enrolled in or accepted to Master of Applied Disability Studies at Brock University or any Master's program specializing in clinical or behavioural psychology or behaviour analysis. **Criteria:** Applicants are selected based on eligibility and compliance with the application process.

Funds Avail.: Up to 12,000 Canadian Dollars. **Duration:** Quarterly. **To Apply:** Applicants must submit a completed application in addition to the following supporting documents: letter of employment from the regional Autism Intervention Program provider or the ABA-based services and supports provider; documented proof of enrolment in

Awards are arranged alphabetically below their administering organizations

or acceptance to a qualifying academic program; and copy of tuition receipts for courses completed to date. **Contact:** Applications must be sent to the Grant Assistance Program Administrator, North Bay Regional Health Centre, 680 Kirkwood Drive, Sudbury, ON P3E 1X3; Phone: 705-675-9193 ext. 8411; Email: info@autismgrantprogram.on.ca.

7194 ■ Grant Assistance Program for Autism Professionals - Professional Certification Programs
(Undergraduate, Professional development/Grant)

Purpose: To support qualified staff in their pursuit of professional certification. **Focus:** Mental health; Psychology. **Qualif.:** Applicants must be full-time or part-time employees working in MCYS funded Autism Intervention Program or Applied Behaviour Analysis (ABA)-based services and support for at least one year continuously at the time of application and employed as members of the program's team involved directly in the provision of IBI and/or ABA-based interventions; legally entitled to live and work in Canada; and enrolled in or accepted to any college, undergraduate or graduate course or courses required by a recognized accreditation authority within the field of behavioural analysis in order to qualify for professional certification under the rules of the accreditation authority. **Criteria:** Applicants are selected based on eligibility and compliance with the application process.

Funds Avail.: Up to 1,000 Canadian Dollars after one year or up to 5,000 Canadian Dollars over two or more years. **Duration:** Quarterly. **To Apply:** Applicants must submit a completed application in addition to the following supporting documents: letter of employment from the regional Autism Intervention Program provider or the ABA-based services and supports provider; documented proof of enrolment in or acceptance to a qualifying academic program; and copy of tuition receipts for courses completed to date. **Contact:** Applications must be sent to the Grant Assistance Program Administrator, North Bay Regional Health Centre, 680 Kirkwood Drive, Sudbury, ON P3E 1X3; Phone: 705-675-9193 ext. 8411; Email: info@autismgrantprogram.on.ca.

7195 ■ Grant Assistance Program for Autism Professionals - Retroactive Assistance *(Advanced Professional, Professional development/Grant)*

Purpose: To support qualified staff who are seeking professional development. **Focus:** Mental health; Psychology. **Qualif.:** Applicants must be individuals who qualify for grant assistance but have already completed a qualifying academic program (any of the following: doctoral; professional certification; master's; undergraduate; college or institutional standards), providing they completed the program within five years prior to application date and they continue in the employment of Autism Intervention Program or ABA-based services and supports for the duration of the funding agreement. **Criteria:** Selection will be based on the applicants' eligibility and compliance with the application process.

Funds Avail.: No specific amount. **To Apply:** Applicants that meet all of the eligibility criteria must submit a completed application in addition to the following supporting documents: letter of employment from the regional Autism Intervention Program provider or the ABA-based services and supports provider; documented proof of enrolment in or acceptance to a qualifying academic program; and, a copy of tuition receipts for courses completed to date. Furthermore, applicants must provide proof of successful completion of course(s) and tuition payment. **Con-**

tact: Applications must be sent to the Grant Assistance Program Administrator, North Bay Regional Health Centre, 680 Kirkwood Drive, Sudbury, ON P3E 1X3; Phone: 705-675-9193 ext. 8411; Email: info@autismgrantprogram.on.ca.

7196 ■ Grant Assistance Program for Autism Professionals - Undergraduate Programs
(Undergraduate/Grant)

Purpose: To assist qualified staff in their professional development and pursuit of a degree in psychology. **Focus:** Mental health; Psychology. **Qualif.:** Applicants must be full-time or part-time employees working in MCYS funded Autism Intervention Program or Applied Behaviour Analysis (ABA)-based services and support for at least one year continuously at the time of application (or cumulatively in the case of applicants from isolated communities) and employed as members of the program's team involved directly in the provision of IBI and/or ABA-based interventions; legally entitled to live and work in Canada; and enrolled in or accepted to any undergraduate degree in psychology or any undergraduate degree with a major in psychology. **Criteria:** Applicants are selected based on eligibility and compliance with the application process.

Funds Avail.: Up to 12,000 Canadian Dollars. **Duration:** Quarterly. **To Apply:** Applicants must submit a completed application in addition to the following supporting documents: letter of employment from the regional Autism Intervention Program provider or the ABA-based services and supports provider; documented proof of enrolment in or acceptance to a qualifying academic program; and copy of tuition receipts for courses completed to date. **Contact:** Applications must be sent to the Grant Assistance Program Administrator, North Bay Regional Health Centre, 680 Kirkwood Drive, Sudbury, ON P3E 1X3; Phone: 705-675-9193 ext. 8411; Email: info@autismgrantprogram.on.ca.

7197 ■ Ontario Native Education Counselling Association (ONECA)
White Fish Lake First Nation
37 A Reserve Rd.
Walden, ON, Canada P0M 2M0
Ph: (705)692-2999
Fax: (705)692-9988
E-mail: oneca@oneca.com
URL: www.oneca.com

7198 ■ ONECA Four Directions Scholarship
(Undergraduate/Scholarship)

Purpose: To support graduating aboriginal secondary school/adult students in their continuing education. **Focus:** General studies/Field of study not specified. **Qualif.:** Applicants must be students of aboriginal ancestry graduating from an Ontario Secondary School with O.S.S.D of the current school year; maintain good academic standing throughout the school year; 75% overall average in graduating year; proceeding into a post-secondary institution full time program; involvement in the community and/or school extra-curricular-activities; recommended by Secondary School, First Nation Community or Education Counsellor; and leadership qualities, dedication and good attendance. **Criteria:** Selection will be based on leadership qualities, dedication and good attendance.

Funds Avail.: 1,000 Canadian Dollars each. **Duration:** Annual. **Number Awarded:** 4. **To Apply:** Applicants should complete and submit the application form available online

Awards are arranged alphabetically below their administering organizations

and must include the following requirements: a copy of letter of acceptance into second year of the program; proof of Aboriginal Ancestry; biography and one paragraph describing how a scholarship would assist you; letter of recommendation from school, First Nation or Education Counselor; copy of final marks for 1st year of the program; copies of awards, diplomas or other supporting documents; a recent photo; signed release form which allows the Association to post the applicants' name and picture to the website; signed authorization form agreeing to allow the post-secondary institution to release information regarding the attendance at the time the awards are selected. **Deadline:** June 30.

7199 ■ Colin Wasacase Scholarship *(Undergraduate/Scholarship)*

Purpose: To support aboriginal post-secondary college students and post-secondary university students who have successfully completed their first year in a full-time program in the field of counseling. **Focus:** Counseling/Guidance. **Qualif.:** Applicants must be full-time post-secondary students of aboriginal ancestry; must have successfully completed their first year in a Counseling program at an Ontario Post Secondary Institution; must have an good academic standing throughout the first school year; must have a 75% overall average in first year; must be proceeding into the second year of the same program; must be involved in the community or school extra-curricular activities. **Criteria:** Selection will be based on leadership qualities, dedication and good attendance.

Funds Avail.: 1,000 Canadian Dollars. **Duration:** Annual. **Number Awarded:** Varies. **To Apply:** Applicants should complete and submit the application form available online and must include the following: a copy of letter of acceptance into second year of the program; proof of Aboriginal Ancestry; biography and one paragraph describing how a scholarship would assist you; letter of recommendation from school, First Nation or Education Counselor; copy of final marks for 1st year of the program; copies of awards, diplomas or other supporting documents; a recent photo; signed release form which allows the Association to post the applicants' name and picture to the website; signed authorization form agreeing to allow the post-secondary institution to release information regarding the attendance at the time the awards are selected; 500-word essay outlining why the applicants have chosen this career path. **Deadline:** June 30. **Remarks:** Established in 2004.

7200 ■ Open Society Foundations
224 W 57th St.
New York, NY 10019-3212
Ph: (212)548-0600
Fax: (212)548-4600
URL: www.opensocietyfoundations.org

7201 ■ Open Society Baltimore Community Fellowships *(Advanced Professional/Fellowship)*

Purpose: To seek dynamic activists and social entrepreneurs interested in implementing projects that address problems in underserved communities in Baltimore city. **Focus:** Economics; Social sciences. **Qualif.:** Applicants may come from any field, including, but not limited to law, medicine, drug addiction solutions, education, the arts, race relations, and juvenile and criminal justice; must be from Baltimore city and knowledgeable about social and

economic justice issues affecting Baltimore's communities; and must be willing to participate fully in meetings scheduled for the Community Fellows. **Criteria:** Selection will be based on the applicants' eligibility and compliance with the application process.

Funds Avail.: $60,000. **To Apply:** Applicants must submit two copies of the application. The application can be found in the Download Files section of the website. **Deadline:** March 2. **Contact:** Applicants may contact Emily Smith at 410-234-1091 for questions regarding the program.

7202 ■ Open Society Fellowships *(Other/Fellowship)*

Purpose: To support individuals seeking innovative and unconventional approaches to fundamental open society challenges. **Focus:** General studies/Field of study not specified. **Qualif.:** Applicants must be innovative professionals working on projects that inspire meaningful public debate, shape public policy, and generate intellectual ferment within the Open Society Foundations. **Criteria:** Criteria for selection include, but are not limited to, the applicant's experience, the project's relevance to the goals of the fellowship, and the applicant's potential to accomplish such goals.

Funds Avail.: $80,000-$100,000. **Duration:** Annual. **To Apply:** Applicants must check the available website to download the application form and learn the application process. **Remarks:** Established in 2008.

7203 ■ Open Society Presidential Fellowships *(Advanced Professional/Fellowship)*

Purpose: To encourage aspiring fellows to pursue work related to human rights, good governance and justice. **Focus:** Business; Law; Public affairs. **Qualif.:** Applicants must be recent J.D., MPA, MPP and MBA graduates from accredited U.S. law, public policy and business schools. **Criteria:** Selection will be based on the applicants' scholarship, leadership and commitment to continued practice in the fields of nonprofit management, human rights, good governance and justice.

Funds Avail.: $65,000. **Number Awarded:** 3. **To Apply:** Applicants who are J.D. or LLM graduates must be able to attach the materials necessary to complete the application which consists of the following items: fellowship application; official law school transcript; resume; two recommendation letters (from any of the following: law school advisor; law school professor; former or current employer). Recent public policy and MBA graduates' application should consist of the following: resume (including the following information on references: name; affiliation/address; position; telephone number); official transcript; personal essay comprised of two parts (one is explaining the background, skills, experience, and personal characteristics that they have that will enable them to serve effectively as Presidential Fellows; the other is on how will the Fellowship impact their plans for the future and their vision of their long-term career); and two recommendation letters from any of the following (university advisor; university professor; former or current employer). Printed materials can be sent to Prof. Jill S. Manny. Application form can be accessed at https://its.law.nyu.edu/ncpl/OpenSociety/index.cfm. **Deadline:** December 11. **Contact:** Prof. Jill S. Manny, Executive Director, National Center for Philanthropy and the Law, 139 MacDougal St., 1st Fl., New York, New York 10012; Email at ncpl.info@nyu.edu. Recommendation letters of public policy or MBA graduates can be included in the single PDF or can be emailed separately to: humanresources@opensocietyfoundations.org with "OOP-Fellow [LAST NAME]" in the subject line.

Awards are arranged alphabetically below their administering organizations

7204 ■ Soros Justice Advocacy Fellowships - Track I (*Professional development/Fellowship*)

Purpose: To advance professional growth, support career development, and both seed and deepen leadership in the field of criminal justice reform. **Focus:** Criminal justice. **Qualif.:** Applicants must have at least two (2) years of relevant advocacy experience, which may include: full-time and part-time employment; paid or unpaid internships; longer term experience as advocates, organizers or researchers; or other pertinent experience (e.g. advocacy while incarcerated). **Criteria:** Applications will be evaluated on the extent to which the applicants possess the vision, drive, and skills required to create and sustain a project that will advance one or more of the Open Society Foundations' U.S. criminal justice reform goals or priorities. In evaluating applications, the program will consider: project need; project approach; project goals, objectives, and activities; and the applicants' eligibility.

Funds Avail.: $75,000 ($50,000 for the 1st year; $25,000 for the remaining 6 months); up to $6,000 student loan repayment assistance; $3,750 health insurance; $1,000 for professional development. **Duration:** 18 months. **To Apply:** Applicants must submit their applications via online. On the online system, applicants will have to provide basic contact information and register with the system. Once registered, applicants will be able to proceed to the application itself. All communications from the Open Society Foundations regarding applications will be sent to the email used to register with the online system, so applicants should ensure that email communications from Open Society Foundations do not end up in their "Junk Mail" folder. Complete applications consist of a number of documents that must be uploaded to the online application system: resume, proposal (single-spaced, no more than 3,000 words), letters of recommendation, and host commitment letter (if applicable). Meanwhile, applicants who are uncertain whether some aspect of their proposed projects fit within the parameters of the Fellowships Program guidelines or whether the projects are otherwise likely to be of interest to the program may submit an email inquiry before proceeding with the full application. The email should provide a brief (no more than 500 words) description of the proposed projects, as well as some background information on the applicants. **Deadline:** October 22. **Contact:** Email inquiry should be sent to sorosjusticefellowships@ opensocietyfoundations.org.

7205 ■ Soros Justice Advocacy Fellowships - Track II (*Professional development/Fellowship*)

Purpose: To support seasoned, established, and accomplished leaders and experts in the field of criminal justice. **Focus:** Criminal justice. **Qualif.:** Applicants must have at least ten (10) years of relevant advocacy experience. **Criteria:** Applications will be evaluated on the extent to which the applicants possess the vision, drive, and skills required to create and sustain a project that will advance one or more of the Open Society Foundations' U.S. criminal justice reform goals or priorities. In evaluating applications, the program will consider: project need; project approach; project goals, objectives, and activities; and the applicants' eligibility.

Funds Avail.: $105,000 ($70,000 for 1st year; $35,000 for the remaining 6 months); $3,750 health insurance. **To Apply:** Applicants must submit their applications via online. On the online system, applicants will have to provide basic contact information and register with the system. Once registered, applicants will be able to proceed to the application itself. All communications from the Open Society

Foundations regarding applications will be sent to the email used to register with the online system, so applicants should ensure that email communications from Open Society Foundations do not end up in their "Junk Mail" folder. Complete applications consist of a number of documents that must be uploaded to the online application system: resume, proposal (single-spaced, no more than 3,000 words), letters of recommendation, and host commitment letter (if applicable). Meanwhile, applicants who are uncertain whether some aspect of their proposed projects fit within the parameters of the Fellowships Program guidelines or whether the projects are otherwise likely to be of interest to the program may submit an email inquiry before proceeding with the full application. The email should provide a brief (no more than 500 words) description of the proposed projects, as well as some background information on the applicants. **Deadline:** October 22. **Contact:** Email inquiry should be sent to sorosjusticefellowships@ opensocietyfoundations.org.

7206 ■ Soros Justice Media Fellowships - Track I (*Professional development/Fellowship*)

Purpose: To support writers, print and broadcast journalists, bloggers, filmmakers, and other individuals with distinctive voices proposing to complete media projects that engage and inform, spur debate and conversation, and catalyze change on important U.S. criminal justice issues. **Focus:** Communications; Criminal justice. **Qualif.:** Applicants are ideally full-time writers, print or broadcast journalists, filmmakers, bloggers, or other media makers, with well-established records of publication, dissemination or broadcast in local, regional or national markets, or among targeted audiences or constituencies. Applicants who are not professional writers, journalists, filmmakers, or other types of media makers must demonstrate that they nonetheless have the experience and capacity to be able to accomplish the project. Applicants must have at least two (2) years of relevant full-time experience. **Criteria:** Selection of applicants will be based on the following criteria: project treatment; project viability; project dissemination; project budget and timeline; and the applicants' eligibility.

Funds Avail.: $50,000; $4,000 project-related expenses; $2,500 health insurance; $700 professional development. **To Apply:** Applicants must submit their applications via online. On the online system, applicants will have to provide basic contact information and register with the system. Once registered, applicants will be able to proceed to the application itself. All communications from the Open Society Foundations regarding applications will be sent to the email used to register with the online system, so applicants should ensure that email communications from Open Society Foundations do not end up in their "Junk Mail" folder. Complete applications consist of a number of documents that must be uploaded to the online application system: resume, proposal (single-spaced, no more than 3,000 words), letters of recommendation, and host commitment letter (if applicable). Meanwhile, applicants who are uncertain whether some aspect of their proposed projects fit within the parameters of the Fellowships Program guidelines or whether the projects are otherwise likely to be of interest to the program may submit an email inquiry before proceeding with the full application. The email should provide a brief (no more than 500 words) description of the proposed projects, as well as some background information on the applicants. **Deadline:** October 22. **Contact:** Email inquiry should be sent to sorosjusticefellowships@ opensocietyfoundations.org.

Awards are arranged alphabetically below their administering organizations

7207 ■ Soros Justice Media Fellowships - Track II
(Professional development/Fellowship)

Purpose: To support writers, print and broadcast journalists, bloggers, filmmakers, and other individuals with distinctive voices proposing to complete media projects that engage and inform, spur debate and conversation, and catalyze change on important U.S. criminal justice issues. **Focus:** Communications; Criminal justice. **Qualif.:** Applicants are ideally full-time writers, print or broadcast journalists, filmmakers, bloggers, or other media makers, with well-established records of publication, dissemination or broadcast in local, regional or national markets, or among targeted audiences or constituencies. Applicants who are not professional writers, journalists, filmmakers, or other types of media makers must demonstrate that they nonetheless have the experience and capacity to be able to accomplish the project. Applicants must have at least ten (10) years of relevant full-time experience. **Criteria:** Selection of applicants will be based on the following criteria: project treatment; project viability; project dissemination; project budget and timeline; and the applicants' eligibility.

Funds Avail.: $70,000 stipend; $4,000 for project-related expenses; $2,500 health insurance. **To Apply:** Applicants must submit their applications via online. On the online system, applicants will have to provide basic contact information and register with the system. Once registered, applicants will be able to proceed to the application itself. All communications from the Open Society Foundations regarding applications will be sent to the email used to register with the online system, so applicants should ensure that email communications from Open Society Foundations do not end up in their "Junk Mail" folder. Complete applications consist of a number of documents that must be uploaded to the online application system: resume, proposal (single-spaced, no more than 3,000 words), letters of recommendation, and host commitment letter (if applicable). Meanwhile, applicants who are uncertain whether some aspect of their proposed projects fit within the parameters of the Fellowships Program guidelines or whether the projects are otherwise likely to be of interest to the program may submit an email inquiry before proceeding with the full application. The email should provide a brief (no more than 500 words) description of the proposed projects, as well as some background information on the applicants. **Deadline:** October 22. **Contact:** Email inquiry should be sent to sorosjusticefellowships@opensocietyfoundations.org.

7208 ■ Opera Foundation (OF)
712 5th Ave., 32nd Fl.
New York, NY 10019
Ph: (212)664-8843
Fax: (212)664-8415
E-mail: gala@operafoundation.org
URL: www.operafoundation.org

7209 ■ Opera Foundation Scholarships *(Other/ Scholarship)*

Purpose: To provide the opportunity for young artists to participate in programs offered by one of our three partnering opera houses in Berlin, Turin, and Munich. **Focus:** Opera. **Qualif.:** Scholarship competition is open to American citizens and permanent residents between the ages of 18 and 30 who are beginning their professional careers. Selected candidates will be invited to participate in auditions at a location to be announced by the Foundation.

Transportation to and from New York is at the candidate's own expense. **Criteria:** Selection will be based on the committee's criteria.

Funds Avail.: $16,000; and $1,300 (travel expenses). **Duration:** Annual. **To Apply:** Applicants may download or request an application online. Applicants can also request an application directly by contacting the Foundation. Applications must be accompanied by all of the following requirements: a photocopy of birth certificate, Green Card or Passport; two letters of recommendation from a music professional (manager, teacher, coach) dated no later than the deadline; a recent photograph; an application processing fee of $40.00 (non-refundable) paid by certified bank check or money order, payable to The Opera Foundation, Inc.

7210 ■ Optical Society of America Foundation (OSAF)
2010 Massachusetts Ave. NW
Washington, DC 20036
Ph: (202)416-1985
Fax: (202)416-6130
E-mail: foundation@osa.org
URL: www.osa.org/en-us/foundation

7211 ■ Jean Bennett Memorial Student Travel Grants *(Graduate, Undergraduate/Grant)*

Purpose: To support students in their educational pursuits. **Focus:** Optics. **Qualif.:** Applicant must be an undergraduate or graduate student of an educational institution of collegiate grade who is devoting more than half-time to studies within the institution at the time the paper or abstract was completed. **Criteria:** Selection is based on the submitted application materials.

Funds Avail.: $1,000. **Duration:** Annual. **Number Awarded:** 1. **To Apply:** Applicant must submit a copy of the paper/abstract; a letter of support from an advisor or professor; statement explaining the value of attending the event; and Resume/CV. **Deadline:** August 1. **Remarks:** Established in 2008.

7212 ■ Corning Outstanding Student Paper Competition *(Graduate, Undergraduate/Award)*

Purpose: To recognize student innovation, research excellence and presentation abilities in optical communications. **Focus:** Optics. **Qualif.:** Student must be an undergraduate or graduate of an educational institution of collegiate grade who is devoting more than half-time to studies within the institution at the time the paper was written. **Criteria:** All properly submitted papers are reviewed and scored according to standard OFC/NFOEC Technical Program Committee review criteria. Finalists are judged on innovation, research excellence and presentation skills.

Funds Avail.: 1st prize - $1,500; Honorable mention - $1,000 each. **Duration:** Annual. **Number Awarded:** 3. **To Apply:** Students must submit their research paper and opt-in to the competition during the submissions process. **Remarks:** Established in 2007.

7213 ■ Robert S. Hilbert Memorial Student Travel Grants *(Graduate, Undergraduate/Grant)*

Purpose: To support the students in the areas of optical engineering, lens design and/or illumination design. **Focus:** Engineering, Optical. **Qualif.:** Applicant must be an undergraduate or graduate student of an educational

Awards are arranged alphabetically below their administering organizations

institution of collegiate grade who is devoting more than half-time to studies within the institution at the time the paper was written. Accepted paper/poster must include research in the areas of optical engineering, lens design and/or illumination design. Applicants are encouraged to include graphics created using either CODE V or Light-Tools. **Criteria:** Selection is based on the submitted application materials.

Funds Avail.: $1,100. **Duration:** Annual. **Number Awarded:** 3. **To Apply:** Applicant must submit a copy of the paper and abstract; a letter of support from an advisor or professor; statement explaining the value of attending the meeting; and CV/Resume. **Remarks:** Established in 2009.

7214 ■ Maiman Student Paper Competition *(Graduate, Undergraduate/Award)*

Purpose: To recognize student innovation, research excellence and presentation skills in the areas of laser technology and electro-optics. **Focus:** Optics. **Qualif.:** Student must be an undergraduate or graduate of an educational institution of collegiate grade who is devoting more than half-time to studies within the institution at the time the paper was written. **Criteria:** All properly submitted papers are reviewed and scored according to standard CLEO/QELS or CLEO/IQEC Technical Program Committee review criteria. Each finalist will present their paper to the Review Committee in a private session, and will be judged on innovation, research excellence and presentation skills.

Funds Avail.: $3,000. **Duration:** Annual. **Number Awarded:** 3. **To Apply:** Students must submit their research paper during the regular "call for papers" and opt-in to the competition during the submissions process. **Deadline:** December 16. **Remarks:** Established in 2008.

7215 ■ Harvey M. Pollicove Memorial Scholarships *(Undergraduate/Scholarship)*

Purpose: To support student pursuing a degree in the field of precision optics manufacturing. **Focus:** Optics. **Qualif.:** Applicant must be a student pursuing a degree in the field of precision optics manufacturing. **Criteria:** Selection is based on the application materials submitted.

Funds Avail.: $4,000. **Duration:** Annual. **To Apply:** Applicants may contact OSA Foundation for the application information. **Deadline:** June 1. **Remarks:** Established in 2007.

7216 ■ Emil Wolf Outstanding Student Paper Competition *(Graduate, Undergraduate/Award)*

Purpose: To recognize innovation, research and excellence in optics students. **Focus:** Optics. **Qualif.:** Student must be an undergraduate or graduate of an educational institution of collegiate grade who is devoting more than half-time to studies within the institution at the time the paper was written. The student must be listed as the presenting author of the paper, and must present the paper at the conference. **Criteria:** All papers submitted to the competition will be reviewed during the standard Technical Program Committee (TPC) review process. Finalists are judged based on their work's technical advances and value to the technical community of interest, and their skill of public presentation.

Funds Avail.: $300. **Duration:** Annual. **Number Awarded:** 1. **To Apply:** Students must submit their research paper and opt-in to the competition during the submissions process. **Deadline:** August 1. **Remarks:** Established in 2008.

7217 ■ Order of Omega
300 E Border St.
Arlington, TX 76010
Ph: (817)265-4074
Fax: (817)459-3355
E-mail: hq@orderofomega.org
URL: www.orderofomega.org

7218 ■ William J. Brennan Graduate Assistant Fellowships *(Graduate/Fellowship)*

Purpose: To provide financial assistance to students who are pursuing graduate program in higher education. **Focus:** Educational administration. **Qualif.:** Applicants must be currently enrolled full-time or part-time in an accredited master's degree program in Higher Education, Student Personnel or related field; must be currently employed part-time or must be graduate assistants with direct or indirect responsibility for advising Greek Life/Order of Omega; must be currently employed and enrolled at a college/university with an Order of Omega chapter and must be in good standing in the headquarter. **Criteria:** Selection will be based on evaluation of submitted documents and specific criteria.

Funds Avail.: $1,000. **Duration:** Annual. **To Apply:** Applicants must submit a completed application form; two recommendation letters from previous college/university supervisor and current college/university supervisor; verification of current graduate enrollment and any previous graduate coursework completed (official or unofficial college transcript); photograph (jpeg or gif).

7219 ■ Jacque Placette Chapman Master's Fellowships *(Graduate, Master's/Fellowship)*

Purpose: To provide financial assistance to students who are pursuing graduate program in higher education. **Focus:** Educational administration. **Qualif.:** Applicants must be currently enrolled full-time or part-time in an accredited master's degree program in Higher Education, Student Personnel or related field; must be employed full-time with direct responsibility for advising Greek Life/Order of Omega; must be currently employed and enrolled at a college/university with an Order of Omega chapter and must be in good standing in the headquarter. **Criteria:** Selection will be based on evaluation of submitted documents and specific criteria.

Funds Avail.: $1,000. **Duration:** Annual. **To Apply:** Applicants must submit a completed application form; two recommendation letters from previous college/university supervisor and current college/university supervisor; verification of current graduate enrollment and any previous graduate coursework completed (official or unofficial college transcript); photograph (jpeg or gif).

7220 ■ Order of Omega Doctoral Fellowships *(Doctorate, Graduate/Fellowship)*

Purpose: To provide financial assistance to students who are pursuing graduate program in higher education. **Focus:** Educational administration. **Qualif.:** Applicants must be currently enrolled full-time or part-time in an accredited doctoral degree program in Higher Education, Student Personnel or related field; must be currently employed part-time or must be graduate assistants with direct and/or previous direct responsibilities for advising Greek Life/Order of Omega; must be currently employed and enrolled at a college/university or previously employed at a college/university with an Order of Omega chapter; must be in

Awards are arranged alphabetically below their administering organizations

good standing in the headquarter. **Criteria:** Selection will be based on evaluation of submitted documents and specific criteria.

Funds Avail.: $2,000. **Duration:** Annual. **To Apply:** Applicants must submit a completed application form; two recommendation letters from previous college/university supervisor and current college/university supervisor; verification of current graduate enrollment and any previous graduate coursework completed (official or unofficial college transcript); photograph (jpeg or gif).

7221 ■ Order Sons of Italy in America (OSIA)
219 E St. NE
Washington, DC 20002-4922
Ph: (202)547-2900
Fax: (202)546-8168
Free: 800-552-OSIA
E-mail: nationaloffice@osia.org
URL: www.osia.org

7222 ■ Italian Language Scholarships
(Undergraduate/Scholarship)

Purpose: To provide financial support for education of US citizens of Italian descent. **Focus:** Foreign languages; General studies/Field of study not specified; Italian studies. **Qualif.:** Applicants must be US citizens of Italian descent (at least one Italian or Italian American grandparent) in their junior or senior year of undergraduate study for the Fall of 2012 term, majoring or minoring Italian language studies at an accredited academic institution. SIF scholarship recipients are not eligible. **Criteria:** Recipients will be selected based on the submitted application.

Funds Avail.: No specific amount. **To Apply:** Applicants must submit cover sheet; official transcript; test scores; resume outlining extracurricular activities, work, experience, volunteer service and honors, especially as they relate to Italian language, culture and heritage; letters of recommendation; an original, typewritten 500-750-word essay in Italian on why learning Italian is important in today's world and plan of how to use the language degree; and the processing fee. **Deadline:** February 28.

7223 ■ Order Sons of Italy Foundation General Scholarships *(Graduate, Undergraduate/Scholarship)*

Purpose: To provide financial support for the education of eligible individuals for the scholarship. **Focus:** General studies/Field of study not specified. **Qualif.:** Applicants must be U.S. citizens of Italian descent enrolled in an undergraduate or graduate program at a four-year, accredited academic institution for the Fall 2012 term. **Criteria:** Recipient of the NELA scholarship must be in a matriculated program of study either on the undergraduate or graduate level.

Funds Avail.: No specific amount. **To Apply:** Applicants must submit a cover sheet; official transcript(s); test scores; resume; letters of recommendation; essay; and the processing fee. **Deadline:** February 28.

7224 ■ Henry Salvatori Scholarships
(Undergraduate/Scholarship)

Purpose: To provide financial support to college-bound high school senior demonstrating exceptional leadership, deep understanding and respect for the principles of the nation - liberty, freedom and equality. **Focus:** General studies/Field of study not specified. **Qualif.:** Applicants

must be U.S. citizens of Italian descent in their senior year of high school and planning to attend a four-year, accredited institution for the Fall 2012 term. Previous SIF scholarship recipients are not eligible. **Criteria:** Recipients will be selected based on the submitted application.

Funds Avail.: No specific amount. **To Apply:** Applicants must submit cover sheet; official transcript; test scores; resume; two letters of recommendation from public figures whose careers have demonstrated a commitment to the principles the scholarship embodies; type-written original essay of 750-1,000 words concerning the declaration of independence, the constitution and the Bill of Rights - discussion of the relevance of these documents to the principles of liberty, freedom and equality in the United States and the processing fee; and submit a type-written cover letter of 150-250 words outlining the academic and professional goals. **Deadline:** February 28.

7225 ■ Order of United Commercial Travelers of America (UCT)
1801 Watermark Dr., Ste. 100
Columbus, OH 43215-7088
Ph: (614)487-9680
Fax: (614)487-9675
Free: 800-848-0123
URL: www.uct.org

7226 ■ UCT Scholarships *(Graduate, Other, Undergraduate/Scholarship)*

Purpose: To provide aid to individuals wishing to teach people with intellectual disabilities. **Focus:** Education, Special. **Qualif.:** Applicants must: be teachers of people with intellectual disabilities who need additional course work to be certified or to retain certification; be experienced teachers who wish to become certified to teach people with intellectual disabilities; have a bachelor's or master's degree and wish to pursue graduate work in special education with an emphasis on teaching people with intellectual disabilities; be college juniors/seniors whose undergraduate course of study is special education, specifically focusing on teaching people with intellectual disabilities; be enrolled in courses to become certified instructors under a structured trade, vocational or recreation program at a facility for people with intellectual disabilities. They must plan to be of service to people with intellectual disabilities in U.S. or Canada, and must demonstrate a justifiable need for financial assistance. **Criteria:** Selection shall be based on the aforementioned qualifications and compliance with the application details.

Funds Avail.: $2,500. **Duration:** Annual. **To Apply:** Applicants may visit the website to verify the application process and other pieces of information. **Deadline:** November 15. **Remarks:** Scholarships are funded by the UCT Charities. **Contact:** Ann Marshall at amarshall@uct.org or at 800-848-0123 ext. 126.

7227 ■ Oregon Association of Broadcasters (OAB)
9020 SW Washington Square Rd., Ste. 140
Portland, OR 97223-4433
Ph: (503)443-2299
Fax: (503)443-2488
E-mail: theoab@theoab.org
URL: www.theoab.org

Awards are arranged alphabetically below their administering organizations

7228 ■ Oregon Association of Broadcasters Scholarships *(Undergraduate/Scholarship)*

Purpose: To promote, enhance, strengthen and defend the broadcast industry. To encourage and promote sound broadcast customs and practices. **Focus:** Broadcasting. **Qualif.:** Applicants must be graduating high school students enrolled in two or four-year college broadcast programs; must be Oregon residents; must be enrolled or intending to enroll at an Oregon college or university; and must have minimum GPA of 3.25 on a 4.0 scale. **Criteria:** Recipients are selected based on academic record and financial need.

Funds Avail.: $2,500 - $3,500. **Number Awarded:** 5. **To Apply:** Applicants must complete the application form; must include an essay explaining the student's reasons for choosing a career in broadcasting or a related field including eventual career goals using the following topics: 1) Broadcast activities in which you have participated. 2) What would be your first job preference after college? 3) What are your 10-year goals? 4) Have you received any other scholarships? 5) If so, list the scholarships and amounts.6) List any other academic honors. 7) Explain, in detail, why you need this scholarship in order to continue your education. **Deadline:** May 29. **Contact:** Oregon Association of Broadcasters Foundation, Attn: Scholarship Committee; E-mail at theoab@theoab.org.

7229 ■ Oregon Association of Independent Accountants (OAIA)

1804 NE 43rd Ave.
Portland, OR 97214
Ph: (503)282-7247
E-mail: info@oaia.net
URL: www.oaia.net

7230 ■ OAIA Scholarships *(Undergraduate, Graduate/Scholarship)*

Purpose: To support the education of accounting students in Oregon. **Focus:** Accounting. **Qualif.:** Applicants must be: residents of the State of Oregon; enrolled in, or accepted by, an accredited school for the study of accounting within the State of Oregon; and, full-time students carrying a minimum of 12 credit hours. **Criteria:** Selection shall be based on financial need, scholastics achievement, personal qualifications and professional promise.

Funds Avail.: Amount varies. **Duration:** Annual. **To Apply:** Applicants must submit a completed scholarship application along with high school and college transcripts. **Deadline:** April 1. **Contact:** Oregon Association of Independent Accountants, at the above address.

7231 ■ Oregon Association of Nurseries (OAN)

29751 SW Town Center Loop W
Wilsonville, OR 97070
Ph: (503)682-5089
Fax: (503)682-5099
Free: 800-342-6401
E-mail: info@oan.org
URL: www.oan.org

7232 ■ Christmas Tree Chapter Scholarship Awards *(Undergraduate/Scholarship)*

Purpose: To provide opportunities for education, research and business development to members, including landscap-ers and allied businesses, that supply goods and services to those who grow, handle and retail ornamental horticultural products in Oregon. **Focus:** Horticulture. **Qualif.:** Applicants must be students pursuing a degree in the field of horticulture. **Criteria:** Recipients are selected based on academic performance and financial need. Preference will be given to a member, his/her child or an employee of a Christmas Tree Chapter member.

Funds Avail.: $500. **To Apply:** Applicants must submit one copy of an official transcript of records and three current letters of reference supporting the applicant's horticulture abilities. **Deadline:** April 1. **Contact:** Oregon Nurseries Foundation, 29751 SW Town Center Loop W, Wilsonville, OR 97070; Fax: 503-682-5099; Email: onf@oan.org.

7233 ■ Clackamas Chapter Scholarship Awards *(Undergraduate/Scholarship)*

Purpose: To provide opportunities for education, research and business development to members, including landscapers and allied businesses, that supply goods and services to those who grow, handle and retail ornamental horticultural products in Oregon. **Focus:** Horticulture. **Qualif.:** Applicants must be freshmen students in an ornamental horticulture field. **Criteria:** Recipients are selected based on academic performance and financial need.

Funds Avail.: $1,000. **To Apply:** Applicants must submit one copy of official transcript of records and three current letters of reference supporting the applicant's horticulture abilities. **Deadline:** April 1.

7234 ■ Bill Egan Scholarship Program *(Undergraduate/Scholarship)*

Purpose: To provide opportunities for education, research and business development to members, including landscapers and allied businesses, that supply goods and services to those who grow, handle and retail ornamental horticultural products in Oregon. **Focus:** Horticulture. **Qualif.:** Applicants must be college students majoring in horticulture with an emphasis on the greenhouse/floriculture areas. **Criteria:** Recipients are selected based on academic performance and financial need.

Funds Avail.: $500. **To Apply:** Applicants must submit one copy of an official transcript of records and three current letters of reference supporting the applicant's horticulture abilities. **Deadline:** April 1. **Contact:** Mail applications to Oregon Nurseries Foundation, 29751 SW Town Ctr., Loop W, Wilsonville, OR 97070.

7235 ■ Emerald Empire Chapter Scholarship Awards *(Undergraduate/Scholarship)*

Purpose: To provide opportunities for education, research and business development to members, including landscapers and allied businesses, that supply goods and services to those who grow, handle and retail ornamental horticultural products in Oregon. **Focus:** Horticulture. **Qualif.:** Applicants must be junior or senior college students majoring in horticulture, landscape architecture or landscape construction who have graduated from an Oregon high school. **Criteria:** Recipients are selected based on academic performance and financial need.

Funds Avail.: $500. **To Apply:** Applicants must submit one copy of official transcript of records and three current letters of reference supporting the applicant's horticulture abilities. **Deadline:** April 1.

7236 ■ Joseph H. Klupenger Scholarship Awards *(Undergraduate/Scholarship)*

Purpose: To provide opportunities for education, research and business development to members, including landscap-

Awards are arranged alphabetically below their administering organizations

ers and allied businesses that supply goods and services to those who grow, handle and retail ornamental horticultural products in Oregon. **Focus:** Horticulture. **Qualif.:** Applicants must be students majoring in ornamental horticulture; must intend to work in the ornamental industry. **Criteria:** Recipients are selected based on academic performance and financial need.

Funds Avail.: $550. **To Apply:** Applicants must submit one copy of official transcript of records and three current letters of reference supporting the applicant's horticulture abilities. **Deadline:** April 1.

7237 ■ Mt. Hood Chapter Scholarship Awards
(Undergraduate/Scholarship)

Purpose: To provide opportunities for education, research and business development to members, including landscapers and allied businesses, that supply goods and services to those who grow, handle and retail ornamental horticultural products in Oregon. **Focus:** Horticulture. **Qualif.:** Applicants must be college students majoring in ornamental horticulture. **Criteria:** Recipients are selected based on academic performance and financial need.

Funds Avail.: $1,000. **To Apply:** Applicants must submit one copy of official transcript of records and three current letters of reference supporting the applicant's horticulture abilities. **Deadline:** April 1.

7238 ■ Nurseries Foundation Scholarship Awards
(Undergraduate/Scholarship)

Purpose: To provide opportunities for education, research and business development to members, including landscapers and allied businesses, that supply goods and services to those who grow, handle and retail ornamental horticultural products in Oregon. **Focus:** Horticulture. **Qualif.:** Applicants must be college students majoring in the field of horticulture. **Criteria:** Recipients are selected based on academic performance and financial need.

Funds Avail.: $1,000. **To Apply:** Applicants must submit one copy of official transcript of an records and three current letters of reference supporting the applicant's horticulture abilities. **Deadline:** April 1. **Contact:** Mail applications to Oregon Nurseries Foundation, 29751 SW Town Ctr., Loop W, Wilsonville, OR 97070.

7239 ■ Nurseries Memorial Scholarship Awards
(Graduate/Scholarship)

Purpose: To provide opportunities for education, research and business development to members, including landscapers and allied businesses, that supply goods and services to those who grow, handle and retail ornamental horticultural products in Oregon. **Focus:** Horticulture. **Qualif.:** Applicants must be graduate students pursuing a research project pertaining to ornamental horticulture. **Criteria:** Recipients are selected based on academic performance and financial need.

Funds Avail.: $1,000. **To Apply:** Applicants must submit one copy of an official transcript of records and three current letters of reference supporting the applicant's horticulture abilities. **Deadline:** April 1. **Contact:** Mail applications to Oregon Nurseries Foundation, 29751 SW Town Ctr., Loop W, Wilsonville, OR 97070.

7240 ■ Oregon Association of Nurseries Scholarship Program *(Undergraduate/Scholarship)*

Purpose: To provide opportunities for education, research and business development to members, including landscap-

ers and allied businesses, that supply goods and services to those who grow, handle and retail ornamental horticultural products in Oregon. **Focus:** Horticulture. **Qualif.:** Applicants must be students preparing for a career in ornamental horticulture and related fields. **Criteria:** Recipients are selected based on academic performance and financial need.

Funds Avail.: Varies. **Duration:** Annual. **To Apply:** Applicants must submit one copy of an official transcript of records and three current letters of reference supporting the applicants' horticulture abilities. Applicants must provide five copies of the application materials. **Deadline:** April 1. **Contact:** Oregon Nurseries Foundation, 29751 SW Town Center Loop W, Wilsonville, OR 97070; Fax: 503-682-5099; Email: onf@oan.org.

7241 ■ Retail Chapter Scholarship Awards
(Undergraduate/Scholarship)

Purpose: To provide opportunities for education, research and business development to members, including landscapers and allied businesses, that supply goods and services to those who grow, handle and retail ornamental horticultural products in Oregon. **Focus:** Horticulture. **Qualif.:** Applicants must be students majoring in ornamental horticulture and related fields. **Criteria:** Recipients are selected based on academic performance and financial need. Preference will be given to a student who is son or daughter of an OAN member retailer, or one of their employees.

Funds Avail.: $1,000. **To Apply:** Applicants must submit one copy of an official transcript of records and three current letters of reference supporting applicant's horticulture abilities. **Deadline:** April 1. **Contact:** Oregon Nurseries Foundation, 29751 SW Town Center Loop W, Wilsonville, OR 97070; Fax: 503-682-5099; Email: onf@oan.org.

7242 ■ Willamette Chapter Scholarship Awards
(Undergraduate/Scholarship)

Purpose: To provide opportunities for education, research and business development to members, including landscapers and allied businesses, that supply goods and services to those who grow, handle and retail ornamental horticultural products in Oregon. **Focus:** Horticulture. **Qualif.:** Applicants must be students majoring in ornamental horticulture and related fields. **Criteria:** Recipients are selected based on academic performance and financial need. Preference will be given to a member, member's child or an employee of a Willamette Chapter member.

Funds Avail.: $1,000. **To Apply:** Applicants must submit one copy of official transcript of records and three current letters of reference supporting the applicant's horticulture abilities. **Deadline:** April 1. **Contact:** Oregon Nurseries Foundation, 29751 SW Town Center Loop W, Wilsonville, OR 97070; Fax: 503-682-5099; Email: onf@oan.org.

7243 ■ Ed Wood Memorial Scholarship Awards
(Undergraduate/Scholarship)

Purpose: To provide opportunities for education, research and business development to members, including landscapers and allied businesses, that supply goods and services to those who grow, handle and retail ornamental horticultural products in Oregon. **Focus:** Horticulture. **Qualif.:** Applicants must be currently enrolled in a college horticulture program in Oregon. **Criteria:** Recipients are selected based on the promise and commitment they show toward making significant future contributions to the nursery industry.

Funds Avail.: $1,500. **To Apply:** Applicants must submit

Awards are arranged alphabetically below their administering organizations

one copy of official transcript of records and three current letters of reference supporting the applicant's horticulture abilities. **Deadline:** April 1.

7244 ■ Oregon Farm Bureau (OFB)
1320 Capitol St. NE, Ste. 200
Salem, OR 97301
Ph: (503)399-1701
Fax: (503)399-8082
Free: 800-334-6323
URL: www.oregonfb.org/home

7245 ■ Clackamas County Farm Bureau Scholarships *(Undergraduate/Scholarship)*

Purpose: To help students pursuing a career in agriculture or related field at a two or four year institution of higher learning. **Focus:** Agriculture, Economic aspects. **Qualif.:** Applicants must be residents of Clackamas County at the time of the application; must be interested in pursuing a career in agriculture or a related field; must have a GPA of at least 2.8. **Criteria:** Recipients are selected based on academic performance.

Funds Avail.: $500-$3,000. **To Apply:** Applicants must submit: two letters of recommendation, from which one must come from an Ag Advisor or teacher and the other from another non-relative; transcript of records from most recent school attended; written statement detailing reasons for interest in an agricultural profession, leadership, community service experience and experience in agriculture. **Deadline:** March 15. **Contact:** Tom Winterrowd; Phone: 503-263-2696; E-mail: tawinterrowd@gmail.com.

7246 ■ Oregon Farm Bureau Memorial Scholarships *(Undergraduate/Scholarship)*

Purpose: To promote educational improvement, economic opportunity and social achievement for its members and the farming, ranching and natural resources industry as a whole. **Focus:** Agriculture, Economic aspects. **Qualif.:** Applicants must be full-time students pursuing an agriculture-related major. **Criteria:** Recipients are selected based on academic performance and financial need.

Funds Avail.: No specific amount. **Duration:** Annual. **To Apply:** Applicants must complete an application form; must submit a transcript of records and three letters of recommendation. **Deadline:** March 15. **Contact:** Andréa Kuenzi, Scholarship Coordinator; Fax: 503-399-8082; E-mail: andrea@oregonfb.org.

7247 ■ Yamhill County Farm Bureau Scholarships *(Undergraduate/Scholarship)*

Purpose: To assist Yamhill County high school graduates in furthering their education. **Focus:** Agriculture, Economic aspects. **Qualif.:** Applicants must be full-time students who have successfully completed at least one year of higher education at an accredited college or university; must have plans to continue their education at an accredited college; must have a major in agriculture or related field; must have a minimum of 2.5 GPA for the last college term; must have a minimum of 12 credits per term; must be graduates of Yamhill County. **Criteria:** Recipients are selected based on academic performance.

Funds Avail.: $1,500. **Duration:** Annual. **Number Awarded:** 2. **To Apply:** Applicants must submit a completed and signed application form, two letters of recommendation from non-related persons and official transcripts from all colleges attended. **Deadline:** August 1. **Contact:** Marie Schmidt; Phone: 503-852-7545; E-mail: mschmidt@linfield.edu.

7248 ■ Oregon Medical Association (OMA)
11740 SW 68th Pkwy., Ste. 100
Portland, OR 97223
Ph: (503)619-8000
Fax: (503)619-0609
E-mail: OMA@theOMA.org
URL: www.theoma.org

7249 ■ Linn-Benton County Scholarships *(Undergraduate/Scholarship)*

Purpose: To provide educational assistance to students who are seeking a career in medicine or nursing. **Focus:** Medicine; Nursing. **Qualif.:** Applicants must be high school seniors or graduates seeking a career in medicine or nursing. **Criteria:** Recipients are selected based on academic performance.

Funds Avail.: $1,000. **To Apply:** Applicants must complete the application form. Applicants must submit their official academic high school transcript in Linn or Benon County; official academic transcript from all subsequent institutions of higher education; letter of recommendation from current academic advisor; one-page essay describing why you are interested in a career in nursing or medicine; and list of all school and community service activities. **Deadline:** March 31.

7250 ■ Oregon Society of Certified Public Accountants (OSCPA)
10206 SW Laurel St.
Beaverton, OR 97005-3209
Ph: (503)641-7200
Fax: (503)626-2942
Free: 800-255-1470
E-mail: oscpa@orcpa.org
URL: www.orcpa.org

7251 ■ OSCPA Educational Foundation College Scholarships *(Community College, Graduate, Undergraduate/Scholarship)*

Purpose: To financially support accounting students. **Focus:** Accounting. **Qualif.:** Applicants must be Oregon high school seniors planning to study accounting or an Oregon undergraduates planning to study accounting. All applicants must have a minimum of 3.5 GPA for high school and 3.2 GPA for college. **Criteria:** Selection is based on scholastic ability and student's interest in the accounting profession.

Funds Avail.: $500 - $3,000. **Duration:** Annual. **To Apply:** Applicant may complete the application online or mail the completed application form. In addition, applicants must submit official transcripts, current resume or vita, and three letters of recommendation (must be completed by the reference listed on the application form). **Deadline:** February 17. **Contact:** Tonna Hollis at 503-597-5471/800-255-1470 x-29; edfound@orcpa.org.

7252 ■ OSCPA Educational Foundation High School Scholarships *(Community College, Undergraduate/Scholarship)*

Purpose: To financially support accounting students. **Focus:** Accounting. **Qualif.:** Applicant must be an Oregon

Awards are arranged alphabetically below their administering organizations

high school senior planning to attend as a full time student at an accredited Oregon college/university offering an accounting major; or an Oregon high school senior planning to attend as a full time student at an Oregon community college to study accounting; must have a minimum GPA of 3.5. **Criteria:** Selection is based on scholastic ability and a student's interest in the accounting profession.

Funds Avail.: $500 - $1,000. **Duration:** Annual. **To Apply:** Applicants may complete the application online or mail the completed application form. In addition, applicants must submit official transcripts and three letters of recommendation (must be completed by the reference listed on the application form). **Deadline:** February 17. **Contact:** Tonna Hollis at 503-597-5471/800-255-1470 x-29; edfound@orcpa.org.

7253 ■ Carl Orff Canada

Box 1 Group 23
RR 1
East Selkirk
Saint Clements, MB, Canada R0E 0M0
Ph: (902)667-0455
E-mail: president@orffcanada.ca
URL: www.orffcanada.ca

7254 ■ Gunild Keetman Scholarships *(Other, Undergraduate/Scholarship)*

Purpose: To financially assist students or teachers to studying in an approved course within a Canadian university. **Focus:** Music. **Qualif.:** Applicants must be members in good standing of Carl Orff Canada who have successfully completed a level 1 Orff course. **Criteria:** Applicants will be judged based on qualifications and submitted documents.

Funds Avail.: No specific amount.. **Duration:** Annual. **To Apply:** Applicants must submit a filled-out application form; must obtain a transcript of grades in level I and/or II; and reference letters from two referees (one from a music education professor or music consultant/supervisor and one from a previous Orff instructor). Subject line of the e-mail should be, "Gunild Keetman Scholarship Application", followed by the applicant's name. Recipients are required to submit an article to the Ostinato Editor reflecting their course experience(s) and must forward a copy of certificate or transcript of completed course to the National Treasurer. **Deadline:** April 15. **Remarks:** Established in 1976. **Contact:** Carl Orff Canada, at the above address.

7255 ■ Organization of American Historians (OAH)

112 N Bryan Ave.
Bloomington, IN 47408-4141
Ph: (812)855-7311
Fax: (812)855-0696
E-mail: oah@oah.org
URL: www.oah.org

7256 ■ John Higham Travel Grants *(Graduate/Grant)*

Purpose: To provide travel grants to graduate students to be used toward costs of attending the OAH/IEHS Annual Meeting. **Focus:** History, American; Immigration. **Qualif.:** Candidates must be graduate students with a preferred area of concentration in American Immigration and/or American Ethnic and/or American Intellectual history. **Crite-**

ria: Selection will be based on the committee's criteria.

Funds Avail.: No specific amount. **Duration:** Annual. **Number Awarded:** 3. **To Apply:** Applicants must provide the following documents: current and permanent addresses; educational background; degrees achieved and expected; current institution attending; current status; travel funds from other sources; publications and papers presented. Applicants will be required to include a short statement of no more than 500 words about how they envision attending the annual meeting will help prepare them for a career in history. Applicants will need to indicate if other travel monies will be made available. One complete copy of each application must be mailed directly to each committee member. **Deadline:** December 2. **Contact:** Andrew K. Sandoval-Strausz, Department of History, MSC06 3760, One University of New Mexico, Albuquerque, NM 87131-1181; Julio Capo, Jr., History Dept., Herter Hall, University of Massachusetts, 161 Presidents Dr., Amherst, MA 01003-9312; Maddalena Marinari, Department of History, Doyle Hall 135, St. Bonaventure University, 3261 W State Rd., St. Bonaventure, NY 14778.

7257 ■ Lerner-Scott Prize *(Doctorate/Prize)*

Purpose: To recognize the best doctoral dissertation in U.S. women's history. **Focus:** History. **Qualif.:** Applicants must be at the doctoral level of study. **Criteria:** Selection will be based on the committee's criteria.

Funds Avail.: No specific amount. **Duration:** Annual. **To Apply:** Applicants must submit an application containing a letter of support from a faculty member at the degree-granting institution, along with an abstract, table of contents and sample chapter from the dissertation. Also include email addresses for both the applicant and the adviser, if available. Finalist will be asked to submit a complete copy of the dissertation at a later date. **Deadline:** October 1. **Contact:** Charlene M. Boyer Lewis at clewis@kzoo.edu; Wendy Gamber at wgamber@indiana.edu; Vivien Rose at verose@lightlink.com.

7258 ■ OAH-IEHS Huggins-Quarles Dissertation Awards *(Doctorate, Graduate/Grant)*

Purpose: To assist qualified individuals with travel expenses related to travel to research collections for the completion of their PhD dissertations. **Focus:** History. **Qualif.:** Applicants must be graduate students of color. **Criteria:** Recipient will be chosen based on the application materials submitted.

Funds Avail.: $1,500. **Duration:** Annual. **Number Awarded:** 1 - 2. **To Apply:** Students should submit a five-page dissertation proposal (which should include a definition of the project, and explanation of the project's significance and contribution to the field, and a description of the most important primary sources), along with a one-page itemized budget explaining travel and research plans. **Deadline:** December 1. **Contact:** William Bauer, Committee Chair; Email: wbauer@unlv.edu.

7259 ■ Louis Pelzer Memorial Awards *(Graduate/Award)*

Purpose: To promote excellence in the scholarship, teaching and presentation of American history. **Focus:** History. **Qualif.:** Applicants must be in their graduate degree of study. **Criteria:** Selection will be based on the committee's criteria.

Funds Avail.: $500. **Duration:** Annual. **To Apply:** Applicants must submit an essay of not more than 10,000

Awards are arranged alphabetically below their administering organizations

words (including endnotes). **Deadline:** December 1. **Remarks:** Established in 1949. **Contact:** Edward T. Linenthal, Exec. Dir., at the above address.

7260 ■ Organization of American States (OAS)

17th St. & Constitution Ave. NW
Washington, DC 20006
Ph: (202)458-3000
E-mail: websection@oas.org
URL: www.oas.org

7261 ■ OAS Academic Scholarships - Graduate
(Graduate/Scholarship)

Purpose: To support graduate students from OAS Member States in their further education. **Focus:** General studies/Field of study not specified. **Qualif.:** Applicants must: be citizens or permanent residents from any OAS Member State; have obtained a university degree by the time of applying for a scholarship; have an above average GPA; and, be in good physical and mental health to successfully complete the program of study. **Criteria:** Selection will be based on the committee's criteria.

Funds Avail.: Up to $30,000. **Duration:** Annual; up to two years. **To Apply:** Interested applicants may visit the website to fill-up an online application. Applicants must also provide the following documents: copy of diploma for the highest degree obtained; copies of transcripts of grades for all academic degrees completed and to be completed; three recommendation letters. Two different letters must be from current or former professors using the OAS Recommendation Statement Form and one letter from a current or previous employer using the Employer Recommendation Form. If unemployed or never employed, obtain a third recommendation using the Recommendation Statement Form; resume, maximum of four pages, including diplomas from conferences, workshops, seminars, etc.; admission letter. Scan all required documents in one single file in PDF format, shouldn't be larger than 8MB. After the applicants submit their application, they will receive an email with the application they filled out in PDF format. Print the application, add the required documents and submit the package to the National Liaison Agency (ONE) in their country. **Deadline:** October 31; May 31.

7262 ■ OAS Scholarships for Professional Development - Disaster Communications Management
(Professional development/Scholarship)

Purpose: To encourage students to complete their short or medium-term, intensive, nonacademic courses and training programs offered by its partner offering institutions around the world. **Focus:** Communications technologies; Telecommunications systems. **Qualif.:** Applicants must be citizens or permanent residents of an OAS Member State who are policymakers, engineers or managers of all levels with at least three years of experience and working on aspects related to disaster relief. **Criteria:** Scholarship will be awarded based on the following criteria: objective and priorities established in the Strategic Plan for Partnership for Development; training priorities of the member states; merits and overall credentials of the candidates, including their academic and professional background; financial need of the candidates; extensive and equitable geographic distribution for the benefit of all member states and that takes into account the greater needs of the smaller and relatively less developed economies.

Funds Avail.: Varies. **To Apply:** Interested applicants may visit the website for an online application. Applicants must

also provide the following documents: copy of diploma for the highest degree obtained; copies of transcripts of grades for all academic degrees completed and to be completed; three recommendation letters. Two different letters must be from current or former professors using the OAS Recommendation Statement Form and one letter from a current or previous employer using the Employer Recommendation Form. If unemployed or never employed, obtain a third recommendation using the Recommendation Statement Form; resume, maximum of four pages, including diplomas from conferences, workshops, seminars, etc.; admission letter. Scan all required documents in one single file in PDF format, shouldn't be larger than 8MB. After the applicants submit their application, they will receive an email with the application they filled out in PDF format. Print the application, add the required documents and submit the package to the National Liaison Agency (ONE) in their country.

7263 ■ OAS Scholarships for Professional Development - Radio Spectrum Monitoring Techniques and Procedures *(Professional development/Scholarship)*

Purpose: To support students who are completing their short or medium-term, intensive, nonacademic courses and training programs offered by its partner offering institutions around the world. **Focus:** Radio and television; Telecommunications systems. **Qualif.:** Applicants must: be citizens or permanent residents of an OAS Member State with the exception of the United States since it is the host country; have earned a Bachelor's degree in economics, law or engineering; be government policy-makers and regulators, executives and managers of telecommunications companies subject to existing or proposed governmental regulations and government and private sector attorneys who advise them with at least three years of experience; and, be proficient in English. **Criteria:** Scholarship will be awarded based on the following criteria: objectives and priorities established in the Strategic Plan for Partnership for Development; training priorities of the member states; merits and overall credentials of the candidates, including their academic and professional background; financial need of the candidates; extensive and equitable geographic distribution for the benefit of all member states and that takes into account the greater needs of the smaller and relatively less developed economies.

Funds Avail.: Varies. **To Apply:** Interested applicants may visit the website for an online application. Applicants must also provide the following documents: copy of diploma for the highest degree obtained; copies of transcripts of grades for all academic degrees completed and to be completed; three recommendation letters. Two different letters must be from current or former professors using the OAS Recommendation Statement Form and one letter from a current or previous employer using the Employer Recommendation Form. If unemployed or never employed, obtain a third recommendation using the Recommendation Statement Form; resume, maximum of four pages, including diplomas from conferences, workshops, seminars, etc.; admission letter. Scan all required documents in one single file in PDF format, shouldn't be larger than 8MB. After the applicants submit their application, they will receive an email with the application they filled out in PDF format. Print the application, add the required documents and submit the package to the National Liaison Agency (ONE) in their country.

7264 ■ OAS Scholarships for Professional Development - Satellite Communications *(Professional development/Scholarship)*

Purpose: To provide support to students for them to complete their short or medium-term, intensive, nonaca-

Awards are arranged alphabetically below their administering organizations

demic courses and training programs offered by its partner offering institutions around the world. **Focus:** Communications technologies; Telecommunications systems. **Qualif.:** Applicants must be: citizens or permanent residents of an OAS Member State with the exception of the United States, since it is the host country; and, policymakers, engineers and managers of all levels with at least three years of experience and working on aspects related to disaster relief. **Criteria:** Selection will be based on the following criteria: objectives and priorities established in the Strategic Plan for Partnership for Development; training priorities of the member states; merits and overall credentials of the candidate, including their academic and professional background; financial need of the candidate; an extensive and equitable geographic distribution for the benefit of all member states and that takes into account the greater needs of the smaller and relatively less developed economies.

Funds Avail.: $750. **To Apply:** Interested applicants may visit the website for an online application. Applicants must also provide the following documents: copy of diploma for the highest degree obtained; copies of transcripts of grades for all academic degrees completed and to be completed; three recommendation letters. Two different letters must be from current or former professors using the OAS Recommendation Statement Form and one letter from a current or previous employer using the Employer Recommendation Form. If unemployed or never employed, obtain a third recommendation using the Recommendation Statement Form; resume, maximum of four pages, including diplomas from conferences, workshops, seminars, etc.; admission letter. Scan all required documents in one single file in PDF format, shouldn't be larger than 8MB. After the applicants submit their application, they will receive an email with the application they filled out in PDF format. Print the application, add the required documents and submit the package to the National Liaison Agency (ONE) in their country.

7265 ■ OAS Scholarships for Professional Development - The ABC of Telecommunications (Professional development/Scholarship)

Purpose: To provide assistance to students to complete their short or medium-term, intensive, nonacademic courses and training programs offered by its partner offering institutions around the world. **Focus:** Telecommunications systems. **Qualif.:** Applicants must be citizens or permanent residents of an OAS Member State with at least two years of telecommunication/ICT experience working for an operator or a regulator, and should have at least Bachelor's degree in Administration, Commerce, Economics, Engineering, Law or Science. **Criteria:** Scholarship will be granted based on the following criteria: the merits and overall credentials of the candidates, including their academic and professional background and an extensive and equitable geographic distribution for the benefit of all member states that takes into account the greater needs of the smaller and relatively less developed economies.

Funds Avail.: No specific amount. **To Apply:** Applicants must complete the following required documents: OAS scholarship application form; copy of transcript of the latest degree obtained; updated resume; one letter of recommendation of current or most recent employer. Scan all required documents in one single file in PDF format, shouldn't be larger than 8MB. After the applicants submit their application, they will receive an email with the application they filled out in PDF format. Print and sign the application, add the required documents and submit the package to the National Liaison Agency (ONE) in their country.

7266 ■ Organization of American States Academic Scholarships (Undergraduate, Graduate/Scholarship)

Purpose: To assist the member states with their domestic efforts in pursuit of integral development goals by supporting human resource development in the priority areas; to promote and support human capacity development and the strengthening of bonds among peoples in the hemisphere by maximizing the number of scholarships awarded in reputable educational institutions in its member states with the resources available. **Focus:** General studies/Field of study not specified. **Qualif.:** Applicants must be involved in undergraduate or graduate studies that lead to a degree and/or graduate research at a university or higher learning institution in a member state. **Criteria:** Recipients are selected based on financial need.

Funds Avail.: No specific amount. **Duration:** Annual. **To Apply:** Applicants must accomplish application form. **Remarks:** Established in 1958. **Contact:** scholarships@aos.org.

7267 ■ Organization of American States AOS-Placed Scholarships (Graduate, Undergraduate/Scholarship)

Purpose: To assist the member states with their domestic efforts in pursuit of integral development goals by supporting human resource development in the priority areas; to promote and support human capacity development and the strengthening of bonds among people in the hemisphere by maximizing the number of scholarships awarded in reputable educational institutions in its member states with the resources available. **Focus:** General studies/Field of study not specified. **Qualif.:** Applicants must be enrolled in a university, college, or institution; must be enrolled in a full-time study or research leading to a graduate or undergraduate degree in any AOS member state except the one who is sponsoring the candidate for this scholarship. **Criteria:** Recipients are selected based on the following criteria: (1) objectives and priorities established in the Strategic Plan for Partnership for Integral Development; (2) training priorities of member states; (3) merits and overall credentials of applicants; (4) quality of the written essay; (5) GPA; (6) completeness of the application and required documents; (7) quality of recommendation letter; (8) geographic distribution based on needs of smaller and less developed economies; (9) gender quality and equity; and (10) financial need.

Funds Avail.: Up to $30,000. **To Apply:** Applicants who will begin their studies between the month of January and April must send their letter of admission to AOS headquarters by October 30. All other candidates must send their letter of admission on July 2. Applicants must submit the following: (1) standardized test results (optional); (2) copy of diploma; (3) original transcript of records for the highest degree completed and for the program of studies in which currently enrolled; and (4) not to exceed four pages curriculum vitae. **Contact:** Application form and other supporting documents may be sent electronically at scholtechassist@oas.org.

7268 ■ Organization of American States Graduate Scholarships (Doctorate, Graduate/Scholarship)

Purpose: To assist the member states with their domestic efforts in pursuit of integral development goals by supporting human resource development in the priority areas; to promote and support human capacity development and the strengthening of bonds among people in the hemisphere by maximizing the number of scholarships awarded in

Awards are arranged alphabetically below their administering organizations

reputable educational institutions in its member states with the resources available. **Focus:** General studies/Field of study not specified. **Qualif.:** Applicants must be enrolled in a master's or doctorate degree program. **Criteria:** Recipients are selected based on financial need.

Funds Avail.: No specific amount. **Duration:** Annual. **To Apply:** Applicants must complete the application form. **Remarks:** Established in 1958. **Contact:** scholarships@aos.org.

7269 ■ Organization of American States Self-Placed Scholarships (Doctorate, Graduate/Scholarship)

Purpose: To assist the member states with their domestic efforts in pursuit of integral development goals by supporting human resource development in the priority areas; to promote and support human capacity development and the strengthening of bonds among peoples in the hemisphere by maximizing the number of scholarships awarded in reputable educational institutions in its member states with the resources available. **Focus:** General studies/Field of study not specified. **Qualif.:** Applicants must be enrolled in a master's or doctorate degree program. **Criteria:** Recipients are selected based on financial need.

Funds Avail.: Up to $30,000. **Duration:** Annual. **To Apply:** Applicants must complete the application form. Candidates may apply directly to the universities or educational institutions where scholarship is being offered. **Contact:** scholarships@aos.org.

7270 ■ Leo S. Rowe Pan American Fund (Graduate, Undergraduate/Loan)

Purpose: To help finance higher educational pursuits in the United States. **Focus:** Arts; Latin American studies; Science. **Qualif.:** Applicants must be undergraduates or graduate students from Latin American or Caribbean AOS member countries; must have been admitted for studies in the United States to a program leading to a university degree in an institution of higher learning accredited by the corresponding regional or national council; or must be students and professionals who are either currently pursuing or wish to pursue advanced studies, research, or technical activities in the arts or sciences in institution in the United States; must be able to meet the Committee's satisfaction by demonstrating their need for assistance, the usefulness and ability to successfully complete their studies; must be nationals of Latin American or Caribbean member state of the AOS; must have a grade point average of at least 3.0 or "B" from their current or most recent academic institution; and must agree to return to their origin after completion of their studies. **Criteria:** Recipients are selected based on academic records and financial need.

Funds Avail.: Up to $15,000. **Duration:** Annual. **To Apply:** Applicants must submit an original, duly sealed, stamped, or notarized transcript of grades; diplomas; and foreign student advisor form. **Contact:** Questions about loans can be e-mailed at rowefund@oas.org.

7271 ■ Organization of Black Aerospace Professionals (OBAP)

1 Westbrook Corporate Ctr., Ste. 300
Westchester, IL 60154
Free: 800-JET-OBAP
E-mail: nationaloffice@obap.org
URL: www.obap.org

Awards are arranged alphabetically below their administering organizations

7272 ■ Edward L. Horne, Jr. Scholarships (Advanced Professional/Scholarship)

Purpose: To promote education in the aviation industry. **Focus:** Aviation. **Qualif.:** Applicants must be OBAP members pursuing a career in the aviation industry. **Criteria:** Selection shall be based on the aforementioned qualifications and compliance with the application details.

Funds Avail.: $2,500. **Duration:** Annual. **To Apply:** Applicants must submit their respective documents via email. Contents of the email shall include in PDF form: application form; essay; two letters of recommendation, and any other required documents as indicated on the scholarship. All documents must be attached to a single email with only the OBAP member number in the subject line. **Contact:** obapscholarships@obap.org.

7273 ■ Organization of Black Aerospace Professionals General Scholarships (All/Scholarship)

Purpose: To promote education in the aviation industry. **Focus:** Aviation. **Qualif.:** Applicant must be an OBAP member pursuing a career in the aviation industry. **Criteria:** Selection is based on achievements; attitude to others; commitment to success; financial need and responsibility.

Funds Avail.: No specific amount. **To Apply:** Applicant must provide an evidence of participation in at least one OBAP event; a copy of Private Pilot's license; a resume; two letters of recommendations (one must be from an OBAP member); a copy of medical permit; (two-page) autobiography with recent photo; and an essay on, "What is/has been your greatest life challenge and how has it enriched you or someone else's life?" **Deadline:** May 20. **Contact:** obapscholarships@obap.org.

7274 ■ Organization for Tropical Studies (OTS)

Duke University
410 Swift Ave.
Durham, NC 27705
Ph: (919)684-5774
Fax: (919)684-5661
E-mail: ots@duke.edu
URL: www.ots.ac.cr

7275 ■ William L. Brown Fellowships (Graduate/Fellowship)

Purpose: To assist thesis-related field research in tropical biology and similar fields. **Focus:** Biology. **Qualif.:** Applicants must be graduate students enrolled in a degree program at OTS member institutions. **Criteria:** Selection will be based on the committee's criteria.

Funds Avail.: $4,200 for 50 days at OTS field stations plus $500 in airfare or other permissible expenses. **To Apply:** Applicants must submit the following items: OTS Fellowship Cover Sheet; project abstract, objectives, methods and significance; project schedule and expected outputs; project budget; project justification; literature cited; name, address, telephone, fax and email of four people who can comment on the scientific merit of the proposal; applicant's curriculum vitae; letter of endorsement from thesis advisor. Materials should be typed in 12-point font and all pages must be numbered. The cover sheet and proposal should be submitted by email. Letter of endorsement from thesis advisor should be sent directly by the applicant's recommender by email. Proposals may be submitted in English or Spanish. **Deadline:** October 1 and March 1. **Contact:** Organization for Tropical Studies, at the above address.

7276 ■ David and Deborah Clark Fellowships (Graduate/Fellowship)

Purpose: To assist thesis-related field research in tropical biology and similar fields. **Focus:** Biology. **Qualif.:** Applicants must be graduate students enrolled in a degree program at OTS member institutions. **Criteria:** Selection will be based on the committee's criteria.

Funds Avail.: $4,200 for 50 days at OTS field stations plus $500 in airfare or other permissible expenses. **To Apply:** Applicants must submit the following items: OTS Fellowship Cover Sheet; project abstract, objectives, methods and significance; project schedule and expected outputs; project budget; project justification; literature cited; name, address, telephone, fax and email of four people who can comment on the scientific merit of the proposal; applicant's curriculum vitae; letter of endorsement from thesis advisor. Materials should be typed in 12-point font and all pages must be numbered. The cover sheet and proposal should be submitted by email. Letter of endorsement from thesis advisor should be sent directly by the applicant's recommender by email. Proposals may be submitted in English or Spanish. **Deadline:** October 1 and March 1. **Contact:** Organization for Tropical Studies, at the above address.

7277 ■ Rexford Daubenmire Fellowships (Graduate/Fellowship)

Purpose: To assist thesis-related field research in tropical biology and similar fields. **Focus:** Biology. **Qualif.:** Applicants must be graduate students enrolled in a degree program at OTS member institutions. **Criteria:** Selection will be based on the committee's criteria.

Funds Avail.: $4,200 for 50 days at OTS field stations plus $500 in airfare or other permissible expenses. **To Apply:** Applicants must submit the following items: OTS Fellowship Cover Sheet; project abstract, objectives, methods and significance; project schedule and expected outputs; project budget; project justification; literature cited; name, address, telephone, fax and email of four people who can comment on the scientific merit of the proposal; applicant's curriculum vitae; letter of endorsement from thesis advisor. Materials should be typed in 12-point font and all pages must be numbered. The cover sheet and proposal should be submitted by email. Letter of endorsement from thesis advisor should be sent directly by the applicant's recommender by email. Proposals may be submitted in English or Spanish. **Deadline:** October 1 and March 1. **Contact:** Organization for Tropical Studies, at the above address.

7278 ■ Dole Food Fellowships (Graduate/Fellowship)

Purpose: To assist thesis-related field research in tropical biology and similar fields. **Focus:** Biology. **Qualif.:** Applicants must be graduate students enrolled in a degree program at OTS member institutions **Criteria:** Selection will be based on the committee's criteria.

Funds Avail.: $4,200 for 50 days at OTS field stations plus $500 in airfare or other permissible expenses. **To Apply:** Applicants must submit the following items: OTS Fellowship Cover Sheet; project abstract, objectives, methods and significance; project schedule and expected outputs; project budget; project justification; literature cited; name, address, telephone, fax and email of four people who can comment on the scientific merit of the proposal; applicant's curriculum vitae; letter of endorsement from thesis advisor. Materials should be typed in 12-point font and all pages must be numbered. The cover sheet and proposal should be submitted by email. Letter of endorsement from thesis advisor should be sent directly by the applicant's recom-

mender by email. Proposals may be submitted in English or Spanish. **Deadline:** October 1 and March 1. **Contact:** Organization for Tropical Studies, at the above address.

7279 ■ Emily P. Foster Fellowships (Graduate/Fellowship)

Purpose: To assist thesis-related field research in tropical biology and similar fields. **Focus:** Biology. **Qualif.:** Applicants must be graduate students enrolled in a degree program at OTS member institutions. **Criteria:** Selection will be based on the committee's criteria.

Funds Avail.: $4,200 for 50 days at OTS field stations plus $500 in airfare or other permissible expenses. **To Apply:** Applicants must submit the following items: OTS Fellowship Cover Sheet; project abstract, objectives, methods and significance; project schedule and expected outputs; project budget; project justification; literature cited; name, address, telephone, fax and email of four people who can comment on the scientific merit of the proposal; applicant's curriculum vitae; letter of endorsement from thesis advisor. Materials should be typed in 12-point font and all pages must be numbered. The cover sheet and proposal should be submitted by email. Letter of endorsement from thesis advisor should be sent directly by the applicant's recommender by email. Proposals may be submitted in English or Spanish. **Deadline:** October 1; March 1. **Contact:** Organization for Tropical Studies, at the above address.

7280 ■ Andrew W. Mellon Foundation Fellowships (Graduate/Fellowship)

Purpose: To support graduate thesis research on plants and ecosystem-oriented projects. **Focus:** Ecology. **Qualif.:** Applicants must be graduate students with a research focusing on plants and ecosystem. **Criteria:** Selection will be based on the committee's criteria.

Funds Avail.: $4,200 for 50 days at OTS field stations plus $500 in airfare or other permissible expenses. **Duration:** Annual. **To Apply:** Applicants must submit the following items: OTS Fellowship Cover Sheet; project abstract, objectives, methods and significance; project schedule and expected outputs; project budget; project justification; literature cited; name, address, telephone, fax and email of four people who can comment on the scientific merit of the proposal; applicant's curriculum vitae; letter of endorsement from thesis advisor. Materials should be typed in 12-point font and all pages must be numbered. The cover sheet and proposal should be submitted by email. Letter of endorsement from thesis advisor should be sent directly by the applicant's recommender by email. **Deadline:** October 1 and March 1. **Contact:** Organization for Tropical Studies, at the above address.

7281 ■ Peace Frogs Fellowships (Graduate/Fellowship)

Purpose: To provide funds for graduate students interested in conducting herpetological research, particularly with threatened or endangered species. **Focus:** Herpetology. **Qualif.:** Applicants must be graduate students enrolled in a degree program at OTS member institutions. **Criteria:** Selection will be based on the committee's criteria.

Funds Avail.: $4,200 for 50 days at OTS field stations plus $500 in airfare or other permissible expenses. **Duration:** Annual. **To Apply:** Applicants must submit the following items: OTS Fellowship Cover Sheet; project abstract, project objectives; project methods; project significance; project schedule and expected outputs; project budget; project justification; literature cited; name, address,

Awards are arranged alphabetically below their administering organizations

telephone, fax and email of four people who can comment on the scientific merit of the proposal; applicant's curriculum vitae; letter of endorsement from thesis advisor. Materials should be typed in 12-point font and all pages must be numbered. The cover sheet and proposal should be submitted by email. Letter of endorsement from thesis advisor should be sent directly by the applicant's recommender by email. Proposals may be submitted in English or Spanish. **Deadline:** October 1 and March 1. **Remarks:** Established in 1995.

7282 ■ Rowe Family Fellowships (Graduate/Fellowship)

Purpose: To enable selected students to conduct their thesis work at an OTS research station in Costa Rica or to receive a post-course award after taking an OTS course. **Focus:** Biology. **Qualif.:** Applicants must be students throughout the United States and Latin America. **Criteria:** Selection will be based on the committee's criteria.

Funds Avail.: $4,200 for 50 days at OTS field stations plus $500 in airfare or other permissible expenses. **To Apply:** Applicants must submit the following items: OTS Fellowship Cover Sheet; project abstract, objectives, methods and significance; project schedule and expected outputs; project budget; project justification; literature cited; name, address, telephone, fax and email of four people who can comment on the scientific merit of the proposal; applicant's curriculum vitae; letter of endorsement from thesis advisor. Materials should be typed in 12-point font and all pages must be numbered. The cover sheet and proposal should be submitted by email. Letter of endorsement from thesis advisor should be sent directly by the applicant's recommender by email. **Deadline:** October 1 and March 1. **Contact:** Organization for Tropical Studies, at the above address.

7283 ■ Lillian and Murray Slatkin Fellowships (Graduate/Fellowship)

Purpose: To assist thesis-related field research in tropical biology and similar fields. **Focus:** Biology. **Qualif.:** Applicants must be graduate students enrolled in a degree program at OTS member institutions. **Criteria:** Selection will be based on the committee's criteria.

Funds Avail.: $4,200 for 50 days at OTS field stations plus $500 in airfare or other permissible expenses. **To Apply:** Applicants must submit the following items: OTS Fellowship Cover Sheet; project abstract, objectives, methods and significance; project schedule and expected outputs; project budget; project justification; literature cited; name, address, telephone, fax and email of four people who can comment on the scientific merit of the proposal; applicant's curriculum vitae; letter of endorsement from thesis advisor. Materials should be typed in 12-point font and all pages must be numbered. The cover sheet and proposal should be submitted by email. Letter of endorsement from thesis advisor should be sent directly by the applicant's recommender by email. Proposals may be submitted in English or Spanish. **Deadline:** October 1 and March 1. **Contact:** Organization for Tropical Studies, at the above address.

7284 ■ Stanley Smith Horticultural Fellowships (Graduate, Undergraduate/Fellowship)

Purpose: To provide funds for horticultural work and systematic research on tropical plants of interest to the Wilson Botanical Garden. **Focus:** Horticulture. **Qualif.:** Applicants must be individuals of all levels who are experts in tropical plant groups. **Criteria:** Selection will be based on the committee's criteria.

Funds Avail.: $4,200 for 50 days at OTS field stations plus $500 in airfare or other permissible expenses. **To Apply:** Applicants must submit the following items: OTS Fellowship Cover Sheet; project abstract, objectives, methods and significance; project schedule and expected outputs; project budget; project justification; literature cited; name, address, telephone, fax and email of four people who can comment on the scientific merit of the proposal; applicant's curriculum vitae; letter of endorsement from thesis advisor. Materials should be typed in 12-point font and all pages must be numbered. The cover sheet and proposal should be submitted by email. Letter of endorsement from thesis advisor should be sent directly by the applicant's recommender by email. **Deadline:** October 1 and March 1. **Contact:** Zak Zahawi at zak.zak.zahawi@ots.cr.

7285 ■ F. Christian and Betty Thompson Fellowships (Graduate/Fellowship)

Purpose: To assist thesis-related field research in tropical biology and similar fields. **Focus:** Biology. **Qualif.:** Applicants must be graduate students enrolled in a degree program at OTS member institutions. **Criteria:** Selection will be based on the committee's criteria.

Funds Avail.: $4,200 for 50 days at OTS field stations plus $500 in airfare or other permissible expenses. **To Apply:** Applicants must submit the following items: OTS Fellowship Cover Sheet; project abstract, objectives, methods and significance; project schedule and expected outputs; project budget; project justification; literature cited; name, address, telephone, fax and email of four people who can comment on the scientific merit of the proposal; applicant's curriculum vitae; letter of endorsement from thesis advisor. Materials should be typed in 12-point font and all pages must be numbered. The cover sheet and proposal should be submitted by email. Letter of endorsement from thesis advisor should be sent directly by the applicant's recommender by email. Proposals may be submitted in English or Spanish. **Deadline:** October 1 and March 1. **Contact:** Organization for Tropical Studies, at the above address.

7286 ■ Orthopaedic Trauma Association (OTA)
9400 W Higgins Rd., Ste. 305
Rosemont, IL 60018-4226
Ph: (847)698-1631
Fax: (847)823-0536
E-mail: ota@aaos.org
URL: ota.org

7287 ■ Orthopaedic Trauma Association Research Grants (Other/Grant)

Purpose: To promote excellence in care for the injured patient, through provision of scientific forums; to provide funds that will promote the research endeavors and interests of the OTA members. **Focus:** Medicine, Orthopedic. **Qualif.:** Applicants must be investigators or co-principal investigators who are OTA or AONA members; must be in good standing and the primary research institution must be located in North America. **Criteria:** Proposals will be reviewed by OTA Research Committee based on scientific merit scores and ranking.

Funds Avail.: Clinical Research Grants: $40,000; Basic Research Grants: $50,000; Resident Research Grants: $20,000. **To Apply:** Research grants pre-proposal applications are available online. All application materials (Word document only), figures, tables, etc. must be part of the single Word document submitted. **Deadline:** June 16.

Awards are arranged alphabetically below their administering organizations

7288 ■ Orthotic and Prosthetic Education and Research Foundation (OPERF)

PO Box 34635
Washington, DC 20043-4635
Ph: (202)380-3663
Fax: (202)380-3447
URL: www.operf.org

7289 ■ OPERF Educator and Student Awards
(Professional development/Grant)

Purpose: To support orthotics and prosthetics educators who currently hold teaching position at CAAHEP-accredited O&P education institutions who are pursuing higher degrees to improve their skills as O&P instructors. **Focus:** Orthotics prosthetics technology. **Qualif.:** Applicants must be employed as faculty members at a CAAHEP-Accredited O&P Program; enrolled in an advanced degree program. **Criteria:** Selection will be based on the Review Panel's criteria.

Duration: Annual. **To Apply:** Completed application must include the following: current faculty position; degree program; plan of study and progress toward degree; letter of recommendation; applicants' statement describing how the students' academic goals will contribute to excellence as an O&P faculty member and how the OPERF Educator Award will assist the students in pursuing their academic goals; Applicants' CV. **Contact:** OPERF Research Committee Chairperson, Andrew Hansen, PhD at andrew.hansen@operf.org.

7290 ■ OPERF Fellowships *(Graduate, Master's, Doctorate/Fellowship)*

Purpose: To support quality graduate education research related to the orthotics and prosthetics profession. **Focus:** Orthotics prosthetics technology. **Qualif.:** Applicants must be students currently enrolled in a Masters and/or PhD educational program within the United States. The project must be relevant to the orthotics and prosthetics profession. **Criteria:** Selection will be based on the committee's criteria.

Funds Avail.: $5,000. **Duration:** Annual. **To Apply:** Applicants must submit a letter of intent, maximum of one page in length and must briefly describe the proposed research. The proposal should be a maximum of five pages in length, 12 point font, one inch borders and single-space. The research proposal must include the following components: application cover page, available at the website; abstract, up to 300 words; specific aims; background and significance; previous research; methodology; project timeline, including milestones and deliverables; anticipated results; references; budget and facilities; list of current/pending support related to the proposed research; list of collaborators (including a short biosketch for each); biosketch for the students; letter of faculty support (from the students' advisor). **Deadline:** January 16. **Contact:** OPERF Research Committee Chairperson, Andrew Hansen, PhD at andrew.hansen@operf.org.

7291 ■ OPERF Resident Travel Awards *(Professional development/Grant)*

Purpose: To support prosthetics and orthotics residents travel to the American Academy of Orthotists and Prosthetists (AAOP) national meeting so that they may present their NCOPE (National Commission on Orthotic and Prosthetic Education) required Directed Study Report. **Focus:** Orthotics prosthetics technology. **Qualif.:** Applicants must be prosthetics and orthotics residents; must be currently involved in or have completed an NCOPE accredited residency within the last 12 months; project must be relevant to the orthotics and prosthetics profession. **Criteria:** Selection will be based upon the merit of the residents' project, as determined by the OPERF Research Committee and OPERF Board of Directors.

Funds Avail.: $1,000. **Duration:** Annual. **To Apply:** The submission must include the following components: application cover page, available at the website; maximum of one page abstract; a one-page brief biosketches for the residents and residency advisor. The abstract should: describe the residents' NCOPE Directed Study project; typed single-space in 10-12 point font on pages with one inch margins; be formatted according to the conventional format of introduction, methods, results, discussion, conclusion and references. Figures may be included in the one-page abstract, if they are legible. **Deadline:** January 16. **Contact:** OPERF Research Committee Chairperson, Andrew Hansen, PhD at andrew.hansen@operf.org.

7292 ■ OPERF Small Grants *(Doctorate/Grant)*

Purpose: To support quality investigator-initiated research related to the orthotics and prosthetics profession. **Focus:** Orthotics prosthetics technology. **Qualif.:** The Principal Investigator must have attained a doctoral degree or provide evidence of prior research experience. The host institution and the primary research site must be located within the United States. The project must be relevant to the orthotics and prosthetics profession. The proposed research must include a clinician trained in prosthetics and orthotics as the principal investigator or co-investigator. **Criteria:** Selection will be based on the committee's criteria.

Funds Avail.: Up to $25,000. **Duration:** Annual. **To Apply:** Applicants must submit a maximum of one page Letter of Intent and must briefly describe the proposed research. The research proposal should be a maximum of 15 pages in length, 12 point font, 1 inch borders, single-spaced. The research proposal should include the following components: application cover page, available at the website; abstract, up to 500 words; specific aims; background and significance; previous research; methodology; project timeline, including milestones and deliverables; anticipated results; references; budget and facilities, current/pending support related to proposed research; list of collaborators, including a short biosketch for each; letters of support; biosketch for the principal investigator. **Deadline:** December 12. **Contact:** OPERF Research Committee Chairperson, Andrew Hansen, PhD at andrew.hansen@operf.org.

7293 ■ Osgoode Society for Canadian Legal History

Osgoode Hall
130 Queen St. W
Toronto, ON, Canada M5H 2N6
Ph: (416)947-3321
Fax: (416)947-3447
E-mail: osgoodesociety@lsuc.on.ca
URL: www.osgoodesociety.ca

7294 ■ R. Roy McMurtry Fellowships in Legal History *(Doctorate, Graduate/Fellowship)*

Purpose: To provide financial assistance for graduate students in the field of Canadian legal history. **Focus:** Law. **Qualif.:** Applicants must be graduate students or those who recently completed their doctoral degree affiliated by

---

Awards are arranged alphabetically below their administering organizations

Ontario University and who must conduct research in the field of Canadian legal history. **Criteria:** Recipients will be selected based on financial need.

Funds Avail.: No specific amount. **Duration:** Annual; one year. **To Apply:** Applicants must submit a curriculum vitae and statement of the research to be conducted. **Deadline:** April 30. **Remarks:** Established in 2007. **Contact:** Curriculum vitae and statement of the research must be submitted to Marilyn Macfarlane at McMurtry Fellowship Selection Committee, Osgoode Society for Canadian Legal History, Osgoode Hall, 130 Queen Street West, Toronto, M5H 2N6.

7295 ■ Our World-Underwater Scholarship Society (OW-USS)

PO Box 6157
Woodridge, IL 60517
Ph: (630)969-6690
Fax: (630)969-6690
URL: www.owuscholarship.org

7296 ■ Our World Underwater Scholarship Society North American Rolex Scholarships
(Undergraduate, Professional development/ Scholarship)

Purpose: To provide hands-on introduction to underwater and other aquatic-related endeavors for a young person considering a career in an underwater-related discipline. **Focus:** Biology, Marine. **Qualif.:** Applicants must be 21-26 years old; North American citizens; have not yet earned a graduate degree; have a high academic standing; certified Rescue Divers or equivalent, with a minimum of 25 dives logged in the past 2 years; and have evidence of adequate health insurance for the duration of scholarship year. **Criteria:** Selection shall be based on the aforementioned applicants' qualifications and compliance with the application details.

Funds Avail.: Maximum of $25,000. **Duration:** Annual. **Number Awarded:** 1. **To Apply:** Applicants must submit a completed application form including execution of Financial Responsibility Statement; a photocopy of both sides of the scuba diving certification card(s); a copy of the dive log for the last 6 months; official transcripts; completed medical form signed by a licensed physician; two letters of recommendation from teachers/professors; two letters of recommendation from persons in the community; statement from certifying agency/school or recent scuba instructor regarding the applicant's diving proficiency; resume; personal biography (double spaced, maximum of 2 pages); and an essay. **Deadline:** December 31 (for both North American and European application); January 31 (Australasian application). **Contact:** Our World Underwater Scholarship Society, at the above address.

7297 ■ Out on Bay Street

20 Bloor St. E
Toronto, ON, Canada M4W 3T3
E-mail: info@outonbayst.org
URL: outonbayst.org

7298 ■ OOBS Student Leadership Scholarships
(Undergraduate/Scholarship)

Purpose: To support students who make a difference in their LGBTQ and other communities by providing resources to help them achieve their educational goals. **Focus:** General studies/Field of study not specified. **Qualif.:** Applicants must be Canadian legal residents; must be current registered students in an accredited Canadian post-secondary program of study; must exemplify leadership, especially within the LGBTQ communities; and must have demonstrated personal and/or academic success. **Criteria:** Selection will be based on the applicants' eligibility and compliance with the application process.

Funds Avail.: 2,500 Canadian Dollars. **To Apply:** Applicants must register as Student Members on the Out On Bay Street Student Portal to gain access to the OOBS Student Leadership Scholarship application; must provide supporting documents such as resume and unofficial transcript, and email address. Other information regarding the application process can be verified at the program website. **Deadline:** May 29.

7299 ■ Outdoor Power Equipment Aftermarket Association (OPEAA)

341 S Patrick St.
Alexandria, VA 22314
Ph: (703)549-7608
Fax: (703)549-7609
URL: www.opeaa.org

7300 ■ Bill Nelson Scholarship Endowment (BNSE)
(Undergraduate, Graduate/Scholarship)

Purpose: To provide financial assistance for the educational pursuits of employees of OPEAA members and their dependents. **Focus:** General studies/Field of study not specified. **Qualif.:** Application will be open to employees of OPEAA members, their children, stepchildren, grandchildren and adopted children. There will be no limitation on who can apply, other than the employees must be working full time upon submission of the application on behalf of themselves or their children, as defined above. Current part-time employees (but not their children) are also eligible to apply for a scholarship. Applicants must be planning to attend, or already be enrolled in an accredited institution of higher learning. **Criteria:** Awards are given based on academic merit and tests results.

Funds Avail.: No specific amount. **Duration:** Annual. **To Apply:** Applicants must fill out an application form available in OPEAA website and submit along with sponsor information, essay (in 250 words) describing academic aspirations, two letters of reference, applicants' ACT and SAT scores and a cumulative GPA and recent photos. **Deadline:** May 29. **Contact:** Jean Hawes, BNSE Administrator; Email: jhawes@opeaa.org.

7301 ■ Outdoor Writers Association of America (OWAA)

615 Oak St., Ste. 201
Missoula, MT 59801
Ph: (406)728-7434
E-mail: info@owaa.org
URL: www.owaa.org

7302 ■ Bodie McDowell Scholarships *(Graduate, Undergraduate/Scholarship)*

Purpose: To provide educational services to members. **Focus:** Writing. **Qualif.:** Applicant must be an undergraduate or graduate student from any discipline and school; must have a career goal in outdoor communications includ-

Awards are arranged alphabetically below their administering organizations

ing print, photography, film, art or broadcasting. **Criteria:** Selection of applicant will be based on talent, promise and firsthand outdoor knowledge and will be rated on clarity, organization and originality. GPA average is also considered.

Funds Avail.: $1,000 to $5,000. **Duration:** Annual. **Number Awarded:** 3. **To Apply:** Applicant must submit a completed application, letter of recommendation from school, transcript, example of outdoor communication work, a one- to two-page statement of career goals, and optional letters of recommendation from others familiar with applicant's work. **Deadline:** March 2.

7303 ■ Overseas Press Club Foundation
40 W 45 St.
New York, NY 10036
Ph: (201)493-9087
Fax: (201)612-9915
E-mail: foundation@opcofamerica.org
URL: www.overseaspressclubfoundation.org

7304 ■ Emanuel R. Freedman Scholarships *(Graduate, Undergraduate/Scholarship)*

Purpose: To support the education of students who aspire to become foreign correspondents. **Focus:** Journalism. **Qualif.:** Applicants must be graduate or undergraduate students, studying at American colleges and universities, who aspire to become foreign correspondents. **Criteria:** The judges respond well to applications showing strong reporting skills, color, and understanding or passion.

Funds Avail.: $2,000. **Number Awarded:** 1. **To Apply:** Applicants must submit a cover letter (should be autobiographical in nature addressing such questions as how the applicant developed an interest in this particular part of the world, or how he or she would use the scholarship to further journalistic ambitions); resume; and essay (approximately 500 words concentrating on an area of the world or an international issue that is in keeping with the applicant's interest). The applicant's name and school should appear at the top of each page.

7305 ■ Alexander Kendrick Memorial Scholarships *(Graduate, Undergraduate/Scholarship)*

Purpose: To support the education of students who aspire to become foreign correspondents. **Focus:** Journalism. **Qualif.:** Applicants must be graduate or undergraduate students, studying at American colleges and universities, who aspire to become foreign correspondents. **Criteria:** The judges respond well to applications showing strong reporting skills, color, and understanding or passion.

Funds Avail.: $2,000. **Duration:** Annual. **To Apply:** Applicants must submit a cover letter (should be autobiographical in nature addressing such questions as how the applicant developed an interest in this particular part of the world, or how he or she would use the scholarship to further journalistic ambitions); resume; and essay (approximately 500 words concentrating on an area of the world or an international issue that is in keeping with the applicant's interest). The applicant's name and school should appear at the top of each page.

7306 ■ Irene Corbally Kuhn Scholarships *(Graduate, Undergraduate/Scholarship)*

Purpose: To support the education of students who aspire to become foreign correspondents. **Focus:** Journalism.

Qualif.: Applicants must be graduate or undergraduate students, studying at American colleges and universities, who aspire to become foreign correspondents. **Criteria:** The judges respond well to applications showing strong reporting skills, color, and understanding or passion.

Funds Avail.: $2,000. **Duration:** Annual. **To Apply:** Applicants must submit a cover letter (should be autobiographical in nature addressing such questions as how the applicant developed an interest in this particular part of the world, or how he or she would use the scholarship to further journalistic ambitions); resume; and essay (approximately 500 words concentrating on an area of the world or an international issue that is in keeping with the applicant's interest). The applicant's name and school should appear at the top of each page. **Contact:** Overseas Press Club Foundation, at the above address.

7307 ■ Flora Lewis Memorial Scholarships *(Graduate, Undergraduate/Scholarship)*

Purpose: To support the education of students who aspire to become foreign correspondents. **Focus:** Journalism. **Qualif.:** Applicants must be graduate or undergraduate students, studying at American colleges and universities, who aspire to become foreign correspondents. **Criteria:** The judges respond well to applications showing strong reporting skills, color, and understanding or passion.

Funds Avail.: $2,000. **Duration:** Annual. **To Apply:** Applicants must submit a cover letter (should be autobiographical in nature addressing such questions as how the applicant developed an interest in this particular part of the world, or how he or she would use the scholarship to further journalistic ambitions); resume; and essay (approximately 500 words concentrating on an area of the world or an international issue that is in keeping with the applicant's interest). The applicant's name and school should appear at the top of each page. **Contact:** Overseas Press Club Foundation, at the above address.

7308 ■ Overseas Press Club Foundation Harper's Magazine Scholarships *(Graduate, Undergraduate/Scholarship)*

Purpose: To support the education of students who aspire to become foreign correspondents. **Focus:** Journalism. **Qualif.:** Applicants must be graduate or undergraduate students, studying at American colleges and universities, who aspire to become foreign correspondents. **Criteria:** The judges respond well to applications showing strong reporting skills, color, and understanding or passion.

Funds Avail.: $2,000. **Duration:** Annual. **To Apply:** Applicants must submit a cover letter (should be autobiographical in nature addressing such questions as how the applicant developed an interest in this particular part of the world, or how he or she would use the scholarship to further journalistic ambitions); resume; and essay (approximately 500 words concentrating on an area of the world or an international issue that is in keeping with the applicant's interest). The applicant's name and school should appear at the top of each page. **Contact:** Overseas Press Club Foundation, at the above address.

7309 ■ Overseas Press Club Foundation Reuters Scholarships *(Graduate, Undergraduate/Scholarship)*

Purpose: To support the education of students who aspire to become foreign correspondents. **Focus:** Journalism. **Qualif.:** Applicants must be graduate or undergraduate students, studying at American colleges and universities, who aspire to become foreign correspondents.

Awards are arranged alphabetically below their administering organizations

Funds Avail.: $2,000. **Duration:** Annual. **To Apply:** Applicants must submit a cover letter (should be autobiographical in nature addressing such questions as how the applicant developed an interest in this particular part of the world, or how he or she would use the scholarship to further journalistic ambitions); resume; and essay (approximately 500 words concentrating on an area of the world or an international issue that is in keeping with the applicant's interest). The applicant's name and school should appear at the top of each page. **Contact:** Jane Reilly, Exec. Dir. at the above address, or Email: opcofamerica.org.

7310 ■ Roy Rowan Scholarships *(Graduate, Undergraduate/Scholarship)*

Purpose: To support the education of students who aspire to become foreign correspondents. **Focus:** Journalism. **Qualif.:** Applicants must be graduate or undergraduate students, studying at American colleges and universities, who aspire to become foreign correspondents. **Criteria:** The judges respond well to applications showing strong reporting skills, color, and understanding or passion.

Funds Avail.: $2,000. **Duration:** Annual. **To Apply:** Applicants must submit a cover Letter (should be autobiographical in nature addressing such questions as how the applicant developed an interest in this particular part of the world, or how he or she would use the scholarship to further journalistic ambitions); resume; and essay (approximately 500 words concentrating on an area of the world or an international issue that is in keeping with the applicant's interest). The applicant's name and school should appear at the top of each page. **Contact:** Overseas Press Club Foundation, at the above address.

7311 ■ David R. Schweisberg Memorial Scholarships *(Graduate, Undergraduate/Scholarship)*

Purpose: To support the education of students who aspire to become foreign correspondents. **Focus:** Journalism. **Qualif.:** Applicants must be graduate or undergraduate students, studying at American colleges and universities, who aspire to become foreign correspondents. **Criteria:** The judges respond well to applications showing strong reporting skills, color, and understanding or passion.

Funds Avail.: $2,000. **Duration:** Annual. **To Apply:** Applicants must submit a cover letter (should be autobiographical in nature addressing such questions as how the applicant developed an interest in this particular part of the world, or how he or she would use the scholarship to further journalistic ambitions); resume; and essay (approximately 500 words concentrating on an area of the world or an international issue that is in keeping with the applicant's interest). The applicant's name and school should appear at the top of each page. **Contact:** Overseas Press Club Foundation, at the above address.

7312 ■ Standard and Poor's Award for Economic and Business Reporting - S&P Scholarships *(Graduate, Undergraduate/Scholarship)*

Purpose: To encourage talented young reporters considering careers in financial journalism. **Focus:** Journalism. **Qualif.:** Applicants must be graduate or undergraduate students, studying at American colleges and universities, who aspire to become foreign correspondents. **Criteria:** The judges respond well to applications showing strong reporting skills, color, and understanding or passion.

Funds Avail.: $2,000. **Duration:** Annual. **To Apply:** Applicants must submit a Cover Letter (should be autobiographical in nature addressing such questions as how the

applicant developed an interest in this particular part of the world, or how he or she would use the scholarship to further journalistic ambitions), Resume and Essay (approximately 500 words concentrating on an area of the world or an international issue that is in keeping with the applicant's interest). The applicant's name and school should appear at the top of each page.

7313 ■ H.L. Stevenson Scholarships *(Graduate, Undergraduate/Scholarship)*

Purpose: To support the education of students who aspire to become foreign correspondents. **Focus:** Journalism. **Qualif.:** Applicants must be graduate or undergraduate students, studying at American colleges and universities, who aspire to become foreign correspondents. **Criteria:** The judges respond well to applications showing strong reporting skills, color, and understanding or passion.

Funds Avail.: $2,000. **Duration:** Annual. **To Apply:** Applicants must submit a cover letter (should be autobiographical in nature addressing such questions as how the applicant developed an interest in this particular part of the world, or how he or she would use the scholarship to further journalistic ambitions); resume; and essay (approximately 500 words concentrating on an area of the world or an international issue that is in keeping with the applicant's interest). The applicant's name and school should appear at the top of each page. **Contact:** Overseas Press Club Foundation, at the above address.

7314 ■ Stan Swinton Scholarships *(Graduate, Undergraduate/Scholarship)*

Purpose: To support the education of students who aspire to become foreign correspondents. **Focus:** Journalism. **Qualif.:** Applicants must be graduate or undergraduate students, studying at American colleges and universities, who aspire to become foreign correspondents. **Criteria:** The judges respond well to applications showing strong reporting skills, color, and understanding or passion.

Funds Avail.: $2,000. **Duration:** Annual. **To Apply:** Applicants must submit a cover letter (should be autobiographical in nature addressing such questions as how the applicant developed an interest in this particular part of the world, or how he or she would use the scholarship to further journalistic ambitions); resume; and essay (approximately 500 words concentrating on an area of the world or an international issue that is in keeping with the applicant's interest). The applicant's name and school should appear at the top of each page. **Contact:** Overseas Press Club Foundation, at the above address.

7315 ■ Theo Wilson Scholarships *(Graduate, Undergraduate/Scholarship)*

Purpose: To support the education of students who aspire to become foreign correspondents. **Focus:** Journalism. **Qualif.:** Applicants must be graduate or undergraduate students, studying at American colleges and universities, who aspire to become foreign correspondents. **Criteria:** The judges respond well to applications showing strong reporting skills, color, and understanding or passion.

Funds Avail.: $2,000. **Number Awarded:** 1. **To Apply:** Applicants must submit a cover letter (should be autobiographical in nature addressing such questions as how the applicant developed an interest in this particular part of the world, or how he or she would use the scholarship to further journalistic ambitions); resume; and essay (approximately 500 words concentrating on an area of the world or an international issue that is in keeping with the applicant's

Awards are arranged alphabetically below their administering organizations

interest). The applicant's name and school should appear at the top of each page.

7316 ■ Owner-Operator Independent Drivers Association (OOIDA)

1 NW OOIDA Dr.
Grain Valley, MO 64029-7903
Ph: (816)229-5791
Fax: (816)229-0518
Free: 800-444-5791
URL: www.ooida.com

7317 ■ OOIDA Mary Johnston Scholarships
(Undergraduate/Scholarship)

Purpose: To assist the children, grandchildren and legal dependents of OOIDA members in their effort to gain higher education. **Focus:** General studies/Field of study not specified. **Qualif.:** Applicants must be immediate family members of OOIDA. Scholarships are available for children, grandchildren and legal dependents of OOIDA members. **Criteria:** Awards are given based on academic merit. Applicants are selected in a blind evaluation conducted by the Scholarship Advisory Committee.

Funds Avail.: Four $1,000; One $2,000. **Duration:** Annual. **Number Awarded:** 5. **To Apply:** Applicants must submit a (500-word) essay; official certified high school (grades 9-12) transcript; proof of enrollment from institution of higher education. Application form and guidelines can be obtained from the OOIDA office or can be downloaded from the OOIDA website. **Deadline:** February 2. **Remarks:** Established in 1998. **Contact:** Andrew King, Email: andrew_king@ooida.com.

7318 ■ Pacific 12 Conference (Pac-12)

1350 Treat Blvd., Ste. 500
Walnut Creek, CA 94597-8853
Ph: (925)932-4411
Fax: (925)932-4601
URL: pac-12.com

7319 ■ The Pac-10 Postgraduate Scholarships
(Graduate/Scholarship)

Purpose: To honor outstanding student-athletes from member institutions who are also outstanding scholars. **Focus:** General studies/Field of study not specified. **Qualif.:** Applicants must have an overall undergraduate minimum cumulative GPA of 3.00 (based on a 4.00 scale) or its equivalent; in the final season of intercollegiate athletics eligibility in all sports or in final year of undergraduate studies; have performed with distinction as a member of the varsity team in the sport in which the student-athlete has been nominated; intend to continue academic work beyond the baccalaureate degree as a full-time graduate student; have behaved, both on and off the field, in a manner that has brought credit to the student-athlete, the institution and intercollegiate athletics. **Criteria:** Selection will be based on participation in campus or community service activities.

Funds Avail.: $3,000. **Duration:** Annual; 3 years. **Number Awarded:** 40. **To Apply:** Applicants must submit data form; student-athlete's statement; and coach endorsement. **Deadline:** June 1.

7320 ■ Pacific Aviation Museum - Pearl Harbor

Historic Ford Island
319 Lexington Boulevard
Honolulu, HI 96818
Ph: (808)441-1000
Fax: (808)441-1010
E-mail: Reservations@PacificAviationMuseum.org
URL: www.pacificaviationmuseum.org

7321 ■ The Frank Der Yuen Aviation Scholarship
(Undergraduate/Scholarship)

Purpose: To provide financial assistance to Hawaii residents who have been accepted or are enrolled in an aviation-related program at an accredited trade school, college or university. **Focus:** Aviation. **Qualif.:** Applicants must be Hawaii residents who have been accepted or are enrolled in an aviation-related program at an accredited trade school, college or university. **Criteria:** Selection will be based on the committee's criteria.

Funds Avail.: No specific amount. **Duration:** Annual. **To Apply:** Applicants must visit the website for the online application process and must provide following: completed application, two recommendations, and written essay. Addition is the proof of acceptance or enrollment in an aviation related-program at an accredited trade school, college or university. Application package must be submitted to the Pacific Aviation Museum Pearl Harbor or via email. **Deadline:** September 30. **Contact:** Pacific Aviation Museum Pearl Harbor, ATTN: Frank Der Yuen Aviation Scholarship, at the above address.

7322 ■ Pacific Institute for the Mathematical Sciences (PIMS)

University of British Columbia
4176-2207 Main Hall
Vancouver, BC, Canada V6T 1Z4
Ph: (604)822-3922
Fax: (604)822-0883
E-mail: reception@pims.math.ca
URL: www.pims.math.ca

7323 ■ PIMS Postdoctoral Fellowships *(Doctorate/Fellowship)*

Purpose: To support young researchers in the field of mathematical sciences. **Focus:** Mathematics and mathematical sciences. **Qualif.:** Applicant must have a PhD or equivalent at the time of the nomination. **Criteria:** Selection is based on the applicant's excellence and potentials.

Funds Avail.: $20,000. **Duration:** Annual; one year (renewable for one year). **To Apply:** Applicants must be nominated by one or more scientist affiliated with PIMS or by a department (or departments) affiliated with PIMS. Nomination process must take place entirely online. **Deadline:** December 1.

7324 ■ David and Lucile Packard Foundation

343 2nd St.
Los Altos, CA 94022-3632
Ph: (650)948-7658
E-mail: communications@packard.org
URL: www.packard.org

7325 ■ Packard Fellowships for Science and Engineering *(Professional development/Fellowship)*

Purpose: To allow the nation's most promising early career professors to pursue their science and engineering research with few funding restrictions and limited paperwork

Awards are arranged alphabetically below their administering organizations

requirements. **Focus:** Engineering; Science. **Qualif.:** Candidates must be faculty members who are eligible to serve as principal investigators engaged in research in the natural and physical sciences or engineering and must be within the first three years of their faculty careers. Disciplines that will be considered include physics, chemistry, mathematics, biology, astronomy, computer science, earth science, ocean science, and all branches of engineering. **Criteria:** Selection will be based on the assessment of nominees. Assessment of nominees shall be made by the Advisory Panel, which makes recommendations to the Foundation's Board of Trustees.

Funds Avail.: $875,000 ($175,000 per year). **Duration:** Annual; up to five years. **Number Awarded:** Up to 18. **To Apply:** Applications will be through nomination and online. The Foundation invites the presidents of 50 universities to nominate two early-career professors each from their institutions. Please note that nominees will not be able to access the online application system until they have been identified to the Packard Foundation. A completed nomination form from the president of the university, which will be mailed to the universities with the request for nominations, should state the nominees' name and contact information including email address, departmental affiliation, sponsoring institutions' name, and president's name and address. Online submission should also include: complete contact information; departmental and institutional affiliation(s); and disciplinary field(s); educational background; professional positions held; honors and awards; current external research support; publications; and research statement describing why the research is important and outline the general goals for the next five years. Additional requirements are four recommendation letters (one from the department head; three from people outside the nominees' universities who are personally familiar with the nominees' work and creative ability. **Deadline:** March 16 (nominations deadline); April 20 (application materials). **Contact:** Email at fellows@packard.org.

7326 ■ Painting and Decorating Contractors of America (PDCA)

2316 Millpark Dr.
Maryland Heights, MO 63043
Ph: (314)514-7322
Fax: (314)890-2068
Free: 800-332-7322
E-mail: rbright@pdca.org
URL: www.pdca.org

7327 ■ A.E. Robert Friedman Scholarships
(Undergraduate/Scholarship)

Purpose: To assist students who wish to further their education. **Focus:** General studies/Field of study not specified. **Qualif.:** Applicants must be at least seniors in high school, no more than 26 years old; nominated by an active PDCA member, unrelated to a PDCA member or employee and otherwise unconnected with the PDCA. **Criteria:** Applicants are selected based on character, financial need and attendance at an educational institution.

Funds Avail.: No specific amount. **Duration:** Annual. **To Apply:** Applicants must submit a completed application form; essay; letters of recommendation and transcripts. **Deadline:** August 19.

7328 ■ Pan-Macedonian Association USA Inc.
149-14 14th Ave.
Whitestone, NY 11357-1730

Ph: (718)747-0488
Fax: (718)747-0489
E-mail: nina@panmacedonian.info
URL: panmacedonian.info

7329 ■ Pan-Macedonian National Scholarships
(Undergraduate, High School/Scholarship)

Purpose: To provide scholarships to high school seniors with Macedonian ancestry. **Focus:** General studies/Field of study not specified. **Qualif.:** Applicants must be members of Pan-Macedonian Association, or be members of the Pan-Macedonian Youth Group; must be high school seniors or equivalent who have planned to enroll in a college or any accredited institution; must have taken the Scholastic Aptitude Test (SAT) or American College Test. **Criteria:** Applicants will be chosen based on merit and demonstrated financial need.

Funds Avail.: $500. **Duration:** Annual. **Number Awarded:** 2. **To Apply:** Applicants must complete the application form. must submit the results of the scholastic exam taken; must attach a complete transcript of records, a handwriting letter stating the professional goals and plans for achieving them; and must submit a proof of membership to a Chapter or Member-Society of the Pan-Macedonian Association. Students can strengthen their application by submitting a one-page essay on the stating the following: a) History of the Macedonian Hellenism; b) How do they feel about their Macedonian ancestry. **Deadline:** May 22.

7330 ■ Paper-Check.Com
703 Market St., Ste. 2100
San Francisco, CA 94103
Free: 866-693-3348
E-mail: support@papercheck.com
URL: www.papercheck.com

7331 ■ Charles Shafae Scholarships *(Undergraduate/Scholarship)*

Purpose: To provide funds for the education of qualified individuals through an essay contest. **Focus:** General studies/Field of study not specified. **Qualif.:** Applicants must: be enrolled at an accredited four-year college or university in the U.S.; be enrolled at the undergraduate level (have taken or are taking an undergraduate course) taking at least 12 credits per semester; be legal residents of the U.S. or hold a valid student visa; carry a status of "good standing"; and, maintain a cumulative Grade Point Average (GPA) of at least 3.2. **Criteria:** Selection shall be based on the Papercheck Essay Contest.

Funds Avail.: $1,000. **Duration:** Annual. **To Apply:** Applicants may visit the website to verify the application process and other pieces of information. **Deadline:** January 18. **Contact:** Paper-Check.Com, at the above address.

7332 ■ Paper Stock Industries
PO Box 2819
Palm Beach, FL 33480
Ph: (561)627-9191
E-mail: info@paperstockindustries.org
URL: www.paperstockindustries.org

7333 ■ Paper Stock Industries/RRF Scholarships
(Undergraduate/Scholarship)

Purpose: To provide financial assistance to students who wish to continue their education. **Focus:** General studies/

Awards are arranged alphabetically below their administering organizations

Field of study not specified. **Qualif.:** Applicant must be any of the following: employee, son, daughter or spouse of an individual who has been employed for at least one year in a member firm of any PSI Chapter; must have at least a C+ average in high school and meet all the qualifications for admission to a regionally accredited two-year or four-year post secondary institution. **Criteria:** Recipient will be evaluated based on merit.

Funds Avail.: $1,500 each. **Duration:** Annual. **Number Awarded:** 4. **To Apply:** Applicant must submit a completed scholarship application; official transcripts of all high school and/or college grades, SAT, and/or ACT scores; two letters of recommendation; resume of the applicant's personal history; and a one-page short essay entitled "Why College is important to Me." **Deadline:** March 31. **Contact:** Crawford Carpenter, PSI Scholarship Chair, at ccarpenter@tngus.com.

7334 ■ Paper Stock Industries Chapter of the Institute of Scrap Recycling Industries
PO Box 2819
Palm Beach, FL 33480
Ph: (214)357-0262
E-mail: info@paperstockindustries.org
URL: www.paperstockindustries.org

7335 ■ Paper Stock Industries Chapter of ISRI Scholarship Program *(Undergraduate, Professional development/Scholarship)*

Purpose: To provide financial assistance for employees of the Paper Stock Industries Chapter and their immediate families intending to pursue education. **Focus:** General studies/Field of study not specified. **Qualif.:** Applicant must be an employee, or an immediate relative (child or spouse) of an individual who has been employed for at least one year by a member firm of the PSI Chapter; and must have at least a C+ average in high school. **Criteria:** Scholarship beneficiaries will be selected by the PSI Chapter Scholarship Committee based on merit.

Funds Avail.: $1,500. **Duration:** Annual. **Number Awarded:** 4. **To Apply:** Applicants must complete the scholarship application (downloadable from PSI website); official transcript of records (high school and college); standardized test scores: SAT and/or ACT; two letters of recommendation; a personal resume; and a one-page minimum essay on "What was a defining moment in my life and how has it shaped my career outlook." Applicants must send an original and two copies of all necessary documents to Paper Stock Industries. **Deadline:** March 31.

7336 ■ Paper Stock Industries Chapter of ISRI (PSI)
PO Box 2819
Palm Beach, FL 33480
E-mail: info@paperstockindustries.org
URL: www.paperstockindustries.org

7337 ■ PSI Scholarships *(Undergraduate/Scholarship)*

Purpose: To support students related to employees of PSI member companies with their college expenses. **Focus:** General studies/Field of study not specified. **Qualif.:** Applicants must be college students related to employees of PSI member companies; must have at least a C+ average in high school and meet all qualifications for admission to a

regionally accredited two-year or four-year post-secondary institution. **Criteria:** Selection of the scholarship recipients will be made by the PSI Chapter Scholarship Committee based on merit.

Funds Avail.: $1,500. **Duration:** Annual. **Number Awarded:** 4. **To Apply:** Applicants must submit the following: completed scholarship application; official transcript of all high school and college grades, SAT and/or ACT scores; two letters of recommendation; resume of the individual's personal history; and short, one page minimum essay answering one of the topics provided by the bestowing organization. **Deadline:** March 31. **Contact:** For more information, contact Crawford Carpenter, PSI Scholarship Chair, at ccarpenter@tngus.com.

7338 ■ Paralyzed Veterans of America (PVA)
801 18th St. NW
Washington, DC 20006-3517
Free: 800-424-8200
E-mail: info@pva.org
URL: www.pva.org

7339 ■ PVA Research Foundation Fellowships *(Postdoctorate/Fellowship)*

Purpose: To support innovative research and fellowships that improve the lives of those with spinal cord injury and disease. **Focus:** Spinal cord injuries and research. **Qualif.:** Applicants must be postdoctoral students who received their PhD or MD within four years or less. Applicants with more than four years of training should apply as principal investigators. Applicants must have a designated and identified mentor/sponsor who is a senior-level investigator of the laboratory in which the research is to be conducted. **Criteria:** Selection will be based on scientific/technical merit and relevance to spinal cord dysfunction issues.

Funds Avail.: $100,000. **Duration:** Two years. **To Apply:** Application can be obtained at the website. Applicants must submit a proposal and must include the following: one letter of support written by the mentor/sponsor. The letter should identify the mentor and must be submitted as an attachment in the supporting documents section of the online application. The letter should include a statement about the applicant, a brief overview of the sponsor's training and number of fellows and students previously trained, a description of the training environment provided by the laboratory and department, such as seminar program and availability of other investigators for discussion and consultation; two additional letters of support from individuals familiar with the qualifications of the fellows; a biosketch of the mentor/sponsor.

7340 ■ Parapsychological Association (PA)
c/o Annalisa Ventola, Executive Director
PO Box 24173
Columbus, OH 43224
Ph: (202)318-2364
Fax: (202)318-2364
E-mail: business@parapsych.org
URL: www.parapsych.org

7341 ■ Parapsychological Association Research Endowments *(All/Grant)*

Purpose: To encourage parapsychological research by students and other researchers. **Focus:** Parapsychology.

Awards are arranged alphabetically below their administering organizations

Qualif.: Applicants must have or interested in doing parapsychological research. **Criteria:** Recipients will be selected based on quality of proposal; and prospects for completion as a useful contribution to the field.

Funds Avail.: $2,000-$5,000. **To Apply:** Applicants must submit a brief but formal proposal (less than 3000 words), in either plain text or a word document. The proposal should have a cover page, contact information and short statement of personal qualifications; must include letter of support from people involved in supervising or helping the work. **Deadline:** June 30. **Contact:** Send materials to Dr. Harvey Irwin or e-mail him at hirwin2@une.edu.au.

7342 ■ Parapsychology Foundation (PF)
PO Box 1562
New York, NY 10021-0043
Ph: (212)628-1550
Fax: (212)628-1559
E-mail: office@parapsychology.org
URL: www.parapsychology.org

7343 ■ Eileen J. Garrett Scholarships *(Undergraduate, Postgraduate/Scholarship)*

Purpose: To assist a student attending an accredited college or university who wishes to pursue the academic study of the science of parapsychology. **Focus:** Parapsychology. **Qualif.:** Applicants must: be currently enrolled full-time in an accredited school or university pursuing academic study in parapsychology; be members of the foundation; and, demonstrate an interest from the chosen field. **Criteria:** Awards are given based on academic record, personal promise, character and financial need. Selection is made by the colleges in accordance with their established procedures.

Funds Avail.: $3,000. **Duration:** Annual. **Number Awarded:** 1. **To Apply:** Applicants must submit an application form together with letters of reference from individuals familiar with the applicants' work or studies in parapsychology. **Deadline:** July 15. **Contact:** office@parapsychology.org.

7344 ■ Parent Cooperative Preschools International (PCPI)
National Cooperative Business Ctr.
1401 New York Ave. NW, Ste. 1100
Washington, DC 20005
E-mail: enquiries@preschools.coop
URL: www.preschools.coop

7345 ■ Katharine Whiteside Taylor Bursary *(Professional development/Scholarship)*

Purpose: To help parents and teachers in Canada about cooperative preschools. **Focus:** Education, Early childhood. **Qualif.:** Eligible applicants must be teaching staff currently employed in a Canadian parent cooperative; must be members of a parent participating co-op schools who wish to pursue professional development in the field of early childhood education or related leadership training. **Criteria:** The KWT bursary committee is made of PCPI board members and selected advisors. The selection committee will use a standardized evaluation scale that lists all the criteria for the application and gives a weighted point value for each area.

Funds Avail.: Up to $500. **Duration:** Annual. **To Apply:**

Application form can be retrieved from the program website. **Deadline:** March 15. **Remarks:** Established in 1995.

7346 ■ Park Law Enforcement Association (PLEA)
c/o Capt. Carl Nielsen, Executive Director
4397 McCullough St.
Port Charlotte, FL 33948
Ph: (941)286-7410
URL: www.myparkranger.org

7347 ■ Newell S. Rand Jr. Memorial Scholarships *(Undergraduate/Scholarship)*

Purpose: To provide scholarships to persons pursuing a bachelor's or master's degree in a Park Law Enforcement related course of study. **Focus:** Law enforcement. **Qualif.:** Applicants must be enrolled in a field of study related to park law enforcement. **Criteria:** Recipients are chosen by the PLEA Board or Committee appointed by the PLEA board.

Funds Avail.: $1,000. **Duration:** Annual. **To Apply:** Applicants must submit current resume including education, work experience and civic activity; a letter showing their interest in the Park Law Enforcement field and explaining why they are worthy of the PLEA Scholarship; three letters of recommendation from an instructor or advisor in their field of study; and proof of enrollment. Applications must be submitted to the PLEA President. **Deadline:** June 1. **Contact:** John Nesbit, Saint Louis County Park Rangers, 41 S Central, Clayton, MO 63105, or e-mail at jnesbit@stlouisco.com.

7348 ■ Parkersburg Area Community Foundation
PO Box 1762
Parkersburg, WV 26102-1762
Ph: (304)428-4438
Free: 866-428-4438
E-mail: info@pacfwv.com
URL: www.pacfwv.com

7349 ■ Martin K. Alsup Scholarships *(Undergraduate/Scholarship)*

Purpose: To provide financial assistance for qualified high school seniors from Parkersburg High School. **Focus:** Music; Musicology. **Qualif.:** Applicant must be a graduating senior from Parkersburg High School; must have a strong commitment to the field of instrumental music and music-related activities as demonstrated by participation in orchestra or the Big Red Band. **Criteria:** Recipients will be selected based on strong commitment to the field of music and related activities. Preference will be given to students majoring in music.

Funds Avail.: No specific amount. **Duration:** Annual. **To Apply:** Applicants must submit a cover sheet (three pages) and application form (four pages); must have a personal essay; high school and/or post- secondary transcripts; must provide a letter of recommendation; copy of the page of their or their parent's most recent tax return that indicates adjusted gross income; and must have a Student Aid Report showing estimated family contribution from FAFSA. Application form and other supporting documents must be sent to the Foundation's office. **Deadline:** March 4.

7350 ■ Ambrose/Ramsey Schoarship Fund *(Undergraduate/Scholarship)*

Purpose: To provide financial assistance for qualified students from Parkersburg, Parkersburg South, Parkers-

Awards are arranged alphabetically below their administering organizations

burg Catholic, or Williamstown High School. **Focus:** Religion. **Qualif.:** Applicant must be a graduate from Parkersburg, Parkersburg South, Parkersburg Catholic, or Williamstown High School with the desire to further their education in the study of the Methodist Ministry. **Criteria:** Selection of applicants will be based on the application requirements and scholarship selection criteria.

Funds Avail.: No specific amount. **Duration:** Annual. **To Apply:** Applicant must submit a cover sheet (three pages) and application form (four pages); a personal essay; a high school and/or post-secondary transcript; a letter of recommendation; signed copy of the page of their or their parent's most recent tax return that indicates adjusted gross income; and a Student Aid Report showing estimated family contribution from FAFSA. Application form and other supporting documents must be sent to the Foundation's office. **Deadline:** March 4.

7351 ■ Joe Barbarow Memorial Scholarships
(Undergraduate/Scholarship)

Purpose: To provide financial support to deserving graduate seniors at Parkersburg High School. **Focus:** General studies/Field of study not specified. **Qualif.:** Applicant must be a high school graduating senior and must have attended Hamilton Junior High in Wood County. **Criteria:** Selection of applicants will be based on academic achievement, school citizenship, moral character and financial need.

Funds Avail.: No specific amount. **Duration:** Annual. **To Apply:** Applicant must submit a cover sheet (3 pages) and application form (4 pages); a personal essay; a high school and/or post-secondary transcripts; a letter of recommendation; a signed copy of the page of their parent's most recent tax return that indicates adjusted gross income; and a Student Aid Report showing estimated family contribution from FAFSA. Application form and other supporting documents must be sent to the Foundation's office. **Deadline:** March 4.

7352 ■ Lewis and Gurry Batten/Sand Plains Educational Trust Scholarships *(Undergraduate/Scholarship)*

Purpose: To provide financial assistance for qualified senior high school at Parkersburg High School. **Focus:** General studies/Field of study not specified. **Qualif.:** Applicant must be a Parkersburg High School graduating senior; must have a minimum of 2.5 GPA; and must be attending a four-year course in college or university. **Criteria:** Selection of recipients will be based on merit and financial need.

Funds Avail.: No specific amount. **To Apply:** Applicant must submit a cover sheet (thee pages) and application form (four pages); a personal essay; a high school and/or post-secondary transcript; a letter of recommendation; a signed copy of the page of their or their parent's most recent tax return that indicates adjusted gross income; and a Student Aid Report showing estimated family contribution from FAFSA. Application form and other supporting documents must be sent to Our Community's Foundation, at the above address.

7353 ■ William (Billbo) Boston/Harold Knopp Scholarship *(Undergraduate/Scholarship)*

Purpose: To provide financial assistance for qualified graduating students from Wood County. **Focus:** Computer and information sciences; Journalism. **Qualif.:** Applicants must be graduating seniors from Wood County; and must be planning to pursue a career in journalism or in computer

science in West Virginia or Ohio. **Criteria:** Selection based on financial need, academic achievement (minimum 3.0 GPA), and school/community activities.

Funds Avail.: No specific amount. **Duration:** Annual. **To Apply:** Applicants must submit the cover sheet (three pages) and application form (four pages); must have personal essay; high school and/or post-secondary transcript; must provide letter of recommendation; copy of the page of their or their parent's most recent tax return that indicates adjusted gross income; and Student Aid Report showing estimated family contribution from FAFSA. Application form and other supporting documents must be sent to the Foundation's office. **Deadline:** March 4. **Remarks:** Established in 2012.

7354 ■ Chester H. Bruce Memorial Scholarships
(Undergraduate, Vocational/Occupational/Scholarship)

Purpose: To provide financial support for qualified students of Wirt County High School. **Focus:** Christian education. **Qualif.:** Applicant must be a graduating senior of Wirt County High School; must be pursuing vocational or trade studies, Christian ministry or service; must be enrolled as a full-time student in an undergraduate two or four-year program or a vocational program or graduate school; must have a minimum of 2.5 GPA; and must have a strong work ethic. **Criteria:** Selection of recipients will be based on scholarship selection criteria.

Funds Avail.: No specific amount. **Duration:** Annual. **To Apply:** Applicant must submit a cover sheet (three pages) and application form (four pages); must have a personal essay; must have a high school and/or post-secondary transcript; must provide a letter of recommendation and a signed copy of the page of their or their parent's most recent tax return that indicates adjusted gross income; and must have a Student Aid Report showing estimated family contribution from FAFSA. Application form and other supporting documents must be sent to Our Community's Foundation, at the above address.

7355 ■ Freda Burge Scholarships *(Undergraduate/Scholarship)*

Purpose: To encourage graduating students of Williamstown High School to pursue their education. **Focus:** General studies/Field of study not specified. **Qualif.:** Applicant must be a Williamstown High School graduating senior; must be planning to attend West Virginia University-Parkersburg full-time; and must have a minimum of 2.5 GPA. **Criteria:** Selection of recipients will be based on financial need and application materials.

Funds Avail.: No specific amount. **To Apply:** Applicant must submit a cover sheet (three pages) and application form (four pages); must have personal essay; high school and/or post-secondary transcript; must provide a letter of recommendation and a signed copy of the page of their or their parent's most recent tax return that indicates adjusted gross income; and Student Aid Report showing estimated family contribution from FAFSA. Application form and other supporting documents must be sent to Our Community's Foundation at the above address.

7356 ■ George H. Clinton Scholarship Fund
(Undergraduate/Scholarship)

Purpose: To provide support for graduating or graduate students from a Wood County, WV high school. **Focus:** Communications. **Qualif.:** Applicants must be graduating or have graduated from a Wood County high school; must be attending college full-time and majoring in the media com-

Awards are arranged alphabetically below their administering organizations

munications field; must have a minimum of 3.0 GPA. **Criteria:** Selection of applicants will be based on the scholarship selection criteria.

Funds Avail.: No specific amount. **To Apply:** Applicants must submit the cover sheet (three pages) and application form (four pages); must have personal essay; high school and/or post-secondary transcript; must provide letter of recommendation and a signed copy of the page of their or their parent's most recent tax return that indicates adjusted gross income; and Student Aid Report showing estimated family contribution from FAFSA. Application form and other supporting documents must be sent to Our Community's Foundation, at the above address.

7357 ■ Dwight O. Conner and Ellen Conner Lepp/ Danhart Scholarships (Undergraduate/Scholarship)

Purpose: To provide financial assistance for qualified graduating high school students at Parkersburg High School. **Focus:** General studies/Field of study not specified. **Qualif.:** Applicant must be a Parkersburg High School graduating senior. **Criteria:** Selection of an applicant will be based on financial need.

Funds Avail.: No specific amount. **To Apply:** Applicant must submit a cover sheet (three pages) and application form (four pages); must have a personal essay; must have a high school and/or post-secondary transcripts; must provide a signed letter of recommendation; copy of the page of their or their parent's most recent tax return that indicates adjusted gross income; and must have a Student Aid Report showing estimated family contribution from FAFSA. Application form and other supporting documents must be sent to Our Community's Foundation, at the above address.

7358 ■ Dave Couch Memorial Scholarships (Undergraduate/Scholarship)

Purpose: To provide financial assistance for qualified individuals intending to pursue studies involving massage therapy or physical or occupational therapy. **Focus:** Occupational therapy; Physical therapy. **Qualif.:** Applicants must be residents of Wood, Wirt, Jackson, Pleasants, Ritchie, Roane, Mason, Calhoun, Gilmer, or Doddridge in West Virginia or Washington County, Ohio; must be actively pursuing a course of study involving massage therapy, physical, or occupational therapy. **Criteria:** Selection of applicants will be based on personal commitment to service for individuals whose lives are affected by ALS or other neuromuscular or disabling disease, as evidenced by related volunteer or community service to individuals whose lives are affected by these diseases or for organizations serving individuals whose lives are affected.

Funds Avail.: No specific amount. **Duration:** Annual. **To Apply:** Applicants must submit the cover sheet (three pages) and application form (four pages); must have personal essay; must have high school and/or post-secondary transcripts; must provide a letter of recommendation in a signed and sealed envelope; a copy of the page of their or their parent's most recent tax return that indicates adjusted gross income; must have Student Aid Report showing estimated family contribution from FAFSA. Application form and other supporting documents must be sent to the Foundation's office. **Deadline:** March 4. **Contact:** Parkersburg Area Community Foundation, info@pacfwv.com.

7359 ■ Jennifer Coulter Memorial Scholarships (Undergraduate/Scholarship)

Purpose: To encourage the graduating seniors of Parkersburg High School to pursue their career in teaching. **Focus:**

Teaching. **Qualif.:** Applicants must be graduating seniors from Parkersburg High School interested in pursuing a career in teaching and must be involved in extracurricular and/or community service activities. **Criteria:** Selection of recipients will be based on academic achievement or potential to achieve academically with evidence of at least a 2.5 GPA and financial need. Preference will be given to students who have displayed interest in foreign language study during their high school career.

Funds Avail.: No specific amount. **To Apply:** Applicants must submit the cover sheet (three pages) and application form (four pages); must have personal essay; high school and/or post-secondary transcript; must provide letter of recommendation and a signed copy of the page of their or their parent's most recent tax return that indicates adjusted gross income; and Student Aid Report showing estimated family contribution from FAFSA. Application form and other supporting documents must be sent to Our Community's Foundation, at the above address.

7360 ■ Cindy Curry Memorial Scholarships (Undergraduate/Scholarship)

Purpose: To encourage the graduating students to pursue their education. **Focus:** General studies/Field of study not specified. **Qualif.:** Applicants must be graduating high school seniors from any Wood County high school; must be planning to attend an accredited West Virginia college or university full-time; must have minimum of 3.0 GPA; and must have strong motivation to attend school. **Criteria:** Recipients will be selected based on scholarship selection criteria.

Funds Avail.: No specific amount. **To Apply:** Applicants must submit a cover sheet (three pages) and application form (four pages); must have a personal essay; must have a high school and/or post-secondary transcript; must provide a letter of recommendation and a signed copy of the page of their or their parent's most recent tax return that indicates adjusted gross income; and must have a Student Aid Report, showing estimated family contribution from FAFSA. Application form and other supporting documents must be sent to Our Community's Foundation, at the above address.

7361 ■ Kenneth D. and Katherine D. Davis Scholarships (Undergraduate/Scholarship)

Purpose: To encourage graduating seniors of Wirt County High School to pursue their education. **Focus:** Business. **Qualif.:** Applicant must be a Wirt County High School graduating senior pursuing a career or major in business. **Criteria:** Recipients will be selected based on financial need, academic achievement, potential and character. Preference will be given to an applicant pursuing a career in business.

Funds Avail.: No specific amount. **To Apply:** Applicant must submit a cover sheet (three pages) and application form (four pages); must have a personal essay; high school and/or post-secondary transcript; letter of recommendation and a signed, copy of the page of their or their parent's most recent tax return that indicates adjusted gross income; and a Student Aid Report showing estimated family contribution from FAFSA. Application form and other supporting documents must be sent to Our Community's Foundation, at the above address.

7362 ■ Lawrence E. Davis Scholarships (Undergraduate/Scholarship)

Purpose: To encourage the graduating seniors of Parkersburg High School to pursue their education in either the

Awards are arranged alphabetically below their administering organizations

state of West Virginia or Ohio. **Focus:** General studies/ Field of study not specified. **Qualif.:** Applicants must be graduating seniors from Parkersburg High School who have been admitted to attend an accredited four-year institution of higher education in either the state of West Virginia or Ohio as full-time students with a minimum 2.5 GPA. **Criteria:** Selection of recipients will be based on financial need.

Funds Avail.: No specific amount. **To Apply:** Applicants must submit a cover sheet (three pages) and application form (four pages); must have a personal essay; must have a high school and/or post-secondary transcript; must provide a letter of recommendation in a signed, copy of the page of their or their parent's most recent tax return that indicates adjusted gross income; and must have a Student Aid Report showing estimated family contribution from FAFSA. Application form and other supporting documents must be sent to Our Community's Foundation, at the above address.

7363 ■ Doddridge County Promise Scholarships
(Undergraduate/Scholarship)

Purpose: To encourage the graduating students of Doddridge County High School to pursue their education. **Focus:** General studies/Field of study not specified. **Qualif.:** Applicants must be graduating high school seniors or graduates of Doddridge County High School who have been admitted to the college of their choice; must have a GPA of 3.2 or above, be in the top 20% of the class, ACT of 21 or above or SAT of 1100 or above; must have followed a college-bound curriculum; and must have financial need. **Criteria:** Recipients will be selected based on the evaluation of the scholarship selection committee.

Funds Avail.: No specific amount. **To Apply:** Applicants must submit a cover sheet (3 pages) and application form (4 pages); must have a personal essay; must have a high school and/or post-secondary transcript; must provide a letter of recommendation and a signed copy of the page of their or their parent's most recent tax return that indicates adjusted gross income; and must have a Student Aid Report showing estimated family contribution from FAFSA. Application form and other supporting documents must be sent to Our Community's Foundation, at the above address.

7364 ■ Deborah Gandee Dudding Memorial Scholarships *(Undergraduate/Scholarship)*

Purpose: To provide financial assistance for qualified graduating seniors at Ravenswood High School. **Focus:** General studies/Field of study not specified. **Qualif.:** Applicant must be a Ravenswood High School graduating senior; must have a minimum of 2.5 GPA. **Criteria:** Preference will be given to students with financial need who have exhibited a record of community service, a balance of academic and extracurricular interest, commitment to the growth, development and/ or the well-being of children.

Funds Avail.: No specific amount. **Duration:** Annual. **To Apply:** Applicant must submit a cover sheet (three pages) and application form (four pages); must have a personal essay; must have high school and/or post-secondary transcripts; must provide a letter of recommendation and a signed copy of the page of their or their parent's most recent tax return that indicates adjusted gross income; and must have a Student Aid Report showing estimated family contribution from FAFSA. Application form and other supporting documents must be sent to the Foundation's office **Deadline:** March 4.

7365 ■ David Edward Farson Scholarships
(Undergraduate/Scholarship)

Purpose: To encourage graduating seniors at Parkersburg High School to pursue their education. **Focus:** General studies/Field of study not specified. **Qualif.:** Applicants must be Parkersburg High School graduating seniors planning to attend Marshall University. **Criteria:** Selection of applicants will be based on financial need and academic achievements.

Funds Avail.: No specific amount. **Duration:** Annual. **To Apply:** Applicants must submit the cover sheet (three pages) and application form (four pages); must have personal essay; high school and/or post-secondary transcripts; must provide letter of recommendation and a signed copy of the page of their or their parent's most recent tax return that indicates adjusted gross income; and Student Aid Report showing estimated family contribution from FAFSA. **Deadline:** March 4.

7366 ■ Fostering Hope Scholarships Fund
(Undergraduate/Scholarship)

Purpose: To provide financial assistance for qualified individuals intending to pursue their education. **Focus:** General studies/Field of study not specified. **Qualif.:** Applicants must be students who are actively enrolled or have been enrolled in the foster care system; must be West Virginia residents; must be admitted to a course of study at a post-high school educational institution for the upcoming year. **Criteria:** Selection of applicants will be based on academic promise, good character, good citizenship and financial need.

Funds Avail.: No specific amount. **Duration:** Annual. **To Apply:** Applicants must submit the cover sheet (three pages) and application form (four pages); must have personal essay; high school and/or post-secondary transcripts; must provide letter of recommendation and signed copy of the page of their or their parent's most recent tax return that indicates adjusted gross income; and Student Aid Report showing estimated family contribution from FAFSA. Application form and other supporting documents must be sent to the Foundation's office. **Deadline:** March 4.

7367 ■ William E. "Bill" Gallagher Scholarships
(Undergraduate/Scholarship)

Purpose: To provide financial assistance for qualified graduating seniors at Parkersburg South High School. **Focus:** Arts; Education; Education, Physical; History. **Qualif.:** Applicants must be graduating seniors at Parkersburg South High School who have been admitted to attend Glenville State College in Glenville, WV, or Alderson Broaddus College in Philippi, WV. **Criteria:** Selection of applicants will be based on the knowledge and a love of people as attested to by the guidance counselors and as evidenced by candidate's participation in extracurricular activities and community service. Preference will be given to students majoring in education, with further preference given to students intending to major in history, fine arts, physical education or middle school education.

Funds Avail.: No specific amount. **Duration:** Annual. **To Apply:** Applicants must submit the cover sheet (three pages) and application form (four pages); must have personal essay; high school and/or post-secondary transcripts; must provide letter of recommendation and a signed copy of the page of their or their parent's most recent tax return that indicates adjusted gross income; and Student Aid Report showing estimated family contribution from

Awards are arranged alphabetically below their administering organizations

FAFSA. Application form and other supporting documents must be sent to the Foundation's office. **Deadline:** March 4.

7368 ■ Laverne L. Gibson Memorial Scholarships
(Undergraduate/Scholarship)

Purpose: To provide financial assistance for qualified graduating seniors intending to pursue their career in education. **Focus:** Education; Education, Special. **Qualif.:** Applicant must be a graduating senior from Wood County West Virginia or Washington County Ohio; must be majoring in education and special education. **Criteria:** Selection of applicants will be based on academic achievement or potential to achieve, honesty and good moral character, involvement in extracurricular and/or community service activities and financial need.

Funds Avail.: No specific amount. **Duration:** Annual. **To Apply:** Applicant must submit a cover sheet (three pages) and application form (four pages); must have a personal essay; must have high school and/or post-secondary transcripts; must provide a letter of recommendation and a signed copy of the page of their or their parent's most recent tax return that indicates adjusted gross income; must have a Student Aid Report showing estimated family contribution from FAFSA. Application form and other supporting documents must be sent to the Foundation's office. **Deadline:** March 4.

7369 ■ Shane Gilbert Memorial Scholarships
(Undergraduate/Scholarship)

Purpose: To encourage graduating students to pursue their post-secondary education. **Focus:** General studies/Field of study not specified. **Qualif.:** Applicant must be a Wood County Technical/Caperton Canter graduating senior intending to pursue post-secondary education. **Criteria:** Selection of applicants will be based on achievements, ability, financial need, citizenship and recommendation.

Funds Avail.: No specific amount. **To Apply:** Applicant must submit a cover sheet (three pages) and application form (four pages); must have a personal essay; must have a high school and/or post-secondary transcript; must provide a letter of recommendation and a signed copy of the page of their or their parent's most recent tax return that indicates adjusted gross income; and must have a Student Aid Report showing estimated family contribution from FAFSA. Application form and other supporting documents must be sent to Our Community's Foundation, at the above address.

7370 ■ Russ Grant Memorial Scholarship for Tennis
(Undergraduate/Scholarship)

Purpose: To encourage graduating seniors to pursue higher level education. **Focus:** General studies/Field of study not specified. **Qualif.:** Applicants must be graduating seniors from Parkersburg High School, Parkersburg South High School or Parkersburg Catholic High School; must have shown evidence of an interest in tennis; must be pursuing higher level education; and must have a minimum of 2.5 GPA. **Criteria:** Selection of recipients will be based on commitment to tennis, academic achievement and financial need.

Funds Avail.: No specific amount. **To Apply:** Applicants must submit a cover sheet (three pages) and application form (four pages); must have a personal essay; must have a high school and/or post-secondary transcript; must provide a letter of recommendation and a signed copy of the page of their or their parent's most recent tax return

that indicates adjusted gross income; and must have a Student Aid Report showing estimated family contribution from FAFSA. Application form and other supporting documents must be sent to Our Community's Foundation, at the above address.

7371 ■ Sara Gwisdalla Memorial Scholarships
(Undergraduate/Scholarship)

Purpose: To encourage the graduating students of Ripley High School to pursue their education. **Focus:** General studies/Field of study not specified. **Qualif.:** Applicant must be a Ripley High School graduating senior with a minimum of 3.0 GPA. **Criteria:** Preference will be given to students with financial need and a strong record of community service.

Funds Avail.: No specific amount. **To Apply:** Applicants must submit a cover sheet (3 pages) and application form (4 pages); must have a personal essay; must have a high school and/or post-secondary transcript; must provide a letter of recommendation in a signed, copy of the page of their or their parent's most recent tax return that indicates adjusted gross income; must have a Student Aid Report, showing estimated family contribution from FAFSA. Application form and other supporting documents must be sent to Our Community's Foundation, at the above address.

7372 ■ Clayburn and Garnet R. Hanna Scholarships
(Undergraduate/Scholarship)

Purpose: To provide financial assistance for the residents or graduates of Wirt County. **Focus:** General studies/Field of study not specified. **Qualif.:** Applicant must be a resident of Wirt County or graduate of Wirt County High School; must be planning to attend a post-secondary educational institution full-time. **Criteria:** Selection of applicants will be based on financial need, likelihood of completion of degree and leadership. Preference will be given to students who are not likely to receive other significant scholarship awards.

Funds Avail.: No specific amount. **To Apply:** Applicant must submit a cover sheet (three pages) and application form (four pages); must have a personal essay; must have a high school and/or post-secondary transcript; must provide a letter of recommendation and a signed copy of the page of their or their parent's most recent tax return that indicates adjusted gross income; and must have a Student Aid Report showing estimated family contribution from FAFSA. Application form and other supporting documents must be sent to Our Community's Foundation, at the above address.

7373 ■ H.G. Hardbarger Science and Mathematics Awards *(Undergraduate/Award)*

Purpose: To provide financial assistance for graduating seniors from Ritchie County High School. **Focus:** Mathematics and mathematical sciences; Science. **Qualif.:** Applicant must be a graduating senior from Ritchie County High School who has demonstrated achievement in the fields of Math/Science; must be planning to attend an accredited college, university or vocational/trade school in West Virginia. **Criteria:** Applicants will be selected based on the scholarship criteria.

Funds Avail.: No specific amount. **Duration:** Annual. **To Apply:** Applicant must submit a cover sheet (three pages) and application form (four pages); must have a personal essay; must have high school and/or post-secondary transcripts; must provide a letter of recommendation and a signed copy of the page of their or their parent's most

Awards are arranged alphabetically below their administering organizations

recent tax return that indicates adjusted gross income; and must have a Student Aid Report showing estimated family contribution from FAFSA. Application form and other supporting documents must be sent to the Foundation's office. **Deadline:** March 4.

7374 ■ Harrisville Lions Club Scholarships
(Undergraduate/Scholarship)

Purpose: To provide financial support for qualified individuals in Ritchie County intending to pursue their studies. **Focus:** Education, Vocational-technical. **Qualif.:** Applicant must be a resident of Ritchie County; must be pursuing vocational, technical, or trade related education through an accredited institution or program; and must have a minimum 2.0 GPA (if a graduating senior or presently enrolled in school). **Criteria:** Preference will be given to students with financial need.

Funds Avail.: No specific amount. **Duration:** Annual. **To Apply:** Applicant must submit a cover sheet (three pages) and application form (four pages); must have a personal essay; must have high school and/or post-secondary transcripts; must provide a letter of recommendation; copy of the page of their or their parent's most recent tax return that indicates adjusted gross income; and must have a Student Aid Report showing estimated family contribution from FAFSA. Application form and other supporting documents must be sent to the Foundation's office. **Deadline:** March 4.

7375 ■ Harry Hartleben Scholarships
(Undergraduate/Scholarship)

Purpose: To provide financial assistance for qualified graduating seniors from Parkersburg High School intending to pursue higher education. **Focus:** General studies/Field of study not specified. **Qualif.:** Applicant must be a graduating senior from Parkersburg High School who plans to pursue higher education; and must have a minimum 3.0 GPA. **Criteria:** Recipients of the scholarships will be selected based on academic achievement, motivation, character and involvement in school and community activities. Financial need is not a primary consideration.

Funds Avail.: No specific amount. **Duration:** Annual. **To Apply:** Applicant must submit a cover sheet (three pages) and application form (four pages); must have a personal essay; must have high school and/or post- secondary transcripts; must provide a letter of recommendation; copy of the page of their or their parent's most recent tax return that indicates adjusted gross income; and must have a Student Aid Report showing estimated family contribution from FAFSA. Application form and other supporting documents must be sent to the Foundation's office. **Deadline:** March 4.

7376 ■ Gail L. Hartshorn Memorial Fund
(Undergraduate/Scholarship)

Purpose: To provide financial assistance for qualified Wood County residents intending to pursue their studies. **Focus:** Emergency and disaster services; Paramedics. **Qualif.:** Applicants must be Wood County residents who are pursuing emergency medical technician or paramedic training. **Criteria:** Selection of applicants will be based on financial need and commitment to career in emergency services.

Funds Avail.: No specific amount. **To Apply:** Applicants must submit the cover sheet (three pages) and application form (four pages); must have personal essay; high school and/or post-secondary transcript; must provide letter of recommendation; copy of the page of their or their parent's

most recent tax return that indicates adjusted gross income; and Student Aid Report, showing estimated family contribution from FAFSA. **Deadline:** March 4.

7377 ■ Gregory Linn Haught Citizenship Awards
(Undergraduate/Award)

Purpose: To encourage the graduating students of Ritchie County High School to pursue their education. **Focus:** General studies/Field of study not specified. **Qualif.:** Applicants must be Ritchie County High School graduating seniors. **Criteria:** Selection of applicants will be based on academic achievement, good moral character, service to others, and service in religious activities and endeavors.

Funds Avail.: No specific amount. **To Apply:** Applicants must submit a cover sheet (3 pages) and application form (4 pages); must have a personal essay; must have a high school and/or postsecondary transcript; must provide a letter of recommendation and a signed copy of the page of their or their parent's most recent tax return that indicates adjusted gross income; and must have a Student Aid Report showing estimated family contribution from FAFSA. Application form and other supporting documents must be sent to Our Community's Foundation, at the above address.

7378 ■ Dorcas Edmonson Haught Scholarships
(Undergraduate/Scholarship)

Purpose: To provide financial support for qualified students intending to attend Marietta College. **Focus:** General studies/Field of study not specified. **Qualif.:** Applicants must be graduating Parkersburg High School seniors who plan to attend Marietta College. **Criteria:** Selection of applicants will be based on financial need, achievements and character.

Funds Avail.: No specific amount. **Duration:** Annual. **To Apply:** Applicants must submit the cover sheet (three pages) and application form (four pages); must have personal essay; high school and/or post-secondary transcript; must provide letter of recommendation; copy of the page of their or their parent's most recent tax return that indicates adjusted gross income; and Student Aid Report showing estimated family contribution from FAFSA. **Deadline:** March 4.

7379 ■ Ella Beren Hersch Scholarships
(Undergraduate/Scholarship)

Purpose: To encourage graduating students to pursue their education. **Focus:** General studies/Field of study not specified. **Qualif.:** Applicants must be a Parkersburg High School graduating senior. **Criteria:** Applicants will be selected based on financial need.

Funds Avail.: No specific amount. **To Apply:** Applicants must submit a cover sheet (3 pages) and application form (4 pages); must have a personal essay; must have a high school and/or post-secondary transcript; must provide a letter of recommendation and a signed copy of the page of their or their parent's most recent tax return that indicates adjusted gross income; and must have a Student Aid Report showing estimated family contribution from FAFSA. Application form and other supporting documents must be sent to Our Community's Foundation, at the above address.

7380 ■ Holly Jackson-Wuller Memorial Scholarships
(Undergraduate/Scholarship)

Purpose: To encourage the graduating seniors of Parkersburg South High School to pursue their college degree. **Focus:** General studies/Field of study not specified. **Qua-

Awards are arranged alphabetically below their administering organizations

lif.: Applicant must be a graduating senior from Parkersburg South High School planning to attend Marshall University, with minimum 2.5 GPA. **Criteria:** Selection of applicants will be based on financial need and participation in school, church and community activities.

Funds Avail.: No specific amount. **To Apply:** Applicants may apply online.

7381 ■ K.A.S.A Memorial Scholarships
(Undergraduate/Scholarship)

Purpose: To provide financial support for graduating high school seniors or graduates of Doddridge County High School. **Focus:** General studies/Field of study not specified. **Qualif.:** Applicant must be a graduating high school senior or graduate of Doddridge County High School; must have a minimum GPA of 2.25. **Criteria:** Preference will be given to a student who has been admitted to attend a public college in West Virginia, and to a well-rounded, hard working individual with financial need who is not receiving substantial scholarship aid from other sources.

Funds Avail.: No specific amount. **Duration:** Annual. **To Apply:** Applicant must submit a cover sheet (three pages) and application form (four pages); must have a personal essay; must have a high school and/or post-secondary transcript; must provide a letter of recommendation; copy of the page of their or their parent's most recent tax return that indicates adjusted gross income; and a Student Aid Report showing estimated family contribution from FAFSA.

7382 ■ Dr. Charles Kelly Memorial Scholarships
(Undergraduate/Scholarship)

Purpose: To provide financial assistance for qualified graduating seniors of Ravenswood High School. **Focus:** General studies/Field of study not specified. **Qualif.:** Applicant must be a Jackson County graduating senior planning to attend Marshall University. **Criteria:** Selection of applicants will be based on financial need.

Funds Avail.: No specific amount. **Duration:** Annual. **To Apply:** Applicant must submit a cover sheet (three pages) and application form (four pages); must have a personal essay; must have a high school and/or post-secondary transcript; must provide a letter of recommendation; copy of the page of their or their parent's most recent tax return that indicates adjusted gross income; and a Student Aid Report showing estimated family contribution from FAFSA. **Deadline:** March 4.

7383 ■ Judge Oliver Kessel Memorial Scholarships - Ripley Rotary *(Undergraduate/Scholarship)*

Purpose: To assist Ripley High School graduating seniors. **Focus:** General studies/Field of study not specified. **Qualif.:** Applicant must be a Ripley High School graduating senior with a minimum GPA of 2.0. **Criteria:** Selection of recipients will be based on financial need and strong record of community service.

Funds Avail.: No specific amount. **Duration:** Annual. **To Apply:** Applicant must submit a cover sheet (three pages) and application form (four pages); must have a personal essay; must have a high school and/or postsecondary transcript; must provide a letter of recommendation; copy of the page of their or their parent's most recent tax return that indicates adjusted gross income; and a Student Aid Report showing estimated family contribution from FAFSA. Application form and other supporting documents must be sent to the Foundation's office. **Deadline:** March 4.

7384 ■ Langfitt/Ambrose Scholarship Fund
(Undergraduate/Scholarship)

Purpose: To provide financial assistance for deserving students intending to pursue their education. **Focus:** English language and literature; Mathematics and mathematical sciences. **Qualif.:** Applicant must be a graduate from Parkersburg, Parkersburg South, Parkersburg Catholic, or Williamstown High School; must have excelled in the combined fields of Mathematics and English desiring to further their education in those fields. **Criteria:** Recipients will be selected based on their application materials.

Funds Avail.: No specific amount. **Duration:** Annual. **To Apply:** Applicant must submit a cover sheet (three pages) and application form (four pages); a personal essay; a high school and/or post-secondary transcripts; a letter of recommendation; copy of the page of their parent's most recent tax return that indicates adjusted gross income; and a Student Aid Report showing estimated family contribution from FAFSA. Application form and other supporting documents must be sent to the Foundation's office. **Deadline:** March 4.

7385 ■ Megan Nicole Longwell Scholarships
(Undergraduate/Scholarship)

Purpose: To encourage the graduating seniors of Parkersburg South High School to pursue their college degree. **Focus:** General studies/Field of study not specified. **Qualif.:** Applicants must be Parkersburg South High School graduating seniors who have been admitted to an accredited institution of higher learning as full-time students with a minimum 2.5 GPA. **Criteria:** Selection of applicants will be based on financial need and participation in school athletics. Special consideration will be given to applicants whose families have experienced extraordinary special need.

Funds Avail.: No specific amount. **To Apply:** Applicants must submit the cover sheet (three pages) and application form (four pages); must have personal essay; high school and/or post-secondary transcript; letter of recommendation and a signed copy of the page of their or their parent's most recent tax return that indicates adjusted gross income; and Student Aid Report showing estimated family contribution from FAFSA. Application form and other supporting documents must be sent to Our Community's Foundation, at the above address.

7386 ■ Bryce-Lietzke Martin Scholarships
(Undergraduate/Scholarship)

Purpose: To provide financial assistance for qualified individuals in Wood County. **Focus:** General studies/Field of study not specified. **Qualif.:** Applicant must be a Wood County resident; must have an interest in golf; must have a minimum of 2.5 GPA; and must be accepted or attending a post-secondary education. **Criteria:** Selection of recipients will be based on good moral character, involvement in extracurricular activities and financial need.

Funds Avail.: No specific amount. **To Apply:** Applicants must submit a cover sheet (three pages) and application form (four pages); must have a personal essay; high school and/or post-secondary transcript; must provide a letter of recommendation and a signed copy of the page of their or their parent's most recent tax return that indicates adjusted gross income; and Student Aid Report showing estimated family contribution, from FAFSA. Application form and other supporting documents must be sent to Our Community's Foundation, at the above address.

Awards are arranged alphabetically below their administering organizations

7387 ■ Dudley Mullins/Cabot Corporation Scholarships *(Undergraduate/Scholarship)*

Purpose: To assist graduating seniors of Williamstown High School in their educational pursuits. **Focus:** General studies/Field of study not specified. **Qualif.:** Applicants must be Williamstown graduating seniors; must have attended Waverly Elementary School for a minimum of one year and graduated from Waverly Elementary; must have minimum of 2.0 GPA. **Criteria:** Selection of applicants will be based on involvement in school and civic activities, academic achievement and potential.

Funds Avail.: No specific amount. **Duration:** Annual. **To Apply:** Applicants must submit the cover sheet (three pages) and application form (four pages);personal essay; high school and/or post-secondary transcript; letter of recommendation; signed copy of the page of their parent's most recent tax return that indicates adjusted gross income; and Student Aid Report showing estimated family contribution from FAFSA. **Deadline:** March 4.

7388 ■ Pennsboro Alumni Scholarship Fund *(Undergraduate/Scholarship)*

Purpose: To provide financial assistance for graduating seniors of Ritchie County High School intending to pursue their education. **Focus:** General studies/Field of study not specified. **Qualif.:** Applicant must be a Ritchie County High School graduating senior who demonstrates financial need. **Criteria:** Preference will be given to students who demonstrated academic promise, good character, good citizenship and financial need.

Funds Avail.: No specific amount. **Duration:** Annual. **To Apply:** Applicant must submit a cover sheet (three pages) and application form (four pages); a personal essay; a high school and/or post-secondary transcript; a letter of recommendation; a signed copy of the page of their or their parent's most recent tax return that indicates adjusted gross income; and a Student Aid Report showing estimated family contribution from FAFSA. Application form and other supporting documents must be sent to the Foundation's office. **Deadline:** March 4.

7389 ■ Pepsi Wood County Technical/Caperton Center Scholarship Fund *(Undergraduate/Scholarship)*

Purpose: To assist graduating seniors in their educational pursuits. **Focus:** General studies/Field of study not specified. **Qualif.:** Applicants must be graduating seniors attending Wood County Technical/Caperton Canter who are admitted to a post-secondary education institution. **Criteria:** Selection of applicants will be based on GPA, financial need, and recommendations.

Funds Avail.: No specific amount. **Duration:** Annual. **To Apply:** Applicants must submit a cover sheet (3 pages) and application form (4 pages); a personal essay; a high school and/or post-secondary transcript; a letter of recommendation; a signed copy of the page of their or their parent's most recent tax return that indicates adjusted gross income; and a Student Aid Report showing estimated family contribution from FAFSA. Application form and other supporting documents must be sent to the Foundation's office. **Deadline:** March 4.

7390 ■ William R. Pfalzgraf Scholarships *(Undergraduate/Scholarship)*

Purpose: To assist graduating students in their educational pursuits. **Focus:** Education, English as a second language; English language and literature; Law; Music; Speech, Debate, and Forensics. **Qualif.:** Applicant must be a Parkersburg High School graduating senior with a minimum of 3.0 GPA. **Criteria:** Selection of applicants will be based on merit, motivation toward higher education, character and financial need. Preference will be given to student with interest in or achievement in the areas of law, debating, English or music.

Funds Avail.: No specific amount. **Duration:** Annual. **To Apply:** Applicant must submit a cover sheet (3 pages) and application form (4 pages); a personal essay; a high school and/or post-secondary transcript; a letter of recommendation; a signed copy of the page of their or their parent's most recent tax return that indicates adjusted gross income; and a Student Aid Report showing estimated family contribution from FAFSA. Application form and other supporting documents must be sent to the Foundation's office. **Deadline:** March 4.

7391 ■ Herschel Pifer Memorial Scholarships *(Undergraduate/Scholarship)*

Purpose: To encourage graduating students to pursue their education. **Focus:** General studies/Field of study not specified. **Qualif.:** Applicants must be Ritchie County High School graduating seniors. **Criteria:** Selection of applicants will be based on financial need, academic achievement and activities. Preference will be given to applicants who have not yet received a scholarship support.

Funds Avail.: No specific amount. **To Apply:** Applicants must submit the cover sheet (three pages) and application form (four pages); must have personal essay; high school and/or post-secondary transcript; must provide a letter of recommendation and a signed copy of the page of their or their parent's most recent tax return that indicates adjusted gross income; and Student Aid Report showing estimated family contribution from FAFSA. Application form and other supporting documents must be sent to Our Community's Foundation, at the above address.

7392 ■ William Reaser Scholarships *(Undergraduate, Vocational/Occupational/Scholarship)*

Purpose: To encourage graduating students to pursue their college post-Secondary education. **Focus:** Education, Vocational-technical. **Qualif.:** Applicant must be a Ritchie County High School graduating senior planning to pursue post-secondary education in a technical or vocational field. **Criteria:** Selection of recipients will be based on academic achievement or potential in the area of vocational/technical studies, honesty and good moral character, community service and financial need.

Funds Avail.: No specific amount. **To Apply:** Applicant must submit a cover sheet (three pages) and application form (four pages); must have a personal essay; must have a high school and/or post-secondary transcript; must provide a letter of recommendation and a signed copy of the page of their or their parent's most recent tax return that indicates adjusted gross income; and must have a Student Aid Report showing estimated family contribution from FAFSA. Application form and other supporting documents must be sent to Our Community's Foundation, at the above address.

7393 ■ James H. Roberts Athletic Scholarships *(Undergraduate/Scholarship)*

Purpose: To encourage graduating students to continue their education. **Focus:** Athletics; Education, Physical; Sports studies. **Qualif.:** Applicant must be a graduating

Awards are arranged alphabetically below their administering organizations

senior from Wirt County High School; must be planning to attend a four-year program of study at a higher education institution in West Virginia; must be a student athlete; and must have a minimum of 2.0 GPA. **Criteria:** Selection of recipients will be based on commitment to athletics, GPA and test scores.

Funds Avail.: No specific amount. **Duration:** Annual. **To Apply:** Applicant must submit a cover sheet (3 pages) and application form (4 pages); a personal essay; a high school and/or post-secondary transcript; a letter of recommendation; a signed copy of the page of their or their parent's most recent tax return that indicates adjusted gross income; and a Student Aid Report showing estimated family contribution from FAFSA. Application form and other supporting documents must be sent to the Foundation's office. **Deadline:** March 4.

7394 ■ Thomas Warren Roberts Scholarships
(Undergraduate/Scholarship)

Purpose: To encourage graduating students to continue their education. **Focus:** General studies/Field of study not specified. **Qualif.:** Applicant must be a Belpre High School graduating senior. **Criteria:** Selection of recipient will be based on financial need, academic achievement, involvement in school activities and character.

Funds Avail.: No specific amount. **Duration:** Annual. **To Apply:** Applicant must submit a cover sheet (3 pages) and application form (4 pages); a personal essay; a high school and/or post-secondary transcript; a letter of recommendation; a signed copy of the page of their or their parent's most recent tax return that indicates adjusted gross income; and a Student Aid Report showing estimated family contribution from FAFSA. Application form and other supporting documents must be sent to the Foundation's office. **Deadline:** March 4.

7395 ■ James Robinson Memorial Scholarship - Ripley Rotary *(Undergraduate/Scholarship)*

Purpose: To provide support for graduating students intending to pursue their education. **Focus:** General studies/Field of study not specified. **Qualif.:** Applicant must be a Ripley High School, Jackson County, graduating senior pursuing full-time enrollment or person of any age currently enrolled full-time at WVU Parkersburg Jackson County Center with a minimum of 2.0 GPA. **Criteria:** Selection of recipients will be based on financial need and records of community service.

Funds Avail.: No specific amount. **Duration:** Annual. **To Apply:** Applicant must submit a cover sheet (3 pages) and application form (4 pages); a personal essay; a high school and/or post-secondary transcript; a letter of recommendation; a signed copy of the page of their or their parent's most recent tax return that indicates adjusted gross income; and a Student Aid Report showing estimated family contribution from FAFSA. Application form and other supporting documents must be sent to the Foundation's office. **Deadline:** March 4.

7396 ■ Carl Rose Memorial Scholarship Fund
(Undergraduate/Scholarship)

Purpose: To encourage graduating students to pursue their education. **Focus:** Education, Secondary; Mathematics and mathematical sciences; Science. **Qualif.:** Applicant must be a Parkersburg South High School graduating senior; must have a 3.0 GPA; and must be planning to pursue a major in secondary education. **Criteria:** Selection will be based on financial need, personal statement and

academic achievement. Consideration will be given to applicant majoring in math and science secondary education.

Funds Avail.: No specific amount. **Duration:** Annual. **To Apply:** Applicant must submit a cover sheet (3 pages) and application form (4 pages); a personal essay; a high school and/or post-secondary transcript; a letter of recommendation; a signed copy of the page of their parent's most recent tax return that indicates adjusted gross income; and a Student Aid Report showing estimated family contribution from FAFSA. Application form and other supporting documents must be sent at the Foundation's office. **Deadline:** March 4.

7397 ■ S. Byrl Ross Memorial Scholarship Fund
(Undergraduate/Scholarship)

Purpose: To encourage graduating students to pursue their education. **Focus:** Music; Music, Vocal. **Qualif.:** Applicant must be a graduating senior of Wood or Ritchie Counties pursuing a major in music or a music-related field at a post-secondary educational institution. **Criteria:** Scholarship recipients are chosen on the basis of financial need, academic achievement, potential and character.

Funds Avail.: No specific amount. **Duration:** Annual. **To Apply:** Applicant must submit a cover sheet (3 pages) and application form (4 pages); a personal essay; a high school and/or post-secondary transcript; a letter of recommendation; a signed copy of the page of their or their parent's most recent tax return that indicates adjusted gross income; and a Student Aid Report showing estimated family contribution from FAFSA. Application form and other supporting documents must be sent to the Foundation's office. **Deadline:** March 4.

7398 ■ The Viking Voices - Mike Ruben Honorarium and John Rice Memorial Scholarship
(Undergraduate/Scholarship)

Purpose: To encourage graduating students to pursue their education. **Focus:** Athletics. **Qualif.:** Applicant must be a Ripley high school graduating senior. **Criteria:** Preference will be given to deserving students who have demonstrated excellence in academics and athletics.

Funds Avail.: No specific amount. **Duration:** Annual. **To Apply:** Applicant must submit a cover sheet (3 pages) and application form (4 pages); a personal essay; a high school and/or post-secondary transcript; a letter of recommendation; a signed copy of the page of their or their parent's most recent tax return that indicates adjusted gross income; and a Student Aid Report showing estimated family contribution from FAFSA. Application form and other supporting documents must be sent to the Foundation's office. **Deadline:** March 4.

7399 ■ St. Joseph's Hospital School of Nursing Alumnae Scholarship *(Undergraduate/Scholarship)*

Purpose: To encourage graduating students to pursue their education. **Focus:** Nursing. **Qualif.:** Applicant must be a resident of Wood, Ritchie, Wirt, Calhoun, Jackson, Gilmer, Roane, Pleasants, or Doddridge in WV or Washington County, OH; must be planning to attend an accredited college/nursing school to become a RN; must have a financial need and a minimum of 2.0 GPA; must be willing to make a written pledge attesting to their intention to return to the area covered by the service region of the Foundation to practice for at least two years. **Criteria:** Recipient will be selected based on financial need and other scholarship selection criteria.

Funds Avail.: No specific amount. **Duration:** Annual. **To**

Awards are arranged alphabetically below their administering organizations

Apply: Applicant must submit a cover sheet (3 pages) and application form (4 pages); a personal essay; a high school and/or post-secondary transcript; a letter of recommendation; a signed copy of the page of their or their parent's most recent tax return that indicates adjusted gross income; and a Student Aid Report showing estimated family contribution from FAFSA. Application form and other supporting documents must be sent to the Foundation's office. **Deadline:** March 4.

7400 ■ Everett Oscar Shimp Memorial Scholarships
(Undergraduate/Scholarship)

Purpose: To encourage graduating students to pursue their education. **Focus:** Agricultural sciences; Computer and information sciences; Education; History; Life sciences; Mathematics and mathematical sciences; Physical therapy; Science. **Qualif.:** Applicants must be graduates of Jackson or Roane County high schools who are currently enrolled full-time and have completed college credits equivalent to junior or senior status; must have a minimum of 3.0 college GPA; and must be majoring in math, science (biology, zoology, chemistry, geology, forestry), physical therapy, computer science, agriculture, or history or pursuing an education degree majoring in math, science, agriculture, or history. **Criteria:** Applicants will be selected based on the scholarship criteria.

Funds Avail.: No specific amount. **Duration:** Annual. **To Apply:** Applicants must submit a cover sheet (3 pages) and application form (4 pages); a personal essay; a high school and/or post-secondary transcript; a letter of recommendation; a signed copy of the page of their or their parent's most recent tax return that indicates adjusted gross income; and a Student Aid Report showing estimated family contribution from FAFSA. Application form and other supporting documents must be sent to the Foundation's office. **Deadline:** March 4.

7401 ■ Pat Shimp Memorial Scholarships
(Undergraduate/Scholarship)

Purpose: To encourage graduating students to pursue their degree in the business or agriculture field. **Focus:** Agriculture, Economic aspects; Business; Health care services; Nursing. **Qualif.:** Applicant must be a Roane County High School graduating senior pursuing a degree in a business, agriculture, nursing, or a health-care related field with a minimum of 2.0 GPA. **Criteria:** Preference will be given to student with record of community service.

Funds Avail.: No specific amount. **Duration:** Annual. **To Apply:** Applicant must submit a cover sheet (3 pages) and application form (4 pages); a personal essay; a high school and/or post-secondary transcript; a letter of recommendation; a signed copy of the page of their or their parent's most recent tax return that indicates adjusted gross income; and a Student Aid Report showing estimated family contribution from FAFSA. Application form and other supporting documents must be sent to the Foundation's office. **Deadline:** March 4.

7402 ■ Simonton Windows Scholarships
(Undergraduate, Vocational/Occupational/Scholarship)

Purpose: To provide educational assistance to high school graduates or the equivalent who demonstrate academic potential. **Focus:** General studies/Field of study not specified. **Qualif.:** Applicants must be currently enrolled in undergraduate studies; must have graduated from high school or the equivalent and shall desire to attend a post-secondary educational institution, such as a college, university, technical or trade school, vocational school, business school; must have a good academic standing with a minimum 2.5 GPA on a 4.0 scale; and must be dependent children of employees of Simonton Windows or SimEx. **Criteria:** Selection of applicants will be based on financial need, academic achievement, leadership abilities and activities.

Funds Avail.: No specific amount. **To Apply:** Applicants must complete the application form available online; must submit personal essay; high school and/or post-secondary transcript(s); must have copy of the page of their or their parent's most recent tax return that indicates adjusted gross income; copy of the page from their Student Aid Report from FAFSA that shows their Estimated Family Contribution; must have financial aid award letter from their top-choice post-secondary educational institution. Application form and other supporting documents must be sent to Our Community's Foundation, at the above address.

7403 ■ Bill Six Memorial Scholarship Fund
(Undergraduate/Scholarship)

Purpose: To encourage graduating seniors to pursue their education. **Focus:** General studies/Field of study not specified. **Qualif.:** Applicants must be graduating seniors or previous high school graduates who are permanent residents of Vienna, West Virginia; must have at least a 2.0 GPA. **Criteria:** Selection of recipients is based on financial need and potential for successful achievement beyond high school. Preference will be given to the students who appears to be a hard worker and is likely to succeed, yet does not necessarily maintain a superior GPA.

Funds Avail.: No specific amount. **Duration:** Annual. **To Apply:** Applicants must submit a cover sheet (3 pages) and application form (4 pages); a personal essay; a high school and/or post-secondary transcript; a letter of recommendation; a signed copy of the page of their or their parent's most recent tax return that indicates adjusted gross income; and a Student Aid Report showing estimated family contribution from FAFSA. Application form and other supporting documents must be sent to the Foundation's office. **Deadline:** March 4.

7404 ■ Mary K. Smith Rector Scholarships
(Undergraduate/Scholarship)

Purpose: To encourage graduating seniors to pursue their education. **Focus:** Education, Vocational-technical. **Qualif.:** Applicants must be graduating seniors from Gilmer County High School; must be planning to attend an accredited college or university in West Virginia or pursue a vocational training; must have a minimum of 2.5 GPA. **Criteria:** Selection of recipients will be based on academic achievement and financial need.

Funds Avail.: No specific amount. **Duration:** Annual. **To Apply:** Applicants must submit the cover sheet (three pages) and application form (four pages); must have personal essay; high school and/or post-secondary transcripts; must provide a letter of recommendation; copy of the page of their or their parent's most recent tax return that indicates adjusted gross income; and Student Aid Report showing estimated family contribution from FAFSA. Application form and other supporting documents must be sent at the Foundation's office. **Deadline:** March 4.

7405 ■ C.R. Thomas Scholarships *(Undergraduate/Scholarship)*

Purpose: To encourage graduating students to pursue their education. **Focus:** General studies/Field of study not speci-

Awards are arranged alphabetically below their administering organizations

fied. **Qualif.:** Applicant must be a graduating senior of Parkersburg High School and must be willing to help the community and others. **Criteria:** Recipient will be selected based on financial need and application materials.

Funds Avail.: No specific amount. **Duration:** Annual. **To Apply:** Applicant must submit a cover sheet (3 pages) and application form (4 pages); a personal essay; a high school and/or post-secondary transcript; a letter of recommendation; a signed copy of the page of parent's most recent tax return that indicates adjusted gross income; and a Student Aid Report showing estimated family contribution from FAFSA. Application form and other supporting documents must be sent to the Foundation's office. **Deadline:** March 4.

7406 ■ Charles A. Townsend Scholarships
(Undergraduate/Scholarship)

Purpose: To encourage graduating students to pursue their career as education professionals. **Focus:** Education. **Qualif.:** Applicant must be a graduating senior of Wood County schools planning to attend an accredited post-secondary school; must be interested in pursuing a career as an education professional; and must be pursuing a degree at St. John's College in Annapolis, MD, or Santa Fe, NM. **Criteria:** Selection of recipients will be based on financial need, achievement and character.

Funds Avail.: No specific amount. **Duration:** Annual. **To Apply:** Applicant must submit a cover sheet (3 pages) and application form (4 pages); a personal essay; a high school and/or post-secondary transcript; a letter of recommendation; a signed copy of the page of their or their parent's most recent tax return that indicates adjusted gross income; and a Student Aid Report showing estimated family contribution from FAFSA. Application form and other supporting documents must be sent to the Foundation's office. **Deadline:** March 4.

7407 ■ Wayne-Meador-Elliott Scholarships
(Undergraduate/Scholarship)

Purpose: To encourage graduating seniors of Ritchie County High School to pursue their education. **Focus:** Education; Engineering, Petroleum; Geology; Music. **Qualif.:** Applicant must be a Ritchie County High School graduating senior; must be enrolled as a fulltime student to attend an accredited four-year college or university; and must have a minimum of 3.0 GPA. **Criteria:** Preference will be given to students planning to major in the field of education administration, music, geology/ petroleum engineering or education. Selection of recipients will be based on ability to overcome obstacles, strong work ethic, interest in community service, leadership ability and financial need.

Funds Avail.: No specific amount. **Duration:** Annual. **To Apply:** Applicant must submit a cover sheet (3 pages) and application form (4 pages); a personal essay; a high school and/or post-secondary transcript; a letter of recommendation; a signed copy of the page of their or their parent's most recent tax return that indicates adjusted gross income; and a Student Aid Report showing estimated family contribution from FAFSA. Application form and other supporting documents must be sent to the Foundation's office. **Deadline:** March 4.

7408 ■ West Virginia Nurses Association District No. 3 Scholarships *(Undergraduate/Scholarship)*

Purpose: To provide support for qualified individuals intending to pursue their nursing degree. **Focus:** Nursing. **Qualif.:** Applicants must reside in Wood, Wirt, Calhoun, Jackson, or Roane Counties and must be pursuing an associate nursing degree as full-time students. **Criteria:** Selection of recipients will be based on merit.

Funds Avail.: No specific amount. **Duration:** Annual. **To Apply:** Applicants must submit a cover sheet (3 pages) and application form (4 pages); a personal essay; a high school and/or post-secondary transcript; a letter of recommendation; a signed copy of the page of their or their parent's most recent tax return that indicates adjusted gross income; and a Student Aid Report showing estimated family contribution from FAFSA. Application form and other supporting documents must be sent to the Foundation's office. **Deadline:** March 4.

7409 ■ Whitaker-Minard Memorial Scholarships
(Undergraduate/Scholarship)

Purpose: To encourage graduating seniors to pursue their degrees in any field specializing in services for individuals with disabilities. **Focus:** Disabilities. **Qualif.:** Applicants must be graduating high school seniors admitted to attend college, or currently enrolled college students; must be pursuing associate or bachelor level degrees in any field specializing in services for individuals with disabilities; must have minimum of 2.5 GPA; must be residents of Wood, Pleasants, Ritchie, Wirt, Gilmer, Calhoun, Jackson, Roane or Tyler Counties, West Virginia or Washington County, Ohio. **Criteria:** Preference will be given to applicants who show willingness to volunteer/participate or has previously volunteered/participated in one of Wood County Society's programs within or the following year after the scholarship is received.

Funds Avail.: No specific amount. **To Apply:** Applicants must submit the cover sheet (three pages) and application form (four pages); must have a personal essay; must have a high school and/or post-secondary transcripts; must provide a letter of recommendation and a signed copy of the page of their or their parent's most recent tax return that indicates adjusted gross income; and must have a Student Aid Report showing estimated family contribution from FAFSA. Application form and other supporting documents must be sent to Our Community's Foundation, at the above address.

7410 ■ S. William and Martha R. Goff Educational Scholarships *(Undergraduate/Scholarship)*

Purpose: To encourage individuals to pursue their career in medical school. **Focus:** Education, Medical. **Qualif.:** Applicants must have attended high school in Wood County and must be entering or currently in medical school. **Criteria:** Selection of applicants will be based on merit and need.

Funds Avail.: No specific amount. **To Apply:** Applicants must submit a cover sheet (three pages) and application form (four pages); must have a personal essay; must have a high school and/or post-secondary transcript; must provide a letter of recommendation and a signed copy of the page of their or their parent's most recent tax return that indicates adjusted gross income; and must have a Student Aid Report showing estimated family contribution from FAFSA. Application form and other supporting documents must be sent to Our Community's Foundation at the above address.

7411 ■ Glenn Wilson Broadcast Journalism Scholarships *(Undergraduate/Scholarship)*

Purpose: To provide financial support for qualified individuals intending to pursue their education. **Focus:** Broadcasting; Communications; Journalism; Marketing and distribu-

Awards are arranged alphabetically below their administering organizations

tion. **Qualif.:** Applicants must be current or previous Wood or Pleasant County, WV, or Washington County, OH, high school students; must be studying broadcast journalism, journalism, communications or marketing; and must have a minimum 2.5 GPA. **Criteria:** Preference will be given to students whose main interest is broadcast journalism as demonstrated by candidate's school activities or through study of this field.

Funds Avail.: No specific amount. **Duration:** Annual. **To Apply:** Applicants must submit a cover sheet (3 pages) and application form (4 pages); a personal essay; a high school and/or post- secondary transcript; a letter of recommendation; a signed copy of the page of their or their parent's most recent tax return that indicates adjusted gross income; and a Student Aid Report showing estimated family contribution from FAFSA. Application form and other supporting documents must be sent to the Foundation's office. **Deadline:** March 4.

7412 ■ Wood County Bar Association Memorial Scholarships (Undergraduate/Scholarship)

Purpose: To provide financial assistance for qualified individuals intending to pursue their law degree. **Focus:** Law. **Qualif.:** Applicant must be a student attending an accredited law school in the United States and must have certain minimal contacts with Wood, Jackson, Ritchie, Wirt, or Pleasant Counties in West Virginia. **Criteria:** Selection of recipients will be based on scholarship selection criteria.

Funds Avail.: No specific amount. **To Apply:** Applicant must submit a cover sheet (three pages) and application form (four pages); a personal essay; a high school and/or post-secondary transcript; a letter of recommendation; a signed copy of the page of their or their parent's most recent tax return that indicates adjusted gross income; and a Student Aid Report showing estimated family contribution from FAFSA. Application form and other supporting documents must be sent to Our Community's Foundation, at the above address.

7413 ■ Parkinson's Disease Foundation (PDF)

1359 Broadway, Ste. 1509
New York, NY 10018
Ph: (212)923-4700
Fax: (212)923-4778
E-mail: info@pdf.org
URL: www.pdf.org

7414 ■ Clinician Scientist Development Awards (Postgraduate/Fellowship)

Purpose: To provide financial assistance to support three years of research training in an environment where talented young clinicians address problems in Parkinson's Disease with the most current scientific tools. **Focus:** Parkinson's disease. **Qualif.:** Applicants must hold an MD, DO, or equivalent clinical degree from an accredited institution; must have completed residency training but be less than seven years from completion of residency when funding begins; and must be neurologists interested in clinical research. **Criteria:** Applicants will be evaluated by the embers of the Clinical Research Subcommittee, Translational Neuroscience Subcommittee, and various ad-hoc reviewers based on the following criteria: ability and promise as a clinician-scientist based on previous training and career plan, letters of reference and curriculum vitae; quality and nature of the training to be provided and the institutional, departmental and mentor-specific training

environment; quality and originality of the research plan.

Funds Avail.: $80,000. **Duration:** Three years. **To Apply:** Applicants must submit a letter of nomination; letter of intent to pursue a three-year program indicating the specific clinical focus, the proposed institution and preceptor and future goals; three-page research plan, including brief statements of aims, background and the contemplated approaches to methodology and data; copy of current curriculum vitae; two letters of reference supporting his/her potential for a clinical, academic research career and qualifications for the fellowship; listing of the applicants' and mentor's current and pending support, other than this award, using NIH format; letter from the proposed mentor detailing his/her support of and commitment to the applicant and the proposed research and training plan, specifically indicating the mentor's role in the development and preparation of the applicants' research plan. The letter should describe: how the proposed research fits into the mentor's research program: expertise and experience in the area of research proposed and the nature of the mentor's proposed time commitment to the supervision and training of the applicant: and the mentor's prior experience in the supervision, training and successful mentoring of clinician scientists; copy of mentor's NIH biosketch; document describing arrangements for formal course work to include: quantitative clinical epidemiology, biostatistics, study design, data analysis and ethics. The documentation must outline: hours and content of the proposed formal instruction; availability of tutorial assistance for the research project; and computer approaches to statistical analysis at the host institution; document describing the level of interaction between the applicants and subjects in their research project. **Deadline:** October 1.

7415 ■ Parkinson's Disease Foundation International Research Grants Program (Postdoctorate/Grant)

Purpose: To provide financial assistance for projects of the highest scientific caliber from around the world; to promote innovative research with high potential to advance the knowledge of Parkinson's disease. **Focus:** Parkinson's disease. **Qualif.:** Applicants must have completed a PhD or MD and qualified to serve as a principal investigator for the project which is basic, translational and clinical research. **Criteria:** Applicant's proposal will be peer-reviewed and competitively evaluated based on the quality of the research proposal and its pertinence to Parkinson's disease. Preference will be given to those applicants who are at any early stage of their professional careers.

Funds Avail.: $75,000. **Duration:** Two years. **To Apply:** Applicants must submit the application package which includes: the completed PDF application form, including the signature of the applicant and the relevant institutional authority; letter of recommendation consisting the background of proposed study, specific aims, details of proposed experiment including methods, statement describing relevance of proposed studies, budget and justification, curriculum vitae and references. **Deadline:** February 1. **Contact:** grants@pdf.org.

7416 ■ PDF-PSG Mentored Clinical Research Awards (Professional development, Advanced Professional/Award)

Purpose: To provide funding for an investigator who has the potential to become an independent researcher. **Focus:** Parkinson's disease. **Qualif.:** Applicants must be clinicians and scientists who are within five years of having completed

Awards are arranged alphabetically below their administering organizations

formal training. Applicants must identify an apporiate mentor or mentors with extensive research experience. Either applicants or mentors must be members of the PSG. Applicants may have co-mentors. **Criteria:** Selection will be based on the committee's criteria.

Funds Avail.: $50,000. **Duration:** Annual. **To Apply:** All applications must include the following elements: a research proposal including an abstract, specific aims, background and significance, preliminary studies and experimental designs and methods; a clear description of the educational plan that will be implemented to educate the candidate in development of appropriate research methodology under the direction of the mentor; a statement of the qualification of the mentor(s) to guide the research program. The focus of the proposal must relate to an area of importance in the field. The research plan should address unmet needs of people living with PD, have the potential for broad application among the PD community, and lead to advances in clinically relevant treatment option. Proposals must met the following requirements: must be in Microsoft Word or PDF format; candidates' proposal should be formatted according to the guidelines indicated on the PSG website; the research plan itself should not exceed five pages and should also include a four-page NIH-style biosketch and other support statement for both the applicants and the mentor(s); the proposal should include a statement from the mentor(s) including information on research qualifications. The statement should include the nature of the supervision that will occur during the award period and an agreement to provide mentorship to the candidates for the award period. The mentor must include information on what skill they plan to teach the mentee and how previous fellows are contributing to Parkinson's research; a budget and brief budget justification; the funding request; clinical research proposals should include a Human Studies section that addresses concerns pertaining to risk, benefit and consent; revised applications should include an introduction of not more than one page that describes how the applicants responded to the reviewers' criticisms. **Deadline:** January 3.

7417 ■ PDF Student Travel Award (Graduate, Undergraduate/Scholarship)

Purpose: To enable eligible students working in Parkinson's disease research to attend and present data at relevant scientific conferences. **Focus:** Education. **Qualif.:** Applicants must be graduates and medical students conducting Parkinson's disease research. **Criteria:** Applications are judged based on the appropriateness of the conference, the applicants' financial and academic needs, and the abstract that will be presented at the conference.

Funds Avail.: $1,000. **Duration:** Annual. **To Apply:** Application form can be obtained at the website. All applications must be submitted online through the Foundation's website at grants.pdf.org. A complete application must be consist of the following items: application form; copy of the abstract submitted to the conference; confirmation of abstract acceptance or abstract submission pending acceptance; statement by the applicants, justifying meeting attendance and potential impact on future research and career; statement by the applicants, describing interest in Parkinson's research, their qualifications and the relevance of this meeting to their career/research interests; letter of support, written by the mentor under whose guidance the applicants completed the research to be presented at the conference. The letter should discuss the qualifications of the students, as well as the academic and financial need for attendance. The letter must be sent separately by the mentor via email with "STUDENT TRAVEL AWARD" in the subject line; travel budget, including any funds to be provided by applicants' home institution. **Deadline:** June 15.

7418 ■ PDF Summer Student Fellowships (Undergraduate, Graduate/Fellowship)

Purpose: To cultivate an early interest in Fellows into the cause and possible treatments for Parkinson's desease. **Focus:** Parkinson's disease. **Qualif.:** Applicants must be undergraduates and medical students. Graduate students who are already conducting research may also apply if they can demonstrate financial need. Applicants must identify a mentor with whom they will conduct the proposed project. **Criteria:** Selection will be based on the committee's criteria.

Funds Avail.: $4,000. **Duration:** Up to 10 weeks. **To Apply:** Application form can be obtained at the website. All applications must be submitted online through the PDF website at grants.pdf.org. A complete application must consist of the following items: application form; brief, two-page proposal describing the research plan and must be written in conjunction with mentor; copy of students' academic transcript; statement by the applicants, describing why they are interested in conducting Parkinson's research, their qualifications and the relevance of this research to their career/research interests; letter of support, written by the mentor under whom the applicants plans to work, discussing qualifications of the students, affirming that facilities and materials will be available and agreeing to actively guide the students' work. This letter must be sent separately by the mentor either via email with "SUMMER FELLOWSHIP" in the subject line. Graduate students should email their eligibility before applying. **Deadline:** January 27.

7419 ■ Postdoctoral Fellowships for Clinical Neurologists (Postdoctorate/Fellowship)

Purpose: To provide financial assistance for young clinicians who have completed their neurology residency and are seeking clinical research experience. **Focus:** Neurology. **Qualif.:** Applicants must possess a M.D. or equivalent and be within three years of having completed a residency in neurology. Applicants may not have their own lab and must identify an individual who will serve as their mentor and supervisor of their research. This program is open to both national and international applicants. **Criteria:** All proposals are peer-reviewed based upon scientific merit and its impact upon Parkinson's disease.

Funds Avail.: $55,000 plus a $5,000 research allowance. **Duration:** Annual. **To Apply:** All applicants must first submit their letter of intent, and if selected by the reviewers, they will be notified by email and may proceed to the next step; applicants must submit their full proposal with maximum of seven pages using the format given on the website. **Deadline:** February 16. **Contact:** Please contact PDF at grants@pdf.org.

7420 ■ Partnership for Public Service (PPS)
1100 New York Ave. NW, Ste. 200 E
Washington, DC 20005
Ph: (202)775-9111
Fax: (202)775-8885
URL: ourpublicservice.org

Awards are arranged alphabetically below their administering organizations

7421 ■ Public Service Fellows Internship Program - Center for Government Leadership (Undergraduate, Graduate/Internship)

Purpose: To allow individuals to contribute to the Partnership's mission of revitalizing federal government by transforming the way government works and inspiring a new generation to serve while developing valuable professional skills. **Focus:** General studies/Field of study not specified. **Qualif.:** Applicants must be undergraduate, graduate and recent graduate students; must be willing to relocate to Washington, D.C. for the duration of the term. **Criteria:** Selection will be based on the following requirements: strong communication, customer service, writing and organizational skills, as well as an ability to adapt and collaborate.

Funds Avail.: $1,000 per month (for full-time fellows with an undergraduate or graduate degree); $800 (for those who are currently undergraduate students). **To Apply:** Applicants may contact the Partnership for Public Service for the available positions and for the application process. **Deadline:** February 27 (summer application); July 10 (fall application); October 24 (spring application). **Contact:** Mollie Allers, Christina Francisco, and Patrick Moniz, Program Coordinators; Phone: (202) 775-9111; Email: fellows@ourpublicservice.org.

7422 ■ Public Service Fellows Internship Program - Communications (Undergraduate, Graduate, Professional development/Internship)

Purpose: To allow individuals to contribute to the Partnership's mission of revitalizing federal government by transforming the way government works and inspiring a new generation to serve while developing valuable professional skills. **Focus:** General studies/Field of study not specified. **Qualif.:** Applicants must be undergraduate, graduate and recent graduate students; must be willing to relocate to Washington, D.C. for the duration of the term. **Criteria:** Selection will be based on the committee's criteria. Ideal applicants are outgoing, detail-oriented, team players and have excellent writing, organization and public speaking skills.

Funds Avail.: $1,000 per month (for full-time fellows with an undergraduate or graduate degree); $800 (for those who are currently undergraduate students). **To Apply:** Applicants may contact the Partnership for Public Service for the available positions and for the application process. **Deadline:** February 27 (summer application); July 10 (fall application); October 24 (spring application). **Contact:** Mollie Allers, Christina Francisco, and Patrick Moniz, Program Coordinators; Phone: (202) 775-9111; Email: fellows@ourpublicservice.org.

7423 ■ Public Service Fellows Internship Program - Development (Undergraduate, Graduate, Professional development/Internship)

Purpose: To allow individuals to contribute to the Partnership's mission of revitalizing federal government by transforming the way government works and inspiring a new generation to serve while developing valuable professional skills. **Focus:** General studies/Field of study not specified. **Qualif.:** Applicants must be undergraduate, graduate and recent graduate students; must be willing to relocate to Washington, D.C. for the duration of the term. **Criteria:** Selection will be based on the committee's criteria. Ideal applicants must also have exceptional written and spoken communication skills which are essential.

Funds Avail.: $1,000 per month (for full-time fellows with

an undergraduate or graduate degree); $800 (for those who are currently undergraduate students). **To Apply:** Applicants may contact the Partnership for Public Service for the available positions and for the application process. **Deadline:** February 27 (summer application); July 10 (fall application); October 24 (spring application). **Contact:** Mollie Allers, Christina Francisco, and Patrick Moniz, Program Coordinators; Phone: (202) 775-9111; Email: fellows@ourpublicservice.org.

7424 ■ Public Service Fellows Internship Program - Education and Outreach (Undergraduate, Graduate, Professional development/Internship)

Purpose: To allow individuals to contribute to the Partnership's mission of revitalizing federal government by transforming the way government works and inspiring a new generation to serve while developing valuable professional skills. **Focus:** General studies/Field of study not specified. **Qualif.:** Applicants must be undergraduate, graduate and recent graduate students; must be willing to relocate to Washington, D.C. for the duration of the term. **Criteria:** Selection will be based on the committee's criteria. Ideal applicants must possess outstanding written and verbal communication skills, strong attention to detail and excellent time-management abilities.

Funds Avail.: $1,000 per month (for full-time fellows with an undergraduate or graduate degree); $800 (for those who are currently undergraduate students). **To Apply:** Applicants may contact the Partnership for Public Service for the available positions and for the application process. **Deadline:** February 27 (summer application); July 10 (fall application); October 24 (spring application). **Contact:** Mollie Allers, Christina Francisco, and Patrick Moniz, Program Coordinators; Phone: (202) 775-9111; Email: fellows@ourpublicservice.org.

7425 ■ Public Service Fellows Internship Program - Government Affairs (Undergraduate, Graduate, Professional development/Internship)

Purpose: To allow individuals to contribute to the Partnership's mission of revitalizing federal government by transforming the way government works and inspiring a new generation to serve while developing valuable professional skills. **Focus:** General studies/Field of study not specified. **Qualif.:** Applicants must be undergraduate, graduate and recent graduate students; must be willing to relocate to Washington, D.C. for the duration of the term. **Criteria:** Selection will be based on the committee's criteria.

Funds Avail.: $1,000 per month (for full-time fellows with an undergraduate or graduate degree); $800 (for those who are currently undergraduate students). **To Apply:** Applicants may contact the Partnership for Public Service for the available positions and for the application process. **Deadline:** February 27 (summer application); July 10 (fall application); October 24 (spring application). **Contact:** Mollie Allers, Christina Francisco, and Patrick Moniz, Program Coordinators; Phone: (202) 775-9111; Email: fellows@ourpublicservice.org.

7426 ■ Public Service Fellows Internship Program - Government Transformation and Agency Partnerships (Undergraduate, Graduate, Professional development/Internship)

Purpose: To allow individuals to contribute to the Partnership's mission of revitalizing federal government by transforming the way government works and inspiring a new generation to serve while developing valuable profes-

Awards are arranged alphabetically below their administering organizations

sional skills. **Focus:** General studies/Field of study not specified. **Qualif.:** Applicants must be undergraduate, graduate and recent graduate students; must be willing to relocate to Washington, D.C. for the duration of the term. **Criteria:** Selection will be based on the committee's criteria.

Funds Avail.: $1,000 per month (for full-time fellows with an undergraduate or graduate degree); $800 (for those who are currently undergraduate students). **To Apply:** Applicants may contact the Partnership for Public Service for the available positions and for the application process. **Deadline:** February 27 (summer application); July 10 (fall application); October 24 (spring application). **Contact:** Mollie Allers, Christina Francisco, and Patrick Moniz, Program Coordinators; Phone: (202) 775-9111; Email: fellows@ourpublicservice.org.

7427 ■ Public Service Fellows Internship Program - Human Resources *(Undergraduate, Graduate, Professional development/Internship)*

Purpose: To allow individuals to contribute to the Partnership's mission of revitalizing federal government by transforming the way government works and inspiring a new generation to serve while developing valuable professional skills. **Focus:** General studies/Field of study not specified. **Qualif.:** Applicants must be undergraduate, graduate or recent graduate students; must be willing to relocate to Washington, D.C. for the duration of the term; must be able to work independently and in a team setting; and must show a demonstrated ability to handle confidential information with discretion and professionalism. **Criteria:** Selection will be based on the committee's criteria. Applicants who are working toward a degree in human resources or a closely related field will be preferred.

Funds Avail.: $1,000 per month (for full-time fellows with an undergraduate or graduate degree); $800 (for those who are currently undergraduate students). **To Apply:** Applicants may contact the Partnership for Public Service for the available positions and for the application process. **Deadline:** February 27 (summer application); July 10 (fall application); October 24 (spring application). **Contact:** Mollie Allers, Christina Francisco, and Patrick Moniz, Program Coordinators; Phone: (202) 775-9111; Email: fellows@ourpublicservice.org.

7428 ■ Public Service Fellows Internship Program - Research *(Undergraduate, Graduate, Professional development/Internship)*

Purpose: To allow individuals to contribute to the Partnership's mission of revitalizing federal government by transforming the way government works and inspiring a new generation to serve while developing valuable professional skills. **Focus:** General studies/Field of study not specified. **Qualif.:** Applicants must be undergraduate, graduate and recent graduate students; must be willing to relocate to Washington, D.C. for the duration of the term. **Criteria:** Selection will be based on the committee's criteria. Preference will be given to those with social science research experiences. Excel and/or SPSS skills will also be considered.

Funds Avail.: $1,000 per month (for full-time fellows with an undergraduate or graduate degree); $800 (for those who are currently undergraduate students). **To Apply:** Applicants may contact the Partnership for Public Service for the available positions and for the application process. **Deadline:** February 27 (summer application); July 10 (fall application); October 24 (spring application). **Contact:** Mollie Allers, Christina Francisco, and Patrick Moniz, Program

Coordinators; Phone: (202) 775-9111; Email: fellows@ourpublicservice.org.

7429 ■ Pasteur Foundation
420 Lexington Ave., Ste. 1654
New York, NY 10170
Ph: (212)599-2050
Fax: (212)599-2047
E-mail: director@pasteurfoundation.org
URL: www.pasteurfoundation.org

7430 ■ Pasteur Foundation Postdoctoral Fellowships *(Postdoctorate/Fellowship)*

Purpose: To support postdoctoral researchers who wants to work in Pasteur laboratories in Paris. **Focus:** General studies/Field of study not specified. **Qualif.:** Applicants must be post-doctoral researchers who are US citizens not currently in France wishing to work in the laboratories of the Institut Pasteur. **Criteria:** Selection will be based on the committee's criteria.

Funds Avail.: 3,750 Euros per month. **Duration:** Annual; 3 years. **To Apply:** Applicants must submit the following in English: letter of introduction of the candidate by the head of the sponsoring laboratory or unit at the Institut Pasteur; sponsoring lab's organizational chart of all current personnel; candidate's Curriculum Vitae (2 pages maximum) including an ID photo. Curriculum Vitae should list source and duration of all current grants and/or funding; list of candidate's publications; a synopsis of candidate's scientific accomplishments (3 pages maximum, Arial 12 point); a brief description of candidate's research project (3 pages maximum, Arial 12 point) emphasizing how it fits into the host laboratory's work-in-progress. The project must be described in the context of international competition in the field and should indicate goals, experiment strategies, feasibility, plus three key bibliographic references; a summary of the research project (title + 15 to 20 line description + 5 key words); reprints of candidate's most significant articles; two letters of recommendation from recognized scientists who have personal knowledge of candidate's scientific qualifications are to be sent directly via email. **Deadline:** September 10. **Contact:** Pasteur Foundation New York; E-mail: director@pasteurfoundation.org.

7431 ■ PATCH
560 N Nimitz Hwy., Ste. 218
Honolulu, HI 96817
Ph: (808)839-1988
Fax: (808)839-1799
E-mail: patch@patchhawaii.org
URL: www.patchhawaii.org

7432 ■ PATCH Early Childhood Education Scholarships *(Other/Scholarship)*

Purpose: To support the quality of care for young people who are entering into the early care and education profession. **Focus:** General studies/Field of study not specified. **Qualif.:** Applicants must have passed college level courses in early childhood, conversion of PACE classes to college credits or award of a CDA Credential. **Criteria:** Selection will be based on the committee's criteria.

Funds Avail.: $750. **To Apply:** Applicants must submit completed application with supporting documentation for Reimbursement and Need-Based Scholarships. **Deadline:**

Awards are arranged alphabetically below their administering organizations

August 31; January 15; May 31. **Contact:** PATCH at the above address, or Email: patch@patch-hi.org.

7433 ■ Patterson, Belknap, Webb and Tyler L.L.P.

1133 Avenue of the Americas
New York, NY 10036-6710
Ph: (212)336-2000
Fax: (212)336-2222
URL: www.pbwt.com

7434 ■ Patterson Belknap Webb & Tyler LLP Diversity Fellowships *(Doctorate/Fellowship)*

Purpose: To help students continue their doctoral degree at an ABA accredited law school. **Focus:** Law. **Qualif.:** Applicants must be rising second year students who show the promise of becoming attorneys and contributing to the diversity of Patterson Belknap and the legal community; must be in good standing pursuing a Juris Doctor at an ABA accredited law school. **Criteria:** Recipients will be selected based on demonstrated academic excellence and leadership abilities, personal and professional accomplishments, and commitment to community service.

Funds Avail.: $15,000. **To Apply:** Applicants must complete the application form; must submit their first-year law school transcript.

7435 ■ Pauahi Foundation

567 S King St., Ste. 160
Honolulu, HI 96813-3036
Ph: (808)534-3966
URL: www.pauahi.org

7436 ■ Bruce T. and Jackie Mahi Erickson Grant *(Graduate, Undergraduate/Grant)*

Purpose: To support the educational needs and goals of people of Hawaiian ancestry. **Focus:** Arts; Crafts; Photography. **Qualif.:** Applicants must be undergraduate or graduate students pursuing studies in the creation of crafts, art and photography and/or independent research relating to historical Hawaiian crafts and arts. Students must be in good academic standing, demonstrate financial need and be pursuing a post-high degree consistent with the purpose of the scholarship. **Criteria:** Selection will be based on the committee's criteria.

Funds Avail.: $950. **Duration:** Annual. **Number Awarded:** 1. **To Apply:** Applicant must submit a College Acceptance Letter if attending a college or university for the first time, or currently enrolled college student changing schools or degree programs; official transcript of grades; and student aid report (SAR). In addition, applicants must also submit two letters of recommendation from a teacher or counselor or other knowledgeable person in Hawaiian arts, crafts, and photography; and one letter of recommendation from an unrelated person that can vouch for the student's character and the likelihood of completing their course of study.

7437 ■ Goldman Sachs/Matsuo Takabuki Commemorative Scholarships *(Graduate/Scholarship)*

Purpose: To support the educational needs and goals of people of Hawaiian ancestry. **Focus:** Business. **Qualif.:** Applicants must be students pursuing graduate degrees in business or financial services related fields; must be resident of Hawaii. **Criteria:** Preference given to those demonstrating financial need.

Funds Avail.: $15,000. **Duration:** Annual. **Number Awarded:** Varies. **To Apply:** Applicant must submit a College Acceptance Letter if attending a college or university for the first time, or currently enrolled college student changing schools or degree programs; official transcript of grades; and student aid report (SAR).

7438 ■ Isaac and Mary Harbottle Scholarships *(Graduate, Undergraduate/Scholarship)*

Purpose: To support the educational needs and goals of people who wants to enrich the learning in areas of education, community organization, and/or spiritual growth. **Focus:** General studies/Field of study not specified. **Qualif.:** Applicants must be undergraduate or graduate students in the areas of education, community organization, and/or spiritual growth. Students are challenged to create and sustain healthy communities, increase healthy relationships in the community, and keep the native Hawaiian culture and the legacy of Isaac Hakuole and Mary Kaimookalani Kamaolipua Okuu Piikoi Harbottle alive. **Criteria:** Selection will be based on the committee's criteria.

Funds Avail.: $800. **Duration:** Annual. **Number Awarded:** 1. **To Apply:** Applicant must submit a College Acceptance Letter; official transcript of grades; and student aid report (SAR).

7439 ■ Daniel Kahikina and Millie Akaka Scholarships *(Graduate, Undergraduate/Scholarship)*

Purpose: To support the educational needs and goals of people of Hawaiian ancestry. **Focus:** General studies/Field of study not specified. **Qualif.:** Applicants must be undergraduate or graduate students that demonstrate a financial need and have a GPA of 3.2 or higher. Recipients are strongly encouraged to provide a minimum of 10 hours of community service to the Council for Native Hawaiian Advancement. **Criteria:** Selection will be based on the committee's criteria.

Funds Avail.: $2,000. **Duration:** Annual. **Number Awarded:** 1. **To Apply:** Applicant must submit a College Acceptance Letter if attending a college or university for the first time, or currently enrolled college student changing schools or degree program; official transcript of grades; and student aid report (SAR). In addition, two letters of recommendation from the school, employer or community organization must be submitted.

7440 ■ Gladys Kamakakūokalani 'Ainoa Brandt Scholarships *(Graduate, Undergraduate/Scholarship)*

Purpose: To support the educational needs and goals of people of Hawaiian ancestry. **Focus:** General studies/Field of study not specified. **Qualif.:** Applicants must be full-time junior, senior or graduate students at an accredited university aspiring to enter the educational profession; must demonstrate financial need; must have a GPA of 2.5 or higher. **Criteria:** Priority will be given to current or former residents of Kaua'i.

Funds Avail.: $2,750. **Duration:** Annual. **Number Awarded:** 4. **To Apply:** Applicant must submit a College Acceptance Letter if attending a college or university for the first time, or currently enrolled college student changing schools or degree programs; official transcript of grades; and student aid report (SAR). Applicants must also submit two letters of recommendation from a teacher or counselor or community organization.

Awards are arranged alphabetically below their administering organizations

7441 ■ Kamehameha Schools Class of 1968 "Ka Poli O Kaiona" Scholarships *(Graduate, Undergraduate/Scholarship)*

Purpose: To support the educational needs and goals of people of Hawaiian ancestry. **Focus:** General studies/Field of study not specified. **Qualif.:** Applicants must be pursuing a two-year, four-year or graduate degree from an accredited post-high institution; must possess a minimum 2.8 GPA and demonstrate a financial need. **Criteria:** Preference will be given to family members (as defined) of KS Class of 1968 graduates.

Funds Avail.: $750. **Duration:** Annual. **Number Awarded:** 2. **To Apply:** Applicant must submit two letters of recommendation from school, employer or community organization; submit essay on how this award would support and extend the legacy of Ke Ali'i Bernice Pauahi Bishop; and student Aid Report (SAR) from the Free Application for Federal Student Aid (FAFSA). **Remarks:** Established in 1968.

7442 ■ Kamehameha Schools Class of 1972 Scholarships *(Graduate, Undergraduate/Scholarship)*

Purpose: To support the educational needs and goals of people of Hawaiian ancestry. **Focus:** General studies/Field of study not specified. **Qualif.:** The first priority, applicants must be classmates of Kamehameha Schools (KS) Class of 1972 to earn a college degree: undergraduate, graduate, or doctoral; second priority, must be children and grandchildren of KS Class of 1972 graduates with a minimum GPA of 2.8; third priority, must be individuals whose lives have been impacted, and maybe traumatized, by challenging circumstances (death of a significant family member; domestics violence; sexual abuse; poverty; major health problems, etc.) but who, because of their motivation, have the potential to be successfully enriched by an educational opportunity. **Criteria:** Selection will be based on the committee's criteria.

Funds Avail.: $600. **Duration:** Annual. **Number Awarded:** 2. **To Apply:** Applicant must submit a College Acceptance Letter if attending a college or university for the first time, or currently enrolled college student changing schools or degree programs; official transcript of grades; and student aid report (SAR). Applicants who wish to be considered in the third priority group should also submit one letter of recommendation from a social service agency or counselor citing the applicant's challenging and extraordinary life circumstances and how they would benefit from this scholarship.

7443 ■ Dan and Rachel Mahi Educational Scholarships *(Graduate, Undergraduate/Scholarship)*

Purpose: To support the educational needs and goals of people of Hawaiian ancestry. **Focus:** General studies/Field of study not specified. **Qualif.:** Applicants must be undergraduate or graduate students that demonstrate a financial need and have a cumulative GPA of 2.0 or higher. **Criteria:** Selection will be based on the committee's criteria.

Funds Avail.: $1,300. **Duration:** Annual. **Number Awarded:** 1. **To Apply:** Applicant must submit two letters of recommendation; one from a teacher or counselor and one from an employer or community organization who can comment on your overall character, achievement and contribution to serve the greater community; Student Aid Report (SAR) from the Free Application for Federal Student Aid (FAFSA).

7444 ■ George Hi'ilani Mills Perpetual Fellowships *(Graduate/Fellowship)*

Purpose: To support the educational needs and goals of people of Hawaiian ancestry. **Focus:** Health sciences. **Qualif.:** Applicants must be graduate students pursuing professional studies in the field of medicine or the allied health-related fields. Applicants must also demonstrate financial need. **Criteria:** Selection will be based on the committee's criteria.

Funds Avail.: $1,000. **Duration:** Annual. **Number Awarded:** 5. **To Apply:** Applicant must submit a College Acceptance Letter if attending a college or university for the first time, or currently enrolled college student changing schools or degree programs; official transcript of grades; and student aid report (SAR). Applicants must also submit a one-page essay demonstrating their balance record of achievement as well as holding the value and tradition of the Hawaiian Civic club movement to perpetuate and preserve language, history, music, dance, and other cultural traditions as well as advocate for improve welfare of native Hawaiians in culture, health, economic development, education, social welfare and nationhood, to name a few.

7445 ■ Native Hawaiian Chamber of Commerce Scholarships *(Graduate, Undergraduate/Scholarship)*

Purpose: To support the educational needs and goals of people of Hawaiian ancestry. **Focus:** Business administration. **Qualif.:** Applicants must be students in an undergraduate or graduate degree-seeking program from an accredited post-high educational institution majoring in Business Administration. A cumulative GPA of 3.0 or higher is required. **Criteria:** Selection will be based on the committee's criteria.

Funds Avail.: $1,000. **Duration:** Annual. **Number Awarded:** 15. **To Apply:** Applicant must submit a College Acceptance Letter if attending a college or university for the first time, or currently enrolled college student changing schools or degree programs; official transcript of grades; and student aid report (SAR).

7446 ■ Native Hawaiian Visual Arts Scholarships *(Graduate, Undergraduate/Scholarship)*

Purpose: To support the educational needs and goals of people of Hawaiian ancestry. **Focus:** Visual arts. **Qualif.:** Applicants must be undergraduate and graduate students majoring in Art to pursue the area of Visual Arts, including but not limited to, drawing, painting, printmaking, graphic design, fiber arts, sculpture, ceramics, digital art (computer), photography, and film-making/video production; must have a GPA of 3.2 or higher. **Criteria:** Selection will be based on artistic merit as demonstrated by an artistic portfolio and academic achievements.

Funds Avail.: $1,600. **Duration:** Annual. **Number Awarded:** 1. **To Apply:** Applicant must submit a College Acceptance Letter if attending a college or university for the first time, or currently enrolled college student changing schools or degree programs; official transcript of grades; and student aid report (SAR). Applicant must also submit a portfolio of artistic works created and a hard-copy photos of artistic works created (CDs and DVDs will not be accepted).

7447 ■ William S. Richardson Commemorative Scholarships *(Graduate/Scholarship)*

Purpose: To support the educational needs and goals of people of Hawaiian ancestry. **Focus:** Law. **Qualif.:** Applicant must be a resident of the State of Hawaii; must be

Awards are arranged alphabetically below their administering organizations

pursuing law degrees from the University of Hawaii-Manoa William S. Richardson School of Law. **Criteria:** Preference will be given to applicants demonstrating financial need and commitment to contributing to the greater community. **Funds Avail.:** $1,000. **Duration:** Annual. **Number Awarded:** 4. **To Apply:** Applicant must submit a College Acceptance Letter if attending a college or university for the first time, or currently enrolled college student changing schools or degree programs; official transcript of grades; and student aid report (SAR).

7448 ■ Iwalani Carpenter Sowa Scholarships
(Graduate/Scholarship)

Purpose: To support the educational needs and goals of people of Hawaiian ancestry. **Focus:** Religion. **Qualif.:** Applicants must be students pursuing a graduate degree in the Protestant Christian ministry and who have a desire to minister in Hawaii. **Criteria:** Preference will be given to a Kamehameha Schools graduate and those demonstrating financial need.

Funds Avail.: $1,600. **Duration:** Annual. **Number Awarded:** 1. **To Apply:** Applicant must submit a College Acceptance Letter if attending a college or university for the first time, or currently enrolled college student changing schools or degree programs; official transcript of grades; and student aid report (SAR). Applicants must also submit two letter of recommendation from applicant's religion professor, college advisor, church minister or community organization.

7449 ■ Denis Wong and Associates Scholarships
(Graduate, Undergraduate/Scholarship)

Purpose: To support the educational needs and goals of people of Hawaiian ancestry. **Focus:** Liberal arts; Science. **Qualif.:** Applicants must be outstanding students pursuing an undergraduate degree in liberal arts or science or a graduate degree in a professional field from an accredited university. Applicants must have a minimum GPA of 3.5. **Criteria:** Selection will be based on the committee's criteria.

Funds Avail.: $1,000. **Duration:** Annual. **Number Awarded:** 3. **To Apply:** Applicant must submit a College Acceptance Letter if attending a college or university for the first time, or currently enrolled college student changing schools or degree programs; official transcript of grades; and student aid report (SAR). Applicants must also submit two letters of recommendation from teachers, counselors, coaches or employers citing the applicant's credentials and potential for success.

7450 ■ PBR Forces Veterans Association (PBR-FVA)
310 W Park St.
Odon, IN 47562-1534
Ph: (812)636-4343
Fax: (812)636-4343
E-mail: membership@pbr-fva.org
URL: www.pbr-fva.org

7451 ■ BM1 James Elliott Williams Memorial Scholarship Fund *(Undergraduate/Scholarship)*

Purpose: To assist the direct descendants of members. **Focus:** Vietnamese studies. **Qualif.:** Candidates must be a direct descent of an active Vietnam Veteran member of PBR Forces Veterans Association; must be enrolled in a two or four-year accredited college/technical school. **Crite-**

ria: Scholarship will be awarded to the student who best meets the criteria.

Funds Avail.: Varies depending on available funds. **To Apply:** Applicants must fill out the application form; form must be printed using blue or black ink; and application must be countersigned by the Sponsor. **Deadline:** August 15.

7452 ■ Pediatric Endocrinology Nursing Society (PENS)
PO Box 14516
Lenexa, KS 66285-4516
Ph: (913)895-4628
Fax: (913)895-4652
Free: 877-936-7367
E-mail: pens@goamp.com
URL: www.pens.org

7453 ■ Pediatric Endocrinology Nursing Society Academic Education Scholarships *(Undergraduate/Scholarship)*

Purpose: To promote the study and development of pediatric endocrine nursing. **Focus:** Nursing, Pediatric. **Qualif.:** Applicant must be an active PENS member for at least three years; currently employed in pediatric endocrine nursing; and pursuing a nursing degree. **Criteria:** Applicants who are pursuing their BS(N) and applying for the scholarship for the first-time will be given preference.

Funds Avail.: $1,000. **Duration:** One year. **To Apply:** Applicant must submit a completed application form; copy of RN License; curriculum vitae or resume; receipt of registration from college or university; transcript of records or acceptance letter. **Deadline:** April 1 and September 1. **Contact:** Questions can be addressed by e-mail to pens@goamp.com.

7454 ■ Pediatric Endocrinology Nursing Society Convention Reimbursement Awards *(Undergraduate/Award)*

Purpose: To promote the study of endocrine and growth disorders, research and current issues in nursing. **Focus:** Nursing, Pediatric. **Qualif.:** Applicant must be an active PENS member for at least three years. **Criteria:** Recipients are selected based on the committee's review of the application materials.

Funds Avail.: $1,000. **Number Awarded:** Up to 16. **To Apply:** Applicants must send a completed application form and a (2-4 page) clinical exemplar. Send documents via email. **Deadline:** March 1. **Contact:** PENS Executive Office 913-895-4628.

7455 ■ Pedrozzi Scholarship Foundation
1040 Florence Rd., Rm. 21
Livermore, CA 94550
Ph: (925)456-3700
Fax: (925)456-3701
E-mail: info@pedrozzifoundation.org
URL: www.pedrozzifoundation.org

7456 ■ Mario Pedrozzi Scholarships *(Undergraduate, Graduate/Scholarship)*

Purpose: To support students in their educational pursuit. **Focus:** General studies/Field of study not specified. **Qualif.:** Applicants must have either graduated from a Liver-

Awards are arranged alphabetically below their administering organizations

more Valley Joint Unified School District high school (Del Valle/Phoenix, Granada, Livermore or Vineyard) or have been residents of Alameda County upon high school graduation and been accepted at St. Patrick's Seminary & University. Students applying for undergraduate or graduate scholarships must have a minimum GPA of 3.0. **Criteria:** Applicants are evaluated anonymously based on the combination of: responses to short essay prompts, school and community activities, work experience, reference responses and academic record.

Funds Avail.: $1,000 each per annum. **Duration:** Annual; up to four years. **Number Awarded:** Varies. **To Apply:** Applicants are required to apply online. Students are to submit official transcript (in an official stamped and sealed envelope) via regular mail. **Deadline:** March 2. **Contact:** Pedrozzi Scholarship Foundation, at the above address.

7457 ■ Pennsylvania Association on Probation, Parole and Corrections (PAPPC)

PO Box 5553
Harrisburg, PA 17110-0553
Ph: (724)662-2380
URL: www.pappc.org

7458 ■ Robert E. Kelsey Annual Scholarship
(Undergraduate/Scholarship)

Purpose: To support and promote best practice methods and professionalism in the field of juvenile and adult probation, parole, corrections institutional care and community supervision. **Focus:** Humanities; Social sciences. **Qualif.:** Applicants must be current PAPPC members or immediate family members; must be currently enrolled or accepted into a two-year or four-year accredited program of higher education with a concentration of studies in the Humanities and Social Sciences; must be in good academic standing; must demonstrate academic success by holding at least a 2.75 GPA or equivalent at the time of application. Students presently enrolled in a college or university must demonstrate academic success by holding a current overall college GPA of 2.75 or better at the time of application. **Criteria:** Selection will be based on the committee's criteria.

Funds Avail.: $1,500. **Duration:** Annual. **Number Awarded:** 2. **To Apply:** Applicants must submit three letters of recommendation at the time of application; must submit a personal statement explaining why they chose their field of study and how that field applies to their future aspirations. Statements should not exceed 500 words, must be type-written and double-spaced. They must submit a copy of their most current transcripts. In addition, applicants must submit the following information: full name; social security number; address; phone number; email address; high school or college GPA; name of college or university that the applicants planning to attend or currently attending; and major; PAPPC member name and relationship. **Deadline:** March 31.

7459 ■ Pennsylvania Dental Hygienists' Association (PDHA)

c/o Margie Mengle, Executive Secretary
PO Box 606
Mechanicsburg, PA 17055
Ph: (717)766-0334
Fax: (717)766-4452
E-mail: pdha@verizon.net
URL: pdhaonline.org

7460 ■ Bailey/Hollister Scholarships *(Graduate, Professional development/Scholarship)*

Purpose: To help students to pursue a career in the dental hygiene profession. **Focus:** Dental hygiene. **Qualif.:** Applicants must be dental hygienists who are completing the first year in an entry level dental hygiene curricula or enrolled in a post-entry level or graduate program complementary to the profession of dental hygiene and consistent with the six roles of the dental hygienist recognized by the ADHA; must be members/student members of the American Dental Hygienists' Association; must be residents of Pennsylvania. **Criteria:** Selection will be based on the committee's criteria.

Funds Avail.: No specific amount. **To Apply:** Applicants must submit the following materials: a completed financial need form; a letter of reference from the director of the dental hygiene program, which includes the current GPA which must be 2.5 or higher; a letter of reference from a clinical instructor; a certified copy of the student's academic record; a letter from the applicant stating why they should be awarded the scholarship; a copy of driver's license as a proof of Pennsylvania residency. **Deadline:** July 1. **Contact:** 717-766-0334, pdha@verizon.net.

7461 ■ Pennsylvania Library Association (PaLA)

220 Cumberland Pkwy., Ste. 10
Mechanicsburg, PA 17055
Ph: (717)766-7663
Fax: (717)766-5440
Free: 800-622-3308
URL: www.palibraries.org

7462 ■ Pennsylvania Library Association MLS Scholarships *(Graduate/Scholarship)*

Purpose: To provide opportunities for professional growth, leadership development and continuing education for librarians. **Focus:** Library and archival sciences. **Qualif.:** Applicants must be Pennsylvania residents who are seeking a master's degree in the Library Science field that will earn them professional status; must have completed 12 credit hours toward the degree during the scholarship year; and must be enrolled in an ALA-accredited institution. **Criteria:** Recipients will be selected based on financial need; scholarship; motivation; civic activities; PALA activities; and previous library experience.

Funds Avail.: $1,500. **Duration:** Annual. **Number Awarded:** 3. **To Apply:** Applicants must submit a completed application form; three letters of recommendation; and verification of enrollment in an ALA-accredited graduate program. Applicants must also submit letters describing purpose for the continuing education; a letter from the individual's immediate supervisor, documenting the value of this specific continuing education; a letter of the applicant's work performance and a description of the course or institution as provided by the sponsoring agency. **Deadline:** May 15.

7463 ■ Pennsylvania Music Educators Association (PMEA)

56 S 3rd St.
Hamburg, PA 19526
Ph: (610)562-9757
Fax: (610)562-9760
Free: 888-919-7632

Awards are arranged alphabetically below their administering organizations

URL: www.pmea.net

7464 ■ Irene R. Christman Scholarship
(Undergraduate/Scholarship)

Purpose: To support students who are planning to pursue music education in college. **Focus:** Music. **Qualif.:** Applicants must be senior student members of a PMEA All-State Ensemble who are planning to attend college with a major in music education. **Criteria:** The scholarship will be based on the student's academic and musical excellence, resume, and letters of recommendation, as determined by the PMEA Scholarship Committee.

Funds Avail.: $1,000. **Duration:** Annual. **Number Awarded:** 1. **To Apply:** Applicants must complete and submit the following requirements: recommendation of high school music director(s); recommendation of high school guidance counselor; verification of college application and acceptance for the study of music curriculum at an accredited college, university or conservatory; an essay on how participation in the school's music program has enriched their lives and influenced their future music aspirations; high school transcript, attached to online application if possible or mailed to PMEA. **Deadline:** February 26.

7465 ■ Pennsylvania Society of Land Surveyors (PSLS)
801 E Park Dr., Ste. 107
Harrisburg, PA 17111
Ph: (717)540-6811
Fax: (717)540-6815
E-mail: psls@psls.org
URL: www.psls.org

7466 ■ Pennsylvania Land Surveyors Foundation Scholarships *(Undergraduate/Scholarship)*

Purpose: To provide financial assistance to individuals pursuing an education in land surveying. **Focus:** Cartography/Surveying. **Qualif.:** Applicants must: be citizens of the United States and be residents of the Commonwealth of Pennsylvania; be enrolled in or accepted in a two-year Surveying Technology Program or a four-year Bachelor of Science Program in Land Surveying; submit copies of SAT scores and high school or college transcripts with completed Transcript Release Form from Guidance Office or Registrar's Office. **Criteria:** Selection will be based on performance factors, applicant's activities, application preparation, Guidance Counselor/Advisor evaluation, applicant's potential as a Professional Land Surveyor.

Funds Avail.: No specific amount. **To Apply:** Application form can be downloaded online. Each portion of the application has a specific point value. Judges will score each section separately. Incomplete applications will not be considered. Forms must be typed or neatly printed. Use of separate paper will be accepted. Points may be lost for poor grammar, incorrect spelling, illegibility, or lack of neatness. Proofread carefully. Applicants must submit a recommendation form to their Guidance Counselor/Advisor. **Deadline:** April 2.

7467 ■ Pennsylvania Society of Professional Engineers (PSPE)
908 N 2nd St.
Harrisburg, PA 17102
Ph: (717)441-6051
Fax: (717)236-2046

E-mail: pspeinfo@pspe.org
URL: pspe.org

7468 ■ Pennsylvania Society of Professional Engineers Scholarships *(Undergraduate/Scholarship)*

Purpose: To provide financial assistance for freshmen students to pursue their academic goals in the engineering field of study. **Focus:** Engineering. **Qualif.:** Applicants must be freshmen attending their first semester of college at an ABET-accredited engineering School in the Commonwealth of Pennsylvania; must be Pennsylvania residents; have minimum of SAT Math scores of 700 and Verbal (600); and have minimum GPA of 3.6. **Criteria:** Applicants are evaluated based on financial need.

Funds Avail.: $1,000. **Duration:** Annual. **Number Awarded:** 3. **To Apply:** Applicants must complete the application form; and must include certified copy of transcripts; include SAT scores with a copy of the official test report. **Deadline:** April 15.

7469 ■ Pennsylvania State System of Higher Education Foundation
2986 N 2nd St.
Harrisburg, PA 17110
Ph: (717)720-4056
URL: www.thepafoundation.org

7470 ■ Wayne G. Failor Scholarships
(Undergraduate/Scholarship)

Purpose: To provide funding to help cover the cost of the students participating in the summer internship program. **Focus:** Business. **Qualif.:** Applicants must be students who are graduating seniors of a West Shore School District high school; full-time undergraduate students who plan to enroll at a State System university; must plan to major in business or a related field; must have a "B" average or better by the end of their junior year in high school. **Criteria:** Recipients are selected on the basis of financial need.

Funds Avail.: $1,000. **Number Awarded:** 1. **To Apply:** Applicants must submit all the required application information.

7471 ■ James Hughes Memorial Scholarship Fund
(Undergraduate/Scholarship)

Purpose: To provide recognition and financial assistance to low-income disadvantaged students residing in the city of Philadelphia who attended any of the public high schools or charter schools in the school district of Philadelphia and who wish to enroll in universities of the Pennsylvania State System of Higher Education. **Focus:** General studies/Field of study not specified. **Qualif.:** Applicants must have graduated from any public high school or charter school in the school district of Philadelphia; must be full-time undergraduate students accepted at a PASSHE university, with priority given to incoming freshmen. **Criteria:** Recipients are selected based on financial need.

Funds Avail.: $1,500. **To Apply:** Applicants must submit the James Hughes Memorial Scholarship (JHMS) application form; two written references using the letter of reference form (one academic/professional and one personal); current high school transcript; 250-word essay on why they feel they are deserving of the Hughes scholarship, their desire to achieve academically and how they have overcome adversities in their lives. **Deadline:** April 30.

Awards are arranged alphabetically below their administering organizations

7472 ■ Robert Noyce Scholarship Program
(Undergraduate/Scholarship)

Purpose: To provide financial assistance to increase the number of basic education teachers with strong content knowledge in science, technology, engineering, and mathematics (STEM). **Focus:** Engineering; Mathematics and mathematical sciences; Science; Technology. **Qualif.:** Applicants must have a qualifying cumulative GPA of 3.00, with preference for those with a GPA of 3.5 or higher; must be transfer students or post-baccalaureates who completed a semester or more of coursework at a State System university to establish the qualifying GPA of 3.00; must be full-time students during each semester for which the award is received. **Criteria:** Applicants will be evaluated by a screening committee. Those with the highest scores will receive the scholarship. year.

Funds Avail.: $7,500-$10,000. **To Apply:** Applicants must submit completed application form; official transcripts from all institutions attended; a two page essay describing personal and professional goals, commitment to teaching and personal philosophy of teaching; three letters of recommendation that must address, but are not limited to: a) the scholarship of the applicant, b) the character of the applicant, c) the interpersonal skills of the applicant relative to teaching, and d) the general interpersonal skills of the applicant; and a resume. **Deadline:** April 20 and October 20.

7473 ■ Minnie Patton Stayman Scholarships
(Undergraduate/Scholarship)

Purpose: To provide educational assistance to all the students who are enrolled at PASSHE universities. **Focus:** General studies/Field of study not specified. **Qualif.:** Applicants must: be residents of Altoona; be full-time undergraduate students who plan to enroll at Indian University of Pennsylvania or Lock Haven University of Pennsylvania. **Criteria:** Recipients are selected based on financial need.

Funds Avail.: $1,000. **To Apply:** Applicants must submit all the required application information. **Deadline:** June 30.

7474 ■ The Penny Hoarder
2637 E Atlantic Blvd., Ste. 19140
Pompano Beach, FL 33062
Ph: (941)323-3178
URL: www.thepennyhoarder.com

7475 ■ "Frugal Student" Scholarships
(Undergraduate/Scholarship)

Purpose: To support students in their pursuit of higher education. **Focus:** General studies/Field of study not specified. **Qualif.:** Applicants must be enrolled in a college or university with an active class schedule. **Criteria:** Selection will be based on the submitted essays.

Funds Avail.: $2,000. **Number Awarded:** 1. **To Apply:** Applicants must write a brief essay (150 words or less) in which they describe an inventive way they have earned or saved extra money. **Deadline:** February 1. **Contact:** scholarships@thepennyhoarder.com.

7476 ■ Pension Real Estate Association (PREA)
100 Pearl St., 13th Fl.
Hartford, CT 06103
Ph: (860)692-6341
Fax: (860)692-6351
E-mail: membership@prea.org

URL: www.prea.org

7477 ■ Pension Real Estate Association Scholarships *(Undergraduate, Graduate/Scholarship)*

Purpose: To promote understanding of institutional investment in real estate. **Focus:** Real estate. **Qualif.:** Applicants must be students studying real estate at the undergraduate and graduate levels. **Criteria:** Recipients are selected based on financial need.

Funds Avail.: Total amount of $30,000. **Duration:** Annual. **To Apply:** Applicants must submit a completed application form. **Deadline:** June 1. **Remarks:** Established in 1994.

7478 ■ PEO International
3700 Grand Ave.
Des Moines, IA 50312-2806
Ph: (515)255-3153
Fax: (515)255-3820
URL: www.peointernational.org

7479 ■ PEO Educational Loan Funds *(Graduate, Undergraduate, Vocational/Occupational, Doctorate/Loan)*

Purpose: To promote educational opportunities for women who desire higher education and are in need of financial assistance. **Focus:** General studies/Field of study not specified. **Qualif.:** Applicants must be recommended by a local chapter of the P.E.O. sisterhood and must be within two years of completing their course of study; must be citizens or legal permanent residents of the United States or Canada. Program is also open for applicants who are graduate students in medical or law schools, seniors seeking a bachelor's degree or students enrolled in a hospital professional nurse training program, a non-collegiate, technical program, or vocational program in a college or university. **Criteria:** Recipients are selected based on financial need.

Funds Avail.: $12,000 (All programs of study); $20,000 (Doctoral degrees). **Duration:** Annual. **To Apply:** Applicants must submit a cover letter; application form with a packet checklist and instructions; school information form or proof of enrollment; transcript of records; request for permission to obtain credit report; acknowledgement of loan terms; and memo of indebtedness. **Remarks:** Established in 1907.

7480 ■ PEO International Peace Scholarships (IPS)
(Graduate, Master's, Doctorate/Scholarship)

Purpose: To provide scholarships for selected women from other countries for study in the United States and Canada. **Focus:** General studies/Field of study not specified. **Qualif.:** Applicants must be qualified for admission to a full-time graduate study, working toward a graduate degree in the college or university. **Criteria:** Recipients are selected based on a non-discriminatory basis without consideration of race, national origin, religious affiliation, or disability.

Funds Avail.: $10,000. **Duration:** Annual. **To Apply:** Applicants must submit completed application form; a copy of confirmation of admission; and a witnessed statement certifying that upon completion of their degree programs they will return to their own country within 60 days. **Deadline:** December 15. **Remarks:** Established in 1949.

7481 ■ People for the Ethical Treatment of Animals (PETA)
501 Front St.
Norfolk, VA 23510

Awards are arranged alphabetically below their administering organizations

Ph: (757)622-7382
Fax: (757)622-0457
E-mail: info@peta.org
URL: www.peta.org

7482 ■ PETA Foundation Law Internships (Graduate/ Internship)

Purpose: To provide assistance to attorneys at the PETA Foundation with a wide range of legal issues that arise in the course of PETA's work to protect animals through public education, cruelty investigations, research, animal rescue, legislation, and protest campaigns. **Focus:** Animal rights; Law. **Qualif.:** Applicants must be 3L or rising 3L students or Juris Doctors with up to three years of legal experience; have desired experience in animal law, administrative law, environmental law, and/or criminal law; have superior legal research and writing skills; have proven ability to be resourceful and innovative; have supportive position vis-a-vis PETA's philosophy and the ability to professionally advocate PETA's positions on issues; and be committed to the objectives of the organization. **Criteria:** Selection will be based on applicants' eligibility and compliance with the application process.

Funds Avail.: No specific amount. **To Apply:** Applicants must send a letter of interest, resume, transcript, legal writing sample, and list of three professional references to Amanda Schwoerke. **Remarks:** The term of employment is temporary, unpaid position. **Contact:** Amanda Schwoerke, counsel, at AmandaSchwoerke@petaf.org.

7483 ■ People to People International (PTPI)

2405 Grand Blvd., Ste. 500
Kansas City, MO 64105-5305
Ph: (816)531-4701
Fax: (816)561-7502
Free: 800-676-7874
E-mail: ptpi@ptpi.org
URL: www.ptpi.org

7484 ■ Joyce C. Hall College Scholarships (Undergraduate/Scholarship)

Purpose: To encourage youth participation in international activities. **Focus:** General studies/Field of study not specified. **Qualif.:** Applicants must be current members of People to People International with experience in at least one of the many programs offered during the past four years. They must also be full-time college students or high school seniors maintaining a 3.0 grade point average on a 4.0 scale. **Criteria:** Recipients will be selected based on the evaluation of all application materials.

Funds Avail.: $2,000 each. **Duration:** Annual. **Number Awarded:** Up to 5. **To Apply:** Applicants must send an application form accompanied by: a statement of the applicant's participation in a People to People International activity, and what that experience meant to increasing his/her understanding of intercultural relations among the peoples of the world; an original essay not more than 1,000 words regarding "Why I believe international friendships are important and how my experiences have improved my understanding of people from other countries/cultures;" Statement of Financial Need Form; three letters of recommendation; transcript. High school seniors must provide proof that they are actively applying to a college or university. **Deadline:** October 15. **Contact:** For further information, applicants may send an e-mail at accounting@ptpi.org.

7485 ■ Pepperdine University School of Law

24255 Pacific Coast Hwy.
Malibu, CA 90263
Ph: (310)506-4611
E-mail: lawadmis@pepperdine.edu
URL: law.pepperdine.edu

7486 ■ Associated Women for Pepperdine Scholarships (AWP) (Undergraduate/Scholarship)

Purpose: To support students to meet the educational costs of attending the School of Law. **Focus:** Education; Law; Psychology. **Qualif.:** Applicants must be admitted at Pepperdine University; and be members of the Church of Christ. **Criteria:** Recipient selection is based financial need, merit, character, and church membership.

Funds Avail.: No specific amount. **Duration:** Annual. **To Apply:** Applicants must submit a completed scholarship application form together with a resume, letter of qualifications, and a letter confirming active membership in a local Church of Christ congregation.

7487 ■ Beck-Pfann Memorial Scholarships (Undergraduate/Scholarship)

Purpose: To support students to meet the educational costs of attending the School of Law. **Focus:** Law. **Qualif.:** Applicants must be second-year students. **Criteria:** Recipient selection is based on community service, academic achievement, financial need, and extracurricular activities.

Funds Avail.: No specific amount. **Duration:** Annual. **To Apply:** Applicants must submit a completed scholarship application form together with a resume and a letter of qualifications.

7488 ■ David and Camille Boatwright Endowed Scholarships (Undergraduate/Scholarship)

Purpose: To support students to meet the educational costs of attending the School of Law. **Focus:** Law. **Qualif.:** Applicants must be Pepperdine University School of Law students. **Criteria:** Recipient of the award is determined by the Scholarship Committee.

Funds Avail.: No specific amount. **Duration:** Annual. **To Apply:** Applicants must submit a completed scholarship application form together with a resume, and letter of qualifications.

7489 ■ Ann Marie Bredefeld Scholarships (Undergraduate/Scholarship)

Purpose: To support students to meet the educational costs of attending the School of Law. **Focus:** Law. **Qualif.:** Applicants must be students who share the Christian values of Pepperdine. **Criteria:** Selection will be based on financial need, academic merit, community involvement and personal achievement.

Funds Avail.: No specific amount. **Duration:** Annual. **To Apply:** Applicants must submit a completed scholarship application form together with a resume and a letter of qualifications.

7490 ■ Margaret Martin Brock Scholarships in Law (Undergraduate/Scholarship)

Purpose: To support students to meet the educational costs of attending the School of Law. **Focus:** Law. **Qualif.:** Applicants must be Pepperdine University School of Law students. **Criteria:** Selection will be based on financial

Awards are arranged alphabetically below their administering organizations

need, academic merit, community involvement and personal achievement.

Funds Avail.: No specific amount. **Duration:** Annual. **To Apply:** Applicants must submit a completed scholarship application form together with a resume and a letter of qualifications.

7491 ■ Kae and Kay Brockermeyer Endowed Scholarships (Undergraduate/Scholarship)

Purpose: To support students to meet the educational costs of attending the School of Law. **Focus:** Law. **Qualif.:** Applicants must be law students interested in trial advocacy. Applicant must also be a resident of the state of Texas. **Criteria:** Selection will be based on financial need, academic merit, community involvement and personal achievement.

Funds Avail.: No specific amount. **Duration:** Annual. **To Apply:** Applicants must submit a completed scholarship application form together with a resume and a letter of qualifications.

7492 ■ Shirley J. Brooke Endowed Scholarships (Undergraduate/Scholarship)

Purpose: To support students to meet the educational costs of attending the School of Law. **Focus:** Law. **Qualif.:** Applicants must be female law students who demonstrate above average academic achievement. **Criteria:** Selection will be based on financial need, academic merit, community involvement and personal achievement.

Funds Avail.: No specific amount. **Duration:** Annual. **To Apply:** Applicants must submit a completed scholarship application form together with a resume and a letter of qualifications.

7493 ■ Athalie Clarke Endowed Scholarships (Undergraduate/Scholarship)

Purpose: To support students to meet the educational costs of attending the School of Law. **Focus:** Law. **Qualif.:** Applicants must be Pepperdine University School of Law students. **Criteria:** Selection will be based on financial need, academic merit, community involvement and personal achievement.

Funds Avail.: No specific amount. **Duration:** Annual. **To Apply:** Applicants must submit a completed scholarship application form together with a resume and a letter of qualifications.

7494 ■ Brian Dane Cleary Memorial Scholarships (Undergraduate/Scholarship)

Purpose: To assist a well-rounded, financially-needy student. **Focus:** Law. **Qualif.:** Applicants must be Pepperdine University School of Law students. **Criteria:** Selection will be based on financial need, academic merit, community involvement and personal achievement.

Funds Avail.: No specific amount. **Duration:** Annual. **To Apply:** Applicants must submit a completed scholarship application form together with a resume and a letter of qualifications. **Deadline:** April 1.

7495 ■ Hugh and Hazel Darling Dean Scholarships (Undergraduate/Scholarship)

Purpose: To encourage students to remain enrolled at the school of law. **Focus:** Law. **Qualif.:** Applicants must be Pepperdine University School of Law students. **Criteria:** Recipients are selected based on academic excellence as

well as school and community involvement.

Funds Avail.: No specific amount. **Duration:** Annual. **To Apply:** Applicants must submit a completed scholarship application form together with a resume and a letter of qualifications.

7496 ■ Darling Foundation Endowed School of Law Scholarships (Undergraduate/Scholarship)

Purpose: To support students to meet the educational costs of attending the School of Law. **Focus:** Law. **Qualif.:** Applicants must be Pepperdine University School of Law students. **Criteria:** Selection will be based on financial need, academic merit, community involvement and personal achievement.

Funds Avail.: No specific amount. **Duration:** Annual. **To Apply:** Applicants must submit a completed scholarship application form together with a resume and a letter of qualifications.

7497 ■ Martha Delman and Milton Arthur Krug Endowed Scholarships (Undergraduate/Scholarship)

Purpose: To support students to meet the educational costs of attending the School of Law. **Focus:** Law. **Qualif.:** Applicants must be Pepperdine University School of Law students. **Criteria:** Recipient of the award is determined by the Scholarship Committee.

Funds Avail.: No specific amount. **Duration:** Annual. **To Apply:** Applicants must submit a completed scholarship application form together with a resume and a letter of qualifications.

7498 ■ Edward D. Di Loreto-Odell S. McConnell Scholarships (Undergraduate/Scholarship)

Purpose: To support students to meet the educational costs of attending the School of Law. **Focus:** Law. **Qualif.:** Applicants must be Pepperdine University School of Law students with high scholastic standing. **Criteria:** Selection will be based on financial need, academic merit, community involvement and personal achievement.

Funds Avail.: No specific amount. **Duration:** Annual. **To Apply:** Applicants must submit a completed scholarship application form together with a resume and a letter of qualifications.

7499 ■ R. Wayne Estes Endowed Scholarships (Undergraduate/Scholarship)

Purpose: To support students to meet the educational costs of attending the School of Law. **Focus:** Law. **Qualif.:** Applicants must be Pepperdine University School of Law students. **Criteria:** Selection will be based on financial need, academic merit, community involvement and personal achievement.

Funds Avail.: No specific amount. **Duration:** Annual. **To Apply:** Applicants must submit a completed scholarship application form together with a resume and a letter of qualifications.

7500 ■ Judge McIntyre Faries Scholarships (Undergraduate/Scholarship)

Purpose: To support students to meet the educational costs of attending the School of Law. **Focus:** Law. **Qualif.:** Applicants must be Pepperdine University School of Law students. **Criteria:** Selection will be based on financial need, academic merit, community involvement and personal achievement.

Awards are arranged alphabetically below their administering organizations

Funds Avail.: No specific amount. **Duration:** Annual. **To Apply:** Applicants must submit a completed scholarship application form together with a resume and a letter of qualifications.

7501 ■ Froberg-Suess JD/MBA Scholarships
(Undergraduate/Scholarship)

Purpose: To support students to meet the educational costs of attending the School of Law. **Focus:** Law. **Qualif.:** Applicants must have successfully completed at least one semester of law school and one semester of business school. **Criteria:** Recipients are selected based on merit.

Funds Avail.: No specific amount. **Duration:** Annual. **To Apply:** Applicants must submit a completed scholarship application form together with a resume and a letter of qualifications.

7502 ■ Gerald Garner Memorial Scholarships
(Undergraduate/Scholarship)

Purpose: To support students to meet the educational costs of attending the School of Law. **Focus:** Law. **Qualif.:** Applicants must be Pepperdine University School of Law students. **Criteria:** Selection will be based on financial need, academic merit, community involvement and personal achievement.

Funds Avail.: No specific amount. **Duration:** Annual. **To Apply:** Applicants must submit a completed scholarship application form together with a resume and a letter of qualifications.

7503 ■ Terry M. Giles Honor Scholarships
(Undergraduate/Scholarship)

Purpose: To support students to meet the educational costs of attending the School of Law. **Focus:** Law. **Qualif.:** Applicants must be third-year students. **Criteria:** Recipients are selected based on scholastic achievement, co-curricular and extracurricular activities, personality and character.

Funds Avail.: No specific amount. **Duration:** Annual. **To Apply:** Applicants must submit a completed scholarship application form together with a resume and a letter of qualifications.

7504 ■ Guy P. Greenwald Jr. Endowed Scholarships
(Undergraduate/Scholarship)

Purpose: To support students to meet the educational costs of attending the School of Law. **Focus:** Law. **Qualif.:** Applicants must be Pepperdine University School of Law students. **Criteria:** Selection will be based on financial need, academic merit, community involvement and personal achievement.

Funds Avail.: No specific amount. **Duration:** Annual. **To Apply:** Applicants must submit a completed scholarship application form together with a resume and a letter of qualifications.

7505 ■ Warren and Rosalie Gummow Endowed Scholarships *(Undergraduate/Scholarship)*

Purpose: To support students to meet the educational costs of attending the School of Law. **Focus:** Law. **Qualif.:** Applicants must be Pepperdine University School of Law students. **Criteria:** Selection will be based on financial need, academic merit, community involvement and personal achievement.

Funds Avail.: No specific amount. **Duration:** Annual. **To Apply:** Applicants must submit a completed scholarship

application form together with a resume and a letter of qualifications.

7506 ■ Mark and Michelle Hiepler Endowed Scholarships *(Undergraduate/Scholarship)*

Purpose: To support students to meet the educational costs of attending the School of Law. **Focus:** Law. **Qualif.:** Applicants must be the writers of the Best Respondent's Brief and Best Petitioner's Brief in the yearly Vincent S. Dalsimer Moot Court Competition. **Criteria:** Scholarships will be awarded based on financial need, academic study, community involvement, and health care law interest or health care background.

Funds Avail.: $1,000. **Duration:** Annual. **To Apply:** Applicants must submit a completed scholarship application form together with a resume and a letter of qualifications. **Remarks:** Established in 1988.

7507 ■ JD/MBA Endowed Scholarships
(Undergraduate/Scholarship)

Purpose: To support students to meet the educational costs of attending the School of Law. **Focus:** Business; Law. **Qualif.:** Applicant must be a student enrolled in the joint JD and MBA program at the School of Law and Graziadio School of Business and Management. Applicant must be in good standing in all areas of the University. **Criteria:** Award is given based on merit.

Funds Avail.: No specific amount. **Duration:** Annual. **To Apply:** Applicants must submit a completed scholarship application form together with a resume and a letter of qualifications.

7508 ■ JSR Foundation Endowed School of Law Scholarships *(Undergraduate/Scholarship)*

Purpose: To assist deserving students with financial need. **Focus:** Law. **Qualif.:** Applicants must be Pepperdine University School of Law students. **Criteria:** Recipients will be selected based on financial need.

Funds Avail.: No specific amount. **Duration:** Annual. **To Apply:** Applicants must submit a completed scholarship application form together with a resume and a letter of qualifications.

7509 ■ Woodrow Judkins Endowed Scholarships
(Undergraduate/Scholarship)

Purpose: To support students to meet the educational costs of attending the School of Law. **Focus:** Law. **Qualif.:** Applicants must be Pepperdine University School of Law students with good academic standing. **Criteria:** Recipient of the award is determined by the Scholarship Committee.

Funds Avail.: No specific amount. **Duration:** Annual. **To Apply:** Applicants must submit a completed scholarship application form together with a resume and a letter of qualifications.

7510 ■ Kerrigan Scholarships *(Undergraduate/ Scholarship)*

Purpose: To support students to meet the educational costs of attending the School of Law. **Focus:** Law. **Qualif.:** Applicant must be a single-parent mother enrolled at the School of Law. **Criteria:** Selection will based on financial need, academic merit, community involvement and personal achievement.

Funds Avail.: No specific amount. **Duration:** Annual. **To Apply:** Applicant must submit a completed scholarship ap-

Awards are arranged alphabetically below their administering organizations

plication form together with a resume and a letter of qualifications. **Remarks:** Established in 1992.

7511 ■ Krist-Reavley Minority Scholarships
(Undergraduate/Scholarship)

Purpose: To support students to meet the educational costs of attending the School of Law. **Focus:** Law. **Qualif.:** Applicant must be an ethnically diverse student. **Criteria:** Selection will be based on financial need, academic merit, community involvement and personal achievement.

Funds Avail.: No specific amount. **Duration:** Annual. **To Apply:** Applicant must submit a completed scholarship application form together with a resume and a letter of qualifications.

7512 ■ Julia Kwan Endowed Scholarships
(Graduate/Scholarship)

Purpose: To assist students with financial need who are pursuing a graduate degree at the School of Law. **Focus:** Law. **Qualif.:** Applicants must be Pepperdine University School of Law students pursuing a graduate degree. **Criteria:** Recipients will be selected based on financial need.

Funds Avail.: No specific amount. **Duration:** Annual. **To Apply:** Applicants must submit a completed scholarship application form together with a resume and a letter of qualifications.

7513 ■ Albert J. and Mae Lee Memorial Scholarships
(Undergraduate/Scholarship)

Purpose: To support students to meet the educational costs of attending the School of Law. **Focus:** Law. **Qualif.:** Applicants must be Pepperdine University School of Law students with above average scholastic ability, and who are in need of financial assistance. **Criteria:** Selection will be based on financial need, academic merit, community involvement and personal achievement.

Funds Avail.: No specific amount. **Duration:** Annual. **To Apply:** Applicants must submit a completed scholarship application form together with a resume and a letter of qualifications. **Remarks:** Established in 2003.

7514 ■ Greg Matthews Memorial Scholarships
(Undergraduate/Scholarship)

Purpose: To support students to meet the educational costs of attending the School of Law. **Focus:** Law. **Qualif.:** Applicants must be Pepperdine University School of Law students. **Criteria:** Recipients will be selected based on financial need.

Funds Avail.: No specific amount. **Duration:** Annual. **To Apply:** Applicants must submit a completed scholarship application form together with a resume and a letter of qualifications.

7515 ■ J. McDonald and Judy Williams School of Law Scholarships
(Undergraduate/Scholarship)

Purpose: To support students to meet the educational costs of attending the School of Law. **Focus:** Law. **Qualif.:** Applicants must be admitted at Pepperdine University; and must be members of the Church of Christ. **Criteria:** Award is given based on merit and financial need.

Funds Avail.: No specific amount. **Duration:** Annual. **To Apply:** Applicants must submit a completed scholarship application form together with a resume, letter of qualifications, and a letter confirming active membership in a local Church of Christ congregation.

7516 ■ John Merrick Law Scholarships
(Undergraduate/Scholarship)

Purpose: To support students to meet the educational costs of attending the School of Law. **Focus:** Law. **Qualif.:** Applicants must be Pepperdine University School of Law students. **Criteria:** Preference is given to those with an interest in public service.

Funds Avail.: No specific amount. **Duration:** Annual. **To Apply:** Applicants must submit a completed scholarship application form together with a resume and a letter of qualifications.

7517 ■ Charles I. Nelson Endowed Scholarships
(Undergraduate/Scholarship)

Purpose: To support students to meet the educational costs of attending the School of Law. **Focus:** Law. **Qualif.:** Applicants must be Pepperdine University School of Law students. **Criteria:** Recipient of the award is determined by the Scholarship Committee.

Funds Avail.: No specific amount. **Duration:** Annual. **To Apply:** Applicants must submit a completed scholarship application form together with a resume and a letter of qualifications.

7518 ■ Gunnar Nicholson Endowed Scholarships
(Undergraduate/Scholarship)

Purpose: To provide scholarships to deserving students. **Focus:** Law. **Qualif.:** Applicants must be Pepperdine University School of Law students. **Criteria:** Recipient of the award is determined by the Scholarship Committee.

Funds Avail.: No specific amount. **Duration:** Annual. **To Apply:** Applicants must submit a completed scholarship application form together with a resume and a letter of qualifications.

7519 ■ Pepperdine University Armenian Student Scholarships
(Undergraduate/Scholarship)

Purpose: To support students to meet the educational costs of attending the School of Law. **Focus:** Law. **Qualif.:** Applicants must be law students of Armenian heritage; and must be admitted at Pepperdine University School of Law. **Criteria:** Selection will be based on financial need, academic merit, community involvement and personal achievement.

Funds Avail.: No specific amount. **Duration:** Annual. **To Apply:** Applicants must submit a completed application form together with a resume and a letter of qualifications.

7520 ■ Pepperdine University Dean's Scholarships
(Doctorate, Graduate/Scholarship)

Purpose: To assist students in the Juris Doctor program at Pepperdine University School of Law. **Focus:** Law. **Qualif.:** Applicants must be admitted as full-time students at the Juris Doctor program at Pepperdine University School of Law in fall or spring semesters only; must have an undergraduate GPA of 3.5 or higher; and an LSAT score in the 88th percentile. **Criteria:** Award is given based on merit.

Funds Avail.: No specific amount. **Duration:** Annual. **To Apply:** Applicants admitted full-time will be automatically considered.

7521 ■ Pepperdine University Diversity Scholarships
(Doctorate, Graduate/Scholarship)

Purpose: To support students to meet the educational costs of attending the School of Law. **Focus:** Law. **Qualif.:**

Awards are arranged alphabetically below their administering organizations

Applicants must be admitted as full-time students of the Juris Doctor program at Pepperdine University School of Law in the fall or spring semesters only. Applicants must have the ability to bring significant diversity to the student body. **Criteria:** Award is given based on merit.

Funds Avail.: No specific amount. **To Apply:** Applicants must submit a completed Diversity Scholarship application to the Admissions Office.

7522 ■ Pepperdine University Faculty Scholarships
(Doctorate, Graduate/Scholarship)

Purpose: To assist students in the Juris Doctor program at Pepperdine University School of Law. **Focus:** Law. **Qualif.:** Applicants must be admitted as full-time students at the Juris Doctor program at Pepperdine University School of Law in the fall or spring semesters only; have a minimum undergraduate GPA of 3.65; and an LSAT score in the 93rd percentile. **Criteria:** Recipients are selected based on academic excellence and personal achievement, without regard to financial need.

Funds Avail.: No specific amount. **Duration:** Annual. **To Apply:** Applicants must submit a complete admission file; faculty scholar application; and a letter to the Office of Admissions.

7523 ■ Jamie Phillips Endowed Scholarships
(Undergraduate/Scholarship)

Purpose: To support students to meet the educational costs of attending the School of Law. **Focus:** Law. **Qualif.:** Applicants must be Pepperdine University School of Law students. **Criteria:** Recipient of the award is determined by the Scholarship Committee.

Funds Avail.: No specific amount. **Duration:** Annual. **To Apply:** Applicants must submit a completed scholarship application form together with a resume and a letter of qualifications.

7524 ■ John Purfield Endowed Scholarships
(Undergraduate/Scholarship)

Purpose: To support students to meet the educational costs of attending the School of Law. **Focus:** Law. **Qualif.:** Applicants must be Pepperdine University School of Law students. **Criteria:** Award is given based on academic excellence.

Funds Avail.: No specific amount. **Duration:** Annual. **To Apply:** Applicants must submit a completed scholarship application form together with a resume and a letter of qualifications.

7525 ■ Barbara A. Shacochis Scholarships
(Undergraduate/Scholarship)

Purpose: To support students to meet the educational costs of attending the School of Law. **Focus:** Law. **Qualif.:** Applicants must be Pepperdine University School of Law students and members of the Law Review. **Criteria:** Preference will be given to third year Law Review students or editors of the Law Review.

Funds Avail.: No specific amount. **Duration:** Annual. **To Apply:** Applicants must submit a completed scholarship application form together with a resume and a letter of qualifications.

7526 ■ Benjamin G. Shatz Scholarships
(Undergraduate/Scholarship)

Purpose: To support students to meet the educational costs of attending the School of Law. **Focus:** Law. **Qualif.:**

Applicants must be second or third-year students and active members of the Jewish Law Student Association. **Criteria:** Award is given based on merit and financial need.

Funds Avail.: No specific amount. **Duration:** Annual. **To Apply:** Applicants must submit a completed scholarship application form together with a resume and a letter of qualifications.

7527 ■ Stuart Silverman Scholarships
(Undergraduate/Scholarship)

Purpose: To support students to meet the educational costs of attending the School of Law. **Focus:** Law. **Qualif.:** Applicants must be Pepperdine University School of Law students pursuing a Juris Doctorate degree at the School of Law; and must have overcome a major tragedy or hardship. **Criteria:** Award is given based on need.

Funds Avail.: No specific amount. **Duration:** Annual. **To Apply:** Applicants must submit a completed scholarship application form together with a resume and a letter of qualifications.

7528 ■ Special Law School Scholarships
(Undergraduate/Scholarship)

Purpose: To support students to meet the educational costs of attending the School of Law. **Focus:** Law. **Qualif.:** Applicants must be Pepperdine University School of Law students with a special financial need. **Criteria:** Award is given based on financial need.

Funds Avail.: No specific amount. **Duration:** Annual. **To Apply:** Applicants must submit a completed scholarship application form together with a resume and a letter of qualifications.

7529 ■ Honorable Raymond Thompson Endowed Scholarships *(Undergraduate/Scholarship)*

Purpose: To support students to meet the educational costs of attending the School of Law. **Focus:** Law. **Qualif.:** Applicants must be Pepperdine University School of Law students. **Criteria:** Award is given based on public service, extracurricular activities, financial need and merit.

Funds Avail.: No specific amount. **Duration:** Annual. **To Apply:** Applicants must submit a completed scholarship application form together with a resume and a letter of qualifications.

7530 ■ Thomas and Glenna Trimble Endowed Scholarships *(Undergraduate/Scholarship)*

Purpose: To support students to meet the educational costs of attending the School of Law. **Focus:** Law. **Qualif.:** Applicants must be admitted at Pepperdine University; and must be members of the Church of Christ. **Criteria:** Award is given based on financial need, merit, character, and church membership.

Funds Avail.: No specific amount. **Duration:** Annual. **To Apply:** Applicants must submit a completed scholarship application form together with a resume, letter of qualifications, and a letter confirming active membership in a local Church of Christ congregation.

7531 ■ Brian J. White Endowed Law Scholarships
(Undergraduate/Scholarship)

Purpose: To support students to meet the educational costs of attending the School of Law. **Focus:** Law. **Qualif.:** Applicants must be practicing Christians committed to pursuing a career in criminal defense; must actively wor-

Awards are arranged alphabetically below their administering organizations

ship with a local congregation and be committed to Christ. **Criteria:** Award is given based on a review of all application materials.

Funds Avail.: No specific amount. **Duration:** Annual. **To Apply:** Applicants must submit a completed scholarship application form together with a resume, letter of qualifications, and a letter of confirmation from a minister or priest.

7532 ■ Howard A. White Endowed Scholarships
(Undergraduate/Scholarship)

Purpose: To support students to meet the educational costs of attending the School of Law. **Focus:** Law. **Qualif.:** Applicants must be Pepperdine University School of Law students. **Criteria:** Award is given based on merit.

Funds Avail.: No specific amount. **Duration:** Annual. **To Apply:** Applicants must submit a completed scholarship application form together with a resume and a letter of qualifications.

7533 ■ Perkins Coie L.L.P.
1201 3rd Ave., Ste. 4800
Seattle, WA 98101
Ph: (206)359-8000
Fax: (206)359-9000
URL: www.perkinscoie.com

7534 ■ Perkins Coie 1L Diversity Fellowships
(Postgraduate/Fellowship)

Purpose: To support students from a diversity of backgrounds in their pursuit of legal education, as well as for their preparation in legal careers. **Focus:** Law. **Qualif.:** Applicants must be first year law students from a diversity of backgrounds. **Criteria:** Selection will be based on the committee's criteria.

Funds Avail.: $7,500. **To Apply:** Interested applicants may contact the Firm for the application process and other information. **Deadline:** January 9.

7535 ■ Perkins Coie 1L Patent Litigation and Patent Fellowships *(Postgraduate/Fellowship)*

Purpose: To allow those law students to further their knowledge and interest in patent litigation and/or patent prosecution. **Focus:** Law. **Qualif.:** Applicants must be students with particular technical backgrounds and an interest in patent litigation and/or patent prosecution. **Criteria:** Selection will be based on the committee's criteria.

Funds Avail.: $7,500. **To Apply:** Interested applicants may contact the Firm for the application process and other information. **Deadline:** January 9.

7536 ■ Perkins Coie 1L Political Law Fellowships
(Postgraduate/Fellowship)

Purpose: To assist students with their political law careers. **Focus:** Law; Political science. **Qualif.:** Applicants must be law students who are interested in political law. **Criteria:** Selection will be based on the committee's criteria.

Funds Avail.: $7,500. **To Apply:** Applicants must contact the Firm for the application process and other information. **Deadline:** January 9.

7537 ■ Petroleum History Society (PHS)
1638 Broadview Rd., NW
Calgary, AB, Canada T2N 3H1
Ph: (403)283-9268

E-mail: info@petroleumhistory.ca
URL: www.petroleumhistory.ca

7538 ■ Petroleum History Society Graduate Scholarships *(Graduate/Scholarship)*

Purpose: To support a graduate student working in a field of study related to petroleum history. **Focus:** History. **Qualif.:** Applicant must be, at the time of tenure, registered full-time in a graduate program in the Faculty of Graduate Studies at the University of Calgary. **Criteria:** Selection is based on the application.

Funds Avail.: $1,500. **Duration:** Annual. **Number Awarded:** 1. **To Apply:** Applicants may contact the Graduate Scholarship Office at University of Calgary for the application information. **Contact:** gsaward@ucalgary.ca.

7539 ■ Petroleum Packaging Council (PPC)
c/o ATD Management Inc.
1519 via Tulipan
San Clemente, CA 92673-3715
Ph: (949)369-7102
Fax: (949)366-1057
E-mail: ppc@atdmanagement.com
URL: www.ppcouncil.org

7540 ■ Petroleum Packaging Council Scholarships
(Undergraduate/Scholarship)

Purpose: To provide technical leadership and education for the petroleum packaging industry. **Focus:** Packaging. **Qualif.:** Must be a child of a PPC member in good standing. **Criteria:** Scholarships are given based on the academic performance of the student.

Funds Avail.: $2,500. **Number Awarded:** 2. **To Apply:** Applications are available online. Applicant must be a member to access the links. **Deadline:** April 1. **Contact:** Brenda Baker at ppc@atdmanagement.com.

7541 ■ Pew Charitable Trusts
1 Commerce Sq., Ste. 2800
2005 Market St.
Philadelphia, PA 19103-7077
Ph: (215)575-9050
Fax: (215)575-4939
E-mail: info@pewtrusts.org
URL: www.pewtrusts.org

7542 ■ Pew Latin American Fellows Program in the Biomedical Sciences *(Other/Fellowship)*

Purpose: To support young scientists from Latin America to receive postdoctoral training in the United States. **Focus:** Biomedical research. **Qualif.:** Applicants must be scientists from Latin America. **Criteria:** Recipients will be selected based on their commitment as outstanding investigators as well as the scientific merit of their research proposal, record training and the match of their interests with those of their host laboratory in the United States.

Funds Avail.: $30,000 stipend plus $35,000 for the purchase of supplies and equipment. **Duration:** Annual. **To Apply:** Applicants must send an e-mail to the Program Manager to request a username and password to be able to access the online application guide. **Remarks:** Established in 1990. **Contact:** Anita Pepper, Director; Email: apepper@pewtrusts.org.

Awards are arranged alphabetically below their administering organizations

7543 ■ Pfizer Epilepsy Scholarship Award

c/o Adeph Eden Health Communications
30 Irving Pl., 10th Fl.
New York, NY 10003
Free: 800-292-7373
URL: www.epilepsy-scholarship.com

7544 ■ Pfizer Epilepsy Scholarships *(Graduate, Undergraduate/Scholarship)*

Purpose: To support students with epilepsy in their educational pursuits. **Focus:** General studies/Field of study not specified. **Qualif.:** Applicant must be under a doctor's care for epilepsy; a high school senior who has applied to college, a freshman, sophomore or junior in college; or a college senior who applied to a graduate school. **Criteria:** Selection is based on the submitted application materials.

Funds Avail.: $2,000. **Duration:** Annual. **Number Awarded:** 40. **To Apply:** Applicants must first register at the website before submitting an application form. **Deadline:** June 15.

7545 ■ Pfizer Inc.

235 E 42nd St.
New York, NY 10017-5703
Ph: (212)733-2323
Fax: (212)573-7851
Free: 800-879-3477
URL: www.pfizer.com

7546 ■ ASPIRE Rheumatology and Dermatology Research Awards *(Postdoctorate/Award)*

Purpose: To support promising investigators with an interest in advancing knowledge in defined disease areas within rheumatology and dermatology. **Focus:** Dermatology; Rheumatology. **Qualif.:** Applicants must be U.S. investigators and must have a professional degree. **Criteria:** The selection committee will evaluate applicants based on the following criteria: the scientific merit of the research proposal and its relevance to the program's mission; evidence of the applicants' commitment to an academic research career; evidence of a suitable research environment; and the qualifications of the applicants.

Funds Avail.: $750,000. **Duration:** Annual. **Number Awarded:** 5. **To Apply:** Interested applicants must complete the online submission. Applicants must also include at least three of the following documentation to no more than six separate uploads: description of available laboratory facilities; listing of other research support; listing of consenting collaborators (including CVs) if applicable; bibliography of relevant references. **Deadline:** July 10.

7547 ■ PFLAG Columbia/Howard County

PO Box 1479
Columbia, MD 21044
Ph: (443)745-8294
E-mail: pflagmd@gmail.com
URL: pflagmd.org

7548 ■ PFLAG Columbia-Howard County Scholarship *(Undergraduate/Scholarship)*

Purpose: To recognize outstanding lesbian, gay, bisexual, transgender and allied students; to encourage the pursuit of post-secondary education for self-identified LGBT and allies; to foster a positive image of the LGBT society. **Focus:** General studies/Field of study not specified. **Qualif.:** Applicant must self-identify as lesbian, gay, bisexual, transgender or as an Ally who demonstrates outstanding support directly and supports equality for all; must be a resident of the state of Maryland who is currently attending or planning to attend a post-secondary educational institution during the current academic year. **Criteria:** The Scholarship Selection Committee will review all applications at once and make their final decision. All applicants will receive written communication of the decisions made by the scholarship committee. All decisions will be sent out in the mail. The scholarship recipient will be publicly announced at the general meeting in May, and attendance at this meeting is mandatory.

Funds Avail.: $2,000. **Duration:** Annual. **Number Awarded:** 2. **To Apply:** Applicants must fully complete a Columbia-Howard County PFLAG scholarship applciation and submit all required supplemental forms.Application forms are available online. **Deadline:** April 11.

7549 ■ Pharmaceutical Research and Manufacturers of America Foundation

950 F St. NW, Ste. 300
Washington, DC 20004
Ph: (202)572-7756
Fax: (202)572-7799
E-mail: foundation@phrma.org
URL: www.phrmafoundation.org

7550 ■ Informatics Post Doctoral Fellowships *(Doctorate/Fellowship)*

Purpose: To support the post doctoral career development of individuals preparing to engage in research that will bridge the gap between experimental and computational approaches in genomic and biomedical studies. **Focus:** General studies/Field of study not specified. **Qualif.:** Applicants must either (1) hold a PhD degree in a field of study logically or functionally related to the proposed post doctoral activities, or (2) expect to receive the PhD before activating the award. Applicants must also have a firm commitment from an accredited U.S. university and be a U.S. citizen or permanent resident. The sponsor (mentor) of the post doctoral program must describe how the multidisciplinary goals of the research training program will be accomplished and provide assurance that key collaborating mentors endorse and are willing to support the training plan. **Criteria:** Selection will be based on the committee's criteria.

Funds Avail.: $40,000. **Duration:** Annual. **To Apply:** Applications must be submitted by an accredited U.S. school via the foundation website. **Deadline:** September 1.

7551 ■ Informatics Pre Doctoral Fellowships *(Doctorate/Fellowship)*

Purpose: To promote the use of informatics in an integrative approach to the understanding of biological and disease processes. **Focus:** General studies/Field of study not specified. **Qualif.:** Applicants must be full-time, in-residence PhD candidates in the fields of informatics who are enrolled in USA schools of medicine, pharmacy, dentistry or veterinary medicine. **Criteria:** Selection will be based on the committee's criteria.

Funds Avail.: $20,000. **Duration:** Annual; 1 - 2 years. **To Apply:** Applications must be submitted by an accredited

Awards are arranged alphabetically below their administering organizations

U.S. school via the foundation website. **Deadline:** September 1.

7552 ■ Informatics Sabbatical Fellowships (Doctorate, Postdoctorate/Fellowship)

Purpose: To enable faculty with active research programs to work outside of their home institutions for periods of six months to one year to learn new skills or develop new collaborations that will enhance their research and research training capabilities in informatics. **Focus:** General studies/Field of study not specified. **Qualif.:** Applicants must: hold a PhD or MD degree in a field of study logically or functionally related to the proposed post doctoral activities; hold a faculty appointment that imparts eligibility for a sabbatical; leave from their home institution; have institutional approval of a sabbatical plan that includes partial salary that matches the PhRMA stipend; hold an endorsement from a mentor who agrees to sponsor the applicant's visiting scientist activity; be a U.S. citizen or permanent resident. **Criteria:** Selection will be based on the committee's criteria.

Funds Avail.: $40,000. **Duration:** Annual. **To Apply:** Applications must be submitted by an accredited U.S. school via the foundation website. **Deadline:** September 1.

7553 ■ Pharmaceutics Post Doctoral Fellowships (Postdoctorate/Fellowship)

Purpose: To assist individuals doing post-doctoral research. **Focus:** Pharmacy. **Qualif.:** Applicants must hold a PhD degree in pharmaceutics or a related discipline from an accredited U.S. university or expect to receive such a degree before activating the fellowship. The mentor of the fellow must be in an accredited school of pharmacy. Alternatively, a student with a PhD from a school of pharmacy may use the fellowship to study with a mentor in any science or engineering department. **Criteria:** Selection will be based on the committee's criteria.

Funds Avail.: $40,000. **Duration:** Annual; up to 2 years. **To Apply:** Applicants must submit their applications via the foundation website. **Deadline:** December 15.

7554 ■ Pharmaceutics Research Starter Grants (Doctorate/Grant)

Purpose: To offer financial support to individuals beginning their independent research careers at the faculty level. **Focus:** Pharmacy. **Qualif.:** Grants are open to those holding an academic, tenure track, rank of instructor or assistant professor, and to investigators at the doctoral level with equivalent positions providing their proposed research is neither directly nor indirectly subsidized to any significant degree by an extramural support mechanism. **Criteria:** Selection will be based on the committee's criteria.

Funds Avail.: $100,000. **Duration:** Annual. **To Apply:** Applicants must submit their applications via the Foundation website. **Deadline:** December 15.

7555 ■ Pharmaceutics Sabbatical Fellowships (Postdoctorate/Fellowship)

Purpose: To provide stipend funding to enable pharmaceutics faculty members at all levels with active research programs the opportunity to work at other institutions. **Focus:** Pharmacy. **Qualif.:** Applicants must hold a PhD, PharmD, MD or ScD degree in a field of study logically or functionally related to the proposed post doctoral activities; hold a faculty appointment that imparts eligibility for a sabbatical leave from their home institution; have institutional approval of a sabbatical plan that includes partial salary

that matches the PhRMA stipend; hold an endorsement from a mentor who agrees to sponsor the applicant's visiting scientist activity; and be a U.S. citizen or permanent resident. **Criteria:** Selection will be based on the committee's criteria.

Funds Avail.: $40,000. **Duration:** Annual. **To Apply:** Applicants must submit their applications via the Foundation website. **Deadline:** December 15.

7556 ■ Pharmacology/Toxicology Pre Doctoral Fellowships (Doctorate/Fellowship)

Purpose: To assist in the candidate's pre doctoral training. **Focus:** Pharmacology; Toxicology. **Qualif.:** Applicant must be full-time student, in-residence PhD candidates in the fields of pharmacology or toxicology who are enrolled in USA schools of medicine, pharmacy, dentistry or veterinary medicine. Applicants must be U.S. citizens or permanent residents. **Criteria:** Selection will be based on the committee's criteria.

Funds Avail.: $20,000. **Duration:** Annual; up 2 years. **To Apply:** Applications must be submitted by an accredited U.S. school through the Foundation website. **Deadline:** December 15.

7557 ■ PhRMA Foundation Health Outcomes Post Doctoral Fellowships (Postdoctorate/Fellowship)

Purpose: To provide stipend support for individuals engaged in a research training program that will create or extend their credentials in health outcomes. **Focus:** Health sciences; Public health. **Qualif.:** Applicants must be PharmD, MD, and PhD graduates; must have a firm commitment from an accredited U.S. university; must be U.S. citizens or permanent residents. **Criteria:** Selection will be based on the committee's criteria.

Funds Avail.: No specific amount. **Duration:** Annual. **To Apply:** Applications must be submitted via the Foundations website. **Deadline:** February 1.

7558 ■ PhRMA Foundation Health Outcomes Pre Doctoral Fellowships (Doctorate/Fellowship)

Purpose: To assist full-time, in-residence PhD candidates in the fields of health outcomes. **Focus:** Health sciences; Public health. **Qualif.:** Applicants must be PhD candidates in the fields of health outcomes who are enrolled in U.S. schools of medicine, pharmacy, dentistry, nursing, or schools of public health; must have a firm commitment from a U.S. university; must be U.S. citizens or permanent residents. **Criteria:** Selection will be based on the committee's criteria.

Funds Avail.: No specific amount. **Duration:** Annual. **To Apply:** Applications must be submitted by an accredited U.S. school. **Deadline:** February 1.

7559 ■ PhRMA Foundation Health Outcomes Research Starter Grants (Doctorate/Grant)

Purpose: To offer financial support to individuals beginning their independent research careers at the faculty level. **Focus:** Health sciences; Public health. **Qualif.:** Grants are open to those holding an academic rank of instructor or assistant professor, and to investigators at the doctoral level with equivalent positions; must be sponsored by the department or unit within which the proposed research is to be undertaken; must have a firm commitment from a U.S. university. **Criteria:** Applicants will be judged on the scientific worthiness of the proposed research, and on the degree of need.

Awards are arranged alphabetically below their administering organizations

Funds Avail.: No specific amount. **To Apply:** Applications should be submitted through the foundation website. **Deadline:** February 1.

7560 ■ PhRMA Foundation Health Outcomes Sabbatical Fellowships (Postdoctorate/Fellowship)

Purpose: To enable faculty with active research programs to work outside of their home institution. **Focus:** Health sciences; Public health. **Qualif.:** Applicants must: hold a PhD, MD, PharmD, or ScD degree in a field of study logically or functionally related to the proposed post doctoral activities; hold a faculty appointment that imparts eligibility for a sabbatical leave from their home institution; have institutional approval of a sabbatical plan that includes partial salary that matches the PhRMA stipend; hold an endorsement from a mentor who agrees to sponsor the applicant's visiting scientist activity; and be a U.S. citizen or permanent resident. **Criteria:** Selection will be based on the committee's criteria.

Funds Avail.: No specific amount. **To Apply:** Applications must be submitted via the Foundation website. **Deadline:** February 1.

7561 ■ PhRMA Foundation Informatics Research Starter Grants (Doctorate/Grant)

Purpose: To provide financial support to individuals beginning their independent research careers at the faculty level. **Focus:** General studies/Field of study not specified. **Qualif.:** Applicants must be holding an academic rank of Assistant Professor (or Research Assistant Professor) within a tenure track (or Research track) appointment. **Criteria:** Preference will be given to individuals whose research combines the application of novel computational methods with experimental validation.

Funds Avail.: $100,000. **Duration:** Annual. **To Apply:** Applications must be submitted by an accredited U.S. school via the foundation website. **Deadline:** September 1.

7562 ■ PhRMA Foundation Pharmaceutics Pre Doctoral Fellowships (Doctorate/Fellowship)

Purpose: To support advanced students who will have completed the bulk of their pre-thesis requirements and are starting their thesis research by the time the award is activated. **Focus:** Pharmacy. **Qualif.:** Applicants must hold a BS, MS or PharmD degree in pharmacy or a related area such as chemistry or biology from an accredited school in the USA. Candidates enrolled in a PharmD/PhD program should not be taking required clinical course work or clinical clerkships during the tenure of the fellowship. **Criteria:** Selection will be based on the committee's criteria.

Funds Avail.: No specific amount. **Duration:** Annual. **To Apply:** Applicants must submit their applications via the foundation website. **Deadline:** September 1.

7563 ■ PhRMA Foundation Pharmacology/ Toxicology Research Starter Grants (Doctorate/ Grant)

Purpose: To provide financial support to individuals beginning their independent research careers at the faculty level. **Focus:** Pharmacology; Toxicology. **Qualif.:** Grants are open to those holding an academic rank of instructor or assistant professor, and to investigators at the doctoral level with equivalent positions; must be in a tenure track position for 3 years or less; must be sponsored by the department or unit in which the proposed research is to be undertaken. The sponsoring unit must have responsibility for pharmacology/toxicology teaching and research as part of its core mission. If the pharmacology/toxicology mission is not apparent on the sponsoring unit's website, the sponsored letter must describe how the academic appointment will support the applicant's career development in pharmacology/toxicology. **Criteria:** Selection will be based on the committee's criteria.

Funds Avail.: No specific amount. **To Apply:** Applicants must submit their applications via the foundation website. **Deadline:** September 1.

7564 ■ PhRMA Foundation Pharmacology/ Toxicology Sabbatical Fellowships (Postdoctorate/ Fellowship)

Purpose: To enable faculty with active research programs to work outside of their home institutions for periods of 6 months to one year to learn new skills or develop new collaborations that will enhance their research training capabilities in pharmacology/toxicology. **Focus:** Pharmacology; Toxicology. **Qualif.:** Applicants must: hold a PhD degree or appropriate terminal doctorate and record of research accomplishment in a field of study logically or functionally related to the proposed post doctoral activities; hold a faculty appointment that imparts eligibility for a sabbatical leave from their home institution; have institutional approval of a sabbatical plan that includes partial salary that matches the PhRMA stipend; hold an endorsement from a mentor who agrees to sponsor the applicant's visiting scientist activity; be a U.S. citizen or permanent resident. **Criteria:** Selection will be based on the committee's criteria.

Funds Avail.: No specific amount. **To Apply:** Applicants must submit their applications via the foundation website. **Deadline:** September 1.

7565 ■ PhRMA Foundaton Pharmacology/ Toxicology Post Doctoral Fellowships (Postdoctorate/Fellowship)

Purpose: To support post-doctoral career development activities of individuals prepared to engage in research that integrates information on molecular or cellular mechanisms of action with information on the effect of an agent in the intact organism. **Focus:** Pharmacology; Toxicology. **Qualif.:** Applicants must either (1) hold a PhD degree or appropriate terminal research doctorate in a field of study logically or functionally related to the proposed post doctoral activities, or (2) expect to receive the PhD before activating the award. Applicants must also have a firm commitment from a mentor at an accredited U.S. university and be a U.S. citizen or permanent resident. **Criteria:** Selection will be based on the committee's criteria.

Funds Avail.: No specific amount. **Duration:** Annual; 2 years. **To Apply:** Applicants must submit their applications via the Foundation website.

7566 ■ Phi Alpha Theta

University of South Florida
4202 E Fowler Ave., SOC107
Tampa, FL 33620-8100
Fax: (813)974-8215
Free: 800-394-8195
E-mail: info@phialphatheta.org
URL: www.phialphatheta.org

7567 ■ Thomas S. Morgan Memorial Scholarship (Graduate, Master's/Scholarship)

Purpose: To support Phi Alpha Theta graduate students and their educational goals. **Focus:** History. **Qualif.:** Ap-

Awards are arranged alphabetically below their administering organizations

plicant must be a Phi Alpha Theta member entering graduate school for the first time and enrolled in a Master's program in History. **Criteria:** Selection is based on the application.

Funds Avail.: $1,000. **To Apply:** Applicants must submit six copies of the completed application form together with six copies of official transcripts (one official copy from each undergraduate and graduate institution where work was credited toward a degree); six copies of curriculum vitae or resume; GRE scores; letter of recommendation from each of the three individuals listed in the application (original only); letter from the Department Chair confirming the student is not enrolled in an online program. **Deadline:** March 1. **Contact:** Phi Alpha Theta History Honor Society, University of South Florida; E-Mail: info@phialphatheta.org.

7568 ■ William E. Parrish Scholarships (Graduate, Master's/Scholarship)

Purpose: To support Phi Alpha Theta graduate students and their educational goals. **Focus:** History. **Qualif.:** Applicant must be a Phi Alpha Theta member entering graduate school for the first time and enrolled in a Master's program in History. **Criteria:** Selection is based on the application.

Funds Avail.: $1,000. **To Apply:** Applicants must submit six copies of the completed application form together with six copies of official transcripts (one official copy from each undergraduate and graduate institution where work was credited toward a degree); six copies of curriculum vitae or resume; GRE scores; letter of recommendation from each of the three individuals listed in the application (original only); letter from the Department Chair confirming the student is not enrolled in an online program. **Deadline:** March 1. **Contact:** Phi Alpha Theta History Honor Society, University of South Florida; E-Mail: info@phialphatheta.org.

7569 ■ Phi Alpha Theta Doctoral Scholarships (Doctorate/Scholarship)

Purpose: To financially support graduate student members who are pursuing a PhD in History. **Focus:** History. **Qualif.:** Applicant must be a graduate student member pursuing a PhD in History and have passed the general examination. **Criteria:** Selection is based on the application.

Funds Avail.: No specific amount. **Duration:** Annual. **To Apply:** Applicants must submit six copies of the completed application and supporting materials (official transcripts; curriculum vitae or resume; writing sample; letter of recommendation; dissertation prospectus of no more than 3 double-spaced pages; letter from the History Department Chair confirming the applicant is not enrolled in an online degree program) **Deadline:** March 1. **Contact:** Doctoral Scholarship Committee, Phi Alpha Theta History Honor Society, University of South Florida at the above address.

7570 ■ Phi Alpha Theta Faculty Advisor Research Grant (Other/Grant)

Purpose: To support the advancement of a faculty advisor's career. **Focus:** History. **Qualif.:** Applicant must be a faculty advisor who has served as a chapter advisor for five or more years and is currently advising. **Criteria:** Selection is based on years of service to Phi Alpha Theta; compliance with honor society procedures and guidelines (i.e. submitting initiates) and the merit of the proposal.

Funds Avail.: $1,000. **To Apply:** Applicant must submit four copies of the completed application form and all supporting materials; four copies of a current curriculum vitae

including a selected list of the applicant's publications; and the original and three copies of a letter of support from Department Chair or Dean. **Deadline:** July1. **Contact:** Phi Alpha Theta History Honor Society, University of South Florida; E-Mail: info@phialphatheta.org.

7571 ■ John Pine Memorial Scholarships (Doctorate, Graduate/Scholarship)

Purpose: To financially support graduate student members who are pursuing a PhD in History. **Focus:** History. **Qualif.:** Applicant must be a graduate student member pursuing a PhD in History and have passed the general examination. **Criteria:** Selection is based on the application.

Funds Avail.: $1,000. **Duration:** Annual. **To Apply:** Applicants must submit six copies of completed application and supporting materials (official transcripts; curriculum vitae or resume; writing sample; letter of recommendation; dissertation prospectus of no more than 3 double-spaced pages; letter from the History Department Chair confirming the applicant is not enrolled in an online degree program) **Deadline:** March 1. **Contact:** Phi Alpha Theta History Honor Society, University of South Florida; E-Mail: info@phialphatheta.org.

7572 ■ Graydon A. Tunstall Undergraduate Student Scholarships (Undergraduate/Scholarship)

Purpose: To support student members and their educational goals. **Focus:** History. **Qualif.:** Applicant must be a student member entering senior year and majoring in Modern European History. **Criteria:** Selection is based on financial need and merit.

Funds Avail.: $1,000. **To Apply:** Applicants must submit three copies of the completed application form together with official transcripts (one official copy from each undergraduate institution where work was credited toward a degree); three copies of curriculum vitae or resume; letter of recommendation from each of the three individuals listed in the application form (original only); and a letter from the Department Chair confirming the applicant is not enrolled in an online program. **Deadline:** March 1. **Contact:** Undergraduate Scholarship Committee, Phi Alpha Theta History Honor Society University of South Florida; E-mail: info@phialphatheta.org.

7573 ■ A.F. Zimmerman Scholarships (Graduate, Master's/Scholarship)

Purpose: To support Phi Alpha Theta graduate students and their educational goals. **Focus:** History. **Qualif.:** Applicant must be a Phi Alpha Theta member entering graduate school for the first time and enrolled in a Master's program in History. **Criteria:** Selection is based on the application.

Funds Avail.: $1,250. **To Apply:** Applicants must submit six copies of the completed application form together with six copies of official transcripts (one official copy from each undergraduate and graduate institution where work was credited toward a degree); six copies of curriculum vitae or resume; GRE scores; letter of recommendation from each of the three individuals listed in the application (original only); letter from the Department Chair confirming the student is not enrolled in an online program. **Deadline:** March 1. **Contact:** Phi Alpha Theta History Honor Society, University of South Florida; E-Mail: info@phialphatheta.org.

7574 ■ Phi Beta Kappa Society
1606 New Hampshire Ave. NW
Washington, DC 20009

Awards are arranged alphabetically below their administering organizations

Ph: (202)265-3808
Fax: (202)986-1601
E-mail: info@pbk.org
URL: www.pbk.org

7575 ■ Walter J. Jensen Fellowships *(Other/Fellowship)*

Purpose: To help educators and researchers improve education in standard French language, literature and culture and in the study of standard French in the United States. **Focus:** French studies. **Qualif.:** Candidates must be U.S. citizens under the age of 40 who can demonstrate their career does or will involve active use of the French language. They must have earned a bachelor's degree from an accredited four-year institution with a 3.0 minimum GPA in French language and literature as a major. They must demonstrate superior competence in French, according to the standards established by the American Association of Teachers of French. **Criteria:** Preference may be given to members of Phi Beta Kappa and educators at the secondary school level or higher.

Funds Avail.: $15,500. **Duration:** Annual. **To Apply:** Applicants must complete an online application form; must submit an official transcript; GPA in French and Literature; list of scholarships, fellowships and prizes received; reference letter; and attach a statement including: description and impact of the study, place where the project would be conducted and expectations when report of studies would be published in France. **Deadline:** February 6. **Contact:** Further questions may send by e-mail at awards@pbk.org or call 202-745-3287.

7576 ■ Mary Isabel Sibley Fellowships *(Doctorate/Fellowship)*

Purpose: To increase interest in the study of Greek language, history, literature or archaeology, or the study of French language or literature. **Focus:** French studies; Greek studies; Linguistics. **Qualif.:** Candidates must be unmarried women 25 to 35 years of age who have demonstrated their ability to carry on with an original research; must hold a doctoral degree or have fulfilled all the requirements for a doctorate except for the dissertation; and must be planning to be full-time working on research during the fellowship year. Award is not restricted to Phi Beta Kappa members or U.S citizens. **Criteria:** Selection of applicants will be based on the criteria of the Fellowship Committee.

Funds Avail.: $20,000. **Duration:** Annual. **To Apply:** Applicants must submit the completed application form; official transcript; list of scholarships, fellowships and prizes received; three letters of reference; and attach a statement including: description/state of the project, place where project would be carried out and expectations with regards to study. Applicants must include four copies of each letter of recommendation in a single envelope signed and sealed by the reference. **Deadline:** January 15. **Remarks:** The fellowship is awarded alternately in the fields of Greek and French. **Contact:** Questions can be addressed to the Director of Society Affairs by calling 202-745-3287 or email awards@pbk.org.

7577 ■ Phi Chi Theta
1508 E Beltline Rd., Ste. 104
Carrollton, TX 75006
Ph: (972)245-7202
E-mail: executivedirector@phichitheta.org
URL: www.phichitheta.org

7578 ■ Anna E. Hall Memorial Scholarships *(Undergraduate, Graduate/Scholarship)*

Purpose: To support students who have made a substantial contribution and impact to the organization or local community intending to pursue a degree in the fields of business and/or economics. **Focus:** Business; Economics. **Qualif.:** Applicants must be national members of Phi Chi Theta in good standing who are students who have completed at least one semester or two quarters of college in United States, and will be enrolled or attending classes during the forthcoming academic year at an approved college or university in United States (in pursuit of a degree in the fields of Business and/or Economics). **Criteria:** Applicants will be selected based on: achievements and contributions to the Phi Chi Theta; scholastic achievement; courses enrolled during the Spring Semester; school and community involvement.

Funds Avail.: $700. **Duration:** Annual. **To Apply:** Applicants must submit a completed application form; one copy of an official transcript (mailed directly from Registrar's Office to the Scholarship Committee); two letters of recommendation from a Phi Chi Theta Fraternity officer; an essay explaining of how they see themselves in the next 3-5 years; resume; and professional or business photo. **Deadline:** March 1. **Remarks:** Established in 1989. **Contact:** Phi Chi Theta Scholarship Committee, c/o Mary Ellen Lewis, 1886 South Poplar Street, Denver, Colorado 80224-2271; Email at PCTEdScholarship@aol.com.

7579 ■ Helen D. Snow Memorial Scholarships *(Undergraduate/Scholarship)*

Purpose: To support students who have made a substantial contribution and impact to the organization or local community pursuing a degree in the fields of business and/or economics. **Focus:** Business; Economics. **Qualif.:** Applicants must be national members of Phi Chi Theta in good standing; must be students who have completed at least one semester or two quarters of college in United States; and must be enrolled or attending classes during the forthcoming academic year at an approved college or university in United States in pursuit of a degree in the fields of business and/or economics. **Criteria:** Candidates will be selected based on: achievements and contributions to the Phi Chi Theta; scholastic achievement as demonstrated in transcript; courses enrolled during the Spring Semester; school and community achievement and activities;

Funds Avail.: $700. **To Apply:** Applicants must submit a completed application form; one copy of an official transcript (mailed directly from Registrar's Office to the Scholarship Committee; two letters of recommendation from a Phi Chi Theta Fraternity officer; an essay explaining of how they see themselves in the next 3-5 years; resume; and professional or business photo. **Deadline:** May 1. **Contact:** For further information, applicants may send an e-mail to Scholarship Committee at pctedscholarship@aol.com.

7580 ■ Phi Delta Gamma
1201 Red Mile Rd.
Lexington, KY 40504-2648
Ph: (859)255-1848
Fax: (859)253-0779
E-mail: phigam@phigam.org
URL: www.phigam.org

Awards are arranged alphabetically below their administering organizations

7581 ■ Academic Achievement Awards
(Undergraduate/Scholarship)

Purpose: To support undergraduate members who need a healthy academic environment for their scholastic aspirations. **Focus:** General studies/Field of study not specified. **Qualif.:** Applicants must be initiated members of a Phi Gamma Delta chapter or colony; must have 3.2 on a 4.0 GPA scale during their pledging semester; must complete a minimum 12 credit hours for the semester. Chapter must have properly pledged and initiated the applicants; must have turned in all pledge and initiation forms and fees to the International Fraternity. Chapter President must verify membership by signing the application. **Criteria:** Selection will be based on the committee's criteria.

Funds Avail.: $250. **To Apply:** Application form can be obtained at the website. Applicants must insure that their application and all attachments are received at the Foundation offices on or before the deadline.

7582 ■ Peale Scholarship Grant *(Professional development/Scholarship)*

Purpose: To support Phi Gamma Delta brothers who have chosen careers in the ministry. **Focus:** Religion. **Qualif.:** Applicants must be members of a Phi Gamma Delta chapter or colony choosing a career in ministry. **Criteria:** Selection will be based on the committee's criteria.

Funds Avail.: No specific amount. **To Apply:** Interested applicants may contact Virginia Miller to request an application and other information.

7583 ■ Phi Eta Sigma
Western Kentucky University
1906 College Heights Blvd., No. 11062
Bowling Green, KY 42101-1062
Ph: (270)745-6540
Fax: (270)745-3893
E-mail: phi.eta.sigma@wku.edu
URL: www.phietasigma.org

7584 ■ Thomas Arkle Clark Scholar-Leader of the Year Endowed Scholarships *(Graduate, Undergraduate/Scholarship)*

Purpose: To support students with their educational goals. **Focus:** General studies/Field of study not specified. **Qualif.:** Applicants must be members of Phi Eta Sigma. **Criteria:** Selection will be based on: high scholastic records with a minimum 3.5 cumulative GPA; participation in local chapter activities; evidence of creative ability; potential for success in chosen field; letters of recommendation, not to exceed three.

Funds Avail.: $10,000. **Duration:** Annual. **To Apply:** Application forms for undergraduate scholarships may be obtained from the chapter adviser. Members applying for graduate scholarships may contact the chapter adviser, or may request an application form by mailing a request to the national office (a self-addressed stamped envelope should be enclosed). **Deadline:** March 1. **Contact:** Phi Eta Sigma, at the above address.

7585 ■ Phi Eta Sigma Distinguished Member Scholarships - Graduate or Professional *(Graduate, Other/Scholarship)*

Purpose: To support members who are pursuing higher education. **Focus:** General studies/Field of study not speci-

fied. **Qualif.:** Applicants must be members of Phi Eta Sigma. **Criteria:** Selection will be based on: high scholastic records with a minimum 3.5 cumulative GPA; participation in local chapter activities; evidence of creative ability; potential for success in chosen field; letters of recommendation, not to exceed three.

Funds Avail.: $7,500. **Duration:** Annual. **Number Awarded:** 6. **To Apply:** Applications may be sent directly to the secretary of the Scholarship Committee at the national office address or may be submitted to the chapter adviser so that all chapter applications may be sent to the national office in one mailing. **Deadline:** March 1. **Contact:** Phi Eta Sigma, at the above address.

7586 ■ Phi Eta Sigma Distinguished Member Scholarships - Undergraduate *(Undergraduate/Scholarship)*

Purpose: To support members who are pursuing higher education. **Focus:** General studies/Field of study not specified. **Qualif.:** Applicants must be full-time undergraduate student members of Phi Eta Sigma. **Criteria:** Selection will be based on: high scholastic records with a minimum 3.5 cumulative GPA; participation in local chapter activities; evidence of creative ability; potential for success in chosen field; letters of recommendation, not to exceed three.

Funds Avail.: $6,000. **Duration:** Annual. **To Apply:** Application forms for undergraduate scholarships may be obtained from the chapter adviser. **Deadline:** March 1. **Contact:** Phi Eta Sigma, at the above address.

7587 ■ Phi Eta Sigma Undergraduate Scholarship Awards *(Undergraduate/Scholarship)*

Purpose: To support members who are pursuing higher education. **Focus:** General studies/Field of study not specified. **Qualif.:** Applicants must be full-time undergraduate student members of Phi Eta Sigma. **Criteria:** Selection will be based on: high scholastic records with a minimum 3.5 cumulative GPA; participation in local chapter activities; evidence of creative ability; potential for success in chosen field; letters of recommendation, not to exceed three.

Funds Avail.: $1,000. **Duration:** Annual. **To Apply:** Application forms for undergraduate scholarships may be obtained from the chapter adviser. **Deadline:** March 1. **Contact:** Phi Eta Sigma, at the above address.

7588 ■ Phi Kappa Phi
7576 Goodwood Blvd.
Baton Rouge, LA 70806
Ph: (225)388-4917
Fax: (225)388-4900
Free: 800-804-9880
E-mail: info@phikappaphi.org
URL: www.phikappaphi.org

7589 ■ Phi Kappa Phi Fellowships *(Graduate, Undergraduate/Fellowship)*

Purpose: To provide financial support for members entering the first year of graduate or professional study. **Focus:** General studies/Field of study not specified. **Qualif.:** Applicants must be active members of Phi Kappa Phi and have applied to enroll as a full-time student in a post-baccalaureate program of study for the current academic year, at an accredited American Institution of higher learning. **Criteria:** Candidates will be evaluated based on academic achievement, including transcripts, honors and

Awards are arranged alphabetically below their administering organizations

awards, relevant research experience, standardized test scores, and samples of creative work, service and leadership experience, on and off campus letters of recommendation, personal statement and career goals, and acceptance at an approved graduate or professional program.

Funds Avail.: $5,000-$15,000. **Duration:** Annual. **Number Awarded:** 57. **To Apply:** Applicants must complete application online, print, and submit it with the other required materials to respective chapters. **Deadline:** April 15.

7590 ■ Phi Kappa Sigma (PKS)

2 Timber Dr.
Chester Springs, PA 19425
Ph: (610)469-3282
Fax: (610)469-3286
URL: www.pks.org

7591 ■ Phi Kappa Sigma Foundation Scholarship
(Undergraduate/Scholarship)

Purpose: To support students with financial needs who want to continue their education. **Focus:** General studies/ Field of study not specified. **Qualif.:** Applicants must be full-time students and active members of Phi Kappa Sigma Fraternity. **Criteria:** Selection will be based on the applicants' financial need, scholastic achievement or applicants' chapter, campus and community involvement.

Funds Avail.: Up to $5,000. **Duration:** Annual. **To Apply:** Applicants must visit the website to complete the online application process. **Deadline:** April 15.

7592 ■ Phi Kappa Sigma Need-Based Scholarships
(Undergraduate/Scholarship)

Purpose: To support student members with their educational pursuits. **Focus:** General studies/Field of study not specified. **Qualif.:** Applicants must be officially registered members of Phi Kappa Sigma Fraternity; with initiation fee having been remitted by the chapter to the Fraternity Headquarters; and must be in undergraduate level, taking up a bachelor's degree. **Criteria:** Selection is based on financial need and scholastic achievement.

Funds Avail.: No specific amount. **Duration:** One academic year. **Number Awarded:** Varies. **To Apply:** Applicants must submit/upload completed application forms along with the required materials: a Resume, Financial Information of the applicant (most recent tax return of the applicant and his/her parents), completed and signed Chapter Advisor check-off form, letter of intent (optional), Official transcript of grades must be forwarded directly by the college registrar. **Deadline:** April 15. **Contact:** All materials must be submitted to Reynold R. Hagel 6701 Sixth Avenue South Seattle, WA 98108, 206-499-2393 or scholarship@pks.org.

7593 ■ Phi Kappa Sigma Participation-Based Scholarships *(Undergraduate/Scholarship)*

Purpose: To support student members with their educational pursuits. **Focus:** General studies/Field of study not specified. **Qualif.:** Applicant must be an officially registered member of Phi Kappa Sigma Fraternity; with initiation fee having been remitted by the chapter to the Fraternity Headquarters; and must be in undergraduate level entering a bachelor's degree. **Criteria:** Selection will be based on the applicant's chapter, campus, and community involvement and scholastic achievement.

Funds Avail.: No specific amount. **Duration:** One aca-

demic year. **Number Awarded:** Varies. **To Apply:** Applicant must submit/upload a completed application form along with the required materials: resume, basic financial information (electronic copy of most recent tax return of the applicant and his/her parents), completed and signed Chapter Advisor check-off form, letter of intent (optional), Official transcript of grades must be forwarded directly by the college registrar. **Deadline:** April 15.

7594 ■ Phi Sigma Epsilon

5217 S 51st St.
Greenfield, WI 53220
Ph: (414)328-1952
Fax: (414)235-3425
E-mail: pse@pse.org
URL: www.pse.org

7595 ■ Anchor Plastics Scholarships *(Graduate, Undergraduate/Scholarship)*

Purpose: To advance education of Pi Sigma Epsilon student member in sales and marketing. **Focus:** Marketing and distribution. **Qualif.:** Applicants must be enrolled in an undergraduate program and working toward an undergraduate degree with at least one semester, two quarters or summer session left before graduation; or enrolled or planning to enroll in a Graduate Program and working toward a post graduate degree (such as an MBA) with at least one semester, two quarters or summer session left before graduation; be students studying abroad; or graduating seniors with outstanding loans to their university. **Criteria:** Selection is based on Pi Sigma Epsilon activities; career objectives/ educational goals; educational financing; overall and major GPA; and non-PSE activities/work experience.

Funds Avail.: $1,000. **Number Awarded:** 3. **To Apply:** Applicants must submit a completed application form together with a one page description of qualifications (Pi Sigma Epsilon activities; Mu Kappa Tau activities; Career objectives; Educational goals; Campus/Community activities; Special achievements/awards; Employment history; Percent of education financed by self, parents, scholarships, other); and two letters of recommendation. Applicants must also submit/bring a college transcript and resume. **Contact:** Send materials electronically to scholarships@ pse.org.

7596 ■ Enterprise Rent-A-Car Scholarships *(Graduate, Undergraduate/Scholarship)*

Purpose: To advance education of Pi Sigma Epsilon student member in sales and marketing. **Focus:** Marketing and distribution. **Qualif.:** Applicants must be enrolled in an undergraduate program and working toward an undergraduate degree with at least one semester, two quarters or summer session left before graduation; or enrolled or planning to enroll in a Graduate Program and working toward a post graduate degree (such as an MBA) with at least one semester, two quarters or summer session left before graduation; be students studying abroad; or graduating seniors with outstanding loans to their university. **Criteria:** Selection is based on Pi Sigma Epsilon activities; career objectives/ educational goals; educational financing; overall and major GPA; and non-PSE activities/work experience.

Funds Avail.: $1,500. **Number Awarded:** 1. **To Apply:** Applicants must submit a completed application form together with a one page description of qualifications (Pi Sigma Epsilon activities; Mu Kappa Tau activities; Career objectives; Educational goals; Campus/Community activi-

Awards are arranged alphabetically below their administering organizations

ties; Special achievements/awards; Employment history; Percent of education financed by self, parents, scholarships, other); and two letters of recommendation. Applicants must also submit/bring a college transcript and resume. **Contact:** Send materials electronically to scholarships@pse.org.

7597 ▪ Federated Insurance Scholarships (Graduate, Undergraduate/Scholarship)

Purpose: To advance education of Pi Sigma Epsilon student member in sales and marketing. **Focus:** Marketing and distribution. **Qualif.:** Applicants must be enrolled in an undergraduate program and working toward an undergraduate degree with at least one semester, two quarters or summer session left before graduation; or enrolled or planning to enroll in a Graduate Program and working toward a post graduate degree (such as an MBA) with at least one semester, two quarters or summer session left before graduation; be students studying abroad; or graduating seniors with outstanding loans to their university. **Criteria:** Selection is based on Pi Sigma Epsilon activities; career objectives/ educational goals; educational financing; overall and major GPA; and non-PSE activities/work experience.

Funds Avail.: $1,000. **Number Awarded:** 1. **To Apply:** Applicants must submit a completed application form together with a one page description of qualifications (Pi Sigma Epsilon activities; Mu Kappa Tau activities; Career objectives; Educational goals; Campus/Community activities; Special achievements/awards; Employment history; Percent of education financed by self, parents, scholarships, other); and two letters of recommendation. Applicants must also submit/bring a college transcript and resume. **Contact:** Send materials electronically to scholarships@pse.org.

7598 ▪ William H. Harris Memorial Scholarships (Graduate, Undergraduate/Scholarship)

Purpose: To advance education of Pi Sigma Epsilon student member in sales and marketing. **Focus:** Marketing and distribution. **Qualif.:** Applicants must be enrolled in an undergraduate program and working toward an undergraduate degree with at least one semester, two quarters or summer session left before graduation; or enrolled or planning to enroll in a Graduate Program and working toward a post graduate degree (such as an MBA) with at least one semester, two quarters or summer session left before graduation; be students studying abroad; or graduating seniors with outstanding loans to their university. **Criteria:** Selection is based on Pi Sigma Epsilon activities; career objectives/ educational goals; educational financing; overall and major GPA; and non-PSE activities/work experience.

Funds Avail.: $1,500. **Number Awarded:** 1. **To Apply:** Applicants must submit a completed application form together with a one page description of qualifications (Pi Sigma Epsilon activities; Mu Kappa Tau activities; Career objectives; Educational goals; Campus/Community activities; Special achievements/awards; Employment history; Percent of education financed by self, parents, scholarships, other); and two letters of recommendation. Applicants must also submit/bring a college transcript and resume.

7599 ▪ Debbie Khalil Memorial Scholarships (Graduate, Undergraduate/Scholarship)

Purpose: To advance education of Pi Sigma Epsilon student member in sales and marketing. **Focus:** Marketing and distribution. **Qualif.:** Applicants must be enrolled in an undergraduate program and working toward an undergradu-

ate degree with at least one semester, two quarters or summer session left before graduation; or enrolled or planning to enroll in a Graduate Program and working toward a post graduate degree (such as an MBA) with at least one semester, two quarters or summer session left before graduation; be students studying abroad; or graduating seniors with outstanding loans to their university. **Criteria:** Selection is based on Pi Sigma Epsilon activities; career objectives/ educational goals; educational financing; overall and major GPA; and non-PSE activities/work experience.

Funds Avail.: $1,000. **Number Awarded:** 1. **To Apply:** Applicants must submit a completed application form together with a one page description of qualifications (Pi Sigma Epsilon activities; Mu Kappa Tau activities; Career objectives; Educational goals; Campus/Community activities; Special achievements/awards; Employment history; Percent of education financed by self, parents, scholarships, other); and two letters of recommendation. **Contact:** Send materials electronically to scholarships@pse.org.

7600 ▪ Northwestern Mutual Financial Network Scholarships (Graduate, Undergraduate/Scholarship)

Purpose: To advance education of Pi Sigma Epsilon student member in sales and marketing. **Focus:** Marketing and distribution. **Qualif.:** Applicants must be enrolled in an undergraduate program and working toward an undergraduate degree who have an interest in a career in finance, sales, or accounting with at least one semester, two quarters or summer session left before graduation; or enrolled or planning to enroll in a Graduate Program and working toward a post graduate degree (such as an MBA) with at least one semester, two quarters or summer session left before graduation; be students studying abroad; or graduating seniors with outstanding loans to their university. **Criteria:** Selection is based on Pi Sigma Epsilon activities; career objectives/ educational goals; educational financing; overall and major GPA; and non-PSE activities/work experience.

Funds Avail.: $1,500. **Number Awarded:** 1. **To Apply:** Applicants must submit a completed application form together with a one page description of qualifications (Pi Sigma Epsilon activities; Mu Kappa Tau activities; Career objectives; Educational goals; Campus/Community activities; Special achievements/awards; Employment history; Percent of education financed by self, parents, scholarships, other); and two letters of recommendation. Applicants must also submit/bring a college transcript and resume. **Contact:** Send materials electronically to scholarships@pse.org.

7601 ▪ Phi Sigma Epsilon Past National President Scholarships (Graduate, Undergraduate/Scholarship)

Purpose: To advance education of Pi Sigma Epsilon student member in sales and marketing. **Focus:** Marketing and distribution. **Qualif.:** Applicants must be enrolled in an undergraduate program and working toward an undergraduate degree majoring in marketing or sales with at least one semester, two quarters or summer session left before graduation; or enrolled or planning to enroll in a Graduate Program and working toward a post graduate degree (such as an MBA) with at least one semester, two quarters or summer session left before graduation; be students studying abroad; or graduating seniors with outstanding loans to their university. **Criteria:** Selection will be based on Pi Sigma Epsilon activities; career objectives/ educational goals; educational financing; overall and major GPA; and non-PSE activities/work experience.

Funds Avail.: $1,000. **Number Awarded:** 1. **To Apply:**

Awards are arranged alphabetically below their administering organizations

Applicants must submit a completed application form together with a one page description of qualifications (Pi Sigma Epsilon activities; Mu Kappa Tau activities; Career objectives; Educational goals; Campus/Community activities; Special achievements/awards; Employment history; Percent of education financed by self, parents, scholarships, other); and two letters of recommendation. Applicants must also submit/bring a college transcript and resume. **Contact:** Send materials electronically to scholarships@pse.org.

7602 ■ Vector Marketing Scholarships (Graduate, Undergraduate/Scholarship)

Purpose: To advance education of Pi Sigma Epsilon student member in sales and marketing. **Focus:** Marketing and distribution. **Qualif.:** Applicants must be enrolled in an undergraduate program and working toward an undergraduate degree with at least one semester, two quarters or summer session left before graduation; or enrolled or planning to enroll in a Graduate Program and working toward a post graduate degree (such as an MBA) with at least one semester, two quarters or summer session left before graduation; be students studying abroad; or graduating seniors with outstanding loans to their university. **Criteria:** Selection is based on Pi Sigma Epsilon activities; career objectives/ educational goals; educational financing; overall and major GPA; and non-PSE activities/work experience.

Funds Avail.: $1,500. **Number Awarded:** 1. **To Apply:** Applicants must submit a completed application form together with a one page description of qualifications (Pi Sigma Epsilon activities; Mu Kappa Tau activities; Career objectives; Educational goals; Campus/Community activities; Special achievements/awards; Employment history; Percent of education financed by self, parents, scholarships, other); and two letters of recommendation. Applicant must also submit/bring a college transcript and resume. **Contact:** Send materials electronically to scholarships@pse.org.

7603 ■ Whan Memorial Scholarships (Graduate, Undergraduate/Scholarship)

Purpose: To advance education of Pi Sigma Epsilon student member in sales and marketing. **Focus:** Marketing and distribution. **Qualif.:** Applicants must be enrolled in an undergraduate program and working toward an undergraduate degree with at least one semester, two quarters or summer session left before graduation; or enrolled or planning to enroll in a Graduate Program and working toward a post graduate degree (such as an MBA) with at least one semester, two quarters or summer session left before graduation; be students studying abroad; or graduating seniors with outstanding loans to their university. **Criteria:** Selection is based on Pi Sigma Epsilon activities; career objectives/ educational goals; educational financing; overall and major GPA; and non-PSE activities/work experience.

Funds Avail.: $1,500. **Number Awarded:** 1. **To Apply:** Applicants must submit a completed application form together with a one page description of qualifications (Pi Sigma Epsilon activities; Mu Kappa Tau activities; Career objectives; Educational goals; Campus/Community activities; Special achievements/awards; Employment history; Percent of education financed by self, parents, scholarships, other); and two letters of recommendation. Applicants must also submit/bring a college transcript and resume. **Remarks:** Established in 1989. **Contact:** Send materials electronically to scholarships@pse.org.

7604 ■ Phi Sigma Pi National Honor Fraternity

2119 Ambassador Cir.
Lancaster, PA 17603
Ph: (717)299-4710
Fax: (717)390-3054
E-mail: pspoffice@phisigmapi.org
URL: www.phisigmapi.org

7605 ■ Richard Cecil Todd and Clauda Pennock Todd Tripod Scholarships (Graduate, Undergraduate/Scholarship)

Purpose: To promote the future academic opportunity of Phi Sigma Pi Brothers. **Focus:** General studies/Field of study not specified. **Qualif.:** Applicant must be an undergraduate student pursuing a Bachelor's Degree; or graduating senior entering a graduate school (must provide a proof of enrollment to a graduate program); an active Phi Sigma Pi member; and have a GPA of 3.00. **Criteria:** Selection is based on application.

Funds Avail.: No specific amount. **To Apply:** Applicants must submit a completed application form; letters of recommendation; official transcript; and notification from the Financial Aid Office (if applicable). **Deadline:** April 15. **Remarks:** All required materials must be typewritten.

7606 ■ Rolla F. Wood Graduate Scholarships (Graduate/Scholarship)

Purpose: To encourage the educational advancement of an alumni member. **Focus:** General studies/Field of study not specified. **Qualif.:** Applicants must be Phi Sigma Pi alumni who have graduated in good standing and pursuing a postgraduate degree or certification (Proof of enrollment in a graduate/professional school program must be submitted); must be members of the National Alumni Association; and have a GPA of 3.0. **Criteria:** Selection will be based on the submitted application.

Funds Avail.: No specific amount. **To Apply:** Applicants must submit a completed application form; three (3) letters of recommendation: two (2) from faculty members and one (1) from the collegiate chapter; official post-secondary transcript; an essay (1,500 words) describing living the ideals of the fraternity since graduation; and notification from the Financial Aid Office (if applicable). **Deadline:** April 15. **Remarks:** Established in 2004.

7607 ■ Phi Upsilon Omicron, Inc. (Phi U)

PO Box 50970
Bowling Green, KY 42102-4270
Ph: (270)904-1340
E-mail: national@phiu.org
URL: www.phiu.org

7608 ■ S. Penny Chappell Scholarships (Undergraduate/Scholarship)

Purpose: To promote education in advance family and consumer sciences and related areas. **Focus:** Fashion design; Textile science. **Qualif.:** Applicants must be Phi U members; pursuing a baccalaureate degree in fashion design and construction, textile design and development and/or textile preservation. **Criteria:** Selection will be based on the applicants' scholastic record; participation in Phi U and other collegiate activities; a statement of professional aims and goals; professional services; and recommendations.

Funds Avail.: No specific amount. **To Apply:** Applicants

Awards are arranged alphabetically below their administering organizations

must submit an application; transcripts; recommendations. Application documents must be assembled in order, clipped together with a paper clip and placed in a 10″ x 13″ envelope. Enclose a self-addressed stamped postcard. **Deadline:** February 1.

7609 ■ Geraldine Clewell Fellowships - Doctoral Student (Graduate/Fellowship)

Purpose: To promote education in advance family and consumer sciences and related areas. **Focus:** Consumer affairs; Family planning. **Qualif.:** Applicants must be Phi U members; must be doctoral students in family and consumer sciences or a related area. **Criteria:** Selection will be based on the applicants' scholastic record; honors and recognitions; participation in honor society, professional, community, and other organizations; scholarly work; statement of professional goals; and recommendations. Preference will be given to students who desires to teach at the college/university level.

Funds Avail.: No specific amount. **To Apply:** Applicants must submit an application; transcripts; recommendations (at least one must be from major advisor). Application documents must be assembled in order, clipped together with a paper clip and placed in a 10″ x 13″ envelope. Enclose a self-addressed stamped postcard. **Deadline:** February 1.

7610 ■ Geraldine Clewell Fellowships - Masteral (Graduate/Fellowship)

Purpose: To promote education in advance family and consumer sciences and related areas. **Focus:** Consumer affairs; Family planning. **Qualif.:** Applicants smust be Phi U members; pursuing a master's degree in family and consumer sciences or related area. **Criteria:** Selection will be based on the applicants' scholastic record; honors and recognitions; participation in honor society, professional, community, and other organizations; scholarly work; statement of professional goals; and recommendations. Preference will be given to students majoring in family and consumer sciences education and who desires to teach at the elementary/secondary level.

Funds Avail.: No specific amount. **To Apply:** Applicants must submit an application; transcripts; recommendations (at least one must be from major advisor). Application documents must be assembled in order, clipped together with a paper clip and placed in a 10″ x 13″ envelope. Enclose a self-addressed stamped postcard. **Deadline:** February 1.

7611 ■ Geraldine Clewell Scholarships - Undergraduate (Undergraduate/Scholarship)

Purpose: To promote education in advance family and consumer sciences and related areas. **Focus:** Consumer affairs; Family planning. **Qualif.:** Applicants must be Phi U members; must be enrolled full-time in a baccalaureate degree program in family and consumer sciences or a related area. **Criteria:** Selection will be based on the applicants' scholastic record; participation in Phi U and other collegiate activities; a statement of professional aims and goals; professional services; and recommendations.

Funds Avail.: No specific amount. **To Apply:** Applicants must submit an application; transcripts; recommendations. Application documents must be assembled in order, clipped together with a paper clip and placed in a 10″ x 13″ envelope. Enclose a self-addressed stamped postcard. **Deadline:** February 1.

7612 ■ Closs/Parnitzke/Clarke Scholarships (Undergraduate/Scholarship)

Purpose: To promote education in advance family and consumer sciences and related areas. **Focus:** Consumer

affairs; Family planning. **Qualif.:** Applicants must be Phi U members; enrolled full-time in a baccalaureate degree program in family and consumer sciences or a related area. **Criteria:** Selection will be based on the applicants' scholastic record; participation in Phi U and other collegiate activities; a statement of professional aims and goals; professional services; and recommendations.

Funds Avail.: No specific amount. **To Apply:** Applicants must submit an application; transcripts; recommendations. Application documents must be assembled in order, clipped together with a paper clip and placed in a 10″ x 13″ envelope. Enclose a self-addressed stamped postcard. **Deadline:** February 1.

7613 ■ Jean Dearth Dickerscheid Fellowships (Graduate/Fellowship)

Purpose: To promote education in advance family and consumer sciences and related areas. **Focus:** Consumer affairs; Family planning. **Qualif.:** Applicant must be a Phi U member; pursuing a Ph.D. in family and consumer sciences or related area and has earned at least one other degree in family and consumer sciences; and interested for a career in academia. **Criteria:** Selection is based on applicant's scholastic record; honors and recognitions; participation in honor society, professional, community, and other organizations; scholarly work; statement of professional goals; and recommendations.

Funds Avail.: No specific amount. **To Apply:** Applicants must submit an application; transcripts; recommendations. Application documents must be assembled in order, clipped together with a paper clip and placed in a 10″ x 13″ envelope. Enclose a self-addressed stamped postcard. **Deadline:** February 1. **Remarks:** Applicants may apply for more than one fellowship.

7614 ■ Margaret Drew Alpha Fellowships (Graduate/Fellowship)

Purpose: To promote education in advance family and consumer sciences and related areas. **Focus:** Consumer affairs; Family planning; Nutrition. **Qualif.:** Applicants must be Phi U members; must be in a graduate study in the field of family and consumer sciences. **Criteria:** Selection will be based on the applicants' scholastic record; honors and recognitions; participation in honor society, professional, community, and other organizations; scholarly work; statement of professional goals; and recommendations. Preference will be given to a dietetics or food and nutrition major.

Funds Avail.: No specific amount. **To Apply:** Applicants must submit an application; transcripts; recommendations. Application documents must be assembled in order, clipped together with a paper clip and placed in a 10″ x 13″ envelope. Enclose a self-addressed stamped postcard. **Deadline:** February 1.

7615 ■ Genevieve Forthun Scholarships (Undergraduate/Scholarship)

Purpose: To promote education in advance family and consumer sciences and related areas. **Focus:** Consumer affairs; Family planning. **Qualif.:** Applicant must be a Phi U member; enrolled full-time in a baccalaureate degree program in family and consumer sciences or a related area. **Criteria:** Selection is based on the applicant's scholastic record; participation in Phi U and other collegiate activities; a statement of professional aims and goals; professional services; and recommendations.

Funds Avail.: $500-$4,000. **To Apply:** Applicants must

Awards are arranged alphabetically below their administering organizations

submit an application; transcripts; recommendations. Application documents must be assembled in order, clipped together with a paper clip and placed in a 10″ x 13″ envelope. Enclose a self-addressed stamped postcard. **Deadline:** February 1. **Remarks:** Applicants may apply for more than one fellowship.

7616 ■ Mary Weiking Franken Scholarships
(Undergraduate/Scholarship)

Purpose: To promote education in advance family and consumer sciences and related areas. **Focus:** Consumer affairs; Family planning. **Qualif.:** Applicant must be a Phi U member; enrolled full-time in a baccalaureate degree program in family and consumer sciences or a related area. **Criteria:** Preference is given to students majoring in child/family or family and consumer sciences education.

Funds Avail.: No specific amount. **To Apply:** Applicants must submit an application; transcripts; recommendations. Application documents must be assembled in order, clipped together with a paper clip and placed in a 10″ x 13″ envelope. Enclose a self-addressed stamped postcard. **Deadline:** February 1. **Remarks:** Applicants may apply for more than one fellowship.

7617 ■ Tommie J. Hamner Scholarships
(Undergraduate/Scholarship)

Purpose: To promote education in advance family and consumer sciences and related areas. **Focus:** Consumer affairs; Family planning. **Qualif.:** Applicants must be Phi U members; enrolled full-time in a baccalaureate degree program in family and consumer sciences or a related area; and have shown exemplary commitment to Phi Upsilon Omicron. **Criteria:** Selection will be based on the applicants' scholastic record; participation in Phi U and other collegiate activities; a statement of professional aims and goals; professional services; and recommendations.

Funds Avail.: No specific amount. **To Apply:** Applicants must submit an application; transcripts; recommendations. Application documents must be assembled in order, clipped together with a paper clip and placed in a 10″ x 13″ envelope. Enclose a self-addressed stamped postcard. **Deadline:** February 1.

7618 ■ Jackman Scholarships *(Undergraduate/Scholarship)*

Purpose: To promote education in advance family and consumer sciences and related areas. **Focus:** Consumer affairs; Family planning. **Qualif.:** Applicants must be Phi U members; enrolled full-time in a baccalaureate degree program in family and consumer sciences or a related area; and have shown exemplary commitment to Phi Upsilon Omicron. **Criteria:** Selection will be based on the applicants' scholastic record; participation in Phi U and other collegiate activities; a statement of professional aims and goals; professional services; and recommendations.

Funds Avail.: No specific amount. **To Apply:** Applicants must submit an application; transcripts; recommendations. Application documents must be assembled in order, clipped together with a paper clip and placed in a 10″ x 13″ envelope. Enclose a self-addressed stamped postcard. **Deadline:** February 1.

7619 ■ Martha Combs Jenkins Scholarships
(Undergraduate/Scholarship)

Purpose: To promote education in advance family and consumer sciences and related areas. **Focus:** Consumer

affairs; Family planning. **Qualif.:** Applicants must be Phi U members; pursuing a baccalaureate degree in family and consumer sciences or one of its related areas; and have shown exemplary commitment to Phi Upsilon Omicron. **Criteria:** Selection will be based on the applicants' scholastic record; participation in Phi U and other collegiate activities; a statement of professional aims and goals; professional services; and recommendations.

Funds Avail.: No specific amount. **To Apply:** Applicants must submit an application; transcripts; recommendations. Application documents must be assembled in order, clipped together with a paper clip and placed in a 10″ x 13″ envelope. Enclose a self-addressed stamped postcard. **Deadline:** February 1.

7620 ■ Treva C. Kintner Scholarships
(Undergraduate/Scholarship)

Purpose: To promote education in advance family and consumer sciences and related areas. **Focus:** Consumer affairs; Family planning. **Qualif.:** Applicant must be a Phi U member; a non-traditional student; completed at least half of the academic work toward a baccalaureate degree in family and consumer sciences or a related area. **Criteria:** Selection is based on the applicant's scholastic record; participation in Phi U and other collegiate activities; a statement of professional aims and goals; professional services; and recommendations.

Funds Avail.: No specific amount. **To Apply:** Applicants must submit an application; transcripts; recommendations. Application documents must be assembled in order, clipped together with a paper clip and placed in a 10″ x 13″ envelope. Enclose a self-addressed stamped postcard. **Deadline:** February 1. **Remarks:** Applicants may apply for more than one fellowship.

7621 ■ Phi Upsilon Omicron Candle Fellowships
(Graduate/Fellowship)

Purpose: To promote education in advance family and consumer sciences and related areas. **Focus:** Consumer affairs; Family planning. **Qualif.:** Applicant must be a Phi U member; enrolled or planning to enroll in a graduate school; and study leading to a master's degree in family and consumer sciences. **Criteria:** Selection is based on applicant's scholastic record; honors and recognitions; participation in honor society, professional, community, and other organizations; scholarly work; statement of professional goals; and recommendations.

Funds Avail.: No specific amount. **To Apply:** Applicants must submit an application; transcripts; recommendations. Application documents must be assembled in order, clipped together with a paper clip and placed in a 10″ x 13″ envelope. Enclose a self-addressed stamped postcard. **Deadline:** February 1. **Remarks:** Applicants may apply for more than one fellowship.

7622 ■ Phi Upsilon Omicron Challenge Scholarships *(Undergraduate/Scholarship)*

Purpose: To promote education in advance family and consumer sciences and related areas. **Focus:** Consumer affairs; Family planning. **Qualif.:** Applicants must be Phi U members; must be enrolled full-time in a baccalaureate degree program in family and consumer sciences or a related area. **Criteria:** Selection will be based on the applicants' scholastic record; participation in Phi U and other collegiate activities; a statement of professional aims and goals; professional services; and recommendations.

Funds Avail.: No specific amount. **To Apply:** Applicants

Awards are arranged alphabetically below their administering organizations

must submit an application; transcripts; recommendations. Application documents must be assembled in order, clipped together with a paper clip and placed in a 10″ x 13″ envelope. Enclose a self-addressed stamped postcard. **Deadline:** February 1.

7623 ■ Phi Upsilon Omicron Diamond Anniversary Fellowships *(Graduate/Fellowship)*

Purpose: To promote education in advance family and consumer sciences and related areas. **Focus:** Consumer affairs; Family planning. **Qualif.:** Applicant must be a Phi U member; accepted into or currently enrolled in a graduate program; studying at the master's or doctoral level in family and consumer sciences or a related area. **Criteria:** Selection is based on applicant's scholastic record; honors and recognitions; participation in honor society, professional, community, and other organizations; scholarly work; statement of professional goals; and recommendations.

Funds Avail.: No specific amount. **To Apply:** Applicants must submit an application; transcripts; recommendations. Application documents must be assembled in order, clipped together with a paper clip and placed in a 10″ x 13″ envelope. Enclose a self-addressed stamped postcard. **Deadline:** February 1. **Remarks:** Applicants may apply for more than one fellowship.

7624 ■ Phi Upsilon Omicron Founders Fellowships *(Graduate/Fellowship)*

Purpose: To promote education in advance family and consumer sciences and related areas. **Focus:** Consumer affairs; Family planning. **Qualif.:** Applicant must be a Phi U member; have completed at least half the credit-hour requirements toward the doctorate in some area of family and consumer sciences and have had several years of successful employment in the profession. **Criteria:** Selection is based on applicant's scholastic record; honors and recognitions; participation in honor society, professional, community, and other organizations; scholarly work; statement of professional goals; and recommendations.

Funds Avail.: $750-$1,500. **To Apply:** Applicants must submit an application; transcripts; recommendations. Application documents must be assembled in order, clipped together with a paper clip and placed in a 10″ x 13″ envelope. Enclose a self-addressed stamped postcard. **Deadline:** February 1. **Remarks:** Applicants may apply for more than one fellowship.

7625 ■ Phi Upsilon Omicron Golden Anniversary Scholarships *(Undergraduate/Scholarship)*

Purpose: To promote education in advance family and consumer sciences and related areas. **Focus:** Consumer affairs; Family planning. **Qualif.:** Applicant must be a Phi U member; enrolled full-time in a baccalaureate degree program in family and consumer sciences or a related area. **Criteria:** Selection is based on the applicant's scholastic record; participation in Phi U and other collegiate activities; a statement of professional aims and goals; professional services; and recommendations.

Funds Avail.: $500-$4,000. **To Apply:** Applicants must submit an application; transcripts; recommendations. Application documents must be assembled in order, clipped together with a paper clip and placed in a 10″ x 13″ envelope. Enclose a self-addressed stamped postcard. **Deadline:** February 1. **Remarks:** Applicants may apply for more than one fellowship.

7626 ■ Phi Upsilon Omicron Past Presidents Scholarships *(Undergraduate/Scholarship)*

Purpose: To promote education in advance family and consumer sciences and related areas. **Focus:** Consumer affairs; Family planning. **Qualif.:** Applicant must be a Phi U member; enrolled full-time in a baccalaureate degree program in family and consumer sciences or a related area. **Criteria:** Selection is based on the applicant's scholastic record; participation in Phi U and other collegiate activities; a statement of professional aims and goals; professional services; and recommendations.

Funds Avail.: No specific amount. **To Apply:** Applicants must submit an application; transcripts; recommendations. Application documents must be assembled in order, clipped together with a paper clip and placed in a 10″ x 13″ envelope. Enclose a self-addressed stamped postcard. **Deadline:** February 1. **Remarks:** Applicants may apply for more than one fellowship.

7627 ■ Phi Upsilon Omicron Presidents Research Fellowships *(Graduate/Fellowship)*

Purpose: To promote education in advance family and consumer sciences and related areas. **Focus:** Consumer affairs; Family planning. **Qualif.:** Applicant must be a Phi U member; on a graduate research at the master's, doctoral or post-doctoral level in family and consumer sciences or a related area. **Criteria:** Selection is based on applicant's scholastic record; honors and recognitions; participation in honor society, professional, community, and other organizations; scholarly work; statement of professional goals; and recommendations.

Funds Avail.: $750-$1,500. **To Apply:** Applicants must submit an application; transcripts; recommendations; and include a research prospectus exhibiting organization and need for the research. Application documents must be assembled in order, clipped together with a paper clip and placed in a 10″ x 13″ envelope. Enclose a self-addressed stamped postcard. **Deadline:** February 1. **Remarks:** Applicants may apply for more than one fellowship.

7628 ■ Nell Bryant Robinson Scholarships *(Undergraduate/Scholarship)*

Purpose: To promote education in advance family and consumer sciences and related areas. **Focus:** Consumer affairs; Family planning; Nutrition. **Qualif.:** Applicants must be Phi U members; must be pursuing a baccalaureate degree in family and consumer sciences or one of its related areas. **Criteria:** Preference is given to students majoring in dietetics or food and nutrition.

Funds Avail.: No specific amount. **To Apply:** Applicants must submit an application; transcripts; recommendations. Application documents must be assembled in order, clipped together with a paper clip and placed in a 10″ x 13″ envelope. Enclose a self-addressed stamped postcard. **Deadline:** February 1.

7629 ■ Lucile Rust Scholarships *(Undergraduate/Scholarship)*

Purpose: To promote education in advance family and consumer sciences and related areas. **Focus:** Consumer affairs; Family planning. **Qualif.:** Applicant must be a Phi U member; enrolled full-time in a baccalaureate degree program in family and consumer sciences or a related area. **Criteria:** Selection is based on the applicant's scholastic record; participation in Phi U and other collegiate activities; a statement of professional aims and goals; professional

Awards are arranged alphabetically below their administering organizations

services; and recommendations.

Funds Avail.: No specific amount. **To Apply:** Applicants must submit an application; transcripts; recommendations. Application documents must be assembled in order, clipped together with a paper clip and placed in a 10" x 13" envelope. Enclose a self-addressed stamped postcard. **Deadline:** February 1. **Remarks:** Applicants may apply for more than one fellowship.

7630 ■ Margaret Jerome Sampson Scholarships
(Undergraduate/Scholarship)

Purpose: To promote education in advance family and consumer sciences and related areas. **Focus:** Consumer affairs; Family planning; Nutrition. **Qualif.:** Applicants must be Phi U members; must be enrolled full-time in a baccalaureate degree program in family and consumer sciences or a related area. **Criteria:** Selection will be based on the applicants' scholastic record; participation in Phi U; professional aims and goals. Preference is given to students majoring in dietetics or food and nutrition.

Funds Avail.: $4,000. **Number Awarded:** 5. **To Apply:** Applicants must submit an application; transcripts; recommendations (one must be from the Phi U chapter advisor). Application documents must be assembled in order, clipped together with a paper clip and placed in a 10" x 13" envelope. Enclose a self-addressed stamped postcard, a financial statement and one double-spaced typewritten page about the reasons for needing an additional financial assistance. **Deadline:** February 1.

7631 ■ Lillian P. Schoephoerster Scholarships
(Undergraduate/Scholarship)

Purpose: To promote education in advance family and consumer sciences and related areas. **Focus:** Consumer affairs; Family planning. **Qualif.:** Applicant must be a Phi U member; a non-traditional student enrolled full-time in a baccalaureate degree program in family and consumer sciences or a related area. **Criteria:** Selection is based on the applicant's scholastic record; participation in Phi U and other collegiate activities; a statement of professional aims and goals; professional services; and recommendations.

Funds Avail.: $2,000. **Number Awarded:** 2. **To Apply:** Applicants must submit an application; transcripts; recommendations. Application documents must be assembled in order, clipped together with a paper clip and placed in a 10" x 13" envelope. Enclose a self-addressed stamped postcard. **Deadline:** February 1. **Remarks:** Applicants may apply for more than one fellowship.

7632 ■ Sutherland/Purdy Scholarships
(Undergraduate/Scholarship)

Purpose: To promote education in advance family and consumer sciences and related areas. **Focus:** Fashion design; Textile science. **Qualif.:** Applicants must be Phi U members; pursuing a baccalaureate degree in clothing and textiles or a related area such as apparel design or fashion merchandising; have held a leadership position in her/his Phi U chapter; and have earned at least a 3.0 out of 4.0 overall point average. **Criteria:** Selection will be based on the applicants' scholastic record; participation in Phi U and other collegiate activities; a statement of professional aims and goals; professional services; and recommendations.

Funds Avail.: No specific amount. **To Apply:** Applicants must submit an application; transcripts; recommendations. Application documents must be assembled in order, clipped together with a paper clip and placed in a 10" x 13"

envelope. Enclose a self-addressed stamped postcard. **Deadline:** February 1.

7633 ■ Philadelphia Bar Association
1101 Market St., 11th Fl.
Philadelphia, PA 19107
Ph: (215)238-6300
Fax: (215)238-1159
URL: www.philadelphiabar.org

7634 ■ Philadelphia Public Interest Fellowships
(Undergraduate/Fellowship)

Purpose: To provide an extraordinary opportunity for new attorneys at participating firms to defer private practice for a year while they perform valuable public service at one of Philadelphia's legal services agencies. **Focus:** Law. **Qualif.:** Candidates must be third year law students who have received and accepted an offer from a participating private law firm employer. **Criteria:** Selection will be based on the committee's criteria.

Funds Avail.: No specific amount. **Duration:** Annual. **To Apply:** The fellow and private employer are encouraged to consider a written agreement that outlines procedures such as payroll, conflicts checking and participation in the firm's own training and other activities during the year of the fellowship. A letter of intent from the agency to the fellow will suffice, with copies to the employer and Bar Foundation.

7635 ■ Philippine Nurses Association of America (PNAA)
656 Canton St.
Westwood, MA 02090
E-mail: info@mypnaa.org
URL: mypnaa.org

7636 ■ PNAA Nursing Scholarship Award *(Master's, Doctorate/Scholarship)*

Purpose: To encourage and provide support to members to obtain a Master's Degree in Nursing, Post Master's Program or Doctoral Program. **Focus:** Nursing. **Qualif.:** Applicant must be a current/active member of PNAA one full year prior to application; currently enrolled and or admitted to an accredited Master's or Doctoral Program; must have a Grade Point Average (G.P.A.) of 3.0 or better. **Criteria:** Selection will be based on the Chair of the PNAA Scholarship Committee's criteria.

Funds Avail.: $2,000. **Duration:** Annual. **To Apply:** Applicant must be endorsed/recommended by the Chapter President; must submit a progress report at the end of each academic year to the PNAA President and to the Chair of the Scholarship Committee (must have served PNAA as an Officer, Board, Committee Member, etc. at the Chapter and/or at the National level); submit brief essay (150 words) describing professional career goals; and include: letter of Acceptance to an accredited program; academic transcript of records; three letters of recommendations (one from employer, one from a faculty or supervisor and one from the Chapter President); resume/curriculum vitae; and passport picture. **Deadline:** May 14.

7637 ■ PHS Commissioned Officers Foundation
8201 Corporate Dr., Ste. 200
Landover, MD 20785
Ph: (301)731-9080

Awards are arranged alphabetically below their administering organizations

Fax: (301)731-9084
URL: www.phscof.org

7638 ■ Scholarship for Junior PHS Commissioned Officers *(Undergraduate/Scholarship)*

Purpose: To provide financial assistance to dependent children or dependent spouses of active duty, retired, or deceased officers of the USPHS Commissioned Corps. **Focus:** General studies/Field of study not specified. **Qualif.:** Applicants must be dependent children or spouses of active duty, retired or deceased officers of the USPHS Commissioned Corps; must be current or entering college/vocational students who have a minimum cumulative grade point average of 3.0 (on a 4.0 scale). **Criteria:** Applicants are evaluated based on criteria designed by the Scholarship Selection Committee.

Funds Avail.: No specific amount. **To Apply:** Applicants must submit all the required application information.

7639 ■ Physical and Health Education Canada (PHE Canada)

301-2197 Riverside Dr.
Ottawa, ON, Canada K1H 7X3
Ph: (613)523-1348
Fax: (613)523-1206
Free: 800-663-8708
E-mail: info@phecanada.ca
URL: www.phecanada.ca

7640 ■ Dr. Andy Anderson Young Professional Awards *(Professional development/Award)*

Purpose: To recognize individuals who epitomize exemplary work on behalf of the physical and health education profession. **Focus:** Education, Physical; Health education. **Qualif.:** Applicants must be 35 years of age or younger who are members of PHE Canada or a Liaison group. **Criteria:** Candidates will be evaluated based on their contribution to the profession.

Funds Avail.: No specific amount. **Duration:** One year. **To Apply:** Applicants must complete the online application form.

7641 ■ R. Tait Mckenzie Awards *(Professional development/Award)*

Purpose: To advance the knowledge and understanding of physical and health education, recreation and dance. **Focus:** Education, Physical; Health education. **Qualif.:** Applicants must be nominated by an individual who is a member of PHE Canada; nominee must be a teacher, coach, supervisor, or administrator with 10 years experience and has performed as a recognized leader locally, regionally, nationally and internationally; nominees need not be members of PHE Canada. **Criteria:** Recipients will be chosen based on completeness and eligibility of the submitted nomination package.

Funds Avail.: Amount not specified. **Number Awarded:** 4. **To Apply:** Nomination package must include candidate and nominator information forms, 500-word biographical sketch, three letters of reference and supporting documents that may showcase the nominee's contribution to the field. **Deadline:** February 28. **Contact:** Brent Gibson at the above address or at brent@phecanada.ca.

7642 ■ National Award for Teaching Excellence in Physical Education *(Professional development/Award, Recognition)*

Purpose: To recognize elementary, middle and secondary teachers who have the ability to motivate students to participate in physical activity. **Focus:** Education, Physical. **Qualif.:** Applicants must hold a bachelor's degree in Education, Physical Education, or Kinesiology; must have minimum five years teaching experience; and must be full-time teaching contract, current at the time of nomination and selection. **Criteria:** Award will be given to applicants who demonstrate the following qualifications: a) conduct a quality physical education program as reflected in PHE Canada's definition; b) serve as role models epitomizing personal health and fitness, enjoyment of activity, sportspersonship and sensitivity to the needs of students; and c) able to participate in professional development related to teaching of physical education.

Funds Avail.: No specific amount. **Duration:** Periodic. **Number Awarded:** 2. **To Apply:** Applicants must submit the candidate and nominator information forms; biographical sketch, three completed and signed letters of reference and supporting documents that may highlight the nominee's professional contributions (optional). **Deadline:** May 23. **Contact:** Brent Gibson at the above address.

7643 ■ North American Society Fellowships *(Professional development/Fellowship)*

Purpose: To recognize outstanding professionals related to health education, physical education, recreation, sport and dance in North America. **Focus:** Education, Physical; Health education. **Qualif.:** Applicants must be members of AAHPERD or PHE Canada who have been active within one or more of the recognized disciplines; must be residents of Canada; must demonstrate outstanding competence through professional involvement over a period of at least 20 years. **Criteria:** Applicants will be evaluated based on completeness and eligibility of the submitted nomination package.

Funds Avail.: No specific amount. **To Apply:** Applicants must visit the website for procedures and required materials. **Remarks:** Established in 1999.

7644 ■ PHE Canada Health Educator Awards *(Professional development/Award)*

Purpose: To honor individuals for their work that aims to further the importance of health education in Canada. **Focus:** Health education. **Qualif.:** Applicants must be directly involved in school-based health education as educators, school administrators, university professors, researchers, physicians or health professionals; must have positive contributions in advancing the field of health education through research curriculum development, program development and/or program delivery within a school setting. **Criteria:** Recipients will be evaluated based on submitted materials.

Funds Avail.: No specific amount. **To Apply:** Applicants must complete the online application form; must submit details about the positive impacts made by the nominee in the area of school-based health education and two letters of support. **Deadline:** May 23.

7645 ■ PHE Canada Student Awards *(Undergraduate/Award)*

Purpose: To recognize undergraduate student leadership in the field of physical education or a related discipline. **Focus:** Education, Physical; Health education. **Qualif.:** Applicants must be second or third year undergraduate students in physical or health education. **Criteria:** Recipients will be selected based on submitted materials.

Funds Avail.: Amount not specified. **To Apply:** Applicants

Awards are arranged alphabetically below their administering organizations

must complete the online application form; must submit curriculum vitae, signed nomination form and one letter of support. **Deadline:** March 31.

7646 ■ Physicians' Services Incorporated Foundation
1006-5160 Yonge St.
Toronto, ON, Canada M2N 6L9
Ph: (416)226-6323
Fax: (416)226-6080
URL: www.psifoundation.org

7647 ■ Educational Fellowships for Practicing Physicians (Advanced Professional, Professional development/Fellowship)

Purpose: To encourage practicing physicians to undertake training to acquire a clinical skill or knowledge currently lacking in the community or to undertake training in research methodology. **Focus:** Medical research. **Qualif.:** Applicants must be Ontario physicians in established practice and residing outside of the teaching center communities. General practitioners and specialists are also eligible but they must have the approval and support of the local medical society or the physicians within their community. **Criteria:** Selection will be based on the Foundation's criteria. Preference is given to a training program involving active participation by the applicants rather than mere observation.

Funds Avail.: No specific amount. **To Apply:** Applications will be considered for support of physicians who have undertaken training courses that commenced up to three months prior to the time the application is considered at a meeting of the Foundation's Grants Committee. For the meeting dates of the Grants Committee please see the website or contact the Foundation.

7648 ■ PSI Graham Farquharson Knowledge Translation Fellowships (Advanced Professional, Professional development/Fellowship)

Purpose: To provide salary support to new Ontario investigators who have demonstrated the ability to successfully complete high impact knowledge translation research. **Focus:** Medical research. **Qualif.:** Candidates must be either within five years of their first academic appointment and have demonstrated potential for high impact research work or who have dedicated at least 50% of a full-time schedule to the Fellowship or practicing physicians having direct patient care responsibilities and an academic appointment. **Criteria:** Selection will be based on the following: candidates' past research productivity; research plan; leveraging PSI fund; and institutional support and in-kind support.

Funds Avail.: No specific amount. **Number Awarded:** Up to 2. **To Apply:** Applicants may visit the website for further information on the application process.

7649 ■ PSI Healthcare Research by Community Physicians Grants (Advanced Professional, Professional development/Grant)

Purpose: To assist physicians practicing in a community setting to undertake a review of their practice patterns which would enhance effectiveness of practice and patient care in their own clinic, hospital or region. **Focus:** Medical research. **Qualif.:** Applicants must be Ontario physicians. **Criteria:** Selection will be based on the committee's criteria.

Funds Avail.: Up to 5,000 Canadian Dollars (500 will be for travel costs). **To Apply:** Applications will be considered for support of physicians who have undertaken training courses that commenced up to three months prior to the time the application is considered at a meeting of the Foundation's Grants Committee. For the meeting dates of the Grants Committee please see the website or contact the Foundation.

7650 ■ Resident Research Grants (Postgraduate, Professional development/Grant)

Purpose: To support professionals in their research. **Focus:** Health education; Medical research. **Qualif.:** Applicants must be resident researchers in one of the following three areas: clinical research, medical education research and health systems research); must have a salary as Residents (such is being provided by the Ontario Ministry of Health and Long-Term Care); must be registered in a recognized program leading to certification by the Royal College of Physicians and Surgeons or the College of Family Physicians; and must be registered as postgraduate students at the university where residency training is being taken. **Criteria:** Selection will be on a competitive basis due to grants allocated.

Funds Avail.: Up to 20,000 Canadian Dollars. **Duration:** Two years. **To Apply:** Applicants may verify the website for further instructions regarding the application.

7651 ■ Physiotherapy Foundation of Canada
955 Green Valley Crescent, Ste. 270
Ottawa, ON, Canada K2C 3V4
Ph: (613)564-5454
Fax: (613)564-1577
Free: 888-387-8679
E-mail: information@physiotherapy.ca
URL: www.physiotherapyfoundation.ca

7652 ■ Dominio of Canada Insurance Scholarships (Graduate/Scholarship)

Purpose: To provide scholarships for students involved in a research project. **Focus:** Physiology. **Qualif.:** Applicants must be post-licensure students at the Master's and PhD level who are involved in a physiotherapy research project that is part of the academic requirements for completion of their program. **Criteria:** Selection will be based on the committee's criteria.

Funds Avail.: Up to $4,500. **Number Awarded:** 1. **To Apply:** Applicants must submit one hard copy and one soft copy of the completed application and all appendices. Applications and appendices should be typed single spaced, minimum font size 11, on 21.5cm x 28cm paper. Appendices include: the applicant's curriculum vitae and applicant's supervisor's curriculum vitae. Applicants must also submit a letter of appraisal from the supervisor, or advisor, of the applicant that also outlines the proposed research programme; two additional letters of appraisal; a letter from the Head of the Department at the university confirming acceptance into one of the programmes described in the Regulations for The Dominion of Canada General Insurance Scholarship. If the applicant is not enrolled at the time of the application, any scholarship will be conditional upon the receipt of written confirmation of enrollment in the programmed is received; certified transcripts from foreign universities must provide the grade conversions used by Graduate Studies in the Canadian university in which they are enrolled. **Deadline:** January 30. **Remarks:** Established

Awards are arranged alphabetically below their administering organizations

in 2007. **Contact:** foundation@physiotherapy.ca.

7653 ■ Physiotherapy Foundation of Canada Research Grant *(Other/Grant)*

Purpose: To fund a physiotherapy research in Canada that aims to improve the mobility, health and well-being of society. **Focus:** Physiology. **Qualif.:** Applicants must be Canadian citizens, landed immigrants, or people who reside in Canada (for the duration of the grant) with a valid work or student visa. **Criteria:** Application will be considered from the standpoint of its scientific merit and budget within the framework of the aforementioned regulations.

Funds Avail.: $4,000. **Number Awarded:** 1. **To Apply:** Applicants must submit one hard copy and one soft copy of the completed application and all appendices which can be obtained from the website. Applications and appendices should be typed single spaced, minimum font size 11, on 21.5cm x 28cm paper. Illustrations should be drawn with clean black lines. **Deadline:** January 30. **Contact:** foundation@physiotherapy.ca.

7654 ■ B.E. Schnurr Memorial Fund Research Grants *(Other/Grant)*

Purpose: To provide grants for students involved in physiotherapy research programs. **Focus:** Physiology. **Qualif.:** Applicants must be Canadian citizens, landed immigrants, or people who reside in Canada (for the duration of the grant) with a valid work or student visa. Special consideration will be given to blind individuals. **Criteria:** Recipients will be selected based on scientific merit, budget within framework of the aforementioned regulations. Priority will be given to research projects that are perceived to be of maximum benefit to the practice of physiotherapy and society as a whole.

Funds Avail.: $3,500. **To Apply:** Applicants must submit one hard copy and one soft copy of the completed application and all attachments. Applications should be prepared in such a manner that they can be read and understood in a general way without reference to any further material that may be provided in the appendices. Applications and attachments should be typed single spaced, minimum font size 11 on 21.5 x 28cm paper. Illustrations should be drawn with clean black lines. **Deadline:** January 30. **Contact:** foundation@physiotherapy.ca.

7655 ■ Ann Collins Whitmore Memorial Scholarship (ACWMS) *(Graduate/Scholarship)*

Purpose: To provide scholarship for students involved in a research project that is part of the academic requirements for completion of their program. **Focus:** Physiology. **Qualif.:** Applicants must have completed a professional physiotherapy program and are enrolled full-time in a PhD or post-professional masters program and who must be Canadian citizens, landed immigrants, or people who reside in Canada (for the duration of the grant) with a valid work or student visa. **Criteria:** Special consideration will be given to visually impaired applicants.

Funds Avail.: Up to $4,000. **To Apply:** Applicants must submit one hard copy and one soft copy of the completed application and all appendices. Applications and appendices should be typed single spaced, minimum font size 11, on 21.5cm x 28cm paper. Appendices include the applicant's and supervisor's curriculum vitae. Applicants must also submit a letter of appraisal from their supervisor, or advisor that also outlines the proposed research programme; two additional letters of appraisal; and a letter from the Head of the Department at the university confirm-

ing acceptance into one of the programmes described in the regulations for The Dominion of Canada General Insurance Scholarship. If the applicant is not enrolled at the time of the application, any scholarship will be conditional upon the receipt of written confirmation of enrollment in the programme in question; and certified transcripts of all university-level courses (graduate and undergraduate). Applicants with transcripts from foreign universities must provide the grade conversions used by Graduate Studies in the Canadian university in which they are enrolled. **Deadline:** January 30. **Contact:** foundation@physiotherapy.ca.

7656 ■ Pi Gamma Mu (PGM)
1001 Millington St., Ste. B
Winfield, KS 67156
Ph: (620)221-3128
Fax: (620)221-7124
E-mail: executivedirector@pigammamu.org
URL: www.pigammamu.org

7657 ■ Pi Gamma Mu Scholarships *(Graduate/Scholarship)*

Purpose: To provide financial support to qualified individuals to pursue graduate education. **Focus:** Anthropology; Criminal justice; Economics; Geography; History; International affairs and relations; Law; Political science; Psychology; Public administration; Social work; Sociology. **Qualif.:** Applicant must be a first or second year graduate student in the areas of sociology, anthropology, political science, history, economics, international relations, public administration, criminal justice, law, social work, psychology and human/cultural geography. **Criteria:** Application will be evaluated based upon the degree to which the social sciences are an integral component of the overall course of study.

Funds Avail.: $1,000 - $2,000. **Duration:** Annual. **Number Awarded:** 11. **To Apply:** Applicant must submit a program description outlining requirements and coursework; must have transcripts, a statement explaining why the scholarship is desired, a resume, and three letters of recommendation from professors or work supervisors in the field in which the applicant intends to work. **Deadline:** February 15.

7658 ■ Pinnacle West Capital Corp.
400 N 5th St.
Phoenix, AZ 85004
Ph: (602)250-1000
Free: 800-457-2983
E-mail: alan.bunnell@pinnaclewest.com
URL: www.pinnaclewest.com

7659 ■ APS/ASU Scholarships *(Undergraduate/Scholarship)*

Purpose: To provide financial assistance to qualified individuals who want to pursue their career. **Focus:** Accounting; Construction; Economics; Education, Elementary; Education, Secondary; Education, Special; Engineering, Chemical; Engineering, Civil; Engineering, Electrical; Engineering, Mechanical; Finance; Information science and technology; Nursing; Telecommunications systems. **Qualif.:** Applicant must be an Arizona resident; must have a cumulative GPA of at least 3.0; must demonstrate financial need. **Criteria:** Recipient will be selected based on the scholarship application requirements.

Awards are arranged alphabetically below their administering organizations

Funds Avail.: $2,000. **Duration:** One year. **Number Awarded:** 10. **To Apply:** Applicant must complete the application form available online and send it to ASU Scholarship Office. **Deadline:** February 1. **Contact:** Louise Moskowitz at louise.moskowitz@aps.com; ASU Scholarship Office, Arizona State University, PO Box 870412, Tempe, AZ 85287-0412.

7660 ■ APS/Maricopa County Community Colleges Scholarships *(Undergraduate/Scholarship)*

Purpose: To provide financial assistance to qualified individuals who want to pursue their career. **Focus:** Accounting; Economics; Education; Education, Vocational-technical; Engineering, Chemical; Engineering, Civil; Engineering, Electrical; Engineering, Mechanical; Finance; Health care services; Information science and technology; Management; Marketing and distribution. **Qualif.:** Applicant must be an Arizona resident; must have a cumulative GPA of at least 3.0; must demonstrate financial need; must be a high school senior or current Maricopa Community College student; must be enrolled in a minimum of nine credit hours per semester. **Criteria:** Recipient will be selected based on the scholarship application requirements.

Funds Avail.: No specific amount. **To Apply:** Applicant must complete the application form available online and must be sent to ASU Scholarship Office. **Contact:** Louise Moskowitz at louise.moskowitz@aps.com; ASU Scholarship Office, Arizona State University, PO BOX 870412, Tempe, AZ 85287-0412.

7661 ■ Pipe Line Contractors Association of Canada
Ste. 201 1075 North Service Road W
Oakville, ON, Canada
Ph: (905)847-9383
Fax: (905)847-7824
E-mail: plcac@pipeline.ca
URL: www.pipeline.ca/

7662 ■ Pipe Line Contractors Association of Canada Student Bursary *(Undergraduate, Postgraduate/Scholarship)*

Purpose: To assist students with their educational expenses. **Focus:** Construction. **Qualif.:** Applicants must provide proof of a full-time enrollment in a program leading to a diploma or degree in any field at a recognized Canadian college or university and must be sons or daughters of a person whose principal income is derived from the pipeline construction industry. The parents or guardians of the applicants must be employed by or have a history of employment with a company who is a member of the Pipe Line Contractors Association of Canada. **Criteria:** Selection will be based on the committee's criteria.

Funds Avail.: No specific amount. **To Apply:** Applicants may contact the Society for the online application process and other required materials.

7663 ■ PKD Foundation
8330 Ward Pkwy., Ste. 510
Kansas City, MO 64114-2027
Ph: (816)931-2600
Fax: (816)931-8655
Free: 800-753-2873
E-mail: pkdcure@pkdcure.org

URL: www.pkdcure.org

7664 ■ PKD Foundation Fellowships *(Doctorate, Graduate/Fellowship)*

Purpose: To foster further research in all hereditary cystic disorders and to address the structure and function of polycystic kidney disease related genes in health and disease. **Focus:** Medicine. **Qualif.:** Applicants must: have a PhD or MD degree; describe a clear career path and explain how their respective projects are relevant to the path; and have approved human experimentation and animal use protocols (if required by project). **Criteria:** Applications are reviewed based on the scientific merit of the project and its relevance to PKD research.

Funds Avail.: $50,000/year. **Duration:** Annual. **Number Awarded:** 2. **To Apply:** Applicants must use the PKD Foundation Research Fellowship application cover page. Attach a Proposal Summary (1 page); Lay Summary (maximum of 150 words); Specific Aims & Rationale (1 page); Background Information (maximum of 3 pages); Research plan & Methods of Study (maximum of 6 page); References (maximum of 2 pages); Career Path Information (1 page); Budget (1 page); NIH BioSketch for Applicant (maximum of 2 pages); NIH BioSketch for Mentor (maximum of 2 pages); Other Support for Applicants (maximum of 2 pages); Other Support for Mentor (maximum of 2 pages); 3 Letters of Support; Animal Protocol approval; Human Subject Certification; and the Checklist. Application materials must be typed, single-spaced, 12-point font, and numbered. All applications must be sent electronically in a pdf file (not more than 1.5 MB in size), or via snail mail. **Deadline:** April 1. **Contact:** research@pkdcure.org.

7665 ■ A Place for Mom
1300 Dexter Ave.
Seattle, WA 98109
Ph: (206)285-4666
Free: 866-333-7935
URL: www.aplaceformom.com

7666 ■ Senior Innovation Scholarships *(Undergraduate, Graduate/Scholarship)*

Purpose: To support the training and education of future senior care leaders. **Focus:** Nursing. **Qualif.:** Applicants must be enrolled in an undergraduate or graduate degree program at an accredited U.S. college; must be permanent resident of the United States; and must have a minimum GPA of 3.0. **Criteria:** Selection will be based on the committee's criteria.

Funds Avail.: $1,000. **Duration:** Annual. **Number Awarded:** 5. **To Apply:** Applicants must submit a 500 words essay as regards to senior care innovations. **Deadline:** April 15.

7667 ■ Platinum Educational Group
2644 Sun Valley
Jenison, MI 49428
Ph: (616)818-7877
E-mail: info@platinumed.com
URL: platinumed.com

7668 ■ EMS Scholarship Awards *(All/Award)*

Purpose: To support students who dedicate their lives to helping others in EMS. **Focus:** Paramedics. **Qualif.:** Ap-

Awards are arranged alphabetically below their administering organizations

plicants must be currently attending a State approved or accredited EMS Program. **Criteria:** Selection will be based on the committee's criteria.

Funds Avail.: $1,000. **Duration:** Annual. **Number Awarded:** 2. **To Apply:** Applicants must email the completed following requirements to Platinum Educational Group: copy of student ID and State Identification Card; letter of recommendation form from program instructor; and brief essay (approximately 500 words) on what the applicants interested in the Medical Services Field and what his/her plans upon graduating. **Deadline:** July 17.

7669 ■ Playwrights' Center

2301 Franklin Ave. E
Minneapolis, MN 55406-1099
Ph: (612)332-7481
Fax: (612)332-6037
E-mail: info@pwcenter.org
URL: pwcenter.org

7670 ■ Jerome Fellowships *(Other/Fellowship)*

Purpose: To provide funds and services to emerging American playwrights and to aid them in the development of their craft. **Focus:** Theater arts. **Qualif.:** Applicants must be citizens or permanent residents of the United States; may not have had more than two different works fully produced by professional theaters at the time of application, defined as productions for which the author and/or primary artists (actors, directors, creative collaborators) were compensated; and received at least three public performances. **Criteria:** Selection is based on artistic excellence, potential and commitment.

Funds Avail.: $16,000 plus $1,500 development support. **Duration:** Annual. **Number Awarded:** 4. **To Apply:** Applicants must download the reference form online and provide it to two people familiar with their work. Applicants must create a single PDF document containing the following elements, arranged in the specified sequence: a cover sheet with name, work sample title, phone number(s), email address and mailing address (including city, state and ZIP code) presented in a clear format. The cover sheet should also include the following statement: "I hereby certify that the information contained in this application is true and correct to the best of my knowledge."; one full-length play script, with name and play title on the cover page; a one-page playwriting resume (listing all reading, s productions, awards, commissions, etc.) and/or autobiographical narrative. **Deadline:** November 20. **Remarks:** Awarded in partnership with the Jerome Foundation. Established in 1976. **Contact:** amandar@pwcenter.org.

7671 ■ Many Voices Fellowships *(Other/Fellowship)*

Purpose: To increase cultural diversity in contemporary theater, both locally and nationally, through cash grants, education and opportunities to develop new work with theater professionals. **Focus:** Theater arts. **Qualif.:** Applicants must be artists of color, 21 years of age or older, who are citizens or permanent residents of the United States. **Criteria:** Selection will be based on the applicant's commitment, proven talent and artistic potential.

Funds Avail.: $1,500 - $10,000. **Duration:** Annual. **Number Awarded:** 2. **To Apply:** Applicants must download the reference form online and provide it to two people familiar with their work. Applicants must create a single document in PDF format, containing the following elements, arranged

in the specified sequence: For the beginning playwright track: a cover sheet with applicant's name, work sample title, phone number(s), email address, and mailing address (including city, state and ZIP code) presented in a clear format; one-page (maximum) biography or resume including name, address, email, and phone number; a writing sample of no more than 30 pages in any genre (play scripts, film scripts, poetry, fiction, and nonfiction); one-page (maximum) description of goals for the fellowship period. For the emerging playwright track: a cover sheet; one-page biography or resume including name, address, email and phone number; a play script. Scripts must be written by the applicant only (no co-written submissions will be accepted). Scripts for musicals may be submitted by the book writer only; one-page (maximum) description of goals for the fellowship period. **Deadline:** February 5. **Contact:** Artistic Administrator Amanda Robbins-Butcher at amandar@pwcenter.org.

7672 ■ McKnight Advancement Grants *(Other/Grant)*

Purpose: To recognize playwrights whose work demonstrates exceptional artistic merit and potential. **Focus:** Theater arts. **Qualif.:** Applicant must be a resident of Minnesota; must have a minimum of one work fully produced by a professional theater at the time of the application. For the purposes of this application, "fully produced" is defined as a production for which the author and primary artists (actors, director, creative collaborators) were compensated and which received at least three public performances. **Criteria:** Selection will be based on artistic excellence, professional achievement, and proposed residency plans.

Funds Avail.: $25,000 stipend; $1,400 travel support; $2,500 to support a play development workshop and other professional expenses. **Number Awarded:** 2. **To Apply:** Applicants must submit a single document in PDF or Microsoft Word format, containing the following elements: a cover sheet with name, play title, home phone, other phone, email address, and complete mailing address; a full-length play script with applicant's name and the play title on the script's cover page; a representative list (maximum two pages) of production credits, indicating whether productions were professional, nonprofessional, or academic and listing name, address, and phone number of each producer/presenter; list of fellowships, grants, prizes, and honors that the applicant has won; brief autobiographical narrative of career history emphasizing artistic and professional accomplishments; a description of plans for the year with specific reference to active participation in the life of The Playwrights Center. **Deadline:** January 8. **Remarks:** Sponsored by the McKnight Foundation Arts Funding Plan. Established in 1990. **Contact:** Amanda Robbins-Butcher at amandar@pwcenter.org.

7673 ■ McKnight Theater Artist Fellowships *(Other/Fellowship)*

Purpose: To support outstanding work by professional artists whose skill and talent contribute to theatrical productions. **Focus:** Theater arts. **Qualif.:** Applicants must be professional artists who have been continuous residents of Minnesota. Fellowship is open to actors, directors, dramaturgs, and theatrical designers. It is also open to choreographers and composers whose main body of work is in theater. Professional artists working in other forms such as visual art or music are eligible to apply if their primary career focus is in work that plays a supporting or collaborative role in creating a theatrical event. **Criteria:** Selection will be based on commitment to theater arts, evidence of professional achievements, and a sustained level of excellence in the applicant's work.

Awards are arranged alphabetically below their administering organizations

Funds Avail.: $25,000 each. **To Apply:** Applicants must declare their intent to apply and inform the Playwrights' Center where and when the performances will take place. In final application, applicants must submit six collated sets of the following items: cover sheet; one-page artist statement; resume (2 pages maximum); statements of working process; work sample information sheet (2 pages maximum); work samples. Submit samples in no more than two of the following formats: video, 3-4 minutes of video in DVD format; photographs, up to 10 images in JPEG or TIFF format on a CD; audio, 3-4 minutes in audio cd format or MP3 format. Applicants must place their name at the top of each page of submitted material. Do not send the originals of work samples and be sure to keep copies of all application materials for applicant's records. **Deadline:** April 16. **Contact:** McKnight Theater Artist Fellowship, The Playwrights' Center; Email: submissions@pwcenter.org.

7674 ■ PWC Internships *(Undergraduate, Graduate/ Internship)*

Purpose: To provide opportunity to individuals to work at the heart of a thriving arts organization while learning multiple aspects of the day-to-day of a non-profit. **Focus:** Performing arts; Theater arts. **Qualif.:** Applicants must be recent graduates, advanced undergraduates, and graduate-level students of playwriting, dramaturgy, directing, stage management, and other theater programs. **Criteria:** Selection will be based on the committee's criteria.

Funds Avail.: No specific amount. **To Apply:** Applicants must download the provided internship application form at the website and such must be submitted with the following: current resume and a cover letter explaining short-term and long-term career goals, what skills they will bring to the Playwrights' Center, and why they are interested in an internship at the Playwrights' Center. **Deadline:** March 13 (for summer internships); May 1 (for 9-month internships). **Contact:** All application materials can be emailed to Hannah Joyce-Hoven at hannahj@pwcenter.org.

7675 ■ D.F. Plett Historical Research Foundation
University of Winnipeg
515 Portage Ave.
Winnipeg, MB, Canada R3B 2E9
Ph: (204)786-9352
E-mail: plettfoundation@gmail.com
URL: www.plettfoundation.org

7676 ■ D.F. Plett Graduate Fellowships *(Graduate/ Fellowship)*

Purpose: To encourage graduate students who are pursuing studies and research in the history of the forerunners and descendants of the 1870s Mennonite migrants to Manitoba. **Focus:** History. **Qualif.:** Applicant must be admitted or applying to complete a master of arts degree in history in the Joint Master's Program of the University of Winnipeg and the University of Manitoba or a PhD in history at the University of Manitoba. **Criteria:** Selection is based on the submitted application and materials.

Funds Avail.: Varies. **Number Awarded:** 2. **To Apply:** Applicants must submit a completed application form along with a photocopy of official transcripts, a summary of the proposed research (not more than 250 words); and sealed letters from two referees. **Deadline:** January 1; March 1; July 1. **Remarks:** Established in 2006. **Contact:** Hans Werner at the above address.

7677 ■ Plumbing-Heating-Cooling Contractors Association (PHCC)
180 S Washington St., Ste. 100
Falls Church, VA 22046
Ph: (703)237-8100
Fax: (703)237-7442
Free: 800-533-7694
E-mail: naphcc@naphcc.org
URL: www.phccweb.org

7678 ■ Delta Faucet Scholarships *(Undergraduate/ Scholarship)*

Purpose: To establish a framework for the industry's first apprenticeship system and to spearhead education programs to keep pace with technological change. **Focus:** Business. **Qualif.:** Applicants must be citizens of the United States or Canada and currently enrolled in or planning to enroll in plumbing, heating, cooling contractors; or must be enrolled full-time in an undergraduate degree program at an accredited four-year college or university with a major directly relating to the plumbing-heating-cooling profession. **Criteria:** Recipients are selected based on academic performance.

Funds Avail.: $2,500. **Number Awarded:** 6. **To Apply:** Applicants must complete the application form; must submit an official transcript of the high school grades; letter of recommendation from high school principal or counselor, college/university dean, academic advisor or apprentice program instructor; letter of recommendation from an active member of the Plumbing-Heating-Cooling Contractors-National Association (active for one year); SAT and ACT scores and cumulative GPA. **Deadline:** May 1. **Contact:** Plumbing-Heating-Cooling Contractors Association at the above address.

7679 ■ Plumbing-Heating-Cooling Contractors Association Educational Foundation Massachusetts Auxiliary Scholarships *(Undergraduate/Scholarship)*

Purpose: To establish a framework for the industry's first apprenticeship system and to spearhead educational programs to keep pace with technological change. **Focus:** Business. **Qualif.:** Applicants must be high school seniors who are citizens of the United States and residents of the Commonwealth of Massachusetts, planning to enroll in a full-time undergraduate degree program at an accredited four-year college or university. **Criteria:** Recipients are selected based on academic performance and financial need.

Funds Avail.: $1,500. **To Apply:** Applicants must complete the application form and submit an official transcript of high school grades; letter of recommendation from high school principal or counselor; SAT and ACT scores and cumulative GPA; and a letter of recommendation from an active member of the Plumbing-Heating-Cooling Contractors Association National Auxiliary. **Deadline:** May 1. **Contact:** Foundation Scholarship Coordinator; E-mail: foundation@naphcc.org.

7680 ■ Plumbing-Heating-Cooling Contractors Association Educational Foundation Need-Based Scholarships *(Undergraduate/Scholarship)*

Purpose: To establish a framework for the industry's first apprenticeship system and to spearhead educational programs to keep pace with technological change. **Focus:** Business. **Qualif.:** Applicants must be citizens of the United States or Canada planning to enroll in a full-time under-

Awards are arranged alphabetically below their administering organizations

graduate degree program at an accredited four-year college or university. **Criteria:** Recipients are selected based on academic performance and financial need.

Funds Avail.: $2,500. **To Apply:** Applicants must complete the application form and submit an official transcript of high school grades; letter of recommendation from high school principal or counselor; SAT and ACT scores and cumulative GPA; and a letter of recommendation from an active member of the Plumbing-Heating-Cooling Contractors Association National Association. **Deadline:** May 1.

7681 ■ Plumbing-Heating-Cooling Contractors Association Educational Foundation Scholarships (Undergraduate/Scholarship)

Purpose: To establish a framework for the industry's first apprenticeship system and to spearhead educational programs to keep pace with technological change. **Focus:** Business. **Qualif.:** Applicants must be citizens of the United States or Canada and must be enrolled full-time in an undergraduate degree program at an accredited four-year college or university with a major directly to plumbing-heating-cooling profession. **Criteria:** Recipients are selected based on academic performance and financial need.

Funds Avail.: No specific amount. **To Apply:** Applicants must complete the application form and submit an official transcript of the high school grades; letter of recommendation from high school principal or counselor; SAT and ACT scores as well as cumulative GPA; and a letter of recommendation from an active member of the Plumbing-Heating-Cooling Contractors Association National Association. **Deadline:** May 1. **Contact:** John Zink, at zink@naphcc.org.

7682 ■ A.O. Smith Scholarships (Undergraduate/Scholarship)

Purpose: To establish a framework for the industry's first apprenticeship system and to spearhead education programs to keep pace with technological change. **Focus:** Business. **Qualif.:** Applicants must be citizens of the United States or Canada and must be enrolled full-time in an undergraduate degree program at an accredited four-year college or university with a major directly to plumbing-heating-cooling profession. **Criteria:** Recipients are selected based on academic performance.

Funds Avail.: No specific amount. **Number Awarded:** 2. **To Apply:** Applicants must complete the application form and must submit an official transcript of the high school grades; letter of recommendation from high school principal or counselor, college/university dean, academic advisor or apprentice program instructor; SAT and ACT scores as well as cumulative GPA; and a letter of recommendation from an active member of the plumbing-heating-cooling contractors. **Deadline:** May 1. **Contact:** Foundation Scholarship Coordinator; E-mail: foundation@naphcc.org.

7683 ■ Bradford White Scholarships (Undergraduate/Scholarship)

Purpose: To establish a framework for the industry's first apprenticeship system and to spearhead education programs to keep pace with technological change. **Focus:** Business. **Qualif.:** Applicants must be citizens of the United States or Canada and must be enrolled full-time in an undergraduate degree program at an accredited two-year community college, technical college or trade school with a major directly related to the plumbing-heating-cooling profession. Applicant must be employed by a PHCC National Association member. **Criteria:** Recipients are

selected based on academic performance.

Funds Avail.: $7,500. **To Apply:** Applicants must complete the application form and submit an official transcript of the high school grades; letter of recommendation from high school principal or counselor, college/university dean, academic advisor or apprentice program instructor; SAT and ACT scores and cumulative GPA; and a letter of recommendation from an active member of the plumbing-heating-cooling contractors. **Deadline:** June 15. **Contact:** Plumbing-Heating-Cooling Contractors Association at the above address.

7684 ■ Plus Foundation
5353 Wayzata Blvd., Ste. 600
Minneapolis, MN 55416
Ph: (952)746-2590
Fax: (952)746-2599
URL: www.plusfoundation.org

7685 ■ Leo Gilmartin Scholarships (Undergraduate/Scholarship)

Purpose: To assist deserving PLUS member students with their college education. **Focus:** General studies/Field of study not specified. **Qualif.:** Applicants must be high school seniors who are children of current PLUS members or children of employees of current PLUS corporate sponsors. **Criteria:** Applicants are evaluated based on scholastic merit and extracurricular activity.

Funds Avail.: $12,000. **To Apply:** Applicants must submit college entrance exam scores; GPA and class rank; essay and letters of recommendation; list of extracurricular and community service activities. **Deadline:** March 13.

7686 ■ PLUS Foundation Financial Aid Grants (Undergraduate/Scholarship)

Purpose: To provide educational assistance to students who wants to advance their education. **Focus:** General studies/Field of study not specified. **Qualif.:** Applicants must be high school seniors who are children of current PLUS members or children of employees of current PLUS corporate sponsors. **Criteria:** Recipients are selected based on family financial need and proof of average to above average high school performance.

Funds Avail.: No specific amount. **To Apply:** Applicants must submit the household adjusted gross income; total number in household and number of dependent children attending college; estimated cost of tuition; GPA, class rank, college entrance exams scores. **Deadline:** March 13.

7687 ■ PMCA: An International Association of Confectioners
2980 Linden St., Ste. E3
Bethlehem, PA 18017
Ph: (610)625-4655
Fax: (610)625-4657
E-mail: info@pmca.com
URL: www.pmca.com

7688 ■ PMCA/Penn State Fellowship in Confectionery Research (Graduate/Fellowship)

Purpose: To recognize and support outstanding graduate students enrolled or planning to enroll in the Department of Food Science at the Pennsylvania State University, as well

Awards are arranged alphabetically below their administering organizations

as to promote and enhance the knowledge and image of the confectionery industry. **Focus:** Food science and technology. **Qualif.:** Applicants must be individuals that have earned an undergraduate degree, have some confectionery experience and are interested in furthering their education. **Criteria:** Selection shall be based on the aforementioned qualifications and compliance with the application details. Preference is given to the candidates who have some experience in confectionery manufacture.

Funds Avail.: No specific amount. **Duration:** Continuous. **To Apply:** Interested applicants may contact the Association for the application process and other details. **Remarks:** Established in 1989. **Contact:** Dr. Swamy Anantheswaran, Professor, Department of Food Science, Penn State University, 202 Food Science Bl. University Park, Pennsylvania 16802; Phone: 814-865-3004; Fax: 814-863-6132; Email: rca3@psu.edu.

7689 ■ Point Foundation (PF)

5055 Wilshire Blvd., Ste. 501
Los Angeles, CA 90036
Ph: (323)933-1234
Free: 866-337-6468
E-mail: info@pointfoundation.org
URL: www.pointfoundation.org

7690 ■ Walter M. Decker Point Scholarships *(Graduate, Undergraduate/Scholarship)*

Purpose: To support the LGBT community. **Focus:** General studies/Field of study not specified. **Qualif.:** Applicant must be LGBT; or have a history of leadership in the LGBT community and plan to be a LGBT leader in the future. **Criteria:** Award is given based on the application.

Funds Avail.: No specific amount. **To Apply:** Applicants must complete the online scholarship application before the deadline. If chosen as semi-finalists, students are requested to submit supplemental materials, in one envelope: two to three letters of recommendation; official transcripts; test score verification; and resume. **Contact:** Claire Walsh; Phone: (212) 512-5339.

7691 ■ HBO Point Scholarships *(Graduate, Undergraduate/Scholarship)*

Purpose: To support the LGBT community. **Focus:** Media arts. **Qualif.:** Applicants must be members of the LGBT or have a history of leadership in the LGBT community and plan to be a LGBT leader in the future and be pursuing a career in the media. **Criteria:** Award will be given based on the application.

Funds Avail.: No specific amount. **To Apply:** Applicants must complete the online scholarship application on or before the deadline. If chosen as semi-finalists, students are requested to submit supplemental materials, in one envelope: two to three letters of recommendation; official transcripts; test score verification; and resume.

7692 ■ Kevin Hummer Point Scholarships *(Graduate, Undergraduate/Scholarship)*

Purpose: To support the LGBT community. **Focus:** General studies/Field of study not specified. **Qualif.:** Applicants must be members of the LGBT; or have a history of leadership in the LGBT community and plan to be LGBT leaders in the future. **Criteria:** Award will be given based on the submitted application.

Funds Avail.: No specific amount. **To Apply:** Applicants

must complete the online scholarship application on or before the deadline. If chosen as semi-finalists, students are requested to submit supplemental materials, in one envelope: two to three letters of recommendation; official transcripts; test score verification; and resume.

7693 ■ Bryan L. Knapp Point Scholarships *(Graduate, Undergraduate/Scholarship)*

Purpose: To support the LGBT community. **Focus:** General studies/Field of study not specified. **Qualif.:** Applicants must be undergraduate LGBT students of distinction from the New York City area attending Cornell University, Ithaca, New York. **Criteria:** Award will be given based on the submitted application.

Funds Avail.: No specific amount. **To Apply:** Applicants must complete the online scholarship application before the deadline. If chosen as semi-finalists, students are requested to submit supplemental materials, in one envelope: two to three letters of recommendation; official transcripts; test score verification; and resume.

7694 ■ Jonathan D. Lewis Point Scholarships *(Graduate, Undergraduate/Scholarship)*

Purpose: To support the LGBT community. **Focus:** General studies/Field of study not specified. **Qualif.:** Applicants must be members of the LGBT or have a history of leadership in the LGBT community and plan to be a LGBT leader in the future. **Criteria:** Award will given based on the submitted application.

Funds Avail.: No specific amount. **To Apply:** Applicants must complete the online scholarship application on or before the deadline. If chosen as semi-finalists, students are requested to submit supplemental materials, in one envelope: two to three letters of recommendation; official transcripts; test score verification; and resume.

7695 ■ Casey Sakir Point Scholarships *(Graduate, Undergraduate/Scholarship)*

Purpose: To support the LGBT community. **Focus:** Arts; Fashion design. **Qualif.:** Applicants must be members of the LGBT; or have a history of leadership in the LGBT community and plan to be a LGBT leader in the future, and planning a future in the fields of design, fashion or the arts. **Criteria:** Award will be given based on the submitted application.

Funds Avail.: No specific amount. **To Apply:** Applicants must complete the online scholarship application onor before the deadline. If chosen as semi-finalists, students are requested to submit supplemental materials, in one envelope: two to three letters of recommendation; official transcripts; test score verification; and resume.

7696 ■ Time Warner Point Scholarships *(Graduate, Undergraduate/Scholarship)*

Purpose: To support the LGBT community. **Focus:** General studies/Field of study not specified. **Qualif.:** Applicants must be members of the LGBT or have a history of leadership in the LGBT community and plan to be a LGBT leader in the future. **Criteria:** Award will be given based on the submitted application.

Funds Avail.: No specific amount. **To Apply:** Applicants must complete the online scholarship application on or before the deadline. If chosen as semi-finalists, students are requested to submit supplemental materials, in one envelope: two to three letters of recommendation; official transcripts; test score verification; and resume.

Awards are arranged alphabetically below their administering organizations

7697 ■ Polish-American Engineers Association

1 Watergate Dr.
South Barrington, IL 60010
E-mail: contact@polishengineers.org
URL: www.polishengineers.org

7698 ■ Ralph Modjeski Scholarships *(Graduate, Undergraduate/Scholarship)*

Purpose: To provide financial assistance for qualified engineering students. **Focus:** Engineering. **Qualif.:** Applicant must be an engineering student at a 4-year college or university or can also be a graduate engineering who demonstrates excellent academic achievements and proven commitment to engineering. **Criteria:** Scholarship committee gives particular consideration to applicants of Polish heritage.

Funds Avail.: No specific amount. **Duration:** Annual. **Number Awarded:** 3. **To Apply:** Applicants must complete the application form, available online; must submit an official transcript, a 200-word letter describing the student's short and long term goals with any other information deemed pertinent; and must have three references with addresses and telephone numbers. **Contact:** Polish-American Engineers Association, c/o Michael Niedzinski; email: contact@polishengineers.org.

7699 ■ Polish Falcons of America (PFA)

381 Mansfield Ave.
Pittsburgh, PA 15220-2751
Ph: (412)922-2244
Fax: (412)922-5029
Free: 800-535-2071
E-mail: info@polishfalcons.org
URL: www.polishfalcons.org

7700 ■ Falcon Achievement Scholarships *(Undergraduate/Scholarship)*

Purpose: To provide financial support for deserving Falcon members aspiring to attend institutions of higher learning. **Focus:** Polish studies. **Qualif.:** Candidates must be graduating high school seniors or presently enrolled undergraduates intending to pursue further education as full time students in an accredited two or four year college, university or trade school; must have a minimum cumulative GPA of 2.0 out of 4.0. **Criteria:** Selection will be based on the academic achievements and leadership qualities.

Funds Avail.: $1,500. **To Apply:** Applicants must complete and sign the application form available online; must provide a community service information, essay, and photo; must submit the official transcript, counselor recommendation, and net information form and letter. **Deadline:** March 1.

7701 ■ General Falcon Scholarships *(Undergraduate/Scholarship)*

Purpose: To provide financial support for deserving Falcon members who are aspiring to attend institutions of higher learning. **Focus:** General studies/Field of study not specified. **Qualif.:** Candidates must be graduating high school seniors or presently enrolled undergraduates intending to pursue further education as full time students in an accredited two- or four-year college, university or trade school; must have a minimum cumulative GPA of 3.0 out of 4.0; must have taken an active participation in the Polish Falcon programs. **Criteria:** Selection will be based on the criteria of the selection committee.

Funds Avail.: $750. **To Apply:** Applicants must complete and sign the application form available online; must provide a community service information, essay and photo; must submit the official transcript, counselor recommendation and net information form and letter. **Deadline:** March 1. **Contact:** Patricia Del Busse, National First Vice President, Phone: 800-535-2071; Email: vptrish@polishfalcons.org.

7702 ■ Richard C. Gorecki Scholarships *(Undergraduate/Scholarship)*

Purpose: To provide financial assistance for deserving individuals intending to pursue their education. **Focus:** General studies/Field of study not specified. **Qualif.:** Applicant must be a PFA member for six years; must have a minimum GPA of 3.0 out of 4.0; Applicant must be enrolled full-time in a four-year college or university, or full-time postgraduate studies. **Criteria:** Selection of applicant will be based on the academic achievements and leadership qualities. Decisions of the selection board are subject to the approval of the National Board of Directors.

Funds Avail.: $15,000. **To Apply:** Applicant must complete the scholarship application; must have a two part essay (minimum 500 words for each part); must provide at least three letters of recommendation. **Deadline:** March 29.

7703 ■ Portable Sanitation Association International (PSAI)

7760 France Ave. S, 11th Fl.
Minneapolis, MN 55435
Ph: (952)854-8300
Fax: (952)854-7560
Free: 800-822-3020
E-mail: info@psai.org
URL: www.psai.org

7704 ■ Portable Sanitation Association International Scholarship Fund *(Undergraduate/Scholarship)*

Purpose: To assist individuals in the portable sanitation industry who have made a commitment to advancing themselves through higher education. **Focus:** Technology. **Qualif.:** Applicants must: be employees of a PSAI Member company, or children or spouses of full-time employees who have been with the Member company for at least two years; be high school senior or college undergraduate students enrolled full-time at a four-year or two-year college, vocational or technical school; have GPA of 3.0 or above; obtain a minimum SAT score of 1000, ACT score of 21, or country equivalent. **Criteria:** Selection is done on the basis of the aforesaid qualifications, academic achievement, community involvement, work experience and recommendations.

Funds Avail.: $5,000 each. **Duration:** Annual. **Number Awarded:** A least 5. **To Apply:** Applicants must submit a copy of transcript; a (500-1,000 words) essay; a completed hard copy of application form; and profile sheet with the PSAI office. **Deadline:** March 15. **Remarks:** Established in 2004.

7705 ■ Portuguese American Leadership Council of the United States (PALCUS)

9255 Center St., Ste. 404
Manassas, VA 20110
Ph: (202)466-4664
Fax: (202)466-4661

Awards are arranged alphabetically below their administering organizations

E-mail: palcus@palcus.org
URL: www.palcus.org

7706 ■ Portuguese-American Scholarship Foundation (Undergraduate/Scholarship)

Purpose: To provide financial assistance to qualified New Jersey students of Portuguese ancestry, who want to further their post-secondary school education and gain greater access to a better way of life. **Focus:** General studies/Field of study not specified. **Qualif.:** Applicants must be New Jersey High School seniors that are Portuguese-born or that have a parent or grandparent that is Portuguese-born; must be a U.S. citizens or U.S. permanent residents; must demonstrate financial need; must be a New Jersey high school senior applying to, or accepted in, a four-year college or university curriculum leading to a baccalaureate degree; must meet the minimum PASF academic standards, including a grade point average of B or better. **Criteria:** Scholarship will be evaluated based on the academic achievement and financial need.

Funds Avail.: $5,000. **Number Awarded:** 10. **Deadline:** February 15.

7707 ■ Portuguese-American Police Association of Massachusetts, Lodge II (PAPA)

56 Holly St.
New Bedford, MA 02746
Ph: (508)994-5390
E-mail: info@papamass.com
URL: papamass.com

7708 ■ Portuguese American Police Association Scholarships (Undergraduate/Scholarship)

Purpose: To provide support for deserving students intending to pursue a career in either Health Care, Social Service, Law Enforcement, or other related fields. **Focus:** Health care services; Law enforcement; Social work. **Qualif.:** Applicants must be Portuguese descents; must be residents of Massachusetts; must be enrolled full-time in an accredited college or university or graduating seniors applying to full-time status in an accredited or another college or university; must be majoring in either health care, social services, law enforcement or another related field; must maintain a GPA of 2.0 or higher. **Criteria:** Candidates will be selected based on their academic standing.

Funds Avail.: $500. **Duration:** One year. **Number Awarded:** 6. **To Apply:** Application forms are available online. Applicants must submit an essay of not more than three paragraphs stating the reasons and their career goals; must have a high school transcript that includes the class rank; must have the current college/university transcript; must have a letter of reference from each of the following: (1) Guidance counselor or advisor and (2) Personal reference, preferably from someone with whom the applicants have work. **Deadline:** August 15.

7709 ■ Poteet Strawberry Festival Association (PSFA)

PO Box 227
Poteet, TX 78065
Ph: (830)742-8144
Fax: (830)742-3608
Free: 888-742-8144
E-mail: info@strawberryfestival.com

URL: www.strawberryfestival.com

7710 ■ Poteet Strawberry Festival Association Scholarships (Graduate, Undergraduate/Scholarship)

Purpose: To increase the number of minority students who want to attain higher education. **Focus:** General studies/Field of study not specified. **Qualif.:** Applicants must be students who are still in college. **Criteria:** Applications will be reviewed by the selection committee.

Funds Avail.: No specific amount. **Duration:** Annual. **Number Awarded:** Varies. **To Apply:** For further information about the scholarship, applicants are advised to contact the Foundation.

7711 ■ Practising Law Institute (PLI)

1177 Avenue of the Americas
New York, NY 10036
Ph: (212)824-5700
Fax: (212)824-5733
Free: 800-260-4PLI
E-mail: info@pli.edu
URL: www.pli.edu

7712 ■ Practising Law Institute Law Student Scholarships (Undergraduate/Scholarship)

Purpose: To provide financial assistance to qualified students who want to pursue their career. **Focus:** Law. **Qualif.:** Applicants must be legal aid and government attorneys, judges, judicial clerks, and employees of nonprofit organizations. **Criteria:** Recipients will be selected based on all application requirements.

Funds Avail.: No specific amount. **To Apply:** Applicants must complete the application forms available online; must have a legible copy of a student ID for the current term; and must complete the Statement of Need on the respective letter head. **Contact:** PLI at the above address.

7713 ■ Presbyterian Association of Musicians (PAM)

100 Witherspoon St.
Louisville, KY 40202-1396
Ph: (502)569-5288
Fax: (502)569-8465
Free: 888-728-7228
URL: www.presbymusic.org

7714 ■ Presbyterian Association of Musicians Scholarships (All/Scholarship)

Purpose: To provide financial assistance for students for summer worship and music conferences. **Focus:** Music. **Qualif.:** Applicants must be adults, children, youth members of the association. **Criteria:** Recipient will be selected based on financial need.

Funds Avail.: No specific amount. **To Apply:** Adult applicants must write and submit a short essay of qualifications and why they would like to attend a PAM conference and a letter of recommendation from pastor or music director. For children and youth applicants, their music director must write an evaluation statement including their musical experience and involvement in the church, how the applicants would benefit from the conference and perception of the applicants' financial need. **Deadline:** March 15.

7715 ■ Presbyterian Church

100 Witherspoon St.
Louisville, KY 40202-1396

Awards are arranged alphabetically below their administering organizations

Fax: (502)569-8005
Free: 888-728-7228
E-mail: info@pcusa.org
URL: www.pcusa.org

7716 ■ Samuel Robinson Awards (Undergraduate/ Award)

Purpose: To stimulate interest in the Westminster shorter Catechism. **Focus:** Religion. **Qualif.:** Applicants must be Presbyterian Church members who are: full time students at a Presbyterian related college or university; a junior or senior of the current school year; and not previously awarded. **Criteria:** Selection will be based on the committee's criteria.

Funds Avail.: $2,000 - $5,000. **Duration:** Annual. **Number Awarded:** 15. **To Apply:** Applicants must submit an essay of at least 2,000 words, double spaced, and prepared on plain white text. Applicants may visit the website for the essay topic. Essays may be faxed or sent by email and may be written in the language of instruction. Students attending Universidad Inter-Americana may submit their essay in Spanish. Completed application should include: a recitation form signed by the applicant's chaplain or campus minister; an essay of at least 2,000 words; W-9 form, completed and signed by the applicant. **Deadline:** April 1. **Contact:** Presbyterian Foundation at the above address.

7717 ■ Prescott Center for the Arts (PCA)

208 N Marina St.
Prescott, AZ 86301
Ph: (928)541-0209
E-mail: director@pca-az.net
URL: www.pfaa.net

7718 ■ Prescott Fine Arts Association Scholarship Program (Undergraduate/Scholarship)

Purpose: To recognize and support the talented young people of Yavapai County. **Focus:** Arts. **Qualif.:** Applicants must be high school students who reside in Yavapai County. **Criteria:** Recipients are selected based on financial need.

Funds Avail.: No specific amount. **Duration:** Annual. **To Apply:** Applicants must complete the application form. **Deadline:** February 24.

7719 ■ President's Commission on White House Fellowships

1900 E St. NW, Rm. B431
Washington, DC 20415
Ph: (202)395-4522
Fax: (202)395-6179
E-mail: whitehousefellows@whf.eop.gov
URL: www.whitehouse.gov/about/fellows/commission

7720 ■ White House Fellows (Other/Fellowship)

Purpose: To provide gifted and highly motivated young Americans with some firsthand experience in the process of governing the Nation and a sense of personal involvement in the leadership of society; to enhance the leadership and other learning experiences in the work assignment. **Focus:** General studies/Field of study not specified. **Qualif.:** Applicants must be U.S. citizens; and must have completed their undergraduate education and be working in their chosen professions. Employees of the federal

government are not eligible unless they are career military personnel. **Criteria:** Selection of applicants will be based on the following criteria: (1) A record of remarkable professional achievement early in one's career; (2) Evidence of leadership skills and the potential for further growth; (3) A demonstrated commitment to public service; (4) The knowledge and skills necessary to contribute successfully at the highest levels of the federal government.

Funds Avail.: No specific amount. **Duration:** Annual. **To Apply:** Application forms are available online and must be sent together with the other supporting documents. **Deadline:** January 15. **Remarks:** Established in 1964 by President Lyndon Johnson. **Contact:** Letters of recommendation should be sent to: Shiela Coates at the above address.

7721 ■ Prevent Cancer Foundation (PCF)

1600 Duke St., Ste. 500
Alexandria, VA 22314-3421
Ph: (703)836-4412
Fax: (703)836-4413
Free: 800-227-2732
E-mail: pcf@preventcancer.org
URL: preventcancer.org

7722 ■ Prevent Cancer Foundation Fellowships (Postdoctorate/Fellowship)

Purpose: To provide funding for innovative projects expected to lead to future funding from other peer-reviewed sources. **Focus:** Oncology. **Qualif.:** Applicants must be postdoctoral students (graduate students who will have their doctoral degree before the project start date); or researchers from non-profit institutions (including academic institutions). **Criteria:** Selection shall be based on: quality of the research training environment; scientific merit of the training project; qualifications of the candidate; qualifications of the mentor; estimated potential of the fellowship candidate to establish a career in cancer prevention; and achievability of the project's specific aims within the two-year time frame.

Funds Avail.: $40,000/year. **Duration:** Annual; up to two years. **Number Awarded:** Varies. **To Apply:** Applicants are required to apply online. There is an application fee of $75. **Deadline:** August 28. **Remarks:** Established in 1985. **Contact:** E-mail pamela.nwoji@preventcancer.org or Jenny.Twesten@preventcancer.org.

7723 ■ Pride Foundation

2014 E Madison St., Ste. 300
Seattle, WA 98122
Ph: (206)323-3318
Free: 800-735-7287
URL: www.pridefoundation.org

7724 ■ Paul Arnold Memorial Scholarships (Undergraduate/Scholarship)

Purpose: To support students studying interior, fashion, or graphic design. **Focus:** Fashion design; Graphic art and design; Interior design. **Qualif.:** Applicants must be young men and women studying interior, fashion, graphic design; must be a resident of Alaska, Idaho, Montana, Oregon or Washington but may study elsewhere. **Criteria:** Preference will be given to students who are self-identified LGBTQ, members of LGBTQ families or straight-allies who have

Awards are arranged alphabetically below their administering organizations

been strongly supportive of the LGBTQ community.

Funds Avail.: No specific amount. **Duration:** Annual. **To Apply:** Qualified students are asked to submit an application to determine eligibility for scholarships. Applicants may download an application form from the Foundation's website. **Deadline:** January 15. **Remarks:** Established in 1996. **Contact:** scholarships@pridefoundation.org.

7725 ■ Asian and Pacific Islander Queers Sisters Scholarships *(Undergraduate/Scholarship)*

Purpose: To provide scholarship to students who have been stigmatized, isolated or closeted because of sexual identity issues. **Focus:** General studies/Field of study not specified. **Qualif.:** Applicants must be Asian/Pacific Islander lesbians, bisexual females, and transgender (both MTF and FTM spectrum) students, and straight ally community from Alaska, Idaho, Montana, Oregon, and Washington. **Criteria:** Preference will be given to students who are self-identified LGBTQ, members of LGBTQ families or straight-allies who have been strongly supportive of the LGBTQ community.

Funds Avail.: No specific amount. **To Apply:** Qualified students are asked to submit an application to determine eligibility for scholarships. Applicants may download an application form from the Foundation's website. **Deadline:** January 15. **Contact:** scholarships@pridefoundation.org.

7726 ■ Associates in Behavioral Health Scholarships *(Graduate/Scholarship)*

Purpose: To support LGBTQ students pursuing graduate education in psychology, psychiatry, social work, or psychiatric nursing. **Focus:** Nursing, Psychiatric; Psychiatry; Psychology; Social work. **Qualif.:** Applicants must be: LGBT students pursuing graduate education in psychology, psychiatry, social work, or psychiatric nursing; residents of Alaska, Idaho, Montana, Oregon or Washington. **Criteria:** Preference given to individuals with demonstrated financial needs and to those entering or already enrolled in an accredited graduate program.

Funds Avail.: No specific amount. **Duration:** Annual. **To Apply:** Qualified students are asked to submit an application to determine eligibility for scholarships. Applicants may download an application form from the Foundation's website. **Deadline:** January 15. **Remarks:** Established in 2007. **Contact:** scholarships@pridefoundation.org.

7727 ■ Barbara Bailey Scholarships *(Undergraduate/Scholarship)*

Purpose: To provide scholarship to the students who have been stigmatized, isolated or closeted because of sexual identity issues. **Focus:** General studies/Field of study not specified. **Qualif.:** Applicant must be lesbians who are residents of Washington. **Criteria:** Preference will be given to students who are self-identified LGBTQ, members of LGBTQ families or straight-allies who have been strongly supportive of the LGBTQ community.

Funds Avail.: No specific amount. **To Apply:** Qualified students are asked to submit an application to determine eligibility for scholarships. Applicants may download an application form from the Foundation's website. **Deadline:** January 15. **Contact:** scholarships@pridefoundation.org.

7728 ■ Bellevue PFLAG Scholarships *(Undergraduate/Scholarship)*

Purpose: To support East King County High School seniors who have demonstrated their ability to promote leadership in the LGBTQ community through their actions as volunteers and/or advocates. **Focus:** General studies/Field of study not specified. **Qualif.:** Applicants must be graduating high school seniors currently attending a greater East King County high school. **Criteria:** Preference will be given to students who are self-identified LGBTQ, members of LGBTQ families or straight-allies who have been strongly supportive of the LGBTQ community.

Funds Avail.: No specific amount. **Duration:** Annual. **To Apply:** Qualified students are asked to submit an application to determine eligibility for scholarships. Applicants may download an application form from the Foundation's website. **Deadline:** January 15. **Remarks:** Established in 1999. **Contact:** scholarships@pridefoundation.org.

7729 ■ Bill Bendiner and Doug Morgenson Scholarships *(Undergraduate/Scholarship)*

Purpose: To support students pursuing a career in human services, health sciences, or visual arts. **Focus:** Health sciences; Human relations; Visual arts. **Qualif.:** Applicants must be students pursuing a career in human services, health sciences, or visual arts. **Criteria:** Preference will be given to students who are self-identified LGBTQ, members of LGBTQ families or straight-allies who have been strongly supportive of the LGBTQ community.

Funds Avail.: No specific amount. **Duration:** Annual. **To Apply:** Qualified students are asked to submit an application to determine eligibility for scholarships. Applicants may download an application form from the Foundation's website. **Deadline:** January 15. **Remarks:** Established in 2001. **Contact:** scholarships@pridefoundation.org.

7730 ■ Robert Browning Scholarships *(Undergraduate/Scholarship)*

Purpose: To support students studying health sciences or health services. **Focus:** Health sciences. **Qualif.:** Applicants must be: majoring in health sciences program; and, resident of Alaska, Idaho, Montana, Oregon or Washington but may study elsewhere. **Criteria:** Preference will be given to students who are self-identified LGBTQ, members of LGBTQ families or straight-allies who have been strongly supportive of the LGBTQ community.

Funds Avail.: No specific amount. **Duration:** Annual. **To Apply:** Qualified students are asked to submit an application to determine eligibility for scholarships. Applicants may download an application form from the Foundation's website. **Deadline:** January 15. **Remarks:** Established in 1993. **Contact:** scholarships@pridefoundation.org.

7731 ■ Deloris Carter Hampton Scholarships *(Undergraduate/Scholarship)*

Purpose: To support the education of those women of color who are advocates of LGBTQ community. **Focus:** Dance; Education. **Qualif.:** Applicants must be women of color who have a demonstrated history of activism and/or leadership in the LGBT community and are pursuing a degree in education, women's health, or dance; and, residents of Alaska, Idaho, Montana, Oregon or Washington but may study elsewhere. **Criteria:** Preference will be given to students who are self-identified LGBTQ, members of LGBTQ families or straight-allies who have been strongly supportive of the LGBTQ community.

Funds Avail.: No specific amount. **Duration:** Annual. **To Apply:** Qualified students are asked to submit an application to determine eligibility for scholarships. Applicants may download an application form from the Foundation's

Awards are arranged alphabetically below their administering organizations

website. **Deadline:** January 15. **Remarks:** Established in 2001. **Contact:** scholarships@pridefoundation.org.

7732 ■ Donald O. Coffman Scholarships
(Undergraduate/Scholarship)

Purpose: To provide scholarship to the students who have been stigmatized, isolated or closeted because of sexual identity issues. **Focus:** General studies/Field of study not specified. **Qualif.:** Applicants must be current and future LGBT and straight-ally leaders and role models that are residents of Alaska, Idaho, Montana, Oregon or Washington but may study elsewhere. **Criteria:** Preference will be given to students who are self-identified LGBTQ, members of LGBTQ families or straight-allies who have been strongly supportive of the LGBTQ community.

Funds Avail.: No specific amount. **To Apply:** Qualified students are asked to submit an application to determine eligibility for scholarships. Applicants may download an application form from the Foundation's website. **Deadline:** January 15. **Contact:** scholarships@pridefoundation.org.

7733 ■ Cole Family Scholarships *(Undergraduate/Scholarship)*

Purpose: To support students whose parents are LGBTQ affiliated. **Focus:** General studies/Field of study not specified. **Qualif.:** Applicants must be Washington residents under age 25 raised by one or more LGBTQ parent. **Criteria:** Preference will be given to students who are self-identified LGBTQ, members of LGBTQ families or straight-allies who have been strongly supportive of the LGBTQ community.

Funds Avail.: No specific amount. **To Apply:** Qualified students are asked to submit an application to determine eligibility for scholarships. Applicants may download an application form from the Foundation's website.

7734 ■ Dennis Coleman Choral Conducting Scholarships *(Undergraduate/Scholarship)*

Purpose: To provide scholarship to the students who have been stigmatized, isolated or closeted because of sexual identity issues. **Focus:** Music. **Qualif.:** Applicants must be LGBT students studying choral conducting or music, and residents of Alaska, Idaho, Montana, Oregon or Washington but may study elsewhere. **Criteria:** Preference will be given to those who are committed to creating social change through music.

Funds Avail.: No specific amount. **To Apply:** Qualified students are asked to submit an application to determine eligibility for scholarships. Applicants may download an application form from the Foundation's website. **Deadline:** January 15. **Contact:** scholarships@pridefoundation.org.

7735 ■ Dennis Coleman Memorial Scholarships
(Undergraduate/Scholarship)

Purpose: To support LGBTQ students that are studying choral conducting or music. **Focus:** Music. **Qualif.:** Applicants must be LGBTQ students studying choral conducting or music. **Criteria:** Preference will be given to those committed to creating social change through music.

Funds Avail.: No specific amount. **To Apply:** Qualified students are asked to submit an application to determine eligibility for scholarships. Applicants may download an application form from the Foundation's website.

7736 ■ Brian M. Day Scholarships *(Undergraduate/Scholarship)*

Purpose: To support Puget Sound area gay men of color in their continuing education. **Focus:** General studies/Field

of study not specified. **Qualif.:** Applicants must be: Puget Sound area gay men of color who have significant financial need and demonstrate activism in the gay/lesbian community and their communities of color; and, residents of Alaska, Idaho, Montana, Oregon or Washington but may study elsewhere. **Criteria:** Preference will be given to students who are self-identified LGBTQ, members of LGBTQ families or straight-allies who have been strongly supportive of the LGBTQ community.

Funds Avail.: No specific amount. **Duration:** Annual. **To Apply:** Qualified students are asked to submit an application to determine eligibility for scholarships. Applicants may download an application form from the Foundation's website. **Deadline:** January 15. **Remarks:** Established in 1993. **Contact:** scholarships@pridefoundation.org.

7737 ■ Derivative Duo Scholarships *(Undergraduate/Scholarship)*

Purpose: To provide scholarship to the students who have been stigmatized, isolated or closeted because of sexual identity issues. **Focus:** Human relations; Mental health. **Qualif.:** Applicants must be residents of Washington studying mental health or human services. **Criteria:** Selection will be based on the committee's criteria.

Funds Avail.: No specific amount. **Duration:** Annual. **To Apply:** Qualified students are asked to submit an application to determine eligibility for scholarships. Applicants may download an application form from the Foundation's website. **Deadline:** January 15. **Remarks:** Established in 2002. **Contact:** scholarships@pridefoundation.org.

7738 ■ Inland Northwest Business Alliance Scholarships (INBA) *(Undergraduate/Scholarship)*

Purpose: To provide scholarship to the students who have been stigmatized, isolated or closeted because of sexual identity issues. **Focus:** General studies/Field of study not specified. **Qualif.:** Applicants must be undergraduate students who are also residents of Eastern Washington and Northern Idaho. **Criteria:** Selection will be based on the committee's criteria.

Funds Avail.: No specific amount. **To Apply:** Qualified students are asked to submit an application to determine eligibility for scholarships. Applicants may download an application form from the Foundation's website. **Deadline:** January 16. **Contact:** scholarships@pridefoundation.org.

7739 ■ Obrzut Ling Scholarships *(Undergraduate/Scholarship)*

Purpose: To provide scholarship to the students who have been stigmatized, isolated or closeted because of sexual identity issues. **Focus:** General studies/Field of study not specified. **Qualif.:** Applicants must be: students enrolled or entering a vocational or technical program at an accredited learning institution; and, residents of Alaska, Idaho, Montana, Oregon or Washington but may study elsewhere. **Criteria:** Preference will be given to students who are self-identified LGBTQ, members of LGBTQ families or straight-allies who have been strongly supportive of the LGBTQ community.

Funds Avail.: No specific amount. **To Apply:** Qualified students are asked to submit an application to determine eligibility for scholarships. Applicants may download an application form from the Foundation's website.

7740 ■ McFarffels Scholarships *(Undergraduate/Scholarship)*

Purpose: To provide scholarship to the students who have been stigmatized, isolated or closeted because of sexual

Awards are arranged alphabetically below their administering organizations

identity issues. **Focus:** General studies/Field of study not specified. **Qualif.:** Applicants must be: lesbians with financial need entering a field that promotes social change and/or social justice; and, residents of Alaska, Idaho, Montana, Oregon or Washington but may study elsewhere. **Criteria:** Preference will be given to students who are self-identified LGBTQ, members of LGBTQ families or straight-allies who have been strongly supportive of the LGBTQ community.

Funds Avail.: No specific amount. **To Apply:** Qualified students are asked to submit an application to determine eligibility for scholarships. Applicants may download an application form from the Foundation's website.

7741 ■ Jack D. Motteler Scholarships
(Undergraduate/Scholarship)

Purpose: To support LGBTQ and allied students in the visual arts. **Focus:** Visual arts. **Qualif.:** Applicant must be undergraduate students in the visual arts; and residents of Alaska, Idaho, Montana, Oregon or Washington but may study elsewhere. **Criteria:** Preference will be given to students who are self-identified LGBTQ, members of LGBTQ families or straight-allies who have been strongly supportive of the LGBTQ community.

Funds Avail.: No specific amount. **Duration:** Annual. **To Apply:** Qualified students are asked to submit an application to determine eligibility for scholarships. Applicants may download an application form from the Foundation's website. **Deadline:** January 15. **Remarks:** Established in 2000. **Contact:** scholarships@pridefoundation.org.

7742 ■ Pride Foundation Political Leadership Scholarships *(Undergraduate/Scholarship)*

Purpose: To provide scholarship to the students who have been stigmatized, isolated or closeted because of sexual identity issues. **Focus:** Law; Political science; Public administration. **Qualif.:** Applicants must be students studying law, political science, public policy, or public administration with the goal of improving rights for LGBTQ people. **Criteria:** Preference is given to LGBTQ students of color and low-income or first-generation college students.

Funds Avail.: No specific amount. **To Apply:** Qualified students are asked to submit an application to determine eligibility for scholarships. Applicants may download an application form from the Foundation's website. **Deadline:** January 15. **Contact:** scholarships@pridefoundation.org.

7743 ■ Pride Foundation Regional Scholarships
(Undergraduate/Scholarship)

Purpose: To provide scholarship to the students who have been stigmatized, isolated or closeted because of sexual identity issues. **Focus:** General studies/Field of study not specified. **Qualif.:** Applicants must be residents of areas outside of King County where Pride Foundation is working to enhance the leadership of the LGBTQ and ally community: Alaska, Idaho, Montana, Oregon, Eastern Washington, and Northwest/Southwest Washington. **Criteria:** Preference will be given to students who are self-identified LGBTQ, members of LGBTQ families or straight-allies who have been strongly supportive of the LGBTQ community.

Funds Avail.: No specific amount. **To Apply:** Qualified students are asked to submit an application to determine eligibility for scholarships. Applicants may download an application form from the Foundation's website. **Deadline:** January 15. **Contact:** scholarships@pridefoundation.org.

7744 ■ Pride Foundation Social Work Scholarships
(Undergraduate/Scholarship)

Purpose: To provide scholarship to the students who have been stigmatized, isolated or closeted because of sexual identity issues. **Focus:** Social work. **Qualif.:** Applicants must be LGBTQ students enrolled or admitted to a Council on Social Work Education baccalaureate or master's program in social work. Students in a doctoral program in Social Work can also apply. **Criteria:** Preference will be given to students of color.

Funds Avail.: No specific amount. **To Apply:** Qualified students are asked to submit an application to determine eligibility for scholarships. Applicants may download an application form from the Foundation's website. **Deadline:** January 15. **Contact:** scholarships@pridefoundation.org.

7745 ■ Don Renschler Scholarships *(Graduate/ Scholarship)*

Purpose: To provide scholarship to the students who have been stigmatized, isolated or closeted because of sexual identity issues. **Focus:** Mental health. **Qualif.:** Applicant must be residents of Washington who are graduate students in the study of mental health. **Criteria:** Selection will be based on the committee's criteria.

Funds Avail.: No specific amount. **To Apply:** Qualified students are asked to submit an application to determine eligibility for scholarships. Applicants may download an application form from the Foundation's website. **Deadline:** January 15. **Contact:** scholarships@pridefoundation.org.

7746 ■ Rosenberg-Ibarra Scholarships
(Undergraduate/Scholarship)

Purpose: To provide scholarship to the students who have been stigmatized, isolated or closeted because of sexual identity issues. **Focus:** General studies/Field of study not specified. **Qualif.:** Applicants must be LGBTQ students who either graduated from a high school in Idaho or will be attending a college or university within the state of Idaho. They must also be residents of Alaska, Idaho, Montana, Oregon or Washington. **Criteria:** Preference will be given to students who are self-identified LGBTQ, members of LGBTQ families or straight-allies who have been strongly supportive of the LGBTQ community.

Funds Avail.: No specific amount. **To Apply:** Qualified students are asked to submit an application to determine eligibility for scholarships. Applicants may download an application form from the Foundation's website. **Deadline:** January 15. **Contact:** scholarships@pridefoundation.org.

7747 ■ Kathy Spadoni Memorial Scholarships
(Undergraduate/Scholarship)

Purpose: To provide scholarship to the students who have been stigmatized, isolated or closeted because of sexual identity issues. **Focus:** General studies/Field of study not specified. **Qualif.:** Applicants must be graduating high school seniors entering a bachelor's degree program who have demonstrated leadership skills and have a passion for making positive social change. They must also be residents of Alaska, Idaho, Montana, Oregon or Washington but may study elsewhere. **Criteria:** Preference will be given to students who are self-identified LGBTQ, members of LGBTQ families or straight-allies who have been strongly supportive of the LGBTQ community.

Funds Avail.: No specific amount. **To Apply:** Qualified students are asked to submit an application to determine eligibility for scholarships. Applicants may download an ap-

Awards are arranged alphabetically below their administering organizations

plication form from the Foundation's website. **Deadline:** January 15. **Contact:** scholarships@pridefoundation.org.

7748 ■ Phil Sullivan Scholarships (Undergraduate/ Scholarship)

Purpose: To provide scholarship to the students who have been stigmatized, isolated or closeted because of sexual identity issues. **Focus:** General studies/Field of study not specified. **Qualif.:** Applicants must be students under the age of 21 who demonstrate significant financial need, with preference to those that have been homeless. **Criteria:** Selection will be based on the committee's criteria.

Funds Avail.: No specific amount. **To Apply:** Qualified students are asked to submit an application to determine eligibility for scholarships. Applicants may download an application form from the Foundation's website.

7749 ■ Ric Ulrich and Chuck Pischke Scholarships (Undergraduate/Scholarship)

Purpose: To support LGBTQ and allied students studying visual arts and design. **Focus:** Visual arts. **Qualif.:** Candidates must intend to study in visual arts and design. **Criteria:** Preference will be given to students who are self-identified LGBTQ, members of LGBTQ families or straight-allies who have been strongly supportive of the LGBTQ community.

Funds Avail.: No specific amount. **To Apply:** Qualified students are asked to submit an application to determine eligibility for scholarships. Candidates may download an application form from the Foundation's website. **Deadline:** January 15. **Remarks:** Established in 1998. **Contact:** scholarships@pridefoundation.org.

7750 ■ Patricia Van Kirk Scholarships (Undergraduate/Scholarship)

Purpose: To support lesbians studyinbg theater or visual arts with a commitment to social justice. **Focus:** Theater arts; Visual arts. **Qualif.:** Applicants must be: lesbians studying theater or visual arts; and, resident of Alaska, Idaho, Montana, Oregon or Washington but may study elsewhere. **Criteria:** Preference will be given to students who are self-identified LGBTQ, members of LGBTQ families or straight-allies who have been strongly supportive of the LGBTQ community.

Funds Avail.: No specific amount. **Duration:** Annual. **To Apply:** Qualified students are asked to submit an application to determine eligibility for scholarships. Applicants may download an application form from the Foundation's website. **Deadline:** January 15. **Remarks:** Established in 2007. **Contact:** scholarships@pridefoundation.org.

7751 ■ Wells Fargo Scholarships (Undergraduate/ Scholarship)

Purpose: To provide scholarship to the students who have been stigmatized, isolated or closeted because of sexual identity issues. **Focus:** General studies/Field of study not specified. **Qualif.:** Applicants must be current or future LGBT and straight-ally leaders and role models and residents of Alaska, Idaho, Montana, Oregon or Washington but may study elsewhere. **Criteria:** Preference will be given to students who are self-identified LGBTQ, members of LGBTQ families or straight-allies who have been strongly supportive of the LGBTQ community.

Funds Avail.: No specific amount. **To Apply:** Qualified students are asked to submit an application to determine eligibility for scholarships. Applicants may download an ap-

plication form from the Foundation's website.

7752 ■ Whidbey Island Giving Circle Scholarships (Undergraduate/Scholarship)

Purpose: To provide scholarship to the students who have been stigmatized, isolated or closeted because of sexual identity issues. **Focus:** General studies/Field of study not specified. **Qualif.:** Applicants must be current and future LGBTQ and ally leaders and role models. **Criteria:** Preference will be given to residents of Whidbey Island.

Funds Avail.: No specific amount. **Duration:** Annual. **To Apply:** Qualified students are asked to submit an application to determine eligibility for scholarships. Applicants may download an application form from the Foundation's website. **Deadline:** January 15. **Remarks:** Established in 2007. **Contact:** Dyanne Sheldon at 206-303-0576 or email at whidbeygivingcircle@whidbey.com.

7753 ■ Wozumi Family Scholarships (Undergraduate/ Scholarship)

Purpose: To provide scholarship to the students who have been stigmatized, isolated or closeted because of sexual identity issues. **Focus:** General studies/Field of study not specified. **Qualif.:** Applicants must be students who are goal-oriented, HIV-positive, and/or focusing on the treatment and/or eradication of HIV. **Criteria:** Selection shall be based on the aforementioned qualifications and compliance with the application details.

Funds Avail.: No specific amount. **To Apply:** Qualified students are asked to submit an application to determine eligibility for scholarships. Applicants may download an application form from the Foundation's website. **Deadline:** January 15. **Contact:** scholarships@pridefoundation.org.

7754 ■ You Go Girl! Scholarships (Undergraduate/ Scholarship)

Purpose: To provide scholarship to the students who have been stigmatized, isolated or closeted because of sexual identity issues. **Focus:** General studies/Field of study not specified. **Qualif.:** Applicants must be lesbians who have completed their sophomore year of college; and residents of Alaska, Idaho, Montana, Oregon or Washington but may study elsewhere. **Criteria:** Preference will be given to students who are self-identified LGBTQ, members of LGBTQ families or straight-allies who have been strongly supportive of the LGBTQ community.

Funds Avail.: No specific amount. **To Apply:** Qualified students are asked to submit an application to determine eligibility for scholarships. Applicants may download an application form from the Foundation's website.

7755 ■ Urashi Zen Scholarships (Undergraduate/ Scholarship)

Purpose: To provide scholarship to the students who have been stigmatized, isolated or closeted because of sexual identity issues. **Focus:** Business administration; Computer and information sciences; Political science. **Qualif.:** Applicants must be: students studying business administration, computer science, or political science; and residents of Alaska, Idaho, Montana, Oregon or Washington but may study elsewhere. **Criteria:** Preference will be given to students who are self-identified LGBTQ, members of LGBTQ families or straight-allies who have been strongly supportive of the LGBTQ community.

Funds Avail.: No specific amount. **To Apply:** Qualified students are asked to submit an application to determine

Awards are arranged alphabetically below their administering organizations

eligibility for scholarships. Applicants may download an application form from the Foundation's website.

7756 ■ Pride Law Fund

PO Box 2602
San Francisco, CA 94126-2602
E-mail: info@pridelawfund.org
URL: www.pridelawfund.org

7757 ■ Tom Steel Post-Graduate Fellowships
(Postgraduate, Other/Fellowship)

Purpose: To provide financial assistance to law advocates of lesbian, gay, bisexual and transgendered (LGBT) community; to ensure that unmet legal needs are recognized and prioritized for the security of the civil rights of the LGBT community in the future. **Focus:** Law. **Qualif.:** Applicants must be law students who are about to graduate in the Spring semester or lawyers within three years of their graduation from law school; must complete full-time work within 12 months. **Criteria:** Selection will be based on the need of the project; anticipated impact of the project; organizational structure of the proposal; stability and supportiveness of the sponsoring organization or supervising attorney; applicant's past community or public service activities; applicant's connection and involvement with the LGBT community

Funds Avail.: $30,000. **Duration:** Annual. **To Apply:** Applicants must submit a cover page; one-page overview of project; full description of the project; applicant's qualifications; estimated budget; resume; law transcript; description of the sponsoring organization and/or Supervising Attorney; list of any other people involved in the project and a description of their respective roles and relevant experiences; letter of support from the sponsoring organization; two additional letters of support; timetable; a signed "usage agreement and certification". **Deadline:** January 12. **Contact:** Completed applications should be sent at info@pridelawfund.org.

7758 ■ Primate Conservation, Inc.

1411 Shannock Rd.
Charlestown, RI 02813-3726
Ph: (401)364-7140
Fax: (401)364-6785
E-mail: nrowe@primate.org
URL: www.primate.org

7759 ■ Primate Conservation Grants *(Graduate, Professional development/Grant)*

Purpose: To fund field research that supports conservation programs for wild populations of primates. **Focus:** Zoology. **Qualif.:** Applicants must be graduate students, qualified conservationists and primatologists to study rare and endangered primates and their conservation in their natural habitat. **Criteria:** Proposals are evaluated on competitive basis. Applications are screened by outside reviewers and the Board of Directors of PCI, All appropriate projects will be considered, but the regions of current interest are Asia and West Africa.

Funds Avail.: $2,500-$5,000. **To Apply:** Applicants must fill out the cover sheet and institutional agreement forms and submit three copies of the complete proposal via regular air mail. Email one digital copy of the proposal with applicants' name and species in the file name in an MS

.doc file or RTF. Proposals must be typed, double spaced, in English, and limited to 20 pages total. Proposal should consist of the following: introduction; background information; project description; methods; post-project follow-up; timetable; budget; bibliography; CV of principal personnel, maximum of two pages; copies of permissions from appropriate governmental agencies, or statement that permits and permissions are not needed; completed and signed institution agreement form; names and addresses of three people qualified to review the applicants' proposal. **Deadline:** February 1 and September 20.

7760 ■ Prince Henry Society (PHS)

PO Box 6726
New Bedford, MA 02742
Ph: (508)991-2623
E-mail: info@princehenrysociety.org
URL: www.princehenrysociety.org

7761 ■ Prince Henry Society Scholarships
(Undergraduate/Scholarship)

Purpose: To provide opportunities for deserving students who want to pursue a higher education. **Focus:** General studies/Field of study not specified. **Qualif.:** Applicants must be graduating seniors of Portuguese descent seeking an undergraduate or associate degree from an accredited college or university; must be residents of the Greater New Bedford area. **Criteria:** Awards will be given based on financial need and academic merit.

Funds Avail.: No specific amount. **Duration:** Annual. **To Apply:** Applicants must complete the application form available online; must submit a copy of their most recent college transcript, including their recent class rank and S.A.T. scores. **Contact:** Prince Henry Society, at the above address.

7762 ■ Printing Industries of America - Center for Technology and Research

301 Brush Creek Rd.
Warrendale, PA 15086
Ph: (412)741-6860
Fax: (412)741-2311
Free: 800-910-4283
E-mail: printingind@printing.org
URL: www.printing.org/ctr

7763 ■ PGSF Scholarships *(Undergraduate/ Scholarship)*

Purpose: To encourage and support talented men and women who are interested in graphic communication careers. **Focus:** Graphic art and design. **Qualif.:** Applicants must be: interested in pursuing a career in graphic communications; high school seniors or high school graduates that have not yet started college, or college students who are enrolled in a two- or four-year college program; studying full-time; and, able to maintain a 3.0 GPA or higher. **Criteria:** Selection shall be based on high school/college academic records, rank in class, recommendations and biographical information, which includes extracurricular interests and academic honors.

Funds Avail.: $2,000 each; $5,000 (Gutenberg level). **Duration:** Annual. **Number Awarded:** Varies. **To Apply:** Applicants may visit the program website for further information regarding the application details/instructions. **Deadline:**

Awards are arranged alphabetically below their administering organizations

April 1. **Remarks:** Established in 1956. **Contact:** Print and Graphics Scholarship Foundation, Attn: Bernie Eckert, 200 Deer Run Road, Sewickley, PA 15143-2600.

7764 ■ Professional Beauty Association (PBA)
15825 N 71st St., No. 100
Scottsdale, AZ 85254
Ph: (480)281-0424
Fax: (480)905-0708
Free: 800-468-2274
E-mail: info@probeauty.org
URL: www.probeauty.org

7765 ■ Sally Beauty Scholarships for High School Graduates *(Undergraduate/Scholarship)*
Purpose: To support high school graduates, desiring to enter the cosmetology profession. **Focus:** Cosmetology. **Qualif.:** Applicants must be high school graduates under the age of 26 who want to enter the cosmetology profession. **Criteria:** Recipients are selected based on academic performance and interest in a cosmetology program.

Funds Avail.: $1,000. **Duration:** Annual. **Number Awarded:** Varies. **To Apply:** Applicants must submit a completed application form along with two letters of recommendation; personal essay; and high school transcript.

7766 ■ Professional Construction Estimators Association of America (PCEA)
PO Box 680336
Charlotte, NC 28216
Ph: (704)489-1494
Free: 877-521-7232
E-mail: pcea@pcea.org
URL: www.pcea.org

7767 ■ Ted G. Wilson Memorial Scholarships *(Undergraduate/Scholarship)*
Purpose: To provide financial assistance for individuals intending to further their education in the construction industry. **Focus:** Construction; Engineering. **Qualif.:** Applicant must be a high school senior, college freshman, sophomore or junior student planning to further his/her education in the construction industry. Applicant must be a resident of, or plan to attend a school or university in North Carolina, South Carolina, Virginia, Georgia and Florida where PCEA has an established chapter. **Criteria:** Applicants are selected based on the academic ability, need and desire to enter the construction industry.

Funds Avail.: $1,000. **Duration:** One Year. **To Apply:** Applicants must submit a completed application form; one evaluation form completed by the high school Guidance Counselor or College Faculty Advisor, whichever is applicable at time of application; one evaluation form completed by an adult not related to the applicant; official transcript of high school/college grades and latest S.A.T. scores if available. Finalists may be interviewed by the Scholarship Committee. **Deadline:** March 15. **Remarks:** Established in May 21, 1988 in memory of Ted Wilson (1932-1987), the first National Executive Director of the PCEA.

7768 ■ Professional Employees Association
505-1207 Douglas St.
Victoria, BC, Canada V8W 2E7

Ph: (250)385-8791
Fax: (250)385-6629
Free: 800-779-7736
URL: www.pea.org

7769 ■ PEA Bursaries *(Undergraduate/Scholarship)*
Purpose: To provide financial assistance to deserving individuals who want to pursue their education. **Focus:** General studies/Field of study not specified. **Qualif.:** Applicants must: be current members of PEA; be registered, or in the process of being registered, in a part-time post-secondary educational program for an upcoming educational session; and, demonstrate financial need. **Criteria:** Recipients will be selected based on the qualifications and compliance with the application details.

Funds Avail.: $500 each. **Duration:** Annual. **Number Awarded:** Up to 10. **To Apply:** Applicants must submit a complete application form available at the website; must include (a) a typed letter setting out the applicants' education and career goals, (b) a statutory declaration that the applicants meet the criteria set out in the qualifications. **Deadline:** March 15.

7770 ■ PEA Scholarships *(Undergraduate/Scholarship)*
Purpose: To support the education of members and/or relatives of the Professional Employees Association. **Focus:** General studies/Field of study not specified. **Qualif.:** Applicants must be current members or relatives of PEA staff; must also be registered, or in the process of being registered, in a full-time post-secondary educational program for an upcoming educational session. **Criteria:** Award is given based on the worthiness of the essay considering content, analysis and literary style, as selected by the scholarships committee.

Funds Avail.: $1,000 each. **Duration:** Annual. **Number Awarded:** Up to 10. **To Apply:** Applicants must submit a 1,500-word essay discussing the impact of provincial government funding cuts on unionized public sector workers and the public they serve. **Deadline:** March 15.

7771 ■ Project 10
115 W California Blvd., Ste. 116
Pasadena, CA 91105
Ph: (626)577-4553
URL: www.project10.org

7772 ■ Friends of Project 10 Models of Excellence Scholarships *(Undergraduate/Scholarship)*
Purpose: To support students who have advanced the civil rights of the lesbian, gay, bisexual, and transgender communities. **Focus:** Sexuality. **Qualif.:** Applicants are limited to graduating senior high school students residing in these Southern California counties: Imperial, Kern, Los Angeles, Orange, Riverside, Santa Barbara, San Bernardino, San Diego, San Luis Obispo, Ventura. They must be from public, private and parochial schools who have advanced the civil rights of the lesbian, gay, bisexual, and transgender (LGBT) population. **Criteria:** Selection shall be based on the aforementioned applicants' qualifications and compliance with the application details.

Funds Avail.: $1,000, $2000 and $3,000. **Duration:** Annual. **Number Awarded:** Varies. **To Apply:** Applicants must submit a completed scholarship application. Applicants must also enclose the following: a transcript of high school

Awards are arranged alphabetically below their administering organizations

grades and grades in progress; a list of activities with particular emphasis on work done in the LGBT community; proposed course of study at college, university, or technical school; one or more letters of recommendation; autobiography describing the background, the aspirations after college, and the connection to the LGBT community (2 pages maximum); and examples of any work that such applicant think would be of interest to the scholarship committee (optional). **Deadline:** May 9. **Remarks:** Established in 1994. **Contact:** Friends of Project 10, Inc., at the above address.

7773 ■ Project Management Association of Canada (PMAC)

1234 Kingston Rd., Ste. 125
Toronto, ON, Canada M1N 1P3
Fax: (416)986-5777
URL: www.pmac-ampc.ca

7774 ■ Fellowships in the PMAC-AGPC *(Professional development/Fellowship)*

Purpose: To recognize individuals who made a significant contribution to the development of the art and science project, program or portfolio management, either as practitioners, teachers, or researchers. **Focus:** General studies/Field of study not specified. **Qualif.:** Applicants must be regular members of the association for at least five years. Interested individuals who have been members with less than five years will be considered depending on the contribution made to the field or the association. **Criteria:** Applicants will be evaluated based on the following criteria: a) evidence of substantial achievement in professional practice; b) evidence of significant contribution to a broad area of professional work or to experience in a very specific and specialized context; c) giving back to the profession through research, publication, teaching, presentations or mentoring; d) active commitment to continuing professional development; e) continued development of a full range of competencies; f) experience in a number of work environments, industries and project types; g) evidence of enhanced professional, interpersonal, evaluative and analytical skills that have been applied on projects; and h) evidence of using innovative approaches to resolving project issues or applying professional skills.

Funds Avail.: No specific amount. **Duration:** Annual. **To Apply:** Applicants must submit a completed application form, curriculum vitae, personal statement, portfolio of evidence, documentary and letter of support.

7775 ■ Property and Environment Research Center (PERC)

2048 Analysis Dr., Ste. A
Bozeman, MT 59718
Ph: (406)587-9591
E-mail: perc@perc.org
URL: www.perc.org

7776 ■ Property and Environment Research Center Graduate Fellowships *(Graduate/Fellowship)*

Purpose: To provide opportunities for those who are interested in researching issues related to natural resources and the environment. **Focus:** Environmental law; Natural resources. **Qualif.:** Applicant must be a graduate or law student interested in natural resources and environmental

issues and show potential for research and writing in these areas. **Criteria:** Preference is given to those who are working on a research paper, thesis or dissertation on a natural resource or environmental topic.

Funds Avail.: $2,250 per month. **Duration:** 3/year. **To Apply:** Applicants must complete the application online. In addition, applicants must provide and upload a cover letter; resume/vita; description of the proposed research project (2-5 pages double-spaced); writing sample, preferably in the applicant's area of expertise; one letter of reference; and undergraduate and graduate transcripts. **Deadline:** March 1.

7777 ■ Property and Environment Research Center Lone Mountain Fellowships *(Other/Fellowship)*

Purpose: To advance understanding of the role of markets and property rights in protecting and enhancing environmental resources. **Focus:** Natural resources. **Qualif.:** Applicant must be a scholar, journalist, policy-maker or environmentalist interested in undertaking a project that advances understanding of the role of markets and property rights in protecting and enhancing environmental resources. **Criteria:** Selection is based on the submitted applications.

Funds Avail.: No specific amount. **To Apply:** Applicants must complete the application online. In addition, applicants must provide and upload a resume/vita; a brief budget statement related to the proposal; a short (2-3 page) research proposal summarizing the work to be undertaken while at PERC; and individuals who are at a relatively early stage of their career (graduate students, post-graduates, untenured faculty, or journalists in the first five years of their career) should have a senior participant in the field write a letter of recommendation on their behalf.

7778 ■ Property and Environment Research Center Media Fellowships *(Other/Fellowship)*

Purpose: To help journalists examine how property rights and markets can improve the environment. **Focus:** Natural resources. **Qualif.:** Applicant must be a reporter, editorial writer, broadcaster, producer or other working in the field of journalism, primarily covering the environment; a journalist who is skeptical but open-minded; or a journalist who is familiar with property rights and markets and their affect on the environment. **Criteria:** Preference may be given to journalists who specialize in environmental reporting.

Funds Avail.: No specific amount. **To Apply:** Applicants must complete the application online. In addition, applicants must provide and upload a statement (one page or less) explaining why they want to be fellows; resume; clippings or other indications of writing or broadcasting experience (may be sent as attachments or URLs or mailed separately); and two references.

7779 ■ Julian Simon Fellowships *(Other/Fellowship)*

Purpose: To develop policy-oriented research on natural resource and environmental conservation. **Focus:** Natural resources. **Qualif.:** Applicant must be an excellent scholar with a focus on empiricism and an imaginative research agenda assessing natural resource and environmental issues. **Criteria:** Selection is based on the submitted application.

Funds Avail.: No specific amount. **To Apply:** Applicants must complete the application online. In addition, applicants must provide and upload a vita; a short (2-3 page) research proposal summarizing the work to undertake while at PERC; and individuals who are at a relatively early stage of

Awards are arranged alphabetically below their administering organizations

their career (untenured faculty) should have a senior scholar in their field write a letter of recommendation on their behalf.

7780 ■ ProQuest L.L.C.
789 E Eisenhower Pkwy.
Ann Arbor, MI 48106-1346
Ph: (734)761-4700
Fax: (734)662-4554
Free: 800-521-0600
E-mail: info@proquest.com
URL: www.proquest.com

7781 ■ Roger K. Summit Scholarships for North America *(Graduate/Scholarship)*

Purpose: To assist students studying library science and related disciplines. **Focus:** Library and archival sciences. **Qualif.:** Applicants must be students who are currently enrolled in an accredited library or information science program. **Criteria:** Selection of recipient shall be based on the following: academic achievement; demonstrated interest in electronic information services, based on course work, research, and experience; and, faculty recommendations.

Funds Avail.: $5,000. **Duration:** Annual. **To Apply:** Applicants may visit the scholarship section of the bestowing organization's website for further information regarding the application details. **Deadline:** March 30. **Remarks:** Established in 1993.

7782 ■ Prostate Cancer Foundation
1250 Fourth St.
Santa Monica, CA 90401
Ph: (310)570-4700
Fax: (310)570-4701
Free: 800-757-2873
E-mail: info@pcf.org
URL: www.pcf.org

7783 ■ PCF Challenge Awards *(Professional development/Grant)*

Purpose: To support cross-disciplinary teams of investigators in strategic areas. **Focus:** Oncology. **Qualif.:** Applicants must be teams of individuals, which may be assembled from one institution or from several institutions, and should be comprised of at least three highly experienced investigators capable of providing unique scientific expertise to the solution of a significant problem in prostate cancer research. **Criteria:** Selection will be based on the committee's criteria.

Funds Avail.: $300,000 to $1,500,000 per year. **Duration:** Three years. **To Apply:** Applicants may visit the website for further information.

7784 ■ PCF Young Investigator Awards *(Professional development/Grant)*

Purpose: To support future research leaders who will keep the field of prostate cancer research vibrant with new ideas. **Focus:** Oncology. **Qualif.:** Applicants must be young (generally 35 and younger) investigators who have achieved junior faculty positions and are committing their lives to the field of prostate cancer. **Criteria:** Selection will be based on the committee's criteria.

Funds Avail.: No specific amount. **To Apply:** Applicants may contact the Foundation for the application process and other information.

7785 ■ Psychology Association of Saskatchewan
PO Box 4528
Regina, SK, Canada S4P 3W7
E-mail: info@psychsask.ca
URL: psychsask.ca/

7786 ■ Psychology Association of Saskatchewan Student Scholarships - Academic Achievement *(Master's, Doctorate/Scholarship)*

Purpose: To support students to further develop psychological research, education and training in the Province of Saskatchewan. **Focus:** Psychology. **Qualif.:** Applicants must be full-time students (Honors, Masters, or Doctoral) who do not currently hold any major scholarships or departmental awards over $10,000. Preference will be given to student representatives of Psychology Association of Saskatchewan (PAS). **Criteria:** Selection will be based on the committee's criteria.

Funds Avail.: $500. **Duration:** Annual. **To Apply:** Applicants must submit all required documents: most recent transcript from an accredited Saskatchewan University; one letter of recommendation from a supervisor; and a written statement, no more than 500 words describing educational and work goals. **Deadline:** April 30.

7787 ■ Psychology Association of Saskatchewan Student Scholarships - Research Based *(Master's, Doctorate/Scholarship)*

Purpose: To support students to further develop psychological research, education and training in the Province of Saskatchewan. **Focus:** Psychology. **Qualif.:** Applicants must be full-time students (Honors, Masters, or Doctoral) who do not currently hold any major scholarships or departmental awards over $10,000 and successfully defended/passed projects, theses or dissertations before the application deadline. Preference will be given to student representatives of Psychology Association of Saskatchewan (PAS). **Criteria:** Selection will be based on the committee's criteria.

Funds Avail.: $500. **Duration:** Annual. **To Apply:** Applicants must submit the following documents: recent transcript from an accredited Saskatchewan University; comprehensive one-page summary of project, thesis or dissertation; and one letter of recommendation from a supervisor. **Deadline:** April 30.

7788 ■ Public Accountants Association of Kansas (PAAK)
PO Box 2732
Salina, KS 67402-2732
Ph: (785)827-7225
Fax: (785)827-0283
E-mail: accountant@paak.org
URL: www.paak.org

7789 ■ The Floyd Lietz Memorial Scholarship *(Undergraduate/Scholarship)*

Purpose: To recognize accounting students in Kansas and assist with their financial education needs at Kansas Universities. **Focus:** Accounting. **Qualif.:** Applicants must

Awards are arranged alphabetically below their administering organizations

be junior or senior students with an accounting major; must have a GPA of 3.0 or better in accounting classes; must be full-time students in Kansas University. **Criteria:** Selection will be based on the committee's criteria.

Funds Avail.: No specific amount. **Duration:** Annual. **To Apply:** Applicants must complete and submit the following requirements: a typewritten or printed application; a copy of most recent transcript; wallet size photo suitable for publication; a one-page essay on the following topics: the outlook of the accounting profession in Kansas, and personal accounting career objectives. **Deadline:** June 30. **Contact:** Victor D. Barbo, chairman; Phone: 785-537-0190; Fax: 785-537-0158; Email: vbarbo@sinkgordon.com.

7790 ■ Public Agency Risk Managers Association (PARMA)
1 Capitol Mall, Ste. 800
Sacramento, CA 95814
Free: 844-467-2762
URL: parma.com

7791 ■ PARMA Scholarships *(Undergraduate/Scholarship)*
Purpose: To promote, develop, and facilitate education and leadership in public agency risk management. **Focus:** Management. **Qualif.:** Applicant should be an employee of a member public agency pursuing an associate in Risk Management, Risk Management for Public Entities, Associate in Risk Pool Management. **Criteria:** The member of the Committee appointed by the president of PARMA will select the candidates based on the statement of his or her ultimate life goals in risk management and other related information.

Funds Avail.: $1,000. **To Apply:** An applicant must fill out the application form; attach a written sponsorship statement by a PARMA member agency; must submit a paper of his/her ultimate own goals in the field of risk management; a description of the participation in PARMA including the local Chapter level; and attach any other related experience or information that will support of the scholarship request. **Contact:** PARMA Secretary Treasurer PO Box 711894 Santee, CA 92072-1894.

7792 ■ Public Education Foundation
4350 S Maryland Pkwy.
Las Vegas, NV 89119
Ph: (702)799-1042
Fax: (702)799-5247
E-mail: info@ccpef.org
URL: ccpef.org

7793 ■ Evelyn Abrams Memorial Scholarships *(Undergraduate/Scholarship)*
Purpose: To support individuals aiming to acquire a degree in education or business. **Focus:** Business; Education. **Qualif.:** Applicants must be CCSD female seniors interested in pursuing a degree in education or business at an accredited college/university; must have a minimum 3.0 unweighted cumulative GPA; and must demonstrate financial need. **Criteria:** Selection is based on merit.

Funds Avail.: $750. **Duration:** Annual. **Number Awarded:** 1. **To Apply:** Applicants must submit a completed application form, essay, letter of recommendation from a teacher, counselor, club advisor, or coach, and transcript of records. **Deadline:** February 28. **Contact:** For further inquiry, please contact Scholarship Office at 702-221-7422; E-mail: csdonnelly@ccpef.org.

7794 ■ Adelson Family Scholarships *(Undergraduate/Scholarship)*
Purpose: To assist the education of the dependents of Venetian Resort Hotel Casino Employees. **Focus:** General studies/Field of study not specified. **Qualif.:** Applicants must: be CCSD seniors; be dependents of a Venetian Resort Hotel Casino employee; be planning to attend any accredited college/university; have a minimum 3.5 cumulative GPA; and, demonstrate financial needs. **Criteria:** Awards are given based on need.

Funds Avail.: $3,000 each. **Duration:** Annual. **Number Awarded:** 3. **To Apply:** Applicants must submit a completed application form together with an essay; two letters of recommendation; transcript; and a resume of awards, **Deadline:** February 25. **Contact:** Kelli Grimm at the above address.

7795 ■ Adelson Scholarships *(Undergraduate/Scholarship)*
Purpose: To support individuals pursuing a career in the field of health services. **Focus:** Health care services. **Qualif.:** Applicants must be CCSD seniors interested in pursuing a career in the field of health services at an accredited college/university; must have a minimum 3.5 cumulative GPA; and must demonstrate financial need. **Criteria:** Selection is based on merit.

Funds Avail.: $3,000 each. **Duration:** Annual. **Number Awarded:** 3. **To Apply:** Applicants must submit a completed application form together with an essay, two letters of recommendation, transcript and a resume of awards. **Deadline:** February 28. **Contact:** For further inquiry, please contact Scholarship Office at 702-221-7422; E-mail: csdonnelly@ccpef.org.

7796 ■ Alliance of Black Culinarians Scholarships *(Undergraduate/Scholarship)*
Purpose: To promote education in culinary arts. **Focus:** Culinary arts. **Qualif.:** Applicants must be CCSD seniors; must have a minimum 2.5 GPA; and must demonstrate financial needs. **Criteria:** Preference is given to minority students and those interested in a career in culinary arts.

Funds Avail.: $1,000. **Duration:** Annual. **Number Awarded:** 1. **To Apply:** Applicants must submit a completed application form together with an essay, two letters of recommendation, transcript and a resume. **Deadline:** February 18. **Contact:** For further inquiry, please contact Scholarship Office at 702-221-7422; E-mail: csdonnelly@ccpef.org.

7797 ■ American Nuclear Society Nevada Section Scholarships *(Undergraduate/Scholarship)*
Purpose: To promote education in the field of nuclear science. **Focus:** Engineering, Nuclear; Nuclear science. **Qualif.:** Applicants must be CCSD seniors planning to major in nuclear engineering or a nuclear science related field at UNLV with a minimum 3.8 cumulative GPA. **Criteria:** Awards are given based on merit.

Funds Avail.: $1,000. **Duration:** Annual. **Number Awarded:** 1. **To Apply:** Applicants must submit a completed application form together with an essay, two letters of recommendation, transcript and a resume of awards. **Deadline:** February 18. **Contact:** For further inquiry, please contact Scholarship Office at 702-221-7422; E-mail: csdonnelly@ccpef.org.

Awards are arranged alphabetically below their administering organizations

7798 ■ Susan Ayers Memorial Scholarships
(Undergraduate/Scholarship)

Purpose: To provide educational opportunities for individuals intending to pursue higher studies. **Focus:** General studies/Field of study not specified. **Qualif.:** Applicants must be CCSD seniors who have attended Estes McDoniel Elementary School; must be planning to attend an accredited post-secondary college/university; and must have a minimum 3.0 unweighted cumulative GPA. **Criteria:** Award is given based on the compliance with submission of the necessary application materials.

Funds Avail.: $500. **Duration:** Annual. **Number Awarded:** 1. **To Apply:** Applicants must submit completed application form together with essay; two letters of recommendation; and transcript. **Contact:** For further inquiry, please contact Scholarship Office at 702-221-7422; E-mail: csdonnelly@ccpef.org.

7799 ■ Susan Brager Occupational Education Scholarships *(Undergraduate/Scholarship)*

Purpose: To provide educational opportunities for individuals intending to pursue higher studies. **Focus:** Education. **Qualif.:** Applicants must be CCSD seniors; must have completed a minimum of two years of an established occupational education program; must have a minimum 2.5 cumulative GPA; and must be planning to attend a school in the Nevada Higher Education System within Clark County. **Criteria:** Selection will be based on the submitted application materials.

Funds Avail.: $1,000. **Duration:** Annual. **Number Awarded:** 1. **To Apply:** Applicants must submit a completed application form together with an essay, a letter of recommendation, transcript and a resume of awards. **Deadline:** February 18. **Contact:** For further inquiry, please contact Scholarship Office at 702-221-7422; E-mail: csdonnelly@ccpef.org.

7800 ■ Agustin C. Cano Memorial Scholarships
(Undergraduate/Scholarship)

Purpose: To provide educational opportunities for individuals intending to pursue higher studies. **Focus:** General studies/Field of study not specified. **Qualif.:** Applicants must be Valley High School seniors planning to attend at any accredited college/university as full-time students. **Criteria:** Selection shall be based on the compliance in submission of the necessary application materials.

Funds Avail.: $500. **Duration:** Annual. **Number Awarded:** 1. **To Apply:** Applicants must submit a completed application form together with two letters of recommendation, a resume, and a 400-500 words essay explaining the topic: "What has impacted your life the most?" **Deadline:** February 18.

7801 ■ John Caoile Memorial Scholarships
(Undergraduate/Scholarship)

Purpose: To provide educational opportunities for individuals intending to pursue higher studies. **Focus:** General studies/Field of study not specified. **Qualif.:** Applicants must be Durango High School AFJROTC program seniors planning to attend at any accredited post-secondary institution and have excelled in the areas of leadership, community service and extra-curricular activities and must have a minimum of 3.0 GPA. **Criteria:** Selection will be based on the submitted application materials.

Funds Avail.: $1,000. **Duration:** Annual. **Number Awarded:** 1. **To Apply:** Applicants must submit a com-

pleted application form together with a letter of recommendation, transcript and a resume. **Deadline:** February 18. **Contact:** For further inquiry, please contact Scholarship Office at 702-221-7422; E-mail: csdonnelly@ccpef.org.

7802 ■ CCSD School Counselors' Scholarships
(Undergraduate/Scholarship)

Purpose: To provide educational opportunities for individuals intending to pursue higher studies. **Focus:** General studies/Field of study not specified. **Qualif.:** Applicants must be CCSD seniors who have met and overcome a serious personal challenge or adversity; must have a minimum 2.5 unweighted GPA; and must be planning to attend an accredited post-secondary institution. **Criteria:** Award is given based on the application materials.

Funds Avail.: $1,000. **Duration:** Annual. **Number Awarded:** 1. **To Apply:** Applicants must submit a completed application form together with an essay, two letters of recommendation, transcript and a resume of awards. **Deadline:** February 18. **Contact:** For further inquiry, please contact Scholarship Office at 702-221-7422; E-mail: csdonnelly@ccpef.org.

7803 ■ Cheyenne High School Desert Shields Scholarship *(Undergraduate/Scholarship)*

Purpose: To provide educational opportunities for individuals intending to pursue higher studies. **Focus:** General studies/Field of study not specified. **Qualif.:** Applicants must be Cheyenne High School seniors planning to attend an accredited post-secondary institution and have a minimum 3.1 unweighted GPA. **Criteria:** Awards are given based on the application materials.

Funds Avail.: $1,000. **Duration:** Annual. **Number Awarded:** 2. **To Apply:** Applicants must submit a completed application form together with an essay, a resume of awards, and two letters of recommendation. **Deadline:** February 18. **Contact:** For further inquiry, please contact Scholarship Office at 702-221-7422; E-mail: csdonnelly@ccpef.org.

7804 ■ Clark High School Academy of Finance Scholarships *(Undergraduate/Scholarship)*

Purpose: To promote education in business, economics or finance. **Focus:** Business; Economics; Finance. **Qualif.:** Applicants must be Clark High School Academy of Finance (AOF) seniors interested in pursuing a degree in business, economics or finance at any accredited college/university and who have a minimum 3.0 GPA. **Criteria:** Award is given based on merit.

Funds Avail.: $1,000. **Duration:** Annual. **Number Awarded:** 1. **To Apply:** Applicants must submit a completed application form together with an essay, three letters of recommendation, transcript, resume of awards, and a copy of AOF Internship Evaluation. **Deadline:** February 18. **Contact:** For further inquiry, please contact Scholarship Office at 702-221-7422; E-mail: csdonnelly@ccpef.org.

7805 ■ Clark HS Brendan Flores Alumni Leadership Circle Scholarship *(Undergraduate/Scholarship)*

Purpose: To promote education in business, economics or finance. **Focus:** Business; Economics; Finance. **Qualif.:** Applicants must be Clark High School Academy of Finance (AOF) seniors interested in pursuing a degree in business, economics or finance at an accredited college/university and who have a minimum 3.0 GPA. **Criteria:** Award is given based on the application materials.

Awards are arranged alphabetically below their administering organizations

Funds Avail.: $500. **Duration:** Annual. **Number Awarded:** 1. **To Apply:** Applicants must submit a completed application form together with an essay, two letters of recommendation, transcript, resume of awards, and a copy of AOF Internship Evaluation. **Deadline:** February 18. **Contact:** For further inquiry, please contact Scholarship Office at 702-221-7422; E-mail: csdonnelly@ccpef.org.

7806 ■ Tsutako Curo Scholarships *(Undergraduate/ Scholarship)*

Purpose: To support single mothers desiring to advance their education. **Focus:** General studies/Field of study not specified. **Qualif.:** Applicants must be CCSD seniors who are single mothers desiring to advance their education at any accredited post-secondary institution; must have a minimum 2.5 cumulative GPA; and must demonstrate financial needs. **Criteria:** Award is given based on need.

Funds Avail.: $1,500. **Duration:** Annual. **Number Awarded:** 1. **To Apply:** Applicants must submit a completed application form together with an essay, two letters of recommendation, and transcript. **Deadline:** March 15. **Contact:** For further inquiry, please contact Scholarship Office at 702-221-7422; E-mail: csdonnelly@ccpef.org.

7807 ■ Mickey Donnelly Memorial Scholarships *(Undergraduate/Scholarship)*

Purpose: To provide educational opportunities for individuals intending to pursue higher studies. **Focus:** General studies/Field of study not specified. **Qualif.:** Applicants must be CCSD seniors who have attended Walter Johnson Junior High School for a minimum of one year and are planning to attend an accredited post-secondary institution in Nevada; must have a minimum 2.5 unweighted cumulative GPA. **Criteria:** Award is given based on merit.

Funds Avail.: $1,000. **Duration:** Annual. **Number Awarded:** 1. **To Apply:** Applicants must submit a completed application form together with an essay; two letters of recommendation; transcript; and resume of awards, employment and community services. **Deadline:** February 18. **Contact:** For further inquiry, please contact Scholarship Office at 702-221-7422; E-mail: csdonnelly@ccpef.org.

7808 ■ Travis Dunning Memorial Scholarships *(Undergraduate/Scholarship)*

Purpose: To provide educational opportunities for individuals intending to pursue higher studies. **Focus:** General studies/Field of study not specified. **Qualif.:** Applicants must be high school seniors from Green Valley, Coronado, Foothill, Silverado or Liberty planning to attend an accredited four-year college/university and who have a 3.0 weighted or unweighted GPA. **Criteria:** Award is given based on need.

Funds Avail.: $1,500. **Duration:** Annual. **Number Awarded:** 1. **To Apply:** Applicants must submit a completed application form together with an essay; two letters of recommendation; transcript; and resume of awards, employment and community services. **Deadline:** February 13. **Contact:** For further inquiry, please contact Scholarship Office at 702-221-7422; E-mail: csdonnelly@ccpef.org.

7809 ■ Palo Verde High School - Barbara Edwards Memorial Scholarships *(Undergraduate/Scholarship)*

Purpose: To provide educational opportunities for individuals intending to pursue higher studies. **Focus:** Foreign languages. **Qualif.:** Applicants must be Palo Verde High School seniors who have completed seven semesters of the same foreign language and demonstrated academic excellence; must be planning to attend an accredited college or university; and must have a minimum 3.5 cumulative GPA. **Criteria:** Award is given based on the application materials.

Funds Avail.: $1,000. **Duration:** Annual. **Number Awarded:** 1. **To Apply:** Applicants must submit a completed application form along with an essay, transcript, resume of awards, and Foreign Language Teacher Evaluation Sheet. **Deadline:** February 18. **Contact:** For further inquiry, please contact Scholarship Office at 702-221-7422; E-mail: csdonnelly@ccpef.org.

7810 ■ Gordy Fink Memorial Scholarships *(Undergraduate/Scholarship)*

Purpose: To provide educational opportunities for individuals intending to pursue higher studies. **Focus:** General studies/Field of study not specified. **Qualif.:** Applicants must be Valley High School seniors planning to attend the University of Nevada, Las Vegas as full-time students. **Criteria:** Consideration is given to students with financial need.

Funds Avail.: $1,000. **Duration:** Annual. **Number Awarded:** 1. **To Apply:** Applicants must submit a completed application form together with an essay, two letters of recommendation, transcript, resume of awards, and letter of admission from UNLV. **Deadline:** February 18. **Contact:** For further inquiry, please contact Scholarship Office at 702-221-7422; E-mail: csdonnelly@ccpef.org.

7811 ■ Fraser Family Scholarships *(Undergraduate/ Scholarship)*

Purpose: To provide educational opportunities for individuals intending to pursue higher studies. **Focus:** General studies/Field of study not specified. **Qualif.:** Applicants must be high school seniors from Durango with 3.5 cumulative GPA planning to attend any accredited college/ university and pursuing a degree in education or related field. **Criteria:** Award is given based on the application materials.

Funds Avail.: $1,000. **Duration:** Annual. **Number Awarded:** 1. **To Apply:** Applicants must submit a completed application form together with an essay, two letters of recommendation, transcript, and resume of awards. **Deadline:** February 18. **Contact:** For further inquiry, please contact Scholarship Office at 702-221-7422; E-mail: csdonnelly@ccpef.org.

7812 ■ Veronica Gantt Memorial Scholarships *(Undergraduate/Scholarship)*

Purpose: To provide educational opportunities for individuals intending to pursue higher studies. **Focus:** Education, Physical; Sports studies. **Qualif.:** Applicants must be: Del Sol High School seniors who are active in sports and community; planning to attend any accredited college or university; and, must have a minimum 3.0 cumulative GPA. **Criteria:** Awards are given based on the application materials.

Funds Avail.: $500 each. **Duration:** Annual. **Number Awarded:** 2. **To Apply:** Applicants must submit a completed application form together with an essay and a recommendation letter. **Deadline:** February 18. **Contact:** For further inquiry, please contact Scholarship Office at 702-221-7422; E-mail: csdonnelly@ccpef.org.

7813 ■ Glazing Industry Scholarships *(Undergraduate/Scholarship)*

Purpose: To support the education of students having a parent or grandparent participating in the glazing industry.

Awards are arranged alphabetically below their administering organizations

Focus: General studies/Field of study not specified. **Qualif.:** Applicants must: be high school seniors or post-secondary students in Nevada who are children or grandchildren of individuals actively participating in the glazing industry; have the desire to achieve excellence through education, planning to attend any post-secondary program; and, have a minimum 2.8 unweighted cumulative GPA. **Criteria:** Awards are given based on application materials.

Funds Avail.: $500 each. **Duration:** Annual. **Number Awarded:** 2. **To Apply:** Applicants must submit a completed application form together with an essay, a letter of recommendation, and transcript. **Deadline:** February 18. **Contact:** For further inquiry, please contact Scholarship Office at 702-221-7422; E-mail: csdonnelly@ccpef.org.

7814 ■ North Las Vegas Firefighters William J. Harnedy Memorial Scholarships (Undergraduate/Scholarship)

Purpose: To provide educational opportunities for individuals intending to pursue higher studies. **Focus:** General studies/Field of study not specified. **Qualif.:** Applicants must: be CCSD seniors who have attended North Las Vegas High School; be enrolled in the Credit Retrieval Program; have a minimum cumulative 2.5 GPA; have demonstrated financial need; and, be planning to attend any accredited post-secondary institution. **Criteria:** Award is given based on the compliance with the submission of necessary application materials.

Funds Avail.: $1,000. **Duration:** Annual. **Number Awarded:** 1. **To Apply:** Applicants must submit a completed application form together with an essay and transcript. **Deadline:** February 18. **Contact:** For further inquiry, please contact Scholarship Office at 702-221-7422; E-mail: csdonnelly@ccpef.org.

7815 ■ Gretchen Hauff Memorial Scholarships (Undergraduate/Scholarship)

Purpose: To promote education in physical education. **Focus:** Education, Physical. **Qualif.:** Applicants must: be CCSD female seniors interested in pursuing a degree in physical education at an accredited college/university; have a minimum 2.5 unweighted cumulative GPA; and, have demonstrated financial needs. **Criteria:** Award is given based on need.

Funds Avail.: $1,000. **Duration:** Annual. **Number Awarded:** 1. **To Apply:** Applicants must submit a completed application form together with an essay, three letters of recommendation, transcript, and resume of awards. **Deadline:** February 18. **Contact:** For further inquiry, please contact Scholarship Office at 702-221-7422; E-mail: csdonnelly@ccpef.org.

7816 ■ Michael J. Hoggard Memorial Scholarships (Undergraduate/Scholarship)

Purpose: To provide educational opportunities for individuals intending to pursue higher studies. **Focus:** General studies/Field of study not specified. **Qualif.:** Applicants must be Green Valley High School seniors who have been on the school's soccer team for at least two years (including senior year); must be planning to attend any accredited post-secondary college/university; and must have a minimum 3.0 cumulative GPA. **Criteria:** Award is given based on need.

Funds Avail.: $1,000. **Duration:** Annual. **Number Awarded:** 1. **To Apply:** Applicants must submit a completed application form with the essay; two letters of recom-

mendation; transcript; and resume of awards, employment and community services. **Deadline:** March 15. **Contact:** For further inquiry, please contact Scholarship Office at 702-221-7422; E-mail: csdonnelly@ccpef.org.

7817 ■ JMA Architecture Studios Scholarships (Undergraduate/Scholarship)

Purpose: To provide educational opportunities for individuals intending to pursue education in architecture. **Focus:** Architecture. **Qualif.:** Applicants must be CCSD seniors interested in pursuing a career in architecture; must be planning to attend a university with an accredited School of Architecture; must demonstrate financial needs; and must have a minimum 3.0 unweighted cumulative GPA. **Criteria:** Preference shall be given to students who have participated in the Clark County School District's drafting program.

Funds Avail.: $5,000. **Duration:** Annual. **Number Awarded:** 1. **To Apply:** Applicants must submit a completed application form along with a work sample, two letters of recommendation, transcript, resume of awards, and a college/university admission acceptance letter. **Deadline:** February 18. **Contact:** For further inquiry, please contact Scholarship Office at 702-221-7422; E-mail: csdonnelly@ccpef.org.

7818 ■ Las Vegas Chinatown Scholarships (Undergraduate/Scholarship)

Purpose: To provide educational opportunities for individuals intending to pursue higher studies. **Focus:** Business. **Qualif.:** Applicants must be CCSD seniors of Asian descent planning to attend any accredited college/university in Nevada and must have a minimum 3.5 cumulative GPA. **Criteria:** Preference will be given to students planning to major in Business.

Funds Avail.: $1,000 each. **Duration:** Annual. **Number Awarded:** 2. **To Apply:** Applicants must submit a completed application form with an essay; two letters of recommendation; transcript; and resume of awards, employment and community services. **Deadline:** February 18. **Contact:** For further inquiry, please contact Scholarship Office at 702-221-7422; E-mail: csdonnelly@ccpef.org.

7819 ■ Nate Mack/Cindi Turner Scholarships (Undergraduate/Scholarship)

Purpose: To provide educational opportunities for individuals intending to pursue higher studies. **Focus:** General studies/Field of study not specified. **Qualif.:** Applicants must be: CCSD seniors who attended Nate Mack Elementary School for at least three years; planning to attend any accredited college/university; and, must have a minimum 3.0 cumulative GPA; and must demonstrate financial need. **Criteria:** Award is given based on the application materials.

Funds Avail.: $1,000. **Duration:** Annual. **Number Awarded:** 1. **To Apply:** Applicants must submit a completed application form along with an essay, two letters of recommendation, transcript, and resume of awards. **Deadline:** February 18. **Contact:** For further inquiry, please contact Scholarship Office at 702-221-7422; E-mail: csdonnelly@ccpef.org.

7820 ■ Corporal Joseph Martinez U.S. Army Memorial Scholarships (Undergraduate/Scholarship)

Purpose: To provide educational opportunities for individuals intending to pursue higher studies. **Focus:** General studies/Field of study not specified. **Qualif.:** Applicants

Awards are arranged alphabetically below their administering organizations

must be Durango High School AFJROTC program seniors planning to attend any accredited post-secondary institution either during or immediately following enlistment in any branch of the U.S. military. **Criteria:** Award is given based on compliance with the submission of necessary application materials. Preference will be given to applicants who have excelled in the areas of leadership, community service and extracurricular activities.

Funds Avail.: $1,000. **Duration:** Annual. **Number Awarded:** 1. **To Apply:** Applicants must submit completed application form along with the letter from military recruiter, one letter of recommendation, transcript, and resume. **Deadline:** February 28. **Contact:** For further inquiry, please contact Scholarship Office at 702-221-7422; E-mail: csdonnelly@ccpef.org.

7821 ■ Mesquite Club Evening Chapter Scholarships (Undergraduate/Scholarship)

Purpose: To provide educational opportunities for individuals intending to pursue higher studies. **Focus:** General studies/Field of study not specified. **Qualif.:** Applicants must be CCSD female seniors planning to attend an accredited post-secondary institution in Nevada as a full-time students; must have a minimum 3.0 GPA; and must have demonstrated financial need. **Criteria:** Award is given based on need.

Funds Avail.: $1,500. **Duration:** Annual. **Number Awarded:** 3. **To Apply:** Applicants must submit a completed application form together with an essay, two letters of recommendation, transcript, and resume of awards. **Deadline:** February 28. **Contact:** For further inquiry, please contact Scholarship Office at 702-221-7422; E-mail: csdonnelly@ccpef.org.

7822 ■ National Security Technologies Engineering and Science Scholarships (Undergraduate/Scholarship)

Purpose: To promote education in the field of engineering or science. **Focus:** Engineering; Science. **Qualif.:** Applicants must be CCSD seniors planning to major in engineering or science at a four-year institution with a minimum 3.5 cumulative GPA. **Criteria:** Awards are given based on the compliance with the submission of necessary application materials.

Funds Avail.: $5,000 each. **Duration:** Annual. **Number Awarded:** Up to 10. **To Apply:** Applicants must submit a completed application form along with an essay, transcript, and three letters of recommendation. **Contact:** For further inquiry, please contact Scholarship Office at 702-221-7422; E-mail: csdonnelly@ccpef.org.

7823 ■ Palo Verde High School Faculty Follies Scholarships (Undergraduate/Scholarship)

Purpose: To provide educational opportunities for individuals intending to pursue higher studies. **Focus:** General studies/Field of study not specified. **Qualif.:** Applicants must be Palo Verde High School seniors who have completed six semesters of theater classes; must be planning to attend any accredited college/university; and must have a minimum 2.5 cumulative GPA. **Criteria:** Award is given based on the compliance with submission of the necessary application materials.

Funds Avail.: $500. **Duration:** Annual. **Number Awarded:** 1. **To Apply:** Applicants must submit completed application form along with essay, transcript, resume of awards, and Leadership, Activities and Achievement Information. **Dead-**

line: March 15. **Contact:** For further inquiry, please contact Scholarship Office at 702-221-7422; E-mail: csdonnelly@ccpef.org.

7824 ■ Panther Cafe Scholarships (Undergraduate/Scholarship)

Purpose: To provide educational opportunities for individuals intending to pursue higher studies. **Focus:** General studies/Field of study not specified. **Qualif.:** Applicants must be Palo Verde High School seniors who have participated in a class that is directly associated with the operation of the Panther Cafe and must be planning to attend any accredited post-secondary college or institution. **Criteria:** Awards are given based on the compliance with the submission of the necessary application materials.

Funds Avail.: $1,000. **Duration:** Annual. **Number Awarded:** 1. **To Apply:** Applicants must submit a completed application form along with an essay, two letters of recommendation, transcript, and resume of awards. **Deadline:** March 15. **Contact:** For further inquiry, please contact Scholarship Office at 702-221-7422; E-mail: csdonnelly@ccpef.org.

7825 ■ Pardee Community Building Scholarships (Undergraduate/Scholarship)

Purpose: To provide educational opportunities for individuals intending to pursue higher studies. **Focus:** Architecture; Business; Construction; Engineering, Civil. **Qualif.:** Applicants must be CCSD seniors who have demonstrated interests in home building and community development; must be planning to attend a Nevada accredited college or university; must be pursuing studies in areas of business, civil engineering, architecture or landscape architecture and construction management; and must have a minimum 2.8 cumulative GPA. **Criteria:** Awards are given based on merit.

Funds Avail.: $1,500 each. **Duration:** Annual. **Number Awarded:** 5. **To Apply:** Applicants must submit completed application form along with essay, two letters of recommendation, transcript, and resume of awards. **Deadline:** February 18. **Remarks:** Established in 2002. **Contact:** For further inquiry, please contact Scholarship Office at 702-221-7422; E-mail: csdonnelly@ccpef.org.

7826 ■ Josef Princ Memorial Scholarships (Undergraduate/Scholarship)

Purpose: To provide educational opportunities for individuals intending to pursue higher studies. **Focus:** Engineering; Mathematics and mathematical sciences. **Qualif.:** Applicants must be: CCSD male seniors of European descent; maintaining a minimum 3.5 cumulative GPA; must be demonstrating financial need; and, planning to attend any accredited post-secondary college/university majoring in engineering, mathematics or science. **Criteria:** Awards are given based on need.

Funds Avail.: $2,000 each. **Duration:** Annual. **Number Awarded:** Up to 4. **To Apply:** Applicants must submit completed application form along with essay, two letters of recommendation, transcript, and resume of awards. **Deadline:** February 28. **Contact:** For further inquiry, please contact Scholarship Office at 702-221-7422; E-mail: csdonnelly@ccpef.org.

7827 ■ R.M. Princ Scholarships (Undergraduate/Scholarship)

Purpose: To provide educational opportunities for individuals intending to pursue higher studies. **Focus:** Education,

Awards are arranged alphabetically below their administering organizations

Elementary; Education, Secondary. **Qualif.:** Applicants must be CCSD female seniors who have maintained a minimum 3.5 cumulative GPA; must demonstrate financial need; and must be planning to attend any accredited post-secondary college or university majoring in the field of education (elementary or secondary). **Criteria:** Awards are given based on need.

Funds Avail.: $2,000 each. **Duration:** Annual. **Number Awarded:** Up to 4. **To Apply:** Applicants must submit completed application form along with essay, two letters of recommendation, transcript, and resume of awards, activities, employment and community service. **Deadline:** February 28. **Contact:** For further inquiry, please contact Scholarship Office at 702-221-7422; E-mail: csdonnelly@ccpef.org.

7828 ■ Elizabeth Shafer Memorial Scholarships
(Undergraduate/Scholarship)

Purpose: To provide educational opportunities for individuals intending to pursue higher studies. **Focus:** Culinary arts. **Qualif.:** Applicants must be CCSD seniors pursuing a degree in the culinary field; must have a minimum 2.0 cumulative GPA; and must be U.S. citizens either by birth or naturalization. **Criteria:** Award is given based on the compliance with submission of the necessary application materials.

Funds Avail.: $1,000. **Duration:** Annual. **Number Awarded:** 1. **To Apply:** Applicants must submit completed application form along with essay, transcript, resume of awards, and a visible sample of artwork or culinary talents. **Deadline:** February 18. **Contact:** For further inquiry, please contact Scholarship Office at 702-221-7422; E-mail: csdonnelly@ccpef.org.

7829 ■ Smith's Personal Best Scholarships
(Undergraduate/Scholarship)

Purpose: To provide educational opportunities for individuals intending to pursue higher studies. **Focus:** General studies/Field of study not specified. **Qualif.:** Applicants must be CCSD seniors who have met and overcome a serious personal challenge or adversity; must plan to attend an accredited post-secondary institution. **Criteria:** Awards are given based on the application materials.

Funds Avail.: $2,000. **Duration:** Annual. **Number Awarded:** 5. **To Apply:** Applicants must submit complete application package which include the Applicant's General Information, the Certifications and Authorizations form, the Short Answer Questionnaire and the nomination form completed by an adult who knows the student well - a teacher, counselor, club advisor, employer, etc. **Deadline:** February 18. **Contact:** For further inquiry, please contact Scholarship Office at 702-221-7422; E-mail: csdonnelly@ccpef.org.

7830 ■ Southern Nevada Sports Hall of Fame Scholarships *(Undergraduate/Scholarship)*

Purpose: To provide educational opportunities for individuals intending to pursue higher studies. **Focus:** General studies/Field of study not specified. **Qualif.:** Applicants must be CCSD seniors who have participated in athletics for the past four years with a minimum 3.2 unweighted cumulative GPA. **Criteria:** Awards are given based on the submitted materials.

Funds Avail.: $2,000. **Number Awarded:** 4. **To Apply:** Applicants must submit a completed application form along with an essay, two letters of recommendation, transcript, and resume. **Deadline:** February 18. **Contact:** For further

inquiry, please contact Scholarship Office at 702-221-7422; E-mail: csdonnelly@ccpef.org.

7831 ■ Spartan Staff Scholarships *(Undergraduate/Scholarship)*

Purpose: To provide educational opportunities for individuals intending to pursue higher studies. **Focus:** General studies/Field of study not specified. **Qualif.:** Applicants must be Cimarron-Memorial High School seniors interested in pursuing a degree at an accredited college or university; must have a minimum 3.0 unweighted cumulative GPA; and must demonstrate financial need. **Criteria:** Awards are given based on need.

Funds Avail.: $500. **Duration:** Annual. **Number Awarded:** 5. **To Apply:** Applicants must submit a completed application form along with an essay, two letters of recommendation, transcript, and resume of awards. **Deadline:** February 18. **Contact:** For further inquiry, please contact Scholarship Office at 702-221-7422; E-mail: csdonnelly@ccpef.org.

7832 ■ Tall Awareness Scholarships *(Undergraduate/Scholarship)*

Purpose: To provide educational opportunities for individuals intending to pursue higher studies. **Focus:** General studies/Field of study not specified. **Qualif.:** Applicants must be CCSD seniors attending an accredited post-secondary school; must have met the minimum height requirement of 5'10" for female students and 6'2" for male students. **Criteria:** Selection is based on height requirement, financial need, academic achievement, volunteer work, school activities and service to the community.

Funds Avail.: $1,000. **Duration:** Annual. **Number Awarded:** 1. **To Apply:** Applicants must submit completed application form along with (500-750 words) essay, letter of recommendation, and transcript. **Deadline:** February 18. **Contact:** For further inquiry, please contact Scholarship Office at 702-221-7422; E-mail: csdonnelly@ccpef.org.

7833 ■ Tarkanian Teacher Education Academy at Clark High School Scholarships (TEACH)
(Undergraduate/Scholarship)

Purpose: To provide educational opportunities for individuals intending to pursue higher studies. **Focus:** Education. **Qualif.:** Applicants must be Teacher Education Academy at Clark High School (TEACH) seniors interested in pursuing a degree in education at any accredited college/university; must have a minimum 2.8 cumulative GPA; and must be currently enrolled in the TEACH Educational Internship and Seminar course. **Criteria:** Awards are given based on the compliance with submission of the necessary application materials.

Funds Avail.: $500-$1,000. **Duration:** Annual. **Number Awarded:** Up to 2. **To Apply:** Applicants must submit completed application form along with essay, transcript, resume of awards, and a copy of recent TEACH Internship Evaluation. **Deadline:** March 15. **Contact:** For further inquiry, please contact Scholarship Office at 702-221-7422; E-mail: csdonnelly@ccpef.org.

7834 ■ Sheila Tarr-Smith Memorial Scholarships
(Undergraduate/Scholarship)

Purpose: To provide educational opportunities for individuals intending to pursue higher studies. **Focus:** Public service. **Qualif.:** Applicants must be CCSD seniors planning to attend the University of Nevada, Las Vegas, as full-time students; must have a major related to public service;

Awards are arranged alphabetically below their administering organizations

must have a minimum 3.4 unweighted cumulative GPA; and must demonstrate community service and financial need. **Criteria:** Awards are given based on the application materials.

Funds Avail.: $2,500. **Duration:** Annual. **Number Awarded:** 1. **To Apply:** Applicants must submit a completed application form along with an essay, two letters of recommendation, transcript, and resume of awards. **Deadline:** February 18. **Contact:** For further inquiry, please contact Scholarship Office at 702-221-7422; E-mail: csdonnelly@ccpef.org.

7835 ■ Judith Warner Memorial Scholarships
(Undergraduate/Scholarship)

Purpose: To provide educational opportunities for individuals intending to pursue higher studies. **Focus:** General studies/Field of study not specified. **Qualif.:** Applicants must be Rancho High School seniors planning to attend the University of Nevada, Las Vegas as full-time students; must have a minimum 2.5 cumulative GPA; and must demonstrate financial needs. **Criteria:** Award is given based on merit.

Funds Avail.: $1,200. **Duration:** Annual. **Number Awarded:** 1. **To Apply:** Applicants must submit completed application form along with essay, two letters of recommendation, transcript, resume of awards, and letter of admission from UNLV. **Deadline:** February 18. **Contact:** For further inquiry, please contact Scholarship Office at 702-221-7422; E-mail: csdonnelly@ccpef.org.

7836 ■ Edwin F. Wiegand Science and Technology Scholarships *(Undergraduate/Scholarship)*

Purpose: To provide educational opportunities for individuals intending to pursue higher studies. **Focus:** Computer and information sciences; Information science and technology. **Qualif.:** Applicants must be CCSD seniors pursuing a degree in science, technology, computer science or related field at the University of Nevada, Las Vegas, or the University of Nevada, or Reno, with a minimum of 3.0 cumulative GPA. **Criteria:** Priority will be given to students who have been involved with CyberCorps or CCSD's Inter-Act Online Learning Community.

Funds Avail.: $1,250. **Duration:** Annual. **Number Awarded:** 1. **To Apply:** Applicants must submit completed application form along with essay, two letters of recommendation, transcript, and resume of awards. **Deadline:** February 18. **Contact:** For further inquiry, please contact Scholarship Office at 702-221-7422; E-mail: csdonnelly@ccpef.org.

7837 ■ Public Library Association (PLA)
50 E Huron St.
Chicago, IL 60611
Ph: (312)280-5752
Fax: (312)280-5029
Free: 800-545-2433
E-mail: bmacikas@ala.org
URL: www.ala.org/pla

7838 ■ DEMCO New Leaders Travel Grants *(Professional development/Grant)*

Purpose: To enhance the professional development and improve the expertise of public librarians new to the field by making possible their attendance at major professional development activities. **Focus:** Library and archival sciences. **Qualif.:** Applicants must be members of the Public Library Association; must be practicing librarians for five years or less; must not be officers or members of the PLA Board of Directors; and must not be members or supervisors of the New Leaders Travel Grant Jury. **Criteria:** Selection is based on quality and appropriateness of the submitted proposals. Preference will be given to applicants who can document the fiscal need for travel fund based on their institution's budget and those whose continuing education falls within the framework of PLA priority concerns.

Funds Avail.: $1,500. **Duration:** Annual. **Number Awarded:** Varies. **To Apply:** Applicants are advised to visit the website for the PLA's awards online application. **Deadline:** December 1.

7839 ■ Public Relations Society of America - Maryland (PRSAMD)
c/o Mariner Management and Marketing
PO Box 1640
Columbia, MD 21044
Free: 866-868-7772
E-mail: info@prsamd.org
URL: www.prsamd.org

7840 ■ Kathleen Kelly Undergraduate Scholarship Award *(Undergraduate, College/Scholarship)*

Purpose: To support students who demonstrates excellent academic credentials and hold promise for successful careers in public relations. **Focus:** Public administration. **Qualif.:** Applicants must be College-level students, sophomore or junior status; must be enrolled in a Maryland college or university; or residents of Maryland attending college outside of the state; concentrated study in an area of communications with the intention to pursue a career in public relations; must have a minimum 3.0 GPA overall and grades of B or better in all public relations English and/or writing courses. **Criteria:** Selection will be based on the following: academic records; commitment to public relations as demonstrated by campus public relations activities; membership in PRSSA and/or other career-related student organizations; public relations work experience (paid, volunteer or internship); active involvement in campus and/or community organizations.

Funds Avail.: No specific amount. **Duration:** Annual. **To Apply:** Applicants must submit a completed application including an essay, along with a resume covering all areas outlined in award criteria; official transcripts from all colleges and universities attended and currently enrolled required. **Deadline:** April 18.

7841 ■ Public Relations Student Society of America (PRSSA)
33 Maiden Ln., 11th Fl.
New York, NY 10038-5150
Ph: (212)460-1474
Fax: (212)995-0757
E-mail: prssa@prsa.org
URL: prssa.prsa.org

7842 ■ Stephen D. Pisinski Memorial Scholarships *(Undergraduate/Scholarship)*

Purpose: To provide educational assistance for qualified students intending to pursue a career in the field of public relations. **Focus:** Communications; Journalism; Public

Awards are arranged alphabetically below their administering organizations

administration; Public relations. **Qualif.:** Applicants must be majoring in journalism, communications, or public relations; must be junior or senior level only; must have at least a 3.3 overall GPA on a 4.0 system; must be members of the Public Relations Student Society of America, and leadership positions are additional credentials. **Criteria:** Applicants will be selected by criteria of the selection committee.

Funds Avail.: $1,500. **Duration:** Annual. **To Apply:** Applicants must submit the following: resume including any academic honors, special projects, activities and/or work experience or training; an official transcript of all college studies, including grades of the preceding semester; an essay of 1,000 words or less stating career goals; two strong writing samples; and two letters of academic and/or professional recommendations. **Deadline:** June 5. **Remarks:** Established in 2002.

7843 ■ Betsy Plank/PRSSA Scholarships
(Undergraduate/Scholarship)

Purpose: To provide educational support for deserving students intending to pursue a career in public relations. **Focus:** Public relations. **Qualif.:** Program is open to PRSSA members who are enrolled in programs of public relations studies and are in their junior or senior year of undergraduate studies. **Criteria:** Applicants will be selected based on their academic achievement in public relations and overall studies, demonstrated leadership, practical experience and commitment to public relations, particularly as expressed in the candidate's statement.

Funds Avail.: $5,000 (First honor); $1,500 (Second honor); $1,000 (Third honor). **Duration:** Annual. **Number Awarded:** 3. **To Apply:** Applicants must complete and submit the following application materials: an application form, available at the website, signed by the applicants, Faculty Adviser and Professional Adviser; a letter of recommendation from the Faculty or Professional Adviser; a signed statement of 300 words or fewer that outlines the commitment to public relations and its ethical practice; a optional additional letters of recommendation from previous employers or professors. **Deadline:** June 5.

7844 ■ PRSA Diversity Multicultural Scholarships
(Undergraduate/Scholarship)

Purpose: To assist and recognize young men and women for outstanding academic achievement and commitment to the practice of public relations. **Focus:** Communications; Public relations. **Qualif.:** Applicant must be a full-time undergraduate student at an accredited four-year college/university; has attained at least junior status or has at least one full term remaining by the time the scholarship will be awarded; maintained a 3.0 GPA on a 4.0 scale in all courses; membership in PRSSA is preferred, but is not a requirement; must have African-American/Black, Hispanic/Latino, Asian, Native American, Alaskan Native or Pacific Islander ancestry. **Criteria:** Selection is based on the submitted application materials.

Funds Avail.: $1,500. **Duration:** Annual. **Number Awarded:** 2. **To Apply:** Applicants must submit a completed application form together with an official transcript; a brief letter of recommendation from a PRSA member or an individual associated with public relations or higher education; a typed, double-spaced essay (maximum of three pages); and statement of Financial Status. **Deadline:** May 22. **Contact:** jessica.espinal@prsa.org.

7845 ■ Gary Yoshimura Scholarships
(Undergraduate/Scholarship)

Purpose: To provide support to qualified PRSSA members who demonstrate a financial need for the pursuit of higher education in the public relations field. **Focus:** Public administration; Public relations. **Qualif.:** Applicants must be pursuing higher education in the public relations field; have a minimum GPA of 3.0; demonstrate financial needs; and, be PRSSA members. **Criteria:** Applicants will be selected based on their academic performance and application materials.

Funds Avail.: $2,400. **Duration:** Annual. **To Apply:** Application forms are available at the website. Applicants must submit the following: official transcript, letter of recommendation from the internship supervisor/employer or faculty advisor; must prepare a 1,000-word essay describing the challenges they have faced, either personally or professionally, and how they overcame it; must complete the statement of intent and financial need section. **Deadline:** January 26.

7846 ■ Public Schools of Hawaii Foundation (PSHF)
PO Box 4148
Honolulu, HI 96812
E-mail: pshf88@gmail.com
URL: pshf.org

7847 ■ PSHF Good Idea Grants *(Other/Grant)*

Purpose: To enhance innovation in the classroom and challenge teachers to think creatively and boldly. **Focus:** General studies/Field of study not specified. **Qualif.:** Applicants must be classroom teachers in a Hawaii public school during the current school year. A team of teachers from the same school may apply, but one teacher on the team must be designated as the team leader/contact. **Criteria:** Selection will be based on the committee's criteria.

Funds Avail.: Maximum of $3,000. **Duration:** Annual. **To Apply:** Applicants may download an application form online. **Deadline:** July 18.

7848 ■ Public Service Alliance of Canada
233 Gilmour St.
Ottawa, ON, Canada K2P 0P1
Ph: (613)560-4200
Free: 888-604-PSAC
URL: psacunion.ca

7849 ■ J.R. (Joe) Power National Scholarships
(Postgraduate/Scholarship)

Purpose: To provide financial assistance to children and dependents of PSAC members. **Focus:** General studies/Field of study not specified. **Qualif.:** Applicants must be PSAC members or their children who are returning to university, college or a recognized institute of higher learning; must have a good standing in PSAC as of March 31 of the current year. **Criteria:** Scholarships are awarded based on the impact of the 800-word essay, scholastic achievement, and community and union involvement as reviewed by the PSAC scholarship committee.

Funds Avail.: 2,000 Canadian dollars. **Number Awarded:** 1. **To Apply:** Applicant must submit an 800-word essay on the topic chosen by the PSAC scholarship committee and

Awards are arranged alphabetically below their administering organizations

a transcript of the most current academic standing. Applicant must also prepare a proof of registration with the name of the university, college or institute of higher learning. Application forms are available from the website and must be completed and mailed to Public Service Alliance of Canada.

7850 ■ PSAC-AGR National Scholarships
(Postgraduate/Scholarship)

Purpose: To provide financial assistance to children and dependents of PSAC members. **Focus:** General studies/ Field of study not specified. **Qualif.:** Applicants must be PSAC members or their children who are returning to university, college or a recognized institute of higher learning; must have a good standing in PSAC as of March 31 of the current year. **Criteria:** Scholarships are awarded based on the impact of the 800-word essay, scholastic achievement, and community and union involvement as reviewed by the PSAC scholarship committee.

Funds Avail.: 2,000 Canadian dollars. **Number Awarded:** 3. **To Apply:** Applicant must submit an 800-word essay on the topic chosen by the PSAC scholarship committee and a transcript of the most current academic standing. Applicant must also prepare a proof of registration with the name of the university, college or institute of higher learning. Application forms are available from the website and must be completed and mailed to: Public Service Alliance of Canada, 233 Gilmour St., Ste. 904, Ottawa, ON K2P OP1.

7851 ■ PSAC - Coughlin National Scholarships
(Postgraduate/Scholarship)

Purpose: To provide financial assistance to children and dependents of PSAC members. **Focus:** General studies/ Field of study not specified. **Qualif.:** Applicants must be PSAC members or their children who are returning to university, college or a recognized institute of higher learning; must have a good standing in PSAC as of May 31 of the current year. **Criteria:** Scholarships are awarded based on the impact of the 800-word essay, scholastic achievement, and community and union involvement as reviewed by the PSAC scholarship committee.

Funds Avail.: 3,000 Canadian dollars - 4,000 Canadian dollars. **Number Awarded:** 3. **To Apply:** Applicant must submit an 800-word essay on the topic chosen by the PSAC scholarship committee and a transcript of the most current academic standing. Applicant must also prepare a proof of registration with the name of the university, college or institute of higher learning. Application forms are available from the website and must be completed and mailed to Public Service Alliance of Canada.

7852 ■ PSAC Regional Scholarships *(Postgraduate/Scholarship)*

Purpose: To provide financial assistance to children and dependents of PSAC members. **Focus:** General studies/ Field of study not specified. **Qualif.:** Applicants must be PSAC members or their children who are returning to university, college or a recognized institute of higher learning; must have a good standing in PSAC as of March 31 of the current year. **Criteria:** Scholarships are awarded based on the impact of the 800-word essay, scholastic achievement, and community and union involvement as reviewed by the PSAC scholarship committee.

Funds Avail.: $1,000. **Number Awarded:** 7. **To Apply:** Applicant must submit an 800-word essay on the topic chosen by the PSAC scholarship committee and a transcript

of the most current academic standing. Applicant must also prepare a proof of registration with the name of the university, college or institute of higher learning. Application forms are available from the website and must be completed and mailed to Public Service Alliance of Canada.

7853 ■ QFD Institute
1140 Morehead Ct.
Ann Arbor, MI 48103-6181
Ph: (734)995-0847
Fax: (206)203-3575
E-mail: qfdi@qfdi.org
URL: www.qfdi.org

7854 ■ Akao Scholarships for QFD *(Undergraduate/ Scholarship)*

Purpose: To encourage students in the United States and other countries who wish to attend the Symposium on QFD for free. **Focus:** Education. **Qualif.:** Applicants must be both full-time and part-time or working students; currently enrolled in an accredited university/college degree program. **Criteria:** Selection is determined by the Akao Scholarship Committee.

Funds Avail.: No specific amount. **To Apply:** Applicants must submit complete application form; proof of enrollment status issued by the school; letter of recommendation from the school professor or academic advisor.

7855 ■ Quarter Century Wireless Association (QCWA)
12967 N Normandy Way
West Palm Beach, FL 33410-1412
Ph: (352)425-1097
URL: www.qcwa.org

7856 ■ Quarter Century Wireless Association Scholarships *(Undergraduate/Scholarship)*

Purpose: To provide financial support for students intending to pursue higher education. **Focus:** Radio and television. **Qualif.:** Applicants must be radio amateurs enrolled or planning to enroll in a full-time course which leads to a degree at an accredited college/university. **Criteria:** Applications will be reviewed by the Foundation for Amateur Radio.

Funds Avail.: No specific amount. **Number Awarded:** 17. **To Apply:** Applications are requested from the Foundation for Amateur Radio Scholarship Committee; applicant must be recommended by a QCWA member. **Deadline:** April 15. **Remarks:** Established in 1977. **Contact:** Timothy G. Donovan, QCWA Memorial Scholarship Fund, 4502 Rachael Manor Drive, phone: 703-323-9207, e-mail: scholarship@qcwa.org.

7857 ■ Queens County Women's Bar Association (QCWBA)
Borough Hall Sta.
Kew Gardens, NY 11424
Ph: (718)595-0585
E-mail: info@qcwba.org
URL: www.qcwba.com

7858 ■ Faith E. O'Neal Scholarships *(Undergraduate/ Scholarship)*

Purpose: To financially assist students who have demonstrated a dedication to public interest. **Focus:** Law. **Qualif.:**

Awards are arranged alphabetically below their administering organizations

Applicants must be students enrolled at an accredited law school who have completed their first full semester and are domiciled in Queens County, or attend a law school in Queens County. **Criteria:** Committees will judge applications based on community service, financial need, academics and written statement.

Funds Avail.: $1,000. **Duration:** Annual. **Number Awarded:** 2. **To Apply:** Application must include college/law school transcript(s) and written personal statement. **Deadline:** October 18. **Remarks:** Established in 2005. **Contact:** Susan L. Borko., 125-10 Queens Boulevard, Suite 311, Jew Gardens, New York 11415.Susan L. Borko.

7859 ■ Queer Foundation

c/o Joseph Dial, Ph.D., Executive Director
3213 W Wheeler St., No. 145
Seattle, WA 98199
Ph: (206)999-8740
E-mail: queerfoundation@queerfoundation.org
URL: queerfoundation.org

7860 ■ Queer Foundation Effective Writing and Scholarships (Undergraduate/Prize, Scholarship)

Purpose: To enable LGBTQA youth, by means of their studies and effective writing, to contribute to building a stable future for queer youth through business/community involvement and self-directed improvement. **Focus:** General studies/Field of study not specified. **Qualif.:** Applicant must be a high school senior and must write an essay dealing with the announced theme. **Criteria:** Judges will evaluate the essays. Authors of winning essays will be invited and must pass the interview.

Funds Avail.: $1,000. **Duration:** Annual. **To Apply:** Applicant must write an essay dealing with the announced theme. **Deadline:** February 14.

7861 ■ Quill and Scroll International Honorary Society (QSS)

University of Iowa
100 Adler Journalism Bldg.
Iowa City, IA 52242
Ph: (319)335-3457
Fax: (319)335-3989
E-mail: quill-scroll@uiowa.edu
URL: quillandscroll.org

7862 ■ Lester G. Benz Memorial Scholarships for College Journalism Study (Other/Scholarship)

Purpose: To identify and reward experienced journalism teachers and publication advisers who seek the opportunity to upgrade journalism skills, teaching methodologies and advising techniques. **Focus:** Journalism. **Qualif.:** Applicants must be high-school journalism teachers and newspaper and yearbook advisers who have had at least six semester hours of journalism courses; a minimum of four years of teaching experience and advising school publications; currently teaching a journalistic writing class; and a definite commitment to return to the high school classroom and publication. **Criteria:** Candidates will be selected by Scholarship Committee.

Funds Avail.: $500 for actual tuition, room, board and transportation costs. **To Apply:** Applicants must submit the completed application form; two letters of recommendation

that will attest to their journalism teaching skills, publication advising, quality of the journalistic writing courses the applicants teach and the quality of the publications the applicant advises. **Deadline:** April 15.

7863 ■ Edward J. Nell Memorial Scholarships in Journalism (Undergraduate/Scholarship)

Purpose: To provide financial assistance to well-qualified individuals who wish to attend any college or university that offers a major in journalism. **Focus:** Journalism. **Qualif.:** Applicant must be a freshman. National winners in either the Yearbook Excellence Contest or the International Writing/Photography Contest are eligible to apply. **Criteria:** Recipients will be selected based on some criteria designed by the Scholarship Committee.

Funds Avail.: No specific amount. **To Apply:** Applicant must submit three separate forms (Form I - Principal or Counselor, Form II - Student and Form III Journalism Adviser) together with the supporting materials (official transcript(s), applicant's letter regarding journalistic experience and five selections of student's published work and letters of endorsement from principal, counselor and/or adviser). **Deadline:** May 10.

7864 ■ Radio Advisory Board of Canada (RABC)

811-116 Albert St.
Ottawa, ON, Canada K1P 5G3
Ph: (613)230-3261
Free: 888-902-5768
E-mail: rabc.gm@on.aibn.com
URL: www.rabc-cccr.ca

7865 ■ Future Leader in Radiocommunications Scholarships (Undergraduate/Scholarship)

Purpose: To encourage careers in telecommunications especially among engineering students. **Focus:** Telecommunications systems. **Qualif.:** Applicants must be enrolled in an accredited Canadian university and must have completed at least the second year in an engineering programme. **Criteria:** Selection of applicants will be based on their academic excellence and community involvement.

Funds Avail.: $3,500. **Duration:** Annual. **To Apply:** Scholarship applications may be obtained by contacting RABC or log on to www.electrofed.com. Completed applications must be submitted to RABC. **Deadline:** July 31. **Remarks:** Administered by the Electro-Federation Canada.

7866 ■ Radio-Television Digital News Association (RTDNA)

529 14th St. NW, Ste. 1240
Washington, DC 20045
Fax: (202)223-4007
URL: rtdna.org

7867 ■ Ken Kashiwahara Scholarships (Undergraduate/Scholarship)

Purpose: To provide financial assistance to students who have demonstrated their interest in the field of radio and television news. **Focus:** Radio and television. **Qualif.:** Applicant must be an officially enrolled college sophomore and have at least one full academic year; must be fully enrolled college sophomore or higher to receive a scholarship; must be enrolled in any major involved in electronic journalism. **Criteria:** Selection is based on the submitted

Awards are arranged alphabetically below their administering organizations

application materials and financial need.

Funds Avail.: No specific amount. **To Apply:** Applicant must submit a completed application form available on the website accompanied by the following materials: (1) copy of resume, (2) one to three examples of their journalistic skills on audio CD or DVD, with scripts, (3) one page statement, with specific career preferences (radio, TC, online, reporting, producing, or newsroom management), and (4) letter of reference from dean or faculty.

7868 ■ Abe Schechter Graduate Scholarships (Graduate/Scholarship)

Purpose: To provide financial assistance to students who have demonstrated their interest in the field of radio and television news. **Focus:** Radio and television. **Qualif.:** Applicants must be enrolled in a graduate program and must be in good standing in the field of radio and television news. **Criteria:** Selection is based on the application materials submitted.

Funds Avail.: No amount specific. **Duration:** Annual. **To Apply:** Applicants must submit a completed application form available online along with a copy of an updated resume, one-page statement stating their merits and career objectives, and letter of reference from dean or faculty.

7869 ■ Radio and Television News Directors Association and Foundation (RTNDA) - Association of Electronic Journalists (RTNDF)

529 14th St. NW, Ste. 1240
Washington, DC 20045-2520
Fax: (202)223-4007
URL: www.rtnda.org

7870 ■ N.S. Beinstock Fellowships (Other/Fellowship)

Purpose: To support a promising minority journalist in radio or television news. **Focus:** Journalism. **Qualif.:** Applicants must be minority journalists who have fewer than 10 years as professionals. **Criteria:** Recipients are selected based on the completed application form and completed requirements.

Funds Avail.: $2,500. **Duration:** Annual. **To Apply:** Applicant must complete the application form online; a cover letter discussing journalism experiences, use of fellowship funds, discussing choosing career in electronic journalism; 3-5 links to your best and most relevant work samples discussing the roles in each of the pieces; a letter of reference news manager or higher. All must be submitted online. **Remarks:** Established in 1999.

7871 ■ Ed Bradley Scholarships (Undergraduate/Scholarship)

Purpose: To help RTNDF members embody and uphold the standards of ethical journalism; to promote leadership in the newsroom. **Focus:** Journalism. **Qualif.:** Applicant must be enrolled in radio and television news; must be a full-time college student with at least one full year of college remaining whose career objective is to enter into the electronic journalism field. **Criteria:** Judges will base their decisions on the applicants' adherence to the stated qualifications.

Funds Avail.: $10,000. **To Apply:** Applicant must complete the application form online and provide evidence proving that he/she is currently enrolled; a cover letter discussing

journalism experiences, use of scholarship, discussing choosing career in electronic journalism; 3-5 links to your best and most relevant work samples discussing the roles in each of the pieces; a letter of reference from the dean, faculty sponsor or internship advisor. All must be submitted online. **Deadline:** April 30. **Remarks:** Established in 1994.

7872 ■ Michele Clark Fellowships (Undergraduate/Fellowship)

Purpose: To honor women journalists in television news. **Focus:** Journalism. **Qualif.:** Recipient of the award is for young, promising minority professionals in television or radio news who have fewer than 10 years as a professional journalist. **Criteria:** Recipients are selected based on the completed application form and completed requirements.

Funds Avail.: $1,000. **Duration:** Annual. **To Apply:** Applicant must complete the application form online; a cover letter discussing journalism experiences, use of fellowship funds, discussing choosing career in electronic journalism; 3-5 links to your best and most relevant work samples discussing the roles in each of the pieces; a letter of reference from news manager or higher. All must be submitted online.

7873 ■ George Foreman Tribute to Lyndon B. Johnson Scholarships (Undergraduate/Scholarship)

Purpose: To help RTNDF members embody and uphold the standards of ethical journalism; to promote leadership in the newsroom. **Focus:** Journalism. **Qualif.:** Applicants must be journalism students at the University of Texas-Austin; must be officially enrolled in college and have at least one full academic year remaining majoring a career in electronic journalism. **Criteria:** Recipients are selected based on academic standing and financial need.

Funds Avail.: $6,000. **To Apply:** Applicant must complete the application form online and provide evidence proving that he/she is currently enrolled; a cover letter discussing journalism experiences, use of scholarship, discussing choosing career in electronic journalism; 3-5 links to your best and most relevant work samples discussing the roles in each of the pieces; a letter of reference from the dean, faculty sponsor or internship advisor. All must be submitted online. **Deadline:** April 30.

7874 ■ Jacque I. Minnotte Health Reporting Fellowships (Other/Fellowship)

Purpose: To promote excellence in health or medical television and radio reporting. **Focus:** Journalism. **Qualif.:** Applicants must have fewer than 10 years of experience in health or medical television and radio reporting. **Criteria:** Recipients are selected based on the completed application form and completed requirements.

Funds Avail.: $2,000. **Duration:** Annual. **To Apply:** Applicant must complete the application form online; a cover letter discussing journalism experiences, use of fellowship funds, discussing choosing career in electronic journalism; 3-5 links to your best and most relevant work samples discussing the roles in each of the pieces; a letter of reference from news manager or higher. All must be submitted online.

7875 ■ Lou and Carole Prato Sports Reporting Scholarships (Undergraduate/Scholarship)

Purpose: To help RTNDF members embody and uphold the standards of ethical journalism. To promote leadership

Awards are arranged alphabetically below their administering organizations

in the newsroom. **Focus:** Journalism. **Qualif.:** Applicant must be a student pursuing a career as a sports reporter in television or radio. **Criteria:** Recipients are selected based on academic standing and strong writing skills.

Funds Avail.: $1,000. **To Apply:** Applicant must complete the application form online and provide evidence proving that he/she is currently enrolled; a cover letter discussing journalism experiences, use of scholarship, discussing choosing career in electronic journalism; 3-5 links to your best and most relevant work samples discussing the roles in each of the pieces; a letter of reference from the dean, faculty sponsor or internship advisor. All must be submitted online. **Deadline:** April 30. **Remarks:** Established in 2001.

7876 ■ Mike Reynolds Journalism Scholarships
(Undergraduate/Scholarship)

Purpose: To help RTNDF members embody and uphold the standards of ethical journalism. To promote leadership in the newsroom. **Focus:** Journalism. **Qualif.:** Applicant must be currently enrolled in journalism school and have good writing abilities, excellent grades and have a dedication to the news business; must have strong interest in pursuing electronic journalism; and have demonstrated financial need. **Criteria:** Recipients are selected based on academic standing and financial need.

Funds Avail.: $1,000. **To Apply:** Applicant must complete the application form online and provide evidence proving that he/she is currently enrolled; a cover letter discussing journalism experiences, use of scholarship, discussing choosing career in electronic journalism; 3-5 links to your best and most relevant work samples discussing the roles in each of the pieces; a letter of reference from the dean, faculty sponsor or internship advisor; list of media-related jobs held and contributions made to funding education. All must be submitted online. **Deadline:** April 30.

7877 ■ RTDNA Presidents Scholarships
(Undergraduate/Scholarship)

Purpose: To help RTNDF members embody and uphold the standards of ethical journalism. To promote leadership in the newsroom. **Focus:** Journalism. **Qualif.:** Applicants must be currently enrolled as college sophomores, juniors and seniors in good standing with career goal in electronic journalism. **Criteria:** Recipients are selected based on academic standing and financial need.

Funds Avail.: $1,000. **Duration:** Annual. **Number Awarded:** 2. **To Apply:** Applicant must complete the application form online and provide evidence proving that he/she is currently enrolled; a cover letter discussing journalism experiences, use of scholarship, discussing choosing career in electronic journalism; 3-5 links to your best and most relevant work samples discussing the roles in each of the pieces; a letter of reference from the dean, faculty sponsor or internship advisor. All must be submitted online. **Deadline:** April 30.

7878 ■ Carole Simpson Scholarships
(Undergraduate/Scholarship)

Purpose: To help RTNDF members embody and uphold the standards of ethical journalism; to promote leadership in the newsroom; to encourage and help minority students overcome hurdles along their career path. **Focus:** Journalism. **Qualif.:** Applicant must be enrolled in radio and television news; applicant must be a full-time college student whose career objective is to enter the electronic journalism field and who has at least one full year of college remaining. **Criteria:** Recipients are selected based on academic standing.

Funds Avail.: $2,000. **To Apply:** Applicant must complete the application form online and provide evidence proving that he/she is currently enrolled; a cover letter discussing journalism experiences, use of scholarship, discussing choosing career in electronic journalism; 3-5 links to your best and most relevant work samples discussing the roles in each of the pieces; a letter of reference from the dean, faculty sponsor or internship advisor. All must be submitted online. **Deadline:** April 30.

7879 ■ Pete Wilson Graduate Scholarships *(Graduate, Undergraduate/Scholarship)*

Purpose: To help RTNDF members embody and uphold the standards of ethical journalism. To promote leadership in the newsroom. **Focus:** Journalism. **Qualif.:** Applicant must be pursuing a career in radio and television news. Applicant must be a graduate or undergraduate student in the San Francisco Bay area, whose career objective is to enter the electronic journalism field. Applicant must be enrolled in college and be in good standing. **Criteria:** Recipients are selected based on academic standing and financial need.

Funds Avail.: $2,000. **To Apply:** Applicant must complete the application form online and provide evidence proving that he/she is currently enrolled; a cover letter discussing journalism experiences, use of scholarship, discussing choosing career in electronic journalism; 3-5 links to your best and most relevant work samples discussing the roles in each of the pieces; a letter of reference from the dean, faculty sponsor or internship advisor. All must be submitted online. **Deadline:** April 30. **Remarks:** Established in 2007.

7880 ■ Pete Wilson Journalism Scholarships
(Graduate, Undergraduate/Scholarship)

Purpose: To help RTNDF members embody and uphold the standards of ethical journalism. To promote leadership in the newsroom. **Focus:** Journalism. **Qualif.:** Applicant must be a full-time undergraduate or graduate student who plans to work in the electronic journalism field in the San Francisco Bay area. **Criteria:** Recipients are selected based on academic standing.

Funds Avail.: $2,000. **To Apply:** Applicant must complete the application form online and provide evidence proving that he/she is currently enrolled; a cover letter discussing journalism experiences, use of scholarship, discussing choosing career in electronic journalism; 3-5 links to your best and most relevant work samples discussing the roles in each of the pieces; a letter of reference from the dean, faculty sponsor or internship advisor. All must be submitted online. **Remarks:** Established in 2007.

7881 ■ Radio-Television News Directors Foundation Canada (RTDNF)
2800-14th Ave., Ste. 210
Markham, ON, Canada L3R 0E4
Ph: (416)491-2886
Fax: (416)491-1670
URL: rtdnfcanada.com/

7882 ■ RTDNF Scholarships *(Undergraduate, Graduate/Scholarship)*

Purpose: To offer financial assistance to students in Canada. **Focus:** Radio and television. **Qualif.:** Applicants must be second year, third year or graduate students enrolled in broadcast journalism course at either a college, university, college or university programs with a broadcast

Awards are arranged alphabetically below their administering organizations

journalism option, or actively involved in news at a radio or TV station on or off campus. **Criteria:** Selection will be based on the committee's criteria.

Funds Avail.: No specific amount. **To Apply:** Applicants must submit a completed entry form online: a radio or TV documentary, feature, newscast, sportscast, or spot news or sports report. The total presentation time must not exceed 10 minutes. **Deadline:** April 10.

7883 ■ Radiological Society of North America (RSNA)

820 Jorie Blvd.
Oak Brook, IL 60523-2251
Ph: (630)571-2670
Fax: (630)571-7837
Free: 800-381-6660
E-mail: mwatson@rsna.org
URL: www.rsna.org

7884 ■ Education Scholar Grant (Professional development/Grant)

Purpose: To provide funding opportunities for individuals with an active interest in radiologic education. **Focus:** Radiology. **Qualif.:** Applicants must be RSNA members at the time of the application. If the applicants' membership category is Member-in-Training or any other non dues-paying category, the scientific advisor or one of the co-investigators must be a dues-paying member. **Criteria:** Selection will be based on the committee's criteria.

Funds Avail.: $75,000. **Duration:** Annual. **To Apply:** Applicants must visit the website and complete the online application using the Online Grant Application System. Applicants must use their RSNA membership username and password to login. Applicants' project must be in any area of research related to the radiologic sciences. Projects may include, but are not limited to: advanced training in the discipline of education, possibly resulting in an advanced degree/certificate; development, dissemination and evaluation of printed or electronic educational materials; research of teaching methods and evaluation processes; education in emerging nations; medical students, residents, fellows, CME participants, allied health professional student education. **Deadline:** January 12.

7885 ■ R&E Foundation Education Scholarships (Graduate, Other/Scholarship)

Purpose: To develop teachers and educational leaders in radiology who can effectively share their knowledge with the radiology community. **Focus:** Education; Medicine, Nuclear; Radiology. **Qualif.:** Applicant must hold a faculty position in a department of radiology, radiation oncology, or nuclear medicine within an educational institution; must hold an MD degree or equivalent; must have completed advanced training and be certified by the American Board of Radiology (ABR) or its equivalent or be on track for certification; must not be an agent of any for-profit, commercial company in the radiologic sciences; and may not have concurrent RSNA grants. **Criteria:** Selection is based on the application materials submitted.

Funds Avail.: $75,000/year. **Duration:** Two years. **To Apply:** Applicants may apply online by creating an account or they may print the application form, obtain original signatures and send the entire document to the Foundation Office. **Deadline:** January 10. **Remarks:** International applicants must be certified by the radiology board in their

countries. **Contact:** Scott A. Walter, MS at swalter@rsna.org; 630-571-7816.

7886 ■ Research Resident/Fellow Grants (Professional development/Grant)

Purpose: To provide young investigators the opportunity to gain further insight into scientific investigation and to gain competence in research techniques and methods in anticipation of establishing a career in academic radiologic science. **Focus:** Radiology. **Qualif.:** Applicants must be RSNA members at the time of application; if the applicants' membership category is Member-in-Training or any other non dues-paying category, the scientific advisor or one of the co-investigators must be a dues-paying member; must hold a full-time faculty position in a department of radiology, radiation oncology or nuclear medicine within a North American educational institution; must be within five years of initial faculty appointment with an academic rank of instructor or assistant professor; must have completed advanced training and be certified by the American Board of Radiology or equivalent or on track for certification. **Criteria:** Selection will be based on the committee's criteria.

Funds Avail.: $30,000 - Research resident project; $50,000 - Research fellow project. **Duration:** Annual. **To Apply:** Applicants must visit the website and complete the online application using the Online Grant Application System. Applicants must use their RSNA membership username and password to login. Applicants' project must: be in any area of research related to the radiologic sciences; describe the unique nature of the research effort independent of existing research efforts and should have well-defined goals for the funding period of the grant. Participation of the recipients in established funded research is encourage, but the responsibility and project of the recipient should be clearly described in the application; focused on advancing imaging science, developing or evaluating medical imaging technology or making innovative use of imaging science to answer important biologic or clinical questions. **Deadline:** January 15.

7887 ■ RSNA/AUR/APDR/SCARD Radiology Education Research Development Grant (Professional development/Grant)

Purpose: To encourage innovation and improvement in health sciences education by providing research opportunities to individuals throughout the world who are in pursuit of advancing the science of radiology education. **Focus:** Radiology. **Qualif.:** Applicants must be individuals, at any level of career development, who have a primary appointment in a radiology department; must be members of one or more of the sponsoring organizations. **Criteria:** Selection will be based on the committee's criteria.

Funds Avail.: $10,000. **Duration:** One year. **To Apply:** Applicants must visit the website to complete the online application using the Online Grant Application System. Applicants must use their RSNA membership username and password to login. Applicants' project must be in the areas of radiology education research including, but not limited to: Development of new educational programs or the improvement of existing programs; pilot studies with respect to methods of teaching and the evaluation of educational techniques, materials or programs; improving methods of student, teacher, course or program evaluation; expanding knowledge of how to provide effective education in the radiologic sciences. **Deadline:** January 12.

Awards are arranged alphabetically below their administering organizations

7888 ■ RSNA Research Scholar Grants *(Professional development/Grant)*

Purpose: To support junior faculty members who have completed the conventional resident/fellowship training program(s) but have not yet been recognized as independent investigators. **Focus:** Radiology. **Qualif.:** Applicants must be RSNA members at the time of application; if the applicants' membership category is Member-in-Training or any other non dues-paying category, the scientific advisor or one of the co-investigators must be a dues-paying member; must hold a full-time faculty position in a department of radiology, radiation oncology or nuclear medicine within a North American educational institution; must be within five years of initial faculty appointment with an academic rank of instructor or assistant professor; must have completed advanced training and be certified by the American Board of Radiology or equivalent or on track for certification. **Criteria:** Selection will be based on the committee's criteria.

Funds Avail.: $75,000. **Duration:** Annual. **To Apply:** Applicants must be nominated by the department chair. Applications must be completed online using the Online Grant Application System. Applicants must use their RSNA membership username and password to login. Applicants' project must: be in any area of research related to the radiologic sciences; describe the unique nature of the research effort independent of existing research efforts and should have well-defined goals for the funding period of the grant. Greater emphasis on the independent nature of the research will be stressed compared to resident/fellowship research efforts; focused on advancing imaging science, developing or evaluating medical imaging technology or making innovative use of imaging science to answer important biologic or clinical questions. **Deadline:** January 15.

7889 ■ RSNA Research Seed Grants *(Professional development/Grant)*

Purpose: To enable all levels of investigators throughout the world in defining objectives and testing hypotheses in preparation of major grant applications to corporation, foundations and governmental agencies. **Focus:** Radiology. **Qualif.:** Applicant must be an RSNA member at the time of application; must hold a full-time faculty position in a department of radiology, radiation oncology, or nuclear medicine within an educational institution. If the applicants is not a full-time faculty member at the time of application but will become a full-time faculty members when the award commences, a letter from the department chair attesting to this appointment must be included; must have completed advanced training and be certified by the American Board of Radiology, or equivalent, or on track for certification. Applicants in institutions outside North America must have completed advanced training and be certified by the radiology board in their country. **Criteria:** Selection will be based on the committee's criteria.

Funds Avail.: $40,000. **Duration:** Annual. **To Apply:** Applicants must visit the website and complete the online application using the Online Grant Application System. Applicants must use their RSNA membership username and password to login. Applicants' project must: be in any area of research related to the radiologic sciences; describe the unique nature of the research effort independent of existing research efforts. Greater emphasis will be place on the likelihood of this research to attract future funding given the nature and extent of the preliminary data collected within the cycle of the grant; focused on advancing imaging science, developing or evaluating medical imaging technology

or making innovative use of imaging science to answer important biologic or clinical questions. **Deadline:** January 15.

7890 ■ Railway Tie Association (RTA)
115 Commerce Dr., Ste. C
Fayetteville, GA 30214-7335
Ph: (770)460-5553
Fax: (770)460-5573
E-mail: ties@rta.org
URL: www.rta.org

7891 ■ John Mabry Forestry Scholarships *(Undergraduate/Scholarship)*

Purpose: To provide financial support for students attending technical schools, colleges and universities. **Focus:** General studies/Field of study not specified. **Qualif.:** Applicants must be students in accredited second year technical schools or juniors and seniors attending four-year colleges and universities. **Criteria:** Recipients are selected based on leadership qualities, career objectives, scholastic achievement, and financial need.

Funds Avail.: $2,000. **Duration:** One year. **Number Awarded:** 2. **To Apply:** Applicants must submit completed application along with personal narrative, letters of reference, one black and white photo, and a copy of transcript. **Deadline:** June 30.

7892 ■ Rainbow Business and Professional Association (RBPA)
PO Box 11148
Portland, ME 04104
Ph: (207)775-0077
URL: www.rbpa.org

7893 ■ RBPA Scholarships *(All/Scholarship)*

Purpose: To promote positive role models for gay, lesbian, bisexual and transgendered individuals in the academic environment and community at large. **Focus:** Sexuality. **Qualif.:** Applicants must be gay, lesbian, bisexual or transgendered students. **Criteria:** Selection is based on the essay application.

Funds Avail.: Up to $3,000 each. **Duration:** Annual. **Number Awarded:** Up to 4. **To Apply:** Applicants must submit a completed scholarship application form to the RBPA Scholarship Fund, Inc. **Deadline:** March 19. **Remarks:** Established in 1997. **Contact:** RBPA Scholarship Fund, Inc. PO Box 3442, Portland, ME 04104-3442, or scholarship@rbpa.org.

7894 ■ Ayn Rand Institute (ARI)
2121 Alton Pkwy., Ste. 250
Irvine, CA 92606
Ph: (949)222-6550
Fax: (949)222-6558
E-mail: mail@aynrand.org
URL: www.aynrand.org

7895 ■ Atlas Shrugged Essay Contest *(Graduate, Undergraduate/Prize)*

Purpose: To encourage students to use and practice their writing skills through essay contests. **Focus:** General

Awards are arranged alphabetically below their administering organizations

studies/Field of study not specified. **Qualif.:** Applicant must be a 12th Grader, a college undergraduates, or a graduate student and not a previous first place winner. **Criteria:** Selection is based on the essay's style and content. Judges will look for writing that is clear, articulate and logically organized, and must demonstrate an outstanding grasp of the philosophic meaning of Atlas Shrugged.

Funds Avail.: First-Prize: $10,000; Second-Prize: $2,000; Third-Prize: $1,000; Finalist: $100; Semi-Finalist: $50. **Duration:** Annual. **To Apply:** No application is required. Applicants must submit the essay (800-1,600 words, double-spaced, typewritten) along with a stapled cover sheet which includes the applicant's name and address, e-mail address, name and address of the applicant's university, the selected topic, and applicant's declared major. Applicants may submit the essay online or mail to above address. **Deadline:** October 23. **Contact:** info@aynrandnovels.com.

7896 ■ Ayn Rand Institute Anthem Essay Contest
(High School, Undergraduate/Prize)

Purpose: To support high school and college students for the best essay on Ayn Rand's fiction. **Focus:** General studies/Field of study not specified. **Qualif.:** Students must be 8th, 9th and 10th Graders. **Criteria:** Essays will be judged on both style and content. Judges will look for writing that is clear, articulate and logically organized. Winning essays must demonstrate an outstanding grasp of the philosophic meaning of Anthem.

Funds Avail.: $2,000 - 1st prize; $500 - 2nd prize; $200 - 3rd prize. **Duration:** Annual. **To Apply:** No application is required. Contest is open to students worldwide. Students must select one of the following topics: 1) Contrast Equality's view of morality at the end of the novel to the morality exemplified by his society's institutions, practices, and officials; 2) Anthem's theme is, in Ayn Rand's own words, "the meaning of man's ego." Explain the ways in which the characters and story in Anthem illustrate this theme; 3) To fully control a man, dictators must not only enslave his body, but also destroy his mind. Discuss how the leaders and society in Anthem seek to accomplish this tyrannical end. To avoid disqualification, mailed in essays must include a stapled cover sheet with the following information: name and address; email address (if available); name and address of school; topic selected; current grade level; and (optional) the name of the teacher who assigned the essay, if the applicant is completing it for classroom credit. Essays must be no fewer than 800 words and no more than 1,600 words in length and must be double-spaced. Essays with stapled cover sheets must be submitted to the above address. **Contact:** essay@aynrand.org.

7897 ■ Ayn Rand Institute Former Participants' Essay Contest *(High School, Undergraduate/Prize)*

Purpose: To award high school and college students for the best essay on Ayn Rand's fiction. **Focus:** General studies/Field of study not specified. **Qualif.:** Participants must be grades 11 through College/Adult. **Criteria:** Essays will be judged on both style and content. Judges will look for writing that is clear, articulate and logically organized. Winning essays must demonstrate an outstanding grasp of the philosophic meaning of Ayn Rand's novels.

Funds Avail.: $2,000 - 1st prize; $500 2nd prize; $100 - 3rd prize; $50 - finalist. **Duration:** Annual. **To Apply:** No application is required. Contest is open to students worldwide. Participants must submit an essay in response the topic question of: What was your initial response to the novel(s)? In what ways has reading Ayn Rand inspired you and the choices you have made in your life? To avoid disqualification, mailed in essays must include a stapled cover sheet with the following information: name and address; email address (if available); name and address of school; topic selected; current grade level; and (optional) the name of the teacher who assigned the essay, if the applicant is completing it for classroom credit. Essay must be no fewer than 700 and no more than 1,500 words in length and must be double-spaced. Essays with stapled cover sheets must be submitted to:PO Box 57044, Irvine, CA 92619-7044 or applicants may visit the website for online submission details. **Deadline:** May 14.

7898 ■ Ayn Rand Institute Fountainhead Essay Contest *(High School, Undergraduate/Prize)*

Purpose: To support high school and college students for the best essay on Ayn Rand's fiction. **Focus:** General studies/Field of study not specified. **Qualif.:** Students must be 11th and 12th graders. **Criteria:** Essays will be judged on both style and content. Judges will look for writing that is clear, articulate and logically organized. Winning essays must demonstrate an outstanding grasp of the philosophic meaning of The Fountainheads.

Funds Avail.: $10,000 - 1st prize; $2,000 - 2nd prize; $1,000 - 3rd prize. **Duration:** Annual. **To Apply:** No application is required. Contest is open to students worldwide. Students must select one of the following three topics: 1) After the Stoddard trial, Dominique Francon marries Peter Keating. Given her love for the integrity of Howard Roark's buildings and person, why does she do this? What is she seeking from the marriage? How does her action of marrying Peter relate to her deeper convictions and conflicts?; 2) In dynamiting Cortlandt Homes, Howard Roark breaks the law. What is his moral and philosophical argument for the rectitude of his action?; 3) Choose the scene in The Fountainhead that is most meaningful to you. Analyze that scene in terms of the wider themes in the book. To avoid disqualification, mailed in essays must include a stapled cover sheet with the following information: name and address; email address (if available); name and address of school; topic selected; current grade level; and (optional) the name of the teacher who assigned the essay, if the applicant is completing it for classroom credit. Essay must be no fewer than 800 and no more than 1,600 words in length and must be double-spaced. Essays with stapled cover sheets must be submitted to the above address or applicants may visit the website for online submission details. **Contact:** essay@aynrand.org.

7899 ■ James Randi Educational Foundation (JREF)
2941 Fairview Park Dr., Ste. 105
Falls Church, VA 22042
Ph: (571)318-6530
Fax: (703)226-3781
E-mail: jref@randi.org
URL: web.randi.org

7900 ■ James Randi Educational Foundation Scholarships *(Graduate, Undergraduate/Scholarship)*

Purpose: To provide fund for qualified graduate or undergraduate students enrolled in any field. **Focus:** General studies/Field of study not specified. **Qualif.:** Applicants must be students who are enrolled, or admitted to, colleges and universities at the graduate or undergraduate level in

Awards are arranged alphabetically below their administering organizations

any field of academic study. **Criteria:** Selection will be based on academic achievement, commitment to enhancing critical thinking skills, potential, and the content and quality of the essay, as well as other criteria designed by the Scholarship Committee.

Funds Avail.: $2,000. **Duration:** Annual. **Number Awarded:** 2. **To Apply:** Applicants must submit a completed application form; copy of academic transcripts and/or records from school that do not use the US-standard A-F; one double spaced essay (500 words maximum) expressing how do they intend to apply critical thinking skills to their chosen area of study, and how does their proposed study include the mission goals of the James Randi Educational Foundation.

7901 ■ Charles B. Rangel International Affairs Program

2218 6th St. NW
Washington, DC 20059
Ph: (202)806-4367
Fax: (202)806-5424
Free: 877-633-0002
E-mail: rangelprogram@howard.edu
URL: www.rangelprogram.org

7902 ■ Rangel Graduate Fellowship *(Graduate/Fellowship)*

Purpose: To attract and prepare outstanding young people for careers in the Foreign Service in which they can help formulate, represent and implement U.S. foreign policy. **Focus:** International affairs and relations. **Qualif.:** Applicant must be a U.S. citizen; seeking admission to enter graduate school for a two-year program at a U.S. university; and have a cumulative GPA of at least 3.2 on a 4.0 scale at the time of application. **Criteria:** Selection is based on the candidate's community, academic, extracurricular and leadership activities. Consideration will be given to qualified applicants who demonstrate outstanding leadership skills and academic achievement in programs relevant to the work of the U.S. Department of State, and also based upon whether a candidate demonstrates financial need.

Funds Avail.: $35,000. **Duration:** Annual; two years. **Number Awarded:** 20. **To Apply:** Applicants must complete the application online. Applicants must submit, in one package, proof of U.S. citizenship with a notarized copy of: birth certificate, certificate of U.S. citizenship, U.S. passport; Student Aid Report (SAR) generated from the Free Application for Federal Student Aid (FAFSA) form; and GRE or GMAT Scores (copy of report sent to student). In addition, the institution or individual must submit the official transcript from all colleges and universities that the applicant has attended (in a sealed/signed envelope either by applicant or by institution); official Financial Aid Statement from applicant's senior year; and two letters of recommendation: (can be sent directly from the recommender or from the applicant in a sealed and signed envelope) one from a faculty member, and one from a community leader or other individual who can comment on the applicant's non-academic accomplishments and his/her potential.

7903 ■ Jeannette Rankin Women's Scholarship Fund

1 Huntington Rd., Ste. 701
Athens, GA 30606
Ph: (706)208-1211

Fax: (706)548-0202
E-mail: info@rankinfoundation.org
URL: www.rankinfoundation.org

7904 ■ Jeannette Rankin Scholarships *(Undergraduate, Vocational/Occupational/Scholarship)*

Purpose: To financially support the education of a low-income female student who wishes to pursue her educational goals. **Focus:** General studies/Field of study not specified. **Qualif.:** Applicant must be a female, age 35 or older; a U.S. citizen; enrolled in, or accepted to an accredited school; pursuing a technical or vocational education, an associate's degree, or a first bachelor's degree; and have low-income according to the U.S. Department of Labor's Lower Living Standard. **Criteria:** Awards are given based on goals; plans in reaching those goals; challenges the applicant may have faced; and financial situation.

Funds Avail.: No specific amount. **To Apply:** Applicants must submit a completed scholarship application along with a personal statement; two letters of recommendation; and proof of enrollment or acceptance. Applicants are requested to submit two complete sets of the application materials.

7905 ■ Rappaport Center for Law and Public Service

Phyllis and Jerome Lyle Rappaport Foundation
75 State St., 12th Fl.
Boston, MA 02109
Ph: (617)573-8644
URL: www.rappaportfoundation.org/initiatives/suffolk.html

7906 ■ Consumer Law Public Service Fellowships *(Undergraduate/Fellowship)*

Purpose: To support a Suffolk law student who demonstrates interest and commitment to issues of consumer law, rights and protection. **Focus:** Law. **Qualif.:** Applicant must be a Suffolk law student in good academic standing and who is not in his/her final semester. **Criteria:** Selection is based on applicant's demonstrated interest and commitment working in the field of consumer law, rights and protection; demonstrated commitment to public service as shown by past paid and volunteer work experiences and extracurricular activities; and academic achievement.

Funds Avail.: $7,000. **Number Awarded:** 1. **To Apply:** Applicants must submit a completed application cover sheet along with a law school transcript; a resume; personal statement on interest and commitment to the area of consumer law, rights and protection (maximum of 2 page, double-spaced); and two references. **Deadline:** March 3.

7907 ■ Thomas J. Drinan Memorial Fellowships *(Undergraduate/Fellowship)*

Purpose: To support a Suffolk student who desires to work in a Massachusetts public office engaged in the prosecution or defence of criminal cases. **Focus:** Criminal justice; Law. **Qualif.:** Applicant must be a Suffolk University Law student who demonstrates a commitment of integrity and advocacy within the criminal justice system. **Criteria:** Selection is based on the applicant's demonstrated interest and commitment in working in the criminal justice system; excellent legal skills; and personal integrity and character.

Funds Avail.: No specific amount. **Duration:** Annual; ten weeks. **Number Awarded:** 1. **To Apply:** Applicants must submit a letter of intent/personal statement, resume and unofficial transcript. **Deadline:** October 3.

Awards are arranged alphabetically below their administering organizations

7908 ■ John E. Fenton, Jr. Public Service Awards
(Postgraduate/Fellowship)

Purpose: To support a graduating student pursuing public interest careers. **Focus:** Law; Public service. **Qualif.:** Applicant must be a graduating Suffolk Law School student or who has recently graduated and pursuing a public interest career. **Criteria:** Selection is based on merit and financial need.

Funds Avail.: $8,000 each. **Number Awarded:** 3-4. **To Apply:** Applicants must submit a completed application form together with the law school transcript; a resume; and a personal statement (maximum of 2 double-spaced pages). **Deadline:** March 17. **Contact:** Applicants must email rappaportcenter@suffolk.edu or hand-deliver a completed application to the Rappaport Center Suite 110.

7909 ■ Paul R. McLaughlin Fellowship
(Undergraduate/Fellowship)

Purpose: To support a Suffolk law student interested in pursuing a career in criminal law in the public sector. **Focus:** Criminal justice; Law. **Qualif.:** Applicant must be a Suffolk University law student interested in pursuing a career in criminal law in the public sector. **Criteria:** Selection is based on the submitted application materials.

Funds Avail.: $7,000. **Number Awarded:** 1. **To Apply:** Applicants must submit a letter of intent/personal statement; a resume; unofficial transcript; and list of three references. **Deadline:** October 3.

7910 ■ Rappaport Fellows Program in Law and Public Policy (Undergraduate/Fellowship)

Purpose: To train and expose law students to the challenging complexities and powerful societal rewards of creating successful public policy. **Focus:** Law. **Qualif.:** Applicant must be a J.D. candidate who is not in the final year of study at one of the six law schools in the Greater Boston region (Boston College, Boston University, Harvard, New England, Northeastern, and Suffolk University). **Criteria:** Selection is based on academic records, demonstrated commitment to public service, and demonstrated capacity for leadership.

Funds Avail.: No specific amount. **Number Awarded:** Varies. **To Apply:** Applicants must submit a completed application cover sheet; a resume; a personal statement (maximum of 2 double-spaced pages); two reference with phone numbers; and unofficial law school transcript. Applicants must send three packets in order.

7911 ■ Suffolk Public Interest Law Group Summer Fellowships (SPILG) (Undergraduate/Fellowship)

Purpose: To support Suffolk Law students who are interested in public service while providing an invaluable service to government agencies and non-profit organizations. **Focus:** Law. **Qualif.:** Applicant must be a Suffolk law student in good academic standing and who is not in his/her final semester. **Criteria:** Selection is based on the applicant's level of demonstrated commitment to public service and the likelihood that the student's summer employment will provide services to traditionally underserved clients.

Funds Avail.: $5,000. **Number Awarded:** Varies. **To Apply:** The application is a two-part process. Applicants must submit a completed SPILG application consisting of an identification sheet, resume, and essay. In addition, applicants must submit an application for summer work study funding and all necessary financial aid forms to the Financial Aid Office. **Deadline:** March 3.

7912 ■ Raytheon Co.
870 Winter St.
Waltham, MA 02451-1449
Ph: (781)522-3000
E-mail: corporatecontributions@raytheon.com
URL: www.raytheon.com

7913 ■ Raytheon Scholarship Program
(Undergraduate/Scholarship)

Purpose: To assist employee's children who plan to continue their education in college. **Focus:** General studies/Field of study not specified. **Qualif.:** Applicants must be under the age of 24; dependent children of active employees who work 20 hours or more per week and have at least one year of service with the company by the application deadline; college freshmen, sophomores and juniors who plan to enroll in a full-time undergraduate course of study at an accredited two-year or four-year college or university. **Criteria:** Recipients are selected on the basis of academic record, demonstrated leadership, and participation in school and community activities, honors, and work experience, statement of goals and aspirations, and unusual personal or family circumstances.

Funds Avail.: $2,000. **To Apply:** Applicants must submit the application and current complete official transcript of grades to Scholarship America. **Deadline:** March 31.

7914 ■ Redlands Community Scholarship Foundation
PO Box 1683
Redlands, CA 92373
Ph: (909)307-9892
E-mail: president@redlandsscholarships.org
URL: www.redlandsscholarships.org

7915 ■ Ruth Adams Memorial Scholarships
(Undergraduate/Scholarship)

Purpose: To encourage educational pursuits among Redlands Unified School District graduates by providing educational assistance. **Focus:** General studies/Field of study not specified. **Qualif.:** Applicant must be a female graduating senior who has been accepted at and will be attending the University of Redlands as a full-time student. **Criteria:** Award is given based on merit.

Funds Avail.: $500. **To Apply:** Applicants must submit: completed application form with the scantron sheet; cover sheet; student activity and community activity sheets; personal essay; and a copy of unofficial transcript (signed by the counselor). **Deadline:** February 7.

7916 ■ Patty Ahearn Victoria Elementary Scholarships (Undergraduate/Scholarship)

Purpose: To encourage educational pursuits among Redlands Unified School District graduates by providing educational assistance. **Focus:** General studies/Field of study not specified. **Qualif.:** Applicant must be a graduating senior; must have a 2.5 GPA or higher; must have attended Victoria Elementary School for at least three years; and must have continued to follow the "Victoria Peace Builder's Pledge." **Criteria:** Award is given based on merit.

Funds Avail.: $500. **Number Awarded:** 1. **To Apply:** Ap-

Awards are arranged alphabetically below their administering organizations

plicant must submit a completed application form together with the scantron sheet; cover sheet; student activity and community activity sheets; personal essay; and a copy of unofficial transcript (signed by the counselor). **Remarks:** No electronic submissions of application will be accepted. Submit two printed copies of the application and use a No. 2 pencil on the scantron sheet.

7917 ■ Robinson G. Allen Athletic Memorial Scholarships (Undergraduate/Scholarship)

Purpose: To encourage educational pursuits among Redlands Unified School District graduates by providing educational assistance. **Focus:** General studies/Field of study not specified. **Qualif.:** Applicant must be a senior whose athletic prowess has been limited, for the most part, to junior varsity teams and who plans to attend an institution of higher learning on a full-time basis. **Criteria:** Award is given based on sportsmanship, citizenship, scholarship and financial need.

Funds Avail.: $500. **Number Awarded:** 1. **To Apply:** Applicant must submit a completed application form together with the scantron sheet; cover sheet; student activity and community activity sheets; personal essay; and a copy of unofficial transcript (signed by the counselor). **Remarks:** No electronic submissions of application will be accepted. Submit two printed copies of the application and use a No. 2 pencil on the scantron sheet.

7918 ■ William A. Allen Memorial Metal Shop/Auto Body Scholarships (Undergraduate/Scholarship)

Purpose: To support the continuing education of an outstanding metal shop or auto body student. **Focus:** General studies/Field of study not specified. **Qualif.:** Applicant must be an outstanding metal shop or auto body student who displays dedication, skill and desire to become a true craftsman. **Criteria:** Selection shall be based on the applicant's demonstration of: creativity, show problem solving abilities, and exhibit good social skills.

Funds Avail.: $400. **Duration:** Annual. **To Apply:** Applicant may visit the scholarship section of the bestowing organization's website for further information regarding the application details. **Deadline:** February 6. **Contact:** Redlands Community Scholarship Foundation, at the above address.

7919 ■ Redlands Rotary Club - Donald C. Anderson Scholarships (Undergraduate/Scholarship)

Purpose: To assist graduate seniors in their pursuit of higher education. **Focus:** General studies/Field of study not specified. **Qualif.:** Applicants must be graduating seniors from Citrus Valley High School, Redlands East Valley High School, and/or Redlands High School who have shown the highest academic achievement, outstanding citizenship, andservice to school and community. **Criteria:** Selection shall be based on the aforementioned applicant's qualifications and compliance with the application details.

Funds Avail.: $2,500 each. **Duration:** Annual. **Number Awarded:** Varies. **To Apply:** Applicants may visit the scholarship section of the bestowing organization's website for further information regarding the application details. **Deadline:** February 6. **Contact:** Redlands Community Scholarship Foundation, at the above address.

7920 ■ Cindy Andrews Educational Scholarships (Undergraduate/Scholarship)

Purpose: To encourage those who want to be at the teaching profession. **Focus:** Educational administration; Teaching. **Qualif.:** Applicants must be graduating seniors from Redlands High School who have been CSF members for at least 4 semesters and plan to be teachers and eventually administrators in the public school system. **Criteria:** Selection shall be based on the aforementioned applicants' qualifications and compliance with the application details.

Funds Avail.: $500. **Duration:** Annual. **To Apply:** Applicants may visit the scholarship section of the bestowing organization's website for further information regarding the application details. **Deadline:** February 6. **Contact:** Redlands Community Scholarship Foundation, at the above address.

7921 ■ Aquatics Booster Club Scholarships (Undergraduate/Scholarship)

Purpose: To encourage educational pursuits among Redlands Unified School District graduates by providing educational assistance. **Focus:** General studies/Field of study not specified. **Qualif.:** Applicants must be graduating seniors from Citrus Valley High School and/or Redlands High School who have participated for at least three consecutive years in the water polo and/or swimming program. They must have maintained at least a 3.0 GPA and be planning to continue in an aquatic program in college. Students from Citrus Valley High School must have a 2-year CVABC membership and planning to attend a 4-year college, community college or accredited trade school. **Criteria:** Selection will be based on merit.

Funds Avail.: $500. **Duration:** Annual. **Number Awarded:** Varies. **To Apply:** Applicants must submit a completed application form together with the scantron sheet; cover sheet; student activity and community activity sheets; personal essay; and a copy of unofficial transcript (signed by the counselor). Applicants from Citrus Valley High School must submit an essay on "How high school swimming/water polo helped me achieve my educational goals and career objectives". **Deadline:** February 6. **Remarks:** No electronic submissions of application will be accepted. Submit two printed copies of the application and use a No. 2 pencil on the scantron sheet. **Contact:** Pam Bibo, Administrative Assistant, at admin@redlandsscholarships.org.

7922 ■ Frank G. Araujo Memorial Scholarships (Undergraduate/Scholarship)

Purpose: To assist Mexican-American graduate seniors in their pursuit of higher education. **Focus:** General studies/Field of study not specified. **Qualif.:** Applicants must be students of Mexican-American descent from Citrus Valley High School, Redlands eAcademy, Redlands East Valley High School, and/or Redlands High School. **Criteria:** Selection shall be based on the premises that students must have a 3.0 or higher GPA, demonstrate good citizenship, and participate in school or community activities.

Funds Avail.: $500 each person. **Duration:** Annual. **Number Awarded:** 2 from each high schools. **To Apply:** Applicants may visit the scholarship section of the bestowing organization's website for further information regarding the application details. **Deadline:** February 6. **Contact:** Redlands Community Scholarship Foundation, at the above address.

7923 ■ Connie "Chelo" Armendariz Memorial Scholarships (Undergraduate/Scholarship)

Purpose: To provide financial assistance to those graduating seniors who are planning to continue their education at a vocational school, junior college, or university. **Focus:** General studies/Field of study not specified. **Qualif.:** Ap-

Awards are arranged alphabetically below their administering organizations

plicants must be graduating seniors from Redlands East Valley High School and/or Redlands High School planning to continue their education at a vocational school, junior college, or university. **Criteria:** Preference shall be given to students who attended the former Saint Mary's Catholic Church in Redlands.

Funds Avail.: $500 each. **Duration:** Annual. **Number Awarded:** Varies. **To Apply:** Applicants must submit a completed application form together with the scantron sheet; cover sheet; student activity and community activity sheets; personal essay; and a copy of unofficial transcript (signed by the counselor). **Deadline:** February 6. **Contact:** Pam Bibo, Administrative Assistant, at admin@ redlandsscholarships.org.

7924 ■ Baha'i Faith Scholarships for Racial Harmony *(Undergraduate/Scholarship)*

Purpose: To support the education of graduating high school students for their promotion of racial and intercultural harmony on campus. **Focus:** General studies/Field of study not specified. **Qualif.:** Applicants must be graduating seniors from Orangewood High School who have promoted racial and intercultural harmony on campus. **Criteria:** Selection will be based on merit.

Funds Avail.: $400 each. **Duration:** Annual. **Number Awarded:** Varies. **To Apply:** Applicants must submit a completed application form together with the scantron sheet; cover sheet; student activity and community activity sheets; personal essay; and a copy of unofficial transcript (signed by the counselor). They should also attach a short statement showing how they have met the promotion of racial and intercultural harmony on campus. **Deadline:** February 6. **Contact:** Pam Bibo, Administrative Assistant, at admin@redlandsscholarships.org.

7925 ■ Timothy Baylink Good Fellowship Awards *(Undergraduate/Fellowship)*

Purpose: To encourage educational pursuits among Redlands Unified School District graduates by providing educational assistance. **Focus:** General studies/Field of study not specified. **Qualif.:** Applicant must be a graduating senior who possesses some of the attributes of Dr. Timothy Baylink, which include athleticism, sense of adventure, friendliness, free spirit, interest in computers and commitment to learning. **Criteria:** Award is given based on merit.

Funds Avail.: $1,000. **To Apply:** Applicant must submit: a completed application form together with the scantron sheet; cover sheet; student activity and community activity sheets; personal essay; and a copy of unofficial transcript (signed by the counselor). **Deadline:** February 7.

7926 ■ Beaver Medical Clinic-Glen Adams Scholarship Awards *(Undergraduate/Scholarship)*

Purpose: To encourage educational pursuits among Redlands Unified School District graduates by providing educational assistance. **Focus:** General studies/Field of study not specified. **Qualif.:** Applicant must be a graduating senior seeking a career in the field of medicine and must be outstanding academically, in leadership skills and in sports participation. **Criteria:** Award is given based on merit.

Funds Avail.: $750. **Number Awarded:** 1. **To Apply:** Applicant must submit a completed application form together with the scantron sheet; cover sheet; student activity and community activity sheets; personal essay; and a copy of

unofficial transcript (signed by the counselor). **Remarks:** No electronic submissions of application will be accepted. Submit two printed copies of the application and use a No. 2 pencil on the scantron sheet.

7927 ■ Beaver Medical Clinic-H.E.A.R.T. Scholarship Awards *(Undergraduate/Scholarship)*

Purpose: To provide financial assistance to a graduating student attending Redlands High School seekinf a career in medical field. **Focus:** General studies/Field of study not specified. **Qualif.:** Applicant must be a graduating senior seeking a career in the field of medicine who participated in the HEART Academy program for three years. **Criteria:** Award is given based on merit.

Funds Avail.: $750. **To Apply:** Applicant must submit a completed application form together with the scantron sheet; cover sheet; student activity and community activity sheets; personal essay; and a copy of unofficial transcript (signed by the counselor). **Remarks:** No electronic submissions of application will be accepted. Submit two printed copies of the application and use a No. 2 pencil on the scantron sheet.

7928 ■ Beaver Medical Clinic-Premed Scholarship Awards *(Undergraduate/Scholarship)*

Purpose: To encourage educational pursuits among Redlands Unified School District graduates by providing educational assistance. **Focus:** General studies/Field of study not specified. **Qualif.:** Applicant must be a graduating senior seeking a career in the field of medicine. Student must be outstanding both academically and in leadership skills. **Criteria:** Award is given based on merit

Funds Avail.: $4,000. **Number Awarded:** 1. **To Apply:** Applicant must submit a completed application form together with the scantron sheet; cover sheet; student activity and community activity sheets; personal essay; and a copy of unofficial transcript (signed by the counselor). **Remarks:** No electronic submissions of application will be accepted. Submit two printed copies of the application and use a No. 2 pencil on the scantron sheet.

7929 ■ Garvin L. Beck Scholarships *(Undergraduate/Scholarship)*

Purpose: To encourage educational pursuits among Redlands Unified School District graduates by providing educational assistance. **Focus:** General studies/Field of study not specified. **Qualif.:** Applicant must be enrolled at a four-year college, junior college or trade school. **Criteria:** Award is given based on merit.

Funds Avail.: $1,000 and $500. **To Apply:** Applicant must submit a completed application form together with the scantron sheet; cover sheet; student activity and community activity sheets; written documentation of registration at the college or a valid registration to a junior college or trade school; proof of a letter of junior varsity sport during the last two years of high school; a one-page essay; and a copy of unofficial transcript (signed by the counselor). **Remarks:** No electronic submissions of application will be accepted. Submit two printed copies of the application and use a No. 2 pencil on the scantron sheet.

7930 ■ Raymond and Donald Beeler Memorial Scholarships *(Undergraduate/Scholarship)*

Purpose: To encourage educational pursuits among Redlands Unified School District graduates by providing educational assistance. **Focus:** General studies/Field of

Awards are arranged alphabetically below their administering organizations

study not specified. **Qualif.:** Applicant must be a student with at least a 3.0 GPA intending to attend a community or four-year college on a full-time basis. **Criteria:** Awards are given based on merit. Financial need is also a consideration.

Funds Avail.: $500. **To Apply:** Applicant must submit a completed application form together with the scantron sheet; cover sheet; student activity and community activity sheets; personal essay; and a copy of unofficial transcript (signed by the counselor). **Remarks:** No electronic submissions of application will be accepted. Submit two printed copies of the application and use a No. 2 pencil on the scantron sheet.

7931 ■ David Beltran Memorial Scholarships
(Undergraduate/Scholarship)

Purpose: To encourage educational pursuits among Redlands Unified School District graduates by providing educational assistance. **Focus:** Theater arts. **Qualif.:** Applicant must be a college-bound graduating senior planning to major in drama, theater arts or thespian studies. **Criteria:** Awards are given based on merit.

Funds Avail.: $500. **To Apply:** Applicant must submit a completed application form together with the scantron sheet; cover sheet; student activity and community activity sheets; personal essay; and a copy of unofficial transcript (signed by the counselor). **Remarks:** No electronic submissions of application will be accepted. Submit two printed copies of the application and use a No. 2 pencil on the scantron sheet.

7932 ■ Barbara Bonnema Memorial Scholarships
(Undergraduate/Scholarship)

Purpose: To encourage educational pursuits among Redlands Unified School District graduates by providing educational assistance. **Focus:** General studies/Field of study not specified. **Qualif.:** Applicant must be a college-bound graduating senior who will be attending school on a full-time basis. **Criteria:** Awards are given based academic excellence and financial need.

Funds Avail.: $500. **To Apply:** Applicant must submit a completed application form together with the scantron sheet; cover sheet; student activity and community activity sheets; personal essay; and a copy of unofficial transcript (signed by the counselor). **Remarks:** No electronic submissions of application will be accepted. Submit two printed copies of the application and use a No. 2 pencil on the scantron sheet.

7933 ■ Boy Scouts of America Troop 3 Scholarships - Art Till/Nathan E. Smith Memorial Scholarships *(Undergraduate, Vocational/Occupational/Scholarship)*

Purpose: To encourage educational pursuits among Redlands Unified School District graduates by providing educational assistance. **Focus:** General studies/Field of study not specified. **Qualif.:** Applicant must be a graduating senior with at least a 2.0 GPA; must be planning to attend an accredited college, university, or vocational program; and must have continuous involvement in scouting and community service. **Criteria:** Preference is given to individuals who have attained the rank of Eagle Scout.

Funds Avail.: $500. **To Apply:** Applicant must submit a completed application form together with the scantron sheet; cover sheet; student activity and community activity sheets; personal essay; and a copy of unofficial transcript

(signed by the counselor). **Remarks:** No electronic submissions of application will be accepted. Submit two printed copies of the application and use a No. 2 pencil on the scantron sheet.

7934 ■ Quincy Brown Memorial Scholarships
(Undergraduate/Scholarship)

Purpose: To encourage educational pursuits among Redlands Unified School District graduates by providing educational assistance. **Focus:** Business; Teaching. **Qualif.:** Applicant must be a graduating senior enrolled as a full-time student in a four-year college or university; must be pursuing a business or teaching career; must have a 3.0 or higher GPA; and must have attended Redlands High School for at least three consecutive years. **Criteria:** Awards are given based on merit.

Funds Avail.: $500 or greater scholarship. **To Apply:** Applicant must submit a completed application form together with the scantron sheet; cover sheet; student activity and community activity sheets; personal essay; and a copy of unofficial transcript (signed by the counselor). **Remarks:** No electronic submissions of application will be accepted. Submit two printed copies of the application and use a No. 2 pencil on the scantron sheet.

7935 ■ Kathy Bush Memorial Scholarships
(Undergraduate/Scholarship)

Purpose: To encourage educational pursuits among Redlands Unified School District graduates by providing educational assistance. **Focus:** General studies/Field of study not specified. **Qualif.:** Applicant must be a graduating senior who has been outstanding in the field of instrumental music. **Criteria:** Award is given based on merit.

Funds Avail.: $500. **To Apply:** Applicant must submit a completed application form together with the scantron sheet; cover sheet; student activity and community activity sheets; personal essay; and a copy of unofficial transcript (signed by the counselor). **Remarks:** No electronic submissions of application will be accepted. Submit two printed copies of the application and use a No. 2 pencil on the scantron sheet.

7936 ■ Robert G. Campbell Scholarships
(Undergraduate/Scholarship)

Purpose: To provide scholarship to an outstanding student who is highly motivated, and plans to attend either a junior college or a vocational school. **Focus:** General studies/Field of study not specified. **Qualif.:** Applicants must be above-average students from Orangewood High School and/or Redlands High School who are highly motivated and planning a career. For those who are from Orangewood High School, they should have the plan to attend either a junior college or a vocational school for the LVN program or a post-secondary education. Those from Redlands High School will attend and remain at the University of Redlands. **Criteria:** Scholarship will be given based on merit.

Funds Avail.: $500 each (for those from Oragewood High School); $7,000 good for 4 years (for those from Redlands High School). **Duration:** Annual. **Number Awarded:** Varies. **To Apply:** Applicants must submit a completed application form together with the scantron sheet; cover sheet; student activity and community activity sheets; personal essay; and a copy of unofficial transcript (signed by the counselor). **Deadline:** February 6. **Contact:** Pam Bibo, Administrative Assistant, at admin@redlandsscholarships.org.

Awards are arranged alphabetically below their administering organizations

7937 ■ Cesar E. Chavez Scholarships
(Undergraduate/Scholarship)

Purpose: To encourage educational pursuits among Redlands Unified School District graduates by providing educational assistance. **Focus:** General studies/Field of study not specified. **Qualif.:** Applicant must be a graduating senior who is in need of financial assistance in order to attend an institution of higher learning. **Criteria:** Award is given based on merit.

Funds Avail.: $750. **To Apply:** Applicant must submit a completed application form together with the scantron sheet; cover sheet; student activity and community activity sheets; personal essay; and a copy of unofficial transcript (signed by the counselor). **Remarks:** No electronic submissions of application will be accepted. Submit two printed copies of the application and use a No. 2 pencil on the scantron sheet.

7938 ■ Community Bank - Lee Guggisberg Foundation Memorial Scholarships *(Undergraduate/Scholarship)*

Purpose: To provide scholarship to those students who are planning to further their education in the field of business management or accounting. **Focus:** Accounting; Business. **Qualif.:** Applicants must: be students from Redlands East Valley High School and Redlands High School; complete the graduation requirements of the Redlands Unified School District; be enrolled as full-time students at an accredited college/university prior to Community Bank releasing the scholarship money; and, plan to further education in the field of business management or accounting. **Criteria:** Selection will be based on merit.

Funds Avail.: $300 each. **Duration:** Annual. **Number Awarded:** 3. **To Apply:** Applicants must submit a completed application form together with the scantron sheet; cover sheet; student activity and community activity sheets; personal essay; and a copy of unofficial transcript (signed by the counselor). **Deadline:** February 6. **Contact:** Pam Bibo, Administrative Assistant, at admin@redlandsscholarships.org.

7939 ■ Contemporary Club Scholarships
(Undergraduate/Scholarship)

Purpose: To encourage educational pursuits among Redlands Unified School District graduates by providing educational assistance. **Focus:** Music. **Qualif.:** Applicant must be a graduating senior intending to continue his/her studies in music. **Criteria:** Award is given based on merit.

Funds Avail.: $500. **To Apply:** Applicant must submit a completed application form together with the scantron sheet; cover sheet; student activity and community activity sheets; personal essay; and a copy of unofficial transcript (signed by the counselor). **Remarks:** No electronic submissions of application will be accepted. Submit two printed copies of the application and use a No. 2 pencil on the scantron sheet.

7940 ■ Cope Middle School PTSA Scholarships
(Undergraduate/Scholarship)

Purpose: To encourage educational pursuits among Redlands Unified School District graduates by providing educational assistance. **Focus:** General studies/Field of study not specified. **Qualif.:** Applicant must be a graduating senior who attended Cope Middle School for two years. **Criteria:** Priority will be given to a student whose parents were PTA volunteers.

Funds Avail.: $300. **To Apply:** Applicant must submit a completed application form together with the scantron sheet; cover sheet; student activity and community activity sheets; personal essay; and a copy of unofficial transcript (signed by the counselor). **Remarks:** No electronic submissions of application will be accepted. Submit two printed copies of the application and use a No. 2 pencil on the scantron sheet.

7941 ■ Crafton Elementary School PTA Scholarships *(Undergraduate/Scholarship)*

Purpose: To encourage educational pursuits among Redlands Unified School District graduates by providing educational assistance. **Focus:** General studies/Field of study not specified. **Qualif.:** Applicant must be a graduating senior who attended Crafton Elementary School for at least a year. **Criteria:** Preference is given to a student living in the school area.

Funds Avail.: $500. **Number Awarded:** 2. **To Apply:** Applicant must submit a completed application form together with the scantron sheet; cover sheet; student activity and community activity sheets; personal essay; and a copy of unofficial transcript (signed by the counselor). **Remarks:** No electronic submissions of application will be accepted. Submit two printed copies of the application and use a No. 2 pencil on the scantron sheet.

7942 ■ Crafton Hills College Foundation Scholarships *(Undergraduate/Scholarship)*

Purpose: To provide scholarship to those students who are in need to achieve their educational goal. **Focus:** General studies/Field of study not specified. **Qualif.:** Applicants must be graduating seniors enrolled at Crafton Hills College; have a minimum 3.0 GPA; and be attending college on a full-time basis. **Criteria:** Scholarship will be given to those who meet the qualifications.

Funds Avail.: $500. **Duration:** Annual. **Number Awarded:** 2. **To Apply:** Applicants must submit a completed application form together with the scantron sheet; cover sheet; student activity and community activity sheets; personal essay; and a copy of unofficial transcript (signed by the counselor). **Deadline:** February 6. **Contact:** Pam Bibo, Administrative Assistant, at admin@redlandsscholarships.org.

7943 ■ Redlands Rotary Club - Ernest L. Cronemeyer Memorial Scholarships *(Undergraduate/Scholarship)*

Purpose: To assist graduating high school students in their continuing education. **Focus:** General studies/Field of study not specified. **Qualif.:** Applicants must be graduating seniors from Citrus Valley High School, Redlands East Valley High School, and/or Redlands High School who have shown the highest in academic achievements, outstanding citizenship, and service to school and community. **Criteria:** Selection will be based on the aforesaid qualifications. Recipients will be selected through an interview process conducted by the Redlands Rotary Club scholarship committee.

Funds Avail.: $4,000 each. **Duration:** Annual. **Number Awarded:** Varies. **To Apply:** Applicants must submit a completed application form together with the scantron sheet; cover sheet; student activity and community activity sheets; personal essay; and a copy of unofficial transcript (signed by the counselor). **Deadline:** February 6. **Contact:** Pam Bibo, Administrative Assistant, at admin@redlandsscholarships.org.

Awards are arranged alphabetically below their administering organizations

7944 ■ Arthur H. Daniels Scholarships *(Undergraduate/Scholarship)*

Purpose: To encourage educational pursuits among Redlands Unified School District graduates by providing educational assistance. **Focus:** General studies/Field of study not specified. **Qualif.:** Applicant must be a graduating senior demonstrating good citizenship, academic accomplishment, contribution to school and community and the intention to attend a college/university on a full-time basis. **Criteria:** Awards are given based on merit.

Funds Avail.: $500. **To Apply:** Applicants must submit a completed application form together with the scantron sheet; cover sheet; student activity and community activity sheets; personal essay; and a copy of unofficial transcript (signed by the counselor). **Remarks:** No electronic submissions of application will be accepted. Submit two printed copies of the application and use a No. 2 pencil on the scantron sheet.

7945 ■ Pat Dermargosian Memorial Scholarships *(Undergraduate/Scholarship)*

Purpose: To encourage educational pursuits among Redlands Unified School District graduates by providing educational assistance. **Focus:** General studies/Field of study not specified. **Qualif.:** Applicant must be a graduating senior whose parent has been actively involved in the PTA throughout his/her school years. **Criteria:** Award is given based on merit.

Funds Avail.: $300. **Number Awarded:** 1. **To Apply:** Applicant must submit a completed application form together with the scantron sheet; cover sheet; student activity and community activity sheets; and a copy of unofficial transcript (signed by the counselor). In addition, applicant must also submit an essay stating the effect of his/her parent's participation in school PTA. **Remarks:** No electronic submissions of application will be accepted. Submit two printed copies of the application and use a No. 2 pencil on the scantron sheet.

7946 ■ Optimist Club of Redlands - Virginia Elliott Scholarships *(Undergraduate/Scholarship)*

Purpose: To encourage educational pursuits among Redlands Unified School District graduates by providing educational assistance. **Focus:** General studies/Field of study not specified. **Qualif.:** Applicant must be a female graduating senior from Redlands High School who has a minimum 3.0 GPA, has a positive attitude, and involved in service to the community. **Criteria:** Selection shall be based on the aforementioned applicant's qualifications and compliance with the application details.

Funds Avail.: $2,000. **Duration:** Annual. **To Apply:** Applicant may visit the scholarship section of the bestowing organization's website for further information regarding the application details. **Deadline:** February 6. **Contact:** Redlands Community Scholarship Foundation, at the above address.

7947 ■ James Mackenzie Fallows Scholarships Honoring Gertrude Baccus *(Undergraduate/Scholarship)*

Purpose: To support students who produce the best piece of expository writing. **Focus:** General studies/Field of study not specified. **Qualif.:** Applicants must be students from Redlands High School who are about to write an essay, article, speech, or some other work of non-fiction designed to explore an idea or explain a situation with the clarity and logic that Mrs. Baccus insisted on from her students. **Criteria:** Scholarships will be given to students who will produce the best piece of expository writing.

Funds Avail.: $1,000. **Duration:** Annual. **To Apply:** Applicants must submit a completed application form together with the scantron sheet; cover sheet; student activity and community activity sheets; personal essay; and a copy of unofficial transcript (signed by the counselor). **Deadline:** February 6. **Contact:** Pam Bibo, Administrative Assistant, at admin@redlandsscholarships.org.

7948 ■ Arthur and Juna Fisher Memorial Track Scholarships *(Undergraduate/Scholarship)*

Purpose: To encourage educational pursuits among Redlands Unified School District graduates by providing educational assistance. **Focus:** General studies/Field of study not specified. **Qualif.:** Applicant must be a graduating senior who has been active in track activities for at least two years and has maintained a 3.0 or better GPA. **Criteria:** Award is given based on merit.

Funds Avail.: $500. **Number Awarded:** 1. **To Apply:** Applicant must submit a completed form together with the scantron sheet; cover sheet; student activity and community activity sheets; personal essay; and a copy of unofficial transcript (signed by the counselor). **Remarks:** No electronic submissions of application will be accepted. Submit two printed copies of the application and use a No. 2 pencil on the scantron sheet.

7949 ■ Franklin Elementary School PTA Scholarships *(Undergraduate/Scholarship)*

Purpose: To encourage educational pursuits among Redlands Unified School District graduates by providing educational assistance. **Focus:** General studies/Field of study not specified. **Qualif.:** Applicants must be students who attended Franklin Elementary School and have extensive volunteer service in both school and community. **Criteria:** Recipients will be selected based on academic standing and financial need.

Funds Avail.: $600. **Number Awarded:** 1. **To Apply:** Applicants must submit a completed application form together with the scantron sheet; cover sheet; student activity and community activity sheets; personal essay; and a copy of unofficial transcript (signed by the counselor). **Remarks:** No electronic submissions of application will be accepted. Submit two printed copies of the application and use a No. 2 pencil on the scantron sheet.

7950 ■ Gail Garner R.I.S.E. Memorial Scholarships *(Undergraduate/Scholarship)*

Purpose: To encourage educational pursuits among Redlands Unified School District graduates by providing educational assistance. **Focus:** General studies/Field of study not specified. **Qualif.:** Applicant must be a student graduating through the Redlands Independent Study Education (R.I.S.E.) program. **Criteria:** Award is given based on merit.

Funds Avail.: $500. **To Apply:** Applicants must submit a completed application form together with the scantron sheet; cover sheet; student activity and community activity sheets; personal essay; and a copy of unofficial transcript (signed by the counselor). **Remarks:** No electronic submissions of application will be accepted. Submit two printed copies of the application and use a No. 2 pencil on the scantron sheet.

Awards are arranged alphabetically below their administering organizations

7951 ■ Ann and Brad Glassco Scholarships
(Undergraduate/Scholarship)

Purpose: To encourage educational pursuits among Redlands Unified School District graduates by providing educational assistance. **Focus:** General studies/Field of study not specified. **Qualif.:** Applicant must be a student who has performed in at least two acts in the YMCA's Great "Y" Circus in junior or senior year of high school. Student must have a 2.75 GPA or better. **Criteria:** Award is given based on merit.

Funds Avail.: $500. **Number Awarded:** 1. **To Apply:** Applicant must submit a completed application form together with the scantron sheet; cover sheet; student activity and community activity sheets; personal essay; and a copy of unofficial transcript (signed by the counselor). **Remarks:** No electronic submissions of application will be accepted. Submit two printed copies of the application and use a No. 2 pencil on the scantron sheet.

7952 ■ Rachel Graham Memorial Scholarships
(Undergraduate/Scholarship)

Purpose: To encourage educational pursuits among Redlands Unified School District graduates by providing educational assistance. **Focus:** General studies/Field of study not specified. **Qualif.:** Applicants must be graduating seniors from Citrus Valley High School, Redlands eAcademy, Redlands East Valley High School, and Redlands High School who will attend a four-year college/university on a full-time basis; must also have maintained at least a 3.0 GPA; shown good citizenship; and participated in school and community activities. **Criteria:** Selection shall be based on merit.

Funds Avail.: $500 each. **Duration:** Annual. **Number Awarded:** Varies. **To Apply:** Applicant must submit a completed application form together with the scantron sheet; cover sheet; student activity and community activity sheets; personal essay; and a copy of unofficial transcript (signed by the counselor). **Deadline:** February 6. **Contact:** Redlands Community Scholarship Foundation, at the above address.

7953 ■ Guzkowski Family Scholarships
(Undergraduate/Scholarship)

Purpose: To support the continuing education of students who want to pursue further learning in the area of government and public policy. **Focus:** Political science; Public administration. **Qualif.:** Applicant must be a graduating student by the Guzkowski Family to recognize critical thinking in the area of government and public policy. **Criteria:** Selection shall be based on the aforementioned applicants' qualifications and compliance with the application details.

Funds Avail.: $600 each. **Duration:** Annual. **Number Awarded:** Varies. **To Apply:** Applicant must submit a 500-word essay that demonstrates an appreciation for and understanding of objective analysis and some of the problems and challenges confronting contemporary society, as well as the role that can be played by government through rational public policy in addressing these issues. Applicant should include the information required by the scholarship using the specific essay listed on the Directory Page. (RCSF web pages 28 through 34). **Deadline:** February 6. **Contact:** Redlands Community Scholarship Foundation, at the above address.

7954 ■ William T. Hartzell Memorial Scholarships
(Undergraduate/Scholarship)

Purpose: To assist outstanding students to obtain further education. **Focus:** General studies/Field of study not specified. **Qualif.:** Applicant must be a graduating student from Orangewood High School or Redlands High School. **Criteria:** Selection shall be based on the aforementioned applicant's qualifications and compliance with the application details. Preference will be given to a student who has participated in school or community activities.

Funds Avail.: $500. **Duration:** Annual. **To Apply:** Applicant may visit the scholarship section of the bestowing organization's website for further information regarding the application details. **Deadline:** February 6. **Remarks:** The scholarship is in memory of William T. Hartzell, a lifetime resident of Redlands who was very active in community affairs. **Contact:** Redlands Community Scholarship Foundation, at the above address.

7955 ■ R. Garn Haycock Memorial Scholarships
(Undergraduate/Scholarship)

Purpose: To encourage educational pursuits among Redlands Unified School District graduates by providing educational assistance. **Focus:** General studies/Field of study not specified. **Qualif.:** Applicant must be a deserving senior who displays good citizenship, character and academic potential; must demonstrate a need for financial assistance and is intending to attend an institution of higher learning on a full-time basis. **Criteria:** Selection shall be based on the aforementioned applicant's qualifications and compliance with the application details.

Funds Avail.: $1,000. **Duration:** Annual. **To Apply:** Applicant may visit the scholarship section of the bestowing organization's website for further information regarding the application details. **Contact:** Redlands Community Scholarship Foundation, at the above address.

7956 ■ Eric L. Jacobson Memorial Scholarships
(Undergraduate/Scholarship)

Purpose: To encourage educational pursuits among Redlands Unified School District graduates by providing educational assistance. **Focus:** General studies/Field of study not specified. **Qualif.:** Applicant must be a graduating student from Redlands High School who has maintained a 3.0 or higher GPA, has participated on the speech or debate team for at least two years (one of which must be the senior year), and plans to attend a four-year college or university on a full-time basis. **Criteria:** Selection shall be based on the aforementioned applicant's qualifications and compliance with the application details. Additional consideration will be given to a student who demonstrates a variety of interests and performs service to school and community.

Funds Avail.: $1,000. **Duration:** Annual. **To Apply:** Applicant may visit the scholarship section of the bestowing organization's website for further information regarding the application details. **Deadline:** February 6. **Contact:** Redlands Community Scholarship Foundation, at the above address.

7957 ■ Brian Jimenez Memorial Scholarships
(Undergraduate/Scholarship)

Purpose: To assist male baseball or soccer athletes planning to take criminal law or criminal justice studies. **Focus:** Criminal justice. **Qualif.:** Applicant must be a senior male from Redlands High School who has participated in baseball or soccer, has a GPA of 2.5 or higher, and is intending to attend an institution of higher learning on a full-time basis. **Criteria:** Preference is given to a student who plans to major in criminal justice or criminal law. Applicant should also demonstrate a love of family, be a strong but quiet role model, be respected by peers, and be goal-oriented in his tasks.

Awards are arranged alphabetically below their administering organizations

Funds Avail.: $500. **Duration:** Annual. **To Apply:** Applicant may visit the scholarship section of the bestowing organization's website for further information regarding the application details. **Deadline:** February 6. **Contact:** Redlands Community Scholarship Foundation, at the above address.

7958 ■ Redlands Council PTA - Dorathy Jolley Memorial Scholarships (Undergraduate/Scholarship)

Purpose: To assist graduate seniors in their pursuit of higher education. **Focus:** General studies/Field of study not specified. **Qualif.:** Applicants must be graduating students from Citrus Valley High School, Orangewood High School, Redlands East Valley High School, and/or Redlands High School who have a minimum 3.0 GPA and are active in a non-school service group such as church, scouts, or a community service club. **Criteria:** Selection shall be based on the aforementioned applicants' qualifications and compliance with the application details.

Funds Avail.: $400 each. **Duration:** Annual. **Number Awarded:** Varies. **To Apply:** Applicants may visit the scholarship section of the bestowing organization's website for further information regarding the application details. **Deadline:** February 6. **Contact:** Redlands Community Scholarship Foundation, at the above address.

7959 ■ Annette and Ernest Keith Scholarships (Undergraduate/Scholarship)

Purpose: To support the continuing education of an exceptional student who wishes to study at California. **Focus:** General studies/Field of study not specified. **Qualif.:** Applicant must be a graduating student from Citrus Valley High School, Redlands eAcademy, Redlands East Valley High School, and/or Redlands High School who is in the top ten percent (10%) of the class and will be attending a four-year California college or university on a full-time basis. **Criteria:** Selection shall be based on the aforementioned applicant's qualifications and compliance with the application details.

Funds Avail.: $500 each. **Duration:** Annual. **Number Awarded:** Varies. **To Apply:** Applicant may visit the scholarship section of the bestowing organization's website for further information regarding the application details. **Deadline:** February 6. **Contact:** Redlands Community Scholarship Foundation, at the above address.

7960 ■ Kimberly Elementary School PTA Scholarships (Undergraduate/Scholarship)

Purpose: To encourage those who attended Kimberly Elementary School to continue learning. **Focus:** General studies/Field of study not specified. **Qualif.:** Applicants must be graduating students from Citrus Valley High School, Redlands eAcademy, Redlands East Valley High School, and/or Redlands High School who attended Kimberly Elementary School for a minimum of three years, are average or above-average achievers, demonstrate good citizenship, and preferably have not received other scholarships. **Criteria:** Selection shall be based on the aforementioned applicant's qualifications and compliance with the application details.

Funds Avail.: $300 each. **Duration:** Annual. **To Apply:** Applicants may visit the scholarship section of the bestowing organization's website for further information regarding the application details. **Deadline:** February 6. **Contact:** Redlands Community Scholarship Foundation, at the above address.

7961 ■ Kingsbury Elementary School PTA Scholarships (Undergraduate/Scholarship)

Purpose: To encourage those who attended Kingsbury Elementary School to continue learning. **Focus:** General studies/Field of study not specified. **Qualif.:** Applicants must be students from Redlands East Valley High School, and/or Redlands High School who attended Kingsbury Elementary School for at least three years, have a minimum of a C average, and have demonstrated good citizenship and leadership. **Criteria:** Selection shall be based on the following grounds: students' financial need, and involvement in extracurricular and community activities.

Funds Avail.: $350 each. **Duration:** Annual. **Number Awarded:** Varies. **To Apply:** Applicants may visit the scholarship section of the bestowing organization's website for further information regarding the application details. **Contact:** Redlands Community Scholarship Foundation, at the above address.

7962 ■ Kiwanis Club of Redlands Foundation Academic Excellence Scholarships (Undergraduate/Scholarship)

Purpose: To encourage educational pursuits among Redlands Unified School District graduates by providing educational assistance. **Focus:** General studies/Field of study not specified. **Qualif.:** Applicant must be a graduating senior with good citizenship, extracurricular activity involvement and demonstrated leadership abilities. **Criteria:** Recipients will be selected through an interview process conducted by the Kiwanis Club Foundation scholarship committee.

Funds Avail.: $6,000. **Duration:** Up to 4 years. **To Apply:** Applicant must submit a completed application form together with the scantron sheet; cover sheet; student activity and community activity sheets; personal essay; and a copy of unofficial transcript (signed by the counselor). **Remarks:** No electronic submissions of application will be accepted. Submit two printed copies of the application and use a No. 2 pencil on the scantron sheet.

7963 ■ Friends and Family of Christopher J. Kohlmeier Scholarships (Undergraduate/Scholarship)

Purpose: To support students who are interested in a career in law enforcement or firefighting. **Focus:** Fires and fire prevention; Law enforcement. **Qualif.:** Applicants must be graduating students from Citrus Valley High School who plan to attend a two-year or four-year college or university and who have strong test scores, but whose C average in high school could easily have been higher. **Criteria:** Preference will be given to students who are interested in a career in law enforcement or firefighting.

Funds Avail.: $750. **Duration:** Annual. **To Apply:** Applicants may visit the scholarship section of the bestowing organization's website for further information regarding the application details. **Deadline:** February 6. **Contact:** Redlands Community Scholarship Foundation, at the above address.

7964 ■ Doreen Legg Memorial Scholarships (Undergraduate/Scholarship)

Purpose: To encourage educational pursuits among Redlands Unified School District graduates by providing educational assistance. **Focus:** Business; Teaching. **Qualif.:** Applicants must be graduating seniors from Citrus Valley High School, Redlands eAcademy, Redlands East Valley High School, and/or Redlands High School who will

Awards are arranged alphabetically below their administering organizations

enroll full-time at a four-year college or university pursuing a business or teaching career. **Criteria:** Preference will be given to those who have a minimum 3.0 GPA and attended a RUSD High School for three consecutive years.

Funds Avail.: $500 each. **Duration:** Annual. **Number Awarded:** Varies. **To Apply:** Applicants may visit the scholarship section of the bestowing organization's website for further information regarding the application details. **Deadline:** February 6. **Contact:** Redlands Community Scholarship Foundation, at the above address.

7965 ■ PCH Architects/Steven J. Lehnhof Memorial Architectural Scholarships (Undergraduate/ Scholarship)

Purpose: To encourage those who want to study architecture or architectural engineering at an accredited college or university. **Focus:** Architecture; Engineering, Architectural. **Qualif.:** Applicants must be graduating seniors from Citrus Valley High School, Redlands East Valley High School, and/or Redlands High School who will be majoring in architecture or architectural engineering at an accredited college or university. **Criteria:** Selection shall be based on the aforementioned applicants' qualifications and compliance with the application details.

Funds Avail.: $500 each. **Duration:** Annual. **Number Awarded:** Varies. **To Apply:** Applicants may visit the scholarship section of the bestowing organization's website for further information regarding the application details. **Deadline:** February 6. **Remarks:** The scholarship is awarded in memory of Steven J. Lehnhof, an architecture and drafting teacher at Redlands High School for many years. **Contact:** Redlands Community Scholarship Foundation, at the above address.

7966 ■ Jack A. and Louise S. Levine Memorial Scholarships (Undergraduate/Scholarship)

Purpose: To support the continuing education of those students from the Redlands Unified School District. **Focus:** General studies/Field of study not specified. **Qualif.:** Applicants must be graduating seniors from Citrus Valley High School, Redlands eAcademy, Redlands East Valley High School, and/or Redlands High School who plan to continue their education, have 3.0 or higher GPA, demonstrate good citizenship, and have participated in school and/or community activities. **Criteria:** Selection shall be based on the aforementioned applicants' qualifications and compliance with the application details.

Funds Avail.: $500. **Duration:** Annual. **Number Awarded:** 1. **To Apply:** Applicants may visit the scholarship section of the bestowing organization's website for further information regarding the application details. **Contact:** Redlands Community Scholarship Foundation, at the above address.

7967 ■ Lugonia Alumni/Harrison Lightfoot Scholarships (Undergraduate/Scholarship)

Purpose: To support the continuing education of those students from the Redlands Unified School District. **Focus:** General studies/Field of study not specified. **Qualif.:** Applicants must be graduating seniors from Citrus Valley High School, Redlands eAcademy, Orangewood High School, and/or Redlands High School who attended Lugonia Elementary School. **Criteria:** Selection shall be based on the following criteria: students must have extensive community service and/or be involved in school activities, demonstrate good citizenship, and have a GPA of 2.5 or higher.

Funds Avail.: $1,500 each. **Duration:** Annual. **Number**

Awarded: Varies. **To Apply:** Applicants may visit the scholarship section of the bestowing organization's website for further information regarding the application details. **Deadline:** February 6. **Contact:** Redlands Community Scholarship Foundation, at the above address.

7968 ■ James Mackenzie Fallows Scholarships Honoring William Cunningham (Undergraduate/ Scholarship)

Purpose: To provide scholarship to those students who are in need to achieve their educational goal. **Focus:** Public service. **Qualif.:** Applicants must be students from Redlands High School who show great promise for public service in their career. Public service could include teaching, medical care, religious or volunteer work, or other expressions of the use of private talent for the public good. **Criteria:** Selection will be based on the qualifications and compliance with the application process.

Funds Avail.: $1,000. **Duration:** Annual. **To Apply:** Applicants must submit a completed application form together with the scantron sheet; cover sheet; student activity and community activity sheets; personal essay; and a copy of unofficial transcript (signed by the counselor). **Deadline:** February 6. **Contact:** Pam Bibo, Administrative Assistant, at admin@redlandsscholarships.org.

7969 ■ Optimist Club Of Redlands - Ralph Maloof Scholarships (Undergraduate/Scholarship)

Purpose: To encourage educational pursuits among Redlands Unified School District graduates by providing educational assistance. **Focus:** General studies/Field of study not specified. **Qualif.:** Applicant must be a male graduating senior from Redlands High School who has a minimum 3.0 GPA, has a positive attitude, and involved in service to the community. **Criteria:** Selection shall be based on the aforementioned applicant's qualifications and compliance with the application details.

Funds Avail.: $2,000. **Duration:** Annual. **To Apply:** Applicant may visit the scholarship section of the bestowing organization's website for further information regarding the application details. **Deadline:** February 6. **Contact:** Redlands Community Scholarship Foundation, at the above address.

7970 ■ Mariposa Elementary School PTA Scholarships (Undergraduate/Scholarship)

Purpose: To assist those students who attended Mariposa Elementary School and want to earn degrees in their desired university. **Focus:** General studies/Field of study not specified. **Qualif.:** Applicants must be graduating seniors from Redlands East Valley High School, and/or Redlands High School who attended Mariposa Elementary School for at least three years, pursuing education at a four-year university and show academic excellence with a minimum 3.5 GPA as well as community service. **Criteria:** Preference will be given to those who meet the criteria and demonstrate financial need.

Funds Avail.: $750 each. **Number Awarded:** Varies. **To Apply:** Applicants may visit the scholarship section of the bestowing organization's website for further information regarding the application details. **Deadline:** February 6. **Contact:** Redlands Community Scholarship Foundation, at the above address.

7971 ■ McKinley Elementary School PTA Scholarships (Undergraduate/Scholarship)

Purpose: To support the continuing education of those students from the Redlands Unified School District. **Focus:**

Awards are arranged alphabetically below their administering organizations

General studies/Field of study not specified. **Qualif.:** Applicant must be a graduating senior who attended McKinley Elementary School for at least three years and plans to attend a college, university, or vocational school. **Criteria:** Selection shall be based on the aforementioned applicant's qualifications and compliance with the application details.

Funds Avail.: $300. **Duration:** Annual. **To Apply:** Applicant may visit the scholarship section of the bestowing organization's website for further information regarding the application details. **Contact:** Redlands Community Scholarship Foundation, at the above address.

7972 ■ Benchwarmers of Redlands-Jess Mercado Football Scholarships *(Undergraduate/Scholarship)*

Purpose: To encourage educational pursuits among Redlands Unified School District graduates by providing educational assistance. **Focus:** General studies/Field of study not specified. **Qualif.:** Applicant must be a three-year member of the Terrier football team who has been a starter for at least one year, exhibits good citizenship, with dedication and has an eligible GPA. **Criteria:** Award is given based on merit.

Funds Avail.: $500. **To Apply:** Applicant must submit a completed application form together with the scantron sheet; cover sheet; student activity and community activity sheets; personal essay; and a copy of unofficial transcript (signed by the counselor). **Remarks:** No electronic submissions of application will be accepted. Submit two printed copies of the application and use a No. 2 pencil on the scantron sheet.

7973 ■ Dorothy Mitchell Scholarships *(Undergraduate/Scholarship)*

Purpose: To assist a graduating senior from Redlands High School who plans to enter the teaching profession. **Focus:** General studies/Field of study not specified. **Qualif.:** Applicant must be a graduating senior from Redlands High School who plans to enter the teaching profession. **Criteria:** Selection shall be based on the aforementioned applicant's qualifications and compliance with the application details.

Funds Avail.: $500. **Duration:** Annual. **To Apply:** Applicant may visit the scholarship section of the bestowing organization's website for further information regarding the application details. **Contact:** Redlands Community Scholarship Foundation, at the above address.

7974 ■ Moore Middle School PTA Scholarships *(Undergraduate/Scholarship)*

Purpose: To support those who attended Moore Middle School for three years and have plan to attend college or a trade school. **Focus:** General studies/Field of study not specified. **Qualif.:** Applicant must be a graduating senior from Citrus Valley High School, Redlands East Valley High School, and/or Redlands High School who attended Moore Middle School for three years and plans to attend college or a trade school. **Criteria:** Selection shall be based on the aforementioned applicant's qualifications and compliance with the application details.

Funds Avail.: $300 each. **Duration:** Annual. **Number Awarded:** Varies. **To Apply:** Applicant may visit the scholarship section of the bestowing organization's website for further information regarding the application details. **Deadline:** February 6. **Contact:** Redlands Community Scholarship Foundation, at the above address.

7975 ■ Robert L. Morlan Redlands Area Interfaith Council Scholarships *(Undergraduate/Scholarship)*

Purpose: To encourage educational pursuits among Redlands Unified School District graduates by providing educational assistance. **Focus:** General studies/Field of study not specified. **Qualif.:** Applicants must be graduating students from Citrus Valley High School, Orangewood High School, Redlands East Valley High School, and/or Redlands High School. **Criteria:** Selection shall be based on the aforementioned applicants' qualifications and compliance with the application details.

Funds Avail.: $300 each. **Duration:** Annual. **Number Awarded:** Varies. **To Apply:** Applicants must provide a one-page essay using the following prompt: How I Can Be an Agent of Peace. Applicants should include the information required by the scholarship using the specific essay listed on the Directory Page (RCSF web pages 28 through 34). **Deadline:** February 6. **Contact:** Redlands Community Scholarship Foundation, at the above address.

7976 ■ Harry Munoz Memorial Scholarships *(Undergraduate/Scholarship)*

Purpose: To provide scholarship to those students who are in need to achieve their educational goal. **Focus:** General studies/Field of study not specified. **Qualif.:** Applicants must be graduate students from Redlands East Valley High School and/or Redlands High School who have demonstrated academic achievement, outstanding citizenship and a desire to continue their education. **Criteria:** Scholarships will be given based on the stated qualifications.

Funds Avail.: $1,000. **Duration:** Annual. **Number Awarded:** Varies. **To Apply:** Applicants must submit a completed application form together with the scantron sheet; cover sheet; student activity and community activity sheets; personal essay; and a copy of unofficial transcript (signed by the counselor). **Deadline:** February 6. **Contact:** Pam Bibo, Administrative Assistant, at admin@ redlandsscholarships.org.

7977 ■ Rick Munoz Memorial Scholarships *(Undergraduate/Scholarship)*

Purpose: To support Redlands Unified School District graduates with their educational pursuit. **Focus:** General studies/Field of study not specified. **Qualif.:** Applicant must be a graduating senior from Citrus Valley High School, Redlands East Valley High School, and/or Redlands High School. **Criteria:** Selection shall be based on the aforementioned applicant's qualifications and compliance with the application details.

Funds Avail.: $500 each. **Duration:** Annual. **Number Awarded:** Varies. **To Apply:** Applicant may visit the scholarship section of the bestowing organization's website for further information regarding the application details. **Deadline:** February 6. **Contact:** Redlands Community Scholarship Foundation, at the above address.

7978 ■ Kiwanis Club of Redlands Foundation - Martin and Dorothy Munz Scholarships *(Undergraduate/Scholarship)*

Purpose: To assist graduate seniors in their pursuit of higher education. **Focus:** General studies/Field of study not specified. **Qualif.:** Applicants must be graduating seniors from Redlands High School. **Criteria:** Selection shall be based on the aforementioned applicant's qualifications and compliance with the application details.

Funds Avail.: $1,250. **Duration:** Annual. **Number Awarded:** 1. **To Apply:** Applicants may visit the scholarship section of the bestowing organization's website for further information regarding the application details. **Deadline:** February 6. **Contact:** Redlands Community Scholar-

Awards are arranged alphabetically below their administering organizations

ship Foundation, at the above address.

7979 ■ Jack Nagasaka Memorial Scholarships
(Undergraduate/Scholarship)

Purpose: To support and encourage those graduating high school students who are outstanding in the field of math or science. **Focus:** General studies/Field of study not specified. **Qualif.:** Applicant must be a graduating senior from Redlands High School who is outstanding in the field of math or science. **Criteria:** Selection shall be based on grades and achievement test scores in chemistry, physics and/or math.

Funds Avail.: $300. **Duration:** Annual. **To Apply:** Applicants may visit the scholarship section of the bestowing organization's website for further information regarding the application details. **Contact:** Redlands Community Scholarship Foundation, at the above address.

7980 ■ Robyn Nance Memorial Scholarships
(Undergraduate/Scholarship)

Purpose: To support the continuing education of those who are active in dramatic arts. **Focus:** General studies/Field of study not specified. **Qualif.:** Applicants must be graduating seniors from Redlands High School who are active in dramatic arts, have utilized their talents to the utmost, display love and enthusiasm for the theater, and participate whenever and wherever needed. **Criteria:** Selection shall be based on the aforementioned applicants' qualifications and compliance with the application details.

Funds Avail.: $500. **Duration:** Annual. **To Apply:** Applicants may visit the scholarship section of the bestowing organization's website for further information regarding the application details. **Deadline:** February 6. **Contact:** Redlands Community Scholarship Foundation, at the above address.

7981 ■ Mike Niemeyer Memorial Football Scholarships
(Undergraduate/Scholarship)

Purpose: To encourage graduating senior students, who are also members of the H.S. football team, to continue their education. **Focus:** Athletics; General studies/Field of study not specified. **Qualif.:** Applicants must be graduating seniors from Redlands High School who are members of the Redlands High School Terrier football team. **Criteria:** Preference will be given to those who are able to demonstrate high academic achievement and good citizenship, as well as those offensive or defensive linemen.

Funds Avail.: $500. **Duration:** Annual. **To Apply:** Applicants may visit the scholarship section of the bestowing organization's website for further information regarding the application details. **Deadline:** February 6. **Contact:** Redlands Community Scholarship Foundation, at the above address.

7982 ■ Marshall Phelps Athletic Memorial Scholarships
(Undergraduate/Scholarship)

Purpose: To encourage educational pursuits among Redlands Unified School District graduates by providing educational assistance. **Focus:** General studies/Field of study not specified. **Qualif.:** Applicants must be graduating male or female from Redlands High School with proven athletic ability and interest in a career involving some phase of athletics, such as sports medicine, coaching, or physical therapy. **Criteria:** Selection will be based upon high school counselors' recommendations.

Funds Avail.: $1,000. **Duration:** Annual. **To Apply:** Ap-

plicants may visit the scholarship section of the bestowing organization's website for further information regarding the application details. **Deadline:** February 6. **Contact:** Redlands Community Scholarship Foundation, at the above address.

7983 ■ Professional Women of Redlands, PoWeR to Continue Learning Scholarships
(Undergraduate/Scholarship)

Purpose: To support women in obtaining their continuing education. **Focus:** General studies/Field of study not specified. **Qualif.:** Applicant must be a graduating young woman from any of the Redlands Unified Schools, except Redlands eAcademy; must have a minimum 2.5 GPA; must have participated in at least one school activity; must have demonstrated some type of community service; and must be planning to attend a two-year or four-year college or a vocational program. **Criteria:** Preference is given to a student who will be the first in her family to obtain a college degree or professional-level training.

Funds Avail.: $1,000 each. **Duration:** Annual. **Number Awarded:** Varies. **To Apply:** Applicant must submit a short essay that attached on the topic "Describe an adversity you have faced and overcome." Applicants should include the information required by the scholarship using the specific essay listed on the Directory Page. (RCSF web pages 28 through 34). **Deadline:** February 6. **Contact:** Redlands Community Scholarship Foundation, at the above address.

7984 ■ Redlands Baseball/Softball for Youth Scholarship
(Undergraduate/Scholarship)

Purpose: To support the continuing education of those who have participated in the Redlands Baseball/Softball for Youth program for a given period of time. **Focus:** General studies/Field of study not specified. **Qualif.:** Applicants must be graduating seniors from Citrus Valley High School, Orangewood High School, Redlands East Valley High School, and Redlands High School who have participated in the Redlands Baseball/Softball for Youth program (including score keepers and/or umpires) for a minimum of three years and have exemplified good sportsmanship and academic achievement. **Criteria:** Selection shall be based on the aforementioned applicants' qualifications and compliance with the application details.

Funds Avail.: $350 each. **Duration:** Annual. **Number Awarded:** Varies. **To Apply:** Applications must include a 200 word essay entitled "How Redlands Baseball/Softball for Youth Has Impacted My Life." Indicate how many years and in what capacity applicants participated (i.e.: Player, Umpire, Scorekeeper). Applicants should include the information required by the scholarship using the specific essay listed on the Directory Page. (RCSF web pages 28 through 34). **Deadline:** February 6. **Contact:** Redlands Community Scholarship Foundation, at the above address.

7985 ■ Redlands Community Scholarship Foundation Awards
(Undergraduate/Scholarship)

Purpose: To assist graduate seniors in their pursuit of higher education. **Focus:** General studies/Field of study not specified. **Qualif.:** Applicant must be graduating senior students from Citrus Valley High School, Redlands eAcademy, Redlands East Valley High School, and/or Redlands High School. **Criteria:** Selection shall be based on the aforementioned applicants' qualifications and compliance with the application details.

Funds Avail.: $500 each. **Duration:** Annual. **Number Awarded:** Varies. **To Apply:** Applicants may visit the

Awards are arranged alphabetically below their administering organizations

scholarship section of the bestowing organization's website for further information regarding the application details. **Deadline:** February 6. **Remarks:** Redlands Community Scholarship Foundation, at the above address.

7986 ■ Redlands High School Academic Decathlon Scholarships (Undergraduate/Scholarship)

Purpose: To assist outstanding seniors who have participated in Academic Decathlon, in their pursuit of higher education. **Focus:** General studies/Field of study not specified. **Qualif.:** Applicants must be outstanding seniors from Redlands High School who participated in the Academic Decathlon program for a minimum of three years, have played on the varsity team at least one year and whose performances have contributed to a successful program. **Criteria:** Selection shall be based on the aforementioned applicants' qualifications and compliance with the application details.

Funds Avail.: $400 each person. **Duration:** Annual. **Number Awarded:** 2 from each high schools. **To Apply:** Applicants may visit the scholarship section of the bestowing organization's website for further information regarding the application details. **Deadline:** February 6. **Contact:** Redlands Community Scholarship Foundation, at the above address.

7987 ■ Redlands High School Boy's Varsity Volleyball Scholarships (Undergraduate/Scholarship)

Purpose: To assist graduate male seniors who are members of the Varsity Volleyball team in their pursuit of higher education. **Focus:** Athletics; General studies/Field of study not specified. **Qualif.:** Applicants must be graduating male seniors from Redlands High School who are members of the Varsity Volleyball team. **Criteria:** Selection shall be based on the aforementioned applicants' qualifications and compliance with the application details.

Funds Avail.: $300 each. **Duration:** Annual. **Number Awarded:** Varies. **To Apply:** Applicants may visit the scholarship section of the bestowing organization's website for further information regarding the application details. **Deadline:** February 6. **Contact:** Redlands Community Scholarship Foundation, at the above address.

7988 ■ Redlands High School Drama Boosters Awards (Undergraduate/Scholarship)

Purpose: To encourage educational pursuits among Redlands Unified School District graduates by providing educational assistance. **Focus:** Performing arts. **Qualif.:** Applicant must be a graduating senior pursuing a performing arts degree in college. **Criteria:** Award is given based on merit.

Funds Avail.: $200. **Number Awarded:** 1. **To Apply:** Applicant must submit: a completed application form together with the scantron sheet; cover sheet; student activity and community activity sheets; personal essay; and a copy of unofficial transcript (signed by the counselor). **Remarks:** No electronic submissions of application will be accepted. Submit two printed copies of the application and use a No. 2 pencil on the scantron sheet.

7989 ■ Redlands High School Girls' Volleyball Boosters Scholarship Awards (Undergraduate/Scholarship)

Purpose: To encourage educational pursuits among Redlands Unified School District graduates by providing educational assistance. **Focus:** General studies/Field of study not specified. **Qualif.:** Applicant must be a graduating senior volleyball player with good academic standing and citizenship; must be a dedicated team player; and must have positive leadership skills and a positive attitude. **Criteria:** Award is given based on the application.

Funds Avail.: No specific amount. **To Apply:** Applicant must submit a completed application form together with the scantron sheet; cover sheet; student activity and community activity sheets; personal essay; and a copy of unofficial transcript (signed by the counselor). **Remarks:** No electronic submissions of application will be accepted. Submit two printed copies of the application and use a No. 2 pencil on the scantron sheet.

7990 ■ Redlands High School Mock Trial Scholarships (Undergraduate/Scholarship)

Purpose: To assist graduate seniors who are also members of Mock Trial team in their pursuit of higher education. **Focus:** General studies/Field of study not specified. **Qualif.:** Applicants must be graduating seniors from Redlands High School and members of the RHS Mock Trial team (either Varsity or Junior Varsity) whose performances have contributed to a successful program. **Criteria:** Selection shall be based on the aforementioned applicants' qualifications and compliance with the application details.

Funds Avail.: $300 each. **Duration:** Annual. **Number Awarded:** 3. **To Apply:** Applicants may visit the scholarship section of the bestowing organization's website for further information regarding the application details. **Deadline:** February 6. **Contact:** Redlands Community Scholarship Foundation, at the above address.

7991 ■ Redlands High School-PTSA Scholarships (Undergraduate/Scholarship)

Purpose: To assist graduate seniors in their pursuit of higher education. **Focus:** General studies/Field of study not specified. **Qualif.:** Applicants must be graduating seniors from Redlands High School pursuing careers in a vocational field and who have a 2.0 or higher GPA. Also eligible are graduating seniors with a 3.0 or higher GPA who plan to pursue careers in a four-year college. **Criteria:** Selection shall be based on the premises that students must demonstrate good citizenship, a high work capacity, and service to school and/or community. PTSA membership is a "strong" consideration.

Funds Avail.: $400 each. **Number Awarded:** Varies. **To Apply:** Applicants may visit the scholarship section of the bestowing organization's website for further information regarding the application details. **Deadline:** February 6. **Contact:** Redlands Community Scholarship Foundation, at the above address.

7992 ■ Redlands High School Softball Booster Scholarship Awards (Undergraduate/Scholarship)

Purpose: To encourage educational pursuits among Redlands Unified School District graduates by providing educational assistance. **Focus:** General studies/Field of study not specified. **Qualif.:** Applicants must be graduating seniors who have earned a varsity letter in senior year and who have a minimum 3.25 weighted GPA. **Criteria:** Award is given based on the application.

Funds Avail.: $300. **To Apply:** Applicants must submit a completed application form together with the scantron sheet; cover sheet; student activity and community activity sheets; personal essay; and a copy of unofficial transcript (signed by the counselor). **Deadline:** February 1.

Awards are arranged alphabetically below their administering organizations

7993 ■ Redlands High School Spiritleaders Scholarships (Undergraduate/Scholarship)

Purpose: To encourage educational pursuits among Redlands Unified School District graduates by providing educational assistance. **Focus:** General studies/Field of study not specified. **Qualif.:** Applicant must be a graduating senior who has been in Spiritleaders for a minimum of two years. **Criteria:** Awards are given based on GPA.

Funds Avail.: $300. **To Apply:** Applicant must submit a completed application form together with the scantron sheet; cover sheet; student activity and community activity sheets; personal essay; and a copy of unofficial transcript (signed by the counselor). **Remarks:** No electronic submissions of application will be accepted. Submit two printed copies of the application and use a No. 2 pencil on the scantron sheet.

7994 ■ Redlands High School Terrier Band Boosters Club Scholarships (Undergraduate/Scholarship)

Purpose: To encourage educational pursuits among Redlands Unified School District graduates by providing educational assistance. **Focus:** Music. **Qualif.:** Applicant must be a graduating senior who participated in the Redlands High School instrumental music program and plans to continue with instrumental music in some capacity (not necessarily majoring in music). **Criteria:** Award is given based on the application.

Funds Avail.: $250. **To Apply:** Applicant must submit a completed application form together with the scantron sheet; cover sheet; student activity and community activity sheets; personal essay; and a copy of unofficial transcript (signed by the counselor).

7995 ■ Redlands High School Vocal Music Boosters Scholarship Awards (Undergraduate/Scholarship)

Purpose: To encourage educational pursuits among Redlands Unified School District graduates by providing educational assistance. **Focus:** Music. **Qualif.:** Applicant must be a graduating senior who has participated in the Redlands High School choral program and plans to continue with music in some capacity. **Criteria:** Awards are given based on the application.

Funds Avail.: $500 and $400. **To Apply:** Applicant must submit a completed application form together with the scantron sheet; cover sheet; student activity and community activity sheets; personal essay; and a copy of unofficial transcript (signed by the counselor). **Remarks:** No electronic submissions of application will be accepted. Submit two printed copies of the application and use a No. 2 pencil on the scantron sheet.

7996 ■ Redlands Morning Kiwanis Club Foundation Scholarships (Undergraduate/Scholarship)

Purpose: To help a deserving graduate pursue his or her training beyond high school. **Focus:** General studies/Field of study not specified. **Qualif.:** Applicants must be graduating seniors from Redlands East Valley High School; must have at least a 3.0 GPA; and must be planning to attend an accredited college, university, or vocational program. **Criteria:** Preference is given to those who were members of Kiwanis Key Club.

Funds Avail.: $300 each. **Duration:** Annual. **Number Awarded:** 3. **To Apply:** Applicants may visit the scholarship section of the bestowing organization's website for further information regarding the application details. **Deadline:** February 6. **Contact:** Redlands Community Scholarship Foundation, at the above address.

7997 ■ Redlands Rotary Club Foundation Discretionary Scholarships (Undergraduate/Scholarship)

Purpose: To assist outstanding students who are pursuing a higher education at a two-year or four-year college. **Focus:** General studies/Field of study not specified. **Qualif.:** Applicants must be graduating seniors from either Citrus Valley High School, Orangewood High School, Redlands East Valley High School and/or Redlands High School pursuing higher education at a two- or four-year college. **Criteria:** Recipients will be selected through an interview process conducted by the Redlands Rotary Club scholarship committee.

Funds Avail.: $500 each. **Duration:** Annual. **Number Awarded:** Varies. **To Apply:** Applicants must submit a completed application form together with the scantron sheet; cover sheet; student activity and community activity sheets; personal essay; and a copy of unofficial transcript (signed by the counselor). **Deadline:** February 6. **Contact:** Pam Bibo, Administrative Assistant, at admin@redlandsscholarships.org.

7998 ■ Redlands Teachers Association Scholarships (Undergraduate/Scholarship)

Purpose: To provide scholarship to graduating seniors who are committed to the profession of teaching. **Focus:** Teaching. **Qualif.:** Applicants must be graduating seniors from either Citrus Valley High School, Orangewood High School, Redlands East Valley High School and/or Redlands High School who are committed to the profession of teaching. **Criteria:** Selection will be based on the premises that the prospect recipients must be in good standing scholastically and have good citizenship. Consideration will be given to qualified children with Redland Teachers Association affiliations.

Funds Avail.: $500 each. **Duration:** Annual. **Number Awarded:** Varies. **To Apply:** Applicants must submit a completed application form together with the scantron sheet; cover sheet; student activity and community activity sheets; personal essay; and a copy of unofficial transcript (signed by the counselor). **Deadline:** February 6. **Contact:** Pam Bibo, Administrative Assistant, at admin@redlandsscholarships.org.

7999 ■ Smiley Elementary School PTA - Beverly Roberts Memorial Scholarships (Undergraduate/Scholarship)

Purpose: To provide scholarship to those students who are in need to achieve their educational goal. **Focus:** General studies/Field of study not specified. **Qualif.:** Applicants must be graduating seniors from Redlands High School who attended Smiley Elementary School and are well-rounded students. **Criteria:** Primary considerations for the selection of recipients are the qualifications stated above, and financial need.

Funds Avail.: $500 each. **Duration:** Annual. **Number Awarded:** 2. **To Apply:** Applicants must submit a completed application form together with the scantron sheet; cover sheet; student activity and community activity sheets; personal essay; and a copy of unofficial transcript (signed by the counselor). **Deadline:** February 6. **Contact:** Pam Bibo, Administrative Assistant, at admin@redlandsscholarships.org.

Awards are arranged alphabetically below their administering organizations

8000 ■ Charles and Ruth Ronin Memorial Scholarships (Undergraduate/Scholarship)

Purpose: To provide scholarship to those students who are in need to achieve their educational goal. **Focus:** Education; History; Political science. **Qualif.:** Applicants must be graduating seniors from Redlands High School with a 3.5 or higher GPA who are going to attend a four-year college/university on a full-time basis in pursuit of a bachelor's degree in political science, history, or education. **Criteria:** Primary considerations for the selection of recipients are the qualifications stated above, and financial need.

Funds Avail.: $1,000. **Duration:** Annual. **Number Awarded:** Varies. **To Apply:** Applicants must submit a completed application form together with the scantron sheet; cover sheet; student activity and community activity sheets; personal essay; and a copy of unofficial transcript (signed by the counselor). **Deadline:** February 6. **Contact:** Pam Bibo, Administrative Assistant, at admin@redlandsscholarships.org.

8001 ■ Michael A. Russo Memorial Scholarships (Undergraduate/Scholarship)

Purpose: To support students who are planning to pursue a career in a medical or medically-allied profession or career. **Focus:** Medicine. **Qualif.:** Applicants must be graduating seniors from Redlands East Valley High School and/or Redlands High School who plan to pursue a career in a medical or medically-allied profession or career. **Criteria:** Selection will be based on the aforesaid qualifications and compliance with the application process.

Funds Avail.: $1,000. **Duration:** Annual. **Number Awarded:** 2. **To Apply:** Applicants must submit a completed application form together with the scantron sheet; cover sheet; student activity and community activity sheets; personal essay; and a copy of unofficial transcript (signed by the counselor). **Deadline:** February 6. **Contact:** Pam Bibo, Administrative Assistant, at admin@redlandsscholarships.org.

8002 ■ Schoolsfirst Federal Credit Union Scholarships (Undergraduate/Scholarship)

Purpose: To encourage educational pursuits among Redlands Unified School District graduates by providing educational assistance. **Focus:** General studies/Field of study not specified. **Qualif.:** Applicants must be high school seniors. **Criteria:** Award is given based on scholarship, participation in school and community activities, and school personnel recommendation.

Funds Avail.: $500. **To Apply:** Applicants must submit a completed application form together with the scantron sheet; cover sheet; student activity and community activity sheets; personal essay; and a copy of unofficial transcript (signed by the counselor). **Remarks:** No electronic submissions of application will be accepted. Submit two printed copies of the application and use a No. 2 pencil on the scantron sheet.

8003 ■ Felix R. Sepulveda Memorial Scholarships - Northside Booster Club (Undergraduate/Scholarship)

Purpose: To support students who have maintain a good academic average. **Focus:** Sports studies. **Qualif.:** Applicants must be graduating male or female senior athletes from Citrus Valley High School, Redlands East Valley High School, and/or Redlands High School who have maintained at least 2.5 GPA and participated in at least one sport. **Criteria:** Selection will be based on the aforesaid qualifica-

tions and compliance with the application process.

Funds Avail.: $500 each. **Duration:** Annual. **Number Awarded:** Varies. **To Apply:** Applicants must submit a completed application form together with the scantron sheet; cover sheet; student activity and community activity sheets; personal essay; and a copy of unofficial transcript (signed by the counselor). **Deadline:** February 6. **Contact:** Pam Bibo, Administrative Assistant, at admin@redlandsscholarships.org.

8004 ■ Soroptimist International of Redlands Scholarships (Undergraduate/Scholarship)

Purpose: To provide scholarship to those students who are in need to achieve their educational goal. **Focus:** General studies/Field of study not specified. **Qualif.:** Applicants must be outstanding graduating female seniors from Citrus Valley High School, Orangewood High School, Redlands East Valley High School and/or Redlands High School who have participated in the community service and will be attending an accredited four-year college or university, community college, or trade school in a full- or part-time basis. **Criteria:** Selection will be based on the applicants' eligibility.

Funds Avail.: $500 each. **Duration:** Annual. **Number Awarded:** Varies. **To Apply:** Applicants must submit a completed application form together with the scantron sheet; cover sheet; student activity and community activity sheets; personal essay; and a copy of unofficial transcript (signed by the counselor). **Deadline:** February 6. **Contact:** Pam Bibo, Administrative Assistant, at admin@redlandsscholarships.org.

8005 ■ Redlands Evening Lions Club - Barbara Westen Memorial Scholarships (Undergraduate/Scholarship)

Purpose: To help a deserving graduate pursue his or her training beyond high school. **Focus:** General studies/Field of study not specified. **Qualif.:** Applicant must be a graduating senior student from Citrus Valley High School, Orangewood High School, Redlands East Valley High School, and/or Redlands High School. **Criteria:** Preference is given to a student with a hearing or sight disability. Financial need is also considered.

Funds Avail.: $350 each. **Duration:** Annual. **Number Awarded:** Varies. **To Apply:** Applicants may visit the scholarship section of the bestowing organization's website for further information regarding the application details. **Deadline:** February 6. **Contact:** Redlands Community Scholarship Foundation, at the above address.

8006 ■ Redlands Footlighters, Inc. - Merle and Peggy Williams Scholarships (Undergraduate/Scholarship)

Purpose: To provide scholarship to those students who have made major contributions in theater. **Focus:** Theater arts. **Qualif.:** Applicants must be graduating seniors from Redlands High School who have made major contributions in theater, either as actors or as theater technicians, and intend to continue involvement in theater activities in the future. **Criteria:** Selection will be based on merit.

Funds Avail.: $1,000. **Duration:** Annual. **To Apply:** Applicants must submit a completed application form together with the scantron sheet; cover sheet; student activity and community activity sheets; personal essay; and a copy of unofficial transcript (signed by the counselor). **Deadline:** February 6. **Contact:** Pam Bibo, Administrative Assistant,

Awards are arranged alphabetically below their administering organizations

at admin@redlandsscholarships.org.

8007 ■ Reflex Sympathetic Dystrophy Syndrome Association (RSDSA)

99 Cherry St.
Milford, CT 06460
Ph: (203)877-3790
Fax: (203)882-8362
Free: 877-662-7737
E-mail: info@rsds.org
URL: www.rsds.org

8008 ■ RSDSA Research Grants *(Other/Grant)*

Purpose: To seek relevant research that will improve understanding and treatment of RSD/CRPS-1. **Focus:** Medicine; Muscular dystrophy. **Qualif.:** Applicants must be: health science professionals with interest in study and treatment of painful conditions; and, residents, fellows and Ph.D. holders who are under the direct sponsorship and supervision of a senior scientist or faculty member. **Criteria:** Recipients are selected based on a committee's review of the proposal.

Funds Avail.: No specific amount. **To Apply:** Applicants may visit the website to verify the application process and other pieces of information.

8009 ■ REFORMA: National Association to Promote Library and Information Services to Latinos and the Spanish-Speaking

PO Box 832
Anaheim, CA 92815-0832
E-mail: info@reforma.org
URL: www.reforma.org

8010 ■ REFORMA Scholarship Program *(Doctorate, Graduate, Other/Scholarship)*

Purpose: To encourage Spanish-speaking individuals to pursue or advance a career in library and information science. **Focus:** Library and archival sciences. **Qualif.:** Applicants must be U.S. citizens; must be Spanish-speaking; must be current or entering graduate library school students; and must show evidence of commitment to a career in librarianship. **Criteria:** Recipients are selected based on educational background, intellectual abilities and personal character.

Funds Avail.: $1,500. **Duration:** One academic year. **Number Awarded:** Varies. **To Apply:** Application materials are available at the website. Applicants must submit a completed application form together with official copies of college transcripts, resume and two letters of reference from professors, employers, librarians or other professionals. **Deadline:** March 15. **Contact:** REFORMA Scholarship Committee, Ramona Grijalva, Chair, 408 W Ohio St., Tucson, AZ 85714; Phone: 520-741-1762; E-mail: ramonagrijalva@yahoo.com.

8011 ■ Regions Financial Corp.

1900 5th Ave. N
Birmingham, AL 35203-2610
Ph: (205)944-1300
Free: 800-734-4667
URL: www.regions.com

8012 ■ Regions Riding Forward Scholarships Essay Contest *(Undergraduate/Scholarship)*

Purpose: To support the education of those who are inspired by the African-American individuals. **Focus:** General studies/Field of study not specified. **Qualif.:** Applicants must either be high school seniors or college students. High school seniors must be legal residents of either Alabama, Arkansas, Florida, Georgia, Iowa, Illinois, Indiana, Kentucky, Louisiana, Mississippi, Missouri, North Carolina, South Carolina, Tennessee, Texas or Virginia; 13 years old or older; enrolled in 12th grade in a public or private school (or home school) in one of the mentioned states; and have a minimum cumulative GPA of 2.0. College students must either be legal residents of or currently attending college or university located in the states mentioned; 16 years old or older; have at least one year (or 18 credit hours) remaining before graduation; and have a minimum cumulative GPA of 2.0. **Criteria:** Selection will be based on the aforesaid qualifications and compliance with the application process.

Funds Avail.: $5,000 each for high school seniors; $3,500 each for college students. **Number Awarded:** 32 (16 high school seniors; 16 college students). **To Apply:** Applicants must submit an essay (in 500 words or less) addressing how African-Americans have been inspirations in their lives, and discussing the contributions of African-American individuals who have served to inspire and motivate them. **Deadline:** February 26.

8013 ■ Registered Psychiatric Nurses Association of Saskatchewan (RPNAS)

2055 Lorne St.
Regina, SK, Canada S4P 2M4
Ph: (306)586-4617
Fax: (306)586-6000
URL: www.rpnas.com

8014 ■ RPNAS Baccalaureate Level Program Scholarships *(Undergraduate/Scholarship)*

Purpose: To provide financial assistance to qualified individuals who want to pursue their Baccalaureate degree in psychiatric nursing. **Focus:** Nursing, Psychiatric. **Qualif.:** Applicant must hold active practicing membership with the registered Psychiatric Nurses Association of Saskatchewan with at least five successive years of psychiatric nursing practice as a Registered Psychiatric Nurse immediately preceding the current membership year; must have made a significant contribution to the profession and/or the Association beyond the responsibilities of his/her job. **Criteria:** Recipient will be selected by the RPNAS Selection Committee.

Funds Avail.: $1,000. **Duration:** Annual. **Number Awarded:** 1. **To Apply:** Applicant must provide a proof of formal enrollment in a recognized, post-diploma program leading to a Baccalaureate related to psychiatric nursing; must provide a full course outline of the program; must complete the attached questionnaire. **Deadline:** May 1.

8015 ■ RPNAS Doctorate Level Program Scholarship *(Doctorate/Scholarship)*

Purpose: To provide financial assistance to qualified individuals who want to pursue their doctorate degree in psychiatric nursing. **Focus:** Nursing, Psychiatric. **Qualif.:** Applicant must hold active practicing membership with the registered Psychiatric Nurses Association of Saskatchewan, with at least five successive years of psychiatric nursing

Awards are arranged alphabetically below their administering organizations

practice as a Registered Psychiatric Nurse immediately preceding the current membership year; must have made a significant contribution to the profession and/or the Association beyond the responsibilities of his/her job. **Criteria:** Recipient will be selected by the RPNAS Selection Committee.

Funds Avail.: $2,000. **Duration:** Annual. **Number Awarded:** 1. **To Apply:** Applicant must provide a proof of formal enrollment in a recognized, doctorate level program leading to a doctorate degree; must provide an overview of how the doctorate will enhance the profession of psychiatric nursing (1,000-1,500 words, 4-6 pages); must provide a copy of his/her dissertation to RPNAS. **Deadline:** May 1.

8016 ■ RPNAS Master's Level Program Scholarship
(Graduate, Master's/Scholarship)

Purpose: To provide financial assistance to qualified individuals who want to pursue their Master's degree in psychiatric nursing. **Focus:** Nursing, Psychiatric. **Qualif.:** Applicant must hold active practicing membership with the registered Psychiatric Nurses Association of Saskatchewan with at least five successive years of psychiatric nursing practice as a Registered Psychiatric Nurse immediately preceding the current membership year; must have made a significant contribution to the profession and/or the Association beyond the responsibilities of his/her job. **Criteria:** Recipient will be selected by the RPNAS Selection Committee.

Funds Avail.: $1,000 each. **Duration:** Annual. **Number Awarded:** 2. **To Apply:** Applicant must provide proof of formal enrollment in a recognized, master level program leading to a Master's degree; must complete attached questionnaire; must have made a significant contribution to the profession and/or the Association beyond the responsibilities of his/her job; must provide a copy of his/her research proposal. **Deadline:** May 1.

8017 ■ Registry of Interpreters for the Deaf (RID)
333 Commerce St.
Alexandria, VA 22314
Ph: (703)838-0030
Fax: (703)838-0454
E-mail: ridinfo@rid.org
URL: www.rid.org

8018 ■ Elizabeth Benson Scholarship Awards
(Undergraduate/Scholarship)

Purpose: To provide financial assistance to members enrolled to ITP or IPP. **Focus:** Hearing and deafness. **Qualif.:** Applicants must have dual memberships; enrolled full-time or nine hours in an interpreter or transliterator program; must have completed at least one semester of ITP or IPP; have 3.0 GPA in ITP or IPP. **Criteria:** Awards are given based on credentials.

Funds Avail.: $500. **Duration:** Annual. **To Apply:** Applicants must submit a letter of interest or video specifying financial need; an application form (can be downloaded from the website); transcripts; three letters of recommendation (must be from an ITP or IPP chair, instructor and personal reference); copies of current RID and affiliate chapter membership card. **Deadline:** May 31.

8019 ■ Daniel H. Pokorny Memorial Scholarship Awards *(Undergraduate/Scholarship)*

Purpose: To provide financial assistance to members applying for certification. **Focus:** Hearing and deafness. **Qua-**

lif.: Applicant must be a member for least one year. **Criteria:** Awards are given based on the committee's votes, submitted application, supporting documents and financial need.

Funds Avail.: No specific amount. **Duration:** 12 months. **To Apply:** Applicant must send eight copies of the application form (can be downloaded from the website).

8020 ■ J.H. Stewart Reid Memorial Fellowship Trust
c/o Canadian Association of University Teachers
2705 Queensview Dr.
Ottawa, ON, Canada K2B 8K2
E-mail: stewartreid@caut.ca
URL: stewartreid.caut.ca

8021 ■ J.H. Stewart Reid Memorial Fellowship Trust
(Doctorate/Fellowship, Award)

Purpose: To support students registered in a doctoral program at a Canadian University. **Focus:** General studies/Field of study not specified. **Qualif.:** Applicants must be Canadian citizens; must be registered in a doctoral program at a Canadian University who have completed their comprehensive examinations or equivalent; must have their doctoral thesis proposal; must have a first-class academic records in a graduate program; and must not be awardees of scholarships exceeding $25,000. **Criteria:** Recipients will be selected based on submitted applications.

Funds Avail.: $5,000. **Duration:** Annual. **To Apply:** Applicants must complete the online application form and must contact the Trustees through postal service, electronic mail and telephone conference call.

8022 ■ Religion Newswriters Association (RNA)
30 Neff Annex
Columbia, MO 65211-2600
Ph: (573)882-9257
URL: www.rna.org

8023 ■ Lilly Scholarships in Religion for Journalists
(Other/Scholarship)

Purpose: To help journalists achieve excellence in writing and reporting in faith, values, ethics and spirituality in the news media. **Focus:** Journalism. **Qualif.:** Applicants must be full-time print and broadcast journalists in the U.S. and Canada. **Criteria:** Recipients are selected based on demonstrated interest in the field of journalism.

Funds Avail.: Up to $5,000. **To Apply:** Applicants may visit the website to verify the application process and other pieces of information. **Contact:** Amy Schiska at 573-355-5201, ext. 3 or email at schiska@rna.org.

8024 ■ Research Center for Alcoholic Liver and Pancreatic Diseases
1333 San Pablo St., MMR 4th Fl.
Los Angeles, CA 90089-9141
Ph: (323)442-5107
Fax: (323)442-3126
URL: keck.usc.edu/Research/Centers_and_Programs/
Research_Center_For_Alcoholic_Liver_and_Pancreatic-
_Disease.aspx

8025 ■ Lee Summer Student Fellowship
(Undergraduate, Master's/Fellowship)

Purpose: To provide hands-on research training for undergraduate and Master students with interest in the sci-

Awards are arranged alphabetically below their administering organizations

ences and exposure to laboratory medicine. **Focus:** Medical research. **Qualif.:** Candidates must be active undergraduate, Master's or medical students or lab volunteers while in transition to graduate or medical school.

Funds Avail.: Varies. **To Apply:** Project must be related to the pathogenesis of alcoholic liver or pancreatic diseases, cirrhosis or related biology. Interested candidates must submit the following: curriculum vitae; title of project; proposed project start and end dates; summary of project; mentor's contact information; mentor's mentorship confirmation. **Deadline:** May 29. **Remarks:** Established in 2001. **Contact:** Jennifer Griffith, MA, Administrator; email: griffitj@usc.edu.

8026 ■ Research Corporation for Science Advancement (RCSA)
4703 E Camp Lowell Dr., Ste. 201
Tucson, AZ 85712
Ph: (520)571-1111
Fax: (520)571-1119
E-mail: awards@rescorp.org
URL: www.rescorp.org

8027 ■ Cottrell Scholar Awards (CSA) *(Graduate, Advanced Professional, Professional development/Grant)*

Purpose: To provide funding for early career faculty in the physical sciences and related fields who are committed to excellence in both research and undergraduate teaching at U.S. research universities. **Focus:** Science. **Qualif.:** Applicants must be tenure-track faculty members at U.S. institutions whose primary appointment is in a Bachelor's and Ph.D.-granting department of astronomy, biochemistry, biophysics, chemistry, or physics, but not in a school of medicine or engineering. **Criteria:** Selection shall be based on the aforesaid qualifications and the respective research proposals of the applicants.

Funds Avail.: Up to $100,000. **Duration:** Annual. **To Apply:** Applicants may visit the program website for further information regarding the application process. **Deadline:** May 15 (pre-proposal); August 15 (proposal). **Remarks:** Established in 1994. **Contact:** Silvia Ronco at sronco@rescorp.org or Richard Wiener at rwiener@rescorp.org.

8028 ■ Research and Development Corporation, Newfoundland and Labrador
68 Portugal Cove Rd.
Saint John, NL, Canada A1B 2L9
Ph: (709)758-0913
E-mail: info@rdc.org
URL: www.rdc.org

8029 ■ Ocean Industries Student Research Awards *(Undergraduate, Graduate, Postdoctorate/Award)*

Purpose: To attract, retain and develop highly qualified people and the next generation of R&D leaders for Newfoundland and Labrador's ocean industries. **Focus:** Engineering; Science; Technology. **Qualif.:** Applicants must be full-time undergraduate students who are enrolled in a Newfoundland and Labrador college, institute or university; or full-time graduate students attending or planning to attend Memorial University of Newfoundland; must have a minimum 75% average in their last 20 courses completed. **Criteria:** Selection will be based on a competitive basis us-

ing the following criteria: academic achievement; technical merits of the research plan; relevance to Newfoundland and Labrador's ocean industries.

Funds Avail.: $5,000-$30,000. **To Apply:** Applicants must submit a PDF, scanned copy of a signed, completed RDC application form (which includes a defined research plan that is relevant to Newfoundland and Labrador's ocean industries; a detailed resume or curriculum vitae outlining their career interests, relevant academic and work experience and extracurricular activities. Applicants' referee must submit a PDF, scanned copy of one signed letter of reference from an academic or industry researcher. An official transcript of academic achievement over the previous 20 courses must be sent directly to the RDC. **Deadline:** February 19 - Master's and Doctoral; May 14 - Diploma and Bachelor's. **Contact:** application@rdc.org.

8030 ■ Resources for the Future (RFF)
1616 P St. NW
Washington, DC 20036
Ph: (202)328-5000
Fax: (202)939-3460
E-mail: rffpress@rff.org
URL: www.rff.org

8031 ■ Joseph L. Fisher Doctoral Dissertation Fellowships *(Graduate/Fellowship)*

Purpose: To support graduate students in the final year of their dissertation research. **Focus:** General studies/Field of study not specified. **Qualif.:** Applicants must be graduate students. **Criteria:** Recipients will be selected based on financial need.

Funds Avail.: $18,000. **Duration:** Annual. **Number Awarded:** 3 in 2014. **To Apply:** Applicants must submit a completed application form, cover letter, curriculum vitae, transcript of records, one-page abstract of the dissertation, 2,500 words technical summary of the dissertation, letter from the department chair or other university officials certifying the student's doctoral candidacy and two letters of recommendation from faculty members on the student's dissertation committee. **Deadline:** February 20. **Remarks:** Established in 1998. **Contact:** Phone: 202-328-5020; E-mail: fisher-award@rff.org.

8032 ■ Restaurant Association of Maryland Education Foundation (RAMEF)
6301 Hillside Ct.
Columbia, MD 21046
Ph: (410)290-6800
Free: 800-874-1313
URL: www.ramef.org

8033 ■ Letitia B. Carter Scholarships *(Undergraduate, Advanced Professional/Scholarship)*

Purpose: To support students in the restaurant and food service industry. **Focus:** Culinary arts; Food science and technology; Food service careers; Hotel, institutional, and restaurant management. **Qualif.:** Applicants must be Maryland residents; high school, college, corporate instructor/teacher or hospitality industry professionals. Applicants must be pursuing hospitality-related coursework; applicants must have applied to an RAMEF-recognized professional development program in hospitality or enrolled in a RAMEF-recognized food service/hospitality program.

Awards are arranged alphabetically below their administering organizations

Criteria: Recipients will be selected on a competitive basis. **Funds Avail.:** $500 to $2,000. **Duration:** Annual. **To Apply:** Applicants must complete the provided application form which can be downloaded from the program website. Such must be submitted together with the other prescribed requirements. Other procedures must also be followed and complied with. **Deadline:** April 15. **Contact:** LaDeana Wentzel, Executive Director, Restaurant Association of Maryland Education Foundation; Email: ladeana@ramef.org.

8034 ■ Marcia S. Harris Legacy Fund Scholarships
(Undergraduate, Advanced Professional/Scholarship)

Purpose: To support students in the restaurant and food service industry. **Focus:** Culinary arts; Food science and technology; Food service careers; Hotel, institutional, and restaurant management. **Qualif.:** Applicants must be Maryland residents; must be high school or college students, or high school or postsecondary instructors who teach culinary arts or hospitality management courses; must be enrolled in a postsecondary or professional development course; must be pursuing hospitality-related coursework in culinary arts, hospitality management or bartending academy programs. **Criteria:** Selection will be on a competitive basis. Preference will be given to those who possess the qualities of passion and dedication and have a strong desire to improve the foodservice industry through the personal pursuit of professionalism.

Funds Avail.: $500 to $2,000. **Duration:** Annual. **To Apply:** Applicants must complete the provided application form which can be downloaded from the program website. Such must be submitted together with the other prescribed requirements. Other procedures must also be followed and complied with. **Deadline:** April 15. **Contact:** LaDeana Wentzel, Executive Director, Restaurant Association of Maryland Education Foundation, at the above address. Email: LaDeana@ramef.org.

8035 ■ RAMEF/NRAEF Co-Branded Scholarships
(Undergraduate/Scholarship)

Purpose: To support students in the restaurant and food service industry. **Focus:** Culinary arts; Food science and technology; Food service careers; Hotel, institutional, and restaurant management. **Qualif.:** Applicants must be high school seniors in the State of Maryland and pursuing hospitality related coursework. **Criteria:** Recipients will be selected on a competitive basis.

Funds Avail.: $500 to $4,000. **Duration:** Annual. **To Apply:** Applicants must complete the provided application form which can be downloaded from the program website. Such must be submitted together with the other prescribed requirements. **Deadline:** April 15. **Contact:** LaDeana Wentzel, Executive Director, Restaurant Association of Maryland Education Foundation; Email: ladeana@ramef.org.

8036 ■ Retail Print Music Dealers Association (RPMDA)
14070 Proton Rd., Ste. 100
Dallas, TX 75244-3601
Ph: (972)233-9107
Fax: (972)490-4219
E-mail: office@printmusic.org
URL: printmusic.org

8037 ■ RPMDA/Ed Adams Memorial Scholarships
(Other/Scholarship)

Purpose: To encourage individuals working for print music retailers to further their education and professional develop-

ment by attending the annual RPMDA convention. **Focus:** Music. **Qualif.:** Applicants must: be currently working for an RPMDA member or associate member establishment; have worked for a minimum of 400 hours in the print music industry; and, exhibit a strong desire to continue to work in the print music industry. They must be under the age of 40. **Criteria:** Scholarship recipients will be selected by RPMDA based on college or high school records; financial need; honors; awards; community service; recommendations; personal qualifications; quality of essay from the applicant; and sponsoring company.

Funds Avail.: No specific amount. **Duration:** Annual. **To Apply:** Applicants must submit a completed RPMDA/Ed Adams Scholarship Award application; three letters of reference; a completed Employment Verification Form a Sponsoring RPDMA members or assistance member; SAT or ACT scores (optional); sponsor statement of endorsement (200 words); a (300-word) essay; and a photo (optional). **Deadline:** March 15. **Remarks:** In memory of Ed Adams, a man whose dedicated service to the print music industry touched lives across the United States.

8038 ■ Retired League Postmasters of the National League of Postmasters (RLP)
National League of Postmasters
1 Beltway Ctr.
5904 Richmond Hwy., Ste. 500
Alexandria, VA 22303-1864
Ph: (703)329-4550
Fax: (703)329-0466
E-mail: Information@Postmasters.og
URL: www.postmasters.org/membership/become

8039 ■ Retired League Postmasters Scholarship Program *(Undergraduate/Scholarship)*

Purpose: To provide financial assistance for the education of children or grandchildren of an active Postmasters or retired postmasters, who are members of the National League of Postmasters. **Focus:** General studies/Field of study not specified. **Qualif.:** Applicants must be high school graduates accepted as first year students, for fall admission to an accredited college, university or trade school; must have a 3.0 GPA over all or a 3.0 average for the last full year of high school; must be children or grandchildren of an active Postmaster or a Retired Postmaster, who are members of the National League of Postmasters. **Criteria:** Applicants will be evaluated based on academic performance by a certain committee for the program.

Funds Avail.: No specific amount. **Duration:** Annual. **To Apply:** Applicants must submit transcript of grades covering the most recent year of school and list of awards or community service during previous school terms. **Deadline:** May 30. **Contact:** H. Ray Boone, Scholarship Committee Chairman RLP, hrayboone@yahoo.com.

8040 ■ The Reymont Foundation
14 Hester St.
Hamilton, ON, Canada L9A 2N2
Ph: (905)574-9212
Fax: (905)574-9212
E-mail: president@reymontfoundation.com
URL: www.reymontfoundation.com

8041 ■ Dulemba Aleksander and Stefania Scholarship *(Undergraduate/Scholarship)*

Purpose: To provide financial support for Polish individuals in Canada who want to pursue their studies. **Focus:** Educa-

Awards are arranged alphabetically below their administering organizations

tion, Medical. **Qualif.:** Applicants must be students of Polish descent; must be either Canadian citizens or landed immigrants; must be registered in at least the second year of a recognized program at a post secondary institution; must be a medical student. **Criteria:** Applicants are selected based on the application materials.

Funds Avail.: No specific amount. **To Apply:** Applicants may apply to the scholarship committee or download an application form from the website. **Deadline:** October 17. **Contact:** Witold Jaroszewski; email: scholarship@ reymontfoundation.com.

8042 ■ Alex Blaski Memorial Scholarships
(Undergraduate/Scholarship)

Purpose: To provide financial support for Polish individuals in Canada who want to pursue their studies. **Focus:** General studies/Field of study not specified. **Qualif.:** Applicants must be students of Polish descent; must be either Canadian citizens or landed immigrants; must be registered in at least the second year of a recognized program at a post secondary institution; must be students from the Barrie area. **Criteria:** Applicants are selected based on the application materials.

Funds Avail.: No specific amount. **To Apply:** Applicants may apply to the scholarship committee or download an application form from the website. **Deadline:** October 17. **Contact:** Witold Jaroszewski; email: scholarship@ reymontfoundation.com.

8043 ■ Maria and Czeslaw Borek Scholarships
(Undergraduate/Scholarship)

Purpose: To provide financial support for Polish individuals in Canada who want to pursue their studies. **Focus:** General studies/Field of study not specified. **Qualif.:** Applicants must be students of Polish descent; must be either Canadian citizens or landed immigrants; must be registered in at least the second year of a recognized program at a post secondary institution; must be students from Durham/ Oshawa area. **Criteria:** Applicants are selected based on the application materials.

Funds Avail.: No specific amount. **To Apply:** Applicants may apply to the scholarship committee or download an application form from the website. **Deadline:** October 17. **Contact:** Applicants may submit their application form and other required documents electronically to scholarship@ reymontfoundation.com.

8044 ■ Julian Dobranowski Memorial Scholarships
(Undergraduate/Scholarship)

Purpose: To provide financial support for Polish individuals in Canada who want to pursue their studies. **Focus:** General studies/Field of study not specified. **Qualif.:** Applicants must be students of Polish descent; must be either Canadian citizens or landed immigrants; must be registered in at least the second year of a recognized program at a post secondary institution. **Criteria:** Applicants are selected based on the application materials.

Funds Avail.: No specific amount. **To Apply:** Applicants may apply to the scholarship committee or download an application form from the website. **Deadline:** October 17. **Contact:** Witold Jaroszewski; email: scholarship@ reymontfoundation.com.

8045 ■ Franciszek Gadzala Memorial Scholarships
(Undergraduate/Scholarship)

Purpose: To provide financial support for Polish individuals in Canada who want to pursue their studies. **Focus:** His-

tory. **Qualif.:** Applicants must be from the University of Toronto Polish history faculty students; must be born in Canada; must be registered in at least the second year of a recognized program at a post secondary institution. **Criteria:** Applicants are selected based on the application materials.

Funds Avail.: No specific amount. **To Apply:** Applicants may apply to the scholarship committee or download an application form from the website. **Deadline:** October 17. **Contact:** Witold Jaroszewski; email: scholarship@ reymontfoundation.com.

8046 ■ Franciszek Glogowski Memorial Scholarships *(Undergraduate/Scholarship)*

Purpose: To provide financial support for Polish individuals in Canada who want to pursue their studies. **Focus:** General studies/Field of study not specified. **Qualif.:** Applicants must be students of Polish descent; must be either Canadian citizens or landed immigrants; must be registered in at least the second year of a recognized program at a post secondary institution. **Criteria:** Applicants are selected based on the application materials.

Funds Avail.: No specific amount. **To Apply:** Applicants may apply to the scholarship committee or download an application form from the website. **Deadline:** October 17. **Contact:** Witold Jaroszewski; email: scholarship@ reymontfoundation.com.

8047 ■ Drzymala Janusz and Roma Scholarship
(Undergraduate/Scholarship)

Purpose: To provide financial support for Polish individuals in Canada who want to pursue their studies. **Focus:** Engineering, Architectural; Science. **Qualif.:** Applicants must be students of Polish descent; must be either Canadian citizens or landed immigrants; must be registered in at least the second year of a recognized program at a post secondary institution; must be science and engineering students. **Criteria:** Applicants are selected based on the application materials.

Funds Avail.: No specific amount. **To Apply:** Applicants may apply to the scholarship committee or download an application form from the website. **Deadline:** October 17. **Contact:** Witold Jaroszewski; email: scholarship@ reymontfoundation.com.

8048 ■ Kazimiera Juchniewicz Memorial Scholarships *(Undergraduate/Scholarship)*

Purpose: To provide financial support for Polish individuals in Canada who want to pursue their studies. **Focus:** General studies/Field of study not specified. **Qualif.:** Applicants must be students of Polish descent; must be either Canadian citizens or landed immigrants; must be registered in at least the second year of a recognized program at a post secondary institution. **Criteria:** Applicants are selected based on the application materials.

Funds Avail.: No specific amount. **To Apply:** Applicants may apply to the scholarship committee or download an application form from the website. **Deadline:** October 17. **Contact:** Witold Jaroszewski; email: scholarship@ reymontfoundation.com.

8049 ■ Stefan and Weronika Kacperski Memorial Scholarships *(Undergraduate/Scholarship)*

Purpose: To provide financial support for Polish individuals in Canada who want to pursue their studies. **Focus:** General studies/Field of study not specified. **Qualif.:** Applicants

Awards are arranged alphabetically below their administering organizations

must be students of Polish descent; must be either Canadian citizens or landed immigrants; must be registered in at least the second year of a recognized program at a post secondary institution. **Criteria:** Applicants are selected based on the application materials.

Funds Avail.: No specific amount. **To Apply:** Applicants may apply to the scholarship committee or download an application form from the website. **Deadline:** October 17. **Contact:** Witold Jaroszewski; email: scholarship@reymontfoundation.com.

8050 ■ Stefan and Janina Klimt Scholarships
(Undergraduate/Scholarship)

Purpose: To provide financial support for Polish individuals in Canada who want to pursue their studies. **Focus:** General studies/Field of study not specified. **Qualif.:** Applicants must be from Cambridge and other local areas; must be either Canadian citizens or landed immigrants; must be registered in at least the second year of a recognized program at a post secondary institution. **Criteria:** Applicants are selected based on the application materials.

Funds Avail.: No specific amount. **To Apply:** Applicants may apply to the scholarship committee or download an application form from the website. **Deadline:** October 17. **Contact:** Witold Jaroszewski; email: scholarship@reymontfoundation.com.

8051 ■ George Kokociński Memorial Scholarships
(Undergraduate/Scholarship)

Purpose: To provide financial support for Polish individuals in Canada who want to pursue their studies. **Focus:** General studies/Field of study not specified. **Qualif.:** Applicants must be students of Polish descent; must be either Canadian citizens or landed immigrants; must be registered in at least the second year of a recognized program at a post secondary institution. **Criteria:** Applicants are selected based on the application materials.

Funds Avail.: No specific amount. **To Apply:** Applicants may apply to the scholarship committee or download an application form from the website. **Deadline:** October 17. **Contact:** Witold Jaroszewski; email: scholarship@reymontfoundation.com.

8052 ■ Krawczyk-Krane Family Scholarships
(Undergraduate/Scholarship)

Purpose: To provide financial support for Polish individuals in Canada who want to pursue their studies. **Focus:** General studies/Field of study not specified. **Qualif.:** Applicants must be students of Polish descent; must be either Canadian citizens or landed immigrants; must be registered in at least the second year of a recognized program at a post secondary institution. **Criteria:** Applicants are selected based on the application materials.

Funds Avail.: No specific amount. **To Apply:** Applicants may apply to the scholarship committee or download an application form from the website. **Deadline:** October 17. **Contact:** Witold Jaroszewski; email: scholarship@reymontfoundation.com.

8053 ■ Jan Kuropas Memorial Scholarships
(Undergraduate/Scholarship)

Purpose: To provide financial support for Polish individuals in Canada who want to pursue their studies. **Focus:** General studies/Field of study not specified. **Qualif.:** Applicants must be open to students of Polish descent; must be either Canadian citizens or landed immigrants; must be registered

in at least the second year of a recognized program at a post secondary institution. **Criteria:** Applicants are selected based on the application materials.

Funds Avail.: No specific amount. **To Apply:** Applicants may apply to the scholarship committee or download an application form from the website. **Deadline:** October 17. **Contact:** Witold Jaroszewski; email: scholarship@reymontfoundation.com.

8054 ■ Tadeusz Maziarz Scholarships
(Undergraduate/Scholarship)

Purpose: To provide financial support for Polish individuals in Canada who want to pursue their studies. **Focus:** General studies/Field of study not specified. **Qualif.:** Applicants must be students of Polish descent; must be either Canadian citizens or landed immigrants; must be registered in at least the second year of a recognized program at a post secondary institution. **Criteria:** Applicants are selected based on the application materials.

Funds Avail.: No specific amount. **To Apply:** Applicants may apply to the scholarship committee or download an application form from the website. **Deadline:** October 17. **Contact:** Witold Jaroszewski; email: scholarship@reymontfoundation.com.

8055 ■ Bronislaw Michno Memorial Scholarships
(Undergraduate/Scholarship)

Purpose: To provide financial support for Polish individuals in Canada who want to pursue their studies. **Focus:** General studies/Field of study not specified. **Qualif.:** Applicants must be students of Polish descent; must be either Canadian citizens or landed immigrants; must be registered in at least the second year of a recognized program at a post secondary institution. **Criteria:** Applicants are selected based on the application materials.

Funds Avail.: No specific amount. **To Apply:** Applicants may apply to the scholarship committee or download an application form from the website. **Deadline:** October 17. **Contact:** Witold Jaroszewski; email: scholarship@reymontfoundation.com.

8056 ■ Marek Nawrot Memorial Scholarships
(Undergraduate/Scholarship)

Purpose: To provide financial support for Polish individuals in Canada who want to pursue their studies. **Focus:** Cartography/Surveying. **Qualif.:** Applicants must be York University students of geography or environment; must be either Canadian citizens or landed immigrants; must be registered in at least the second year of a recognized program at a post secondary institution. **Criteria:** Applicants are selected based on the application materials.

Funds Avail.: No specific amount. **To Apply:** Applicants may apply to the scholarship committee or download an application form from the website. **Deadline:** October 17. **Contact:** Witold Jaroszewski; email: scholarship@reymontfoundation.com.

8057 ■ Eleonora Pidperyhora Scholarship
(Undergraduate/Scholarship)

Purpose: To provide financial support for Polish individuals in Canada who want to pursue their studies. **Focus:** General studies/Field of study not specified. **Qualif.:** Applicants must be students of Polish descent; must be either Canadian citizens or landed immigrants; must be registered in at least the second year of a recognized program at a post secondary institution. **Criteria:** Applicants are selected

Awards are arranged alphabetically below their administering organizations

based on the application materials.

Funds Avail.: No specific amount. **To Apply:** Applicants may apply to the scholarship committee or download an application form from the website. **Deadline:** October 17. **Contact:** Witold Jaroszewski; email: scholarship@reymontfoundation.com.

8058 ■ Dr. Adolph Piotrowski Memorial Art Scholarships *(Undergraduate/Scholarship)*

Purpose: To provide financial support for Polish individuals in Canada who want to pursue their studies. **Focus:** Visual arts. **Qualif.:** Applicants must be paint and sculpture students; must be either Canadian citizens or landed immigrants; must be registered in at least the second year of a recognized program at a post secondary institution. **Criteria:** Applicants are selected based on the application materials.

Funds Avail.: No specific amount. **To Apply:** Applicants may apply to the scholarship committee or download an application form from the website. **Deadline:** October 17. **Contact:** Witold Jaroszewski; email: scholarship@reymontfoundation.com.

8059 ■ W. Reymont Scholarships *(Undergraduate/Scholarship)*

Purpose: To provide financial support for Polish individuals in Canada who want to pursue their studies. **Focus:** General studies/Field of study not specified. **Qualif.:** Applicants must be students of Polish descent; must be either Canadian citizens or landed immigrants; must be registered in at least the second year of a recognized program at a post secondary institution. **Criteria:** Applicants are selected based on the application materials.

Funds Avail.: No specific amount. **To Apply:** Applicants may apply to the scholarship committee or download an application form from the website. **Deadline:** October 17. **Contact:** Witold Jaroszewski; email: scholarship@reymontfoundation.com.

8060 ■ Chester & Maria Sadowski Memorial Scholarships *(Undergraduate/Scholarship)*

Purpose: To provide financial support for Polish individuals in Canada who want to pursue their studies. **Focus:** Science. **Qualif.:** Applicants must be female science students; must be either Canadian citizens or landed immigrants; must be registered in at least the second year of a recognized program at a post secondary institution. **Criteria:** Applicants are selected based on the application materials.

Funds Avail.: No specific amount. **To Apply:** Applicants may apply to the scholarship committee or download an application form from the website. **Deadline:** October 17. **Contact:** Witold Jaroszewski; email: scholarship@reymontfoundation.com.

8061 ■ Boleslaw & Irena Sobczak Scholarships *(Undergraduate/Scholarship)*

Purpose: To provide financial support for Polish individuals in Canada who want to pursue their studies. **Focus:** General studies/Field of study not specified. **Qualif.:** Applicants must be students of Polish descent; must be either Canadian citizens or landed immigrants; must be registered in at least the second year of a recognized program at a post secondary institution. **Criteria:** Applicants are selected based on the application materials.

Funds Avail.: No specific amount. **To Apply:** Applicants

may apply to the scholarship committee or download an application form from the website. **Deadline:** October 17. **Contact:** Witold Jaroszewski; email: scholarship@reymontfoundation.com.

8062 ■ Lasek Stanisław and Aniela Scholarship *(Undergraduate/Scholarship)*

Purpose: To provide financial support for Polish individuals in Canada who want to pursue their studies. **Focus:** General studies/Field of study not specified. **Qualif.:** Applicants must be students of Polish descent; must be either Canadian citizens or landed immigrants; must be registered in at least the second year of a recognized program at a post secondary institution. **Criteria:** Applicants are selected based on the application materials.

Funds Avail.: No specific amount. **To Apply:** Applicants may apply to the scholarship committee or download an application form from the website. **Deadline:** October 17. **Contact:** Witold Jaroszewski; email: scholarship@reymontfoundation.com.

8063 ■ Flis Walter and Anna Memorial Scholarship *(Undergraduate/Scholarship)*

Purpose: To provide financial support for Polish individuals in Canada who want to pursue their studies. **Focus:** General studies/Field of study not specified. **Qualif.:** Applicants must be students of Polish descent; must be either Canadian citizens or landed immigrants; must be registered in at least the second year of a recognized program at a post secondary institution. **Criteria:** Applicants are selected based on the application materials.

Funds Avail.: No specific amount. **To Apply:** Applicants may apply to the scholarship committee or download an application form from the website. **Deadline:** October 17. **Contact:** Witold Jaroszewski; email: scholarship@reymontfoundation.com.

8064 ■ Reynoldsburg-Pickerington Rotary Club
PO Box 1155
Reynoldsburg, OH 43068-6155
E-mail: info@rprotaryclub.com
URL: www.rprotaryclub.com

8065 ■ Reynoldsburg-Pickerington Rotary Club High School Scholarship *(Undergraduate/Scholarship)*

Purpose: To support graduating seniors at high schools in Reynoldsburg and Pickerington. **Focus:** General studies/Field of study not specified. **Qualif.:** Applicants must be graduating seniors in the Reynoldsburg or Pickerington high schools. **Criteria:** Selection will be based on the committee's criteria.

Funds Avail.: $10,000 (three $2,000 and two $2,000 to graduating high school students from Reynoldsburg HS and Pickerington HS, respectively). **Duration:** Annual. **Number Awarded:** 5. **To Apply:** Interested applicants may contact the Rotary Club of Reynoldsburg - Pickerington for the application process and other related information.

8066 ■ The Rho Chi Society
c/o UNC Eshelman School of Pharmacy
University of North Carolina
3210 Kerr Hall, CB 7569
Chapel Hill, NC 27599-7569
Ph: (919)843-9001

Awards are arranged alphabetically below their administering organizations

Fax: (919)962-0644
E-mail: rhochi@unc.edu
URL: www.rhochi.org

8067 ■ Rho Chi, AFPE First Year Graduate Fellowships (Doctorate, Graduate/Fellowship)

Purpose: To defray the cost in conducting student's research. **Focus:** Pharmacy. **Qualif.:** Applicants must be members of Rho Chi Honor Society; must be pharmacy students in their final year of professional studies or a professional pharmacy degree program; must be graduates entering pharmaceutical sciences or a PhD program in an accredited U.S. school or college of pharmacy as full-time students; must be U.S. citizens or permanent residents. **Criteria:** Applicants will be judged based on academic achievement.

Funds Avail.: $7,500. **Duration:** Annual. **Number Awarded:** 1. **To Apply:** Applicants must submit three letters of recommendation, and must provide on a separate sheet the detailed resume and brief narrative. Applicants may also submit supporting documents such as official transcripts from all colleges or universities attended; official record or photocopy of GRE scores and must provide names of those individuals who will provide letters of reference. **Deadline:** February 1.

8068 ■ Rho Chi Society Clinical Research Scholarships (Postdoctorate/Scholarship)

Purpose: To help post-doctoral members pursue their education. **Focus:** Pharmacy. **Qualif.:** Applicants must be clinical research fellows who have completed professional studies in an ACPE accredited school or college of pharmacy; must be members of the Rho Chi Honor Society; must be U.S. citizens or permanent residents. **Criteria:** Selection will be based on academic achievement.

Funds Avail.: $7,500. **Duration:** Annual. **To Apply:** Applicants must submit three letters of recommendation, narrative statement. On a separate sheet, applicants must provide the title, affiliation and abbreviated description of the fellowship program, curriculum vitae, maximum of two pages description of the research project and list of any research-related posters or platform presentations, published abstracts and/or published articles. Applicants may also submit supporting documents such as transcript of records, names of three individuals who will provide letters of reference/recommendation. Three copies each of completed application, supporting documents and letters of recommendation should be mailed. **Deadline:** February 1. **Contact:** The Rho Chi Society, C/O UNC School of Pharmacy, Attn: Clinical Research Scholarship Committee, at the above address.

8069 ■ Rhode Island Bar Association

41 Sharpe Dr.
Cranston, RI 02920
Ph: (401)421-5740
Fax: (401)421-2703
E-mail: info@ribar.com
URL: www.ribar.com

8070 ■ Thomas F. Black, Jr. Memorial Scholarships (Undergraduate/Scholarship)

Purpose: To provide financial assistance to aspiring lawyers who desire to continue their study at quality law schools. **Focus:** Law. **Qualif.:** Applicants must be Rhode Island residents; must be full-time students in programs leading to the award of the LLB or JD degree offered by law schools located in the United States and accredited by the American Bar Association. **Criteria:** Applicants will be selected based on financial need, academic performance, community and public service, and demonstrated contacts with and commitment to the State of Rhode Island.

Funds Avail.: $20,000. **Duration:** Annual. **Number Awarded:** 2. **To Apply:** Applicants must submit the completed application form together with their personal statement, official transcripts, SAR report from FAFSA, copies of their parents' tax return and two letter of recommendation. **Deadline:** March 23. **Remarks:** Established in 1989. **Contact:** Rhode Island Bar Association, at the above address.

8071 ■ Rhode Island Foundation

1 Union Sta.
Providence, RI 02903
Ph: (401)274-4564
E-mail: info@rifoundation.org
URL: www.rifoundation.org/Home.aspx

8072 ■ Bach Organ Scholarship (Undergraduate/ Scholarship)

Purpose: To provide financial assistance for promising music students to pursue their career. **Focus:** Education, Music. **Qualif.:** Applicant must be a Rhode Island resident enrolled in college as a music major; must be a church organist and an American Guild of Organists member; and must demonstrate financial need. **Criteria:** Selection will be based on financial need.

Funds Avail.: $800 - $1,000. **Duration:** Annual. **To Apply:** Applicant must complete the application form, available online; must submit one essay, recent high school or college transcript (music majors); must have a copy of their final Student Aid Report, financial aid award letter, and one recommendation from their organ/keyboard teacher or church official. Application forms and other supporting documents must be sent to Rhode Island Foundation. **Deadline:** April 24.

8073 ■ Antonio Cirino Memorial Art Education Fellowships (Undergraduate/Fellowship)

Purpose: To provide financial assistance for qualified individuals pursuing graduate education toward a master's or doctorate in order to pursue a teaching career in the arts. **Focus:** Arts. **Qualif.:** Applicant must be a Rhode Island resident; must be an artist pursuing graduate education toward a master's or doctorate in order to pursue a teaching career in the arts; must demonstrate financial need; and must have lived in Rhode Island for at least five years prior to applying for the award. **Criteria:** Preference will be given to visual art artists.

Funds Avail.: $2,000 - $12,000. **Duration:** Annual. **To Apply:** Application form and other supporting documents must be sent to Rhode Island Foundation. **Deadline:** May 1.

8074 ■ Constant Memorial Scholarship (Undergraduate/Scholarship)

Purpose: To provide support for deserving visual art or music major students intending to pursue their education. **Focus:** Education, Music; Visual arts. **Qualif.:** Applicants must be Aquidneck Island residents for at least three years; must demonstrate a serious interest in visual arts and/or

Awards are arranged alphabetically below their administering organizations

music; must have a proof of enrollment in an arts or music major at an accredited institution of higher education; and must be able to demonstrate financial need. **Criteria:** Selection of applicants will be based on the scholarship selection criteria.

Funds Avail.: $2,000 - $5,000. **Duration:** Annual. **To Apply:** Applicants must complete the application form, available online; must have a copy of their financial aid award letter; must submit a recent official college transcript; three proofs of Rhode Island residency; one essay; copy of their final Student Aid Report; one letter of recommendation; and a sample of work done within the last 12 months. Application forms and other supporting documents must be sent to Rhode Island Foundation. **Deadline:** April 24.

8075 ■ Edward Leon Duhamel Freemasons Scholarships (Undergraduate/Scholarship)

Purpose: To provide financial assistance to descendants of members of the Franklin Lodge of Freemasons in Wesley, RI. **Focus:** General studies/Field of study not specified. **Qualif.:** Applicants must be descendants of a member of Franklin Lodge in Wesley, Rhode Island, or descendants of other freemasons who are RI residents; must be able to demonstrate scholastic achievement and good citizenship; and must be enrolled in an accredited post-secondary institution. **Criteria:** Applicants will be selected based on the scholarship selection criteria. Preference will be given to prior year's recipients.

Funds Avail.: Range from $500 to $1,000. **Duration:** Annual. **To Apply:** Interested applicant may contact Edward Lowe for the application process and other information. **Contact:** Edward Lowe at ed01lowe@aol.com.

8076 ■ GFWC Women's Club of South County Scholarships (Undergraduate/Scholarship)

Purpose: To provide support for females living in Washington County who need financial assistance in order to pursue education or job training. **Focus:** General studies/Field of study not specified. **Qualif.:** Applicants must be women of 21 years of age and Washington County, Rhode Island residents who are able to obtain education or training of becoming self-supporting. **Criteria:** Preference will be given to highly motivated, low-income single women with children.

Funds Avail.: No specific amount. **Duration:** Annual. **To Apply:** Interested applicant may contact Daryl Anderson for the application process and other information. **Contact:** Daryl Anderson at ramptda@aol.com.

8077 ■ Rhode Island Commission on Women/Freda H. Goldman Education Awards (Undergraduate/Award)

Purpose: To provide support for individuals intending to pursue their education or job training. **Focus:** General studies/Field of study not specified. **Qualif.:** Applicants must be enrolled or registered in an educational or job skills training program; must be Rhode Island residents; and must be able to demonstrate financial need. **Criteria:** Preference will be given to highly motivated, self-supporting low-income women who are completing their first undergraduate degree or certificate program.

Funds Avail.: $500 - $2,000. **Duration:** Annual. **To Apply:** Applicants must complete the application form, available online; must have their financial aid award letter, a copy of their final Student Aid Report, one essay, most recent official academic transcript, letter of recommendation, and resume. Application forms and other supporting documents must be sent to Rhode Island Foundation. **Deadline:** May 15.

8078 ■ Rhode Island Association of Former Legislators Scholarships (Undergraduate/Scholarship)

Purpose: To provide financial assistance for promising students with a distinguished record of public services. **Focus:** General studies/Field of study not specified. **Qualif.:** Applicant must be a graduating high school senior and resident of Rhode Island; must have a history of substantial voluntary involvement in community service; must have been accepted into an accredited post-secondary institution; must be able to demonstrate financial need. **Criteria:** Selection of applicants will be based on Scholarship selection criteria.

Funds Avail.: $1,500. **Duration:** Annual. **Number Awarded:** 8. **To Apply:** Applicants must complete the application form, available online; must submit a copy of financial aid award letter, most recent official high school transcript, one letter of recommendation, one essay, and a copy of their final Student Aid Report. Application forms and other supporting documents must be sent to Rhode Island Foundation. **Remarks:** Established in 1996.

8079 ■ Lily and Catello Sorrentino Memorial Scholarships (Undergraduate/Scholarship)

Purpose: To encourage older students to return to undergraduate school for further education. **Focus:** General studies/Field of study not specified. **Qualif.:** Applicant must be a Rhode Island resident who is 25 years of age or older; must be attending any degree-conferring, non-parochial educational college or university within Rhode Island towards an undergraduate degree; must be able to demonstrate financial need; must not have any relationship with the Sorrentino family or the Rhode Island Foundation that can be construed in any way as influencing the fund's recommendation. **Criteria:** Selection of applicants will be based on the selection criteria. Preference will be given to first-time applicants

Funds Avail.: No specific amount. **Duration:** Annual. **To Apply:** Applicants must complete the application form, available online; must have a copy of their financial aid award letter, official transcript, one essay, copy of their final student aid report, and two letters of recommendation. Application form and other supporting documents must be sent to Rhode Island Foundation. **Deadline:** May 1.

8080 ■ Bruce and Marjorie Sundlun Scholarships (Undergraduate/Scholarship)

Purpose: To assist single parents in the pursuit of education beyond high school. **Focus:** General studies/Field of study not specified. **Qualif.:** Applicants must be single parents, either male or female, who are currently enrolled in a Rhode Island institution of higher learning or continuing education; must be Rhode Island residents and able to demonstrate financial need. **Criteria:** Preference will be given to applicants who are completing their first degree or certificate program.

Funds Avail.: $1,500. **Duration:** Annual. **To Apply:** Applicants must complete the application form, available online; must submit a copy of their financial aid award letter, and a recent official transcript; must prepare one essay; must have a copy of their final Student Aid Report and letter of recommendation. Application forms and other supporting documents must be sent to Rhode Island Foundation. **Deadline:** May 15.

Awards are arranged alphabetically below their administering organizations

8081 ■ Marilynne Graboys Wool Scholarships
(Undergraduate/Scholarship)

Purpose: To provide tuition support to women with financial need planning to attend graduate school to attain a law degree at an accredited institution. **Focus:** Law. **Qualif.:** Applicants must be females planning to attend or registered in an accredited law school; must be Rhode Island residents; must be accepted into an accredited law school; and must be able to demonstrate financial need. **Criteria:** Selection of applicants will be based on the scholarship selection criteria.

Funds Avail.: $2,000. **Duration:** Annual. **To Apply:** Applicants must complete the application form, available online; must have a copy of their financial aid award letter and a recent official transcript; and must provide one essay, a copy of their Student Aid Report, and letter of recommendation. Application forms and other supporting documents must be sent to Rhode Island Foundation. **Deadline:** June 5.

8082 ■ Rhode Island Student Loan Authority
560 Jefferson Blvd., Ste. 200
Warwick, RI 02886
Ph: (401)468-1700
Fax: (401)468-2196
Free: 800-758-7562
E-mail: info@risla.com
URL: www.risla.com

8083 ■ RISLA Student Loans *(Undergraduate, Graduate/Loan)*

Purpose: To cover the educational expenses of students attending eligible Rhode Island schools. **Focus:** General studies/Field of study not specified. **Qualif.:** Applicants must be Rhode Island residents attending eligible in-state schools or out-of-state schools and students from outside of Rhode Island who are attending eligible Rhode Island schools; must be either undergraduate or graduate students; must be full-time, half-time, less than half-time, matriculating or non-matriculating students. International students may apply if they have a social security number and cosigner that is a US citizen. **Criteria:** Selection will be based on credit check approval and other eligibility requirements.

Funds Avail.: Varies. **To Apply:** Interested applicants must visit the website for the online application process and to choose the loan term.

8084 ■ Bryon Riesch Paralysis Foundation (BRPF)
PO Box 1388
Waukesha, WI 53187-1388
Ph: (262)547-2083
E-mail: info@brpf.org
URL: www.brpf.org

8085 ■ Bryon Riesch Paralysis Foundation Research Grants *(Professional development/Grant)*

Purpose: To promote new and exciting research in the field of paralysis. **Focus:** Spinal cord injuries and research. **Qualif.:** Applicants must be American investigators located at institutions that have established lines of accountability and fiscal responsibility. The following area of research are of primary interest to the Bryon Riesch Paralysis Foundation: factors relating to re-myelination, axonal preservation or growth and cell differentiation that may lead to acute or chronic recovery in spinal cord injured individuals; drug therapies or other interventions that would limit secondary damage after a spinal cord injury; activities that investigate underlying problems associated with neurological disorders such as spasticity, chronic pain, bladder/bowel function or sexual function. **Criteria:** Selection will be based on the submitted applications.

Funds Avail.: No specific amount. **To Apply:** Applicants must submit an application in the following order: title of research; principal investigator; title (title and degrees of PI and co-investigator if applicable); principal investigator present appointment; signature of principal investigator; fiscal officer; contract officer; check payable to; personnel; equipment; animal and supplies; nontechnical abstract; key words; relationship to BROF priorities; narrative describing the specific objective of the project and hypothesis, the prior research/theory behind the project; the methods and experimental design; and equipment/facilities to be used. Applications must be maximum of five pages, single-space and 12 pt. font. Applicants must also include references. **Deadline:** December 19.

8086 ■ Rising Farmworker Dream Fund (RFDF)
9512 Rachel St.
Live Oak, CA 95953
E-mail: info@risingfarmworkers.org
URL: www.rfdf.org

8087 ■ RFDF MBA Preparation Fellowships *(Graduate, Undergraduate/Fellowship)*

Purpose: To encourage the sons and daughters of farmworkers to purse MBA degrees and in turn, develop more leaders who will channel resources to the U.S. farmworking community. **Focus:** Business. **Qualif.:** Applicant must be a son/daughter of a farmworker and/or has worked in the agricultural sector as a farm laborer for a minimum of five years and a junior or senior in college or a graduate student intending to pursue an MBA degree in the next 5 years. **Criteria:** Selection is based on the online application submitted by the applicants.

Funds Avail.: No specific amount. **To Apply:** Applicants must complete the application online.

8088 ■ RFDF Pre-MBA Fellowships *(Graduate/Fellowship)*

Purpose: To encourage the sons and daughters of farmworkers to purse MBA degrees and in turn, develop more leaders who will channel resources to the U.S. farmworking community. **Focus:** Business. **Qualif.:** Applicant must be a son/daughter of a farmworker and/or has worked in the agricultural sector as a farm laborer for a minimum of five years; willing to commit a minimum of 50 community service hours within the farm working community; and applying to a top business school. **Criteria:** Preference will be given to applicants of Top 30 business schools.

Funds Avail.: No specific amount. **To Apply:** Applicants must complete the application online.

8089 ■ Riverside Sheriffs Association (RSA)
6215 River Crest Dr., Ste. A
Riverside, CA 92507
Ph: (951)653-5152

Awards are arranged alphabetically below their administering organizations

Fax: (951)653-1943
Free: 800-655-4772
URL: www.rcdsa.org

8090 ■ Riverside Sheriffs Association Member Scholarship Program *(Graduate, Undergraduate/ Scholarship)*

Purpose: To assist members of the Riverside Sheriffs' Association (RSA) who have plans to continue their education in college or university. **Focus:** General studies/Field of study not specified. **Qualif.:** Applicants must be members of RSA; have earned at least an associate or equivalent degree; and must be accepted or plan to enroll in an undergraduate or graduate course of study on a full-time or part-time basis. **Criteria:** Awards will be given to applicants who meet the required qualifications.

Funds Avail.: $5,000. **Number Awarded:** 4. **To Apply:** Applicants must complete the application form and mail it along with a current transcript of grades. **Deadline:** March 31. **Contact:** Riverside Sheriffs' Association Member Scholarship Program, Scholarship Management Services, at the above address.

8091 ■ Roanoke Bar Association (RBA)

PO Box 18183
Roanoke, VA 24014
Ph: (540)342-4905
Fax: (540)342-1252
E-mail: roanokebar@earthlink.net
URL: roanokebar.com

8092 ■ James N. Kincanon Scholarships *(Undergraduate/Scholarship)*

Purpose: To provide financial assistance to those students who want to pursue legal education. **Focus:** Law. **Qualif.:** Applicants must: be residents of the City of Roanoke, the City of Salem, or the County of Roanoke, or graduates of a high school located in those jurisdictions; have a grade point average of at least 3.0 during high school (and college or law school, if applicable); and, be accepted, or expect to be accepted prior to the fall semester, into post-secondary training, pursuing education in the law. **Criteria:** Selection shall be based on demonstrated diligence in and commitment to studies, academic excellence and an interest in the pursuit of law.

Funds Avail.: No specific amount. **Duration:** Annual. **To Apply:** An original application, typewritten or completed in black ink, which must be postmarked no later than the deadline, and must be accompanied by the following: two letters of recommendation dated during the current school year, one of which must be from a teacher or instructor; a statement of 250 words or less on why the applicant has chosen to pursue an education in the law; and an official copy of the applicant's latest grade transcript (3.0 GPA minimum required). **Deadline:** March 31. **Remarks:** Established in 1997.

8093 ■ Robert Wood Johnson Foundation (RWJF)

College Rd. E, Rte. 1
Princeton, NJ 08543-2316
Free: 877-843-7953
E-mail: mail@rwjf.org
URL: www.rwjf.org

8094 ■ Robert Wood Johnson Clinical Scholarships *(Graduate, Professional development/Fellowship)*

Purpose: To integrate scholars' clinical expertise with training in program development and research methods to help them find solutions for the challenges posed by the U.S. health care system and the health of U.S. communities, as well as to augment clinical training of physicians by providing new skills and perspectives necessary to achieving leadership positions within and outside academia. **Focus:** Medical research. **Qualif.:** Applicants must be: U.S. Citizens or permanent residents who complete the clinical requirements of their residency training by the date of entry into the program; highly regarded by those responsible for their clinical training; and, committed to a career in academic medicine, public health, health policy or another career congruent with the program's purposes and priorities of developing physician leaders and skilled researchers. **Criteria:** Selection shall be based on the aforementioned applicants' qualifications and compliance with the application details.

Funds Avail.: No specific amount. **Duration:** Annual; up to two years. **Number Awarded:** Varies. **To Apply:** Applicants may visit the program website for further information regarding the application details. **Remarks:** Established in 1972. **Contact:** Robert Wood Johnson Foundation, at the above address.

8095 ■ Jackie Robinson Foundation (JRF)

One Hudson Sq.
75 Varick St., 2nd Fl.
New York, NY 10013-1917
Ph: (212)290-8600
Fax: (212)290-8081
E-mail: general@jackierobinson.org
URL: www.jackierobinson.org

8096 ■ Jackie Robinson Scholarships *(Undergraduate/Scholarship)*

Purpose: To financially support minority students in attaining higher educational pursuits. **Focus:** General studies/ Field of study not specified. **Qualif.:** Applicant must be a minority high school student showing leadership potential and demonstrating financial need to attend an accredited 4-year college or university. **Criteria:** Awards are given based on merit and need.

Funds Avail.: Up to $24,000. **Duration:** Up to 4 years. **To Apply:** Applicants must submit a letter of recommendation, official transcript (with raised seal), and SAT or ACT scores. **Deadline:** February 15. **Contact:** Infosnap, Inc., Email: customerservice@infosnap.com.

8097 ■ Rocky Mountain Coal Mining Institute (RMCMI)

3500 S Wadsworth Blvd., Ste. 211
Lakewood, CO 80235
Ph: (303)948-3300
Fax: (303)954-9004
URL: www.rmcmi.org

8098 ■ Rocky Mountain Coal Mining Institute Engineering/Geology Scholarships *(Undergraduate/ Scholarship)*

Purpose: To provide financial aid for junior and senior year students who are career-pathed in mining related industries.

Awards are arranged alphabetically below their administering organizations

Focus: Engineering; Engineering, Geological. **Qualif.:** Applicant must be a full-time college sophomore or junior at the time of selection; must be both a U.S. citizen and a legal resident of one of the Rocky Mountain Coal Mining Institute member states Arizona, Colorado, Montana, New Mexico, North Dakota, Texas, Utah, or Wyoming; pursuing a degree in a mining-related field or in the engineering disciplines; and must be interested in coal as a career path. **Criteria:** Recipients are selected based on Scholarship committee's review of the application materials.

Funds Avail.: $2,750 per year. **Duration:** Annual. **To Apply:** Applicants must submit a completed application form that can be downloaded from www.rmcmi.org. **Deadline:** February 1.

8099 ■ Rocky Mountain Coal Mining Institute Technical Scholarships (Undergraduate/Scholarship)

Purpose: To provide financial aid for students enrolled in technical programs who would like to pursue their education in the coal industry. **Focus:** Energy-related areas. **Qualif.:** Applicant must be a first-year student at a two-year Technical/Trade School in a good standing at the time of selection; both a U.S. citizen and a legal resident of one of the Rocky Mountain Coal Mining Institute member states - Arizona, Colorado, Montana, New Mexico, North Dakota, Texas, Utah, or Wyoming; studying an applicable trade; and interested in coal as a career path. **Criteria:** Recipients are selected based on the scholarship committee's review of the application materials.

Funds Avail.: $1,000. **Duration:** Annual. **To Apply:** Applicants must submit a completed application form downloadable from www.rmcmi.org. **Deadline:** February 1.

8100 ■ Rocky Mountain Mineral Law Foundation (RMMLF)

9191 Sheridan Blvd., Ste. 203
Westminster, CO 80031-3020
Ph: (303)321-8100
Fax: (303)321-7657
E-mail: info@rmmlf.org
URL: www.rmmlf.org

8101 ■ Joe Rudd Scholarships (Graduate/Scholarship)

Purpose: To encourage the study of natural resources law by well-qualified law students who have the potential to make significant contributions to scholarship in natural resources law. **Focus:** Law. **Qualif.:** Applicants must be a law student enrolled at one of the foundation's governing law schools and can demonstrate a commitment to study natural resources law. **Criteria:** Recipients are selected based on potential to make a significant contribution to the field of natural resources law, academic ability, leadership ability, year in law school and financial need.

Funds Avail.: $4,500-$15,000. **Duration:** Annual. **Number Awarded:** Varies. **To Apply:** Applicants must submit the requirements. **Deadline:** February 28 (JD Applicants); March 15 (LLM Applicants). **Remarks:** Established in 1979. **Contact:** Rocky Mountain Mineral Law Foundation; Phone: 303-321-8100 ext. 107; or scholarships@rmmlf.org.

8102 ■ Roofing Industry Alliance for Progress

c/o Rob McNamara, President
10255 W Higgins Rd., Ste. 600
Rosemont, IL 60018-5607

Fax: (847)493-7959
Free: 800-323-9545
URL: www.roofingindustryalliance.net

8103 ■ Melvin Kruger Endowed Scholarships (Graduate, Undergraduate/Scholarship)

Purpose: To assist individuals seeking to further their education to pursue careers in the roofing or building construction industries. **Focus:** Construction. **Qualif.:** Applicants must be dependents of full-time employees or spouses of NRCA contractor members or companies that have been NRCA members for at least one year; high school seniors or graduates or undergraduates who plan to enroll or students who are already enrolled full-time in a course of study in an accredited two- or four-year college/university or vocational school. **Criteria:** Awards are given based on academic record, potential to succeed, leadership and participation in school and community, honors, work experience, statement of educational and career goals and outside appraisal.

Funds Avail.: No specific amount. **Duration:** Annual. **To Apply:** Applicant must send a completed application form together with a transcript.

8104 ■ Roothbert Fund

475 Riverside Dr., Rm. 1622
New York, NY 10115
Ph: (212)870-3116
E-mail: mail@roothbertfund.org
URL: www.roothbertfund.org

8105 ■ Roothbert Fund Scholarships (Undergraduate/Scholarship)

Purpose: To provide financial assistance to both men and women who wants to further their education. **Focus:** General studies/Field of study not specified. **Qualif.:** Scholarship is open to all people in the United States regardless of sex, age, color, nationality or religious background. **Criteria:** Preference will be given to those who can satisfy high scholastic requirements and are considering careers in education.

Funds Avail.: $2,000-$3,000. **Duration:** Annual. **To Apply:** Applicants may obtain a copy of the current application form by submitting a written request with a stamped, self-addressed envelope to The Roothbert Fund, Inc., or may download a current copy of the form online. Applicants must include autobiographical essays, supporting transcripts and letters of recommendation.

8106 ■ Travis Roy Foundation

60 State St., 8th Fl.
Boston, MA 02109
Ph: (617)619-8257
E-mail: info@travisfoundation.org
URL: www.travisfoundation.org

8107 ■ Travis Roy Foundation Individual Grants (All/Grant)

Purpose: To provide assistance to spinal cord injury survivors. **Focus:** Spinal cord injuries and research. **Qualif.:** Applicants must be spinal cord injury survivors with paraplegia and quadriplegia; must demonstrate financial need and may be required to provide documentation; must be US residents. **Criteria:** Selection will be based on the committee's criteria.

Awards are arranged alphabetically below their administering organizations

Funds Avail.: No specific amount. **Duration:** Annual. **To Apply:** Applicants must complete all questions of the applications in order to be considered for a Travis Roy Foundation Individual Grant, including contact information and estimates from at least two suppliers and/or contractors for the equipment or renovations requested in the application. **Remarks:** Established in 1989. **Contact:** Travis Roy Foundation, at the above address.

8108 ■ Lucille and Edward R. Roybal Foundation
5253 E Beverly Blvd.
Los Angeles, CA 90022-2020
Ph: (323)725-3960
E-mail: dnevarez@roybalfoundation.org
URL: www.roybalfoundation.org

8109 ■ Lucille and Edward R. Roybal Foundation Public Health Scholarships *(Graduate, Undergraduate/Scholarship)*

Purpose: To support graduate and undergraduate Hispanic students pursuing degrees in public health related programs. **Focus:** Nursing; Optometry; Pharmacy; Public health. **Qualif.:** Applicants must be Hispanic students in their junior or senior year or in a graduate program of an accredited college or university in Pharmacy, Optometry, Nursing, or Public Health; must have a minimum GPA of 2.5. **Criteria:** Applicants will be selected based on their commitment to serve the interest on low-income Latino communities in the United States, and on financial need.

Funds Avail.: $5,000 for graduate students and $2,500 for undergraduate students. **Number Awarded:** 2. **To Apply:** Applicants must submit a completed application form available online; must provide two letters of recommendation, one from an academic source and another from a community leadership source, resume, and school transcript with current GPA. **Deadline:** May 14. **Contact:** Lucille and Edward R. Roybal Foundation, at the above address or Email: mgroybalfoundation@att.net.

8110 ■ Damon Runyon Cancer Research Foundation
1 Exchange Plz.
55 Broadway, Ste. 302
New York, NY 10006-3720
Ph: (212)455-0500
Free: 877-7CA-NCER
E-mail: info@damonrunyon.org
URL: www.damonrunyon.org

8111 ■ Damon Runyon Cancer Research Foundation Fellowships *(Doctorate, Graduate, Postdoctorate/ Fellowship)*

Purpose: To support the training of the brightest postdoctoral scientists as they embark upon their research careers. **Focus:** Medical research. **Qualif.:** Applicants must have completed one or more degrees or its equivalent: MD, PhD, MD/Phd, DDS, DVM (applicants must include a copy of their diploma to confirm date of conferral); application must be under the guidance of a Sponsor - a scientist (tenured, tenure-track or equivalent position); applicants who have already accepted a postdoctoral research fellowship award are not eligible. **Criteria:** Selection is based on the quality of the research proposal; qualifications, experience and productivity of both the candidate and the Sponsor; and the

quality of the research training environment in which the proposed research is to be conducted.

Funds Avail.: $50,000 to $60,000. **Duration:** Three years. **Number Awarded:** Varies. **To Apply:** Applicants must submit an application cover sheet with all required original signatures; the Sponsor's biographical sketch in NIH format and a list of current funding; sponsor's letter including: a)description of training plan for the candidate, b) track record of mentorship with list of graduate and postdoctoral fellows trained, c) percentage of proposal written by the candidate (numerical percentage); applicant's curriculum vitae, including a bibliography of all published works; a letter from the applicant describing his/her previous research and teaching experience (the letter must state that the applicant is committed to a career in cancer research); and the research proposal, which shall not exceed five pages of single-spaced 12-point type with at least 0.5 inch margins. **Deadline:** March 17 and August 15. **Contact:** awards@ damonrunyon.org.

8112 ■ Damon Runyon Clinical Investigator Awards *(Doctorate, Graduate, Postdoctorate/Fellowship, Award)*

Purpose: To increase the number of physicians capable of moving seamlessly between the laboratory and the patient's bedside in search of breakthrough treatments. **Focus:** Medical research. **Qualif.:** Applicants must be U.S. citizens or permanent legal residents; must be nominated by their institution; must have received an MD or MD/PhD degree(s) from an accredited institution and are board-eligible; must be committed to spending 80% of their time conducting research; must apply in conjunction with a mentor who is established in the field of clinical translational cancer research. **Criteria:** Recipients are chosen based on excellence of the applicant and the mentor; innovation, creativity, quality and originality of research proposal; commitment of the mentor and institution to the development and training of the applicant as an independent clinical research investigator; evidence of the applicant's commitment to clinical translational and/or cancer prevention research and their ability to apply these advances; importance of the proposed research; and adherence of the proposal to the definition of clinical research.

Funds Avail.: $450,000. **Duration:** Three years. **To Apply:** Applicants submit a curriculum vitae; cover sheet; At-a-Glance form; nomination letter from institution/department; applicant's letter and accomplishments; mentor's biographical sketch and letter of support; mentor's proposal training; applicant's research proposal; human subjects, radiation safety and environmental health issues statement; summary of research form; and two letters of recommendation. All application materials should be sent in a CD/DVD. **Deadline:** February 20.

8113 ■ Damon Runyon Physician-Scientist Training Awards *(Postdoctorate, Professional development/ Award)*

Purpose: To provide funds to developing physician-scientists to pursue research intensively. **Focus:** General studies/Field of study not specified. **Qualif.:** Applicants must be physician-scientist; must be completed his/her residency and clinical training; must be U.S. Specialty Board eligible at the time of the application; and must be able to devote at least 80% of his/her time and effort to Damon Runyon-supported research. **Criteria:** Selection is based on the following: quality of a format research proposal written by the applicants; commitment of the institution to the development and training of future physician-scientists, including providing the necessary

Awards are arranged alphabetically below their administering organizations

protected time for research; importance of the proposed research to the understanding of cancer and/or prevention, diagnosis or treatment of cancer; and capacity of the mentor to provide a robust training experience that will accelerate the development of the applicants' scientific skills and prepare him/her to independently conduct high quality, innovative cancer-related research.

Funds Avail.: $460,000. **Duration:** Annual. **Number Awarded:** 3. **To Apply:** Applicants must propose a research together with the help of his/her mentor and submit a letter of commitment from Institution/Department. A letter endorsed by both the Dean or Center Director, and the Head/Chair of the Department, should confirm the applicant's and mentor's academic appointments, state the institution's commitment to support the applicant's research efforts, the nature of the support that will be provided, and guarantee a minimum of 80% protected time for the applicant's research to fulfill the terms of the award. **Deadline:** December 1.

8114 ■ Damon Runyon-Rachleff Innovation Awards
(Postdoctorate/Fellowship)

Purpose: To provide funding for extraordinary early career researchers who have an innovative new idea but lack sufficient preliminary data to obtain traditional funding. **Focus:** Medical research. **Qualif.:** Applicants, including non-U.S. citizens, must be conducting independent research at a U.S. research institution; institutional nominations are not required; basic and translational/clinical projects will be considered; applicants with a background in multiple disciplines are encouraged to apply; joint submission from collaborators working in different disciplines will be considered; applicants must belong to either: tenure-track Assistant Professors within the first four years of obtaining the position, Clinical Instructors and Senior Clinical Fellows (with an MD) pursuing a period of independent research before taking a faculty position, or Postdoctoral Fellows and highly motivated recent PhD and MD graduates pursuing a period of independent research before taking a faculty position; must commit 80% of their time to conducting research; and must demonstrate access to the resources and infrastructures necessary to conduct the research. **Criteria:** Recipients are chosen based on the applicant's capacity to conduct bold, exceptionally creative research; the novelty and potential for breakthrough innovation of the proposed research; the likelihood of impact to cancer understanding if research is successful; and the applicant's lack of resources to pursue the proposed research.

Funds Avail.: $150,000 per year. **To Apply:** Applicants must submit the pre-proposal materials including the following: (1) a completed cover sheet; (2) one-page description of the proposed research; (3) one paragraph description of the resources and core facilities; (4) NIH biosketch; (5) three reference letters from a Tenure-track Assistant professor and clinical instructors and/or Senior Clinical Fellows. Semi finalist applicants will be asked to submit a full proposal including the following: (1) an expanded description of the research proposal (maximum of three pages); (2) full curriculum vitae; (3) a proposed budget for the term of the award; (4) a written statement guaranteeing adequate safety precautions and approved by the appropriate Institutional Review Board; and two letters of reference.

8115 ■ Damon Runyon-Sohn Pediatric Cancer Fellowship Awards *(Master's, Doctorate/Fellowship)*

Purpose: To provide funds to basic scientists and clinicians who conduct research with the potential to significantly impact the prevention, diagnosis or treatment of one or more pediatric cancers. **Focus:** Medical research. **Qualif.:** Applicants must have completed one or more of the following degrees or its equivalent: MD, PHD, MD/PHD,DDS, and DVM. **Criteria:** Applicants are evaluated based on the following criteria: potential impact of the research on pediatric cancer; the quality of the research proposal (importance of the problem, originality of approach, and appropriateness of techniques and clarity of presentation); the qualifications, experience and productivity of both the candidate and the sponsor; the quality of the research training environment in which the proposed research is to be conducted and its potential for broadening and strengthening the applicants' ability to conduct innovative and substantive research.

Funds Avail.: $50,000-$60,000. **To Apply:** Applicants must propose a research that conducted at a university, hospital or research institution.

8116 ■ Russian Brotherhood Organization of the U.S.A. (RBOUSA)
1733 Spring Garden St.
Philadelphia, PA 19130-3915
Ph: (215)563-2537
Fax: (215)563-8106
E-mail: info@rbo.org
URL: www.rbo.org

8117 ■ Mihaly Russin Scholarship Awards
(Graduate/Scholarship)

Purpose: To offer aid to students seeking higher education. **Focus:** General studies/Field of study not specified. **Qualif.:** Applicants must have life insurance policy of $10,000 or more with the RBO; remained active within the society; must be a Christian. **Criteria:** Selection is based on the application.

Funds Avail.: $1,000. **Duration:** Annual. **To Apply:** Applicants must submit a completed application form together with two letters of recommendation, a picture, a copy of transcripts and acceptance letter. **Deadline:** September 30.

8118 ■ Saints Cyril and Methodius Scholarships
(Undergraduate/Scholarship)

Purpose: To support the education of a student member. **Focus:** General studies/Field of study not specified. **Qualif.:** Applicant must be a high school graduate or prep school; hold a Russian Brotherhood Organization life insurance certificate of not less than $10000; and a member of the society in good standing. **Criteria:** Recipients are selected by an independent scholarship committee.

Funds Avail.: Depends on the financial need of the student's family. **Duration:** Annually. **To Apply:** Applicants must submit a completed application form, photograph and copy of college acceptance letter to SS. Cyril and Methodius Scholarships. **Deadline:** September 30.

8119 ■ Safe Schools Coalition (SSC)
c/o Equal Rights Washington
PO Box 2388
Seattle, WA 98111
Fax: (206)325-2689
Free: 877-723-3723
URL: www.safeschoolscoalition.org

8120 ■ Davis-Putter Scholarships Fund *(Undergraduate, Graduate/Scholarship)*

Purpose: To provide scholarships for individuals who are able to do academic work at the university level and who

Awards are arranged alphabetically below their administering organizations

are part of the progressive movement on the campus and in the community. **Focus:** General studies/Field of study not specified. **Qualif.:** Applicants must be students actively working for peace and justice; must be enrolled in an accredited school and receiving college credit for the time period covered by their grants; and must be living in the United States and planning to enroll in school in the U.S. in order to apply. **Criteria:** Selection will be based on academic merit and financial need.

Funds Avail.: No specific amount. **To Apply:** Applicants must submit a completed application form with a short personal statement, transcripts, letters of support from two people able to evaluate the applicant's current political work, an official financial statement (i.e., FAFSA or SAR), and a passport-like photograph suitable for reproduction. **Contact:** Davis-Putter Scholarship Fund; Email: davisputter@davisputter.org.

8121 ■ LEAGUE Foundation Scholarships
(Undergraduate/Scholarship)

Purpose: To provide financial assistance for lesbian, gay, bisexual and transgender high school seniors. **Focus:** General studies/Field of study not specified. **Qualif.:** Applicants must be lesbian, gay, bisexual and transgender college-bound students; must have a GPA of at least 3.0 on a 4.0 scale; and must be actively and substantially involved in community service. **Criteria:** Selection of scholars will be based on criteria.

Funds Avail.: $1,500 - $2,500. **To Apply:** Applicants must check the available website for the required materials.

8122 ■ Minnesota GLBT Educational Fund
(Undergraduate/Scholarship)

Purpose: To support outstanding gay, lesbian, bisexual and transgender youth and friends and to support their continuing education. **Focus:** General studies/Field of study not specified. **Qualif.:** Applicants must be GLBT or allied student (post-secondary); Resident of Minnesota or attending a qualifying Minnesota academic institution; Enrolled in a post-secondary program; Not a current PFund board member or partner of a current PFund board member. **Criteria:** Awards will be given to those who meet the criteria.

Funds Avail.: No specific amount. **To Apply:** Applicants must check the available website for the required materials.

8123 ■ Point Foundation Scholarships *(Graduate, Postgraduate, Undergraduate/Scholarship)*

Purpose: To provide financial support and hope for meritorious undergraduate, graduate and postgraduate students who are marginalized because of their sexual orientation or gender identity. **Focus:** General studies/Field of study not specified. **Qualif.:** Applicants must be LGBT students. **Criteria:** Awards will be based on need and criteria.

Funds Avail.: No specific amount. **To Apply:** Applicants must check the available contact information for more inquiries.

8124 ■ Pride Foundation Scholarships
(Undergraduate/Scholarship)

Purpose: To provide financial assistance for gay, lesbian, bisexual and transgender students pursuing higher education. **Focus:** General studies/Field of study not specified. **Qualif.:** Applicants must be gay, lesbian, bisexual, transgender, queer and straight-ally students as well as students

raised by LGBT families. Must be residents of Alaska, Idaho , Montana , Oregon and Washington. **Criteria:** Preference will be given to those who meet the scholarship criteria; Seattle-area gay men of color, Latin youth involved in athletics, students of health sciences; interior, fashion or graphic arts; design; or performing arts and former TRIO students from a NASP member program.

Funds Avail.: Up to $10,000. **Number Awarded:** Varies. **To Apply:** Applicants must check the available website for the required materials.

8125 ■ University of Puget Sound LGBT Leadership Scholarships Fund *(Undergraduate/Scholarship)*

Purpose: To support students who have demonstrated leadership and involvement in the lesbian, gay, bisexual, and transgender (LGBT) community at the University of Puget Sound. **Focus:** General studies/Field of study not specified. **Qualif.:** Applicants who demonstrated leadership and involvement in the lesbian, gay, bisexual, transgender community at the University of Puget Sound are welcome and eligible for this award. Applicants must be a sophomore, junior or senior during the current academic year; must be enrolled, planning to enroll at the University of Puget Sound; and must be in good academic standing. **Criteria:** Preference will be given to those who meet the criteria.

Funds Avail.: No specific amount. **Duration:** Annual. **To Apply:** Applicants must check the available website for the required materials. **Remarks:** Established in 2000.

8126 ■ Safelink Internet
1895 N Wildwood
Boise, ID 83713
Ph: (208)331-9822
E-mail: info@safelink.net
URL: www.safelinkinternet.com

8127 ■ Safelink Internet Scholarships
(Undergraduate/Scholarship)

Purpose: To assist Idaho community students in their pursuit of higher education. **Focus:** General studies/Field of study not specified. **Qualif.:** Applicants must be graduates from Idaho and have 3.0 GPA. **Criteria:** Applicants will be judged primarily on need basis, but does not exclude achievement standards.

Funds Avail.: $1,000. **Number Awarded:** 1. **To Apply:** Applicants must visit the scholarship website to fill out the application. Additional requirements are transcripts (such must be attached with counselor or school representative signature) and student aid report showing income status of their households. All applications must be submitted electronically. **Deadline:** March 31. **Contact:** community@ safelink.net.

8128 ■ Russell Sage Foundation (RSF)
112 E 64th St.
New York, NY 10065
Ph: (212)750-6000
Fax: (212)371-4761
Free: 800-666-2211
E-mail: info@rsage.org
URL: www.russellsage.org

8129 ■ Russell Sage Foundation Visiting Scholars
(Postdoctorate/Fellowship)

Purpose: To promote writing and research in the social sciences. **Focus:** Behavioral sciences; Social sciences.

Awards are arranged alphabetically below their administering organizations

Qualif.: Applicant must be at least several years beyond the PhD. **Criteria:** Selection is based on the applicant's demonstrated record of accomplishment, the merit of the proposed project, and its relevance to the foundation's current programs.

Funds Avail.: $110,000. **Duration:** Up to 10 months. **Number Awarded:** 19. **To Apply:** Applicants must write and submit a 4-5 page letter describing the project to be undertaken while in the residence at the foundation along with an up-to-date CV and the questionnaire. Include 4 copies each of the materials. **Deadline:** September 30.

8130 ■ Saint Andrew's Society of the State of New York

150 E 55th St., 3rd Fl.
New York, NY 10022
Ph: (212)223-4248
E-mail: office@standrewsny.org
URL: www.standrewsny.org

8131 ■ Saint Andrews Scholarships (Undergraduate/ Scholarship)

Purpose: To promote cultural interchange and goodwill between Scotland and the United States. **Focus:** General studies/Field of study not specified. **Qualif.:** Applicants must be senior undergraduate students who will obtain a Bachelor's degree from an accredited college or university and who can demonstrate the significance of studying in Scotland; must reside or attend school within 250 miles of New York State. **Criteria:** Recipients are selected based on academic achievement, extracurricular activities, financial need, statement of personal objectives, Scottish descent and proof of citizenship.

Funds Avail.: No specific amount. **To Apply:** Applicants must submit application and letters of reference from appropriate professors.

8132 ■ St. Louis Paralegal Association (SPA)

PO Box 69218
Saint Louis, MO 63169-0218
URL: stlpa.org

8133 ■ CLA/CP Scholarship (Other/Scholarship)

Purpose: To support legal assistants with their CLE exam fees. **Focus:** Paralegal studies. **Qualif.:** Applicants must be legal assistants who are members of the SLALA. **Criteria:** Recipients will be selected based on submitted references, recommendations and participation in the community.

Funds Avail.: $750. **Duration:** Annual. **Number Awarded:** 1. **To Apply:** Applicants must submit a letter of recommendation from a supervisor or employer; and a typewritten statement (maximum of three pages, double-spaced) indicating career objectives. **Deadline:** April 1.

8134 ■ St. Louis Paralegal Association Student Scholarships (Undergraduate/Scholarship)

Purpose: To assist students with the cost of required books for legal assistants program classes. **Focus:** Paralegal studies. **Qualif.:** Applicants must be enrolled in a study leading to a position as a legal assistant; must be members of the St. Louis Association of Legal Assistants (SLALA); and must maintain at least a "B" average in all legal assistant program classes. **Criteria:** Recipients will be

selected based on scholastic achievement; participation in campus, paralegal and community activities; and review of the writing sample. Applicants who have demonstrated a financial need will be given consideration.

Funds Avail.: $500. **Duration:** Annual. **Number Awarded:** 2. **To Apply:** Applicants must submit the following: a letter of recommendation from a director, faculty member, Legal Assistant Program, or employer; an official transcript of records; and personal statement (maximum of three pages, double-spaced) indicating the applicant's career objectives. **Deadline:** April 1.

8135 ■ Saint Paul University Canada

223 Main St.
Ottawa, ON, Canada K1S 1C4
Ph: (613)236-1393
Fax: (613)782-3005
Free: 800-637-6859
E-mail: info@ustpaul.ca
URL: www.ustpaul.ca

8136 ■ Saint Paul University Excellence Scholarships (Undergraduate/Scholarship, Medal)

Purpose: To provide educational assistance for the students of Saint Paul University. **Focus:** General studies/ Field of study not specified. **Qualif.:** Program is open to all students in Saint Paul University. **Criteria:** Scholarships are awarded by a committee upon reception of recommended candidacies from the various academic units.

Funds Avail.: $1,000. **Duration:** Annual. **Number Awarded:** 8. **To Apply:** Applicants must submit a request for scholarships to a national council. **Contact:** Saint Paul University at the above address.

8137 ■ Saint Paul University Financial Aid Bursaries (Undergraduate, Graduate/Scholarship)

Purpose: To provide educational assistance for all students in Saint Paul University. **Focus:** General studies/Field of study not specified. **Qualif.:** Applicants must be full-time students enrolled in a program of 1st, 2nd and 3rd cycles of Saint Paul University. Bursaries are offered to Canadian citizens, permanent residents and foreign students alike. **Criteria:** Requests are evaluated by a committee according to financial necessity or very special conditions.

Funds Avail.: No specific amount. **Duration:** Annual. **Number Awarded:** Varies. **To Apply:** Applicants may get an application form six weeks before the deadline at the Scholarships Office or at the Saint Paul University website.

8138 ■ Salvadoran American Leadership and Education Fund (SALEF)

1625 W Olympic Blvd., Ste. 718
Los Angeles, CA 90015
Ph: (213)480-1052
Fax: (213)487-2530
URL: www.salef.org

8139 ■ SALEF Health Career Scholarships (Undergraduate, Graduate/Scholarship)

Purpose: To support students pursuing health related fields. **Focus:** Health care services; Health education. **Qualif.:** Applicants must: be pursuing health related degrees and careers; be of Central American or other Latino ethnic-

Awards are arranged alphabetically below their administering organizations

ity; demonstrate proven financial need; demonstrate a history of community involvement; possess a minimum 2.5 GPA; and, be either of the following: graduating high school seniors; current undergraduate, graduate, MPH, MD or Dentistry School students; community college students; or enrolled/studying at vocational/trade schools. They must also reside in the following areas: Los Angeles Area (specifically from those who are from Pico Union, South Los Angeles, Central LA, and surrounding schools). **Criteria:** Selection shall be based on the aforementioned applicants' qualifications and compliance with the application details.

Funds Avail.: Range from $1,000to $2,250. **Duration:** Annual. **Number Awarded:** Varies. **To Apply:** Applicants must submit a completed application form along with two letters of recommendation (on official letterhead when applicable); a personal statement (maximum of 800 words); resume; official transcripts (have school seal and/or authorized signature); copy of applicants' or applicants' parents' Federal Tax Return or Proof of Family Income (include a written statement with explanation, if not applicable); and a colored photograph (wallet size, 3 1/2 x 5) and the attached Release Authorization Form. **Deadline:** May 31. **Contact:** Ever Hilleprandt, Education and Academic Programs Manager at 213-480-1052 or via email at ehilleprandt@salef.org.

8140 ■ SAMFund

89 S St., Ste. LL02
Boston, MA 02111
Ph: (617)938-3484
Fax: (866)496-8070
E-mail: info@thesamfund.org
URL: www.thesamfund.org

8141 ■ SAMFund Scholarships *(Advanced Professional/Scholarship)*

Purpose: To provide financial assistance to young adults as they move forward with their lives after cancer. **Focus:** General studies/Field of study not specified. **Qualif.:** Applicant must be a young adult between the ages of 17 and 35, finished with active cancer treatment and a resident of the United States. **Criteria:** Selection is based on the submitted application materials.

Funds Avail.: No specific amount. **To Apply:** Applicants must first submit a Letter of Intent (LOI) and after a review period, selected applicants will then be invited to submit a full application. **Contact:** Michelle Zeitler at michelle@thesamfund.org.

8142 ■ San Angelo Area Foundation (SAAF)

221 S Irving St.
San Angelo, TX 76903-6421
Ph: (325)947-7071
Fax: (325)947-7322
E-mail: infosaaf@saafound.org
URL: www.saafound.org

8143 ■ San Angelo Area Foundation Scholarships *(All/Scholarship)*

Purpose: To support the education of students from the San Angelo area. **Focus:** General studies/Field of study not specified. **Qualif.:** Applicant must be from San Angelo area. **Criteria:** Selection is based on submitted application materials.

Funds Avail.: No specific amount. **Duration:** Annual. **Number Awarded:** Varies. **To Apply:** Applicants must submit a completed application form along with the essay entitled "Why I need this Scholarship;" high school transcript (high school senior) or college transcript; SAT and/or ACT score sheets (if both have been taken); two letters of recommendation (one from a teacher and one from a non-school source not related to the applicant); and social security number and/or student ID on page 1. **Deadline:** March 2. **Contact:** Questions can be addressed at scholarship@saafound.org.

8144 ■ San Diego Foundation

2508 Historic Decatur Rd., Ste. 200
San Diego, CA 92106
Ph: (619)235-2300
E-mail: info@sdfoundation.org
URL: www.sdfoundation.org

8145 ■ Marvin Arnold and Irene Jaquetta Heye Scholarships *(Undergraduate/Scholarship)*

Purpose: To provide financial assistance to graduating high school seniors planning to attend, or current students who are attending California Polytechnic State University - San Luis Obispo. **Focus:** Engineering. **Qualif.:** Applicants must be graduating high school seniors planning to attend California Polytechnic State University or current students attending California Polytechnic State University. Students must be majoring in engineering (aerospace, civil and environmental, electrical, general, industrial and manufacturing, materials or mechanical engineering); have a minimum 3.33 grade point average on a 4.0 scale; have a demonstrated financial need; and be actively involved in extra-curricular activities, community service, or work experience. **Criteria:** Preference will be given to students with a high financial need, former military personnel and dependents of active military personnel.

Funds Avail.: No specific amount. **Duration:** Annual; up to four years. **To Apply:** Applicants may obtain an application form online. Applicants must submit their letters of recommendation, transcripts of record and personal statement together with their completed application form. **Deadline:** March 25. **Contact:** scholarships@sdfoundation.org.

8146 ■ Luis Arreola Memorial Scholarships *(Undergraduate/Scholarship)*

Purpose: To support the education of students from California. **Focus:** General studies/Field of study not specified. **Qualif.:** Applicants must be graduating seniors from Sweetwater Union High School District who plan to attend an accredited four-year university, community college or licensed career/technical school in the United States. They must also have a minimum GPA of 3.0 on an 4.0 scale, have demonstrated both commitment to serving their community and financial need. **Criteria:** Preference will be given to students who are ambitious, have shown success and potential in the courses related to their chosen career and persevere in spite of their obstacles.

Funds Avail.: No specific amount. **Duration:** Annual. **To Apply:** Applicants may visit the website to verify the application process and other pieces of information. **Deadline:** February 4.

8147 ■ Frank H. Ault Scholarships *(Undergraduate/Scholarship)*

Purpose: To support the education of students from California. **Focus:** Accounting. **Qualif.:** Applicants must be

Awards are arranged alphabetically below their administering organizations

graduating high school students or junior college students planning to major in accounting or finance at an accredited four-year university; or a current college student (sophomore, junior, or senior year) have declared a major in finance or accounting. Students must have a minimum of 3.0 GPA on a 4.0 scale; and have participated in extracurricular or community service activities. **Criteria:** Preference will be given to students who are active members of or have taken leadership in their school's accounting society.

Funds Avail.: No specific amount. **Duration:** Annual. **To Apply:** Applicants may visit the website to verify the application process and other pieces of information. Required additional materials: Unofficial copy of current transcript. **Deadline:** February 4.

8148 ■ Ballard Family Foundation Scholarships
(Undergraduate/Scholarship)

Purpose: To support the education of students from California. **Focus:** General studies/Field of study not specified. **Qualif.:** Applicants must be students between the ages of 17-25 who are or have been in foster care; have demonstrated financial need; have a minimum high school GPA of 2.50 on a 4.0 scale or a 2.75 college GPA on a 4.0 scale; and be attending an accredited four-year university, two-year college or licensed trade/vocational school in the U.S. **Criteria:** Special consideration will be given to African-American students.

Funds Avail.: No specific amount. **To Apply:** Applicants must submit a completed Common Scholarship Application together with personal statement; two letters of recommendation on official letterhead (written within the last six months); official transcript in an official and sealed envelope; and a letter of recommendation from the applicant's social worker indicating the applicant is or has been in foster care.

8149 ■ Barta-Lehman Musical Scholarships
(Undergraduate/Scholarship)

Purpose: To support the education of students from California. **Focus:** Music. **Qualif.:** Applicants must be graduating high school seniors, or current undergraduate or graduate college students who are serious and talented musicians planning to pursue a career in music and/or play professionally (string instruments preferred) and plan to enroll full-time at an accredited four-year university or music academy in the United States. They must have a minimum of 3.0 GPA on a 4.0 scale. **Criteria:** Selection will be based on the submitted application materials.

Funds Avail.: No specific amount. **To Apply:** Applicants must submit the completed application. Required additional materials are: letter of recommendation on official letterhead from applicants' music teacher indicating their level of talent and seriousness about pursuing music as a career and a CD or DVD of applicants' music. Materials will not be returned.

8150 ■ Ray and Mary Bell Memorial Scholarships
(Undergraduate/Scholarship)

Purpose: To support the education of students from California. **Focus:** General studies/Field of study not specified. **Qualif.:** Applicants must be graduating high school seniors from Fallbrook High School who will attend an accredited two-year college or four-year university in the U.S; have a minimum 3.0 GPA on a 4.0 scale; and have a commitment to serving the community through involvement in community service, church or extra-curricular activities.

Criteria: Selection will be based on the aforesaid qualifications.

Funds Avail.: No specific amount. **Duration:** Annual. **To Apply:** Applicants may visit the website to verify the application process and other pieces of information. **Deadline:** February 4.

8151 ■ James R. and Geraldine F. Bertelsen Scholarships *(Undergraduate/Scholarship)*

Purpose: To support the education of students from California. **Focus:** General studies/Field of study not specified. **Qualif.:** Applicants must be practicing Roman Catholics who are: graduating high school seniors who have applied to, been accepted by, and will attend a four-year Roman Catholic college/university in the U.S.; or students currently enrolled at a Catholic college/university in the United States. They must also be residents of Carlsbad, CA for a minimum of one full year enrolling in or currently enrolled in a course of instruction that will enable to obtain an undergraduate degree within four years. **Criteria:** Award is given based on achievement with need being a secondary consideration.

Funds Avail.: No specific amount. **Duration:** Annual. **To Apply:** Applicants may visit the website to verify the application process and other pieces of information. **Contact:** scholarships@sdfoundation.org.

8152 ■ Dorothy M. Bolyard Memorial Scholarships
(Undergraduate/Scholarship)

Purpose: To support the education of students from California. **Focus:** General studies/Field of study not specified. **Qualif.:** Applicants must be San Diego residents (age 25 years and older) pursuing a degree at an accredited two-year college or four-year university in San Diego County; have a minimum 3.0 GPA on a 4.0 scale; and demonstrated financial need. **Criteria:** Preference is given to applicants who have a record of involvement in their community as demonstrated by their extra-curricular activities, community or church service, or work experience.

Funds Avail.: No specific amount. **Duration:** Annual. **To Apply:** Applicants may visit the website to verify the application process and other pieces of information. **Deadline:** February 4.

8153 ■ Breslauer Family Scholarships
(Undergraduate/Scholarship)

Purpose: To support the education of students from California. **Focus:** General studies/Field of study not specified. **Qualif.:** Applicants must: be San Diego county residents; be graduating seniors from San Diego High School (in downtown San Diego only) who plan to attend an accredited four-year university in the United States; have a minimum unweighted GPA of 3.5 on a 4.0 scale; show a strong commitment to their community as demonstrated by their involvement in extra-curricular activities and/or work/volunteer experience; and, have a demonstrated financial need, as evidenced by an adjusted gross family income of equal to or less than $40,000. **Criteria:** Selection shall be based on the aforementioned qualifications and compliance with the application details.

Funds Avail.: No specific amount. **Duration:** Annual. **To Apply:** Applicants may visit the website to verify the application process and other pieces of information. Required additional materials: 1) Unofficial copy of your current transcript. 2) At least one letter of reference from a teacher at your high school or school employee. **Deadline:** February 4.

Awards are arranged alphabetically below their administering organizations

8154 ■ Louise A. Broderick San Diego County Scholarships *(Undergraduate/Scholarship)*

Purpose: To support the education of students from California. **Focus:** General studies/Field of study not specified. **Qualif.:** Applicants must be single parents with dependent children who are re-entering college or are already in college. They must have a minimum of 2.0 GPA on a 4.0 scale; demonstrated financial need; and plan to attend a two-year community college, four-year university, or trade and vocational school. **Criteria:** Selection shall be based on the aforementioned qualifications and compliance with the application details.

Funds Avail.: No specific amount. **Duration:** Annual. **To Apply:** Applicants may visit the website to verify the application process and other pieces of information. Applicants must also submit the first page of the prior year federal tax form showing their filing status and their dependent child(ren). **Deadline:** February 4.

8155 ■ California Association of Family and Consumer Sciences - San Diego Chapter Scholarships (CAFCS) *(Undergraduate, Graduate/Scholarship)*

Purpose: To support the education of students from California. **Focus:** Fashion design; Food science and technology; Food service careers; Home Economics; Housing; Management; Nutrition; Textile science. **Qualif.:** Applicants must be graduating high school seniors, current college students, or graduate students majoring in Food Sciences; Dietetics; Nutrition; Food Services; Hospitality; Human, Child and Family Development; Apparel, Fashion and Textile Services; Housing and Interiors; Consumer Economics; Management and Resources; or Family and Consumer Science Education. Students must have a minimum 2.50 GPA on a 4.0 scale; planning to attend an accredited two-year college, four-year university, or licensed trade-vocational school in the U.S. Undergraduate students must be enrolled in school full-time (12 units per semester or 9 per quarter). Graduate students may be enrolled full-time or part-time with awards allocated appropriately based upon enrollment units. **Criteria:** Selection shall be based on the aforementioned qualifications and compliance with the application details.

Funds Avail.: No specific amount. **Duration:** Annual. **To Apply:** Applicants may visit the website to verify the application process and other pieces of information. Required additional materials: Letter of recommendation on official letterhead from an instructor or other professional indicating interest in pursuing a career in one of above listed fields. **Deadline:** February 4.

8156 ■ Cheerful Giver Scholarships *(Undergraduate/ Scholarship)*

Purpose: To support the education of students from California. **Focus:** General studies/Field of study not specified. **Qualif.:** Applicants must be graduating high school seniors who are children of single parents and plan to enroll full-time at an accredited four-year university in the United States; have a minimum unweighted GPA of 3.5 on a 4.0 scale and a minimum SAT score of 1600 or a minimum ACT score of 29. **Criteria:** Selection will be based on aforesaid qualifications.

Funds Avail.: No specific amount. **Duration:** Annual. **To Apply:** Applicants must submit the completed application. Required additional materials are: essay (maximum 250 words) addressing how being the children of single parents have influenced them; unofficial copy of their current transcript; and, unofficial copy of their SAT or ACT scores.

Deadline: February 4. **Contact:** scholarships@ sdfoundation.org.

8157 ■ The Club at Morningside Scholarships *(Undergraduate, Graduate/Scholarship)*

Purpose: To support the education of students from California. **Focus:** General studies/Field of study not specified. **Qualif.:** Applicants must be: employees (full- or part-time) and children of employees at The Club at Morningside who have been employed for a minimum of two consecutive years on a seasonal or year-round basis; graduating high school seniors, current college students or those planning to attend an accredited career/technical school. community college, four-year university or graduate school in the United States. High school seniors and students currently enrolled in school must have a minimum unweighted GPA of 2.5 on a 4.0 scale. **Criteria:** Factors that may be considered include academic achievement, involvement in extra-curricular activities and community service, work experience, and financial need.

Funds Avail.: No specific amount. **Duration:** Annual. **To Apply:** Applicants must submit the completed application. Required additional material is a letter on official letterhead from the Human Resources department verifying them or their parents are employed at The Club at Morningside, including position held, length of employment and a description of job responsibilities. **Deadline:** February 4.

8158 ■ Madison and Edith Cooper Scholarships *(Undergraduate/Scholarship)*

Purpose: To support the education of students from California. **Focus:** General studies/Field of study not specified. **Qualif.:** Applicants must be young adults in San Diego County (up to age 24); have been in the foster care system; planning to attend an accredited two-year college, four-year university, or licensed trade/vocational school in the U.S.; have a minimum of 2.50 GPA on a 4.0 scale; demonstrated financial need; and involved in serving the community through extra-curricular activities, community service, or work experience. **Criteria:** Awards are given based on the application materials.

Funds Avail.: No specific amount. **To Apply:** Applicants may visit the website to verify the application process and other pieces of information. Additional material(s) required: letter on official letterhead from a social worker verifying applicants are currently or have been in foster care.

8159 ■ Crawford Scholarships *(Undergraduate/ Scholarship)*

Purpose: To support the education of students from California. **Focus:** General studies/Field of study not specified. **Qualif.:** Applicants must be: graduating seniors of Crawford Educational Complex who plan to attend an accredited community college or four-year university in the United States; previous Crawford Scholarship recipients who had to forfeit their scholarship who are attending an accredited community college or four-year university in the United States; have a minimum 2.50 GPA on a 4.0 scale (high school GPAs are unweighted); those who are engaged in their community through their involvement in extracurricular, church, volunteer activities or work experience. They must have a demonstrated financial need. **Criteria:** Selection shall be based on the aforementioned qualifications and compliance with the application details.

Funds Avail.: No specific amount. **Duration:** Annual. **To Apply:** Applicants may visit the website to verify the application process and other pieces of information. **Deadline:** February 4.

Awards are arranged alphabetically below their administering organizations

8160 ■ Davis Family Scholarships (Undergraduate/ Scholarship)

Purpose: To support the education of students from California. **Focus:** General studies/Field of study not specified. **Qualif.:** Applicants must be graduating Latino high school seniors from a San Diego County public school; planning to attend an accredited four-year public university in the state of California; have demonstrated financial need; and have an unweighted GPA between 3.25 to 3.50 GPA on a 4.0 scale. **Criteria:** Special consideration will be given to applicants who are committed to their communities through their involvement in community service, extracurricular activities and/or work experience.

Funds Avail.: No specific amount. **Duration:** Annual. **To Apply:** Applicants may visit the website to verify the application process and other pieces of information. **Deadline:** February 4.

8161 ■ Ruth DeMoss Scholarships (Undergraduate/ Scholarship)

Purpose: To support the education of students from California. **Focus:** General studies/Field of study not specified. **Qualif.:** Applicants must be African-American, Native American, or Latino students who are currently attending an accredited two-year college in San Diego County and will transfer to a four-year university in San Diego County. Students must have a minimum of 2.50 GPA on a 4.0 scale; have demonstrated financial need, and a commitment to the community as shown by leadership and volunteer activities. **Criteria:** Selection will be based on aforesaid qualifications.

Funds Avail.: No specific amount. **To Apply:** Applicants may visit the website to verify the application process and other pieces of information.

8162 ■ Herman H. Derksen Scholarships (Undergraduate/Scholarship)

Purpose: To support the education of students from California. **Focus:** General studies/Field of study not specified. **Qualif.:** Applicant must be San Diego residents pursuing a trade or vocation who will attend an accredited two-year college or licensed trade/vocational school in San Diego County; have a minimum of 2.0 GPA on a 4.0 scale; and demonstrated financial need. **Criteria:** Special consideration is given to applicants who have a record of involvement in their community as demonstrated by their extracurricular activities, community or church service, or work experience.

Funds Avail.: No specific amount. **Duration:** Annual. **To Apply:** Applicants may visit the website to verify the application process and other pieces of information. **Deadline:** February 4.

8163 ■ Hans H. and Margaret B. Doe Scholarships (Graduate, Undergraduate/Scholarship)

Purpose: To support the education of students from California. **Focus:** Law; Medicine. **Qualif.:** Applicants must be biological, adopted or stepchildren of the employees at the Vista Irrigation District. Students may attend a career/technical school, community college, four-year university or graduate school, including medicine and law. **Criteria:** Selection shall be made on the basis of academic achievement, financial need, extra-curricular activities/work experience, demonstrated leadership, good citizenship and potential for future development.

Funds Avail.: No specific amount. **To Apply:** Applicants

must contact The San Diego Foundation for obtaining the application form and guidelines. **Contact:** scholarships@ sdfoundation.org.

8164 ■ Drinkwater Family Scholarships (Undergraduate/Scholarship)

Purpose: To support the education of students from California. **Focus:** General studies/Field of study not specified. **Qualif.:** Applicants must be graduating high school seniors; be the first in the family to attend an accredited four-year university in the U.S.; have a minimum unweighted GPA of 3.25 on a 4.0 scale; demonstrated financial need; and actively involved in serving the community as shown by participation in extra-curricular, church activities, or community service. **Criteria:** Selection shall be based on the aforementioned qualifications and compliance with the application details.

Funds Avail.: No specific amount. **To Apply:** Applicants may visit the website to verify the application process and other pieces of information.

8165 ■ Reuben H. Fleet Memorial Scholarships (Undergraduate/Scholarship)

Purpose: To support the education of students from California. **Focus:** Engineering; Mathematics and mathematical sciences; Science. **Qualif.:** Applicants must be college students pursuing an undergraduate degree in science, engineering or math; have completed 54 semester units or 72 quarter units; have maintained a minimum of 3.0 GPA on a 4.0 scale; be enrolled at a four-year university in San Diego County; or be San Diego County residents attending a four-year university in the U.S. **Criteria:** Selection will be based on aforesaid qualifications.

Funds Avail.: No specific amount. **Duration:** Annual. **To Apply:** Applicants may visit the website to verify the application process and other pieces of information. **Deadline:** February 4.

8166 ■ Leslie Jane Hahn Memorial Scholarships (Undergraduate/Scholarship)

Purpose: To support the education of students from California. **Focus:** General studies/Field of study not specified. **Qualif.:** Applicants must be graduating high school senior females from a public school who plan to enroll full-time at an accredited four-year college/university in the U.S.; have at least a 3.75 GPA on a 4.0 scale; demonstrated financial need; and have a history of active involvement in athletics, other extracurricular activities, community service or work experience. **Criteria:** Preference will be given to applicants who most closely embody Jane's qualities and reflect her background described above.

Funds Avail.: No specific amount. **Duration:** Annual. **To Apply:** Applicants may visit the website to verify the application process and other pieces of information. **Deadline:** February 4.

8167 ■ Helm Family Scholarships (Undergraduate/ Scholarship)

Purpose: To support the education of students from California. **Focus:** Biology; Chemistry; Computer and information sciences; Engineering; Physics; Technology. **Qualif.:** Applicants must be entering junior or senior students at San Diego State University or the University of California, San Diego; have declared a major in mathematics or a scientific field such as, but not limited to, biology, computer science, chemistry, technology, engineering,

Awards are arranged alphabetically below their administering organizations

physics, etc.; have a minimum of 3.0 GPA on a 4.0 scale; and have demonstrated financial need. **Criteria:** Consideration will be given to students who are employed or have participated in extra-curricular activities or community service.

Funds Avail.: No specific amount. **Duration:** Annual. **To Apply:** Applicants may visit the website to verify the application process and other pieces of information. **Deadline:** February 4.

8168 ■ Doris Hendren Memorial Scholarships *(Undergraduate/Scholarship)*

Purpose: To support the education of students from California. **Focus:** Liberal arts. **Qualif.:** Applicants must be students attending an accredited two-year college or four-year university in San Diego County; pursuing a degree in a field of liberal arts; have a minimum 3.0 GPA on a 4.0 scale; demonstrated financial need; have commitment to the San Diego community through work experience, community, church, or school activities. **Criteria:** Selection shall be based on the aforementioned qualifications and compliance with the application details.

Funds Avail.: No specific amount. **Duration:** Annual. **To Apply:** Applicants may visit the website to verify the application process and other pieces of information. Required additional materials: Unofficial copy of current transcript. **Deadline:** February 4.

8169 ■ Albert W. and Mildred Hubbard Scholarships *(Undergraduate/Scholarship)*

Purpose: To support the education of students from California. **Focus:** General studies/Field of study not specified. **Qualif.:** Applicants must be graduating seniors attending high school in Escondido or Valley Center; residents of Escondido or Valley Center already in college; or students currently attending the San Pasqual Academy in Escondido, CA. They must have a minimum of 2.50 GPA on a 4.0 scale; residents of Escondido, CA or Valley Center, CA for the past four years (excluding students attending San Pasqual Academy); have demonstrated financial need; and plan to attend an accredited two-year college or four-year university in the U.S. **Criteria:** Selection shall be based on the aforementioned qualifications and compliance with the application details.

Funds Avail.: No specific amount. **Duration:** Annual. **To Apply:** Applicants may visit the website to verify the application process and other pieces of information. Applicants must also submit the following required materials: unofficial copy of current transcript, and unofficial copy of the SAT or ACT scores. **Deadline:** February 4.

8170 ■ Ruth E. Jenkins Scholarships *(Undergraduate/Scholarship)*

Purpose: To support the education of African-American students from California. **Focus:** General studies/Field of study not specified. **Qualif.:** Applicants must be graduating African-American high school seniors from San Diego County who will enroll full-time at an accredited four-year university in San Diego county or a historically African-American college or university in the United States. They must have a 3.0 GPA on a 4.0 scale; have demonstrated financial need; and be involved in serving the communities through extra-curricular activities, work, church, or community service. **Criteria:** Preference is given to applicants who will attend a historically African-American college or university.

Funds Avail.: No specific amount. **Duration:** Annual. **To

Apply: Applicants may visit the website to verify the application process and other pieces of information. **Deadline:** February 4.

8171 ■ Napoleon A. Jones, III Memorial Scholarships *(Undergraduate/Scholarship)*

Purpose: To support the education of students from California. **Focus:** General studies/Field of study not specified. **Qualif.:** Applicants must be graduating high school senior residing within the zip codes of 92113, 92114 and 92115; or a graduating senior attending one of the following public high schools: Crawford, Hoover, Lincoln, Morse, San Diego High (located in downtown San Diego), and School for the Creative and Performing Arts. They must have a minimum 3.0 GPA on a 4.0 scale; planning to attend an accredited four-year university in the U.S.; have financial need; and engaged in serving the community as demonstrated by involvement in extra-curricular, work, church, or volunteer activities. **Criteria:** Selection shall be based on the aforementioned qualifications and compliance with the application details.

Funds Avail.: No specific amount. **Duration:** Annual. **To Apply:** Applicants may visit the website to verify the application process and other pieces of information. **Deadline:** February 4.

8172 ■ Kawano Family Scholarships *(Undergraduate/Scholarship)*

Purpose: To support the education of students with arthritis from California. **Focus:** General studies/Field of study not specified. **Qualif.:** Applicants must be students from San Diego County who have arthritis or have an immediate family member affected by arthritis, which impact the applicants on a daily basis. They must have a minimum of 3.0 GPA on a 4.0 scale; demonstrated financial need; and planning to attend, or attending an accredited four-year university in the U.S. **Criteria:** Selection shall be based on the aforementioned qualifications and compliance with the application details.

Funds Avail.: No specific amount. **To Apply:** Applicants may visit the website to verify the application process and other pieces of information.

8173 ■ Kiwanis Club of Escondido Scholarships *(Undergraduate/Scholarship)*

Purpose: To support the education of students from California. **Focus:** General studies/Field of study not specified. **Qualif.:** Applicants must be graduating high school seniors in the Escondido High School District planning to attend a two-year college or licensed trade/vocational school in the U.S.; have a minimum of 2.0 GPA on a 4.0 scale; active members of a Key Club (sponsored by an Escondido Kiwanis Club); have demonstrated financial need; and actively involved in serving the community through involvement in extra-curricular activities, community service, sports, or work experience. **Criteria:** Selection shall be based on the aforementioned qualifications and compliance with the application details.

Funds Avail.: No specific amount. **Duration:** Annual. **To Apply:** Applicants may visit the website to verify the application process and other pieces of information. Required additional materials: letter of recommendation from their respective Key Club advisors indicating their degree of involvement. **Deadline:** February 4. **Contact:** Arzo Mansury, Dir. Scholarships at 619-814-1343, or scholarships@sdfoundation.org.

Awards are arranged alphabetically below their administering organizations

8174 ■ Judith Keller Marx Krumholz Scholarships
(Undergraduate/Scholarship)

Purpose: To support the education of students from California. **Focus:** General studies/Field of study not specified. **Qualif.:** Applicants must be students currently attending San Diego City College who have completed one full academic semester and will continue attending San Diego City College in the fall of the current year; enrolled in at least 6 credits a semester; pursuing a Certificate of Achievement, an Associate degree, planning to transfer to a four-year university or, in some cases, a Certificate of Completion with a Vocational emphasis at San Diego City College; and have a minimum of 2.50 GPA on a 4.0 scale. **Criteria:** Selection shall be based on the aforementioned qualifications and compliance with the application details.

Funds Avail.: No specific amount. **Duration:** Annual. **To Apply:** Applicants may visit the website to verify the application process and other pieces of information. **Deadline:** February 4.

8175 ■ Patrick Ledden Honorary Scholarships
(Undergraduate/Scholarship)

Purpose: To support the education of students from California. **Focus:** General studies/Field of study not specified. **Qualif.:** Applicants must be graduating seniors at The Preuss School, UCSD; have a minimum 3.50 GPA on a 4.0 scale; and planning to attend a public or private four-year university in the state of California. **Criteria:** Special consideration is given to students who have participated in extra-curricular activities and community service or have work experience.

Funds Avail.: No specific amount. **To Apply:** Applicants may visit the website to verify the application process and other pieces of information. Required additional materials: essay (typed, double-spaced, maximum one page) answering "What have you learned from your experience at The Preuss School, UCSD that you feel will best benefit you in college?"

8176 ■ Lehman Family Scholarships *(Undergraduate/Scholarship)*

Purpose: To support the education of students from California. **Focus:** General studies/Field of study not specified. **Qualif.:** Applicants must be graduating seniors from Lincoln, Morse, or San Diego (downtown San Diego) high schools; have a minimum of 3.00 GPA on a 4.0 scale; planning to attend an accredited four-year university in the U.S; have financial need; and have demonstrated commitment to the through involvement in extra-curricular activities, work or volunteer experience, or church activities. **Criteria:** Preference will be given to foreign born children of immigrant parents.

Funds Avail.: No specific amount. **Duration:** Annual. **To Apply:** Applicants may visit the website to verify the application process and other pieces of information. **Deadline:** February 4.

8177 ■ The Lemon Grove Education Foundation Scholarships *(Undergraduate/Scholarship)*

Purpose: To support the education of students from California. **Focus:** General studies/Field of study not specified. **Qualif.:** Applicants must be graduating high school seniors or adults (ages 18 or over) reside within the boundaries of the Lemon Grove School District; have a minimum of 2.0 GPA on a 4.0 scale; and, planning to attend a four-year public university, two-year community college, licensed trade/vocational school, or regional occupational program in San Diego County. **Criteria:** Selection shall be based on the aforementioned qualifications and compliance with the application details.

Funds Avail.: No specific amount. **Duration:** Annual. **To Apply:** Applicants may visit the website to verify the application process and other pieces of information. **Deadline:** February 4.

8178 ■ Mission Bay Hospital Auxiliary Scholarships
(Undergraduate/Scholarship)

Purpose: To support the education of students from California. **Focus:** Medicine. **Qualif.:** Applicants must be graduating college seniors pursuing a career in medicine; residents of San Diego County planning to attend an accredited medical school in the U.S.; have a minimum 3.50 GPA on a 4.0 scale; and demonstrate financial need. **Criteria:** Award is given based on the application materials. Special consideration will be given to applicants who are involved in their community.

Funds Avail.: No specific amount. **Duration:** Annual. **To Apply:** Applicants may visit the website to verify the application process and other pieces of information. **Deadline:** February 4.

8179 ■ MKC/Preuss Scholarship Fund
(Undergraduate/Scholarship)

Purpose: To support the education of students from California. **Focus:** General studies/Field of study not specified. **Qualif.:** Applicants must be current graduating seniors and students who have already graduated from The Preuss School, UCSD. Student must have financial need; planning to attend an accredited two-year college or four-year university in the U.S.; have a minimum 3.0 GPA on a 4.0 scale; and involved in the community through participation in extra-curricular or religious activities or volunteer or work experience. **Criteria:** Selection will be based on the committee's criteria.

Funds Avail.: No specific amount. **Duration:** Annual. **To Apply:** Applicants should submit the completed application, and must provide the additional materials: unofficial copy of their current transcript and letter of recommendation on official letterhead from someone who knows them from an academic perspective. If selected, recipients must agree to identify a personal mentor during their freshman college year. The mentor might be a professor, club advisor, upperclassman attending the college of your choice, etc. **Deadline:** February 3.

8180 ■ Stuart L. Noderer Memorial Scholarships
(Undergraduate/Scholarship)

Purpose: To support the education of students from California. **Focus:** Architecture; Engineering; Science. **Qualif.:** Applicants must be graduating seniors from Mission Bay High School; planning to attend an accredited four-year university in the U.S.; have a minimum of 3.50 GPA on a 4.0 scale; and will major in science, engineering or architecture. **Criteria:** Selection will be based on aforesaid qualifications.

Funds Avail.: No specific amount. **Duration:** Annual. **To Apply:** Applicants may visit the website to verify the application process and other pieces of information. **Deadline:** February 4.

8181 ■ Pearman Family Scholarships
(Undergraduate/Scholarship)

Purpose: To support the education of students from California. **Focus:** General studies/Field of study not speci-

Awards are arranged alphabetically below their administering organizations

fied. **Qualif.:** Applicants must be graduating African-American high school seniors from San Diego County; must have a minimum of 3.4 GPA on a 4.0 scale; planning to attend an accredited four-year university in the U.S.; and have demonstrated financial need. **Criteria:** Preference may be given to applicants whose parents have not graduated from college.

Funds Avail.: No specific amount. **Duration:** Annual. **To Apply:** Applicants may visit the website to verify the application process and other pieces of information. **Deadline:** February 4.

8182 ■ Steve Petix Journalism Scholarships
(Undergraduate/Scholarship)

Purpose: To support the education of students from California. **Focus:** Journalism. **Qualif.:** Applicants must be graduating seniors attending schools in the Grossmont Union High School District who are interested in pursuing a career in journalism or related writing career; have a minimum of 2.50 GPA on a 4.0 scale; and planning to attend an accredited two-year college or four-year university in the U.S. **Criteria:** Preference will be given to students who have been involved in their school newspaper or serve as yearbook staff.

Funds Avail.: No specific amount. **Duration:** Annual. **To Apply:** Applicants may visit the website to verify the application process and other pieces of information. **Deadline:** February 4.

8183 ■ Pollard-Bailey Scholarships *(Undergraduate/ Scholarship)*

Purpose: To support the education of students from California. **Focus:** General studies/Field of study not specified. **Qualif.:** Applicants must be graduating high school seniors who will attend an accredited two-year community college in San Diego County; must have a minimum 2.50 GPA on a 4.0 scale; have a demonstrated financial need; and be engaged in serving the community through involvement in extra-curricular activities, church/volunteer activities or work experience. **Criteria:** Selection shall be based on the aforementioned qualifications and compliance with the application details.

Funds Avail.: No specific amount. **Duration:** Annual. **To Apply:** Applicants may visit the website to verify the application process and other pieces of information. **Deadline:** February 4.

8184 ■ Qualcomm San Diego Science, Technology, Engineering and Mathematics Scholarships
(Undergraduate/Scholarship)

Purpose: To support the education of students from California. **Focus:** General studies/Field of study not specified. **Qualif.:** Applicants must be graduating high school seniors; or students currently attending a local community college and transferring to either the University of California, San Diego, San Diego State University or California State University, San Marcos. Students must have a minimum of 3.50 GPA on a 4.0 scale and demonstrated financial need. **Criteria:** Awards are given based on the application materials. Consideration will be given to students who have participated in extra-curricular activities, community service, or work experience.

Funds Avail.: No specific amount. **Duration:** Annual. **To Apply:** Applicants may visit the website to verify the application process and other pieces of information. **Deadline:** February 4.

8185 ■ Rancho Bernardo/Smith Scholarships
(Undergraduate/Scholarship)

Purpose: To support the education of students from California. **Focus:** General studies/Field of study not specified. **Qualif.:** Applicants must be graduating high school senior from Rancho Bernardo who will attend an accredited, public four-year university in the state of California; have a minimum of 3.50 GPA on a 4.0 scale; and demonstrate commitment to the Rancho Bernardo community through involvement in extra-curricular activities, community service, sports, or work experience. **Criteria:** Special consideration will be given to applicants who have lost one or both parents while in high school.

Funds Avail.: No specific amount. **Duration:** Annual. **To Apply:** Applicants may visit the website to verify the application process and other pieces of information. **Deadline:** February 4.

8186 ■ The Rotary Club of Rancho Bernardo Sunrise Community Service Scholarships
(Undergraduate/Scholarship)

Purpose: To support the education of students from California. **Focus:** General studies/Field of study not specified. **Qualif.:** Applicants must be one of the following: graduating high school seniors living in or attending high school in Rancho Bernardo or Poway who plan to attend an accredited four-year university; current community college students whose high school home residence would have qualified them as graduating high school seniors who will transfer to a four-year college/university; current four-year university students whose high school hime residence would have qualified them as graduating high school seniors; or current Interact or Rotoract members residing in the communities of Scripps Ranch, Rancho Penasquitos or Rancho Bernardo, CA and/or who attend Abraxas High School, Del Norte High School, Mount Carmel High School, Poway High School, Scripps Ranch High School, or Westview High School. Furthermore, they must meet all of the following criteria: have a GPA of 3.25 on a 4.0 scale (high school GPAs are unweighted); be actively involved (more than 500 hours total during high school) in serving their community through their involvement in in extra-curricular activities, community service, or work experience in areas benefiting the greater San Diego community; and have demonstrated financial need. **Criteria:** Selection will be based on the submitted application materials.

Funds Avail.: No specific amount. **To Apply:** Applicants may visit the website to verify the application process and other pieces of information.

8187 ■ The San Diego Foundation Community Scholarships I *(Undergraduate/Scholarship)*

Purpose: To support the education of students from California. **Focus:** General studies/Field of study not specified. **Qualif.:** Applicants must be graduating seniors from a San Diego County continuation high school who plan to enroll part-time or full-time (taking at least 6 credits a semester) at an accredited four-year university, community college, or licensed career/technical school in the United States; have a minimum GPA of 2.0 on a 4.0 scale; have contributed to their community as demonstrated by their involvement in extra-curricular, work, religious, or volunteer activities; and have demonstrated financial need. **Criteria:** Selection will be based on aforesaid qualifications.

Funds Avail.: No specific amount. **Duration:** Annual. **To Apply:** Applicants may visit the website to verify the application process and other pieces of information. **Deadline:** February 4.

Awards are arranged alphabetically below their administering organizations

8188 ■ The San Diego Foundation Community Scholarships II *(Undergraduate/Scholarship)*

Purpose: To support the education of students from California. **Focus:** General studies/Field of study not specified. **Qualif.:** Applicants must be graduating high school seniors; have a minimum of 2.50 GPA on a 4.0 scale; and will attend an accredited two-year college in San Diego County. **Criteria:** Selection will be based on aforesaid qualifications.

Funds Avail.: No specific amount. **Duration:** Annual. **To Apply:** Applicants may visit the website to verify the application process and other pieces of information. **Deadline:** February 4.

8189 ■ San Pasqual Academy Scholarships *(Undergraduate/Scholarship)*

Purpose: To support the education of students from California. **Focus:** General studies/Field of study not specified. **Qualif.:** Applicants must be graduating high school seniors at San Pasqual Academy who plan to attend a four-year university, community college, or licensed career/technical school in he United States; and, have a minimum unweighted GPA of 3.0 on a 4.0 scale. **Criteria:** Awards are given based on the application materials.

Funds Avail.: No specific amount. **Duration:** Annual. **To Apply:** Applicants must submit the completed application. Required additional material is letter of recommendation on official letterhead from staff or faculty at San Pasqual Academy. **Deadline:** February 4.

8190 ■ Malini E. Sathyadev Memorial Scholarships *(Undergraduate/Scholarship)*

Purpose: To support the education of students from California. **Focus:** General studies/Field of study not specified. **Qualif.:** Applicants must be graduating high school seniors from Horizon High School and Cathedral Catholic High School; have a minimum of 3.50 GPA on a 4.0 scale; attending an accredited four-year university in the U.S.; and involved in serving the community as demonstrated by involvement in community service and extra-curricular activities such as sports and music. **Criteria:** Selection shall be based on the aforementioned qualifications and compliance with the application details.

Funds Avail.: No specific amount. **Duration:** Annual. **To Apply:** Applicants may visit the website to verify the application process and other pieces of information. Applicants must also submit an essay (maximum 500 words) on the role that Jesus Christ plays in their lives. **Deadline:** February 4.

8191 ■ Harvey L. Simmons Memorial Scholarships *(Undergraduate/Scholarship)*

Purpose: To support the education of students from California. **Focus:** General studies/Field of study not specified. **Qualif.:** Applicants must be graduating high school seniors who will attend an accredited two-year college or four-year university in the U.S.; have a minimum of 3.0 GPA on a 4.0 scale; have demonstrated financial need; and committed in serving the community through involvement in community service, church or extra-curricular activities. **Criteria:** Preference will be given to applicants who have participated in high school sports for at least three years, two at the varsity level, and are intending to play at the college level.

Funds Avail.: No specific amount. **Duration:** Annual. **To Apply:** Applicants may visit the website to verify the ap-

plication process and other pieces of information. Required additional materials: letter on official letterhead from their coach detailing the sport(s) played, level, years of participation and achievements. **Deadline:** February 4.

8192 ■ Step Up Scholarships *(Undergraduate, Graduate/Scholarship)*

Purpose: To support the education of students from California. **Focus:** Education; Teaching. **Qualif.:** Applicants must be students currently pursuing a teaching credential, current undergraduate students in their junior or senior year pursuing a career in teaching or students pursuing a Master's degree in education at a four-year university in San Diego county; and have a minimum of 3.20 GPA on a 4.0 scale. **Criteria:** Selection will be based on aforesaid qualifications.

Funds Avail.: No specific amount. **To Apply:** Applicants may visit the website to verify the application process and other pieces of information.

8193 ■ Mark and Karla Stuart Family Scholarship *(Undergraduate/Scholarship)*

Purpose: To support the education of students from California. **Focus:** General studies/Field of study not specified. **Qualif.:** Applicants must be U.S. citizens who are graduating high school seniors from Mission Bay High School planning to attend an accredited community college or four-year university in the United States; have a minimum unweighted GPA of 3.0 on a 4.0 scale; have a commitment to helping others and serving their community through their involvement in community service, academic clubs, sports, church or extra-curricular activities. **Criteria:** Selection shall be based on the aforementioned qualifications and compliance with the application details.

Funds Avail.: No specific amount. **Duration:** Annual. **To Apply:** Applicants may visit the website to verify the application process and other pieces of information. **Deadline:** February 4.

8194 ■ Raymond A. Tice Scholarships I *(Undergraduate/Scholarship)*

Purpose: To support the education of students from California. **Focus:** General studies/Field of study not specified. **Qualif.:** Applicants must be graduating high school seniors who will attend an accredited two-year college or four-year university in San Diego County; have a minimum of 2.25 to 3.50 GPA on a 4.0 scale and demonstrate financial need. They must be actively involved in serving the community as demonstrated by involvement in extra-curricular activities, community/church service, or work experience. **Criteria:** Selection will be based on aforesaid qualifications.

Funds Avail.: No specific amount. **To Apply:** Applicants may visit the website to verify the application process and other pieces of information.

8195 ■ Raymond A. Tice Scholarships II *(Undergraduate/Scholarship)*

Purpose: To support the education of students from California. **Focus:** General studies/Field of study not specified. **Qualif.:** Applicants must be students already attending an accredited two-year college or four-year university in San Diego County who will continue their college education in San Diego. They must have a minimum of 2.75 to 3.75 GPA on a 4.0 scale; have demonstrated financial need; and be involved in serving the community as demonstrated by

Awards are arranged alphabetically below their administering organizations

their involvement in extra-curricular activities, community/ church service, or work experience. **Criteria:** Selection will be based on aforesaid qualifications.

Funds Avail.: No specific amount. **To Apply:** Applicants may visit the website to verify the application process and other pieces of information.

8196 ■ Vincent Trotter Health Care Scholarships
(Undergraduate/Scholarship)

Purpose: To support the education of students from California. **Focus:** Health care services. **Qualif.:** Applicants must be current college students or adult re-entry students pursuing a career in the health care field (nurse practitioner, nurse, paramedic, health care aide or hospice aide) who plan to attend an accredited four-year university, community college or licensed career/technical school in the United States; and have a minimum GPA of 2.5 or better on a 4.0 scale. **Criteria:** Selection will be based on aforesaid qualifications.

Funds Avail.: No specific amount. **To Apply:** Applicants may visit the website to verify the application process and other pieces of information.

8197 ■ The UCSD Black Alumni Scholarship for Arts and Humanities *(Undergraduate/Scholarship)*

Purpose: To support the education of African-American students from California. **Focus:** Arts; Humanities. **Qualif.:** Applicants must be African-American students currently attending the University of California, San Diego (UCSD); or prospective African-American students enrolling at UCSD. Students must be majoring in the arts or humanities. High school students must have a 3.0 GPA on a 4.0 scale while current UCSD students must maintain at least a 2.70 GPA on a 4.0 scale. **Criteria:** Selection will be based on the students' involvement in the community.

Funds Avail.: No specific amount. **Duration:** Annual. **To Apply:** Applicants may visit the website to verify the application process and other pieces of information.

8198 ■ The UCSD Black Alumni Scholarships for Engineering, Mathematics and Science
(Undergraduate/Scholarship)

Purpose: To support the education of African-American students from California. **Focus:** Engineering; Mathematics and mathematical sciences; Science. **Qualif.:** Applicants must be African-American students currently enrolled full-time at the University of California, San Diego (UCSD); or prospective African-American students who are current California residents and will be enrolling at UCSD. Students must be majoring in engineering, mathematics or science. High school students must have a 3.0 GPA on a 4.0 scale while current UCSD students must have maintained at least a 2.7 GPA on a 4.0 scale. **Criteria:** Selection will be based on the students' involvement in the community.

Funds Avail.: No specifc amount. **Duration:** Annual. **To Apply:** Applicants may visit the website to verify the application process and other pieces of information. **Deadline:** February 4.

8199 ■ U.S. Bank Scholarships *(Undergraduate/ Scholarship)*

Purpose: To support the education of students from California. **Focus:** General studies/Field of study not specified. **Qualif.:** Applicants must be adults (ages 25 or older) with income levels less than or equal to 50% of the prevailing San Diego County Metropolitan Statistical Area HUD

median income level (currently $37,950); have earned a high school diploma or GED; have demonstrated financial need; working either full-time or part-time; either re-entering college after a break or are starting college for the first time in fall of the current year. **Criteria:** Selection will be based on aforesaid qualifications.

Funds Avail.: No specific amount. **Duration:** Annual. **To Apply:** Applicants may visit the website to verify the application process and other pieces of information. **Deadline:** February 4.

8200 ■ USA Freestyle Martial Arts Scholarships
(Undergraduate/Scholarship)

Purpose: To support the education of students from California. **Focus:** General studies/Field of study not specified. **Qualif.:** Applicants must be students who have attended USA Freestyle Martial Arts for at least two years and have earned a minimum of a Red Belt; must have a minimum 2.50 GPA on a 4.0 scale; and either be graduating high school seniors or current college students planning to attend an accredited two-year college, four-year university, or licensed career/technical school in the U.S. **Criteria:** Preference will be given to students with a demonstrated financial need and/or have persevered in spite of any obstacles.

Funds Avail.: No specific amount. **Duration:** Annual. **To Apply:** Applicants may visit the website to verify the application process and other pieces of information. **Deadline:** February 4.

8201 ■ Weissbuch Family Scholarships
(Undergraduate/Scholarship)

Purpose: To support the education of students from California. **Focus:** General studies/Field of study not specified. **Qualif.:** Applicants must be students enrolled at the University of California, San Diego (UCSD) in their freshman, sophomore or junior year and have a minimum of 2.50 GPA on a 4.0 scale. Students must be employed part-time and have a demonstrated financial need. They must also be residents of San Diego county for a minimum of four years. **Criteria:** Selection will be based on aforesaid qualifications.

Funds Avail.: No specific amount. **Duration:** Annual. **To Apply:** Applicants may visit the website to verify the application process and other pieces of information. **Deadline:** February 4.

8202 ■ Leon Williams Scholarships *(Undergraduate/ Scholarship)*

Purpose: To support the education of students from California. **Focus:** Health care services. **Qualif.:** Applicants must be graduating African-American high school seniors from San Diego County; have a minimum of 2.50 GPA on a 4.0 scale; attending an accredited four-year university in the U.S.; involved in communities as demonstrated by extra-curricular, work, church, or volunteer activities; have demonstrated financial need; and pursuing a career in health or the healthcare field. **Criteria:** Selection shall be based on the aforementioned qualifications and compliance with the application details.

Funds Avail.: No specific amount. **Duration:** Annual. **To Apply:** Applicants may visit the website to verify the application process and other pieces of information. Required additional materials: essay (maximum 500 words) on "Improving the Health of our Underserved Community." **Deadline:** February 4.

Awards are arranged alphabetically below their administering organizations

8203 ■ Randy Williams Scholarships
(Undergraduate/Scholarship)

Purpose: To support the education of students from California. **Focus:** General studies/Field of study not specified. **Qualif.:** Applicants must be graduating high school seniors; have participated in high school and/or club competitive swimming programs; be planning to attend an accredited two-year college, four-year university or licensed trade/vocational school in the U.S.; and have a minimum of 2.50 GPA on a 4.0 scale. **Criteria:** Selection will be based on the submitted application materials.

Funds Avail.: No specific amount. **Duration:** Annual. **To Apply:** Applicants must submit the following: completed application; letter of recommendation on official letterhead from swimming coach; essay (maximum of 250 words) describing the benefits they have enjoyed from being involved in competitive swimming and emphasizing how they will utilize the skills they learned in swimming to reach their goals. **Deadline:** February 4.

8204 ■ Jean Wright-Elson Scholarships *(Doctorate, Graduate, Undergraduate/Scholarship)*

Purpose: To support the education of students from California. **Focus:** Nursing. **Qualif.:** Applicants must be U.S. citizens and permanent residents; San Diego county residents; college students who have already completed two full academic years (60 semester units or 72 quarter units) pursuing a career in nursing or students pursuing their Master's degree or Ph.D. in nursing who will be enrolled fulltime at a community college or four-year university in San Diego; have a minimum of 3.0 GPA on a 4.0 scale. **Criteria:** Selection shall be based on demonstrated financial need.

Funds Avail.: No specific amount. **Duration:** Annual. **To Apply:** Applicants may visit the website to verify the application process and other pieces of information. Required additional materials: unofficial copy of current transcript. **Deadline:** February 4.

8205 ■ San Diego Pan-Pacific Law Enforcement Association (PANPAC)
PO Box 122924
San Diego, CA 92112
E-mail: sdpanpac@gmail.com
URL: www.sdpanpac.org

8206 ■ Pan Pacific Law Enforcement Scholarships
(Undergraduate/Scholarship)

Purpose: To provide financial assistance to San Diego students interested in law enforcement careers. **Focus:** Law enforcement. **Qualif.:** Applicants must be graduating high school seniors with a full time attendance record at a San Diego County High School; must be dependents of a PANPAC member or a member of the San Diego Asian Youth Organization; must have maintained a minimum GPA of 3.0 throughout high school. **Criteria:** Applicants are selected based on committee's review of the application materials.

Funds Avail.: No specific amount. **To Apply:** Applicants must submit a completed application form available online; must provide an autobiography (one-page maximum, 12-Font, 1 inch margins), high school transcript, two recommendation letters (community, school, government agency) and a 250-word essay describing, "How can Law Enforcement better serve the Asian and Pacific Island Community."

8207 ■ San Francisco Foundation
1 Embarcadero Ctr., Ste. 1400
San Francisco, CA 94111
Ph: (415)733-8500
Fax: (415)477-2783
E-mail: info@sff.org
URL: sff.org

8208 ■ Edwin Anthony and Adelaide Boudreaux Cadogan Scholarships *(Graduate/Fellowship)*

Purpose: To provide financial assistance to Bay area Fine Arts students in their academic studies. **Focus:** Art. **Qualif.:** Applicants must be MFA students currently pursuing a graduate degree at the California College of the Arts, Mills College, San Francisco Art Institute, San Francisco State University, Stanford University, or the University of California, Berkeley; must have completed at least one semester of graduate study, must be continuously enrolled in the same program, and be in good academic standing. **Criteria:** Selection will be based on evaluation of the submitted requirements and specific criteria.

Funds Avail.: $5,000. **To Apply:** Applicants must submit a completed online application form; work samples; description of work submitted; numbered list or work samples as detailed in the online application. **Deadline:** May 6. **Remarks:** Established in 1986. **Contact:** San Francisco Foundation, at the above address.

8209 ■ Jack K. and Gertrude Murphy Fellowships
(Graduate/Fellowship)

Purpose: To provide financial assistance to Bay area Fine Arts students in their academic studies. **Focus:** Art. **Qualif.:** Applicants must be MFA students currently pursuing a graduate degree at the California College of the Arts, Mills College, San Francisco Art Institute, San Francisco State University, Stanford University, or the University of California, Berkeley; must have completed at least one semester of graduate study, must be continuously enrolled in the same program, and be in good academic standing. **Criteria:** Selection will be based on the evaluation of the submitted requirements and specific criteria.

Funds Avail.: $5,000. **To Apply:** Applicants must submit a completed online application form; work samples; description of work submitted; numbered list or work samples as detailed in the online application. **Deadline:** May 6. **Remarks:** Established in 1986. **Contact:** San Francisco Foundation, at the above address.

8210 ■ San Francisco State University Disability Programs and Resource Center
Student Service Bldg., Rm. 110
1600 Holloway Ave.
San Francisco, CA 94132
Ph: (415)338-2472
Fax: (415)338-1041
E-mail: dprc@sfsu.edu
URL: www.sfsu.edu/~dprc

8211 ■ Ethel Louise Armstrong Foundation Scholarships *(Graduate/Scholarship)*

Purpose: To provide financial assistance for female students with physical disabilities for their educational expenses. **Focus:** Disabilities. **Qualif.:** Applicants must be graduate female students with disability; must be active in

Awards are arranged alphabetically below their administering organizations

a local, state or national disability organization; and must be willing to network as an ELA Scholar. **Criteria:** Selection will be based on the committee's criteria.

Funds Avail.: $500-$2,000. **To Apply:** Applicants may contact the Foundation for the application process and other information. **Deadline:** June.

8212 ■ California Council of the Blind Scholarships
(Undergraduate, Graduate/Scholarship)

Purpose: To provide financial assistance to students with disabilites for their educational expenses. **Focus:** Disabilities. **Qualif.:** Applicants must be students who will enter or continue undergraduate or graduate studies with good academic achievements; must be registered as legally blind; must be permanent California residents; and must be enrolled on a full-time basis. **Criteria:** Selection will be based on the committee's criteria.

Funds Avail.: No specific amount. **To Apply:** Applicants may contact the Foundation for the application process and other information. **Deadline:** June.

8213 ■ P. Johnson and C. Kolb Memorial Scholarships *(Undergraduate, Graduate, Master's, Doctorate/ Scholarship)*

Purpose: To provide financial support for students with disabilities to achieve their academic goals. **Focus:** Disabilities. **Qualif.:** Applicants must be students with disabilities who will be entering or are currently enrolled in graduate school with a minimum of 4 units; can be undergraduate, graduating senior, graduate, masters/ credential or in PhD level of study (undergraduate and graduate applicants must have a minimum of 3.0 for their GPA). **Criteria:** Selection will be based on the committee's criteria.

Funds Avail.: $1,000. **To Apply:** Applicants must contact the Center for the application process and other information. **Deadline:** May 15.

8214 ■ Dale M. Schoettler Scholarships
(Undergraduate, Graduate/Scholarship)

Purpose: To assist visually impaired students with their educational expenses. **Focus:** Disabilities. **Qualif.:** Applicants must be currently enrolled in 6.1 units or more as CSU undergraduate or graduate students in any major field and must remain enrolled in 6.1 units during the academic year in which the award is received; must currently have a minimum cumulative GPA of 2.8 on a 4.0 scale and must maintain a minimum GPA of 2.8 on a 4.0 scale during the academic year in which the award is received; and must have a visual disabilities and provide verification from a medical health professional. **Criteria:** Selection will be based on the committee's criteria.

Funds Avail.: $8,500. **Number Awarded:** 40. **To Apply:** Applicants must submit the following application requirements: completed scholarship applicant information form (typed); calculation of unmet financial need and calculation of grade point average to be verified by the Financial Aid before submission to DPRC; medical health professional's verification of visual disability, which includes the best corrected visual acuity notations using the "Confirmation of Visual Disability"; brief personal statement of the students describing the applicants' background, personal achievements, challenges encountered, educational pursuits and goals and aspirations for the future; and complete application checklist with initials from the Financial Aid office before submission to the DPRC. Be sure to print out and complete

both the Scholarship Applicant Information Form and the Application Checklist. Do not leave any line blank on the Applicant Information Form. If there is no information to provide, "N/A" should be used. Each item submitted with the application packet (i.e., "Personal Statement") should be clearly labeled. All application requirements must be submitted to the DPRC, no fax submissions will be accepted. **Remarks:** Established in 1991.

8215 ■ Timothy Wiese Memorial Scholarships
(Undergraduate, Graduate/Scholarship)

Purpose: To provide financial support for continuing SFSU students with disabilities who are in good academic standing. **Focus:** Disabilities. **Qualif.:** Applicants must be a continuing graduate or undergraduate students at SFSU; enrolled in at least 6 units for undergraduates and 4 units for graduate students; able to demonstrate financial need as determined by the Office of Student Financial Aid at SFSU, if the applicant have not done this he/she need to complete a Free Application for Federal Aid (FAFSA); able to either demonstrate some measure of academic achievement (2.5 GPA for undergraduates; 3.0 for graduate students) or show potential for eventual academic progress by virtue of non-academic accomplishments; and registered with the Disability Programs and Resource Center at SFSU. **Criteria:** Selection will be based on the committee's criteria.

Funds Avail.: $800. **To Apply:** Applicants must submit the following requirements: completed and signed application form; copy of most recent academic transcript (unofficial accepted); and application form of Free Application for Federal Aid (FAFSA). Applicants must also submit no more than three pages in response to the following topics: academic and career objectives; personal, academic or financial information; and list and brief narrative about the applicants' involvement with any schools, communities, or volunteer organizations. **Deadline:** November 15.

8216 ■ San Jose American GI Forum
322 S 1st St.
San Jose, CA 95113
Ph: (408)288-9470
Fax: (408)288-9473
E-mail: sjgif@sjgif.org
URL: www.sjgif.org

8217 ■ American GI Forum of San Jose Scholarships *(Undergraduate/Scholarship)*

Purpose: To provide financial assistance to qualified students of Hispanic descent who reside in the County of Santa Clara, California. **Focus:** General studies/Field of study not specified. **Qualif.:** Applicants must be graduating high school students located in Santa Clara County; must be enrolled or plan to enroll in an accredited college or university leading to an associate or bachelor's degree; and must have a minimum grade point average of 2.5. **Criteria:** Recipients are selected based on academic achievement, career goals and aspirations, community school activities and financial need; and quality of the essay based on its content, clarity, grammar and experience. Priority will be given to students of Mexican-American Descent.

Funds Avail.: No specific amount. **To Apply:** Applicants must submit completed application form; wallet size senior picture; official copy of high school transcript; biographical data sheet; an autobiographical essay; and a copy of parent's most recent Federal Income Tax or Student Aid

Awards are arranged alphabetically below their administering organizations

Application for California. Essay must be typed and not exceeding two pages. **Deadline:** March. **Contact:** San Jose GI Forum, Scholarship Foundation, Inc.; Address: 322 South First Street, San Jose, CA 95113; Phone: (408) 288-9470; Fax: (408) 288-9473.

8218 ■ Bert Saperstein Communications Scholarship Fund

PO Box 42
New Rochelle, NY 10804
Ph: (914)636-1281
E-mail: info@bsc-scholarshipfund.org
URL: www.bsc-scholarshipfund.org

8219 ■ Bert Saperstein Communication Scholarships *(Undergraduate/Scholarship)*

Purpose: To promote and increase interest in the field of Communication Arts which include film and television, creative writing, advertising, public relations and communication design. **Focus:** Communications. **Qualif.:** Applicants must be enrolled full-time in any college/university. **Criteria:** Selection will be based on the criteria set by the Board of Trustees.

Funds Avail.: No specific amount. **To Apply:** Applicants may submit their application letters and other requirements to the office. **Remarks:** Established in 1983.

8220 ■ Saratoga County Bar Association

PO Box 994
Saratoga Springs, NY 12866
Ph: (518)280-1974
URL: www.saratogacountybar.org

8221 ■ Saratoga County Bar Association Law Student Scholarships *(Undergraduate/Scholarship)*

Purpose: To provide assistance to students who made an effort in studying to enter the legal profession. **Focus:** Law. **Qualif.:** Applicants must be residents of Saratoga County who are in their second or third year of law school. **Criteria:** Recipients are selected based on class rank, demonstrated leadership, community involvement and financial need.

Funds Avail.: $1,000 each. **Duration:** Annual. **Number Awarded:** 2. **To Apply:** Applicants must submit a completed application form; and must attach Graduate and Professional School Financial Aid Report, if available **Deadline:** March 20. **Contact:** pclute@saratogacountybar.org.

8222 ■ Saskatchewan Association of Recreation Professionals

2205 Victoria Ave.
Regina, SK, Canada S4P 0S4
Ph: (306)780-9267
Fax: (306)525-4009
Free: 800-667-7780
E-mail: sarp.sk@sasktel.net
URL: sarp-online.ca

8223 ■ SARP Education Assistance Grants *(Professional development/Grant)*

Purpose: To provide professional, affiliate and student members funding to further develop their knowledge, skills and abilities through attending conferences, workshops, and post-secondary education classes. **Focus:** General studies/Field of study not specified. **Qualif.:** Applicants must be either professional, affiliate or student members in good standing. **Criteria:** Applications are reviewed based on the following criteria: volunteer involvement in the Association (past 5 years); significance to individual's professional development; location of professional development; years of membership; and previous education assistance received.

Funds Avail.: Maximum of $1,000. **Duration:** Annual. **To Apply:** Applicants must complete the application form and send it in to the provincial office mailed in or electronic. For further information, applicants may contact the Society for online application process and other required materials. **Deadline:** March 15; July 15; November 15.

8224 ■ SARP Professional Development Grants *(Professional development/Grant)*

Purpose: To provide opportunities for members to access financial assistance to host conferences, workshops and seminars in their community. **Focus:** General studies/Field of study not specified. **Qualif.:** Applicants must be either professional, affiliate, associate or student members in good standing that have host groups or organizations. **Criteria:** Application forms will be forwarded to the PDG Committee for review and scoring. Applications are scored according to the following criteria: significance to the professional development of the group(s) targeted; location of event (urban or rural); estimated number of participants; estimated number of SARP members participating; number of membership sectors targeted; and number of hosting partnerships.

Funds Avail.: Maximum of $500. **Duration:** Biennial. **To Apply:** Applicants must obtain a PD grant application form, complete and sign it then send it in to the provincial office. **Deadline:** March 15; July 15; November 15.

8225 ■ Saskatchewan Government Insurance (SGI)

2260 - 11th Ave.
Regina, SK, Canada S4P 0J9
Ph: (306)775-6900
Free: 800-667-9868
E-mail: sgiinquiries@sgi.sk.ca
URL: www.sgi.sk.ca

8226 ■ Auto Body Technician Certificate Scholarships *(Undergraduate/Scholarship)*

Purpose: To help Saskatchewan students accomplish their education goals. **Focus:** Automotive technology. **Qualif.:** Applicants must be students enrolled in the Auto Body Technician Certificate program at SIAST Wascana Campus and SIAST Kelsey Campus. **Criteria:** Selection will be based on academic achievement and financial need.

Funds Avail.: $2,500 each. **Duration:** Annual. **Number Awarded:** 2. **To Apply:** Students apply directly to SIAST. Students may download the application from the SIAST website or pick up applications at the Wascana and Kelsey Campuses. **Contact:** Human Resources, Scholarships, 2260 11th Avenue Regina, Saskatchewan S4P 0J9; Email: scholarships@sgi.sk.ca.

8227 ■ Business Insurance Diploma Scholarships *(Undergraduate/Scholarship)*

Purpose: To help Saskatchewan students accomplish their education goals. **Focus:** Business. **Qualif.:** Applicants must

Awards are arranged alphabetically below their administering organizations

be enrolled full-time in the Business Insurance Diploma Program - Year 2 at the SIAST Palliser campus; must have earned a minimum 70% average in their 1st year (Business Certificate Program); must self-declare as a diversity student with SIAST (for the diversity scholarship). **Criteria:** Selection will be based on the following criteria: academic achievement, as reflected in their overall GPA of all classes required to complete their Business Certificate (75% Weighting); financial need (25% Weighting).

Funds Avail.: $2,500. **Duration:** Annual. **Number Awarded:** 4. **To Apply:** Students may download the application from the SIAST website or pick up applications at the Palliser Campus. **Contact:** scholarships@sgi.sk.ca.

8228 ■ Stan Hamilton Scholarships *(Undergraduate/ Scholarship)*

Purpose: To help Saskatchewan aboriginal students for them to accomplish their education goals. **Focus:** General studies/Field of study not specified. **Qualif.:** Applicants must: be aboriginal (First Nations - Treaty or non-status, Metis or Inuit); be full-time students at FNUC; be enrolled in the last 12 credit hour classes in Administration Qualifying, Faculty of Administration, or in at least the second year of a computer science degree; maintain an overall average of at least 65%; and, show their contribution to the community, extracurricular activities or commitments made in balancing work, education and home responsibilities. **Criteria:** Selection shall be based on the aforementioned qualifications and compliance with the application details.

Funds Avail.: $2,500. **Duration:** Annual. **Number Awarded:** 1. **To Apply:** Applicants must complete and submit the application form. Applications can be obtained from the FNUC website or from the FNUC Student Success Services. **Deadline:** October 31. **Remarks:** The scholarship is awarded in the name of Stan Hamilton, SGI Vice President of Human Resources.

8229 ■ Insurance and Risk Management Scholarships - Grant MacEwan *(Undergraduate/Scholarship)*

Purpose: To help Saskatchewan students accomplish their education goals. **Focus:** Insurance and insurance-related fields; Risk management. **Qualif.:** Students must be enrolled full-time in the Insurance and Risk Management program (minimum 9 credit hours per term); must be Alberta, Saskatchewan or Manitoba residents; maintain a GPA of 3.0 by the end of the 2nd term. Scholarships will be awarded to the students achieving the highest cumulative GPA; must be receiving no other Insurance and Risk Management scholarships; must demonstrate involvement or leadership in the community and/or at the college. **Criteria:** Selection will be based on the Student Resource Centre Selection Committee's criteria.

Funds Avail.: $1,000. **Number Awarded:** 2. **To Apply:** There is no application for this scholarship. Students in the Insurance and Risk Management faculty that meet the criteria will automatically be considered. **Contact:** scholarships@sgi.sk.ca.

8230 ■ Risk Management and Insurance Scholarships - University of Calgary *(Undergraduate/ Scholarship)*

Purpose: To provide an ideal opportunity for students to gain professional and academic knowledge directly related to the insurance industry. **Focus:** Insurance and insurance-related fields; Risk management. **Qualif.:** Applicants must: be students that are residents of Saskatchewan, Alberta, or Manitoba; be egistered in the 2nd, 3rd or 4th year of stud-

ies in Risk Management and Insurance (RMIN) or Risk Management and Insurance/Finance (RMIF) at the University of Calgary; and have a GPA of 3.20. **Criteria:** Selection will be based on the Insurance and Risk Management faculty's criteria.

Funds Avail.: $3,000. **Duration:** Annual. **To Apply:** No application is required for this scholarship. Eligible students will automatically be considered by their faculty. **Contact:** Human Resources at: scholarships@sgi.sk.ca.

8231 ■ Saskatchewan Government Insurance Actuarial Science Scholarships *(Undergraduate/ Scholarship)*

Purpose: To help Saskatchewan students accomplish their education goals in the field of actuarial science. **Focus:** Actuarial science. **Qualif.:** Applicants must: be students enrolled in the third, fourth or fifth year of studies in the Faculty of Science, actuarial science program; have successfully completed 60 or more credit hours towards a Bachelor of Science Degree, major in Actuarial Science; have completed or enrolled in ASC 116, 216 and 317 and have a GPA of 80% or higher inte completed course stated; and, be registered in a minimum of 12 credit hours in the semester the scholarship is paid. **Criteria:** Selection shall be based on the aforementioned qualifications.

Funds Avail.: $2,000. **Duration:** Annual. **Number Awarded:** 1. **To Apply:** There is no application for this scholarship. Students are considered through recommendation of the University of Regina Department of Mathematics and Statistics.

8232 ■ Saskatchewan Government Insurance Anniversary Scholarships *(Undergraduate/Scholarship)*

Purpose: To help Saskatchewan students accomplish their education goals. **Focus:** General studies/Field of study not specified. **Qualif.:** Applicants must be children/legal dependents of an employee of SGI or its wholly-owned subsidiaries; be enrolled full-time in a certificate, diploma or degree program at an accredited post-secondary campus. **Criteria:** Selection will be based on the committee's criteria.

Funds Avail.: $2,500. **Duration:** Annual. **Number Awarded:** 4. **To Apply:** Applicants must complete and submit the application form together with proof of enrollment of the current academic year and a transcript demonstrating a minimum average of 70% in the last academic year of study. **Deadline:** September 30. **Contact:** scholarships@sgi.sk.ca.

8233 ■ Saskatchewan Government Insurance Corporate Scholarships *(Undergraduate/Scholarship)*

Purpose: To help Saskatchewan students accomplish their education goals. **Focus:** General studies/Field of study not specified. **Qualif.:** Applicants must be residents of Saskatchewan, Alberta or Manitoba; not be legal dependents of an employee of SGI or its wholly owned subsidiaries (legal dependents of SGI employees are eligible for the SGI Anniversary Scholarships only); be enrolled full-time in a certificate, diploma or degree program (related to the business needs of SGI) at an accredited post-secondary campus in Saskatchewan, Alberta or Manitoba. Business needs of SGI are defined broadly to include all aspects and departments in the corporation; must demonstrate contribution to community, extracurricular activities or commitments made in balancing work, education and home responsibilities. **Criteria:** Selection will be based on the committee's criteria.

Funds Avail.: $2,500. **Duration:** One year. **Number**

Awards are arranged alphabetically below their administering organizations

Awarded: 7. **To Apply:** Applicants must complete and submit the application form together with proof of enrollment of the current academic year and a transcript demonstrating a minimum average of 70% in the last academic year of study. **Deadline:** September 30. **Contact:** scholarships@sgi.sk.ca.

8234 ■ SGI Research Scholarships *(Graduate/Scholarship)*

Purpose: To support development of ideas which may be applied to the solution of problems in traffic safety in Saskatchewan. **Focus:** Engineering; Social sciences. **Qualif.:** Applicant must be a University of Regina graduate student who meets the following criteria: has a proposed research which involves engineering or human factors issues related to traffic safety; has a minimum cumulative grade point average (CGPA) of 80%; and, be registered full-time (minimum 6 credit hours) in the semester the award is presented. Continuing students must be in good standing and have demonstrated satisfactory achievement in course work as well as appropriate progress toward the completion of the research requirement. **Criteria:** Selection shall be based on the aforementioned qualifications and compliance with the application details.

Funds Avail.: $5,000. **Duration:** Annual. **To Apply:** Applications for the award are available on the University of Regina website and are to be submitted to the Faculty of Graduate Studies and Research. Applications should include a proposal for carrying out the research along with an outline of relevant experience that would have a bearing on the project proposed. Applications must also be supported by a confidential letter of reference from the faculty member who may be designated to supervise the student's research. **Deadline:** September 30.

8235 ■ Saskatchewan Hockey Association

No. 2 - 575 Park St.
Regina, SK, Canada S4N 5B2
Ph: (306)789-5101
Fax: (306)789-6112
E-mail: kellym@sha.sk.ca
URL: www.sha.sk.ca

8236 ■ Saskatchewan Hockey Association Scholarships *(Undergraduate/Scholarship)*

Purpose: To provide financial assistance to the SHA registered member to further their education. **Focus:** Sports studies. **Qualif.:** Each applicant must: have been registered for three years; be a registrant in good standing in the SHA; be a graduating Grade 12 student during that year for Junior A, B and C players or Senior players 20 years of age or under as of December 31 of the current year; be going to attend a Saskatchewan based University, affiliate College or SIAST; and, attend an institution within four years to take advantage of the grant. **Criteria:** Selection will be based on the committee's criteria.

Funds Avail.: $1,000 each. **Duration:** Annual. **Number Awarded:** Minimum of 11. **To Apply:** Application form can be obtained from the SHA office. Each applicant will be required to fill out and return an application on or before the deadline. **Deadline:** August 31.

8237 ■ Saskatchewan Pulse Growers (SPG)

207-116 Research Dr.
Saskatoon, SK, Canada S7N 3R3

Ph: (306)668-5556
Fax: (306)668-5557
E-mail: pulse@saskpulse.com
URL: www.saskpulse.com

8238 ■ Don Jaques Memorial Fellowships *(Graduate/Fellowship)*

Purpose: To recognize and support outstanding academic achievement and research interests in pulse crops. **Focus:** Agricultural sciences. **Qualif.:** Applicants must be either Canadian citizens or landed immigrants who are full-time, post-graduate students in a MSc or PhD degree program at the University of Saskatchewan, and are conducting thesis research on some aspect of pulse crop development **Criteria:** Selection will be made on the basis of a proven record of outstanding academic achievement and research interest in pulse crops development. Preference will be given to Saskatchewan residents.

Funds Avail.: $20,000. **Duration:** Annual. **Number Awarded:** 1. **To Apply:** Applicants may verify the application process through the program website.

8239 ■ Saskatchewan Pulse Growers Undergraduate Scholarships *(Undergraduate/Scholarship)*

Purpose: To promote the interest in pursuing a career related to agriculture and pulse industry. **Focus:** Agricultural sciences; Engineering; Natural sciences; Nutrition. **Qualif.:** Applicants must: be students in which they, or their parents, are registered as Saskatchewan pulse growers; not be immediate family members of current SPG staff or directors; have a minimum average of 70% on five high school average; and, be accepted as full-time students in a Saskatchewan-based post-secondary program that is associated with the pulse industry or agriculture (e.g. agriculture, natural sciences, nutrition, and engineering). **Criteria:** Selection shal be based on the premises that students must: have an interest in pursuing a career related to agriculture and the pulse industry; have a history of demonstrated leadership; and, have made contributions to school and community life.

Funds Avail.: $5,000. **Duration:** Annual. **Number Awarded:** 5. **To Apply:** Applicants must submit the following application requirements: unofficial transcript at the time of application followed by Official Transcript upon receipt; proof of acceptance (conditional or otherwise) to a post-secondary program, followed by proof of registration; one headshot photo; written permission to use photo and name in promotional materials (if candidate is successful). Applicants must also submit a maximum of 500 words essay on: career plans and how applicants plan to contribute to the pulse industry; situations where the applicant has demonstrated leadership; contributions the applicants have made to school and community life. **Deadline:** May 8.

8240 ■ Dr. Alfred E. Slinkard Scholarships *(Graduate/Scholarship)*

Purpose: To promote academic excellence within the area of pulse crop research in Saskatchewan. **Focus:** Agricultural sciences. **Qualif.:** Applicants must be full-time students entering or continuing studies pursuing a Masters of Science degree or Doctor of Philosophy degree who are conducting pulse crop research at the University of Saskatchewan. **Criteria:** Selection will be based on academic achievement, as determined by the Award Committee.

Funds Avail.: $20,000. **Duration:** Annual. **Number**

Awards are arranged alphabetically below their administering organizations

Awarded: 1. **To Apply:** Applicants may verify the application process through the program website.

8241 ■ Saskatchewan School Boards Association

400 - 2222 13th Ave.
Regina, SK, Canada S4P 3M7
Ph: (306)569-0750
Fax: (306)352-9633
E-mail: admin@saskschoolboards.ca
URL: www.saskschoolboards.ca

8242 ■ Saskatchewan School Boards Association Education Scholarships *(Undergraduate/Scholarship)*

Purpose: To support students who remain in Saskatchewan for acquiring post-secondary education. **Focus:** Science technologies. **Qualif.:** Applicants must be graduating high school students who remain in Saskatchewan in post-secondary study, and they should be either: entering university in Saskatchewan; or, entering a recognized institute of applied science and technology in Saskatchewan. **Criteria:** Selection will be based on demonstrated good character, community leadership, financial need and a 500-word essay.

Funds Avail.: $2,500 (University); $2,500 (Applied Science and Technoology). **Duration:** Annual. **Number Awarded:** 2. **To Apply:** Applicants may verify the application process through the program website. **Deadline:** August 31. **Remarks:** The scholarships are awarded in two categories: University Scholarships, and Applied Science and Technology Scholarships. **Contact:** admin@saskschoolboards.ca.

8243 ■ Saskatchewan School Boards Association Graduate Student Awards *(Graduate/Monetary)*

Purpose: To recognize leadership in education and to advance informed decision making in education. **Focus:** General studies/Field of study not specified. **Qualif.:** Applicants should be individuals who have recently completed a doctoral dissertation, master's thesis or project in education. Such study must contribute to advancing K-12 education in Saskatchewan. **Criteria:** Selection shall be based on the aforementioned qualifications and compliance with the application details.

Funds Avail.: $2,000 each. **Duration:** Annual. **Number Awarded:** Up to 4. **To Apply:** Applicants may verify the application process through the program website. **Deadline:** September 1.

8244 ■ Saskatchewan Trucking Association

1335 Wallace St.
Regina, SK, Canada S4N 3Z5
Ph: (306)569-9696
Fax: (306)569-1008
Free: 800-563-7623
URL: www.sasktrucking.com

8245 ■ Saskatchewan Trucking Association Scholarships *(Undergraduate/Scholarship)*

Purpose: To provide support children of employees for their post-secondary education. **Focus:** General studies/Field of study not specified. **Qualif.:** Applicant must be a grade 12 graduate who is an employee or a child of an employee, a carrier or associate trade member of the as-sociation; must be a student returning to post-secondary education after an absence of more than five years. **Criteria:** Applicants will be selected based on financial need and scholastic ability. Scholarship will be awarded without regards to sex, race, color, national origin or religion.

Funds Avail.: $1,000 each. **Number Awarded:** 7. **To Apply:** Applicants must submit a transcript of record and the application form and must send it to Scholarship Selection Committee. **Deadline:** June 30.

8246 ■ Savoy Foundation

230 Foch St.
Saint-Jean-sur-Richelieu, QC, Canada J3B 2B2
Ph: (450)358-9779
Fax: (450)346-1045
E-mail: epilepsy@savoy-foundation.ca
URL: www.savoy-foundation.ca

8247 ■ Savoy Foundation Postdoctoral and Clinical Research Fellowships *(Postdoctorate/Fellowship)*

Purpose: To support study and research in the field of epilepsy. **Focus:** Epilepsy. **Qualif.:** Applicant must be a scientist or medical specialist (PhD or MD) who wish to carry out a full-time research project in the field of epilepsy. **Criteria:** Selection is based on the submitted application.

Funds Avail.: $30,000; plus additional $1,500 for the fellow with the highest mark. **Duration:** 1 year. **To Apply:** Applicants must submit a completed application form. Two letters of reference must be sent directly by the writers to the foundation. **Deadline:** January 15.

8248 ■ Scandinavian Society of Cincinnati (SSOC)

1279 Sweetwater Dr.
Cincinnati, OH 45215
URL: www.scandinaviansoc.org

8249 ■ SSOC Scholarships *(Undergraduate/Scholarship)*

Purpose: To foster the development of ideas, knowledge, culture and understanding between the people of the United States of America and Scandinavian countries. **Focus:** General studies/Field of study not specified. **Qualif.:** Applicants must be persons/students from the Greater Cincinnati area, students from Scandinavia studying in the Greater Cincinnati, or persons or groups putting on Scandinavian cultural events in this area. **Criteria:** Recipients will be selected based on submitted materials.

Funds Avail.: $1,000. **To Apply:** Applicants must complete the application form and must prepare a 10-page, double-spaced reviewed paper. **Contact:** Shirley Ekvall; 549 Tohatchi Dr., Cincinnati, OH 45215.

8250 ■ Leopold Schepp Foundation

551 Fifth Ave., Ste. 3000
New York, NY 10176
Ph: (212)692-0191
URL: www.scheppfoundation.org

8251 ■ Leopold Schepp Foundation Scholarships *(Undergraduate, Graduate/Scholarship)*

Purpose: To provide educational support for students pursuing higher education. **Focus:** General studies/Field of

Awards are arranged alphabetically below their administering organizations

study not specified. **Qualif.:** Applicants must: be undergraduate students (under 30 years of age) or graduates (under 40 years of age) at the time of application; have a minimum GPA of 3.2 on a 4.0 scale and enroll full-time in a four year bachelor degree or approved graduate program; and, be citizens or permanent residents of the United States. High school seniors are eligible to apply during their senior year in high school for their first year in college. **Criteria:** Selection shall be based on the following: character; ability; and financial need.

Funds Avail.: No specific amount. **Duration:** Annual. **Number Awarded:** Varies. **To Apply:** Applicants may visit the scholarship section of the bestowing organization's website for further information regarding the application details. **Contact:** The Leopold Schepp Foundation, at the above address.

8252 ■ Schmeelk Canada Foundation
Sta. B
Montreal, QC, Canada H3B 3K5
E-mail: contact@schmeelk.ca
URL: www.schmeelk.ca

8253 ■ Richard J. Schmeelk Fellowships *(Graduate/Fellowship)*

Purpose: To promote intercultural awareness and interprovincial studies. **Focus:** Foreign languages. **Qualif.:** Applicant must be a Canadian citizen or landed immigrant; must have completed a bachelor's degree; and pursuing studies in Canada's other official language at one of the Richard J. Schmeelk Fellowship partner universities. **Criteria:** Selection is based on applicant's likelihood of contributing to the development of tolerance and understanding between Anglophone and Francophone Canadians and Canada's regional differences east and west; applicant's academic merit; and applicant's maturity, ability and character as reflected by the application and letters of reference.

Funds Avail.: $10,000 per semester, maximum of $40,000. **To Apply:** Applicants must submit a completed application form and attach the required supporting documents. Submit complete application package to the participating university of the applicant's choice. **Deadline:** April 15.

8254 ■ Scholarship Foundation of the Pacific
PO Box 505
Little Fort, BC, Canada V0E 2C0
Ph: (604)638-1802
URL: www.sfotp.com

8255 ■ Fernandez Earle Undergraduate Entrance Scholarships *(Undergraduate/Scholarship)*

Purpose: To support the education of undergraduate students from a high school in the Queens Charlotte Islands. **Focus:** General studies/Field of study not specified. **Qualif.:** Applicant must be a graduating student with scholastic achievement as well as strong leadership qualities and concern for their community. **Criteria:** Preference will be based on merit and need.

Funds Avail.: No specific amount. **To Apply:** Applicant must provide a transcript, letter of recommendation from school officials and community representatives, and a letter from the applicant describing their educational and career goals.

8256 ■ The Scholarship Foundation of St. Louis
8215 Clayton Rd.
Saint Louis, MO 63117
Ph: (314)725-7990
Fax: (314)725-5231
E-mail: info@sfstl.org
URL: www.sfstl.org

8257 ■ The Scholarship Foundation of St. Louis Scholarships *(Graduate, Undergraduate/Scholarship)*

Purpose: To provide financial assistance to members who want to pursue their educational goals. **Focus:** General studies/Field of study not specified. **Qualif.:** Applicant must be a student seeking a second baccalaureate degree; must be a graduate student applying to the foundation for the first time; must not be attending to a non accredited school by North Central or its regional equivalent. **Criteria:** Selection will be based on submitted application and financial need.

Funds Avail.: No specific amount. **To Apply:** Applicant must complete the application form available in the website; must submit a written statement describing the applicant's professional and personal goals in no more than the equivalent of one type page; must provide a Federal Income Tax Returns, Student Aid Report, Recommendation Form, Official Academic Transcripts and Financial Aid Award Letter. **Deadline:** November 15.

8258 ■ Scholarship Foundation of Santa Barbara
2253 Las Positas Rd.
Santa Barbara, CA 93105
Ph: (805)687-6065
E-mail: info@sbscholarship.org
URL: www.sbscholarship.org

8259 ■ Scholarship Foundation of Santa Barbara Art Scholarship Program *(Undergraduate/Scholarship)*

Purpose: To provide financial assistance to students who are planning to major in Art or an art-related major at college. **Focus:** Arts. **Qualif.:** Applicants must be Santa Barbara County area graduating high school seniors who have attended at least four of the six secondary grade school years in Southern Santa Barbara County, comprised of Goleta, Santa Barbara and Carpinteria; must be planning to major in art or an art-related field in college. **Criteria:** Applicants will be assessed based on academic merit.

Funds Avail.: No specific amount. **Duration:** Annual. **To Apply:** Applicants must complete the online application, including the questionnaire; they must also upload their high school transcripts to their online application. **Deadline:** November 15. **Contact:** info@sbscholarship.org.

8260 ■ Scholarship Foundation of Santa Barbara General Undergraduate, Vocational and Graduate/Medical Scholarships and Loans Program *(Undergraduate, Graduate/Scholarship)*

Purpose: To assist applicants studying in standard academic programs on a traditional academic calendar. **Focus:** General studies/Field of study not specified. **Qualif.:** Applicants must be U.S. citizens or documented legal permanent U.S. residents; have attended at least four of the six secondary grade school years at a Santa Barbara County school and have graduated or will graduate from a

---

Awards are arranged alphabetically below their administering organizations

Santa Barbara County high school; be planning to attend full-time (12 units minimum per term) at an approved vocational school, two or four-year college; and must maintain a minimum 2.0 GPA. **Criteria:** Applicants are evaluated based on financial need, potential and motivation.

Funds Avail.: $500 to $5,000 per academic year. **Duration:** Annual. **To Apply:** Applicants must submit all the required application information. **Deadline:** January 31. **Contact:** info@sbscholarship.org.

8261 ■ South Coast Area High School Senior Honors Scholarship Program (Undergraduate/Scholarship)

Purpose: To provide assistance to those students who are pursuing their chosen education. **Focus:** General studies/Field of study not specified. **Qualif.:** Applicants must be graduating high school seniors who have attended at least four of the six secondary grade school years in Southern Santa Barbara County (Goleta, Santa Barbara, Carpinteria); must be U.S. citizens or legal permanent residents. Students and their families must be residents of Santa Barbara County. **Criteria:** Applicants are evaluated based on academic achievement.

Funds Avail.: No specific amount. **Duration:** Annual. **To Apply:** Applicants must submit completed application form; personal statement/essay; academic transcript; academic recommendation letter; copy of SAT/ACT scores; and employer/supervisor recommendation letter in order to qualify for an interview. Only qualified applicants will be considered for a personal interview. **Deadline:** November 15. **Contact:** info@sbscholarship.org.

8262 ■ The Scholarship Foundation of Wakefield
467 Main St., Main Fl.
Wakefield, MA 01880
Ph: (781)245-4890
Fax: (781)245-6761
E-mail: tsfofwakefield@earthlink.net
URL: www.csfofwakefield.org

8263 ■ The Scholarship Foundation of Wakefield Scholarships (All/Scholarship)

Purpose: To support the education of Wakefield students. **Focus:** General studies/Field of study not specified. **Qualif.:** Applicants must be residents of Wakefield who will attend school in a full-time basis and must demonstrate financial need. **Criteria:** Selection is based on financial need and merit.

Funds Avail.: Amount varies. **Duration:** Annual. **Number Awarded:** Varies. **To Apply:** Applicants may visit the scholarship section of the Foundation's website for further information regarding the application details. **Deadline:** March 31. **Contact:** The Scholarship Foundation of Wakefield, at the above address.

8264 ■ ScholarshipExpert.com
3020 Hartley Rd., Ste. 220
Jacksonville, FL 32257
E-mail: info@scholarshipexperts.com
URL: www.scholarshipexperts.com

8265 ■ All About Education Scholarships
(Undergraduate, Graduate/Scholarship)

Purpose: To serve the needs of college undergraduate and graduate students and college-bound high school seniors as they look for ways to pay for their education. **Focus:** General studies/Field of study not specified. **Qualif.:** Applicants must be 13 years of age or older at the time of application; must be legal residents of the 50 United States or the District of Columbia; must be currently enrolled in an accredited post-secondary institution of higher education. **Criteria:** Selection will be based on the committee's criteria.

Funds Avail.: $3,000. **Number Awarded:** 1. **To Apply:** Applicants must visit the website for the online application and must submit a short written response, 250 words or less, for the topic: "How will a $3,000 scholarship for education make a difference in your life?" **Deadline:** April 30.

8266 ■ Do-Over Scholarships (Undergraduate, Graduate/Scholarship)

Purpose: To serve the needs of college undergraduate and graduate students and college-bound high school seniors as they look for ways to pay for their education. **Focus:** General studies/Field of study not specified. **Qualif.:** Applicants must be 13 years of age or older at the time of application; must be legal residents of the 50 United States or the District of Columbia; must be currently enrolled in an accredited post-secondary institution of higher education. **Criteria:** Selection will be based on the committee's criteria.

Funds Avail.: $1,500. **Number Awarded:** 1. **To Apply:** Applicants must visit the website for the online application and must submit a short written response, 250 words or less, for the question: "If you could get one 'Do-Over' in life, what would it be and why?" **Deadline:** June 30.

8267 ■ Education Matters Scholarships (High School, Undergraduate, Graduate/Scholarship)

Purpose: To serve the needs of college undergraduate and graduate students and college-bound high school seniors as they look for ways to pay for their education. **Focus:** General studies/Field of study not specified. **Qualif.:** Applicants must be 13 years of age or older at the time of application; must be legal residents of the 50 United States or the District of Columbia; must be currently enrolled in an accredited post-secondary institution of higher education. **Criteria:** Selection will be based on the committee's criteria.

Funds Avail.: $5,000. **Duration:** Annual. **Number Awarded:** 1. **To Apply:** Applicants must visit the website for the online application and must submit a short written response, 250 words or less, for the question: "What would you say to someone who thinks education doesn't matter, or that college is a waste of time and money?" **Deadline:** November 30.

8268 ■ Fifth Month Scholarships (Undergraduate, Graduate/Scholarship)

Purpose: To serve the needs of college undergraduate and graduate students and college-bound high school seniors as they look for ways to pay for their education. **Focus:** General studies/Field of study not specified. **Qualif.:** Applicants must be 13 years of age or older at the time of application; must be legal residents of the 50 United States or the District of Columbia; must be currently enrolled in an accredited post-secondary institution of higher education. **Criteria:** Selection will be based on the committee's criteria.

Funds Avail.: $1,500. **Number Awarded:** 1. **To Apply:** Applicants must visit the website for the online application

Awards are arranged alphabetically below their administering organizations

and must submit a short written response, 250 words or less, for the question: "May is the fifth month of the year. Write a letter to the number five explaining why five is important. Be serious or be funny. Either way, here's a high five to you just for being original." **Deadline:** May 31.

8269 ■ Flavor of the Month Scholarship
(Undergraduate, Graduate/Scholarship)

Purpose: To serve the needs of college undergraduate and graduate students and college-bound high school seniors as they look for ways to pay for their education. **Focus:** General studies/Field of study not specified. **Qualif.:** Applicants must be 13 years of age or older at the time of application; must be legal residents of the 50 United States or the District of Columbia; must be currently enrolled in an accredited post-secondary institution of higher education. **Criteria:** Selection will be based on the committee's criteria.

Funds Avail.: $1,500. **Number Awarded:** 1. **To Apply:** Applicants must visit the website for the online application and must submit a short written response, 250 words or less, for the question: "Summer and ice cream go hand-in-hand. In fact, July is National Ice Cream Month and that's the inspiration behind this award. We think people are very similar to ice cream; some are nutty, others a little exotic, while some are very comforting. If you were an ice cream flavor, which would you be and why?" **Deadline:** July 31.

8270 ■ Good Deeds Scholarships *(High School, Undergraduate/Scholarship)*

Purpose: To serve the needs of college undergraduate and graduate students and college-bound high school senior as they look for ways to pay for their education. **Focus:** General studies/Field of study not specified. **Qualif.:** Applicants must be current high school students (freshman, sophomore, junior or senior) at the time of application; must be legal residents of the 50 United States or the District of Columbia; must have plans to enroll in an accredited post-secondary institution of higher education. **Criteria:** Selection will be based on the committee's criteria.

Funds Avail.: $1,000. **Duration:** Annual. **Number Awarded:** 1. **To Apply:** Applicants must visit the website for the online application and must submit a short written response, 250 words or less, for the topic: "Have you ever volunteered, done community service or helped others in a way that changed the world for the better? If not, what would you do in the future to make a difference? Explain how your good deed positively contributed or will contribute to society." **Deadline:** December 31.

8271 ■ Make Me Laugh Scholarships *(High School, Undergraduate, Graduate/Scholarship)*

Purpose: To serve the needs of college undergraduate and graduate students and college-bound high school seniors as they look for ways to pay for their education. **Focus:** General studies/Field of study not specified. **Qualif.:** Applicants must be 13 years of age or older at the time of application; must be legal resident of the 50 United States or the District of Columbia; must be currently enrolled in an accredited post-secondary institution of higher education. **Criteria:** Selection will be based on the committee's criteria.

Funds Avail.: $1,500. **Duration:** Annual. **Number Awarded:** 1. **To Apply:** Applicants must visit the website for the online application and must submit a short written response, 250 words or less, for the topic: "OMG... finding and applying for scholarships is serious business, but it's

time to lighten things up a little. We don't want to know why you deserve $1,500 or how great your grades are, we simply want to LOL. Describe an incident in your life, funny or embarrassing (fact or fiction) and make us laugh!" **Deadline:** August 31.

8272 ■ Next Big Thing Scholarships *(Undergraduate, Graduate/Scholarship)*

Purpose: To serve the needs of college undergraduate and graduate students and college-bound high school seniors as they look for ways to pay for their education. **Focus:** General studies/Field of study not specified. **Qualif.:** Applicants must be 13 years of age or older at the time of application; must be legal residents of the 50 United States or the District of Columbia; must be currently enrolled in an accredited post-secondary institution of higher education. **Criteria:** Selection will be based on the committee's criteria.

Funds Avail.: No specific amount. **To Apply:** Applicants must visit the website for the online application and must submit a short written response, 250 words or less, for the question: "If you could create the next big thing, what would it be, what would it do and why is it needed?"

8273 ■ Shout It Out Scholarships *(High School, Undergraduate, Graduate/Scholarship)*

Purpose: To serve the needs of college undergraduate and graduate students and college-bound high school seniors as they look for ways to pay for their education. **Focus:** General studies/Field of study not specified. **Qualif.:** Applicants must be 13 years of age or older at the time of application; must be legal resident of the 50 United States or the District of Columbia; must be currently enrolled in an accredited post-secondary institution of higher education. **Criteria:** Selection will be based on the committee's criteria.

Funds Avail.: $1,500. **Duration:** Annual. **Number Awarded:** 1. **To Apply:** Applicants must visit the website for the online application and must submit a short written response, 250 words or less, for the question: "If you could say one thing to the entire world at once, what would it be and why?" **Deadline:** September 30.

8274 ■ Superpower Scholarships *(Undergraduate, Graduate/Scholarship)*

Purpose: To serve the needs of college undergraduate and graduate student as they look for ways to pay for their education. **Focus:** General studies/Field of study not specified. **Qualif.:** Applicants must be 13 years of age or older at the time of application; must be legal residents of the 50 United States or the District of Columbia; must be currently enrolled in an accredited post-secondary institution of higher education. **Criteria:** Selection will be based on the committee's criteria.

Funds Avail.: $2,500. **Number Awarded:** 1. **To Apply:** Applicants must visit the website for the online application and must submit a short written response, 250 words or less, for the question: "Which superhero or villain would you want to changes places with for a day and why?" **Deadline:** March 31.

8275 ■ Top Ten List Scholarships *(High School, Undergraduate, Graduate/Scholarship)*

Purpose: To serve the needs of college undergraduate and graduate students and college-bound high school senior as they look for ways to pay for their education.

Awards are arranged alphabetically below their administering organizations

Focus: General studies/Field of study not specified. **Qualif.:** Applicants must be 13 years of age or older at the time of application; must be legal residents of the 50 United States or the District of Columbia; must be currently enrolled in an accredited post-secondary institution of higher education. **Criteria:** Selection will be based on the committee's criteria.

Funds Avail.: $1,500. **Duration:** Annual. **Number Awarded:** 1. **To Apply:** Applicants must visit the website for the online application and must submit a short written response, 250 words or less, for the topic: "Create a top ten list of the top ten reasons you should get this scholarship." **Deadline:** December 31.

8276 ▪ Zombie Apocalypse Scholarships (High School, Undergraduate, Graduate/Scholarship)

Purpose: To serve the needs of college undergraduate and graduate students and college-bound high school seniors as they look for ways to pay for their education. **Focus:** General studies/Field of study not specified. **Qualif.:** Applicants must be 13 years of age or older at the time of application; must be legal residents of the 50 United States or the District of Columbia; must be currently enrolled in an accredited post-secondary institution of higher education. **Criteria:** Selection will be based on the committee's criteria.

Funds Avail.: $2,000. **Duration:** Annual. **Number Awarded:** 1. **To Apply:** Applicants must visit the website for the online application and must submit a short written response, 250 words or less, for the question: "Imagine that your high school/college has been overrun with zombies... Your math professor, the cafeteria ladies and even your best friend have all joined the walking dead. Use your brain to flesh out a plan to avoid the zombies, including where you would hide and the top five things you would bring with you to stay alive." **Deadline:** October 31.

8277 ▪ School Nutrition Association (SNA)

120 Waterfront St., Ste. 300
National Harbor
Oxon Hill, MD 20745-1142
Ph: (301)686-3100
Fax: (301)686-3115
Free: 800-877-8822
E-mail: servicecenter@schoolnutrition.org
URL: www.schoolnutrition.org

8278 ▪ Nancy Curry Scholarships (Postgraduate, Vocational/Occupational/Scholarship)

Purpose: To provide School Nutrition Association members with the opportunity to explore higher education options with the help of financial assistance. **Focus:** Food service careers. **Qualif.:** Applicant must be a member or dependent of a member of SNA for at least one year; pursuing a school food service related field; accepted at technical/vocational institution or university/college; have a satisfactory academic record; and must express the desire to make school foodservice a career. **Criteria:** Selection is based on the submitted application.

Funds Avail.: $500. **Duration:** Annual; One academic year. **Number Awarded:** 1. **To Apply:** Applicant must submit a completed application along with the required materials and information. **Deadline:** April 9.

8279 ▪ GED Jump Start Scholarships (Undergraduate/Scholarship)

Purpose: To empower SNA members to stay in school foodservice and advance their careers, and make members eligible for college-level scholarships. **Focus:** Food service careers. **Qualif.:** Applicants must be members of the SNA; have not yet received a high school diploma or a GED; planning on getting GED within one year of receiving the scholarship; and must not have received a GED Jump Start Scholarship in the past. **Criteria:** Selection will be based on the Financial Aid Committee's criteria.

Funds Avail.: $200. **Duration:** Annual. **Number Awarded:** 20. **To Apply:** Applicants must submit a completed application form along with the required materials and information. **Contact:** 800-877-8822 x-104, or scholarships@schoolnutrition.org.

8280 ▪ Schwan's Food Service Scholarships (Undergraduate, Vocational/Occupational/Scholarship)

Purpose: To provide School Nutrition Association members with the opportunity to explore higher education options with the help of financial assistance. **Focus:** Food service careers. **Qualif.:** Applicant must be a member or dependent of a member of SNA for at least one year; pursuing a school food service related field; accepted at technical/vocational institution or university/college; have a satisfactory academic record; and must express the desire to make school foodservice a career. **Criteria:** Selection is based on the application.

Funds Avail.: Up to $2,500. **Duration:** One academic year. **To Apply:** Applicants must submit a completed application along with the required materials and information. **Remarks:** Funded by Schwan's Food Service.

8281 ▪ SNF Professional Growth Scholarships (Graduate, Undergraduate/Scholarship)

Purpose: To provide School Nutrition Association members with the opportunity to explore higher education options with the help of financial assistance. **Focus:** Food service careers. **Qualif.:** Applicant must be a member or dependent of a member of SNA for at least one year; pursuing undergraduate or graduate studies; have a satisfactory academic record; and must express the desire to make school foodservice a career. **Criteria:** Selection will be based on the submitted application.

Funds Avail.: $2,500. **Duration:** Annual; One academic year. **To Apply:** Applicant must submit a completed application along with the required materials and information. **Deadline:** April 9.

8282 ▪ Winston Scholarships (Graduate, Undergraduate, Vocational/Occupational/Scholarship)

Purpose: To provide School Nutrition Association members with the opportunity to explore higher education options through financial assistance. **Focus:** Food service careers. **Qualif.:** Applicant must be employed as a School Food Service Professional; or a dependent of an employee, employed as a School Food Service Professional; a registered at, or have plans to attend an accredited college, university or vocational/technical institution. **Criteria:** Selection will be based on the submitted application.

Funds Avail.: $2,500. **To Apply:** Applicant must submit a completed Winston Scholarship application form along with the required materials and information.

8283 ▪ School Nutrition Association of Kansas (SNA-KS)

c/o Elaine Harris, President
12538 Prestwick Dr.
Kansas City, KS 66109

Awards are arranged alphabetically below their administering organizations

Ph: (913)294-8005
URL: www.sna-ks.org

8284 ■ School Nutrition Association of Kansas Education Scholarship *(Undergraduate/Scholarship)*

Purpose: To support school food service personnel who have an interest in furthering their career and refining their skills in school food service. **Focus:** Food science and technology. **Qualif.:** Applicants must be school food service personnel who have an interest in furthering their career and refining their skills in school food service; must be current members of SNA-KS. **Criteria:** Applications are accepted for classes or courses taken in the current year only. The number of scholarships awarded will be determined by the funds available annually by the SNA-KS Board.

Funds Avail.: No specific amount. **Duration:** Annual. **To Apply:** Applicant must submit the following requirements: a copy of the applicants' current membership card; personal information; course information; education history; essay. **Deadline:** May 31.

8285 ■ Evalee C. Schwarz Charitable Trust for Education

c/o Private Foundation Services, Inc.
4265 San Felipe, Ste. 1100
Houston, TX 77027-2913
E-mail: pfs@privatefoundationservices.com
URL: www.evaleeschwarztrust.org

8286 ■ Evalee C. Schwarz Educational Loans *(Undergraduate, Graduate/Loan)*

Purpose: To provide interest-free loans to undergraduate and graduate students who demonstrate exceptional academic performance and significant financial need. **Focus:** General studies/Field of study not specified. **Qualif.:** Applicants must: be U.S. citizens; qualify for financial need in the form of government grants (Please complete the Free Application for Federal Student Aid); be enrolled in a school in the state in which the students reside; demonstrate outstanding combination of class rank and standardized test scores (scores must be in the top 10% of nationwide scores); and, not be seeking a law degree. **Criteria:** Selection shall be based on academic performance and financial need.

Funds Avail.: Range from $5,000 to $15,000, with a $60,000 lifetime cap per student. **Duration:** Annual. **Number Awarded:** Varies. **To Apply:** Applicants must submit a completed typed or printed application form along with a copy of official picture I.D.; official transcripts; copy of admission test scores; copy of brochure or other document stating current school cost; copy of Student Aid Report (SAR); three letters of recommendation; and a personal essay. **Deadline:** April 10. **Contact:** Evalee C. Schwarz Charitable Trust for Education, at the above address.

8287 ■ Science Foundation Arizona (SFAz)

400 E Van Buren St., Ste. 200
Phoenix, AZ 85004
Ph: (602)682-2800
Fax: (602)682-2890
URL: www.sfaz.org

8288 ■ Science Foundation Arizona Graduate Research Fellowships (GRF) *(Graduate/Fellowship)*

Purpose: To strengthen existing research programs at universities in Arizona. **Focus:** Engineering, Aerospace/

Aeronautical/Astronautical. **Qualif.:** Applicant must be a VP of Research at a 501(C)(3) educational institution that grants PhD or higher-level degrees or a Master's degree in aeronautical sciences. Applicant must be selected by the educational institution where he/she has performed undergraduate or some post-graduate studies. **Criteria:** Submitted proposals are reviewed by a panel of expert outside reviewers.

Funds Avail.: No specific amount. **Duration:** Annual. **To Apply:** Applicants must complete the application online.

8289 ■ Scleroderma Foundation (SF)

300 Rosewood Dr., Ste. 105
Danvers, MA 01923
Ph: (978)463-5843
Fax: (978)463-5809
Free: 800-722-4673
E-mail: sfinfo@scleroderma.org
URL: www.scleroderma.org

8290 ■ Scleroderma Foundation Established Investigator Grants *(Doctorate/Grant)*

Purpose: To provide assistance for established investigators in areas of research related to SSc who are pursuing highly innovative and meritorious pilot projects; to facilitate highly innovative and meritorious pilot projects in areas of research related to scleroderma. **Focus:** Medicine, Osteopathic. **Qualif.:** Applicants must have a doctoral degree in Medicine, Osteopathy, Veterinary Medicine or one of the sciences and must have completed a postdoctoral fellowship. **Criteria:** Recipients are selected based on a committee's review of the proposal.

Funds Avail.: $150,000. **To Apply:** Applicants must submit one original copy in PDF format via CD and five hard copies of completed application along with five sets of appendices. **Deadline:** September 15. **Contact:** Tracey O. Sperry at tsperry@scleroderma.org.

8291 ■ Scleroderma Foundation New Investigator Grants *(Doctorate/Grant)*

Purpose: To provide financial assistance to promising new investigators in areas of research related to SSc. **Focus:** Medicine, Osteopathic. **Qualif.:** Applicants must have a doctoral degree in Medicine, Osteopathy, Veterinary Medicine or one of the sciences and must have completed a postdoctoral fellowship. **Criteria:** Recipients are selected based on a committee's review of the proposal.

Funds Avail.: $150,000. **Duration:** Annual. **To Apply:** Applicants must submit one original copy in PDF format via CD and five hard copies of completed application and five sets of appendices. **Deadline:** September 15. **Contact:** Tracey O. Sperry at tsperry@scleroderma.org.

8292 ■ Scleroderma Research Foundation (SRF)

220 Montgomery St., Ste. 1411
San Francisco, CA 94104
Free: 800-441-CURE
URL: www.srfcure.org

8293 ■ SRF Post-doctoral Fellowships *(Postdoctorate/Fellowship)*

Purpose: To raise interest in exploring new approaches and hypotheses on the pathogenesis of scleroderma

Awards are arranged alphabetically below their administering organizations

among young scientists by providing funding support. **Focus:** Biomedical research. **Qualif.:** Applicants must be U.S. citizens or permanent residents and must be Ph.D. or M.D. degree holders. Applicants must also identify a sponsoring private or public non-profit institution and an individual who will serve as a sponsor and will directly supervise and document everything that are involved in the training and research experience of the candidate. **Criteria:** Award is given based on merit.

Funds Avail.: $35,000-$55,000. **Duration:** Two years. **Number Awarded:** 2. **To Apply:** Applicants must submit completed and signed application along with letter from sponsoring principle investigator; relevant supplemental material appended to application; research proposal; and three letters of recommendation. **Deadline:** November 30 for new applications and December 30 for continuing grants. **Contact:** Application form and all supporting documents must be submitted to Victoria Slotfeldt at the above address; E-mail: vslotfeldt@sclerodermaresearch.org.

8294 ■ Scottish Rite Foundation of Colorado

c/o Scottish Rite Masonic Center
1370 Grant St.
Denver, CO 80203-2347
Ph: (303)861-2410
Fax: (303)861-2411
Free: 866-289-6797
E-mail: ritecare@scottishfoundation.org
URL: www.scottishritefoundation.org

8295 ■ Dwight A. Hamilton Scottish Rite Foundation of Colorado Graduate Scholarships *(Graduate/ Scholarship)*

Purpose: To provide scholarship to graduate students in speech-language pathology who are in need of educational assistance. **Focus:** Speech and language pathology/ Audiology. **Qualif.:** Applicants must have successfully completed the first year of graduate study in speech-language pathology with a grade point average of 3.5 (B+) or higher; must be enrolled as second-year graduate students in speech-language pathology at either the University of Colorado-Boulder or the University of Northern Colorado; must be recognized as Colorado residents by the university; must be committed to a career in treating children with childhood language disorders; must be planning to remain in Colorado after graduation to serve children in the state. **Criteria:** Applicants who are interested in serving children in rural or underserved areas of Colorado are given preference.

Funds Avail.: No specific amount. **Duration:** Annual. **To Apply:** Applicants must submit official transcript or academic progress report (first year graduate study); proof of Colorado residency as defined by the university's criteria; one-page, double-spaced statement on career goals and aspirations including a description of students' interest in serving children with language disorders and intention to remain in Colorado; one letter of recommendation from university faculty; one letter of recommendation from clinical supervisor; one-page professional resume; application checklist showing application completeness. **Deadline:** June 15. **Remarks:** Established in 2005.

8296 ■ Scouts Canada (SC)

1345 Baseline Rd.
Ottawa, ON, Canada K2C 0A7

Ph: (613)224-5134
Free: 888-855-3336
E-mail: helpcentre@scouts.ca
URL: www.scouts.ca

8297 ■ Reginald K. Groome Memorial Scholarships *(Undergraduate/Scholarship)*

Purpose: To enhance the mission of Scouts Canada through recognition of scholastic and other achievement by youth members of Scouts Canada; to encourage continuous self-development on the part of active youth members of Scouts Canada through institutions of post secondary education. **Focus:** General studies/Field of study not specified. **Qualif.:** Program is open to individuals who have not reached their 25th birthday; must have the leadership contribution to scouting; and must have scholastic achievements up to the time of application. **Criteria:** Candidates will be selected based on leadership contribution; scholastic achievement; attitude and aptitude.

Funds Avail.: $1,500. **Duration:** Annually. **Number Awarded:** Each year a minimum of 17. **To Apply:** Application form is available at the website. Applicants must submit an official transcript of records; must attach a typed statement (200 words) discussing the value of scouting in their life; authorised report card; one passport/school-sized photo; and two letters of recommendation from Scouting and outside organization. **Deadline:** April 1.

8298 ■ Herbert Scoville Jr. Peace Fellowship

322 4th St. NE
Washington, DC 20002
Ph: (202)446-1565
E-mail: info@scoville.org
URL: www.scoville.org

8299 ■ Herbert Scoville Jr. Peace Fellowships *(Graduate/Fellowship)*

Purpose: To provide an opportunity for college graduates to gain practical knowledge and experience by contributing to the efforts of nonprofit, public-interest organizations working on peace and security issues. **Focus:** Peace studies. **Qualif.:** Applicants must be graduate students and residents of the United States. **Criteria:** Selection shall be based on academic accomplishments and interest in issues of peace and security.

Funds Avail.: Amount varies. **Duration:** Annual. **Number Awarded:** Varies. **To Apply:** Application materials must include: a cover sheet (applicant's name, semester for which they are applying, contact details); a signed letter indicating the applicants' desire to apply, addresses and telephone numbers of two references (letter should indicate how the applicant first learned of the Scoville Peace Fellowship); a full CV (educational and professional data, and extracurricular activities); a personal essay discussing the applicants' qualifications, interests, Fellowship objectives and career goals (should also list 5-6 organizations they would like to work with); a policy/opinion essay of no more than 1,000 words relevant to the field of peace and security taking a position on a contemporary, contentious issue (must be titled); official transcript(s) detailing the candidates' entire college academic record including undergraduate, graduate and foreign study; and two signed letters of reference. Electronic applications must be submitted as one compiled Adobe PDF file or Microsoft Word, subject must be: Scoville Application-name of the applicant. Paper ap-

Awards are arranged alphabetically below their administering organizations

plications must be submitted in a single envelope (each page must be numbered, do not staple pages together). **Deadline:** October 1 (Spring); January 4 (Fall). **Contact:** Paul Revsine, at the above address.

8300 ■ Screen Actors Guild - American Federation of Television and Radio Artists (SAG-AFTRA)

5757 Wilshire Blvd., 7th Fl.
Los Angeles, CA 90036
Ph: (323)954-1600
Free: 855-724-2387
URL: www.sagaftra.org

8301 ■ The John L. Dales Scholarship Fund
(Undergraduate, Vocational/Occupational/Scholarship)

Purpose: To assist students in their chosen field. **Focus:** Performing arts. **Qualif.:** The scholarship applies only to accredited and licensed universities, colleges, junior colleges, adult specialty schools or trade/vocational schools. **Criteria:** Applicant for scholarship awards of the John L. Dales Scholarship Fund will be selected in accordance of the criteria.

Funds Avail.: No specific amount. **Duration:** Annual. **To Apply:** Applicant shall submit a transcript of all high school, college and university course and evaluations, SAT scores, and any other relevant information; applicant shall submit the Confidential Financial Aid Form for applicant and a copy of their most recent Federal Income Tax Returns for applicant and parent. If either applicant or parents are incorporated, the Corporate Tax Return must be submitted. All submitted tax returns must be complete; Applicant shall submit an essay of 350 to 750 words on one of the topics provided with the application and two personal letters of recommendation. **Deadline:** March 15. **Remarks:** Established in 1973. **Contact:** Davidson Lloyd, Managing Director, 323-549-6649.

8302 ■ Scrollsaw Association of the World (SAW)

PO Box 340
Botkins, OH 45306
Ph: (937)693-3309
URL: www.saw-online.com

8303 ■ Patrick Spielman Memorial Scholarship Program *(Undergraduate, Vocational/Occupational/Scholarship)*

Purpose: To promote activities within Local Chapter that will enhance the group's scrolling knowledge. **Focus:** Arts. **Qualif.:** Applicant must be undergraduate or a senior high school student; he/she is at least 24 age and under-enrolled in a full-time undergraduate course study at an accredited two- or four-year college, university, or vocational-technical school; and must be a U.S. or Canadian resident. Applicant must be sponsored by a SAW member whose membership is active. **Criteria:** Recipient is selected based on consideration of past academic performance and future potential; leadership and participation in school and community activities; work experience; statement of career and educational aspirations and goals; unusual personal or family circumstances; and an outside proposal.

Funds Avail.: $1,000. **Duration:** One year. **Number Awarded:** 2. **To Apply:** Applicant must complete an application form with appraisal; complete transcript of grades;

and essay. Application of a Canadian citizen must be written in English. **Deadline:** March 31. **Contact:** The Patrick Spielman Memorial Scholarship Program, Scholarship Management Services, One Scholarship Way, PO Box 297, St. Peter, MN 56082.

8304 ■ Seldovia Native Association

PO Drawer L
Seldovia, AK 99663
Ph: (907)234-7625
Fax: (907)234-7637
Free: 800-478-7898
E-mail: info@snai.com
URL: www.snai.com

8305 ■ Seldovia Native Association Achievement Scholarships *(Undergraduate, Graduate/Scholarship)*

Purpose: To financially assist Alaska Natives to pursue their education. **Focus:** General studies/Field of study not specified. **Qualif.:** Applicants must be Alaska Natives who are shareholders and their lineal descendants (children, grandchildren, natural or adopted and spouses); must be enrolled at an accredited college or university and must maintain 3.0 GPA. Undergraduate applicants must have enrolled 12 or more credit hours per semester and nine or more credit hours per semester for graduate students. **Criteria:** Recipients will be evaluated based on the following categories: a) scholastic achievement; b) previous work performance, education and community involvement; c) financial need; d) recommendations and demonstrated potential to succeed in a chosen career; e) seriousness of purpose; f) major field of study; and g) practicality of education, professional goals and completeness of the application.

Funds Avail.: $2,500. **To Apply:** Applicants must submit a completed, signed and dated application form, an official copy of transcript, two letters of recommendation, proof of acceptance and photo. **Deadline:** July 1.

8306 ■ Seldovia Native Association General Scholarships *(Undergraduate, Graduate/Scholarship)*

Purpose: To financially assist Alaska Natives to pursue their education. **Focus:** General studies/Field of study not specified. **Qualif.:** Applicants must be Alaska Natives who are shareholders and their lineal descendants (children, grandchildren, natural or adopted and spouses); must be enrolled at an accredited college or university and must maintain 2.0 GPA. Undergraduate applicants must have enrolled 12 or more credit hours per semester and nine or more credit hours per semester for graduate students. **Criteria:** Recipients will be evaluated based on the following categories: a) scholastic achievement; b) previous work performance, education and community involvement; c) financial need; d) recommendations and demonstrated potential to succeed in a chosen career; e) seriousness of purpose; f) major field of study; and g) practicality of education, professional goals and completeness of the application.

Funds Avail.: $500. **To Apply:** Applicants must submit a completed, signed and dated application form, an official copy of transcript, two letters of recommendation, proof of acceptance and photo. **Deadline:** July 1.

8307 ■ Semiconductor Research Corporation - Global Research Collaboration (SRC-GRC)

PO Box 12053
Research Triangle Park, NC 27709

Awards are arranged alphabetically below their administering organizations

Ph: (919)941-9400
Fax: (919)941-9450
E-mail: students@src.org
URL: www.src.org/program/grc

8308 ■ Graduate Fellowship Program - Robert M. Burger Fellowships *(Doctorate, Graduate/Fellowship)*

Purpose: To encourage academically gifted students to pursue doctoral degrees relevant to microelectrics. **Focus:** Engineering; Science; Technology. **Qualif.:** Applicant must be a U.S. citizen; has completed a Master's degree; pursuing, or planning to pursue a doctoral program in an academic area appropriate to the Fellowship; and has the required recommendation from the proposed university advisor. **Criteria:** Selection is based on quality, relevance and timeliness of the proposed research; demonstrated academic and leadership ability; and on the appropriateness of the institutional environment for the research.

Funds Avail.: No specific amount. **Duration:** No more than four years. **Number Awarded:** Varies. **To Apply:** Applicants must submit a completed Personal Information Form (may be submitted electronically from the applicant's university e-mail address or in hard copy) along with official transcripts of all accredited baccalaureate and graduate work completed; three Reference Report Forms completed by scientists, engineers or faculty members; and official report of test results from the Graduate Record Examination (SRC institution code 2800). **Contact:** apply@src.org.

8309 ■ Graduate Fellowship Program - Research Fellowships (GFP) *(Doctorate, Graduate/Fellowship)*

Purpose: To encourage academically gifted students to pursue doctoral degrees relevant to microelectrics. **Focus:** Engineering; Science; Technology. **Qualif.:** Applicant must be a U.S. citizen or have a permanent resident, refugee, or political asylum status in the U.S.; pursuing or planning to pursue a PhD degree with research relevant to microelectronics under the guidance of an GRC/SRCEA-approved faculty member and with at least two years to completion of the doctoral degree; will be performing research under a sponsored research program approved by the GRC/SRCEA; and willing to provide a copy of his/her PhD dissertation to GRC for publication. **Criteria:** Selection is based on outstanding academic achievement in the field of microelectronics and the relevance of the proposed research to GRC's goals.

Funds Avail.: No specific amount. **Duration:** Annual. **Number Awarded:** 35. **To Apply:** Applicants must submit a completed Personal Information Form (may be submitted electronically from the applicant's university e-mail address or in hard copy) along with official transcripts of all accredited baccalaureate and graduate work completed; three Reference Report Forms completed by scientists, engineers or faculty members; and official report of test results from the Graduate Record Examination (SRC institution code 2800). **Deadline:** February. **Contact:** apply@src.org.

8310 ■ Graduate Fellowship Program - Mahboob Khan/Advanced Micro Devices Fellowships *(Doctorate, Graduate/Fellowship)*

Purpose: To encourage academically gifted students to pursue doctoral degrees relevant to microelectrics. **Focus:** Engineering; Science; Technology. **Qualif.:** Applicant must be a U.S. citizen or have permanent resident, refugee or political asylum status in the United States; pursuing or planning to pursue a PhD degree with research relevant to microelectronics under the guidance of an GRC/SRCEA-approved faculty member and with at least two years to completion of the doctoral degree; will be performing research under a sponsored research program approved by the GRC/SRCEA; and willing to provide a copy of his/her PhD dissertation to GRC for publication. **Criteria:** Selection is based on outstanding academic achievement in the field of microelectronics and the relevance of the proposed research to GRC's goals.

Funds Avail.: No specific amount. **To Apply:** Applicants must submit a completed Personal Information Form (may be submitted electronically from the applicant's university e-mail address or in hard copy) along with official transcripts of all accredited baccalaureate and graduate work completed; three Reference Report Forms completed by scientists, engineers or faculty members; and official report of test results from the Graduate Record Examination (SRC institution code 2800). **Contact:** apply@src.org.

8311 ■ Master's Scholarships Program (MSP) *(Graduate, Master's/Scholarship)*

Purpose: To attract qualified students who are also in underrepresented minority categories to graduate study in areas of interest to the semiconductor industry. **Focus:** Engineering; Science; Technology. **Qualif.:** Applicant must be a female; a member of an underrepresented minority category (African-American, Hispanic, Native American); meet admission requirements for graduate school at an GRC/SRCEA participating university; a U.S. citizen or with permanent resident, refugee or political asylum status in the United States; planning to pursue a Master's degree with research relevant to microelectronics under the guidance of an SRC/SRCEA approved faculty member and under a GRC/SRCEA approved research program; and willing to provide a copy of his/her master's thesis to GRC for publication. **Criteria:** Selection is based on minority or female status and outstanding academic achievement.

Funds Avail.: No specific amount. **Duration:** Annual; Up to two years. **Number Awarded:** 12. **To Apply:** Applicants must submit a completed Personal Information Form (may be submitted electronically from the applicant's university e-mail address or in hard copy) along with official transcripts of all accredited baccalaureate and graduate work completed; three Reference Report Forms completed by scientists, engineers or faculty members; and official report of test results from the Graduate Record Examination (SRC institution code 2800). **Deadline:** February. **Contact:** apply@src.org.

8312 ■ Graduate Fellowship Program - Peter Verhofstadt Fellowships *(Graduate/Fellowship)*

Purpose: To encourage academically gifted students to pursue doctoral degrees relevant to microelectrics. **Focus:** Biophysics; Chemistry; Mathematics and mathematical sciences; Physical sciences; Physics. **Qualif.:** Applicant must be a graduate student who will have completed a bachelor's degree by the time the Fellowship begins; pursuing or planning to undertake either a master's or doctoral program in an academic area appropriate to the Fellowship; and must hold citizenship in the United States or any country not defined by the government as export controlled or embargoed. **Criteria:** Selection is based on quality, relevance and timeliness of the proposed research; on demonstrated academic and leadership ability; and on the appropriateness of the institutional environment for the research.

Funds Avail.: No specific amount. **To Apply:** Applicants must submit a completed Personal Information Form (may

Awards are arranged alphabetically below their administering organizations

be submitted electronically from the applicant's university e-mail address or in hard copy) along with official transcripts of all accredited baccalaureate and graduate work completed; three Reference Report Forms completed by scientists, engineers, or faculty members; and official report of test results from the Graduate Record Examination (SRC institution code 2800). **Contact:** apply@src.org.

8313 ■ Semiconductor Research Corporation - Nanoelectronics Research Initiative (SRC-NRI)
PO Box 12053
Research Triangle Park, NC 27709
Ph: (919)941-9400
Fax: (919)941-9450
E-mail: students@src.org
URL: www.src.org/program/nri

8314 ■ SRC NRI Hans J. Coufal Fellowships
(Graduate/Fellowship)

Purpose: To increase the number of graduate students being educated to enter the semiconductor and nanoelectronics fields. **Focus:** Electronics; Physics. **Qualif.:** Applicant must be a U.S. citizen or have permanent resident, refugee, or political asylum status in the United States; pursuing or planning to pursue a PhD degree with research relevant to microelectronics, preferably nanoelectronic device technologies, physics or materials, under the guidance of an NRI-approved faculty member with at least two years remaining to completion of the doctoral degree; be performing research under a sponsored research program approved by NRI; and willing to provide a copy of his/her PhD dissertation to NRI for publication to NRI sponsoring organizations. **Criteria:** Selection is based on quality, relevance and timeliness of the proposed research; on demonstrated academic and leadership ability; and on the appropriateness of the institutional environment for the research.

Funds Avail.: Full tuition and fees and stipend $2,000 a year. **Duration:** Annual; No more than five years. **Number Awarded:** 1. **To Apply:** Applicants must submit a completed Personal Information Form (may be submitted electronically from the applicant's university e-mail address or in hard copy) along with official transcripts of all accredited baccalaureate and graduate work completed; three Reference Report Forms completed by scientists, engineers, or faculty members; and official report of test results from the Graduate Record Examination. **Deadline:** February. **Remarks:** Established in 2006. **Contact:** apply@src.org.

8315 ■ Sentinels of Freedom
PO Box 1316
San Ramon, CA 94583
Ph: (925)380-6342
Fax: (925)867-1078
E-mail: info@sentinelsoffreedom.org
URL: www.sentinelsoffreedom.org

8316 ■ Sentinels of Freedom Scholarships
(Advanced Professional/Scholarship)

Purpose: To provide life-changing opportunities for men and women of the U.S. Armed Forces who have suffered severe injuries and need the support of grateful communities to realize their dreams. **Focus:** General studies/Field of study not specified. **Qualif.:** Applicant must be a member of the U.S. Air Force, Army, Coast Guard, Marines or Navy (including Reserves) who on or after Sept. 11, 2001, sustained injuries in the line of duty resulting in one or a combination of the conditions resulting in 60% or higher permanent disability. Injuries may include: Amputation, Blindness, Deafness, Paraplegia, Severe Burns, TBI, PTSD and other severe mental injuries. **Criteria:** Selection is based on the applicant's attitude, motivation, and high morals.

Funds Avail.: No specific amount. **Duration:** Semiannual. **To Apply:** Applicant must provide detailed information to the Sentinels of Freedom Scholarship Foundation using the website questionnaire. Once the Foundation receive the form, the applicant will be emailed an Authorization for Disclosure of Information form that must be signed and returned before the Foundation can create an application file on behalf of the applicant. Other information about the scholarship can be found at the program website. **Deadline:** June 1 (Fall school enrollment); November 1 (Spring school enrollment). **Contact:** Program Director at 925-380-6342 ext. 3.

8317 ■ SEO Optimizers
1509 Westmount Dr.
San Pedro, CA 90732
Ph: (310)940-9463
E-mail: info@seooptimizers.com
URL: seooptimizers.com

8318 ■ SEO Optimizers Scholarships *(All/Scholarship)*

Purpose: To provide students the opportunity of gaining real-working experience in a chosen field. **Focus:** General studies/Field of study not specified. **Qualif.:** Applicants must be American citizens, permanent residents, or hold a valid student visa; must be currently enrolled as high school or college/university students within the United States; must have a cumulative GPA of at least 3.0 (or the equivalent); and must have designed an innovative project that makes a difference in the lives of others (could be a website, series of blogs, an app, fundraising event, etc.). **Criteria:** Selection will be based on the applicants' qualifications and compliance with the application process.

Funds Avail.: No specific amount. **Duration:** Annual. **To Apply:** Applicants must submit an essay describing the goal of the particular project and provide supporting documentation. The essay, idea, or creation must be the applicants' original work. **Deadline:** 20th of each month.

8319 ■ Serbian Bar Association of America (SBAA)
20 S Clark St., Ste. 700
Chicago, IL 60603
Ph: (312)782-8500
E-mail: sbaa@serbbar.org
URL: www.serbbar.org

8320 ■ Serbian Bar Association of America Scholarships *(Undergraduate/Scholarship)*

Purpose: To promote the best interests of the Serbian American community. **Focus:** Law. **Qualif.:** Applicants must be of Serbian birth or ancestry and/or their spouses who are enrolled in an accredited law school in the US. **Criteria:** Selection is based on merit.

Awards are arranged alphabetically below their administering organizations

Funds Avail.: $500 - $2,000. **Duration:** Annual. **Number Awarded:** 4. **To Apply:** Applicants must submit a typed essay of no more than 250 words detailing how they plan to use their legal education within the Serbian American community and submit a certified copy of their law school transcript. **Deadline:** March 20.

8321 ■ SERTOMA
1912 E Meyer Blvd.
Kansas City, MO 64132
Ph: (816)333-8300
Fax: (816)333-4320
E-mail: infosertoma@sertomahq.org
URL: www.sertoma.org

8322 ■ Sertoma Communicative Disorders Scholarship *(Graduate/Scholarship)*

Purpose: To provide scholarships to hard of hearing and deaf students. **Focus:** Hearing and deafness. **Qualif.:** Applicants must be US citizens accepted into a graduate level program in speech language pathology and/or audiology at a college or university in the United Sates, accredited by ASHA's Council on Academic Accreditation; must have a minimum cumulative 3.2 on a 4.0 scale for all undergraduate and graduate level course work. **Criteria:** Selection will be based on the committee's criteria.

Funds Avail.: $1,000. **Duration:** Annual. **To Apply:** Applicants must submit the following in a single envelope in the order listed: application, which must be on the original form, typed and signed; statement of purpose stating how this scholarships will help you achieve your goals; two letters of recommendation from hearing professional, teacher or school official; high school or college transcript; recent audiogram or statement from hearing health professional. Hearing loss level on application must be verifiable from an audiogram or statement; one additional copy of all items must be included. Copy must blank out all references to the student's personal information including the name, address, phone, e-mail and social security number. **Deadline:** March 30. **Contact:** Bridget Almond, at balmond@sertomahq.org.

8323 ■ Sertoma Hard of Hearing and Deaf Scholarships *(Undergraduate/Scholarship)*

Purpose: To provide scholarships to hard of hearing and deaf students. **Focus:** Hearing and deafness. **Qualif.:** Applicants must have a minimum 40dB bilateral hearing loss as evidenced on audiogram by an SRT of 40dB or greater in both ears; must be citizens of the United States of America; must be either entering college on a full time basis or currently attending college in a full time basis at a college or university in the United States of America; must be pursuing a bachelor's degree in any discipline; must have a minimum unweighted GPA of 3.2 on a 4.0 scale or be at least 85% in all courses. **Criteria:** Scholarship will be given to the applicants who best meet the criteria.

Funds Avail.: $1,000. **Duration:** Annual. **To Apply:** Applicants must submit the following in a single envelope in the order listed: Application - must be on the original form, typed and signed; statement of purpose stating how this scholarships will help you achieve your goals; two letters of recommendation from hearing professional, teacher or school official; high school or college transcript; recent audiogram or statement from hearing health professional. Hearing loss level on application must be verifiable from audiogram or statement; one additional copy of all items,

except for audiogram, must be included. Copy must blank out all references to the student's personal information including the name, address, phone, e-mail and social security number. **Deadline:** May 1. **Remarks:** Established in 1994. **Contact:** Bridget Almond, at balmond@sertomahq.org.

8324 ■ Seton Hall University School of Law
1 Newark Ctr.
1109 Raymond Blvd.
Newark, NJ 07102
Ph: (973)642-8500
Free: 888-415-7271
E-mail: admitme@shu.edu
URL: law.shu.edu

8325 ■ Seton Hall Law School Merit Scholarships Program *(Undergraduate/Scholarship)*

Purpose: To reward the hard work and academic success of students. **Focus:** Law. **Qualif.:** Prospective recipients must be incoming law students of the university. **Criteria:** Recipients are selected based on the Law School Admission Test (LSAT) scores, undergraduate academic performance, and academic promise.

Funds Avail.: $8,000 to full tuition. **Duration:** Annual. **To Apply:** All applications for school admission are considered as application for the program since no separate application is required.

8326 ■ SHAPE America
1900 Association Dr.
Reston, VA 20191
Fax: (703)476-9527
Free: 800-213-7193
URL: www.shapeamerica.org

8327 ■ Ruth Abernathy Presidential Scholarships *(Graduate, Undergraduate/Scholarship)*

Purpose: To honor and support deserving students in their educational pursuit. **Focus:** Education, Physical; Health education. **Qualif.:** Applicants must be undergraduate or graduate student members majoring in a field related to one or more of the disciplines represented by SHAPE America and its associations; and have a cumulative GPA of 3.5. **Criteria:** Selection of applicants will be based on scholastic proficiency, evidence of leadership, school, community, professional activity services and character attributes.

Funds Avail.: $1,250 each for undergraduates; $1,750 each for graduates. **Duration:** Annual. **Number Awarded:** 5 (3 undergraduate; 2 graduate). **To Apply:** Applicants must submit a completed application from together with the required materials. Application materials should be submitted by U.S. mail (fax copies will not be accepted). **Deadline:** October 15. **Remarks:** Established in 1995. **Contact:** Patti Hartle at phartle@shapeamerica.org.

8328 ■ Shastri Indo-Canadian Institute
1418 Education Tower
2500 University Dr. NW
Calgary, AB, Canada T2N 1N4
Ph: (403)220-7467
Fax: (403)289-0100

Awards are arranged alphabetically below their administering organizations

URL: www.sici.org

8329 ■ Shastri Scholar Travel Subsidy Grants (SSTSG) *(Graduate, Professional development/Grant)*

Purpose: To assist faculty members and graduate students with travel subsidies. **Focus:** Canadian studies; Indian studies (Asia). **Qualif.:** Applicants must be citizens or permanent residents of India and Canada; must have been invited to participate by an academic institution and be affiliated with, or travelling to a Shastri Institute member institutions. **Criteria:** An adjudicating committee will make the final decision concerning successful applicants based upon the following criteria and marking system: Institution/ Event; contribution to own development; contribution to promoting/building academic linkages between India-Canada; and professional background.

Funds Avail.: Up to $1,250. **To Apply:** Applicants must submit the completed electronic application form to Shastri Institute's Canada office along with the following documents: curriculum vitae that is not more than three pages; letter of invitation from the host institution/organization; and proof of residency either copy of passport or permanent resident card. **Deadline:** August 31.

8330 ■ Sheet Metal and Air Conditioning Contractors' National Association (SMACNA)

4201 Lafayette Center Dr.
Chantilly, VA 20151-1209
Ph: (703)803-2980
Fax: (703)803-3732
E-mail: info@smacna.org
URL: www.smacna.org

8331 ■ Sheet Metal And Air Conditioning Contractors' National Association College of Fellows Scholarships *(Undergraduate/Scholarship)*

Purpose: To provide financial assistance for the discovery, interpretation and dissemination of new knowledge that promotes leadership development and personal growth. **Focus:** Metallurgy. **Qualif.:** Applicants must be SMACNA contractors, employees of Chapter, National and National Associate Member or their family members who are entering their first year at an accredited institution of higher education; and must be planning to pursue any course of study, however, studies in a field related to the sheet metal industry are preferred. **Criteria:** Recipients are selected based on demonstrated academic excellence; academic goals; involvement in extracurricular activities; community involvement; leadership ability; and good character.

Funds Avail.: $3,000 per year. **Duration:** Annual; four years. **To Apply:** Applicants must complete the application form; must submit an essay; high school transcripts; three letters of recommendation; college aptitude scores; indication of an acceptance at an accredited four-year college or university; and recent photograph. **Deadline:** March 31. **Contact:** SMACNA College of Fellows Scholarship Program at the above address.

8332 ■ Shell Oil Co.

PO Box 2463
Houston, TX 77252-2463
Ph: (713)241-6161
Free: 888-467-4355
E-mail: ShellCustomerCare@shell.com

URL: www.shell.us

8333 ■ Shell Incentive Scholarship Fund *(Undergraduate/Scholarship)*

Purpose: To support under-represented students pursuing undergraduate degree in a specific technical field at certain colleges. **Focus:** Engineering; Geosciences. **Qualif.:** Applicants must be US citizens or authorized to work on a full-time basis in the United States; enrolled full-time as sophomores, juniors, seniors or fifth year students in one of the specified institutions (full list available at website); have a minimum 3.2 cumulative GPA (on 4.0 scale), which must be maintained throughout the participation in the program; major in one of the following disciplines: geology, geophysics or physics, chemical, civil, electrical, mechanical, petroleum, geological, or geophysical engineering; and members of an under-represented race/ethnicity in the technical/science academic areas. (Black - Not of Hispanic Origin, Hispanic/Latino, American Indian, or Alaskan Native). **Criteria:** Recipients are selected based on financial need.

Funds Avail.: $5,000. **Duration:** Annual. **Number Awarded:** 1. **To Apply:** Applicants must complete an online application. Candidates should include a resume and an unofficial transcript as attachments to the online application. **Deadline:** March 2.

8334 ■ Shell Oil Company Technical Scholarships *(Undergraduate/Scholarship)*

Purpose: To support students pursuing undergraduate degree in a specific technical field at certain colleges. **Focus:** Engineering; Geosciences. **Qualif.:** Applicants must be US citizens or authorized to work on a full-time basis in the United States; enrolled full-time as sophomores, juniors, seniors or fifth year students in one of the specified institutions (full list available at website); have a minimum 3.2 cumulative GPA (on 4.0 scale), which must be maintained throughout the participation in the program; major in one of the following disciplines: geology, geophysics or physics; chemical, civil, electrical, mechanical, geological, petroleum, or geophysical engineering. **Criteria:** Recipients are selected based on academic performance and financial need.

Funds Avail.: $5,000. **Duration:** Annual. **Number Awarded:** 1. **To Apply:** Applicants must complete the online application for student opportunities. They should include a resume and an unofficial transcript as attachments to the online application. **Deadline:** March 2.

8335 ■ Shell Process Technology Scholarships *(Undergraduate/Scholarship)*

Purpose: To aid students who seek an education to obtain employment in the industries that use and control mechanical, physical or chemical processes to produce a final product. **Focus:** Engineering; Geosciences. **Qualif.:** Applicants must be US citizens or authorized to work on a full-time basis in the United States; enrolled full or part-time in a Process Technology (or Instrumentation Technology) two-year degree program or be high school seniors planning to enroll in the Process Technology (or Instrumentation Technology) two-year degree program; and enrolled in at least one Process Technology or Instrumentation Technology course per semester unless pursuing a four-year degree. **Criteria:** Recipients are selected based on financial need.

Funds Avail.: Amount varies. **Duration:** Annual. **To Apply:** Applicants must submit a completed application form. **Deadline:** April 1.

Awards are arranged alphabetically below their administering organizations

8336 ■ Sheriff's Law Enforcement Association of McLennan County (SLEAMC)

PO Box 23475
Waco, TX 76702-3475
URL: sleamc.org

8337 ■ SLEAMC Scholarships *(Graduate, Undergraduate/Scholarship)*

Purpose: To provide financial assistance to those students with good scholastic records. **Focus:** General studies/Field of study not specified. **Qualif.:** Applicants must be U.S. citizens; must be high school seniors, graduates, or GED recipients at time of application; must be enrolled in a college or university in an academic course of study; must be 25 years of age or less at time of application; must have a cumulative GPA of at least 2.5; must be enrolled as full-time students during semester for which the application is submitted; must not have been convicted of a crime. **Criteria:** Preference will be given to those students residing in McLennan County, Texas and will be based on academic achievement.

Funds Avail.: $3,000. **Duration:** Annual. **To Apply:** Applicants must complete the application form available online; must submit the following application requirements: (1) Official high school transcript or GED certification; (2) Current official college transcript; (3) Work history (summer and/or part time, volunteer; indicate number of hours worked).

8338 ■ Joseph Shinoda Memorial Scholarship Foundation

c/o Pat Broering, Executive Assistant
962 Pecho St.
Morro Bay, CA 93442
Ph: (805)704-2408
URL: www.shinodascholarship.org

8339 ■ Joseph Shinoda Memorial Scholarships *(Undergraduate/Scholarship)*

Purpose: To encourage creative young talent to pursue careers in floriculture. **Focus:** Floriculture. **Qualif.:** Applicant must be an undergraduate student enrolled in an accredited four-year college/university in the U.S. (or in a California community college) majoring in a degree program related to the field of floriculture. **Criteria:** Selection is based on the application materials submitted.

Funds Avail.: $1,000 - $5,000. **Duration:** Annual; One academic year. **To Apply:** Applicants must submit a completed application form together with a letter of recommendation from the faculty evaluating the applicant as a student; another letter of recommendation from an employer or community service organization evaluating the applicant as a worker or volunteer; and transcript of grades. **Deadline:** March 30.

8340 ■ Shoreline Community College Foundation

Admin Bldg., Ste. 1005
16101 Greenwood Ave. N
Shoreline, WA 98133-5696
Ph: (206)546-4101
Fax: (206)546-4630
URL: www.shoreline.edu/foundation

8341 ■ Beta Sigma Phi Visual Arts Scholarship *(Undergraduate/Scholarship)*

Purpose: To increase access and success of Shoreline Community College students; to attract, encourage and assist talented students enrolled in Fine Arts programs at SCC. **Focus:** Art. **Qualif.:** Applicants must be Washington state residents; must have a cumulative 2.5 GPA from previous schools and/or maintain a cumulative 2.5 GPA at SCC; and have a minimum 3.0 GPA in visual studio art courses at SCC; must be part-time or full-time students; must have applied or be currently enrolled SCC students. **Criteria:** Recipients are selected based on the academic performance and financial needs.

Funds Avail.: $500. **Duration:** Annual. **Number Awarded:** 1. **To Apply:** Applicants must submit 4 copies of the following materials: application form; budget worksheet; class schedule; high school or college transcripts; artist statement; artist biography; references; five to seven images of most recent art; and annotated list of images. **Deadline:** April 8.

8342 ■ Boeing Company Scholarships *(Undergraduate/Scholarship)*

Purpose: To provide financial assistance to students who are in need. **Focus:** Engineering; Information science and technology; Manufacturing. **Qualif.:** Applicants must be full-time or part-time students at the Shoreline/Lake Forest Park area who are enrolling at SCC; must be Washington state resident; must have a minimum 3.0 GPA; must display good academic performance and involvement in school and/or community activities. **Criteria:** Recipients are selected based on academic performance and financial needs.

Funds Avail.: $500. **Duration:** Annual. **Number Awarded:** 1. **To Apply:** Applicants must complete the application form. **Deadline:** April 8.

8343 ■ Carli Edwards Memorial Scholarships *(Undergraduate/Scholarship)*

Purpose: To provide Shoreline Community College students who are survivors of domestic abuse with financial assistance toward the purchase of textbooks. **Focus:** Criminal justice. **Qualif.:** Applicants must be returning or part-time students at Shoreline Community College; must be survivors of domestic abuse; must be Washington State residents for a minimum of one year; must not have previous two or four year college degree; must be criminal justice majors; must earn and maintain a minimum cumulative GPA of 3.0 (GPA of 3.5 in criminal justice coursework); and must not be currently included on the Scholarship Selection Committee or related (first degree) to a person on the Selection Committee. **Criteria:** Recipients are selected based on academic standing and financial needs.

Funds Avail.: $200. **Duration:** Quarterly. **To Apply:** Applicants must complete application form; must submit letter of recommendation from teacher, professor or employer (excluding criminal justice faculty); statement or documentation of income and need; and unofficial SCC transcript.

8344 ■ Friends of Mary Automotive Scholarships *(Undergraduate/Scholarship)*

Purpose: To provide financial assistance to women who are taking automotive program. **Focus:** Automotive technology. **Qualif.:** Applicants must be returning female students at Shoreline Community College; must be Washington State residents (as defined by the college), must completed a minimum of two quarters in the SCC automotive program and earned and maintain a minimum cumulative GPA of 2.0 at SCC. **Criteria:** Recipients will be selected based on academic performance and financial needs.

Funds Avail.: $750. **Duration:** Annual. **To Apply:** Ap-

Awards are arranged alphabetically below their administering organizations

plicants must complete and submit the application form. **Deadline:** April 30.

8345 ■ High School Academic Scholarship
(Undergraduate/Scholarship)

Purpose: To provide financial assistance to students who are in need. **Focus:** General studies/Field of study not specified. **Qualif.:** Applicants must be graduating Washington State high school seniors in the Shoreline area who are enrolling at SCC; must have demonstrated strong academic improvement. **Criteria:** Recipients are selected based on academic performance and financial needs.

Funds Avail.: $1,500. **Duration:** Annual. **To Apply:** Applicants must complete the application form; submit two letters of recommendation from non-related adults, of which at least one is from a school counselor or teacher; copy of high school transcripts; and one page personal essay. **Deadline:** April 8.

8346 ■ Professor Emeritus Dr. Bill Johnson Memorial Scholarship. *(Undergraduate/Scholarship)*

Purpose: To provide financial support to students who are in need. **Focus:** Mathematics and mathematical sciences. **Qualif.:** Applicant must be a U.S. citizen or legal U.S. resident or permanent U.S. resident with an I-551 Card or a student in F-1 nonimmigrant status; completed a minimum of 25 credits at SCC and plan on transferring to a four-year university or college. **Criteria:** Recipient will be selected based on academic performance and financial needs.

Funds Avail.: $1,500. **Duration:** Annual. **Number Awarded:** 2. **To Apply:** Applicant must submit 4 copies of the following: application form; budget worksheet; class schedule; Un-official Shoreline Community College transcripts; copy of Permanent U.S. Resident (I-551) Card or passport, I-20 and I-94 documents; and essay. **Deadline:** April 9.

8347 ■ Ina Knutsen Scholarships *(Undergraduate/Scholarship)*

Purpose: To provide financial support to students who are in need. **Focus:** General studies/Field of study not specified. **Qualif.:** Applicants must be full-time or part-time students at the Shoreline/Lake Forest Park area who are enrolling at SCC. Applicants must be single parents with child/children under the age of 18 living at home; must have a cumulative SCC grade point average of 3.0 or better. **Criteria:** Recipients will be selected based on academic performance and financial needs.

Funds Avail.: $2,000. **Duration:** Annual. **To Apply:** Applicants must complete and submit the application form. **Deadline:** April 30.

8348 ■ Ken LaFountaine First Nations Scholarships
(Undergraduate/Scholarship)

Purpose: To provide First Nation students (indigenous to the Americas and associated territories) with financial assistance in times of need. **Focus:** Dental hygiene. **Qualif.:** Applicants must be returning or part-time students at Shoreline Community College; must have demonstrated active involvement in the First Nation community in the Puget Sound area, either on campus or in the broader community; and must not be currently included on the Scholarship Selection Committee or related (first degree) to a person on the Selection Committee. **Criteria:** Recipients are selected based on academic standing and financial needs.

Funds Avail.: Maximum of $500. **To Apply:** Applicants must submit evidence of likelihood of academic success with a minimum of 2.0 GPA or 2.0 during most recent quarter attended; evidence of the other venues of financial support; letter of recommendation from a teacher, professor, or employer.

8349 ■ Ron LaFreniere Business Administration Scholarship *(Undergraduate/Scholarship)*

Purpose: To provide students they need like tuition fees, books, and/or any class related fees. **Focus:** Business administration. **Qualif.:** Applicants must be Washington state residents (as defined by the college), must have completed a minimum of two quarters at SCC and taken at least 12 credits in Business Administration, have a strong emphasis of study in Business Administration, have a minimum SCC cumulative grade point average of 3.0, and must have applied for Financial Aid. **Criteria:** Recipients will be selected based on academic performance and financial needs.

Funds Avail.: $1,000. **Duration:** Annual. **Number Awarded:** 1. **To Apply:** Applicants must complete and submit the application form. **Deadline:** April 30.

8350 ■ Margaret Mallett Nursing Scholarship
(Undergraduate/Scholarship)

Purpose: To provide financial support to students who are in need. **Focus:** Nursing. **Qualif.:** Applicants must be part-time or full-time students who are currently enrolled at Shoreline Community College. **Criteria:** Recipients are selected based on academic performance, financial needs, merit and community involvement.

Funds Avail.: $1,000. **Duration:** Annual. **Number Awarded:** 7. **To Apply:** Applicants must complete the application form.

8351 ■ Eric Niemitalo Scholarships in Earth and Environmental Science *(Undergraduate/Scholarship)*

Purpose: To provide financial support to students who are pursuing a degree in sciences. **Focus:** Environmental science; Geography; Geology. **Qualif.:** Applicants must be full-time or part-time students at the Shoreline/Lake Forest Park area who are enrolling at SCC; must be Washington state residents; needs to have completed at least 15 credits at Shoreline Community College; must be presently enrolled as SCC for at least 12 credits; must have completed at least one curse at Shoreline Community College in one of the following subjects areas (Geology, Environmental Science, Geography or Oceanography); must be in Good Academic Standing; must demonstrate financial need. **Criteria:** Recipients will be selected based on academic performance and financial needs.

Funds Avail.: $500. **Duration:** Annual. **To Apply:** Interested applicants may contact the Foundation for the applicatioin process and other required materials. **Deadline:** April 8.

8352 ■ Joseph Wood Rogers Memorial Scholarships *(Undergraduate/Scholarship)*

Purpose: To provide financial support to students who are in need. **Focus:** Mathematics and mathematical sciences. **Qualif.:** Applicants must be Washington state residents (as defined by the college). Completed at least 30 credits at Shoreline Community College; must have completed at least two mathematic courses at or above the calculus level at SCC; must have at least a 3.5 grade point average in

Awards are arranged alphabetically below their administering organizations

mathematic courses taken at SCC; must Intend to pursue a degree in "pure" mathematics at an accredited college or university; must show promise of continued growth in mathematics. **Criteria:** Recipients will be selected based on academic performance and financial needs.

Funds Avail.: $1,000. **Duration:** Annual. **To Apply:** Applicants must complete and submit the application form. **Deadline:** April 30.

8353 ■ Shoreline Community College Full-Time Continuing Students Scholarships (Undergraduate/Scholarship)

Purpose: To provide financial assistance to students who are in need. **Focus:** General studies/Field of study not specified. **Qualif.:** Applicants must be Washington state residents; must have a minimum SCC cumulative GPA of 3.0; must display good academic performance and involvement in school and/or community activities; must be currently enrolled at SCC with at least 12 credits. **Criteria:** Recipients are selected based on academic performance, financial needs, involvement in school and community activities.

Funds Avail.: $2,500. **Duration:** Annual. **Number Awarded:** 12. **To Apply:** Applicants must submit five copies of the following in collated packets: completed application; Shoreline Community College unofficial transcripts; one page personal essay stating the applicants' qualifications, including career interests, personal background and educational goals; one page essay answering the question: How is Shoreline Community College preparing you for the future? **Deadline:** April 8.

8354 ■ Shoreline Community College Part-Time Students Scholarships (Undergraduate/Scholarship)

Purpose: To provide financial assistance to students who are in need. **Focus:** General studies/Field of study not specified. **Qualif.:** Applicants must be part-time students who are currently enrolled at Shoreline Community College. Applicants must demonstrate good academic performance while working 25-40 hours a week. **Criteria:** Recipients are selected based on the academic performance, financial needs, involvement in school and community activities.

Funds Avail.: $1,000. **Duration:** Annual. **Number Awarded:** 3. **To Apply:** Applicants must complete the application form. **Deadline:** April 9.

8355 ■ Shoreline - Lake Forest Park High School Scholarship (Undergraduate/Scholarship)

Purpose: To provide financial assistance to students who are in need. **Focus:** General studies/Field of study not specified. **Qualif.:** Applicants must be graduating high school seniors in the Shoreline/Lake Forest Park area who are enrolling at SCC; must have demonstrated strong academic performance. **Criteria:** Recipients are selected based on academic performance, leadership qualities and involvement in school and community activities.

Funds Avail.: $2,000. **Duration:** Annual. **To Apply:** Applicants must complete the application form. **Deadline:** April 8.

8356 ■ Margaret Svec Scholarships (Undergraduate/Scholarship)

Purpose: To provide financial support to students who are in need. **Focus:** Mathematics and mathematical sciences. **Qualif.:** Applicants must be part-time or full-time female

students who are currently enrolled at Shoreline Community College and who demonstrate financial need; must have earned a minimum of 24 credits at SCC; must have earned an SCC cumulative GPA of 3.0 or higher. **Criteria:** Recipients are selected based on academic performance and financial needs.

Funds Avail.: $4,000. **Duration:** Annual. **To Apply:** Applicants must complete the application form. **Deadline:** April 9. **Contact:** SCC Foundation Office; Phone: (206) 533-6783.

8357 ■ Elizabeth R. Thomas Alumni Nursing Scholarship (Undergraduate/Scholarship)

Purpose: To provide financial assistance to students who are in need. **Focus:** General studies/Field of study not specified. **Qualif.:** Applicants must be full-time or part-time students at the Shoreline/Lake Forest Park area who are enrolling at SCC. **Criteria:** Recipients are selected based on academic performance and financial needs.

Funds Avail.: $500. **Duration:** Annual. **Number Awarded:** 2. **To Apply:** Applicants must complete the application form.

8358 ■ SHPE Foundation
1765 Duke St.
Alexandria, VA 22314
Ph: (703)647-2122
Fax: (323)622-1046
E-mail: shpefoundation@shpe.org
URL: www.shpefoundation.org

8359 ■ AHETEMS/ExxonMobil Scholarships (Undergraduate/Scholarship)

Purpose: To enhance and achieve the potential of students pursuing degrees in engineering. **Focus:** Engineering, Civil; Engineering, Electrical; Engineering, Mechanical; Engineering, Petroleum. **Qualif.:** Applicant must be a U.S. citizen; enrolled full-time (12 hrs undergraduate) during the academic year at an accredited university in the U.S. or Puerto Rico; have a minimum GPA of 3.0 on a 4.0 scale; majoring in civil, chemical, electrical, mechanical, or petroleum engineering. **Criteria:** Selection is based on demonstrated significant motivation and aptitude for a career in science, technology, engineering or mathematics.

Funds Avail.: Amount varies. **Duration:** Annual. **To Apply:** Applicant must complete the application form online. In addition, applicants must submit via mail the Scholarship Certification Form along with the personal statement, official transcript, letter of recommendation, and a resume to AHETEMS. **Deadline:** April 1. **Contact:** SHPE Foundation, at the above address.

8360 ■ AHETEMS General Scholarships (Undergraduate, Graduate/Scholarship)

Purpose: To enhance and achieve the potential of Latino students pursuing degrees in engineering, math and science. **Focus:** Engineering; Mathematics and mathematical sciences; Science; Technology. **Qualif.:** Applicant must be of Hispanic-descent; accepted into or attending an accredited 2-year or 4-year college/university in the U.S. or Puerto Rico; enrolled full-time (12 hrs undergraduate, 9 hrs graduate) during the academic year; or a high school graduating senior graduating from an accredited U.S. high school with a diploma; have a minimum GPA of 3.00 on a 4.0 (high school senior and undergraduate), or 3.25 on a 4.0 scale (graduate student); majoring in science, technol-

Awards are arranged alphabetically below their administering organizations

ogy, engineering, mathematics or a related field; and pursuing first bachelors, masters or doctoral degree (students pursuing a second bachelors, etc. are not eligible). **Criteria:** Selection is based on demonstrated significant motivation and aptitude for a career in science, technology, engineering or mathematics.

Funds Avail.: $1,000 to $5,000. **Duration:** Annual. **To Apply:** Applicant must complete the application form online. In addition, applicants must submit via mail the Scholarship Certification Form along with the personal statement, official transcript, letter of recommendation, and a resume to AHETEMS. **Deadline:** April 1. **Contact:** SHPE Foundation, at the above address.

8361 ■ AHETEMS Professional Scholarships
(Graduate/Scholarship)

Purpose: To enhance and achieve the potential of Latino students pursuing degrees in engineering, math and science. **Focus:** Engineering; Mathematics and mathematical sciences; Science; Technology. **Qualif.:** Applicant must be employed full-time in the U.S. or Puerto Rico in a technical career field; enrolled in a science, technology, engineering, or mathematics graduate degree program at an accredited university in the U.S. or Puerto Rico at least half-time (6 hrs/credits) throughout the academic year; have a minimum 3.25 on a 4.0 GPA; be a SHPE member in good standing both at the time of application and throughout the academic year (non-member may become member at the time of application); pursuing a first masters or doctoral degree. **Criteria:** Selection is based on demonstrated significant motivation and aptitude for a career in science, technology, engineering or mathematics.

Funds Avail.: Amount varies. **Duration:** Annual. **To Apply:** Applicant must complete the application form online. In addition, applicants must submit via mail the Scholarship Certification Form along with the personal statement, official transcript, letter of recommendation, and a resume to AHETEMS. **Deadline:** April 1. **Contact:** SHPE Foundation, at the above address.

8362 ■ Purdue Krannert School of Management SHPE Scholarships *(Undergraduate, Master's/Scholarship)*

Purpose: To help master's and undergraduate students pursue their education. **Focus:** Engineering; Mathematics and mathematical sciences; Science; Technology. **Qualif.:** Applicants must be undergraduate students or master's degree in science, technology, engineering, or math; must be SHPE members who are U.S. citizens, U.S. nationals, permanent resident aliens and aliens lawfully present in and able to establish domicile in the United States per federal immigration laws; must be admitted to one of the following Krannert Master's program: MBA, Master of Science Degree in Human Resource Management program (MSHRM), Master of Science in Industrial Administration (MSIA), Weekend MBA, Executive MBA and International Master's in Management (IMM). **Criteria:** Recipients will be selected based on submitted materials.

Funds Avail.: $1,000-$5,000. **To Apply:** Applicants must complete the online application form; must submit a scholarship certification form, personal statement, transcript of records, recommendation letter and resume. **Deadline:** May 1.

8363 ■ SHPE Foundation Dissertation Scholarships
(Doctorate/Scholarship)

Purpose: To financially assist doctoral candidates who demonstrate both significant motivation and aptitude for a

career in science, technology, engineering or mathematics. **Focus:** Engineering; Mathematics and mathematical sciences; Science; Technology. **Qualif.:** Applicants must be pursuing a PhD or Eng.D. in a science, technology, engineering or math-related field; must have a minimum GPA of 3.50 on a 4.0 scale; must be currently enrolled as doctoral candidates at an accredited university in the United States or Puerto Rico; must have advanced to candidacy (passed all oral and written exams, proposal stages, completed all required coursework and making satisfactory progress on the dissertation). **Criteria:** Applicants will be selected based on merit and financial need.

Funds Avail.: $5,000. **Number Awarded:** 1. **To Apply:** Applicants must complete the online application form; must submit a scholarship certification form, personal statement, transcript of records, recommendation letter, resume, dissertation abstract and an official statement of advancement to candidacy from a graduate college/department. **Deadline:** May 1.

8364 ■ SHPE Foundation General Scholarships
(High School, Undergraduate, Graduate/Scholarship)

Purpose: To financially assist students who demonstrate both significant motivation and aptitude for a career in science, technology, engineering or mathematics. **Focus:** Engineering; Mathematics and mathematical sciences; Science; Technology. **Qualif.:** Applicants must be high school graduating seniors, undergraduate and graduate students majoring in science, technology, engineering, mathematics or a related field; must be of Hispanic descent; must be accepted into or attending an accredited two- or four-year college/university in the United States or Puerto Rico; must be enrolled full-time (12 hours undergraduate, nine hours graduate); or must be pursuing their first bachelor's, master's or doctoral degree; must have 3.0 on a 4.0 scale (high school seniors and undergraduates), 3.25 on a 4.0 scale (graduate students). **Criteria:** Candidates will be selected on a merit-based and financial need.

Funds Avail.: $1,000-$3,000. **To Apply:** Applicants must complete the online application form; must submit a scholarship certification form, personal statement, transcript of records, recommendation letter and resume. **Deadline:** May 1.

8365 ■ SHPE Foundation Northrop Grumman Scholarships *(Undergraduate/Scholarship)*

Purpose: To support undergraduate students who demonstrate both significant motivation and aptitude for a career in science, technology, engineering or mathematics. **Focus:** Engineering; Mathematics and mathematical sciences; Science; Technology. **Qualif.:** Applicants must be incoming sophomore, junior or senior students; must have minimum GPA of 3.0 on a 4.0 scale; must be U.S. citizens; must be enrolled full-time (12 hours undergraduate) during the academic year at an accredited university in the United States or Puerto Rico; must be majoring Aerospace, Computer, Electrical, Industrial, Mechanical or Systems Engineering, Computer Science, Math, Naval Architecture, or Physics; must attend any Hispanic Serving Institution (HSI), Historically Black College or University (HBCU) or any of the following institutions: California Polytechnic San Luis Obispo; California Institute of Technology; Georgia Institute of Technology; Massachusetts Institute of Technology; North Carolina State University; Ohio State University; Pennsylvania State University; Purdue University; University of California, Los Angeles; University of Illinois, Urbana-Champaign; University of Maryland; University of Michigan; University of Southern California; University of Virginia;

Awards are arranged alphabetically below their administering organizations

Virginia Polytechnic University. **Criteria:** Candidates will be chosen based on merit.

Funds Avail.: $5,000. **To Apply:** Applicants must complete the online application form; must submit a scholarship certification form, personal statement, transcript of records, recommendation letter and resume. **Deadline:** May 1.

8366 ■ SHPE Foundation Professional Scholarships
(Master's, Doctorate/Scholarship)

Purpose: To help defray the cost of SHPE professionals who demonstrate significant motivation in pursuing their graduate education. **Focus:** Engineering; Mathematics and mathematical sciences; Science; Technology. **Qualif.:** Applicants must be pursuing their first master's or doctoral degree; must be employed full-time in the United States or Puerto Rico in a technical career field; must be enrolled in a science, technology, engineering, mathematics graduate degree program at an accredited university in the United States or Puerto Rico at least half-time (six hours/credits) throughout the academic year; must have a minimum GPA of 3.25 on a 4.0 scale; must be SHPE members in good standing at the time of application. **Criteria:** Recipients will be selected based on merit.

Funds Avail.: $2,000. **To Apply:** Applicants must complete the online application form; must submit a scholarship certification form, personal statement, transcript of records, recommendation letter and resume. **Deadline:** May 1.

8367 ■ SHPE Foundation Verizon Scholarships
(Undergraduate/Scholarship)

Purpose: To support undergraduate students who demonstrate both significant motivation and aptitude for a career in civil engineering, computer engineering and computer science. **Focus:** Computer and information sciences; Engineering, Civil; Engineering, Computer. **Qualif.:** Applicants must be undergraduate students completing their sophomore credit hours and entering their junior classification year; must be attending a university with an active SHPE student chapter in the United States or Puerto Rico; must be enrolled full-time (12 hours undergraduate) during the academic year at an accredited university; must have minimum GPA of 3.0 on a 4.0 scale; must be majoring in civil engineering, computer engineering or computer science. **Criteria:** Candidates will be selected based on merit and financial need.

Funds Avail.: $5,000. **To Apply:** Applicants must complete the online application form; must submit a scholarship certification form, personal statement, transcript of records, recommendation letter and resume.

8368 ■ Sickle Cell Disease Association of America (SCDAA)
3700 Koppers St., Ste. 570
Baltimore, MD 21227-1019
Ph: (410)528-1555
Fax: (410)528-1495
Free: 800-421-8453
E-mail: scdaa@sicklecelldisease.org
URL: www.sicklecelldisease.org

8369 ■ Kermit B. Nash Academic Scholarships
(Undergraduate/Scholarship)

Purpose: To promote educational pursuits of individuals with sickle cell disease. **Focus:** General studies/Field of study not specified. **Qualif.:** Applicants must be individuals with sickle cell disease (individuals with sickle cell trait are not eligible); must be graduating high school seniors; must be U.S. citizens and permanent residents; must have a minimum of 3.0 GPA; must be members of SCDAA. **Criteria:** Award is given based on applicant's GPA, academic achievement, SAT scores, community service, quality of essay and academic obstacles caused by the disease.

Funds Avail.: $5,000 per academic year. **Duration:** 4 years. **Number Awarded:** 1. **To Apply:** Applicants must submit an application form; transcripts; physician's certification of sickle cell status; and an essay.

8370 ■ SCDAA Post-Doctoral Research Fellowships
(Doctorate/Fellowship)

Purpose: To provide financial support for young investigators conducting research in sickle cell disease. **Focus:** specific diseases. **Qualif.:** Applicants must have completed a doctoral degree (MD, PhD or equivalent); must have completed clinical training; must not have more than a total of five years of post-doctoral research experience by the award date; and must be affiliated with a non-profit institution of higher learning or non-profit research facility in the United States. **Criteria:** Awards will be given based on evidence of the applicant's commitment to a research career in sickle cell disease, quality and originality of the proposed research, and importance of the research to the field.

Funds Avail.: $25,000 ($20,000 salary and $5,000 supplies) per year. **Duration:** Two years. **To Apply:** Applicants must submit three copies of application and research mentor's supporting documents including a letter of commitment and the biographical sketch of the mentor. The research proposal must address the broad subject of sickle cell disease in basic laboratory, clinical or psychosocial research areas.

8371 ■ Sidley Austin LLP - North America
One S Dearborn
Chicago, IL 60603
Ph: (312)853-7000
Fax: (312)853-7036
E-mail: cdouglas@sidley.com
URL: www.sidley.com

8372 ■ Sidley Diversity and Inclusion Scholarships
(Undergraduate/Scholarship)

Purpose: To promote diversity within the legal profession and within the firm. **Focus:** Law. **Qualif.:** Applicants must: have demonstrated ability to contribute meaningfully to the diversity of the law school, the firm, and the legal profession; be second year law students; have demonstrated academic achievement and leadership qualities. Preference is given to students at schools where Sidley conducts on-campus interviews or participates in resume collections. **Criteria:** Selection will be based on the committee's criteria.

Funds Avail.: $15,000. **To Apply:** Interested applicants should submit an application, including resume, official law school transcript, legal writing sample and personal statement; an optional letter of recommendation from a professor, employer or personal acquaintance who can meaningfully comment on applicant's academic and intellectual strengths, demonstrated commitment to diversity, and/or ability to contribute to Sidley's diversity efforts. **Deadline:** September 1. **Contact:** Jenny Connelly; Email: scholarship@sidley.com.

Awards are arranged alphabetically below their administering organizations

8373 ■ Sidley Prelaw Scholars Initiative
(Undergraduate/Scholarship)

Purpose: To increase diversity in law schools by subsidizing the cost of applying to law school for talented, financially needy minority students. **Focus:** Law. **Qualif.:** Applicant must be a second semester junior or senior graduating from college in good standing; a native-born or naturalized U.S. citizen; and has demonstrated financial need. **Criteria:** Selection is based on merit and need.

Funds Avail.: $2,500. **Duration:** Annual. **To Apply:** Applicants must submit a completed scholarship application form along with a copy of most recent FAFSA SAR; a copy of current transcript; resume or CV (maximum of two pages); and completed recommendation form from one academic reference. Send application packet via express mail. **Deadline:** January 17. **Contact:** Lisa LeTourneau; Phone:312-853-4144; Fax:312-853-7036; Email:lletourneau@sidley.com.

8374 ■ Sigma Delta Chi Foundation (SDX)
3909 N Meridian St.
Indianapolis, IN 46208
Ph: (317)927-8000
Fax: (317)920-4789
URL: www.spj.org/sdxabout.asp

8375 ■ Eugene C. Pulliam Fellowships for Editorial Writing *(Other/Fellowship)*

Purpose: To provide financial assistance to outstanding editorial writers to help broaden their journalistic horizons and knowledge of the world. **Focus:** Editors and editing. **Qualif.:** Applicants must be part-time or full-time editorial writers at a news publication located in the United States; with at least three years experience as an editorial writer; demonstrate outstanding writing and analytical abilities and ability and intent to publish work within 18 months of selection. **Criteria:** Applicants entry will be reviewed and evaluated by a panel of judges.

Funds Avail.: $75,000. **To Apply:** Applicants must submit a cover letter (containing complete contact information) stating the purpose and nature of the proposed study, a timeline for accomplishing the work and a plan for how the stipend will be used; editor's endorsement; a (one-page) professional biography and summary of professional experience; and five samples of editorials. **Deadline:** June 22. **Contact:** awards@spj.org.

8376 ■ Sigma Delta Epsilon, Graduate Women in Science (SDE/GWIS)
PO Box 240607
Saint Paul, MN 55124-0607
Ph: (952)236-9112
E-mail: gwised@mac.com
URL: www.gwis.org

8377 ■ Eloise Gerry Fellowships *(Graduate, Postdoctorate/Fellowship)*

Purpose: To encourage research careers in the sciences for women. **Focus:** Science. **Qualif.:** Applicant must be enrolled as a graduate student, or engaged in post-doctoral or early-stage junior faculty academic research, and demonstrates financial need. **Criteria:** Selection is based on scientific merit, fields of study and requested funding amounts.

Funds Avail.: $2,500. **Number Awarded:** 2. **To Apply:** Applicants must submit a completed application form together with the abstract of the proposed project (maximum of 200 words, 12 point font, 0.75 in margins); a project proposal description; a proposed budget; two letters of recommendation (sent directly by the authors to fellowships applications@gwis.org, with the name of the applicant as the subject line); copies of animal/human subjects approval or collecting permits; an application process fee of $25. Entire application (except the recommendation letters and fee) must be sent electronically as a single, complete PDF document with "SDE/GWIS Application" and applicant's name in the subject line to fellowships applications@gwis.org. **Deadline:** January 15. **Contact:** Dr. Julie Gros-Louis, PhD, 11 Seashore Hall E, University of Iowa, Iowa City, IA 52242-1407; Phone: 319-384-1816; Fax: 319-335-0191; Email: julie-gros-louis@uiowa.edu.

8378 ■ Nell I. Mondy Fellowships *(Graduate, Postdoctorate/Fellowship)*

Purpose: To encourage research careers in the sciences for women. **Focus:** Science. **Qualif.:** Applicant must be enrolled as a graduate student, or engaged in post-doctoral or early-stage junior faculty academic research, and demonstrates financial need. **Criteria:** Selection is based on scientific merit, fields of study and requested funding amounts.

Funds Avail.: No specific amount. **Duration:** Annual. **To Apply:** Applicant must submit a completed application form together with the abstract of the proposed project (maximum of 200 words, 12 point font, 0.75 in margins); a project proposal description; a proposed budget; two letters of recommendation (sent directly by the authors with the name of the applicant as the subject line); copies of animal/human subjects approval or collecting permits; an application process fee of $25. Entire application (except the recommendation letters and fee) must be sent electronically as a single, complete PDF document with "SDE/GWIS Application" and applicant's name in the subject line. **Deadline:** January 15. **Contact:** Dr. Julie Gros-Louis, PhD, 11 Seashore Hall E, University of Iowa, Iowa City, IA 52242-1407; Phone: 319-384-1816; Fax: 319-335-0191; Email: julie-gros-louis@uiowa.edu.

8379 ■ Vessa Notchev Fellowships *(Graduate, Postdoctorate/Fellowship)*

Purpose: To encourage research careers in the sciences for women. **Focus:** Science. **Qualif.:** Applicant must be enrolled as a graduate student, or engaged in post-doctoral or early-stage junior faculty academic research and demonstrates financial need. **Criteria:** Selection is based on scientific merit, fields of study and requested funding amounts.

Funds Avail.: $4,000. **Duration:** Annual; One year. **Number Awarded:** 1. **To Apply:** Applicant must submit a completed application from together with the abstract of the proposed project (maximum of 200 words, 12 point font, 0.75 in margins); a project proposal description; a proposed budget; two letters of recommendation (sent directly by the authors with the name of the applicant as the subject line); copies of animal/human subjects approval or collecting permits; an application process fee of $25. Entire application (except the recommendation letters and fee) must be sent electronically as a single, complete PDF document with "SDE/GWIS Application" and applicant's name in the subject line. **Deadline:** January 15. **Contact:** Dr. Julie Gros-Louis, PhD, 11 Seashore Hall E, University of Iowa, Iowa City, IA 52242-1407; Phone: 319-384-1816; Fax: 319-335-

Awards are arranged alphabetically below their administering organizations

0191; Email: julie-gros-louis@uiowa.edu.

8380 ■ Sigma Delta Epsilon Fellowships (Graduate, Postdoctorate/Fellowship)

Purpose: To encourage research careers in the sciences for women. **Focus:** Science. **Qualif.:** Applicant must be enrolled as a graduate student, or engaged in post-doctoral or early-stage junior faculty academic research, and demonstrates financial need. **Criteria:** Selection is based on scientific merit, fields of study and requested funding amounts.

Funds Avail.: $2,500. **Duration:** One year. **To Apply:** Applicants must submit a completed application form together with the abstract of the proposed project (maximum of 200 words, 12 point font, 0.75 in margins); a project proposal description; a proposed budget; two letters of recommendation (sent directly by the authors to fellowships applications@gwis.org, with the name of the applicant as the subject line); copies of animal/human subjects approval or collecting permits; an application process fee of $25. Entire application (except the recommendation letters and fee) must be sent electronically as a single, complete PDF document with "SDE/GWIS Application" and applicant's name in the subject line to fellowships applications@gwis.org. **Deadline:** January 15. **Contact:** Dr. Julie Gros-Louis, PhD, 11 Seashore Hall E, University of Iowa, Iowa City, IA 52242-1407; Phone: 319-384-1816; Fax: 319-335-0191; Email: julie-gros-louis@uiowa.edu.

8381 ■ Sigma Kappa Foundation
695 Pro Med Ln., Ste. 300
Carmel, IN 46032
Ph: (317)381-5531
Fax: (317)872-0716
E-mail: foundation@sigmakappa.org
URL: www.sigmakappafoundation.org

8382 ■ Margaret J. Andrew Memorial Scholarships (Undergraduate/Scholarship)

Purpose: To encourage and support the scholastic development of the collegiate and alumnae sisters of the foundation. **Focus:** Food science and technology. **Qualif.:** Applicant must be in good standing as a junior, senior, or graduate student; must be studying food science/food technology or a related major (nutrition, dietetics); must have a minimum cumulative GPA: 3.0. **Criteria:** Selection will be based on GPA and other basic demographic criteria.

Funds Avail.: No specific amount. **To Apply:** Application forms are available online. Applicant must submit the transcript and recommendation letter through online.

8383 ■ Francis Warren Baker Memorial Scholarships (Undergraduate/Scholarship)

Purpose: To encourage and support the scholastic development of the collegiate and alumnae sisters of the foundation. **Focus:** Communications; Journalism. **Qualif.:** Applicant must be a member in good standing enrolled in an undergraduate program in the fields of journalism or communication (print media); must have a minimum cumulative GPA: 3.0. **Criteria:** Preference will be given to sophomores and juniors with at least one year's study remaining.

Funds Avail.: No specific amount. **To Apply:** Application forms are available online. Applicant must submit the transcript and recommendation letter through online.

8384 ■ Beta Omega Scholarships (Undergraduate/Scholarship)

Purpose: To encourage and support the scholastic development of the collegiate and alumnae sisters of the foundation. **Focus:** General studies/Field of study not specified. **Qualif.:** Applicants must be initiated, active members in good standing of Beta Omega Chapter (University of Nebraska, Omaha); must be juniors or seniors class status (mid-year graduating seniors are eligible); must have a minimum cumulative GPA of 3.0; must be in need of financial assistance. **Criteria:** Applicants will be judge based on their active participation in a variety of the foundation and academic activities.

Funds Avail.: No specific amount. **To Apply:** Application forms are available online. Applicants must submit the transcript and recommendation letter through online.

8385 ■ Beta Sigma Scholarships (Undergraduate/Scholarship)

Purpose: To encourage and support the scholastic development of the collegiate and alumnae sisters of the foundation. **Focus:** General studies/Field of study not specified. **Qualif.:** Applicant must be an active, initiated members in good standing of Beta Sigma Chapter (Purdue University); must be a sophomore, junior, or senior class status (mid-year graduating seniors are eligible); must have a minimum cumulative GPA: 2.5; must be in need of financial assistance; must be Residing in the chapter house; must demonstrate leadership in their chapter and on campus. **Criteria:** Applicant will be judge based on their active participation in a variety of the foundation and academic activities.

Funds Avail.: No specific amount. **To Apply:** Application forms are available online. Applicant must submit the transcript and recommendation letter through online.

8386 ■ Walta Wilkinson Carmichael Scholarships (Undergraduate/Scholarship)

Purpose: To encourage and support the scholastic development of the collegiate and alumnae sisters of the foundation. **Focus:** General studies/Field of study not specified. **Qualif.:** Applicant must be a alumnae member in good standing, enrolled in a graduate program, who have demonstrated participation in collegiate chapter activities from their beginning year and continuing through the senior year of membership; must have a minimum undergraduate GPA of 3.0. **Criteria:** Candidate will be selected based on his/her academic standing.

Funds Avail.: No specific amount. **To Apply:** Application forms are available online. Applicant must submit the transcript and recommendation letter through online.

8387 ■ Christine Kerr Cawthorne Scholarships (Undergraduate/Scholarship)

Purpose: To encourage and support the scholastic development of the collegiate and alumnae sisters of the foundation. **Focus:** General studies/Field of study not specified. **Qualif.:** Applicants must be initiated collegiate members in good standing of Alpha Chi Chapter (Georgetown College); must be a matriculated rising sophomore at the time the application is completed, and therefore a matriculated junior in the academic year for which the scholarship is issued; must have a minimum cumulative GPA: 3.0. **Criteria:** Applicants will be judged on leadership and service provided to the chapter and campus community.

Awards are arranged alphabetically below their administering organizations

Funds Avail.: No specific amount. **To Apply:** Application forms are available online. Applicants must submit the transcript and recommendation letter through online.

8388 ■ Maridell Braham Condon Scholarships
(Undergraduate/Scholarship)

Purpose: To encourage and support the scholastic development of the collegiate and alumnae sisters of the foundation. **Focus:** Education. **Qualif.:** Applicants must be initiated, active members in good standing; must be majoring in education; must have a minimum cumulative GPA of 3.0. **Criteria:** Applicants will be judged based on the demonstrated financial need and active participation in a variety of Sigma Kappa and academic activities. Preference will be given to juniors and seniors with at least one year study remaining.

Funds Avail.: No specific amount. **To Apply:** Application forms are available online. Applicants must submit the transcript and recommendation letter through online.

8389 ■ Beta Nu/Caryl Cordis D'hondt Scholarships
(Undergraduate/Scholarship)

Purpose: To encourage and support the scholastic development of the collegiate and alumnae sisters of the foundation. **Focus:** General studies/Field of study not specified. **Qualif.:** Applicants must be initiated members in good standing (scholastic, financial, membership) of Beta Nu Chapter (Bradley University); must be in need of financial assistance; must be involved in Sigma Kappa and the Bradley University campus. **Criteria:** Applicants will be judge based on their active participation in a variety of the foundation and academic activities.

Funds Avail.: No specific amount. **To Apply:** Application forms are available online. Applicants must submit the transcript and recommendation letter through online.

8390 ■ Theta/Caryl Cordis D'hondt Scholarships
(Undergraduate/Scholarship)

Purpose: To encourage and support the scholastic development of the collegiate and alumnae sisters of the foundation. **Focus:** General studies/Field of study not specified. **Qualif.:** Applicants must be initiated, active members in good standing with Theta Tau Chapter (Kansas State University); must be a junior or senior class status (mid-year graduating seniors are also eligible); must have a minimum cumulative GPA of 3.25; must be in need of financial assistance. **Criteria:** Financial need will be considered.

Funds Avail.: No specific amount. **To Apply:** Application forms are available online. Applicants must submit the transcript and recommendation letter through online.

8391 ■ Delta Chi Alumnae Memorial Scholarships
(Undergraduate/Scholarship)

Purpose: To encourage and support the scholastic development of the collegiate and alumnae sisters of the foundation. **Focus:** General studies/Field of study not specified. **Qualif.:** Applicants must be initiated members of Delta Chi Chapter (University of Central Oklahoma); must be a junior or senior class status; must have a minimum cumulative GPA: 3.25; must be currently enrolled in 12 hours or more. **Criteria:** Consideration will be given for leadership and service provided to the chapter and to the campus community.

Funds Avail.: No specific amount. **To Apply:** Application forms are available online. Applicants must submit the

transcript and recommendation letter through online.

8392 ■ Wilma Sackett Dressel Scholarships
(Undergraduate/Scholarship)

Purpose: To encourage and support the scholastic development of the collegiate and alumnae sisters of the foundation. **Focus:** General studies/Field of study not specified. **Qualif.:** Applicant must be an initiated member in good standing of Alpha Tau Chapter (Michigan State University); must demonstrate financial need. **Criteria:** Selection of applicant will be based on their financial need.

Funds Avail.: No specific amount. **To Apply:** Application forms are available online. Applicant must submit the transcript and recommendation letter through online.

8393 ■ Epsilon Epsilon Scholarships
(Undergraduate/Scholarship)

Purpose: To encourage and support the scholastic development of the collegiate and alumnae sisters of the foundation. **Focus:** General studies/Field of study not specified. **Qualif.:** Applicant must be an initiated member in good standing of Epsilon Epsilon Chapter (University of Georgia); must be a junior or senior class status; must have a minimum cumulative GPA 3.00. **Criteria:** Candidate will be selected based on his/her leadership qualities as an officer or former officer of the chapter and financial need.

Funds Avail.: No specific amount. **To Apply:** Application forms are available online. Applicant must submit the transcript and recommendation letter through online.

8394 ■ Epsilon Tau Scholarships *(Undergraduate/Scholarship)*

Purpose: To encourage and support the scholastic development of the collegiate and alumnae sisters of the foundation. **Focus:** General studies/Field of study not specified. **Qualif.:** Applicant must be an initiated member in good standing (scholastic, financial, membership) of Epsilon Tau Chapter (California State University at Fullerton); must demonstrate financial need and involvement in Sigma Kappa, campus, and the community. **Criteria:** Candidates will be selected based on their financial need and involvement to the foundation.

Funds Avail.: No specific amount. **To Apply:** Application forms are available online. Applicant must submit the transcript and recommendation letter through online.

8395 ■ Marian Johnson Frutiger Scholarships
(Undergraduate/Scholarship)

Purpose: To encourage and support the scholastic development of the collegiate and alumnae sisters of the foundation. **Focus:** General studies/Field of study not specified. **Qualif.:** Candidates must be initiated members in good financial standing of the foundation; must have a minimum cumulative GPA of 3.0; must exemplify the ideals and standards of Sigma Kappa; must exhibit outstanding sisterhood and must demonstrate leadership in the Greek system. **Criteria:** Candidates will be judged based on leadership, academic excellence and financial standing.

Funds Avail.: No specific amount. **Number Awarded:** 1. **To Apply:** Application forms are available online. Applicants must submit the transcript and recommendation letter through online.

8396 ■ Gamma Iota Scholarships - Gamma Tau
(Undergraduate/Scholarship)

Purpose: To encourage and support the scholastic development of the collegiate and alumnae sisters of the

Awards are arranged alphabetically below their administering organizations

foundation. **Focus:** General studies/Field of study not specified. **Qualif.:** Applicants must be initiated members attending Kappa Eta (Texas Christian University), Zeta Nu (University of Texas at San Antonio), Gamma Tau (Midwestern State), or Zeta Kappa (Angelo State); must have a minimum cumulative GPA of 3.0; must held or currently hold a Sorority position; must demonstrate involvement in campus and community activities; must be in need of financial assistance. **Criteria:** Candidates will be selected based on their financial need and involvement to the foundation.

Funds Avail.: No specific amount. **To Apply:** Application forms are available online. Applicants must submit the transcript and recommendation letter through online.

8397 ■ Gamma Iota Scholarships - Kappa Eta
(Undergraduate/Scholarship)

Purpose: To encourage and support the scholastic development of the collegiate and alumnae sisters of the foundation. **Focus:** General studies/Field of study not specified. **Qualif.:** Applicants must be initiated members attending Kappa Eta (Texas Christian University), Zeta Nu (University of Texas at San Antonio), Gamma Tau (Midwestern State), or Zeta Kappa (Angelo State); must have a minimum cumulative GPA: 3.0; must have held or currently hold a Sorority position; must demonstrate involvement in campus and community activities; must be in need of financial assistance. **Criteria:** Candidates will be selected based on their financial need and involvement to the foundation.

Funds Avail.: No specific amount. **To Apply:** Application forms are available online. Applicants must submit the transcript and recommendation letter through online.

8398 ■ Gamma Iota Scholarships - Zeta Kappa
(Undergraduate/Scholarship)

Purpose: To encourage and support the scholastic development of the collegiate and alumnae sisters of the foundation. **Focus:** General studies/Field of study not specified. **Qualif.:** Applicants must be initiated members attending Kappa Eta (Texas Christian University), Zeta Nu (University of Texas at San Antonio), Gamma Tau (Midwestern State), or Zeta Kappa (Angelo State); must have a minimum cumulative GPA of 3.0; must have held or currently hold a Sorority position; must demonstrate involvement in campus and community activities; must be in need of financial assistance. **Criteria:** Candidates will be selected based on their financial need and involvement to the foundation.

Funds Avail.: No specific amount. **To Apply:** Application forms are available online. Applicants must submit the transcript and recommendation letter through online.

8399 ■ Gamma Iota Scholarships - Zeta Nu
(Undergraduate/Scholarship)

Purpose: To encourage and support the scholastic development of the collegiate and alumnae sisters of the foundation. **Focus:** General studies/Field of study not specified. **Qualif.:** Applicants must be initiated members attending Kappa Eta (Texas Christian University), Zeta Nu (University of Texas at San Antonio), Gamma Tau (Midwestern State), or Zeta Kappa (Angelo State); must have a minimum cumulative GPA of 3.0; must have held or currently hold a Sorority position; must have demonstrate involvement in campus and community activities; must be in need of financial assistance. **Criteria:** Candidates will be selected based on their financial need and involvement to the foundation.

Funds Avail.: No specific amount. **To Apply:** Application forms are available online. Applicants must submit the transcript and recommendation letter through online.

8400 ■ Lucille Cheever Graubart/Lambda Scholarships
(Undergraduate/Scholarship)

Purpose: To encourage and support the scholastic development of the collegiate and alumnae sisters of the foundation. **Focus:** General studies/Field of study not specified. **Qualif.:** Applicants must be initiated members of Lambda Chapter (University of California, Berkeley) in good standing; must be in need of financial assistance. **Criteria:** Candidates will be selected based on their financial need.

Funds Avail.: No specific amount. **To Apply:** Application forms are available online. Applicants must submit the transcript and recommendation letter through online.

8401 ■ Elise Reed Jenkins Memorial Scholarships - Gamma Lambda
(Undergraduate/Scholarship)

Purpose: To encourage and support the scholastic development of the collegiate and alumnae sisters of the foundation. **Focus:** General studies/Field of study not specified. **Qualif.:** Applicants must be an undergraduate member of either Alpha Delta Chapter (University of Tennessee, Knoxville), Gamma Lambda Chapter (East Tennessee State University), or Gamma Psi Chapter (Tennessee Wesleyan); must be a loyal members of Sigma Kappa for at least two, and preferably three years; must have a minimum cumulative GPA of: 3.0. **Criteria:** Applicants will be selected based on their performance and service provided to the chapter and to the campus community.

Funds Avail.: No specific amount. **To Apply:** Application forms are available online. Applicant must submit the transcript and recommendation letter through online.

8402 ■ Elise Reed Jenkins Memorial Scholarships - Gamma Psi
(Undergraduate/Scholarship)

Purpose: To encourage and support the scholastic development of the collegiate and alumnae sisters of the foundation. **Focus:** General studies/Field of study not specified. **Qualif.:** Applicants must be an undergraduate member of either Alpha Delta Chapter (University of Tennessee, Knoxville), Gamma Lambda Chapter (East Tennessee State University), or Gamma Psi Chapter (Tennessee Wesleyan); must be loyal members of Sigma Kappa for at least two, and preferably three years; must have a minimum cumulative GPA of: 3.0. **Criteria:** Consideration will be given for leadership and service provided to the chapter and to the campus community.

Funds Avail.: No specific amount. **To Apply:** Application forms are available online. Applicants must submit the transcript and recommendation letter through online.

8403 ■ Kappa Zeta Scholarships *(Undergraduate/Scholarship)*

Purpose: To encourage and support the scholastic development of the collegiate and alumnae sisters of the foundation. **Focus:** General studies/Field of study not specified. **Qualif.:** Applicants must be initiated members of Kappa Zeta Chapter (Elon University) in good standing; must demonstrate outstanding leadership and service to the chapter, Panhellenic, and the University; must have a minimum cumulative GPA: 3.4. **Criteria:** Candidates will be selected based on their academic achievements and involvement to the foundation.

Funds Avail.: No specific amount. **To Apply:** Application

Awards are arranged alphabetically below their administering organizations

forms are available online. Applicants must submit the transcript and recommendation letter through online.

8404 ■ Joan Reagin McNeill Scholarships - Alpha Theta *(Undergraduate/Scholarship)*

Purpose: To encourage and support the scholastic development of the collegiate and alumnae sisters of the foundation. **Focus:** General studies/Field of study not specified. **Qualif.:** Applicants must be an active sophomore, junior, or senior members of Alpha Theta Chapter (University of Louisville) or Theta Phi Chapter (University of Tennessee, Chattanooga) in good standing with at least one year remaining for completion of an undergraduate degree; must have a minimum cumulative GPA: 3.25. **Criteria:** Financial need will be considered.

Funds Avail.: No specific amount. **To Apply:** Application forms are available online. Applicants must submit the transcript and recommendation letter through online.

8405 ■ Joan Reagin McNeill Scholarships - Theta Phi *(Undergraduate/Scholarship)*

Purpose: To encourage and support the scholastic development of the collegiate and alumnae sisters of the foundation. **Focus:** General studies/Field of study not specified. **Qualif.:** Applicants must be a active sophomore, junior, or senior members of Alpha Theta Chapter (University of Louisville) or Theta Phi Chapter (University of Tennessee, Chattanooga) in good standing with at least one year remaining for completion of an undergraduate degree; must have a minimum cumulative GPA: 3.25. **Criteria:** Financial need will be considered.

Funds Avail.: No specific amount. **To Apply:** Application forms are available online. Applicants must submit the transcript and recommendation letter through online.

8406 ■ Evelyn S. Nish Scholarships *(Undergraduate/Scholarship)*

Purpose: To encourage and support the scholastic development of the collegiate and alumnae sisters of the foundation. **Focus:** General studies/Field of study not specified. **Qualif.:** Applicants must be initiated, active members in good standing of the Theta Chapter (University of Illinois); must be junior or senior students enrolled during the academic year that the scholarship is granted; must have a minimum cumulative GPA: 3.0. **Criteria:** Consideration will be given for leadership and service provided to the chapter and to the campus community.

Funds Avail.: No specific amount. **To Apply:** Application forms are available online. Applicants must submit the transcript and recommendation letter through online.

8407 ■ Mary Turnbull Schacht Memorial Scholarships *(Undergraduate/Scholarship)*

Purpose: To encourage and support the scholastic development of the collegiate and alumnae sisters of the foundation. **Focus:** General studies/Field of study not specified. **Qualif.:** Applicants must be initiated, active members in good standing of the Lambda Chapter (University of California, Berkeley); must demonstrate outstanding leadership and service provided to the chapter, panhellenic and the University of California, Berkeley; must have a minimum cumulative GPA of 3.0. **Criteria:** Candidates will be selected based on their involvement to the foundation.

Funds Avail.: No specific amount. **To Apply:** Application forms are available online. Applicants must submit the transcript and recommendation letter through online.

8408 ■ Sigma Kappa Foundation Alumnae Continuing Education Scholarships *(Undergraduate/Scholarship)*

Purpose: To encourage and support the scholastic development of the collegiate and alumnae sisters of the foundation. **Focus:** General studies/Field of study not specified. **Qualif.:** Applicant must be a alumnae currently possessing an undergraduate degree from a four-year institution and having been accepted/enrolled in an advanced degree program; must have a minimum cumulative GPA: 3.0. **Criteria:** Selection will be based on applicant's academic standing.

Funds Avail.: No specific amount. **To Apply:** Application forms are available online. Applicant must submit the transcript and recommendation letter through online.

8409 ■ Sigma Kappa Foundation Alzheimer's/Gerontology Scholarships *(Graduate/Scholarship)*

Purpose: To encourage and support the scholastic development of the collegiate and alumnae sisters of the foundation. **Focus:** Alzheimer's disease; Gerontology. **Qualif.:** Applicant must be a graduate student or alumnae studying Alzheimer, Gerontology (the study of aging), or a related field. **Criteria:** Selection of candidate will be based on the scholarship criteria.

Funds Avail.: No specific amount. **To Apply:** Application forms are available online. Applicant must submit the transcript and recommendation letter through online.

8410 ■ Sigma Kappa Foundation Founders' Scholarships *(Undergraduate/Scholarship)*

Purpose: To encourage and support the scholastic development of the collegiate and alumnae sisters of the foundation. **Focus:** General studies/Field of study not specified. **Qualif.:** Applicants should be active, initiated, continuing members in good standing; must have a minimum cumulative GPA of 3.0; must demonstrate a leadership role on campus (student government, chapter officer, Panhellenic officer). **Criteria:** Preference will be given to sophomores and juniors with at least one year study remaining.

Funds Avail.: No specific amount. **To Apply:** Application forms are available online. Applicants must submit the transcript and recommendation letter through online. **Deadline:** March 15.

8411 ■ Sigma Kappa Foundation Gerontology Scholarships *(Undergraduate/Scholarship)*

Purpose: To encourage and support the scholastic development of the collegiate and alumnae sisters of the foundation. **Focus:** Gerontology. **Qualif.:** Applicant must be a junior, senior, or graduate student with at least one year study remaining; must be a member in good standing, majoring in Gerontology (the study of aging) or a related field; must have a minimum cumulative GPA: 3.0. **Criteria:** Selection of candidates will be based on GPA and other basic demographic criteria.

Funds Avail.: No specific amount. **To Apply:** Application forms are available online. Applicant must submit the transcript and recommendation letter through online.

8412 ■ Sigma Kappa Foundation Michigan Scholarships *(Undergraduate/Scholarship)*

Purpose: To encourage and support the scholastic development of the collegiate and alumnae sisters of the

---

Awards are arranged alphabetically below their administering organizations

foundation. **Focus:** General studies/Field of study not specified. **Qualif.:** Applicant must be a Michigan resident as defined by the university of attendance; must be initiated in Sigma Kappa, currently active, and in good standing with the chapter at a College or University in Michigan; must have at least two semesters of undergraduate study remaining at the time of the award; must have a minimum GPA: 2.5 and in good standing with the university of enrollment. Applicant may not have received the scholarship previously. **Criteria:** Candidate will be selected based on their academic achievements and involvement to the foundation.

Funds Avail.: No specific amount. **To Apply:** Application forms are available online. Applicants must submit the transcript and recommendation letter through online.

8413 ■ Elin J. Stene/Xi Scholarships *(Undergraduate/ Scholarship)*

Purpose: To encourage and support the scholastic development of the collegiate and alumnae sisters of the foundation. **Focus:** General studies/Field of study not specified. **Qualif.:** Applicants must be initiated, active members in good standing of Xi Chapter (University of Kansas); must be juniors or seniors class status (mid-year graduating seniors are eligible); must have a minimum cumulative GPA: 3.0; must be in need of financial assistance. **Criteria:** Consideration will be given for leadership and service provided to the chapter and to the campus community.

Funds Avail.: No specific amount. **To Apply:** Application forms are available online. Applicants must submit the transcript and recommendation letter through online.

8414 ■ Lorraine E. Swain Scholarships *(Undergraduate/Scholarship)*

Purpose: To encourage and support the scholastic development of the collegiate and alumnae sisters of the foundation. **Focus:** General studies/Field of study not specified. **Qualif.:** Applicants must initiated in Sigma Kappa, currently active, and in good standing with the chapter at a College or University in Colorado. **Criteria:** Consideration will be given for leadership and service provided to the chapter and to the campus community.

Funds Avail.: No specific amount. **To Apply:** Application forms are available online. Applicants must submit the transcript and recommendation letter through online.

8415 ■ Theta Tau Scholarships *(Undergraduate/ Scholarship)*

Purpose: To encourage and support the scholastic development of the collegiate and alumnae sisters of the foundation. **Focus:** General studies/Field of study not specified. **Qualif.:** Applicants must be initiated, active members in good standing with Theta Tau Chapter (Kansas State University); must be a junior or senior class status (mid-year graduating seniors are also eligible); must have a minimum cumulative GPA of 3.0; must be in need of financial assistance. **Criteria:** Candidates will be selected based on their merit and financial need.

Funds Avail.: No specific amount. **To Apply:** Application forms are available online. Applicants must submit the transcript and recommendation letter through online.

8416 ■ Barber Owen Thomas Scholarships *(Undergraduate/Scholarship)*

Purpose: To encourage and support the scholastic development of the collegiate and alumnae sisters of the foundation. **Focus:** General studies/Field of study not specified. **Qualif.:** Applicants must be active members in good standing of the Beta Sigma Chapter (Purdue University); must be juniors or seniors in class status (mid-year graduating seniors are also eligible); must have a minimum cumulative GPA of 2.5; must be in need of financial assistance; must be residing in the chapter house. **Criteria:** Applicants will be judge based on their active participation in a variety of the foundation and academic activities.

Funds Avail.: No specific amount. **To Apply:** Application forms are available online. Applicants must submit the transcript and recommendation letter through online.

8417 ■ Irma E. Voigt Memorial Scholarships *(Undergraduate/Scholarship)*

Purpose: To encourage and support the scholastic development of the collegiate and alumnae sisters of the foundation. **Focus:** General studies/Field of study not specified. **Qualif.:** Applicants must be initiated members of Beta Upsilon Chapter (Ohio University) in good standing; must be a junior class status, currently enrolled in 12 or more hours; must have a minimum cumulative GPA of 3.0; must be actively involved in her chapter, on campus, and in the community. **Criteria:** Candidates will be selected based on their academic achievements and involvement to the foundation.

Funds Avail.: No specific amount. **To Apply:** Application forms are available online. Applicants must submit the transcript and recommendation letter through online.

8418 ■ Alice Hersey Wick Scholarships *(Undergraduate/Scholarship)*

Purpose: To encourage and support the scholastic development of the collegiate and alumnae sisters of the foundation. **Focus:** General studies/Field of study not specified. **Qualif.:** Applicant must be initiated collegiate members in good standing; must have a minimum cumulative GPA of 3.0. **Criteria:** Applications will be judged based on leadership and service provided to the chapter, campus, and community.

Funds Avail.: No specific amount. **To Apply:** Application forms are available online. Applicant must submit the transcript and recommendation letter through online.

8419 ■ Andrea Will Memorial Scholarships *(Undergraduate/Scholarship)*

Purpose: To encourage and support the scholastic development of the collegiate and alumnae sisters of the foundation. **Focus:** General studies/Field of study not specified. **Qualif.:** Applicants must be new initiates in good standing of Gamma Mu Chapter, matriculating at Eastern Illinois University; must have a minimum cumulative GPA of 3.0; must demonstrate involvement in co-curricular activities, and evidence of leadership qualities and experience. **Criteria:** Applicants will be judge based on their active participation in a variety of the foundation and academic activities.

Funds Avail.: No specific amount. **To Apply:** Application forms are available online. Applicants must submit the transcript and recommendation letter through online.

8420 ■ Silicon Valley Community Foundation

2440 W El Camino Real, Ste. 300
Mountain View, CA 94040-1498
Ph: (650)450-5400
Fax: (650)450-5401

Awards are arranged alphabetically below their administering organizations

E-mail: info@siliconvalleycf.org
URL: www.siliconvalleycf.org

8421 ■ Hazel Reed Baumeister Scholarship Program *(Undergraduate/Scholarship)*

Purpose: To support high school graduates of high academic achievement who would be unable to pursue higher education without financial assistance. **Focus:** General studies/Field of study not specified. **Qualif.:** Applicants must be current graduating seniors or graduates of a public or private high school in San Mateo County or Santa Clara County; must be United States citizens; must have demonstrated financial hardship; must have earned a minimum cumulative grade point average of 3.5. **Criteria:** Preference will be given to those students who meet the criteria.

Funds Avail.: Up to $5,000. **Number Awarded:** Up to 15. **To Apply:** Applicants must check the available website for the required materials. **Remarks:** Established in 2001. **Contact:** scholarships@siliconvalleycf.org.

8422 ■ Crain Educational Grant Program *(Undergraduate/Scholarship)*

Purpose: To enable high school graduates to pursue courses of study they would otherwise be unable to follow due to limited financial means. **Focus:** General studies/Field of study not specified. **Qualif.:** Applicants must be current graduating seniors or graduates of a public or private high school in San Mateo County or Santa Clara County; must be U.S. citizens; must have demonstrated financial hardship; must have a minimum cumulative grade point average of 3.3. **Criteria:** Applicants will be evaluated based on demonstrated academic promise, documented perseverance in activities outside the classroom, quality of the personal statement and personal characteristics. Finalists will undergo an interview.

Funds Avail.: $5,000. **Number Awarded:** Up to 10. **To Apply:** Applicants must check the available website to download the application form online. **Deadline:** February 25. **Remarks:** Established in 1987. **Contact:** scholarships@siliconvalleycf.org.

8423 ■ Curry Awards for Girls and Young Women *(Undergraduate/Scholarship)*

Purpose: To provide financial support to those students who are in need. **Focus:** General studies/Field of study not specified. **Qualif.:** Applicants must be current residents of San Mateo County; must be U.S. citizens or legal residents; must be young women 16 to 26 years old. **Criteria:** Recipients will be evaluated based on demonstrated financial need.

Funds Avail.: $1,000. **Number Awarded:** Up to 10. **To Apply:** Applicants must check the available website to download the application form online. **Contact:** scholarships@siliconvalleycf.org.

8424 ■ Eustace-Kwan Family Foundation Scholarships *(Undergraduate/Scholarship)*

Purpose: To help promising high school and junior college students pursue higher education at an accredited two or four-year college or vocational school. **Focus:** General studies/Field of study not specified. **Qualif.:** Applicants must be current residents of San Mateo County or Northern Santa Clara County; must be current graduating high school seniors planning to attend an accredited two or four-year college or vocational school or current community college students planning to transfer to a four-year college; must

be United States citizens or legal residents; must have a cumulative grade point average of 3.5 or 3.7 and on a 4.0 scale; must have demonstrated community involvement. **Criteria:** Selection committee looks for students who are focused, able to articulate clear goals, determined to succeed in their chosen field and career, financial need, overall quality of the personal statement and whether student's activities align with stated goals. Special consideration will be given to working students.

Funds Avail.: Up to $10,000. **Number Awarded:** Up to 10. **To Apply:** Applicants must submit a completed application form; two letters of reference, one of which must be from a teacher or academic advisor and another one from a work or volunteer supervisor, youth leader or personal acquaintance; an official transcript of grades; signed and dated personal statement at least 500 words, but no longer than 850 words; evidence of financial need; and proof of citizenship or legal residency. Detailed information are available at the website. **Remarks:** Established in 2006. **Contact:** scholarships@siliconvalleycf.org.

8425 ■ Bobette Bibo Gugliotta Memorial Scholarships for Creative Writing *(Undergraduate/Scholarship)*

Purpose: To provide financial assistance to those students who are in need. **Focus:** General studies/Field of study not specified. **Qualif.:** Applicants must be current graduating seniors or graduates of a public or private high school in San Mateo County or Northern Santa Clara County; must be accepted to or awaiting acceptance to a two- or four-year college or university; must be United States citizens. **Criteria:** Preference will be given to those students who meet the criteria.

Funds Avail.: Up to $1,000. **Number Awarded:** Up to 2. **To Apply:** Applicants must check the available website for the required materials. **Contact:** scholarships@siliconvalleycf.org.

8426 ■ Dr. James L. Hutchinson and Evelyn Ribbs Hutchinson Medical School Scholarship Fund *(Undergraduate/Scholarship)*

Purpose: To support students who demonstrate excellence in both character and academic achievement by giving them scholarships. **Focus:** Medicine. **Qualif.:** Applicants must be United States citizens; must be college seniors and accepted to medical school, or currently enrolled full-time in an accredited medical school program; must demonstrate personal motivation for excellence in both character and academic achievement. Personal integrity, as exemplified by leadership, community involvement, and concern for others, will be considered. **Criteria:** Preference will be given to those students who meet the criteria.

Funds Avail.: Up to $2,000. **Number Awarded:** 1. **To Apply:** Applicants must check the available website for the required materials. **Deadline:** March 23. **Contact:** scholarships@siliconvalleycf.org.

8427 ■ Kumin Scholars Program *(Undergraduate/Scholarship)*

Purpose: To support current community college students who wish to transfer to a four-year institution. **Focus:** General studies/Field of study not specified. **Qualif.:** Applicants must be United States citizens or legal residents; must be enrolled part-time or full-time in a community college; must have completed at least 20 graded semester or quarter units; must have earned a minimum GPA of 2.5.

Awards are arranged alphabetically below their administering organizations

Criteria: Preference will be given to those students who meet the criteria.

Funds Avail.: Up to $2,000 for Community College students; and up to $4,000 when students transfer to a four-year institution. **To Apply:** Applicants must check the available website for the required materials. **Remarks:** Established in 2004. **Contact:** scholarships@ siliconvalleycf.org.

8428 ■ Fauneil J. Rinn Scholarships (Undergraduate/ Scholarship)

Purpose: To provide financial assistance to those students who are in need. **Focus:** Political science; Public administration. **Qualif.:** Applicants must be women who are current students in good standing in the Political Science or Master of Public Administration programs at San Jose State University. **Criteria:** Selection will be based on their achievements and abilities as reflected in a brief application form, a resume and a 500-word essay on a subject relevant to the political or governmental role of women.

Funds Avail.: Up to $1,250. **Number Awarded:** 1. **To Apply:** Applicants must check the available website for the required materials. **Contact:** Peter Kenneth at kenneth.peter@sjsu.edu.

8429 ■ Ruppert Educational Grant Program (Undergraduate/Grant)

Purpose: To provide financial assistance to those students who are in need. **Focus:** General studies/Field of study not specified. **Qualif.:** Applicants must be U.S. citizens; must be current graduating seniors attending high schools in San Mateo County or Northern Santa Clara County (Daly City through Mountain View). Applicants must demonstrate: financial hardship; evidence of partial self-support (e.g., savings from summer jobs, part-time work, etc.); community involvement; must show academic promise; must have 3.3 GPA on a 4.0 scale during high school years. **Criteria:** Recipients will be chosen based on demonstrated financial need.

Funds Avail.: up to $10,000. **Number Awarded:** 30. **To Apply:** Applicants must check the available website for the required materials. **Contact:** scholarships@ siliconvalleycf.org.

8430 ■ Leo and Trinidad Sanchez Scholarships (Undergraduate/Scholarship)

Purpose: To provide financial support to those students who are in need. **Focus:** Architecture. **Qualif.:** Applicants must be Hispanic/American (with at least one parent of Hispanic or Hispanic/American heritage); must be residents of Santa Clara or Santa Cruz County; must be seniors in high school or students at West Valley College enrolled in a program leading to a degree in architecture, or students in any architectural school. **Criteria:** Preference will be given to those who meet the criteria.

Funds Avail.: Up to $4,500. **Number Awarded:** 1. **To Apply:** Applicants must check the available website for more information regarding this award. **Contact:** April Becerra; Phone: 408-298-0611; E-mail: abecerra@aiascv.org.

8431 ■ Sand Hill Scholars Program (Undergraduate/ Scholarship)

Purpose: To provide financial assistance to those students who are in need. **Focus:** General studies/Field of study not specified. **Qualif.:** Applicants must be eighth-grade graduates of the Ravenswood City School District; must be cur-

rent graduating seniors attending a high school in San Mateo County or Northern Santa Clara County; and must be U.S. citizens or legal residents. **Criteria:** Preference is given to students who have shown motivation and leadership, have overcome hardships to remain in school, or have been involved in educational, job-related, or community activities outside the school environment.

Funds Avail.: Up to $12,000. **Duration:** Up to four years. **Number Awarded:** Up to 2. **To Apply:** Applicants must check the available website for the required materials. **Contact:** scholarships@siliconvalleycf.org.

8432 ■ Simon Youth Foundation (SYF)
225 W Washington St.
Indianapolis, IN 46204
Free: 800-509-3676
E-mail: syf@simon.com
URL: www.syf.org

8433 ■ Simon Youth Foundation Community Scholarships (Undergraduate/Scholarship)

Purpose: To provide scholarships to the promising students in communities that host Simon properties. **Focus:** General studies/Field of study not specified. **Qualif.:** Scholarship is available to students who plan to enroll in a full-time undergraduate course of study at an accredited two- or four-year college, university, or vocational/technical school. **Criteria:** Selection will be based on the committee's criteria. In addition, four-year renewable Awards of Excellence are awarded in eight communities: Atlanta, Boston, Dallas, Indianapolis, Miami, New York, Orange County and Orlando.

Funds Avail.: $1,500. **To Apply:** Applicants may submit an application and other required documents to the Foundation.

8434 ■ The Simons Foundation
PO Box 2163 Station Terminal
Vancouver, BC, Canada V6B 3V3
Ph: (778)782-7779
Fax: (778)782-7781
E-mail: info@thesimonsfoundation.ca
URL: www.thesimonsfoundation.ca/

8435 ■ Graduate Research Awards for Disarmament, Arms Control and Non-Proliferation (Master's, Doctorate/Award)

Purpose: To enhance Canadian graduate level scholarship on disarmament, arms control and non-proliferation issues. **Focus:** Law. **Qualif.:** Applicants must be citizens, permanent residents, or landed immigrants of Canada including Canadian graduate students currently studying abroad; must be in a masters or doctoral program. **Criteria:** Committee will select eight winners on a competitive basis.

Funds Avail.: $3,000. **Number Awarded:** 8. **To Apply:** Applicants must submit the following documents: an introductory letter of interest that supports their candidacy for the GRA program; a writing sample (up to 1,500 words) that addresses non-proliferation, arms control and disarmament (NACD) issues; resume, including proof of citizenship status; a complete, official transcript of grades; letter of reference from the applicants' supervisor; and second letter of reference. **Remarks:** Established in 2003.

Awards are arranged alphabetically below their administering organizations

8436 ■ DW Simpson Global Actuarial Recruitment

4121 N Ravenswood Ave.
Chicago, IL 60613
Ph: (312)867-2300
Fax: (312)951-8386
Free: 800-837-8338
E-mail: actuaries@dwsimpson.com
URL: www.dwsimpson.com

8437 ■ DW Simpson Actuarial Science Scholarship Program *(Undergraduate/Scholarship)*

Purpose: To provide financial support for deserving students who are pursuing study in actuarial science. **Focus:** Actuarial science. **Qualif.:** Applicants must be entering their senior year of undergraduate study in actuarial science, have maintained a GPA of 3.2 or higher in their major and an overall GPA of 3.0 or better and have passed at least 1 actuarial examination, and be eligible to work in the United States. **Criteria:** Applicants will be evaluated on the basis of academic performance.

Funds Avail.: $1,000. **Duration:** Annual. **Number Awarded:** 2. **To Apply:** Applicants must complete the application form available online at the DW Simpsons Global Actuarial Recruitment. **Deadline:** April 30 for the Fall scholarship; October 31 for the Spring scholarship.

8438 ■ Sindhi Association of North America

12881 Knott St., Ste. 219
Garden Grove, CA 92841-3925
Ph: (714)271-9947
Fax: (714)373-3702
E-mail: president@sanalist.org
URL: www.sanalist.org/sana/newsite

8439 ■ Dr. Feroz Ahmed Memorial Educational Post-Graduate Scholarships *(Doctorate, Postgraduate/Scholarship)*

Purpose: To financially support the education of meritorious Sindhi students who are pursuing higher degrees in research topics at a university in Pakistan. **Focus:** History; Humanities; Nursing; Pharmaceutical sciences; Social sciences; Sociology. **Qualif.:** Applicants must be currently enrolled in M.A., M. Phil. or PhD program in any recognized university in Pakistan. **Criteria:** Selection will be based on academic excellence and financial need.

Funds Avail.: No specific amount. **To Apply:** Applicants must submit a completed application form; attendance record of the current semester; proof of admission in the university; attested mark sheets for Class X, Class XII and university examinations mentioned in this form; two recommendation letters; original family income certificate; autobiographical essay stating why do applicants deserve the award.

8440 ■ SINFONIA Educational Foundation (SEF)

10600 Old State Rd.
Evansville, IN 47711
Ph: (812)867-2433
Fax: (812)867-0633
Free: 800-473-2649
E-mail: sef@sinfonia.org
URL: www.sinfonia.org

8441 ■ Delta Iota Alumni Scholarships *(Undergraduate/Scholarship)*

Purpose: To provide educational assistance for American college students. **Focus:** General studies/Field of study not specified. **Qualif.:** Applicants must have been college students for at least two semesters; must be in good standing; must maintain good standing status during the academic year of scholarship. **Criteria:** Applicants will be evaluated based on merit.

Funds Avail.: $500. **To Apply:** Applicants must submit a typed or computer-generated application with 1-2 page essay on the topic: How has your membership in Phi Mu Alpha developed in you the tools to instill in others an awareness of music's important role in the enrichment of the human spirit?; minimum of three letters and a maximum of five letters of support, one from a Sinfonian and one from a non-Sinfonian, that address evidence of the applicants' integrity, ethics, initiative and overall devotion to the Object of Phi Mu Alpha Sinfonia Fraternity; composite style coat and tie photo for promotional purposes only; name and address of hometown newspaper for promotional purposes.

8442 ■ W. Eldridge and Emily Lowe Scholarships *(Undergraduate/Scholarship)*

Purpose: To provide educational assistance for American college students. **Focus:** General studies/Field of study not specified. **Qualif.:** Applicants must have been college students for at least two semesters; must be in good standing; must maintain good standing status during the academic year of scholarship. **Criteria:** Applicants will be evaluated based on merit.

Funds Avail.: $1,000. **Duration:** Annual. **To Apply:** Applicants must submit a typed or computer-generated application with 1-2 page essay on the topic: How has your membership in Phi Mu Alpha developed in you the tools to instill in others an awareness of music's important role in the enrichment of the human spirit?; minimum of three letters and maximum of five letters of support, one from a Sinfonian and one from a non-Sinfonian, that address evidence of the applicants' integrity, ethics, initiative and overall devotion to the Object of Phi Mu Alpha Sinfonia Fraternity; composite style coat and tie photo for promotional purposes only; name and address of hometown newspaper for promotional purposes.

8443 ■ James H. Patrenos Memorial Scholarships *(Undergraduate/Scholarship)*

Purpose: To provide educational assistance for American college students. **Focus:** General studies/Field of study not specified. **Qualif.:** Must be a collegiate member in good standing of Phi Mu Alpha Sinfonia as of the date of application and have been in good standing for at least one complete semester. Must maintain status as a collegiate member in good standing throughout the complete academic year toward which the scholarship is applied. Must maintain full-time enrollment during the complete academic year toward which the scholarship is applied. **Criteria:** Applicants are evaluated based on merit.

Funds Avail.: $2,500. **Duration:** Annual. **To Apply:** Applicants must submit typed or computer-generated application with 1-2 page essay on the topic: How has your membership in Phi Mu Alpha developed in you the tools to instill in others an awareness of music's important role in the enrichment of the human spirit?; minimum of three letters and a maximum of five letters of support, one from a Sinfonian and one from a non-Sinfonian, that address

Awards are arranged alphabetically below their administering organizations

evidence of the applicant's integrity, ethics, initiative and overall devotion to the Object of Phi Mu Alpha Sinfonia Fraternity; composite style coat and tie photo for promotional purposes only; name and address of hometown newspaper for promotional purposes. **Deadline:** April 17.

8444 ■ Sino-American Pharmaceutical Professionals Association (SAPA)

PO Box 282
Nanuet, NY 10954
E-mail: information@sapaweb.org
URL: www.sapaweb.org

8445 ■ Sino-American Pharmaceutical Professionals Association Scholarships *(Undergraduate/Scholarship)*

Purpose: To recognize and support excellence on the part of outstanding high school students and to encourage the finest high school graduates to develop careers in life science. **Focus:** Life sciences. **Qualif.:** Applicant must be a full-time high school graduate who plans full-time undergraduate study at an accredited four-year college in the upcoming academic year; must have GPA above 3.3, a minimum SAT 1400 and be in the top tenth of the class; must be a United States citizen, or a legal resident alien; must demonstrated a potential and commitment to a career in life sciences. **Criteria:** Applicant will be evaluated based on their merit and outstanding potential to pursue careers in life sciences. SAPA Scholars are selected by the Board of SAPA Scholarship and Excellence in Education for Life Science Foundation.

Funds Avail.: $1,000. **Duration:** One year. **To Apply:** Applicant must submit an essay of approximately 600 words; two letters of recommendation from teachers who can discuss the nominee's potential for a career in life sciences including a teacher in the applicant's field of study and another who can attest the nominee's potential; must have a list of awards received; must have a list of Advanced Placement of Honors courses with grades and awards received. **Deadline:** April 30. **Remarks:** Established in 1999. **Contact:** sapa_scholarship@yahoo.com.

8446 ■ Sjogren's Syndrome Foundation (SSF)

6707 Democracy Blvd., Ste. 325
Bethesda, MD 20817
Ph: (301)530-4420
Fax: (301)530-4415
Free: 800-475-6473
E-mail: tms@sjogrens.org
URL: www.sjogrens.org

8447 ■ SSF Research Grants *(Other/Grant)*

Purpose: To encourage therapeutic development in Sjogren's syndrome by funding potential researches on further treatment and understanding of the disease. **Focus:** Medical research. **Qualif.:** Applicant must be a basic scientist and clinical investigator; or a junior or senior investigator conducting research at an institution in the United States. **Criteria:** Applicants are selected based on the application package.

Funds Avail.: $15,000 to $50,000 for two years. **Duration:** Two years. **To Apply:** Applicants must submit a complete application package which includes: an Application Face page; abstract for the research proposal; publications;

budget; letters of recommendation; statement of guarantee of adequate facilities and budget for the research proposal; and a principal investigators signed statement of responsibility. Applicants may send the documents electronically with a subject line: (Applicant Name) Research Grant Application, or send on a CD. **Deadline:** February 1.

8448 ■ SSF Student Fellowships *(Doctorate, Undergraduate/Fellowship)*

Purpose: To provide financial support for students working on a semester or summer research project in Sjogren's Syndrome. **Focus:** Medical research. **Qualif.:** Applicants must be medical, dental, or PhD graduates and undergraduate students and must be conducting research at an institution in the United States. **Criteria:** Applicants are selected based on the application package.

Funds Avail.: No specific amount. **Duration:** Annual. **Number Awarded:** 1. **To Apply:** Applicants must submit a complete application package which includes: an Application Face page; abstract for the research proposal; publications; budget; letters of recommendation; statement of guarantee of adequate facilities and budget for the research proposal; and a principal investigators signed statement of responsibility. Applicants must send the documents electronically with a subject line: (Applicant Name) Research Grant Application, or send on a CD.

8449 ■ Skadden Fellowship Foundation

c/o Susan B. Plum, Secretary
4 Times Sq., Office 40-126
New York, NY 10036
Ph: (212)735-2956
URL: www.skaddenfellowships.org

8450 ■ Skadden Fellowships *(Graduate/Fellowship)*

Purpose: To provide funding for graduating law students who wish to devote their professional lives to providing legal services to the poor (including the working poor), the elderly, the homeless and the disabled, as well as those deprived of their civil or human rights. **Focus:** Law. **Qualif.:** Applicants must be law school graduates or outgoing judicial law clerks. **Criteria:** Selection shall be based on the aforementioned applicants' qualifications and compliance with the application details.

Funds Avail.: No specific amount. **Duration:** Annual; up to two years. **Number Awarded:** Varies. **To Apply:** Applicants must submit a completed application form with the official law school transcripts; two letters of recommendation (from former employer, and law school professor); a commitment letter from a potential sponsoring organization; and three essays. **Deadline:** October 5. **Remarks:** Established in 1988. **Contact:** Susan Butler Plum, Director, Skadden Fellowship Foundation, at susan.plum@skadden.com.

8451 ■ Skidmore, Owings and Merrill Foundation

224 S Michigan Ave., Ste. 1000
Chicago, IL 60604
Ph: (312)427-4202
Fax: (312)360-4545
E-mail: somfoundation@som.com
URL: www.somfoundation.som.com

8452 ■ Architecture, Design and Urban Design Prize *(Graduate, Undergraduate/Prize)*

Purpose: To identify and nurture emerging talent by sponsoring prestigious research awards and traveling study

Awards are arranged alphabetically below their administering organizations

grants to students of architecture, design and urban design. **Focus:** Architecture; Design. **Qualif.:** Applicants must have graduated or be graduating with a bachelor's or master's degree from an accredited U.S. school of architecture, design or urban design; should be academically accomplished, demonstrate the highest design aspirations, and intend to enter the professional practice of architecture, design or urban design. **Criteria:** Selection will be based on the committee's criteria.

Funds Avail.: $50,000. **Duration:** Annual. **To Apply:** Applicants must submit the following in an enclosed 9 x 12 envelope and placed inside the front cover of the portfolio binder: a cover sheet; a sealed letter of recommendation on school letterhead from a thesis advisor or senior faculty member addressing the student's specific strengths and how the award will further his/her growth; the authorization form signed by the department chair or dean; the copyright release statement; a portfolio; a research abstract and travel itinerary. **Deadline:** April 20.

8453 ■ Structural Engineering Travel Fellowships (Doctorate, Graduate, Master's, Undergraduate/ Fellowship)

Purpose: To foster an appreciation of the aesthetic potential in the structural design of buildings and bridges by enabling a gifted graduate to experience works of architecture and engineering first hand. **Focus:** Engineering, Architectural; Engineering, Civil. **Qualif.:** Applicants must be graduating with a bachelor's degree, master's degree, or PhD in Civil or Architectural Engineering with a specialization in Structural Engineering from a U.S. school. **Criteria:** Selection will be based on the committee's criteria.

Funds Avail.: $20,000. **Duration:** Annual. **To Apply:** Applicants may contact the foundation for the application process. **Deadline:** October.

8454 ■ Travel Fellowships in Architecture, Design and Urban Design (Graduate, Undergraduate/ Fellowship)

Purpose: To support students with the highest design aspirations and enable them, through research and travel, to broaden their horizons and achieve excellence in their professional or academic careers. **Focus:** Architecture; Design. **Qualif.:** Applicants must have graduated or be graduating with a bachelor's or master's degree from an accredited U.S. school of architecture, urban design or design; should be academically accomplished, demonstrate the highest design aspirations, and intend to enter the professional practice of architecture, design or urban design. **Criteria:** Selection will be based on the committee's criteria.

Funds Avail.: $20,000. **To Apply:** Applicants must submit the following in an enclosed 9 x 12 envelope and placed inside the front cover of the portfolio binder: a cover sheet; a sealed letter of recommendation on school letterhead from a thesis advisor or senior faculty member. The letter should address the student's specific strengths and how the award will further his/her growth; the authorization form signed by the department chair or dean; the copyright release statement; a portfolio; a research abstract and travel itinerary. **Deadline:** July 20.

8455 ■ Skooblie
PO Box 1165
Wheeling, IL 60090-4756
Free: 866-705-3581

URL: www.skooblie.com

8456 ■ Skooblie Scholarships (Undergraduate/ Scholarship)

Purpose: To provide assistance to students who are pursuing higher education. **Focus:** Education. **Qualif.:** Applicants must be students who successfully complete six credit hours at a college that they were matched with through the college match process. **Criteria:** Selection will be based on the committee's criteria.

Funds Avail.: Varies. **Duration:** One-time. **Number Awarded:** Varies. **To Apply:** Applicants must accomplish the following steps: complete a profile, match and save a Skooblie Scholarship; enroll and notify Skooblie by sending an email along with class schedule of credits intended; complete the six hours credit hours within one year of enrolling and send via scanning and emailing or mailing a final report card showing credits earned to Skooblie within 60 days of completion.

8457 ■ Sleeping Angels Co.
528 Arizona Ave., Ste. 300
Santa Monica, CA 90401
Ph: (310)451-5692
E-mail: info@sleepingangelsco.com
URL: www.sleepingangelsco.com

8458 ■ Sleeping Angels Co. Scholarships (All/ Scholarship)

Purpose: To provide opportunities for gaining real-working experience in a chosen field, and giving students the chance to connect with adults outside their circle who might be able to help them get into their top choice college or secure an internship. **Focus:** General studies/Field of study not specified. **Qualif.:** Applicants must be currently enrolled as high school or college/university students within the United States; must have a cumulative GPA of at least 3.0; must be American citizens, permanent residents or hold a valid student visa; must have designed an innovative project that makes a difference in the lives of others (this could be a website, series of blogs, an app, fundraising event, etc.). **Criteria:** The winning project will be judged on the basis of its creativity, innovation and user experience.

Funds Avail.: $500. **Number Awarded:** 1. **To Apply:** Applicants must provide an essay describing the goal of the particular project. The essay, idea or creation must be the applicants original work. Applicants are advised to visit the website to upload their essay, letter of recommendation and their photo. **Deadline:** 20th of each month.

8459 ■ Alfred P. Sloan Foundation
45 Rockefeller Plz., Ste. 2200
New York, NY 10111
Ph: (212)649-1649
Fax: (212)757-5117
URL: www.sloan.org

8460 ■ Sloan Research Fellowships (Doctorate/ Fellowship)

Purpose: To stimulate fundamental research by early-career scientists and scholars of outstanding promise. **Focus:** Biology, Molecular; Chemistry; Computer and information sciences; Economics; Mathematics and mathematical sciences; Neuroscience; Physics. **Qualif.:** Applicant must

Awards are arranged alphabetically below their administering organizations

hold a PhD (or equivalent) in chemistry, physics, mathematics, computer science, economics, neuroscience or computational and evolutionary molecular biology, or in a related interdisciplinary field; must be a member of the regular faculty (tenure track) of a college/university in the United States or Canada; be no more than six years from completion of the most recent PhD or equivalent and must be nominated by department heads or other senior researchers for the fellowship. **Criteria:** Selection is based on the nominations.

Funds Avail.: $50,000. **Duration:** Two years. **Number Awarded:** 126. **To Apply:** Materials for nomination must include: a completed nomination form; nominee's curriculum vitae; a list of the nominee's publications (if not included in the CV); a brief (1 page) statement by the nominee describing his/her significant scientific work and immediate research plans; a letter from the nominator describing the nominee's qualifications and a copy of no more than two representative articles written by the nominee. In addition, three letters of support from other researchers (from different institutions) must be mailed directly to the foundation. **Deadline:** September 16. **Contact:** Daniel Goroff-Program Director.

8461 ■ SmileMarketing
PO Box 37
Palmer Lake, CO 80133
Free: 800-381-0228
URL: www.smilemarketing.com

8462 ■ SmileMarketing Dental Scholarships
(Doctorate/Scholarship)

Purpose: To help students ease some financial burdens in attending dental school. **Focus:** Dentistry. **Qualif.:** Applicants must be currently enrolled in an accredited dental school. **Criteria:** Selection will be based on the committee's criteria.

Funds Avail.: $1,000. **Duration:** One-time. **Number Awarded:** 1. **To Apply:** Applicants must send a completed email of 500-word essay response to the question: "What role do you believe the Internet will play in your dental career?" including their name, address, email, phone number, dental school and year of graduation in the header of their essay. Submission file name should be firstname.lastname.scholarship. **Deadline:** September 15.

8463 ■ The Smith Companies
PO Box 560219
Orlando, FL 32856
Fax: (866)859-6660
E-mail: ryan.smith@smithcompanies.com
URL: www.smithcompanies.com

8464 ■ Ryan and Jamie Smith Essay Contest
(Graduate, Postgraduate/Scholarship)

Purpose: To support individuals who have a desire to better others. **Focus:** General studies/Field of study not specified. **Qualif.:** Applicants must be continuing education, graduate or post-graduate students who are enrolled in an accredited institution; must be 18 years of age or older. U.S. citizens and international students are eligible. **Criteria:** Selection will be based on the submitted application.

Funds Avail.: No specific amount. **To Apply:** Applicants must submit an essay of less than 1000 words answering

the question "What do you feel is an appropriate balance between being successful financially and the need to serve others by giving back?" Applicants must check the website www.smithcompanies.com for the complete application process.

8465 ■ Robert H. Smith International Center for Jefferson Studies (ICJS)
PO Box 316
Charlottesville, VA 22902
Ph: (434)984-9800
Free: 800-243-0743
E-mail: info@monticello.org
URL: www.monticello.org/site/research-and-collections/robert-h-smith-international-center-jefferson-studies

8466 ■ ICJS Short-Term Fellowships (Doctorate, Postdoctorate, Advanced Professional/Fellowship)

Purpose: To support research on Jefferson-related projects. **Focus:** History, American.

Funds Avail.: Varies. **Duration:** Monthly. **Number Awarded:** Varies. **To Apply:** Applicants must submit a succinct description of the research project (500 words), a one-paragraph summary of the project, and a resume; two letters of reference should be emailed directly to the Center. **Deadline:** November 1; April 1.

8467 ■ Smith Scholarship Foundation
400 Caldwell Trace
Birmingham, AL 35242
Ph: (205)202-4076
Fax: (205)202-4171
URL: www.smithscholarships.com

8468 ■ J. Craig and Page T. Smith Scholarships
(Undergraduate/Scholarship)

Purpose: To support the education of Alabama high school seniors. **Focus:** General studies/Field of study not specified. **Qualif.:** Applicant must be a graduating Alabama high school senior entering an Alabama 4-year college; must have a minimum grade of C+. **Criteria:** Special consideration is given to applicants who would be the first in either their mother's or father's (or both) families to attend college hence the name "First In Family."

Funds Avail.: Full tuition. **Duration:** One year. **Number Awarded:** Varies. **To Apply:** Applicants must submit a completed application form along with the checklist; official high school transcript; ACT or SAT scores; an essay on future plans or goals of accomplishments; an essay documenting community and civic-oriented activities or assistance to family; and three signed personal recommendation letters.

8469 ■ Smithsonian Institution Archives of American Art
750 9th St. NW
Victor Bldg., Ste. 2200
Washington, DC 20013-7012
Ph: (202)633-7940
Fax: (202)633-7994
URL: www.aaa.si.edu

8470 ■ Minority Visiting Students Awards
(Undergraduate, Graduate/Award, Internship)

Purpose: To provide undergraduate and beginning graduate students the opportunity to learn more about the Smith-

Awards are arranged alphabetically below their administering organizations

sonian and their academic fields through direct experience in research or museum-related internship projects under the supervision of research and professional staff members at the Institution's many museums, research institutes and offices. **Focus:** Animal science and behavior; Anthropology; Arts; Culture; Earth sciences; Social sciences. **Qualif.:** Applicants must be currently engaged in undergraduate or graduate study, and an overall GPA of 3.0 or its equivalent generally is expected. **Criteria:** Selection will be based on the committee's criteria.

Funds Avail.: $600 per week (10 weeks). **To Apply:** Applicants must visit the website for the online application process. **Deadline:** February 1; October 1.

8471 ■ Molecular Evolution Fellowships (Doctorate/Fellowship)

Purpose: To support research on molecular evolution and analytical methods in evolution at the Smithsonian Institution. **Focus:** General studies/Field of study not specified. **Qualif.:** Applicants must have completed or be near completion of the PhD. Recipients who have not completed the PhD at the time of application must provide proof of completion of the degree before the fellowship begins. **Criteria:** Selection will be based on the proposal's merit, the applicant's ability to carry out the proposed research and study, the likelihood that the research could be completed in the requested time, and the extent to which the Smithsonian, through its research staff members and resources, could contribute to the proposed research.

Funds Avail.: $45,000. **Duration:** Annual. **To Apply:** Applicants must visit the website for the online application process. **Deadline:** January 15.

8472 ■ Native American Community Scholars Awards (Graduate/Award)

Purpose: To provide students and scholars with opportunities to pursue independent research projects in association with members of the Smithsonian professional research staff. **Focus:** General studies/Field of study not specified. **Qualif.:** Applicants must be Native Americans who are formally or informally related to a Native American community, to undertake projects on a Native American subject and utilize the Native American resources of the Institution. **Criteria:** Selection will be based on the committee's criteria.

Funds Avail.: $175 per day up to 21 days. **Duration:** Annual. **To Apply:** Applicants must visit the website for the online application process and must upload the following files: an essay for internships or research proposal for visiting students and community scholars; transcripts; resume; names and email addresses of two references. **Deadline:** February 1; October 1. **Contact:** Pamela Hudson Veenbaas at siofg@si.edu; Phone: 202-633-7070.

8473 ■ Native American Visiting Student Awards (Graduate/Fellowship)

Purpose: To support research on molecular evolution and analytical methods in evolution at the Smithsonian Institution. **Focus:** General studies/Field of study not specified. **Qualif.:** Applicants must be currently enrolled advanced Native American graduate students who are formally or informally related to a Native American community. **Criteria:** Selection will be based on the committee's criteria.

Funds Avail.: $175 per day or $600 per week (21 days and 3 to 10 weeks). **Duration:** Annual. **To Apply:** Applicants must visit the website for the online application process and must upload the following files: an essay for

internships or research proposal for visiting students and community scholars; transcripts; resume; names and email addresses of two references. **Deadline:** February 1; October 1. **Contact:** Pamela Hudson Veenbaas at siofg@si.edu or 202-633-7070.

8474 ■ Smithsonian Institution Graduate Student Fellowships (Graduate/Fellowship)

Purpose: To provide students and scholars with opportunities to pursue independent research projects in association with members of the Smithsonian professional research staff. **Focus:** Natural resources. **Qualif.:** Applicants must be formally enrolled in a graduate program of study at a degree granting institution; must have completed at least one full-time semester or its equivalent; and must have not yet been advanced to candidacy in a doctoral program. **Criteria:** Selection will be based on the proposal's merit, the applicant's ability to carry out the proposed research and study, the likelihood that the research could be completed in the requested time, and the extent to which the Smithsonian, through its research staff members and resources, could contribute to the proposed research.

Funds Avail.: A stipend of $6,500. **Duration:** 10 weeks. **To Apply:** Interested applicants must visit the website for the online application process and other application requirements. Applicants are strongly encouraged to contact staff members to help identify potential advisors, determine the feasibility of the proposed research being conducted at the Smithsonian Institution, and the availability of relevant resources such as staff, collections, archives and library materials during the proposed tenure dates. **Deadline:** January 15.

8475 ■ Smithsonian Institution Postdoctoral Fellowships (Doctorate/Fellowship)

Purpose: To provide students and scholars with opportunities to pursue independent research projects in association with members of the Smithsonian professional research staff. **Focus:** Natural resources. **Qualif.:** Applicants must be scholars who have held the doctoral degree or equivalent for fewer than seven years as of the application deadline. **Criteria:** Selection will be based on the proposal's merit, the applicant's ability to carry out the proposed research and study, the likelihood that the research could be completed in the requested time, and the extent to which the Smithsonian, through its research be its staff members and resources, could contribute to the proposed research.

Funds Avail.: $48,000. **Duration:** 3 to 12 months. **To Apply:** Interested applicants must visit the website for the online application process and other application requirements. Applicants are strongly encouraged to contact staff members to help identify potential advisors, determine the feasibility of the proposed research being conducted at the Smithsonian Institution, and the availability of relevant resources such as staff, collections, archives and library materials during the proposed tenure dates. **Deadline:** January 15.

8476 ■ Smithsonian Institution Predoctoral Fellowships (Doctorate/Fellowship)

Purpose: To provide students and scholars with opportunities to pursue independent research projects in association with members of the Smithsonian professional research staff. **Focus:** Natural resources. **Qualif.:** Applicants must be students enrolled in a university as candidates for the PhD or equivalent. Applicants must have completed coursework and preliminary examinations for the doctoral

Awards are arranged alphabetically below their administering organizations

degree, and must be engaged in dissertation research. In addition, applicants must have the approval of their universities to conduct their doctoral research at the Smithsonian Institution. **Criteria:** Selection will be based on the proposal's merit, the applicant's ability to carry out the proposed research and study, the likelihood that the research could be completed in the requested time, and the extent to which the Smithsonian, through its research staff members and resources, could contribute to the proposed research.

Funds Avail.: $32,700. **Duration:** 3 to 12 months. **To Apply:** Interested applicants must visit the website for the online application process and other application requirements. Applicants are strongly encouraged to contact staff members to help identify potential advisors, determine the feasibility of the proposed research being conducted at the Smithsonian Institution, and the availability of relevant resources such as staff, collections, archives and library materials during the proposed tenure dates. **Deadline:** January 15.

8477 ■ Smithsonian Institution Senior Fellowships
(Doctorate/Fellowship)

Purpose: To provide students and scholars with opportunities to pursue independent research projects in association with members of the Smithsonian professional research staff. **Focus:** Natural resources. **Qualif.:** Applicants must be scholars who have held the doctoral degree or equivalent for more than seven years as of the application deadline. **Criteria:** Selection will be based on the proposal's merit, the applicants' ability to carry out the proposed research and study, the likelihood that the research could be completed in the requested time, and the extent to which the Smithsonian, through its research staff members and resources, could contribute to the proposed research.

Funds Avail.: $53,000. **Duration:** 3 to 12 months. **To Apply:** Interested applicants must visit the website for the online application process and other application requirements. Applicants are strongly encouraged to contact staff members to help identify potential advisors, determine the feasibility of the proposed research being conducted at the Smithsonian Institution, and the availability of relevant resources such as staff, collections, archives and library materials during the proposed tenure dates. **Deadline:** January 15.

8478 ■ Smithsonian Postgraduate Fellowships in Conservation of Museum Collection Program
(Postgraduate/Fellowship)

Purpose: To provide students and scholars with opportunities to pursue independent research projects in association with members of the Smithsonian professional research staff. **Focus:** Archeology; Art. **Qualif.:** Applicants must be recent graduates of masters programs in art conservation or the equivalent or conservation scientists, including those at the postdoctoral level, who wish to conduct research and gain further training in Smithsonian conservation laboratories for a period of one year. **Criteria:** Selection will be based on the proposal's merit, the applicant's ability to carry out the proposed research and study, the likelihood that the research could be completed in the requested time, and the extent to which the Smithsonian, through its research staff members and resources, could contribute to the proposed research.

Funds Avail.: $4,000. **To Apply:** Interested applicants must visit the website for the online application process and other application requirements. Applicants are strongly encour-

aged to contact staff members to help identify potential advisors, determine the feasibility of the proposed research being conducted at the Smithsonian Institution, and the availability of relevant resources such as staff, collections, archives and library materials during the proposed tenure dates. **Deadline:** December 1.

8479 ■ Smithsonian Institution - National Air and Space Museum
National Air & Space Museum, Rm. 3100
Independence Ave. SW & 6th St.
Washington, DC 20560-0314
Ph: (202)633-2320
Fax: (202)786-2835
E-mail: libmail@si.edu
URL: library.si.edu/libraries/air-and-space

8480 ■ Guggenheim Fellowships *(Doctorate/ Fellowship)*

Purpose: To promote research into, and writing about, the history of aviation and space flight. **Focus:** Aviation. **Qualif.:** Fellowships are for pre-doctoral or postdoctoral applicants. Predoctoral applicants should have completed preliminary course work and examinations and be engaged in dissertation research. Postdoctoral applicants should have received their PhD within the past seven years. **Criteria:** Selection will be based on the following criteria: the potential contribution of the project to the field of aviation and space history; its utilization of National Air and Space Museum and Smithsonian resources and staff; and its potential contribution to National Air and Space Museum program.

Funds Avail.: $30,000 for predoctoral candidates and $45,000 for postdoctoral candidates. **To Apply:** Applicants must apply through the Smithsonian Online Academic Appointment system. As part of the application, applicants will be required to include the following supplemental files: a maximum of 250 words summary description of the proposed research; a maximum of 1,500 words of a research proposal. This statement should set forth the applicants' research plan, indicating the importance of the work both in relation to the larger discipline and to their own intellectual goals; a research budget for equipment, supplies, travel costs and other support required to conduct the research itself; a bibliography of literature relevant to the applicants' proposed research, especially that cited in the research proposal; an estimated schedule for each phase of the proposed research; a curriculum vitae or resume, not longer than three pages, including pertinent publications, fellowships or accomplishments relevant to their proposal. **Deadline:** January 15. **Contact:** Ms. Collette Williams at nasm-fellowships@si.edu.

8481 ■ Charles A. Lindbergh Fellowships *(Graduate/ Fellowship)*

Purpose: To promote research into, and writing about, the history of aviation and space flight. **Focus:** Aviation. **Qualif.:** Fellowship is open to senior scholars with distinguished records of publication who are at work on, or anticipate being at work on, books in aerospace history. **Criteria:** Selection will be based on the following criteria: the potential contribution of the project to the field of aviation and space history; its utilization of National Air and Space Museum and Smithsonian resources and staff; and its potential contribution to National Air and Space Museum program.

Funds Avail.: Maximum of $100,000. **Duration:** Annual.

Awards are arranged alphabetically below their administering organizations

To Apply: Applicants must apply through the Smithsonian Online Academic Appointment system. As part of the application, applicants will be required to include the following supplemental files: a maximum of 250 words summary description of the proposed research; a maximum of 1,500 words of a research proposal. This statement should set forth the applicants' research plan, indicating the importance of the work both in relation to the larger discipline and to their own intellectual goals; a research budget for equipment, supplies, travel costs and other support required to conduct the research itself; a bibliography of literature relevant to the applicants' proposed research, especially that cited in the research proposal; an estimated schedule for each phase of the proposed research; a curriculum vitae or resume, not longer than three pages, including pertinent publications, fellowships or accomplishments relevant to their proposal. **Deadline:** January 15. **Contact:** Dominick A. Pisano at pisanod@si.edu or Allan Needell at needella@si.edu.

8482 ■ A. Verville Fellowships *(All/Fellowship)*

Purpose: To promote research into, and writing about, the history of aviation and space flight. **Focus:** Aviation. **Qualif.:** Fellowship is open to all interested candidates who can provide a critical analytical approach to major trends, developments and accomplishments in some aspect of aviation and/or space history. **Criteria:** Selection will be based on the following criteria: the potential contribution of the project to the field of aviation and space history; its utilization of National Air and Space Museum and Smithsonian resources and staff; and its potential contribution to National Air and Space Museum program.

Funds Avail.: $55,000. **Duration:** 12 months. **To Apply:** Applicants must apply through the Smithsonian Online Academic Appointment system. As part of the application, applicants will be required to include the following supplemental files: a maximum of 250 words summary description of the proposed research; a maximum of 1,500 words of a research proposal. This statement should set forth the applicants' research plan, indicating the importance of the work both in relation to the larger discipline and to their own intellectual goals; a research budget for equipment, supplies, travel costs and other support required to conduct the research itself; a bibliography of literature relevant to the applicants' proposed research, especially that cited in the research proposal; an estimated schedule for each phase of the proposed research; a curriculum vitae or resume, not longer than three pages, including pertinent publications, fellowships or accomplishments relevant to their proposal. **Deadline:** January 15. **Contact:** Ms. Collette Williams at nasm-fellowships@si.edu.

8483 ■ Smithsonian Institution - National Museum of American History

PO Box 37012
MRC 619
Washington, DC 20013-7012
Ph: (202)633-1000
E-mail: info@si.edu
URL: americanhistory.si.edu

8484 ■ Lemelson Center Fellowships *(Doctorate, Postdoctorate, Professional development/Fellowship)*

Purpose: To support projects that present creative approaches to the study of invention and innovation in American society. **Focus:** General studies/Field of study not specified. **Qualif.:** Applicants must be pre-doctoral graduate students, post-doctoral scholars and other professional who have completed advanced training. Fellows are expected to reside in the Washington, DC area, to participate in the Center's activities, and to make presentations on their work to colleagues at the museum. **Criteria:** Selection will be based on the committee's criteria.

Funds Avail.: $630/week (pre-doctoral); $925/week (post-doctoral/professional). **Duration:** Annual. **Number Awarded:** 2-3. **To Apply:** Applicants must visit the website for the online application process. Researchers must consult with the Fellowship Coordinator prior to submitting a proposal. A complete application must consists of: an abstract; bibliography, curriculum vitae; project/research proposal; and three references who are familiar with their work. **Deadline:** December 1. **Contact:** Eric S. Hintz, PhD; Phone: 202-633-3734; Fax: 202-633-4593; Email: hintze@si.edu.

8485 ■ Lemelson Center Travel to Collections Awards *(Graduate, Professional development/Award)*

Purpose: To support research on the history of invention and innovation based on the holding of the Museum's Archives Center and curatorial divisions. **Focus:** General studies/Field of study not specified. **Qualif.:** Applicants must be scholars, graduate students and independent researchers not residing or attending school within commuting distance of the National Museum of American History. **Criteria:** Selection will be based on the committee's criteria.

Funds Avail.: $150 per day for 10 days. **Duration:** Annual. **To Apply:** Applicants must visit the website for the Smithsonian Online Application System. Applicants must also provide the following: application form and current curriculum vitae or resume; bibliography of relevant secondary sources; statement of purpse summarizing their project and detailing why the Archives Center's collections are essential to their research; list of specific collections or resources to be consulted. Applicants must consult with the Travel Award Coordinator prior to submitting a proposal. **Remarks:** Established in 1995. **Contact:** Alison L. Oswald at 202-633-3726 or oswalda@si.edu.

8486 ■ Smithsonian Institution - National Museum of the American Indian

Fourth St. and Independence Ave., SW
Washington, DC 20560
Ph: (202)633-1000
Fax: (202)287-2033
E-mail: nin@si.edu
URL: nmai.si.edu

8487 ■ Conservation Department Program Fellowships *(Graduate/Fellowship)*

Purpose: To cultivate practical skills as well as foster a solid understanding of the contexts of material culture, the philosophies of conservation at the NMAI, and the ethics of the conservation profession. **Focus:** Archeology; Culture; Ethnography. **Qualif.:** Applicants must be currently enrolled in a conservation training program or recent graduate. Applicants should have a proven record of research, writing ability and proficient English language skills. **Criteria:** Selection will be based on the committee's criteria.

Funds Avail.: No specific amount. **Duration:** One year. **To Apply:** Applicants must visit the website for the Smithso-

Awards are arranged alphabetically below their administering organizations

nian Online Application System. Applicants must also prepare the following materials: a no more than two pages cover letter explaining candidate's interests and intent; curriculum vitae including basic biographical information, current and permanent addresses, phone numbers and email address; at least two examples of pertinent publications, lectures or other written materials; unofficial transcripts of both undergraduate and graduate courses of academic study with an explanation of the evaluation system if it is not equivalent to that of the United States; three letters of recommendation. Two are from conservation professionals familiar with the candidate's work and one letter of personal reference. **Deadline:** March 15.

8488 ■ Smithsonian Institution - National Museum of Natural History

SI Bldg., Rm. 153, MRC 010
Washington, DC 20013-7012
Ph: (202)633-1000
E-mail: naturalexperience@si.edu
URL: www.mnh.si.edu

8489 ■ American Indian Program Fellowships
(Graduate/Fellowship)

Purpose: To encourage participation of Native Americans in Smithsonian activities and to support collection research, exhibitions and public programming as they relate to Native peoples. **Focus:** Culture; History. **Qualif.:** Applicants must be students of Native American history and culture. **Criteria:** Selection will be based on the committee's criteria.

Funds Avail.: No specific amount. **To Apply:** Interested applicants must visit the website for the online application process and other application requirements. **Remarks:** Established in 1986. **Contact:** JoAllyn Archambault at 202-633-1936; archambj@si.edu.

8490 ■ Global Volcanism Program for Visiting Scientist/Postdoctoral Fellowships *(Postdoctorate/Fellowship)*

Purpose: To understand global patterns in volcanism in space and time. **Focus:** Geosciences. **Qualif.:** Applicants must be postdoctoral or visiting senior scientist position. **Criteria:** Selection will be based on the committee's criteria.

Funds Avail.: $50,000. **Duration:** Annual. **To Apply:** Interested applicants must email their project proposal (maximum of 5 pages), resume and names of at least two references familiar with the applicant's work. **Contact:** Elizabeth Cottrell at cottrelle@si.edu; Benjamin Andrews at andrewsb@si.edu.

8491 ■ Link Foundation/Smithsonian Graduate Fellowships in Marine Science *(Graduate/Fellowship)*

Purpose: To support and conduct of scholarly research in the marine sciences, including collection, documentation and preservation of south Florida's marine biodiversity and ecosystems, as well as education, training and public service. **Focus:** Biology, Marine. **Qualif.:** Applicants must be students enrolled in a graduate program of study at a degree-granting institution and who have completed at least one semester before the appointment period. **Criteria:** Selection will be based on the committee's criteria.

Funds Avail.: $6,500. **Duration:** Annual; 12 weeks. **To Apply:** Interested applicants must visit the website for the online application process. **Deadline:** February 15. **Remarks:** Established in 1998. **Contact:** Dr. Valerie Paul,

Smithsonian Marine Station, 701 Seaway Drive, Ft. Pierce, FL 34949; Phone: 772-462-0982; email: paul@si.edu.

8492 ■ Peter Buck Fellowships Program - Graduate
(Graduate/Fellowship)

Purpose: To provide opportunities to pursue independent research projects in association with members of the Smithsonian professional research staff. **Focus:** General studies/Field of study not specified. **Qualif.:** Applicants must be any students enrolled in or admitted to a PhD program, as long as their advisor/co-advisor is one of the staff of NMNH and the project involves full-time residency at the Museum and/or its permanent facilities during the fellowship period. **Criteria:** Selection will be based on the committee's criteria.

Funds Avail.: No specific amount. **Duration:** Annual; up to two years. **To Apply:** Interested applicants must contact the Smithsonian Institution - National Museum of Natural History for the application process and requirements. **Deadline:** January 15. **Contact:** Scott Wing, 202-633-1361; wings@si.edu.

8493 ■ Peter Buck Fellowships Program - Postdoctoral *(Postdoctorate/Fellowship)*

Purpose: To provide opportunities to pursue independent research projects in association with members of the Smithsonian professional research staff. **Focus:** General studies/Field of study not specified. **Qualif.:** Applicants must be scientists who have received their PhD or equivalent degree in the last five years. Fellowships are open to citizens of any country. **Criteria:** Selection will be based on the committee's criteria.

Funds Avail.: $4,000. **Duration:** Annual. **To Apply:** Interested applicants must contact the Smithsonian Institution - National Museum of Natural History for the application process and requirements. **Deadline:** January 15. **Contact:** Scott Wing, 202-633-1361; wings@si.edu.

8494 ■ Smithsonian Institution - Smithsonian Center for Education and Museum Studies (SCEMS)

600 Maryland Ave., Ste. 1005
Washington, DC 20024
Ph: (202)633-5330
Fax: (202)633-5489
E-mail: learning@si.edu
URL: smithsonianeducation.org

8495 ■ Smithsonian Fellowships in Museum Practice *(Professional development/Fellowship)*

Purpose: To serve as a catalyst for helping expand the intellectual resources and networking capacities of museums and their personnel - conditions necessary for fostering inspiration, innovation and ultimately, the production of new scholarship. **Focus:** Museum science. **Qualif.:** The program is open to mid- and senior-level museum personnel, researchers and training providers. Applicants must be employed by a not-for-profit cultural or educational institution that deals directly with the public or be an independent scholar. **Criteria:** Fellowships are awarded through a competitive process. Applications are evaluated by an external committee of museum professionals on the following factors: the range and depth of the applicant's knowledge and experience about the topic; evidence of the applicant's ability to produce quality work; rationale and coherence of the proposed plan of action; extent to which

Awards are arranged alphabetically below their administering organizations

research on the topic would contribute to improved museum practices or impact institutional decisions; extent to which access to resources at the Smithsonian and in Washington, D.C. are needed to produce the product; Degree to which the proposal advances the fellowship program's goals and the priorities of the Smithsonian Institution.

Funds Avail.: $3,500. **Duration:** Annual; six months. **To Apply:** Interested applicants must visit the website for the online application process. The following materials and requirements must be uploaded online: title of the study; discussion of the topic to be investigated including the thesis statement and key issues; description of the nature and scope of the topic relative to the needs of museums and cultural institutions and an explanation of how this proposal will add knowledge to the topic; plan of action including a description of the research methodology to be used and a list of preliminary questions to be explored; review of existing literature specific to the study; description of the format for disseminating the research and the rationale for the choice; resume/curriculum vitae, not to exceed two pages; two confidential letters of reference submitted on behalf of the applicants by their referees. **Deadline:** February 15.

8496 ■ Smithsonian Tropical Research Institute
Quad Ste. 3123, 705
PO Box 37012
Washington, DC 20013-7012
Ph: (202)633-4700
Fax: (202)786-2557
URL: www.stri.si.edu

8497 ■ CTFS Research Grants Program (Graduate, Postdoctorate, Professional development/Grant)

Purpose: To provide opportunities for senior researchers, postdoctoral fellows and graduate students to use existing CTFS plots to conduct research with scientists affiliated with them. **Focus:** Environmental science; Natural sciences. **Qualif.:** Applicants must be senior researchers, postdoctoral fellows and graduate students. Applicants of all nationalities are welcome to apply. **Criteria:** Preference will be given to scientists in the countries with CTFS (Center for Tropical Forest Science) site and to all graduate students and postdoctoral researchers. Awards are made on the basis of the proposal's merit, the applicant's ability to carry out the proposed research, the likelihood that the research can be carried out in the proposed time frame, and the extent to which CTFS plots contribute to the proposed research.

Funds Avail.: $3,000-$40,000. **Duration:** three months to three years. **To Apply:** Applicants must submit a completed application. Completed application must consist the following: (1) Cover sheet. Include project title, name, contact information and nationality of principal investigator(s), duration of project, and status of PI(s); (2) Maximum of 1500 words research proposal. The proposal must describe the proposed research, indicate its relevance to one or more CTFS plots, and explain the significance of the work to a broader discipline. The general format of the proposal should include introduction, description of research project with clearly stated hypotheses, significance of research, detailed methods, anticipated outcomes and bibliography/references; (3) List of collaborators; (4) Curriculum vitae; (5) Proposed referees; (6) Detailed budget and timeline. Proposals can be sent electronically or by mail. **Contact:** Delaney Rakosnik, CTFS-ForestGEO Program Assistant; email: RakosnikD@si.edu.

8498 ■ A. Stanley Rand Fellowships Program
(Undergraduate, Doctorate, Postdoctorate/Fellowship)

Purpose: To support and carry out short-term research projects in the tropics. **Focus:** Animal science and behavior; Biology; Ecology; Environmental science; History. **Qualif.:** Any undergraduate, predoctoral and postdoctoral researchers may apply. **Criteria:** Applications are evaluated on the scientific merits of the proposed research relative to its costs; the applicant's ability to conduct the proposed research in the time available; and the relevance of the proposed research to STRI research programs and interests. Availability of space at the particular facility will also be considered.

Funds Avail.: $800 per month; $2,000. **Duration:** Annual; three months. **To Apply:** A complete application must include the following components, compiled in the following order: a two-page application form available online with the requested information, including the names of main advisors and consultants; a non-technical abstract of not more than 250 words; a research proposal with a narrative of not more than 1,500 words, plus a bibliography that is not included in the word count. The narrative should include a description of the research to be undertaken at STRI, including a general introduction to the research topic, the methodology to be used, and expected results; a detailed 3-month timetable for the proposed research; research budget and justification; curriculum vitae; copies of academic transcripts. Additionally, applicants must arrange to have two letters of recommendation sent directly to STRI's Office of Academic Programs. Before submitting a formal application, all applicants should consult with STRI scientific staff, who will serve as potential advisors, to confirm that they are willing to supervise and support the proposed project. **Deadline:** March 15; May 15; August 15; November 15. **Contact:** STRI/Office of Academic Programs, Unit 0948, APO AA 34002-0948; Phone: 507-212-8031; Fax: 507-212-8150; Email: fellows@si.edu.

8499 ■ Short-Term Fellowships (Undergraduate, Graduate, Postdoctorate/Fellowship)

Purpose: To support and carry out short-term research projects in the tropics. **Focus:** Animal science and behavior; Anthropology; Biology; Ecology; Neuroscience; Paleontology; Physiology; Soil science. **Qualif.:** Applicants must be undergraduate, graduate and postdoctoral students. Fellowships are awarded to graduate students, but awards are occasionally made to outstanding undergraduate. **Criteria:** Applications are evaluated on the scientific merits of the proposed research relative to its costs; the applicant's ability to conduct the proposed research in the time available; and the relevance of the proposed research to STRI research programs and interests. Availability of space at the particular facility will also be considered.

Funds Avail.: $800 per month. **Duration:** Annual; three months. **To Apply:** A complete application must include the following components, compiled in the following order: a two-page application form available online with the requested information, including the names of main advisors and consultants; a non-technical abstract of not more than 250 words; a research proposal with a narrative of not more than 1,500 words, plus a bibliography that is not included in the word count. The narrative should include a description of the research to be undertaken at STRI, including a general introduction to the research topic, the methodology to be used, and expected results; a detailed 3-month timetable for the proposed research; research budget and justification; curriculum vitae; copies of academic transcripts. Additionally, applicants must arrange to have two

Awards are arranged alphabetically below their administering organizations

letters of recommendation sent directly to STRI's Office of Academic Programs. Before submitting a formal application, all applicants should consult with STRI scientific staff, who will serve as potential advisors, to confirm that they are willing to supervise and support the proposed project. **Deadline:** January 15; April 15; July 15; October 15. **Contact:** STRI/Office of Academic Programs, Unit 0948, APO AA 34002-0948; Phone: 507-212-8031; Fax: 507-212-8150; Email: fellows@si.edu.

8500 ■ Earl S. Tupper 3-year Postdoctoral Fellowships in Tropical Biology *(Postdoctorate/Fellowship)*

Purpose: To promote biological diversity. **Focus:** Animal science and behavior; Anthropology; Biology; Ecology; Neuroscience; Paleontology; Physiology; Soil science. **Qualif.:** Candidates must be any individuals who already have their postdoctoral degree. **Criteria:** Selection will be based on the committee's criteria.

Funds Avail.: $40,000. **Duration:** Annual. **To Apply:** Applicants must submit a detailed research proposal with one page abstract and budget (less than 10 pages), curriculum vitae, two letters of reference, names and telephone numbers of three additional professional references and reprints of most important papers. Applicants must consult with the STRI scientific staff member who will serve as their host/advisor before submitting final application. Candidates must designate the most appropriate staff member who serves as STRI host/advisor and two additional co-advisors than can review the proposal. Applications consist of one printed copy, plus one electronic copy of all requested materials. The electronic copy should be submitted on a CD or by e-mail, as a single file in Word or preferably PDF, including proposal with budget and CV. Reference letters may also be submitted electronically. **Deadline:** January 15. **Contact:** Adriana Bilgray, STRI/Office of Academic Programs, Unit 0948, APO AA 34002-0948; Phone: 507-212-8031; Fax: 507-212-8150; Email: fellows@si.edu; or Apartado 0843-03092, Balboa, Panama.

8501 ■ Smithsonian Tropical Research Institute (STRI) - Center for Tropical Forest Science - ForestGEO (CTFS-ForestGEO)
CTFS-SIGEO NMNH-MRC 166
West Loading Dock
10th and Constitution Ave, NW
Washington, DC 20560
Ph: (202)633-1836
Fax: (202)786-2563
URL: www.stri.si.edu

8502 ■ CTFS-ForestGEO Research Grants Program *(Graduate, Postdoctorate, Advanced Professional/Grant)*

Purpose: To provide opportunities for researchers, post doctorate fellows, and graduate students to use existing CTFS-ForestGEO plots to conduct research with scientists affiliated with them. **Focus:** Natural sciences; Social sciences. **Qualif.:** Application is open to all researchers, from graduate students to senior scientists. In some cases, advanced undergraduates will also be considered. Applicants of all nationalities are welcome to apply. Everyone working directly in CTFS-ForestGEO plots, analyzing plot data, or generating complementary data that strengthen CTFS-ForestGEO programs are eligible. **Criteria:** Preference will be given to scientists in the countries with CTFS-ForestGEO sites and to all graduate students and postdoctoral researchers.

Funds Avail.: $2,000 to $15,000. **Duration:** Up to 2 years. **To Apply:** Applicants must submit application form including the following: CTFS-ForestGEO cover letter; research proposal of 1,000 words; list of collaborators; two-page curriculum vitae; contact references;and detailed budget and time. All of these are needed to be submitted to Delaney Rakosnik. **Deadline:** June 20. **Contact:** Delaney Rakosnik, at the above address.

8503 ■ SMSA Scholarship
PO Box 6574
Silver Spring, MD 20916
Ph: (301)570-2850
E-mail: smsa@seabee.org
URL: www.seabee.org

8504 ■ Seabee Memorial Scholarship Association Scholarships *(Undergraduate/Scholarship)*

Purpose: To provide educational assistance to children and grandchildren of Seabees. **Focus:** General studies/Field of study not specified. **Qualif.:** Applicants must be the children or grandchildren of regular, reserve, retired, or deceased officers or enlisted members who have served the Naval Construction Force (Seabees) or Navy Civil Engineer Corps; or members who have served but honorably discharged; and must be attending a four year baccalaureate degree. **Criteria:** Recipients will be selected based on financial need, scholastic record, leadership, good citizenship and character.

Funds Avail.: No specific amount. **Duration:** Annual. **To Apply:** Applicants must attach a copy of an official document that verifies the rate/rank, service number and a Seabee/CEC unit in which the sponsor served; two pages of military sponsor's information; Student Aid Report (SAR); complete list of extracurricular activities and awards; list of work experiences; and high school or college transcript. **Deadline:** April 15. **Contact:** Applications and transcripts must be sent to Sheryl Chiogioji at the above address.

8505 ■ Snowmobile Association of Massachusetts (SAM)
PO Box 386
Conway, MA 01341
Ph: (413)369-8092
Fax: (413)369-0203
E-mail: sledmass@aol.com
URL: www.sledmass.com

8506 ■ Snowmobile Association of Massachusetts Scholarships *(Undergraduate, Vocational/Occupational/Scholarship)*

Purpose: To develop and maintain an expanding interconnected snowmobile trail system, allowing snowmobile enthusiasts to travel from Worcester County. **Focus:** Transportation. **Qualif.:** Applicants must be parents or students who are members of Snowmobile Association of Massachusetts and local clubs. **Criteria:** Recipients are selected based on academic performance and financial need.

Funds Avail.: $5,000. **Duration:** Annual. **Number Awarded:** 3. **To Apply:** Applicants must submit a completed application form; an official high school or college transcript; recommendations in writing by at least two teachers; recommendations in writing by one or two friends,

Awards are arranged alphabetically below their administering organizations

employers or clergy; proof of acceptance at the listed college, university or vocational school; a written essay about snowmobiling in the state (500 words or less); overview of extracurricular activity or snow mobile associated volunteerism (within the last year of application). All required documents must be provided in five copies. **Deadline:** March 1.

8507 ■ Sobeys Inc.
115 King St.
Stellarton, NS, Canada B0K 1S0
Ph: (902)752-8371
Fax: (902)928-1101
URL: www.sobeys.com

8508 ■ D&R Sobey Scholarships *(Undergraduate/ Scholarship)*

Purpose: To help young people attain the education needed to succeed today. **Focus:** General studies/Field of study not specified. **Qualif.:** Applicants must be students from Atlantic Canada pursuing a commerce degree at Queens University. **Criteria:** Selection will be based on the committee's criteria.

Funds Avail.: A total of $60,000. **Duration:** Annual. **Number Awarded:** 6. **To Apply:** Applicants may contact the company for the application process and other requirements.

8509 ■ Frank H. Sobey Awards for Excellence in Business Studies *(Undergraduate/Award)*

Purpose: To help young people attain the education needed to succeed today. **Focus:** Business. **Qualif.:** Applicants must be full-time students attending business schools in Atlantic Canada. **Criteria:** Selection will be based on the committee's criteria.

Funds Avail.: $10,000. **Duration:** Annual. **Number Awarded:** 6. **To Apply:** Applicants may contact the company for the application process and other requirements.

8510 ■ Sobeys & Empire Work Experience & Scholarship Program - Future Leaders Awards *(Other/Award)*

Purpose: To help young people attain the education needed to succeed today. **Focus:** General studies/Field of study not specified. **Qualif.:** Applicants must be employees of Sobeys across Canada. **Criteria:** Selection will be based on the committee's criteria.

Funds Avail.: Up to $10,000. **Duration:** Annual. **To Apply:** Applicants may contact the company for the application process and other requirements.

8511 ■ Social Equity Venture Fund
1770 Massachusetts Ave., No. 247
Cambridge, MA 02140
E-mail: info@sevenfund.org
URL: www.sevenfund.org

8512 ■ SEVEN Fund Teaching Fellowships *(Other/ Fellowship)*

Purpose: To provide financial assistance to fellows that will travel to Rwanda and work with scientists. **Focus:** General studies/Field of study not specified. **Qualif.:** Applicants

must be administrators or teachers in K-12 public or faith-based schools within the United States; must travel to Rwanda and study enterprise solutions to poverty; and can be from any field of study or discipline. **Criteria:** Selection will be based on a confidential jury review; three fellows will be selected from public schools in the United States and one fellow will be from a faith-based school.

Funds Avail.: $1,000. **To Apply:** Applicants must submit a resume or curriculum vitae; two recommendation letters including one from a person who can attest the impact of the applicant's teaching or leadership; a sample lesson plan; contact information of current supervisor for employment verification; a personal statement of no more than 1000 words addressing how the fellowship will help integrate the enterprise solutions to poverty into teaching, understanding of what to learn, both personally and as educators from participating in the fellowship and specific factors that differentiate applicants among others. **Deadline:** March. **Contact:** Ms. Jessica Ullrich at the above address.

8513 ■ Social Science Research Council (SSRC)
300 Cadman Plz. W
1 Pierrepont Plz., 15th Fl.
Brooklyn, NY 11201
Ph: (212)377-2700
Fax: (212)377-2727
E-mail: info@ssrc.org
URL: www.ssrc.org

8514 ■ Abe Fellowship Program *(Professional development/Fellowship)*

Purpose: To foster the development of a new generation of researchers who are interested in policy-relevant topics of long-range importance and who are willing to become key members of a bilateral and global research network built around international multidisciplinary research on topics of pressing global concern. **Focus:** Social sciences. **Qualif.:** Applicants must: be citizens of the United States and Japan, as well as thoseo nationals of other countries who can demonstrate strong and serious long-term affiliations with research communities in Japan or the United States; and, hold a Ph.D. or the terminal degree in their field or have attained an equivalent level of professional experience. **Criteria:** Selection shall be based on the applicants' submitted proposals for research in the social sciences and related disciplines relevant to any one or any combination of the three themes which are: 1) traditional and nontraditional approaches to security and diplomacy; 2) global and regional economic issues; and, 3) social and cultural issues.

Funds Avail.: No specific amount. **Duration:** Annual; every 3 to 12 months. **To Apply:** Interested applicants may visit the website at http://soap.ssrc.org for the online application process. **Deadline:** September 1. **Contact:** Fellowships Coordinator and Special Projects Associate, Abe Fellowship Program; E-mail: rojas@ssrc.org, Phone: 718-517-3640.

8515 ■ Abe Fellowships for Journalists *(Professional development/Fellowship)*

Purpose: To encourage in-depth coverage of topics of pressing concern to the United States and Japan through individual short-term policy-related projects. **Focus:** Journalism. **Qualif.:** Applicants must be citizens of the United States and Japan with at least five years of professional

Awards are arranged alphabetically below their administering organizations

journalistic experience with newspapers, news magazines, wire services and online news organizations. Freelancers are also eligible. Nationals of other countries must be permanent residents of the United States or Japan, or have a long-term affiliation with the American or Japanese journalistic communities; US-based applicants with no previous journalistic employment in Japan or Japan-based applicants with no previous journalistic employment in the United States will be given priority. Proposals must be non-partisan. **Criteria:** Selection will be based on the committee's criteria.

Funds Avail.: $23,500. **To Apply:** Interested applicants may visit the website at http://soap.ssrc.org for the online application process. **Deadline:** September 15.

8516 ■ Dissertation Proposal Development Fellowships (Doctorate/Fellowship)

Purpose: To support early-stage graduate students in formulating successful doctoral dissertation proposals. **Focus:** Humanities; Social sciences. **Qualif.:** Applicant must be a student in the humanities and social sciences undertaking doctoral dissertation research; must be a second or third year PhD student enrolled in a U.S. institution who has not yet submitted and will not submit his/her dissertation proposal until after the fall workshop; must be a student who have completed their comprehensive, general and qualifying exams. Faculty must apply as teams; must be tenured at the time of application; must be trained in different disciplines; must be experienced supervisor of dissertation research. **Criteria:** Student applications will be evaluated based on the following criteria: (1) Originality and appropriateness of the topic; (2) Preparation of the student; (3) Summer Pre-dissertation Research Plan; (4) Summer Funding. Research directors and their proposed research fields are evaluated based on the following criteria: (1) Originality; (2) Appropriateness; (3) Research Directors; (4) Impact.

Funds Avail.: $5,000. **Duration:** Annual. **Number Awarded:** 60. **To Apply:** Applicant must submit a proposed research about the dissertation topic. Applications have to be submitted by two tenured faculty from different US universities and, as relevant, different disciplines. **Contact:** dpdf@ssrc.org.

8517 ■ International Dissertation Research Fellowship (IDRF) (Graduate, Doctorate/Fellowship)

Purpose: To provide assistance in fostering innovative research and mobilizing necessary knowledge on important public issues to new generations of social scientists. **Focus:** Humanities; Social sciences. **Qualif.:** Applicants must be graduates of humanities and social sciences enrolled in PhD programs in the United States. **Criteria:** Preference will be given to applicants who write their prose clearly and intelligibly; proposal that shows major concepts, theories, and methods; and applicants who will provide evidence of having attained an appropriate level of training to do the proposed research.

Funds Avail.: Amount varies. **Duration:** Annual. **Number Awarded:** 80. **To Apply:** Applicants must be filled out the online application through the SSRC Online Application Portal; must complete the research relevance section must upload their research proposal and bibliography; and must send reminders to referees and language evaluators.

8518 ■ Japan Society for the Promotion of Science Fellowship Program (Doctorate/Fellowship)

Purpose: To encourage and to advance recent PhD recipients and ABDs' own research and at the same time closely collaborate with young Japanese researchers and contribute to Japanese research communities. **Focus:** Humanities; Social sciences. **Qualif.:** Candidates for the long-term and short-term fellowships must possess US citizenship or permanent residency status and must provide a copy of a permanent resident card. Citizens of other countries may be eligible if they have completed a master's or PhD course at a US university, and upon completing the course, have at least three continuous years conducted high-level research in the US. **Criteria:** Fellows are selected by the Japan Society for the Promotion of Science based on nominations made by the SSRC Japan Advisory Board.

Funds Avail.: No specific amount. **Duration:** Annual. **To Apply:** Interested applicants must submit the following: an application form, a project description; two letters of recommendation; a letter of invitation from a host institution in Japan. Applicants must also submit a copy of PhD diploma from a university outside Japan dated no more than six years or, for a short-term fellowship, a letter from their institution stating that the applicants is a PhD candidate within two years of receiving a PhD. **Deadline:** December 1.

8519 ■ Korean Studies Dissertation Workshop Funds (Graduate/Fellowship, Grant)

Purpose: To foster a sustained network of advanced graduate students and faculty engaged in research on Korea. **Focus:** Humanities; Social sciences. **Qualif.:** Applicant must be a full-time advanced graduate student enrolled at a U.S. or Canadian institution; must have an approved dissertation prospectus at the time of application, but cannot have completed writing for final submission. **Criteria:** Special consideration will be given to students from universities that are not major Korea Studies institutions. Selection of applicant will be based on the narrative project descriptions as part of the application.

Funds Avail.: No specific amount. **To Apply:** Applicant must complete and sign a two-page application form; must have a summary of the dissertation proposal; must submit a curriculum vitae. **Deadline:** May 1.

8520 ■ Next Generation Social Sciences in Africa: Doctoral Dissertation Completion Fellowships (Doctorate/Fellowship)

Purpose: To support the advancement of social science faculty toward completion of doctoral degrees and to promote next generation social science research in Ghana, Nigeria, South Africa, Tanzania and Uganda. **Focus:** Social sciences. **Qualif.:** Applicants must be citizens of and reside in a sub-Saharan African country while holding a current faculty position at an accredited college or university in Ghana, Nigeria, South Africa, Tanzania, or Uganda; must have a master's degree and be working toward completion of a doctoral degree; must be in the final year of writing and have completed at least one dissertation chapter. **Criteria:** Selection will be based on the committee's criteria.

Funds Avail.: $15,000. **Duration:** Annual. **To Apply:** All applications must be submitted using the online application portal. Strong proposals will offer clear and concise descriptions of the project and its significance. Proposals should display thorough knowledge of the relevant social science literature that applicants will engage and the methodologies relevant to the project. In addition, applicants must demonstrate that all proposed activities are feasible and can be completed in a timely manner. Fellows must be willing to attend two workshops sponsored by the SSRC each

Awards are arranged alphabetically below their administering organizations

year that are intended to help early-career faculty produce scholarly publications. **Deadline:** December 1. **Contact:** Natalie Reinhart, nextgenafrica@ssrc.org.

8521 ■ Next Generation Social Sciences in Africa: Doctoral Dissertation Proposal Fellowships
(Doctorate/Fellowship)

Purpose: To support short-term research costs to develop a doctoral dissertation proposal. **Focus:** Social sciences. **Qualif.:** Applicants must be citizens of and reside in a sub-Saharan African country while holding a current faculty position at an accredited college or university in Ghana, Nigeria, South Africa, Tanzania or Uganda; must have a master's degree and be working toward completion of a doctoral degree; must be admitted to a graduate program but have yet to undertake dissertation research. **Criteria:** Selection will be based on the committee's criteria.

Funds Avail.: $3,000. **Duration:** Annual. **To Apply:** All applications must be submitted using the online application portal. Strong proposals will offer clear and concise descriptions of the project and its significance. Proposals should display thorough knowledge of the relevant social science literature that applicants will engage and the methodologies relevant to the project. In addition, applicants must demonstrate that all proposed activities are feasible and can be completed in a timely manner. Fellows must be willing to attend two workshops sponsored by the SSRC each year that are intended to help early-career faculty produce scholarly publications. **Deadline:** December 1. **Contact:** Natalie Reinhart, nextgenafrica@ssrc.org or E-mail at:reinhart@ssrc.org.

8522 ■ Next Generation Social Sciences in Africa: Doctoral Dissertation Research Fellowship
(Doctorate/Fellowship)

Purpose: To support the advancement of social science faculty toward completion of doctoral degrees and to promote next generation social science research in Ghana, Nigeria, South Africa, Tanzania and Uganda. **Focus:** Social sciences. **Qualif.:** Applicants must be citizens of and reside in a sub-Saharan African country while holding a current faculty position at an accredited college or university in Ghana, Nigeria, South Africa, Tanzania or Uganda; must have a master's degree and be working toward completion of a doctoral degree; must have an approved dissertation proposal but will not yet have undertaken research of nine months or more. **Criteria:** Selection will be based on the committee's criteria.

Funds Avail.: $15,000. **Duration:** Annual. **To Apply:** All applications must be submitted using the online application portal. Strong proposals will offer clear and concise descriptions of the project and its significance. Proposals should display thorough knowledge of the relevant social science literature that applicants will engage and the methodologies relevant to the project. In addition, applicants must demonstrate that all proposed activities are feasible and can be completed in a timely manner. Fellows must be willing to attend two workshops sponsored by the SSRC each year that are intended to help early-career faculty produce scholarly publications. **Deadline:** December 1. **Contact:** Natalie Reinhart, nextgenafrica@ssrc.org or E-mail at:reinhart@ssrc.org.

8523 ■ Societe des designers graphiques du Canada
Arts Ct.
2 Daly Ave.
Ottawa, ON, Canada K1N 6E2
Ph: (613)567-5400
Fax: (613)564-4428
Free: 877-496-4453
E-mail: director@gdc.net
URL: www.gdc.net

8524 ■ Society of Graphic Designers of Canada Adobe Scholarships *(Undergraduate/Scholarship)*

Purpose: To encourage and support students in taking their design education to a level that will prepare them for professional practice. **Focus:** Graphic art and design. **Qualif.:** Applicants must be full-time students enrolled in a two, three, or four-year design degree or diploma program; must be members of Graphic Designers of Canada (GDC), SDGQ, or RGD Ontario. **Criteria:** Recipients will be selected based on qualifications and submitted materials.

Funds Avail.: $2,000. **Duration:** Annual. **To Apply:** Applicants must provide a transcript of grades, letter of reference from an instructor, one sample of work to be accompanied by a detailed rationale, photo and electronic files of their work. Applicants must also draft a personal letter (250 words) describing their design history, previous design education, reason(s) for applying, career aspirations and goals. **Deadline:** April 20. **Contact:** GDC National Scholarship Program, c/o Hudson Design Group, at the above address.

8525 ■ Society of Graphic Designers of Canada Applied Arts Scholarships *(Undergraduate/Scholarship)*

Purpose: To encourage and support students in taking their design education that will prepare them for professional practice. **Focus:** Graphic art and design. **Qualif.:** Applicants must be full-time students enrolled in a two, three, or four-year design degree or diploma program; must be members of Graphic Designers of Canada (GDC), SDGQ, or RGD Ontario. **Criteria:** Recipients will be selected based on qualifications and submitted materials.

Funds Avail.: $1,000. **Duration:** Annual. **To Apply:** Applicants must provide a transcript of grades, letter of reference from an instructor, one sample of work to be accompanied by a detailed rationale, photo and electronic files of their work. Applicants must also draft a personal letter (250 words) describing their design history, previous design education, reason(s) for applying, career aspirations and goals. **Contact:** GDC National Scholarship Program, c/o Hudson Design Group, at the above address.

8526 ■ Society of Graphic Designers of Canada Veer Scholarships *(Undergraduate/Scholarship)*

Purpose: To encourage and support students in taking their design education to a level that will prepare them for professional practice. **Focus:** Graphic art and design. **Qualif.:** Applicants must be full-time students enrolled in a two, three, or four-year design degree or diploma program; must be members of Graphic Designers of Canada (GDC), SDGQ, or RGD Ontario. **Criteria:** Recipients will be selected based on qualifications and submitted materials.

Funds Avail.: $2,500. **Duration:** Annual. **To Apply:** Applicants must provide a transcript of grades, letter of reference from an instructor, one sample of work to be accompanied by a detailed rationale, photo and electronic files of their work. Applicants must also draft a personal letter (250 words) describing their design history, previous design education, reason(s) for applying, career aspirations and goals. **Deadline:** April 20. **Contact:** GDC National

Awards are arranged alphabetically below their administering organizations

Scholarship Program, c/o Hudson Design Group, at the above address.

8527 ■ Society of Allied Weight Engineers (SAWE)

5734 E Lucia Walk
Long Beach, CA 90803-4015
Ph: (562)596-2873
Fax: (562)596-2874
URL: www.sawe.org

8528 ■ Frank Fong Scholarships *(Undergraduate/ Scholarship)*

Purpose: To provide financial assistance for the education of the dependents of SAWE members. **Focus:** Computer and information sciences; Engineering; Mathematics and mathematical sciences; Physics. **Qualif.:** Applicants must be children or grandchildren (age 25 or below) of SAWE members (living or deceased) that are students enrolled in a technical course of study (e.g. engineering, physics, mathematics, computer sciences, etc.). **Criteria:** Awards are given based on academic merit; work experience; extracurricular activities; and goal for the application.

Funds Avail.: $1,000 each. **Duration:** Annual. **Number Awarded:** Up to 3. **To Apply:** Applicants must complete and submit the application form available at the website together with their transcript of grades. **Deadline:** April 1.

8529 ■ Society of Allied Weight Engineers Scholarships *(Undergraduate/Scholarship)*

Purpose: To provide financial assistance for the education of the dependents of SAWE members. **Focus:** General studies/Field of study not specified. **Qualif.:** Applicants must be children or grandchildren of SAWE members; must be aged 25 or below; and must be full-time undergraduate students. **Criteria:** Awards are given based on academic merit; work experience; extracurricular activities; and goal for the application.

Funds Avail.: $1,000. **Number Awarded:** 3. **To Apply:** Application forms are available at the website. Applicants must submit completed application form and send together with a complete transcript of grades. **Deadline:** April 1. **Contact:** Scholarship Management Services, One Scholarship Way, St. Peter, MN 56082; Telephone: 507-931-1682, Tollfree: 800-537-4180.

8530 ■ Society for American Archaeology (SAA)

1111 14th St. NW, Ste. 800
Washington, DC 20005
Ph: (202)789-8200
Fax: (202)789-0284
E-mail: headquarters@saa.org
URL: www.saa.org

8531 ■ SAA Native American Scholarships *(Undergraduate, Graduate, Professional development/ Scholarship)*

Purpose: To support archaeological training for Native American students. **Focus:** Archeology. **Qualif.:** Applicants must be current high school seniors, college undergraduates and graduate students, or personnels of a Tribal or other Native cultural preservation programs. High school students must be enrolled as seniors. Undergraduate and graduate students must be enrolled in an accredited college/university. Native Americans and Pacific Islanders from the U.S., including U.S. Trust Territories, and Indigenous peoples from Canada are also eligible. **Criteria:** Selection is based on the application or nomination.

Funds Avail.: Amount varies. **Duration:** Annual. **Number Awarded:** Varies. **To Apply:** Applicant must submit a completed application/nomination form together with a letter of nomination or recommendation; a 1-page personal statement; a 1-page brief description of the archaeological methods training program; an itemized budget; and a documentation of Native identity. Applicant may apply or may be nominated by a current professor, high school teacher, or cultural preservation program supervisor. **Deadline:** December 16. **Remarks:** The SAA Native American Scholarships are offered in the following: the SAA Arthur C. Parker Scholarship or NSF Scholarship for Archaeological Training; SAA Native American Undergraduate Archaeology Scholarship; SAA Native American Graduate Archaeology Scholarship. Established in 1998. **Contact:** nasf@saa.org.

8532 ■ Society for Applied Anthropology (SfAA)

PO Box 2436
Oklahoma City, OK 73101-2436
Ph: (405)843-5113
Fax: (405)843-8553
E-mail: info@sfaa.net
URL: www.sfaa.net

8533 ■ Margaret Mead Award *(Other/Award)*

Purpose: To support young scholars for a book, film, monograph or service which interprets anthropological data and principles in ways that make them meaningful to a broadly concerned public. **Focus:** Anthropology. **Qualif.:** Applicants must have received their PhD degree after January 1 (ten years or less). **Criteria:** Nominees contributions will be judged based on intellectual quality, clarity and understandability, extent or depth of the impact and breadth of the impact.

Funds Avail.: No specific amount. **Duration:** Annual. **To Apply:** Applicants must include a curriculum vitae, two letters of recommendation and must submit a four copies of the book or film. **Deadline:** March 15. **Remarks:** Offered jointly by the American Anthropological Association (AAA) and the Society for Applied Anthropology (SfAA). Established in 1979. **Contact:** Nominations and four copies of supporting materials must be submitted to the Society of Applied Anthropology, at the above address; E-mail: info@sfaa.net.

8534 ■ Society of Architectural Historians (SAH)

1365 N Astor St.
Chicago, IL 60610-2144
Ph: (312)573-1365
URL: www.sah.org

8535 ■ Edilia and Francois Auguste de Montequin Fellowships *(Doctorate/Fellowship)*

Purpose: To provide support for travel related to research on Spanish, Portuguese, or Ibero-American architecture. **Focus:** Engineering, Architectural. **Qualif.:** Applicant must be a member of the Society of Architectural Historians; a full-time junior graduate student engaged in a doctoral dissertation research; or a senior graduate student with a

Awards are arranged alphabetically below their administering organizations

completed PhD or equivalent with a research focusing on Spanish, Portuguese, or Ibero-American architecture. **Criteria:** Awards are given based on the submitted applications. **Funds Avail.:** $2,000 for junior scholars and $6,000 for senior scholars. **Duration:** Annual. **Number Awarded:** 1. **To Apply:** Application form is available at the SAH office and at the website. **Deadline:** September 8.

8536 ■ Samuel H. Kress Foundation Dissertation Fellowships *(Doctorate/Fellowship)*

Purpose: To provide assistance for the professional development of graduate students in architectural history. **Focus:** Architecture. **Qualif.:** Applicants must be U.S. citizens; must be enrolled at an American university; must be doctoral candidates with a dissertation that focuses on European architecture before 1850. **Criteria:** Selection will be based on the committee's criteria.

Funds Avail.: No specific amount. **To Apply:** Applicants must complete the online registration and must provide the following materials: a summary or abstract; a budget detailing the use of the funds (one to two pages); curriculum vitae; and two letters of recommendation. All materials must in Word document and sent via electronically.

8537 ■ SAH Study Tour Fellowships *(Graduate/ Fellowship)*

Purpose: To provide travel opportunities that focus on the history of architecture and landscapes. **Focus:** Architecture. **Qualif.:** Applicant must be a member of the Society of Architectural Historians and a PhD student. **Criteria:** Recipients are selected by a committee by the SAH President.

Funds Avail.: $200. **To Apply:** Applicants are advised to visit the website for the online Study Tour Fellowship application. Applicants must submit maximum of five pages curriculum vitae and a 300-word statement explaining how this fellowship will advance their studies or interests. **Deadline:** May 6. **Contact:** Materials should be submitted in a Word format to beifrig@sah.org.

8538 ■ Beverly Willis Architecture Foundation Travel Fellowship *(Doctorate/Fellowship)*

Purpose: To support travel expenses of a speaker whose paper has been accepted for delivery at the SAH annual conference. **Focus:** Architecture. **Qualif.:** Applicants must be enrolled in a PhD program conducting a dissertation research about the contribution of women to the production of architecture in the United States in the mid-twentieth century (should be submitted in English). **Criteria:** Recipient is selected based on the submitted materials.

Funds Avail.: $1,500. **Duration:** Annual. **To Apply:** Applicants are advised to visit the website for the online Fellowship Application. Applicants must also submit a Word document which contains a summary or abstract; a budget detailing the use of the funds (one to two pages); a curriculum vitae; and letters of recommendation. **Remarks:** Established in 2004.

8539 ■ Society for the Arts in Healthcare (SAH)
2647 Connecticut Ave. NW, Ste. 200
Washington, DC 20008
Ph: (202)299-9770
Fax: (202)299-9887
URL: www.thesah.org

8540 ■ Society for the Arts in Healthcare Environmental Arts Research Grants *(Other/Grant)*

Purpose: To help investigators conduct research in the field of Arts in Healthcare. **Focus:** Health care services.

Qualif.: Principal investigators must be members of the Society for the Arts in Healthcare and must not be winners of the research grant in the preceding year. The applicant's proposal must be focused on research and conducted within a health-related facility. **Criteria:** Selection will be made on the basis of merit, innovation and feasibility of the research proposal. The following categories will be included in judging criteria: 1) clarity of the research; 2) rigorous research methodology; 3) availability of the site and feasible implementation plan; 4) expertise of the research team and strength of partnerships; 5) benefit to healthcare facility and fields of art in healthcare; 6) contributions to advance the new knowledge in the field; and 7) proof of IRB approval.

Funds Avail.: $1,000. **To Apply:** Applicants must submit a project proposal, curriculum vitae of the principal investigator, names and contact information for two references.

8541 ■ Society for the Arts in Healthcare Student Scholarships *(Doctorate, Graduate, Undergraduate/ Scholarship)*

Purpose: To support the education of students enrolled in the field of Arts in Healthcare curriculum. **Focus:** Health care services. **Qualif.:** Applicants must be undergraduate, graduate or doctoral student members of Society for the Arts in Healthcare who are in good standing; must show a documentation of at least part-time enrollment; and must demonstrate specific contributions to the field through development of student activities, community outreach and/or similar actions that support the integration of the arts in the healthcare experience. **Criteria:** Applications will be judged based on creativity, uniqueness and ability to implement thoughts and ideas regarding the future of the field.

Funds Avail.: $1,000. **Duration:** Annual. **To Apply:** Applicants must submit an application form, references and proof of enrollment. Materials must be submitted in Word or PDF file and should be written in English. **Deadline:** November 15.

8542 ■ Society of Broadcast Engineers (SBE)
9102 N Meridian St., Ste. 150
Indianapolis, IN 46260
Ph: (317)846-9000
Fax: (317)846-9120
E-mail: mclappe@sbe.org
URL: www.sbe.org

8543 ■ Harold E. Ennes Scholarships *(Graduate, Other/Award, Scholarship)*

Purpose: To provide educational fund to deserving candidates who aspire to a career in the technical aspects of broadcasting. **Focus:** Broadcasting; Engineering. **Qualif.:** Applicants must be SBE members; have work experience in broadcasting engineering; and interested in continuing their education in order to advance their careers. **Criteria:** Preference will be given to those who are SBE members and employed in broadcast engineering.

Funds Avail.: $1,000-$1,500. **Number Awarded:** 1. **To Apply:** Application forms are available at the website. Complete only the A and C sections of the application form and send together with a brief autobiography; a summary of technical changes; and a copy of recent college transcripts (if applicable). **Deadline:** July 1. **Remarks:** Established in memory of Harold E. Ennes.

Awards are arranged alphabetically below their administering organizations

8544 ■ Robert D. Greenberg Scholarships *(Graduate, Other/Scholarship)*

Purpose: To provide educational fund to deserving candidates who aspire to a career in the technical aspects of broadcasting. **Focus:** Broadcasting; Engineering. **Qualif.:** Applicants must be SBE members; have work experience in broadcasting engineering; and interested in continuing their education in order to advance their careers. **Criteria:** Preference will be given to those who are SBE members and employed in broadcasting engineering.

Funds Avail.: Varies from $1,000 to $1,500. **Duration:** Annual. **Number Awarded:** 1. **To Apply:** Applicants must submit an application (or copy) obtained from SBE. **Deadline:** July 1.

8545 ■ SBE/Ennes Youth Scholarships
(Undergraduate/Scholarship)

Purpose: To provide educational fund to deserving candidates who aspire to a career in the technical aspects of broadcasting. **Focus:** Broadcasting; Technical communications. **Qualif.:** Candidates must: be in their senior year of high school, anticipating graduation by the spring of the current year; intend to enroll at a technical school, college or university in the fall of the current year; and, have a serious interest in pursuing studies leading to a career in broadcast engineering or closely related technical field. **Criteria:** Recipients are selected based on the committee's review of application materials.

Funds Avail.: Varies from $1,000 to $1,500. **Duration:** Annual. **Number Awarded:** 1. **To Apply:** Applicants must submit an application (or copy) obtained from SBE. **Deadline:** July 1.

8546 ■ Society for Cinema and Media Studies (SCMS)
Wallace Old Science Hall, Rm. 300
640 Parrington Oval
Norman, OK 73019
Ph: (405)325-8075
Fax: (405)325-7135
E-mail: office@cmstudies.org
URL: www.cmstudies.org

8547 ■ Anne Friedberg Innovative Scholarship Awards *(Other/Scholarship)*

Purpose: To recognize innovative works that expand the discipline of film and media studies, emphasizing its relationship to other visual fields, including architect, art history and digital media. **Focus:** Filmmaking; Media arts. **Qualif.:** Applicants must be authors of books or media projects. It should be written or translated in English and published between August 1 and July 31. **Criteria:** Evaluation will be based on submitted materials.

Funds Avail.: $1,000. **Duration:** Annual. **To Apply:** Applicants must complete the nomination form and send four copies of eligible books or include instructions for accessing online media projects to the SCMS office. **Deadline:** August 3. **Remarks:** Established in 2010. **Contact:** Society for Cinema and Media Studies, Anne Friedberg Award, at the above address.

8548 ■ Society for Classical Studies (SCS)
University of Pennsylvania
220 S 40th St., Ste. 201E
Philadelphia, PA 19104-3512

Ph: (215)898-4975
Fax: (215)573-7874
E-mail: apaclassics@sas.upenn.edu
URL: www.apaclassics.org

8549 ■ American Philological Association Minority Student Summer Fellowships *(Undergraduate/Fellowship)*

Purpose: To provide financial assistance for undergraduate students who wish to pursue their preparation for graduate work in classical archeology. **Focus:** Archeology; Classical studies. **Qualif.:** Applicant must have (but not limited to) participated in classical summer programs or field schools in Italy, Greece or Egypt or language training at institutions in the U.S., Canada or Europe. **Criteria:** Candidates will be judged based on academic qualifications, quality of proposal and financial need.

Funds Avail.: No specific amount. **Duration:** Annual. **To Apply:** Applicants must complete the application form together with a letter of application describing the applicant's career goals and plans with a list of other programs applied to; must have an undergraduate transcript; must provide two letters of recommendation by a faculty member or other professionals who have worked with the applicant during the past two years (at least one must be an APA or AIA member).

8550 ■ Thesaurus Linguae Latinae Fellowships (TTL) *(Doctorate/Fellowship)*

Purpose: To support American scholars who wish to broaden their knowledge in the work of Thesaurus Linguae Latinae Institute in Munich. **Focus:** Latin American studies; Philology. **Qualif.:** Applicant must be a U.S. citizen or permanent resident; must have a PhD. degree or anticipate the degree in the next few months. **Criteria:** Fellowships will be awarded to applicants who possess a thorough familiarity and special interest in the Latin languages, as well as advanced competence in Greek.

Funds Avail.: No specific amount. **Duration:** Annual. **To Apply:** Applicant must submit a curriculum vitae and a statement of what benefits the applicant expects to derive from the fellowship for his or her research and teaching. Applicant must also provide three references.

8551 ■ Society for Conservation Biology (SCB)
1017 O St. NW
Washington, DC 20001
Ph: (202)234-4133
Fax: (703)995-4633
E-mail: info@conbio.org
URL: www.conbio.org

8552 ■ David H. Smith Conservation Research Fellowships *(Postdoctorate/Fellowship)*

Purpose: To identify and support early-career scientists who will shape the field of applied conservation biology. **Focus:** Biology. **Qualif.:** Applicants must be postdoctoral researchers affiliated with a United States institution, proposing research that addresses pressing conservation issues for the United States; must have completed their doctorate within the past five years. Applicants who have not yet completed their doctorate must clearly indicate on the application the date the degree is expected. **Criteria:** Selection will be based on the following criteria: professional record, perceived potential for innovation and leader-

Awards are arranged alphabetically below their administering organizations

ship, commitment to biological conservation and the strength of their proposal.

Funds Avail.: $32,000 research fund; $50,000 annual salary; $8,000 travel budget. **Duration:** Two years. **To Apply:** All materials must be submitted electronically and must be in PDF or MS Word format. Please include the applicants' last name in some part of the file name. Research approaches may include comparative studies, synthetic analyses across sites, experimentation or observational studies, applied modeling or any combination. Proposed research may include intensive work at one site, work at multiple sites, or comparative evaluations of studies by other scientists across many sites. In all cases, the central questions of the inquiry must be clearly articulated. Proposed study sites must be noted; an explanation of how the results will inform conservation practice is required. The research plan, excluding literature cited, must not under any circumstances exceed 8 pages. Font size must be at least 11 point, 2.5 cm margins; at least 1.5 line spacing. The cover letter, literature cited, personal statement, and curriculum vitae are not included in the 8-page limit for the research plan. The research plan should include the following: abstract, background section, statement of objectives, approaches and methods, anticipated results, research schedule and relevance to conservation science and practice. The complete application must include the following: cover letter; title page; research plan; applicants' curriculum vitae; personal statement; three letters of recommendation addressing the merits of the candidate and the candidate's proposal; sponsor support letter; sponsor's abbreviated curriculum vitae; support letter from practitioner mentor; indirect cost waiver. The personal statement should address the following questions, in at least 200 words: Give an example(s) of an accomplishment you believe demonstrates your leadership skills or entrepreneurial abilities; How is your research cutting edge or innovative?; What will be the greatest impact of your research? Who or what will be most greatly affected? **Deadline:** September 20. **Contact:** smithfellows@conbio.org; smithinfo@smithfellows.org.

8553 ■ Society of Dance History Scholars (SDHS)

3416 Primm Ln.
Birmingham, AL 35216
Ph: (205)978-1404
Fax: (205)823-2760
E-mail: office@sdhs.org
URL: sdhs.org

8554 ■ Graduate Student Travel Grants *(Graduate, Other/Grant)*

Purpose: To help graduate students to defray costs of attending the annual conference. **Focus:** Dance. **Qualif.:** Applicants must be student members of SDHS; must be enrolled in a graduate degree program; and must be engaged in dance research. **Criteria:** Recipients are selected based on the committee's review of application materials.

Funds Avail.: No specific amount. **To Apply:** Applicants must submit application form; estimated budget; proposal of maximum 250 words; and a curriculum vitae. **Deadline:** September 1. **Contact:** Ashanti Pretlow, Accounts Manager; info@sdhs.org.

8555 ■ Society for Economic Botany

PO Box 299
Saint Louis, MO 63166-0299
Fax: (314)577-9515
E-mail: seb@botany.org
URL: www.econbot.org

8556 ■ Richard E. Schultes Research Awards *(Graduate/Grant, Award)*

Purpose: To provide funding support for research related to economic botany. **Focus:** Botany. **Qualif.:** Applicants must be graduate students who have received their degree within a year and must be members of the society. **Criteria:** Recipients are selected based on the submitted proposal.

Funds Avail.: $2,500. **Duration:** Annual. **To Apply:** Applicants' major advisor must confirm current MS, PhD or Post-doctoral status of the applicant through email message and must also provide a recommendation letter. Applicants must prepare in MS Word a 2-page description of the proposed research; a 1-page tabular budget; and a 1-page resume. Files must be named using first initial_lastname and must be sent electronically. If selected, recipients must submit a 1-2-page, double-spaced narrative of their project within nine months of receiving the award. **Deadline:** March 15. **Remarks:** Founded in honor of Dr. Richard Evans Schultes, the society's economic botanist. Established in 2001. **Contact:** schultesaward@econbot.org.

8557 ■ Society of Emergency Medicine Physician Assistants (SEMPA)

1125 Executive Cir.
Irving, TX 75038-2522
Fax: (972)580-2816
Free: 877-297-7594
E-mail: sempa@sempa.org
URL: www.sempa.org

8558 ■ Paul S. Robinson Scholarships *(Undergraduate/Scholarship)*

Purpose: To financially support students who are pursuing a career in emergency medicine. **Focus:** Medicine. **Qualif.:** Applicants must be Physician Assistant students who plan to pursue a career in emergency medicine; must be current SEMPA members; a student in good standing of an ARC-PA accredited PA training program or a student in a post-graduate emergency medicine training program; should be in the final year of training; should be nominated by a program director or could be self-nomination. **Criteria:** Recipients will be selected based on the submitted applications;

Funds Avail.: $2,000. **Duration:** Annual. **To Apply:** Applicants must submit a completed application form; endorsement letter form the program director; curriculum vitae; recommendation letter; summary of leadership positions; a brief description of involvement on any community service. **Deadline:** January 31. **Contact:** Applicants may submit their application form and other required documents electronically to scholarship@sempa.org.

8559 ■ Society of Exploration Geophysicists (SEG)

8801 S Yale, Ste. 500
Tulsa, OK 74137-3575
Ph: (918)497-5500

Awards are arranged alphabetically below their administering organizations

Fax: (918)497-5557
E-mail: membership_online@seg.org
URL: www.seg.org

8560 ■ Society of Exploration Geophysicists Foundation Scholarships *(Graduate, Undergraduate/ Scholarship)*

Purpose: To encourage the study of geophysics and related seoscienceTo provide financial support to students who are studying geophysics.s. **Focus:** Geosciences. **Qualif.:** Applicant must be a student pursuing a college curriculum directed toward a career in applied geophysics, or a closely related field such as geosciences, physics, geology, or earth and environmental sciences; must be attending high school and planning to enter college next fall or be an undergraduate or graduate college student whose grades are above average. **Criteria:** Awards are given based on the application materials.

Funds Avail.: $500-$14,000. **To Apply:** Applicants must submit a completed scholarship application form and materials. **Deadline:** March 1.

8561 ■ Society for Family Planning (SFP)

255 S 17th St., Ste. 1102
Philadelphia, PA 19103
Free: 866-584-6758
E-mail: info@societyfp.org
URL: www.societyfp.org

8562 ■ SFP Junior Investigator's Career Development Awards *(Other/Grant)*

Purpose: To provide research support and protected time for junior investigators and mentors. **Focus:** Family planning. **Qualif.:** Applicants must be faculty-level clinical and translational scientists near the beginning of their investigative careers. **Criteria:** Selection will be based on academic and intellectual background; motivation; commitment to pursue clinical and translational research; assessment of candidate's potential; dedication to the clinical or translational research; the degree of support from the department.

Funds Avail.: Varies. **To Apply:** Applicants must submit a completed form including signature page; copy of full curriculum vitae; nine-page narrative plus budget (font must be at least 11 points, all margins at least one inch and 1.5 spacing - applications that do not adhere to these requirements will be disqualified); preliminary studies (if available); IRB documentation; letter from the Department Chair; letter from mentors; copy of the agency's federal 501(c) 3 status determination letter or proof of tax-exempt status.

8563 ■ SFP Mid-Career/Mentor Awards for Family Planning *(Other/Grant)*

Purpose: To support junior researchers conducting clinical/ social science research in family planning and provides additional funding for pilot studies. **Focus:** Biological and clinical sciences; Family planning; Social sciences. **Qualif.:** Applicants should be at the Associate Professor level with independent peer-reviewed research support; must commit 10% full-time professional effort to the research, training and mentoring proposed. **Criteria:** Selection will be based on academic and intellectual background; motivation; commitment to pursue clinical and translational research; assessment of candidate's potential; dedication to the clinical or translational research; the degree of support from the department.

Funds Avail.: $40,000. **Duration:** Annual. **To Apply:** Applicants must submit a completed form including signature page; copy of full curriculum vitae; eight-page narrative plus budget (font must be at least 11 points, all margins at least one inch and 1.5 spacing applications that do not adhere to these requirements will be disqualified); half-page commitment statement; IRB documentation; biographical sketch; copy of the agency's federal 501(c)3 status determination letter or proof of tax-exempt status.

8564 ■ SFP Student and Resident Research Grants *(Graduate/Grant)*

Purpose: To aid the development of graduate-level students who want to pursue research-oriented careers in the field of family planning. **Focus:** Family planning. **Qualif.:** Applicants must be actively pursuing their medical degree; enrolled in a residency or graduate program at the time of application and award. **Criteria:** Selection will be based on the evaluation of the submitted documents and specific criteria.

Funds Avail.: $30,000. **Duration:** 12 months. **Number Awarded:** 6. **To Apply:** Applicants must submit a completed application form; a narrative with a maximum of four pages (font must be at least 11 points, all margins at least one inch and 1.5 spacing - applications that do not adhere to these requirements will be disqualified); letter from project supervisor; IRB documentation. **Deadline:** April 12. **Contact:** mpolonsky@societyfp.org.

8565 ■ Society of Georgia Archivists (SGA)

PO Box 688
Decatur, GA 30031
Ph: (404)712-7051
E-mail: president@soga.org
URL: www.soga.org

8566 ■ Brenda S. Bank Educational Workshop Scholarships *(Undergraduate/Scholarship)*

Purpose: To provide funding to attend the SGA-sponsored Spring/Summer Workshop as scheduled by the Education Committee. **Focus:** General studies/Field of study not specified. **Qualif.:** Eligible applicants are those who are engaged in compensated or volunteer archival work at any level in an institution in the state of Georgia, SGA members employed outside the state of Georgia, graduate students preparing for a career in archives at a college or university in Georgia or SGA students studying outside of Georgia. **Criteria:** Recipients are selected based on the academic performance and financial need.

Funds Avail.: No specific amount. **Duration:** Annual. **To Apply:** Applicants must submit: completed application form; a cover letter; letter of recommendation; resume; 500-word or less essay discussing how scholarship will enhance their overall professional development and/or what they hope to bring back to their current and/or anticipated work from the experience. **Deadline:** May 15. **Contact:** SGA at scholarships@soga.org.

8567 ■ Anthony R. Dees Educational Workshop Scholarships *(Undergraduate/Scholarship)*

Purpose: To provide funding to attend the SGA-sponsored Pre-Conference Workshop. **Focus:** General studies/Field of study not specified. **Qualif.:** Eligible applicants are those who are engaged in compensated or volunteer archival work at any level in an institution in the state of Georgia,

Awards are arranged alphabetically below their administering organizations

SGA members employed outside the state of Georgia, graduate students preparing for a career in archives at a college or university in Georgia or SGA students studying outside of Georgia. **Criteria:** Recipients are selected based on the academic performance and financial need.

Funds Avail.: No specific amount. **Duration:** Annual. **To Apply:** Applicants must submit: completed application form; a cover letter; letter of recommendation; resume; a 500-word or less essay discussing how scholarship will enhance their overall professional development and/or what they hope to bring back to their current and/or anticipated work from the experience. **Deadline:** July 24. **Contact:** SGA at scholarships@soga.org.

8568 ■ Larry Gulley Scholarships (Undergraduate/Scholarship)

Purpose: To provide funding to attend the SGA Annual Meeting. **Focus:** General studies/Field of study not specified. **Qualif.:** Eligible applicants are those who are engaged in compensated or volunteer archival work at any level in an institution in the state of Georgia, SGA members employed outside the state of Georgia, graduate students preparing for a career in archives at a college or university in Georgia or SGA students studying outside of Georgia. **Criteria:** Recipients are selected based on the academic performance and financial need.

Funds Avail.: Varies. **Duration:** Annual. **To Apply:** Applicants must submit: completed application form; a cover letter; letter of recommendation; resume; a 500-word or less essay discussing how scholarship will enhance their overall professional development and/or what they hope to bring back to their current and/or anticipated work from the experience. **Deadline:** July 24. **Contact:** SGA at scholarships@soga.org.

8569 ■ Carroll Hart Scholarship (Graduate/Scholarship)

Purpose: To provide funding to attend the Georgia Archives Institute **Focus:** General studies/Field of study not specified. **Qualif.:** Eligible applicants are those engaged in compensated or volunteer archival work at any level in an institution in the state of Georgia, SGA members employed outside the state of Georgia, graduate students preparing for a career in archives at a college or university in Georgia or SGA students studying outside of Georgia. **Criteria:** Recipients are selected based on the academic performance and financial need.

Funds Avail.: $500. **Duration:** Annual. **To Apply:** Applicants must submit: completed application form; a cover letter; letter of recommendation; resume; 500 or less word essay discussing how scholarship will enhance their overall professional development and/or what they hope to bring back to their current and/or anticipated work from the experience. **Deadline:** March 1. **Contact:** SGA at scholarships@soga.org.

8570 ■ Society for Historians of American Foreign Relations (SHAFR)

106 Dulles Hall
Dept. of History
Ohio State University
230 W 17th Ave.
Columbus, OH 43210-1367
Ph: (614)292-1951
Fax: (614)292-2282
E-mail: shafr@osu.edu

URL: www.shafr.org

8571 ■ Samuel Flagg Bemis Dissertation Research Grants (Doctorate, Graduate/Grant)

Purpose: To promote dissertation research on significant scholarly projects. **Focus:** International affairs and relations. **Qualif.:** Applicants must be working on a dissertation dealing with some aspect of U.S. foreign relations history and must have completed all requirements for the doctoral degree except the dissertation. Membership in SHAFR is required. **Criteria:** Selection will be based on the committee's criteria.

Funds Avail.: Up to $2,000. **Duration:** Annual. **To Apply:** Complete application can be downloaded at the website. Applicants must submit a cover sheet (available at website) with project narrative; budget and justification; one-page CV; and a letter of recommendation. All application materials (including the cover sheet but excluding letters of recommendation), should be in a single document (.doc, .pdf, .rtf) and submit it via e-mail with a subject line which contains the last name of the applicant only. Letters of recommendation should be sent separately. **Deadline:** October 1. **Contact:** fellowships@shafr.org.

8572 ■ Stuart L. Bernath Dissertation Grants (Doctorate, Graduate/Grant)

Purpose: To help graduate students defray expenses encountered in the writing of their dissertations. **Focus:** International affairs and relations. **Qualif.:** Applicants must be working on dissertations dealing with some aspect of U.S. foreign relations history and have completed all requirements for the doctoral degree except the dissertation. Membership in SHAFR is required. **Criteria:** Selection will be based on merit.

Funds Avail.: $4,000. **Duration:** Annual. **To Apply:** Application form can be downloaded at the website. Applicants must submit a cover sheet (available at website) with project narrative; budget and justification; one-page CV; and a letter of recommendation. All application materials (including the cover sheet but excluding letters of recommendation), should be in a single document (.doc, .pdf, .rtf) and submit it via e-mail with a subject line which contains the last name of the applicant only. Letters of recommendation should be sent separately. **Deadline:** October 1. **Contact:** Application materials must be submitted via e-mail at fellowships@shafr.org.

8573 ■ Myrna F. Bernath Fellowships (Doctorate, Graduate/Fellowship)

Purpose: To promote scholarship in U.S. foreign relations history by women. **Focus:** International affairs and relations. **Qualif.:** Applicants must be women from U.S. universities or women abroad pursuing a research in the United States. **Criteria:** Preference will be given to graduate students who will be completing their Ph.D. within five years.

Funds Avail.: Up to $5,000. **Duration:** Biennial; in odd-numbered years. **To Apply:** Application form can be downloaded at the website. Applicants must submit a cover sheet (available at website) with project narrative; budget and justification; one-page CV; and a letter of recommendation. All application materials (including the cover sheet but excluding letters of recommendation), should be in a single document (.doc, .pdf, .rtf) and submit it via e-mail with a subject line which contains the last name of the applicant only. Letters of recommendation should be sent separately. **Deadline:** October 1. **Contact:** myrnabernath-committee@shafr.org.

Awards are arranged alphabetically below their administering organizations

8574 ■ Robert A. and Barbara Divine Graduate Student Travel Grants (Graduate/Grant)

Purpose: To assist graduate students who present papers at the conference. **Focus:** International affairs and relations. **Qualif.:** Applicants must be graduate students who will present papers at the annual meetings of SHAFR. **Criteria:** Program committee shall evaluate applications and allocate the available funds. Selection is based on merit and not on financial need. Priority will be given to graduate students who receive no or limited funds from their home institutions.

Funds Avail.: up to $300 per student. **Duration:** Annual. **To Apply:** Applications should consist of a concise letter from the prospective participant requesting funds and an accompanying letter from the graduate advisor confirming the unavailability of departmental funds to cover travel to the conference. These two items should be submitted via the online interface at the time the panel or paper proposal is submitted.

8575 ■ Lawrence Gelfand - Armin Rappaport - Walter LaFeber Dissertation Fellowships (Doctorate, Graduate/Fellowship)

Purpose: To help defray the costs of travel in conducting a research on a significant dissertation project. **Focus:** International affairs and relations. **Qualif.:** Applicants must be working on a dissertation dealing with some aspect of United States foreign relations history and have completed all requirements for the doctoral degree except the dissertation and be members of SHAFR. **Criteria:** Selection shall be based on the aforementioned qualifications and compliance with the application details.

Funds Avail.: Up to $4,000. **Duration:** Annual. **To Apply:** Complete application can be downloaded at the website. Applicants must submit a cover sheet (available at website) with project narrative; budget and justification; one-page CV; and a letter of recommendation. All application materials (including the cover sheet but excluding letters of recommendation), should be in a single document (.doc, .pdf, .rtf) and submit it via e-mail with a subject line which contains the last name of the applicant only. Letters of recommendation should be sent separately. **Deadline:** October 1. **Contact:** Electronic submission should be forwarded to fellowships@shafr.org.

8576 ■ Michael J. Hogan Language Fellowships (Graduate/Fellowship)

Purpose: To promote research in foreign language sources. **Focus:** Foreign languages. **Qualif.:** Applicants must be graduate students conducting research on some aspect of U.S. foreign relations history, and be members of SHAFR. **Criteria:** Recipients will be selected based on submitted application.

Funds Avail.: Up to $4,000. **Duration:** Annual. **To Apply:** Application form can be downloaded at the website. Applicants must submit a cover sheet (available at website) with project narrative; budget and justification; one-page CV; and a letter of recommendation. All application materials (including the cover sheet but excluding letters of recommendation), should be in a single document (.doc, .pdf, .rtf) and submit it via e-mail with a subject line which contains the last name of the applicant only. Letters of recommendation should be sent separately. **Deadline:** November 15. **Contact:** hogan-fellowships@shafr.org.

8577 ■ W. Stull Holt Dissertation Fellowships (Doctorate, Graduate/Fellowship)

Purpose: To defray the costs of travel in conducting a research on a significant dissertation project. **Focus:** International affairs and relations. **Qualif.:** Applicants must be working on a dissertation dealing with some aspect of U.S. foreign relations history and must have completed all requirements for the doctoral degree except the dissertation. **Criteria:** Selection will be based on the committee's criteria.

Funds Avail.: Up to $4,000. **Duration:** Annual. **To Apply:** Application can be downloaded at the website. Applicants must submit a cover sheet (available at website) with project narrative; budget and justification; one-page CV; and a letter of recommendation. All application materials (including the cover sheet but excluding letters of recommendation), should be in a single document (.doc, .pdf, .rtf) and submit it via e-mail with a subject line which contains the last name of the applicant only. Letters of recommendation should be sent separately. **Deadline:** October 1. **Contact:** fellowships@shafr.org.

8578 ■ SHAFR Dissertation Completion Fellowships (Doctorate/Fellowship)

Purpose: To support the writing and completion of doctoral dissertation. **Focus:** Humanities; International affairs and relations; Social sciences. **Qualif.:** Applicants must be candidates for the Ph.D. in a humanities or social science doctoral program (most likely history), must have been admitted to candidacy, and must be at the writing stage, with all substantial research completed by the time of the award. Also, they must be working on a topic in the field of U.S. foreign relations history or international history, broadly defined, and must be current members of SHAFR. **Criteria:** Selection will be based on the committee's criteria.

Funds Avail.: $20,000 each. **Duration:** Up to two years. **Number Awarded:** 2. **To Apply:** Applicants must submit an application letter stating the project's significance, applicants' status and other received support; a statement of research (3 pages, 750 words); a curriculum vitae; and a recommendation letter from the doctoral advisor. **Deadline:** April 1. **Remarks:** Letters of recommendation must be submitted separately indicating the last name of the applicant at the subject line. **Contact:** Application form and other supporting documents must be submitted by e-mail at dissertation-fellowships@shafr.org.

8579 ■ Society for the History of Technology (SHOT)

Dept. of History
310 Thach Hall
Auburn University, AL 36849-5207
Ph: (334)844-6770
Fax: (334)844-6673
E-mail: shotsec@auburn.edu
URL: www.historyoftechnology.org

8580 ■ Brooke Hindle Postdoctoral Fellowships (Postdoctorate/Fellowship)

Purpose: To promote the history of technology as a field of scholarly endeavor. **Focus:** History. **Qualif.:** Applicants must hold a doctorate in the history of technology or a related field. **Criteria:** Selection of awardees is based on the committee's criteria.

Funds Avail.: $10,000. **Duration:** Biennial. **To Apply:** Ap-

Awards are arranged alphabetically below their administering organizations

plicants must submit their 2,500-word summary of the dissertation and a sample chapter; a plan of work (1000-1500 words) for the period of the fellowship; two letters of recommendation. For applicants in full-time employment, one letter must include confirmation that an appropriate period of release will be granted. **Deadline:** April 1.

8581 ■ Melvin Kranzberg Dissertation Fellowships
(Doctorate/Fellowship)

Purpose: To promote the history of technology as a field of scholarly endeavor. **Focus:** History. **Qualif.:** Applicants must be working on projects in the history of technology and have completed all requirements for their doctorate except for the dissertation by September 1 of the year of the award is made. **Criteria:** Recipients will be selected based on the committee's criteria.

Funds Avail.: $4,000. **Duration:** Annual. **To Apply:** Applicants must submit their curriculum vitae; a 3-5 page (750-1250 words) summary of abstract of the proposed dissertation which applicants should describe how their research contributes to the history of technology; a 1-2 page (250-500 words) description of how the applicants intend to use the funds; and letter of recommendation from the students' respective dissertation director. **Deadline:** April 15.

8582 ■ SHOT-NASA Fellowships *(Doctorate, Postdoctorate/Fellowship)*

Purpose: To promote the history of technology as a field of scholarly endeavor. **Focus:** Indian studies (Asia). **Qualif.:** Applicant must possess a doctorate in history of technology or in a closely related field, or be enrolled as a student in a doctoral degree program and have completed all requirements for the Ph.D., except the dissertation in history of technology or a related field. **Criteria:** Selection will be based on the committee's criteria.

Funds Avail.: $21,500. **Duration:** Annual. **To Apply:** Applicant must submit an application form, curriculum vitae, two letters of recommendation and a research proposal of not more than six pages, double-spaced. **Deadline:** April 1.

8583 ■ Society for Human Resource Management (SHRM)
1800 Duke St.
Alexandria, VA 22314
Ph: (703)548-3440
Fax: (703)535-6490
Free: 800-253-7476
E-mail: shrm@shrm.org
URL: www.shrm.org

8584 ■ Susan R. Meisinger Fellowship for Graduate Study in HR *(Graduate, Master's, Advanced Professional/Fellowship)*

Purpose: To support master's degree students who are either members of SHRM or certified HR professionals. **Focus:** Personnel administration/human resources; Resource management. **Qualif.:** Applicants must be members of SHRM; must be master's degree students or certified HR professionals. **Criteria:** Selection will be based on the committee's criteria.

Funds Avail.: Up to $20,000. **Duration:** Annual; Up to 2 years. **Number Awarded:** 1. **To Apply:** Interested applicants may download the application form online. Compile all required materials and must be submitted in one package. **Deadline:** August 17. **Contact:** Meisinger Fellowship,

SHRM Foundation Administrator, at the above address.

8585 ■ SHRM Certification Scholarships - Individual
(Professional development/Scholarship)

Purpose: To provide education scholarships to individuals pursuing study in Human Resource Management. **Focus:** Personnel administration/human resources. **Qualif.:** Applicants must be current members of SHRM that are preparing to sit for the SHRM-CP or SHRM-SCP certification exam. **Criteria:** Recipients are selected based on work experience/progression (HR involvement and future career plans); volunteer activity; and financial need.

Funds Avail.: $750 each. **Duration:** Annual. **Number Awarded:** Varies. **To Apply:** Applicants may visit the website to verify the application process and other pieces of information. **Deadline:** July 15. **Remarks:** Members who have already taken a SHRM certification exam in the current calendar year are also eligible to apply. Student members are however, not eligible.

8586 ■ SHRM Foundation Academic Scholarships
(Graduate, Undergraduate/Scholarship)

Purpose: To encourage interest and education in the field of human resources. **Focus:** Personnel administration/human resources. **Qualif.:** Applicants must be: SHRM members enrolled in a degree-seeking program pursuing an undergraduate, masters or doctorate in an HR-related field (includes business, psychology, organizational development, etc.) through an accredited institution of higher learning; and, accepted and ready to begin their studies within six months following notification of the award. **Criteria:** Scholarship recipients will be selected based primarily on merit and will be evaluated according to the criteria set by the reviewing committee.

Funds Avail.: $2,000 each. **Duration:** Annual. **Number Awarded:** Varies. **To Apply:** Applicants must complete and submit the online application using the link at the end of the scholarship web page. Such includes contact information and a series of short answer questions about their volunteer experience and their career aspirations. They will also be asked to upload a current resume that includes their SHRM/SHRM Foundation volunteer experience, and two letters of references. Reference letters should be addressed to the "SHRM Foundation Scholarship Review Committee" and should provide insight into their character, career and volunteer accomplishments, work ethic, values and need for the scholarship. **Deadline:** July 15.

8587 ■ Society for Imaging Science and Technology
7003 Kilworth Ln.
Springfield, VA 22151
Ph: (703)642-9090
Fax: (703)642-9094
E-mail: info@imaging.org
URL: www.imaging.org

8588 ■ Raymond Davis Scholarships *(Undergraduate, Graduate/Scholarship)*

Purpose: To support students who pursue full time study, in a field related to imaging, leading to an academic degree. **Focus:** Engineering, Optical; Photography. **Qualif.:** Applicant must be a graduate or undergraduate student; completed or will complete two academic years of college before the term of the scholarship; a full-time student pursu-

Awards are arranged alphabetically below their administering organizations

ing work at an accredited institution; and a student of photographic or imaging science or engineering. **Criteria:** Selection is based on the application materials submitted.

Funds Avail.: $1,000. **Duration:** Annual. **Number Awarded:** Varies. **To Apply:** Applicant must submit a completed scholarship application form together with the letters of nomination from at least two faculty members; an official transcript of college record; and a letter stating the applicant's goals and interests. **Deadline:** October 1. **Contact:** info@imaging.org.

8589 ■ Society for Industrial and Organizational Psychology (SIOP)
440 E Poe Rd., Ste. 101
Bowling Green, OH 43402-1355
Ph: (419)353-0032
Fax: (419)352-2645
E-mail: siop@siop.org
URL: www.siop.org

8590 ■ Lee Hakel Graduate Student Scholarship
(Doctorate, Graduate/Scholarship)

Purpose: To support the research of graduate students pursuing doctoral study in industrial-organizational psychology. **Focus:** Psychology. **Qualif.:** Applicants must be student affiliates of SIOP; must have an approved plan for their dissertation; must have not previously received a SIOP Graduate Student Scholarship. **Criteria:** Applicant proposals will be evaluated by the Graduate Student Scholarship Subcommittee and will be based on the following criteria: (1) expressed understanding of the field of inquiry; (2) ability of the research design to provide meaningful answers to questions posed by the researcher; (3) potential of the proposed study to make significant theoretical and application contributions to the field of industrial organization psychology.

Funds Avail.: $3,500. **Duration:** Annual. **Number Awarded:** 1. **To Apply:** Applicants must submit a 12-page maximum summary of the dissertation research, including an explanation of research design and other important aspects of the project; must provide a two-page maximum curriculum vitae including scientific publications and presentations; must have a letter from the advisor indicating that the dissertation plan has been approved; must have a letter of endorsement from the chair or director of the program in which the applicant is enrolled. **Deadline:** June 30. **Remarks:** The Lee Hakel Graduate Student Scholarship is reserved for the highest ranked student.

8591 ■ Leslie W. Joyce and Paul W. Thayer Graduate Fellowship in I-O Psychology *(Doctorate, Graduate/Fellowship)*

Purpose: To provide financial support to doctoral students in industrial-organizational (I-O) psychology who are specializing in training and development and/or selection and placement. **Focus:** Psychology. **Qualif.:** Applicants must be PhD students in I-O psychology; must specialize in training and development and/or selection and placement; must be committed to a practitioner career as evidenced by work experience and/or statement of career goals; must have some experience in an applied setting relevant to I-O. **Criteria:** Applicants will be selected based on the following criteria: (1) the quality of the undergraduate or graduate record, including appropriateness of coursework to specialization in training and development

and/or selection and placement; (2) the quality of the master's thesis or research summary, both scientifically and practically; (3) the clarity and realism of the statement of goals and aspirations; (4) relevance of any applied experience to career specialization; (5) appropriateness of faculty recommendation.

Funds Avail.: $10,000. **Duration:** Annual. **Number Awarded:** 1. **To Apply:** Applicants must submit an official copy of undergraduate and graduate transcripts; statement of graduate program goals and career aspirations; summary of the nominee's master's thesis or summary of the other completed research not to exceed 10 pages; resume that includes work assignments, paid or unpaid, related to I-O psychology; letter of recommendation from the graduate faculty and endorsement letter from the university. **Deadline:** June 30.

8592 ■ Mary L. Tenopyr Graduate Student Scholarships *(Doctorate, Graduate/Scholarship)*

Purpose: To support the research of graduate students pursuing doctoral study in industrial-organizational psychology. **Focus:** Psychology. **Qualif.:** Applicants must be student affiliates of SIOP; must have an approved plan for their dissertation; must have not previously received a SIOP Graduate Student Scholarship. **Criteria:** Applicant proposals will be evaluated by the Graduate Student Scholarship Subcommittee and will be based on the following criteria: (1) expressed understanding of the field of inquiry; (2) ability of the research design to provide meaningful answers to questions posed by the researcher; (3) potential of the proposed study to make significant theoretical and application contributions to the field of industrial organization psychology.

Funds Avail.: $3,000. **Duration:** Annual. **Number Awarded:** 1. **To Apply:** Applicants must submit a 12-page maximum summary of the dissertation research, including an explanation of research design and other important aspects of the project; a two-page maximum curriculum vitae including scientific publications and presentations; a letter from the advisor indicating that the dissertation plan has been approved; a letter of endorsement from the chair or director of the program in which the applicant is enrolled. **Deadline:** June 30. **Contact:** The Mary L. Tenopyr Graduate Student Scholarship is reserved for the author/writer of the second highest ranked paper.

8593 ■ Society for Integrative and Comparative Biology (SICB)
1313 Dolley Madison Blvd., Ste. 402
McLean, VA 22101
Ph: (703)790-1745
Fax: (703)790-2672
Free: 800-955-1236
E-mail: questions@sicb.org
URL: www.sicb.org

8594 ■ Libbie H. Hyman Memorial Scholarships
(Graduate, Undergraduate/Scholarship)

Purpose: To provide assistance to students to take courses or to pursue research on invertebrates at a marine, freshwater, or terrestrial field station. **Focus:** Zoology. **Qualif.:** Applicant must be a first or second year graduate student currently enrolled in degree programs or an advanced undergraduate. **Criteria:** Selection is based on submitted proposals.

Funds Avail.: No specific amount. **To Apply:** Applicants

Awards are arranged alphabetically below their administering organizations

must submit a research proposal. Grant applications must be filed electronically using the forms provided at the website.

8595 ■ SICB Fellowships of Graduate Student Travel (FGST) (Graduate/Fellowship)

Purpose: To provide funds for travel and other expenses for students to work at distant research laboratories, museums, or field sites. **Focus:** Biology. **Qualif.:** Applicant must be a graduate student currently enrolled in a degree program and an active member of SICB. **Criteria:** Selection is based on submitted proposals.

Funds Avail.: $2,000. **Number Awarded:** 2-3. **To Apply:** Applicants must submit a research proposal. Grant applications must be filed electronically using the forms provided at the website. All fields in the electronic form must be completed unless noted otherwise. **Remarks:** Established in 2002. **Contact:** Prof. Ryan Earley, University of Alabama; Email: rlearley@ua.edu.

8596 ■ SICB Grants-in-Aid of Research Program (GIAR) (Graduate/Grant)

Purpose: To support graduate students who conduct research in the fields of integrated and comparative biology. **Focus:** Biology. **Qualif.:** Applicant must be a graduate student currently enrolled in degree program and an active member of SICB. **Criteria:** Selection is based on submitted proposals.

Funds Avail.: No specific amount. **To Apply:** Applicants must submit a research proposal. Grant applications must be filed electronically using the forms provided at the website. All fields in the electronic form must be completed unless noted otherwise. **Deadline:** October. **Remarks:** Established in 1996. **Contact:** Prof. Ryan Earley, University of Alabama; rlearley@ua.edu.

8597 ■ Society for Judgment and Decision Making (SJDM)

c/o Bud Fennema, Secretary-Treasurer
Florida State University
College of Business
Tallahassee, FL 32306-1110
Ph: (850)644-8231
Fax: (850)644-8234
URL: www.sjdm.org

8598 ■ Jane Beattie Memorial Scholarships (Graduate, Advanced Professional, Professional development/Scholarship)

Purpose: To provide funds to subsidize travel to the U.S. for purposes of scholarly activity by foreign scholars in the area of judgment and decision research. **Focus:** General studies/Field of study not specified. **Qualif.:** Applicants should be scholars living and working outside the destination who will use the award to help pay for travel for scholarly activities associated with research in judgment and decision making. Most awards will be granted to early-career faculty or advanced graduate students at colleges and universities, but others will also be considered. **Criteria:** Awards will be granted on the basis of the committee's estimate of the prospective value of the proposed activity, its relevance to the field of judgment and decision research, the scholarly credentials of the applicant, and the extent to which the award would contribute to the applicants' success (including considerations of financial and academic need).

Funds Avail.: $625 each. **Duration:** Annual. **Number Awarded:** Maximum of 2. **To Apply:** Applicants should submit the application form, along with a one page (single-spaced) description of the planned scholarly activity and a copy of their curriculum vitae. The activity may consist of attendance at a relevant conference, or a visit to a North American or European institution. The description of activities should indicate the nature of the planned scholarly activity, with whom the applicant plans to work (if applicable), what the applicant hopes to accomplish with the visit, and why travel to North America is important to its accomplishment. Submit applications via E-mail via attachments in Word, .rtf, or .pdf format to the contact provided, with the subject "Beattie Application". **Contact:** Jonathan Baron at: baron@psych.upenn.edu.

8599 ■ Hillel Einhorn New Investigator Award (Doctorate/Award)

Purpose: To encourage outstanding work by new researchers. **Focus:** General studies/Field of study not specified. **Qualif.:** Applicants must have not yet completed their PhD, or if completed, it should be within the last five years. **Criteria:** Applicants will be evaluated based on their submitted journal-style manuscript on any topic related to judgment and decision making.

Funds Avail.: No specific amount. **Duration:** Annual. **To Apply:** Applicants must submit four copies of a journal-style manuscript on any topic related to judgment and decision making accompanied by: (1) four copies of a summary or extended abstract of the paper, not to exceed four pages in length and (2) a cover letter that includes the name of the investigator's graduate advisor and the date that the Ph.D. was awarded (if applicable). In the case of co-authored papers, if the authors are all new investigators they can be considered jointly; otherwise, the new investigator(s) must be the primary author(s) and should be the primary source of ideas. **Deadline:** June 30. **Remarks:** Established in 1988.

8600 ■ Society for Linguistic Anthropology (SLA)

c/o Prof. Brigittine M. French, Editor
Grinnell College
Dept. of Anthropology
306 Goodnow Hall
1118 Park St.
Grinnell, IA 50112
URL: www.linguisticanthropology.org

8601 ■ Society for Linguistic Anthropology Student Essay Prize (Graduate, Undergraduate/Prize)

Purpose: To promote Linguistic Anthropology. **Focus:** Anthropology. **Qualif.:** Applicants must be either undergraduate or graduate students in a degree-granting program when the paper was written; must be the sole author of the paper; and must submit the paper no more than two years after it was written. **Criteria:** Submitted essay will be evaluated on the basis of clarity, significance to the field and substantive contribution.

Funds Avail.: $500 prize and a grant of $300. **Duration:** Annual. **To Apply:** The paper must be an original work based on original research conducted by the author. The paper should be suitable for submission to the Journal of Linguistic Anthropology and must not exceed 25 double-spaced pages, not including bibliography. The paper must be submitted electronically in either .pdf or .doc format to Jillian Cavanaugh at jcavanaugh@brooklyn.cuny.edu. The

Awards are arranged alphabetically below their administering organizations

cover sheet should include the title of the paper; the author's name; the author's email address; the author's college or university affiliation; the prize category (undergraduate or graduate) for which the paper is being submitted; and the name of the faculty member who served as the student's advisor with respect to the writing of the paper.

8602 ■ Society of Louisiana Certified Public Accountants (LCPA)

2400 Veterans Memorial Blvd., Ste. 500
Kenner, LA 70062-4739
Ph: (504)464-1040
Free: 800-288-5272
URL: www.lcpa.org

8603 ■ Society of Louisiana Certified Public Accountants Scholarships *(Undergraduate/Scholarship)*

Purpose: To further develop the accounting education and the accounting profession. **Focus:** Accounting. **Qualif.:** Applicants must have 2.5 academic GPA; must be Louisiana domiciled; must be enrolled in an accounting program in a Louisiana four-year college or university; and must be at least fifth semester students. **Criteria:** Recipients are selected based on academic achievement and financial need. Preference to students in doctoral program.

Funds Avail.: $500 - 2,500. **Duration:** Annual. **Number Awarded:** Varies. **To Apply:** Applicants must complete the application form; must submit an official college transcript; essay; and Faculty Scholarship Form. **Deadline:** November 14. **Contact:** Ann Lupo, at alupo@lcpa.org.

8604 ■ Society of Manufacturing Engineers Education Foundation (SME)

1 SME Dr.
Dearborn, MI 48121-0930
Ph: (313)425-3300
Fax: (313)425-3411
E-mail: foundation@sme.org
URL: www.smeef.org

8605 ■ Walt Bartram Memorial Education Award, Region 12 and Chapter 119 *(Undergraduate/ Scholarship)*

Purpose: To provide assistance to students who are pursuing manufacturing engineering. **Focus:** Manufacturing. **Qualif.:** Applicant must be a graduating high school senior enrolling as a full-time college or university student; must be a current SME Chapter member (except high school students); must have a GPA of 2.5 on a 4.0 scale. **Criteria:** Preference is given to the applicants who will best meet the requirements.

Funds Avail.: No specific amount. **To Apply:** Interested applicants may visit the website for the application process and other details.

8606 ■ Arthur and Gladys Cervenka Scholarships *(Undergraduate/Scholarship)*

Purpose: To provide assistance to students who are pursuing manufacturing engineering. **Focus:** Manufacturing; Technology. **Qualif.:** Applicant must be an undergraduate student enrolled fulltime in a degree program in manufacturing engineering or technology; have completed a minimum of 30 college credit hours; have a GPA of 3.0 on a 4.0

scale. **Criteria:** Preference is given, but not limited to, the students in the state of Florida.

Funds Avail.: No specific amount. **To Apply:** Interested applicants may visit the website for the application process and other details.

8607 ■ Chapter 17 - St. Louis Scholarships *(Undergraduate/Scholarship)*

Purpose: To provide assistance to students who are pursuing manufacturing engineering. **Focus:** Engineering, Industrial; Manufacturing. **Qualif.:** Applicants must be enrolled full-time or part-time undergraduates in a manufacturing engineering, industrial technology or other manufacturing related degree program with a GPA of 2.5 on a 4.0 scale. **Criteria:** Recipient selection is based on: First preference: residing within the boundaries of St. Lewis Chapter 17; Second preference: residing within the state of Missouri.

Funds Avail.: No specific amount. **To Apply:** Interested applicants may visit the website for the online scholarship application process. Applicants must complete an application form and must provide a statement explaining the following: 1) applicant's career and educational objectives; 2) how this scholarship will help attain the objectives; and 3) reasons why applicants are interested in entering the manufacturing field; one copy of high school or college transcript of records; and two letters of recommendation from which one must come from a current faculty.

8608 ■ Chapter 198 - Downriver Detroit Scholarships *(Graduate, Undergraduate/Scholarship)*

Purpose: To provide students the assistance they need in their studies. **Focus:** Engineering, Industrial; Engineering, Mechanical; Manufacturing. **Qualif.:** Applicants must be enrolled full-time seeking an associate's degree, bachelor's degree or graduate degree in manufacturing, mechanical or industrial engineering, engineering technology, or industrial technology at an accredited public or private college/university in the state of Michigan; have a GPA of 2.5 on a 4.0 scale. **Criteria:** Recipients are selected based on: First preference: a child/grandchild of a current SME Downriver Chapter No. 198 member; Second preference: a SME student member of student chapter that SME Downriver Chapter No. 198 sponsors; Third preference: applicants who are residents of Michigan; Fourth preference: applicants who plan to attend a college/university in the state of Michigan.

Funds Avail.: No specific amount. **To Apply:** Interested applicants may visit the website for the online scholarship application process. Applicants must complete an application form and must provide a statement explaining the following: 1) applicants' career and educational objectives; 2) how this scholarship will help attain the objectives; and 3) reasons why applicants are interested in entering the manufacturing field; one copy of high school or college transcript of records; and two letters of recommendation from which one must come from a current faculty.

8609 ■ Chapter 23 - Quad Cities Iowa/Illinois Scholarships *(Undergraduate/Scholarship)*

Purpose: To provide assistance to students who are pursuing manufacturing engineering. **Focus:** Manufacturing. **Qualif.:** Applicant must be an undergraduate student or entering freshman pursuing a bachelor's degree in manufacturing engineering or related field on an accredited college or university in Iowa or Illinois with a GPA of 2.5 on a 4.0 scale. **Criteria:** Recipient is selected based on: First

Awards are arranged alphabetically below their administering organizations

preference: a child/grandchild/step child of a registered SME member or student member; Second preference: residing and attending college or university at Iowa or Illinois; Third preference: attending a college located in Iowa or Illinois.

Funds Avail.: No specific amount. **To Apply:** Visit the website for the online scholarship application process.

8610 ■ Chapter 31 - Peoria Endowed Scholarships
(Undergraduate/Scholarship)

Purpose: To provide assistance to students who are pursuing manufacturing engineering. **Focus:** Engineering, Industrial; Manufacturing. **Qualif.:** Applicants must be pursuing a bachelor's degree in manufacturing engineering, industrial engineering, manufacturing technology or a manufacturing related degree program at Bradley University (Peoria, Illinois) or Illinois University (Normal, Illinois); have a GPA of 3.0 on a 4.0 scale. **Criteria:** Recipient is selected based on: First preference: a North Central Peoria-Chapter 31 member (spouse/child/grandchild); Second preference: an Illinois Central College transfer student; Third preference: SME student chapter members.

Funds Avail.: No specific amount. **To Apply:** Interested applicants may visit the website for the online scholarship application process. Applicants must complete an application form and must provide a statement explaining the following: 1) applicant's career and educational objectives; 2) how this scholarship will help attain the objectives; and 3) reasons why applicants are interested in entering the manufacturing field; one copy of high school or college transcript of records; and two letters of recommendation from which one must come from a current faculty.

8611 ■ Chapter 311 - Tri City Scholarships
(Undergraduate/Scholarship)

Purpose: To promote higher education in the state of Michigan. **Focus:** Engineering, Industrial; Manufacturing. **Qualif.:** Applicants must pursue a bachelor's degree in manufacturing engineering, industrial engineering, manufacturing technology engineering or related field; have a GPA of 3.0 on a 4.0 scale. **Criteria:** Scholarship committee will give consideration to: First preference: residents of Michigan; Second preference: students enrolled in a college or university in Michigan.

Funds Avail.: No specific amount. **To Apply:** Interested applicants may visit the website for the online scholarship application process.

8612 ■ Chapter 52 - Wichita Scholarships *(Graduate, Undergraduate/Scholarship)*

Purpose: To provide students the assistance they need with their studies. **Focus:** Engineering, Industrial; Manufacturing. **Qualif.:** Applicants must pursue an associate's degree, bachelor's degree or graduate degree in manufacturing, mechanical or industrial engineering, engineering technology or industrial technology at an accredited public or private college or university in Kansas, Oklahoma or Missouri with a GPA of 2.5 on a 4.0 scale. **Criteria:** Recipients are selected based on: First preference: a child/grandchild/relative of a current SME Wichita Chapter No. 52 member; Second preference: resident of Kansas, Oklahoma or Missouri; Third preference: applicants planning to attend college or university at the state of Kansas.

Funds Avail.: No specific amount. **To Apply:** Interested applicants may visit the website for the online scholarship application process. Applicants must complete an applica-

tion form and must provide a statement explaining the following: 1) applicants' career and educational objectives; 2) how this scholarship will help attain the objectives; and 3) reasons why applicants are interested in entering the manufacturing field; one copy of high school or college transcript of records; and two letters of recommendation from which one must come from a current faculty.

8613 ■ Chapter 56 - Fort Wayne Scholarships
(Graduate, Undergraduate/Scholarship)

Purpose: To provide students the assistance they need in their studies. **Focus:** Engineering, Industrial; Manufacturing. **Qualif.:** Applicant must pursue an associate's degree, bachelor's degree or graduate degree in manufacturing, mechanical or industrial engineering, engineering technology or industrial technology at an accredited public or private college or university in Indiana with a GPA of 2.5 on a 4.0 scale. **Criteria:** Recipient is selected based on: First preference: a child/grandchild of a current SME Fort Wayne Chapter No. 56 member; Second preference: a SME student member of student chapters that SME Fort Wayne Chapter No. 56 sponsor; Third preference: residents of Indiana; Fourth preference: planning to attend a college or university in the state of Indiana.

Funds Avail.: No specific amount. **To Apply:** Interested applicants may visit the website for the online scholarship application process.

8614 ■ Chapter 6 Fairfield County Scholarships
(Undergraduate/Scholarship)

Purpose: To provide assistance to students who are pursuing manufacturing engineering. **Focus:** Manufacturing; Technology. **Qualif.:** Applicants must be undergraduate students enrolled full-time in a degree program in manufacturing, technology, or a closely related field in the United States or Canada; have a GPA of 3.0 on a 4.0 scale. **Criteria:** Preference is given, but not limited to, applicants residing in the eastern part of the United States.

Funds Avail.: No specific amount. **To Apply:** Interested applicants may visit the website for the online scholarship application process. Applicants must complete an application form and must provide a statement explaining the following: 1) applicant's career and educational objectives; 2) how this scholarship will help attain the objectives; and 3) reasons why applicants are interested in entering the manufacturing field; one copy of high school or college transcript of records; and two letters of recommendation from which one must come from a current faculty.

8615 ■ Chapter 67 - Phoenix Scholarships
(Undergraduate/Scholarship)

Purpose: To provide students the assistance they need in their studies. **Focus:** Engineering, Industrial; Manufacturing. **Qualif.:** Applicant must be a high school senior planning to enroll in a manufacturing program technology course; or an undergraduate student currently enrolled in a manufacturing engineering technology, manufacturing technology, industrial technology or related program at an accredited college or university in Arizona; have a GPA of 3.0 on a 4.0 scale. **Criteria:** Preference is given to applicants who best meet the requirements.

Funds Avail.: No specific amount. **To Apply:** Interested applicants may visit the website for the online scholarship application process.

8616 ■ Chapter 93 - Albuquerque Scholarships
(Undergraduate/Scholarship)

Purpose: To promote higher education in the local area. **Focus:** Manufacturing. **Qualif.:** Applicant must be a fresh-

Awards are arranged alphabetically below their administering organizations

man or undergraduate student pursuing a bachelor's degree in manufacturing engineering or related field at an accredited college or university in New Mexico; have a GPA of 2.5 on a 4.0 scale. **Criteria:** Scholarship committee will give consideration to: First preference: a child/grandchild/step child of a current Chapter 93 member; Second preference: an SME student member attending New Mexico university; Third preference: resident of the state of New Mexico; Fourth preference: student planning to attend an engineering college or university in the state of New Mexico.

Funds Avail.: No specific amount. **To Apply:** Interested applicants may visit the website for the online scholarship application process.

8617 ■ Chapter One - Detroit Founding Chapter Undergraduate Scholarships (Undergraduate/Scholarship)

Purpose: To provide assistance to students who are pursuing manufacturing engineering. **Focus:** Manufacturing. **Qualif.:** Applicants must be graduate or undergraduate students enrolled full-time or part-time in a manufacturing, manufacturing engineering technology or any related degree or certificate program in the following institutions: Wayne State University, Student Chapter S004; Lawrence Technological University, Student Chapter S011; University of Detroit-Mercy, Student Chapter S081; Focus: Hope, Center for Advanced Technologies, Student Chapter S279; Henry Ford Community College, Student Chapter S331; Macomb Community College, Student Chapter S071; University of Michigan - Dearborn, Student Chapter S326. Applicants must have a minimum GPA of 3.0 on a 4.0 scale; and must demonstrate good character and leadership. **Criteria:** Preference is given to applicants who are active in SME Student Chapter activities at their respective institutions or SME-Detroit Chapter One - The Founding Chapter.

Funds Avail.: No specific amount. **To Apply:** Interested applicants may visit the website for the online scholarship application process. Applicants must complete an application form and must provide a statement explaining the following: 1) applicant's career and educational objectives; 2) how this scholarship will help attain the objectives; and 3) reasons why applicants are interested in entering the manufacturing field; one copy of high school or college transcript of records; and two letters of recommendation from which one must come from a current faculty.

8618 ■ Chapter 116 - Kalamazoo - Roscoe Douglas Scholarships (Undergraduate/Scholarship)

Purpose: To provide students the assistance they need in their studies. **Focus:** Manufacturing. **Qualif.:** Applicants must be full-time undergraduate students at the Western Michigan University; must have completed at least 30 college credit hours; be pursuing a career in manufacturing engineering or manufacturing engineering technology; have a GPA of 3.0 on a 4.0 scale. **Criteria:** Preference is given to applicants who will best meet the requirements.

Funds Avail.: No specific amount. **To Apply:** Interested applicants may visit the website for the online scholarship application process. Applicants must complete an application form and must provide a statement explaining the following: 1) applicants' career and educational objectives; 2) how this scholarship will help attain the objectives; and 3) reasons why applicants are interested in entering the manufacturing field; one copy of high school or college transcript of records; and two letters of recommendation from which one must come from a current faculty.

8619 ■ Future Leaders of Manufacturing Scholarships (Graduate, Undergraduate/Scholarship)

Purpose: To provide students the assistance they need in their education. **Focus:** Engineering; Engineering, Industrial; Manufacturing. **Qualif.:** Candidates must be SME Student Chapter members; must be nominated by their faculty advisors; must be enrolled full-time undergraduate or graduate students; must be in manufacturing engineering, engineering technology, industrial technology, technical or related majors. **Criteria:** Preference is given to candidates who best meet the requirements.

Funds Avail.: No specific amount. **To Apply:** Candidates must submit a completed Nomination/Application form; a recommendation letter from the faculty advisor; a resume; transcripts.

8620 ■ SME Education Foundation Connie and Robert T. Gunter Scholarships (Undergraduate/Scholarship)

Purpose: To provide students the assistance they need in education. **Focus:** Manufacturing. **Qualif.:** Applicants must be enrolled as full-time undergraduate students in a degree program in manufacturing engineering or technology; must have completed a minimum of 30 college credit hours; must have a GPA of 3.5 on a 4.0 scale. **Criteria:** Preference is given to applicants who best meet the requirements.

Funds Avail.: No specific amount. **Duration:** Annual. **To Apply:** Visit the website for the online scholarship application process. Applicants must complete an application form; must provide a statement explaining the following: 1) applicant's career and educational objectives; 2) how this scholarship will help attain the objectives; and 3) reasons why applicants are interested in entering the manufacturing field; one copy of high school or college transcript of records; and two letters of recommendation from which one must come from a current faculty.

8621 ■ Clinton J. Helton Manufacturing Scholarships (Undergraduate/Scholarship)

Purpose: To provide students with the assistance they need in furthering their education. **Focus:** Manufacturing. **Qualif.:** Applicants must be enrolled as full-time undergraduate students in a degree seeking program in manufacturing engineering, technology or related field at an approved Colorado college (Colorado State University or University of Colorado); must have completed a minimum of 30 college credit hours; must have a GPA of 3.0 on a 4.0 scale. **Criteria:** Preference is given to applicants who best meet the requirements.

Funds Avail.: No specific amount. **Duration:** Annual. **To Apply:** Visit the website for the online scholarship application process. Applicants must complete an application form; must provide a statement explaining the following: 1) applicant's career and educational objectives; 2) how this scholarship will help attain the objectives; and 3) reasons why applicants are interested in entering the manufacturing field; one copy of high school or college transcript of records; and two letters of recommendation from which one must come from a current faculty.

8622 ■ Lucile B. Kaufman Women's Scholarships (Undergraduate/Scholarship)

Purpose: To provide students with the assistance they need in furthering their education. **Focus:** Manufacturing; Technology. **Qualif.:** Applicants must be enrolled full-time undergraduate students in a degree program in manufactur-

Awards are arranged alphabetically below their administering organizations

ing engineering, technology, or related field in the United States or Canada; must be female; have a GPA of 3.0 on a 4.0 scale; have completed at least 30 college credits. **Criteria:** Preference is given to applicants who best meet the requirements.

Funds Avail.: No specific amount. **To Apply:** Visit the website for the online scholarship application process. Applicants must complete an application form; must provide (300 words) statement explaining the following: 1) applicant's career and educational objectives; 2) how this scholarship will help attain the objectives; and 3) reasons why applicants are interested in entering the manufacturing field; one copy of high school or college transcript of records; and two letters of recommendation from which one must come from a current faculty.

8623 ■ E. Wayne Kay Co-op Scholarships
(Undergraduate/Award, Scholarship)

Purpose: To financially support students in their education. **Focus:** Manufacturing. **Qualif.:** Applicant must be enrolled as a full-time undergraduate student in a manufacturing engineering or technology degree program in the United States or Canada; must be working through a co-op program in a manufacturing related environment; must have completed a minimum of 30 college credit hours; have a GPA of 3.0 on a 4.0 scale; must provide an evidence of demonstrated excellence related to manufacturing engineering or technology that may include a project completed for the applicant's employer. **Criteria:** Preference is given to applicants who best meet the requirements.

Funds Avail.: $1,000. **To Apply:** Visit the website for the online scholarship application process. Applicant must complete an application form; must provide a statement explaining the following: 1) applicant's career and educational objectives; 2) how this scholarship will help attain the objectives; and reasons why an applicant is interested in entering the manufacturing field; one copy of high school or college transcript of records; and must present a letter of recommendation from his/her employer and a letter of support from a current faculty.

8624 ■ E. Wayne Kay Community College Scholarships *(Undergraduate/Scholarship)*

Purpose: To provide students the assistance they need in studying. **Focus:** Manufacturing. **Qualif.:** Applicant must be a graduating high school senior or a full-time undergraduate student enrolled in a degree program in manufacturing or related field at a two-year community college or trade school in the U.S. or Canada; freshman or sophomore with less than 60 college credit hours completed and pursuing a career in manufacturing engineering or technology; have a GPA of 3.0 on a 4.0 scale. **Criteria:** Preference is given to applicants who best meet the requirements.

Funds Avail.: No specific amount. **Duration:** Annual. **To Apply:** Interested applicants may visit the website for the online scholarship application process.

8625 ■ E. Wayne Kay High School Scholarships
(Undergraduate/Scholarship)

Purpose: To provide students the assistance they need in attending at an accredited college or university. **Focus:** Manufacturing. **Qualif.:** Applicant must be a graduating high school senior with an overall GPA of 3.0 on a 4.0 scale for high school senior year. **Criteria:** Preference is given to applicants who best meet the requirements.

Funds Avail.: No specific amount. **To Apply:** Interested

applicants may visit the website for the online scholarship application process.

8626 ■ Giuliano Mazzetti Scholarships
(Undergraduate/Scholarship)

Purpose: To provide students the assistance they need in studying manufacturing engineering or technology in the United States or Canada. **Focus:** Manufacturing; Technology. **Qualif.:** Program is open to undergraduate students enrolled full-time in a degree program in manufacturing engineering, technology, or related field in the United States or Canada; must have completed at least 30 college credit hours; must have a GPA of 3.0 on a 4.0 scale. **Criteria:** Preference is given to applicants who best meet the requirements.

Funds Avail.: No specific amount. **Duration:** Annual. **To Apply:** Interested applicants may visit the website for the online scholarship application process. Applicants must complete the application form and must provide (300 words) statement explaining the following: 1) applicants' career and educational objectives in manufacturing engineering or any related field; 2) how this scholarship will help attain the objectives; and 3) reasons why applicants are interested in entering this field; one copy of high school or college transcript of records; two letters of recommendation from which one must come from current school faculty.

8627 ■ Chapter 63 - Portland James E. Morrow Scholarships *(Graduate, Undergraduate/Scholarship)*

Purpose: To promote higher education in the local area. **Focus:** Manufacturing. **Qualif.:** Applicants must be students pursuing a career in manufacturing or any related field; have a GPA of 2.5 on a 4.0 scale. **Criteria:** Recipients are selected based on: First preference: a child/grandchild/step child of a current Chapter 63 member; Second preference: SME student chapter members in Oregon or southwest Washington; Third preference: applicants planning to attend school in Oregon or southwest Washington; Fourth preference: applicants residing within Oregon and Washington.

Funds Avail.: No specific amount. **To Apply:** Interested applicants may visit the website for the online scholarship application process. Applicants must complete an application form and must provide a statement explaining the following: 1) applicants' career and educational objectives; 2) how this scholarship will help attain the objectives; and 3) reasons why applicants are interested in entering the manufacturing field; one copy of high school or college transcript of records; and two letters of recommendation from which one must come from a current faculty.

8628 ■ Clarence and Josephine Myers Scholarships
(Graduate, Undergraduate/Scholarship)

Purpose: To provide students the assistance they need in their education. **Focus:** Engineering, Industrial; Engineering, Mechanical; Manufacturing. **Qualif.:** Applicant must be a graduate or undergraduate student pursuing an associate, bachelor or graduate degree in manufacturing, machinable or industrial engineering in the state of Indiana; have a GPA of 3.0 on a 4.0 scale. **Criteria:** Applicants who plan to attend or are currently attending a college/university in Indiana; who attended Arsenal Technological High School in Indianapolis; SME student members of SME Chapter 37 sponsored chapters; children/grandchildren of a current SME Chapter 37 member, will be given special consideration by the Scholarships Committee.

Funds Avail.: No specific amount. **To Apply:** Interested

Awards are arranged alphabetically below their administering organizations

applicants may visit the website for the online scholarship application process. Applicants must complete an application form and must provide a statement explaining the following: 1) applicants' career and educational objectives; 2) how this scholarship will help attain the objectives; and 3) reasons why applicants are interested in entering the manufacturing field; one copy of high school or college transcript of records; and two letters of recommendation from which one must come from a current faculty.

8629 ■ North Central, Region 9 Scholarships (Undergraduate/Scholarship)

Purpose: To provide students the assistance they need in education. **Focus:** Engineering, Industrial; Engineering, Mechanical; Manufacturing. **Qualif.:** Applicant must be an enrolled full-time undergraduate student pursuing a bachelor's degree or associate's degree in manufacturing, mechanical, industrial engineering or industrial engineering or industrial technology at a two- or four-year college/university within the North Central Region (Iowa, Minnesota, Nebraska, North Dakota, South Dakota, Wisconsin and upper peninsula of Michigan); have a GPA of 3.0 on a 4.0 scale. **Criteria:** Preference is based on: First preference: applicants who are SME members, their spouses or children/grandchildren from the North Central Region; Second Preference: applicants who reside in North Central Region (Iowa, Minnesota, Nebraska, North Dakota, South Dakota, Wisconsin and upper peninsula of Michigan).

Funds Avail.: No specific amount. **To Apply:** Interested applicants may visit the website for the online scholarship application process.

8630 ■ Edward S. Roth Manufacturing Engineering Scholarships (Graduate, Undergraduate/Scholarship)

Purpose: To provide assistance to students who are pursuing manufacturing engineering. **Focus:** Manufacturing. **Qualif.:** Applicant must be a U.S. citizen; must be a graduating high school senior or a current full-time graduate or undergraduate student pursuing a bachelor's or master's degree in manufacturing engineering from an ABET-accredited school (California Polytechnic State University, CA; California State Polytechnic University, CA; University of Miami, FL; Bradley University, IL; Central State University, OH; Miami University, OH; Boston University, MA; Worcester Polytechnic Institute, MA; University of Massachusetts, MA; St. Cloud State University, MN; The University of Texas - Pan American, TX; Brigham Young University, UT; Utah State University, UT); must have a GPA of 3.0 on a 4.0 scale. **Criteria:** Preference is given to applicants with demonstrated financial need, minority students, and students participating in a Co-Op program.

Funds Avail.: No specific amount. **To Apply:** Interested applicants may contact the SMEEF for the application process and other information.

8631 ■ Prof. George Schneider, Jr. Manufacturing Technology Education Scholarships (Undergraduate/Scholarship)

Purpose: To provide students the assistance they need in education. **Focus:** Manufacturing. **Qualif.:** Applicants must be enrolled at least 6 credit hours per semester; pursuing a bachelor's degree in manufacturing engineering, manufacturing engineering technology or related field at the Lawrence Technological University; have a GPA of 2.5 on a 4.0 scale; have completed at least 60 college credit hours. **Criteria:** Preference is given to applicants who best meet the requirements.

Funds Avail.: No specific amount. **Number Awarded:** 2. **To Apply:** The College of Engineering Dean at Lawrence Technological University will recommend two to three candidates for the scholarship annually. A letter of recommendation for the nominated student is provided by the Chair of the School of Technology at Lawrence Technological University.

8632 ■ SME Directors Scholarships (Undergraduate/Scholarship)

Purpose: To provide students the assistance they need in education. **Focus:** Manufacturing. **Qualif.:** Applicants must be undergraduate students enrolled full-time in a manufacturing degree program at a U.S. or Canadian college; have completed at least 30 college credit hours; pursuing a career in manufacturing; have a GPA of 3.5 on a 4.0 scale. **Criteria:** Preference is given to applicants who demonstrate leadership skills in a community, academic, or professional environment.

Funds Avail.: No specific amount. **Duration:** Annual. **To Apply:** Interested applicants may visit the website for the online scholarship application process.

8633 ■ SME Education Foundation Family Scholarships (Undergraduate/Scholarship)

Purpose: To support the children or grandchildren of SME members. **Focus:** Manufacturing. **Qualif.:** Applicant must pursue a degree in manufacturing engineering, manufacturing engineering technology, or a related manufacturing field of study; must be a resident and attending in an accredited institution in the United States or Canada; must have at least one parent or grandparent that became an SME member for two years in good standing; must be graduating high school senior or undergraduate with up to 30 credit hours completed; enrolling full-time at a college or university; have a GPA of 3.0 on a 4.0 scale; have a minimum 1000 SAT score and/or 21 ACT score. **Criteria:** Recipient selection is based on academic excellence; communication and interpersonal skills; interest in manufacturing engineering, manufacturing engineering technology, or related field; and on extracurricular activities.

Funds Avail.: No specific amount. **To Apply:** Applicants must complete the Scholarship Application Process; and submit a 300-word student statement letter explaining: career objectives in manufacturing engineering, manufacturing engineering technology, or related fields; educational objectives; how the scholarship will help with the objectives; reason for entering this field. Applicants must also include a two-page resume; official transcripts; two letters of recommendation from current or former employers or teachers; a copy of SAT or ACT test results; an essay about the applicant's favorite manufacturing engineer.

8634 ■ Chapter 63 - Portland Uncle Bud Smith Scholarships (Graduate, Undergraduate/Scholarship)

Purpose: To promote higher education in the local area. **Focus:** Manufacturing. **Qualif.:** Applicant must be a student pursuing a career in manufacturing or any related field; have a GPA of 2.5 on a 4.0 scale. **Criteria:** selection is based on: First preference: a child/grandchild/step child of a current Chapter 63 member; Second preference: a SME student chapter member in Oregon or southwest Washington; Third preference: planning to attend school in Oregon or southwest Washington; Fourth preference: applicants residing within Oregon and Washington.

Funds Avail.: No specific amount. **To Apply:** Interested applicants may visit the website for the online scholarship application process.

Awards are arranged alphabetically below their administering organizations

8635 ■ Society of Manufacturing Engineers Ford PAS Scholarships (SME) *(Undergraduate/Scholarship)*

Purpose: To provide assistance to students who are pursuing manufacturing engineering. **Focus:** Engineering; Technology. **Qualif.:** Applicant must be a current or former student of a Ford PAS program at their high school or in a Ford PAS after-school/weekend/summer/college program; must be pursuing a bachelor/associate degree in engineering or technology at an accredited college or university in the United States; must have a GPA of 3.0 on a 4.0 scale. **Criteria:** Preference will be given to applicants who attend University of Michigan-Dearborn.

Funds Avail.: No specific amount. **To Apply:** Applicant must submit two reference letters, one from a Ford PAS instructor.

8636 ■ Chapter 4 - Lawrence A. Wacker Memorial Awards *(Undergraduate/Scholarship)*

Purpose: To provide students the assistance they need in studying. **Focus:** Engineering, Industrial; Engineering, Mechanical; Manufacturing. **Qualif.:** Applicant must pursue a bachelor's degree in manufacturing, mechanical or industrial engineering; have a GPA of 3.0 on a 4.0 scale; must reside and attend an accredited institution in the U.S. or Canada. **Criteria:** Scholarship committee will give special considerations for: First preference: applicants who are Chapter 4 members (spouses, children or grandparents); Second preference: applicants who reside within Wisconsin counties (Milwaukee, Ozaukee, Washington and Waukesha); Third preference: applicants who reside within the state of Wisconsin.

Funds Avail.: No specific amount. **To Apply:** Interested applicants may visit the website for the online scholarship application process.

8637 ■ Myrtle and Earl Walker Scholarships *(Undergraduate/Scholarship)*

Purpose: To provide students the assistance they need in studying manufacturing engineering or technology. **Focus:** Manufacturing; Technology. **Qualif.:** Applicant must be an undergraduate student enrolled full-time in a degree program in manufacturing engineering or technology in the U.S. or Canada; must have completed at least 15 college credit hours or one semester; must be pursuing a career in manufacturing engineering or technology; must have a GPA of 3.0 on a 4.0 scale. **Criteria:** Preference is given to applicants who best meet the requirements.

Funds Avail.: $2,500 per recipient. **Duration:** Annual. **To Apply:** Interested applicants may visit the website for the online scholarship application process.

8638 ■ Allen and Loureena Weber Scholarships *(Undergraduate/Scholarship)*

Purpose: To provide assistance to those students who are pursuing degree program in Manufacturing Engineering/Technology, Mechanical Engineering, Industrial Engineering/Technology or Engineering Technology. **Focus:** Engineering; Engineering, Industrial; Engineering, Mechanical; Manufacturing. **Qualif.:** Applicant must be a student of the University of Northern Kentucky with a satisfactory GPA; should reflect the interest of the donor in "individuals who possess technical aptitude and desire for education and practical learning". **Criteria:** Recipients are selected based on: First preference: graduates of Dayton High School (Dayton, KY); Second preference: other high schools in the Dayton, KY area including Newport High School (Newport, KY).

Funds Avail.: No specific amount. **To Apply:** Interested applicants may visit the website for the application process and other details.

8639 ■ William E. Weisel Scholarships *(Undergraduate/Scholarship)*

Purpose: To provide students the with assistance they need in furthering their education. **Focus:** Engineering; Technology. **Qualif.:** Applicants must be U.S. citizens; undergraduate students enrolled full-time in an engineering or technology program in the U.S. or Canada; have completed at least 30 college credit hours; have a GPA of 3.0 on a 4.0 scale. **Criteria:** Preference is given to applicants who intend to apply their knowledge in the sub-specialty of medical robotics.

Funds Avail.: No specific amount. **Duration:** Annual. **To Apply:** Interested applicants may visit the website for the online scholarship application process. **Remarks:** Established in 1985.

8640 ■ Albert E. Wischmeyer Memorial Scholarships *(Undergraduate/Scholarship)*

Purpose: To provide assistance to students who are pursuing manufacturing engineering. **Focus:** Engineering, Mechanical; Manufacturing. **Qualif.:** Applicants must be graduating high school seniors or undergraduates pursuing a degree in manufacturing engineering, manufacturing engineering technology, or mechanical technology; attending an accredited institution in New York State; must be residents of Western New York; must have a GPA of 2.5 on a 4.0 scale. **Criteria:** Recipients will be selected based on the application materials submitted.

Funds Avail.: No specific amount. **To Apply:** Students must write for applications. Applicants must complete an application form; must provide a statement explaining the following: 1) applicant's career and educational objectives; 2) how this scholarship will help attain the objectives; and 3) reasons why applicants are interested in entering the manufacturing field; one copy of high school or college transcript of records; and two letters of recommendation from which one must come from a current faculty.

8641 ■ Society of Marine Port Engineers (SMPE)
111 Broad St.
Eatontown, NJ 07724
Ph: (732)389-2009
Fax: (732)389-2264
URL: www.smpe.org

8642 ■ Society of Marine Port Engineers Scholarship Loans *(Undergraduate/Scholarship loan, Loan)*

Purpose: To assist members of SMPE and their families in pursuing higher studies. **Focus:** General studies/Field of study not specified. **Qualif.:** Program is open to children of SMPE members with a minimum of three years membership; and must be attending or accepted as full-time students in the next regular term of indicated institutions of higher education. **Criteria:** Recipients are selected based on merit.

Funds Avail.: No specific amount. **To Apply:** Application forms and instructions are available at the SMPE website.

8643 ■ Society for Maternal-Fetal Medicine (SMFM)
409 12th St. SW
Washington, DC 20024

Awards are arranged alphabetically below their administering organizations

Ph: (202)863-2476
Fax: (202)554-1132
E-mail: smfm@smfm.org
URL: www.smfm.org

8644 ■ SMFM/AAOGF Scholarship Awards
(Graduate/Scholarship)

Purpose: To support a single scholarship in maternal-fetal medicine. **Focus:** Medicine, Gynecological and obstetrical. **Qualif.:** Applicants must be a member of SMFM. **Criteria:** Scholarship is awarded based on the committee's criteria.

Funds Avail.: $100,000 per year of which at least $5,000 but not more than $15,000 must be used for employee benefits where the scholarship is awarded. **Duration:** One year. **Deadline:** July 1. **Remarks:** With the enthusiastic support of the Board of Directors of the SMFM and the Council of the American Association of Obstetrical Society and the Endowment Fund Committee of the American Association of Obstetricians and Gynecologists Foundation (AAOGF), the SMFM and AAOGF has entered into a partnership to support a single scholarship in maternal-fetal medicine. **Contact:** SMFM at the above address.

8645 ■ Society for Military History (SMH)
George C. Marshall Library
Virginia Military Institute
Lexington, VA 24450-1600
Ph: (540)464-7468
Fax: (540)464-7330
E-mail: jmhsmh@vmi.edu
URL: www.smh-hq.org

8646 ■ ABC-Clio Research Grants *(Graduate/Grant)*

Purpose: To support the work of advanced graduate students and those scholars who do not hold a doctoral degree but are employed full-time as historians. **Focus:** History, Military. **Qualif.:** Applicant must be a member of the Society for Military History; a graduate student enrolled in a doctoral program; or employed full-time as a professional historian without a doctoral degree. **Criteria:** Grant recipients will be selected based on the jury's review of the application materials.

Funds Avail.: $500. **Duration:** Annual. **To Apply:** Applicants must submit a curriculum vita (maximum of 5 pages) which includes a statement of 500 words about the project description, uses of funds, and other sources of financial support already received. Applicants must also submit a one-page bibliography of the recent relevant secondary work on the topic. **Deadline:** January 16.

8647 ■ Society for Mining, Metallurgy, and Exploration (SME)
12999 E Adam Aircraft Cir.
Englewood, CO 80112
Ph: (303)948-4200
Fax: (303)973-3845
Free: 800-763-3132
URL: www.smenet.org

8648 ■ SME Coal and Energy Division Scholarships
(Undergraduate/Scholarship)

Purpose: To provide support to students of Mining Engineering program. **Focus:** Engineering, Mining and Mineral;

Metallurgy; Mineralogy; Mining. **Qualif.:** Applicants must be junior or senior students majoring in mining or mineral engineering programs that are accredited by the Accreditation Board for Engineering and Technology (ABET). Applicants must be student members of SME and must have a minimum cumulative 2.50 GPA. Applicants who have received a previous Coal and Energy Division Scholarship may, upon submitting a new application, be granted a scholarship, subject to the recommendations of the college or university the recipient is attending and review by the Scholarship Committee. **Criteria:** Scholarship recipients are selected based on the academic record, character and financial need.

Funds Avail.: No specific amount. **Duration:** Annual. **Number Awarded:** 1. **To Apply:** Applicants must submit a completed application form, transcript and two letters of recommendation, one of which must be from the Program Chair or Department Head. Application form should include a brief outline of the applicant's participation in mining industry-related activities (such as the student chapter or local section of SME), coal industry employment or employment commitment, scholastic achievements and an explanation why the applicant is interested in a career in coal and is deserving of Coal and Energy Division support. **Deadline:** October 15. **Contact:** Scholarship Coordinator, SME Member Services Department; Phone: 303-948-4208; E-mail: scholarships@smenet.org.

8649 ■ SME Environmental Division Scholarships
(Undergraduate, Graduate/Scholarship)

Purpose: To support promising college students who have chosen as a career path the field of mining and the environment. **Focus:** Engineering, Mining and Mineral; Metallurgy; Mineralogy; Mining. **Qualif.:** Candidates must be promising college students who desire to develop their skills related to mining and the environment. Candidates must be of good character and must have demonstrated scholastic aptitude; must be members of SME, attending a college or university of their choice that provides a curriculum leading to an undergraduate degree related to mining and the environment and a faculty advisor with special interests in an environmentally oriented program. **Criteria:** Scholarship recipients are selected based on scholastic ability, potential, professional interest, character and financial need.

Funds Avail.: $2,000. **Duration:** Annual. **Number Awarded:** Varies. **To Apply:** Applicants must submit a completed application form, transcript and two references from faculty members, people from industry, or others who can write about their academic potential and professional interests. **Deadline:** October 15. **Contact:** Scholarship Coordinator, SME Member Services Department; Phone: 303-948-4208; E-mail: scholarships@smenet.org.

8650 ■ Society of Naval Architects and Marine Engineers (SNAME)
601 Pavonia Ave.
Jersey City, NJ 07306
Ph: (201)798-4800
Fax: (201)798-4975
Free: 800-798-2188
E-mail: ccali-poutre@sname.org
URL: www.sname.org

8651 ■ Robert N. Herbert Undergraduate Scholarships
(Undergraduate/Scholarship)

Purpose: To encourage study in naval architecture, marine engineering, ocean engineering or marine industry-related

Awards are arranged alphabetically below their administering organizations

fields. **Focus:** Architecture, Naval; Engineering, Marine; Engineering, Ocean. **Qualif.:** Applicants must be planning to study in the U.S. or Canada; applicants must study toward a degree in naval architecture, marine engineering, ocean engineering or marine industry related fields at an accredited school; applicants must be entering junior or senior year. **Criteria:** Recipients are selected based on/or in accordance with the colleges' established procedures.

Funds Avail.: $5,000. **Duration:** Annual. **To Apply:** Applicants must complete the online application form; applicants must submit a transcript of records or any proof that he/she is currently enrolled or have been accepted by the school, college, or university. **Deadline:** June 1 - application; June 15 - supporting documents. **Contact:** Brittany Greer at bgreer@sname.org.

8652 ■ Mandell and Lester Rosenblatt Undergraduate Scholarships (Undergraduate/Scholarship)

Purpose: To encourage study in naval architecture, marine engineering, ocean engineering or marine industry-related fields. **Focus:** Architecture, Naval; Engineering, Marine; Engineering, Ocean. **Qualif.:** Applicants must be U.S. or Canadian citizens who are actively involved with SNAME and other professional organizations. **Criteria:** Recipients are selected based on the scholarship committee's recommendations and the executive committee's approval.

Funds Avail.: $6,000. **Duration:** Annual. **To Apply:** Applicants must complete the application form; must provide an evidence of sound academic achievement; a 500-600 word application essay; three letters of professional recommendations in which the two must be NA/ME/OE faculty who have had the student in class and at least two of whom are SNAME members. **Deadline:** June 1 - application; June 15 - supporting documents. **Contact:** Brittany Greer at bgreer@sname.org.

8653 ■ John V. Wehausen Graduate Scholarships for Advanced Study in Ship Hydrodynamics and Wave Theory (Graduate/Scholarship)

Purpose: To support students of naval architecture and marine engineering with their educational expenses. **Focus:** Engineering, Marine. **Qualif.:** Applicants must be graduate students and members of SNAME or another recognized marine society. **Criteria:** Selection will be based on the committee's criteria.

Funds Avail.: Up to $15,000. **To Apply:** Application form is available on the website by downloading.

8654 ■ Society of Nuclear Medicine and Molecular Imaging (SNMMI)

1850 Samuel Morse Dr.
Reston, VA 20190
Ph: (703)708-9000
Fax: (703)708-9015
URL: www.snmmi.org

8655 ■ Mitzi and William Blahd, MD Pilot Research Grants (Doctorate/Grant)

Purpose: To help basic or clinical scientists in the early stages of their career conduct research that may lead to further funding. **Focus:** Medicine, Nuclear. **Qualif.:** Applicants must be basic or clinical scientists with an advanced degree, such as MD, PhD or equivalent; must hold a full-time position in an educational institution when the award starts; must be no more than five years post

nuclear medicine/molecular imaging training; must not have served as the principal investigator of a peer-reviewed grant for more than $50,000 in a single calendar year; must be members of SNMMI at the time of award. **Criteria:** Preference will be given to individuals who have demonstrated great potential for a research career in the field of nuclear medicine/molecular imaging and whose research focuses on translational in vivo studies that include radionuclide imaging or therapy.

Funds Avail.: $25,000. **Duration:** Annual.

8656 ■ Paul Cole Scholarships (Undergraduate/Scholarship)

Purpose: To provide financial support to students for educational careers in line with nuclear medicine technology. **Focus:** Medicine, Nuclear. **Qualif.:** Applicants must demonstrate financial need; be enrolled or accepted in an institution accredited through the Joint Review Committee on Educational Programs in Nuclear Medicine Technology (JRCNMT); have a minimum cumulative GPA of 2.5 or better (on a 4.0 scale) or B average in a nuclear medicine technology core curriculum. **Criteria:** Applicants will be evaluated based on financial need, statement of goals, academic performance and program director evaluation.

Funds Avail.: $1,000. **To Apply:** Applicants must submit completed application including statement and program director's signature; official transcripts of all formal education; and complete evaluation from the program director whose signature verifies the applicant's acceptance into or enrollment in the nuclear medicine technology program. **Contact:** Any questions can be directed to Nicole Mitchell at the above address. or e-mail her at nmitchell@snm.org.

8657 ■ SNMMI Robert E. Henkin, MD, Government Relations Fellowship (Professional development/Fellowship)

Purpose: To provide young professionals in nuclear medicine and molecular imaging direct personal exposure to government relations activities of the SNMMI as well as the state and federal legislative and regulatory process. **Focus:** Medicine, Nuclear. **Qualif.:** Applicants must be young professionals who are resident or fellow physicians, scientists or technologists who have been completed their training within the last 10 years. **Criteria:** Selection will be based on a combination of the following criteria: record of professional achievement in one's career; evidence of leadership skills and the potential for further growth; demonstrated commitment to public service evidenced by prior government relations positions; sincere desire to achieve the goals and objectives of the Fellowship in the form of an essay on why the applicant thinks they should be selected; skills to succeed at the highest levels in nuclear medicine and molecular imaging, and the ability to work effectively as part of a team; exceptional writing ability, a positive attitude, and strong leadership skills.

Funds Avail.: No specific amount. **To Apply:** Applicants will be asked to provide curriculum vitae and a written statement of their interest in health policy and regulatory affairs. Two letters of recommendation in support of the application may be submitted, but will not be required. **Deadline:** December 31. **Remarks:** Established in 2013.

8658 ■ Professional Development and Education Fund (PDEF) Professional Development Scholarships (Professional development/Scholarship)

Purpose: To support students who are employed as technologists and actively pursuing an advanced degree

Awards are arranged alphabetically below their administering organizations

related to their nuclear medicine career. **Focus:** Medicine, Nuclear. **Qualif.:** Candidates must: be active members of the SNMMI Technologist Section; have completed eight or more hours in the last three years matriculating toward an accredited advanced degree program that is intended to further their career in nuclear medicine; have maintained a GPA of 3.0 or better on a 4.0 scale; have worked in the nuclear medicine profession for at least one of the past five years in a clinical or didactic setting. **Criteria:** Selection will be based on the committee's criteria.

Funds Avail.: $5,000. **Duration:** Annual. **To Apply:** Candidates must complete and submit the following requirements: a completed application, which includes personal and financial information and the advanced degree program information; current resume or curriculum vitae; official transcripts of all formal education issued directly from the institution's registrar office; a statement, not to exceed two pages. The brief statement should detail their activity level in the SNMMI Technologist Section and should address their professional achievements and their career and educational goals, and how their advanced degree in the field of nuclear medicine will help them to achieve their goals; a completed evaluation from the program dean/director/advisor; a completed evaluation from their professional supervisor. **Deadline:** August 1.

8659 ■ SNMMI-TS Advanced Practitioner Program Scholarship *(Professional development/Scholarship)*

Purpose: To support students who are pursuing an advanced practitioner program to advance their career in nuclear medicine. **Focus:** Medicine, Nuclear. **Qualif.:** Candidates must: demonstrate financial need; be currently accepted into the Nuclear Medicine Advanced Associate Degree Program offered by the University of Arkansas for Medical Sciences; be members of the SNMMI-TS. **Criteria:** Selection will be based on the committee's criteria.

Funds Avail.: No specific amount. **Duration:** Annual. **To Apply:** Candidates must complete and submit the following requirements: a completed application, which includes personal and financial information; current resume or curriculum vitae; official transcripts of all formal education issued directly from the institution's registrar office; a statement, not to exceed two pages. The brief statement should detail their activity level in the SNMMI Technologist Section and should address their professional achievements and their career and educational goals, and how the advanced practitioner program in the field of nuclear medicine will help them to achieve their goals; a scanned copy of original program acceptance notification. **Deadline:** January 28.

8660 ■ SNMTS Bachelor's Degree Completion Scholarships *(Undergraduate/Scholarship)*

Purpose: To support students pursuing a Bachelor's degree completion program related to their nuclear medicine career. **Focus:** General studies/Field of study not specified. **Qualif.:** Applicants must demonstrate financial need; hold a certificate or associate's degree in nuclear medicine technology; currently enrolled in a bachelor's level program to advance their career in nuclear medicine; have a minimum cumulative GPA of 2.5 or better (on 4.0 scale) or B average in the program's core curriculum, and member of the SNMTS. **Criteria:** Candidates will be judged based on the criteria designed by the Scholarship Committee.

Funds Avail.: $4,000. **Duration:** Annual. **Number Awarded:** 2. **To Apply:** Applicants must submit a completed application, which includes applicant's statement and recommenders' signature; official transcripts of all

formal education (high school transcripts are not necessary if transcripts of college level work are submitted); a letter of recommendation from an educational or professional reference; an official transcript or letter from the institution's registrar's office verifying the applicant's enrollment or acceptance in the Bachelor's degree program.

8661 ■ SNMTS Clinical Advancement Scholarships *(Other/Scholarship)*

Purpose: To support technologists who are pursuing clinical advancement through didactic educational programs. **Focus:** Biological and clinical sciences. **Qualif.:** Applicants must demonstrate financial need; be currently enrolled in didactic educational programs (ex. CT, DEXA, physics, statistics); complete the said class or program; and members of the SNMTS. **Criteria:** Candidates will be judged based on the criteria designed by the Scholarship Committee.

Funds Avail.: $500. **Duration:** Annual. **Number Awarded:** 3. **To Apply:** Applicants must submit a completed application, which includes applicant's statement and recommenders' signature; official transcripts of all formal education (high school transcripts are not necessary if transcripts of college level work are submitted); letter of recommendation from an educational or professional reference; an official transcript or letter from the institution's registrar's office verifying the applicant's enrollment or acceptance in the educational programs. **Deadline:** May 31. **Contact:** Nicole Mitchell, Program Manager, 703-652-6795 or e-mail at nmitchell@snm.org.

8662 ■ SNNMI Predoctoral Molecular Imaging Scholar Program *(Doctorate/Scholarship)*

Purpose: To be used for salary support of the principal investigator, as well as direct costs of supplies and equipment. **Focus:** Medicine, Nuclear. **Qualif.:** Applicants must have advanced to candidacy in PhD or MD or equivalent; must be full-time students in an educational setting when the award starts; must be members of SNMMI at the time of award. Preference will be given to individuals who have demonstrated great potential for a research career in the field of molecular imaging. The research may be done in any country. **Criteria:** Applicants will be evaluated on the following: Relevance - proposal is highly relevant to the grant description; Originality - how innovative is the proposed project; Importance - advances clinical care or makes a significant contribution to scientific knowledge or understanding of disease; Methods - sound methodology that is likely to prove the hypothesis; Likelihood of Success - applicants have the knowledge/skills, resources to successfully conclude the project.

Funds Avail.: $22,500. **Duration:** Annual. **To Apply:** Applicants must complete and submit their applications together with the following: Principal investigator's current curriculum vitae; a research abstract and a detailed research proposal not to exceed 7 pages, excluding references; one letter of recommendation from the program director or research supervisor; one letter of recommendation from a professional colleague. **Deadline:** January 31.

8663 ■ Marc Tetalman, MD, Memorial Award *(Professional development, Doctorate/Recognition)*

Purpose: To honor the research accomplishments of a young investigator who is pursuing a career in nuclear medicine. **Focus:** Medicine, Nuclear. **Qualif.:** Applicants must be 36 years of age or younger and no more than seven years from having obtained certification in nuclear

Awards are arranged alphabetically below their administering organizations

medicine or nuclear radiology or in completing a PhD program. **Criteria:** Selection will be based on the committee's criteria.

Funds Avail.: $5,000 award check and plaque . **Duration:** Biennial. **To Apply:** Applicants may be nominated by a member of the SNMMI or they may apply themselves.

8664 ■ Wagner-Torizuka Fellowships *(Professional development/Fellowship)*

Purpose: To provide experience and training in nuclear medicine/molecular imaging modalities in the areas of cardiology, neurology, and oncology. **Focus:** Medicine, Cardiology; Neurology; Oncology. **Qualif.:** Applicants must be permanent residents of Japan and must have received their Japanese MD license no more than 15 years from the time of application. **Criteria:** Selection will be based on the committee's criteria.

Funds Avail.: $24,000 each (will be paid in three installments) per annum. **Duration:** Annual. **Number Awarded:** Varies. **To Apply:** All applications must be completed online. In addition, two letters of support are required, one from the applicants' supervisor or mentor in Japan and the other from an independent, qualified source from the applicants' US/Canadian institution. **Deadline:** January 31. **Contact:** Development Department at developmenttemp@snmmi.org, or 703-652-6780.

8665 ■ Society for Obstetric Anesthesia and Perinatology (SOAP)

6737 W Washington St., Ste. 1300
Milwaukee, WI 53214
Ph: (414)389-8611
Fax: (414)276-7704
E-mail: soap@soap.org
URL: www.soap.org

8666 ■ SOAP/Kybele International Outreach Grant *(Advanced Professional, Professional development/Grant)*

Purpose: To provide funding needed to get involved with international outreach projects in order to identify and train future leaders in international outreach from SOAP members; to encourage research in collaboration with host countries with the goal of enhancing the practice of obstetric anasthesia in those countries. **Focus:** Anesthesiology. **Qualif.:** Applicants must be members of SOAP in good standing with a commitment to obstetric anesthesia. A proposal for a research project to be conducted in one of the countries where a Kybele or another outreach program must be currently active. It is anticipated that some applicants may have a specific research project in mind, while others might not yet have a concrete plan. **Criteria:** Selection will be based on the committee's criteria.

Funds Avail.: $5,000. **Duration:** Annual. **Number Awarded:** 1. **To Apply:** All documents should be in 12-point font, Word ford, with at least 0.75-inch margins and must include the following: a letter from the chair of the department confirming the department commitment to granting the time needed to fulfill the requirements of the grant; if the applicants are fellows, a letter from the fellowship director is needed highlighting the fellows' suitability for the program; curriculum vitae of the applicants; one page highlighting previous experience and motivation for seeking the grant; 1-3 pages for a proposed research project; letter of support from at least one SOAP member

with international outreach experience. The letter must address the applicants' suitability for the program; and budget. The proposed research project should include the following section: title; specific aims; significance; methods; anticipated impact; potential collaborators; country of proposed work. Application materials to be submit by either email or mail. **Deadline:** April 10. **Contact:** SOAP; Phone: 414-389-8611; E-mail: soap@soap.org.

8667 ■ Society of Otorhinolaryngology and Head-Neck Nurses (SOHN)

207 Downing St.
New Smyrna Beach, FL 32168
Ph: (386)428-1695
Fax: (386)423-7566
E-mail: info@sohnnurse.com
URL: www.sohnnurse.com

8668 ■ SOHN Scholarship *(Undergraduate/Scholarship)*

Purpose: To provide opportunities for professional interaction, education and growth. **Focus:** Medicine; Nursing. **Qualif.:** Applicants must be current members of SOHN. **Criteria:** Selection will be based on the committee's criteria.

Funds Avail.: No specific amount. **Duration:** Annual. **To Apply:** Applicants must complete and submit the application form and must include the following: a copy of current enrollment in a graduate in nursing program (min.6 hours/semester); recent transcripts (must be min. 3.0 GPA on a 4.0 scale); tuition cost per hour; a statement/documentation of need for financial assistance and current assistance received; letters of recommendation from: SOHN member, an instructor or manager (not the same person as SOHN member), any person you may wish to select (letters should contain statements identifying the commitment, learning ability, and quality of performance of the applicant); Narrative (750-1000 words) describing your past or current SOHN involvement, future SOHN goals and desire for advancing your degree in Nursing. **Deadline:** July 1.

8669 ■ Society of Outdoor Recreation Professionals (SORP)

PO Box 221
Marienville, PA 16239
Ph: (814)927-8212
Fax: (814)927-6659
URL: www.narrp.org

8670 ■ SORP Student Conference Scholarship *(Graduate, Undergraduate/Scholarship)*

Purpose: To support undergraduate or graduate students enrolled full-time in an outdoor recreation research, planning, management, policy or closely related degree program. **Focus:** General studies/Field of study not specified. **Qualif.:** Applicants must be undergraduate or graduate students enrolled full-time in an SORP accredited recreation management, planning or closely related degree program. **Criteria:** Applicants will be evaluated based on their clear and compelling statement of career goals related to the recreation planning profession; degree that the scholarship will help the person achieve their career goals; quality of past work performance and future potential as judged by university advisor; extent of other contributing financial support or in-kind contributions from other sources

Awards are arranged alphabetically below their administering organizations

(e.g., university, personal, third party organizations); degree that the requested financial support is appropriate and reasonable. **Funds Avail.:** $763. **Number Awarded:** Up to 10. **To Apply:** Applicants must complete the application form along with the current resume and transcript; 500-word narrative statement of academic and career goals, and how attending the SORP Conference will be helpful towards achieving these goals; and letter of recommendation from Major Professor/Academic Advisor. **Deadline:** January 16.

8671 ■ Society of Pediatric Nurses (SPN)
330 N Wabash Ave., Ste. 2000
Chicago, IL 60611-7621
Ph: (312)321-5154
Fax: (312)673-6754
E-mail: info@pedsnurses.org
URL: www.pedsnurses.org

8672 ■ Society of Pediatric Nurses Educational Scholarships *(Graduate, Other/Scholarship)*
Purpose: To help SPN members further their professional education. **Focus:** Nursing. **Qualif.:** Applicant must be a member engaged in a BSN completion program or a graduate program that will advance the health of children. **Criteria:** Applicants will be evaluated by the Scholarship Selection Committee.

Funds Avail.: No specific amount. **To Apply:** Applicant must submit a complete application which includes the following: documentation of current enrollment/acceptance in BSN completion or graduate program; a curriculum vitae; a letter of recommendation from an SPN member. The letter must address the following: the nominator's relationship to the nominee, the nominee's position and responsibility, the nominee's interest in and/or commitment to the care of children and their families, a letter of recommendation from a faculty member who can evaluate the nominee's potential to meet professional goals.

8673 ■ Society for Pediatric Radiology (SPR)
1891 Preston White Dr.
Reston, VA 20191-4397
Ph: (703)648-0680
E-mail: spr@acr.org
URL: www.pedrad.org

8674 ■ Society for Pediatric Radiology Research Fellows *(Graduate, Other/Fellowship)*
Purpose: To provide young investigators an opportunity to gain further insight into scientific investigation and to develop competence in research techniques and methods. **Focus:** Radiology. **Qualif.:** Applicant must be a member of the Society for the Pediatric Radiology (SPR); holds a full-time faculty position in an educational institution; and in a department of diagnostic radiology, radiation oncology or nuclear medicine and have completed all advanced training. **Criteria:** Selection is based on scientific merit and appropriateness.

Funds Avail.: $30,000. **Duration:** One year. **To Apply:** Applicants must submit one printed copy (with signatures) and one electronic version of the completed application submitted to jboylan@acr.org. **Deadline:** March 15.

8675 ■ Society for Pediatric Radiology Seed Grants *(Graduate, Other/Grant)*
Purpose: To foster research and education in pediatric radiology. **Focus:** Radiology. **Qualif.:** One of the member

of the investigator team must be a member of the Society for the Pediatric Radiology (SPR); holds a full-time faculty position in an educational institution; and in a department of diagnostic radiology, radiation oncology or nuclear medicine and have completed all advanced training. **Criteria:** Selection is based on scientific merit and appropriateness.

Funds Avail.: Maximum of $10,000. **Duration:** One year. **To Apply:** Applicants must submit one printed copy (with signatures) and one electronic version of the completed application submitted to jboylan@acr.org. **Deadline:** March 15. **Contact:** Jennifer Boylan, jboylan@acr.org.

8676 ■ Society for Pediatric Urology (SPU)
500 Cummings Ctr., Ste. 4550
Beverly, MA 01915
Ph: (978)927-8330
Fax: (978)524-0498
URL: www.spuonline.org

8677 ■ John W. Duckett Jr., AFUD Pediatric Research Scholarships *(Undergraduate/Scholarship)*
Purpose: To promote pediatric urology, appropriate practice, education as well as exchanges between practitioners involved in the treatment of genito urinary disorders of children. **Focus:** Medicine, Pediatric. **Qualif.:** Applicant must be taking up pediatric medicine. **Criteria:** Application will be evaluated by the Scholarship Committee.

Funds Avail.: $10,000. **To Apply:** Applicant must fill out the application form and submit to the American Foundation of Urologic Disease. **Contact:** 1000 Corporate Blvd., Ste. 410, Linthicum, MD 21090, Phone: 410-689-3990, Fax: 410-689-3998, Toll free: 800-828-7866.

8678 ■ Society for Pediatric Urology Research Grant Program *(Undergraduate/Grant)*
Purpose: To promote pediatric urology, appropriate practice, education as well as exchanges between practitioners involved in the treatment of genito urinary disorders in children. **Focus:** Medicine, Pediatric. **Qualif.:** Applicants must have knowledge in pediatric urology and must be officially enrolled in an accredited institution; must be sponsored by SPU member. **Criteria:** Recipients will be selected based on the synopsis of the research plan.

Funds Avail.: $30,000. **Duration:** Annual; One year. **To Apply:** Applicants must attach the copy of Principal Investigator's Curriculum Vitae; a letter of commitment from the Chair of the Principal Investigator's Department; must attach an abstract of the research plan which summarizes the long-term objectives, scientific aims and methodology; a grant budget; and must provide a justification which describes any large or unusual expenses in any category or any cost of the need which may not be obvious. **Deadline:** March 2. **Contact:** All originals and four copies each must be forwarded to David A. Diamond, MD, Children's Hospital, Department of Urology located at 300 Longwood Ave., Boston, MA 02115.

8679 ■ Society of Petroleum Engineers - Evangeline Section (SPE)
PO Box 52356
Lafayette, LA 70505-2356
Ph: (337)521-2115
URL: www.spe-laf.org

Awards are arranged alphabetically below their administering organizations

8680 ■ Children of Evangeline Section Scholarships
(Graduate, Undergraduate/Scholarship)

Purpose: To support the education of eligible children of Evangeline Section members. **Focus:** General studies/Field of study not specified. **Qualif.:** Applicant must be a child of an SPE Evangeline Section member in good standing; attending a four-year accredited college, working towards a Bachelor's or Master's degree or an advanced degree; have a declared field of study; be a full-time student with a minimum of 12 semester hours; and have a minimum overall GPA of 3.0. **Criteria:** Selection is based on the submitted application and materials.

Funds Avail.: $1,000 each (paid in two installments). **Duration:** One school year. **Number Awarded:** 15. **To Apply:** Applicant must submit a completed application form along with a certified college (last semester available) or high school transcript (ACT/SAT score reports are also required for entering freshmen). **Deadline:** July 15. **Contact:** John Moore at 337-322-0154 or john.moore@graywireline.com; John Lee at 337-344-1770.

8681 ■ Petroleum Engineering Scholarships *(Graduate, Undergraduate/Scholarship)*

Purpose: To support the education of students majoring in petroleum engineering at Louisiana State University (LSU) or the University of Louisiana at Lafayette (ULL). **Focus:** Engineering, Petroleum. **Qualif.:** Applicant must be a petroleum engineering student at LSU or ULL. **Criteria:** Selection is based on academic excellence and application materials.

Funds Avail.: $20,000. **Duration:** Annual. **To Apply:** Applicants must submit a completed application form along with a certified college (last semester available) or high school transcript (ACT/SAT score reports are also required for entering freshmen). **Contact:** Dr. Fathi Boukadia at 337-482-6148; John Lee at 337-237-4406.

8682 ■ Society for Photographic Education (SPE)
2530 Superior Ave., No. 403
Cleveland, OH 44114
Ph: (216)622-2733
Fax: (216)622-2712
E-mail: vmorrison@spenational.org
URL: www.spenational.org

8683 ■ SPE Student Award for Innovations in Imaging *(Undergraduate, Graduate/Scholarship)*

Purpose: To offset the cost of attending SPE's national conference. **Focus:** Photography. **Qualif.:** Applicants must be SPE member students (undergraduate or graduate) working primarily with digital technology and is designated for work only possible because of emerging digital technologies. **Criteria:** Selection will be based on the committee's criteria and on merits of submitted portfolios.

Funds Avail.: $550 travel stipend. **Duration:** Annual. **To Apply:** Applicants are required to submit a portfolio consist of a project description describing how the work is possible as a result of emerging digital technologies. Other requirements can be found at the program website. **Deadline:** November 1.

8684 ■ Society of Physics Students
1 Physics Ellipse
College Park, MD 20740

Ph: (301)209-3007
Fax: (301)209-0839
E-mail: sps@aip.org
URL: www.spsnational.org

8685 ■ Peggy Dixon Two-Year Scholarships
(Undergraduate/Scholarship)

Purpose: To support students from a two-year college transitioning into a physics bachelor's degree program. **Focus:** Physics. **Qualif.:** Applicants must: be undergraduate members of the SPS national organization; have completed at least one semester or quarter of the introductory physics sequence; and, be transitioning from a two-year college into a physics bachelor's degree program. **Criteria:** Applicants are selected based on high scholarship performance both in physics and overall studies; exhibition of the potential and intention for continued scholastic development in physics; active participation in SPS programs.

Funds Avail.: $2,000. **Duration:** Annual. **Number Awarded:** 1. **To Apply:** Application forms are available online. Applicants must submit completed application form; certified and official transcript (submitted directly by the applicant's college/university); letters from at least two full-time members of the faculty. **Deadline:** February 17. **Remarks:** The scholarship is established in memory of Dr. Peggy A. Dixon, SPS and Sigma Pi Sigma Historian from 1992-2003.

8686 ■ Herbert Levy Memorial Scholarship
(Undergraduate/Scholarship)

Purpose: To encourage the study of physics and the pursuit of high scholarship. **Focus:** Physics. **Qualif.:** Applicants must be full-time undergraduate students applying in their junior year (except for two-year college applicants who should apply after completing one semester of physics); and must be SPS members. **Criteria:** Applicants are selected based on high scholarship performance both in physics and overall studies; exhibition of the potential and intention for continued scholastic development in physics; and active participation in SPS programs.

Funds Avail.: $2,000. **Duration:** Annual. **To Apply:** Application forms are available online. Applicants must submit completed application form; certified and official transcript (submitted directly by the applicant's college/university); letters from at least two full-time members of the faculty; and a statement of financial need. **Deadline:** February 15.

8687 ■ SPS Future Teacher Scholarships
(Undergraduate/Scholarship)

Purpose: To support an SPS member who is participating in a teacher education program and who plans to pursue a career in physics education. **Focus:** Physics. **Qualif.:** Applicants must be: undergraduate members of the SPS national organization; participating in a teacher education program. **Criteria:** Applicants are selected based on high scholarship performance both in physics and overall studies; exhibition of the potential and intention for continued scholastic development in physics; and active participation in SPS programs.

Funds Avail.: $2,000. **Duration:** Annual. **Number Awarded:** 1. **To Apply:** Application forms are available online. Applicants must submit completed application form; certified and official transcript (submitted directly by the applicant's college/university); letters from at least two full-time members of the faculty; and a statement from an SPS advisor that certifies the applicant's participation in a

Awards are arranged alphabetically below their administering organizations

teacher education program. **Deadline:** February 17.

8688 ■ SPS Leadership Scholarships
(Undergraduate/Scholarship)

Purpose: To encourage the students to pursue their career in study of physics. **Focus:** Physics. **Qualif.:** Applicants must be full-time undergraduate students applying in their junior year (except for two-year college applicants who should apply after completing one semester of physics); and must be SPS members. **Criteria:** Applicants are selected based on high scholarship performance both in physics and overall studies; exhibition of the potential and intention for continued scholastic development in physics; and active participation in SPS programs.

Funds Avail.: $2000 and $5000. **Duration:** Annual. **Number Awarded:** Varies. **To Apply:** Application forms are available online. Applicants must submit completed application form; certified and official transcript (submitted directly by the applicant's college/university); letters from at least two full-time members of the faculty. **Deadline:** February 15.

8689 ■ Society of Plastics Engineers (SPE)
6 Berkshire Blvd., Ste. 306
Bethel, CT 06801
Ph: (203)775-0471
Fax: (203)775-8490
URL: www.4spe.org

8690 ■ Blow Molding Division Memorial Scholarships *(Undergraduate/Scholarship)*

Purpose: To promote scientific and engineering knowledge relating to plastics. **Focus:** Engineering, Chemical; Engineering, Industrial; Engineering, Materials; Science. **Qualif.:** Applicants must have demonstrated or expressed interest in the plastic industry; must be completing the second year of a 4-year undergraduate plastics engineering program; be a member of an SPE Student Chapter. **Criteria:** Recipients are selected based on financial need and academic standing.

Funds Avail.: $6,000. **Duration:** Annual. **Number Awarded:** 2. **To Apply:** Applicants must complete the application form; applicants must submit three letters of recommendation, two of which are from a teacher or school official and one from an employer or non-relative; a high school and/or college transcript for the past two years; a list of current and past school activities, community activities, and honors; a listing of employment history; a one-to-two-page typewritten statement telling why they are applying for the scholarship, qualifications, educational and career goals in the plastic industry; and an essay on the importance of blow molding. **Deadline:** May 1. **Contact:** SPE Foundation at foundation@4spe.org.

8691 ■ Robert E. Cramer Product Design and Development Scholarship *(Undergraduate, Graduate/Scholarship)*

Purpose: To promote scientific and engineering knowledge relating to plastics. **Focus:** Engineering, Chemical; Engineering, Industrial; Engineering, Materials; Science. **Qualif.:** Applicants must be undergraduate and graduate students in institutions, colleges, or universities; applicants must have demonstrated or expressed interest in the plastic industry; applicants must be in good academic standing. **Criteria:** Recipients are selected based on financial need and academic standing.

Funds Avail.: $1,000. **Duration:** Annual. **Number Awarded:** 1. **To Apply:** Applicants must complete the application form; applicants must submit three letters of recommendation, two of which are from a teacher or school official and one from an employer or non-relative; a high school and/or college transcript for the past two years; a list of current and past school activities, community activities, and honors; A listing of employment history; a one-to-two-page typewritten statement telling why they are applying for the scholarship, qualifications, educational and career goals in the plastic industry. **Deadline:** May 1. **Contact:** SPE Foundation at foundation@4spe.org.

8692 ■ Detroit Section/Robert G. Dailey Scholarship
(Undergraduate/Scholarship)

Purpose: To promote scientific and engineering knowledge relating to plastics. **Focus:** Engineering, Biomedical; Engineering, Industrial; Engineering, Materials; Science. **Qualif.:** Applicants must be undergraduate students in institutions, colleges, or universities; Applicants must have demonstrated or expressed interest in the plastic industry; applicants must be in good academic standing. **Criteria:** Recipients are selected based on financial need and academic standing.

Funds Avail.: $3,000. **Duration:** Annual. **Number Awarded:** 1. **To Apply:** Applicants must complete the application form; applicants must submit three letters of recommendation, two of which are from a teacher or school official and one from an employer or non-relative; a high school and/or college transcript for the past two years; a list of current and past school activities, community activities, and honors; a listing of employment history; a one-to-two-page typewritten statement telling why they are applying for the scholarship, qualifications, educational and career goals in the plastic industry. **Deadline:** May 1. **Contact:** SPE Foundation at foundation@4spe.org.

8693 ■ Extrusion Division/Lew Erwin Memorial Scholarship *(Graduate, Doctorate/Scholarship)*

Purpose: To promote scientific and engineering knowledge relating to plastics. **Focus:** Engineering, Chemical; Engineering, Industrial; Engineering, Materials; Science. **Qualif.:** Applicants must be Ph.D. candidates, or be working on a Senior or MS project which the scholarship will help support. **Criteria:** Recipients are selected based on financial need and academic standing.

Funds Avail.: $5,000. **Duration:** Annual. **Number Awarded:** 1. **To Apply:** Applicants must complete the application form; three letters of recommendation, two of which are from a teacher or school official and one from an employer or non-relative; a high school and/or college transcript for the past two years; a list of current and past school activities, community activities, and honors; a listing of employment history; a one-to-two-page typewritten statement telling why they are applying for the scholarship, qualifications, educational and career goals in the plastic industry. **Deadline:** March 1. **Contact:** SPE Foundation at foundation@4spe.org.

8694 ■ Fleming/Blaszcak Scholarships *(Undergraduate, Graduate/Scholarship)*

Purpose: To promote scientific and engineering knowledge relating to plastics. **Focus:** Engineering, Chemical; Engineering, Industrial; Engineering, Materials; Science. **Qualif.:** Applicants must be full-time undergraduate students at a 4-year college or students enrolled in a graduate program; applicants must have demonstrated or expressed interest

Awards are arranged alphabetically below their administering organizations

in the plastic industry; applicants must be in good academic standing; applicants must be of Mexican descent and citizens or legal residents of the United States. **Criteria:** Recipients are selected based on financial need and academic standing.

Funds Avail.: $2,000. **Duration:** Annual. **Number Awarded:** 1. **To Apply:** Applicants must complete the application form; applicants must submit three letters of recommendation, two of which are from a teacher or school official and one from an employer or non-relative; a high school and/or college transcript for the past two years; a list of current and past school activities, community activities, and honors; a listing of employment history; a one-to-two-page typewritten statement telling why they are applying for the scholarship, qualifications, educational and career goals in the plastic industry; applicants must provide a documentation of their Mexican heritage and their citizenship status such as a birth certificate or a U.S. passport. **Deadline:** May 1. **Contact:** SPE Foundation at foundation@4spe.org.

8695 ■ Composites Division/Harold Giles Scholarship (Undergraduate, Graduate/Scholarship)

Purpose: To promote scientific and engineering knowledge relating to plastics. **Focus:** Engineering, Chemical; Engineering, Industrial; Engineering, Materials; Science. **Qualif.:** Applicants must be undergraduate and graduate students in institutions, colleges, or universities; applicants must have demonstrated or expressed interest in the plastic industry; applicants must be in good academic standing; applicants must have experience in the composites industry such as courses taken, research conducted, or jobs held. **Criteria:** Recipients are selected based on financial need and academic standing.

Funds Avail.: $1,000. **Duration:** Annual. **Number Awarded:** 1. **To Apply:** Applicants must complete the application form; applicants must submit three letters of recommendation, two of which are from a teacher or school official and one from an employer or non-relative; a high school and/or college transcript for the past two years; a list of current and past school activities, community activities, and honors; a listing of employment history; a one-to-two-page typewritten statement telling why they are applying for the scholarship, qualifications, educational and career goals in the plastic industry. **Deadline:** May 1. **Contact:** SPE Foundation at foundation@4spe.org.

8696 ■ Gulf Coast Hurricane Scholarships (Undergraduate/Scholarship)

Purpose: To promote scientific and engineering knowledge relating to plastics. **Focus:** Engineering, Chemical; Engineering, Industrial; Engineering, Materials; Science. **Qualif.:** Applicants must be: residents of, and attending college in Florida, Alabama, Mississippi, Louisiana, or Texas; and four-year university or two-year junior college or technical institute students. **Criteria:** Recipients are selected based on financial need and academic standing.

Funds Avail.: $6,000 for four-year university student; $2,000 for two-year junior college student. **Duration:** Annual. **Number Awarded:** 2. **To Apply:** Applicants must complete the application form; applicants must submit three letters of recommendation, two of which are from a teacher or school official and one from an employer or non-relative; a high school and/or college transcript for the past two years; a list of current and past school activities, community activities, and honors; a listing of employment history; a one-to-two-page typewritten statement telling why they are

applying for the scholarship, qualifications, educational and career goals in the plastic industry; applicants must provide proof of residence in any Gulf Coast states **Deadline:** May 1. **Contact:** SPE Foundation at foundation@4spe.org.

8697 ■ Injection Molding Division Scholarships (Undergraduate, Graduate/Scholarship)

Purpose: To promote scientific and engineering knowledge relating to plastics. **Focus:** Engineering, Chemical; Engineering, Industrial; Engineering, Materials; Science. **Qualif.:** Applicants must be undergraduate and graduate students in institutions, colleges, or universities; applicants must have demonstrated or expressed interest in the plastic industry; applicants must be in good academic standing; applicants must have experience in the molding industry such as courses taken, research conducted or jobs held. **Criteria:** Recipients are selected based on financial need and academic standing.

Funds Avail.: $3,000. **Duration:** Annual. **Number Awarded:** 1. **To Apply:** Applicants must complete the application form; Applicants must submit three letters of recommendation, two of which are from a teacher or school official and one from an employer or non-relative; a high school and/or college transcript for the past two years; a list of current and past school activities, community activities, and honors; a listing of employment history; a one-to-two-page typewritten statement telling why they are applying for the scholarship, qualifications, educational and career goals in the plastic industry. **Deadline:** May 1. **Contact:** SPE Foundation at foundation@4spe.org.

8698 ■ Thermoset Division/James I. Mackenzie and James H. Cunningham Scholarships (Undergraduate, Graduate/Scholarship)

Purpose: To promote scientific and engineering knowledge relating to plastics. **Focus:** Engineering, Chemical; Engineering, Industrial; Engineering, Materials; Science. **Qualif.:** Applicants must be undergraduate and graduate students in institutions, colleges, or universities. Applicants must have demonstrated or expressed interest in the plastic industry; applicants must be in good academic standing; applicants must have experience in the thermoplastic elastomers industry, such as courses taken, research conducted, or jobs held. **Criteria:** Recipients are selected based on financial need and academic standing.

Funds Avail.: $2,500. **Duration:** Annual. **Number Awarded:** 2. **To Apply:** Applicants must complete the application form; applicants must submit three letters of recommendation, two of which are from a teacher or school official and one from an employer or non-relative; a high school and/or college transcript for the past two years; a list of current and past school activities, community activities, and honors; a listing of employment history; a one-to-two-page typewritten statement telling why they are applying for the scholarship, qualifications, educational and career goals in the plastic industry; applicants must include a statement detailing their exposure to the thermoset industry. **Deadline:** May 1. **Contact:** SPE Foundation at foundation@4spe.org.

8699 ■ Ted and Ruth Neward Scholarships (Undergraduate, Graduate/Scholarship)

Purpose: To promote scientific and engineering knowledge relating to plastics. **Focus:** Engineering, Chemical; Engineering, Industrial; Engineering, Materials; Science. **Qualif.:** Applicants must be U.S. citizens and undergraduate or graduate students in institutions, colleges, or universities;

Awards are arranged alphabetically below their administering organizations

applicants must have demonstrated or expressed interest in the plastic industry; applicants must be in good academic standing. **Criteria:** Recipients are selected based on financial need and academic standing.

Funds Avail.: $3,000. **Duration:** Annual. **Number Awarded:** 4 (1 is restricted to a female student). **To Apply:** Applicants must complete the application form; applicants must submit three letters of recommendation, two of which are from a teacher or school official and one from an employer or non-relative; a high school and/or college transcript for the past two years; a list of current and past school activities, community activities, and honors; a listing of employment history; a one-to-two-page typewritten statement telling why they are applying for the scholarship, qualifications, educational and career goals in the plastic industry. **Deadline:** May 1. **Contact:** SPE Foundation at foundation@4spe.org.

8700 ■ Plastics Pioneers Association Scholarships
(Undergraduate/Scholarship)

Purpose: To promote scientific and engineering knowledge relating to plastics. **Focus:** Engineering, Civil; Engineering, Industrial; Engineering, Materials; Science. **Qualif.:** Applicants must: be U.S. citizens; be undergraduate students in institutions, colleges, or universities including those enrolled in associate degree or technical degree programs who are committed to becoming hands-on workers in the plastics industry and who are dedicated to careers as plastics technicians or engineers; have demonstrated or expressed interest in the plastic industry; and, be in good academic standing. **Criteria:** Recipients are selected based on financial need and academic standing.

Funds Avail.: $3,000. **Duration:** Annual. **Number Awarded:** Varies. **To Apply:** Applicants must complete the application form; applicants must submit three letters of recommendation, two of which are from a teacher or school official and one from an employer or non-relative; a high school and/or college transcript for the past two years; a list of current and past school activities, community activities, and honors; a listing of employment history; A one-to-two-page typewritten statement telling why they are applying for the scholarship, qualifications, educational and career goals in the plastic industry. **Deadline:** May 1. **Contact:** SPE Foundation at foundation@4spe.org.

8701 ■ Polymer Modifiers and Additives Division Scholarships *(Undergraduate, Graduate/Scholarship)*

Purpose: To promote scientific and engineering knowledge relating to plastics. **Focus:** Engineering; Science. **Qualif.:** Applicants must be undergraduate and graduate students in institutions, colleges, or universities; applicants must have demonstrated or expressed interest in the plastic industry; applicants must be in good academic standing. **Criteria:** Recipients are selected based on financial need and academic standing.

Funds Avail.: $4,000. **Duration:** Annual. **Number Awarded:** 4. **To Apply:** Applicants must complete the application form; applicants must submit three letters of recommendation, two of which are from a teacher or school official and one from an employer or non-relative; a high school and/or college transcript for the past two years; a list of current and past school activities, community activities, and honors; a listing of employment history; a one-to-two-page typewritten statement telling why they are applying for the scholarship, qualifications, educational and career goals in the plastic industry. **Deadline:** March 1. **Contact:** SPE Foundation at foundation@4spe.org.

8702 ■ Society of Plastics Engineers General Scholarships *(Undergraduate, Graduate/Scholarship)*

Purpose: To support students who have demonstrated or expressed an interest in the plastics industry. **Focus:** Engineering, Chemical; Engineering, Industrial; Science. **Qualif.:** Applicants must be undergraduate and graduate students in institutions, colleges, or universities; applicants must have demonstrated or expressed interest in the plastic industry; applicants must be in good academic standing. **Criteria:** Recipients are selected based on financial need and academic standing.

Funds Avail.: Varies. **Duration:** Annual. **To Apply:** Applicants must complete the application form; applicants must submit three letters of recommendation, two of which are from a teacher or school official and one from an employer or non-relative; a high school and/or college transcript for the past two years; a list of current and past school activities, community activities, and honors; a listing of employment history; a one-to-two-page typewritten statement telling why they are applying for the scholarship, qualifications, educational and career goals in the plastic industry. **Deadline:** March 1 (Extrusion, PMAD or Vinyl scholarship); May 1. **Contact:** SPE Foundation at foundation@4spe.org.

8703 ■ Thermoforming Division Memorial Scholarships *(Undergraduate, Graduate/Scholarship)*

Purpose: To promote scientific and engineering knowledge relating to plastics. **Focus:** Engineering, Chemical; Engineering, Industrial; Engineering, Materials; Science. **Qualif.:** Applicants must be undergraduate and graduate students in institutions, colleges, or universities including those enrolled in associate degree or technical degree programs. Applicants must have demonstrated or expressed interest in the plastic industry; applicants must be in good academic standing; applicants must have experience in the thermoplastic elastomers industry, such as courses taken, research conducted, or jobs held. **Criteria:** Recipients are selected based on financial need and academic standing.

Funds Avail.: Up to $5,000. **Duration:** Annual. **Number Awarded:** Varies. **To Apply:** Applicants must complete the application form; applicants must submit three letters of recommendation, two of which are from a teacher or school official and one from an employer or non-relative; a high school and/or college transcript for the past two years; a list of current and past school activities, community activities, and honors; a listing of employment history; a one-to-two-page typewritten statement telling why they are applying for the scholarship, qualifications, educational and career goals in the plastic industry. **Deadline:** May 1. **Contact:** SPE Foundation at foundation@4spe.org.

8704 ■ Thermoplastic Elastomers Special Interest Group Scholarship *(Undergraduate, Graduate/Scholarship)*

Purpose: To promote scientific and engineering knowledge relating to plastics. **Focus:** Engineering, Chemical; Engineering, Industrial; Engineering, Materials; Science. **Qualif.:** Applicants must be undergraduate and graduate students in institutions, colleges, or universities. Applicants must have demonstrated or expressed interest in the plastic industry; applicants must be in good academic standing; applicants must have experience in the thermoplastic elastomers industry, such as courses taken, research conducted, or jobs held. **Criteria:** Recipients are selected based on financial need and academic standing.

Awards are arranged alphabetically below their administering organizations

Funds Avail.: $1,000 - undergraduate student; $1,500 - graduate student. **Duration:** Annual. **Number Awarded:** 2. **To Apply:** Applicants must complete the application form; applicants must submit three letters of recommendation, two of which are from a teacher or school official and one from an employer or non-relative; a high school and/or college transcript for the past two years; a list of current and past school activities, community activities, and honors; a listing of employment history; a one-to-two-page typewritten statement telling why they are applying for the scholarship, qualifications, educational and career goals in the plastic industry. **Deadline:** May 1. **Contact:** SPE Foundation at foundation@4spe.org.

8705 ■ Thermoplastic Materials and Foams Division Scholarships (Undergraduate/Scholarship)

Purpose: To promote scientific and engineering knowledge relating to plastics. **Focus:** Engineering; Science. **Qualif.:** Applicants must be undergraduate students in institutions, colleges, or universities; applicants must have demonstrated or expressed interest in the plastic industry; applicants must be in good academic standing. **Criteria:** Recipients are selected based on financial need and academic standing.

Funds Avail.: $2,500. **Duration:** Annual. **Number Awarded:** 1. **To Apply:** Applicants must complete the application form; applicants must submit three letters of recommendation, two of which are from a teacher or school official and one from an employer or non-relative; a high school and/or college transcript for the past two years; a list of current and past school activities, community activities, and honors; a listing of employment history; a one-to-two-page typewritten statement telling why they are applying for the scholarship, qualifications, educational and career goals in the plastic industry. **Deadline:** May 1. **Contact:** SPE Foundation at foundation@4spe.org.

8706 ■ Vinyl Plastics Division Scholarships (Undergraduate/Scholarship)

Purpose: To promote scientific and engineering knowledge relating to plastics. **Focus:** Engineering, Chemical; Engineering, Industrial; Engineering, Materials; Science. **Qualif.:** Applicants must be undergraduate students in institutions, colleges, or universities; applicants must have demonstrated or expressed interest in the plastic industry; applicants must be in good academic standing; must be majoring in or taking courses that are beneficial to a career in the plastics/polymer industry. **Criteria:** Recipients are selected based on financial need and academic standing. Preference will be given to applicants with experience in the vinyl industry, such as courses taken, research conducted, or jobs held.

Funds Avail.: $3,000. **Duration:** Annual. **Number Awarded:** 1. **To Apply:** Applicants must complete the application form; applicants must submit three letters of recommendation, two of which are from a teacher or school official and one from an employer or non-relative; a high school and/or college transcript for the past two years; a list of current and past school activities, community activities, and honors; a listing of employment history; a one-to-two-page typewritten statement telling why they are applying for the scholarship, qualifications, educational and career goals in the plastic industry. **Deadline:** March 1. **Contact:** SPE Foundation at foundation@4spe.org.

8707 ■ Society for the Preservation of Old Mills (SPOOM)

PO Box 422
Great Falls, VA 22066
Ph: (860)423-2033
URL: www.spoom.org

8708 ■ SPOOM Research Grants (Graduate/Grant)

Purpose: To provide financial assistance to researches on mills or milling-related subjects. **Focus:** Preservation. **Qualif.:** Program is open to individuals seeking support for their research on mills or milling-related subject. Applicants must be active members of SPOOM; must be full-time students and in good standing. **Criteria:** Awards are granted based on the significance of the contribution that the proposed project will make to the preservation or understanding of mills or milling; conception, definition, organization and description of the requested project; likelihood that the applicants will complete the entire project; and support of a mill-related group with the eligibility criteria.

Funds Avail.: No specific amount. **Duration:** Annual. **Number Awarded:** Varies. **To Apply:** Applicants must prepare a one-page outline of the project; official graduate transcript; resume detailing applicable work experiences; and must complete application form available in the SPOOM office or website. **Deadline:** August 1. **Contact:** Ivan Lurfriu at 717-359-4363 or ivamar@netzero.net.

8709 ■ Society of Professional Journalists (SPJ)

Eugene Pulliam National Journalism Center
3909 N Meridian St.
Indianapolis, IN 46208
Ph: (317)927-8000
Fax: (317)920-4789
E-mail: spj@spj.org
URL: www.spj.org

8710 ■ Archibald Communications Internships (Undergraduate/Internship)

Purpose: To encourage the free practice of journalism and stimulate high standards of ethical behavior. **Focus:** Journalism. **Qualif.:** Applicants must be journalism students, concentrating in communications or public relations, who have completed at least their junior year. **Criteria:** Recipients are selected based on academic performance.

Funds Avail.: No specific amount. **To Apply:** Applicants must submit a completed application form and attach a cover letter, current resume, three to five writing samples and a one-page essay detailing their future goals and objectives.

8711 ■ Pulliam/Kilgore Freedom of Information Internships (Undergraduate/Award, Internship)

Purpose: To encourage the free practice of journalism and stimulate high standards of ethical behavior. **Focus:** Journalism. **Qualif.:** Applicants must be journalism students who are entering or just completing their senior year, graduate journalism students or law students with a journalism background. **Criteria:** Recipients are selected based on strong background in writing and reporting and academic performance.

Funds Avail.: $400 per week. **Duration:** Annual; Ten weeks. **Number Awarded:** 2. **To Apply:** Applicants must submit completed application form along with resume and

Awards are arranged alphabetically below their administering organizations

one-page essay that illustrates their understanding of Freedom of Information issues and what they expect to gain from the internship (not more than five writings). **Deadline:** January 22.

8712 ■ Society for Psychological Anthropology (SPA)

Dept. of Global Health and Social Medicine
Harvard Medical School
641 Huntington Ave.
Boston, MA 02115
Ph: (617)432-2612
URL: www.aaanet.org/sections/SPA

8713 ■ Condon Prize for Best Student Essay in Psychological Anthropology *(Graduate, Undergraduate/Prize, Recognition)*

Purpose: To promote the study of adolescence, family and change among the Canadian Inuit. **Focus:** Anthropology. **Qualif.:** Applicants must be graduate or undergraduate students. **Criteria:** Selection will be based on the submitted essays.

Funds Avail.: $500. **Duration:** Annual. **To Apply:** Papers submitted for consideration should follow these guidelines: No evidence of the author's identity may be provided in any way through the text or by reference in the paper; the author's name and address, student affiliation, and the title of the paper must be provided on a separate cover sheet accompanying the manuscript, which should be identified by the title; all authors of papers submitted for this prize must either be in Doctoral, Master's or undergraduate degree programs at the time of submission. An entry should be accompanied by a photocopy of each author's student identification card or a photocopy of each author's most recent diploma. Only one entry is allowed per author; Papers must not exceed 35 double-spaced pages and must follow the style of Ethos; an electronic version of the paper must be submitted too. **Deadline:** August 1. **Remarks:** Established in 1997.

8714 ■ Lemelson Student Fellowships *(Graduate/ Award)*

Purpose: To provide graduate students working in the field of psychological anthropology with funding to pursue exploratory research on their dissertation research. **Focus:** Anthropology; Psychology. **Qualif.:** Applicants must student members of SPA enrolled in a graduate program at the time and during the period of fellowship. Graduate students must work in the field of psychological anthropology. **Criteria:** Selection will be based on the committee's criteria.

Funds Avail.: $4,000 - $6,000. **Duration:** Annual. **Number Awarded:** 6. **To Apply:** Interested applicants must file a brief report on the results of their completed research projects; must attend either the Saturday night banquet or the SPA Business Meeting so that they may be recognized. All components of the application including letter of recommendation, application form, project statement, and budget are to be submitted via email as two files with their last name in the title of both. The first file should be the completed application form, and the second should include the project statement and budget. **Deadline:** February 14. **Contact:** Harold Odden at oddenh@ipfw.edu.

8715 ■ Society for the Psychological Study of Lesbian, Gay, Bisexual and Transgender Issues (SPSLGBTI)

Cornell University
Human Sexuality Collection and Library Women's Studies Selector
2B Carl A Kroch Library
Ithaca, NY 14853
Ph: (607)255-3530
Fax: (607)255-9524
E-mail: lgbtc@apa.org
URL: www.apadivision44.org

8716 ■ Bisexual Foundation Scholarships *(Graduate/Scholarship)*

Purpose: To support emerging scholars who are researching about the growing bisexuality to the field of LGBT issues in psychology. **Focus:** Psychology. **Qualif.:** Applicant must be a full-time graduate student in a Department of Psychology. **Criteria:** Recipients are selected based on the application materials submitted.

Funds Avail.: $1,000. **Duration:** Annual. **To Apply:** Applicants must submit an application consisting of: one cover sheet; curriculum vitae; one copy of the project description; and a letter from the applicant's supervisor addressing their qualifications and quality/feasibility of the project. **Deadline:** February 1.

8717 ■ Malyon-Smith Scholarship Award *(Graduate/ Scholarship)*

Purpose: To support the advancement of research about psychology of sexual orientation and gender identity. **Focus:** Psychology. **Qualif.:** Applicant must be a full-time graduate student in a Department of Psychology. **Criteria:** Recipients are selected based on the proposal.

Funds Avail.: $1,000. **Duration:** Annual. **To Apply:** Applicants must submit an application consisting of: one cover sheet; curriculum vitae; one copy of the project description; and a letter from the applicant's supervisor addressing their qualifications and quality/feasibility of the project. **Deadline:** February 1.

8718 ■ Society for the Psychological Study for Social Issues (SPSSE)

208 I St. NE
Washington, DC 20002-4340
Ph: (202)675-6956
Fax: (202)675-6902
Free: 877-310-7778
E-mail: spssi@spssi.org
URL: www.spssi.org

8719 ■ SPSSI Grants-In-Aid Program *(Graduate, Postdoctorate/Grant)*

Purpose: To support scientific research in social problem areas related to the basic interests and goals of SPSSI. **Focus:** Psychology. **Qualif.:** Applicanst must be SPSSI members. **Criteria:** Preference will be given to students at the dissertation stage of their graduate careers.

Funds Avail.: $1,000 - $2,000. **Duration:** Annual; Twice a year. **To Apply:** Applicants must submit the following: a cover letter with name, address, phone number, e-mail address and title for the proposal; an abstract of 100 words or

Awards are arranged alphabetically below their administering organizations

less summarizing the proposed research; project purposes, theoretical rationale, and research methodology and analytical procedures to be employed; relevance of research to SPSSI goals and grants-in-aid criteria; status of human subjects review process (which must be satisfactorily completed before grant funds can be forwarded); resume of investigator (a faculty sponsor's recommendation must be provided if the investigator of a graduate student; support is seldom awarded to students who have not yet reached the dissertation stage); specific amount requested including a budget. For co-authored submissions, please indicate only one name and institution to whom a check should be jointly issured if selected for funding. **Deadline:** May 15 Spring; October 25 Fall.

8720 ■ Society for the Psychological Study of Social Issues (SPSSI)

208 I St. NE
Washington, DC 20002-4340
Ph: (202)675-6956
Fax: (202)675-6902
Free: 877-310-7778
E-mail: spssi@spssi.org
URL: www.spssi.org

8721 ■ Gordon Allport Intergroup Relations Prize
(Professional development/Monetary, Award)

Purpose: To recognize the best paper or article of the year on intergroup relations. **Focus:** Psychology; Social sciences. **Qualif.:** Entries must be works published during the calendar year preceding the year of submission. Submissions are limited to articles, chapters, or other works published in their primary form (e.g., appearing in print for print journals or books or online for online-only journals or other volumes). **Criteria:** Originality of the contribution, whether theoretical or empirical, will be given special weight. The research area of intergroup relations includes such dimensions as age, gender, and socioeconomic status, as well as ethnicity.

Funds Avail.: $1,000. **Duration:** Annual. **To Apply:** Online submissions are the preferred method. For hard copy submissions, send five copies to SPSSI, 208 "I" (Eye) St NE, Washington, DC 20002-4340. Attn: Allport Award. **Deadline:** June 15. **Remarks:** The prize was established to honor the memory of the late Dr. Gordon W. Allport, a founder and past president of SPSSI.

8722 ■ Clara Mayo Grants Program *(Graduate/Grant)*

Purpose: To support masters' theses or pre-dissertation research on aspects of sexism, racism or prejudice. **Focus:** Psychology; Social sciences. **Qualif.:** Applicants must be SPSSI members; matriculated in graduate programs in psychology, applied social science and related disciplines. **Criteria:** Preference will be given to students enrolled in a terminal master's program.

Funds Avail.: $1,000. **Duration:** Annual. **Number Awarded:** 6. **To Apply:** Applicants are advised to visit the website for the online scholarship application. For hard copy submission, applicants must send five copies of cover sheet stating title of thesis proposal, name of investigator, address, phone, and if possible, fax and e-mail; an abstract of no more than 100 words summarizing the proposed research; project purposes, theoretical rationale, research methodology, and analytic procedures to be employed; relevance of research to SPSSI goals and funding criteria;

status of human subjects review process (which must be satisfactorily completed before grant funds can be forwarded); clear statement of type of degree program applicants is enrolled in; faculty advisor's recommendation, including certification that the proposal is for a master's thesis or for pre-dissertation research; specific amount requested, including a budget; and if available, an institutional letter of agreement to match the funds requested. **Deadline:** May 10 Spring; October 15 Fall.

8723 ■ Society for Public Health Education (SOPHE)

10 G St. NE, Ste. 605
Washington, DC 20002-4242
Ph: (202)408-9804
Fax: (202)408-9815
E-mail: info@sophe.org
URL: www.sophe.org

8724 ■ SOPHE/ATSDR Student Fellowships in Environmental Health or Emergency Preparedness
(Doctorate, Graduate, Master's/Fellowship)

Purpose: To recognize, assist and train students working on projects that address environmental health or emergency preparedness from the perspective of health education or the behavioral sciences. **Focus:** Behavioral sciences; Health education. **Qualif.:** Applicant must be enrolled as a full-time student (9 credit hours or more) in a Master's or Doctoral degree program in environmental health, health education, health promotion, behavioral sciences or a related field. Proposed projects should be either research or practice-based and focus on environmental health education/health promotion or environmental justice from the perspective of health education or the behavioral sciences. Proposed projects may be new or on-going, and the applicant must have the primary role in conducting the project. Projects may be related to surveillance, risk factor identification, or intervention development, evaluation, or dissemination. Projects related to the development or use of theory in environmental health are also acceptable. **Criteria:** Proposals will be reviewed by a SOPHE/ATSDR Environmental Health Promotion Fellowship Selection Committee for their scientific and/or theoretical basis, originality and potential contribution to health education's role in environmental health promotion.

Funds Avail.: $1,500. **Duration:** Annual. **To Apply:** Applicants must submit a completed application form; a current resume or curriculum vitae; and a project proposal describing the rationale, intended purpose, process/methodology, and potential contribution or impact of the project in 800 words or less. In addition, applications should include one letter of recommendation (from an internship coordinator, preceptor, faculty member or other professional); and one letter of support from a designated faculty member who plans to work with the applicant on the proposed project and can verify that the student is following a course of study. Letters should be sealed in envelopes with authors' signatures across the seal. **Deadline:** February 25. **Contact:** Application form and supporting documents must be submitted to Nicolette Warren at nwarren@sophe.org.

8725 ■ SOPHE/CDC Student Fellowships in Child, Adolescent and School Health *(Doctorate, Graduate, Master's/Fellowship)*

Purpose: To recognize, assist and train students working on projects that address aspects of child, adolescent, and

Awards are arranged alphabetically below their administering organizations

school health from the perspective of health education, health promotion or the behavioral sciences. **Focus:** Behavioral sciences; Health education. **Qualif.:** Applicant must be enrolled as a full time student in a Master's or Doctoral degree program in health education, health promotion, behavioral sciences, or a related field. **Criteria:** Proposals will be reviewed by a SOPHE/CDC Child and Adolescent School Health Committee for their scientific and/or theoretical basis, originality, and potential contribution to health education's role in promoting Child, Adolescent and School Health.

Funds Avail.: $1,500. **Duration:** Annual. **To Apply:** Applicants must submit a completed application including resume/CV and project proposal; one letter of recommendation; and one letter of support. **Deadline:** September 20. **Contact:** Bryan Damis at bdamis@sophe.org, 202-408-9804.

8726 ■ SOPHE/CDC Student Fellowships in Injury Prevention (Graduate/Fellowship)

Purpose: To assist and train graduate students working on unintentional injury prevention projects from the perspective of health education or behavioral sciences. **Focus:** Behavioral sciences; Health education. **Qualif.:** Applicant must be a SOPHE member and a graduate student working on unintentional injury prevention projects from the perspective of health education or behavioral sciences. **Criteria:** Selection is based on the application.

Funds Avail.: $2,000. **Duration:** Annual. **To Apply:** Applicants must submit the original and three copies of the complete application (including resume/CV and project proposal); one letter of recommendation; and one letter of support. **Deadline:** September 12. **Contact:** Deborah Gordon-Messer at dgordonmesser@sophe.org.

8727 ■ Society of Punjabi Engineers and Technologists of British Columbia (SPEATBC)

PO Box 104
Surrey, BC, Canada V3V 7H7
E-mail: speatbc@gmail.com
URL: www.speatbc.org

8728 ■ SPEATBC Scholarships (Undergraduate, High School/Scholarship)

Purpose: To provide financial assistance to qualified students pursuing a degree in Technical Engineering or any related fields of study. **Focus:** Engineering; Technology. **Qualif.:** Applicants must be high school students planning to pursue post-secondary studies upon graduation; post-secondary students enrolled in an engineering or technology related field of study at a recognized university, college, or technical school in British Columbia; or new immigrants (maximum of one year in Canada) pursuing post-secondary studies in an engineering or technology-related field of study at a recognized university, college, or technical school in British Columbia. **Criteria:** Applicants will be evaluated based on academic achievement, financial needs and involvement in extra-curricular activities.

Funds Avail.: $700 each. **Duration:** Annual. **Number Awarded:** 4. **To Apply:** Applicants must submit a completed application form; an official transcript; proof of registration at their current program of study; must provide an official list of courses currently registered in and a SPEATBC membership form. **Deadline:** January 31. **Contact:** SPEATBC c/o GS Brar & Co.; Email: speatbc@gmail.com.

8729 ■ Society for Range Management (SRM)

6901 S Pierce St., Ste. 225
Littleton, CO 80128
Ph: (303)986-3309
Fax: (303)986-3892
E-mail: info@rangelands.org
URL: www.rangelands.org

8730 ■ Masonic-Range Science Scholarships (Undergraduate/Scholarship)

Purpose: To financially assist students with their education. **Focus:** Science. **Qualif.:** Applicant must be a high school senior, or college freshman or sophomore planning to major in/currently majoring in range science or a closely related field; and must be sponsored by a member of the Society for Range Management (SRM), the National Association of Conservation Districts (NACD), or the Soil and Water Conservation Society (SWCS). **Criteria:** Selection will be based on the submitted application.

Funds Avail.: Varies. **Duration:** Annual; maximum of 8 semesters. **To Apply:** Applicant must submit a completed application form together with a copy of high school and college transcripts; official copy of SAT and ACT scores; two letters of references. **Deadline:** January 10. **Contact:** Paul Loeffler, Texas General Land Office 500 West Ave H, Suite 101, Box 2 Alpine, TX 79830-6008; vtrujillo@rangelands.org.

8731 ■ Society of Satellite Professionals International (SSPI)

The New York Information Technology Ctr.
250 Park Ave., 7th Fl.
New York, NY 10177-0799
Ph: (212)809-5199
Fax: (212)825-0075
URL: www.sspi.org

8732 ■ The SSPI Mid-Atlantic Chapter Scholarships (Graduate, Undergraduate/Scholarship)

Purpose: To provide financial assistance for student who are studying telecommunications systems. **Focus:** Telecommunications systems. **Qualif.:** Applicant must be a SSPI member; pursue education in the satellite industry or a field making direct use of satellite technology; have academic and leadership achievement; show potential for significant contribution to the satellite communications industry; enrolled in an accredited college or university in United States of Delaware, Maryland, West Virginia or the District of Columbia. **Criteria:** Applicant will be selected based on: 1) commitment to pursue education in the field of satellite industry; 2) academic and leadership achievement; 3) potential for significant contributions to the satellite communications industry; and 4) quality of scientific, engineering, business and research.

Funds Avail.: No specific amount. **To Apply:** Applicant may mail or fax their applications together with a current transcript.

8733 ■ Society for the Scientific Study of Sexuality (SSSS)

881 3rd St., Ste. B5
Whitehall, PA 18052
Ph: (610)443-3100
Fax: (610)443-3105

Awards are arranged alphabetically below their administering organizations

E-mail: thesociety@sexscience.org
URL: www.sexscience.org

8734 ■ Society for the Scientific Study of Sexuality Student Research Grants *(Undergraduate/Grant)*

Purpose: To advance knowledge of sexuality; to advance the quality and quantity of the knowledge based in sexual science; to foster the recognition of sexual science within the scientific community, public policy makers and the general public; to communicate the implications of sexual science. **Focus:** Sexuality. **Qualif.:** Applicants must be students enrolled in a degree-granting program and a student member of SSSS who are doing human sexuality research. **Criteria:** Recipients are selected based on submitted requirements.

Funds Avail.: $1,000. **Duration:** Annual. **Number Awarded:** 2. **To Apply:** Applicants must obtain IRB approval for the project; applicants must prepare a 150-word abstract of the proposed research; prepare a short biographical sketch suitable for the use of the society's newsletter; applicants must prepare a ten-page, double-spaced abstract of the proposed research and bibliography in MS Word; applicants must prepare a proposed budget for the project. **Deadline:** February 1 and June 1. **Contact:** Mandy Peters at mlpeters@sexscience.org.

8735 ■ Society for Technical Communication (STC)

9401 Lee Hwy., Ste. 300
Fairfax, VA 22031
Ph: (703)522-4114
Fax: (703)522-2075
URL: www.stc.org

8736 ■ Marian Norby Scholarships *(Other/ Scholarship)*

Purpose: To assist U.S. federal government employees interested in obtaining training in technical communication to improve their employment opportunities. **Focus:** Technical communications. **Qualif.:** Applicants must be female; working full- or part-time for the federal government as a secretary or administrative assistant; and interested in enrolling in a training or academic class related to technical communication. **Criteria:** Selection is based on applicants' expressed interest in technical communication, experience with technical communication and potential for contributing to the profession of technical communication. Consideration will also be given to financial need.

Funds Avail.: No specific amount. **To Apply:** Applicants must submit a completed application form along with an essay on interests and achievements, and letters of recommendation from two co-workers (such as a supervisor and a peer).

8737 ■ STC Scholarships *(Graduate, Undergraduate/ Scholarship)*

Purpose: To assist students who are pursuing established degree programs in some area of technical communication. **Focus:** Technical communications. **Qualif.:** Applicants must have completed at least one year of post-secondary education; full-time students; either graduate students working toward a Master's or Doctor's degree, or undergraduate students working toward a Bachelor's degree; have at least one full year of academic work remaining to complete the degree programs; and studying communication of informa-

tion about technical subjects. **Criteria:** Selection is based on applicants' academic records, experience with technical communication and potential for contributing to the profession of technical communication. Consideration will also be given to financial need.

Funds Avail.: No specific amount. **To Apply:** Applicants must submit a completed application form together with an essay on interests and achievements; a certified copy of the latest transcript from the school currently or last attended; and letters of recommendation from two faculty members in the field of technical communication.

8738 ■ Society for Technical Communication - Canada West Coast Chapter

597-4974 Kingsway St.
Burnaby, BC, Canada V5H 4M9
Ph: (604)440-0262
E-mail: info@stcwestcoast.ca
URL: stcwestcoast.ca

8739 ■ Julia Broderick Scholarships *(Undergraduate/ Scholarship)*

Purpose: To help students to establish their career in the profession after graduation. **Focus:** Technical communications. **Qualif.:** Applicant must be a technical writing student in the final year of study; pursuing a career in technical communication; and must have a first-class standing or equivalent. **Criteria:** Selection is based on the strength of the instructors' recommendations in combination with the applicant's academic standing and achievements.

Funds Avail.: $500. **Duration:** Annual. **Number Awarded:** 1. **To Apply:** Applicants must submit a completed application form along with a copy of current transcripts (in PDF); a one-to-two page description (in MS Word format) of academic and career goals and achievements; and two letters of recommendation from faculty members in the field of technical communications (in PDF).

8740 ■ Society for Technical Communication Lone Star Community (STC LSC)

PO Box 515571
Dallas, TX 75251
E-mail: prez@stc-dfw.org
URL: www.stc-dfw.org

8741 ■ STC-Lone Star Chapter Traditional Education Scholarships *(Graduate, Undergraduate/ Scholarship)*

Purpose: To support students pursuing a traditional bachelor's or continued education degree/certificate in a technical communications field. **Focus:** Technical communications. **Qualif.:** Applicant must be a graduate or undergraduate student working toward a degree or certificate in the technical communications field; pursuing a career in the technical communications field; and living or attending school in the DFW area, or be a member of the Lone Star Chapter of STC. **Criteria:** Selection is based on the completeness and accuracy of the application; demonstration of excellent writing skills; presentation-usage of whitespace, color and graphical elements and financial need.

Funds Avail.: No specific amount. **Duration:** Annual. **To Apply:** Applicant must submit an application that would demonstrate excellent organization, writing and design

Awards are arranged alphabetically below their administering organizations

skills. Applications (maximum of 1500 words and three graphics) must explain how the student meets the eligibility requirements (degree/certificate plan, and plans to accomplish with the degree/certificate); special honors/ achievements; other degrees held; and professional experiences in the technical communications field (if any); applicant's name, address, student ID No. , phone No. , email address; name of college and department; expected graduation date; expected hours for the upcoming semester; estimation of tuition, fees, and book expenses for the following semester; estimation of funds to offset the above costs; information on where to send funds to the school on the student's behalf; Office/Department name, address, Phone No. . In addition applicants must include two school faculty member letters of recommendation (or one faculty member and one employer letter of recommendation) on official letterhead; an unofficial current transcript; degree/ certificate plan (from school's website or catalog); and tuition estimate for the current year (from school's website or catalog). Applications are only accepted in electronic format (PDF or HTML) by email to the Lone Star Chapter of STC. **Deadline:** October 31 (Spring); March 31 (Fall). **Contact:** scholarships@stc-dfw.org.

8742 ■ Society for Technical Communication - Orlando Central Florida Chapter

PO Box 540444
Orlando, FL 32854-0444
E-mail: president@stc-orlando.org
URL: www.stc-orlando.org

8743 ■ Melissa Pellegrin Memorial Scholarships
(Undergraduate, Graduate/Scholarship)

Purpose: To support the education of undergraduate and graduate UCF Technical Communications students. **Focus:** Technical communications; Writing. **Qualif.:** Applicants must be full-time or part-time undergraduate or graduate technical writing students at the University of Central Florida (UCF). **Criteria:** Selection is based on the students' overall GPA and GPA in the major, the quality of the letter expressing the students' interest in technical communication, the students' activities in technical communication, and financial need.

Funds Avail.: Amount varies. **Duration:** Annual. **Number Awarded:** Varies. **To Apply:** Applicants must submit a completed scholarship application form along with a copy of transcripts, and a letter to the STC Orlando Chapter Education Committee. Send application and supporting materials to the contact provided. **Deadline:** February 23. **Remarks:** Established in 1997. **Contact:** Dan Voss, Education Committee Manager, at education@stc-orlando.org.

8744 ■ Society for Technical Communication - Puget Sound Chapter (STC-PSC)

8512 122nd Ave. NE, No. 85
Kirkland, WA 98033
E-mail: president@stc-psc.org
URL: www.stc-psc.org

8745 ■ STC-PSC Scholarships *(Undergraduate, Graduate/Scholarship)*

Purpose: To support students who wish to further their education in technical communication. **Focus:** Technical communications. **Qualif.:** Applicant must be enrolled in an approved two-year, four-year, or graduate program in

colleges/universities in the Puget Sound area (Edmonds Community College: A.T.A., Visual Communications; Art Institute of Seattle: B.F.A., Graphic Design; Shoreline Community College: A.A.A.S., Graphic Design; UW College of Engineering: B.S., M.S.T.C., PhD. in Technical Communication, Certificates in User-Centered Design, Tech Writing & Editing; UW College of Education: M.Ed., Educational Communication & Technology; UW School of Art: B.A., Visual Communication Design; Western Washington University: B.S., Industrial Design). **Criteria:** Selection will be based on the submitted application materials.

Funds Avail.: $1,000 each. **Duration:** Annual. **Number Awarded:** 2. **To Apply:** Applicant must submit a completed scholarship application form. **Deadline:** June 1. **Remarks:** Established in 1986. **Contact:** scholarships@stc-psc.org.

8746 ■ Society for Underwater Technology Houston

5090 Richmond Ave., Ste. 489
Houston, TX 77056
Ph: (713)995-5156
Fax: (713)995-5539
URL: www.suthouston.com

8747 ■ SUT Houston Graduate Scholarships
(Graduate/Scholarship)

Purpose: To support students who wish to pursue their studies with a relevant component area of marine science, underwater technology or offshore engineering. **Focus:** Engineering, Marine. **Qualif.:** Applicant must have completed at least one academic year of full-time graduate work, and must continue as a full-time student; must have a 3.5 on a 4.0 GPA scale as evidenced by an official college transcript; must be enrolled in an accredited college or university located in the United States of America; must provide proof of entry into some field of science or engineering encompassed by the technical activities of the SUT. **Criteria:** Selection of applicants will be based on the following criteria: (1) applicant's GPA or its equivalent, (2) career goals, (3) recommendation letters, (4) extracurricular activities, and (5) applicant's latest GRE score report.

Funds Avail.: $10,000. **To Apply:** Applicants must submit complete application form available online with career essays (500- 1000 word typewritten essay), official transcript and three letters of recommendation. Application material must be addressed to: Scholarship Program, SUT Houston, 8266 Golf Green Circle, Houston, TX 77036. **Deadline:** June 15.

8748 ■ SUT Houston Undergraduate Scholarships
(Undergraduate/Scholarship)

Purpose: To support students who with to pursue their studies with a relevant component area of marine science, underwater technology or offshore engineering. **Focus:** Engineering, Marine. **Qualif.:** Applicant must have completed at least one academic year of full-time graduate work, and must continue as a full-time student; must have a 3.3 on a 4.0 GPA scale as evidenced by an official college transcript; must be enrolled in an accredited college or university located in the United States of America; must provide proof of entry into some field of science or engineering encompassed by the technical activities of the SUT. **Criteria:** Selection of applicants will be based on the following criteria: (1) applicant's GPA or its equivalent, (2) career goals, (3) recommendation letters, (4) extracurricular activities, and (5) applicant's latest GRE score report.

Awards are arranged alphabetically below their administering organizations

Funds Avail.: $3,000. **Duration:** Annual. **To Apply:** Applicants must submit complete application form available online with career essays (500- 1000 word typewritten essay), official transcript and three letters of recommendation. Application material must be addressed to: Scholarship Program, SUT Houston, 8266 Golf Green Circle, Houston, TX 77036. **Deadline:** September 1.

8749 ■ Society of University Surgeons (SUS)

11300 W Olympic Blvd., Ste. 600
Los Angeles, CA 90064
Ph: (310)986-6442
Fax: (310)437-0585
E-mail: info@susweb.org
URL: www.susweb.org

8750 ■ SUS Foundation Junior Faculty Grants
(Other/Grant)

Purpose: To support the research of surgeons whose works involve the basic science that underlies a surgical disease. **Focus:** Surgery. **Qualif.:** Applicants must be tenure-track faculty members in a Department of Surgery; and within three years of their first facility appointment. Individuals with research suite such as national extramural grants are eligible. **Criteria:** Grant is awarded based on the eligibility of the applicants. Officers and members of the SUS Committee are excluded from mentioning Fallow.

Funds Avail.: $30,000. **Duration:** One year. **To Apply:** Applicants must also fill out an authorization form online. **Deadline:** August 1.

8751 ■ Wyeth-SUS Clinical Scholar Awards *(Other/ Award)*

Purpose: To support the research of surgeons whose works involve the basic science that underlies a surgical disease. **Focus:** Surgery. **Qualif.:** Applicant must be a faculty member in a Department of Surgery; and within three years of his/her first faculty appointment. **Criteria:** Selections are based on the scientific merit of the proposal and the potential of the applicant.

Funds Avail.: No specific amount. **Duration:** Annual. **To Apply:** Applicant must submit his/her application online using the submission system. Applicant must download and print a hard-copy of the Award Authorizations Form which will verify various institutional requirements and approvals. A completed Award Authorization form must be submitted via mail to the Society offices prior to the application deadline. **Contact:** SUS at the above address.

8752 ■ Society of Vacuum Coaters Foundation

8100 M-4 Wyoming Blvd. NE, No. 243
Albuquerque, NM 87113
URL: www.svcfoundation.org

8753 ■ Society of Vacuum Coaters Foundation Scholarships *(Vocational/Occupational, Two Year College, Undergraduate, Graduate/Scholarship)*

Purpose: To further the education of people entering or already participating in a course of study related to vacuum coating technology at an accredited institution. **Focus:** Vacuum science and technology. **Qualif.:** Applicants must be students attending an accredited technical, vocational, two-year, undergraduate or graduate school. Students and practitioners already working in the vacuum coating

technology field may apply. **Criteria:** Applicants will be evaluated based on academic achievement, personal qualities, financial need and applicant's field of study to vacuum coating technology. Preference will be given to practitioners, undergraduate and graduate students whose major is Engineering, Physics, Material Science and other fields related to vacuum coating.

Funds Avail.: No specific amount. **Duration:** Annual. **Number Awarded:** Varies. **To Apply:** Applicants must complete and sign the application form; must submit one current official certified transcript and two recommendation forms (at least one from a professor). **Deadline:** December 1.

8754 ■ Society for Vascular Surgery (SVS)

633 N St. Clair St., 22nd Fl.
Chicago, IL 60611
Ph: (312)334-2300
Fax: (312)334-2320
Free: 800-258-7188
E-mail: vascular@vascularsociety.org
URL: www.vascularweb.org

8755 ■ International Scholars Program for Young Vascular Surgeons *(Graduate/Scholarship)*

Purpose: To defray the travel costs and living expenses to visit various universities and clinics in the U.S. and attend the Vascular annual meeting. **Focus:** Medicine; Medicine, Cardiovascular; Medicine, Cerebrovascular. **Qualif.:** Applicants must: be graduates of school of medicine; be at least 35 to 40 years of age on the date that the completed application is filed; have demonstrated a commitment to teaching and/or research in accordance with the standards of the applicants' country. **Criteria:** Selection will be based on the submitted applications.

Funds Avail.: $5,000. **Duration:** Annual. **Number Awarded:** 4. **To Apply:** Applicants must submit the following: applications from their intended permanent location; completed application form; lists of all of their publications and three complete publications (reprints or manuscripts) of their choice from that list; letters of recommendation from three of their colleagues; curriculum vitae of no more than 10 pages; and photograph. **Deadline:** June 14. **Contact:** Application materials should be emailed to the membership staff at membership@vascularsociety.org.

8756 ■ Vascular Surgery Trainee Advocacy Travel Scholarship *(Advanced Professional, Professional development/Scholarship, Grant)*

Purpose: To enhance the health policy and advocacy development of the vascular surgery trainee's career. **Focus:** Medicine; Medicine, Cardiovascular; Medicine, Cerebrovascular. **Qualif.:** Applicants must be SVS candidate members currently enrolled in a vascular surgery training program, and have earnest interests in health policy and advocacy issues relating to vascular surgery. **Criteria:** Selection will be based on the committee's criteria.

Funds Avail.: $1,500. **Duration:** Annual. **To Apply:** Applicants must submit the necessary application materials which include curriculum vitae and 300-word essay describing interest in health policy/advocacy and why the applicants wish to receive the scholarship. Application materials should be submitted to the SVS Resident and Student Outreach Committee. **Contact:** SVS Resident and Student Outreach Committee; Email: studentresident@vascularsociety.org.

Awards are arranged alphabetically below their administering organizations

8757 ■ Women's Leadership Training Grant
(Advanced Professional, Professional development/ Grant)

Purpose: To enhance the health policy and advocacy development of the vascular surgery trainee's career. **Focus:** Medicine; Medicine, Cardiovascular; Medicine, Cerebrovascular. **Qualif.:** Applicants must be female U.S. citizens engaging in vascular surgery profession. **Criteria:** Selection will be based on the committee's criteria.

Funds Avail.: $15,000. **Duration:** Annual. **Number Awarded:** 3. **To Apply:** Applicants must submit the following: completely answered application form; two-page letter of intent that indicates how applicants would use the award to advance personal leadership training and specific career goals; curriculum vitae; three complete publications (reprints or manuscripts); and two letters of recommendation (from the chair of the department in which an academic appointment is held and the other from a colleague). **Deadline:** April 6. **Contact:** Society for Vascular Surgery, at the above address; or email to education@vascularsociety.org.

8758 ■ Society of Women Engineers (SWE)
203 N La Salle St., Ste. 1675
Chicago, IL 60601
Ph: (312)596-5223
Fax: (312)596-5252
Free: 877-SWE-INFO
E-mail: hq@swe.org
URL: societyofwomenengineers.swe.org

8759 ■ Society of Women Engineers Scholarships (SWE) *(Undergraduate, Graduate/Scholarship)*

Purpose: To help individuals achieve full potential in careers as engineers and leaders; to expand the image of the engineering profession as a positive force improving the quality of life; to demonstrate the value of diversity. **Focus:** Computer and information sciences; Engineering; Information science and technology. **Qualif.:** Applicants must be incoming freshmen women who are accepted for enrollment in a baccalaureate ABET/CSAB accredited engineering or computer science degree program; must have a minimum GPA of 3.5/4.0 scale for freshmen applicants; must not be the current recipients of a renewable SWE Scholarship; must be full-time students; must be U.S. citizens or permanent residents of the United States for some scholarships; and must not be receiving full funding for education from another organization. **Criteria:** Recipients are selected based on academic standing.

Funds Avail.: $1,000 - $20,000. **Duration:** Annual. **Number Awarded:** Varies. **To Apply:** Applicants must fill out the online application form and provide the following materials: a current school stamp and signature official transcript from high school or where the applicants have taken courses; a copy of letter of acceptance from ABET accredited college or university indicating acceptance into an engineering or computer science curriculum for the coming academic year; and two letters of recommendation of which one must be from a high school teacher and the other must be from a person who has known the applicants for two or more years and who is not a relative or member of the applicants' family. **Deadline:** Sophomores through Graduate students: February 15; Freshmen: May 15.

8760 ■ Sociologists for Women in Society (SWS)
1415 Jayhawk Blvd.
University of Kansas

Department of Sociology, Rm. 716
Lawrence, KS 66045
Ph: (785)864-9405
E-mail: swseo@ku.edu
URL: www.socwomen.org

8761 ■ Beth B. Hess Memorial Scholarships *(Doctorate, Graduate/Fellowship, Award)*

Purpose: To support graduate students who are pursuing doctoral degrees in sociology. **Focus:** Sociology. **Qualif.:** Applicant must be a student in an accredited PhD program in sociology in the United States; must have a commitment to teaching, especially at a community college or other institution serving less-privileged students; must be doing research and/or activism in social inequality, social justice, or social problems, with a focus on gender and/or gerontology being especially positive; must have a service to the academic and/or local community, including mentoring. **Criteria:** Selection of applicants will be based on the criteria given by the scholarship committee.

Funds Avail.: $15,000. **To Apply:** Applicants must submit a letter of application that describes the student's decision to study sociology, career goals, research, activism and service; must provide a letter confirming enrollment in or admission to a sociology PhD program; must enclose a recommendation letter from a sociologist, full curriculum vitae, including schools, degrees awarded, years of study and full or part-time status in each; must provide a one-page letter describing a community college faculty member who particularly contributed in a significant way to the decision to study sociology or pursue higher education; must provide a cover sheet with the following: (1) name and full contact information, including phone and email address;(2) current academic or organizational affiliation, with years;(3) if not currently enrolled, future PhD program and proposed entry date;(4) community college attended, with years and credits taken, or transcripts;(6) name and contact information for graduate faculty reference; (7) if included, name of honored faculty member. **Deadline:** April 1. **Contact:** Myra Marx Ferree; Email: mferree@ssc.wisc.edu.

8762 ■ Cheryl Allyn Miller Award *(Doctorate, Graduate/Award)*

Purpose: To recognize a sociology graduate student or a recent doctorate who have made outstanding contribution to the field of women and work. **Focus:** Sociology. **Qualif.:** Applicants must be graduate students or have received their Ph.D within the last two years; must be belong to SWS (Sociologists for Women in Society) and may join at the same time they apply for the award. **Criteria:** Selection of applicants will be based on research or activism in the field of women and work.

Funds Avail.: $500. **Duration:** Annual. **To Apply:** Applicants must submit a 2-3 page curriculum vitae; a cover page with the author's name, affiliation and contact information; an abstract and paper of article length (no more than 30 double-spaced pages)in a style suitable for submission to a scholarly journal (should include applicant's name, address, telephone number, email address and, for applicants with PhD, the date the PhD was completed). **Deadline:** April 1.

8763 ■ Barbara Rosenblum Cancer Dissertation Scholarships *(Doctorate/Fellowship, Scholarship)*

Purpose: To encourage doctoral research on women's experience of breast cancer and other reproductive

Awards are arranged alphabetically below their administering organizations

cancers. **Focus:** Oncology. **Qualif.:** Applicant must be a woman with feminist orientation who is sensitive to studying breast cancer and its impact on women of color as well as white women, on lesbians as well as heterosexuals and women from diverse social classes and cultural backgrounds; must have an approval of prospectus for doctoral research on breast cancer that will be useful not only academically but which will have pragmatic and practical applications; must be planning to present research findings and applications to lay audiences as well as to social scientists. **Criteria:** Selection of applicants will be based on the criteria of the scholarship committee.

Funds Avail.: $1,500. **Duration:** Biennial; in odd-numbered years. **Number Awarded:** 1. **To Apply:** Applicants must have use electronic copy of the application form available online; must provide an electronic copy of the CV and a copy of the dissertation proposal or prospectus. **Deadline:** April 1. **Contact:** Chair, Gayle Sulik at gayle.sulik@gmail.com.

8764 ■ SOKOL U.S.A.
276 Prospect St.
East Orange, NJ 07017-2889
Ph: (973)676-0280
Fax: (973)676-3348
Free: 888-253-0362
E-mail: SOKOLUSAHQS@aol.com
URL: www.sokolusa.org

8765 ■ Milan Getting Scholarships *(Undergraduate/ Scholarship)*

Purpose: To support Sokol USA student members in furthering their education. **Focus:** General studies/Field of study not specified. **Qualif.:** Applicant must be a Sokol USA member; furthering education in a four-year college or university. **Criteria:** Selection is based on the application.

Funds Avail.: $500. **Duration:** Four years. **To Apply:** Applicants must request scholarship application at the Sokol USA Headquarters. **Deadline:** March 1.

8766 ■ Solid Waste Association of North America (SWANA)
1100 Wayne Ave., Ste. 650
Silver Spring, MD 20910
Fax: (301)589-7068
Free: 800-467-9262
URL: swana.org/default.aspx

8767 ■ Grant H. Flint International Scholarships - Category I *(Undergraduate/Scholarship)*

Purpose: To promote education and professional development of dependents of SWANA members. **Focus:** General studies/Field of study not specified. **Qualif.:** Applicants must be graduating high school seniors or graduate equivalent certified candidates who have been accepted for enrollment in a junior college, a four-year college, or a university (any program). **Criteria:** Awards are given based on academic achievement, participation in community activities, extracurricular activities and quality of written discussion.

Funds Avail.: $20,000 total fund (amounts to be determined). **Duration:** Annual. **To Apply:** Applicants may visit SWANA website for scholarship forms and instructions.

Deadline: May 1. **Contact:** Kathy Callaghan at: kcallaghan@swana.org.

8768 ■ Grant H. Flint International Scholarships - Category II *(Undergraduate/Scholarship)*

Purpose: To promote education and professional development of dependents of SWANA members. **Focus:** Engineering; Environmental science. **Qualif.:** Applicants must be currently enrolled full-time college or university students who are entering their junior or senior undergraduate year and pursuing a degree in environmental science, engineering, or other suitable major related to the field of solid waste management. **Criteria:** Recipients are selected based on merit.

Funds Avail.: $20,000 total fund (amounts to be determined). **Duration:** Annual. **To Apply:** Application forms and instructions are available at SWANA website. **Deadline:** May 1. **Contact:** Kathy Callaghan at: kcallaghan@swana.org.

8769 ■ Robert P. Stearns/SCS Engineers Scholarships *(Graduate/Scholarship)*

Purpose: To promote education and professional development in areas of solid waste management by providing financial aid. **Focus:** Engineering; Environmental science. **Qualif.:** Applicants must be full-time students who are entering or are in graduate school pursuing a degree in environmental science, engineering or other suitable major related to the field of solid waste management. They also must be sons, daughters, grandsons or granddaughters of a SWANA member (sponsor) in good standing. **Criteria:** Recipients are selected based on merit.

Funds Avail.: $5,000. **Duration:** Annual. **Number Awarded:** 1. **To Apply:** Application forms and instructions are available at SWANA website. **Deadline:** May 1. **Contact:** Kathy Callaghan at: kcallaghan@swana.org.

8770 ■ Sonoma County Mycological Association (SOMA)
PO Box 7147
Santa Rosa, CA 95407
E-mail: somapresident@somamushrooms.org
URL: www.somamushrooms.org

8771 ■ Herbert M. Saylor Memorial Scholarship *(Graduate/Scholarship)*

Purpose: To recognize student achievement and stimulate further interest and study in the world of fungi. **Focus:** Agricultural sciences; Biology. **Qualif.:** Applicants must be graduate students.

Funds Avail.: $1,500. **Duration:** Annual. **To Apply:** Interested applicants must complete and submit the following materials: application form; a brief letter on what you are studying, your major, and whom you are working under. This should also include a list of college courses taken about fungi; a statement confirming your willingness to present a talk/slide show at a monthly meeting of SOMA in Santa Rosa, CA; a brief letter or recommendation from someone connected to your academic pursuits. Bring in application materials to a monthly SOMA meeting or mail to: SOMA Scholarship Committee, PO Box 7147, Santa Rosa, CA 95407. **Deadline:** May 31.

8772 ■ Sons of Confederate Veterans (SCV)
PO Box 59
Columbia, TN 38402-0059

Awards are arranged alphabetically below their administering organizations

Fax: (931)381-6712
Free: 800-380-1896
URL: www.scv.org

8773 ■ Stand Watie Scholarships *(Undergraduate/Scholarship)*

Purpose: To encourage educational pursuits by providing educational assistance. **Focus:** General studies/Field of study not specified. **Qualif.:** Applicants must be members of: Sons of Confederate Veterans, Children of the Confederacy, or United Daughters of the Confederacy; must be sophomores, juniors, or senior students enrolled in a four-year college or university. **Criteria:** Decision by the selection committee is based on information provided in the application letter and associated documents.

Funds Avail.: $1,000. **Duration:** Annual. **To Apply:** Application package includes a personal letter of application; proof of membership in one of the organizations named; a complete personal data; three letters of recommendation; and copies of transcripts, diplomas and/or certificates. Send complete application package to. **Contact:** Stand Watie Scholarship, PO Box 59, Columbia, TN, 38402.

8774 ■ Sons of Norway Foundation (SOFN)
1455 W Lake St.
Minneapolis, MN 55408-2666
Ph: (612)827-3611
Fax: (612)827-0658
Free: 800-945-8851
E-mail: foundation@sofn.com
URL: www.sofn.com/foundation

8775 ■ Nancy Lorraine Jensen Memorial Scholarships *(Undergraduate/Scholarship)*

Purpose: To encourage young women to enter the field of science and engineering. **Focus:** Engineering; Science. **Qualif.:** Applicant must be an American citizen not younger than 17 and not older than 35 on the date the scholarship application is submitted. Applicant must be a current female member or the daughter or granddaughter of a current member of the Sons of Norway, and have held such membership for at least three years duration, on the date the application is submitted. Applicants must be full-time undergraduates who have completed at least one term (quarter, semester) of her studies. **Criteria:** Recipients are selected based on their long-term career goals and clarity of their study plan; academic potential and evidence of ability to succeed; and letters of recommendation giving specific evidence of good character, eagerness, earnestness and ambition in the field of science and engineering.

Funds Avail.: No specific amount. **To Apply:** Applicants must submit an application form. Applicants must send SAT or ACT scores; a 500-word essay giving proof of their accomplishments and describing how they intend to pursue their career; a sealed, official copy of their latest grade transcript; and three sealed letters of recommendation. **Deadline:** April 1.

8776 ■ Sons of Norway Foundation Scholarships to Oslo International School *(Undergraduate/Scholarship)*

Purpose: To support students who attend Oslo International Summer School. **Focus:** Engineering; Science. **Qualif.:** Applicants must be admitted to Oslo International Summer School. Applicants must be current members of the Sons of Norway, children or grandchildren of current members. **Criteria:** Recipients are selected based on financial need, essay, GPA and letters of recommendation. Scholarship winners will bemade by a scholarship committee appointed by the President of the Sons of Norway Foundation.

Funds Avail.: $1,500. **Number Awarded:** 2. **To Apply:** Applicants must submit an application form; essay; two letters of recommendation; academic potential/grade transcripts (ACT/SAT) **Deadline:** March 1.

8777 ■ Sons of Union Veterans of the Civil War (SUVCW)
National Civil War Museum
1 Lincoln Circle at Reservoir Park, Ste. 240
Harrisburg, PA 17103
Ph: (717)232-7000
Fax: (717)412-7492
E-mail: execdir@suvcw.org
URL: www.suvcw.org

8778 ■ Sons of Union Veterans of the Civil War Scholarships *(Undergraduate/Scholarship)*

Purpose: To inspire higher learning by providing educational opportunities. **Focus:** General studies/Field of study not specified. **Qualif.:** Male applicants must be current members or Associate of Sons of Union Veterans of the Civil War; female applicants must be the daughters or granddaughters of a current member or Associate of Sons of Union Veterans of the Civil War and must be current members of at least one of the following organizations: Woman's Relief Corps, Ladies of the Grand Army of the Republic, Daughters of Union Veterans of the Civil War 1861-1865, or Auxiliary to the Sons of Union Veterans of the Civil War; must rank in the upper one-fourth of high school graduating class, preferably in the upper one-tenth; must have a record of performance in activities both in school and in the community; must have a sound interest and positive attitude toward college work. **Criteria:** Recipients are chosen based on merit.

Funds Avail.: $2,500. **Duration:** One year. **Number Awarded:** 2. **To Apply:** Applicants may download forms at the website; must provide three letters of recommendation; photocopies of current membership cards; and transcripts. **Deadline:** March 31. **Contact:** Completed applications and references should be mailed to John R. Ertell, 654 Grace Ave., Spring City, PA 19475; Phone: 610-948-1278; E-mail: jertell@verizon.net.

8779 ■ Paul and Daisy Soros Fellowships for New Americans
224 W 57th St.
New York, NY 10019
Ph: (212)547-6926
Fax: (212)548-4623
E-mail: pdsoros@sorosny.org
URL: www.pdsoros.org

8780 ■ Paul and Daisy Soros Fellowships *(Graduate/Fellowship)*

Purpose: To provide opportunities for continuing generations of able and accomplished New Americans to achieve leadership in their chosen fields. **Focus:** General studies/Field of study not specified. **Qualif.:** Applicants must: be New Americans (either naturalized as U.S. citizens, or

Awards are arranged alphabetically below their administering organizations

children of two parents who are both naturalized citizens); either have a bachelor's degree or be in the final year of undergraduate study; and must not yet be 31 years old as of the application deadline. Those who have a bachelor's degree may already be pursuing graduate studies and may receive fellowship support to continue that study. **Criteria:** Successful candidates must have at least two of the three attributes or criteria for selection: (1) creativity, originality, and initiative, demonstrated in any area of her/his life; (2) a capacity for accomplishment, demonstrated through an activity that has required drive and sustained effort; and (3) a commitment to the values expressed in the U.S. Constitution and the Bill of Rights.

Funds Avail.: Up to $25,000 in maintenance grants and up to $20,000 in tuition. **Duration:** Annual; up to two years. **Number Awarded:** Varies. **To Apply:** Applicants are required to complete the online application form. Applicants must submit two essays on specified topics; a 1-2 page resume; three recommendation letters; an institutional status form from the institution attended indicating when and whether the present degree program will be completed; a copy of transcripts; a documentary evidence that the applicant meets the definition of New American; and a copy of the score report (GMAT, MCAT, GRE, LSAT). **Deadline:** November 1. **Remarks:** Established in 1997. **Contact:** Paul and Daisy Soros Fellowships for New Americans, at the above address.

8781 ■ South Asian Bar Association of Northern California (SABA-NC)
PO Box 2733
San Francisco, CA 94126
E-mail: president@southasianbar.org
URL: www.southasianbar.org

8782 ■ SABA NC - Organizational Fellowships
(Undergraduate/Fellowship)

Purpose: To provide financial assistance to organizations in the Bay area that promote activities within the South Asian community. **Focus:** Law. **Qualif.:** Applicants must be community service organizations working in the Bay area. **Criteria:** Selection may be based on commitment to public service, financial need, academic achievement, and other personal circumstances.

Funds Avail.: No specific amount. **Duration:** Annual. **To Apply:** Applicants may visit the website to verify the application process and other pieces of information. **Deadline:** April 15.

8783 ■ SABA NC - Pro Bono Fellowships
(Undergraduate/Fellowship)

Purpose: To support law school students by sponsoring a fellowship stipend. **Focus:** Law. **Qualif.:** Applicants must be law school students. **Criteria:** Selection will be based on the committee's criteria.

Funds Avail.: No specific amount. **To Apply:** Applicants must submit a copy of their resume, two references and a short statement of interest including the following details: whether you are currently a law student in good academic standing; why you are interested in being a SABA Pro Bono Fellow; any prior or current pro bono activities; any other activities you are involved in at your law school and the approximate time commitment. **Deadline:** June 15. **Contact:** Pro Bono Committee at probono@southasianbar.org.

8784 ■ SABA NC - Public Interest Fellowships
(Undergraduate/Fellowship)

Purpose: To provide stipend for law students to spend a summer working with public interest law organizations in the San Francisco Bay area. **Focus:** Law. **Qualif.:** Applicants must be current law students in good standing and must plan to be employed or intern with a public interest organization or government agency; must have demonstrated commitment to serve the South Asian community. **Criteria:** Selection will be based on the submitted application with particular weight given to the applicants' essay. Other factors that may consider include commitment to public service, financial need, academic achievement and other personal circumstances. Preference will be given to applicants who are enrolled in a Northern California law school and employed at a Northern California organizations doing work that directly impacts the South Asian community.

Funds Avail.: No specific amount. **To Apply:** Applicants must submit the following materials: completed application form; essay responses; resume with two references; completed employer form; completed financial information form; unofficial law school transcript. Applicants may also submit the following optional materials: letters of recommendation and any additional evidence of financial need. **Deadline:** April 15. **Contact:** Siraj Hussain, SABA-NC Foundation Secretary, at foundation.sabanc@gmail.com.

8785 ■ South Asian Journalists Association (SAJA)
Columbia Graduate School of Journalism
New York, NY 10027-7060
Ph: (212)854-5979
E-mail: president@saja.org
URL: www.saja.org

8786 ■ SAJA Journalism Scholarships *(Undergraduate, Graduate/Scholarship)*

Purpose: To help graduate, undergraduate and high school students pursue their education and future careers in journalism. **Focus:** Journalism. **Qualif.:** Applicants must be South Asian descents; must be high school seniors, college undergraduate and graduate students; must be enrolled or current students in an accredited college or university in the United States or Canada and/or entering a graduate-level program in the United States or Canada. **Criteria:** Recipients are selected based on: applicants' interest in journalism; writing skills; reasons for entering journalism; and financial need.

Funds Avail.: $2,500 (high school students); $3,000 (undergraduate college students); $5,000 (graduate-level students). **Duration:** Annual. **Number Awarded:** Varies. **To Apply:** Applicants must fill out the online application form available at the website.

8787 ■ South Carolina Association for Financial Professionals (SCAFP)
c/o Alex Guzman, Membership Chairperson
PO Box 5272
Columbia, SC 29250-5275
Ph: (803)264-5048
E-mail: admin@scafponline.org
URL: www.scafponline.org

Awards are arranged alphabetically below their administering organizations

8788 ■ South Carolina Association for Financial Professionals Certified Treasury Professional Scholarships (Other/Scholarship)

Purpose: To establish an additional scholarship award for students to obtain Treasury Professional certification. **Focus:** Finance. **Qualif.:** Applicants must be employed in South Carolina; must be prepared to lead the treasury and finance profession in pursuit of excellence. **Criteria:** Recipients are selected based on their performance and demonstrated interest in the field of treasury and finance.

Funds Avail.: No specific amount. **Duration:** Annual. **Number Awarded:** 2. **To Apply:** Applicants must complete the application form; must submit a one page summary of specific treasury qualifications; must provide resume of work history; must provide a three-to-five page, double-spaced discussion document based on the latest developments in the Treasury Management field and why they should be awarded the scholarship. **Deadline:** March 31. **Contact:** Will Taylor, President, SCAFP; Phone: 843-937-4573; E-mail: will.taylor@wellsfargo.com.

8789 ■ South Carolina Association for Financial Professionals College Education Scholarships (Undergraduate/Scholarship)

Purpose: To provide a forum for the exchange of ideas and discussion of legislative, regulatory, and banking issues and developments and the opportunity to network with other Treasury Management professionals; to award an academic scholarship to an outstanding undergraduate student pursuing a degree in business in the areas including, but not limited to, accounting, economics, finance, business administration and management. **Focus:** Finance. **Qualif.:** Applicants must be South Carolina residents; must be U.S. citizens or legal permanent residents; must earn a cumulative 3.0 GPA on a 4.0 scale and a GPA in their major area of 3.5 on a 4.0 scale; must be enrolled as degree-seeking students at eligible South Carolina public or independent (private) institutions; must not be current recipients of a full-tuition scholarship. **Criteria:** Recipients are selected based on their academic performance.

Funds Avail.: No specific amount. **To Apply:** Applicants must complete the application form; must submit a one page summary of academic achievement including the applicant's GPA (overall and major area) and a list of all relevant courses in the Treasury Management field; must submit a letter of recommendation from their major field faculty member; must provide a three-to-five page, double-spaced discussion of the Treasury Management field.

8790 ■ South Carolina Law Enforcement Officers Association (SCLEOA)

PO Box 210709
Columbia, SC 29221-0709
Ph: (803)781-5913
Fax: (803)781-9208
Free: 800-922-0038
E-mail: ryan@scleoa.org
URL: www.scleoa.org

8791 ■ SCLEOA Scholarships (Undergraduate/Scholarship)

Purpose: To provide financial assistance to those students who are in need. **Focus:** General studies/Field of study not specified. **Qualif.:** Applicants must be graduating high school seniors in South Carolina; must have been legal residents of South Carolina for at least one year; must have a recommendation from their principal, headmaster, or guidance counselor; must attend a college, university, or technical school in South Carolina; must have a good moral character and reputation. **Criteria:** Applicants will be selected by the Scholarship Committee of the SCLEOA based on the application requirements submitted by the student.

Funds Avail.: Varies. **Duration:** Annual. **To Apply:** Applicants must complete the application form and must submit an essay with a minimum of 1000 words, double-spaced, on the following topics given in the website; must provide a bibliography of cited sources; must attach a copy of high school transcript to the application.

8792 ■ South Carolina Public Health Association (SCPHA)

PO Box 11061
Columbia, SC 29211
Ph: (803)736-9461
Fax: (803)788-0128
E-mail: scpha@scpha.com
URL: www.scpha.com

8793 ■ Malcolm U. Dantzler Scholarships (Other/Scholarship)

Purpose: To protect and promote personal, community and environmental health; to exercise leadership in health policy development and action; to foster scientific and professional development among its members. **Focus:** Public health. **Qualif.:** Applicants must be current members in good standing of the South Carolina Public Health Association for at least the year in which the scholarship application is submitted; must be enrolled in a course of study leading to a degree in a health-related field; must have documentation of at least six hours of study remaining before graduation; must demonstrate great academic and professional promise; must achieve and maintain a GPA of 3.5 or better based on the 4.0 scale; must exhibit significant commitment to the public health profession through volunteer and/or professional activity such as involvement in community and scholarly activities and participation in related professional and/or student organizations. **Criteria:** Recipients are selected based on academic performance and demonstrated involvement in community activities.

Funds Avail.: $500. **To Apply:** Applicants must complete the application form; must write a personal statement of 250 words or less about their career goals and professional aspirations; must include current official transcript of records; must include proof of hours remaining before graduation. **Deadline:** April 24. **Contact:** Brenda Y. Martin, SCPHA Scholarship Committee Chair; Phone: 803-517-2038; E-mail: brendamartin111@yahoo.com.

8794 ■ South Carolina Public Health Association Scholarships (Undergraduate/Scholarship)

Purpose: To financially support students with their studies. **Focus:** Public health. **Qualif.:** Applicants must be students enrolled in an accredited School of Public Health; must be current members in good standing of the South Carolina Public Health Association for at least the year in which the scholarship application is submitted; must have documentation of at least six hours of study remaining before graduation; must demonstrate great academic and professional promise; must achieve and maintain a GPA of 3.5 or better based on the 4.0 scale; must exhibit significant commit-

Awards are arranged alphabetically below their administering organizations

ment to the public health profession through volunteer and/or professional activity such as involvement in community and scholarly activities and participation in related professional and/or student organizations. **Criteria:** Recipients are selected based on academic performance and demonstrated involvement in community activities.

Funds Avail.: $500. **To Apply:** Applicants must complete the application form; must write a personal statement of 250 words or less about their career goals and professional aspirations; must include current official transcript of records; must include proof of hours remaining before graduation. **Deadline:** April 24. **Contact:** Brenda Y. Martin, SCPHA Scholarship Committee Chair; Phone: 803-517-2038; E-mail: brendamartin111@yahoo.com.

8795 ■ South Carolina Restaurant and Lodging Association (SCRLA)
1122 Lady St., Ste. 1210
Columbia, SC 29201
Ph: (803)765-9000
Fax: (803)252-7136
E-mail: info@scrla.org
URL: www.scrla.org

8796 ■ South Carolina Tourism and Hospitality Educational Foundation Scholarships
(Undergraduate/Scholarship)

Purpose: To provide educational assistance for students who demonstrate an interest in and commitment to the hospitality (restaurant, lodging tourism) industry. **Focus:** Travel and tourism. **Qualif.:** Applicants must be students seeking post-secondary education and careers in the restaurant/hospitality industry. **Criteria:** Recipients are selected based on presentation of application; strength of letters of recommendation; a well-written and within word count essay; industry-related work experience and GPA. Preference will be given to applicants who will be classified as full-time students.

Funds Avail.: No specific amount. **To Apply:** Applicants must submit a completed application form; three letters of reference; three completed Character Reference Forms; current official transcript; and a double-spaced essay (minimum of 500 words and maximum of 1,000 words). Scholarship application can be downloaded and filled-out at the website. **Deadline:** May 7.

8797 ■ South Carolina Undergraduate Scholarships
(Undergraduate/Scholarship)

Purpose: To assist students who demonstrate an interest in and commitment to the hospitality (restaurant, foodservice, lodging, tourism) industry. **Focus:** Culinary arts. **Qualif.:** Applicants must be enrolled in a post-secondary restaurant/hospitality program and must be attending an accredited post college or university in South Carolina. **Criteria:** Recipients are selected based on financial need and academic performance.

Funds Avail.: No specific amount. **To Apply:** Applicants must submit a completed application form; three letters of reference; three completed character reference forms; current official transcript; and (minimum of 500 words and maximum of 1,000 words, double-spaced) essay. Scholarship application can be downloaded and filled out at the website. **Deadline:** May 1.

8798 ■ South Carolina Scholastic Press Association (SCSPA)
600 Assembly St.
School of Journalism and Mass Communications
University of South Carolina
Columbia, SC 29208
Ph: (803)777-6284
Fax: (803)777-4103
URL: scspa.sc.edu

8799 ■ McClatchy Scholarships *(Undergraduate/ Scholarship)*

Purpose: To provide financial assistance to those students who are in need. **Focus:** Journalism. **Qualif.:** Applicants must be minority students pursuing print journalism careers in the School of Journalism and Mass Communications. **Criteria:** Scholarships will be awarded based on need and merit as determined by the School of Journalism.

Funds Avail.: $1,000. **To Apply:** Applicants may contact the Association for the scholarship application process. **Deadline:** March 15. **Contact:** South Carolina Scholastic Press Association at the above address.

8800 ■ South Carolina Scholastic Press Association Scholarships *(Undergraduate/Scholarship)*

Purpose: To provide financial support to deserving students. **Focus:** Journalism. **Qualif.:** Applicants must be graduating seniors who have been admitted and plan to attend the USC School of Journalism and Mass Communications; and must be student members of SCSPA. **Criteria:** Awards will be based on scholastic journalism involvement as well as applicants' academic achievements while in high school.

Funds Avail.: $1,000. **Duration:** One year. **To Apply:** Applicants must send a completed application form; a copy of high school transcript; two letters of recommendation from advisers, teachers, principals or superintendents; and must provide a 250-500 words personal essay emphasizing the things and accomplishments in the field of journalism in the future. **Deadline:** February 6. **Contact:** South Carolina Scholastic Press Association at the above address.

8801 ■ South Carolina Scholastic Press Association Yearbook Scholarships *(Undergraduate/Scholarship)*

Purpose: To provide financial assistance to deserving students. **Focus:** Journalism. **Qualif.:** Applicants must be graduating high school seniors who have shown academic excellence; must have plan to attend the University of South Carolina main campus in Columbia; must be student members of SCSPA; and must have worked on the school's yearbook for at least two years or have taken the Journalism 1 class and worked at least one year on the yearbook. **Criteria:** Preference will be given to those students who meet the criteria.

Funds Avail.: $500. **Duration:** One year. **To Apply:** Applicants must submit a completed application form; a copy of high school transcript; two letters of recommendation which may be from advisers, teachers, principals or superintendents; and 250-500 words personal essay emphasizing the accomplishments in the field of journalism in the future. **Deadline:** February 6. **Contact:** Application form and other supporting documents should be sent to College of Mass Communications and Information Studies, University of South Carolina, Columbia, SC 29208.

8802 ■ South Central Power Co.
PO Box 250
Lancaster, OH 43130

Awards are arranged alphabetically below their administering organizations

Ph: (740)653-4422
Fax: (740)681-4488
Free: 800-282-5064
URL: www.southcentralpower.com

8803 ■ South Central Power Scholarships
(Undergraduate/Scholarship)

Purpose: To support high school seniors who are pursuing their education at a college, vocational or technical school. **Focus:** General studies/Field of study not specified. **Qualif.:** Applicants must be graduating seniors who have basic credits for entering college or a proper vocational or technical school; have current career GPA of at least 3.6 on a 4.0 scale and a combined ACT score of at least 22; must be accepted or will be accepted at an accredited college or proper vocational or technical school; and must live at the South Central Power account location. Parents/guardians of the students must be members/consumers of South Central Power Company. **Criteria:** Scholarships will be given based on scholastic record; personal achievement, school and community activities; poise, personality and appearance; and knowledge of cooperatives based on an OREC fact book provided by South Central Power Company.

Funds Avail.: $1,000 each. **Duration:** Annual. **Number Awarded:** Varies. **To Apply:** Applicants must complete the official application form (typed in order to be accepted). They should also submit complete high school transcript. All applications must be submitted to Liz Bainter. **Deadline:** December 31. **Contact:** Liz Bainter, at 1-800-282-5064 ext. 6252.

8804 ■ South Dakota Nurses Association (SDNA)
PO Box 1015
Pierre, SD 57501-1015
Ph: (605)945-4265
Free: 888-425-4265
E-mail: contactus@sdnurses.org
URL: www.sdnursesassociation.org

8805 ■ Marianne M. Stenvig Scholarships *(Master's, Doctorate/Scholarship)*

Purpose: To support male registered nurses in pursuit of their educational goals. **Focus:** Nursing. **Qualif.:** Applicants must be South Dakota residents and RN licensed; must be pursuing a master's or doctoral degree in nursing or related field; must be SDNA members. **Criteria:** Selection will be based on the committee's criteria.

Funds Avail.: $1,000. **To Apply:** Scholarship application form can be downloaded at the website. Applicants must provide the following materials: evidence of current student status, either copy of admission letter if admitted but not yet enrolled, or current transcript if enrolled; two letters of recommendation describing the personal qualities and activities that exemplify leadership, compassion, and involvement in professional organizations(s), professional activities and community service. At least one letter of recommendation should be from a faculty member and one letter may be from a professional colleague; current resume; personal statement addressing career goals, personal qualities that affect their nursing practice, and how their career goals and personal qualities reflect South Dakota Nurses Foundation purposes of education, research, and service. Please limit personal statement to 500 words or less. **Deadline:** July 15.

8806 ■ South Dakota Retailers Association (SDRA)
320 E Capitol Ave.
Pierre, SD 57501
Ph: (605)224-5050
Free: 800-658-5545
URL: www.sdra.org

8807 ■ Jerry Wheeler Scholarships *(Undergraduate/ Scholarship)*

Purpose: To assist students who wish to pursue studies in a retail field. **Focus:** Business. **Qualif.:** Applicants must be enrolled full-time in a retail-related course at an accredited educational institution; must be graduates of South Dakota High School or GED program; or enrolled in a South Dakota post-secondary school. Previous applicants may reapply. **Criteria:** Recipients will be selected based on submitted applications.

Funds Avail.: No specific amount. **To Apply:** Applicants must submit a completed application form; copy of their most recent transcript; two letters of reference from a retailer or other businessperson. **Contact:** Application form and other supporting documents may be sent electronically to donna@sdra.org.

8808 ■ South Jersey Golf Association (SJGA)
PO Box 884
North Cape May, NJ 08204
Ph: (609)760-7779
E-mail: SJGABusinessOffice@gmail.com
URL: www.sjgolf.org

8809 ■ South Jersey Golf Association Scholarships
(Undergraduate/Scholarship)

Purpose: To provide support for deserving high school seniors intending to pursue their education. **Focus:** General studies/Field of study not specified. **Qualif.:** Applicant must be a graduating high school senior who has been a member in good standing of his/her golf team and who plans to enroll as a full-time undergraduate student at an accredited college or university within the United States. **Criteria:** Selection of applicants will be based on academic standing.

Funds Avail.: $400 - $1,000. **Duration:** Annual. **To Apply:** Applicants must have a copy of their college/university letter of acceptance or waitlist deferral; must provide a copy of their transcript which must include mid-year grades through the fall semester of senior year; must provide a copy of their SATI or ACT Score Reports; must have a typed essay, three letters of recommendation, completed resume and a senior yearbook photograph. **Deadline:** May 11. **Contact:** Ms. Gail Reilly; Email: gareilly@aol.com.

8810 ■ South Kentucky Rural Electric Cooperative Corporation (SKRECC)
PO Box 910
Somerset, KY 42502
Ph: (606)678-4121
Fax: (606)679-8279
Free: 800-264-5112
E-mail: skrecc@skrecc.com
URL: www.skrecc.com

8811 ■ Sam J. Hord Memorial Scholarships
(Undergraduate/Scholarship)

Purpose: To provide financial assistance to those who are pursuing higher education. **Focus:** General studies/Field of

Awards are arranged alphabetically below their administering organizations

study not specified. **Qualif.:** Applicants must be members of South Kentucky Rural Electric Cooperative, or whose parents are members, or dependent students whose parents are members. **Criteria:** Applicants are evaluated based on the criteria designed by the Scholarship Selection Committee.

Funds Avail.: No specific amount. **To Apply:** Applicants must submit a completed scholarship application; copy of grade transcript; copy of most recent family federal tax return; and, ACT, SAT or COMPASS results. For further information, applicants may call the Somerset Community College. **Deadline:** March 1 (fall scholarships); July 1 (additional scholarships awarded for fall); January 5 (additional scholarships awarded for spring).

8812 ■ South Kentucky RECC High School Senior Scholarships *(Undergraduate/Scholarship)*

Purpose: To provide financial assistance to those who are pursuing higher education. **Focus:** General studies/Field of study not specified. **Qualif.:** Applicants must be full-time high school seniors whose principal residences are active accounts of South Kentucky RECC. **Criteria:** Applicants are evaluated based on criteria of the Scholarship Committee without regard to race, religion, sex, age or physical capability.

Funds Avail.: $1,000. **Duration:** Annual. **To Apply:** Applicants must submit a completed application form along with an essay (between 350 and 500 words) about "Why Energy Efficiency and Conservation is Important". **Contact:** Alan Coffey, at the above address.

8813 ■ Woman In Rural Electrification Scholarships *(Undergraduate/Scholarship)*

Purpose: To provide financial assistance to those who are pursuing higher education. **Focus:** General studies/Field of study not specified. **Qualif.:** Applicants must be students whose immediate family is served by a Kentucky rural electric cooperative, such as South Kentucky RECC; must be full-time juniors or seniors with at least 60 hours of credits at a Kentucky college or university by the start of the fall term. **Criteria:** Applicants will be evaluated based on criteria designed by the committee of the Kentucky W.I.R.E. and chosen applicants will be notified.

Funds Avail.: $1,000 each. **Duration:** Annual. **Number Awarded:** 3. **To Apply:** Applicants must contact their local South Kentucky RECC office or call the toll-free number found in the cooperative's website, for further information.

8814 ■ Southeastern Library Association (SELA)

PO Box 950
Rex, GA 30273
Ph: (678)466-4334
Fax: (678)466-4349
E-mail: webmaster@selaonline.org
URL: selaonline.org

8815 ■ The Ginny Frankenthaler Memorial Scholarships *(Undergraduate/Scholarship)*

Purpose: To recruit beginning professional librarians who have potential for leadership and have made a commitment to service in the libraries of the Southeastern United States; to provide financial assistance towards the completion of their graduate degree in library science from an institution accredited by the American Library Association. **Focus:** Science. **Qualif.:** Applicants must be completing their

senior year at an accredited college or university or be graduates of such an institution; must be accepted as students in a degree program accredited by the American Library Association; must be ready to begin the program of study no later than the fall term of the year in which the scholarship is awarded; must indicate their intention to complete the degree requirements within three years; must maintain a "B" GPA throughout the program and must agree to work within one year following the graduation from library school. **Criteria:** Recipients are selected based on academic performance, financial need and interest in work and study related to library science.

Funds Avail.: $1,000. **Duration:** Two years. **To Apply:** Applicants must submit an official application form; three letters of acceptance from a library school accredited by the American Library Association; three letters of reference sent directly by the references; and an official transcript of all academic works. **Deadline:** May 1.

8816 ■ Southeastern Theatre Conference

1175 Revolution Mill Dr., Ste. 14
Greensboro, NC 27405
Ph: (336)272-3645
Fax: (336)272-8810
E-mail: dslusser@camden.k12.ga.us
URL: www.setc.org

8817 ■ Leighton M. Ballew Directing Scholarships *(Undergraduate/Scholarship)*

Purpose: To provide services and educational programs for those individuals and organizations engaged in theatre in the southeast. **Focus:** Theater arts. **Qualif.:** Applicants must have completed their undergraduate work at an accredited institution within the SETC region; and be entering graduate school in any region for the time or be currently enrolled in a graduate directing program in a college or university in any region. **Criteria:** Selections will be based on the replies and recommendations as candidates for the award.

Funds Avail.: $3,300. **To Apply:** Applicants should provide: a personal letter outlining plans and objectives for graduate work or internship; a complete resume, including work in stage management or play direction; names, addresses, and telephone numbers of three references who have had agreed, at the request of the award committee, to write letters recommending the applicant; complete undergraduate and graduate transcripts; letter of acceptance by an accredited graduate program in directing. **Deadline:** January 15. **Contact:** Paul Crook, Louisiana Tech University, PO Box 8608, Ruston, LA 71272, pcrook@latech.edu, 318-257-2062.

8818 ■ Polly Holliday Scholarships *(Undergraduate/ Scholarship)*

Purpose: To provide services and educational programs for those individuals and organizations engaged in theatre in the southeast. **Focus:** Theater arts. **Qualif.:** Any high school senior in the southeastern Theatre Conference Region who is planning to attend a college or university with the intent of majoring in theatre arts. **Criteria:** Selection is based on the financial need, talent and the potential for academic success in college.

Funds Avail.: $1,000. **To Apply:** Applicants must provide the following: an official transcript, along with verification of class rank and available SAT or ACT scores from the high

Awards are arranged alphabetically below their administering organizations

school guidance counselor or principal; three completed recommendation forms, with one being from the nominee's high school principal; The students completed nominee resume form. **Deadline:** January 21. **Contact:** Gary Weatherly, 2148 Brookdale Lane, Birmingham, AL 35216; weatherlyg@mtnbrook.k12.al.us.

8819 ■ Robert Porterfield Graduate Scholarships (Graduate/Scholarship)

Purpose: To provide services and educational programs for those individuals and organizations engaged in theatre in the southeast. **Focus:** Theater arts. **Qualif.:** Applicant must have completed undergraduate work at an institution within the SETC region; and be attending or entering an accredited graduate school the fall term following the convention at which the award is announced. **Criteria:** Applicants may be selected as finalists on the basis of their materials.

Funds Avail.: $3,000. **To Apply:** Applicant must provide the following materials: completed application form; personal letter outlining plans and objectives; a complete resume; three reference letters speaking specifically to the applicant's potential as a graduate student; complete official transcripts from all colleges/universities attended. **Deadline:** January 15. **Contact:** Abby Kiker, am_wurster@yahoo.com.

8820 ■ Marian A. Smith Scholarships (Graduate/Scholarship)

Purpose: To provide services and educational programs for those individuals and organizations engaged in theatre in the southeast. **Focus:** Theater arts. **Qualif.:** Applicants must have completed undergraduate work at an institution within the SETC region; and be entering graduate school for the first time. **Criteria:** Selection will be based on their replies and recommendations as the candidates for the award.

Funds Avail.: $2,000. **Duration:** One year. **To Apply:** Applicants should provide via email or standard mail: a completed application form; a personal letter outlining plans and objectives; a complete resume; ten slides or photographs of completed work or renderings; names, addresses and phone numbers of three to five references; complete college transcripts. **Deadline:** January 21. **Contact:** Carey Hanson, University of Mississippi, Department of Theatre, Isom Hall, Room 110 A, University, MS 38677; 662-915-6990; costumes@olemiss.edu.

8821 ■ Southeastern Theatre Conference Secondary School Scholarships (Undergraduate/Scholarship)

Purpose: To provide services and educational programs for those individuals and organizations engaged in theatre in the southeast. **Focus:** Theater arts. **Qualif.:** Any high school senior in the southeastern theatre conference region who is planning to attend a college or university in the SETC region with the intent of majoring in Theatre Arts. **Criteria:** Selection is based on the aptitude in theatrical practices and the potential for academic success in college.

Funds Avail.: $1,500. **To Apply:** Applicant must provide the following: an official transcript, along with verification of class rank and available SAT or ACT scores from the high-school guidance counselor or principal; three completed recommendation forms, with one being from the nominee's high-school principal; the student's completed nominee resume form. **Deadline:** January 15. **Contact:** Jesse Bates, Chair, jbates@asfa.k12.al.us.

8822 ■ William E. Wilson Scholarships (Graduate/Scholarship)

Purpose: To provide services and educational programs for those individuals and organizations engaged in theatre in the southeast. **Focus:** Theater arts. **Qualif.:** Applicants must be legal residents of a state in the SETC region, and must have at least one year of experience as a full-time teacher and director of theatre in a regionally accredited secondary school in the SETC region. The award recipient must enroll in a regionally accredited graduate program within one year of being selected for the scholarship. **Criteria:** Selection will be based on their replies and recommendations as the candidates for the award.

Funds Avail.: $6,000. **To Apply:** Applicants must provide the following: complete application form; official transcript; resume. **Deadline:** January 15. **Contact:** Dean Slusser, 813 Devon Drive, St. Mary's, Georgia 31558, dslusser@camden.k12.ga.us.

8823 ■ Southern Alberta Curling Association (SACA)

720-3rd St. NW
Calgary, AB, Canada T2N 1N9
Ph: (403)246-9300
Fax: (403)246-9349
E-mail: curling@saca.ca
URL: www.saca.ca

8824 ■ Glenn Watson Scholarships (Undergraduate/Scholarship)

Purpose: To financially support junior curlers who want to pursue their studies. **Focus:** General studies/Field of study not specified. **Qualif.:** Applicant must be a resident for a period of 24 months immediately prior to the date of application in the Province of Alberta; must be a Canadian citizen or permanent resident; must have participated regularly with an organized curling league at a curling club associated with SACA at any time within 5 years preceding the date of the application and for not less than two full seasons of curling. **Criteria:** Selection is based on merit and need.

Funds Avail.: $1,250. **Duration:** Annual. **Number Awarded:** 1. **To Apply:** Applicant must provide proof of high school diploma or written notice of diploma pending completion of grade 12; must have proof of acceptance to an accredited post-secondary educational institution for full-time studies; must provide an anticipated income and expenses for the coming year while in school; must have a short description (1-2 pages) of why they think they should be chosen; must have a minimum of two letters of reference with at least one from their curling community; must have written evidence of participation in their curling club. **Deadline:** April 1.

8825 ■ Southern Arizona Environmental Management Society (SAEMS)

PO Box 41433
Tucson, AZ 85717
Ph: (520)882-5880
E-mail: communications@saems.org
URL: www.saems.org

8826 ■ SAEMS Environmental Scholarships (Undergraduate, Graduate/Scholarship)

Purpose: To encourage students pursuing a career in an environmental field who are planning to work on solutions

Awards are arranged alphabetically below their administering organizations

to environmental problems. **Focus:** Environmental science. **Qualif.:** Applicants must be undergraduate or graduate students. **Criteria:** Selection will be based on the committee's criteria.

Funds Avail.: No specific amount. **Duration:** Annual. **To Apply:** Interested applicants may contact the Society for the application process and other information. **Contact:** B.J. Cordova; Phone: 520-481-3223 or bj.cordova@tucsonaz.gov.

8827 ■ Southern California Chinese Lawyers Association (SCCLA)

PO Box 861959
Terminal Annex
Los Angeles, CA 90086-1959
E-mail: info@sccla.org
URL: www.sccla.org

8828 ■ SCCLA Fellowships *(Graduate/Fellowship)*

Purpose: To provide an opportunity for local Asian/Pacific American law students to work with an organization serving the Asian and Pacific Islander (API) community. **Focus:** Law. **Qualif.:** Program is open to Asian/Pacific American law students at all levels. **Criteria:** Selection is based on need, academic accomplishments, and/or potential contribution to the Chinese-American community.

Funds Avail.: $2,000. **Number Awarded:** 2-4. **To Apply:** Interested applicants may visit the website to obtain an application form and other details. **Deadline:** March 20. **Contact:** Faith Santoso at fsantoso@apalc.org; Phone: 213-977-7500; Nate Law Email: nlaw29@yahoo.com.

8829 ■ SCCLA Scholarships *(Graduate/Scholarship)*

Purpose: To support the education of local Asian/Pacific American law students. **Focus:** Law. **Qualif.:** Applicant must be an Asian/Pacific American law student at all levels. **Criteria:** Selection is based on need, academic accomplishments, and/or potential contribution to the Chinese-American community.

Funds Avail.: $1,000. **Duration:** Annual. **To Apply:** Interested applicants may visit the website to obtain an application form and other details. **Deadline:** March 20. **Contact:** Faith Santoso at fsantoso@apalc.org; Phone: 213-977-7500; Nate Law Email: nlaw29@yahoo.com.

8830 ■ Southern California Lambda Medical Association (SCLMA)

5219 Cedros Ave.
Sherman Oaks, CA 91411
URL: www.sclma.org

8831 ■ SCLMA Student Scholarships *(Undergraduate, Graduate/Scholarship)*

Purpose: To support gay, lesbian, and bisexual physicians-in-training. **Focus:** Medicine. **Qualif.:** Applicant must be either a gay, lesbian, bisexual, or transgendered medical student and must be attending UCLA, USC, UCI, Loma Linda University, or Western University of Health Sciences or other medical schools in Southern California. **Criteria:** Selection is based on the application materials submitted.

Funds Avail.: No specific amount. **Duration:** Annual. **To Apply:** Applicant is required to apply online. **Deadline:** November 12. **Contact:** SCLMA, at the above address.

8832 ■ Southern Maine Women's Golf Association (SMWGA)

58 Val Halla Rd.
Cumberland, ME 04021
Ph: (207)829-4442
E-mail: smwga@gwi.net
URL: www.smwga.com

8833 ■ Southern Maine Women's Golf Association Scholarships *(All/Scholarship)*

Purpose: To assist Southern Maine women who wish to further their education. **Focus:** General studies/Field of study not specified. **Qualif.:** Applicants must be residents of Southern Maine including York, Cumberland, Androscoggin and Sagadahoc, or a portion of Oxford County which includes the towns of Boothbay and Boothbay Harbor in Lincoln County. **Criteria:** Applicants will be evaluated based on their level of interests, participation in the sport of golf, scholastic achievement and participation in community activities.

Funds Avail.: No specific amount. **Duration:** Annual. **To Apply:** Applicants must submit a completed application form and two letters of recommendation from individuals who can attest to their participation and performance in any area. **Deadline:** July 15.

8834 ■ Southern Nursing Research Society

10200 W 44th Ave., Ste. 304
Wheat Ridge, CO 80033
Ph: (303)327-7548
Free: 877-314-7677
E-mail: info@snrs.org
URL: www.snrs.org

8835 ■ CANS/SNRS Dissertation Research Grants *(Doctorate/Grant)*

Purpose: To support doctoral students in the Southern region enrolled in research-focused programs as they initiate a program of nursing research to advance nursing science and practice. **Focus:** Nursing. **Qualif.:** Applicants must be: current SNRS members (students or regulars) when the application is received; currently enrolled in doctoral study at a School or College of Nursing in the southern region; and current members (full or student members) of The Council for the Advancement of Nursing Science (CANS). They must also show evidence that the proposed study has met the requirements for the dissertation (proposal has been successfully defended) and that it can be supported at the institution/facility proposed. **Criteria:** Recipients will be selected through a peer review process using the following criteria: significance to nursing; scientific merit; innovation; appropriateness of methodology given the research question; qualifications of the investigators (research teams) to conduct study; adequacy of human subjects/animal protection; and appropriate environment, budget, and time frame.

Funds Avail.: $5,000. **To Apply:** Applicants may visit the website for the online application and submission process. **Deadline:** September 1. **Remarks:** The grant is a joint program of Council for the Advancement of Nursing Science and the Southern Nursing Research Society.

8836 ■ SNRS Dissertation Research Grants *(Doctorate/Grant)*

Purpose: To support doctoral students in the Southern region enrolled in research-focused programs as they initi-

---

Awards are arranged alphabetically below their administering organizations

ate a program of nursing research to advance nursing science and practice. **Focus:** Nursing. **Qualif.:** Applicants must be current SNRS members (student or regular) when the application is received; must be currently enrolled in doctoral study at a School or College of Nursing in the southern region; and must provide evidence that their proposed studies have met the requirements for the dissertation (proposals have been successfully defended) and that can be supported at the institution/facility proposed. **Criteria:** Recipients will be selected through a peer review process using the following criteria: significance to nursing; scientific merit; innovation; appropriateness of methodology given the research question; qualifications of the investigators (research teams) to conduct study; adequacy of human subjects/animal protection; and appropriate environment, budget, and time frame.

Funds Avail.: $5,000. **To Apply:** Applicants must submit a proposal and all required materials as one electronic document through the Society's website and are required to pay the application fee. **Deadline:** March 1.

8837 ■ SNRS Research Grants (Professional development/Grant)

Purpose: To support and promote new investigators in initiating or building a program of research, which advances nursing science and practice. **Focus:** Nursing. **Qualif.:** Applicants must be current SNRS members (students or regulars) when the application is received; or individuals who have received no more than a cumulative $30,000 research funding during the past two years; or individuals who have never served on a SNRS Research Grant as principal investigators. **Criteria:** Recipients will be selected through a peer review process using the following criteria: significance to nursing; scientific merit; innovation; appropriateness of methodology given the research question; qualifications of the investigators (research teams) to conduct study; adequacy of human subjects/animal protection; and appropriate environment, budget, and time frame.

Funds Avail.: $7,500. **To Apply:** Applicants must submit a proposal and all required materials as one electronic document through the Society's website and are required to pay the application fee. **Deadline:** October 1.

8838 ■ SNRS/STTI Research Grants (Professional development/Grant)

Purpose: To encourage qualified nurses to contribute to the advancement of nursing through research. **Focus:** Nursing. **Qualif.:** Applicants must be members in good standing of both STTI and SNRS who are registered nurse with a current license and hold at minimum a master's degree or its equivalent and/or be enrolled in a doctoral program. **Criteria:** Selection will be based on the committee's criteria.

Funds Avail.: Up to $5,000. **To Apply:** Applicants may visit the website for the online application and submission process. **Deadline:** April 1. **Remarks:** The grant is jointly administered and bestowed by the Southern Nursing Research Society, and Sigma Theta Tau International. **Contact:** Research Services, Sigma Theta Tau International; Phone: 888-634-7575 (US/Canada) or (+1) 317-634-8171 (International); Fax: (+1) 317-634-8188; Email: research@stti.iupui.edu.

8839 ■ Southern Regional Education Board (SREB)

592 10th St. NW
Atlanta, GA 30318-5776

Ph: (404)875-9211
Fax: (404)872-1477
E-mail: info@sreb.org
URL: www.sreb.org

8840 ■ SREB-State Doctoral Scholars Program - Doctoral Awards (Doctorate, Graduate/Scholarship)

Purpose: To increase the number of minority students who earn their respective doctoral degrees and wanting to become college/university professors. **Focus:** Engineering; Mathematics and mathematical sciences; Science; Technology. **Qualif.:** Applicants should be those who: are U.S. citizens or have legal permanent resident status; are applying to or enrolled in a Ph.D. program; are expecting admission into a Ph.D. program before the academic year begins or are within a first year of Ph.D. program; are accepted into or enrolled in a full-time, campus-based Ph.D. program (not online or distance learning) at a particular institution in a participating state by August, the start of the academic year; hold or are scheduled to receive a bachelor's or master's degree from a regionally accredited college or university by the beginning of the fall semester (the program particularly encourages applicants who seek Ph.D. in in the STEM disciplines (science, technology, engineering and math which have a particularly low minority representation); are members of a racial or ethnic minority (including African-American, Asian-American, Hispanic/Latin American, Native American, or others); are not employed outside department or discipline; and, plan to become full-time college or university faculty members after earning their Ph.D. **Criteria:** Selection is based on the letter of interest (including statement of teaching goals), letters of recommendation and the area of study (STEM disciplines-science, technology, engineering and math).

Funds Avail.: $20,000 stipend. **Duration:** Annual; up to 3-5 years. **Number Awarded:** 1. **To Apply:** Applicant must submit a completed Doctoral Awards application form along with the application checklist; letter of interest; three letters of recommendation; transcript(s); verification of U.S. citizenship or permanent U.S. resident status; verification from the university of in-state residency status if applying in GA, MS, SC, TN or VA; and verification from the university of passing score on preliminary/comprehensive exams. **Deadline:** March 31. **Contact:** Chanell Turner at chanell.turner@sreb.org.

8841 ■ Southern Scholarship Foundation (SSF)

322 Stadium Dr.
Tallahassee, FL 32304
Ph: (850)222-3833
Fax: (850)222-6750
E-mail: mmahovetz@southernscholarship.org
URL: www.southernscholarship.org

8842 ■ Southern Scholarship Foundation Scholarships (Undergraduate/Scholarship)

Purpose: To support students attending the four major universities in Florida. **Focus:** General studies/Field of study not specified. **Qualif.:** Applicants must be attending one of the four major universities in Florida (Florida A&M University, Florida Gulf Coast University, Florida State University, and the University of Florida); demonstrate financial need (submit the FAFSA); and have at least a 3.00 GPA. **Criteria:** Recipients will be selected based on the application materials.

Funds Avail.: No specific amount. **Duration:** Annual. **To**

Awards are arranged alphabetically below their administering organizations

Apply: Applicants must submit a completed scholarship application form, recent photograph, an acceptance letter, a list of honors and activities, transcript, three letters of recommendation, the essay, financial information, and resume. **Deadline:** March 1 for fall semester; October 31 for spring semester. **Contact:** SSF at admissions@southernscholarship.org.

8843 ■ Southern Section Air and Waste Management Association (SSAWMA)

c/o Justice A. Manning, Administrative Assistant
133 Rolling Hill Dr.
Daphne, AL 36526
Ph: (251)625-0513
URL: www.ss-awma.org

8844 ■ SSAWMA Scholarships *(Graduate/ Scholarship)*

Purpose: To assist students pursuing careers in the areas of air and water pollution control and hazardous waste management, such as transportation control measures, acidic deposition, indoor air quality, new or improved control technology, and physical or chemical characterization of pollutants. **Focus:** Air pollution; Environmental law; Waste management. **Qualif.:** Applicants must be pursuing a graduate-level course of study and research leading to a career related to air or water quality, waste management, pollution prevention, environmental policy/compliance/law, or sustainability. **Criteria:** Awards will be given based on academic records and career goals.

Funds Avail.: $1,500 each. **Duration:** Annual. **Number Awarded:** 2. **To Apply:** Applicants must submit a completed scholarship application form along with the statement of professional goals, transcripts, verification of graduate school attendance, TOEFL or MELAB scores (optional), professional or non-professional work experience and two letters of recommendation. Submit application package in duplicate (must be clipped, not stapled). **Deadline:** May 15. **Contact:** Justice Manning, 251-625-0513 or via e-mail at jmanning1@bellsouth.net.

8845 ■ Southwest Florida Community Foundation

Bldg. 2
8771 College Pkwy., Ste. 201
Fort Myers, FL 33919
Ph: (239)274-5900
Fax: (239)274-5930
URL: www.floridacommunity.com

8846 ■ Jordan Abdo Memorial Scholarship *(Undergraduate/Scholarship)*

Purpose: To fund scholarships for a North Fort Myers High School male or female student athlete. **Focus:** General studies/Field of study not specified. **Qualif.:** Applicants must have graduated from North Fort Myers High School; must be student athletes with a GPA of at least 3.0. **Criteria:** Scholarship recipients are selected based upon the specific criteria made by each fund's donor. Scholarship application is reviewed by the Scholarship Committee. Selection of applicants will be based on academic standing and financial need.

Funds Avail.: $1,000. **Duration:** Annual. **Number Awarded:** 1. **To Apply:** Applicants must complete the ap-

plication form available online and submit a personal essay, transcript, and letter of recommendation. **Deadline:** March 1.

8847 ■ Judge Isaac Anderson, Jr. Scholarships *(Undergraduate/Scholarship)*

Purpose: To provide a two-year regionally accredited college or university to Lee County high school senior who can demonstrate financial need. **Focus:** General studies/Field of study not specified. **Qualif.:** Applicants must be graduates from public or private high school in Lee County; be minority students; maintain a GPA of 3.0 or higher; demonstrate strong community ties, preferably to the local Dunbar community, through extracurricular activities, religious endeavors or community service; plan to attend a two- or four-year regionally accredited college or university; and, document financial need. **Criteria:** Selection will be based on the committee's criteria.

Funds Avail.: $1,300. **Duration:** Annual. **To Apply:** Applicants must complete the application forms available online and must have a personal essay, financial need documentation, transcript and letter of recommendation. **Deadline:** March 2.

8848 ■ Lewis B. Barber Memorial Scholarships *(Undergraduate/Scholarship)*

Purpose: To fund books and tuition for students pursuing either of the following educational paths: (1) certification to teach the deaf and blind; (2) seminary or pre-seminary school to study church, Christian music or Christian education. **Focus:** Christian education; Religion. **Qualif.:** Applicants must graduate from public or private high school in Charlotte, Collier, Glades, Hendry or Lee County; must maintain satisfactory grades; must acknowledge and express Jesus Christ as Lord and Savior; and must demonstrate financial need. **Criteria:** Scholarship recipients are selected based upon the specific criteria made by each fund's donor. Scholarship application is reviewed by the Scholarship Committee. Selection of applicants will be based on academic standing and financial need.

Funds Avail.: $1,000. **Duration:** Annual. **Number Awarded:** 1. **To Apply:** Application forms are available online. Applicants must submit a personal essay, transcript, financial need documentation, and letter of recommendation. **Deadline:** March 1.

8849 ■ James Bilder Scholarships *(Undergraduate, Vocational/Occupational/Scholarship)*

Purpose: To fund tuition for high school students intending to pursue vocational or technical studies. **Focus:** General studies/Field of study not specified. **Qualif.:** Applicants must have graduated from public high school in Lee County; must demonstrate financial need. **Criteria:** Scholarship recipients are selected based upon the specific criteria made by each fund's donor. Scholarship application is reviewed by the Scholarship Committee. Selection of applicants will be based on academic standing and financial need.

Funds Avail.: No specific amount. **Duration:** Annual. **To Apply:** Applicants must submit a personal essay, financial need documentation, transcript, and letter of recommendation. **Deadline:** March 1.

8850 ■ Carl E. Brooks Scholarships *(Undergraduate/ Scholarship)*

Purpose: To fund tuition for college-bound students of one or more immigrant parents. **Focus:** General studies/Field

Awards are arranged alphabetically below their administering organizations

of study not specified. **Qualif.:** Applicants must have graduated from public or private high school in Charlotte, Collier, Glades, Hendry or Lee County. **Criteria:** Scholarship recipients are selected based upon the specific criteria made by each fund's donor. Scholarship application is reviewed by the Scholarship Committee. Selection of applicants will be based on academic standing and financial need.

Funds Avail.: $2,500. **Duration:** Annual. **To Apply:** Applicants must provide proof of parent's immigrant status and must submit a letter of interest, transcript, and letter of recommendation. **Deadline:** March 1.

8851 ■ John and Ruth Childe Scholarships
(Undergraduate/Scholarship)

Purpose: To fund education of students with physical disability intending to pursue higher education in a college, university or technical school. **Focus:** General studies/Field of study not specified. **Qualif.:** Applicants must be graduates from a public or private high school in Lee county; must have a disability; and must have good academic standing. **Criteria:** Consideration is made for middle-income families.

Funds Avail.: $1,000. **Duration:** Annual. **To Apply:** Applicants must complete application form, available online and must have a letter of interest, transcript and letter of recommendation. Application form and other supporting documents must be sent to Southwest Florida, Community Foundation. **Deadline:** March 1. **Contact:** Southwest Florida, Community Foundation; address: 8260 College Pkwy., Ste. 101, Fort Myers, FL 33919.

8852 ■ City of Sanibel Employee Dependent Scholarships *(Undergraduate/Scholarship)*

Purpose: To provide financial assistance for qualified dependents of Sanibel City employees to attend a college or university. **Focus:** General studies/Field of study not specified. **Qualif.:** Applicant must be a dependent of a Sanibel City Employee (includes City Clerk's office, finance, legal, legislative, planning, police, building, natural resources, public works, management information systems, utility, recreation, and administrative services); must demonstrate financial need and academic achievement. **Criteria:** Scholarship recipients are selected based upon the specific criteria made by each fund's donor. Scholarship application is reviewed by the Scholarship Committee.

Funds Avail.: $1,000. **Duration:** Annual. **To Apply:** Applicants must complete the application form, available online; must have a student letter of interest, financial need documentation, transcript, and two letters of recommendation. Application form and other supporting documents must be sent to Community Foundation of Sanibel-Captiva, 8260 College Pkwy., Ste. 101, Fort Myers, FL 33919. **Deadline:** March 1. **Contact:** Kathryn Cintron; address: 8260 College parkway, suite 101, Fort Myers, FL 33919; Phone: 239-274-5900; Fax: 239-274-5930.

8853 ■ COUSE-Gram Scholarships *(Undergraduate/Scholarship)*

Purpose: To provide educational assistance for Moore Haven High School students pursuing post-secondary education. **Focus:** Education, Secondary. **Qualif.:** Applicant must be a Moore Haven High School senior; must pursue post-secondary education. **Criteria:** Application materials are reviewed by a member of the Community Foundation's Scholarship Reading Committee. Selection of applicants will be based on academic standing and financial need.

Funds Avail.: $950. **Duration:** Annual. **To Apply:** Applicant must submit an application, transcript, personal essay and letter of recommendation. Application forms are available online. **Deadline:** March 2.

8854 ■ D&A Florida Scholarships *(Undergraduate/ Scholarship)*

Purpose: To fund a student who will attend: FGCU, university of Florida/ Gainesville, Florida State University/ Tallahassee, Flagler College, Stetson University/Deland, University of Miami, University of Tampa, or Embry Riddle Aeronautical University/Daytona Beach. **Focus:** Architecture; Business; Chemistry; Computer and information sciences; Engineering; International affairs and relations; Journalism; Law; Literature; Medicine; Physics; Political science. **Qualif.:** Applicants must have graduated from a public or private high school in Charlotte, Glades, Hendry or Lee County; must pursue a degree in Architecture, Business, Engineering, International affairs and relations, Journalism, Computer and information sciences, Law, Literature, Medicine, Physics, Chemistry, or Political science; must document financial need; must possess a 3.5 GPA or higher; must be 23 years of age or younger and a first-time college student. **Criteria:** Scholarship recipients are selected based upon the specific criteria made by each fund's donor. Scholarship application is reviewed by the Scholarship Committee. Selection of applicants will be based on academic standing and financial need.

Funds Avail.: $800. **Duration:** Annual. **Number Awarded:** 1. **To Apply:** Application forms are available online. Applicants must submit a personal essay and letter of recommendation, a transcript and financial need documentation. **Deadline:** March 2.

8855 ■ Doctors Ira and Udaya Dash Nursing Scholarships *(Undergraduate, Graduate/Scholarship)*

Purpose: To assist students studying nursing at Florida Southwestern or Florida Gulf Coast University. **Focus:** Nursing. **Qualif.:** Applicants must plan to attend or be attending Edison College or Florida Gulf Coast University; must be enrolled in a nursing program; and must demonstrate financial need. **Criteria:** Selection will be based on the committee's criteria.

Funds Avail.: $850. **Duration:** Annual. **To Apply:** Applicants must submit a personal essay, documentation of financial need, transcript, and letter of recommendation. **Deadline:** March 2.

8856 ■ Dunbar Heritage Scholarships *(Undergraduate/Scholarship)*

Purpose: To fund a Dunbar High School graduating student of African-American descent in pursuing a bachelor's degree at an accredited college. **Focus:** General studies/ Field of study not specified. **Qualif.:** Applicant must be a graduating member of Dunbar High School; must be of African-American descent; must have financial need; must have a GPA of 2.5 or higher; and must enter college within the year following high school graduation. **Criteria:** Scholarship recipients are selected based upon the specific criteria made by each fund's donor. Scholarship application is reviewed by the Scholarship Committee. Selection of applicants will be based on academic standing and financial need.

Funds Avail.: No specific amount. **Duration:** Annual. **To Apply:** Applicants must submit a letter of interest, transcript, and letter of recommendation. Application forms are available online. **Deadline:** March 1.

Awards are arranged alphabetically below their administering organizations

8857 ■ Anne M. Fassett Scholarships (*Undergraduate, Graduate/Scholarship*)

Purpose: To fund post-high school educational opportunities at the college, community college, or technical school level for males and females with a physical disability and who use a wheelchair. **Focus:** General studies/Field of study not specified. **Qualif.:** Applicants must have graduated from a public or private high school in Charlotte, Collier, Glades, Hendry or Lee County; must be currently enrolled or planning to attend a Florida state college, community college or technical school; must have a physical disability and use a wheelchair; and must demonstrate financial need. **Criteria:** Scholarship recipients are selected based upon the specific criteria made by each fund's donor. Scholarship application is reviewed by the Scholarship Committee. Selection of applicants will be based on academic standing and financial need.

Funds Avail.: $3,700. **Duration:** Annual. **To Apply:** Application forms are available online. Applicants must submit a letter of recommendation, letter of interest, financial need documentation, and transcript. **Deadline:** March 2.

8858 ■ Paul B. and Aline Flynn Scholarships (*Undergraduate/Scholarship*)

Purpose: To fund high school or undergraduate/graduate students planning to study at a 4-year accredited college in the area of Communications or Journalism. **Focus:** Communications; Journalism. **Qualif.:** Applicants must have graduated from a public or private high school in Charlotte, Collier, Glades, Hendry or Lee County; must pursue a degree in Communications, English or Journalism; and must have a 3.0 or higher GPA. **Criteria:** Scholarship recipients are selected based upon the specific criteria made by each fund's donor. Scholarship application is reviewed by the Scholarship Committee. Selection of recipients will be based on academic standing and financial need.

Funds Avail.: $1,000. **Duration:** Annual. **To Apply:** Application forms are available online. Applicants must submit a personal essay, high school/college transcript, and letter of recommendation. **Deadline:** March 1.

8859 ■ Doris W. Frey Memorial Scholarships (*Undergraduate, Graduate/Scholarship*)

Purpose: To support students studying Christian ministry/ youth ministry, Christian counseling, nursing, or medicine. **Focus:** Christian education; Medicine; Nursing; Religion. **Qualif.:** Applicants must be graduates from public or private high school in Charlotte, Collier, Hendry, Glades or Lee counties; pursue a degree in any of the following fields (Christian ministry/youth ministry, Christian counseling, nursing, or medicine); maintain satisfactory grades; be committed to a life of Christian service; demonstrate a commitment through action in ministering to others; and have recognized ability and academic performance with standard measures of grades and appropriate test scores. **Criteria:** Selection will be based on the committee's criteria.

Funds Avail.: $2,700. **Duration:** Annual. **To Apply:** Applicants must submit an essay of future commitment, transcript, and references. **Deadline:** March 2.

8860 ■ American Association of University Women Sue Gottcent Memorial Scholarship Fund (*Undergraduate/Scholarship*)

Purpose: To support Lee county women in their education. **Focus:** General studies/Field of study not specified. **Qua-**

lif.: Applicants must be female residents of Lee County who demonstrate financial need. **Criteria:** Preference will be given to females over 25 years of age.

Funds Avail.: $1,000. **To Apply:** Application forms are available online. Applicants must submit a personal statement essay, proof of financial need, high school/college transcript, and three letters of recommendation. **Deadline:** March 2.

8861 ■ William L. Graddy Law School Scholarships (*Graduate/Scholarship*)

Purpose: To fund scholarships for students who have completed their first year of course load at an accredited law school. **Focus:** Law. **Qualif.:** Applicants must have completed first year of law school; must have a GPA of 2.8 or above and be in the top 25% of class; must have been a resident of Charlotte, Collier, Glades, Hendry or Lee for at least 3 years; and must demonstrate financial need. **Criteria:** Scholarship recipients are selected based upon the specific criteria made by each fund's donor. Scholarship application is reviewed by the Scholarship Committee. Selection of applicants will be based on academic standing and financial need.

Funds Avail.: $800. **Duration:** Annual. **To Apply:** Application forms are available online. Applicants must submit a personal essay, letter of recommendation from college instructor, transcript, financial need documentation and financial need documentation. **Deadline:** March 2.

8862 ■ Frances Harris Gresham Scholarships (*Undergraduate/Scholarship*)

Purpose: To fund tuition for college-bound seniors from Lee County high schools. **Focus:** General studies/Field of study not specified. **Qualif.:** Applicants must have graduated from a public or private high school in Lee County. **Criteria:** Scholarship recipients are selected based upon the specific criteria made by each fund's donor. Scholarship application is reviewed by the Scholarship Committee. Selection of applicants will be based on academic standing and financial need.

Funds Avail.: $1,000. **Duration:** Annual. **To Apply:** Applicants must submit a personal essay, transcript, and letter of recommendation. Application forms are available online. **Deadline:** March 1.

8863 ■ Matt Harmon Memorial Scholarships (*Undergraduate/Scholarship*)

Purpose: To fund books and tuition for college-bound male baseball players. **Focus:** General studies/Field of study not specified. **Qualif.:** Applicants must be graduates of a public school in Lee County; must be male; must demonstrate financial need; and must have played baseball in high school. **Criteria:** Scholarship recipients are selected based upon the specific criteria made by each fund's donor. Scholarship application is reviewed by the Scholarship Committee.

Funds Avail.: $500. **Duration:** Annual. **To Apply:** Applicants must submit a personal essay, financial need documentation, transcript, and letter of recommendation. Application forms are available online. **Deadline:** January 29.

8864 ■ Chip Johnson Scholarships (*Undergraduate/Scholarship*)

Purpose: To fund scholarships for students who have completed 60 hours of college and plan to attend one of

Awards are arranged alphabetically below their administering organizations

named colleges. **Focus:** General studies/Field of study not specified. **Qualif.:** Applicants must have completed 60 semester hours of college and plan to continue study toward a 4-year degree at Barry University, FGCU, Nova, Edison College or International College, or a regionally-accredited college in the 5-county area; must have a GPA of 3.5 or above and an outstanding record of academic achievement; must have lived in the 5-county area served by the Community Foundation (Charlotte, Collier, Glades, Hendry and Lee); and must have demonstrated leadership, community service and service to school. **Criteria:** Scholarship recipients are selected based upon the specific criteria made by each fund's donor. Scholarship application is reviewed by the scholarship committee. Selection of applicants will be based on academic standing and financial need.

Funds Avail.: $5,750. **Duration:** Annual. **To Apply:** Applicants must complete the application forms available online; must submit a letter of recommendation from college instructor and personal essay; must have a transcript of record. **Deadline:** March 2.

8865 ■ George E. Judd Scholarships
(Undergraduate/Scholarship)

Purpose: To fund tuition for graduating seniors pursuing higher education in the fine or performing arts. **Focus:** Art; Performing arts. **Qualif.:** Applicants must graduate from public or private high school in Lee County and must pursue a degree in the fine or performing arts. **Criteria:** Scholarship recipients are selected based upon the specific criteria made by each fund's donor. Scholarship application is reviewed by the scholarship Committee.

Funds Avail.: $5,000. **Duration:** Annual. **To Apply:** Applicants must submit a personal essay, transcript, and letter of recommendation. Application forms are available online. **Deadline:** March 1.

8866 ■ Doc Keen Memorial Scholarships
(Undergraduate/Scholarship)

Purpose: To assist students who were active members of 4-H or a FFA Organization for two consecutive years. **Focus:** General studies/Field of study not specified. **Qualif.:** Applicant must be a graduate from a Moore Haven, Clewinston or LaBelle high school; must pursue higher education; must maintain satisfactory grades; and must have been an active member of 4-H or a FFA Organization for two consecutive years. **Criteria:** Application materials are reviewed by a member of the Community Foundation's Scholarship Reading Committee. Selection of applicants will be based on academic standing and financial need.

Funds Avail.: $750. **Duration:** Annual. **To Apply:** Application forms are available online. Applicants must submit a letter of interest, transcript, list of 4-H or FFA activities, and letter of recommendation. **Deadline:** March 2.

8867 ■ Isabel Mayer Kirkpatrick Scholarships
(Undergraduate/Scholarship)

Purpose: To fund tuition for high school graduates with a "B" average of 3.03.7. **Focus:** General studies/Field of study not specified. **Qualif.:** Applicants must graduate from public or private high school in Lee County; must be well-rounded in terms of education, community service, sports and leadership activities; and must have a GPA of 3.0-3.7 (anything higher will disqualify the student). **Criteria:** Application materials must be reviewed by a member of the Community Foundation's Scholarship Reading Committee. Selection of applicants will be based on academic standing and financial need.

Funds Avail.: $1,000. **Duration:** Annual. **To Apply:** Applicants must submit a personal essay, transcript, and letter of recommendation. Application forms are available online. **Deadline:** March 1.

8868 ■ Robert A. Kleckner Scholarships
(Undergraduate, Graduate/Scholarship)

Purpose: To assist financially needy high school, undergraduate, or graduate students pursuing a career in finance or accounting. **Focus:** Accounting; Finance. **Qualif.:** Applicants must be residents of Charlotte, Glades, Hendry or Lee Counties pursuing a degree in finance or accounting. **Criteria:** Selection will be based on the committee's criteria.

Funds Avail.: $1,750. **Duration:** Annual. **To Apply:** Application forms are available online. Applicants must submit a personal essay, high school/college transcript, and letter of recommendation. **Deadline:** March 2.

8869 ■ Love of Bonita Empowerment Scholarships
(Undergraduate/Scholarship)

Purpose: To provide books, tuition, and/or course fees for Bonita Springs residents who have been out of school for at least two years to attend a college or technical school. **Focus:** General studies/Field of study not specified. **Qualif.:** Applicants must be residents of Bonita Springs who are able to document financial need. **Criteria:** Selection will be based on the committee's criteria.

Funds Avail.: $950. **Duration:** Annual. **To Apply:** Applicants may contact the Foundation for more information. **Deadline:** March 2.

8870 ■ Ruth Messmer Memorial Scholarships
(Undergraduate/Scholarship)

Purpose: To provide support for students who are in need. **Focus:** Business. **Qualif.:** Applicants must have graduated from a public or private high school in Lee, Charlotte, Glades, Hendry or Collier Counties with a documented "B" average; must be females pursuing a business career in college. **Criteria:** Scholarship recipients are selected based upon the specific criteria made by each fund's donor. Scholarship application is reviewed by the scholarship committee. Selection of recipients will be based on academic standing and financial need.

Funds Avail.: $1,100. **Duration:** Annual. **To Apply:** Applicants must submit a personal essay, transcript, and letter of recommendation. Application forms are available online. **Deadline:** March 2.

8871 ■ Judge William J. Nelson Scholarships
(Undergraduate/Scholarship)

Purpose: To provide financial assistance for qualified high school seniors who will be attending the University of Florida. **Focus:** General studies/Field of study not specified. **Qualif.:** Applicant must be a resident of Charlotte, Collier, Glades, Hendry or Lee County; must have overcome adversity in some way; and must attend the University of Florida. **Criteria:** Scholarship recipients are selected based upon the specific criteria made by each fund's donor. Scholarship application is reviewed by the Scholarship Committee. Selection of applicants will be based on academic standing and financial need.

Funds Avail.: $1,650. **Duration:** Annual. **To Apply:** Applicant must submit a personal essay detailing how you have overcome adversity, transcript, and letter of recommendation. Application forms are available online. **Deadline:** March 2.

Awards are arranged alphabetically below their administering organizations

8872 ■ Robert B. and Dorothy Pence Scholarships
(Undergraduate/Scholarship)

Purpose: To fund tuition for economically-disadvantaged students to attend college or technical school. **Focus:** General studies/Field of study not specified. **Qualif.:** Applicants must have graduated from a public or private high school in Lee County and must be an industrious student with good moral character and document financial need. **Criteria:** Scholarship recipients are selected based upon the specific criteria made by each fund's donor. Scholarship application is reviewed by the Scholarship Committee. Selection of applicants will be based on academic standing and financial need.

Funds Avail.: $1,800. **Duration:** Annual. **To Apply:** Applicants must submit a personal essay, financial need documentation, transcript, and letter of recommendation. Application forms are available online. **Deadline:** March 2.

8873 ■ Chet and Jannett Perry Scholarships
(Undergraduate/Scholarship)

Purpose: To provide funding support for students pursuing a career in accounting. **Focus:** Accounting. **Qualif.:** Applicant must be graduating from a public or private high school in Charlotte, Hendry, Glades or Lee County; must pursue a degree in accounting; and must enter college within a year following high school graduation. **Criteria:** Scholarship recipients are selected based upon the specific criteria made by each fund's donor. Scholarship application is reviewed by the Scholarship Committee. Selection of applicants will be based on academic standing and financial need.

Funds Avail.: $900. **Duration:** Annual. **To Apply:** Applicant must submit an application, transcript, personal essay and letter of recommendation. Application forms are available online. **Deadline:** March 2.

8874 ■ Faye Lynn Roberts Educational Scholarships
(Undergraduate, Graduate/Scholarship)

Purpose: To fund scholarships for female students pursuing a career in technical studies, court reporting, computer training or nursing. **Focus:** Computer and information sciences; Education, Vocational-technical; Nursing. **Qualif.:** Applicants must be women of 21 years of age or older who are residents of Lee County, and able to demonstrate financial need. **Criteria:** Scholarship recipients are selected based upon the specific criteria made by each fund's donor. Scholarship application is reviewed by the Scholarship Committee. Selection of applicants will be based on academic standing and financial need.

Funds Avail.: $700. **Duration:** Annual. **To Apply:** Application forms are available online. Applicants must submit a personal essay, financial need documentation, high school/college transcript and letter of recommendation.

8875 ■ David G. Robinson Arts Scholarships
(Undergraduate/Scholarship)

Purpose: To fund tuition for high school seniors who plan to study the arts in an accredited school. **Focus:** Art. **Qualif.:** Applicants must graduate from a public school in Lee County; must be an industrious student with good moral character; must document financial need; and must show leadership and community service. **Criteria:** Scholarship recipients are selected based upon the specific criteria made by each fund's donor. Scholarship application is reviewed by the Scholarship Committee. Selection of applicants will be based on academic standing and financial need.

Funds Avail.: $2,250. **Duration:** Annual. **To Apply:** Applicants must submit an application, transcript, personal essay, financial need documentation and letter of recommendation. Application forms are available online. **Deadline:** March 2.

8876 ■ Robert C. and Margaret A. Schikora Scholarships
(Undergraduate/Scholarship)

Purpose: To provide tuition for high school graduates' post-secondary educational opportunities, including trade/technical school, undergraduate work, post-graduate work, and professional education. **Focus:** General studies/Field of study not specified. **Qualif.:** Applicants must graduate from public or private high school in Lee County; must be an industrious student with good moral character; and must demonstrate financial need. **Criteria:** Scholarship recipients are selected based upon the specific criteria made by each fund's donor. Scholarship application is reviewed by the scholarship committee. Selection of applicants will be based on academic standing and financial need.

Funds Avail.: $1,200. **Duration:** Annual. **To Apply:** Applicants must submit an application, transcript, personal essay, financial need documentation and letter of recommendation. Application forms are available online. **Deadline:** March 2.

8877 ■ John M. and Mary A. Shanley Memorial Scholarships
(Undergraduate, Graduate/Scholarship)

Purpose: To fund students pursuing degrees or advanced degrees in medicine, law, dentistry, teaching (math and science), ministry, engineering, accounting, architecture and computer science. **Focus:** Accounting; Agriculture, Economic aspects; Architecture; Computer and information sciences; Dentistry; Engineering; Law; Medicine; Religion; Teaching. **Qualif.:** Applicant must be a resident of Charlotte, Hendry or Lee County; must demonstrate service to school, church and community; must have a GPA of 3.0 or higher. **Criteria:** Selection will be based on the committee's criteria.

Funds Avail.: $5,000. **Duration:** up to four years. **To Apply:** Application forms are available online. Applicants must submit a personal essay, financial need documentation, letter of recommendation and transcript.

8878 ■ Southwest Florida Community Foundation College Assistance Scholarships
(Undergraduate/Scholarship)

Purpose: To fund books, laboratory fees, or any expenses related to student's academic costs. **Focus:** General studies/Field of study not specified. **Qualif.:** Applicants must reside in Charlotte, Lee, Glades, Hendry or Collier County and must demonstrate financial need. **Criteria:** Application materials are reviewed by a member of the Community Foundation's Scholarship Reading Committee. Selection of applicants will be based on academic standing and financial need.

Funds Avail.: No specific amount. **Duration:** Annual. **To Apply:** Applicants must submit a letter of interest, transcript, personal essay and financial need documentation.

8879 ■ Anne Sturrock Nursing Scholarships
(Undergraduate, Graduate/Scholarship)

Purpose: To endow nursing scholarships for members or children of members of St. Andrew Catholic Church in Cape Coral. **Focus:** Nursing. **Qualif.:** Applicants must be members or children of members of St. Andrew Catholic Church; must pursue a career in nursing; and must

Awards are arranged alphabetically below their administering organizations

demonstrate financial need. **Criteria:** Scholarship recipients are selected based upon the specific criteria made by each fund's donor. Scholarship application is reviewed by the Scholarship Committee. Selection of applicants will be based on academic standing and financial need.

Funds Avail.: $7,300. **Duration:** Annual. **To Apply:** Application forms are available online. Applicants must submit a letter of interest, letter of recommendation from pastor of St. Andrew, transcript and financial need documentation. **Deadline:** March 2.

8880 ■ SWFL Deputy Sheriffs Association Fund Scholarships *(Undergraduate/Scholarship)*

Purpose: To provide financial funds for qualified high school students who are dependents of law enforcement officers. **Focus:** General studies/Field of study not specified. **Qualif.:** Applicant must be a graduate from high school in Charlotte, Collier, Lee, Hendry or Glades Counties; must be a dependent of a law enforcement officer in the above counties; and must list name of law enforcement officer. **Criteria:** Scholarship recipients are selected based upon the specific criteria made by each fund's donor. Scholarship application is reviewed by the scholarship committee.

Funds Avail.: $1,500. **Duration:** Annual. **To Apply:** Applicant must complete the application form, available online, and submit a letter of interest, transcript, and letter of recommendation. **Deadline:** March 2.

8881 ■ John I. and Madeleine R. Taeni Scholarships *(Undergraduate/Scholarship)*

Purpose: To support students pursuing degrees in teaching, nursing, paramedic training, or emergency medical technician training. **Focus:** Emergency and disaster services; Nursing; Paramedics; Teaching. **Qualif.:** Applicants must be residents of Charlotte, Collier, Glades, Hendry or Lee County; highly motivated; and pursue teaching, nursing paramedic training, or emergency medical technician training. **Criteria:** Selection will be based on the committee's criteria.

Funds Avail.: $4,500. **Duration:** Annual. **To Apply:** Application forms are available online. Applicants must submit a personal essay, letter of recommendation, and transcript. **Deadline:** March 2.

8882 ■ Southwest Movers Association (SMA)

700 E 11th St.
Austin, TX 78701-2623
Ph: (512)476-0107
Fax: (512)476-6494
Free: 800-759-2305
E-mail: info@southwestmovers.org
URL: www.mytexasmover.com

8883 ■ Southwest Movers Association Scholarships *(Undergraduate/Scholarship)*

Purpose: To provide financial assistance to college and trade school student members or dependents of SMA employees. **Focus:** General studies/Field of study not specified. **Qualif.:** Applicants must be high school seniors or college students; must be employees or dependents of someone who is currently employed. **Criteria:** Recipients will be selected based on academic achievement, community involvement and financial need.

Funds Avail.: No specific amount. **Duration:** Annual. **To**

Apply: Applicants must complete an application form; attach a recent black and white photo; certified copy of transcript; one-to-three letters of recommendation; and an accompanying letter of intent. Letter must include the following information: current and planned studies; career goals; interests; and reasons for applying for this scholarship. **Deadline:** March 2.

8884 ■ Specialized Carriers and Rigging Association (SC&RA)

5870 Trinity Pkwy., Ste. 200
Centreville, VA 20120
Ph: (703)698-0291
Fax: (703)698-0297
E-mail: info@scranet.org
URL: www.scranet.org

8885 ■ SC and R Foundation Grant Program *(Undergraduate/Grant)*

Purpose: To support students and employees in the specialized carriers and rigging industry. **Focus:** Transportation. **Qualif.:** Application is open to the public. Children, grandchildren, employees, spouses of SC&RA member companies as well as anyone looking to pursue a career in the industry are eligible to apply. **Criteria:** Scholarship committee performed blind evaluations of all the applications.

Funds Avail.: $1,500. **Duration:** Annual. **To Apply:** Applicants must complete the application form together with two letters of recommendation (one letter from an academic advisor or employer); official transcripts; recent photograph; and contact information. **Deadline:** January 31.

8886 ■ SC and R Foundation Scholarships *(Undergraduate/Scholarship)*

Purpose: To provide career opportunities and scholarship to its members. **Focus:** Transportation. **Qualif.:** Applicants must have at least one term of undergraduate study remaining or have applied to a college/university; must have study leading to bachelor degree in fields related to specialized carriers and rigging industry; must be employees or relatives of employees of SC and RA Member Company. **Criteria:** Scholarship committee performed blind evaluations of all the applications.

Funds Avail.: $3,000. **To Apply:** Applicants must complete the application form together with two letters of recommendation (one letter from an academic advisor or employer); official transcripts; recent photograph; and contact information. **Contact:** mbaehr@scranet.org.

8887 ■ Specialty Equipment Market Association (SEMA)

1575 S Valley Vista Dr.
Diamond Bar, CA 91765-0910
Ph: (909)610-2030
Fax: (909)860-0184
E-mail: sema@sema.org
URL: www.sema.org

8888 ■ Loan Forgiveness Scholarships *(Graduate, Undergraduate/Loan, Scholarship)*

Purpose: To foster industry leadership by supporting the education of students pursuing careers in the automotive aftermarket. **Focus:** Automotive technology. **Qualif.:** Ap-

Awards are arranged alphabetically below their administering organizations

plicants must be post-graduate students with one year minimum employment by a SEMA member company. **Criteria:** Recipients are selected based on the review of the completed application.

Funds Avail.: $2,000-$5,000. **Duration:** Annual. **To Apply:** Applicants must submit a completed application form; resume; official, sealed transcripts for all college or post-secondary course work completed through the first quarter or semester of the current year; must provide documentation of outstanding student loans; personal essay; two letters of recommendation from professors, career counselors or employers; must submit a current photo for publication and promotional use. **Deadline:** November 1.

8889 ■ SEMA Memorial Scholarships *(Graduate, Undergraduate/Scholarship)*

Purpose: To support educational goals for students pursuing careers in the automotive aftermarkets. **Focus:** Automotive technology. **Qualif.:** Applicants must be graduate-level students at an accredited university or college; four-year accredited university or college; three-year accredited university or community college; or vocational/technical school. **Criteria:** Applications are reviewed and scored by an independent panel comprised of business professionals.

Funds Avail.: $2,000-$3,000 depending on the category. **To Apply:** Applicants must submit an official transcript; two letters of recommendation from a non employer, career counselors or professor on company letterhead; current photographs (head shot) for publication and promotional use; personal essay outlining reasons for pursuing a career in the automotive aftermarker or related field. **Deadline:** April 1. **Remarks:** Established in 1984.

8890 ■ Specialty Equipment Market Association Scholarships *(Graduate, Undergraduate, Vocational/ Occupational/Scholarship)*

Purpose: To foster industry leadership by supporting the education of students pursuing careers in the automotive aftermarket; to foster leadership in the specialty equipment marketplace. **Focus:** Automotive technology. **Qualif.:** Applicants must be graduates or undergraduate sophomores, juniors or seniors, in a vocational or technical degree program in a two-to-four year accredited university or college in the United States or Canada; must have a minimum 2.5 grade point average; must be pursuing studies leading to a career in the automotive aftermarket or a related field. **Criteria:** Recipients are selected based on academic performance.

Funds Avail.: $2,000 - $3,000; with $5,000 going to the top student. **Duration:** Annual. **To Apply:** Applicants must submit a completed application form; must submit a personal essay outlining reasons the applicant wants to pursue a career in the automotive aftermarket or related fields; must submit an official sealed transcript from all college or post-secondary course work completed; two letters of recommendation from a non-family member on company letterhead. **Deadline:** November 1.

8891 ■ SPIE

PO Box 10
Bellingham, WA 98227-0010
Ph: (360)685-5580
Fax: (360)647-1445
Free: 888-902-0894
E-mail: sdlinfo@spie.org
URL: spiedigitallibrary.org

Awards are arranged alphabetically below their administering organizations

8892 ■ BACUS Scholarships *(Graduate, Undergraduate/Scholarship)*

Purpose: To provide education assistance to students in field of microlithography. **Focus:** Engineering, Optical; Optics. **Qualif.:** Applicants must be student members of SPIE; must be enrolled full-time, undergraduate or graduate students in the field of microlithography emphasizing on optical tooling or semiconductor manufacturing technologies. **Criteria:** Applicants are selected based on merit, experiences and education level.

Funds Avail.: $5,000. **Duration:** Annual. **To Apply:** Applicants must submit a completed scholarship application form (available on the website); a 450-word essay; and two letters of recommendation sent separately by the recommender. Application materials must not exceed more than ten pages. **Deadline:** February 15. **Remarks:** Scholarships are sponsored by BACUS, the International Technical Group of SPIE dedicated to the advancement of photomask technology. **Contact:** scholarships@spie.org.

8893 ■ Michael Kidger Memorial Scholarships in Optical Design *(Undergraduate/Scholarship)*

Purpose: To provide education assistance to a student in optical design. **Focus:** Engineering, Optical; Optics. **Qualif.:** Applicants must be students of optical design; must meet the entry criteria for the chosen course of study or research; must have at least one year after the award to completion of their chosen course of study. **Criteria:** Applicants are selected based on merit, experiences and education level.

Funds Avail.: $5,000. **Duration:** Annual. **To Apply:** Applicants must submit a summary (five pages maximum) of their academic background and interest in pursuing training or research in optical design; and two letters of recommendation. **Deadline:** March 31. **Remarks:** Established in honor of Michael John Kidger, a well-respected educator and member of the optical science and engineering community. **Contact:** scholarships@spie.org.

8894 ■ Laser Technology, Engineering and Applications Scholarships *(Graduate, Undergraduate/ Scholarship)*

Purpose: To promote education in laser technology, engineering, or applications. **Focus:** Engineering; Technology. **Qualif.:** Applicants must be student members of SPIE; must be enrolled full-time in an optics photonics imaging or optoelectronics program or related discipline at an accredited school; must be in high school or secondary school, undergraduate or post-secondary school, or graduate school. **Criteria:** Applicants are selected based on merit, experiences and education level.

Funds Avail.: $5,000. **Duration:** Annual. **To Apply:** Applicants must submit a completed scholarship application form (available on the website); a 450-word essay; and two letters of recommendation sent separately by the recommender. Application materials must not exceed more than ten pages. Completed application must be sent electronically. **Deadline:** February 15. **Remarks:** Sponsored in part by a gift from the former Forum for Military Applications of Directed Energy. **Contact:** scholarships@spie.org.

8895 ■ D.J. Lovell Scholarships *(Graduate, Undergraduate/Scholarship)*

Purpose: To provide education assistance to a student in optical design. **Focus:** Engineering, Optical; Optics. **Qualif.:** Applicants must be student members of SPIE; must be enrolled full-time in an optics photonics imaging or optoelectronics program or related discipline at an accredited school; must be in high school or secondary school, undergraduate or post-secondary school, or graduate school. **Criteria:** Applicants are selected based on merit, experiences and education level.

Funds Avail.: $11,000. **Duration:** Annual. **To Apply:** Applicants must submit a completed scholarship application form (available on the website); a 450-word essay; and two letters of recommendation sent separately by the recommender. Application materials must not exceed more than ten pages. Completed application must be sent electronically. **Deadline:** February 15. **Remarks:** The scholarship is sponsored in part by SPIE with contributions from Labsphere Inc. **Contact:** scholarships@spie.org.

8896 ■ Optical Design and Engineering Scholarships (Graduate, Undergraduate/Scholarship)

Purpose: To provide education assistance to a student in optical design and engineering. **Focus:** Engineering, Optical; Optics. **Qualif.:** Applicants must be student members of SPIE; must be enrolled full-time, undergraduate or graduate in an optical design and engineering. **Criteria:** Applicants are selected based on merit, experiences and education level.

Funds Avail.: No specific amount. **To Apply:** Applicants must submit a completed scholarship application form (available at the website); a 450-word essay; and two letters of recommendation sent separately by the recommender. Application materials must not exceed more than ten pages. **Deadline:** February 15. **Remarks:** Established in honor of Bill Price, a well-respected member of the SPIE technical community. **Contact:** scholarships@spie.org.

8897 ■ SPIE Student Travel Author Grants (Graduate, Undergraduate/Grant)

Purpose: To provide supplement travel support for students presenting a paper at any of SPIE's meetings. **Focus:** Engineering, Optical; Optics. **Qualif.:** Applicants must be fulltime student members of SPIE; must be authors of an accepted paper presented at the conference; and must have not received any SPIE funding in the past 12 months. **Criteria:** The conference chair will indicate if the applicant's paper presentation is necessary to the success of the conference.

Funds Avail.: $250-$500 (domestic traveler); $300-$750 (international traveler). **Duration:** Annual. **To Apply:** Applicant must submit a student travel grant application form (available on the website); a letter of recommendation from faculty advisor or head department; and a written support from the chair of the conference which the paper will be presented. **Contact:** scholarships@spie.org.

8898 ■ Spina Bifida & Hydrocephalus Association of Ontario (SB&H)

555 Richmond St. W, Ste. 1006
Toronto, ON, Canada M5V 3B1
Ph: (416)214-1056
Fax: (416)214-1446
Free: 800-387-1575
E-mail: provincial@sbhao.on.ca
URL: www.sbhao.on.ca

8899 ■ Dr. E. Bruce Hendrick Scholarships (All/Scholarship)

Purpose: To encourage students with spina bifida and/or hydrocephalus to continue their education. **Focus:** General

studies/Field of study not specified. **Qualif.:** Applicant must be a Canadian citizen with spina bifida and/or hydrocephalus residing in the province of Ontario. **Criteria:** Selection is based on applicant's motivation, self-awareness and goal setting, as well as potential for success.

Funds Avail.: Varies each year. **Duration:** Annual. **To Apply:** Applicants must submit a completed application form along with academic transcripts; completed medical assessment form; one letter of reference from an adult other than a family; one letter of reference from a teacher, principal or guidance counselor; and a personal letter. **Deadline:** April 30.

8900 ■ Spinal Cord Injury BC

780 SW Marine Dr.
Vancouver, BC, Canada V6P 5Y7
Ph: (604)324-3611
Fax: (604)326-1229
Free: 877-324-3611
E-mail: info@sci-bc.ca
URL: sci-bc.ca

8901 ■ BCPF Bursaries (Undergraduate/Scholarship)

Purpose: To provide educational funds to deserving students with disabilities. **Focus:** General studies/Field of study not specified. **Qualif.:** Applicants must be a students with a spinal cord injury; must be a Canadian citizen or landed immigrant, resident of BC and must be attending or planning to attend a post-secondary educational institution in BC. **Criteria:** Recipient will be selected based on merit.

Funds Avail.: No specific amount. **To Apply:** Applicant must submit the completed application form available from the website; must include an official transcript of records, and a letter of reference from either an employer or educator. **Deadline:** June 6.

8902 ■ Sports Turf Managers Association (STMA)

805 New Hampshire St., Ste. E
Lawrence, KS 66044
Fax: (785)843-2977
Free: 800-323-3875
URL: www.stma.org

8903 ■ Safer Athletic Field Environments Scholarships (SAFE) (Graduate, Undergraduate/Scholarship)

Purpose: To assist those within the industry who are outstanding within the sports turf industry, both in sports turf management and research. **Focus:** Sports studies. **Qualif.:** Applicants must be students who are planning a career in the sports turf industry. **Criteria:** Scholarship is based on merit, not the basis of need. Applicants will be evaluated on the basis of academic skills, potential within the industry, employment history, extracurricular activities, and the recommendations of faculty advisors and employers.

Funds Avail.: $1,000 each. **Duration:** Annual. **Number Awarded:** 3. **To Apply:** Applicants must submit a completed typed and printed application form including the following: professional resume; essay describing career aspirations, educational goals and influencing factors; completed Employer Reference Form which must be submitted with application and other materials in sealed envelope(s); and transcripts from all post-secondary institution attended. **Deadline:** October 15. **Remarks:** SAFE

Awards are arranged alphabetically below their administering organizations

awards three named scholarships: the Dr. James Watson Graduate Scholarship, the Dr. James Watson Undergraduate Scholarship, and the Dr. Fred Grau Scholarship. The Watson Scholarships are named in honor of long-time green industry researcher and consultant Dr. James Watson, are funded by the Toro Giving Program, and are presented to the top graduate and undergraduate scholarship recipients. The top recipient from a two-year program receives the Dr. Fred Grau scholarship, which is named in honor of the first turfgrass extension specialist in the United States. There is not a separate application for these named scholarships; they are awarded to the top graduate and undergraduate applicants. Established in 2000.

8904 ■ Spotlight on Nursing

1302 N. Meridian St., Ste. 350
Indianapolis, IN 46202
Ph: (317)254-1132
Fax: (317)254-1159
Free: 800-892-9364
URL: spotlightonnursing.org

8905 ■ Spotlight on Nursing Graduate Nursing Student Scholarships (Graduate/Scholarship)

Purpose: To provide financial assistance to graduate nursing students with the expressed purpose of increasing nurse faculty in Indiana. **Focus:** Nursing. **Qualif.:** Applicants must be with unencumbered Indiana RN license; must be full-time or part-time graduate nursing students enrolled in a NLNAC or CCNE accredited program that qualifies them to teach in a School of Nursing in Indiana; must have good standing in the enrolled graduate nursing program; must be committed to teach in a NLNAC or CCNE nationally accredited School of Nursing in Indiana for the equivalent of one academic year. **Criteria:** Selection is based on the evaluation of submitted documents and specific criteria.

Funds Avail.: No specific amount. **Duration:** Annual. **To Apply:** Applicants should submit a completed application form; proof of an encumbered Indiana RN license; documentation of admission into a graduate nursing program and evidence of current enrollment; one page resume; recommendation letter from an active faculty member recognizing the commitment to teach nursing; one page narrative. **Contact:** Spotlight On Nursing, at the above address.

8906 ■ StaffordLoan.com

c/o The Student Loan Network
1250 Hancock St., Ste. 703N
Quincy, MA 02169
URL: www.staffordloan.com

8907 ■ Stafford Loan for Graduate Students - Unsubsidized Stafford Loans (Graduate/Loan)

Purpose: To address the needs of graduate students enrolled in a college or university. **Focus:** General studies/Field of study not specified. **Qualif.:** Applicants must be graduate students attending a college or university at least half time. **Criteria:** Selection will be based on submitted application.

Funds Avail.: Varies. **To Apply:** Students must file the free application for Federal Student Aid. Once the application is complete, the school's financial aid office will send an award letter, detailing the amount of aid available.

8908 ■ Stanford University Knight Fellowships

Bldg. 120, Rm. 422
450 Serra Mall
Stanford University
Stanford, CA 94305-2050
Ph: (650)723-4937
Fax: (650)725-6154
E-mail: info@kf.stanford.edu
URL: knight.stanford.edu

8909 ■ John S. Knight Fellowships (Other/Fellowship)

Purpose: To provide financial assistance for U.S. journalists who have already done first-rate work and who have the potential of reaching the top ranks in their specialties. **Focus:** Journalism. **Qualif.:** Applicants must have at least seven years of full-time professional experience; (there are no educational prerequisites; no college degree is required); must be currently working full-time as journalists: employees of newspapers, wire services, television or radio news departments, websites, magazines covering news, commentary, or public affairs, and full-time freelancers. Eligible journalists include those who write or edit news, commentary or editorials; critics and reviewers, photojournalists, editorial cartoonists and supervising editors, anchors and producers; journalism business and management executives whose decisions affect editorial quality - for example, publishers, general managers, news directors and station managers - or who are likely to be in such positions are also eligible. Such applicants must be committed to improving editorial quality in their news organizations and not merely in improving a particular business skill or specialty. Fellows must agree to spend the academic terms in residence at Stanford to participate in the seminars and activities of the fellowship program. **Criteria:** Applicants will be evaluated by three reviewers - the Program Director, the Deputy Director and a third experienced journalist.

Funds Avail.: No specific amount. **Duration:** Ten months. **Number Awarded:** Varies. **To Apply:** Applicants must submit written essays: an intellectual autobiography, and a statement of how they propose to spend the fellowship year, indicating specific areas of study; must submit a letter from their employer endorsing their application and granting a leave of absence if chosen for a fellowship. Three letters of recommendation, including one from the applicant's immediate supervisor, are required as well as work samples. **Deadline:** December 1 for International applicants; January 15 for U.S. applicants. **Contact:** info@kf.stanford.edu.

8910 ■ Stark Community Foundation

400 Market Ave. N, Ste. 200
Canton, OH 44702
Ph: (330)454-3426
Fax: (330)454-5855
E-mail: info@starkcf.org
URL: www.starkcf.org

8911 ■ Wayne D. Ackerman Family Scholarship Fund (Undergraduate/Scholarship)

Purpose: To provide scholarship assistance to qualified individuals who want to pursue their studies. **Focus:** Gen-

Awards are arranged alphabetically below their administering organizations

eral studies/Field of study not specified. **Qualif.:** Applicants must be senior students attending high school in Stark County, OH; must be enrolled as full-time students; must have GPA of at least 3.0 on 4.0 scale; must demonstrate outstanding involvement both in academics and extracurricular activities; must have been accepted into a four-year college or university. **Criteria:** Selection shall be based on the aforementioned qualifications and compliance with the application details.

Funds Avail.: No specific amount. **Duration:** Annual. **To Apply:** Applicants may visit the website to verify the application process and other pieces of information. **Deadline:** May 1.

8912 ■ American Guild of Organists, Canton Chapter Charitable Fund (Undergraduate/Scholarship)

Purpose: To provide scholarship assistance to qualified individuals who want to pursue their studies. **Focus:** Music. **Qualif.:** Applicants must be students residing in Stark County who are pursuing a four-year bachelor degree program at an accredited college or university in music majoring an instrument; must show an evidence of competent technique and musicianship. **Criteria:** Selection of applicants will be based on the scholarship selection criteria.

Funds Avail.: No specific amount. **To Apply:** Application forms are available online. Applicants must submit a letter of reference; recording tape; and audition including one Bach work or movement, one French work or movement and a third work of applicant's choice. **Remarks:** Established in 1992.

8913 ■ Joan Blend Scholarship Fund
(Undergraduate/Scholarship)

Purpose: To provide scholarship assistance to qualified individuals who want to pursue their studies. **Focus:** Nursing. **Qualif.:** Applicants must be attending or planning to attend university or nursing school offering a Registered Nursing Degree; must have GPA of 2.5 or higher; and must demonstrate financial need. **Criteria:** Recipients are selected based on academic standing and financial need.

Funds Avail.: No specific amount. **Duration:** Annual. **Number Awarded:** Varies. **To Apply:** Applicants may visit the website to verify the application process and other pieces of information. **Deadline:** April 15. **Contact:** Mr. Dan Blend, Joan Blend Nursing Scholarship, P.O. Box 36699 Canton, OH 44735 or email at dblend@wgfairfield.com.

8914 ■ Sheriff W. Bruce Umpleby Law Enforcement Scholarship Fund (Undergraduate/Scholarship)

Purpose: To provide scholarship assistance to qualified individuals who want to pursue their studies. **Focus:** Law enforcement. **Qualif.:** Applicants must be students who are seniors attending high school either inside or outside Stark County, who will graduate with their class, or are graduates of a high school either inside or outside Stark County; must be enrolled as full-time students; must have achieved cumulative GPA of at least 3.0 on a 4.0 scale; must have demonstrated outstanding involvement both in academics and extracurricular activities; must have been accepted, into a post secondary institution with plans to major in law enforcement. **Criteria:** Recipient will be selected based on academic standing and extracurricular activities.

Funds Avail.: No specific amount. **Duration:** Annual. **Number Awarded:** Varies. **To Apply:** Applicants must submit a written statement (at least 2 paragraphs) and three letters of recommendations from their teacher and/or teacher. Application form and other supporting documents must be sent to W. Bruce Umpleby Law Enforcement Scholarship Fund. **Deadline:** March 15. **Contact:** W. Bruce Umpleby Law Enforcement Scholarship Fund; Phone: 330-430-3800.

8915 ■ Harry D. Callahan Educational Trust
(Undergraduate/Scholarship)

Purpose: To provide scholarship assistance to qualified individuals who want to pursue their studies. **Focus:** General studies/Field of study not specified. **Qualif.:** Applicants must be residents of Stark County, in the last year of a Stark County High School or Stark County High School graduates, and must have applied to or been accepted by a college or recognized educational institution of higher learning, in the state of Ohio or within a 150 mile radius of the center of Canton, Ohio. They may already be enrolled in college. **Criteria:** Selection shall be made on the basis of satisfactory evidence of scholarship ability, character, and need. Minimum scholastic requirement for consideration for the scholarship will be a 2.6 accumulative average.

Funds Avail.: $500. **Duration:** Annual. **To Apply:** Applicants must submit: completed application form; answered character reference questionnaires from at least four persons of recognized standing in the community; a written paragraph or two attached to the application form explaining the need for funding for college and aims in life; and transcript of high school credits and all credits earned from an institution of higher learning. **Deadline:** April 30.

8916 ■ George H. and Anna Casper Fund
(Undergraduate/Scholarship)

Purpose: To provide scholarship assistance to qualified individuals who want to pursue their studies. **Focus:** General studies/Field of study not specified. **Qualif.:** Applicants must be students residing in Stark County; must be attending college full or part-time; must demonstrate financial need and academic excellence. **Criteria:** Recipients will be selected based on financial need and academic standing.

Funds Avail.: No specific amount. **Duration:** Annual. **To Apply:** Applicants must complete and submit the application form. **Deadline:** June 1. **Remarks:** Established in 1973. **Contact:** info@cantonstudentloan.org.

8917 ■ Ruth M. Cogan Scholarship Fund
(Undergraduate/Scholarship)

Purpose: To provide scholarship assistance to qualified applicants from Stark County, Ohio in obtaining a college education, particularly in the field of music. **Focus:** Music. **Qualif.:** Applicants must be residents of Stark County, Ohio pursuing college-level study in the field of music, have scholastic aptitude, and have demonstrated financial need. **Criteria:** Selection shall be based on the aforementioned applicants' qualifications and compliance with the application details.

Funds Avail.: Amount varies. **Duration:** Annual. **To Apply:** Applicants may retrieve a copy of provided application form at the scholarship website. **Deadline:** April 15. **Contact:** The Ruth Cogan Scholarship, c/o John Hayward, 3427 Shepherd Street NW, N. Canton, Ohio 44720.

8918 ■ Julio C. Diaz Academic Scholarship
(Undergraduate/Scholarship)

Purpose: To provide scholarship assistance to qualified individuals who want to pursue their studies. **Focus:** General studies/Field of study not specified. **Qualif.:** Applicants

Awards are arranged alphabetically below their administering organizations

must be students attending Saint Thomas Aquinas High School who have completed at least one year at the said institution and have achieved minimum cumulative GPA of at least 3.5 on a 4.0 scale. **Criteria:** Selection shall be based on the following grounds: aforesaid qualifications; demonstration of involvement in extracurricular activities at St. Thomas Aquinas HS; demonstration of commitment to anti-tobacco use; and compliance with the application process.

Funds Avail.: $2,500 each. **Duration:** Annual. **Number Awarded:** 2. **To Apply:** Applicants should submit the following: provided application form; a record of school and/or community service; and a letter of recommendation from a current St. Thomas Aquinas teacher. **Deadline:** April 15. **Contact:** St. Thomas Aquinas High School, c/o Victoria Frustaci/Business Office, 2121 Reno Drive, Louisville, OH 44641; Phone: 330-875-1631; Email: vfrustaci@stahs.org.

8919 ■ Robert Martz DiGiacomo Memorial Scholarship Fund (Undergraduate/Scholarship)

Purpose: To provide scholarship assistance to qualified individuals who want to pursue their studies. **Focus:** General studies/Field of study not specified. **Qualif.:** Applicants must be graduating seniors residing at the Lake Local School District; must demonstrate commitment to excellence in academic and athletic accomplishments; must have exceptional moral and personal characteristics; must have leadership skills; and must demonstrate devotion to family. **Criteria:** Selection shall be based on the aforementioned applicants' qualifications and compliance with the application details.

Funds Avail.: $600. **Duration:** Annual. **Number Awarded:** 1. **To Apply:** Applicants may retrieve a copy of provided application form at the scholarship website. **Deadline:** April 15. **Contact:** Edmond and Sandra E. DiGiacomo, 755 Oneida Trail, Hartville, Ohio 44632; Phone: 330-877-2025; E-mail: eands@att.net.

8920 ■ Emergency Medicine Physician Scholarships for Health Information Management Program (Undergraduate/Scholarship)

Purpose: To provide scholarship assistance to qualified individuals who want to pursue their studies. **Focus:** Health education. **Qualif.:** Applicants must be students beginning the second year of study at Stark State College and enrolled full time in the Health Information Management Technology program; must have minimum GPA of 3.0 on a 4.0 scale; must complete his/her education at the conclusion of spring semester; must have interview with the EMP Manager of Coding and Senior Executives. **Criteria:** Selection shall be based on the aforementioned applicants' qualifications and compliance with the application details.

Funds Avail.: No specific amount. **Duration:** Annual. **To Apply:** Applicants may visit the scholarship section of the bestowing organization's website for further information regarding the application details. **Deadline:** May 31. **Contact:** Paula Warren, EMP Scholarship Program, Emergency Medicine Physicians, 4535 Dressler Road, NW Canton, Ohio 44718; Phone: 330-492-4559 ext. 1383; E-mail: pwarren@emp.com.

8921 ■ Jack B. Fisher Scholarship Fund (Undergraduate/Scholarship)

Purpose: To provide scholarship assistance to qualified individuals who want to pursue their studies. **Focus:** Fisheries sciences/management. **Qualif.:** Applicants must be graduates of Stark County High school and current

employees of Fisher Foods in good standing (if employed during high school, a minimum of one year of employment is required. If employed after graduation from high school, a minimum of 2 years of employment is required). must have **Criteria:** Selection shall be based on the following: above average accomplishment in high school; demonstration of good moral and personal characteristics; and recommendation of store manager.

Funds Avail.: $500 each. **Duration:** Annual. **Number Awarded:** 2. **To Apply:** Applicants must submit a recommendation letter from a store manager, and application form to Fisher Foods Marketing, Inc. **Deadline:** June 28. **Contact:** Mr. John Halkias, Fisher Foods Marketing, Inc. 4855 Frank Rd. NW, North Canton, OH 44720; Phone: 330-497-3003, Email: john.halkias@fisherfoods.com.

8922 ■ Alice J. Foit Scholarships (Undergraduate/Scholarship)

Purpose: To provide scholarship assistance to qualified individuals who want to pursue their studies. **Focus:** General studies/Field of study not specified. **Qualif.:** Applicants must be high school graduates or seniors residing in Carroll County, German Township, Harrison County, OH; must be enrolled as full time students; must have achieved high school cumulative GPA of at least 2.5 on a 4.0 scale, and if attending college a cumulative GPA of at least 2.0 on a 4.0 scale; must have demonstrated involvement, both in extracurricular activities or community and religious activities; must have been accepted into a two or four year college on university program leading to a degree; must intend to live or work in either Carroll or Harrison County, OH for a minimum of two years after completion of their education. **Criteria:** Selection of applicants will be based on financial need and potential.

Funds Avail.: No specific amount. **Duration:** Annual. **Number Awarded:** Varies. **To Apply:** Applicants must complete and submit the application form. **Deadline:** December 1. **Contact:** Richard Lee Rumbaugh, 63 E Main St., Carrollton, OH 44615; Phone: 330-627-2918.

8923 ■ Thomas W. Gallagher Scholarships Fund (Undergraduate/Scholarship)

Purpose: To provide scholarship assistance to qualified individuals who want to pursue their studies. **Focus:** Pharmacy. **Qualif.:** Applicants must be: seniors attending Minerva High School who will be graduated with their class in June; full-time students who have been accepted into a four-year college or university to pursue a degree in pharmacy; and, full-time students who have been accepted into a four-year college or university to study in the field of science (if no students pursuing a degree in pharmacy have applied). **Criteria:** Consideration will be given to students pursuing a degree in pharmacy.

Funds Avail.: Amont varies. **Duration:** Annual. **Number Awarded:** Varies. **To Apply:** Applicants must complete and submit the application form available online at Guidance High School. **Deadline:** April 10. **Contact:** Minerva High School, Guidance Office, 501 Minerva Ave., Minerva OH 44657; Phone: 330-868-4134.

8924 ■ David A. and Pamela A. Gault Charitable Fund (Undergraduate/Scholarship)

Purpose: To provide scholarship assistance to qualified individuals who want to pursue their studies. **Focus:** General studies/Field of study not specified. **Qualif.:** Applicants must be graduates of Stark County High School with residency in Stark County for a minimum of five years;

Awards are arranged alphabetically below their administering organizations

enrolled at Otterbein College or Walsh University, pursuing a graduate or undergraduate degree in business; and maintaining a minimum of 2.5 GPA on a 4.0 scale. **Criteria:** Recipients will be selected based on the scholarship selection criteria.

Funds Avail.: Amount varies. **Duration:** Annual. **Number Awarded:** Varies. **To Apply:** Applicants must have a recommendation letter by Otterbein College or Walsh University. **Deadline:** May 1. **Contact:** scholarships@starkcf.org.

8925 ■ Margaret S. Gilbert Scholarship Fund
(Undergraduate/Scholarship)

Purpose: To provide scholarship assistance to qualified individuals who want to pursue their studies. **Focus:** History; Mathematics and mathematical sciences; Natural sciences. **Qualif.:** Applicants must be Stark County public high school female graduates who attend or will attend Oberlin College; must have a major in one of the natural sciences, mathematics, or history; must have extracurricular activities, especially those demonstrating interest in science; must demonstrate diligent effort, responsibility and financial need. **Criteria:** Selection shall be based on the aforementioned qualifications and compliance with the application details.

Funds Avail.: Amount varies. **Duration:** Annual. **Number Awarded:** Varies. **To Apply:** Interested applicants must complete and submit the application form and other requirements on or before the deadline. **Deadline:** May 1. **Contact:** scholarships@starkcf.org.

8926 ■ James H. and Shirley L. Green Scholarship Fund *(Undergraduate/Scholarship)*

Purpose: To provide scholarship assistance to qualified individuals who want to pursue their studies. **Focus:** General studies/Field of study not specified. **Qualif.:** Applicants must be seniors attending Canton South High School, Canton, OH; must have been accepted into a two-year or four-year college or university; must demonstrate financial need; must have achieved a cumulative GPA of at least 2.5; and must demonstrate an outstanding involvement in extracurricular activities and/or outside job activities. **Criteria:** Selection of applicants will be based on the scholarship selection criteria.

Funds Avail.: No specific amount. **Duration:** Annual. **Number Awarded:** Varies. **To Apply:** Interested applicants may visit the website for the online application and other application details. **Deadline:** April 1. **Contact:** Barbra Tscholl, Canton South High School, 600 Faircrest St. SE Canton, OH 44707; Phone: 330-484-8000; Email: Tscholl@cantonlocal.org.

8927 ■ Velma Shotwell Griffin Memorial Scholarship Fund *(Undergraduate/Scholarship)*

Purpose: To provide scholarship assistance to qualified individuals who want to pursue their studies. **Focus:** History; Music; Writing. **Qualif.:** Applicants must be graduates of Conotton Valley High School or Carrollton High School; must be planning to enroll, or currently enrolled, at an accredited college or university to pursue further education in the following fields: (1) History; (2) Writing, not limited to, English Journalism, Language Arts, Communications and programs in Mass Media; (3) Music, not limited to vocal music, instrumental music, music history, music education and music performance; (4) Any other program or field of study approved by the selection committee. **Criteria:** Recipients will be selected based on the following criteria: (1)

Academic merit; (2) Participation in extracurricular school and civic activities related to History, Writing or Music, good moral and personal characteristics; (3) Good moral and personal characteristics, including integrity and an interest in their communities; (4) Demonstrated interest in History, Writing or Music and commitment to the further study of these subject; (5) Demonstrate financial need.

Funds Avail.: $1,000. **Duration:** Annual. **Number Awarded:** 1. **To Apply:** Applicants must submit completed application form and are advised to contact Carrollton High School Guidance Office, Conotton Valley High School Guidance Office. **Deadline:** April 25.

8928 ■ Dr. James H. Heckman Memorial Scholarship Fund *(Undergraduate/Scholarship)*

Purpose: To provide scholarship assistance to qualified individuals who want to pursue their studies. **Focus:** General studies/Field of study not specified. **Qualif.:** Applicants must be Hoover High School graduating seniors; must have above average accomplishment in high school; must have demonstrated financial need; must be planning to a four-year degree program in any field of study; must demonstrate good moral and personal characteristics. **Criteria:** Selection shall be based on the aforementioned qualifications and compliance with the application details.

Funds Avail.: No specific amount. **Duration:** Annual. **Number Awarded:** Varies. **To Apply:** Application forms are available online. **Deadline:** April 1. **Contact:** Jason Downey, Guidance Counselor, Hoover High School 525 Seventh NE North Canton, OH 44720; Phone: 330-497-5627.

8929 ■ Dale O. Heimberger CRNA Memorial Scholarship Fund *(Graduate/Scholarship)*

Purpose: To provide scholarship assistance to qualified individuals who want to pursue their studies. **Focus:** Anesthesiology. **Qualif.:** Applicants must be accepted into the University of Akron, College of Nursing-Graduate Anesthesia Program; must have scholastic aptitude; must demonstrate financial need. **Criteria:** Selection of applicants will be based on financial need and academic excellence.

Funds Avail.: No specific amount. **Number Awarded:** Varies. **To Apply:** Applicants must complete and submit the application form. **Deadline:** November 1. **Contact:** Dennis C. Ross, CRNA Aultman Hospital, Department of Anesthesia 2600 6th Street SW Canton, OH 44710.

8930 ■ Raymond T. Hoge Scholarship Fund
(Undergraduate/Scholarship)

Purpose: To provide scholarship assistance to qualified individuals who want to pursue their studies. **Focus:** Business; Education. **Qualif.:** Applicants must be graduating senior members of Perry High School or alumni who plan to attend an institution of higher learning; must be in good academic standing; must be planning to pursue a degree in the field of business or education; must demonstrate financial need. **Criteria:** Recipients will be selected based on community service and work experience.

Funds Avail.: No specific amount. **Duration:** Annual. **Number Awarded:** Varies. **To Apply:** Applicants must complete and submit the application. Application form must be obtained at Perry High School Guidance Office. **Deadline:** April 15. **Contact:** Perry High School Guidance Office, 3737 13th St. SW Massillon OH 44646; Phoe: 330-477-3486.

Awards are arranged alphabetically below their administering organizations

8931 ■ Minnie Hopkins Memorial Scholarship Fund of Lathrop/Compton School (Undergraduate/Scholarship)

Purpose: To provide scholarship assistance to qualified individuals who want to pursue their studies. **Focus:** General studies/Field of study not specified. **Qualif.:** Applicants must have graduated from Lathrop/Compton School and attended Lathrop/Compton for at least three years; must have graduated from Stark County public high school and been accepted into a college, university, or technical school; must have leadership skills; must have academic ability and achievement; must have initiative and motivation; and must demonstrate financial need. **Criteria:** Recipients will be selected based on the following criteria: (a) leadership skills; (b) academic ability and achievement; (c) initiative and motivation; (d) extracurricular activities; (e) family background; and (f) financial need.

Funds Avail.: Amount varies. **Duration:** Annual. **Number Awarded:** Varies. **To Apply:** Applicants may visit the website to verify the application process and other pieces of information. **Deadline:** May 1.

8932 ■ Judge and Mrs. Robert D. Horowitz Legal Scholarship Fund (Graduate/Scholarship)

Purpose: To provide scholarship assistance to qualified individuals who want to pursue their studies. **Focus:** Paralegal studies. **Qualif.:** Applicants must be graduates of high school in Stark, Columbiana, Carroll, Tuscarawas, Wayne or Holmes County, OH; must be enrolled or accepted as full-time or part-time students in a doctorate program; must demonstrate public service through volunteer activities or work experience; must demonstrate financial need. **Criteria:** Selection of applicants will be based on the scholarship application criteria.

Funds Avail.: No specific amount. **Duration:** Annual. **To Apply:** Applicants must have at least two letter of reference documenting their public service and/or volunteer activities and have completed a short essay on their personal public service and/or volunteer experience. **Deadline:** April 30. **Contact:** Jennifer Saniuk, 59 Deerfield Road, Needham, MA 02492.

8933 ■ Virginia C. Jack and Ralph L. Jack Scholarships (Undergraduate/Scholarship)

Purpose: To provide scholarship assistance to qualified individuals who want to pursue their studies. **Focus:** Education, Vocational-technical; Nursing. **Qualif.:** Applicants must be Stark County residents; must be admitted to technical school, college or university, or school of nursing; must be full or part time students; must be traditional or non-traditional students; must have 2.50 or higher GPA on a 4.0 scale. **Criteria:** Selection of applicants will be based on financial need and academic excellence.

Funds Avail.: $2,000. **Duration:** Annual. **Number Awarded:** Varies. **To Apply:** Applicants must submit the application form, two letters of recommendation and transcripts to Stark Community Foundation. **Deadline:** May 1.

8934 ■ Jackson High School Alumni Scholarship Fund (Undergraduate/Scholarship)

Purpose: To provide scholarship assistance to qualified individuals who want to pursue their studies. **Focus:** General studies/Field of study not specified. **Qualif.:** Applicants must be graduating seniors at Jackson High School or Jackson High School graduates who are currently enrolled as full-time college students; must have minimum GPA of 2.5 or above. **Criteria:** Selection of applicants will be based on their demonstration of community service, involvement in extracurricular activities, academic standing and personal interview with Selection Committee.

Funds Avail.: No specific amount. **To Apply:** Application forms are available online.

8935 ■ Junior Achievement of East Central Ohio, Inc. Scholarship Fund (Undergraduate/Scholarship)

Purpose: To provide scholarship assistance to qualified individuals who want to pursue their studies. **Focus:** General studies/Field of study not specified. **Qualif.:** Applicants must be 12th grade students in Stark, Tuscarawas, or Carroll County high school. **Criteria:** Recipients will be selected based on the following criteria: (1) Participation in J.A.; (2) Demonstrated support of free enterprise system; (3) Academic achievement; (4) Extracurricular activities; (5) Service to school and community; (6) Service to school and community; (7) Anticipated ability to succeed in college.

Funds Avail.: $1,000 each. **Duration:** Annual. **Number Awarded:** 3. **To Apply:** Applicants must complete and submit the application form. **Deadline:** May 21. **Contact:** Scholarship Selection Committee, Junior Achievement of East Central Ohio, Inc. 4353 Executive Circle NW Canton, OH 44718; Phone: 330-433-0063; Email: staff@jaonline.org.

8936 ■ David A. Kaiser Memorial Scholarship Fund (Undergraduate/Scholarship)

Purpose: To provide scholarship assistance to qualified individuals who want to pursue their studies. **Focus:** General studies/Field of study not specified. **Qualif.:** Applicants must be full-time students in high school in the Canton City School District; must be accepted into an accredited college or university; must be planning to pursue a four-year degree. **Criteria:** Selection of applicants will be based on the following criteria: (1) Minimum GPA of 3.8; (2) Personal integrity; (3) Evidence of leadership skills; (4) participation in extracurricular activities.

Funds Avail.: $3,000. **Duration:** Annual. **Number Awarded:** 1. **To Apply:** Applicants may visit the website to verify the application process and other pieces of information. **Deadline:** March 15.

8937 ■ Samuel Krugliak Legal Scholarship Fund (Undergraduate/Scholarship)

Purpose: To provide scholarship assistance to qualified individuals who want to pursue their studies. **Focus:** Paralegal studies. **Qualif.:** Applicants must be currently enrolled and attending law school accredited by the American Bar Association or have enrolled and will be attending in the fall; must have shown an active commitment to their community; must display strong academic achievement; must reside or have formerly resided in the Stark, Wayne, Carroll, Holmes, Summit, Tuscarawas, Columbiana, or Mahoning Counties when not attending law school; must desire to pursue the practice of law in the Stark County Region. **Criteria:** Selection of applicants will be based on the scholarship application criteria.

Funds Avail.: No specific amount. **Duration:** Annual. **Number Awarded:** Varies. **To Apply:** Applicants must attach transcript of records and resume. **Deadline:** June 9. **Contact:** Kelly Osborn at 330-497-0700.

Awards are arranged alphabetically below their administering organizations

8938 ■ Lake Dollars for Scholars Endowment Fund
(Undergraduate/Scholarship)

Purpose: To provide scholarship assistance to qualified individuals who want to pursue their studies. **Focus:** Education, Vocational-technical; Nursing. **Qualif.:** Applicants must be graduating seniors residing within the boundaries of the Lake Local District, Lake Township and Stark County, OH; must have been accepted into a two-year or four-year college or university, nursing school, or other post high school vocational education program; must meet the requirements of the application form provided by Lake Dollars For Scholars. **Criteria:** Selection of applicants will be based on the scholarship application criteria.

Funds Avail.: No specific amount. **Number Awarded:** Varies. **To Apply:** Applicants must submit completed application form and are advised to contact the Lake High School Guidance Office.

8939 ■ Jay C. and B. Nadine Leggett Charitable Scholarship Fund *(Undergraduate/Scholarship)*

Purpose: To assist qualified individuals who want to pursue their studies. **Focus:** General studies/Field of study not specified. **Qualif.:** Applicants must be graduates of Conotton Valley High School or high school seniors who applied to and have been accepted by college, university, or recognized educational institution of higher learning, or presently enrolled in college; must be above average in accomplishments and have participated in extracurricular activities. **Criteria:** Recipients are selected based on academic excellence, character and financial need.

Funds Avail.: No specific amount. **Duration:** Annual. **Number Awarded:** Varies. **To Apply:** Applicants must complete and submit the application form and requirements. **Deadline:** April 25. **Contact:** Judson Lada, Guidance Counselor, Conotton Valley High School, 7205 Cumberland Rd. SW Bowerston, OH 44695.

8940 ■ Lillian Grace Mahan Scholarship Fund
(Graduate/Scholarship)

Purpose: To provide scholarship assistance to qualified individuals who want to pursue their studies. **Focus:** Library and archival sciences. **Qualif.:** Applicants must be graduate students of library science who are residents of Stark County; must have an outstanding academic performance, aptitude and/or in need of financial assistance to pursue a degree in library science; must have demonstrated academic performance record and other activities. **Criteria:** Selection shall be based on the aforementioned qualifications and compliance with the application details.

Funds Avail.: No specific amount. **Duration:** Annual. **Number Awarded:** Varies. **To Apply:** Applicants may visit the website to verify the application process and other pieces of information. **Deadline:** April 1. **Contact:** Executive Director, The Canton Student Loan Foundation 4974 Higbee Avenue NW Canton, OH 44718; Phone 330-493-0020; Email: info@cantonstudentloan.org.

8941 ■ Manzer-Keener-Wefler Scholarships
(Undergraduate/Scholarship)

Purpose: To provide scholarship assistance to qualified individuals who want to pursue their studies. **Focus:** Photography; Visual arts. **Qualif.:** Applicants must have been accepted by or currently attending a two-year or four-year college or university, or art institute within the United States; must have chosen the field related to photography or visual arts; either seniors attending a high school in Stark County, OH, or counties contiguous to Stark who will graduate the year the scholarship is awarded; college undergraduate students originally from Stark County, OH, or counties contiguous to Stark who are currently attending a two-year or four-year college or university or art institute as full time; or non-traditional college students originally from Stark County, OH, or counties contiguous to Stark who are currently attending a two-year or four-year college or university or art institute as part-time; and first time applicants must have a minimum GPA of at least 2.5 on a 4.0. Applicants applying for annual award must achieve a GPA of 3.0 on a 4.0 scale. **Criteria:** Recipients are selected based on financial need; and demonstrated involvement both in academics and extracurricular activities related to their chosen field of study.

Funds Avail.: No specific amount. **Duration:** Annual; up to four years. **Number Awarded:** Varies. **To Apply:** Applicants must submit a two letters of recommendation, recent transcript, and examples of work. **Deadline:** May 1.

8942 ■ Markley Family Scholarship Fund
(Undergraduate/Scholarship)

Purpose: To provide scholarship assistance to qualified individuals who want to pursue their studies. **Focus:** General studies/Field of study not specified. **Qualif.:** Applicants must be full time undergraduate students of Walsh University, North Canton, OH. Both residents and commuters are eligible to apply. **Criteria:** Applicants will be selected based on academic performance and financial need.

Funds Avail.: No specific amount. **Duration:** Annual. **Number Awarded:** Varies. **To Apply:** Applicants may visit the website to verify the application process and other pieces of information. **Deadline:** April 1. **Contact:** Application form and other supporting documents should be sent to Assistant Director of Financial Aid, Walsh University, 2020 Easton NW North Canton, OH 44720; Phone: 330-499-7090.

8943 ■ Bill McCarthy Scout Scholarship Fund
(Undergraduate/Scholarship)

Purpose: To provide scholarship assistance to qualified individuals who want to pursue their studies. **Focus:** General studies/Field of study not specified. **Qualif.:** Applicants must be male students who are or have been Boy Scouts; having belonged to a troop in the Tuslaw District; and who have attained at least the rank of a First Class Scout; and who ranks at least among the highest ten boys in his graduating class in high school. **Criteria:** Selection shall be based on the aforementioned qualifications and compliance with the application details.

Funds Avail.: No specific amount. **Duration:** Annual. **Number Awarded:** Varies. **To Apply:** Applicants may visit the website to verify the application process and other pieces of information. **Deadline:** April 1. **Contact:** Mr. Andy McGeee, Tuslaw High School Guidance Counselor, 1847 Manchester NW, Massillon, OH 44647.

8944 ■ Sanders J. Mestel Legal Scholarship Fund
(Undergraduate/Scholarship)

Purpose: To provide scholarship assistance to qualified individuals who want to pursue their studies. **Focus:** Law. **Qualif.:** Applicants must be law students whose residence is in Stark County. **Criteria:** Selection of applicants will be based on financial need, academic standing and written statement.

Funds Avail.: No specific amount. **Duration:** Annual. **To Apply:** Applicants must submit a written statement of 250-

Awards are arranged alphabetically below their administering organizations

300 words by the applicant indicating his/her special interest, extracurricular activities and future career aspirations in law. **Deadline:** May 1. **Contact:** scholarships@starkcf.org.

8945 ■ Harry Mestel Memorial Accounting Scholarship Fund *(Undergraduate/Scholarship)*

Purpose: To provide scholarship assistance to qualified individuals who want to pursue their studies. **Focus:** Accounting. **Qualif.:** Applicants must be accounting students enrolled in an Ohio college or university in their final year, in pursuit of a Bachelor of Science in Accounting Degree; must be residents of Stark County; must demonstrate financial need; must demonstrate involvement in community activities; and must have achieved a cumulative GPA of at least 3.0 on a 4.0 scale. **Criteria:** Selection will be based on financial need and academic standing.

Funds Avail.: No specific amount. **Duration:** Annual. **Number Awarded:** Varies. **To Apply:** Applicants may visit the website to verify the application process and other pieces of information. **Deadline:** May 1.

8946 ■ John G. and Betty J. Mick Scholarship Fund *(Undergraduate/Scholarship)*

Purpose: To provide scholarship assistance to qualified individuals who want to pursue their studies. **Focus:** Engineering. **Qualif.:** Applicants must be seniors attending a high school in Stark County, OH; must have been accepted as full-time students in Stark State College of Technology engineering Program for a two-year degree which will also transfer to a four-year degree program at another university at the discretion of the students; must have been accepted as full-time students into the Engineering program at any university or college in the State of Ohio; non-traditional students furthering their education after entering the workforce will be considered secondarily; must have cumulative GPA of at least 2.0 on a 4.0 scale. **Criteria:** Recipients will be selected based on academic achievement, personal interview and recommendation by at least one of their teachers, counselors, or principals.

Funds Avail.: No specific amount. **Duration:** Annual; up to four years. **To Apply:** Applicants may visit the website to verify the application process and other pieces of information. **Deadline:** May 1.

8947 ■ Lt. Colonel Robert G. Moreland Vocational/Technical Fund *(Undergraduate/Scholarship)*

Purpose: To provide scholarship assistance to qualified individuals who want to pursue their studies. **Focus:** Education, Vocational-technical. **Qualif.:** Applicants must be residents of Stark County, OH; must have a high school diploma or G.E.D. certification; must intend to pursue vocational or technical education or training in a school or college within the State of Ohio which will lead to an associate degree; must demonstrate financial assistance; must demonstrate desire and ability for vocational, technical education or training. **Criteria:** Selection shall be based on the aforementioned qualifications and compliance with the application details.

Funds Avail.: No specific amount. **Duration:** Annual. **Number Awarded:** Varies. **To Apply:** Applicants must submit their recent transcripts. They may also visit the website to verify the application process and other pieces of information. **Deadline:** May 1.

8948 ■ Notre Dame Club of Canton Scholarships *(Undergraduate/Scholarship)*

Purpose: To provide scholarship assistance to qualified individuals who want to pursue their studies. **Focus:** General studies/Field of study not specified. **Qualif.:** Applicants must be students who have attended Stark County or Tuscarawas County, Ohio High School, Dalton High School, or Orville High School in Wayne County, Ohio, or Central Kidron Christian School in Kidron, OH; must have GPA of at least 3.0 on a 4.0 scale while in high school; must demonstrate an outstanding involvement both in academics and extracurricular activities; must have been accepted to attend the University of Notre Dame, Notre Dame, Indiana. **Criteria:** Recipients will be selected based on academic standing and extracurricular activities.

Funds Avail.: No specific amount. **Duration:** Annual. **Number Awarded:** Varies. **To Apply:** Applicants must complete and submit the application form. To download an application, applicants must log on to www.starkcf.org. **Deadline:** May 1.

8949 ■ O'Jays Scholarship Fund *(Undergraduate/Scholarship)*

Purpose: To provide scholarship assistance to qualified individuals who want to pursue their studies. **Focus:** General studies/Field of study not specified. **Qualif.:** Applicants must be seniors attending high school in Stark County who will graduate the year the scholarship is awarded, or residents of Stark County who have previously attained high school diploma or Graduate Equivalency Diploma; must be accepted by or presently attending a two-year college or university, nursing school, or other post high school vocational educational program; must have cumulative GPA of 2.5 on a 4.0 scale; must demonstrate extracurricular activities or community activities; must demonstrate financial need. **Criteria:** Selection of applicants will be based on the scholarship application criteria.

Funds Avail.: No specific amount. **Duration:** Annual. **Number Awarded:** Varies. **To Apply:** Applicants must complete and submit the application form. **Deadline:** May 1.

8950 ■ Perry Township School Memorial Scholarship Fund *(Undergraduate/Scholarship)*

Purpose: To provide scholarship assistance to qualified individuals who want to pursue their studies. **Focus:** General studies/Field of study not specified. **Qualif.:** Applicants must be high school graduates or high school seniors who have permanent residency in Perry Township, Carroll County, OH or who have permanent residency on the date they began their post high school education; must have been accepted, currently enrolled, or planning to enroll at an accredited college, university, or technical school with at least a two year course of study to pursue further education; must have good moral and personal characteristics; must demonstrate involvement in community and religious activities; must demonstrate financial need. **Criteria:** Recipients will be selected based on the criteria of the Scholarship Selection Committee.

Funds Avail.: No specific amount. **Duration:** Annual. **Number Awarded:** Varies. **To Apply:** Applicants must submit a completed application form; biographical essay; and references from teachers, school counselors, school principal and/or church. **Deadline:** March 1. **Contact:** Carrollton High School at 330-627-7606.

8951 ■ August M. Rocco Scholarship Fund *(Undergraduate/Scholarship)*

Purpose: To provide scholarship assistance to qualified individuals who want to pursue their studies. **Focus:** General studies/Field of study not specified. **Qualif.:** Applicants must be male or female graduates of Canton Central

Awards are arranged alphabetically below their administering organizations

Catholic High School or St. Thomas Aquinas High School and of the Catholic faith; must be accepted to attend college at University of Notre Dame, South Bend, IN; must have good scholastic record and character traits. **Criteria:** Selection shall be based on the aforementioned qualifications and compliance with the application details.

Funds Avail.: No specific amount. **Duration:** Annual. **To Apply:** Applicants must complete and submit the application form and other supporting documents to Stark Community Foundation. **Deadline:** May 1. **Contact:** scholarships@starkcf.org.

8952 ■ Aaron Seesan Memorial Scholarship Fund
(Undergraduate/Scholarship)

Purpose: To provide scholarship assistance to qualified individuals who want to pursue their studies. **Focus:** General studies/Field of study not specified. **Qualif.:** Applicants must be graduating seniors from Massillon Washington High School and any other Stark County High Schools; must demonstrate financial need; must have a minimum of 3.0 cumulative GPA on a 4.0 scale; must demonstrate an involvement in extracurricular activities or community service. **Criteria:** Selection will be based on the committee's criteria.

Funds Avail.: No specific amount. **Duration:** Annual. **Number Awarded:** 2. **To Apply:** Applicants must submit an essay and letter of recommendation from the following: one from school personnel and one from outside source such as employer, community service organization, church official. **Deadline:** April 1. **Contact:** Massillon Washington High School at 330-830-3900 or fax: 330-875-8469.

8953 ■ Don and Madalyn Sickafoose Educational Trust *(Undergraduate/Scholarship)*

Purpose: To provide scholarship assistance to qualified individuals who want to pursue their studies. **Focus:** General studies/Field of study not specified. **Qualif.:** Applicants must be students living in Southeastern Stark County, Northwestern Carroll County and Northern Tuscarawas County which would include the following district: Brown Local, Canton Local, Osnaburg Local, Fairless Local, Sandy Valley, Tusky Valley and Carrollton Exempted Village. Award is renewable for those students who can maintain a 2.5 GPA or better. **Criteria:** Recipients will be selected based on financial need, demonstrated aptitude for college work and academic standing.

Funds Avail.: No specific amount. **Duration:** Annual. **Number Awarded:** Varies. **To Apply:** Applicants must complete and submit the application form. **Deadline:** April 1.

8954 ■ Ruth Skeeles Memorial Scholarship Fund
(Undergraduate/Scholarship)

Purpose: To provide scholarship assistance to qualified individuals who want to pursue their studies. **Focus:** General studies/Field of study not specified. **Qualif.:** Applicants must have attended Worley School for at least four years; must have good academic accomplishment in high school; must have good moral and personal characteristic. **Criteria:** Recipients are selected based on Scholarship Selection Committee's review of application.

Funds Avail.: No specific amount. **Duration:** Annual. **Number Awarded:** Varies. **To Apply:** Applicants must complete and submit the application form. **Deadline:** April 1. **Contact:** Principal of Worley Elementary School PTA, 1340 23rd Street, NW Canton, OH 44709.

8955 ■ Stark County Bar Association Fund
(Undergraduate/Scholarship)

Purpose: To provide scholarship assistance to qualified individuals who want to pursue their studies. **Focus:** Law. **Qualif.:** Applicants must be law students enrolled at accredited law schools; must be from the Stark County area. **Criteria:** Selection of applicants will be based on the demonstration of financial need.

Funds Avail.: No specific amount. **Duration:** Annual. **To Apply:** Applicants must complete and submit the application form. **Deadline:** April 15. **Contact:** Tina McCort, Executive Director, at 330-453-0685.

8956 ■ Stark County Dairy Promoters Scholarships
(Undergraduate/Scholarship)

Purpose: To provide scholarship assistance to qualified individuals who want to pursue their studies. **Focus:** Animal science and behavior; Dairy science; Food science and technology; Nutrition; Veterinary science and medicine. **Qualif.:** Applicants must be residents of Stark County, OH; must be pursuing college-level study in the field of dairy science, animal science, veterinary medicine, human nutrition, or food science; must have 2.5 high school GPA; must have demonstrated financial need. **Criteria:** Selection shall be based on the aforementioned qualifications and compliance with the application details.

Funds Avail.: No specific amount. **Duration:** Annual. **Number Awarded:** Varies. **To Apply:** Applicants must complete the application form provided at the program website and such should be submitted along with three letters of reference (non-family) and recent transcript. **Deadline:** May 1.

8957 ■ Jeffrey Tyler Sweitzer Wrestling Memorial Scholarship Fund *(Undergraduate/Scholarship)*

Purpose: To provide scholarship assistance to qualified individuals who want to pursue their studies. **Focus:** General studies/Field of study not specified. **Qualif.:** Applicants must be male residents of Stark County, OH; must have achieved passing GPA on a 4.0 scale; must be graduating students from Hoover High School, North Canton, OH, have participated in the wrestling program; must be students attending West Liberty College, Wheeling, WV; must be students graduating from any Stark County area high school who have participated in a wrestling program. **Criteria:** Recipients will be selected based on the Scholarship Selection Criteria.

Funds Avail.: No specific amount. **Duration:** Annual. **Number Awarded:** Varies. **To Apply:** Applicants must submit completed application form and requirements to Canton Hoover High School Wrestling Booster Club. **Deadline:** January 24.

8958 ■ Timothy S. Sweterlitsch Memorial Scholarship Fund *(Undergraduate/Scholarship)*

Purpose: To provide scholarship assistance to qualified individuals who want to pursue their studies. **Focus:** General studies/Field of study not specified. **Qualif.:** Applicants must be graduates of Washington High School, Massillon, OH; must have an academic accomplishment; must have good moral and personal characteristics. **Criteria:** Recipients will be selected based on academic standing and character.

Funds Avail.: No specific amount. **Duration:** Annual. **Number Awarded:** Varies. **To Apply:** Applicants must complete and submit the application form. **Deadline:** April 15. **Contact:** Frank Sweterlitsch at sweterlitschf@gmail.com.

Awards are arranged alphabetically below their administering organizations

8959 ■ Tim Triner Letter Carriers Scholarship Fund
(Undergraduate/Scholarship)

Purpose: To provide scholarship assistance to qualified individuals who want to pursue their studies. **Focus:** General studies/Field of study not specified. **Qualif.:** Applicants must be seniors enrolled as full-time students; must have scholastic achievements; must be children or legal wards of Donor's active, retired or deceased members of Branch No. 238, National Association of Letter; must have a proof of acceptance into a post-secondary college, university or technical training program. **Criteria:** Recipients are selected based on the Scholarship Selection Committee's review of application.

Funds Avail.: No specific amount. **Duration:** Annual. **Number Awarded:** Varies. **To Apply:** Applicants must complete and submit the application form; and must provide a proof of acceptance into a post-secondary college, university or technical training program. **Deadline:** May 31.

8960 ■ Norman J. Tschantz/Walter C. Deuble Scholarships *(Undergraduate/Scholarship)*

Purpose: To provide scholarship assistance to qualified individuals who want to pursue their studies. **Focus:** General studies/Field of study not specified. **Qualif.:** Applicants must have served at least one year as a caddy at Congress Lake Country Club; must have academic achievement in high school, college, or trade school; must have extracurricular activities. **Criteria:** Selection of applicants will be based on academic standing, extracurricular activities, overall character and demonstration of responsibility and diligent effort.

Funds Avail.: No specific amount. **Duration:** Annual. **Number Awarded:** Varies. **To Apply:** Applicants must submit completed application form. **Deadline:** June 1. **Contact:** Congress Lake Pro Shop at 330-877-0576.

8961 ■ Ira G. Turpin Scholars Fund *(Undergraduate/Scholarship)*

Purpose: To provide scholarship assistance to qualified individuals who want to pursue their studies. **Focus:** General studies/Field of study not specified. **Qualif.:** Applicants must be minority students attending Stark Country schools. **Criteria:** Selection of applicants will be based on their perseverance, high standards and hard work toward achieving their career goals.

Funds Avail.: No specific amount. **Duration:** Annual. **Number Awarded:** Varies. **To Apply:** Application forms are available online. **Deadline:** March 14.

8962 ■ Lester and Eleanor Webster Foundation Scholarships *(Undergraduate/Scholarship)*

Purpose: To provide scholarship assistance to qualified individuals who want to pursue their studies. **Focus:** General studies/Field of study not specified. **Qualif.:** Applicants must be students residing in Stark County who are pursuing a two-year or four-year college degree at an accredited school within the State of Ohio and who have attained sophomore status in college at time of award. They must also have a minimum GPA of 2.75. **Criteria:** Recipients will be selected based on financial need, high school and/or college activities, scholastic aptitude and competence.

Funds Avail.: No specific amount. **Duration:** Annual. **Number Awarded:** Varies. **To Apply:** Applicants must complete and submit the application form. **Deadline:** May 1. **Contact:** scholarships@starkcf.org.

8963 ■ John R. and Joan F. Werren Scholarships Fund *(Undergraduate/Scholarship)*

Purpose: To provide scholarship assistance to qualified individuals who want to pursue their studies. **Focus:** General studies/Field of study not specified. **Qualif.:** Applicants must be students planning to enroll or are presently enrolled at Grove City College. **Criteria:** Preferences are given to freshmen and current students who are Stark County residents. Recipients will be selected based on scholarship standards established by Grove City College.

Funds Avail.: $500 to $1,000. **Duration:** Annual. **Number Awarded:** 1. **To Apply:** Applicants must contact the school's Financial Aid Office for more information. **Deadline:** April 15.

8964 ■ Mary Kean White Memorial Scholarship Fund *(Undergraduate/Scholarship)*

Purpose: To provide scholarship assistance to qualified individuals who want to pursue their studies. **Focus:** Education, Elementary. **Qualif.:** Applicants must be graduates of Malvern High School or Carrollton High School; must be currently enrolled as full time students at an accredited college or university; must have cumulative GPA of at least 3.0 on a 4.0 scale; must be pursuing a career in elementary education or related field; must demonstrate financial need. **Criteria:** Recipients will be selected based on academic standing and financial need.

Funds Avail.: No specific amount. **Duration:** Annual. **Number Awarded:** Varies. **To Apply:** Applicants must complete and submit the application form and requirements to Carrollton High School Guidance Office, Malvern High School Guidance Office. **Deadline:** April 1.

8965 ■ Workshops, Inc. and Stark MRDD Fostering Diversity Through Special Needs Scholarship Fund *(Undergraduate/Scholarship)*

Purpose: To provide scholarship assistance to qualified individuals who want to pursue their studies. **Focus:** Education, Special. **Qualif.:** Applicants must be residents of Stark County; must have at least a 3.0 cumulative GPA; must be majoring in Special Education or related field; must be juniors or seniors at a college or university. **Criteria:** Recipients will be selected based on academic achievement, volunteer/paid work experience and/or involvement in campus/community activities or organizations, essay review and personal interview.

Funds Avail.: No specific amount. **Duration:** Annual. **Number Awarded:** Varies. **To Apply:** Applicants must submit a 500-word essay which describes "Why you chose to major in special education or related field" and an essay review. **Deadline:** June 15. **Remarks:** Established in 1998. **Contact:** Connie Poulton at poultonc@starkdd.org.

8966 ■ State of Idaho, Board of Education
650 W State St., Ste. 307
Boise, ID 83720
Ph: (208)332-1595
Fax: (208)334-2632
URL: www.boardofed.idaho.gov

8967 ■ Idaho Opportunity Scholarships
(Undergraduate/Scholarship)

Purpose: To support students from Idaho in their pursuit of higher education. **Focus:** General studies/Field of study not specified. **Qualif.:** Applicants must be Idaho residents

Awards are arranged alphabetically below their administering organizations

who have graduated from an Idaho high school or its equivalent (GED from Idaho); and must be enrolled as full-time undergraduate students at Lewis-Clark State College, University of Idaho, Boise State University, Idaho State University, Brigham Young University-Idaho, Northwest Nazarene University, or College of Idaho, or enrolled of at least quarter-time at College of Western Idaho, College of Southern Idaho, Eastern Idaho Technical College, or North Idaho College. **Criteria:** Applicants are selected based on financial need and GPA requirements.

Funds Avail.: $3,000. **Duration:** Annual. **Number Awarded:** 1,500. **To Apply:** Applicants may visit the scholarship website for further application information. **Deadline:** March 1. **Contact:** Joy LaRue at joy.larue@osbe.idaho.gov.

8968 ■ State of Wisconsin Higher Educational Aids Board (HEAB)

131 W Wilson St., Ste. 902
Madison, WI 53703
Ph: (608)267-2206
Fax: (608)267-2808
E-mail: heabmail@wisconsin.gov
URL: www.heab.state.wi.us

8969 ■ Minority Teacher Loans *(Undergraduate, Graduate/Loan)*

Purpose: To address the needs of Wisconsin students enrolled in a program leading to teacher licensure. **Focus:** Education; Teaching. **Qualif.:** Candidates must be Wisconsin residents, minorities, undergraduate juniors or seniors or graduate students who are enrolled at least half-time in programs leading to teacher licensure at the University of Wisconsin or an independent institution; must not currently possess a Wisconsin teacher's license; must have a GPA of 2.5 or higher based on a 4.0 scale. **Criteria:** Selection will be based on the committee's criteria.

Funds Avail.: $2,500-$5,000. **To Apply:** Students must be nominated by the financial aid office at their school. Nominated students must complete a Minority Teacher Loan Recipient Agreement and Minority Teacher Loan Information Sheet. The completed paperwork must be submitted to the Higher Educational Aids Board for processing. Only original documents will be accepted.

8970 ■ Nursing Student Loans *(Graduate/Loan)*

Purpose: To address the needs of nursing students enrolled at an eligible Wisconsin institution that prepares them to be licensed as nurses, either RN or LPN. **Focus:** Nursing. **Qualif.:** Applicants must be students enrolled in a participating UW, Wisconsin Technical College or private, nonprofit post-secondary institution in the state; must be Wisconsin residents; must be enrolled at least half-time in a degree or certificate program leading to a nursing license, master's degree in nursing or doctoral degree in nursing; must make satisfactory academic progress; must demonstrate financial need. Applicants must agree to practice full-time as a licensed nurse and/or as a nurse educator in Wisconsin for the term of the forgiveness period. **Criteria:** Selection will be based on the committee's criteria.

Funds Avail.: $250-$3,000. **Duration:** Annual. **To Apply:** Students must complete and submit a FAFSA form each year; students should inform financial aid administrators of their interest in receiving a nursing student loan each year, so administrators will consider them when allocating this

loan. The school financial aid administrator will designate students who show eligibility for the nursing student loan and will offer them a loan. The school financial aid administrator will forward to the higher educational aids board all student information and a signed loan agreement from each student.

8971 ■ Teacher of the Visually Impaired Loans *(Undergraduate, Graduate/Loan)*

Purpose: To provide loans to individuals for their preparation to become licensed teachers of the visually impaired or orientation and mobility instructors. **Focus:** Education; Teaching; Visual impairment. **Qualif.:** Applicants must be undergraduate or graduate students enrolled at least half-time at an in-state or eligible out-of-state institution in a program that prepares them to be licensed as teachers of the visually impaired or as orientation and mobility instructors; must be Wisconsin residents. For each of the first two years the students teaches and meets the eligibility criteria, 25% of the loan is forgiven. For the third year, 50% is forgiven. If the student does not teach and meet the eligibility criteria, the loan must be repaid at an interest rate of 5%. **Criteria:** Selection will be based on the committee's criteria.

Funds Avail.: $250-$10,000. **Duration:** Annual. **To Apply:** Interested applicants may contact Nancy Wilkison for the application process and other information.

8972 ■ Steuben County Community Foundation

1701 N Wayne St.
Angola, IN 46703-2356
Ph: (260)665-6656
Fax: (260)665-8420
URL: www.steubenfoundation.org

8973 ■ Clifford V. Abbott Memorial Scholarships *(Undergraduate/Scholarship)*

Purpose: To provide financial support to outstanding students. **Focus:** General studies/Field of study not specified. **Qualif.:** Applicants must be: residents of Steuben County; graduating seniors from Fremont High School. **Criteria:** Applicants are selected based on the committee's review of the application materials.

Funds Avail.: No specific amount. **Duration:** Annual. **To Apply:** Applicants must submit one character statement from an individual outside of the school environment, and one academic statement from a person at your school. Applicants must also submit their copy of school transcripts. **Deadline:** February 15. **Contact:** Steuben County Community Foundation, at the above address.

8974 ■ Tara Lynn Arnold Scholarships *(Undergraduate/Scholarship)*

Purpose: To provide financial support to those students who will be entering a four-year college or university with intent of pursuing a Bachelor of Arts Degree. **Focus:** Psychology; Women's studies. **Qualif.:** Applicants must attend or have attended Angola High School, and be in good academic standing. **Criteria:** Preference will be given to those students who will take up psychology or women's studies.

Funds Avail.: No specific amount. **Duration:** Annual. **To Apply:** Applicants may visit the website to verify the application process and other pieces of information. **Deadline:** February 15. **Contact:** Steuben County Community Foundation, at the above address.

Awards are arranged alphabetically below their administering organizations

8975 ■ Richard L. Baker Memorial Scholarships
(Undergraduate/Scholarship)

Purpose: To provide financial support to those graduating students of Fremont High School for their academic achievements. **Focus:** General studies/Field of study not specified. **Qualif.:** Applicants must be: graduating seniors from Fremont High School; residing within the Fremont Community School District; and, admitted to a college or university as full-time students. They must also receive Academic Honors from Fremont High School. **Criteria:** Selection shall be based on the aforementioned applicants' qualifications and compliance with the application details.

Funds Avail.: No specific amount. **Duration:** Annual. **To Apply:** Applicants must submit a completed application form; a 250-word essay; and high school transcripts. **Deadline:** February 15. **Contact:** Steuben County Community Foundation, at the above address.

8976 ■ Verna Curry Boyer Scholarships
(Undergraduate/Scholarship)

Purpose: To provide financial assistance to those students who are pursuing teaching. **Focus:** Teaching. **Qualif.:** Applicants must be graduates of any Steuben County High School, including Prairie Heights, Fremont, Hamilton or MSD of Steuben County, and have a 3.0 or better GPA on a 4.0 scale. **Criteria:** Selection shall be based on the aforementioned applicants' qualifications and compliance with the application details.

Funds Avail.: No specific amount. **Duration:** Annual. **To Apply:** Applicants must submit any supporting statements from former teachers or supervisors of any paid or volunteer work in your chosen field; copy of school transcripts; and an essay answering the question, "What characteristics are necessary to be a successful teacher?" **Deadline:** February 15. **Contact:** Steuben County Community Foundation, at the above address.

8977 ■ Ellen Eberhardt Memorial Scholarships
(Undergraduate/Scholarship)

Purpose: To provide support for students pursuing degree in environmental education. **Focus:** Environmental conservation. **Qualif.:** Applicants must be: residents of Steuben County; graduating seniors from a Steuben County High School; entering a four-year college or university with the intent to pursue a career in environmental education, biology, earth science or elementary education. They must also demonstrate financial need. **Criteria:** Selection shall be based on the aforementioned applicants' qualifications and compliance with the application details.

Funds Avail.: No specific amount. **Duration:** Annual. **To Apply:** Applicants may visit the website to verify the application process and other pieces of information. **Deadline:** February 15. **Contact:** Steuben County Community Foundation, at the above address.

8978 ■ Don and Eileen Fulton Nursing Scholarships
(Undergraduate/Scholarship)

Purpose: To provide financial assistance to those students who will be continuing their education through an accredited nursing program at any Indiana institution of higher education. **Focus:** Nursing. **Qualif.:** Applicants must be graduating seniors or have graduated from a Steuben County High School **Criteria:** Applicants are selected based on the committee's review of the application materials.

Funds Avail.: No specific amount. **Duration:** Annual. **To Apply:** Applicants must submit two references, copy of

school transcripts and an essay answering the question, "Why have you chose nursing as a career?" **Deadline:** February 15. **Contact:** Steuben County Community Foundation, at the above address.

8979 ■ Helen R. Greenamyer Memorial Scholarships
(Undergraduate/Scholarship)

Purpose: To provide financial support to those students who are pursuing a career in Nursing. **Focus:** Nursing. **Qualif.:** Applicants must be graduates of any Steuben County High School, including Prairie Heights, Fremont, Hamilton or MSD of Steuben County pursuing a career in Nursing. **Criteria:** Applicants are selected based on the committee's review of the application materials.

Funds Avail.: No specific amount. **Duration:** Annual. **To Apply:** Application forms are available on-line. Applicants must attach a typed 200-400 words essay that includes the information on what the applicants plan to do with their career in nursing; any letters of recommendation; and a copy of school transcripts. **Contact:** Steuben County Community Foundation, at the above address.

8980 ■ Ed Haas Memorial Scholarships
(Undergraduate/Scholarship)

Purpose: To provide financial assistance to those who are pursuing degrees in education, humanities or the arts. **Focus:** Arts; Education--Curricula; Humanities. **Qualif.:** Applicants must be: residents of Steuben County; graduating seniors from Angola High School; and, pursuing degree in the field of Education, Humanities or Arts. **Criteria:** Applicants are selected based on the committee's review of the application materials.

Funds Avail.: No specific amount. **Duration:** Annual. **To Apply:** Applicants must submit any supporting statements from former teachers or supervisors of any paid or volunteer work in your chosen field; copy of school transcripts; an essay answering the questions "why do you want to pursue a career in Education, Humanities or the Arts?" and "what influenced your decision?" Applicants must check the website for the application process and required materials. **Deadline:** February 15. **Contact:** Steuben County Community Foundation, at the above address.

8981 ■ Pauline Hand Memorial Scholarships
(Undergraduate/Scholarship)

Purpose: To provide financial support to Steuben County students going to a full-time university or college. **Focus:** General studies/Field of study not specified. **Qualif.:** Applicants must be residents of Steuben County who are full-time students at any accredited college or university. **Criteria:** Recipients will be selected based on academic achievement, leadership abilities and character.

Funds Avail.: No specific amount. **Duration:** Annual. **To Apply:** Applicants may visit the website to verify the application process and other pieces of information. **Deadline:** February 15. **Contact:** Steuben County Community Foundation, at the above address.

8982 ■ M.G. "Doc" Headley Scholarships
(Undergraduate/Scholarship)

Purpose: To provide support for students pursuing a degree in agricultural. **Focus:** Agriculture, Economic aspects; Veterinary science and medicine. **Qualif.:** Applicants must be pursuing a certified or degreed agricultural or veterinarian program at an institution of higher education. They must also be graduating students from Angola,

Awards are arranged alphabetically below their administering organizations

Fremont, Hamilton or Prairie Heights High School. **Criteria:** Priority will be given to those students in the field of veterinary medicine.

Funds Avail.: No specific amount. **Duration:** Annual. **To Apply:** Applicants may visit the website to verify the application process and other pieces of information. **Deadline:** February 15. **Contact:** Steuben County Community Foundation, at the above address.

8983 ■ Dale Hughes, Jr. Memorial Scholarships
(Undergraduate/Scholarship)

Purpose: To provide support to Prairie Heights students in their continuing education. **Focus:** General studies/Field of study not specified. **Qualif.:** Applicants must be residents of Steuben County and graduating from Prairie Heights High School. They must also be continuing their education through an accredited program at any institution of higher education. **Criteria:** Applicants are selected based on the committee's review of the application materials. Preference will be given to students pursuing agricultural education opportunities.

Funds Avail.: No specific amount. **Duration:** Annual. **To Apply:** Applicants must check the website for the application form and must submit their copy of school transcripts and one-page essay describing the career goals and potential for success. **Deadline:** February 15. **Contact:** Steuben County Community Foundation, at the above address.

8984 ■ John W. Kelley Memorial Scholarships
(Undergraduate/Scholarship)

Purpose: To provide financial support to those students who are interested in earning a degree in Law Enforcement Education. **Focus:** Law enforcement. **Qualif.:** Applicants must be: residents of Steuben County; graduating seniors from any Steuben County High School; and, pursuing a degree in Law Enforcement Education. **Criteria:** Preference will be given to the following manner: children of active duty Steuben County Sheriff's office employees; children of any active duty law enforcement affiliation such as State Police, local Police Officers of Steuben County jurisdiction, DNR, Conservation officers, etc.

Funds Avail.: No specific amount. **Duration:** Annual. **To Apply:** Application forms are available on-line. Applicants must attached their copy of school transcripts; one-page essay answering the question, "Why does the law enforcement field appeal to me?"; and if related to an active duty Steuben County Sheriff's office employee or an active duty law enforcement employee, applicants must attach a letter stating the relationship and the person's name and position. **Deadline:** February 15. **Contact:** Steuben County Community Foundation, at the above address.

8985 ■ Mandel and Lauretta Abrahamer Scholarships *(Undergraduate/Scholarship)*

Purpose: To provide financial support to those students pursuing education in health-related fields. **Focus:** Nursing. **Qualif.:** Applicants must be residents of Steuben County entering in a Nursing School, and have a cumulative 3.0 GPA. They must also demonstrate financial need. **Criteria:** Selection shall be based on the aforementioned applicants' qualifications and compliance with the application details.

Funds Avail.: No specific amount. **Duration:** Annual. **To Apply:** Applicants must submit the following: copy of school transcripts; any supporting statement from former teachers or supervisors of any paid or volunteer work in your chosen field will be considered; an essay answering the question, "What characteristics are necessary to be a successful nurse?" **Deadline:** February 15. **Contact:** Steuben County Community Foundation, at the above address.

8986 ■ Paul and Inger Friend 4-H Scholarships
(Undergraduate/Scholarship)

Purpose: To provide support to 4-H members attending a 2 or 4 year college. **Focus:** General studies/Field of study not specified. **Qualif.:** Applicants must have: graduated from Angola, Hamilton, Fremont or Prairie Heights High School; and, completed at least 7 years in the 4-H program (minimum of 5 years in Steuben County, Indiana). **Criteria:** Selection shall be based on the aforementioned applicants' qualifications and compliance with the application details.

Funds Avail.: No specific amount. **Duration:** Annual. **To Apply:** Application forms are available on-line. Applicants must attach the following to their application: supporting statements from former teachers or supervisors of any paid or volunteer work in chosen field; high school and college transcripts; copy of 4-H record of Achievement; and a 200-word essay on how 4-H has influenced your career choice. **Deadline:** February 15. **Contact:** Steuben County Community Foundation, at the above address.

8987 ■ Dr. J. Glenn Radcliffe Memorial Scholarships
(Undergraduate/Scholarship)

Purpose: To provide financial assistance to those students who are planning to attend Trine University. **Focus:** General studies/Field of study not specified. **Qualif.:** Applicants must be: residents of Steuben County; graduating high school seniors; and, attending TSU to receive a baccalaureate degree. They must also have a cumulative of 3.5 GPA. **Criteria:** Recipients will be selected based on community involvement, scholastic ability and financial need.

Funds Avail.: No specific amount. **Duration:** Annual. **To Apply:** Applicants may visit the website to verify the application process and other pieces of information. **Deadline:** February 15. **Contact:** Steuben County Community Foundation, at the above address.

8988 ■ Nettie and Edward Shelah Scholarships
(Undergraduate/Scholarship)

Purpose: To provide financial assistance to graduates of Hamilton High School. **Focus:** General studies/Field of study not specified. **Qualif.:** Applicants must be Hamilton High School graduating seniors; must be enrolled in an accredited Indiana College or University. **Criteria:** Recipients will be selected based on academic achievement, scholastic aptitude, financial need and character.

Funds Avail.: No specific amount. **Duration:** Annual. **To Apply:** Applicants may visit the website to verify the application process and other pieces of information. **Deadline:** February 15. **Contact:** Steuben County Community Foundation, at the above address.

8989 ■ Stickler Involved People (SIP)
15 Angelina Dr.
Augusta, KS 67010-2207
Ph: (316)259-5194
E-mail: sip@sticklers.org
URL: www.sticklers.org

8990 ■ Dr. Gunnar B. Stickler Scholarships
(Undergraduate, Vocational/Occupational/Scholarship)
Purpose: To assist deserving college-bound adults afflicted with Stickler Syndrome to pursue their dreams and educa-

---

Awards are arranged alphabetically below their administering organizations

tion goals. **Focus:** General studies/Field of study not specified. **Qualif.:** Applicants must be graduating students who have a minimum GPA of 3.0 on a 4.0 scale or equivalent from any American high school students who plan to enter any accredited public or private community, junior, or four-year college or university or vocational-technical school. **Criteria:** Applicants must be diagnosed with Stickler Syndrome by a primary care physicians or Geneticists.

Funds Avail.: $500. **Duration:** One year. **Number Awarded:** 1. **To Apply:** Applicants must fill out the application form (available on the website); must provide a physician letter diagnosing their Stickler Syndrome; and must enclose a high school transcript (sealed). **Deadline:** June 15.

8991 ■ The Richard Stockton College of New Jersey Foundation, Inc.
101 Vera King Farris Dr.
Galloway, NJ 08205-9441
Ph: (609)626-3491
Fax: (609)626-3481
URL: intraweb.stockton.edu/eyos/
page.cfm?siteID=221&pageID=63

8992 ■ The Achieve Physical Therapy and Fitness Scholarship *(Doctorate/Scholarship)*

Purpose: To provide financial assistance to qualified individuals who wish to pursue a doctoral degree. **Focus:** Physical therapy. **Qualif.:** Applicants must be enrolled in the doctorate level of a physical therapy course. **Criteria:** Recipients will be selected based on the scholarship application materials.

Funds Avail.: No specific amount. **Duration:** Annual. **To Apply:** Applicants must complete the application form; submit two letters of recommendation (one must be from a Stockton faculty member), transcripts; and statement essay. **Deadline:** March 20. **Contact:** Stockton Foundation Scholarship; E-mail: foundationscholarships@stockton.edu.

8993 ■ The Joseph Berkman, and Michael and Sarah Chipkin Holocaust/Genocide Studies Award *(Graduate/Scholarship)*

Purpose: To provide financial assistance to qualified individuals who wish to pursue Holocaust genocide studies. **Focus:** General studies/Field of study not specified. **Qualif.:** Applicant must be a student enrolled in a Master's Program in Holocaust genocide studies. **Criteria:** Recipients will be selected based on the scholarship application materials.

Funds Avail.: No specific amount. **To Apply:** Applicants must complete the application form; submit two letters of recommendation (one must be from a Stockton faculty member), transcript and statement essay. **Deadline:** March 20. **Contact:** Stockton Foundation Scholarship; E-mail: foundationscholarships@stockton.edu.

8994 ■ Dr. Richard E. Bjork Memorial Graduate Study Award *(Graduate/Scholarship)*

Purpose: To provide financial assistance to qualified individuals who want to pursue a graduate degree. **Focus:** General studies/Field of study not specified. **Qualif.:** Applicant must be a student pursuing a graduate studies work. **Criteria:** Recipients will be selected based on the scholarship application materials.

Funds Avail.: No specific amount. **To Apply:** Applicants

must complete the application form available on the website; submit two letters of recommendation (one must be from a Stockton faculty member), transcript and statement essay. **Deadline:** March 20. **Contact:** Stockton Foundation Scholarship; E-mail: foundationscholarships@stockton.edu.

8995 ■ Frances N. Christian Memorial Endowment Nursing Scholarship *(Graduate, Undergraduate/Scholarship)*

Purpose: To provide financial assistance to qualified individuals who want to pursue a degree in the nursing profession. **Focus:** Nursing. **Qualif.:** Applicant must have a minimum cumulative GPA of 3.5 and must demonstrate commitment to the profession of nursing. **Criteria:** Recipients will be selected based on the scholarship application materials.

Funds Avail.: No specific amount. **To Apply:** Applicants must complete the application form available on the website; must submit two letters of recommendation (one must be from a Stockton faculty member), transcript and statement essay. **Deadline:** March 20. **Contact:** Stockton Foundation Scholarship; E-mail: foundationscholarships@stockton.edu.

8996 ■ The Shanon Newberry Physical Therapy Scholarship Endowment *(Doctorate/Scholarship)*

Purpose: To provide financial assistance to qualified individuals who want to pursue a degree in physical therapy. **Focus:** Physical therapy. **Qualif.:** Applicant must be in his/her fifth or sixth year of study in the Doctorate in a Physical Therapy Program. **Criteria:** Recipients will be selected based on the scholarship application materials.

Funds Avail.: No specific amount. **To Apply:** Applicants must complete the application form available in the website; must submit two letters of recommendation (one must be from a Stockton faculty member), transcript and statement essay. **Deadline:** March 20. **Contact:** Stockton Foundation Scholarship; E-mail: foundationscholarships@stockton.edu.

8997 ■ The Physical Therapy Faculty Scholarship Endowment *(Graduate/Scholarship)*

Purpose: To provide financial assistance to qualified individuals who want to pursue a degree in physical therapy. **Focus:** Physical therapy. **Qualif.:** Applicant must be in his/her final year of a physical therapy program and must exhibit a commitment to community service. **Criteria:** Recipients will be selected based on the scholarship application materials.

Funds Avail.: No specific amount. **To Apply:** Applicants must complete the application form available in the website; must submit two letters of recommendation (one must be from a Stockton faculty member), transcript and statement essay. **Deadline:** March 20. **Contact:** Stockton Foundation Scholarship; E-mail: foundationscholarships@stockton.edu.

8998 ■ The Bea and Harry Ross Scholarship Endowment *(Graduate/Scholarship)*

Purpose: To provide financial assistance to qualified individuals who want to pursue their education. **Focus:** General studies/Field of study not specified. **Qualif.:** Applicants must be graduate or upper class students. **Criteria:** Recipients will be selected based on the scholarship application materials.

Funds Avail.: No specific amount. **To Apply:** Applicants must complete the application form available in the website;

Awards are arranged alphabetically below their administering organizations

must submit two letters of recommendation (one must be from a Stockton faculty member), transcript and statement essay. **Deadline:** March 20. **Contact:** Stockton Foundation Scholarship; E-mail: foundationscholarships@stockton.edu.

8999 ■ The Richard Stockton College of New Jersey Foundation Alumni Association Graduate Awards
(Graduate/Scholarship)

Purpose: To provide financial assistance to qualified individuals who wish to pursue their education. **Focus:** General studies/Field of study not specified. **Qualif.:** Applicant must be a student who is pursuing a Master's Degree at Stockton. **Criteria:** Recipients will be selected based on the scholarship application materials.

Funds Avail.: No specific amount. **To Apply:** Applicants must complete the application form available on the website; submit two letters of recommendation (one must be from a Stockton faculty member), transcript and statement essay. **Deadline:** March 20. **Contact:** Stockton Foundation Scholarship; E-mail: foundationscholarships@stockton.edu.

9000 ■ Stonewall Community Foundation
446 W 33rd St.
New York, NY 10001
Ph: (212)367-1155
Fax: (212)367-1157
E-mail: stonewall@stonewallfoundation.org
URL: stonewallfoundation.org

9001 ■ The Gene and John Athletic Scholarships
(Undergraduate/Scholarship)

Purpose: To provide emerging gay and lesbian athletes with a reliable pool of resources (both monetary and community-based) to help them reach their potential and realize their dreams. **Focus:** Athletics. **Qualif.:** Applicants must be LGBT athlete students who are looking to continue their education while pursuing athletics. **Criteria:** Recipients are selected based on financial need.

Funds Avail.: $2,500 - $5,000. **To Apply:** Applicants must submit a completed application form. **Deadline:** August 1.

9002 ■ Traub-Dicker Rainbow Scholarships
(Undergraduate/Scholarship)

Purpose: To encourage and supports LGBT students in their quest for higher education. **Focus:** General studies/Field of study not specified. **Qualif.:** Applicants must be lesbians who are graduating high school seniors; must plan to attend a recognized college or university or be currently enrolled. **Criteria:** Recipients are selected based on demonstrated academic excellence and community service.

Funds Avail.: $3,000. **Duration:** Annual. **Number Awarded:** 3. **To Apply:** Applicants must submit a completed application form; three essays; transcript of records; and two letters of reference. **Deadline:** April 15. **Contact:** stonewall@stonewallfoundation.org.

9003 ■ The Bee Winkler Weinstein Scholarship Fund *(Undergraduate, Vocational/Occupational/ Scholarship)*

Purpose: To promote growth and self-sufficiency in young women by providing grants covering vocational/technical training, licensing fees, college application fees and the like. **Focus:** General studies/Field of study not specified.

Qualif.: Applicants must be lesbians, female bisexuals or transgenders; must be between the ages of 18 to 25 and reside within the United States. **Criteria:** Recipients are selected based on financial need.

Funds Avail.: No specific amount. **To Apply:** Applicants must submit a completed application form and letter of recommendation. **Contact:** stonewall@ stonewallfoundation.org.

9004 ■ StraightForward Media
508 7th St., Ste. 202
Rapid City, SD 57701
Ph: (605)348-3042
Fax: (605)348-3043
E-mail: info@straightforwardmedia.com
URL: www.straightforwardmedia.com

9005 ■ Dale E. Fridell Memorial Scholarships
(Undergraduate, Vocational/Occupational/Scholarship)

Purpose: To financially assist students in their educational pursuits. **Focus:** General studies/Field of study not specified. **Qualif.:** Applicant must be a student currently enrolled or planning to enroll in a university, college, trade school, technical institute, vocational training or other post-secondary education program. **Criteria:** Selection will be based on the submitted application.

Funds Avail.: $1,000. **Duration:** Quarterly. **Number Awarded:** 1. **To Apply:** Applicant must complete the Online Scholarship Application. **Deadline:** January 14.

9006 ■ Mesothelioma Memorial Scholarships
(Undergraduate, Vocational/Occupational/Scholarship)

Purpose: To financially assist students in their educational pursuits. **Focus:** General studies/Field of study not specified. **Qualif.:** Applicant must be a student currently enrolled or planning to enroll in a university, college, trade school, technical institute, vocational training or other post-secondary education program. **Criteria:** Selection will be based on merit.

Funds Avail.: $500. **Duration:** Annual; every three months. **Number Awarded:** 4. **To Apply:** Applicant must complete scholarship application online. **Deadline:** February 15. **Remarks:** Established in 2003.

9007 ■ Outlaw Student's Medical Professions Scholarships *(Undergraduate/Scholarship)*

Purpose: To financially assist students in their educational pursuits. **Focus:** Health care services. **Qualif.:** Applicant must be a student majoring in the medical field. **Criteria:** Selection will be based on merit.

Funds Avail.: $500. **Duration:** Quarterly. **Number Awarded:** 4. **To Apply:** Applicants must complete scholarship application online. **Deadline:** December 30.

9008 ■ Outlaw Student's Nursing School Scholarships *(Undergraduate/Scholarship)*

Purpose: To financially assist students in their educational pursuits. **Focus:** Nursing. **Qualif.:** Applicant must be a nursing student. **Criteria:** Selection will be based on merit.

Funds Avail.: $500. **Duration:** Annual; every three months. **Number Awarded:** 4. **To Apply:** Applicants must complete the scholarship application online. **Deadline:** January 14.

9009 ■ Outlaw Student's Teacher Scholarships
(Undergraduate/Scholarship)

Purpose: To financially assist students in their educational pursuits. **Focus:** Teaching. **Qualif.:** Applicants must be

Awards are arranged alphabetically below their administering organizations

students planning to be a teacher. **Criteria:** Awards will be given based on merit.

Funds Avail.: $500. **Duration:** Annual; every three months. **Number Awarded:** 4. **To Apply:** Applicants must complete the Online Scholarship Application. **Deadline:** January 14.

9010 ■ StraightForward Media Minority Scholarships *(Undergraduate/Scholarship)*

Purpose: To financially assist students in their educational pursuits. **Focus:** General studies/Field of study not specified. **Qualif.:** Applicant must be a minority student. **Criteria:** Selection will be based on merit.

Funds Avail.: $500. **Duration:** Quarterly. **Number Awarded:** 4. **To Apply:** Applicant must complete scholarship application online. **Deadline:** June 30. **Remarks:** Established in 2005.

9011 ■ StraightForward Media's Art School Scholarships *(Undergraduate/Scholarship)*

Purpose: To financially assist students in their educational pursuits. **Focus:** Arts. **Qualif.:** Applicant must be an art student. **Criteria:** Award will be given based on merit.

Funds Avail.: $500. **Duration:** Quarterly. **Number Awarded:** 1. **To Apply:** Applicants must complete scholarship application online. **Deadline:** November 30; February 28; May 31; August 31.

9012 ■ StraightForward Media's Business School Scholarships *(Undergraduate/Scholarship)*

Purpose: To financially assist students in their educational pursuits. **Focus:** Business. **Qualif.:** Applicants must be students attending business schools, including students getting MBAs. **Criteria:** Awards will be given based on merit.

Funds Avail.: $500. **Duration:** Annual; every three months. **Number Awarded:** 4. **To Apply:** Applicants must complete the online scholarship application. **Deadline:** September 30. **Remarks:** Established in 2005.

9013 ■ StraightForward Media's Engineering Scholarships *(Undergraduate/Scholarship)*

Purpose: To financially assist students in their educational pursuits. **Focus:** Engineering. **Qualif.:** Applicant must be an engineering student. **Criteria:** Awards will be given based on merit.

Funds Avail.: $500. **Duration:** Quarterly. **Number Awarded:** 1. **To Apply:** Applicant must complete the Online Scholarship Application. **Deadline:** March 31; June 30; September 30; December 31.

9014 ■ StraightForward Media's Law Enforcement Scholarships *(Other, Undergraduate/Scholarship)*

Purpose: To financially assist students in their educational pursuits. **Focus:** Law enforcement. **Qualif.:** Applicant must be a law enforcement professional or a student studying to become a law enforcement officer. **Criteria:** Award will be given based on merit.

Funds Avail.: $500. **Duration:** Quarterly. **Number Awarded:** 1. **To Apply:** Applicant must complete the Online Scholarship Application. **Deadline:** March 31; February 28; September 30; December 31. **Remarks:** Established in 2005.

9015 ■ StraightForward Media's Law School Scholarships *(Undergraduate/Scholarship)*

Purpose: To financially assist students in their educational pursuits. **Focus:** Law. **Qualif.:** Applicant must be a law student. **Criteria:** Awards will be given based on the submitted application.

Funds Avail.: $500. **Duration:** Quarterly. **Number Awarded:** 1. **To Apply:** Applicant must complete the scholarship application online. **Deadline:** March 31, June 30, September 30, December 31. **Remarks:** Established in 2005.

9016 ■ StraightForward Media's Liberal Arts Scholarships *(Undergraduate/Scholarship)*

Purpose: To financially assist students in their educational pursuits. **Focus:** Liberal arts. **Qualif.:** Applicant must be a liberal arts student. **Criteria:** Award will be given based on the submitted application.

Funds Avail.: $500. **Duration:** Quarterly. **Number Awarded:** 1. **To Apply:** Applicants must complete scholarship application online. **Deadline:** March 31, June 30, September 30, December 31. **Remarks:** Established in 2005.

9017 ■ StraightForward Media's Media and Communications Scholarships *(Undergraduate/Scholarship)*

Purpose: To financially assist students in their educational pursuits. **Focus:** Communications; Media arts. **Qualif.:** Applicant must be a student majoring in communications or media. **Criteria:** Selection will be based on merit.

Funds Avail.: $500. **Duration:** Quarterly. **Number Awarded:** 1. **To Apply:** Applicants must complete scholarship application online. **Deadline:** March 31, June 30, September 30, December 31. **Remarks:** Established in 2005.

9018 ■ StraightForward Media's Science Scholarships *(Undergraduate/Scholarship)*

Purpose: To financially assist students in their educational pursuits. **Focus:** Science. **Qualif.:** Applicant must be a student pursuing a degree in a science-related field. **Criteria:** Selection will be based on merit.

Funds Avail.: $500. **Duration:** Quarterly. **Number Awarded:** 4. **To Apply:** Applicant must complete scholarship application online.

9019 ■ StraightForward Media's Vocational-Technical School Scholarships *(Undergraduate, Vocational/Occupational/Scholarship)*

Purpose: To financially assist students in their educational pursuits. **Focus:** Education, Vocational-technical. **Qualif.:** Applicants must be students pursuing degrees, licenses or certificates at vocational schools. **Criteria:** Awards are given based on merit.

Funds Avail.: $500. **Duration:** Annual; every three months. **Number Awarded:** 4. **To Apply:** Applicants must complete the Online Scholarship Application. **Deadline:** November 30; February 28; May 31; August 31. **Remarks:** Established in 2004.

9020 ■ Student Osteopathic Medical Association (SOMA)
142 E Ontario St.
Chicago, IL 60611-2864
Ph: (312)202-8193
Fax: (312)202-8200
Free: 800-621-1773
E-mail: president@studentdo.com

Awards are arranged alphabetically below their administering organizations

URL: www.studentdo.com

9021 ■ Humanism in Medicine Scholarships
(Undergraduate/Scholarship)

Purpose: To help medical students pursue their studies. **Focus:** Medicine, Osteopathic. **Qualif.:** Applicants must be third- or fourth-year osteopathic medical students attending any accredited osteopathic medical colleges; must be members of SOMA; and must not be previous recipients of the scholarship. **Criteria:** Applicants will be judged on how well they demonstrate their character in the philosophy of osteopathic medicine, love for their community and peers, leadership and dedication, compassion and empathy, spirit and enthusiasm.

Funds Avail.: $1,000. **Number Awarded:** 1. **To Apply:** Applicants must complete and upload the following: application form together with an essay, curriculum vitae and official transcript of records. **Contact:** E-mail completed applications to scholarships-grants@studentdo.com.

9022 ■ Student Osteopathic Medical Student Fellowships and Research *(Undergraduate/Fellowship)*

Purpose: To provide funds for medical students who are currently or will be conducting a research project in the field of osteopathy. **Focus:** Medicine, Osteopathic. **Qualif.:** Applicants must be osteopathic medical students; must be members of Student Osteopathic Medical Association; and must have proposed research related to osteopathic manipulated research. **Criteria:** Recipients are selected based on the significance of their research project.

Funds Avail.: $2,000. **Duration:** Annual. **To Apply:** Applicants must submit the following: (1) research plan; (2) Institutional Review Board approval; (3) budget justification; (4) identification of key personnel; (5) letter of support; and (6) biosketch or curriculum vitae for both applicants and mentors. **Deadline:** March 1. **Contact:** Completed applications and signed documents should be sent to: Elizabeth Hodor at the above address or e-mail rd@studentdo.com and administration@studentdo.com.

9023 ■ Marvin H. and Kathleen G. Teget Leadership Scholarships *(Undergraduate/Scholarship)*

Purpose: To benefit students pursuing a career in specialty medicine. **Focus:** Medicine; Medicine, Osteopathic. **Qualif.:** Applicants must be pursuing specialty medicine career; must be members of SOMA; and must not be previous recipients of the scholarship. **Criteria:** The selection is based on the students demonstrating leadership in a specialty field.

Funds Avail.: $500. **Number Awarded:** 2. **To Apply:** Applicants must complete the application form and must submit their personal statement; curriculum vitae; and official transcript of grades. **Deadline:** January 22. **Contact:** E-mail completed applications to scholarships-grants@ studentdo.com.

9024 ■ Hatton W. Sumners Foundation, Inc.
325 N St. Paul St., Ste. 3920
Dallas, TX 75201
Ph: (214)220-2128
E-mail: info@hattonsumners.org
URL: www.hattonsumners.org

9025 ■ Hatton W. Sumners Endowed Law Schools Scholarships *(Undergraduate, Graduate/Scholarship)*
Purpose: To support worthy students enrolled in a law school. **Focus:** Law. **Qualif.:** Applicants must be law students enrolled at the Oklahoma City University School of Law or Southern Methodist University's Dedman School of Law. **Criteria:** Selection will be based on merit.

Funds Avail.: No specific amount. **Duration:** Annual. **To Apply:** Interested students may contact their school for the application process.

9026 ■ Hatton W. Sumners Endowed Undergraduate School Scholarships *(Undergraduate/Award)*

Purpose: To provide educational assistance to students beginning their junior year. **Focus:** Education; History; Journalism; Law; Political science. **Qualif.:** Applicants must be students beginning their junior year at Austin College, Howard Payne University's Douglas MacArthur Academy of Freedom, Schreiner University, Southern Methodist University's John G. Tower for Political Studies or Texas Wesleyan University. Preferred majors are in the area of political science, although scholarships have been granted in education, history, journalism, pre-law and other disciplines. **Criteria:** Selection will be based on the committee's criteria.

Funds Avail.: No specific amount. **Duration:** Annual. **To Apply:** Interested applicants may contact their school for the application process.

9027 ■ Hatton W. Sumners Non-Endowed Undergraduate and Graduate Scholarships *(Undergraduate, Graduate/Scholarship)*

Purpose: To provide students with a unique educational experience. **Focus:** Education; History; Journalism; Law; Political science. **Qualif.:** Applicants must be junior or senior students enrolled at Southwestern University, Huston-Tillotson University, St. Edwards University, The University of Dallas or Texas Christian University. Preferred majors are in the area of political science, although scholarships have been granted in education, history, journalism, pre-law and other disciplines. The Foundation also supports Masters Students of Public Administration scholarships at the University of North Texas. **Criteria:** Selection will be based on the committee's criteria.

Funds Avail.: No specific amount. **Number Awarded:** Varies. **To Apply:** Interested applicants may contact their school for the application process.

9028 ■ Sun Country Amateur Golf Association (SCAGA)
2316 Southern Blvd., Ste. D
Rio Rancho, NM 87124
Ph: (505)897-0864
Fax: (505)897-3494
Free: 800-346-5319
E-mail: info@suncountrygolfhouse.com
URL: www.suncountrygolf.org

9029 ■ Dwight Teed Scholarships *(Undergraduate/ Scholarship)*

Purpose: To support students that achieved excellence in the classroom, present themselves as excellent citizens, have a connection with the game of golf, need financial assistance and are come highly recommended by credible sources. **Focus:** General studies/Field of study not specified. **Qualif.:** Applicants must have: completed their junior year in high school or at least one year in college; achieved 3.0 or higher cumulative grade point average; and, a connection to golf. **Criteria:** Recipients are selected based on personal character as evidenced by students' participation

Awards are arranged alphabetically below their administering organizations

in extracurricular activities or involvement in the local community; and financial need.

Funds Avail.: $1,500 each. **Duration:** Annual. **Number Awarded:** 4. **To Apply:** Applicants must submit a completed application form together with a letter outlining applicant's goals and objectives for college; three letters of recommendation, at least one must be from a SCAGA member; a copy of parents' most current year tax return (form 1040, 1040A, or 1040EZ). Current high school or college transcripts must be sent directly from the school to the SCAGA office (must include most current SAT or ACT exam results). Submit all the mentioned application to the contact provided. **Deadline:** Last Friday of April. **Remarks:** Established in 1984. **Contact:** Barbara Saia, 2316 Southern Blvd. Suite D Rio Rancho, New Mexico 87124.

9030 ■ The Sunshine Lady Foundation, Inc. (SLF)

103 S 11th St.
Morehead City, NC 28557
URL: www.sunshinelady.org

9031 ■ Women's Independence Scholarship Programs *(Undergraduate/Scholarship)*

Purpose: To help survivors of domestic violence obtain an education that will in turn offer them the chance to secure employment, personal independence and self-sufficiency. To help battered women overcome barriers to the education necessary for their becoming employable and financially stable. To help single mothers with young children who have the greatest financial challenges to gain work so they can support their families. **Focus:** General studies/ Field of study not specified. **Qualif.:** Applicants must be direct survivors of domestic violence or partner abuse. Applicants must be citizens or legal residents of the United States. Applicants must be officially accepted into an accredited course of study at a United States institution. **Criteria:** Recipients are selected based on the demonstrated critical need for financial assistance and determination to complete a training and/or academic program. They should demonstrate a definite plan to use the desired training to upgrade skills for career advancement, to train for new career field, or to enter or re-enter the job market.

Funds Avail.: No specific amount. **To Apply:** Applicants must complete the application form and provide the necessary documents such as transcripts. **Remarks:** Established in 1999.

9032 ■ Super Kutz Scholarship Foundation

1665 Avenue Dollard
Montreal, QC, Canada H8N 1T7
Ph: (438)388-2837
URL: www.superkutzfoundation.com

9033 ■ SuperKutz Scholarships *(Undergraduate/ Scholarship)*

Purpose: To provide financial assistance to students who are pursuing post-secondary education. **Focus:** General studies/Field of study not specified. **Qualif.:** Applicant must be less than 25 years old and a Canadian citizen or landed immigrant residing in Quebec; must be registered for full-time post-secondary academic or vocational studies at the college level (CEGEP), or in an undergraduate university program for the Fall/Winter sessions in the year the application is made; and must demonstrate the need for

financial assistance to pursue post-secondary studies by providing, among other proof, information on the applicant's expected sources of funding (e.g. student loans, bursaries, family). **Criteria:** Selection is based both academic achievement and financial need.

Funds Avail.: No specific amount. **Duration:** Annual. **To Apply:** Applicants must submit a letter of application with supporting documentation, including an official transcript of the last full academic year and a 1-2 page essay; a copy of the document certifying registration at a post-secondary institution; two letters of reference. **Contact:** Super Kutz Scholarship Foundation, at the above address or Email: applications@superkutzfoundation.com.

9034 ■ Surety & Fidelity Association of America (SFAA)

1101 Connecticut Ave. NW, Ste. 800
Washington, DC 20036
Ph: (202)463-0600
Fax: (202)463-0606
E-mail: information@surety.org
URL: www.surety.org

9035 ■ Surety and Fidelity Industry Intern and Scholarship Program for Minority Students *(Undergraduate/Scholarship)*

Purpose: To support minority students whose studies are in the areas of insurance/risk management, accounting, or business/finance and to encourage their consideration of the surety industry and surety/fidelity underwriting as a career choice. **Focus:** Accounting; Business; Finance; Insurance and insurance-related fields; Management. **Qualif.:** Applicants must be majoring in insurance/risk management, accounting, or business/finance; must have an overall and major grade point average (GPA) of at least 3.0 on 4.0 scale; must be minority students who have satisfactorily completed at least 30 semester hours and at least 6 semester hours in their declared major; must be enrolled as full-time undergraduate students (minimum of 12 semester hours or equivalent) at an accredited four-year institution. **Criteria:** Applicants are evaluated based on academic achievement and financial need.

Funds Avail.: Up to $5,000. **Duration:** Annual. **To Apply:** Applicants must submit all the required application information. **Deadline:** January 31. **Remarks:** Established in 2003.

9036 ■ Surface Officers' Spouses of Norfolk

PO Box 9902
Norfolk, VA 23505-9902
Ph: (757)277-9468
E-mail: sos.norfolk@gmail.com
URL: sosnorfolk.org

9037 ■ Anchor Scholarships *(Undergraduate/ Scholarship)*

Purpose: To provide scholarships to eligible dependents (i.e. children and spouses) of active duty or retired Surface Navy personnel. **Focus:** General studies/Field of study not specified. **Qualif.:** Applicants must be students pursuing four year degree (BA or BS) at a college or university in the United States. **Criteria:** Recipients are selected on the basis of four equally weighted criteria: academic performance, character, extracurricular, and financial need.

Funds Avail.: No specific amount. **Duration:** Annual. **To**

Awards are arranged alphabetically below their administering organizations

Apply: Applicants must submit all the needed materials for the scholarship. **Contact:** Anchor Scholarship Foundation, www.anchorscholarship.com.

9038 ■ Swiss Benevolent Society of New York (SBS)

500 5th Ave., Rm. 1800
New York, NY 10110-1804
Ph: (212)246-0655
Fax: (212)246-1366
E-mail: info@sbsny.org
URL: www.sbsny.org

9039 ■ Sonia S. Maguire Outstanding Scholastic Achievement Awards *(Graduate, Undergraduate/ Scholarship)*

Purpose: To provide financial support to college seniors or graduate students who are in need. **Focus:** General studies/Field of study not specified. **Qualif.:** Applicants or one of their parents must be Swiss nationals; must be domiciled in New York, New Jersey, Connecticut, Pennsylvania or Delaware; must demonstrate the need for financial support; must be in good academic standing and show aptitude in their chosen fields of study; must be college senior or graduate student who demonstrates sustained academic excellence (cumulative GPA of at least 3.8) in a demanding study program. **Criteria:** Applicants are selected based on the committee's review of the application materials.

Funds Avail.: No specific amount. **Duration:** Annual. **To Apply:** Application forms can be downloaded at the SB-SNY web site. Applicants must submit the following required documents: general and scholastic pages of application packet; official transcripts of all high school, college and graduate grades when applying for the first time, official updates thereafter; SAT or GRE results when applying for the first time; proof of Swiss citizenship of applicant or one parent when applying for the first time; proof of U.S. citizenship or visa status when applying for the first time; two letters of recommendation from professors in the applicant's major area of study, on official letterhead. **Deadline:** March 31.

9040 ■ Medicus Student Exchange Scholarships *(Graduate, Undergraduate/Scholarship)*

Purpose: To provide partial financial support for U.S. residents at the junior, senior or graduate college level who have been accepted to study at a Swiss University or Federal Institute of Technology. **Focus:** General studies/Field of study not specified. **Qualif.:** Applicants must be residents of the United States; must be in good academic standing and show aptitude in their chosen fields of study; must be junior, senior or graduate college level students who have been accepted to study at a Swiss University or Federal Institute of Technology. **Criteria:** Applicants are selected based on the committee's review of the application materials.

Funds Avail.: No specific amount. **Duration:** Annual. **To Apply:** Application forms can be downloaded at the SB-SNY web site. Applicants must submit the following required documents: general and scholastic pages of application packet; official transcripts of all high school, college and graduate grades when applying for the first time, official updates thereafter; SAT or GRE results when applying for the first time; proof of Swiss citizenship of applicant or one parent when applying for the first time; proof of U.S. citizenship or visa status when applying for the first time; letter of acceptance from Swiss University or Federal Institute of Technology or Technical College; two letters of recommendation from professors in the applicant's major area of study, on official letterhead; proof of proficiency in the language of instruction; statement of sufficient total funding. For studies in the U.S.: official transcript of records of at least one year of study in the U.S.; transcripts of education in Switzerland; letter of recommendation from a professor in the applicant's major area of study, on official letterhead. **Deadline:** March 31.

9041 ■ Pellegrini Scholarships *(Graduate, Undergraduate, Vocational/Occupational/Scholarship)*

Purpose: To provide financial support to students who needs regular payment for their education. **Focus:** General studies/Field of study not specified. **Qualif.:** Applicants or one of their parents must be Swiss nationals; must be domiciled in New York, New Jersey, Connecticut, Pennsylvania or Delaware; must demonstrate the need for financial support; must be in good academic standing and show aptitude in their chosen fields of study. **Criteria:** Applicants are selected based on need and academic merit.

Funds Avail.: No specific amount. **Duration:** Annual. **To Apply:** Application forms can be downloaded at the SB-SNY web site. Applicants must submit the following required documents: general and scholastic pages of application packet; official transcripts of all high school, college and graduate grades when applying for the first time, official updates thereafter; SAT or GRE results when applying for the first time; proof of Swiss citizenship of applicant or one parent when applying of the first time; proof of U.S. citizenship or visa status when applying for the first time; financial pages of application packet, including all requested information, unless applying for merit portion only; signed copy of all pages and schedules of Federal Income Tax returns and of W-2 forms of applicant and supporting party and/or spouse, where applicable; proof of cost for tuition and room and board, copy of bursar's bill (high school applicants provide figures of anticipated cost); letter of reference from a high school principal or a guidance counselor or from a professor in the applicant's major area of study, on official letterhead.

9042 ■ Zimmermann Scholarships *(Graduate/ Scholarship)*

Purpose: To provide financial support to students who are in need. **Focus:** General studies/Field of study not specified. **Qualif.:** Applicants or one of their parents must be Swiss nationals. Applicants must be domiciled in New York, New Jersey, Connecticut, Pennsylvania or Delaware. Applicants must be in good academic standing and show aptitude in their chosen fields of study. Applicants must be graduate students with the highest cumulative GPA of at least 3.8. **Criteria:** Applicants are selected based on the committee's review of the application materials.

Funds Avail.: No specific amount. **Duration:** Annual. **To Apply:** Application forms can be downloaded at the SB-SNY web site. Applicants must submit the following required documents: general and scholastic pages of application packet; official transcripts of all high school, college and graduate grades when applying for the first time, official updates thereafter; SAT or GRE results when applying for the first time; proof of Swiss citizenship of applicant or one parent when applying for the first time; proof of U.S. citizenship or visa status when applying for the first time; two letters of recommendation from professors. **Deadline:** March 31.

Awards are arranged alphabetically below their administering organizations

9043 ■ Robert and Patricia Switzer Foundation

PO Box 293
Belfast, ME 04915
Ph: (207)338-5654
Fax: (207)338-5655
E-mail: info@switzernetwork.org
URL: switzernetwork.org

9044 ■ Switzer Environmental Fellowships
(Graduate/Fellowship)

Purpose: To support highly talented graduate students in New England and California whose studies are directed toward improving environmental quality and who are able to demonstrate potential leadership in their field. **Focus:** Environmental conservation; Environmental law; Environmental science; Environmental technology. **Qualif.:** Applicants must be U.S. citizens; must be enrolled full-time in an accredited graduate institution in California or New England; must have strong academic qualifications; must have academic and career goals focused on environmental improvement, regardless of the school, major or program in which they are enrolled. **Criteria:** Selection will be based on leadership experience and potential; applied focus; career goals and commitment; communication and critical thinking; prior work and volunteer experience in an environmental field.

Funds Avail.: $15,000. **Duration:** Annual. **Number Awarded:** 20. **To Apply:** Applicants must submit a completed application form; original essay (maximum of three pages); two professional recommendation letters; resume; most recent academic transcripts; brief outline of general course of study; evidence of financial need. **Deadline:** January 9. **Remarks:** Established in 1986. **Contact:** For eligibility and general questions, applicants must contact Erin Lloyd at erin@switzernetwork.org; for technical assistance with online applications: Don Brackett, Administrative Officer - don@switzernetwork.org.

9045 ■ Symantec Corp.

350 Ellis St.
Mountain View, CA 94043
Ph: (650)527-8000
Fax: (650)527-2908
Free: 800-327-2232
URL: www.symantec.com

9046 ■ Symantec Research Labs Graduate Fellowships *(Doctorate, Graduate/Fellowship)*

Purpose: To fund innovative research that has real-world value, in areas of Symantec's business interests in information security, availability, and integrity. **Focus:** Information science and technology. **Qualif.:** Applying students must be enrolled in a Ph.D. program. **Criteria:** Recipients will be selected based on their overall potential for research excellence and their academic progress to date as evidenced by publications.

Funds Avail.: Up to $20,000. **To Apply:** Applicants must submit a single compressed file (.zip file) and must include the following: a completed fellowship application form including a personal statement of research interests not to exceed 500 words. Applicants are strongly encouraged to articulate the practical value to customers of their proposed research areas; a curriculum vitae and thesis proposal; three letters of recommendation from professors or industry researchers who can evaluate the applicant's scientific

aptitude and potential for research. **Contact:** Please direct any additional questions about the Symantec Graduate Fellowship Program to: srlfellowship@symantec.com.

9047 ■ Syncrude Canada

PO Box 4023
Fort McMurray, AB, Canada T9H 3H5
Ph: (780)790-5911
E-mail: info@syncrude.com
URL: www.syncrude.ca

9048 ■ Syncrude/Athabasca University Aboriginal Scholarships *(Undergraduate/Scholarship)*

Purpose: To support the education of Aboriginal students. **Focus:** Computer and information sciences; Industry and trade; Information science and technology; Management; Nursing. **Qualif.:** Applicant must be an Alberta resident who is an Aboriginal student studying in the following degree programs through Athabasca University: Bachelor of Arts, Bachelor of Administration, Bachelor of Administration-Post Diploma, Bachelor of Commerce, Bachelor of Science in Computing and Information Systems or Bachelor of Science-Post Diploma in Computing and Information Systems, and Bachelor of Nursing. **Criteria:** Selection is based on financial need, academic performance and potential and community/extracurricular activities. Preference will be given to applicants entering the first year of full-time studies.

Funds Avail.: No specific amount. **To Apply:** Applicants must submit a completed application form.

9049 ■ Tag and Label Manufacturers Institute (TLMI)

1 Blackburn Ctr.
Gloucester, MA 01930
Ph: (978)282-1400
Fax: (978)282-3238
E-mail: office@tlmi.com
URL: www.tlmi.com

9050 ■ Tag and Label Manufacturers Institute Scholarships - Four-Year Colleges *(Undergraduate/Scholarship)*

Purpose: To assist full-time college students in pursuing a degree to prepare for a career in the tag and label manufacturing industry. **Focus:** Graphic art and design; Management; Marketing and distribution. **Qualif.:** Applicant must be a second or third year full-time college student with a 3.00 or higher GPA. **Criteria:** Applicants are selected based on demonstrated interest in the field of tag and label industry.

Funds Avail.: $5,000. **Number Awarded:** Up to 6. **To Apply:** Applicants must fill out the application online; must prepare a one-page personal statement on information sheet, work experiences, family financial report, career and educational goals and reasons why they deserve the award; a school transcript; three references; and samples of work (not mandatory). **Deadline:** March 31.

9051 ■ Tag and Label Manufacturers Institute Scholarships - Two-Year Colleges *(Undergraduate/Scholarship)*

Purpose: To provide students the assistance they need in seeking career in the flexographic industry. **Focus:** Indus-

Awards are arranged alphabetically below their administering organizations

trial design. **Qualif.:** Applicants must be enrolled full-time in a flexographic printing program at a two-year college or technical program that grants degrees; and must maintain a 3.00 or higher GPA. **Criteria:** Applicants will be selected based on the application materials and demonstrated interest in the chosen field.

Funds Avail.: $1,000 per school year. **Number Awarded:** Up to 4. **To Apply:** Application forms are available at the website. Committee will not accept applications direct from a student, applicants must present the application form, official college transcript and a personal statement to their educators who will submit to TLMI office. **Deadline:** March 31.

9052 ■ Tailhook Association (TA)

9696 Businesspark Ave.
San Diego, CA 92131-1643
Free: 800-322-4665
URL: www.tailhook.net

9053 ■ Tailhook Educational Foundation Scholarship Program *(Undergraduate/Scholarship)*

Purpose: To support the education of people who are interested in learning about history and present day activities of US navy carrier aviation. **Focus:** Aviation. **Qualif.:** Applicants must be high school graduates and dependents of current or former (US Navy/US Marines Corps/US Coast Guards) Naval Aviators, Naval Flight Officers, or Naval Aircrew men; must be dependents of individuals who are serving or have served on board as US Navy Aircraft carriers. **Criteria:** Recipients are selected based on their application materials.

Funds Avail.: No specific amount. **Duration:** Annual. **To Apply:** Application forms are available on the website. Applicants must complete the application form together with a certified copy of high school transcript; documentation of SAT or ACT score; an essay on career goals (1 page); endorsement letter; letter of acceptance at a college/university; and an aircrew designation letter (if applicable). **Deadline:** March 15. **Contact:** Application form and supporting documents should be submitted to Capt. Marc Ostertag at the above address.

9054 ■ Taiwanese American Citizens League (TACL)

3001 Walnut Grove Ave., No. 7
Rosemead, CA 91770
Ph: (626)551-0227
E-mail: tacl@tacl.org
URL: tacl.org

9055 ■ Taiwanese American Community Scholarships *(Undergraduate/Scholarship)*

Purpose: To support students with leadership qualities committed to public service. **Focus:** General studies/Field of study not specified. **Qualif.:** Applicants should be of the college bound senior graduating class from one of the ten high schools: Irvine High School, Northwood High School, Canyon High School, University High School, Woodbridge High School, Villa Park High School, Laguna High School, Aliso Niguel High School, Troy High School and Fountain Valley High School. **Criteria:** Awards are given based on the committee's criteria.

Funds Avail.: $500. **To Apply:** Applicant may download an application form from the website. Applicant must submit a one-page biography that includes activities and volunteer work during the high school years; a typed essay of no more than 1000 words on the topic: "Indicate a person who has as a significant influence on you and describe that influence"; one recommendation letter from school teachers or counselors; a copy of the official high school transcript. **Deadline:** April 15.

9056 ■ Robert M. Takasugi Public Interest Fellowship

c/o Dale Minami
Minami Tamaki LLP
360 Post St., 8th Fl.
San Francisco, CA 94108
URL: takasugifellowship.org

9057 ■ Robert M. Takasugi Public Interest Fellowships *(Postgraduate/Fellowship)*

Purpose: To encourage dedicated lawyers to pursue public interest careers. **Focus:** Law. **Qualif.:** Applicant must be a post-graduate law student pursuing public interest careers. **Criteria:** Selection is based on the application.

Funds Avail.: $5,000. **Duration:** 10 weeks. **To Apply:** Applicants must submit a cover letter; resume; three references (without letters); and answers (no more than three pages) to the questions posted at the website. **Deadline:** March 28. **Contact:** Edwin Prather at edwin@pratherlawoffices.com.

9058 ■ Tall Clubs International (TCI)

PO Box 20197
Rochester, NY 14602
Fax: (800)889-9898
Free: 888-468-2552
E-mail: tci-president@tall.org
URL: www.tall.org

9059 ■ Tall Clubs International Student Scholarships *(Undergraduate/Scholarship)*

Purpose: To promote tall awareness among tall men and women, and in the community. **Focus:** General studies/Field of study not specified. **Qualif.:** Applicant must be under 21 years of age and attending their first year of college in the following fall. The recipient must also meet the TCI height requirement minimums of 5'10 for women and 6'2 for men. **Criteria:** Selections are based on the academic performance of an applicant.

Funds Avail.: $1,000. **To Apply:** Candidates must be selected by the closest Member Clubs. TCI forms downloadable in the Member Services Console. **Deadline:** March 1.

9060 ■ Tall Ships America

Bldg. 2, Ste. 101
221 3rd St.
Newport, RI 02840-1088
Ph: (401)846-1775
Fax: (401)849-5400
E-mail: asta@tallshipsamerica.org
URL: tallships.sailtraining.org

9061 ■ Henry H. Anderson, Jr. Sail Training Scholarship *(Undergraduate/Scholarship)*

Purpose: To assist those who are genuinely interested in experiencing sail training and education under sail. **Focus:**

Awards are arranged alphabetically below their administering organizations

Sports studies. **Qualif.:** Eligible applicants for the award are categorized into two: individuals and organized groups. Qualifications for the individual category are: must be 14 to 19 years of age. For the organized groups: school classes, youth groups, scout troops, religious groups or community organizations are accepted. **Criteria:** Selection will be based on the desire of the applicants, whether individuals or groups, to undergo sail training which the main theme of the award is. Applicants must also show a demonstrated need for financial assistance.

Funds Avail.: Maximum awards of $750 for individuals; $1,500 for organized groups. **Duration:** Annual. **To Apply:** Applicants must first select a sail training program to participate in. Individuals or group leaders must then contact that program, request a copy of its registration or application form, and advise that organization that they are applying for a Tall Ships American Financial Assistance Scholarship. It is important for the applicants to establish a good, working contact with he selected sail training program and to be aware of that program's registration requirements. Applicants must complete both the scholarship application and the sail training program application and submit copies of each to both Tall Ships America and the sail training program. Applications should be typewritten or legibly printed. Applicants may also use a computer to download an application form from the Tall Ships America website. Scholarship applications must be completed in full and include the required signatures.

9062 ■ Alex Tanous Foundation
PO Box 3818
Portland, ME 04104-3818
Ph: (207)773-8328
URL: www.alextanous.org

9063 ■ Alex Tanous Scholarship Award
(Undergraduate/Scholarship)

Purpose: To provide financial assistance to qualified students who want to pursue their academic study and or research in science related in the areas of physical and spiritual development. **Focus:** Parapsychology. **Qualif.:** Applicant must be a student attending an accredited college or university and must be a participant in a Psychological Studies program. **Criteria:** Recipients will be selected based on submitted applications.

Funds Avail.: $500. **Duration:** Annual. **To Apply:** Applicant must have two reference forms along with self-addressed envelopes; must have a brief description of the purpose of the application and how the funds would be used; must complete the application form available online. Application forms must be sent to The Alex Tanous Foundation for Scientific Research. **Deadline:** May 1.

9064 ■ Tarkio College Alumni Association
PO Box 111
Tarkio, MO 64491
Ph: (660)736-4208
E-mail: tcaa@tarkio.net
URL: www.tarkioalumni.org

9065 ■ Charles "Chuck" McAdams Memorial Scholarships *(Graduate, Undergraduate/Scholarship)*

Purpose: To provide financial assistance to the children or grandchildren of Tarkio College graduates in attending either an accredited undergraduate baccalaureate or graduate institution in the United States of America. **Focus:** General studies/Field of study not specified. **Qualif.:** Applicants must be directly related to Tarkio College graduates as either sons, daughters or grandchildren. Verification will be made by the submission of a Tarkio College graduation certificate and birth certificate. Undergraduate applicants must have graduated from an accredited United States high school or have a certificate of graduation from a local school district (verify with an official transcript). Graduate applicants must have completed a baccalaureate degree from an accredited United States college or university and to be verified by an official transcript. **Criteria:** Selection is based on the evaluation of submitted documents and specific criteria.

Funds Avail.: No specific amount. **Duration:** Annual. **To Apply:** Applicants must submit a completed application form; copy of high school transcript or certification of high school graduation; college transcript or certificate of baccalaureate degree; birth certificate showing that a parent or grandparent had graduated from Tarkio College; two reference letters; statement of academic goals; essay on how to interpret and plan to fulfill the "Tarkio Experience". **Deadline:** February 15. **Contact:** Tarkio College Alumni Association, at the above address.

9066 ■ Teachers Insurance and Annuity Association of America - College Retirement Equities Fund (TIAA-CREF)
730 3rd Ave.
New York, NY 10017-3206
Ph: (212)490-9000
Fax: (212)916-6088
Free: 866-842-2442
E-mail: cpeterson@tiaa-cref.org
URL: www.tiaa-cref.org

9067 ■ TIAA-CREF Ruth Simms Hamilton Research Fellowships *(Graduate/Fellowship)*

Purpose: To support cutting-edge, graduate-level research to further the study of African diaspora. **Focus:** African studies; Social sciences. **Qualif.:** Applicants must be graduate students enrolled in a social science program at an accredited U.S. college/university and studying the African Diaspora. **Criteria:** Selection is based on evaluation of submissions by an objective panel of judges.

Funds Avail.: No specific amount. **To Apply:** Applicants may visit the website to verify the application process and other pieces of information. **Remarks:** Established to honor the memory and outstanding work of the late Dr. Ruth Simms Hamilton, the former Michigan State University professor and TIAA Trustee.

9068 ■ Technical Women's Organization (TWO)
PO Box 950208
Oklahoma City, OK 73195-0208
E-mail: info@mytwo.org
URL: www.technicalwomen.org

9069 ■ Technical Women's Organization Education Scholarships (TWO) *(Undergraduate/Scholarship)*

Purpose: To encourage students to take every opportunity to participate in training and education that will enhance or advance careers. **Focus:** General studies/Field of study

Awards are arranged alphabetically below their administering organizations

not specified. **Qualif.:** Applicants must be in a training program that will advance or enhance the individual's career in a technical area. **Criteria:** Preference will be given to those students who meet the criteria.

Funds Avail.: $1,000. **Number Awarded:** 3. **To Apply:** Applicants must check the available website for more information. **Deadline:** May 23.

9070 ■ Technology Student Association (TSA)
1914 Association Dr.
Reston, VA 20191-1540
Ph: (703)860-9000
Fax: (703)758-4852
Free: 888-860-9010
E-mail: general@tsaweb.org
URL: www.tsaweb.org

9071 ■ William P. Elrod Memorial Scholarships
(Undergraduate, Vocational/Occupational/Scholarship)

Purpose: To provide financial support for the outstanding service in the field of technology to a TSA student who is college or vocational/tech school bound and who is in good academic standing. **Focus:** Technology. **Qualif.:** Applicants must be: TSA graduating high school seniors or alumni still enrolled in an undergraduate program or vocational/ technical school with a GPA of 3.0 or better; must have performed services on the local, state and national level and active member of an affiliated TSA chapter; able to express financial need for the scholarship; accepted or enrolled in a four-year college, university, or vo/tech school to receive the funds; and able to describe their future educational goals. **Criteria:** Candidates will be evaluated by the Awards Committee.

Funds Avail.: $3,500. **Duration:** Annual. **To Apply:** Applicants must submit a completed application to the TSA Awards Committee. **Deadline:** May 10.

9072 ■ Future STEM Teacher Scholarship
(Undergraduate/Scholarship)

Purpose: To support the STEM education profession by encouraging promising TSA students to pursue careers as K-12 STEM teachers. **Focus:** Technology. **Qualif.:** Applicants must have participated in an active TSA chapter for a minimum of two (2) consecutive years; served as a TSA officer at the local, state and/or national level for a minimum of one (1) academic year; attended and participated in at least one (1) TSA conference at the state or national level. Participated in an active TSA chapter for a minimum of two (2) consecutive years; served as a TSA officer at the local, state and/or national level for a minimum of one (1) academic year; attended and participated in at least one (1) TSA conference at the state or national level. **Criteria:** Selection shall be based on the aforementioned applicants' qualifications and compliance with the application details.

Funds Avail.: $3,500. **Duration:** Annual. **Number Awarded:** 1. **To Apply:** Applicants must submit: a signed cover letter that includes a detailed description of the applicant's involvement in TSA, based on the above criteria; SAT score and/or ACT score: high school class rank (indicate how many in the class); no more than three (3) letters of reference, one of which must come from a technology teacher; a single-sided, one-page typed essay on his/her career plans for becoming a teacher in the technology education profession. **Deadline:** May 8.

9073 ■ Techology First
714 E Monument Ave., Ste. 106
Dayton, OH 45402

Ph: (937)229-0054
E-mail: ahickey@technologyfirst.org
URL: www.technologyfirst.org

9074 ■ Robert V. McKenna Scholarships
(Undergraduate/Scholarship)

Purpose: To provide financial support to those deserving students. **Focus:** Information science and technology. **Qualif.:** Applicant must have at least sophomore standing (30 semester hours or 45 quarter hours) at his/her respective university or college and currently be enrolled as an undergraduate student as defined by the applicant's institution; must be able to prove that his/her major's relation to the information technology field; must have a minimum cumulative GPA of 2.5 and a minimum major GPA of 3.0 on a 4.0 scale at the date of submission; must have a strong interest in pursuing a career in the Miami Valley IT field; must be a permanent resident of or attend an accredited IT degree-granting college within the 11 county Miami Valley region: Champaign, Clark, Darke, Greene, Logan, Miami, Montgomery, Northern Warren, Northern Butler, Northern Clinton, and Shelby. **Criteria:** Preference will be based on criteria.

Funds Avail.: No specific amount. **To Apply:** Application forms are available online. Applicants must complete and submit their official copy of transcript or official college documentation of their GPA and a letter of recommendation from college/university faculty. **Contact:** Ann Gallaher, agallaher@technologyfirst.org.

9075 ■ TELACU
5400 E Olympic Blvd., 3rd Fl.
Los Angeles, CA 90022
Ph: (323)721-1655
Fax: (323)724-3372
URL: telacu.com

9076 ■ Citi/TELACU Scholars Mentoring Program
(Undergraduate/Scholarship)

Purpose: To assist undergraduate students pursuing careers in business-related fields with much more than financial resources. **Focus:** Business. **Qualif.:** Applicant must be a seniors in last year of undergraduate studies; pursuing degrees in business-related disciplines; 3.0 GPA; demonstrate academic excellence; proven leadership qualities. **Criteria:** Selection is based on extracurricular involvement demonstrating a commitment to the community and a need for financial and academic support in order to successfully complete a post-secondary program.

Funds Avail.: No specific amount. **To Apply:** Applicants must submit a completed application form along with a written statement; two letters of recommendation (on organization letterhead, maximum of two pages); and official transcripts of all completed college coursework.

9077 ■ David C. Lizárraga Graduate Fellowships
(Graduate, Master's/Fellowship)

Purpose: To support students pursuing advanced degrees in business or engineering. **Focus:** Business; Engineering. **Qualif.:** Applicant must be a permanent resident of unincorporated East Los Angeles, Bell Gardens, Commerce, Huntington Park, City of Los Angeles, Montebello, Monterey Park, Pico Rivera, Pomona and the Inland Empire, Santa Ana, South Gate, or other communities selected by the TELACU Education Foundation for inclu-

Awards are arranged alphabetically below their administering organizations

sion in the Program; a first-generation college student; from a low-income family; have a minimum GPA of 2.5; pursuing a Master's degree in Business Administration or Engineering (students pursuing other graduate degrees may also be considered); and enrolled in a graduate program full-time for the entire academic year. **Criteria:** Selection is based on outstanding leadership potential; remarkable record of professional/extracurricular achievement; commitment to the development and economic empowerment of communities; and need for financial support in order to successfully complete a graduate program.

Funds Avail.: No specific amount. **To Apply:** Applicants must submit a completed application form along with a written statement; two letters of recommendation (on organization letterhead, maximum of two pages); official transcripts (from most recent college only); and a copy of a document reflecting applicant's parents' finances (Student Aid Report, FAFSA Form, Tax Return). **Deadline:** February 27. **Contact:** Jonathan Garcia at 323-721-1655 or jogarcia@telacu.com.

9078 ■ Toyota/TELACU Scholarships
(Undergraduate/Scholarship)

Purpose: To support Latino students in their educational pursuits. **Focus:** Business; Engineering. **Qualif.:** Applicant must be a first-generation college student; pursuing a career in business or engineering; have a minimum GPA of 2.5; must be attending a partnering college/university and enrolled full-time; a permanent resident of unincorporated East Los Angeles, Bell Gardens, Commerce, Huntington Park, City of Los Angeles, Montebello, Monterey Park, Pico Rivera, Pomona & the Inland Empire, Santa Ana, South Gate, or other communities selected by the TELACU Education Foundation for inclusion in the Scholarship Program. **Criteria:** Selection is based on extracurricular involvement demonstrating a commitment to the community and a need for financial and academic support in order to successfully complete a post-secondary program.

Funds Avail.: $5,000. **To Apply:** Applicants must submit a completed application form along with a written statement; two letters of recommendation (on organization letterhead, maximum of two pages); and official transcripts of all completed college coursework.

9079 ■ Telecommunications Association of Michigan (TAM)
600 W Shiawassee St.
Lansing, MI 48933
Ph: (517)482-4166
Fax: (517)482-3548
URL: www.telecommich.org

9080 ■ Telecommunications Association of Michigan Scholarship Fund *(Undergraduate/ Scholarship)*

Purpose: To elevate the technical and business competence of young people by providing them with assistance to acquire meaningful and marketable skills; to provide educational incentive to deserving students who will ultimately provide leadership for the professions in business, education and public service. **Focus:** General studies/Field of study not specified. **Qualif.:** Applicants must be members of a non-Michigan high school or enrolled in an accredited, degree-granting, non-Michigan college or university. **Criteria:** Selection is based on academic excellence, financial need and ability.

Funds Avail.: No specific amount. **Number Awarded:** 4 (3 for students of Michigan Institutions; 1 for Students of Non-Michigan Institution). **To Apply:** Applicants must check the available website for the required materials. **Contact:** Kelle M. DuBay at the above address.

9081 ■ Telluride Association (TA)
217 West Ave.
Ithaca, NY 14850-3911
Ph: (607)273-5011
Fax: (607)272-2667
E-mail: telluride@tellurideassociation.org
URL: www.tellurideassociation.org

9082 ■ Telluride Association Summer Program Scholarships *(Undergraduate/Scholarship)*

Purpose: To bring together young people from around the world who share a passion for learning. **Focus:** General studies/Field of study not specified. **Qualif.:** Applicant must be a junior high school and must be nominated by a teacher, counselor and other educators. **Criteria:** Applicants who will meet the requirements will be prioritized.

Funds Avail.: Stipend of $500. **Duration:** 6 week. **To Apply:** Teachers, educators, or counselors can nominate up to five candidates. TASP Nomination Form is available at the website.

9083 ■ Telugu Association of North America (TANA)
5 Glenwood Rd.
Southborough, MA 01772
Ph: (508)612-6676
E-mail: president@tana.org
URL: www.tana.org

9084 ■ Guthikonda BasavapunnaRao and Umadevi Scholarships *(Graduate/Scholarship)*

Purpose: To provide financial support to deserving Telugu students who want to pursue their education in the United States. **Focus:** General studies/Field of study not specified. **Qualif.:** Applicants must be Telugu students who are currently residing in Andhra Pradesh; must have been admitted to a graduate school in a U.S. university; must demonstrate financial need. **Criteria:** Selection of applicants will be based on the following criteria: (a) need; (b) merit, grades and recommendations; (c) scores in standardized tests like GRE, TOEFL; (d) reputation of the college/ university in India from which the applicant is graduating; (e) reputation of the school in North America in which the applicant is planning to pursue the education; (f) the field of study in which the applicant is planning higher education; (g) extra curricular activities the applicant is proficient in, and (h) only if the applicant is a Telugu student from Andhra Pradesh.

Funds Avail.: $2,000. **Number Awarded:** 1. **To Apply:** Applicants must complete the following information: (1) name, address with pin code and phone number; (2) profession and annual income; (3) name, address, and phone number of parents; (4) professions and annual incomes of parents; (5) net worth of all assets of applicant and parents combined; (6) high school and college educational qualifications and work experience of the applicant (enclose a copy of the transcripts); (7) name, address and phone number of the department and the university in the United States

Awards are arranged alphabetically below their administering organizations

where the applicant intends to enroll. **Deadline:** July 25. **Contact:** Prasad Choudary Kakarala; E-mail: prasadkakarala@yahoo.com.

9085 ■ Chereddi NarayanaRao and Radhamanohari Scholarships (Graduate/Scholarship)

Purpose: To provide financial support to deserving Telugu students who want to pursue their education in the United States. **Focus:** General studies/Field of study not specified. **Qualif.:** Applicants must be Telugu students who are currently residing in Andhra Pradesh; must have been admitted to a graduate school in a U.S. university; must demonstrate financial need. **Criteria:** Selection will be based on the following criteria: (a) need; (b) merit, grades and recommendations; (c) scores in standardized tests like GRE, TOEFL; (d) reputation of the college/university in India from which the applicant is graduating; (e) reputation of the school in North America in which the applicant is planning to pursue the education; (f) the field of study in which the applicant is planning higher education; (g) extra curricular activities the applicant is proficient in, and (h) only if the applicant is a Telugu student from Andhra Pradesh.

Funds Avail.: $2,000. **Number Awarded:** 1. **To Apply:** Applicants must complete the following information: (1) name, address with pin code and phone number; (2) profession and annual income; (3) name, address, and phone number of parents; (4) professions and annual incomes of parents; (5) net worth of all assets of applicant and parents combined; (6) high school and college educational qualifications and work experience of the applicant (enclose a copy of the transcripts); (7) name, address and phone number of the department and the university in the United States where the applicant intends to enroll. **Deadline:** July 25. **Contact:** Prasad Choudary Kakarala; E-mail: prasadkakarala@yahoo.com.

9086 ■ Guthikonda Ramabrahmam and Balamani (Graduate/Scholarship)

Purpose: To provide financial support to deserving Telugu students who want to pursue their education in the United States. **Focus:** General studies/Field of study not specified. **Qualif.:** Applicants must be Telugu students who are currently residing in Andhra Pradesh; must have been admitted to a graduate school in a U.S. university; must demonstrate financial need. **Criteria:** Selection of applicants will be based on the following criteria: (a) need; (b) merit, grades and recommendations; (c) scores in standardized tests like GRE, TOEFL; (d) reputation of the college/university in India from which the applicant is graduating; (e) reputation of the school in North America in which the applicant is planning to pursue the education; (f) the field of study in which the applicant is planning higher education; (g) extra curricular activities the applicant is proficient in, and (h) only if the applicant is a Telugu student from Andhra Pradesh.

Funds Avail.: $2,000. **Number Awarded:** 1. **To Apply:** Applicants must complete the following information: (1) name, address with pin code and phone number; (2) profession and annual income; (3) name, address, and phone number of parents; (4) professions and annual incomes of parents; (5) net worth of all assets of applicant and parents combined; (6) high school and college educational qualifications and work experience of the applicant (enclose a copy of the transcripts); (7) name, address and phone number of the department and the university in the United States where the applicant intends to enroll. **Deadline:** July 25. **Contact:** Prasad Choudary Kakarala; E-mail: prasadkakarala@yahoo.com.

9087 ■ Gadde Sitaramamma and Tirupataiah Scholarships (Graduate/Scholarship)

Purpose: To provide financial support to deserving Telugu students who want to pursue their education in the United States. **Focus:** General studies/Field of study not specified. **Qualif.:** Applicants must be Telugu students who are currently residing in Andhra Pradesh; must have been admitted to a graduate school in a U.S. university; must demonstrate financial need. **Criteria:** Selection of applicants will be based on the following criteria: (a) need; (b) merit, grades and recommendations; (c) scores in standardized tests like GRE, TOEFL; (d) reputation of the college/university in India from which the applicant is graduating; (e) reputation of the school in North America in which the applicant is planning to pursue the education; (f) the field of study in which the applicant is planning higher education; (g) extra curricular activities the applicant is proficient in, and (h) only if the applicant is a Telugu student from Andhra Pradesh.

Funds Avail.: $2,000. **Number Awarded:** 1. **To Apply:** Applicants must complete the following information: (1) name, address with pin code and phone number; (2) profession and annual income; (3) name, address, and phone number of parents; (4) professions and annual incomes of parents; (5) net worth of all assets of applicant and parents combined; (6) high school and college educational qualifications and work experience of the applicant (enclose a copy of the transcripts); (7) name, address and phone number of the department and the university in the United States where the applicant intends to enroll. **Deadline:** July 25. **Contact:** Prasad Choudary Kakarala; E-mail: prasadkakarala@yahoo.com.

9088 ■ Vallabhaneni Sukundamma and Lakshmaiah Scholarships (Graduate/Scholarship)

Purpose: To provide financial support to deserving Telugu students who want to pursue their education in the United States. **Focus:** General studies/Field of study not specified. **Qualif.:** Applicants must be Telugu students who are currently residing in Andhra Pradesh; must have been admitted to a graduate school in a U.S. university; must demonstrate financial need. **Criteria:** Selection of applicants will be based on the following criteria: (a) need; (b) merit, grades and recommendations; (c) scores in standardized tests like GRE, TOEFL; (d) reputation of the college/university in India from which the applicant is graduating; (e) reputation of the school in North America in which the applicant is planning to pursue the education; (f) the field of study in which the applicant is planning higher education; (g) extra curricular activities the applicant is proficient in, and (h) only if the applicant is a Telugu student from Andhra Pradesh.

Funds Avail.: $2,000. **Number Awarded:** 1. **To Apply:** Applicants must complete the following information: (1) name, address with pin code and phone number; (2) profession and annual income; (3) name, address, and phone number of parents; (4) professions and annual incomes of parents; (5) net worth of all assets of applicant and parents combined; (6) high school and college educational qualifications and work experience of the applicant (enclose a copy of the transcripts); (7) name, address and phone number of the department and the university in the United States where the applicant intends to enroll. **Deadline:** July 25. **Contact:** Prasad Choudary Kakarala; E-mail: prasadkakarala@yahoo.com.

Awards are arranged alphabetically below their administering organizations

9089 ■ TANA Foundation Graduate Scholarships
(Graduate/Scholarship)

Purpose: To provide financial support to deserving Telugu students who want to pursue their education in the United States. **Focus:** General studies/Field of study not specified. **Qualif.:** Applicants must be Telugu students who are currently residing in Andhra Pradesh; must have been admitted to a graduate school in a U.S. university; must demonstrate financial need. **Criteria:** Selection of applicants will be based on the following criteria: (a) need; (b) merit, grades and recommendations; (c) scores in standardized tests like GRE, TOEFL; (d) reputation of the college/university in India from which the applicant is graduating; (e) reputation of the school in North America in which the applicant is planning to pursue the education; (f) the field of study in which the applicant is planning higher education; (g) extra curricular activities the applicant is proficient in, and (h) only if the applicant is a Telugu student from Andhra Pradesh.

Funds Avail.: $2,000. **Number Awarded:** 1. **To Apply:** Applicants must complete the following information: (1) name, address with pin code and phone number; (2) profession and annual income; (3) name, address, and phone number of parents; (4) professions and annual incomes of parents; (5) net worth of all assets of applicant and parents combined; (6) high school and college educational qualifications and work experience of the applicant (enclose a copy of the transcripts); (7) name, address and phone number of the department and the university in the United States where the applicant intends to enroll. **Deadline:** July 25. **Contact:** Prasad Choudary Kakarala; E-mail: prasadkakarala@yahoo.com.

9090 ■ Kodali Veeraiah and Sarojini Scholarships
(Graduate/Scholarship)

Purpose: To provide financial support to deserving Telugu students who want to pursue their education in the United States. **Focus:** General studies/Field of study not specified. **Qualif.:** Applicants must be Telugu students who are currently residing in Andhra Pradesh; must have been admitted to a graduate school in a U.S. university; must demonstrate financial need. **Criteria:** Selection of applicants will be based on the following criteria: (a) need; (b) merit, grades and recommendations; (c) scores in standardized tests like GRE, TOEFL; (d) reputation of the college/university in India from which the applicant is graduating; (e) reputation of the school in North America in which the applicant is planning to pursue the education; (f) the field of study in which the applicant is planning higher education; (g) extra curricular activities the applicant is proficient in, and (h) only if the applicant is a Telugu student from Andhra Pradesh.

Funds Avail.: $2,000. **Number Awarded:** 1. **To Apply:** Applicants must complete the following information: (1) name, address with pin code and phone number; (2) profession and annual income; (3) name, address, and phone number of parents; (4) professions and annual incomes of parents; (5) net worth of all assets of applicant and parents combined; (6) high school and college educational qualifications and work experience of the applicant (enclose a copy of the transcripts); (7) name, address and phone number of the department and the university in the United States where the applicant intends to enroll. **Deadline:** July 25. **Contact:** Prasad Choudary Kakarala; E-mail: prasadkakarala@yahoo.com.

9091 ■ Temecula Valley Wine Society (TVWS)
PO Box 890598
Temecula, CA 92589-0598
E-mail: tvwscrush@gmail.com
URL: www.tvwinesociety.org

9092 ■ Nancy Johnston Memorial Scholarships
(Graduate, Undergraduate/Scholarship)

Purpose: To provide financial assistance to students majoring in Enology, Entomology, Viticulture or Wine Marketing. **Focus:** Enology; Entomology; Viticulture. **Qualif.:** Applicants must be upper division and graduate-level students at California Universities, who are majoring in Viticulture, Enology or Wine Marketing; California State College students pursuing two-year certification or A.S. Degrees in Winemaking. Previous recipients may apply. **Criteria:** Selection will be based on submitted documents; grade point average; financial need; school and community involvement; work experience; and post-graduation goals.

Funds Avail.: No specific amount. **Duration:** Annual. **To Apply:** Applicants must submit a completed application form; a letter of recommendation from advisor or professor and an official copy of college transcript(s) including high school transcripts for A.S. candidates. **Deadline:** October 28. **Contact:** Mail applications to Alma Lyon, c/o TVWS Scholarships, PO Box 890598, Temecula CA 92589-0598.

9093 ■ Tennessee Education Association (TEA)
801 2nd Ave. N
Nashville, TN 37201-1099
Ph: (615)242-8392
Fax: (615)259-4581
Free: 800-342-8367
E-mail: membership@tea.nea.org
URL: www.teateachers.org

9094 ■ Don Sahli-Kathy Woodall Graduate Scholarships *(Graduate/Scholarship)*

Purpose: To provide financial assistance to qualified students who wish to pursue a teaching profession. **Focus:** Teaching. **Qualif.:** Applicant must be a student pursuing a degree in the teaching profession; must be involved or have past activities in the United Education Profession. **Criteria:** Selection of applicants will be based on past activities in the United Education Profession and on academic ability, need, leadership and potential as a leader and association leader within the teaching profession.

Funds Avail.: $1,000. **To Apply:** Applicants must complete the application form available on the website and must be submitted to the TEA Headquarters, Attn: Wanda Dickens. **Deadline:** June 1. **Remarks:** Established in 1971. **Contact:** Sahli-Woodall Scholarship Fund, Tennessee Education Association at the above address.

9095 ■ Sons and Daughters Don Sahli-Kathy Woodall Scholarships *(Graduate, Undergraduate/Scholarship)*

Purpose: To provide support to undergraduate and graduate level students who wish to pursue a teaching profession. **Focus:** Teaching. **Qualif.:** Applicant must be a TEA member's child who is a high school senior, undergraduate or graduate student planning to major in education. **Criteria:** Awards will be given to students who have demonstrated their commitment to the teaching profession. Applicants will

Awards are arranged alphabetically below their administering organizations

be selected based on academic excellence, leadership, economic need and recommendations.

Funds Avail.: $1,000. **Number Awarded:** 1. **To Apply:** Applicants must complete the application form available on the website; attach two recommendation letters, transcript of record, and a short essay of no more than 200 words on why they want to be a teacher. **Deadline:** March 1. **Contact:** Jeanette DeMain, Don Sahli-Kathy Woodall Scholarships, Tennessee Education Association at the above address.

9096 ■ Terra Foundation for American Art

120 E Erie St.
Chicago, IL 60611
Ph: (312)664-3939
Fax: (312)664-2052
E-mail: contact@terraamericanart.org
URL: www.terraamericanart.org

9097 ■ Terra Foundation Fellowships at the Smithsonian American Art Museum *(Postdoctorate/Fellowship)*

Purpose: To support full-time independent and dissertation research by scholars from abroad or by US scholars. **Focus:** Arts; History. **Qualif.:** Applicants must be predoctoral, senior or postdoctoral fellows from US or abroad. **Criteria:** Selection will be based on the committee's criteria.

Funds Avail.: Varies. **Duration:** Annual. **To Apply:** Interested applicants may contact the Foundation for the application process and other information. **Contact:** Amy Gunderson at grants@terraamericanart.org.

9098 ■ Terra Foundation Postdoctoral Teaching Fellowships at the Courtauld Institute of Art, London *(Postdoctorate/Fellowship)*

Purpose: To support advance inquiry in the history of art, conservation, and museum studies. **Focus:** Arts; History. **Qualif.:** Applicants must be postdoctoral fellows. **Criteria:** Selection will be based on the committee's criteria.

Funds Avail.: Varies. **To Apply:** Interested applicants must contact the Foundation for the application process and other information. **Deadline:** January 15. **Contact:** Amy Gunderson at grants@terraamericanart.org.

9099 ■ Terra Foundation Postdoctoral Teaching Fellowships at the Institut National d'Histoire de l'Art, Paris *(Postdoctorate/Fellowship)*

Purpose: To promote education taught in English on the history of American art and transatlantic exchange, and structure a corresponding field of research. **Focus:** Arts; History. **Qualif.:** Applicants must be postdoctoral fellows to teach four semester-long courses to undergraduate and master's-level students at a French university. **Criteria:** Selection will be based on the committee's criteria.

Funds Avail.: No specific amount. **To Apply:** Interested applicants may contact the Foundation for the application process and other information. **Contact:** Amy Gunderson at grants@terraamericanart.org.

9100 ■ Terra Foundation Research Travel Grants *(Doctorate, Undergraduate/Grant)*

Purpose: To enable scholars outside the United States to consult resources that are only available within the United States. **Focus:** Art. **Qualif.:** Applicants must be doctoral students and scholars who received their degree within ten years of the application deadline, outside the United States. **Criteria:** Selection will be based on the committee's criteria.

Funds Avail.: $6,000-$9,000. **Duration:** One year. **Number Awarded:** Six to nine. **To Apply:** Research travel grant application can be downloaded online. The travel should be undertaken within one calendar year after the announcement of the selection results. The final report must be submitted within three months of completion of travel. The report should include a description of the travel undertaken as a result of the grant, an assessment of the research accomplished and a financial report detailing grant expenditures. **Deadline:** January 15. **Contact:** travelgrants@terraamericanart.eu.

9101 ■ Terra Summer Residency Fellowships *(Master's, Doctorate/Fellowship)*

Purpose: To provide an opportunity for participants to widen their academic and creative horizons, explore international cultural perspectives, and forge lifelong exchanged and professional networks. **Focus:** Arts; History. **Qualif.:** Applicants must be either visual artists with a master's degree or its equivalent at the time of application or doctoral candidates researching American art and visual culture or its role in a context of international artistic exchange prior to 1980. All applicants are expected to be fluent in English. Knowledge of French is desirable but not required. Preference will be given to applicants who have completed their degree within the past five years. Doctoral candidates should be at an advanced stage of their doctoral research and writing. **Criteria:** Selection will be based on the committee's criteria.

Funds Avail.: A stipend of $5,000. **Duration:** Annual. **To Apply:** Applicants must be nominated by their dissertation advisor, professor, or previous art school supervisor. Each professor may nominate a maximum of two students each year. Selected fellows are required to give a presentation outlining their research/artistic project; attend the seminars/lectures of all senior scholars and artists and other required meetings; and present their accomplishments at the end of the program. Application form can be obtained at the website. **Deadline:** January 15. **Remarks:** Established in 2001. **Contact:** E-mail: tsr@terraamericanart.eu.

9102 ■ Texas Association of Community Schools (TACS)

1011 San Jacinto Blvd., Ste. 204
Austin, TX 78701-2431
Ph: (512)440-8227
Fax: (512)442-6705
URL: www.tacsnet.org

9103 ■ Student Scholarships *(Undergraduate/Scholarship)*

Purpose: To support students and develop excellence in student achievement through the collaboration of member schools. **Focus:** Education. **Qualif.:** Applicants must be members of TACS. **Criteria:** Selection will be based on the committee's criteria.

Funds Avail.: $1,000. **Duration:** Annual. **Number Awarded:** 2. **To Apply:** Interested applicants may contact the Association for the application process and other details.

Awards are arranged alphabetically below their administering organizations

9104 ■ Texas Association of Developing Colleges (TADC)

1140 Empire Central Dr., Ste. 550
Dallas, TX 75247
Ph: (214)630-2511
Fax: (214)631-2030
E-mail: info@txadc.org
URL: www.txadc.org

9105 ■ The Urban Scholarship Fund (Undergraduate/Scholarship)

Purpose: To strategically plan, organize and direct cooperative opportunities and programs for its members and serve as administrator of educational and community programs. **Focus:** General studies/Field of study not specified. **Qualif.:** Applicants must be U.S. citizens; must be Texas residents; and must be full-time undergraduate students in good standing or graduates of a high school in one of the following 19 cities: Abilene, Amarillo, Arlington, Austin, Beaumont, Corpus Christi, Dallas, El Paso, Forth Worth, Garland, Houston, Irving, Laredo, Lubbock, Meaquito, Plano, San Antonio and Waco. **Criteria:** Recipients are selected based on financial need.

Funds Avail.: $700 - $2,000. **Duration:** One year. **To Apply:** Applicants must submit a completed application form and a copy of high school or college transcript. **Deadline:** July 7.

9106 ■ Texas Choral Directors Association (TCDA)

7900 Centre Park Dr., Ste. A
Austin, TX 78754
Ph: (512)474-2801
Fax: (512)474-7873
URL: www.tcda.net

9107 ■ TCDA Carroll Barnes Student Scholarships (Undergraduate/Scholarship)

Purpose: To support active TCDA student members in their continuing education. **Focus:** Education, Music; Religion. **Qualif.:** Applicants must be Texas college/university undergraduate students in music education or church music majors with 60+ credit hours and must have maintained at least 3.0 GPA on a 4.0 system. **Criteria:** Selection shall be based on the aforementioned qualifications and compliance with the application details.

Funds Avail.: No specific amount. **To Apply:** Applicants must submit a current transcript; two sealed letters of recommendation (one from a current TCDA member); letter of application (typed or printed) detailing musical contributions and accomplishments, potential for success in the choral music profession, and professional qualifications.

9108 ■ TCDA Jim and Glenda Casey Professional Scholarships (Other/Scholarship)

Purpose: To support active TCDA members in their professional development. **Focus:** Education, Music. **Qualif.:** Applicants must be enrolled in a Texas college/university and have three years of continuous active membership. **Criteria:** Selection shall be based on the aforementioned qualifications and compliance with the application details.

Funds Avail.: $500. **Duration:** Annual. **Number Awarded:** 1. **To Apply:** Applicants must submit a letter of application describing their qualifications, professional goals, and a description of the higher education or workshop certification sought. They must also submit their respective resume or curriculum vitae. **Deadline:** April 24. **Contact:** Sharon Lutz at sharon@tcda.net or call 512-474-2801.

9109 ■ TCDA Bill Gorham Student Scholarships (Undergraduate/Scholarship)

Purpose: To support active TCDA student members in their continuing education. **Focus:** Education, Music; Religion. **Qualif.:** Applicants must be Texas college/university undergraduate students in music education or church music majors with 60+ credit hours and must have maintained at least 3.0 GPA on a 4.0 system. **Criteria:** Selection shall be based on the aforementioned qualifications and compliance with the application details.

Funds Avail.: $1,000. **Duration:** Annual. **Number Awarded:** 1. **To Apply:** Applicants must submit a current transcript; two sealed letters of recommendation (one from a current TCDA member); letter of application (typed or printed) detailing musical contributions and accomplishments, potential for success in the choral music profession, and professional qualifications. **Deadline:** April 24. **Contact:** Sharon Lutz at sharon@tcda.net or call 512-474-2801.

9110 ■ TCDA Abbott IPCO Professional Scholarships (Other/Scholarship)

Purpose: To support active TCDA members in their professional development. **Focus:** Education, Music. **Qualif.:** Applicants must be enrolled in a Texas college/university and have three years of continuous active membership. **Criteria:** Selection shall be based on the aforementioned qualifications and compliance with the application details.

Funds Avail.: $1,000. **Duration:** Annual. **Number Awarded:** 1. **To Apply:** Applicants must submit a letter of application describing their qualifications, professional goals, and a description of the higher education or workshop certification sought. They must also submit their respective resume or curriculum vitae. **Deadline:** April 24. **Contact:** Sharon Lutz at sharon@tcda.net or call 512-474-2801.

9111 ■ TCDA Gandy Ink Professional Scholarships (Professional development/Scholarship)

Purpose: To support active TCDA members in their professional development. **Focus:** Education, Music; Religion. **Qualif.:** Applicants must be enrolled in a Texas college/university and have three years of continuous active membership. **Criteria:** Selection shall be based on the aforementioned qualifications and compliance with the application details.

Funds Avail.: $1,000. **Duration:** Annual. **Number Awarded:** 1. **To Apply:** Applicants must submit a letter of application describing their qualifications, professional goals, and a description of the higher education or workshop certification sought. They must also submit their respective resume or curriculum vitae. **Deadline:** April 24. **Contact:** Sharon Lutz at sharon@tcda.net or call 512-474-2801.

9112 ■ TCDA General Fund Scholarships (Undergraduate/Scholarship)

Purpose: To support active TCDA student members in their continuing education. **Focus:** Education, Music; Religion. **Qualif.:** Applicants must be Texas college/university undergraduate students in music education or church music majors with 60+ credit hours and must have maintained at

Awards are arranged alphabetically below their administering organizations

---

least 3.0 GPA on a 4.0 system. **Criteria:** Selection shall be based on the aforementioned qualifications and compliance with the application details.

Funds Avail.: $1,000. **Duration:** Annual. **Number Awarded:** 1. **To Apply:** Applicants must submit a current transcript; two sealed letters of recommendation (one from a current TCDA member); letter of application (typed or printed) detailing musical contributions and accomplishments, potential for success in the choral music profession, and professional qualifications. **Deadline:** April 24. **Contact:** Sharon Lutz at sharon@tcda.net or call 512-474-2801.

9113 ■ TCDA Past Presidents Student Scholarships
(Undergraduate/Scholarship)

Purpose: To support active TCDA student members in their continuing education. **Focus:** Education, Music; Religion. **Qualif.:** Applicants must be Texas college/university undergraduate students in music education or church music majors with 60+ credit hours and must have maintained at least 3.0 GPA on a 4.0 system. **Criteria:** Selection shall be based on the aforementioned qualifications and compliance with the application details.

Funds Avail.: $1,000. **Duration:** Annual. **Number Awarded:** 1. **To Apply:** Applicants must submit a current transcript; two sealed letters of recommendation (one from a current TCDA member); letter of application (typed or printed) detailing musical contributions and accomplishments, potential for success in the choral music profession, and professional qualifications. **Deadline:** April 24. **Contact:** Sharon Lutz at sharon@tcda.net or call 512-474-2801.

9114 ■ TCDA Cloys Webb Student Scholarships
(Undergraduate/Scholarship)

Purpose: To support active TCDA student members in their continuing education. **Focus:** Education, Music; Religion. **Qualif.:** Applicants must be Texas college/university undergraduate students in music education or church music majors with 60+ credit hours and must have maintained at least 3.0 GPA on a 4.0 system. **Criteria:** Selection shall be based on the aforementioned qualifications and compliance with the application details.

Funds Avail.: $1,000. **Duration:** Annual. **Number Awarded:** 1. **To Apply:** Applicants must submit a current transcript; two sealed letters of recommendation (one from a current TCDA member); letter of application (typed or printed) detailing musical contributions and accomplishments, potential for success in the choral music profession, and professional qualifications. **Deadline:** April 24. **Contact:** Sharon Lutz at sharon@tcda.net or call 512-474-2801.

9115 ■ Texas Computer Education Association (TCEA)
3100 Alvin Devane Blvd., Bldg. B
Austin, TX 78741
Ph: (512)476-8500
Fax: (512)476-8574
Free: 800-282-8232
E-mail: tceaoffice@tcea.org
URL: www.tcea.org

9116 ■ Richard A. Brown Student Scholarships
(Undergraduate/Scholarship)

Purpose: To encourage and enhance learning and professional growth in educational technology for practicing and pre-service educators. **Focus:** Computer and information

sciences. **Qualif.:** Applicants must be full time students at an accredited college/university (12 hours or more); have successfully completed at least 24 hours of college; pursuing a career in education; have a cumulative GPA of at least 2.75 on a scale of 4.0; and have not previously received the scholarship. **Criteria:** Selection will be based on the submitted application materials.

Funds Avail.: $1,000. **To Apply:** Applicants must submit a completed Awards Entry Form together with a statement of personal and family information including financial need, if any; three letters of recommendation (not to exceed one page); a copy of college transcript to date; and a one page personal profile. Each entry form must be accompanied with four copies of the supporting documents. **Deadline:** October 31. **Contact:** Katie Treat; E-mail: treat@tcea.org.

9117 ■ Robert E. Knight Professional Scholarships
(Doctorate, Graduate/Scholarship)

Purpose: To encourage and enhance learning and professional growth in educational technology for practicing and pre-service educators. **Focus:** Computer and information sciences. **Qualif.:** Applicants must be members of TCEA (non-members may submit membership and dues at the time of entry); be employed full time in the field of education; use the money for expenses incurred in achieving a higher education degree (master's or doctorate) in the field of educational technology; and have not previously received the scholarship. **Criteria:** Selection is based on the submitted application materials.

Funds Avail.: $1,000. **Duration:** Annual. **Number Awarded:** 1. **To Apply:** Applicants must submit a completed Awards Entry Form along with two letters of recommendation (not to exceed one page); a one page personal profile including; and proof of enrollment in master's or doctoral program in the field of educational technology. Each entry form must be accompanied with four copies of the supporting documents. **Deadline:** October 31. **Remarks:** Established in 2007. **Contact:** Katie Treat; E-mail: treat@tcea.org.

9118 ■ Texas Computer Education Association Professional Educator Grants *(Other/Grant)*

Purpose: To encourage and enhance learning and professional growth in educational technology for practicing and pre-service educators. **Focus:** Computer and information sciences. **Qualif.:** Applicant must be a member of TCEA (non-members may submit membership and dues at the time of entry); be employed full time in the field of education; use the money to attend professional development activities that will increase knowledge of educational technology; and have not received the scholarship previously. **Criteria:** Selection is based on the submitted application materials.

Funds Avail.: No specific amount. **To Apply:** Applicants must submit a completed Awards Entry Form together with two letters of recommendation (not to exceed one page), and a one page personal profile. Each entry form must be accompanied with four copies of the supporting documents. **Deadline:** October 21.

9119 ■ Texas Counseling Association (TCA)
1204 San Antonio St., Ste. 201
Austin, TX 78701-1870
Ph: (512)472-3403
Fax: (512)472-3756
Free: 800-580-8144

Awards are arranged alphabetically below their administering organizations

URL: www.txca.org/tca/default.asp

9120 ■ TCA Outstanding Graduate Student Awards
(Graduate/Award)

Purpose: To support graduate students who are showing dedication and academic excellence in the theory and practice of some significant area of counseling and exhibiting outstanding scholarships. **Focus:** Counseling/Guidance. **Qualif.:** Applicants must be students pursuing graduate degrees in counseling; must have compiled an outstanding academic record of their graduate studies in some significant area of counseling; must demonstrate a commitment to issue of counseling. **Criteria:** Evaluations will be based on academic excellence and commitment to the advancement of the profession of counseling.

Funds Avail.: No specific amount. **To Apply:** Applicants must have their work submitted by a colleague or professor or applicants may submit nominations on their behalf. Nomination submissions include nomination form; one-page summary that provides documentation of academic excellence; two-page summary of independent work that demonstrates commitment to the issues of counseling. **Deadline:** June 1. **Contact:** Texas Counseling Association, ATTN: Awards Coordinator, at the above address.

9121 ■ Texas Elks State Association (TESA)
c/o Diane Martin, Chairperson
PO Box 5531
Borger, TX 79008
URL: texaselks.org

9122 ■ Texas Elks State Association Eagle Scout Scholarships *(High School/Scholarship)*

Purpose: To help students pursue their education. **Focus:** General studies/Field of study not specified. **Qualif.:** Applicants must be graduating high school seniors currently enrolled in an accredited Texas High School. **Criteria:** Recipients will be selected based on financial need, extracurricular events and leadership participation and academics.

Funds Avail.: $2,500. **Duration:** Annual. **To Apply:** Applicants must fill out the application form; must enclose a sealed copy of a high school transcript; attach copies of awards and honors; two letters of recommendation from persons in school, community, church, or scouting; and a copy of Eagle Scout certificate. **Deadline:** March 20.

9123 ■ Texas Elks State Association Girl Scout Gold Award Scholarships *(High School, Undergraduate/Scholarship)*

Purpose: To help students pursue their education. **Focus:** General studies/Field of study not specified. **Qualif.:** Applicants must be graduating seniors who have earned a Girl Scout Gold Award; and have plans to attend a Texas college, university, trade or vocation school for the coming academic year. **Criteria:** Applications will be evaluated based on leadership, achievements, recommendations and financial need.

Funds Avail.: $2,500. **Duration:** Annual. **Number Awarded:** 1. **To Apply:** Applicants must fill out an application form; must provide a sealed copy of high school transcript; three letters of recommendation from: a) non-relative Girl Scout; b) school; c) church or community representatives; and a copy of Girl Scout Gold Award Final Report. **Deadline:** March 15.

9124 ■ Texas Elks State Association Scholarships
(Undergraduate/Scholarship)

Purpose: To help students pursue their education. **Focus:** General studies/Field of study not specified. **Qualif.:** Applicants must be in the current graduating class of a Texas High School; must be U.S. citizens and residents of Texas; and be enrolled full-time in a four year degree program at an accredited junior college, college, or university in Texas. **Criteria:** Applicants will be evaluated based on financial need, scholarship, leadership and extracurricular activities, and character.

Funds Avail.: No specific amount. **To Apply:** Applicants must: complete the application form; prepare a statement of their professional goals(maximum of 300 words); include a guardian's statement (maximum of 200 words); include official transcript of high school grades; include SAT and/or ACT scores; and copies of achievements and awards for leadership, extracurricular activities, or any type of activities. **Deadline:** March 5.

9125 ■ Texas Health Information Management Association (TxHIMA)
18382 FM 306, Ste. 103
Canyon Lake, TX 78133-3336
Ph: (512)215-4261
Fax: (512)607-6437
E-mail: txhima@txhima.org
URL: www.txhima.org

9126 ■ Evelyn L. Cockrell Memorial Scholarship Award *(Undergraduate/Scholarship)*

Purpose: To support the professional development of individuals engaged in the undergraduate study of health information teachnology, health information management, and/or graudate study in health information management or related fields. **Focus:** Health education. **Qualif.:** Applicants must be: active student members of AHIMA with TxHIMA membership; citizens of the United States or hold resident status in the United States; and, enrolled in an AHIMA accredited educational program pursuing an HIT or HIA degree which leads to the RHIT or RHIA certification. **Criteria:** Selection will be based on the Board's criteria.

Funds Avail.: No specific amount. **Duration:** Annual. **To Apply:** Applicants must complete and submit the application form; must provide a copy of official transcript or a copy of high school transcript if a first semester freshman; must have two (2) individuals to complete a letter of recommendation. One letter must be from an educational advisor or professor while the other letter of recommendation must also address perceived financial need of the student and how receiving this scholarship will benefit the student to continue their health information education; must submit an essay of 350-400 words about personal goals and how the scholarship money will help them to reach the goals. Enclose one current digital photograph which will be published with the winner's name at the discretion of the Board of Directors. The photograph will not be circulated to the Board of Directors until the recipient has been chosen. Sign and date each item on the agreement form. **Deadline:** May 1.

9127 ■ Peggy P. Starks Scholarship *(Postgraduate/Scholarship)*

Purpose: To support students who demonstrate academic achievement and commitment to the field of health informa-

Awards are arranged alphabetically below their administering organizations

tion management in Texas. **Focus:** Health sciences. **Qualif.:** Applicants must be post-graduate students; must be active members of AHIMA; must be residents of the state of Texas for at least one year prior to application date; must be citizens of the United States or hold permanent resident status in the U.S.; must have a minimum of a 3.50 GPA on a 4.00 scale within graduate school. **Criteria:** Selection will be based on the following criteria: leadership; scholarship; essay.

Funds Avail.: No specific amount. **Duration:** Annual. **To Apply:** Applicants must visit the website for the online application process and must provide the following requirements: a copy of applicants' graduate degree plan; a university transcript (official or unofficial) showing earned baccalaureate degree; a copy of the last semester grade report showing GPA; letters of recommendation. Both letters should be from either work supervisor or university instructor; a written essay of 350-400 words about personal goals and how the scholarship money will help them to reach the goals; one (1) current photograph, approximately 2" X 2" which will be published with the winner's names at the discretion of the Board of Directors; the photograph will not be circulated to the Board of Directors until the recipient has been chosen. **Deadline:** April 10.

9128 ■ TxHIMA HIA-HIT Scholarship *(Undergraduate/ Scholarship)*

Purpose: To support the professional development of individuals engaged in the undergraduate study of health information teachnology, health information management and/or graduate study in health information management or related fields. **Focus:** Health education. **Qualif.:** Applicants must: be active student members of AHIMA with TxHIMA membership; be residents of the state of Texas for at least one year; be citizens of U.S. or hold permanent resident status in the said country; have a major of Health Information Administration or Technology and a minimum GPA of 3.5 (on a 4.00 scale) in that major and a minimum cumulative GPA of 3.5 on a 4.0 scale. **Criteria:** Preference will be given to active student members of AHIMA.

Funds Avail.: No specific amount. **Duration:** Annual. **Number Awarded:** 2. **To Apply:** Applicants must complete and submit the application form together with their college transcript and letters of recommendation. Applicants must obtain the signature of the Program Director for the purpose of eligibility to apply for the scholarship; must submit their essay of 500 words or less, on a separate sheet of paper, on how they will use the scholarship money and why they feel they deserve it and must discuss what personal attributes, training, experience or goals that will make them an asset to the health information management profession. At the bottom of the essay in own handwriting, write the following statement: "This essay is my work and has not been written, composed, or edited for me by anyone." plus the signature and date the statement; lastly is current wallet-size photo for use in the TxHIMA Journal and the photo will not be shared with the Board of Directors until after the recipients have been selected. **Deadline:** May 1.

9129 ■ TxHIMA Outstanding Student Scholarship *(College/Scholarship)*

Purpose: To identify and honor an outstanding Health Information Technology and Health Information Administration student in Texas. **Focus:** Health education; Health services administration. **Qualif.:** Applicants must be graduating students in the last year of a HIA or HIT program; must have an overall cumulative grade point average (GPA) minimum of 3.0. and an overall major GPA of 3.5; must be full-time students in a health information program (12-semester hours minimum). **Criteria:** Selection will be based on the following criteria: leadership (35 points); scholarship (40 points); student essay (500 words - 25 points) topic: "Why I Chose the HIM Profession?".

Funds Avail.: No specific amount. **Duration:** Annual. **To Apply:** Applicants must visit the website for the online application process and must submit the following requirements: at least two (2) letters of recommendation written by a faculty member, clinical site sponsor, co-worker or peer. One letter of recommendation must be written by the Program Director; a certified transcript of grades to be submitted with the online nomination form; a wallet size photo for recognition in the TxHIMA Newsletter and website. **Deadline:** April 3.

9130 ■ Texas Music Educators Association (TMEA)
7900 Centre Park Dr.
Austin, TX 78754
Ph: (512)452-0710
Fax: (512)451-9213
Free: 888-318-8632
URL: www.tmea.org

9131 ■ Bill Cormack Scholarships *(Undergraduate/ Scholarship)*

Purpose: To provide professional growth opportunities; to encourage interaction among music education professionals; to foster public support for music in school; to offer quality musical experiences for students; to cultivate universal appreciation and lifetime involvement in music; to develop and maintain productive working relationships with other professional organizations. **Focus:** Music. **Qualif.:** Applicants must be entering freshmen in a Texas college or university; must major in a music degree program leading to Texas teacher-certification with music as the primary teaching field. **Criteria:** Recipients are selected based on academic performance.

Funds Avail.: $3,000 per year for up to five years. **To Apply:** Applicants must submit: completed application form; a high school transcript; a one-to-two page essay that describes their reasons for becoming a teacher, commitment to music education and future career goals; three-to-five evaluations from individuals who can assess the applicant's potential for success in an undergraduate music education program and as a music educator, music skills and abilities, work ethic and other personal qualities; must submit a verification from student's advisor that the applicant will teach within the semester indicated on the application. **Deadline:** November 16. **Contact:** Kay Vanlandingham, at the above address.

9132 ■ Texas Music Educators Association Past-Presidents Memorial Scholarships *(Undergraduate/ Scholarship)*

Purpose: To provide professional growth opportunities; to encourage interaction among music education professionals; to foster public support for music in school; to offer quality musical experiences for students; to cultivate universal appreciation and lifetime involvement in music; to develop and maintain productive working relationships with other professional organizations. **Focus:** Music. **Qualif.:** Applicants must be entering freshmen at a Texas college or university; must major in a music degree program leading

Awards are arranged alphabetically below their administering organizations

to Texas teacher-certification with music as the primary teaching field. **Criteria:** Recipients are selected based on academic performance.

Funds Avail.: $2,500 per year for up to five years. **To Apply:** Applicants must submit: completed application form; high school transcript; a one-to-two-page essay that describes their reasons for becoming a teacher, commitment to music education and future career goals; three-to-five evaluations from individuals who can assess the applicant's potential for success in an undergraduate music education program and as a music educator, music skills and abilities, work ethic and other personal qualities; must submit a verification by student's advisor that the applicant will teach within the semester indicated on the application. **Deadline:** November 16. **Contact:** Kay Vanlandingham, at the above address.

9133 ■ Texas Mutual Insurance Company

6210 E Hwy. 290
Austin, TX 78723-1098
Ph: (512)224-3800
Free: 800-859-5995
E-mail: information@texasmutual.com
URL: www.texasmutual.com

9134 ■ Texas Mutual Scholarship Program
(Undergraduate, Vocational/Occupational/Scholarship)

Purpose: To provide financial support for the surviving family members of employees who died from an on-the-job accident, and/or whose injuries qualify for lifetime income benefits, to have the chance to pursue education and training to help them build better futures. **Focus:** Education, Vocational-technical. **Qualif.:** Applicants must be unmarried surviving children of an individual who died as a result of a work-related injury or whose severe injuries qualify them for a lifetime income benefits (LIBs) under the Texas Worker's Compensation Act. **Criteria:** Applicants will be evaluated based on age (must be unmarried and be between the ages of 16 and 25) and academic performance.

Funds Avail.: Up to $4,000. **Duration:** Annual. **To Apply:** Applicants must complete the application form available at the website of Texas Mutual Insurance Company and submit along with the other materials needed to qualify for the scholarship. **Contact:** Texas Mutual Insurance Company at the above address.

9135 ■ Texas Society of Professional Engineers (TSPE)

1001 Congress Ave., Ste. 260
Austin, TX 78701
Ph: (512)472-9286
Free: 800-580-8973
E-mail: info@tspe.org
URL: www.tspe.org

9136 ■ Texas Society of Professional Engineers Scholarships *(Undergraduate/Scholarship)*

Purpose: To provide financial assistance to students studying to become engineers in an engineering program at an ABET-accredited college or university. **Focus:** Engineering. **Qualif.:** Applicants must be United States citizens; high school seniors with a 3.0 or higher GPA entering college in the coming school year; have scored at least 600 in math,

550 in critical reading and 500 in writing on the SAT or a 29 in math and 25 in English on the ACT; and enrolled in an ABET program. **Criteria:** Applicants are evaluated based on academic performance, achievements, leadership, and career goals.

Funds Avail.: No specific amount. **To Apply:** Applicants must submit the completed application form; essay; two recommendations from non-relatives (high school teachers preferred); and an official transcript. **Deadline:** January 9. **Contact:** Applicants may e-mail their application to scholarships@tspe.org.

9137 ■ Texas State Historical Association (TSHA)

3001 Lake Austin Blvd., Ste. 3.116
Austin, TX 78703
Ph: (512)471-2600
Fax: (512)473-8691
URL: www.tshaonline.org

9138 ■ Catarino and Evangelina Hernández Research Fellowships in Latino History *(Professional development/Fellowship)*

Purpose: To provide support for the research proposal relating to the history of Latinos in Texas. **Focus:** History. **Qualif.:** Individuals must have a research proposal relating to the history of Latinos in Texas State. **Criteria:** Recipients will be selected based on submitted research proposal.

Funds Avail.: $500. **Duration:** Annual. **Number Awarded:** 1 in 2014. **To Apply:** Applicants must submit a complete vita and four copies of the research proposal. Application should specify the purpose of the research, the need for money and description of the end product.

9139 ■ Mary M. Hughes Research Fellowships in Texas History *(Professional development/Fellowship)*

Purpose: To financially assist individuals doing research relating to Texas history. **Focus:** History. **Qualif.:** Applicants must be individuals who have a research proposal on twentieth-century Texas history. **Criteria:** Recipients will be chosen based on submitted materials.

Funds Avail.: $1,000. **Duration:** Annual. **Number Awarded:** 1 in 2014. **To Apply:** Candidates must include a complete vita and four copies of the research proposal. Application should be no longer than one page, should specify the purpose of the research, the need for money and description of the end product. **Remarks:** Established in 1999.

9140 ■ John H. Jenkins Research Fellowships in Texas History *(Professional development/Fellowship)*

Purpose: To financially assist individuals doing research having to do with Texas history. **Focus:** History. **Qualif.:** Individuals must have a research proposal relating to Texas history. **Criteria:** Applicants will be evaluated based on submitted research proposal.

Funds Avail.: $1,000. **Duration:** Annual. **Number Awarded:** 1 in 2014. **To Apply:** Applicants must submit four copies of the proposal. Application should be no longer than two pages, should specify the purpose of the research, the need for money and description of the end product. **Remarks:** Established in 1994.

9141 ■ Mary Jon and J. P. Bryan Leadership in Education Awards *(Professional development/Award)*

Purpose: To recognize outstanding teachers in Texas. **Focus:** History. **Qualif.:** Applicants must be full-time teachers

Awards are arranged alphabetically below their administering organizations

at the middle school, high school and college levels presently teaching history in a Texas school or college. **Criteria:** Award will be given to applicants who best meet the judges' criteria and based on submitted materials.

Funds Avail.: $5,000. **Duration:** Annual. **Number Awarded:** 1 in 2014. **To Apply:** Applicants must submit resume or vita, a list of activities and accomplishments, awards/honors, publications, and description of programs. **Remarks:** Established in 1985. **Contact:** Nomination and supporting materials must be submitted to: Chairman Mary Jon and J. P. Bryan Leadership in Education Award Texas State Historical Association 1155 Union Circle #311580 Denton, TX 76203-5017.

9142 ■ Cecilia Steinfeldt Fellowships for Research in the Arts and Material Culture (Professional development/Fellowship)

Purpose: To support research proposal in Arts and Material Culture. **Focus:** Art. **Qualif.:** Individuals must have a research proposal on decorative and fine arts, material culture, preservation and architecture in Texas from the seventh century to present. **Criteria:** Fellowship will be given to applicants whose research proposal best meet the judges' criteria.

Funds Avail.: $1,000. **To Apply:** Applicants must submit four copies of the proposal. Application should be no longer than two pages, should specify the purpose of the research, the need for money and description of the end product. **Deadline:** December 31.

9143 ■ Texas Telephone Association (TTA)
1717 W 6th St., Ste. 370
Austin, TX 78703
Ph: (512)472-1183
Fax: (512)472-1293
URL: www.tta.org

9144 ■ Texas Telephone Association Foundation Scholarships (Undergraduate/Scholarship)

Purpose: To provide financial assistance to those students with financial hardship. **Focus:** General studies/Field of study not specified. **Qualif.:** Applicants must be U.S citizens; must have earned a cumulative GPA of 3.0 or higher; must plan to attend a Texas college or university. **Criteria:** Special consideration will be given to students who will be pursuing a college degree in fields of study relevant to telecommunications (math, business, engineering, and computer science).

Funds Avail.: $1,500. **Duration:** Annual; up to four years. **To Apply:** Applicants must submit completed application. Application must include a current transcript; a letter of acceptance from a Texas college or university; a copy of student's SAR (Student Aid Report). **Deadline:** March 15. **Contact:** JoAnn Kamerman at joannkam@tta.org.

9145 ■ Texas Vegetation Management Association (TVMA)
145 W Travis St.
La Grange, TX 78945
Ph: (979)968-5612
Fax: (979)968-5624
URL: www.tvma.net

9146 ■ Craig Johnson Family Scholarships (CJFS) (Undergraduate/Scholarship)

Purpose: To promote education and help students pursue their careers at an accredited college or university. **Focus:**

Vegetarianism. **Qualif.:** Applicants must be accepted at an accredited Texas college or university. Non-members may apply but have to declare their major field. **Criteria:** Applicants will be judged based on academic achievements, leadership and extracurricular activities and personal traits.

Funds Avail.: $2,000. **To Apply:** Application form must be accompanied by an official transcript of records, resume, three copies of (one-page) letter of reference, and a photo. **Deadline:** April 1. **Contact:** Texas Vegetation Management Association (TVMA), Craig Johnson Family Scholarship, at the above address.

9147 ■ Textile Care Allied Trades Association (TCATA)
271 Rte. 46 W, Ste. C106
Fairfield, NJ 07004
Ph: (973)244-1790
Fax: (973)244-4455
E-mail: info@tcata.org
URL: www.tcata.org/i4a/pages/index.cfm?pageid=1

9148 ■ TCATA College Scholarship Program (Undergraduate/Scholarship)

Purpose: To provide financial support for students interested in pursuing a degree at any accredited U.S. college or university on a full-time basis. **Focus:** General studies/ Field of study not specified. **Qualif.:** Applicant must be a full-time employee, or a son or daughter of a full-time employee, of a member company in good standing of the Textile Care Allied Trades Association for three years. **Criteria:** Recipient will be selected based on academic achievement, leadership qualities and courses of study.

Funds Avail.: $1,000. **To Apply:** Applicants must complete an application form and provide a copy of Scholarship Aptitude Test (SAT) or American College Test (ACT) scores; transcripts of all high school grades and any college grades if applicable; a letter from their high school principal - or other highest official equivalent - describing their leadership qualities, extra-curricular activities and other relevant information; and a letter describing past personal accomplishments, immediate goals and future academic and career objectives. **Deadline:** April 30.

9149 ■ ThanksUSA
1390 Chain Bridge Rd., No. 260
McLean, VA 22101
Fax: (703)641-3767
Free: 888-849-8720
URL: www.thanksusa.org

9150 ■ ThanksUSA Scholarships (Undergraduate, Vocational/Occupational/Scholarship)

Purpose: To support the dependents and spouses of active duty U.S. military service personnel with their educational pursuits. **Focus:** General studies/Field of study not specified. **Qualif.:** Applicants must be dependent children, age 24 and under or spouses of active-duty U.S. military service personnel; planning to enroll full-time in an accredited two-year or four-year college, university, vocational school or technical school; have at least a 2.0 cumulative GPA on a 4.0 scale, or its equivalent, on relevant academic record (high-school record for incoming freshmen or post-secondary school record for those already enrolled in a college, university or vocational/technical school). **Criteria:**

Awards are arranged alphabetically below their administering organizations

Recipients are selected based on financial need, academic record and demonstrated leadership and participation in school and community activities. Preference is given to children or spouses of service personnel killed or injured during active duty.

Funds Avail.: $3,000. **Duration:** Annual. **To Apply:** Applicants must submit a completed application along with transcripts and evidence of active military duty to verify eligibility. Copies of military I.D. are not acceptable. Mail completed application to ThanksUSA Scholarship Program. **Deadline:** May 15.

9151 ■ Theatre Guild of Simsbury (TGS)

PO Box 92
Simsbury, CT 06070
Ph: (860)658-0666
E-mail: theatreguildsimsbury@gmail.com
URL: www.theatreguildsimsbury.org

9152 ■ Theatre Guild Scholarship (Undergraduate/ Scholarship)

Purpose: To recognize high school students who are excellent in performing arts. **Focus:** Performing arts; Theater arts.

Duration: Annual.

9153 ■ Theatre for Young Audiences USA (TYA/ USA)

Theatre School at DePaul University
2350 N Racine Ave.
Chicago, IL 60614
Ph: (773)325-7981
Fax: (773)325-7920
E-mail: info@tyausa.org
URL: www.assitej-usa.org

9154 ■ Anne Shaw Fellowships (Graduate/ Fellowship)

Purpose: To support career development opportunities for theater artists and administrators committed to Theatre for Young Audiences. **Focus:** Theater arts. **Qualif.:** All active ASSITEJ/USA members are eligible to apply. **Criteria:** Priority is given to those applicants (at any stage of their TYA and theatre career) who state clear objectives for career developments and thoughtfully describe a process for active participation with another person, institution or organization.

Funds Avail.: $2,000. **To Apply:** Individuals may submit their proposal specifying a particular host or partner, or may request assistance matching their project proposal with a member of organization. Once an application has been given, the applicant should submit a one-page narrative, a budget, letters of support, and a professional resume. Applicants should articulate the purpose of the project and how it relates to their personal mission or the mission of the theater. **Deadline:** January 9. **Contact:** annshawfellowship@gmail.com.

9155 ■ Third Wave Fund

PO Box 1159
Brooklyn, NY 11238
Ph: (917)387-1262
E-mail: info@thirdwavefund.org

URL: thirdwavefund.org

9156 ■ Lela Breitbart Memorial Fund (Other/ Scholarship)

Purpose: To support organizations working on issues of reproductive justice around the country. **Focus:** Environmental law. **Qualif.:** Applicants must be women and transgender people between the ages of 15 and 30. **Criteria:** Recipients are selected based on financial need.

Funds Avail.: $3,000. **Duration:** Annual. **To Apply:** Applicants complete and submit the application form together with their resume. **Remarks:** Established in 1995.

9157 ■ Thunder Bay Community Foundation

101 N Syndicate Ave., Ste. 312
Thunder Bay, ON, Canada P7C 3VA
Ph: (807)475-7279
Fax: (807)684-0793
E-mail: admin.tbcf@tbaytel.net
URL: www.tbcf.org

9158 ■ Helen L. Dewar Scholarships (Undergraduate/ Scholarship)

Purpose: To provide scholarship assistance to qualified graduating students from Hammarskjold, Hillcrest and Superior Schools. **Focus:** General studies/Field of study not specified. **Qualif.:** Applicant must be from Hammerskfold High School, St. Ignatius High School and Superior Collegiate and Vocational Institute; must have a minimum overall average of 80% in grade 12 credits; must be seeking full-time admission to a Canadian university that is accredited by the Association of Universities and Colleges of Canada. **Criteria:** Applicant will be evaluated based on marks, community involvement, reference letter and the response to the essay question.

Funds Avail.: 2,500 Canadian Dollars. **Number Awarded:** 3. **To Apply:** Applicant must furnish four copies of application package containing: one reference from an adult in the community using criteria in the Reference Format section (stapled to the back of the application), one high school transcript with semester's mid-term marks, bullet point list of community volunteer activities and work experience, bullet point list of school related leadership and volunteer activities, and one 800-word essay in response to one questions included in the package, and must submit to the Thunder Bay Community Foundation. **Deadline:** April 20; April 27. **Remarks:** Established in 1991.

9159 ■ Joshua Dyke Family Scholarships (Undergraduate/Scholarship)

Purpose: To provide scholarship assistance to qualified graduating students from Churchill, St. Patrick and Westgate Schools. **Focus:** General studies/Field of study not specified. **Qualif.:** Applicants must be from Sir Winston Churchill C&VI, St. Patrick High School or Westgate C&VI; must be in their graduating year of secondary school; must have a minimum overall average of 80% in grade 12 credits; must be seeking full-time admission to a Canadian university that is accredited by the Association of Universities and Colleges of Canada. **Criteria:** Applicant will be evaluated based on marks, community involvement, reference letter and the response to the essay question.

Funds Avail.: 3,000 Canadian Dollars. **Number Awarded:** 2. **To Apply:** Applicant must furnish four copies of application package containing: one reference from an adult in the

Awards are arranged alphabetically below their administering organizations

community using criteria in the Reference Format section (stapled to the back of the application), one high school transcript with semester's mid-term marks, bullet point list of community volunteer activities and work experience, bullet point list of school related leadership and volunteer activities, and one 800-word essay in response to one questions included in the package, and must submit to the Thunder Bay Community Foundation. **Deadline:** April 20; April 27.

9160 ■ John Alexander McLean Scholarships
(Undergraduate/Scholarship)

Purpose: To provide scholarship assistance to qualified graduating students from the Bachelor of Education program at Lakehead University. **Focus:** Education. **Qualif.:** Applicant must be a student from Ecole secondaire catholique de La Verendrye, Geraldton Composite School, Hammarskjold High School, Lake Superior High School, Manitouwadge High School, Marathon High School, Nipigon Red Rock District High School, Sir Winston Churchill C&VI, St. Ignatius High School, St. Patrick High School, Superior C&VI and Westgate C&VI. Applicant must be in their final year before graduation from the Bachelor of Education program at Lakehead University; must be pursuing a career in education; must have a minimum overall average of 80% in all Grade 12 credits. **Criteria:** Applicant will be evaluated based on marks, community involvement, reference letter and the response to the essay question.

Funds Avail.: 2,500 Canadian Dollars. **Number Awarded:** 1. **To Apply:** Applicant must furnish four copies of application package containing: one reference from an adult in the community using criteria in the Reference Format section (stapled to the back of the application), one high school transcript with semester's mid-term marks, bullet point list of community volunteer activities and work experience, bullet point list of school related leadership and volunteer activities, and one 800-word essay in response to one questions included in the package, and must submit to the Thunder Bay Community Foundation. **Deadline:** April 20; April 27.

9161 ■ Roy Seymour Rogers and Geraldine Ruth Rogers Scholarships *(Undergraduate/Scholarship)*

Purpose: To provide scholarship assistance to qualified graduating students from Geraldton Composite, La Verendrye, Lake Superior, Manitouwadge, Marathon, and Nipigon-Red Rock District High School. **Focus:** General studies/Field of study not specified. **Qualif.:** Applicants must be from Geraldton Composite High School, Ecole secondaire catholique de la Verendrye, Lake Superior High School, Manitouwadge High School, Marathon High School or Nipigon-Red Rock District High School; must be in their graduating year of secondary school; must have a minimum overall average of 80% in Grade 12 credits; must be seeking full-time admission to a Canadian university that accredited by the Association of Universities and Colleges of Canada. **Criteria:** Applicant will be evaluated based on marks, community involvement, reference letter and the response to the essay question.

Funds Avail.: 3,000 Canadian Dollars. **To Apply:** Applicant must furnish four copies of application package containing: one reference from an adult in the community using criteria in the Reference Format section (stapled to the back of the application), one high school transcript with semester's mid-term marks, bullet point list of community volunteer activities and work experience, bullet point list of school related leadership and volunteer activities, and one 800-word essay in response to one questions included in the

package, and must submit to the Thunder Bay Community Foundation. **Deadline:** April 20; April 27.

9162 ■ Ross A. Wilson Science Scholarships
(Undergraduate/Scholarship)

Purpose: To provide scholarship assistance to qualified graduating students at Hammarskjold High School who excel in science. **Focus:** Science. **Qualif.:** Applicant must be: from Hammarskjold High School; pursuing a university degree and career in the sciences; in their graduating year of secondary school. Applicant must have a minimum overall average of 80% in Grade 12 credits; must be seeking full-time admission to a Canadian university that is accredited by the Association of Universities and Colleges of Canada. **Criteria:** Applicant will be evaluated based on marks, community involvement, reference letter and the response to the essay question.

Funds Avail.: 5,000 Canadian Dollars. **Number Awarded:** 4. **To Apply:** Applicant must furnish four copies of application package containing: one reference from an adult in the community using criteria in the Reference Format section (stapled to the back of the application), one high school transcript with semester's mid-term marks, bullet point list of community volunteer activities and work experience, bullet point list of school related leadership and volunteer activities, and one 800-word essay in response to one questions included in the package, and must submit to the Thunder Bay Community Foundation. **Deadline:** April 20; April 27.

9163 ■ Tidewater Builders Association (TBA)
2117 Smith Ave.
Chesapeake, VA 23320-2515
Ph: (757)420-2434
Fax: (757)424-5954
URL: www.tbaonline.org

9164 ■ Tidewater Builders Association Scholarships
(Undergraduate/Scholarship)

Purpose: To support deserving students in the Tidewater area who have a genuine need and want to further their education. **Focus:** General studies/Field of study not specified. **Qualif.:** Applicants must be local high school seniors residing in Chesapeake, Eastern Shore of Virginia, Franklin,Southampton County, Norfolk, Portsmouth, Suffolk or Virginia Beach; must be U.S. citizens; and must attend an accredited four-year undergraduate degree program as full-time students during the four-year period of continual and uninterrupted studies. **Criteria:** Recipients are selected based on financial need; academic standing; and community involvement.

Funds Avail.: $5,000. **Number Awarded:** 6. **To Apply:** Applicants must complete the application form; must attach an official transcript of high school records including SAT scores; evaluations and recommendations made by teachers, counselors and/or community service providers; page one of parents' or guardians' latest Federal Income Tax Return, W-2 forms or other financial statement; and written description explaining why the applicants deserve the scholarship. **Deadline:** March 18. **Remarks:** Established in 1965.

9165 ■ Tiftickjian Law Firm, P.C.
600 S Cherry St., No. 1105
Denver, CO 80246

Awards are arranged alphabetically below their administering organizations

Ph: (303)991-5896
Fax: (303)544-1919
URL: www.criminallawdenver.com

9166 ■ Tiftickjian Law Firm, P.C. Juvenile Justice Law School Scholarships *(Postgraduate/Scholarship)*

Purpose: To encourage and assist students with attending law school with an interest in juvenile justice, as well as raise awareness of the issue of prison sentences and reduced rights for minors that place youths on an institutionalized path towards spending a large part of their life in the criminal justice system. **Focus:** Criminal justice; Law; Youth. **Qualif.:** Applicants must be U.S. citizens or permanent residents; must be enrolled or accepted to an accredited law school within the United States; and must have a cumulative GPA of 3.50 or higher. **Criteria:** Selection will be based on the applicants' eligibility and compliance with the application process.

Funds Avail.: $1,000. **Number Awarded:** 1. **To Apply:** Applicants must be able to provide the following documents for consideration: proof of Legal Residency in the United States (i.e. birth certificate, passport, permanent resident card, etc.); a completed application; an official copy of a current academic transcript; and an essay of not more than three pages describing how they think juvenile justice could be improved to rehabilitate juveniles and keep them out of the criminal justice system. **Deadline:** July 31. **Contact:** Application materials should be emailed to publicrelations@ CriminalLawDenver.com.

9167 ■ Tikvah Center for Law and Jewish Civilization

NYU Institutes on the Park
22 Washington Sq. N
New York, NY 10011
Ph: (212)992-8910
E-mail: tikvah@nyu.edu
URL: www.nyutikvah.org

9168 ■ Berkowitz Fellowships *(Professional development/Fellowship)*

Purpose: To facilitate research and scholarship into areas that examine historical, cultural and political forces that helped shape the intellectual atmosphere in which the integration of varying traditions of law into an operative jurisprudential system was affected. **Focus:** Jewish studies; Law. **Qualif.:** Applicants must be senior scholars. **Criteria:** Selection will be based on the committee's criteria.

Funds Avail.: No specific amount. **Number Awarded:** 1. **To Apply:** Applicants must complete and submit the following materials: completed online application; full detailed curriculum vitae; personal statement; two letters of recommendation; research proposal with one page abstract which corresponds to the mission statement of The Tikvah Center, or the Annual Theme; one or two sample publications, including a recent publication in English, and accompanied by a list of all publications. **Deadline:** January 18.

9169 ■ Furman-Tikvah Scholarships *(Graduate/ Scholarship)*

Purpose: To promote the study of law and Jewish civilization. **Focus:** Jewish studies; Law. **Qualif.:** Applicants must be outstanding J.D. or J.S.D. graduates of American law schools who are actively pursuing an academic and teaching career and are interested in spending a year research-

ing, writing and learning in the company of some of the best scholars in the field. **Criteria:** Selection will be based on the committee's criteria.

Funds Avail.: No specific amount. **To Apply:** Applicants must submit the following materials: a curriculum vitae; transcripts from all educational institutions from which a degree was awarded; a research proposal for a writing project totaling maximum of 1,200 words and consistent with the mission of The Tikvah Center; writing samples; documents concerning additional funding from other sources; one-page summary of applicants' Bio and Research Proposal (maximum 300 words in total). Applicants must arrange for two reference letters submitted via the online application. Applicants must also indicate four out of the ten Tikvah Fellows who shall be in residence for the upcoming academic year with whom they would wish to work, based on similar areas of research and interest. **Deadline:** January 18.

9170 ■ J.D. Graduate Tikvah Scholarships *(Graduate/Scholarship)*

Purpose: To promote the study of law and Jewish civilization. **Focus:** Jewish studies; Law. **Qualif.:** Applicants must be recent J.D. graduates from NYU Law and other leading law schools who wish to go into teaching and seek to use their time at the Center to engage in intensive research and writing preparing their portfolio for the competitive law teaching market. **Criteria:** Selection will be based on the committee's criteria.

Funds Avail.: No specific amount. **To Apply:** Applicants must submit the following materials: a curriculum vitae; transcripts from all educational institutions from which a degree was awarded; a research proposal for a writing project totaling maximum of 1,200 words and consistent with the mission of The Tikvah Center; writing samples; documents concerning additional funding from other sources; one-page summary of applicants' Bio and Research Proposal (maximum 300 words in total). Applicants must arrange for two reference letters submitted via the online application. Applicants must also indicate four out of the ten Tikvah Fellows who shall be in residence for the upcoming academic year with whom they would wish to work, based on similar areas of research and interest. **Deadline:** January 18.

9171 ■ J.D. or LL.M. Tikvah Scholarships *(Graduate/ Scholarship)*

Purpose: To promote the study of law and Jewish civilization. **Focus:** Jewish studies; Law. **Qualif.:** Applicants must be NYU School of Law J.D. or LL.M. **Criteria:** Selection will be based on the committee's criteria.

Funds Avail.: No specific amount. **To Apply:** Applicants must submit the following materials: a curriculum vitae; transcripts from all educational institutions from which a degree was awarded; a research proposal for a writing project totaling maximum of 1,200 words and consistent with the mission of The Tikvah Center; writing samples; documents concerning additional funding from other sources; one-page summary of applicants' Bio and Research Proposal (maximum 300 words in total). Applicants must arrange for two reference letters submitted via the online application. Applicants must also indicate four out of the ten Tikvah Fellows who shall be in residence for the upcoming academic year with whom they would wish to work, based on similar areas of research and interest. **Deadline:** January 18.

Awards are arranged alphabetically below their administering organizations

9172 ■ Post-Doctoral Tikvah Scholarships
(Postdoctorate/Scholarship)

Purpose: To promote the study of law and Jewish civilization. **Focus:** Jewish studies; Law. **Qualif.:** Applicants must be individuals who have already completed their doctoral degree. **Criteria:** Selection will be based on need.

Funds Avail.: No specific amount. **To Apply:** Applicants must submit the following materials: a curriculum vitae; transcripts from all educational institutions from which a degree was awarded; a research proposal for a writing project totaling maximum of 1,200 words and consistent with the mission of The Tikvah Center; writing samples; documents concerning additional funding from other sources; one-page summary of applicants' Bio and Research Proposal (maximum 300 words in total). Applicants must arrange for two reference letters submitted via the online application. Applicants must also indicate four out of the ten Tikvah Fellows who shall be in residence for the upcoming academic year with whom they would wish to work, based on similar areas of research and interest.

9173 ■ Visiting Doctoral Tikvah Scholarships
(Doctorate/Scholarship)

Purpose: To promote the study of law and Jewish civilization. **Focus:** Jewish studies; Law. **Qualif.:** Applicants must be individuals currently pursuing a doctoral degree at NYU Law, NYU Skirball or other institutions. **Criteria:** Selection will be based on the committee's criteria.

Funds Avail.: No specific amount. **To Apply:** Applicants must submit the following materials: a curriculum vitae; transcripts from all educational institutions from which a degree was awarded; a research proposal for a writing project totaling maximum of 1,200 words and consistent with the mission of The Tikvah Center; writing samples; documents concerning additional funding from other sources; one-page summary of applicants' Bio and Research Proposal (maximum 300 words in total). Applicants must arrange for two reference letters submitted via the online application. Applicants must also indicate four out of the ten Tikvah Fellows who shall be in residence for the upcoming academic year with whom they would wish to work, based on similar areas of research and interest.

9174 ■ Tikvah Fund
745 Fifth Ave., Ste. 1400
New York, NY 10151
Ph: (212)796-1672
Fax: (646)794-0172
E-mail: info@tikvahfund.org
URL: tikvahfund.org

9175 ■ Tikvah Fellowships *(Graduate, Professional development/Fellowship)*

Purpose: To promote serious Jewish thought about the enduring questions of human life and the pressing challenges that confront the Jewish people. **Focus:** Jewish studies. **Qualif.:** Fellowship is open to anyone with at least a completed undergraduate degree, whether from US, Israeli or international colleges and universities. **Criteria:** Selection will be based on the committee's criteria.

Funds Avail.: $25,000 - $75,000. **Number Awarded:** 18 in 2014. **To Apply:** Applicants must complete the online registration form consisting of their basic personal and academic information. Applicants will be asked to upload a Word or PDF file that includes the following: a curriculum

vitae or resume; a personal statement, including the reasons why you would like to participate in the fellowships; a 500-word statement on a book, course, teacher or event that prompted the applicants to change their mind about a major issue, with an explanation of why; two recommendation letters. Applicants must include their name at the top of each page of the application and page numbers at the bottom of each page of the application. **Deadline:** January 31. **Contact:** fellowship@tikvahfund.org.

9176 ■ Robert Toigo Foundation (RTF)
180 Grand Ave., Ste. 450
Oakland, CA 94612
Ph: (510)763-5771
Fax: (510)763-5778
E-mail: info@toigofoundation.org
URL: www.toigofoundation.org

9177 ■ Robert Toigo Foundation Fellowships
(Master's/Fellowship)

Purpose: To support students committed to a career in finance. **Focus:** Finance. **Qualif.:** Applicant must be a U.S. citizen or a permanent resident; a minority, as defined by the U.S. Department of Labor (African American, Asian American/Pacific Islander, U.S. Latino, Native American/ Alaska Native and/or South Asian American); planning a career in financial services after graduation including, but not limited to: Investment Management, Investment Banking, Corporate Finance (non-Investment Banking), Real Estate, Private Equity, Venture Capital, Sales & Trading, Research or Financial Services Consulting; and entering an accredited U.S.-based MBA program. **Criteria:** Selection is based on leadership potential, academic excellence and demonstrated commitment to social change and community responsibility.

Funds Avail.: No specific amount. **Duration:** Annual. **To Apply:** Applicants must complete the application form online. **Deadline:** March 15.

9178 ■ Toronto and Region Conservation Authority (TRCA)
5 Shoreham Dr.
Downsview, ON, Canada M3N 1S4
Ph: (416)661-6600
Fax: (416)661-6898
Free: 888-872-2344
E-mail: info@trca.on.ca
URL: www.trca.on.ca

9179 ■ B. Harper Bull Conservation Fellowships
(Graduate/Fellowship)

Purpose: To further the science of natural heritage management within the boundaries of Toronto and Region Conservation's (TRCA) jurisdiction. **Focus:** Ecology; Fisheries sciences/management; Forestry; Hydrology; Water resources; Wildlife conservation, management, and science. **Qualif.:** Applicant must be working towards a post graduate degree. **Criteria:** Selection is based on submitted application materials.

Funds Avail.: $1,500. **Duration:** Annual. **Number Awarded:** 1. **To Apply:** Applicants must submit an application form available from the Conservation Foundation of Greater Toronto. Submit completed application form along with two letters of reference (each in a sealed envelope). In

Awards are arranged alphabetically below their administering organizations

addition, a verification of enrollment and status must be submitted by the registrar's office directly to the Foundation under separate cover. Successful applicants will be required to submit an abstract from the thesis outlined in the application. **Deadline:** March 31. **Contact:** The Conservation Foundation of Greater Toronto at 416-667-6279, 416-667-6275 (fax) or fdn@trca.on.ca.

9180 ■ Toronto Rehabilitation Institute

550 University Ave., 3rd Fl.
Toronto, ON, Canada M5G 2A2
Ph: (416)597-3040
Fax: (416)597-6201
E-mail: trf@uhn.ca
URL: torontorehabfoundation.com/Contact-Us/
Overview.aspx

9181 ■ Annie Kirshenblatt Memorial Scholarships
(Graduate, Undergraduate/Scholarship)

Purpose: To provide encouragement, recognition and assistance to aspiring persons who are studying in the field of Gerontology. **Focus:** Gerontology. **Qualif.:** Applicant must be a Canadian citizen or landed immigrant; has plan to work in Canada and be enrolled in a course or is conducting a research project within a program that is related to the field of Gerontology that will lead to a certificate, diploma or degree. **Criteria:** Selection is based on submitted application materials.

Funds Avail.: $2,000. **Duration:** Annual. **To Apply:** Applicants must submit a completed application form and references to The Kirshenblatt Memorial Scholarships, Toronto Rehabilitation Institute.

9182 ■ Shoshana Philipp (Kirshenblatt) R.N. Memorial Scholarships *(Graduate, Undergraduate/Scholarship)*

Purpose: To provide encouragement, recognition and assistance to aspiring persons who are studying in the field of Gerontology. **Focus:** Gerontology; Nursing. **Qualif.:** Applicant must be a Canadian citizen or landed immigrant; has plan to work in Canada and be enrolled in a course or is conducting a research project within a program that is related to the field of Gerontology that will lead to a certificate, diploma or degree. **Criteria:** Selection is based on submitted application materials.

Funds Avail.: $2,000. **Duration:** Annual. **To Apply:** Applicants must submit a completed application form and references to The Kirshenblatt Memorial Scholarships, Toronto Rehabilitation Institute. **Deadline:** March 31.

9183 ■ Toronto Rehab Scholarships in Rehabilitation-Related Research *(Graduate/Scholarship)*

Purpose: To further the active involvement of people with disabilities in rehabilitation-related research. **Focus:** Medical research. **Qualif.:** Applicants must have a disability; planning to enroll in a rehabilitation-related graduate program leading to a masters or doctoral degree at an eligible university (McMaster University, Ryerson University, University of Toronto, University of Waterloo, Wilfrid Laurier University, York University); be supervised by an investigator at Toronto Rehab appointed to the School of Graduate Studies at one of the eligible universities; and must be in good standing with an ambition to pursue a career in rehabilitation-related research. Scholarship is also open to

international students admitted to one of the eligible universities. **Criteria:** Selection is based on applicant's research and academic achievements, letters of recommendation, quality of the proposed research and evidence of ambition to pursue a career in rehabilitation-related research.

Funds Avail.: $20,000. **Duration:** Annual. **Number Awarded:** Varies. **To Apply:** Applicants must submit a completed application form along with their transcripts. **Deadline:** February 11. **Contact:** Lois Ward at 416-597-3422 x-7600 or lois.ward@uhn.ca.

9184 ■ Toronto Rehabilitation Institute Graduate Student Scholarships - Ontario Student Opportunities Trust Fund (OSOTF) *(Graduate/Scholarship)*

Purpose: To provide financial support for doctoral stream (MSc/PhD) thesis degree program students at University of Toronto. **Focus:** Engineering; Health services administration. **Qualif.:** Applicants must be graduate students enrolled at the University of Toronto; must have a financial need; and must be in a research training either at Toronto Rehab or another suitable institution. **Criteria:** Selection will be based on the submitted application materials.

Funds Avail.: No specific amount. **To Apply:** Applicants must submit a completed application form and required materials to Office of the Vice Dean, Graduate Affairs, Faculty of Medicine, University of Toronto. **Deadline:** May 1. **Contact:** Lois Ward at 416-597-3422 x-7600 or lois.ward@uhn.ca; Debbie Chau at 416-946-7317 or debbie.chau@utoronto.ca.

9185 ■ Tortuga Backpacks

340 S, Lemon Ave., No. 7616
Walnut, CA 91789
Ph: (310)692-4680
E-mail: contact@tortugabackpacks.com
URL: www.tortugabackpacks.com

9186 ■ Tortuga Backpacks Study Abroad Scholarships *(Undergraduate/Scholarship)*

Purpose: To help students explore and learn from other cultures. **Focus:** Education. **Qualif.:** Applicants must be U.S. citizens or students with visa holder; must be full-time undergraduate student in good academic standing at a four-year, degree-granting college or university in the United States; and must have applied to or been accepted into a study abroad program eligible for credit by the applicants' college or university. **Criteria:** Selection will be based on the committee's criteria.

Funds Avail.: $1,000. **Duration:** Semiannual. **Number Awarded:** 1. **To Apply:** Applicants must submit an application together with their 500-word essay. **Deadline:** December 19.

9187 ■ Tourette Syndrome Association (TSA)

42-40 Bell Blvd.
Bayside, NY 11361
Ph: (718)224-2999
Fax: (718)279-9596
URL: www.tsa-usa.org

9188 ■ Tourette Association of America Research Grant Awards *(Master's, Doctorate/Grant)*

Purpose: To promote, enhance, and support the research regarding Tourette Syndrome. **Focus:** Tourette syndrome.

Awards are arranged alphabetically below their administering organizations

Qualif.: Candidates must have a M.D., Ph.D., or equivalent. Previous experience in the field of movement disorders is desirable, but not essential. Applicants may reside outside the United States. **Criteria:** Applications are evaluated based on: candidate's qualifications and objectives; experience relevant to the project; methodology; significance/relevance to the TS field; percentage of time to be devoted to project; adequacy and availability of research facilities and other project support; and ability to complete project in stated time-frame.

Funds Avail.: Up to $75,000 for one year or up to $150,000 for two years. **Duration:** Annual. **To Apply:** For preliminary screening, a pre-proposal briefly describing the scientific basis and relevance of the proposed project is required. Pre-proposal application forms can be downloaded from the website. **Deadline:** September 12 (pre-proposal); November 14 (full proposal). **Remarks:** Established in 1984. **Contact:** For additional information: http://tourette.org/research.html.

9189 ■ Tourism Industry Association of Canada (TIAC)
116 Lisgar St., Ste. 600
Ottawa, ON, Canada K2P 0C2
Ph: (613)238-3883
E-mail: info@tiac.travel
URL: tiac.travel

9190 ■ TIAC / Parks Canada Sustainable Tourism Scholarships *(Undergraduate, Master's/Scholarship)*

Purpose: To improve and enhance the quality and sustainability of natural and cultural heritage-based tourism experiences. **Focus:** Travel and tourism. **Qualif.:** Applicants must be Canadian students in a university program in hospitality or tourism field; must be enrolled in or entering the 3rd or 4th year of an undergraduate university program, final year of a college diploma program, or a Master's level graduate program. **Criteria:** Recipients will be chosen based on academic achievement and submitted materials.

Funds Avail.: No specific amount. **To Apply:** Applicants must submit a completed application form; must provide a one-page covering letter, curriculum vitae and one letter of reference from a member of the student's academic faculty, department, or an employer. Applications should be submitted either in English or French.

9191 ■ Touro Synagogue Foundation (TSF)
85 Touro St.
Newport, RI 02840
Ph: (401)847-4794
URL: www.tourosynagogue.org

9192 ■ The Aaron and Rita Slom Scholarships *(Undergraduate/Scholarship)*

Purpose: To educate future generations. **Focus:** Historic preservation. **Qualif.:** Applicants must be high school graduating students. **Criteria:** The scholarships are for high school seniors who plan to enroll in an institute of higher learning for a minimum of six credits. The institution can be public or private, and has no geographic limitations.

Funds Avail.: $500. **Number Awarded:** 2. **To Apply:** Students must submit an interpretative work (i.e. written submission, audio visual, documentary, film, PowerPoint) focusing on the George Washington letter in context with the present time. Written submissions such as essays, stories, poems (no less than 500 words and no more than 1000 words), or audio-visual submissions such as documentaries, films or computer presentations (no more than 10 minutes) will be considered. **Deadline:** April 22. **Contact:** Touro Synagogue Foundation at the above address.

9193 ■ Toyota Earth Day Scholarship Program
111 Peter St., Ste. 503
Toronto, ON, Canada M5V 2H1
E-mail: scholarship@earthday.ca
URL: www.earthday.ca/scholarship

9194 ■ Toyota Earth Day Scholarships *(Undergraduate/Scholarship)*

Purpose: To acknowledge and financially assist graduating Canadian high school students who have achieved academic excellence and distinguished themselves in environmental community service. **Focus:** General studies/Field of study not specified. **Qualif.:** Applicant must be graduating or graduated within the last two years from a Canadian high school or Quebec CEGEP; entering the first year of full-time studies at an accredited Canadian college/university or a Quebec accredited collegial institution; a Canadian citizen or permanent resident (landed immigrant); has demonstrated outstanding environmental commitment, community service and leadership during the course of studies; maintained a high level of academic achievement; and not an employee or an immediate family member of an employee of Toyota Canada Inc. and its Dealers, Earth Day Canada or Panasonic Canada Inc. **Criteria:** Selection is based on demonstrated commitment and service to community environmental issues, academic achievement, record of participation in volunteer and extracurricular activities at school and in the community, demonstrated capacity for leadership, letters of recommendation, evaluation of essay and self-assessment and candidate's outstanding potential as an environmental leader.

Funds Avail.: $5,000 each. **Duration:** Annual. **Number Awarded:** 20. **To Apply:** Applicants must submit a completed, typed application form along with the letters of reference and high school academic transcripts to the Toyota Earth Day Scholarship Program. **Deadline:** February 15. **Contact:** For further information, applicants may send an email at scholarship@earthday.ca.

9195 ■ Transport Workers Union of America (TWU)
501 3rd St. NW, 9th Fl.
Washington, DC 20001
Ph: (202)719-3900
Fax: (202)347-0454
URL: www.twu.org

9196 ■ Michael J. Quill Scholarships *(Undergraduate/Scholarship)*

Purpose: To provide professional legal, education, research and public relations services to the local and divisions. **Focus:** General studies/Field of study not specified. **Qualif.:** Applicants must be senior high school students of son, daughter, dependent brothers and sisters of present, retired, or deceased TWU members who will enter an accredited college of their own choice. **Criteria:** Recipients are selected based on applicant's capability to do the college work under the High School Principal certification.

Awards are arranged alphabetically below their administering organizations

Funds Avail.: $4,800 ($1,200 each). **Duration:** Annual; every May. **Number Awarded:** 15. **To Apply:** Applicants must fill out the coupon on the back page of the January, February or March TWU Express. **Deadline:** April 17. **Remarks:** Established in 1969. **Contact:** Michael J. Quill Scholarship Fund at the above address.

9197 ■ Transportation Association of Canada (TAC)

2323 St. Laurent Blvd.
Ottawa, ON, Canada K1G 4J8
Ph: (613)736-1350
Fax: (613)736-1395
E-mail: secretariat@tac-atc.ca
URL: www.tac-atc.ca

9198 ■ TAC Foundation-3M Canada Company Scholarships *(Graduate, Undergraduate/Scholarship)*

Purpose: To provide support and encouragement to those interested in pursuing a career in transportation planning or transportation engineering. **Focus:** Transportation. **Qualif.:** Applicants must be Canadian citizens or landed immigrants; and must be enrolled for the entire academic year. **Criteria:** Preference will be given to candidates with relevant work experience.

Funds Avail.: 4,500 Canadian Dollars. **To Apply:** Applicants must complete the application form available online; must provide academic references and relevant employment information; must have an electronic version of their transcript of records. Application form and requirements must be sent to the TAC Foundation. **Deadline:** March 2. **Contact:** Foundation's Executive Director at foundation@tac-atc.ca.

9199 ■ TAC Foundation-407 ETR Scholarships *(Undergraduate, Graduate/Scholarship)*

Purpose: To support transportation education in Canada, such as promoting careers in transportation to skilled students, and assisting transportation educators and researchers. **Focus:** Transportation. **Qualif.:** Applicants must be undergraduate or graduate students with transportation engineering disciplines as field of their studies. For community college students, they must be enrolled in full-time studies, entering their final year of a certified community college program and intend to pursue a career in the transportation field, as it relates to the Foundation's primary focus. For University undergraduates, they must be enrolled in at least two semesters of full-time studies. For Graduate students, they must be admissible to a full-time transportation-related graduate studies program or already registered as a full-time graduate student in the field. All applicants must be Canadian citizens or permanent residents and have achieved an overall B average or equivalent in their previous academic year. **Criteria:** TAC Foundation Scholarship Committee evaluates and scores all qualifying applications. Preference may be given to candidates with relevant work experience.

Funds Avail.: $5,000. **To Apply:** Applicants must submit the following documents together with the application form: official copy of the current academic transcript with official letterhead in an unalterable format; maximum two-page resume summarizing the education, employment experi-

ence, achievements and interests; and academic reference form. **Deadline:** March 2.

9200 ■ TAC Foundation-Amec Foster Wheeler Scholarships *(Undergraduate, Graduate/Scholarship)*

Purpose: To support transportation education in Canada, such as promoting careers in transportation to skilled students, and assisting transportation educators and researchers. **Focus:** Transportation. **Qualif.:** Applicants must be undergraduate or graduate students with transportation-related disciplines as field of their studies. For community college students, they must be enrolled in full-time studies, entering their final year of a certified community college program and intend to pursue a career in the transportation field, as it relates to the Foundation's primary focus. For University undergraduates, they must be enrolled in at least two semesters of full-time studies. For Graduate students, they must be admissible to a full-time transportation-related graduate studies program or already registered as a full-time graduate student in the field. All applicants must be Canadian citizens or permanent residents and have achieved an overall B average or equivalent in their previous academic year. **Criteria:** TAC Foundation Scholarship Committee evaluates and scores all qualifying applications. Preference may be given to candidates with relevant work experience.

Funds Avail.: $5,000. **To Apply:** Applicants must submit the following documents together with the application form: official copy of the current academic transcript with official letterhead in an unalterable format; maximum two-page resume summarizing the education, employment experience, achievements and interests; and academic reference form. **Deadline:** March 2.

9201 ■ TAC Foundation-ATS Traffic Group of Companies Scholarships *(Undergraduate, Graduate/Scholarship)*

Purpose: To support transportation education in Canada, such as promoting careers in transportation to skilled students, and assisting transportation educators and researchers. **Focus:** Transportation. **Qualif.:** Applicants must be undergraduate or graduate students with traffic engineering and planning (specializing in Intelligent Transportation System) as field of their studies. For community college students, they must be enrolled in full-time studies, entering their final year of a certified community college program and intend to pursue a career in the transportation field, as it relates to the Foundation's primary focus. For University undergraduates, they must be enrolled in at least two semesters of full-time studies. For Graduate students, they must be admissible to a full-time transportation-related graduate studies program or already registered as a full-time graduate student in the field. All applicants must be Canadian citizens or permanent residents and have achieved an overall B average or equivalent in their previous academic year. **Criteria:** TAC Foundation Scholarship Committee evaluates and scores all qualifying applications. Preference may be given to candidates with relevant work experience.

Funds Avail.: $5,000. **To Apply:** Applicants must submit the following documents together with the application form: official copy of the current academic transcript with official letterhead in an unalterable format; maximum two-page resume summarizing the education, employment experience, achievements and interests; and academic reference form. **Deadline:** March 2.

Awards are arranged alphabetically below their administering organizations

9202 ■ TAC Foundation-Canadian Council of Independent Laboratories Graduate Student Scholarships *(Graduate/Scholarship)*

Purpose: To support transportation education in Canada, such as promoting careers in transportation to skilled students, and assisting transportation educators and researchers. **Focus:** Transportation. **Qualif.:** Applicants must be graduate students with materials engineering, concrete or asphalt technology, as field of their studies; must be admissible to a full-time transportation-related graduate studies program or already registered as a full-time graduate student in the field; must be Canadian citizens or permanent residents; and have achieved an overall B average or equivalent in their previous academic year. **Criteria:** TAC Foundation Scholarship Committee evaluates and scores all qualifying applications. Preference may be given to candidates with relevant work experience.

Funds Avail.: $5,000. **To Apply:** Applicants must submit the following documents together with the application form: an official copy of the applicants' most current academic transcript provided on official letterhead in an unalterable format; a maximum two-page resume summarizing the applicant's education, relevant employment experience, achievements and interests; and academic reference form. **Deadline:** March 2.

9203 ■ TAC Foundation-CCMTA Road Safety Scholarships *(Undergraduate, Graduate/Scholarship)*

Purpose: To support transportation education in Canada, such as promoting careers in transportation to skilled students, and assisting transportation educators and researchers. **Focus:** Transportation. **Qualif.:** Applicants must be undergraduate or graduate students with road safety disciplines as field of their studies. For community college students, they must be enrolled in full-time studies, entering their final year of a certified community college program and intend to pursue a career in the transportation field, as it relates to the Foundation's primary focus. For University undergraduates, they must be enrolled in at least two semesters of full-time studies. For Graduate students, they must be admissible to a full-time transportation-related graduate studies program or already registered as a full-time graduate student in the field. All applicants must be Canadian citizens or permanent residents and have achieved an overall B average or equivalent in their previous academic year. **Criteria:** TAC Foundation Scholarship Committee evaluates and scores all qualifying applications. Preference may be given to candidates with relevant work experience.

Funds Avail.: $5,000. **To Apply:** Applicants must submit the following documents together with the application form: official copy of the current academic transcript with official letterhead in an unalterable format; maximum two-page resume summarizing the education, employment experience, achievements and interests; and academic reference form. **Deadline:** March 2.

9204 ■ TAC Foundation-Cement Association of Canada Scholarships *(Graduate, Undergraduate/Scholarship)*

Purpose: To provide support and encouragement to those interested in pursuing a career in transportation planning or transportation engineering. **Focus:** Transportation. **Qualif.:** Applicants must be Canadian citizens or landed immigrants; and must be enrolled for the entire academic year. **Criteria:** Preference will be given to candidates with relevant work experience.

Funds Avail.: 5,000 Canadian Dollars. **To Apply:** Applicants must complete the application form available online; must provide academic references and relevant employment information; must have an electronic version of their transcript of records. Application form and requirements must be sent to the TAC Foundation. **Deadline:** March 2. **Contact:** Foundation's Executive Director at foundation@tac-atc.ca.

9205 ■ TAC Foundation-Dillon Consulting Scholarships *(Undergraduate, Graduate/Scholarship)*

Purpose: To provide support and encouragement to those interested in pursuing a career in transportation planning or transportation engineering. **Focus:** Transportation. **Qualif.:** Applicant must be entering third or fourth year studies; must intend to pursue a career in some aspect of the transportation field and meet the conditions of the scholarships; must have achieved an overall B level or equivalent average mark in their previous academic year. **Criteria:** Preference will be given to candidates with relevant work experience.

Funds Avail.: 5,000 Canadian Dollars. **To Apply:** Applicant must complete the application form (available online); must provide academic references and relevant employment information; must have an electronic version of his/her transcript of records. Application form and requirements must be sent to the TAC Foundation. **Deadline:** March 2. **Contact:** Foundation's Executive Director at foundation@tac-atc.ca.

9206 ■ TAC Foundation-Dr. Ralph Haas Graduate Student Scholarships *(Graduate/Scholarship)*

Purpose: To support transportation education in Canada, such as promoting careers in transportation to skilled students, and assisting transportation educators and researchers. **Focus:** Transportation. **Qualif.:** Applicants must be graduate students with transportation-related disciplines as field of their studies; must be admissible to a full-time transportation-related graduate studies program or already registered as a full-time graduate student in the field; must be Canadian citizens or permanent residents; and have achieved an overall B average or equivalent in their previous academic year. **Criteria:** TAC Foundation Scholarship Committee evaluates and scores all qualifying applications. Preference may be given to candidates with relevant work experience.

Funds Avail.: $5,000. **To Apply:** Applicants must submit the following documents together with the application form: an official copy of the applicants' most current academic transcript provided on official letterhead in an unalterable format; a maximum two-page resume summarizing the applicant's education, relevant employment experience, achievements and interests; and academic reference form. **Deadline:** March 2.

9207 ■ TAC Foundation-EllisDon Community College/CEGEP Scholarships *(Undergraduate/Scholarship)*

Purpose: To support transportation education in Canada, such as promoting careers in transportation to skilled students, and assisting transportation educators and researchers. **Focus:** Transportation. **Qualif.:** Applicants must be college students enrolled in full-time studies, entering their final year of a certified community college program and intend to pursue a career in the transportation field, as it relates to the Foundation's primary focus; must be Canadian citizens or permanent residents; and have

Awards are arranged alphabetically below their administering organizations

achieved an overall B average or equivalent in their previous academic year. **Criteria:** TAC Foundation Scholarship Committee evaluates and scores all qualifying applications. Preference may be given to candidates with relevant work experience.

Funds Avail.: $2,500. **To Apply:** Applicants must submit the following documents together with the application form: an official copy of the applicants' most current academic transcript provided on official letterhead in an unalterable format; a maximum two-page resume summarizing the applicant's education, relevant employment experience, achievements and interests; and academic reference form. **Deadline:** March 2.

9208 ■ TAC Foundation-exp Scholarships
(Undergraduate, Graduate/Scholarship)

Purpose: To support transportation education in Canada, such as promoting careers in transportation to skilled students, and assisting transportation educators and researchers. **Focus:** Transportation. **Qualif.:** Applicants must be undergraduate or graduate students with transportation planning and engineering disciplines as field of their studies. For community college students, they must be enrolled in full-time studies, entering their final year of a certified community college program and intend to pursue a career in the transportation field, as it relates to the Foundation's primary focus. For University undergraduates, they must be enrolled in at least two semesters of full-time studies. For Graduate students, they must be admissible to a full-time transportation-related graduate studies program or already registered as a full-time graduate student in the field. All applicants must be Canadian citizens or permanent residents and have achieved an overall B average or equivalent in their previous academic year. **Criteria:** TAC Foundation Scholarship Committee evaluates and scores all qualifying applications. Preference may be given to candidates with relevant work experience.

Funds Avail.: $5,000. **To Apply:** Applicants must submit the following documents together with the application form: official copy of the current academic transcript with official letterhead in an unalterable format; maximum two-page resume summarizing the education, employment experience, achievements and interests; and academic reference form. **Deadline:** March 2.

9209 ■ TAC Foundation-Golder Associates Ltd. Scholarships *(Undergraduate, Graduate/Scholarship)*

Purpose: To support transportation education in Canada, such as promoting careers in transportation to skilled students, and assisting transportation educators and researchers. **Focus:** Transportation. **Qualif.:** Applicants must be undergraduate or graduate students with transportation related disciplines as field of their studies preferably in the ground engineering or environmental sciences area. For community college students, they must be enrolled in full-time studies, entering their final year of a certified community college program and intend to pursue a career in the transportation field, as it relates to the Foundation's primary focus. For University undergraduates, they must be enrolled in at least two semesters of full-time studies. For Graduate students, they must be admissible to a full-time transportation-related graduate studies program or already registered as a full-time graduate student in the field. All applicants must be Canadian citizens or permanent residents and have achieved an overall B average or equivalent in their previous academic year. **Criteria:** TAC Foundation Scholarship Committee evaluates and scores all qualifying applications. Preference may be given to

candidates with relevant work experience.

Funds Avail.: $5,000. **To Apply:** Applicants must submit the following documents together with the application form: official copy of the current academic transcript with official letterhead in an unalterable format; maximum two-page resume summarizing the education, employment experience, achievements and interests; and academic reference form. **Deadline:** March 2.

9210 ■ TAC Foundation-HDR Corporation Graduate Student Scholarships *(Graduate/Scholarship)*

Purpose: To support transportation education in Canada, such as promoting careers in transportation to skilled students, and assisting transportation educators and researchers. **Focus:** Transportation. **Qualif.:** Applicants must be graduate students with transportation-related disciplines as field of their studies; must be admissible to a full-time transportation-related graduate studies program or already registered as a full-time graduate student in the field; must be Canadian citizens or permanent residents; and have achieved an overall B average or equivalent in their previous academic year. **Criteria:** TAC Foundation Scholarship Committee evaluates and scores all qualifying applications. Preference may be given to candidates with relevant work experience.

Funds Avail.: $5,000. **To Apply:** Applicants must submit the following documents together with the application form: an official copy of the applicants' most current academic transcript provided on official letterhead in an unalterable format; a maximum two-page resume summarizing the applicant's education, relevant employment experience, achievements and interests; and academic reference form. **Deadline:** March 2.

9211 ■ TAC Foundation-IBI Group Scholarships *(Undergraduate, Graduate/Scholarship)*

Purpose: To provide scholarship to students who are pursuing a degree in transportation. **Focus:** Transportation. **Qualif.:** Applicants must be Canadian citizens or landed immigrants; and must be enrolled for the entire academic year. **Criteria:** Preference will be given to candidates with relevant work experience.

Funds Avail.: 4,500 Canadian Dollars. **To Apply:** Applicants must complete the application form (available online); must provide academic references and relevant employment information; must have an electronic version of their transcript of records. Application form and requirements must be sent to the TAC Foundation. **Deadline:** March 2.

9212 ■ TAC Foundation-ISL Engineering Scholarships *(Undergraduate, Graduate/Scholarship)*

Purpose: To support transportation education in Canada, such as promoting careers in transportation to skilled students, and assisting transportation educators and researchers. **Focus:** Transportation. **Qualif.:** Applicants must be undergraduate or graduate students with transportation engineering as field of their studies. For community college students, they must be enrolled in full-time studies, entering their final year of a certified community college program and intend to pursue a career in the transportation field, as it relates to the Foundation's primary focus. For University undergraduates, they must be enrolled in at least two semesters of full-time studies. For Graduate students, they must be admissible to a full-time transportation-related graduate studies program or already registered as a full-time graduate student in the field. All applicants must be

Awards are arranged alphabetically below their administering organizations

Canadian citizens or permanent residents and have achieved an overall B average or equivalent in their previous academic year. **Criteria:** TAC Foundation Scholarship Committee evaluates and scores all qualifying applications. Preference may be given to candidates with relevant work experience.

Funds Avail.: $5,000. **To Apply:** Applicants must submit the following documents together with the application form: official copy of the current academic transcript with official letterhead in an unalterable format; maximum two-page resume summarizing the education, employment experience, achievements and interests; and academic reference form. **Deadline:** March 2. **Remarks:** In recognition of Gary W. Mack.

9213 ■ TAC Foundation-LEA Consulting Ltd. Scholarships *(Undergraduate, Graduate/Scholarship)*

Purpose: To support transportation education in Canada, such as promoting careers in transportation to skilled students, and assisting transportation educators and researchers. **Focus:** Transportation. **Qualif.:** Applicants must be undergraduate or graduate students with transportation-related disciplines as field of their studies. For community college students, they must be enrolled in full-time studies, entering their final year of a certified community college program and intend to pursue a career in the transportation field, as it relates to the Foundation's primary focus. For University undergraduates, they must be enrolled in at least two semesters of full-time studies. For Graduate students, they must be admissible to a full-time transportation-related graduate studies program or already registered as a full-time graduate student in the field. All applicants must be Canadian citizens or permanent residents and have achieved an overall B average or equivalent in their previous academic year. **Criteria:** TAC Foundation Scholarship Committee evaluates and scores all qualifying applications. Preference may be given to candidates with relevant work experience.

Funds Avail.: $5,000. **To Apply:** Applicants must submit the following documents together with the application form: official copy of the current academic transcript with official letterhead in an unalterable format; maximum two-page resume summarizing the education, employment experience, achievements and interests; and academic reference form. **Deadline:** March 2.

9214 ■ TAC Foundation-MMM Group Limited Scholarships *(Undergraduate, Graduate/Scholarship)*

Purpose: To provide scholarship to students who are pursuing a degree in transportation. **Focus:** Transportation. **Qualif.:** Applicants must be Canadian citizens or landed immigrants; and must be enrolled for the entire academic year. **Criteria:** Preference will be given to a student who intends to pursue a career in the private sector.

Funds Avail.: 5,000 Canadian Dollars. **To Apply:** Applicants must complete the application form (available online); must provide academic references and relevant employment information; must have an electronic version of their transcript of records. Application form and requirements must be sent to the TAC Foundation. **Deadline:** March 2. **Contact:** Foundation's Executive Director at foundation@tac-atc.ca.

9215 ■ TAC Foundation-Municipalities Scholarships *(Undergraduate, Graduate/Scholarship)*

Purpose: To provide scholarship to students who are pursuing a degree in transportation. **Focus:** Transportation.

Qualif.: Applicants must be Canadian citizens or landed immigrants; and must be enrolled for the entire academic year. **Criteria:** Preference will be given to candidates with relevant work experience.

Funds Avail.: 3,000 Canadian Dollars. **To Apply:** Applicants must complete the application form (available online); must provide academic references and relevant employment information; must have an electronic version of their transcript of records. Application form and requirements must be sent to the TAC Foundation. **Deadline:** March 2. **Contact:** Foundation's Executive Director at foundation@tac-atc.ca.

9216 ■ TAC Foundation-Parsons Scholarships *(Undergraduate, Graduate/Scholarship)*

Purpose: To support transportation education in Canada, such as promoting careers in transportation to skilled students, and assisting transportation educators and researchers. **Focus:** Transportation. **Qualif.:** Applicants must be undergraduate or graduate students with transportation-related disciplines as field of their studies. For community college students, they must be enrolled in full-time studies, entering their final year of a certified community college program and intend to pursue a career in the transportation field, as it relates to the Foundation's primary focus. For University undergraduates, they must be enrolled in at least two semesters of full-time studies. For Graduate students, they must be admissible to a full-time transportation-related graduate studies program or already registered as a full-time graduate student in the field. All applicants must be Canadian citizens or permanent residents and have achieved an overall B average or equivalent in their previous academic year. **Criteria:** TAC Foundation Scholarship Committee evaluates and scores all qualifying applications. Preference may be given to candidates with relevant work experience.

Funds Avail.: $5,000. **To Apply:** Applicants must submit the following documents together with the application form: official copy of the current academic transcript with official letterhead in an unalterable format; maximum two-page resume summarizing the education, employment experience, achievements and interests; and academic reference form. **Deadline:** March 2. **Remarks:** In recognition of W.J. Malone.

9217 ■ TAC Foundation-Peto MacCallum Undergraduate & College Scholarships *(Undergraduate/Scholarship)*

Purpose: To support transportation education in Canada, such as promoting careers in transportation to skilled students, and assisting transportation educators and researchers. **Focus:** Transportation. **Qualif.:** Applicants must be university undergraduates enrolled in at least two semesters of full-time transportation-related disciplines studies; must be Canadian citizens or permanent residents; and have achieved an overall B average or equivalent in their previous academic year. **Criteria:** TAC Foundation Scholarship Committee evaluates and scores all qualifying applications. Preference may be given to candidates with relevant work experience.

Funds Avail.: $5,000. **To Apply:** Applicants must submit the following documents together with the application form: an official copy of the applicants' most current academic transcript provided on official letterhead in an unalterable format; a maximum two-page resume summarizing the applicant's education, relevant employment experience, achievements and interests; and academic reference form. **Deadline:** March 2.

Awards are arranged alphabetically below their administering organizations

9218 ■ TAC Foundation-Provinces and Territories Scholarships (Undergraduate, Graduate/Scholarship)

Purpose: To provide scholarship to students who are pursuing a degree in transportation. **Focus:** Transportation. **Qualif.:** Applicants must be Canadian citizens or landed immigrants; and must be enrolled for the entire academic year. **Criteria:** Preference will be given to candidates with relevant work experience.

Funds Avail.: 3,000-4,000 Canadian Dollars. **To Apply:** Applicants must complete the application form (available online); must provide academic references and relevant employment information; must have an electronic version of their transcript of records. Application form and requirements must be sent to the TAC Foundation. **Deadline:** March 2. **Contact:** Foundation's Executive Director at foundation@tac-atc.ca.

9219 ■ TAC Foundation-SNC Lavalin Scholarships (Undergraduate, Graduate/Scholarship)

Purpose: To support transportation education in Canada, such as promoting careers in transportation to skilled students, and assisting transportation educators and researchers. **Focus:** Transportation. **Qualif.:** Applicants must be undergraduate or graduate students with transportation-related disciplines as field of their studies. For community college students, they must be enrolled in full-time studies, entering their final year of a certified community college program and intend to pursue a career in the transportation field, as it relates to the Foundation's primary focus. For University undergraduates, they must be enrolled in at least two semesters of full-time studies. For Graduate students, they must be admissible to a full-time transportation-related graduate studies program or already registered as a full-time graduate student in the field. All applicants must be Canadian citizens or permanent residents and have achieved an overall B average or equivalent in their previous academic year. **Criteria:** TAC Foundation Scholarship Committee evaluates and scores all qualifying applications. Preference may be given to candidates with relevant work experience.

Funds Avail.: $5,000. **To Apply:** Applicants must submit the following documents together with the application form: official copy of the current academic transcript with official letterhead in an unalterable format; maximum two-page resume summarizing the education, employment experience, achievements and interests; and academic reference form. **Deadline:** March 2.

9220 ■ TAC Foundation-Stantec Consulting Scholarships (Graduate/Scholarship)

Purpose: To encourage students to continue their post-graduate studies in the field of transportation engineering and to contribute to the cost-effective mobility upon which our society is based. **Focus:** Transportation. **Qualif.:** Applicants must be admitted to a postgraduate studies program or already registered as full-time graduate students; must be studying in the field of transportation and meet the conditions which apply to the scholarships; must be in the top quarter of their class in addition to having a minimum GPA of B. **Criteria:** Selection of applicants will be based on academic standing and application requirements. Preference will be given to candidates with relevant work experience.

Funds Avail.: 5,000 Canadian Dollars. **Number Awarded:** 2. **To Apply:** Applicants must complete the application form available online; must provide academic references and relevant employment information; must have an electronic

version of their transcript of records. Application form and requirements must be sent to the TAC Foundation. **Deadline:** March 2. **Contact:** Foundation's Executive Director at foundation@tac-atc.ca.

9221 ■ TAC Foundation-Tetra Tech EBA Inc. Scholarships (Undergraduate, Graduate/Scholarship)

Purpose: To support transportation education in Canada, such as promoting careers in transportation to skilled students, and assisting transportation educators and researchers. **Focus:** Transportation. **Qualif.:** Applicants must be undergraduate or graduate students with transportation engineering as field of their studies. For community college students, they must be enrolled in full-time studies, entering their final year of a certified community college program and intend to pursue a career in the transportation field, as it relates to the Foundation's primary focus. For University undergraduates, they must be enrolled in at least two semesters of full-time studies. For Graduate students, they must be admissible to a full-time transportation-related graduate studies program or already registered as a full-time graduate student in the field. All applicants must be Canadian citizens or permanent residents and have achieved an overall B average or equivalent in their previous academic year. **Criteria:** TAC Foundation Scholarship Committee evaluates and scores all qualifying applications. Preference may be given to candidates with relevant work experience.

Funds Avail.: $5,000. **To Apply:** Applicants must submit the following documents together with the application form: official copy of the current academic transcript with official letterhead in an unalterable format; maximum two-page resume summarizing the education, employment experience, achievements and interests; and academic reference form. **Deadline:** March 2.

9222 ■ Transportation Association of Canada Foundation Scholarships (Graduate, Undergraduate/Scholarship)

Purpose: To provide support and encouragement to those interested in pursuing a career in transportation planning or transportation engineering. **Focus:** Transportation. **Qualif.:** Applicants must be Canadian citizens or landed immigrants; and must be enrolled for the entire academic year. **Criteria:** Preference will be given to candidates with relevant work experience.

Funds Avail.: Amount varies. **To Apply:** Applicants must complete the application form available online; must provide academic references and relevant employment information; must have an electronic version of their transcript of records. Application form and requirements must be sent to the TAC Foundation. **Deadline:** March 2. **Contact:** Foundation's Executive Director at foundation@tac-atc.ca.

9223 ■ Transportation Clubs International (TCI)
PO Box 2223
Ocean Shores, WA 98569
Fax: (360)289-3188
Free: 877-858-8627
E-mail: info@transportationclubsinternational.com
URL: www.transportationclubsinternational.com

9224 ■ Ginger and Fred Deines Canada Scholarships (Undergraduate, Vocational/Occupational/Scholarship)

Purpose: To create, stimulate, and perpetuate discussion of topics relating to local and national transportation issues;

Awards are arranged alphabetically below their administering organizations

to promote member clubs, companies, and individuals the importance of transportation and transportation logistics; to promote the general welfare of member clubs and their membership; to provide an international forum for local transportation and logistics organizations; to stimulate and perpetuate dialogue among its members on subjects of national and international transportation importance; and to promote education in the transportation industry. **Focus:** Logistics; Transportation. **Qualif.:** Applicants must be enrolled in an accredited institution of higher learning in a vocational or degree program in the fields of Transportation, Logistics or Traffic Management or related fields intending to prepare for a career in these areas. They must be of Canadian nationality and enrolled in a school in Canada or in the United States. **Criteria:** Recipients are selected based on scholastic ability, potential, professional interest, character, and financial need.

Funds Avail.: No specific amount. **To Apply:** Applicants must submit a certified copy of the college/university transcript; three letters of recommendation; a small, current photograph to be used for publication; an essay of not more than 500-words, explaining why you have chosen transportation or an allied field as a career path; and outline of the objectives. **Deadline:** May 31. **Contact:** Lynn Donovick, Martin Midstream Partners, Three Riverway, Suite 400, Houston, Texas 77056; Email: lynn.donovick@ martinmlp.com.

9225 ■ Ginger and Fred Deines Mexico Scholarships *(Undergraduate, Vocational/Occupational/ Scholarship)*

Purpose: To create, stimulate, and perpetuate discussion of topics relating to local and national transportation issues; to promote member clubs, companies, and individuals the importance of transportation and transportation logistics; to promote the general welfare of member clubs and their membership; to provide an international forum for local transportation and logistics organizations; to stimulate and perpetuate dialogue among its members on subjects of national and international transportation importance; and to promote education in the transportation industry. **Focus:** Logistics; Transportation. **Qualif.:** Applicants must be enrolled in an accredited institution of higher learning in a vocational or degree program in the fields of Transportation, Logistics or Traffic Management or related fields intending to prepare for a career in these areas. They must be of Mexican nationality and enrolled in a school in Mexico or the U.S. **Criteria:** Recipients are selected based on scholastic ability, potential, professional interest, character, and financial need.

Funds Avail.: No specific amount. **To Apply:** Applicants must submit a certified copy of the college/university transcript; three letters of recommendation; a small, current photograph to be used for publication; an essay of not more than 500 words explaining why you have chosen transportation or an allied field as a career path; and outline of the objectives. **Deadline:** May 31. **Contact:** Lynn Donovick, Martin Midstream Partners, Three Riverway, Suite 400, Houston, Texas 77056; Email: lynn.donovick@ martinmlp.com.

9226 ■ Hooper Memorial Scholarships *(Undergraduate/Scholarship)*

Purpose: To create, stimulate, and perpetuate discussion of topics relating to local and national transportation issues; to promote member clubs, companies, and individuals the importance of transportation and transportation logistics; to promote the general welfare of member clubs and their

membership; to provide an international forum for local transportation and logistics organizations; to stimulate and perpetuate dialogue among its members on subjects of national and international transportation importance; and to promote education in the transportation industry. **Focus:** Logistics; Management; Transportation. **Qualif.:** Applicants must be enrolled in an accredited institution of higher learning in a vocational or degree program in the fields of Transportation, Logistics or Traffic Management or related fields intending to prepare for a career in these areas. **Criteria:** Selection is vested to TCI Scholarship Trustees who assess applications on the following criteria: GPA through certified transcript; field of study; community involvement/extracurricular activities and honors/awards; written essay of 500 words; and three recommendation letters.

Funds Avail.: No specific amount. **Duration:** Annual. **To Apply:** Applicants must submit a certified copy of the college/university transcript; three letters of recommendation; a small, current photograph to be use for publication; an essay of not more than 500-words, explaining why have to choose transportation or an allied field as a career path; and outline of the objectives.

9227 ■ LTNA Scholarship Awards *(Undergraduate/ Scholarship)*

Purpose: To support students pursuing undergraduate degrees in transportation programs. **Focus:** Logistics; Management; Transportation. **Qualif.:** Applicants must be graduating high school seniors and college undergraduate students accepted to or currently enrolled at accredited institutions of higher learning in degree programs in the fields of transportation logistics, supply-chain management, traffic management, transportation safety and/or related transportation. **Criteria:** Selection will be based on the following criteria: scholastic ability; character; potential; professional interest; and financial need as determined by TCI Scholarship Trustees.

Funds Avail.: No specific amount. **Duration:** Annual. **To Apply:** Applicants must visit the website to obtain the scholarship application form. In addition to a completed application form, applicants must include the following supporting documents: certified transcript directly obtained from applicants' college/university; three letters of recommendation; current 4" x 6" colored photograph; 500-word essay explaining why the applicants have chosen transportation or an allied field as a career path, and outline their objectives. **Deadline:** May 31.

9228 ■ Denny Lydic Scholarships *(Undergraduate/ Scholarship)*

Purpose: To promote education in the transportation industry. **Focus:** Logistics; Management; Transportation. **Qualif.:** Applicants must be enrolled in an accredited institution of higher learning in a vocational or degree program in the fields of Transportation, Logistics or Traffic Management or related fields intending to prepare for a career in these areas. **Criteria:** Selection is vested to TCI Scholarship Trustees who assess applications on the following criteria: GPA through certified transcript; field of study; community involvement/extracurricular activities and honors/ awards; written essay of 500 words; and three recommendation letters.

Funds Avail.: No specific amount. **Duration:** Annual. **Number Awarded:** Varies. **To Apply:** Applicants must submit a certified copy of the college/university transcript; three letters of recommendation; a small, current photograph to be

Awards are arranged alphabetically below their administering organizations

use for publication; an essay of not more than 500-words, explaining why have to choose transportation or an allied field as a career path; and outline of the objectives. **Deadline:** May 31. **Remarks:** Awarded in appreciation and recognition for his dedication to the field of transportation. Mr. Lydic is a Past President of TCI and continues to be very active and supportive. **Contact:** Lynn Donovick, Martin Midstream Partners, Three Riverway, Suite 400, Houston, Texas 77056; Email: lynn.donovick@martinmlp.com.

9229 ■ Texas Transportation Scholarships
(Undergraduate/Scholarship)

Purpose: To create, stimulate, and perpetuate discussion of topics relating to local and national transportation issues; to promote member clubs, companies, and individuals the importance of transportation and transportation logistics; to promote the general welfare of member clubs and their membership; to provide an international forum for local transportation and logistics organizations; To stimulate and perpetuate dialogue among members on subjects of national and international transportation importance; and to promote education in the transportation industry. **Focus:** Logistics; Management; Transportation. **Qualif.:** Applicants must be: enrolled in any accredited institution of higher learning in a vocational or degree program in the fields of Transportation, Logistics or Traffic Management or related fields intending to prepare for a career in these areas; and, students who have been enrolled in any school in Texas during some phase of their education (elementary, secondary, or high school). **Criteria:** Selection is vested to TCI Scholarship Trustees who assess applications on the following criteria: GPA through certified transcript; field of study; community involvement/extracurricular activities and honors/awards; written essay of 500 words; and three recommendation letters.

Funds Avail.: No specific amount. **Duration:** Annual. **To Apply:** Applicants must submit a certified copy of the college/university transcript; three letters of recommendation; a small, current photograph to be use for publication; an essay of not more than 500-words, explaining why have to choose transportation or an allied field as a career path; and outline of the objectives. **Deadline:** May 31. **Remarks:** The scholarship is awarded in memory of Gene Landis of Houston, Texas, to a student who has been enrolled in a school in Texas during some phase of their education (elementary, secondary, or high school). **Contact:** Lynn Donovick, Martin Midstream Partners, Three Riverway, Suite 400, Houston, Texas 77056; Email: lynn.donovick@martinmlp.com.

9230 ■ Alice Glaisyer Warfield Scholarships
(Undergraduate/Scholarship)

Purpose: To create, stimulate, and perpetuate discussion of topics relating to local and national transportation issues; to promote member clubs, companies, and individuals the importance of transportation and transportation logistics; to promote the general welfare of member clubs and their membership; to provide an international forum for local transportation and logistics organizations; To stimulate and perpetuate dialogue among its members on subjects of national and international transportation importance; and to promote education in the transportation industry. **Focus:** Logistics; Management; Transportation. **Qualif.:** Applicants must be enrolled in an accredited institution of higher learning in a vocational or degree program in the fields of Transportation, Logistics or Traffic Management or related fields intending to prepare for a career in these areas. **Criteria:** Selection is vested to TCI Scholarship Trustees

who assess applications on the following criteria: GPA through certified transcript; field of study; community involvement/extracurricular activities and honors/awards; written essay of 500 words; and three recommendation letters.

Funds Avail.: No specific amount. **Duration:** Annual. **To Apply:** Applicants must submit a certified copy of the college/university transcript; three letters of recommendation; a small, current photograph to be use for publication; an essay of not more than 500-words, explaining why have to choose transportation or an allied field as a career path; and outline of the objectives. **Deadline:** May 31. **Remarks:** Awarded in appreciation and memory for the dedication of TCI. Ms. Glaisyer, who was the Past President of TCI and a TCI Scholarship Trustee. **Contact:** Lynn Donovick, Martin Midstream Partners, Three Riverway, Suite 400, Houston, Texas 77056; Email: lynn.donovick@martinmlp.com.

9231 ■ Triangle Coalition for STEM Education
1840 Wilson Blvd., Ste. 201
Arlington, VA 22201
Ph: (703)516-5960
Fax: (703)516-5969
Free: 800-582-0115
URL: www.trianglecoalition.org

9232 ■ Albert Einstein Distinguished Educator Fellowships (AEF) *(Graduate, Other/Fellowship)*

Purpose: To provide a unique professional development opportunity for accomplished K-12 educators in the fields of science, technology, engineering, and mathematics (STEM) to serve in the national education arena. **Focus:** Education, Elementary; Education, Secondary. **Qualif.:** Applicant must be a U.S. citizen; have a minimum of five years full-time classroom teaching experience prior to completing the application; have been teaching full-time in a public or private elementary or secondary school for at least five of the last seven years in a STEM discipline; and be currently employed full-time in a public or private elementary or secondary school or school district. **Criteria:** Selection is based on: excellence in teaching science, mathematics, or technology; experimental and innovative attitude in the approach to teaching; sustained professional growth in science or mathematics in the art of teaching; professional involvement and leadership; interpersonal and communication skills needed to serve in the public policy environment and knowledge of national, state and local policies which affect education.

Funds Avail.: $6,000 monthly stipend plus $1,000 monthly cost of living allowance. **Duration:** 11/year. **Number Awarded:** Varies. **To Apply:** Applicants may visit the website to verify the application process and other pieces of information. **Remarks:** Established in 1994.

9233 ■ Tribeca Film Institute
32 Ave. of the Americas, 27th Fl.
New York, NY 10013
Ph: (212)274-8080
Fax: (212)274-8081
E-mail: institute@tribecafilminstitute.org
URL: www.tribecafilminstitute.org

9234 ■ TFI Latin America Media Arts Fund *(Professional development/Award)*

Purpose: To support Mexican media artists who are working in documentary, narrative, experimental, video installa-

Awards are arranged alphabetically below their administering organizations

tion or new media. **Focus:** Media arts. **Qualif.:** Applicants must be Mexican individuals working in media-related fields; must be nominated by a committee member. **Criteria:** Applicants will be evaluated based on submitted application and supporting materials.

Funds Avail.: $10,000. **To Apply:** Applicants must submit a completed application form available at mediaartists.org.

9235 ■ Charlie Trotter Culinary Education Foundation

816 West Armitage
Chicago, IL 60614
Ph: (773)248-6228
E-mail: info@charlietrotters.com
URL: www.charlietrotters.com

9236 ■ Charlie Trotters's Culinary Education Foundation Culinary Study Scholarships *(Other, Undergraduate/Scholarship)*

Purpose: To support students in pursuing their career in culinary arts. **Focus:** Culinary arts. **Qualif.:** Applicants must reside in Illinois; be currently enrolled or career professionals toward any Culinary Arts degree or certificate program at any accredited national culinary school; have a GPA of 3.0 or higher (for applicants who have been students during the five years prior to the application). **Criteria:** Recipients will be selected based on merit, work experience, culinary goals and skills and references.

Funds Avail.: No specific amount. **To Apply:** Applicants must submit a completed Culinary Trust Scholarship application form; a project proposal (two-page, double-spaced) illustrating their culinary goals; two letters of reference on business or personal letterhead; a current academic transcript; a non-refundable application fee of $35. **Deadline:** March 1.

9237 ■ Truck Renting and Leasing Association (TRLA)

675 N Washington St., Ste. 410
Alexandria, VA 22314
Ph: (703)299-9120
Fax: (703)299-9115
URL: www.trala.org

9238 ■ TRALA Industry Scholarship Awards *(Undergraduate/Scholarship)*

Purpose: To assist TRALA-member company employees or their dependents to pursue vocational training as diesel maintenance technicians. **Focus:** General studies/Field of study not specified. **Qualif.:** Applicants must be employees of TRALA member companies in North America, or dependents/children of full-time employees of TRALA member companies in North America pursuing a course of study related to the truck transportation industry at an accredited two-year vocational program. **Criteria:** Selection of recipients will be administered by Scholarship America.

Funds Avail.: $5,000 each. **Duration:** Annual. **Number Awarded:** 4. **To Apply:** Application forms are available at the scholarship website. **Deadline:** June 1.

9239 ■ Truckload Carriers Association (TCA)

555 E Braddock Rd.
Alexandria, VA 22314-2182

Ph: (703)838-1950
Fax: (703)836-6610
E-mail: tca@truckload.org
URL: www.truckload.org

9240 ■ TCA Scholarship *(Undergraduate/Scholarship)*

Purpose: To support students associated with the truckload industry to reach their dreams. **Focus:** General studies/Field of study not specified. **Qualif.:** Applicant must be a student in good standing who will be attending an accredited four-year college or university as a freshman, sophomore, junior, or senior and who is either the child, grandchild, or spouse of an employee, or an employee of a TCA member; or, the child, grandchild or spouse of an independent contractor or an independent contractor affiliated with a TCA member; must have a minimum grade point average of 3.0. **Criteria:** Selection will be based on the following criteria: financial need; scholastic achievement; student status; character and integrity.

Funds Avail.: Up to $6,000. **Duration:** Annual. **To Apply:** Applicant must complete the online application process and submit the following requirements: official transcript of all courses and grades; a course schedule (if available) for the upcoming term; provided the name, department, address and telephone number of the person at the college or university to which the scholarship check should be sent for disbursement; a headshot photo that must be a 300 dpi resolution or 1 MB in size. **Deadline:** June 20. **Remarks:** Established in 1973. **Contact:** TCA Scholarship Fund, at the above address.

9241 ■ Truckload Carriers Association Scholarships *(Undergraduate/Scholarship)*

Purpose: To help students associated with the truckload industry reach their dreams. **Focus:** General studies/Field of study not specified. **Qualif.:** Applicant must be a college junior or senior in good standing, who is a child, grandchild, spouse of an employee, or an employee of TCA member; must either be the child, grandchild or spouse of an independent contractor or an independent contractor affiliated with a trucking company and attending an accredited four-year college or university. **Criteria:** The recipient will be selected based on financial need, excellence in scholastic achievement in freshman and sophomore years (minimum of 3.3 cumulative GPA), full-time student status with high character and integrity. Students pursuing transportation and business degrees will be given special consideration.

Funds Avail.: $2,000 up to $6,500. **To Apply:** Applicants must send their complete application, official complete transcript of all college courses and grades, course schedule including tuition and fees for upcoming term. **Deadline:** June 20.

9242 ■ Pierre Elliott Trudeau Foundation

600 - 1980 Sherbrooke St. W
Montreal, QC, Canada H3H 1E8
Ph: (514)938-0001
Fax: (514)938-0046
E-mail: tfinfo@trudeaufoundation.ca
URL: www.trudeaufoundation.ca

9243 ■ Trudeau Fellowships - Regular *(Advanced Professional, Professional development/Fellowship)*

Purpose: To support individuals in their research and professional development. **Focus:** General studies/Field of

Awards are arranged alphabetically below their administering organizations

study not specified. **Qualif.:** Candidates must be Canadian citizens or permanent residents or legally allowed to reside in Canada for the period that they will benefit from the funding; must be active in the social sciences and humanities and work in an area related to one or more of the Foundation's four themes; must be committed to contribute the equivalent of at least one day a week for an academic term to the Foundation's intellectual leadership; and must be nominated by a Canadian university or other entity whom the Foundation has invited to submit a nomination. **Criteria:** Selection will be based on the following: productivity; leadership and innovation; communication and engagement; and Trudeau projects. Moreover, Trudeau fellows will be selected through a rigorous process comprised of the following stages: evaluation of all nominations files by an internal committee; selection of finalists by an external committee; approval of the finalists by the Application and Nomination Review Committee; and final approval by the Foundation's Board of Directors.

Funds Avail.: 225,000 Canadian Dollars. **To Apply:** Candidates must provide the following materials: a two-page backgrounder on the candidate (may visit the website for the template); a detailed letter from the nominator, outlining the candidates' academic achievements and their record of public engagement; a detailed project proposal from the candidates, outlining their proposal for a Trudeau project. The proposal is not required to include a budget, but if the candidate feels that a budget would help illustrate the proposal, a summary budget may be included. the proposal, including the budget if desired, should be between 5 and 10 pages; candidates' current resume; up to three publications, articles or book chapters written by the candidates; an optional, one or two testimonies or articles about the candidate containing substantially different elements than those contained in the letter of recommendation. **Deadline:** November 27 (electronic nomination file); November 30 (two hard copies of nomination file).

9244 ▪ Trudeau Fellowships - Visiting *(Advanced Professional, Professional development/Fellowship)*

Purpose: To support individuals in their research and professional development. **Focus:** General studies/Field of study not specified. **Qualif.:** Candidates must be nominated by a Canadian university whom the Foundation has invited to submit a nomination; must be active in the social sciences and humanities and work in an area related to one or more of the Foundation's four themes; and must be recognized for his/her achievements, creativity and engagement in the field of research and creation. **Criteria:** Selection will be based on the applicants' eligibility and other criteria of the committee.

Funds Avail.: 225,000 Canadian Dollars. **Number Awarded:** 1. **To Apply:** Candidates must provide the following materials: a two-page backgrounder on the candidate (may visit the website for the template); a detailed letter from the nominator, outlining the candidates' academic achievements and their record of public engagement; a detailed project proposal from the candidates, outlining their proposal for a Trudeau project. The proposal is not required to include a budget, but if the candidate feels that a budget would help illustrate the proposal, a summary budget may be included. the proposal, including the budget if desired, should be between 5 and 10 pages; candidates' current resume; up to three publications, articles or book chapters written by the candidates; an optional, one or two testimonies or articles about the candidate containing substantially different elements than those contained in the letter of recommendation; an outline of fellows' plan while

in residence at the host university and how the university plans to incorporate the visiting fellow into its academic activities during the fellows' tenure; a statement outlining how the fellowship will benefit the university and the candidate; a detailed budget including the expected use of the visiting fellowship. **Deadline:** December 11 (electronic nomination file); December 14 (two hard copies of nomination file).

9245 ▪ Trudeau Foundation Doctoral Scholarships *(Doctorate/Scholarship)*

Purpose: To support qualified individuals who want to pursue their research on a present-day concern. **Focus:** Humanities; Social sciences. **Qualif.:** Applicants must be Canadian citizens and landed immigrants pursuing fulltime doctoral studies in Canada; must be applying for the first year of a doctoral program, or be registered in the first or second year of such a program. **Criteria:** Selection of candidates will be based on the following criteria: (1) Academic achievement; (2) Outstanding ability to engage in lively exchange with other researchers and scholars; and (3) Intention to work in an area related to one or more of the four themes of the foundation and a desire to contribute to public dialogue about those themes.

Funds Avail.: Up to $60,000 Canadian Dollars. **Duration:** Annual. **Number Awarded:** Up to 15. **To Apply:** Applicant must complete the application form available online; must submit the official transcript and reference letters.

9246 ▪ Harry S. Truman Scholarship Foundation (HSTSF)
712 Jackson Pl. NW
Washington, DC 20006
Ph: (202)395-4831
E-mail: office@truman.gov
URL: www.truman.gov

9247 ▪ Harry S. Truman Scholarships *(Postgraduate/Scholarship)*

Purpose: To provide financial assistance for students pursuing graduate degrees in public service fields. **Focus:** Public service. **Qualif.:** Candidates must be nominated by their current institution of higher education or by their two-year institution if they are transfer students from community colleges or junior colleges; must be full-time junior-level students at a four-year institution pursuing a bachelor's degree; must be students in their second or third year of collegiate study expecting to graduate, or senior-level students who are residents of Puerto Rico or the Islands; committed to a career in public service; in the upper quarter of their class; U.S. citizens or United States nationals from American Samoa or the Commonwealth of the Northern Mariana Islands. **Criteria:** Applicants are selected based on the jury's review of the application materials.

Funds Avail.: $30,000 merit-based. **Number Awarded:** 55-65. **To Apply:** Applicants must submit a completed application form which can be downloaded at www.truman.gov; three additional letters of recommendation; recent transcript of records; and a policy proposal. **Deadline:** February 4.

9248 ▪ TrustedPros Inc.
5201 Great America Pkwy., Ste. 320
Santa Clara, CA 95054
Free: 855-890-7767

Awards are arranged alphabetically below their administering organizations

URL: trustedpros.com

9249 ■ TrustedPros Scholarships (Undergraduate/Scholarship)

Purpose: To help lessen educational expenses of deserving students. **Focus:** General studies/Field of study not specified. **Qualif.:** Applicants must be students enrolled in an accredited American college, university or trade school. The major focus of studies is any of the following: Architectural Design and Building Technician; Brick and Stone Mason; Carpentry or Cabinet Making; Home Renovations Technology; Cement (concrete) Finisher; Contractor/Construction Management; Construction Technician; Construction Craft Worker; Construction Millwright; Drywall Finisher and Plasterer; Drywall, Acoustic and Lathing Applicator; Electrician; Exterior Insulated Finish Systems Mechanic; Floor Covering Installer; General Carpenter; Painter and Decorator; Plumbing; Refrigeration and Air Conditioning Systems Mechanic; Residential Air Conditioning Systems Mechanic; HVAC; Restoration Mason; Roofing; Sprinkler and Fire Protection Installer; Terrazzo; Tile and Marble. Applicants must be U.S. residents and have a minimum GPA of 3.0. **Criteria:** Selection will be based on the committee's criteria.

Funds Avail.: $1,000. **Duration:** Annual. **Number Awarded:** 1. **To Apply:** Applicants must submit a letter demonstrating financial needs and 1,000 minimum words essay about "how your field might be improved?" **Deadline:** December 15.

9250 ■ TSHP Research and Education Foundation

3000 Joe DiMaggio, No. 30-A
Round Rock, TX 78665
Ph: (512)906-0546
Fax: (512)852-8514
Free: 800-242-8747
E-mail: foundation@tshp.org
URL: www.tshp-foundation.org

9251 ■ TSHP R&E Foundation Scholarship Program (Undergraduate, Graduate/Scholarship)

Purpose: To help students pursue their education in pharmacy field. **Focus:** Pharmacy. **Qualif.:** Applicants must be undergraduate and graduate students who are interested in pharmacy field. **Criteria:** Applicants will be selected based on financial need, academic ability and career interest.

Funds Avail.: No specific amount. **To Apply:** Applicants must complete the application form; must submit a letter of application explaining how to meet the required criteria, future pharmacy practice goals and philosophy of pharmacy practice; must submit a copy of the latest grade report verifying their current GPA; must provide proof of residency for El Paso, Gene Lake and Central Texas; and must submit three letters of reference.

9252 ■ Turf and Ornamental Communicators Association (TOCA)

605 Columbus Ave. S
New Prague, MN 56071-1935
Ph: (952)758-6340
Fax: (952)758-5813
URL: www.toca.org

9253 ■ Turf and Ornamental Communicators Association Scholarship Program (Undergraduate/Scholarship)

Purpose: To provide financial support for undergraduate college students pursuing a career in green industry communications. **Focus:** Communications. **Qualif.:** Applicants must major or minor in technical communications or a green industry related field such as horticulture, plant sciences, botany, agronomy, plant pathology, etc; must demonstrate an interest in using this course of study in the field of communications; must have overall GPA of 2.5 or above and a 3.0 in the major area of study (based on 4.0 scale). **Criteria:** Applicants will be evaluated by the Scholarship Committee.

Funds Avail.: $2,500. **Number Awarded:** 1. **To Apply:** Applicants must submit complete application form together with references, writing/editing sample, essay, resume, and transcript. **Deadline:** March 1. **Contact:** Barb Ulschmid at barbulschmid@gardnerandgardnercommunications.com.

9254 ■ Turkish Coalition of America (TCA)

1510 H St. NW, Ste. 900
Washington, DC 20005
Ph: (202)370-1399
Fax: (202)370-1398
E-mail: info@tc-america.org
URL: www.turkishcoalitionofamerica.org

9255 ■ American Turkish Society Arif Mardin Music Fellowships (Other/Fellowship)

Purpose: To provide financial assistance for promising musicians from Turkey and to give them the chance to study in the United States. **Focus:** Music. **Qualif.:** Applicants must be promising musicians from Turkey which will further the education of promising musicians from Turkey and give them a chance to study in the United States. **Criteria:** Consideration for the fellowship will be based on merit and potential to benefit from the program in current or future music career.

Funds Avail.: $500. **To Apply:** Applicants must check the available website for more information.

9256 ■ TCA-ACBH Scholarships (Undergraduate/Scholarship)

Purpose: To provide financial assistance to students who are pursuing their educational goal. **Focus:** General studies/Field of study not specified. **Qualif.:** Applicants full-time Bosnian-American undergraduates accepted to a study abroad program at a Turkish university. **Criteria:** Selection is based on merit.

Funds Avail.: $2,000. **Number Awarded:** 10. **To Apply:** Applicants must send a resume and a cover letter to ACBH with subject title "TCA Scholarship" via email. **Contact:** baacbh@gmail.com.

9257 ■ TCA-UMD Scholarships (Undergraduate/Scholarship)

Purpose: To provide financial assistance to students who are pursuing their educational goal. **Focus:** General studies/Field of study not specified. **Qualif.:** Applicants must be full-time Macedonian-American undergraduates accepted to a study abroad program at a Turkish university. **Criteria:** Preference will be given to those who meet the criteria.

Funds Avail.: $2,000. **Number Awarded:** 10. **To Apply:**

Awards are arranged alphabetically below their administering organizations

Applicants must check the available website for the required materials.

9258 ■ TCAdvance Scholarships (Undergraduate/Scholarship)

Purpose: To fulfill the objective of engaging and cultivating a new generation of Young Turkish American leaders. **Focus:** Communications; International affairs and relations; Political science; Printing trades and industries; Public affairs; Public relations. **Qualif.:** Applicants must meet the following criteria: be a U.S. citizens or permanent residents (green card holder); have, and maintain through the course of the scholarship period, a cumulative minimum 3.3 GPA on a 4.0 scale; evidence of leadership commitment through participation in community service, particularly within the Turkish American community; and be a high school seniors applying to an accredited college or university, or college student who plans to continue undergraduate study; or a college senior or graduate enrolled or about to enroll in graduate school. Graduate students who apply for the TCA must plan to pursue studies and a career in public affairs. **Criteria:** Candidates will be selected on the basis of academic achievement, interest in Turkish American issues as demonstrated by involvement in Turkish American community affairs, and individual leadership qualities conducive to pursuing a career in public affairs, media and public relations. Priority will be given to students who are admitted to top national universities or liberal arts schools.

Funds Avail.: No specific amount. **To Apply:** Applicants must submit three (3) collated, non-stapled, paperclipped copies of each of the following items: (1) Completed Application Form (2) Resume: each copy should be submitted on one single-sided 8.5" x 11" sheet of paper. (3) Short essay: the essay should not exceed 500 words and must be typed and double-spaced.

9259 ■ J.L. Turner Legal Association (JLTLA)

2101 Ross Ave.
Dallas, TX 75201
Ph: (214)997-4073
Fax: (214)296-9694
URL: www.jltla.org/jltla

9260 ■ Fred Finch Scholarships (Undergraduate/Scholarship)

Purpose: To award scholarship to male minority law students. **Focus:** Law. **Qualif.:** Applicants must be male minority law students; must be currently enrolled in an ABA accredited law school in the United States; must be in good academic standing at the law school; must be either second year or third year minority law students that is from the DFW Metroplex or a second or third year minority law students that attend law school in the DFW Metroplex. **Criteria:** Scholarship award will be based on merit.

Funds Avail.: No specific amount. **Duration:** Annual. **To Apply:** Scholarship application form can be obtained at the website. Applicants must submit the application together with the following materials: financial statement and student aid report (if applicable), resume, essay and letter of reference; certified copy of law school transcript; short biographical sketch; photograph. **Deadline:** October 1.

9261 ■ JLTLA Scholarships (Undergraduate/Scholarship)

Purpose: To inspire educational pursuits in the field of law among law students. **Focus:** Law. **Qualif.:** Program is open to minority, second or third year law students that are from or attending law school in the Dallas-Fort Worth Metroplex. Applicants must be U.S. citizens or permanent legal residents; must be in good academic standing. **Criteria:** Selection will be based on financial need and merit.

Funds Avail.: No specific amount. **Duration:** Annual. **To Apply:** Applicants must submit the following requirements: application; a short biographical sketch (5-7 sentences, written in third person for inclusion in gala booklet if selected); photograph (3x5 or larger of head and shoulders, photograph should be suitable for inclusion in gala booklet if selected); a certified copy of law school transcript; letters of reference; and a brief essay. Applicants may download an application form at J.L Turner website. **Deadline:** October 1. **Remarks:** Established in 1982.

9262 ■ Barbara Jordan Scholarships (Undergraduate/Scholarship)

Purpose: To award scholarship to minority law students. **Focus:** Law. **Qualif.:** Applicants must be female minority students; must be currently enrolled in an ABA accredited law school in the United States; must be in good academic standing at the law school; must be either second year or third year minority law students that is from the DFW Metroplex or a second or third year minority law students that attend law school in the DFW Metroplex. **Criteria:** Scholarship award will be based on merit.

Funds Avail.: No specific amount. **Duration:** Annual. **To Apply:** Scholarship application form can be obtained at the website. Applicants must submit the application together with the following materials: financial statement and student aid report (if applicable), resume, essay and letter of reference; certified copy of law school transcript; short biographical sketch; photograph.

9263 ■ Judge's Scholarships (Undergraduate/Scholarship)

Purpose: To award scholarship to a minority law student who has excelled academically. **Focus:** Law. **Qualif.:** Applicants must be either male or female law students; must be currently enrolled in an ABA accredited law school in the United States; must be in good academic standing at the law school; must be either second year or third year minority law students that is from the DFW Metroplex or a second or third year minority law students that attend law school in the DFW Metroplex. **Criteria:** Scholarship award will be based on merit.

Funds Avail.: No specific amount. **Duration:** Annual. **To Apply:** Scholarship application form can be obtained at the website. Applicants must submit the application together with the following materials: financial statement and student aid report (if applicable), resume, essay and letter of reference; certified copy of law school transcript; short biographical sketch; photograph. **Deadline:** October 1.

9264 ■ Marie Trahan/Susman Godfrey Scholarships (Undergraduate/Scholarship)

Purpose: To support outstanding African-American male or female law student in continuing their studies. **Focus:** Law. **Qualif.:** Applicants must be African-American law students from the state of Texas; must be currently enrolled in an ABA accredited law school in the United States; must be in good academic standing at the law school; must be either second or third year minority law students that are from the DFW Metroplex or a second or third year minority law student that attends law school in the DFW Metroplex. **Criteria:** Selection will be based on the committee's criteria.

Funds Avail.: No specific amount. **To Apply:** Scholarship

Awards are arranged alphabetically below their administering organizations

application forms can be obtained at the website. Applicants must submit the application together with the following materials: financial statement and student aid report (if ap-plicable), resume, essay and letter of reference; certified copy of law school transcript; short biographical sketch; photograph. **Deadline:** October 1.

Awards are arranged alphabetically below their administering organizations